8th International Workshop on Semantic Evaluation

(SemEval 2014)

Held with SEM 2014 at COLING 2014

Dublin, Ireland
23 – 24 August 2014

ISBN: 978-1-63439-234-1

Printed from e-media with permission by:

Curran Associates, Inc.
57 Morehouse Lane
Red Hook, NY 12571

Some format issues inherent in the e-media version may also appear in this print version.

Printed by Curran Associates, Inc. (2014)

Association for Computational Linguistics
209 N. Eighth Street
Stroudsburg, Pennsylvania 18360

Phone: 1-570-476-8006
Fax: 1-570-476-0860

acl@aclweb.org

Additional copies of this publication are available from:

Curran Associates, Inc.
57 Morehouse Lane
Red Hook, NY 12571 USA
Phone: 845-758-0400
Fax: 845-758-2634
Email: curran@proceedings.com
Web: www.proceedings.com

Welcome to SemEval-2014

The Semantic Evaluation (SemEval) series of workshops focuses on the evaluation and comparison of systems that can analyse diverse semantic phenomena in text with the aim of extending the current state-of-the-art in semantic analysis and creating high quality annotated datasets in a range of increasingly challenging problems in natural language semantics. SemEval provides an exciting forum for researchers to propose challenging research problems in semantics and to build systems/techniques to address such research problems.

SemEval-2014 is the eighth workshop in the series. The first three workshops, SensEval-1 (1998), SensEval-2 (2001), and SensEval-3 (2004), focused on word sense disambiguation, each time growing in the number of languages offered in the tasks and in the number of participating teams. In 2007, the workshop was renamed as SemEval, and in the next four workshops SemEval-2007/2010/2012/2013 the nature of the tasks evolved to include semantic analysis tasks outside of word sense disambiguation. Starting in 2012, SemEval turned into a yearly event.

This volume contains papers accepted for presentation at the SemEval-2014 International Workshop on Semantic Evaluation Exercises. SemEval-2014 was co-located with the 25th International Conference on Computational Linguistics (COLING) in Dublin.

SemEval-2014 included the following 10 shared tasks:

1. Evaluation of Compositional Distributional Semantic Models on Full Sentences through Semantic Relatedness and Entailment
2. Grammar Induction for Spoken Dialogue Systems
3. Cross-Level Semantic Similarity
4. Aspect Based Sentiment Analysis
5. L2 Writing Assistant
6. Supervised Semantic Parsing of Spatial Robot Commands
7. Analysis of Clinical Text
8. Broad-Coverage Semantic Dependency Parsing
9. Sentiment Analysis in Twitter
10. Multilingual Semantic Textual Similarity

About 185 teams submitted more than 500 systems for the 10 tasks of SemEval-2014. This volume contains both Task Description papers that describe each of the above tasks and System Description papers that describe the systems that participated in the above tasks. A total of 10 task description papers and 139 system description papers are included in this volume.

We are grateful to all program committee members for their high quality, elaborate and thoughtful reviews. The papers in this proceedings have surely benefited from this feedback. We also thank the COLING'2014 conference organizers for the local organization and the forum. Finally, we most gratefully acknowledge the support of our sponsor, the ACL Special Interest Group on the Lexicon (SIGLEX).

Welcome to SemEval-2014,
Preslav Nakov and Torsten Zesch

SemEval Chairs:

- Preslav Nakov, Qatar Computing Research Institute
- Torsten Zesch, University of Duisburg-Essen

Reviewing Track Chairs:

- Carmen Banea, University of Michigan
- Raffaella Bernardi, University of Trento
- Mona Diab, The George Washington University
- Kais Dukes, University of Leeds
- Maarten van Gompel, Radboud University Nijmegen
- Elias Iosif, Athena Research and Innovation Center
- David Jurgens, Sapienza University of Rome
- Marco Kuhlmann, Linköping University
- Preslav Nakov, Qatar Computing Research Institute
- Stephan Oepen, Universitetet i Oslo
- Maria Pontiki, Institute for Language and Speech Processing
- Sameer Pradhan, Harvard University
- Sara Rosenthal, Columbia University
- Mohammad Taher Pilehvar, Sapienza University of Rome

Reviewers:

- Naveed Afzal, King Abdulaziz University North Branch Jeddah
- Apoorv Agarwal, Columbia University
- Eneko Agirre, University of the Basque Country
- Željko Agić, University of Zagreb
- Ameeta Agrawal, York University
- Mariana S. C. Almeida, Priberam / Instituto de Telecomunicações
- Miguel A. Alonso, Universidade da Coruña
- Ana Alves, CISUC - University of Coimbra and Polythecnic Institute of Coimbra
- Silvio Amir, INESC-ID, IST
- Beakal Gizachew Assefa, Koc University
- Georgia Athanasopoulou, Technical University of Crete
- Giuseppe Attardi, Università di Pisa
- Pedro Balage Filho, University of São Paulo
- Timothy Baldwin, The University of Melbourne
- Sivaji Bandyopadhyay, Jadavpur University

- Carmen Banea, University of Michigan
- Pierpaolo Basile, University of Bari
- Roberto Basili, University of Roma, Tor Vergata
- Osman Baskaya, Koç University
- Frederic Bechet, Aix Marseille Universite - LIF/CNRS
- Islam Beltagy, The University of Texas at Austin
- Gabor Berend, University Of Szeged
- Raffaella Bernardi, University of Trento
- Yves Bestgen, Université Catholique de Louvain
- Steven Bethard, University of Alabama at Birmingham
- Ergun Biçici, Centre for Next Generation Localisation, Dublin City University
- Johannes Bjerva, Center for Language and Cognition Groningen, University of Groningen
- Pavel Blinov, VSHU
- Bernd Bohnet, University Birmingham
- Fritjof Bornebusch, University of Bremen
- Houda Bouamor, Carnegie Mellon University
- Caroline Brun, Xerox Research Centre Europe
- Tomáš Brychcín, University of West Bohemia
- Paul Buitelaar, INSIGHT, National University of Ireland, Galway
- Davide Buscaldi, LIPN, Université Paris 13
- Glaucia Cancino, Universität Bremen
- Yenier Castañeda, University of Matanzas, Cuba
- Giuseppe Castellucci, University of Rome, Tor Vergata
- Tawunrat Chalothorn, University of Northumbria at Newcastle
- Maryna Chernyshevich, IHS Inc. / IHS Global Belarus
- Arodami Chorianopoulou, Technical University of Crete
- Mark Cieliebak, Zurich University of Applied Sciences
- Philipp Cimiano, University of Bielefeld
- Francisco Couto, University of Lisbon
- Daniel Dahlmeier, SAP
- Hong-Jie Dai, Taipei Medical University
- Alexandre Denis, LORIA/University of Lorraine
- Mona Diab, The George Washington University
- Cicero dos Santos, IBM Research
- Yantao Du, Institute of Computer Science and Technology of Peking University
- Kais Dukes, University of Leeds
- Asif Ekbal, IIT Patna
- Kilian Evang, University of Groningen
- Stefan Evert, FAU Erlangen-Nürnberg
- Richárd Farkas, University of Szeged
- Javi Fernández, University of Alicante

- Lorenzo Ferrone, University of Rome, Tor Vergata
- Oliver Ferschke, UKP Lab, Technische Universität Darmstadt
- Tim Finin, University of Maryland
- Lucie Flekova, UKP Lab, Technische Universität Darmstadt
- Dan Flickinger, Stanford University
- Jennifer Foster, Dublin City University
- Dimitris Galanis, Institute for Language and Speech Processing, Athena Research Center
- Pablo Gamallo, CITIUS, University of Santiago de Compostela
- Björn Gambäck, Norwegian University of Science and Technology
- Marcos Garcia, University of Santiago de Compostela
- Aitor García Pablos, Vicomtech-IK4
- Georgi Georgiev, Ontotext AD
- Swarnendu Ghosh, Jadavpur University
- Daniel Gildea, University of Rochester
- Filip Ginter, University of Turku
- Paulo Gomes, CISUC - University of Coimbra
- Hugo Gonçalo Oliveira, CISUC, University of Coimbra
- Anubhav Gupta, Université de Franche-Comté
- Rohit Gupta, University of Wolverhampton
- Iryna Gurevych, UKP Lab, Technische Universität Darmstadt
- Yoan Gutiérrez, University of Matanzas
- Tobias Günther, Retresco GmbH
- Hussam Hamdan, Aix-Marseille Université
- Lushan Han, University of Maryland
- Viktor Hangya, University of Szeged
- Eva Hasler, University of Edinburgh
- Iris Hendrickx, Center for Language Studies, Radboud University Nijmegen
- Nora Hollenstein, University of Zurich
- Veronique Hoste, Ghent University
- Estevam Hruschka, Federal University of São Carlos
- Pingping Huang, Peking University
- Elias Iosif, Athena Research and Innovation Center
- Angelina Ivanova, University of Oslo
- Martin Jaggi, ETH Zurich
- Arun kumar Jayapal, Trinity College Dublin
- Sergio Jiménez, National University of Colombia
- Salud María Jiménez-Zafra, University of Jaén
- Richard Johansson, University of Gothenburg
- David Jurgens, Sapienza University of Rome
- Magdalena Kacmajor, IBM
- Suwisa Kaewphan, University of Turku

- Rafael - Michael Karampatsis, Athens University of Economics and Business
- Abhay Kashyap, University of Maryland
- Rohit Kate, University of Wisconsin-Milwaukee
- Melinda Katona, University of Szeged
- Svetlana Kiritchenko, National Research Council Canada
- Ioannis Klasinas, Technical University of Crete
- Manfred Klenner, University of Zurich
- Evgeniy Kotelnikov, Vyatka State University of Humanities at Kirov
- Milen Kouylekov, University of Oslo
- Marco Kuhlmann, Linköping University
- Alice Lai, University of Illinois at Urbana-Champaign
- Man Lan, East China Normal University
- Joseph Le Roux, Université Paris Nord
- Els Lefever, LT3, Ghent University
- Maria Liakata, University of Warwick
- Pengfei Liu, The Chinese University of Hong Kong
- Peter Ljunglöf, University of Gothenburg and Chalmers University of Technology
- André Lynum, Norwegian University of Science and Technology
- Nikolaos Malandrakis, Signal Analysis and Interpretation Laboratory (SAIL), USC
- Suresh Manandhar, University of York
- Soumik Mandal, Jadavpur University
- Morgane Marchand, CEA-LIST / CNRS-LIMSI
- Marco Marelli, University of Trento
- Patricio Martinez-Barco, Universidad de Alicante
- André F. T. Martins, Priberam, Instituto de Telecomunicacoes
- Eugenio Martínez-Cámara, University of Jaén
- Sérgio Matos, DETI/IEETA, University of Aveiro, Portugal
- Willem Mattelaer, Katholieke Universiteit Leuven
- Kathy McKeown, Columbia University
- Helen Meng, The Chinese University of Hong Kong
- Todor Mihaylov, Sofia University
- Yasuhide Miura, Research & Technology Group, Fuji Xerox Co., Ltd.
- Saif Mohammad, National Research Council Canada
- Behrang Mohit, Carnegie Mellon University
- Andres Montoyo, University of Alicante
- Jose G. Moreno, Normandie University - GREYC
- Rafael Muñoz-Guillena, University of Alicante
- Preslav Nakov, Qatar Computing Research Institute
- Naveen Nandan, SAP Research & Innovation
- Shrikanth Narayanan, University of Southern California
- Roberto Navigli, Sapienza University of Rome

- Sapna Negi, National University of Ireland, Galway
- Max Nitze, University of Bremen
- Stephan Oepen, Universitetet i Oslo
- Maite Oronoz, University of the Basque Country
- Reynier Ortega Bueno, CERPAMID, Cuba
- Woodley Packard, University of Washington
- Partha Pakray, Norwegian University of Science and Technology
- Thiago Pardo, University of São Paulo
- Parth Pathak, ezDI
- Braja Gopal Patra, Jadavpur University
- John Pavlopoulos, Athens University of Economics and Business
- Ted Pedersen, University of Minnesota, Duluth
- Viktor Pekar, University of Birmingham
- Mohammad Taher Pilehvar, Sapienza University of Rome
- David Pinto, Benemérita Universidad Autónoma de Puebla
- Maria Pontiki, Institute for Language and Speech Processing
- Alexandros Potamianos, National Technical University of Athens
- Sameer Pradhan, Harvard University
- Thomas Proisl, FAU Erlangen-Nürnberg
- Avinesh PVS, IBM India Pvt Ltd, IBM Software Group, Watson
- SV Ramanan, RelAgent Private Lrd
- German Rigau, UPV/EHU
- Miguel Rios, University of Wolverhampton
- Alejandro Riveros, Universidad Nacional de Colombia
- Sara Rosenthal, Columbia University
- Alex Rudnick, Indiana University
- José Saias, Universidade de Evora
- Kim Schouten, Erasmus University Rotterdam
- Clemens Schulze Wettendorf, FAU Erlangen Nürnberg
- Djamé Seddah, Université Paris Sorbonne (Paris IV)
- Nádia Silva, University of São Paulo
- Mario J. Silva, IST/INESC-ID
- Emilio Silva-Schlenker, Universidad Nacional de Colombia, Universidad de los Andes
- Michel Simard, National Research Council Canada
- Vikram Singh, Indian Institute of Technology-Patna
- Noah A. Smith, Carnegie Mellon University
- Josef Steinberger, University of West Bohemia
- Svetlana Stoyanchev, AT&T Labs Research
- Veselin Stoyanov, Facebook
- Md Arafat Sultan, University of Colorado Boulder
- Anders Søgaard, University of Copenhagen

- Aleš Tamchyna, Charles University in Prague, UFAL MFF
- Liling Tan, Universität des Saarlandes
- Duyu Tang, Harbin Institute of Technology
- Cindi Thompson, University of San Francisco
- Zhu Tiantian, East China Normal University
- Zhiqiang Toh, Institute for Infocomm Research
- Lamia Tounsi, Dublin City University
- David Townsend, Montclair State University
- L. Alfonso Urena Lopez, University of Jaén
- Fatih Uzdilli, ZHAW Zurich University of Applied Sciences
- Antal van den Bosch, Radboud University Nijmegen
- Maarten van Gompel, Radboud University Nijmegen
- Cynthia Van Hee, Ghent University
- Kateřina Veselovská, Charles University in Prague
- Akriti Vij, SAP Research & Innovation, Singapore, and Nanyang Technological University, Singapore
- David Vilares, Universidade da Coruña
- Julio Villena-Román, Daedalus, S.A.
- Ngoc Phuoc An Vo, HLT-FBK, Trento
- Joachim Wagner, Centre for Next Generation Localisation, Dublin City University
- Wenting Wang, NA
- Andy Way, Centre for Next Generation Localisation, Dublin City University
- Janyce Wiebe, University of Pittsburgh
- Deniz Yuret, Koç University
- Roberto Zamparelli, Universitá di Trento
- Kalliopi Zervanou, University of Southern California
- Torsten Zesch, Language Technology Lab, University of Duisburg-Essen
- Yaoyun Zhang, University of Texas
- Fangxi Zhang, East China Normal University
- Jiang Zhao, East China Normal University
- Ming Zhou, Microsoft Research Asia
- Xiaodan Zhu, National Research Council Canada

Invited Speakers (jointly for SemEval and *SEM):

- Mark Steedman, University of Edinburgh
- Tim Baldwin, The University of Melbourne

Table of Contents

SemEval-2014 Task 1: Evaluation of Compositional Distributional Semantic Models on Full Sentences through Semantic Relatedness and Textual Entailment

Marco Marelli(1) **Luisa Bentivogli**(2) **Marco Baroni**(1)
Raffaella Bernardi(1) **Stefano Menini**(1,2) **Roberto Zamparelli**(1)
(1) University of Trento, Italy
(2) FBK - Fondazione Bruno Kessler, Trento, Italy
{name.surname}@unitn.it, {bentivo,menini}@fbk.eu

Abstract

This paper presents the task on the evaluation of Compositional Distributional Semantics Models on full sentences organized for the first time within SemEval-2014. Participation was open to systems based on any approach. Systems were presented with pairs of sentences and were evaluated on their ability to predict human judgments on *(i)* semantic relatedness and *(ii)* entailment. The task attracted 21 teams, most of which participated in both subtasks. We received 17 submissions in the relatedness subtask (for a total of 66 runs) and 18 in the entailment subtask (65 runs).

1 Introduction

Distributional Semantic Models (DSMs) approximate the meaning of words with vectors summarizing their patterns of co-occurrence in corpora. Recently, several compositional extensions of DSMs (CDSMs) have been proposed, with the purpose of representing the meaning of phrases and sentences by composing the distributional representations of the words they contain (Baroni and Zamparelli, 2010; Grefenstette and Sadrzadeh, 2011; Mitchell and Lapata, 2010; Socher et al., 2012). Despite the ever increasing interest in the field, the development of adequate benchmarks for CDSMs, especially at the sentence level, is still lagging. Existing data sets, such as those introduced by Mitchell and Lapata (2008) and Grefenstette and Sadrzadeh (2011), are limited to a few hundred instances of very short sentences with a fixed structure. In the last ten years, several large data sets have been developed for various computational semantics tasks, such as Semantic Text Similarity (STS)(Agirre et al., 2012) or Recognizing Textual Entailment (RTE) (Dagan et al., 2006). Working with such data sets, however, requires dealing with issues, such as identifying multiword expressions, recognizing named entities or accessing encyclopedic knowledge, which have little to do with compositionality *per se*. CDSMs should instead be evaluated on data that are challenging for reasons due to semantic compositionality (e.g. context-cued synonymy resolution and other lexical variation phenomena, active/passive and other syntactic alternations, impact of negation at various levels, operator scope, and other effects linked to the functional lexicon). These issues do not occur frequently in, e.g., the STS and RTE data sets.

With these considerations in mind, we developed SICK (Sentences Involving Compositional Knowledge), a data set aimed at filling the void, including a large number of sentence pairs that are rich in the lexical, syntactic and semantic phenomena that CDSMs are expected to account for, but do not require dealing with other aspects of existing sentential data sets that are not within the scope of compositional distributional semantics. Moreover, we distinguished between generic semantic knowledge about general concept categories (such as knowledge that a couple is formed by a bride and a groom) and encyclopedic knowledge about specific instances of concepts (e.g., knowing the fact that the current president of the US is Barack Obama). The SICK data set contains many examples of the former, but none of the latter.

2 The Task

The Task involved two subtasks. (i) *Relatedness*: predicting the degree of semantic similarity between two sentences, and (ii) *Entailment*: detecting the entailment relation holding between them

Proceedings of the 8th International Workshop on Semantic Evaluation (SemEval 2014), pages 1–8,
Dublin, Ireland, August 23-24, 2014.

(see below for the exact definition). Sentence relatedness scores provide a direct way to evaluate CDSMs, insofar as their outputs are able to quantify the degree of semantic similarity between sentences. On the other hand, starting from the assumption that understanding a sentence means knowing when it is true, being able to verify whether an entailment is valid is a crucial challenge for semantic systems.

In the semantic relatedness subtask, given two sentences, systems were required to produce a relatedness score (on a continuous scale) indicating the extent to which the sentences were expressing a related meaning. Table 1 shows examples of sentence pairs with different degrees of semantic relatedness; gold relatedness scores are expressed on a 5-point rating scale.

In the entailment subtask, given two sentences A and B, systems had to determine whether the meaning of B was entailed by A. In particular, systems were required to assign to each pair either the ENTAILMENT label (when A entails B, viz., B cannot be false when A is true), the CONTRADICTION label (when A contradicted B, viz. B is false whenever A is true), or the NEUTRAL label (when the truth of B could not be determined on the basis of A). Table 2 shows examples of sentence pairs holding different entailment relations.

Participants were invited to submit up to five system runs for one or both subtasks. Developers of CDSMs were especially encouraged to participate, but developers of other systems that could tackle sentence relatedness or entailment tasks were also welcome. Besides being of intrinsic interest, the latter systems' performance will serve to situate CDSM performance within the broader landscape of computational semantics.

3 The SICK Data Set

The SICK data set, consisting of about 10,000 English sentence pairs annotated for relatedness in meaning and entailment, was used to evaluate the systems participating in the task. The data set creation methodology is outlined in the following subsections, while all the details about data generation and annotation, quality control, and inter-annotator agreement can be found in Marelli et al. (2014).

3.1 Data Set Creation

SICK was built starting from two existing data sets: the 8K ImageFlickr data set[1] and the SemEval-2012 STS MSR-Video Descriptions data set.[2] The 8K ImageFlickr dataset is a dataset of images, where each image is associated with five descriptions. To derive SICK sentence pairs we randomly chose 750 images and we sampled two descriptions from each of them. The SemEval-2012 STS MSR-Video Descriptions data set is a collection of sentence pairs sampled from the short video snippets which compose the Microsoft Research Video Description Corpus. A subset of 750 sentence pairs were randomly chosen from this data set to be used in SICK.

In order to generate SICK data from the 1,500 sentence pairs taken from the source data sets, a 3-step process was applied to each sentence composing the pair, namely *(i) normalization*, *(ii) expansion* and *(iii) pairing*. Table 3 presents an example of the output of each step in the process.

The *normalization* step was carried out on the original sentences (S0) to exclude or simplify instances that contained lexical, syntactic or semantic phenomena (e.g., named entities, dates, numbers, multiword expressions) that CDSMs are currently not expected to account for.

The *expansion* step was applied to each of the normalized sentences (S1) in order to create up to three new sentences with specific characteristics suitable to CDSM evaluation. In this step syntactic and lexical transformations with predictable effects were applied to each normalized sentence, in order to obtain *(i)* a sentence with a similar meaning (S2), *(ii)* a sentence with a logically contradictory or at least highly contrasting meaning (S3), and *(iii)* a sentence that contains most of the same lexical items, but has a different meaning (S4) (this last step was carried out only where it could yield a meaningful sentence; as a result, not all normalized sentences have an (S4) expansion).

Finally, in the *pairing* step each normalized sentence in the pair was combined with all the sentences resulting from the expansion phase and with the other normalized sentence in the pair. Considering the example in Table 3, *S1a* and *S1b* were paired. Then, *S1a* and *S1b* were each combined with *S2a*, *S2b*,*S3a*, *S3b*, *S4a*, and *S4b*, lead-

[1] http://nlp.cs.illinois.edu/HockenmaierGroup/data.html

[2] http://www.cs.york.ac.uk/semeval-2012/task6/index.php?id=data

Relatedness score	Example
1.6	A: "*A man is jumping into an empty pool*" B: "*There is no biker jumping in the air*"
2.9	A: "*Two children are lying in the snow and are making snow angels*" B: "*Two angels are making snow on the lying children*"
3.6	A: "*The young boys are playing outdoors and the man is smiling nearby*" B: "*There is no boy playing outdoors and there is no man smiling*"
4.9	A: "*A person in a black jacket is doing tricks on a motorbike*" B: "*A man in a black jacket is doing tricks on a motorbike*"

Table 1: Examples of sentence pairs with their gold relatedness scores (on a 5-point rating scale).

Entailment label	Example
ENTAILMENT	A: "*Two teams are competing in a football match*" B: "*Two groups of people are playing football*"
CONTRADICTION	A: "*The brown horse is near a red barrel at the rodeo*" B: "*The brown horse is far from a red barrel at the rodeo*"
NEUTRAL	A: "*A man in a black jacket is doing tricks on a motorbike*" B: "*A person is riding the bicycle on one wheel*"

Table 2: Examples of sentence pairs with their gold entailment labels.

ing to a total of 13 different sentence pairs.

Furthermore, a number of pairs composed of completely unrelated sentences were added to the data set by randomly taking two sentences from two different pairs.

The result is a set of about 10,000 new sentence pairs, in which each sentence is contrasted with either a (near) paraphrase, a contradictory or strongly contrasting statement, another sentence with very high lexical overlap but different meaning, or a completely unrelated sentence. The rationale behind this approach was that of building a data set which encouraged the use of a compositional semantics step in understanding when two sentences have close meanings or entail each other, hindering methods based on individual lexical items, on the syntactic complexity of the two sentences or on pure world knowledge.

3.2 Relatedness and Entailment Annotation

Each pair in the SICK dataset was annotated to mark *(i)* the degree to which the two sentence meanings are related (on a 5-point scale), and *(ii)* whether one entails or contradicts the other (considering both directions). The ratings were collected through a large crowdsourcing study, where each pair was evaluated by 10 different subjects, and the order of presentation of the sentences was counterbalanced (i.e., 5 judgments were collected for each presentation order). Swapping the order of the sentences within each pair served a two-fold purpose: (i) evaluating the entailment relation in both directions and (ii) controlling possible bias due to priming effects in the relatedness task. Once all the annotations were collected, the relatedness gold score was computed for each pair as the average of the ten ratings assigned by participants, whereas a majority vote scheme was adopted for the entailment gold labels.

3.3 Data Set Statistics

For the purpose of the task, the data set was randomly split into training and test set (50% and 50%), ensuring that each relatedness range and entailment category was equally represented in both sets. Table 4 shows the distribution of sentence pairs considering the combination of relatedness ranges and entailment labels. The "total" column

Original pair	
S0a: *A sea turtle is hunting for fish*	**S0b:** *The turtle followed the fish*
Normalized pair	
S1a: *A sea turtle is hunting for fish*	**S1b:** *The turtle is following the fish*
Expanded pairs	
S2a: *A sea turtle is hunting for food*	**S2b:** *The turtle is following the red fish*
S3a: *A sea turtle is not hunting for fish*	**S3b:** *The turtle isn't following the fish*
S4a: *A fish is hunting for a turtle in the sea*	**S4b:** *The fish is following the turtle*

Table 3: Data set creation process.

indicates the total number of pairs in each range of relatedness, while the "total" row contains the total number of pairs in each entailment class.

SICK Training Set				
relatedness	CONTRADICT	ENTAIL	NEUTRAL	TOTAL
1-2 range	0 (0%)	0 (0%)	471 (10%)	471
2-3 range	59 (1%)	2 (0%)	638 (13%)	699
3-4 range	498 (10%)	71 (1%)	1344 (27%)	1913
4-5 range	155 (3%)	1344 (27%)	352 (7%)	1851
TOTAL	712	1417	2805	4934
SICK Test Set				
relatedness	CONTRADICT	ENTAIL	NEUTRAL	TOTAL
1-2 range	0 (0%)	1 (0%)	451 (9%)	452
2-3 range	59 (1%)	0 (0%)	615(13%)	674
3-4 range	496 (10%)	65 (1%)	1398 (28%)	1959
4-5 range	157 (3%)	1338 (27%)	326 (7%)	1821
TOTAL	712	1404	2790	4906

Table 4: Distribution of sentence pairs across the Training and Test Sets.

4 Evaluation Metrics and Baselines

Both subtasks were evaluated using standard metrics. In particular, the results on entailment were evaluated using accuracy, whereas the outputs on relatedness were evaluated using Pearson correlation, Spearman correlation, and Mean Squared Error (MSE). Pearson correlation was chosen as the official measure to rank the participating systems.

Table 5 presents the performance of 4 baselines. The Majority baseline always assigns the most common label in the training data (NEUTRAL), whereas the Probability baseline assigns labels randomly according to their relative frequency in the training set. The Overlap baseline measures word overlap, again with parameters (number of stop words and ENTAILMENT/NEUTRAL/CONTRADICTION thresholds) estimated on the training part of the data.

Baseline	Relatedness	Entailment
Chance	0	33.3%
Majority	NA	56.7%
Probability	NA	41.8%
Overlap	0.63	56.2%

Table 5: Performance of baselines. Figure of merit is Pearson correlation for relatedness and accuracy for entailment. NA = *Not Applicable*

5 Submitted Runs and Results

Overall, 21 teams participated in the task. Participants were allowed to submit up to 5 runs for each subtask and had to choose the primary run to be included in the comparative evaluation. We received 17 submissions to the relatedness subtask (for a total of 66 runs) and 18 for the entailment subtask (65 runs).

We asked participants to pre-specify a primary run to encourage commitment to a theoretically-motivated approach, rather than post-hoc performance-based assessment. Interestingly, some participants used the non-primary runs to explore the performance one could reach by exploiting weaknesses in the data that are not likely to hold in future tasks of the same kind (for instance, run 3 submitted by The Meaning Factory exploited sentence ID ordering information, but it was not presented as a primary run). Participants could also use non-primary runs to test smart baselines. In the relatedness subtask six non-primary runs slightly outperformed the official winning primary entry,[3] while in the entailment task all ECNU's runs but run 4 were better than ECNU's primary run. Interestingly, the differences between the ECNU's runs were

[3]They were: The_Meaning_Factory's run3 (Pearson 0.84170) ECNU's runs2 (0.83893) run5 (0.83500) and StanfordNLP's run4 (0.83462) and run2 (0.83103).

due to the learning methods used.

We present the results achieved by primary runs against the Entailment and Relatedness subtasks in Table 6 and Table 7, respectively.[4] We witnessed a very close finish in both subtasks, with 4 more systems within 3 percentage points of the winner in both cases. 4 of these 5 top systems were the same across the two subtasks. Most systems performed well above the best baselines from Table 5.

The overall performance pattern suggests that, owing perhaps to the more controlled nature of the sentences, as well as to the purely linguistic nature of the challenges it presents, SICK entailment is "easier" than RTE. Considering the first five RTE challenges (Bentivogli et al., 2009), the median values ranged from 56.20% to 61.75%, whereas the average values ranged from 56.45% to 61.97%. The entailment scores obtained on the SICK data set are considerably higher, being 77.06% for the median system and 75.36% for the average system. On the other hand, the relatedness task is more challenging than the one run on MSRvid (one of our data sources) at STS 2012, where the top Pearson correlation was 0.88 (Agirre et al., 2012).

ID	Compose	ACCURACY
Illinois-LH_run1	P/S	84.6
ECNU_run1	S	83.6
UNAL-NLP_run1		83.1
SemantiKLUE_run1		82.3
The_Meaning_Factory_run1	S	81.6
CECL_ALL_run1		80.0
BUAP_run1	P	79.7
UoW_run1		78.5
Uedinburgh_run1	S	77.1
UIO-Lien_run1		77.0
FBK-TR_run3	P	75.4
StanfordNLP_run5	S	74.5
UTexas_run1	P/S	73.2
Yamraj_run1		70.7
asjai_run5	S	69.8
haLF_run2	S	69.4
RTM-DCU_run1		67.2
UANLPCourse_run2	S	48.7

Table 6: Primary run results for the entailment subtask. The table also shows whether a system exploits composition information at either the phrase (P) or sentence (S) level.

6 Approaches

A summary of the approaches used by the systems to address the task is presented in Table 8. In the table, systems in bold are those for which the authors submitted a paper (Ferrone and Zanzotto, 2014; Bjerva et al., 2014; Beltagy et al., 2014; Lai and Hockenmaier, 2014; Alves et al., 2014; León et al., 2014; Bestgen, 2014; Zhao et al., 2014; Vo et al., 2014; Biçici and Way, 2014; Lien and Kouylekov, 2014; Jimenez et al., 2014; Proisl and Evert, 2014; Gupta et al., 2014). For the others, we used the brief description sent with the system's results, double-checking the information with the authors. In the table, "E" and "R" refer to the entailment and relatedness task respectively, and "B" to both.

Almost all systems combine several kinds of features. To highlight the role played by composition, we draw a distinction between compositional and non-compositional features, and divide the former into 'fully compositional' (systems that compositionally computed the meaning of the full sentences, though not necessarily by assigning meanings to intermediate syntactic constituents) and 'partially compositional' (systems that stop the composition at the level of phrases). As the table shows, thirteen systems used composition in at least one of the tasks; ten used composition for full sentences and six for phrases, only. The best systems are among these thirteen systems.

Let us focus on such compositional methods. Concerning the relatedness task, the fine-grained analyses reported for several systems (Illinois-LH, The Meaning Factory and ECNU) shows that purely compositional systems currently reach performance above 0.7 r. In particular, ECNU's compositional feature gives 0.75 r, The Meaning Factory's logic-based composition model 0.73 r, and Illinois-LH compositional features combined with Word Overlap 0.75 r. While competitive, these scores are lower than the one of the best

[4] ITTK's primary run could not be evaluated due to technical problems with the submission. The best ITTK's non-primary run scored 78,2% accuracy in the entailment task and 0.76 r in the relatedness task.

ID	Compose	r	ρ	MSE
ECNU_run1	S	0.828	0.769	0.325
StanfordNLP_run5	S	0.827	0.756	0.323
The_Meaning_Factory_run1	S	0.827	0.772	0.322
UNAL-NLP_run1		0.804	0.746	0.359
Illinois-LH_run1	P/S	0.799	0.754	0.369
CECL_ALL_run1		0.780	0.732	0.398
SemantiKLUE_run1		0.780	0.736	0.403
RTM-DCU_run1		0.764	0.688	0.429
UTexas_run1	P/S	0.714	0.674	0.499
UoW_run1		0.711	0.679	0.511
FBK-TR_run3	P	0.709	0.644	0.591
BUAP_run1	P	0.697	0.645	0.528
UANLPCourse_run2	S	0.693	0.603	0.542
UQeResearch_run1		0.642	0.626	0.822
ASAP_run1	P	0.628	0.597	0.662
Yamraj_run1		0.535	0.536	2.665
asjai_run5	S	0.479	0.461	1.104

Table 7: Primary run results for the relatedness subtask (r for Pearson and ρ for Spearman correlation). The table also shows whether a system exploits composition information at either the phrase (P) or sentence (S) level.

purely non-compositional system (UNAL-NLP) which reaches the 4th position (0.80 r UNAL-NLP vs. 0.82 r obtained by the best system). UNAL-NLP however exploits an ad-hoc "negation" feature discussed below.

In the entailment task, the best non-compositional model (again UNAL-NLP) reaches the 3rd position, within close reach of the best system (83% UNAL-NLP vs. 84.5% obtained by the best system). Again, purely compositional models have lower performance. haLF CDSM reaches 69.42% accuracy, Illinois-LH Word Overlap combined with a compositional feature reaches 71.8%. The fine-grained analysis reported by Illinois-LH (Lai and Hockenmaier, 2014) shows that a full compositional system (based on point-wise multiplication) fails to capture contradiction. It is better than partial phrase-based compositional models in recognizing entailment pairs, but worse than them on recognizing neutral pairs.

Given our more general interest in the distributional approaches, in Table 8 we also classify the different DSMs used as 'Vector Space Models', 'Topic Models' and 'Neural Language Models'. Due to the impact shown by learning methods (see ECNU's results), we also report the different learning approaches used.

Several participating systems deliberately exploit *ad-hoc* features that, while not helping a true understanding of sentence meaning, exploit some systematic characteristics of SICK that should be controlled for in future releases of the data set. In particular, the Textual Entailment subtask has been shown to rely too much on negative words and antonyms. The Illinois-LH team reports that, just by checking the presence of negative words (the Negation Feature in the table), one can detect 86.4% of the contradiction pairs, and by combining Word Overlap and antonyms one can detect 83.6% of neutral pairs and 82.6% of entailment pairs. This approach, however, is obviously very brittle (it would not have been successful, for instance, if negation had been optionally combined with word-rearranging in the creation of S4 sentences, see Section 3.1 above).

Finally, Table 8 reports about the use of external resources in the task. One of the reasons we created SICK was to have a compositional semantics benchmark that would not require too many external tools and resources (e.g., named-entity recognizers, gazetteers, ontologies). By looking at what the participants chose to use, we think we succeeded, as only standard NLP pre-processing tools (tokenizers, PoS taggers and parsers) and relatively few knowledge resources (mostly, WordNet and paraphrase corpora) were used.

7 Conclusion

We presented the results of the first task on the evaluation of compositional distributional semantic models and other semantic systems on full sentences, organized within SemEval-2014. Two subtasks were offered: (i) predicting the degree of relatedness between two sentences, and (ii) detecting the entailment relation holding between them. The task has raised noticeable attention in the community: 17 and 18 submissions for the relatedness and entailment subtasks, respectively, for a total of 21 participating teams. Participation was not limited to compositional models but the majority of systems (13/21) used composition in at least one of the subtasks. Moreover, the top-ranking systems in both tasks use compositional features. However, it must be noted that all systems also ex-

Participant ID	Non composition features									Comp features		Learning Methods							External Resources				
	Vector Semantics Model	Topic Model	Neural Language Model	Denotational Model	Word Overlap	Word Similarity	Syntactic Features	Sentence difference	Negation Features	Sentence Composition	Phrase composition	SVM and Kernel methods	K-Nearest Neighbours	Classifier Combination	Random Forest	FoL/Probabilistic FoL	Curriculum based learning	Other	WordNet	Paraphrases DB	Other Corpora	ImageFlicker	STS MSR-Video Description
ASAP	R	R				R	R	R	R		R			R					R				
ASJAI	B		B	B	B	B	B	B		B		E		B				R		B			
BUAP	B		B			B	B		E		B	E							B				
UEdinburgh	B				B		B		B	B		E	R								B		
CECL	B				B	B		B										B			B		
ECNU	B		B		B	B	B	B		B		B	B	B	B				B		B		
FBK-TR		R			R	R	E	B	E	E	B	R		E					R		R		E
haLF	E					E				E		E											
IITK	B				B	B	B	B	B		B	B							B				
Illinois-LH	B			B	B	B	B		B	B	B							B	B			B	B
RTM-DCU	B						B					B			B						B		
SemantiKLUE	B				B	B	B		B			B							B		B		
StandfordNLP	B		B		R	R			R	B							E						
The Meaning Factory	R		R	R	R		R	R		B		E			R	E			B	B	R		
UANLPCourse	B				B	B				B		B											
UIO-Lien									E										E				
UNAL-NLP						B	B		B									B	R	B	B		
UoW				B	B		B		B			B								B			
UQeRsearch					R	R	R	R	R									R	R				
UTexas	B			B					B	B	B					B					B		
Yamarj	B				B	B						B											

Table 8: Summary of the main characteristics of the participating systems on R(elatedness), E(ntailment) or B(oth)

ploit non-compositional features and most of them use external resources, especially WordNet. Almost all the participating systems outperformed the proposed baselines in both tasks. Further analyses carried out by some participants in the task show that purely compositional approaches reach accuracy above 70% in entailment and 0.70 r for relatedness. These scores are comparable with the average results obtained in the task.

Acknowledgments

We thank the creators of the ImageFlickr, MSR-Video, and SemEval-2012 STS data sets for granting us permission to use their data for the task. The University of Trento authors were supported by ERC 2011 Starting Independent Research Grant n. 283554 (COMPOSES).

References

Eneko Agirre, Daniel Cer, Mona Diab, and Aitor Gonzalez-Agirre. 2012. Semeval-2012 task 6: A pilot on semantic textual similarity. In *Proceedings of the Sixth International Workshop on Semantic Evaluation (SemEval 2012)*, volume 2.

Ana O. Alves, Adirana Ferrugento, Mariana Lorenço, and Filipe Rodrigues. 2014. ASAP: Automatica semantic alignment for phrases. In *Proceedings of SemEval 2014: International Workshop on Semantic Evaluation.*

Marco Baroni and Roberto Zamparelli. 2010. Nouns are vectors, adjectives are matrices: Representing adjective-noun constructions in semantic space. In *Proceedings of EMNLP*, pages 1183–1193, Boston, MA.

Islam Beltagy, Stephen Roller, Gemma Boleda, Katrin Erk, and Raymon J. Mooney. 2014. UTexas: Natural language semantics using distributional semantics and probablisitc logic. In *Proceedings of SemEval 2014: International Workshop on Semantic Evaluation.*

Luisa Bentivogli, Ido Dagan, Hoa T. Dang, Danilo Giampiccolo, and Bernardo Magnini. 2009. The fifth PASCAL recognizing textual entailment challenge. In *The Text Analysis Conference (TAC 2009)*.

Yves Bestgen. 2014. CECL: a new baseline and a non-compositional approach for the Sick benchmark. In *Proceedings of SemEval 2014: International Workshop on Semantic Evaluation*.

Ergun Biçici and Andy Way. 2014. RTM-DCU: Referential translation machines for semantic similarity. In *Proceedings of SemEval 2014: International Workshop on Semantic Evaluation*.

Johannes Bjerva, Johan Bos, Rob van der Goot, and Malvina Nissim. 2014. The Meaning Factory: Formal Semantics for Recognizing Textual Entailment and Determining Semantic Similarity. In *Proceedings of SemEval 2014: International Workshop on Semantic Evaluation*.

Ido Dagan, Oren Glickman, and Bernardo Magnini. 2006. The PASCAL recognising textual entailment challenge. In *Machine learning challenges. Evaluating predictive uncertainty, visual object classification, and recognising textual entailment*, pages 177–190. Springer.

Lorenzo Ferrone and Fabio Massimo Zanzotto. 2014. haLF:comparing a pure CDSM approach and a standard ML system for RTE. In *Proceedings of SemEval 2014: International Workshop on Semantic Evaluation*.

Edward Grefenstette and Mehrnoosh Sadrzadeh. 2011. Experimental support for a categorical compositional distributional model of meaning. In *Proceedings of EMNLP*, pages 1394–1404, Edinburgh, UK.

Rohit Gupta, Ismail El Maarouf Hannah Bechara, and Costantin Orasăn. 2014. UoW: NLP techniques developed at the University of Wolverhampton for Semantic Similarity and Textual Entailment. In *Proceedings of SemEval 2014: International Workshop on Semantic Evaluation*.

Sergio Jimenez, George Duenas, Julia Baquero, and Alexander Gelbukh. 2014. UNAL-NLP: Combining soft cardinality features for semantic textual similarity, relatedness and entailment. In *Proceedings of SemEval 2014: International Workshop on Semantic Evaluation*.

Alice Lai and Julia Hockenmaier. 2014. Illinois-lh: A denotational and distributional approach to semantics. In *Proceedings of SemEval 2014: International Workshop on Semantic Evaluation*.

Saúl León, Darnes Vilarino, David Pinto, Mireya Tovar, and Beatrice Beltrán. 2014. BUAP:evaluating compositional distributional semantic models on full sentences through semantic relatedness and textual entailment. In *Proceedings of SemEval 2014: International Workshop on Semantic Evaluation*.

Elisabeth Lien and Milen Kouylekov. 2014. UIO-Lien: Entailment recognition using minimal recursion semantics. In *Proceedings of SemEval 2014: International Workshop on Semantic Evaluation*.

Marco Marelli, Stefano Menini, Marco Baroni, Luisa Bentivogli, Raffaella Bernardi, and Roberto Zamparelli. 2014. A SICK cure for the evaluation of compositional distributional semantic models. In *Proceedings of LREC*, Reykjavik.

Jeff Mitchell and Mirella Lapata. 2008. Vector-based models of semantic composition. In *Proceedings of ACL*, pages 236–244, Columbus, OH.

Jeff Mitchell and Mirella Lapata. 2010. Composition in distributional models of semantics. *Cognitive Science*, 34(8):1388–1429.

Thomas Proisl and Stefan Evert. 2014. SemantiKLUE: Robust semantic similarity at multiple levels using maximum weight matching. In *Proceedings of SemEval 2014: International Workshop on Semantic Evaluation*.

Richard Socher, Brody Huval, Christopher Manning, and Andrew Ng. 2012. Semantic compositionality through recursive matrix-vector spaces. In *Proceedings of EMNLP*, pages 1201–1211, Jeju Island, Korea.

An N. P. Vo, Octavian Popescu, and Tommaso Caselli. 2014. FBK-TR: SVM for Semantic Relatedness and Corpus Patterns for RTE. In *Proceedings of SemEval 2014: International Workshop on Semantic Evaluation*.

Jiang Zhao, Tian Tian Zhu, and Man Lan. 2014. ECNU: One Stone Two Birds: Ensemble of Heterogenous Measures for Semantic Relatedness and Textual Entailment. In *Proceedings of SemEval 2014: International Workshop on Semantic Evaluation*.

SemEval-2014 Task 2: Grammar Induction for Spoken Dialogue Systems

Ioannis Klasinas[1], **Elias Iosif**[2,4], **Katerina Louka**[3], **Alexandros Potamianos**[2,4]
[1] School of ECE, Technical University of Crete, Chania 73100, Greece
[2] School of ECE, National Technical University of Athens, Zografou 15780, Greece
[3] Voiceweb S.A., Athens 15124, Greece
[4] Athena Research Center, Marousi 15125, Greece
iklasinas@isc.tuc.gr,{iosife,potam}@telecom.tuc.gr,klouka@voiceweb.eu

Abstract

In this paper we present the SemEval-2014 Task 2 on spoken dialogue grammar induction. The task is to classify a lexical fragment to the appropriate semantic category (grammar rule) in order to construct a grammar for spoken dialogue systems. We describe four subtasks covering two languages, English and Greek, and three speech application domains, travel reservation, tourism and finance. The classification results are compared against the groundtruth. Weighted and unweighted precision, recall and f-measure are reported. Three sites participated in the task with five systems, employing a variety of features and in some cases using external resources for training. The submissions manage to significantly beat the baseline, achieving a f-measure of 0.69 in comparison to 0.56 for the baseline, averaged across all subtasks.

1 Introduction

This task aims to foster the application of computational models of lexical semantics to the field of spoken dialogue systems (SDS) for the problem of grammar induction. Grammars constitute a vital component of SDS representing the semantics of the domain of interest and allowing the system to correctly respond to a user's utterance.

The task has been developed in tight collaboration between the research community and commercial SDS grammar developers, under the auspices of the EU-IST PortDial project[1]. Among the project aims is to help automate the grammar development and localization process. Unlike previous approaches (Wang and Acero, 2006; Cramer, 2007) that have focused on full automation, PortDial adopts a human-in-the-loop approach were a developer bootstraps each grammar rule or request type with a few examples (use cases) and then machine learning algorithms are used to propose grammar rule enhancements to the developer. The enhancements are post-edited by the developer and new grammar rule suggestions are proposed by the system, in an iterative fashion until a grammar of sufficient quality is achieved. In this task, we focus on a snapshot of this process, where a portion of the grammar is already induced and post-edited by the developer and new candidate fragments are rolling in order to be classified to an existing rule (or rejected). The goal is to develop machine learning algorithms for classifying candidate lexical fragments to the correct grammar rule (semantic category). The task is equally relevant for both finite-state machine and statistical grammar induction.

In this task the semantic hierarchy of SDS grammars has two layers, namely, low- and high-level. Low-level rules are similar to gazetteers referring to terminal concepts that can be as represented as sets of lexical entries. For example, the concept of city name can be represented as <CITY> = ("London", "Paris", ...). High-level rules are defined on top of low-level rules, while they can be lexicalized as textual fragments (or chunks), e.g., <TOCITY> = ("fly to <CITY>", ...). Using the above examples the sentence "I want to fly to Paris" will be first parsed as "I want to fly to <CITY>" and finally as "I want to <TOCITY>".

In this task, we focus exclusively on high-level rule induction, assuming that the low-level rules are known. The problem of fragment extraction and selection is simplified by investigating the

[1]http://www.portdial.eu/

Proceedings of the 8th International Workshop on Semantic Evaluation (SemEval 2014), pages 9–16,
Dublin, Ireland, August 23-24, 2014.

binary classification of (already extracted) fragments into valid and non-valid. The task boils down mainly to a semantic similarity estimation problem for the assignment of valid fragments into high-level rules.

2 Prior Work

The manual development of grammars is a time-consuming and tedious process that requires human expertise, posing an obstacle to the rapid porting of SDS to new domains and languages. A semantically coherent workflow for SDS grammar development starts from the definition of low-level rules and proceeds to high-level ones. This process is also valid for the case of induction algorithms. Automatic or machine-aided grammar creation for spoken dialogue systems can be broadly divided in two categories (Wang and Acero, 2006): knowledge-based (or top-down) and data-driven (or bottom-up) approaches.

Knowledge-based approaches rely on the manual or semi-automatic development of domain-specific grammars. They start from the domain ontology (or taxonomy), often in the form of semantic frames. First, terminal concepts in the ontology (that correspond to low-level grammar rules) get populated with values, e.g., <CITY>, and then high-level concepts (that correspond to high-level grammar rules) get lexicalized creating grammar fragments. Finally, phrase headers and trailers are added to create full sentences. The resulting grammars often suffer from limited coverage (poor recall). In order to improve coverage, regular expressions and word/phrase order permutations are used, however at the cost of over-generalization (poor precision). Moreover, knowledge-based grammars are costly to create and maintain, as they require domain and engineering expertise, and they are not easily portable to new domains. This led to the development of grammar authoring tools that aim at facilitating the creation and adaptation of grammars. SGStudio (Semantic Grammar Studio), (Wang and Acero, 2006), for example, enables 1) example-based grammar learning, 2) grammar controls, i.e., building blocks and operators for building more complex grammar fragments (regular expressions, lists of concepts), and 3) configurable grammar structures, allowing for domain-adaptation and word-spotting grammars. The Grammatical Framework Resource Grammar Library (GFRGL) (Ranta, 2004) enables the creation of multilingual grammars adopting an abstraction formalism, which aims to hide the linguistic details (e.g., morphology) from the grammar developer.

Data-driven approaches rely solely on corpora (bottom-up) of transcribed utterances (Meng and Siu, 2002; Pargellis et al., 2004). The induction of low-level rules consists of two steps dealing with the 1) identification of terms, and 2) assignment of terms into rules. Standard tokenization techniques can be used for the first step, however, different approaches are required for the case of multiword terms, e.g., "New York". In such cases, gazetteer lookup and named entity recognition can be employed (if the respective resources and tools are available), as well as corpus-based collocation metrics (Frantzi and Ananiadou, 1997). Typically, the identified terms are assigned into low-level rules via clustering algorithms operating over a feature space that is built according to the term semantic similarity. The distributional hypothesis of meaning (Harris, 1954) is a widely-used approach for estimating term similarity. A comparative study of similarity metrics for the induction of SDS low-level rules is presented in (Pargellis et al., 2004), while the combination of metrics was investigated in (Iosif et al., 2006). Different clustering algorithms have been applied including hard- (Meng and Siu, 2002) and soft-decision (Iosif and Potamianos, 2007) agglomerative clustering.

High-level rule induction is a less researched area that consists of two main sub-problems: 1) the extraction and selection of candidate fragments from a corpus, and 2) assignment of terms into rules. Regarding the first sub-problem, consider the fragments "I want to depart from <CITY> on" and "depart from <CITY>" for the air travel domain. Both express the meaning of departure city, however, the (semantics of the) latter fragment are more concise and generalize better. The application of syntactic parsers for segment extraction is not straightforward since the output is a full parse tree. Moreover, such parsers are typically trained over annotated corpora of formal language usage, while the SDS corpora often are ungrammatical due to spontaneous speech. There are few statistical parsing algorithms that rely only on plain lexical features (Ponvert et al., 2011; Bisk and Hockenmaier, 2012) however, as other algorithms, one needs to decide where to prune the parse tree. In (Georgiladakis et al., 2014), the explicit extraction and selection of fragments is investigated following an example-driven approach where few rule seeds are provided by the grammar developer. The second sub-problem of high-level rule induction deals with the formulation of rules using the selected fragments. Each rule is meant to consist of semantically similar fragments. For this purpose, clustering algorithms can be employed exploiting the semantic similarity between fragments as features. This is a challenging problem since the fragments are multi-word structures whose overall meaning is composed according to semantics of the individual constituents. Recently, several models have been proposed regarding phrase (Mitchell and Lapata, 2010) and sentence similarity (Agirre et al., 2012), while an approach towards addressing the issue of semantic compositionality is presented in (Milajevs and Purver, 2014).

The main drawback of data-driven approaches is the problem of data sparseness, which may affect the coverage of the grammar. A popular solution to the data sparseness bottleneck is to harvest in-domain data from the web. Recently, this has been an active research area both for SDS systems and language modeling in general. Data harvesting is performed in two steps: (i) query formulation, and (ii) selection of relevant documents or sentences (Klasinas et al., 2013). Posing the appropriate queries is important both for obtaining in-domain and linguistically diverse sentences. In (Sethy et al., 2007), an in-domain language model was used to identify the most appropriate n-grams to use as web queries. An in-domain language model was used in (Klasinas et al., 2013) for the selection of relevant sentences. A more sophisticated query formulation was proposed in (Sarikaya, 2008), where from each in-domain utterance a set of queries of varying length and complexity was generated. These approaches assume the availability of in-domain data (even if limited) for the successful formulation of queries; this dependency is also not eliminated when using a mildly lexicalized domain ontology to formulate the queries, as in (Misu and Kawahara, 2006). Selecting the most relevant sentences that get returned from web queries is typically done using statistical similarity metrics between in domain data and retrieved documents, for example the BLEU metric (Papineni et al., 2002) of n-gram similarity in (Sarikaya, 2008) and a metric of relative entropy (Kullback-Leibler) in (Sethy et al., 2007). In cases where in-domain data is not available, cf. (Misu and Kawahara, 2006), heuristics (pronouns, sentence length, wh-questions) and matches with out-of-domain language models can be used to identify sentences for training SDS grammars. In (Sarikaya, 2008), the produced grammar fragments are also parsed and attached to the domain ontology. Harvesting web data can produce high-quality grammars while requiring up to 10 times less in-domain data (Sarikaya, 2008).

Further, data-driven approaches induce syntactic grammars but do not learn their corresponding meanings, for this purpose an additional step is required of parsing the grammar fragments and attaching them to the domain ontology (Sarikaya, 2008). Also, in many cases it was observed that the fully automated bottom-up paradigm results to grammars of moderate quality (Wang and Acero, 2006), especially on corpora containing longer sentences and more lexical variety (Cramer, 2007). Finally, algorithms focusing on crosslingual grammar induction, like CLIoS (Kuhn, 2004), are often even more resource-intensive, as they require training corpora of parallel text and sometimes also a grammar for one of the languages. Grammar quality can be improved by introducing a human in the loop of grammar induction (Portdial, 2014a); an expert that validates the automatically created results (Meng and Siu, 2002).

3 Task Description

Next we describe in detail the candidate grammar fragment classification SemEval task. This task is part of a grammar rule induction scenario for high-level rules. The evaluation focuses in spoken dialogue system grammars for multiple domains and languages.

3.1 Task Design

The goal of the task is to classify a number fragment to the rules available in the grammar. For each grammar we provide a training and development set, i.e., a set of rules with the associated fragments and the test set which is composed of plain fragments. An excerpt of the train set for the rule "<TOCITY>" is "ARRIVE AT <CITY>, ARRIVES AT <CITY>, GOING TO <CITY>" and of the test set "GOING INTO <CITY>, AR-

RIVES INTO <CITY>".

In preliminary experiments during the task design we noticed that if the test set consists of valid fragments only, good classification performance is achieved, even when using the naive baseline system described later in this paper. To make the task more realistic we have included a set of *"junk"* fragments not corresponding to any specific rule. Junk fragments were added both in the train set where they are annotated as such and in the test set. For this task we have artificially created the junk fragments by removing or adding words from legitimate fragments. Example junk fragments used are "HOLD AT AT <TIME> TRY" and "ANY CHOICE EXCEPT <AIRLINE> OR", the first one having a repetition of the word "AT" while the second one should include one more time the concept "<AIRLINE>" in the end to be meaningful.

Junk fragments help better model a real-world scenario, where the candidate fragments will include irrelevant examples too. For example, if web corpora are used to extract the candidate fragments grammatical mistakes and out-of-domain sentences might appear. Similarly, if the transcriptions from a deployed SDS system are used for grammar induction, transcription errors might introduce noise (Bechet et al., 2014).

Junk fragments account for roughly 5% of the train test and 15% of the test set. The discrepancy between train and test set ratios is due to a conscious effort to model realistic train/test conditions, where train data is manually processed and does not include errors, while candidate fragments are typically more noisy.

3.2 Datasets

We have provided four datasets, travel English, travel Greek, tourism English and finance English. The travel domain grammar covers flight, car and hotel reservation utterances. The tourism domain covers touristic information including accommodation, restaurants and movies. The finance domain covers utterances of a bank client asking questions about his bank account as well as reporting problems. In Table 1 are presented typical examples of fragments for every subtask.

All grammars have been manually constructed by a grammar developer. For the three English grammars, a small corpus (between 500 and 2000 sentences) was initially available. The grammar developer first identified terminal concepts, which correspond to low-level rules. Typical examples include city names for the travel domain, restaurant names for the tourism domain and credit card names in the finance domain. After covering all low-level rules the grammar developer proceeded to identify high-level rules present in the corpus, like the departure city in the travel domain, or the user request type for a credit card. The grammar developer was instructed to identify all rules present in the corpus, but also spend some effort to include rules not appearing in the corpus so that the resulting grammar better covers the domain at hand. For the case of Greek travel grammar no corpus was initially available. The Greek grammar was instead produced by manually translating the English one, accounting for the differences in syntax between the two languages. The grammars have been developed as part of the PortDial FP7 project and are explained in detail in (Portdial, 2014b).

For the first three datasets that have been available from the beginning of the campaign we have split the release into train, development and test set. For the finance domain which was announced when the test sets were released we only provided the train and test set, to simulate a resource poor scenario. The statistics of the datasets for all language/domain pairs are given in Table 2.

In addition to the high-level rules we made available the low-level rules for each grammar, which although not used in the evaluation, can be useful for expanding the high-level rules to cover all lexicalizations expressed by the grammar.

3.3 Evaluation

For the evaluation of the task we have used precision, recall and f-measure, both weighted and unweighted.

If R_j denotes the set of fragments for one rule and C_j the set of fragments classified to this rule by a system then per-rule precision is computed by the equation:

$$Pr_j = \frac{|R_j \cap C_j|}{|C_j|}$$

and per-rule recall by:

$$Rc_j = \frac{|R_j \cap C_j|}{|R_j|}$$

F-measure is then computed by:

Grammar	Rule	Fragment
Travel English	<FLIGHTFROM>	FLIGHT FROM <CITY>
Travel Greek	<FLIGHTFROM>	ΠΤΗΣΗ ΑΠΟ <CITY>
Tourism English	<TRANSFERQ>	TRANSFERS FROM <airportname> TO <cityname>
Finance English	<CARDNAME>	<BANKNAME> CARD

Table 1: Example grammar fragments for each application domain.

Grammar	Rules	Fragments		
		Train set	Dev set	Test set
Travel English	32	623	331	284
Travel Greek	35	616	340	324
Tourism English	24	694	334	285
Finance English	9	136	-	37

Table 2: Number of rules in the training, development and test sets for each application domain.

$$F_j = \frac{2Pr_jRc_j}{Pr_j + Rc_j}$$

.

Precision for all the J rules $R_j, 1 \leq j \leq J$ is computed by the following equation:

$$Pr = \sum_j Pr_j w_j$$

In the unweighted case the weight w_j has a fixed value for all rules, so $w_j = \frac{1}{J}$. Taking into account the fact that the rules are not balanced in terms of fragments, a better way to compute for the weight is $w_j = \frac{|R_j|}{\sum_j |R_j|}$. In the latter, weighted, case the total precision will better describe the results.

Recall is similarly computed using the same weighting scheme as:

$$Rc = \sum_j Rc_j w_j$$

3.4 Baseline

For comparison purposes we have developed a naive baseline system. To classify a test fragment, first its similarity with all the train fragments is computed, and it is classified to the rule where the most similar train fragment belongs. Fragment similarity is computed as the ratio of their Longest Common Substring (LCS) divided by the sum of their lengths:

$$Sim(s,t) = \frac{|LCS(s,t)|}{|s| + |t|}$$

where s and t are two strings, $|s|$ and $|t|$ their length in characters and $|LCS(s,t)|$ the length of their LCS. This is a very simple baseline, computing similarity without taking into account context or semantics.

4 Participating Systems

Three teams have participated in the task with five systems. All teams participated in all subtasks with the exception of travel Greek, where only two teams participated. An overview of core system features is presented in Table 3. The remainder of this section briefly describes each of the submissions and then compares them. A brief description for each system is provided in the following paragraphs.

tucSage. The core of the tucSage system is a combination of two components. The first component is used for the selection of candidate rule fragments from a corpus. Specifically, the posterior probability of a candidate fragment belonging to a rule is computed using a variety of features. The feature set includes various lexical features (e.g., the number of tokens), the fragment perplexity computed using n-gram language modeling, and features based on lexical similarity. The second component is used for computing the similarity between a candidate fragment and a grammar rule. In total, two different types of similarity metrics are used relying on the overlap of character bigrams and contextual features. These similarities are fused with the posterior probabilities produced by the fragment selection model. The contribution of the two components is adjusted using an exponential weight.

SAIL-GRS. The SAIL-GRS system is based on the well-established term frequency–inverse document frequency ($TF-IDF$) measurement. This metric is adapted to the present task by considering each grammar rule as a "document". For each rule, all its fragments are aggregated

System acronym	Use of machine learn.	Features used	Similarity metrics	External corpora	Language-specific
Baseline	no	lexical	Longest Common Substring	no	no
tucSage	yes: random forests	lexical, perplexity, similarity-based , heuristic	character overlap, cosine similarity	web documents	no
SAIL-GRS	no	lexical	cosine similarity	no	no
Biel	no	lexical, expansion of low-level rules	cosine similarity	Wikipedia articles	yes

Table 3: Overview of the characteristics of the participating systems.

and the frequency of the respective n-grams (constituents) is computed. The inverse document frequency is casted as inverse rule frequency and it is computed for the extracted n-grams. The process is performed for both unigrams and bigrams.

Biel. The fundamental idea behind the Biel system is the encoding of domain semantics via topic modeling. For this purpose a background document space is constructed using thousands of Wikipedia articles. Particular focus is given to the transformation of the initial document space according to the paradigm of explicit semantic analysis. For each domain, a topic space is defined and a language-specific function is employed for the mapping of documents. In essence, the mapping function is an association measurement that is based on $TF\!-\!IDF$ scores. An approximation regarding the construction of the topic space is investigated in order to reduce data sparsity, while a number of normalization schemes are also presented.

Overall, only the tucSage system employs a machine learning-based approach (random forests), while an unsupervised approach is followed by the SAIL-GRS and Biel systems. All systems exploit lexical information extracted from rule fragments. This information is realized as the lexical surface form of the constituents of fragments. For example, consider the "depart for <CITY>" fragment that corresponds to the high-level rule referring to the notion of departure city. The following set of lexical features can be extracted from the aforementioned fragment: ("depart", "from", "<CITY>"). Unlike the other systems, the Biel system utilizes low-level rules to expand high-level rules with terminal concept instances. For example, the "<CITY>" rule is not processed as is, but it is represented as a list of city names ("New York", "Boston", ...). The most rich feature set is used by the tucSage system which combines lexical, perplexity and similarity features with a set of heuristic rules. All three systems employ the widely-used cosine similarity metric. Both SAIL-GRS and Biel systems rely solely on this metric during the assignment of an unknown fragment to a high-level rule. A more sophisticated approach is presented by tucSage, where first a classifier is built for every grammar rule, computing the probability of a fragment belonging to this rule and then the similarity between the fragment and the rule is computed. Classification is then performed by combining the two scores. Also, another difference regarding the employment of the cosine similarity deals with the computation of the vectorial feature values. A simple binary scheme is used in the tucSage system, while variations of the term frequency-inverse document frequency scheme are used in SAIL-GRS and Biel. Besides cosine similarity, a similarity metric based on the overlap of character bigrams is used by the tucSage system. External corpora (i.e., corpora that were not provided as part of the official task data) were used by the tucSage and Biel systems. Such corpora were meant as an additional source of information with respect to the domains under investigation. Regarding tucSage, the training data were exploited in order to construct web search queries for harvesting a collection of web documents from which a number of sentences were selected for corpus creation. In the case of the Biel system, a set of Wikipedia articles was exploited. Language specific resources where used for the Biel system, while the other two teams used language agnostic methods.

5 Results

The results for all participating teams and the baseline system are given in Table 4. The tucSage team submitted three runs, the first one being the primary, indicated with an asterisk in the results.

Focusing on the weighted F-measure we see that in all domains but the tourism English, at least one submission manages to outperform the baseline provided by the organizers. In travel English the baseline system achieves 0.51 weighted f-measure, with two out of the three systems achieving 0.68 and 0.58. The improvement over the baseline is greater for the travel Greek subtask, where the baseline score of 0.26 is much lower than the achieved 0.52 from tucSage. In the tourism English subtask the best submitted systems managed to match the performance of the baseline system, but not to exceed it. This can be attributed to the good performance of the baseline system, due to the fact that the tourism grammar is composed of longer fragments than the rest, helping the naive baseline system achieve top performance exploiting lexical similarity only. We can however assume that more complex systems would beat the baseline if the test set fragments were built using different lexicalizations, as would be the case in unannotated data coming from deployed SDS.

In the finance domain, even though the amount of training data is quite smaller than in all other subtasks the submitted systems still manage to outperform the baseline system. This means that the submitted systems display robust performance both in resource-rich and resource-poor conditions.

team	Weighted			Unweighted		
	Pr.	Rec.	F-m.	Pr.	Rec.	F-m.
			Travel English			
Baseline	0.40	0.69	0.51	0.38	0.67	0.48
tucSage1*	0.60	**0.73**	0.66	0.59	**0.74**	0.66
tucSage2	0.59	0.72	0.65	0.59	**0.74**	0.65
tucSage3	**0.69**	0.67	**0.68**	**0.66**	0.69	**0.67**
SAIL-GRS	0.54	0.62	0.58	0.57	0.66	0.61
Biel	0.13	0.39	0.20	0.09	0.34	0.14
			Travel Greek			
Baseline	0.17	**0.65**	0.26	0.16	**0.73**	0.26
tucSage1*	0.47	0.58	**0.52**	**0.55**	0.72	**0.62**
tucSage2	0.46	0.53	0.49	0.50	0.59	0.54
tucSage3	**0.51**	0.48	0.49	0.52	0.56	0.54
SAIL-GRS	0.46	0.51	0.49	0.49	0.62	0.55
Biel	-	-	-	-	-	-
			Tourism English			
Baseline	**0.80**	**0.94**	**0.87**	**0.82**	**0.94**	**0.87**
tucSage1*	0.79	**0.94**	0.86	0.76	0.91	0.83
tucSage2	0.78	0.93	0.85	0.73	0.90	0.80
tucSage3	**0.80**	0.93	0.86	0.77	0.90	0.83
SAIL-GRS	0.75	0.90	0.82	0.75	0.90	0.82
Biel	0.04	0.14	0.06	0.02	0.08	0.04
			Finance English			
Baseline	0.48	0.78	0.60	0.40	**0.63**	0.49
tucSage1*	0.61	**0.81**	0.70	0.43	0.54	0.48
tucSage2	0.55	0.74	0.63	0.40	0.51	0.45
tucSage3	0.52	0.67	0.58	0.39	0.43	0.41
SAIL-GRS	**0.78**	0.78	**0.78**	**0.67**	0.62	**0.65**
Biel	0.22	0.30	0.25	0.06	0.18	0.09
			Average over all four tasks			
Baseline	0.46	0.73	0.56	0.44	**0.74**	0.53
tucSage1*	0.62	**0.77**	**0.69**	0.58	0.73	0.65
tucSage2	0.60	0.73	0.66	0.56	0.69	0.61
tucSage3	**0.63**	0.69	0.65	0.59	0.65	0.61
SAIL-GRS	**0.63**	0.70	0.67	**0.62**	0.70	**0.66**
Biel	0.13	0.28	0.17	0.06	0.20	0.09

Table 4: Weighted and unweighted precision, recall and f-measure for all systems. Best performance per metric and dataset shown in bold.

6 Conclusion

The tucSage and SAIL-GRS systems are shown to be portable across domains and languages, achieving performance that exceeds the baseline for three out of four datasets. The highest performance of the tucSage system compared to the SAIL-GRS system may be attributed to the use of a model for fragment selection. Interestingly, the simple variation of the *TF−IDF* scheme used by the SAIL system achieved very good results being a close second performer. The UNIBI system proposed a very interesting new application of the framework of topic modeling to the task of grammar induction, however, the respective performance does not exceed the state-of-the-art. The combination of the tucSage and SAIL-GRS systems could give better results.

Acknowledgements

The task organizers wish to thank Maria Giannoudaki and Maria Vomva for the editing of the hand-crafted grammars used in this evaluation task. The authors would like to thank the anonymous reviewer for the valuable comments and suggestions to improve the quality of the paper. This work has been partially funded by the SpeDial and PortDial projects, supported by the EU Seventh Framework Programme (FP7), with grant number 611396 and 296170 respectively.

References

Eneko Agirre, Daniel Cer, Mona Diab, and Aitor Gonzalez-Agirre. 2012. SemEval-2012 Task 6: A pilot on semantic textual similarity. In *Proceedings of the First Joint Conference on Lexical and Computational Semantics*, pages 385–393.

Frederic Bechet, Benoit Favre, Alexis Nasr, and Mathieu Morey. 2014. Retrieving the syntactic structure of erroneous ASR transcriptions for open-domain spoken language understanding. In *Proceedings of the International Conference on Acoustics, Speech, and Signal Processing (ICASSP)*, pages 4125–4129.

Yonatan Bisk and Julia Hockenmaier. 2012. Simple robust grammar induction with combinatory categorial grammars. In *Proceedings of the 26th Conference on Artificial Intelligence*, pages 1643–1649.

Bart Cramer. 2007. Limitations of current grammar induction algorithms. In *Proceedings of the 45th annual meeting of the ACL: Student Research Workshop*, pages 43–48.

Katerina T. Frantzi and Sophia Ananiadou. 1997. Automatic term recognition using contextual cues. In *Proceedings of the International Joint Conference on Artificial Intelligence*, pages 41–46.

Spiros Georgiladakis, Christina Unger, Elias Iosif, Sebastian Walter, Philipp Cimiano, Euripides Petrakis, and Alexandros Potamianos. 2014. Fusion of knowledge-based and data-driven approaches to grammar induction. In *Proceedings of Interspeech (accepted)*.

Zellig Harris. 1954. Distributional structure. *Word*, 10(23):146–162.

Elias Iosif and Alexandros Potamianos. 2007. A soft-clustering algorithm for automatic induction of semantic classes. In *Proceedings of Interspeech*, pages 1609–1612.

Elias Iosif, Athanasios Tegos, Apostolos Pangos, Eric Fosler-Lussier, and Alexandros Potamianos. 2006. Unsupervised combination of metrics for semantic class induction. In *Proceedings of the International Workshop on Spoken Language Technology (SLT)*, pages 86–89.

Ioannis Klasinas, Alexandros Potamianos, Elias Iosif, Spiros Georgiladakis, and Gianluca Mameli. 2013. Web data harvesting for speech understanding grammar induction. In *Proceedings of Interspeech*, pages 2733–2737.

Jonas Kuhn. 2004. Experiments in parallel-text based grammar induction. In *Proceedings of the 42nd annual meeting of the ACL*, pages 470–477.

Helen M. Meng and Kai-chung Siu. 2002. Semi-automatic acquisition of semantic structures for understanding domain-specific natural language queries. *IEEE Transactions on Knowledge and Data Engineering*, 14(1):172–181.

Dmitrijs Milajevs and Matthew Purver. 2014. Investigating the contribution of distributional semantic information for dialogue act classification. In *Proceedings of the 2nd Workshop on Continuous Vector Space Models and their Compositionality*, pages 40–47.

Teruhisa Misu and Tatsuya Kawahara. 2006. A bootstrapping approach for developing language model of new spoken dialogue systems by selecting web texts. In *Proceedings of Interspeech*, pages 9–12.

Jeff Mitchell and Mirella Lapata. 2010. Composition in distributional models of semantics. *Cognitive Science*, 34(8):1388–1429.

Kishore Papineni, Salim Roukos, Todd Ward, and Wei-Jing Zhu. 2002. BLEU: A method for automatic evaluation of machine translation. In *Proceedings of the 40th annual meeting of the ACL*, pages 311–318.

Andrew N. Pargellis, Eric Fosler-Lussier, Chin-Hui Lee, Alexandros Potamianos, and Augustine Tsai. 2004. Auto-induced semantic classes. *Speech Communication*, 43(3):183–203.

Elias Ponvert, Jason Baldridge, and Katrin Erk. 2011. Simple unsupervised grammar induction from raw text with cascaded finite state models. In *Proceedings of the 49th annual meeting of the ACL*, pages 1077–1086.

Portdial. 2014a. PortDial project, final report on automatic grammar induction and evaluation D3.3. Technical report, https://sites.google.com/site/portdial2/deliverables-publications.

Portdial. 2014b. PortDial project, free data deliverable D3.2. Technical report, https://sites.google.com/site/portdial2/deliverables-publications.

Aarne Ranta. 2004. Grammatical framework: A type-theoretical grammar formalism. *Journal of Functional Programming*, 14(2):145–189.

Ruhi Sarikaya. 2008. Rapid bootstrapping of statistical spoken dialogue systems. *Speech Communication*, 50(7):580–593.

Abhinav Sethy, Shrikanth S. Narayanan, and Bhuvana Ramabhadran. 2007. Data driven approach for language model adaptation using stepwise relative entropy minimization. In *Proceedings of the International Conference on Acoustics, Speech, and Signal Processing (ICASSP)*, pages 177–180.

Ye-Yi Wang and Alex Acero. 2006. Rapid development of spoken language understanding grammars. *Speech Communication*, 48(3-4):390–416.

SemEval-2014 Task 3: Cross-Level Semantic Similarity

David Jurgens, Mohammad Taher Pilehvar, and **Roberto Navigli**
Department of Computer Science
Sapienza University of Rome
{jurgens,pilehvar,navigli}@di.uniroma1.it

Abstract

This paper introduces a new SemEval task on Cross-Level Semantic Similarity (CLSS), which measures the degree to which the meaning of a larger linguistic item, such as a paragraph, is captured by a smaller item, such as a sentence. High-quality data sets were constructed for four comparison types using multi-stage annotation procedures with a graded scale of similarity. Nineteen teams submitted 38 systems. Most systems surpassed the baseline performance, with several attaining high performance for multiple comparison types. Further, our results show that comparisons of semantic representation increase performance beyond what is possible with text alone.

1 Introduction

Given two linguistic items, semantic similarity measures the degree to which the two items have the same meaning. Semantic similarity is an essential component of many applications in Natural Language Processing (NLP), and similarity measurements between all types of text as well as between word senses lend themselves to a variety of NLP tasks such as information retrieval (Hliaoutakis et al., 2006) or paraphrasing (Glickman and Dagan, 2003).

Semantic similarity evaluations have largely focused on comparing similar types of lexical items. Most recently, tasks in SemEval (Agirre et al., 2012) and *SEM (Agirre et al., 2013) have introduced benchmarks for measuring Semantic Textual Similarity (STS) between similar-sized sentences and phrases. Other data sets such as that of Rubenstein and Goodenough (1965) measure similarity between word pairs, while the data sets of Navigli (2006) and Kilgarriff (2001) offer a binary similar-dissimilar distinction between senses. Notably, all of these evaluations have focused on comparisons between a single type, in contrast to application-based evaluations such as summarization and compositionality which incorporate textual items of different sizes, e.g., measuring the quality of a paragraph's sentence summarization.

Task 3 introduces a new evaluation where similarity is measured between items of different types: paragraphs, sentences, phrases, words and senses. Given an item of the lexically-larger type, a system measures the degree to which the meaning of the larger item is captured in the smaller type, e.g., comparing a paragraph to a sentence. We refer to this task as Cross-Level Semantic Similarity (CLSS). A major motivation of this task is to produce semantic similarity systems that are able to compare all types of text, thereby freeing downstream NLP applications from needing to consider the type of text being compared. Task 3 enables assessing the extent to which the meaning of the sentence "do u know where i can watch free older movies online without download?" is captured in the phrase "streaming vintage movies for free", or how similar is "circumscribe" to the phrase "beating around the bush." Furthermore, by incorporating comparisons of a variety of item sizes, Task 3 unifies in a single task multiple objectives from different areas of NLP such as paraphrasing, summarization, and compositionality.

Because CLSS generalizes STS to items of different types, successful CLSS systems can directly be applied to all STS-based applications. Furthermore, CLSS systems can be used in other similarity-based applications such as text simplification (Specia et al., 2012), keyphrase identification (Kim et al., 2010), lexical substitution (McCarthy and Navigli, 2009), summariza-

Proceedings of the 8th International Workshop on Semantic Evaluation (SemEval 2014), pages 17–26,
Dublin, Ireland, August 23-24, 2014.

tion (Spärck Jones, 2007), gloss-to-sense mapping (Pilehvar and Navigli, 2014b), and modeling the semantics of multi-word expressions (Marelli et al., 2014) or polysemous words (Pilehvar and Navigli, 2014a).

Task 3 was designed with three main objectives. First, the task should include multiple types of comparison in order to assess each type's difficulty and whether specialized resources are needed for each. Second, the task should incorporate text from multiple domains and writing styles to ensure that system performance is robust across text types. Third, the similarity methods should be able to operate at the sense level, thereby potentially uniting text- and sense-based similarity methods within a single framework.

2 Task Description

2.1 Objective

Task 3 is intended to serve as an initial task for evaluating the capabilities of systems at measuring all types of semantic similarity, independently of the size of the text. To accomplish this objective, systems were presented with items from four comparison types: (1) paragraph to sentence, (2) sentence to phrase, (3) phrase to word, and (4) word to sense. Given a pair of items, a system must assess the degree to which the meaning of the larger item is captured in the smaller item. WordNet 3.0 was chosen as the sense inventory (Fellbaum, 1998).

2.2 Rating Scale

Following previous SemEval tasks (Agirre et al., 2012; Jurgens et al., 2012), Task 3 recognizes that two items' similarity may fall within a range of similarity values, rather than having a binary notion of similar or dissimilar. Initially a six-point (0–5) scale similar to that used in the STS tasks was considered (Agirre et al., 2012); however, annotators found difficulty in deciding between the lower-similarity options. After multiple revisions and feedback from a group of initial annotators, we developed a five-point Likert scale for rating a pair's similarity, shown in Table 1.[1]

The scale was designed to systematically order a broad range of semantic relations: synonymy, similarity, relatedness, topical association, and unrelatedness. Because items are of different sizes, the highest rating is defined as very similar rather than identical to allow for some small loss in the overall meaning. Furthermore, although the scale is designed as a Likert scale, annotators were given flexibility when rating items to use values between the defined points in the scale, indicating a blend of two relations. Table 2 provides examples of pairs for each scale rating for all four comparison type.

[1]Annotation materials along with all training and test data are available on the task website `http://alt.qcri.org/semeval2014/task3/`.

3 Task Data

Though several data sets exist for STS and comparing words and senses, no standard data set exists for CLSS. Therefore, we created a pilot data set designed to test the capabilities of systems in a variety of settings. The task data for all comparisons but word-to-sense was created using a three-phase process. First, items of all sizes were selected from publicly-available data sets. Second, the selected items were used to produce a second item of the next-smaller level (e.g., a sentence inspires a phrase). Third, the pairs of items were annotated for their similarity. Because of the expertise required for working with word senses, the word-to-sense data set was constructed by the organizers using a separate but similar process. In the training and test data, each comparison type had 500 annotated examples, for a total of 2000 pairs each for training and test. We first describe the corpora used by Task 3 followed by the annotation process. We then describe the construction of the word-to-sense data set.

3.1 Corpora

Test and training data were constructed by drawing from multiple publicly-available corpora and then manually generating a paired item for comparison. To achieve our second objective for the task, the data sets used to create item pairs included texts from specific domains, social media, and text with idiomatic or slang language. Table 3 summarizes the corpora and their distribution across the test and training sets for each comparison type, with a high-level description of the genre of the data. We briefly describe the corpora next.

The WikiNews, Reuters 21578, and Microsoft Research (MSR) Paraphrase corpora are all drawn from newswire text, with WikiNews being authored by volunteer writers and the latter two corpora written by professionals. Travel Guides was drawn from the Berlitz travel guides data in the Open American National Corpus (Ide and Suderman, 2004) and includes very verbose sentences

4 – Very Similar	The two items have very similar meanings and the most important ideas, concepts, or actions in the larger text are represented in the smaller text. Some less important information may be missing, but the smaller text is a very good summary of the larger text.
3 – Somewhat Similar	The two items share many of the same important ideas, concepts, or actions, but include slightly different details. The smaller text may use similar but not identical concepts (e.g., car vs. vehicle), or may omit a few of the more important ideas present in the larger text.
2 – Somewhat related but not similar	The two items have dissimilar meaning, but share concepts, ideas, and actions that are related. The smaller text may use related but not necessarily similar concepts (window vs. house) but should still share some overlapping concepts, ideas, or actions with the larger text.
1 – Slightly related	The two items describe dissimilar concepts, ideas and actions, but may share some small details or domain in common and might be likely to be found together in a longer document on the same topic.
0 – Unrelated	The two items do not mean the same thing and are not on the same topic.

Table 1: The five-point Likert scale used to rate the similarity of item pairs. See Table 2 for examples.

with many named entities. Wikipedia Science was drawn from articles tagged with the category *Science* on Wikipedia. Food reviews were drawn from the SNAP Amazon Fine Food Reviews data set (McAuley and Leskovec, 2013) and are customer-authored reviews for a variety of food items. Fables were taken from a collection of Aesop's Fables. The Yahoo! Answers corpus was derived from the Yahoo! Answers data set, which is a collection of questions and answers from the Community Question Answering (CQA) site; the data set is notable for having the highest degree of ungrammaticality in our test set. SMT Europarl is a collection of texts from the English-language proceedings of the European parliament (Koehn, 2005); Europarl data was also used in the PPDB corpus (Ganitkevitch et al., 2013), from which phrases were extracted. Wikipedia was used to generate two phrase data sets from (1) extracting the definitional portion of an article's initial sentence, e.g., "An [article name] is a [definition]," and (2) captions for an article's images. Web queries were gathered from online sources of real-world queries. Last, the first and second authors generated slang and idiomatic phrases based on expressions contained in Wiktionary.

For all comparison types, the test data included one genre that was not seen in the training data in order to test the generalizability of the systems on data from a novel domain. In addition, we included a new type of challenge genre with Fables; unlike other domains, the sentences paired with the fable paragraphs were potentially semantic interpretations of the intent of the fable, i.e., the moral of the story. These interpretations often have little textual overlap with the fable itself and require a deeper interpretation of the paragraph's meaning in order to make the correct similarity judgment.

Prior to the annotation process, all content was filtered to ensure its size and format matched the desired text type. By average, a paragraph in our dataset consists of 3.8 sentences. Typos and grammatical mistakes in the community-produced content were left unchanged.

3.2 Annotation Process

A two-phase process was used to produce the test and training data sets for all but word-to-sense. Phase 1 generates the item pairs from source texts and Phase 2 rates the pairs' similarity.

Phase 1 In this phase, annotators were shown the larger text of a comparison type and then asked to produce the smaller text of the pair at a specified similarity; for example an annotator may be shown a paragraph and asked to write a sentence that is a "3" rating. Annotators were instructed to leave the smaller text blank if they had difficulty understanding the larger text.

The requested similarity ratings were balanced to create a uniform distribution of similarity values. Annotators were asked only to generate ratings of 1–4; pairs with a "0" rating were automatically created by pairing the larger item with random selections of text of the appropriate size from the same corpus. The intent of Phase 1 is to produce varied item pairs with an expected uniform distribution of similarity values along the rating scale.

Four annotators participated in Phase 1 and were paid a bulk rate of €110 for completing the work. In addition to the four annotators, the first two organizers also assisted in Phase 1: Both completed items from the SCIENTIFIC genre and the first organizer produced 994 pairs, including all

Paragraph to Sentence	
Paragraph: Teenagers take aerial shots of their neighbourhood using digital cameras sitting in old bottles which are launched via kites - a common toy for children living in the favelas. They then use GPS-enabled smartphones to take pictures of specific danger points - such as rubbish heaps, which can become a breeding ground for mosquitoes carrying dengue fever.	
Rating	**Sentence**
4	Students use their GPS-enabled cellphones to take birdview photographs of a land in order to find specific danger points such as rubbish heaps.
3	Teenagers are enthusiastic about taking aerial photograph in order to study their neighbourhood.
2	Aerial photography is a great way to identify terrestrial features that aren't visible from the ground level, such as lake contours or river paths.
1	During the early days of digital SLRs, Canon was pretty much the undisputed leader in CMOS image sensor technology.
0	Syrian President Bashar al-Assad tells the US it will "pay the price" if it strikes against Syria.

Sentence to Phrase	
Sentence: Schumacher was undoubtedly one of the very greatest racing drivers there has ever been, a man who was routinely, on every lap, able to dance on a limit accessible to almost no-one else.	
Rating	**Phrase**
4	the unparalleled greatness of Schumacher's driving abilities
3	driving abilities
2	formula one racing
1	north-south highway
0	orthodontic insurance

Phrase to Word	
Phrase: loss of air pressure in a tire	
Rating	**Word**
4	flat-tire
3	deflation
2	wheel
1	parking
0	butterfly

Word to Sense	
Word: automobile$_n$	
Rating	**Sense**
4	car^1_n (a motor vehicle with four wheels; usually propelled by an internal combustion engine)
3	vehicle^1_n (a conveyance that transports people or objects)
2	bike^1_n (a motor vehicle with two wheels and a strong frame)
1	highway^1_n (a major road for any form of motor transport)
0	pen^1_n (a writing implement with a point from which ink flows)

Table 2: Example pairs and their ratings.

those for the METAPHORIC genre, and those that the other annotators left blank.

Phase 2 Here, the item pairs produced in Phase 1 were rated for their similarity according to the scale described in Section 2.2. An initial pilot study showed that crowdsourcing was only moderately effective for producing these ratings with high agreement. Furthermore, the texts used in Task 3 came from a variety of genres, such as scientific domains, which some workers had difficulty understanding. While we note that crowdsourcing has been used in prior STS tasks for generating similarity scores (Agirre et al., 2012; Agirre et al., 2013), both tasks' efforts encountered lower worker score correlations on some portions of the dataset (Diab, 2013), suggesting that crowdsourcing may not be reliable for judging the similarity of certain types of text. See Section 3.5 for additional details.

Therefore, to ensure high quality, the first two organizers rated all items independently. Because the sentence-to-phrase and phrase-to-word comparisons contain slang and idiomatic language, a third American English mother tongue annotator was added for those data sets. The third annotator was compensated €250 for their assistance.

Annotators were allowed to make finer-grained distinctions in similarity using multiples of 0.25. For all items, when any two annotators disagreed by one or more scale points, we performed an adjudication to determine the item's rating in the gold standard. The adjudication process revealed that nearly all disagreements were due to annotator mistakes, e.g., where one annotator had overlooked a part of the text or had misunderstood the text's meaning. The final similarity rating for an unadjudicated item was the average of its ratings.

3.3 Word-to-Sense

Word-to-sense comparison items were generated in three phases. To increase the diversity and challenge of the data set, the word-to-sense was created for four types of words: (1) a word and its intended meaning are in WordNet, (2) a word was not in the WordNet vocabulary, e.g., the verb "zombify," (3) the word is in WordNet, but has a novel meaning that is not in WordNet, e.g., the adjective "red" referring to Communist, and (4) a set of challenge words where one of the word's senses and a second sense are directly connected by an edge in the WordNet network, but the two senses are not always highly similar.

Corpus	Genre	Paragraph-to-Sentence		Sentence-to-Phrase		Phrase-to-Word	
		Train	Test	Train	Test	Train	Test
WikiNews	Newswire	15.0	10.0	9.2	6.0		
Reuters 21578	Newswire	20.2	15.0			5.0	
Travel Guides	Travel	15.2	10.0	15.0	9.8		
Wikipedia Science	Scientific	–	25.6	–	14.8		
Food Reviews	Review	19.6	20.0				
Fables	Metaphoric	9.0	5.2				
Yahoo! Answers	CQA	21.0	14.2	17.6	17.4		
SMT Europarl	Newswire			35.4	14.4		
MSR Paraphrase	Newswire			10.0	10.0	8.8	6.0
Idioms	Idiomatic			12.8	12.6	20.0	20.0
Slang	Slang			–	15.0	–	25.0
PPDB	Newswire					10.0	10.0
Wikipedia Glosses	Lexicographic					28.2	17.0
Wikipedia Image Captions	Descriptive					23.0	17.0
Web Search Queries	Search					5.0	5.0

Table 3: Percentages of the training and test data per source corpus.

In Phase 1, to select the first type of word, lemmas in WordNet were ranked by frequency in Wikipedia; the ranking was divided into ten equally-sized groups, with words sampled evenly from groups in order to control for word frequency in the task data. For the second type, words not present in WordNet were drawn from two sources: examining words in Wikipedia, which we refer to as out-of-vocabulary (OOV), and slang words. For the third type, to identify words with a novel sense, we examined Wiktionary entries and chose novel, salient senses that were distinct from those in WordNet. We refer to words with a novel meaning as out-of-sense (OOS). Words of the fourth type were chosen by hand. The part-of-speech distributions for all four types of items were balanced as 50% noun, 25% verb, 25% adjective.

In Phase 2, each word was associated with a particular WordNet sense for its intended meaning, or the closest available sense in WordNet for OOV or OOS items. To select a comparison sense, we adopted a neighborhood search procedure: All synsets connected by at most three edges in the WordNet semantic network were shown. Given a word and its neighborhood, the corresponding sense for the item pair was selected by matching the sense with an intended similarity for the pair, much like how text items were generated in Phase 1. The reason behind using this neighborhood-based selection process was to minimize the potential bias of consistently selecting lower-similarity items from those further away in the WordNet semantic network.

In Phase 3, given all word-sense pairs, annotators were shown the definitions associated with the intended meaning of the word and of the sense. Definitions were drawn from WordNet or from Wiktionary, if the word was OOV or OOS. Annotators had access to the WordNet structure for the compared sense in order to take into account its parents and siblings.

3.4 Trial Data

The trial data set was created using a separate process. Source text was drawn from WikiNews; we selected the text for the larger item of each level and then generated the text or sense of the smaller. A total of 156 items were produced. After, four fluent annotators independently rated all items. Inter-annotator agreement rates varied in 0.734–0.882, using Krippendorff's α (Krippendorff, 2004) on the interval scale.

3.5 Data Set Discussion

The resulting annotation process produced a high-quality data set. First, Table 4 shows the inter-annotator agreement (IAA) statistics for each comparison type on both the full and unadjudicated portions of the data set. IAA was measured using Krippendorff's α for interval data. Because the disagreements that led to lower α in the full data were resolved via adjudication, the quality of the full data set is expected to be on par with that of the unadjudicated data. The annotation quality for Task 3 was further improved by manually adjudicating all significant disagreements.

In contrast, the data sets of current STS tasks aggregated data from annotators with moderate correlation with each other (Diab, 2013); STS-2012 (Agirre et al., 2012) saw inter-annotator Pearson correlations of 0.530–0.874 per data set and STS-2013 (Agirre et al., 2013) had average

	Training		Test	
Data	All	Unadj.	All	Unadj.
Para.-to-Sent.	0.856	0.916	0.904	0.971
Sent.-to-Phr.	0.773	0.913	0.766	0.980
Phr.-to-Word	0.735	0.895	0.730	0.988
Word-to-Sense	0.681	0.895	0.655	0.952

Table 4: IAA rates for the task data.

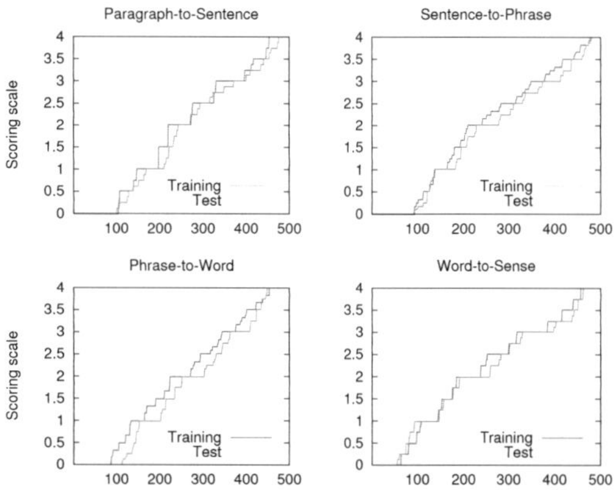

Figure 1: Similarity ratings distributions.

inter-annotator correlations of 0.377–0.832. However, we note that Pearson correlation and Krippendorff's α are not directly comparable (Artstein and Poesio, 2008), as annotators' scores may be correlated, but completely disagree.

Second, the two-phase construction process produced values that were evenly distributed across the rating scale, shown in Figure 1 as the distribution of the values for all data sets. However, we note that this creation procedure was very resource intensive and, therefore, semi-automated or crowdsourcing-based approaches for producing high-quality data will be needed to expand the size of the data in future CLSS-based evaluations. Nevertheless, as a pilot task, the manual effort was essential for ensuring a rigorously-constructed data set for the initial evaluation.

4 Evaluation

Participation The ultimate goal of Task 3 is to produce systems that can measure similarity for multiple types of items. Therefore, we strongly encouraged participating teams to submit systems that were capable of generating similarity judgments for multiple comparison types. However, to further the analysis, participants were also permitted to submit systems specialized to a single domain. Teams were allowed at most three system submissions, regardless of the number of comparison types supported.

Scoring Systems were required to provide similarity values for all items within a comparison type. Following prior STS evaluations, systems were scored for each comparison type using Pearson correlation. Additionally, we include a second score using Spearman's rank correlation, which is only affected by differences in the ranking of items by similarity, rather than differences in the similarity values. Pearson correlation was chosen as the official evaluation metric since the goal of the task is to produce similar scores. However, Spearman's rank correlation provides an important metric for assessing systems whose scores do not match human scores but whose rankings might, e.g., string-similarity measures. Ultimately, a global ranking was produced by ordering systems by the sum of their Pearson correlation values for each of the four comparison levels.

Baselines The official baseline system was based on the Longest Common Substring (LCS), normalized by the length of items using the method of Clough and Stevenson (2011). Given a pair, the similarity is reported as the normalized length of the LCS. In the case of word-to-sense, the LCS for a word-sense pair is measured between the sense's definition in WordNet and the definitions of each sense of the pair's word, reporting the maximal LCS. Because OOV and slang words are not in WordNet, the baseline reports the average similarity value of non-OOV items. Baseline scores were made public after the evaluation period ended.

Because LCS is a simple procedure, a second baseline based on Greedy String Tiling (GST) (Wise, 1996) was added after the evaluation period concluded. Unlike LCS, GST better handles the transpositions of tokens across the two texts and can still report high similarity when encountering reordered text. The minimum match length for GST was set to 6.

5 Results

Nineteen teams submitted 38 systems. Of those systems, 34 produced values for paragraph-to-sentence and sentence-to-phrase comparisons, 22 for phrase-to-word, and 20 for word-to-sense. Two teams submitted revised scores for their systems after the deadline but before the test set had

Team	System	Para-2-Sent	Sent-2-Phr	Phr-2-Word	Word-2-Sense	Official Rank	Spearman Rank
Meerkat Mafia	pairingWords†	0.794	0.704	**0.457**	**0.389**		
SimCompass	run1	0.811	0.742	0.415	0.356	1	1
ECNU	run1	0.834	0.771	0.315	0.269	2	2
UNAL-NLP	run2	0.837	0.738	0.274	0.256	3	6
SemantiKLUE	run1	0.817	0.754	0.215	0.314	4	4
UNAL-NLP	run1	0.817	0.739	0.252	0.249	5	7
UNIBA	run2	0.784	0.734	0.255	0.180	6	8
RTM-DCU	run1†	**0.845**	0.750	0.305			
UNIBA	run1	0.769	0.729	0.229	0.165	7	10
UNIBA	run3	0.769	0.729	0.229	0.165	8	11
BUAP	run1	0.805	0.714	0.162	0.201	9	13
BUAP	run2	0.805	0.714	0.142	0.194	10	9
Meerkat Mafia	pairingWords	0.794	0.704	-0.044	0.389	11	12
HULTECH	run1	0.693	0.665	0.254	0.150	12	16
GST Baseline		0.728	0.662	0.146	0.185		
HULTECH	run3	0.669	0.671	0.232	0.137	13	15
RTM-DCU	run2†	0.785	0.698	0.221			
RTM-DCU	run3	0.780	0.677	0.208		14	17
HULTECH	run2	0.667	0.633	0.180	0.169	15	14
RTM-DCU	run1	0.786	0.666	0.171		16	18
RTM-DCU	run3†	0.786	0.663	0.171			
Meerkat Mafia	SuperSaiyan	0.834	**0.777**			17	19
Meerkat Mafia	Hulk2	0.826	0.705			18	20
RTM-DCU	run2	0.747	0.588	0.164		19	22
FBK-TR	run3	0.759	0.702			20	23
FBK-TR	run1	0.751	0.685			21	24
FBK-TR	run2	0.770	0.648			22	25
Duluth	Duluth2	0.501	0.450	0.241	0.219	23	21
AI-KU	run1	0.732	0.680			24	26
LCS Baseline		0.527	0.562	0.165	0.109		
UNAL-NLP	run3	0.708	0.620			25	27
AI-KU	run2	0.698	0.617			26	28
TCDSCSS	run2	0.607	0.552			27	29
JU-Evora	run1	0.536	0.442	0.090	0.091	28	31
TCDSCSS	run1	0.575	0.541			29	30
Duluth	Duluth1	0.458	0.440	0.075	0.076	30	5
Duluth	Duluth3	0.455	0.426	0.075	0.079	31	3
OPI	run1		0.433	0.213	0.152	32	36
SSMT	run1	0.789				33	34
DIT	run1	0.785				34	32
DIT	run2	0.784				35	33
UMCC DLSI SelSim	run1		0.760			36	35
UMCC DLSI SelSim	run2		0.698			37	37
UMCC DLSI Prob	run1				0.023	38	38

Table 5: Task results. Systems marked with a † were submitted after the deadline but are positioned where they would have ranked.

been released. These systems were scored and noted in the results but were not included in the official ranking.

Table 5 shows the performance of the participating systems across all the four comparison types in terms of Pearson correlation. The two right-most columns show system rankings by Pearson (Official Rank) and Spearman's ranks correlation.

The SimCompass system attained first place, partially due to its superior performance on phrase-to-word comparisons, providing an improvement of 0.10 over the second-best system. The late-submitted version of the Meerkat Mafia pairingWords† system corrected a bug in the phrase-to-word comparison, which ultimately would have attained first place due to large performance improvements over SimCompass on phrase-to-word and word-to-sense. ENCU and UNAL-NLP systems rank respectively second and third while the former being always in top-4 and the latter being among the top-7 systems across the four comparison types. Most systems were able to surpass the naive LCS baseline; however, the more sophisticated GST baseline (which accounts for text transposition) outperforms two-thirds of the systems. Importantly, both baselines perform poorly on smaller text, highlighting the importance of performing a *semantic* comparison, as opposed to a string-based one.

Within the individual comparison types, specialized systems performed well for the larger text sizes. In the paragraph-to-sentence type, the run1 system of UNAL-NLP provides the best official result, with the late RTM-DCU run1† system surpassing its performance slightly. Meerkat Mafia provides the best performance in sentence-to-phrase with its SuperSaiyan system and the best performances in phrase-to-word and word-to-sense with its late pairingWords† system.

Comparison-Type Analysis Performance across the comparison types varied considerably, with systems performing best on comparisons between longer textual items. As a general trend, both the baselines' and systems' performances tend to decrease with the size of lexical items in the comparison types. A main contributing factor to this is the reliance on textual similarity measures (such as the baselines), which perform well when two items' may share content. However, as the items' content becomes smaller, e.g., a word or phrase, the textual similarity does not necessarily provide a meaningful indication of the *semantic* similarity between the two. This performance discrepancy suggests that, in order to perform well, CLSS systems must rely on comparisons between semantic representations rather than textual representations. The two top-performing systems on these smaller levels, Meerkat Mafia and SimCompass, used additional resources beyond WordNet to expand a word or sense to its definition or to represent words with distributional representations.

Per-genre results and discussions Task 3 includes multiple genres within the data set for each comparison type. Figure 2 shows the correlation of each system for each of these genres, with systems ordered left to right according to their official ranking in Table 5. An interesting observation is that a system's official rank does not always match the rank from aggregating its correlations for each genre individually. This difference suggests that some systems provided good similarity judgments on individual genres, but their range of similarity values was not consistent between genres leading to lower overall Pearson correlation. For instance, in the phrase-to-word comparison type, the aggregated per-genre performance of Duluth-1 and Duluth-3 are among the best whereas their overall Pearson performance puts these systems among the worst-performing ones in the comparison type.

Among the genres, CQA, SLANG, and IDIOMATIC prove to be the more difficult for systems to interpret and judge. These genres included misspelled, colloquial, or slang language which required converting the text into semantic form in order to meaningfully compare it. Furthermore, as expected, the METAPHORIC genre was the most difficult, with no system performing well; we view the METAPHORIC genre as an open challenge for future systems to address when interpreting larger text. On the other hand, SCIENTIFIC, TRAVEL, and NEWSWIRE tend to be the easiest genres for paragraph-to-sentence and sentence-to-phrase. All three genres tend to include many named entities or highly-specific language, which are likely to be more preserved in the more-similar paired items. Similarly, DESCRIPTIVE and SEARCH genres were easiest in phrase-to-word, which also often featured specific words that were preserved in highly-similar pairs. In the case of word-to-sense, REGULAR proves to be the least difficult genre. Interestingly, in word-to-sense, most systems attained moderate performance for comparisons with words not in WordNet (i.e., OOV) but had poor performance for slang words, which were also OOV. This difference suggests that systems could be improved with additional semantic resources for slang.

Spearman Rank Analysis Although the goal of Task 3 is to have systems produce similarity judgments, some applications may benefit from simply having a ranking of pairs, e.g., ranking summarizations by goodness. The Spearman rank correlation measures the ability of systems to perform such a ranking. Surprisingly, with the Spearman-based ranking, the Duluth1 and Duluth3 systems attain the third and fifth ranks – despite being among the lowest ranked with Pearson. Both systems were unsupervised and produced similarity values that did not correlate well with those of humans. However, their Spearman ranks demonstrate the systems ability to correctly identify relative similarity and suggests that such unsupervised systems could improve their Pearson correlation by using the training data to tune the range of similarity values to match those of humans.

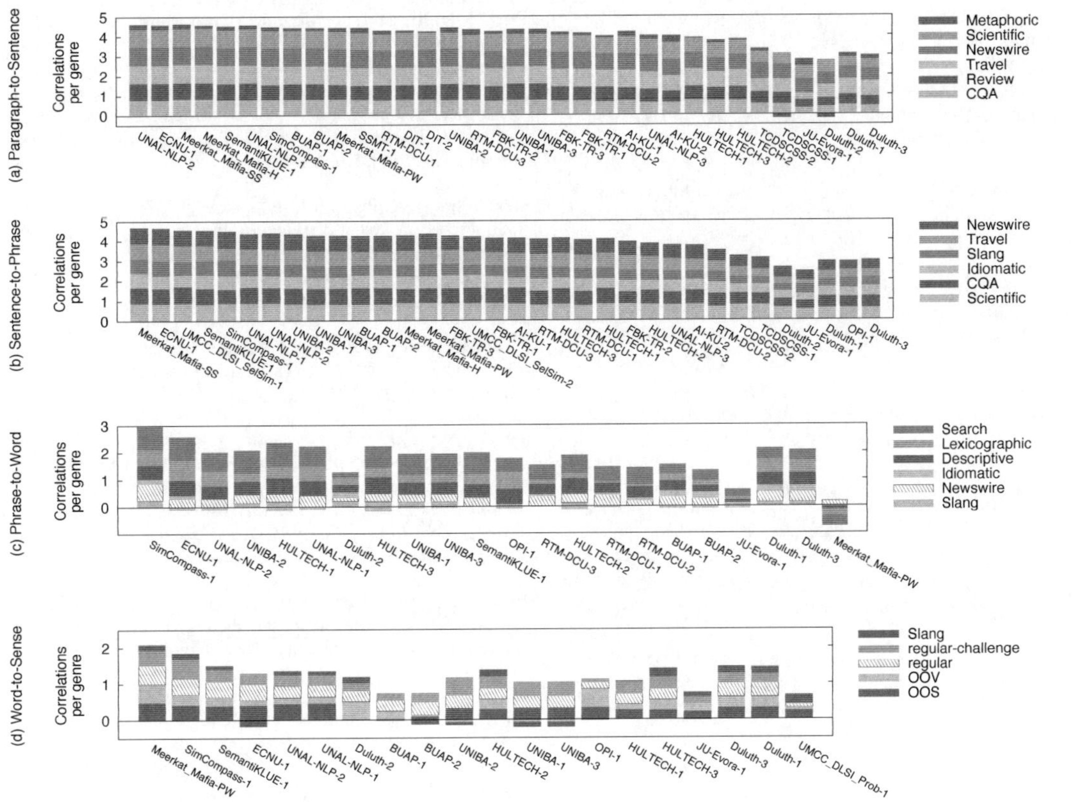

Figure 2: A stacked histogram for each system, showing its Pearson correlations for genre-specific portions of the gold-standard data, which may also be negative.

6 Conclusion

This paper introduces a new similarity task, Cross-Level Semantic Similarity, for measuring the semantic similarity of lexical items of different sizes. Using a multi-phase annotation procedure, we have produced a high-quality data set of 4000 items comprising of various genres, evenly-split between training and test with four types of comparison: paragraph-to-sentence, sentence-to-phrase, phrase-to-word, and word-to-sense. Nineteen teams submitted 38 systems, with most teams surpassing the baseline system and several systems achieving high performance in multiple types of comparison. However, a clear performance trend emerged where systems perform well only when the text itself is similar, rather than its underlying meaning. Nevertheless, the results of Task 3 are highly encouraging and point to clear future objectives for developing CLSS systems that operate on more semantic representations rather than text. In future work on CLSS evaluation, we first intend to develop scalable annotation methods to increase the data sets. Second, we plan to add new evaluations where systems are tested according to their performance in an application related to each comparison-type, such as measuring the quality of a paraphrase or summary.

Acknowledgments

We would like to thank Tiziano Flati, Marc Franco Salvador, Maud Erhmann, and Andrea Moro for their help in preparing the trial data; Gaby Ford, Chelsea Smith, and Eve Atkinson for their help in generating the training and test data; and Amy Templin for her help in generating and rating the training and test data.

The authors gratefully acknowledge the support of the ERC Starting Grant MultiJEDI No. 259234.

References

Eneko Agirre, Daniel Cer, Mona Diab, and Aitor Gonzalez-Agirre. 2012. SemEval-2012 task 6: A pilot on semantic textual similarity. In *Proceedings of the 6th International Workshop on Semantic Evaluation (SemEval-2012)*, pages 385–393, Montréal, Canada.

Eneko Agirre, Daniel Cer, Mona Diab, Aitor Gonzalez-Agirre, and Weiwei Guo. 2013. *SEM 2013 Shared Task: Semantic textual similarity, including a pilot on typed-similarity. In *Proceedings of the Second Joint Confer-*

*ence on Lexical and Computational Semantics (*SEM)*, Atlanta, Georgia.

Ron Artstein and Massimo Poesio. 2008. Inter-coder agreement for computational linguistics. *Computational Linguistics*, 34(4):555–596.

Paul Clough and Mark Stevenson. 2011. Developing a corpus of plagiarised short answers. *Language Resources and Evaluation*, 45(1):5–24.

Mona Diab. 2013. Semantic textual similarity: past present and future. In *Joint Symposium on Semantic Processing*. Keynote address. `http://jssp2013.fbk.eu/sites/jssp2013.fbk.eu/files/Mona.pdf`.

Christiane Fellbaum, editor. 1998. *WordNet: An Electronic Database*. MIT Press, Cambridge, MA.

Juri Ganitkevitch, Benjamin Van Durme, and Chris Callison-Burch. 2013. PPDB: The paraphrase database. In *Proceedings of the 2013 Conference of the North American Chapter of the Association for Computational Linguistics: Human Language Technologies (NAACL-HLT)*, pages 758–764, Atlanta, Georgia.

Oren Glickman and Ido Dagan. 2003. Acquiring lexical paraphrases from a single corpus. In *Proceedings of the International Conference on Recent Advances in Natural Language Processing (RANLP)*, pages 81–90, Borovets, Bulgaria.

Angelos Hliaoutakis, Giannis Varelas, Epimenidis Voutsakis, Euripides GM Petrakis, and Evangelos Milios. 2006. Information retrieval by semantic similarity. *International Journal on Semantic Web and Information Systems*, 2(3):55–73.

Nancy Ide and K. Suderman. 2004. The American National Corpus First Release. In *Proceedings of the 4th Language Resources and Evaluation Conference (LREC)*, pages 1681–1684, Lisbon, Portugal.

David Jurgens, Saif Mohammad, Peter Turney, and Keith Holyoak. 2012. SemEval-2012 Task 2: Measuring Degrees of Relational Similarity. In *Proceedings of the 6th International Workshop on Semantic Evaluation (SemEval-2012)*, pages 356–364, Montréal, Canada.

Adam Kilgarriff. 2001. English lexical sample task description. In *The Proceedings of the Second International Workshop on Evaluating Word Sense Disambiguation Systems (SENSEVAL-2)*, pages 17–20, Toulouse, France.

Su Nam Kim, Olena Medelyan, Min-Yen Kan, and Timothy Baldwin. 2010. SemEval-2010 Task 5: Automatic Keyphrase Extraction from Scientific Articles. In *Proceedings of the 5th International Workshop on Semantic Evaluation (SemEval-2010)*, pages 21–26, Los Angeles, California.

Philipp Koehn. 2005. Europarl: A parallel corpus for statistical machine translation. In *Proceedings of Machine Translation Summit X*, pages 79–86, Phuket, Thailand.

Klaus Krippendorff. 2004. *Content Analysis: An Introduction to Its Methodology*. Sage, Thousand Oaks, CA, second edition.

Marco Marelli, Stefano Menini, Marco Baroni, Luisa Bentivogli, Raffaella Bernardi, and Roberto Zamparelli. 2014. SemEval-2014 Task 1: Evaluation of compositional distributional semantic models on full sentences through semantic relatedness and textual entailment. In *Proceedings of the 8th International Workshop on Semantic Evaluation (SemEval-2014)*, Dublin, Ireland.

Julian John McAuley and Jure Leskovec. 2013. From amateurs to connoisseurs: modeling the evolution of user expertise through online reviews. In *Proceedings of the 22nd International Conference on World Wide Web (WWW)*, pages 897–908, Rio de Janeiro, Brazil.

Diana McCarthy and Roberto Navigli. 2009. The English lexical substitution task. *Language Resources and Evaluation*, 43(2):139–159.

Roberto Navigli. 2006. Meaningful clustering of senses helps boost Word Sense Disambiguation performance. In *Proceedings of the 21st International Conference on Computational Linguistics and the 44th Annual Meeting of the Association for Computational Linguistics (COLING-ACL)*, pages 105–112, Sydney, Australia.

Mohammad Taher Pilehvar and Roberto Navigli. 2014a. A large-scale pseudoword-based evaluation framework for state-of-the-art Word Sense Disambiguation. *Computational Linguistics*, 40(4).

Mohammad Taher Pilehvar and Roberto Navigli. 2014b. A robust approach to aligning heterogeneous lexical resources. In *Proceedings of the 52nd Annual Meeting of the Association for Computational Linguistics*, pages 468–478, Baltimore, USA.

Herbert Rubenstein and John B. Goodenough. 1965. Contextual correlates of synonymy. *Communications of the ACM*, 8(10):627–633.

Karen Spärck Jones. 2007. Automatic summarising: The state of the art. *Information Processing and Management*, 43(6):1449–1481.

Lucia Specia, Sujay Kumar Jauhar, and Rada Mihalcea. 2012. SemEval-2012 Task 1: English Lexical Simplification. In *Proceedings of the Sixth International Workshop on Semantic Evaluation (SemEval-2012)*, pages 347–355.

Michael J. Wise. 1996. YAP3: Improved detection of similarities in computer program and other texts. In *Proceedings of the twenty-seventh SIGCSE technical symposium on Computer science education*, SIGCSE '96, pages 130–134, Philadelphia, Pennsylvania, USA.

SemEval-2014 Task 4: Aspect Based Sentiment Analysis

Maria Pontiki
Institute for Language
and Speech Processing,
"Athena" Research Center
mpontiki@ilsp.gr

Dimitrios Galanis
Institute for Language
and Speech Processing,
"Athena" Research Center
galanisd@ilsp.gr

John Pavlopoulos
Dept. of Informatics,
Athens University of
Economics and Business
annis@aueb.gr

Haris Papageorgiou
Institute for Language
and Speech Processing,
"Athena" Research Center
xaris@ilsp.gr

Ion Androutsopoulos
Dept. of Informatics
Athens University of
Economics and Business
ion@aueb.gr

Suresh Manandhar
Dept. of Computer Science,
University of York
suresh@cs.york.ac.uk

Abstract

Sentiment analysis is increasingly viewed as a vital task both from an academic and a commercial standpoint. The majority of current approaches, however, attempt to detect the overall polarity of a sentence, paragraph, or text span, irrespective of the entities mentioned (e.g., laptops) and their aspects (e.g., battery, screen). SemEval-2014 Task 4 aimed to foster research in the field of aspect-based sentiment analysis, where the goal is to identify the aspects of given target entities and the sentiment expressed for each aspect. The task provided datasets containing manually annotated reviews of restaurants and laptops, as well as a common evaluation procedure. It attracted 163 submissions from 32 teams.

1 Introduction

With the proliferation of user-generated content on the web, interest in mining sentiment and opinions in text has grown rapidly, both in academia and business. Early work in sentiment analysis mainly aimed to detect the overall polarity (e.g., positive or negative) of a given text or text span (Pang et al., 2002; Turney, 2002). However, the need for a more fine-grained approach, such as aspect-based (or 'feature-based') sentiment analysis (ABSA), soon became apparent (Liu, 2012). For example, laptop reviews not only express the overall sentiment about a specific model (e.g., *"This is a great laptop"*), but also sentiments relating to its specific aspects, such as the hardware, software, price, etc. Subsequently, a review may convey opposing sentiments (e.g., *"Its performance is ideal, I wish I could say the same about the price"*) or objective information (e.g., *"This one still has the CD slot"*) for different aspects of an entity.

ABSA is critical in mining and summarizing opinions from on-line reviews (Gamon et al., 2005; Titov and McDonald, 2008; Hu and Liu, 2004a; Popescu and Etzioni, 2005). In this setting, ABSA aims to identify the aspects of the entities being reviewed and to determine the sentiment the reviewers express for each aspect. Within the last decade, several ABSA systems of this kind have been developed for movie reviews (Thet et al., 2010), customer reviews of electronic products like digital cameras (Hu and Liu, 2004a) or netbook computers (Brody and Elhadad, 2010), services (Long et al., 2010), and restaurants (Ganu et al., 2009; Brody and Elhadad, 2010).

Previous publicly available ABSA benchmark datasets adopt different annotation schemes within different tasks. The restaurant reviews dataset of Ganu et al. (2009) uses six coarse-grained aspects (e.g., FOOD, PRICE, SERVICE) and four overall sentence polarity labels (positive, negative, conflict, neutral). Each sentence is assigned one or more aspects together with a polarity label for each aspect; for example, "*The restaurant was expensive, but the menu was great.*" would be assigned the aspect PRICE with negative polarity and FOOD with positive polarity. In the product reviews dataset of Hu and Liu (2004a; 2004b), *aspect terms*, i.e., terms naming aspects (e.g., 'radio', 'voice dialing') together with strength scores (e.g., 'radio': +2, 'voice dialing': −3) are pro-

Proceedings of the 8th International Workshop on Semantic Evaluation (SemEval 2014), pages 27–35,
Dublin, Ireland, August 23-24, 2014.

vided. No predefined inventory of aspects is provided, unlike the dataset of Ganu et al.

The SemEval-2014 ABSA Task is based on laptop and restaurant reviews and consists of four subtasks (see Section 2). Participants were free to participate in a subset of subtasks and the domains (laptops or restaurants) of their choice.

2 Task Description

For the first two subtasks (SB1, SB2), datasets on both domains (restaurants, laptops) were provided. For the last two subtasks (SB3, SB4), datasets only for the restaurant reviews were provided.

Aspect term extraction (SB1): Given a set of review sentences, the task is to identify all aspect terms present in each sentence (e.g., 'wine', 'waiter', 'appetizer', 'price', 'food'). We require all the aspect terms to be identified, including aspect terms for which no sentiment is expressed (neutral polarity). These will be useful for constructing an ontology of aspect terms and to identify frequently discussed aspects.

Aspect term polarity (SB2): In this subtask, we assume that the aspect terms are given (as described in SB1) and the task is to determine the polarity of each aspect term (positive, negative, conflict, or neutral). The conflict label applies when both positive and negative sentiment is expressed about an aspect term (e.g., "*Certainly not the best sushi in New York, however, it is always fresh*"). An alternative would have been to tag the aspect term in these cases with the dominant polarity, but this in turn would be difficult to agree on.

Aspect category detection (SB3): Given a predefined set of aspect categories (e.g., PRICE, FOOD) and a set of review sentences (but without any annotations of aspect terms and their polarities), the task is to identify the aspect categories discussed in each sentence. Aspect categories are typically coarser than the aspect terms as defined in SB1, and they do not necessarily occur as terms in the sentences. For example, in *"Delicious but expensive"*, the aspect categories FOOD and PRICE are not instantiated through specific aspect terms, but are only inferred through the adjectives 'delicious' and 'expensive'. SB1 and SB3 were treated as separate subtasks, thus no information linking aspect terms to aspect categories was provided.

Aspect category polarity (SB4): For this subtask, aspect categories for each review sentence are provided. The goal is to determine the polarity (positive, negative, conflict, or neutral) of each aspect category discussed in each sentence.

Subtasks SB1 and SB2 are useful in cases where no predefined inventory of aspect categories is available. In these cases, frequently discussed aspect terms of the entity can be identified together with their overall sentiment polarities. We hope to include an additional *aspect term aggregation* subtask in future (Pavlopoulos and Androutsopoulos, 2014b) to cluster near-synonymous (e.g., 'money', 'price', 'cost') or related aspect terms (e.g., 'design', 'color', 'feeling') together with their averaged sentiment scores as shown in Fig. 1.

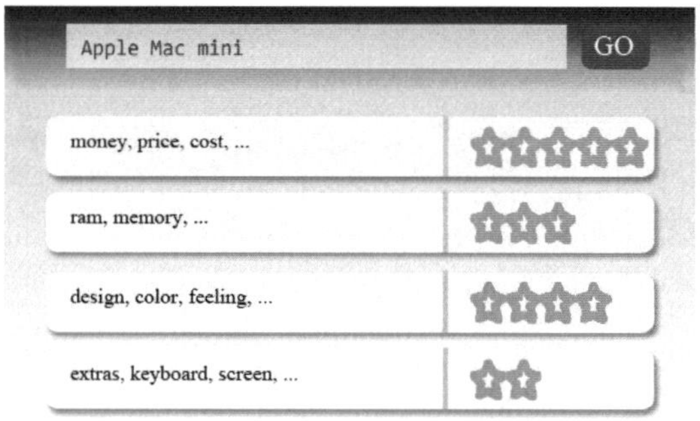

Figure 1: Aggregated aspect terms and average sentiment polarities for a target entity.

Subtasks SB3 and SB4 are useful when a predefined inventory of (coarse) aspect categories is available. A table like the one of Fig. 1 can then also be generated, but this time using the most frequent aspect categories to label the rows, with stars showing the proportion of reviews expressing positive vs. negative opinions for each aspect category.

3 Datasets

3.1 Data Collection

The training and test data sizes are provided in Table 1. The restaurants training data, consisting of 3041 English sentences, is a subset of the dataset from Ganu et al. (2009), which included annotations for coarse aspect categories (as in SB3) and overall sentence polarities. We added annotations for aspect terms occurring in the sentences (SB1), aspect term polarities (SB2), and aspect category polarities (SB4). Additional restaurant reviews were collected and annotated (from scratch) in the same manner and used as test data (800 sentences). The laptops dataset contains 3845 English sentences extracted from laptop custumer reviews. Human annotators tagged the aspect terms (SB1) and their polarities (SB2); 3045 sentences were used for training and 800 for testing (evaluation).

Domain	Train	Test	Total
Restaurants	3041	800	3841
Laptops	3045	800	3845
Total	6086	1600	7686

Table 1: Sizes (sentences) of the datasets.

3.2 Annotation Process

For a given target entity (a restaurant or a laptop) being reviewed, the annotators were asked to provide two types of information: aspect terms (SB1) and aspect term polarities (SB2). For the restaurants dataset, two additional annotation layers were added: aspect category (SB3) and aspect category polarity (SB4).

The annotators used BRAT (Stenetorp et al., 2012), a web-based annotation tool, which was configured appropriately for the needs of the ABSA task.[1] Figure 2 shows an annotated sentence in BRAT, as viewed by the annotators.

Stage 1: Aspect terms and polarities. During a first annotation stage, the annotators tagged all the single or multiword terms that named particular aspects of the target entity (e.g., *"I liked the service and the staff, but not the food"* $\rightarrow$ {'service', 'staff', 'food'}, *"The hard disk is very noisy"* $\rightarrow$ {'hard disk'}). They were asked to tag only aspect terms explicitly naming particular aspects (e.g., *"everything about it"* or *"it's expensive"* do not name particular aspects). The aspect terms were annotated as they appeared, even if misspelled (e.g., *'warrenty'* instead of *'warranty'*). Each identified aspect term also had to be assigned a polarity label (positive, negative, neutral, conflict). For example, *"I hated their fajitas, but their salads were great"* $\rightarrow$ {'fajitas': negative, 'salads': positive}, *"The hard disk is very noisy"* $\rightarrow$ {'hard disk': negative}.

Each sentence of the two datasets was annotated by two annotators, a graduate student (annotator A) and an expert linguist (annotator B). Initially, two subsets of sentences (300 from each dataset) were tagged by annotator A and the annotations were inspected and validated by annotator B. The disagreements between the two annotators were confined to borderline cases. Taking into account the types of these disagreements (discussed below), annotator A was provided with additional guidelines and tagged the remainder of the sentences in both datasets.[2] When A was not confident, a decision was made collaboratively with B. When A and B disagreed, a decision was made collaboratively by them and a third expert annotator. Most disagreements fall into one of the following three types:

Polarity ambiguity: In several sentences, it was unclear if the reviewer expressed positive or negative opinion, or no opinion at all (just reporting a fact), due to lack of context. For example, in *"12.44 seconds boot time"* it is unclear if the reviewer expresses a positive, negative, or no opinion about the aspect term 'boot time'. In future challenges, it would be better to allow the annotators (and the participating systems) to consider the entire review instead of each sentence in isolation.

Multi-word aspect term boundaries: In several cases, the annotators disagreed on the exact boundaries of multi-word aspect terms when they appeared in conjunctions or disjunctions (e.g., *"selection of meats and seafoods"*, *"noodle and rices dishes"*, *"school or office use"*). In such cases, we asked the annotators to tag as a single aspect term the maximal noun phrase (the entire conjunction or disjunction). Other disagreements concerned the extent of the aspect terms when adjectives that may or may not have a subjective meaning were also present. For example, if 'large' in *"large whole shrimp"* is part of the dish name, then the guidelines require the adjective to be included in the aspect term; otherwise (e.g., in *"large portions"*) 'large' is a subjectivity indicator not to be included in the aspect term. Despite the guidelines, in some cases it was difficult to isolate and tag the exact aspect term, because of intervening words, punctuation, or long-term dependencies.

Aspect term vs. reference to target entity: In some cases, it was unclear if a noun or noun phrase was used as the aspect term or if it referred to the entity being reviewed as whole. In "*This place is awesome*", for example, 'place' most probably refers to the restaurant as a whole (hence, it should not be tagged as an aspect term), but in "*Cozy*

[1] Consult `http://brat.nlplab.org/` for more information about BRAT.

[2] The guidelines are available at: `http://alt.qcri.org/semeval2014/task4/data/uploads/`.

Figure 2: A sentence in the BRAT tool, annotated with four aspect terms ('appetizers', 'salads', 'steak', 'pasta') and one aspect category (FOOD). For aspect categories, the whole sentence is tagged.

place and good pizza" it probably refers to the ambience of the restaurant. A broader context would again help in some of these cases.

We note that laptop reviews often evaluate each laptop as a whole, rather than expressing opinions about particular aspects. Furthermore, when they express opinions about particular aspects, they often do so by using adjectives that refer implicitly to aspects (e.g., 'expensive', 'heavy'), rather than using explicit aspect terms (e.g., 'cost', 'weight'); the annotators were instructed to tag only explicit aspect terms, not adjectives implicitly referring to aspects. By contrast, restaurant reviews contain many more aspect terms (Table 2, last column).[3]

Dataset	Pos.	Neg.	Con.	Neu.	Tot.
LPT-TR	987	866	45	460	2358
LPT-TE	341	128	16	169	654
RST-TR	2164	805	91	633	3693
RST-TE	728	196	14	196	1134

Table 2: Aspect terms and their polarities per domain. LPT and RST indicate laptop and restaurant reviews, respectively. TR and TE indicate the training and test set.

Another difference between the two datasets is that the neutral class is much more frequent in (the aspect terms of) laptops, since laptop reviews often mention features without expressing any (clear) sentiment (e.g., "*the latest version does not have a disc drive*"). Nevertheless, the positive class is the majority in both datasets, but it is much more frequent in restaurants (Table 2). The majority of the aspect terms are single-words in both datasets (2148 in laptops, 4827 in restaurants, out of 3012 and 4827 total aspect terms, respectively).

Stage 2: Aspect categories and polarities. In this task, each sentence needs to be tagged with the aspect categories discussed in the sentence. The aspect categories are FOOD, SERVICE, PRICE, AMBIENCE (the atmosphere and environment of a restaurant), and ANECDOTES/MISCELLANEOUS (sentences not belonging in any of the previous aspect categories). [4] For example, *"The restaurant was expensive, but the menu was great"* is assigned the aspect categories PRICE and FOOD. Additionally, a polarity (positive, negative, conflict, neutral) for each aspect category should be provided (e.g., *"The restaurant was expensive, but the menu was great"* $\rightarrow$ {PRICE: negative, FOOD: positive}.

One annotator validated the existing aspect category annotations of the corpus of Ganu et al. (2009). The agreement with the existing annotations was 92% measured as average F_1. Most disagreements concerned additions of missing aspect category annotations. Furthermore, the same annotator validated and corrected (if needed) the existing polarity labels per aspect category annotation. The agreement for the polarity labels was 87% in terms of accuracy and it was measured only on the common aspect category annotations. The additional 800 sentences (not present in Ganu et al.'s dataset) were used for testing and were annotated from scratch in the same manner. The distribution of the polarity classes per category is presented in Table 3. Again, 'positive' is the majority polarity class while the dominant aspect category is FOOD in both the training and test restaurant sentences.

Determining the aspect categories of the sentences and their polarities (Stage 2) was an easier task compared to detecting aspect terms and their polarities (Stage 1). The annotators needed less time in Stage 2 and it was easier to reach agreement. Exceptions were some sentences where it was difficult to decide if the categories AMBIENCE or ANECDOTES/MISCELLANEOUS applied (e.g., *"One of my Fav spots in the city"*). We instructed the annotators to classify those sentences only in ANECDOTES/MISCELLANEOUS, if they conveyed

[3] We count aspect term *occurrences*, not distinct terms.

[4] In the original dataset of Ganu et al. (2009), ANECDOTES and MISCELLANEOUS were separate categories, but in practice they were difficult to distinguish and we merged them.

	Positive		Negative		Conflict		Neutral		Total	
Category	Train	Test	Train	Test	Train	Test	Train	Test	Train	Test
FOOD	867	302	209	69	66	16	90	31	1232	418
PRICE	179	51	115	28	17	3	10	1	321	83
SERVICE	324	101	218	63	35	5	20	3	597	172
AMBIENCE	263	76	98	21	47	13	23	8	431	118
ANECD./MISC.	546	127	199	41	30	15	357	51	1132	234
Total	2179	657	839	159	163	52	500	94	3713	1025

Table 3: Aspect categories distribution per sentiment class.

general views about a restaurant, without explicitly referring to its atmosphere or environment.

3.3 Format and Availability of the Datasets

The datasets of the ABSA task were provided in an XML format (see Fig. 3). They are available with a non commercial, no redistribution license through META-SHARE, a repository devoted to the sharing and dissemination of language resources (Piperidis, 2012).[5]

4 Evaluation Measures and Baselines

The evaluation of the ABSA task ran in two phases. In Phase A, the participants were asked to return the aspect terms (SB1) and aspect categories (SB3) for the provided test datasets. Subsequently, in Phase B, the participants were given the gold aspect terms and aspect categories (as in Fig. 3) for the sentences of Phase A and they were asked to return the polarities of the aspect terms (SB2) and the polarities of the aspect categories of each sentence (SB4).[6] Each participating team was allowed to submit up to two runs per subtask and domain (restaurants, laptops) in each phase; one constrained (C), where only the provided training data and other resources (e.g., publicly available lexica) excluding additional annotated sentences could be used, and one unconstrained (U), where additional data of any kind could be used for training. In the latter case, the teams had to report the resources they used.

To evaluate aspect term extraction (SB1) and aspect category detection (SB3) in Phase A, we used the F_1 measure, defined as usually:

$$F_1 = \frac{2 \cdot P \cdot R}{P + R} \quad (1)$$

where precision (P) and recall (R) are defined as:

$$P = \frac{|S \cap G|}{|S|}, R = \frac{|S \cap G|}{|G|} \quad (2)$$

Here S is the set of aspect term or aspect category annotations (in SB1 and SB3, respectively) that a system returned for all the test sentences (of a domain), and G is the set of the gold (correct) aspect term or aspect category annotations.

To evaluate aspect term polarity (SB2) and aspect category polarity (SB4) detection in Phase B, we calculated the accuracy of each system, defined as the number of correctly predicted aspect term or aspect category polarity labels, respectively, divided by the total number of aspect term or aspect category annotations. Recall that we used the gold aspect term and category annotations in Phase B.

We provided four baselines, one per subtask:[7]

Aspect term extraction (SB1) baseline: A sequence of tokens is tagged as an aspect term in a test sentence (of a domain), if it is listed in a dictionary that contains all the aspect terms of the training sentences (of the same domain).

Aspect term polarity (SB2) baseline: For each aspect term t in a test sentence s (of a particular domain), this baseline checks if t had been encountered in the training sentences (of the domain). If so, it retrieves the k most similar to s training sentences (of the domain), and assigns to the aspect term t the most frequent polarity it had in the k sentences. Otherwise, if t had not been encountered in the training sentences, it is assigned the most frequent aspect term polarity label of the

[5]The datasets can be downloaded from `http://metashare.ilsp.gr:8080/`. META-SHARE (`http://www.meta-share.org/`) was implemented in the framework of the META-NET Network of Excellence (`http://www.meta-net.eu/`).

[6]Phase A ran from 9:00 GMT, March 24 to 21:00 GMT, March 25, 2014. Phase B ran from 9:00 GMT, March 27 to 17:00 GMT, March 29, 2014.

[7]Implementations of the baselines and further information about the baselines are available at: `http://alt.qcri.org/semeval2014/task4/data/uploads/`.

```
<sentence id="11351725#582163#9">
   <text>Our waiter was friendly and it is a shame that he didnt have a supportive
staff to work with.</text>
        <aspectTerms>
            <aspectTerm term="waiter" polarity="positive" from="4" to="10"/>
            <aspectTerm term="staff" polarity="negative" from="74" to="79"/>
        </aspectTerms>
        <aspectCategories>
            <aspectCategory category="service" polarity="conflict"/>
        </aspectCategories>
</sentence>
```

Figure 3: An XML snippet that corresponds to the annotated sentence of Fig. 2.

training set. The similarity between two sentences is measured as the Dice coefficient of the sets of (distinct) words of the two sentences. For example, the similarity between "*this is a demo*" and "*that is yet another demo*" is $\frac{2 \cdot 2}{4+5} = 0.44$.

Aspect category extraction (SB3) baseline: For every test sentence s, the k most similar to s training sentences are retrieved (as in the SB2 baseline). Then, s is assigned the m most frequent aspect category labels of the k retrieved sentences; m is the most frequent number of aspect category labels per sentence among the k sentences.

Aspect category polarity (SB4): This baseline assigns to each aspect category c of a test sentence s the most frequent polarity label that c had in the k most similar to s training sentences (of the same domain), considering only training sentences that have the aspect category label c. Sentence similarity is computed as in the SB2 baseline.

For subtasks SB2 and SB4, we also use a majority baseline that assigns the most frequent polarity (in the training data) to all the aspect terms and aspect categories. The scores of all the baselines and systems are presented in Tables 4–6.

5 Evaluation Results

The ABSA task attracted 32 teams in total and 165 submissions (systems), 76 for phase A and 89 for phase B. Based on the human-annotation experience, the expectations were that systems would perform better in Phase B (SB3, SB4, involving aspect categories) than in Phase A (SB1, SB2, involving aspect terms). The evaluation results confirmed our expectations (Tables 4–6).

5.1 Results of Phase A

The aspect term extraction subtask (SB1) attracted 24 teams for the laptops dataset and 24 teams for the restaurants dataset; consult Table 4.

Laptops		Restaurants	
Team	F_1	Team	F_1
IHS_RD.	74.55†	DLIREC	84.01*
DLIREC	73.78*	XRCE	83.98
DLIREC	70.4	NRC-Can.	80.18
NRC-Can.	68.56	UNITOR	80.09
UNITOR	67.95*	UNITOR	79.96*
XRCE	67.24	IHS_RD.	79.62†
SAP_RI	66.6	UWB	79.35*
IITP	66.55	SeemGo	78.61
UNITOR	66.08	DLIREC	78.34
SeemGo	65.99	ECNU	78.24
ECNU	65.88	SAP_RI	77.88
SNAP	62.4	UWB	76.23
DMIS	60.59	IITP	74.94
UWB	60.39	DMIS	72.73
JU_CSE.	59.37	JU_CSE.	72.34
lsis_lif	56.97	Blinov	71.21*
USF	52.58	lsis_lif	71.09
Blinov	52.07*	USF	70.69
UFAL	48.98	EBDG	69.28*
UBham	47.49	UBham	68.63*
UBham	47.26*	UBham	68.51
SINAI	45.28	SINAI	65.41
EBDG	41.52*	V3	60.43*
V3	36.62*	UFAL	58.88
COMMIT.	25.19	COMMIT.	54.38
NILCUSP	25.19	NILCUSP	49.04
iTac	23.92	SNAP	46.46
		iTac	38.29
Baseline	35.64	Baseline	47.15

Table 4: Results for aspect term extraction (SB1). Stars indicate unconstrained systems. The † indicates a constrained system that was not trained on the in-domain training dataset (unlike the rest of the constrained systems), but on the union of the two training datasets (laptops, restaurants).

Restaurants		Restaurants	
Team	F_1	Team	Acc.
NRC-Can.	88.57	NRC-Can.	82.92
UNITOR	85.26*	XRCE	78.14
XRCE	82.28	UNITOR	76.29*
UWB	81.55*	SAP_RI	75.6
UWB	81.04	SeemGo	74.63
UNITOR	80.76	SA-UZH	73.07
SAP_RI	79.04	UNITOR	73.07
SNAP	78.22	UWB	72.78
Blinov	75.27*	UWB	72.78*
UBham	74.79*	lsis_lif	72.09
UBham	74.24	UBham	71.9
EBDG	73.98*	EBDG	69.75
SeemGo	73.75	SNAP	69.56
SINAI	73.67	COMMIT.	67.7
JU_CSE.	70.46	Blinov	65.65*
lsis_lif	68.27	Ualberta.	65.46
ECNU	67.29	JU_CSE.	64.09
UFAL	64.51	ECNU	63.41
V3	60.20*	UFAL	63.21
COMMIT.	59.3	iTac	62.73*
iTac	56.95	ECNU	60.39*
		SINAI	60.29
		V3	47.21
		Baseline	65.65
Baseline	63.89	Majority	64.09

Table 5: Results for aspect category detection (SB3) and aspect category polarity (SB4). Stars indicate unconstrained systems.

Overall, the systems achieved significantly higher scores (+10%) in the restaurants domain, compared to laptops. The best F_1 score (74.55%) for laptops was achieved by the IHS_RD. team, which relied on Conditional Random Fields (CRF) with features extracted using named entity recognition, POS tagging, parsing, and semantic analysis. The IHS_RD. team used additional reviews from Amazon and Epinions (without annotated terms) to learn the sentiment orientation of words and they trained their CRF on the union of the restaurant and laptop training data that we provided; the same trained CRF classifier was then used in both domains.

The second system, the unconstrained system of DLIREC, also uses a CRF, along with POS and dependency tree based features. It also uses features derived from the aspect terms of the training data and clusters created from additional reviews from YELP and Amazon. In the restaurants domain, the unconstrained system of DLIREC ranked first with an F_1 of 84.01%, but the best unconstrained system, that of XRCE, was very close (83.98%). The XRCE system relies on a parser to extract syntactic/semantic dependencies (e.g., 'dissapointed'–'food'). For aspect term extraction, the parser's vocabulary was enriched with the aspect terms of the training data and a term list extracted from Wikipedia and Wordnet. A set of grammar rules was also added to detect multiword terms and associate them with the corresponding aspect category (e.g., FOOD, PRICE).

The aspect category extraction subtask (SB3) attracted 18 teams. As shown in Table 5, the best score was achieved by the system of NRC-Canada (88.57%), which relied on five binary (one-vs-all) SVMs, one for each aspect category. The SVMs used features based on various types of n-grams (e.g., stemmed) and information from a lexicon learnt from YELP data, which associates aspect terms with aspect categories. The latter lexicon significantly improved F_1. The constrained UNITOR system uses five SVMs with bag-of-words (BoW) features, which in the unconstrained submission are generalized using distributional vectors learnt from Opinosis and TripAdvisor data. Similarly, UWB uses a binary MaxEnt classifier for each aspect category with BoW and TF-IDF features. The unconstrained submission of UWB also uses word clusters learnt using various methods (e.g., LDA); additional features indicate which clusters the words of the sentence being classified come from. XRCE uses information identified by its syntactic parser as well as BoW features to train a logistic regression model that assigns to the sentence probabilities of belonging to each aspect category. A probability threshold, tuned on the training data, is then used to determine which categories will be assigned to the sentence.

5.2 Results of Phase B

The aspect term polarity detection subtask (SB2) attracted 26 teams for the laptops dataset and 26 teams for the restaurants dataset. DCU and NRC-Canada had the best systems in both domains (Table 6). Their scores on the laptops dataset were identical (70.48%). On the laptops dataset, the DCU system performed slightly better (80.95% vs. 80.15%). For SB2, both NRC-Canada and DCU relied on an SVM classifier with features mainly based on n-grams, parse trees, and several out-of-domain, publicly available sentiment lexica (e.g., MPQA, SentiWordnet and Bing Liu's Opinion Lexicon). NRC-Canada also used two automatically compiled polarity lexica for restaurants and laptops, obtained from YELP and Amazon data, respectively. Furthermore, NRC-Canada showed by ablation experiments that the most useful features are those derived from the sentiment lexica. On the other hand, DCU used only publicly available lexica, which were manually adapted by filtering words that do not express sentiment in laptop and restaurant reviews (e.g., 'really') and by adding others that were missing and do express sentiment (e.g., 'mouthwatering').

The aspect category polarity detection subtask (SB4) attracted 20 teams. NRC-Canada again had the best score (82.92%) using an SVM classifier. The same feature set as in SB2 was used, but it was further enriched to capture information related to each specific aspect category. The second team, XRCE, used information from its syntactic parser, BoW features, and an out-of-domain sentiment lexicon to train an SVM model that predicts the polarity of each given aspect category.

6 Conclusions and Future Work

We provided an overview of Task 4 of SemEval-2014. The task aimed to foster research in aspect-based sentiment analysis (ABSA). We constructed and released ABSA benchmark datasets containing manually annotated reviews from two domains (restaurants, laptops). The task attracted 163 submissions from 32 teams that were evaluated in four subtasks centered around aspect terms (detecting aspect terms and their polarities) and coarser aspect categories (assigning aspect categories and aspect category polarities to sentences). The task will be repeated in SemEval-2015 with additional datasets and a domain-adaptation subtask.[8] In the future, we hope to add an aspect term aggregation subtask (Pavlopoulos and Androutsopoulos, 2014a).

Laptops		Restaurants	
Team	Acc.	Team	Acc.
DCU	70.48	DCU	80.95
NRC-Can.	70.48	NRC-Can.	80.15†
SZTE-NLP	66.97	UWB	77.68*
UBham	66.66	XRCE	77.68
UWB	66.66*	SZTE-NLP	75.22
lsis_lif	64.52	UNITOR	74.95*
USF	64.52	UBham	74.6
SNAP	64.06	USF	73.19
UNITOR	62.99	UNITOR	72.48
UWB	62.53	SeemGo	72.31
IHS_RD.	61.62	lsis_lif	72.13
SeemGo	61.31	UWB	71.95
ECNU	61.16	SA-UZH	70.98
ECNU	61.16*	IHS_RD.	70.81
SINAI	58.71	SNAP	70.81
SAP_RI	58.56	ECNU	70.72
UNITOR	58.56*	ECNU	70.72*
SA-UZH	58.25	INSIGHT.	70.72
COMMIT	57.03	SAP_RI	69.92
INSIGHT.	57.03	EBDG	68.6
UMCC.	57.03*	UMCC.	66.84*
UFAL	56.88	UFAL	66.57
UMCC.	56.11	UMCC.	66.57
EBDG	55.96	COMMIT	65.96
JU_CSE.	55.65	JU_CSE.	65.52
UO_UA	55.19*	Blinov	63.58*
V3	53.82	iTac	62.25*
Blinov	52.29*	V3	59.78
iTac	51.83*	SINAI	58.73
DLIREC	36.54	DLIREC	42.32*
DLIREC	36.54*	DLIREC	41.71
IITP	66.97	IITP	67.37
Baseline	51.37	Baseline	64.28
Majority	52.14	Majority	64.19

Table 6: Results for the aspect term polarity subtask (SB2). Stars indicate unconstrained systems. The † indicates a constrained system that was not trained on the in-domain training dataset (unlike the rest of the constrained systems), but on the union of the two training datasets. IITP's original submission files were corrupted; they were resent and scored after the end of the evaluation period.

Acknowledgements

We thank Ioanna Lazari, who provided an initial version of the laptops dataset, Konstantina Papanikolaou, who carried out a critical part of the annotation process, and Juli Bakagianni, who supported our use of the META-SHARE platform. We are also very grateful to the participants for their feedback. Maria Pontiki and Haris Papageorgiou were supported by the IS-HELLEANA (09-

[8]Consult `http://alt.qcri.org/semeval2015/task12/`.

72-922) and the POLYTROPON (KRIPIS-GSRT, MIS: 448306) projects.

References

Samuel Brody and Noemie Elhadad. 2010. An unsupervised aspect-sentiment model for online reviews. In *Proceedings of NAACL*, pages 804–812, Los Angeles, California.

Michael Gamon, Anthony Aue, Simon Corston-Oliver, and Eric K. Ringger. 2005. Pulse: Mining customer opinions from free text. In *IDA*, pages 121–132, Madrid, Spain.

Gayatree Ganu, Noemie Elhadad, and Amélie Marian. 2009. Beyond the stars: Improving rating predictions using review text content. In *Proceedings of WebDB*, Providence, Rhode Island, USA.

Minqing Hu and Bing Liu. 2004a. Mining and summarizing customer reviews. In *Proceedings of KDD*, pages 168–177, Seattle, WA, USA.

Minqing Hu and Bing Liu. 2004b. Mining opinion features in customer reviews. In *Proceedings of AAAI*, pages 755–760, San Jose, California.

Bing Liu. 2012. *Sentiment Analysis and Opinion Mining*. Synthesis Lectures on Human Language Technologies. Morgan & Claypool Publishers.

Chong Long, Jie Zhang, and Xiaoyan Zhu. 2010. A review selection approach for accurate feature rating estimation. In *Proceedings of COLING (Posters)*, pages 766–774, Beijing, China.

Bo Pang, Lillian Lee, and Shivakumar Vaithyanathan. 2002. Thumbs up? sentiment classification using machine learning techniques. In *Proceedings of EMNLP*, pages 79–86, Philadelphia, Pennsylvania, USA.

John Pavlopoulos and Ion Androutsopoulos. 2014a. Aspect term extraction for sentiment analysis: New datasets, new evaluation measures and an improved unsupervised method. In *Proceedings of LASM-EACL*, pages 44–52, Gothenburg, Sweden.

John Pavlopoulos and Ion Androutsopoulos. 2014b. Multi-granular aspect aggregation in aspect-based sentiment analysis. In *Proceedings of EACL*, pages 78–87, Gothenburg, Sweden.

Stelios Piperidis. 2012. The META-SHARE language resources sharing infrastructure: Principles, challenges, solutions. In *Proceedings of LREC-2012*, pages 36–42, Istanbul, Turkey.

Ana-Maria Popescu and Oren Etzioni. 2005. Extracting product features and opinions from reviews. In *Proceedings of HLT/EMNLP*, pages 339–346, Vancouver, British Columbia, Canada.

Pontus Stenetorp, Sampo Pyysalo, Goran Topić, Tomoko Ohta, Sophia Ananiadou, and Jun'ichi Tsujii. 2012. BRAT: a web-based tool for NLP-assisted text annotation. In *Proceedings of EACL*, pages 102–107, Avignon, France.

Tun Thura Thet, Jin-Cheon Na, and Christopher S. G. Khoo. 2010. Aspect-based sentiment analysis of movie reviews on discussion boards. *J. Information Science*, 36(6):823–848.

Ivan Titov and Ryan T. McDonald. 2008. A joint model of text and aspect ratings for sentiment summarization. In *Proceedings of ACL*, pages 308–316, Columbus, Ohio, USA.

Peter Turney. 2002. Thumbs up or thumbs down? semantic orientation applied to unsupervised classification of reviews. In *Proceedings of ACL*, pages 417–424, Philadelphia, Pennsylvania, USA.

SemEval-2014 Task 5: L2 Writing Assistant

Maarten van Gompel, Iris Hendrickx, Antal van den Bosch
Centre for Language Studies,
Radboud University Nijmegen,
The Netherlands
proycon@anaproy.nl,
i.hendrickx@let.ru.nl,
a.vandenbosch@let.ru.nl

Els Lefever and Véronique Hoste
LT3,
Language and Translation Technology Team,
Ghent University,
Belgium
els.lefever@ugent.be,
veronique.hoste@ugent.be

Abstract

We present a new cross-lingual task for SemEval concerning the translation of L1 fragments in an L2 context. The task is at the boundary of Cross-Lingual Word Sense Disambiguation and Machine Translation. It finds its application in the field of computer-assisted translation, particularly in the context of second language learning. Translating L1 fragments in an L2 context allows language learners when writing in a target language (L2) to fall back to their native language (L1) whenever they are uncertain of the right word or phrase.

1 Introduction

We present a new cross-lingual and application-oriented task for SemEval that is situated in the area where Word Sense Disambiguation and Machine Translation meet. Finding the proper translation of a word or phrase in a given context is much like the problem of disambiguating between multiple senses.

In this task participants are asked to build a translation/writing assistance system that translates specifically marked L1 fragments in an L2 context to their proper L2 translation. This type of translation can be applied in writing assistance systems for language learners in which users write in a target language, but are allowed to occasionally back off to their native L1 when they are uncertain of the proper lexical or grammatical form in L2. The task concerns the NLP back-end rather than any user interface.

Full-on machine translation typically concerns the translation of complete sentences or texts from L1 to L2. This task, in contrast, focuses on smaller fragments, side-tracking the problem of full word reordering.

We focus on the following language combinations of L1 and L2 pairs: *English-German*, *English-Spanish*, *French-English* and *Dutch-English*. Task participants could participate for all language pairs or any subset thereof.

2 Task Description

We frame the task in the context of second language learning, yielding a specific practical application.

Participants build a *translation assistance system* rather than a full machine translation system. The L1 expression, a word or phrase, is translated by the system to L2, given the L2 context already present, including right-side context if available. The aim here, as in all translation, is to carry the semantics of the L1 fragment over to L2 and find the most suitable L2 expression given the already present L2 context.

Other than a limit on length (6 words), we do not pose explicit constraints on the kinds of L1 fragments allowed. The number of L1 fragments is limited to one fragment per sentence.

The task addresses both a core problem of WSD, with cross-lingual context, and a sub-problem of Phrase-based Statistical Machine Translation; that of finding the most suitable translation of a word or phrase. In MT this would be modelled by the translation model. In our task the full complexity of full-sentential translation is bypassed, putting the emphasis on the semantic aspect of translation. Our task has specific practical applications and a specific intended audience, namely intermediate and advanced second language learners, whom one generally wants to encourage to use their target language as much as possible, but who may often feel the need to fall back to their native language.

Proceedings of the 8th International Workshop on Semantic Evaluation (SemEval 2014), pages 36–44,
Dublin, Ireland, August 23-24, 2014.

Currently, language learners are forced to fall back to a bilingual dictionary when in doubt. Such dictionaries do not take the L2 context into account and are generally more constrained to single words or short expressions. The proposed application would allow more flexible context-dependent lookups as writing progresses. The task tests how effectively participating systems accomplish this.

The following examples illustrate the task for the four language pairs we offer:

- Input (L1=English,L2=Spanish): *"Todo ello, **in accordance** con los principios que siempre hemos apoyado."*
  Desired output: *"Todo ello, **de conformidad** con los principios que siempre hemos apoyado."*

- Input (L1-English, L2=German): *"Das, was wir heute machen, **is essentially** ein Ärgernis."*
  Desired output: *"Das, was wir heute machen, **ist im Grunde genommen** ein Ärgernis."*

- Input (L1=French,L2=English): *"I **rentre à la maison** because I am tired."*
  Desired output: *"I **return home** because I am tired."*

- Input (L1=Dutch, L2=English): *"Workers are facing a massive **aanval op** their employment and social rights."*
  Desired output: *"Workers are facing a massive **attack on** their employment and social rights."*

The task can be related to two tasks that were offered in previous years of SemEval: Lexical Substitution (Mihalcea et al., 2010) and most notably Cross-lingual Word Sense Disambiguation (Lefever and Hoste, 2013).

When comparing our task to the Cross-Lingual Word-Sense Disambiguation task, one notable difference is the fact that our task concerns not just words, but also phrases. Another essential difference is the nature of the context; our context is in L2 instead of L1. Unlike the Cross-Lingual Word Sense Disambiguation task, we do not constrain the L1 words or phrases that may be used for translation, except for a maximum length which we set to 6 tokens, whereas Lefever and Hoste (2013) only tested a select number of nouns. Our task emphasizes a correct meaning-preserving choice of words in which translations have to fit in the L2 context. There is thus a clear morphosyntactic aspect to the task, although less prominent than in full machine translation, as the remainder of the sentence, already in L2, does not need to be changed. In the Cross-Lingual Word Sense Disambiguation tasks, the translations/senses were lemmatised. We deliberately chose a different path that allows for the envisioned application to function directly as a translation assistance system.

A pilot study was conducted to test the feasibility of the proposed translation system (van Gompel and van den Bosch, 2014). It shows that L2 context information can be a useful cue in translation of L1 fragments to L2, improving over a non-context-informed baseline.

3 Data

We did not provide training data for this task, as we did not want to bias participating systems by favouring a particular sort of material and methodology. Moreover, it would be a prohibitively large task to manually collect enough training data of the task itself. Participants were therefore free to use any suitable training material such as parallel corpora, wordnets, or bilingual lexica.

Trial and test data has been collected for the task, both delivered in a simple XML format that explicitly marks the fragments. System output of participants adheres to the same format. The trial set, released early on in the task, was used by participants to develop and tune their systems on. The test set corresponds to the final data released for the evaluation period; the final evaluation was conducted on this data.

The trial data was constructed in an automated fashion in the way described in our pilot study (van Gompel and van den Bosch, 2014). First a phrase-translation table is constructed from a parallel corpus. We used the Europarl parallel corpus (Koehn, 2005) and the Moses tools (Koehn et al., 2007), which in turn makes use of GIZA++ (Och and Ney, 2000). Only strong phrase pairs (exceeding a set threshold) were retained and weaker ones were pruned. This phrase-translation table was then used to create input sentences in which the L2 fragments are swapped for their L1 counterparts, effectively mimicking a fall-back to L1 in an L2 context. The full L2 sentence acts as reference sentence. Finally, to ensure all fragments are correct and sensible, a manual selection from this automatically generated corpus constituted the final trial set.

In our pilot study, such a data set, even without the manual selection stage, proved adequate to demonstrate the feasibility of translating L1 fragments in an L2 context (van Gompel and van den Bosch, 2014). One can, however, rightfully argue whether such data is sufficiently representative for the task and whether it would adequately cover instances where L2 language learners might experience difficulties and be inclined to fall back to L1. We therefore created a more representative test set for the task.

The actual test set conforms to much more stringent constraints and was composed entirely by hand from a wide variety of written sources. Amongst these sources are study books and grammar books for language learners, short bilingual on-line stories aimed at language learners, gap-exercises and cloze tests, and contemporary written resources such as newspapers, novels, and Wikipedia. We aimed for actual learner corpora, but finding suitable learner corpora with sufficient data proved hard. For German we could use the the Merlin corpus (Abel et al., 2013). In example (a) we see a real example of a fragment in a fallback language in an L2 context from the Merlin corpus.

(a) **Input:** Das Klima hier ist **Tropical** und wir haben fast keinen Winter
Reference: Das Klima hier ist **tropisch** und wir haben fast keinen Winter.

For various sources bilingual data was available. For the ones that were monolingual (L2) we resorted to manual translation. To ensure our translations were correct, these were later independently verified, and where necessary corrected by native speakers.

A large portion of the test set comes from offline resources because we wanted to make sure that a substantial portion of the test set could not be found verbatim on-line. This was done to prevent systems from solving the actual problem by just attempting to just look up the sources through the available context information.

Note that in general we aimed for the European varieties of the different languages. However, for English we did add the US spelling variants as alternatives. A complete list of all sources used in establishing the test set is available on our website[1].

We created a trial set and test set/gold standard of 500 sentence pairs per language pair. Due to the detection of some errors at a later stage, some of which were caused by the tokenisation process, we were forced to remove some sentences from the test set and found ourselves slightly below our aim for some of the language pairs. The test set was delivered in both tokenised[2] and untokenised form. The trial set was delivered only in tokenised form. Evaluation was conducted against the tokenised version, but our evaluation script was designed to be as lenient as possible regarding differences in tokenisation. We explicitly took cases into account where participant's tokenisers split contractions (such as Spanish "del" to "de" + "el"), whereas our tokeniser did not.

For a given input fragment, it may well be possible that there are multiple correct translations possible. In establishing our test set, we therefore paid special attention to adding alternatives. To ensure no alternatives were missed, all participant output was aggregated in one set, effectively anonymising the systems, and valid but previously missed alternatives were added to the gold standard.

4 Evaluation

Several metrics are available for automatic evaluation. First, we measure the absolute accuracy $a = c/n$, where c is the number of fragment translations from the system output that precisely match the corresponding fragments in the reference translation, and n is the total number of translatable fragments, including those for which no translation was found. We also introduce a word-based accuracy, which unlike the absolute accuracy gives some credits to mismatches that show partial overlap with the reference translation. It assigns a score according to the longest consecutive matching substring between output fragment and reference fragment and is computed as follows:

$$wac = \frac{|longestsubmatch(output, reference)|}{max(|output|, |reference|)} \quad (1)$$

The system with the highest word-based accuracy wins the competition. All matching is case-sensitive.

[1]https://github.com/proycon/semeval2014task5

[2]Using ucto, available at https://github.com/proycon/ucto

Systems may decide not to translate fragments if they cannot find a suitable translation. A recall metric simply measures the number of fragments for which the system generated a translation, regardless of whether that translation is correct or not, as a proportion of the total number of fragments.

In addition to these task-specific metrics, standard MT metrics such as BLEU, NIST, METEOR and error rates such as WER, PER and TER, are included in the evaluation script as well. Scores such as BLEU will generally be high (> 0.95) when computed on the full sentence, as a large portion of the sentence is already translated and only a specific fragment remains to be evaluated. Nevertheless, these generic metrics are proven in our pilot study to follow the same trend as the more task-specific evaluation metrics, and will be omitted in the result section for brevity.

It regularly occurs that multiple translations are possible. As stated, in the creation of the test set we have taken this into account by explicitly encoding valid alternatives. A match with any alternative in the reference counts as a valid match. For word accuracy, the highest word accuracy amongst all possible alternatives in the reference is taken. Likewise, participant system output may contain multiple alternatives as well, as we allowed two different types of runs, following the example of the Cross-Lingual Lexical Substitution and Cross-Lingual Word Sense Disambiguation tasks:

- **Best** - The system may only output one, its best, translation;
- **Out of Five** - The system may output up to five alternatives, effectively allowing 5 guesses. Only the best match is counted. This metric does *not* count how many of the five are valid.

Participants could submit up to three runs per language pair and evaluation type.

5 Participants

Six teams submitted systems, three of which participated for all language pairs. In alphabetic order, these are:

1. **CNRC** - Cyril Goutte, Michel Simard, Marine Carpuat - National Research Council Canada – *All language pairs*
2. **IUCL** - Alex Rudnick, Liu Can, Levi King, Sandra Kübler, Markus Dickinson - Indiana University (US) – *all language pairs*
3. **UEdin** - Eva Hasler - University of Edinburgh (UK) – *all language pairs except English-German*
4. **UNAL** - Sergio Jiménez, Emilio Silva - Universidad Nacional de Colombia – *English-Spanish*
5. **Sensible** - Liling Tan - Universität des Saarlandes (Germany) and Nanyang Technological University (Singapore) – *all language pairs*
6. **TeamZ** - Anubhav Gupta - Université de Franche-Comté (France) – *English-Spanish, English-German*

Participants implemented distinct methodologies and implementations. One obvious avenue of tackling the problem is through standard Statistical Machine Translation (SMT). The CNRC team takes a pure SMT approach with few modifications. They employ their own Portage decoder and directly send an L1 fragment in an L2 context, corresponding to a partial translation hypothesis with only one fragment left to decode, to their decoder (Goutte et al., 2014). The UEdin team applies a similar method using the Moses decoder, marking the L2 context so that the decoder leaves this context as is. In addition they add a context similarity feature for every phrase pair in the phrase translation table, which expresses topical similarity with the test context. In order to properly decode, the phrase table is filtered per test sentence (Hasler, 2014). The IUCL and UNAL teams do make use of the information from word alignments or phrase translation tables, but do not use a standard SMT decoder. The IUCL system combines various information sources in a log-linear model: phrase table, L2 Language Model, Multilingual Dictionary, and a dependency-based collocation model, although this latter source was not finished in time for the system submission (Rudnick et al., 2014). The UNAL system extracts syntactic features as a means to relate L1 fragments with L2 context to their L2 fragment translations, and uses memory-based classifiers to achieve this (Silva-Schlenker et al., 2014). The two systems on the lower end of the result spectrum use different techniques altogether. The Sensible team approaches the problem by attempting to emulate the manual post-editing process human translators employ to correct MT output (Tan et al., 2014), whereas TeamZ relies on Wiktionary as the sole source (Gupta, 2014).

6 Results

The results of the six participating teams can be viewed in consensed form in Table 1. This table shows the highest word accuracy achieved by the participants, in which multiple system runs have been aggregated. A ranking can quickly be distilled from this, as the best score is marked in bold. The system by the University of Edinburgh emerges as the clear winner of the task. The full results of the various system runs by the six participants are shown in Tables 2 and 3, two pages down, all three aforementioned evaluation metrics are reported there and the systems are sorted by word accuracy per language pair and evaluation type.

Team	**en-es**	oof	**en-de**	oof
CNRC	0.745	0.887	0.717	**0.868**
IUCL	0.720	0.847	**0.722**	0.857
UEdin	**0.827**	**0.949**	-	-
UNAL	0.809	0.880	-	-
Sensible	0.351	0.231	0.233	0.306
TeamZ	0.333	0.386	0.293	0.385
	fr-en	oof	**nl-en**	oof
CNRC	0.694	0.839	0.610	0.723
IUCL	0.682	0.800	0.679	0.753
UEdin	**0.824**	**0.939**	**0.692**	**0.811**
UNAL	-	-	-	-
Sensible	0.116	0.14	0.152	0.171
TeamZ	-	-	-	-

Table 1: Highest word accuracy per team, per language pair, and per evaluation type (out-of-five is include in the "oof" column). The best score in each column is marked in bold.

For the lowest-ranking participants, the score is negatively impacted by the low recall; their systems could not find translations for a large number of fragments.

Figures 1 (next page) and 2 (last page) show the results for the *best* evaluation type for each system run. Three bars are shown; from left to right these represent *accuracy* (blue), *word-accuracy* (green) and *recall* (red). Graphs for *out-of-five* evaluation were omitted for brevity, but tend to follow the same trend with scores that are somewhat higher. These scores can be viewed on the result website at `http://github.com/proycon/semeval2014task5/`. The result website also holds the system output and evaluation scripts with which all graphs and tables can be reproduced.

We observe that the best scoring team in the task (UEdin), as well as the CNRC team, both employ standard Statistical Machine Translation and achieve high results. From this we can conclude that standard SMT techniques are suitable for this task. Teams IUCL and UNAL achieve similarly good results, building on word and phrase alignment data as does SMT, yet not using a traditional SMT decoder. TeamZ and Sensible, the two systems ranked lowest do not rely on any techniques from SMT. To what extent the context-informed measures of the various participants are effective can not be judged from this comparison, but can only be assessed in comparison to their own baselines. For this we refer to the system papers of the participants.

7 Discussion

We did not specify any training data for the task. The advantage of this is that participants were free to build a wider variety of systems from various sources, rather than introducing a bias towards for instances statistical systems. The disadvantage, however, is that a comparison of the various systems does not yield conclusive results regarding the merit of their methodologies. Discrepancies might at least be partly due to differences in training data, as it is generally well understood in MT that more training data improves results. The baselines various participants describe in their system papers provide more insight to the merit of their approaches than a comparison between them.

In the creation of the test set, we aimed to mimic intermediate to high-level language learners. We also aimed at a fair distribution of different part-of-speech categories and phrasal length. The difficulty of the task differs between language pairs, though not intentionally so. We observe that the Dutch-English set is the hardest and the Spanish-English is the easiest in the task. One of the participants implicitly observes this through measurement of the number of Out-of-Vocabulary words (Goutte et al., 2014). This implies that when comparing system performance between different language pairs, one can not simply ascribe a lower result to a system having more difficulty with said

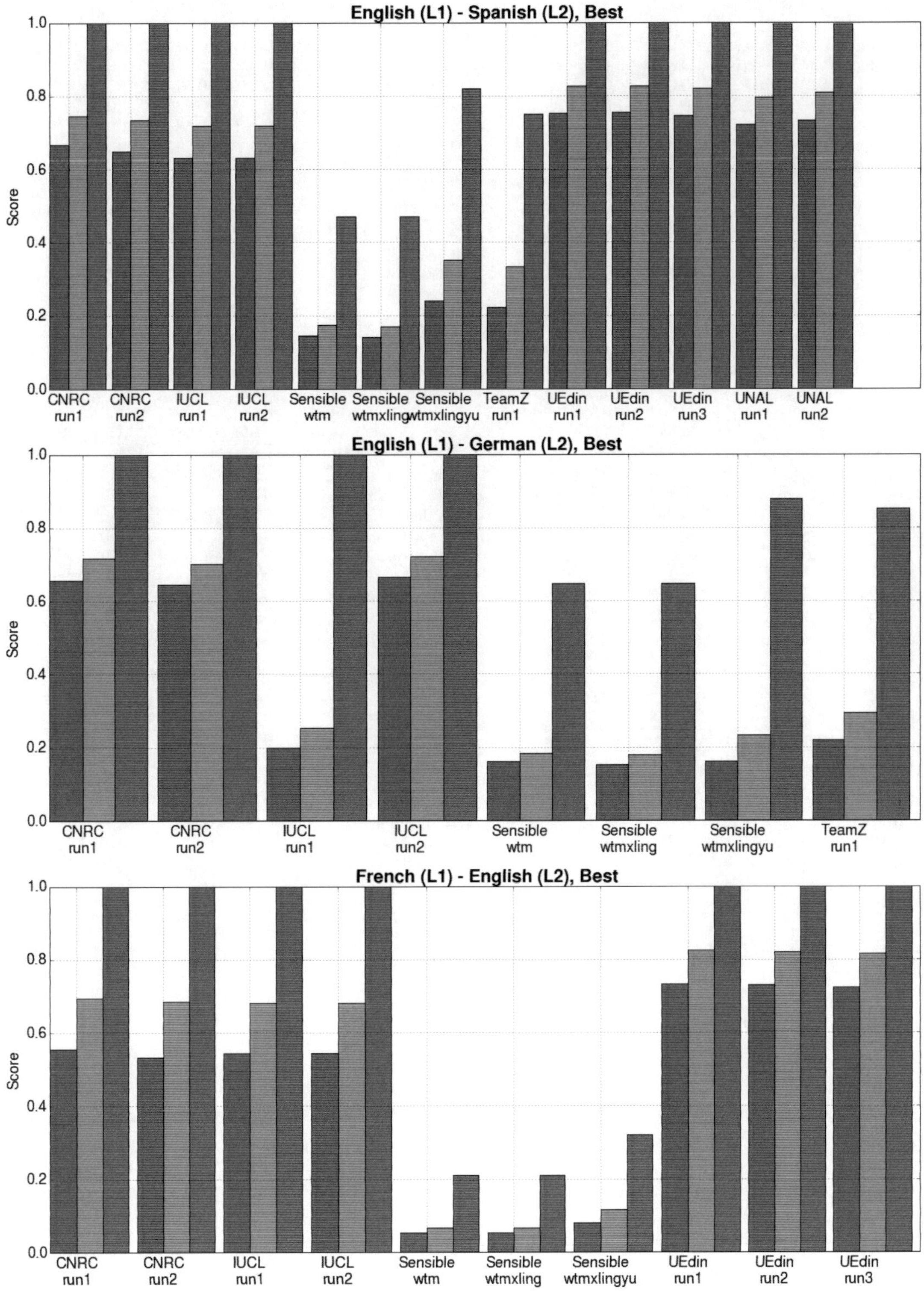

Figure 1: English to Spanish (top), English to German (middle) and French to English (bottom). The three bars, left-to-right, represent Accuracy (blue), Word Accuracy (green) and Recall (red).

System	Acc	W.Acc.	Recall
English-Spanish (best)			
UEdin-run2	0.755	0.827	1.0
UEdin-run1	0.753	0.827	1.0
UEdin-run3	0.745	0.82	1.0
UNAL-run2	0.733	0.809	0.994
UNAL-run1	0.721	0.794	0.994
CNRC-run1	0.667	0.745	1.0
CNRC-run2	0.651	0.735	1.0
IUCL-run1	0.633	0.72	1.0
IUCL-run2	0.633	0.72	1.0
Sensible-wtmxlingyu	0.239	0.351	0.819
TeamZ-run1	0.223	0.333	0.751
Sensible-wtm	0.145	0.175	0.470
Sensible-wtmxling	0.141	0.171	0.470
English-Spanish (out-of-five)			
UEdin-run3	0.928	0.949	1.0
UEdin-run1	0.924	0.946	1.0
UEdin-run2	0.92	0.944	1.0
CNRC-run1	0.843	0.887	1.0
CNRC-run2	0.837	0.884	1.0
UNAL-run1	0.823	0.88	0.994
IUCL-run1	0.781	0.847	1.0
IUCL-run2	0.781	0.847	1.0
Sensible-wtmxlingyu	0.263	0.416	0.819
TeamZ-run1	0.277	0.386	0.751
Sensible-wtm	0.173	0.231	0.470
Sensible-wtmxling	0.169	0.228	0.470
English-German (best)			
IUCL-run2	0.665	0.722	1.0
CNRC-run1	0.657	0.717	1.0
CNRC-run2	0.645	0.702	1.0
TeamZ-run1	0.218	0.293	0.852
IUCL-run1	0.198	0.252	1.0
Sensible-wtmxlingyu	0.162	0.233	0.878
Sensible-wtm	0.16	0.184	0.647
Sensible-wtmxling	0.152	0.178	0.647
English-German (out-of-five)			
CNRC-run1	0.834	0.868	1.0
CNRC-run2	0.828	0.865	1.0
IUCL-run2	0.806	0.857	1.0
TeamZ-run1	0.307	0.385	0.852
IUCL-run1	0.228	0.317	1.0
Sensible-wtmxlingyu	0.18	0.306	0.878
Sensible-wtm	0.182	0.256	0.647
Sensible-wtmxling	0.174	0.25	0.647

Table 2: Full results for English-Spanish and English-German.

System	Acc	W.Acc.	Recall
French-English (best)			
UEdin-run1	0.733	0.824	1.0
UEdin-run2	0.731	0.821	1.0
UEdin-run3	0.723	0.816	1.0
CNRC-run1	0.556	0.694	1.0
CNRC-run2	0.533	0.686	1.0
IUCL-run1	0.545	0.682	1.0
IUCL-run2	0.545	0.682	1.0
Sensible-wtmxlingyu	0.081	0.116	0.321
Sensible-wtm	0.055	0.067	0.210
Sensible-wtmxling	0.055	0.067	0.210
French-English (out-of-five)			
UEdin-run2	0.909	0.939	1.0
UEdin-run1	0.905	0.938	1.0
UEdin-run3	0.907	0.937	1.0
CNRC-run1	0.739	0.839	1.0
CNRC-run2	0.731	0.834	1.0
IUCL-run1	0.691	0.8	1.0
IUCL-run2	0.691	0.8	1.0
Sensible-wtmxlingyu	0.085	0.14	0.321
Sensible-wtmxling	0.061	0.09	0.210
Sensible-wtm	0.061	0.089	0.210
Dutch-English (best)			
UEdin-run1	0.575	0.692	1.0
UEdin-run2	0.567	0.688	1.0
UEdin-run3	0.565	0.688	1.0
IUCL-run1	0.544	0.679	1.0
IUCL-run2	0.544	0.679	1.0
CNRC-run1	0.45	0.61	1.0
CNRC-run2	0.444	0.609	1.0
Sensible-wtmxlingyu	0.115	0.152	0.335
Sensible-wtm	0.092	0.099	0.214
Sensible-wtmxling	0.088	0.095	0.214
Dutch-English (out-of-five)			
UEdin-run1	0.733	0.811	1.0
UEdin-run3	0.727	0.808	1.0
UEdin-run2	0.725	0.808	1.0
IUCL-run1	0.634	0.753	1.0
IUCL-run2	0.634	0.753	1.0
CNRC-run1	0.606	0.723	1.0
CNRC-run2	0.602	0.721	1.0
Sensible-wtmxlingyu	0.123	0.171	0.335
Sensible-wtm	0.099	0.115	0.214
Sensible-wtmxling	0.096	0.112	0.214

Table 3: Full results for French-English and Dutch-English.

language pair. This could rather be an intrinsic property of the test set or the distance between the languages.

Distance in syntactic structure between languages also defines the limits of this task. During composition of the test set it became clear that backing off to L1 was not always possible when syntax diverged to much. An example of this is separable verbs in Dutch and German. Consider the German sentence *"Er **ruft** seine Mutter **an**"* (translation: *"He **calls** his mother"*). Imagine a German language learner wanting to compose such a sentence but wanting to fall back to English for the verb *"to call"*, which would translate to German as *"anrufen"*. The possible input sentence may still be easy to construe: *"Er **calls** seine Mutter"*, but the solution to this problem would require insertion at two different points, whereas the task currently only deals with a substitution of a single fragment. The reverse is arguably even more complex and may stray too far from what a language learner may do. Consider an English language learner wanting to fall back to her native German, struggling with the English translation for *"anrufen"*. She may compose a sentence such as *"He **ruft** his mother **an**"*, which would require translating two dependent fragments into one.

We already have interesting examples in the gold standard, such as example (b), showing syntactic word-order changes confined to a single fragment.

(b) **Input:** I always wanted **iemand te zijn** , but now I realize I should have been more specific.
Reference: I always wanted **to be somebody** , but now I realize I should have been more specific.
Participant output (aggregated): to be a person; it to be; someone to his; to be somebody; person to be; someone to; someone to be; to be anybody; to anyone; to be someone; a person to have any; to be someone else

Another question we can ask, but have not investigated, is whether a language learner would insert the proper morphosyntactic form of an L1 word given the L2 context, or whether she may be inclined to fall back to a normal form such as an infinitive. Especially in the above case of separable verbs someone may be more inclined to circumvent the double fragments and provide the input: *"He **anrufen** his mother"*, but in simpler cases the same issue arises as well. Consider an English learner falling back to her native Croatian, a Slavic language which heavily declines nouns. If she did not know the English word *"book"* and wanted to write *"He gave the book to him"*, she could use either the Croatian word *"knjigu"* in its accusative declension or fall back to the normal form *"knjiga"*. A proper writing assistant system would have to account for both options.

We can analyse which of the sentences in the test data participants struggled with most. First we look at the number of sentences that produce an average word accuracy of zero, measured per sentence over all systems and runs in the out-of-five metric. This means no participant was close to the correct output. There were 6 such sentences in English-Spanish, 17 in English-German, 6 in French-English, and 32 in Dutch-English.

A particularly difficult context from the Spanish set is when a subjunctive verb form was required, but an indicative verb form was submitted by the systems, such as in the sentence: *"Espero que los frenos del coche **funcionen** bien."*. Though this may be deduced from context (the word *"Espero"*, expressing hope yet doubt, being key here), it is often subtle and hard to capture. Another problematic case that recurs in the German and Dutch data sets is compound nouns. The English fragment *"work motivation"* should translate into the German compound *"Arbeitsmotivation"* or *"Arbeitsmoral"*, yet participants were not able to find the actual compound noun. Beside compound nouns, other less frequent multi-word expressions are also amongst the difficult cases. Sparsity or complete absence in training data of these expressions is why systems struggle here.

Another point of discussion is the fact that we enriched the test set by adding previously unavailable alternative translations from an aggregated pool of system output. This might draw criticism for possibly introducing a bias, also considering the fact that the decision to include a particular alternative for a given context is not always straightforward and at times subjective. We, however, contend that this is the best way to ensure that valid system output is not discarded and reduce the number of false negatives. The effect of this measure has been an increase in (word) accuracy for all systems, without significant impact on ranking.

8 Conclusion

In this SemEval task we showed that systems can translate L1 fragments in an L2 context, a task that finds application in computer-assisted translation and computer-assisted language learning. The localised translation of a fragment in a cross-lingual context makes it a novel task in the field. Though the task has its limits, we argue for its practical application in a language-learning setting: as a writing assistant and dictionary replacement. Six contestants participated in the task, and used an ensemble of techniques from Statistical Machine Translation and Word Sense Disambiguation. Most of the task organizers' time went into manually establishing a gold standard based on a wide variety of sources, most aimed at language learners, for each of the four language pairs in the task. We have been positively surprised by the good results of the highest ranking systems.

9 Acknowledgements

We would like to thank Andreu van Hooft and Sarah Schulz for their manual correction work, and Sean Banville, Geert Joris, Bernard De Clerck, Rogier Crijns, Adriane Boyd, Detmar Meurers, Guillermo Sanz Gallego and Nils Smeuninx for helping us with the data collection.

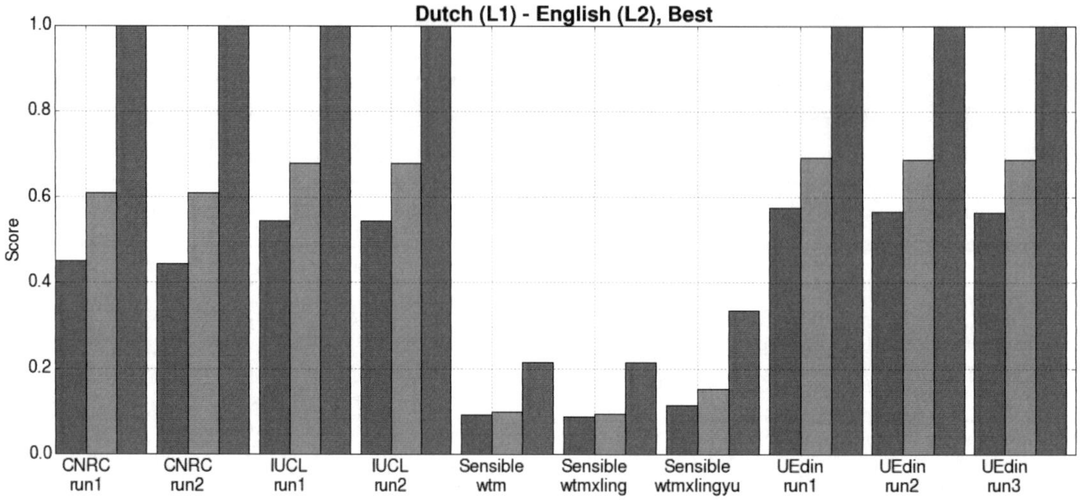

Figure 2: Dutch to English.

References

Andrea Abel, Lionel Nicolas, Jirka Hana, Barbora Štindlová, Katrin Wisniewski, Claudia Woldt, Detmar Meurers, and Serhiy Bykh. 2013. A trilingual learner corpus illustrating european reference levels. In *Proceedings of the Learner Corpus Research Conference*, Bergen, Norway, 27-29 September.

Cyril Goutte, Michel Simard, and Marine Carpuat. 2014. CNRC-TMT: Second language writing assistant system description. In *Proceedings of the 8th International Workshop on Semantic Evaluation (SemEval-2014)*, Dublin, Ireland.

Anubhav Gupta. 2014. Team Z: Wiktionary as L2 writing assistant. In *Proceedings of the 8th International Workshop on Semantic Evaluation (SemEval-2014)*, Dublin, Ireland.

Eva Hasler. 2014. UEdin: Translating L1 phrases in L2 context using context-sensitive smt. In *Proceedings of the 8th International Workshop on Semantic Evaluation (SemEval-2014)*, Dublin, Ireland.

Philipp Koehn, Hieu Hoang, Alexandra Birch, Chris Callison-Burch, Marcello Federico, Nicola Bertoldi, Brooke Cowan, Wade Shen, Christine Moran, Richard Zens, Chris Dyer, Ohttp://www.aclweb.org/anthology/P/P07/P07 2045ndrej Bojar, Alexandra Constantin, and Evan Herbst. 2007. Moses: Open source toolkit for statistical machine translation. In *Proceedings of the 45th Annual Meeting of the Association for Computational Linguistics Companion Volume Proceedings of the Demo and Poster Sessions*, pages 177–180, Prague, Czech Republic, June.

Philipp Koehn. 2005. Europarl: A parallel corpus for statistical machine translation. In *In Proceedings of the Machine Translation Summit X ([MT]'05).*, pages 79–86.

Els Lefever and Veronique Hoste. 2013. SemEval-2013 Task 10: Cross-Lingual Word Sense Disambiguation. In *Proceedings of the 7th International Workshop on Semantic Evaluation (SemEval 2013), in conjunction with the Second Joint Conference on Lexical and Computational Semantics.*

Rada Mihalcea, Ravi Sinha, and Diana McCarthy. 2010. Semeval 2010 task 2: Cross-lingual lexical substitution. In *Proceedings of the 5th International Workshop on Semantic Evaluations (SemEval-2010)*, Uppsala, Sweden.

Franz Josef Och and Hermann Ney. 2000. Giza++: Training of statistical translation models. Technical report, RWTH Aachen, University of Technology.

Alex Rudnick, Levi King, Can Liu, Markus Dickinson, and Sandra Kübler. 2014. IUCL: Combining information sources for semeval task 5. In *Proceedings of the 8th International Workshop on Semantic Evaluation (SemEval-2014)*, Dublin, Ireland.

Emilio Silva-Schlenker, Sergio Jimenez, and Julia Baquero. 2014. UNAL-NLP: Cross-lingual phrase sense disambiguation with syntactic dependency trees. In *Proceedings of the 8th International Workshop on Semantic Evaluation (SemEval-2014)*, Dublin, Ireland.

Liling Tan, Anne Schumann, José Martinez, and Francis Bond. 2014. Sensible: L2 translation assistance by emulating the manual post-editing process. In *Proceedings of the 8th International Workshop on Semantic Evaluation (SemEval-2014)*, Dublin, Ireland.

Maarten van Gompel and Antal van den Bosch. 2014. Translation assistance by translation of L1 fragments in an L2 context. In *To appear in Proceedings of ACL 2014.*

SemEval-2014 Task 6: Supervised Semantic Parsing of Robotic Spatial Commands

Kais Dukes
School of Computing, University of Leeds
Leeds LS2 9JT, United Kingdom
sckd@leeds.ac.uk

Abstract

SemEval-2014 Task 6 aims to advance semantic parsing research by providing a high-quality annotated dataset to compare and evaluate approaches. The task focuses on contextual parsing of robotic commands, in which the additional context of spatial scenes can be used to guide a parser to control a robot arm. Six teams submitted systems using both rule-based and statistical methods. The best performing (hybrid) system scored 92.5% and 90.5% for parsing with and without spatial context. However, the best performing statistical system scored 87.35% and 60.84% respectively, indicating that generalized understanding of commands given to a robot remains challenging, despite the fixed domain used for the task.

1 Introduction

Semantic parsers analyze sentences to produce formal meaning representations that are used for the computational understanding of natural language. Recently, state-of-the-art semantic parsing methods have used for a variety of applications, including question answering (Kwiatkowski et al., 2013; Krishnamurthy and Mitchell, 2012), dialog systems (Artzi and Zettlemoyer, 2011), entity relation extraction (Kate and Mooney, 2010) and robotic control (Tellex, 2011; Kim and Mooney, 2012).

Different parsers can be distinguished by the level of supervision they require during training. Fully supervised training typically requires an annotated dataset that maps natural language (NL) to a formal meaning representation such as logical form. However, because annotated data is often not available, a recent trend in semantic parsing research has been to eschew supervised training in favour of either unsupervised or weakly-supervised methods that utilize additional information. For example, Berant and Liang (2014) use a dataset of 5,810 question-answer pairs without annotated logical forms to induce a parser for a question-answering system. In comparison, Poon (2013) converts NL questions into formal queries via indirect supervision through database interaction.

In contrast to previous work, the shared task described in this paper uses the Robot Commands Treebank (Dukes, 2013a), a new dataset made available for supervised semantic parsing. The chosen domain is robotic control, in which NL commands are given to a robot arm used to manipulate shapes on an 8 x 8 game board. Despite the fixed domain, the task is challenging as correctly parsing commands requires understanding spatial context. For example, the command in Figure 1 may have several plausible interpretations, given different board configurations.

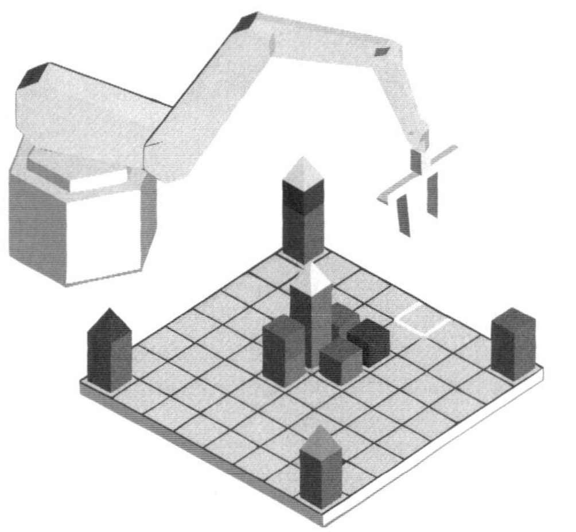

'Move the pyramid on the blue cube on the gray one.'

Figure 1: Example scene with a contextual spatial command from the Robot Commands Treebank.

Proceedings of the 8th International Workshop on Semantic Evaluation (SemEval 2014), pages 45–53, Dublin, Ireland, August 23-24, 2014.

The task is inspired by the classic AI system SHRLDU, which responded to NL commands to control a robot for a similar game board (Winograd, 1972), although that system is reported to not have generalized well (Dreyfus, 2009; Mitkov, 1999). More recent research in command understanding has focused on parsing jointly with *grounding*, the process of mapping NL descriptions of entities within an environment to a semantic representation. Previous work includes Tellex et al. (2011), who develop a small corpus of commands for a simulated fork lift robot, with grounding performed using a factor graph. Similarly, Kim and Mooney (2012) perform joint parsing and grounding using a corpus of navigation commands. In contrast, this paper focuses on parsing using additional situational context for disambiguation and by using a larger NL dataset, in comparison to previous robotics research.

In the remainder of this paper, we describe the task, the dataset and the metrics used for evaluation. We then compare the approaches used by participant systems and conclude with suggested improvements for future work.

2 Task Description

The long term research goal encouraged by the task is to develop a system that will robustly execute NL robotic commands. In general, this is a highly complex problem involving computational processing of language, spatial reasoning, contextual awareness and knowledge representation. To simplify the problem, participants were provided with additional tools and resources, allowing them to focus on developing a semantic parser for a fixed domain that would fit into an existing component architecture. Figure 2 shows how these components interact.

Semantic parser: Systems submitted by participants are *semantic parsers* that accept an NL command as input, mapping this to a formal Robot Control Language (RCL), described further in section 3.3. The Robot Commands Treebank used for the both training and evaluation is an annotated corpus that pairs NL commands with contextual RCL statements.

Spatial planner: A *spatial planner* is provided as an open Java API[1]. Commands in the treebank are specified in the context of spatial scenes. By interfacing with the planner, participant systems

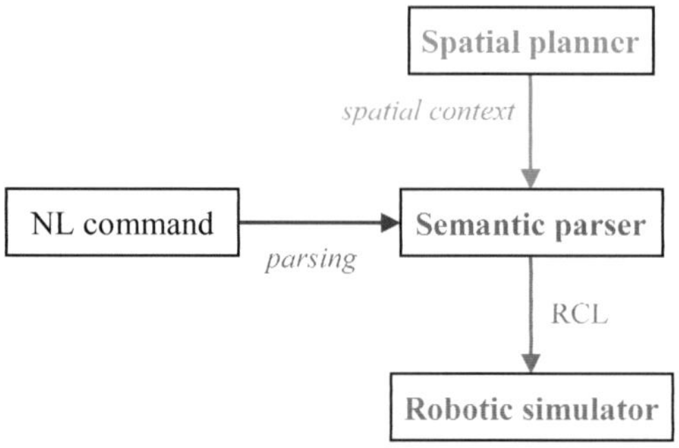

Figure 2: Integrated command understanding system.

have access to this additional information. For example, given an RCL fragment for the expression '*the red cube on the blue block*', the planner will ground the entity, returning a list of zero or more board coordinates corresponding to possible matches. The planner also validates commands to determine if they are compatible with spatial context. It can therefore be used to constrain the search space of possible parses, as well as enabling early resolution of attachment ambiguity during parsing.

Robotic simulator: The simulated environment consists of an 8 x 8 board that can hold prisms and cubes which occur in eight different colors. The robot's gripper can move to any discrete position within an 8 x 8 x 8 space above the board. The planner uses the simulator to enforce physical laws within the game. For example, a block cannot remain unsupported in empty space due to gravity. Similarly, prisms cannot lie below other block types. In the integrated system, the parser uses the planner for context, then provides the final RCL statement to the simulator which executes the command by moving the robot arm to update the board.

3 Data

3.1 Data Collection

For the shared task, 3,409 sentences were selected from the treebank. This data size compares with related corpora used for semantic parsing such as the ATIS (Zettlemoyer and Collins, 2007), GeoQuery (Kate et al., 2005), Jobs (Tang and Mooney, 2001) and RoboCup (Kuhlmann et al., 2004) datasets, consisting of 4,978; 880; 640 and 300 sentences respectively.

The treebank was developed via a game with a purpose (`www.TrainRobots.com`), in which players were shown *before* and *after* configurations

[1] `https://github.com/kaisdukes/train-robots`

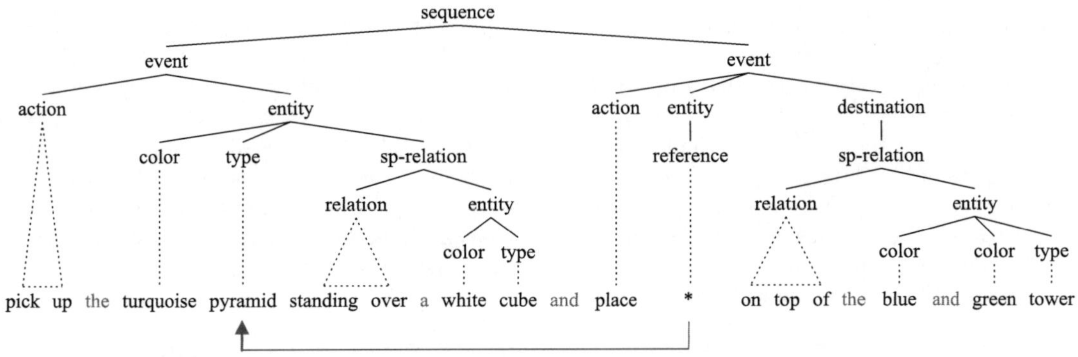

Figure 3: Semantic tree from the treebank with an elliptical anaphoric node and its annotated antecedent.

and asked to give a corresponding command to a hypothetical robot arm. To make the game more competitive and to promote data quality, players rated each other's sentences and were rewarded with points for accurate entries (Dukes, 2013b).

3.2 Annotation

In total, over 10,000 commands were collected through the game. During an offline annotation phase, sentences were manually mapped to RCL. However, due to the nature of the game, players were free to enter arbitrarily complex sentences to describe moves, not all of which could be represented by RCL. In addition, some commands were syntactically well-formed, but not compatible with the corresponding scenes. The 3,409 commands selected for the task had RCL statements that were both understood by the planner and when given to the robotic simulator resulted in the expected move being made between *before* and *after* board configurations. Due to this extra validation step, all RCL statements provided for the task were contextually well-formed.

```
(sequence:
  (event:
    (action: take)
    (entity:
      (id: 1)
      (color: cyan)
      (type: prism)
      (spatial-relation:
        (relation: above)
        (entity:
          (color: white)
          (type: cube)))))
  (event:
    (action: drop)
    (entity:
      (type: reference)
      (reference-id: 1))
    (destination:
      (spatial-relation:
        (relation: above)
        (entity:
          (color: blue)
          (color: green)
          (type: stack))))))
```

Figure 4: RCL representation with co-referencing.

3.3 Robot Control Language

RCL is a novel linguistically-oriented semantic representation. An RCL statement is a semantic tree (Figure 3) where leaf nodes generally align to words in the corresponding sentence, and non-leaves are tagged using a pre-defined set of categories. RCL is designed to annotate rich linguistic structure, including ellipsis (such as 'place [it] on'), anaphoric references ('it' and 'one'), multi-word spatial expressions ('on top of') and lexical disambiguation ('one' and 'place'). Due to ellipsis, unaligned words and multi-word expressions, a leaf node may align to zero, one or more words in a sentence. Figure 4 shows the RCL syntax for the tree in Figure 3, as accepted by the spatial planner and the simulator. As these components do not require NL word alignment data, this additional information was made available to task participants for training via a separate Java API.

The tagset used to annotate RCL nodes can be divided into general tags (that are arguably applicable to other domains) and specific tags that were customized for the domain in the task (Tables 1 and 2 overleaf, respectively). The general elements are typed *entities* (labelled with semantic features) that are connected using *relations* and *events*. This universal formalism is not domain-specific, and is inspired by semantic frames (Fillmore and Baker, 2001), a practical representation used for NL understanding systems (Dzikovska, 2004; UzZaman and Allen, 2010; Coyne et al., 2010; Dukes, 2009).

In the remainder of this section we summarize aspects of RCL that are relevant to the task; a more detailed description is provided by Dukes (2013a; 2014). In an RCL statement such as Figure 4, a preterminal node together with its child leaf node correspond to a feature-value pair (such as the feature *color* and the constant *blue*). Two special features which are distinguished by the planner are *id* and *reference-id*, which are used for co-referencing such as for annotating anaphora and their antecedents. The remaining features model the simulated robotic domain. For example, the values of the *action* feature are the moves used to control the robotic arm, while values of the *type* and *relation* features are the entity and relation types understood by the spatial planner (Table 2). As well as qualitative relations (such as 'below' or 'above'), the planner also accepts spatial relations that include quantitative measurements, such as in 'two squares left of the red prism' (Figure 5).

RCL Element	Description
action	Aligned to a verbal group in NL, e.g. 'drop' or 'pick up'.
cardinal	Number (e.g. 2 or 'three').
color	Colored attribute of an entity.
destination	A spatial destination.
entity	Entity within the domain.
event	Specification of a command.
id	Id for anaphoric references.
indicator	Spatial attribute of an entity.
measure	Used for distance metrics.
reference-id	A resolved reference.
relation	Relation type (e.g. 'above').
sequence	Used to specify a sequence of events or statements.
spatial-relation	Used to specify a spatial relation between two entities or to describe a location.
type	Used to specify an entity type.

Table 1: Universal semantic elements in RCL.

Category	Values
Actions	move, take, drop
Relations	left, right, above, below, forward, backward, adjacent, within, between, nearest, near, furthest, far, part
Indicators	left, leftmost, right, rightmost, top, highest, bottom, lowest, front, back, individual, furthest, nearest, center
entity types	cube, prism, corner, board stack, row, column, edge, tile, robot, region, reference, type-reference
Colors	blue, cyan, red, yellow, green, magenta, gray, white

Table 2: Semantic categories customized for the task.

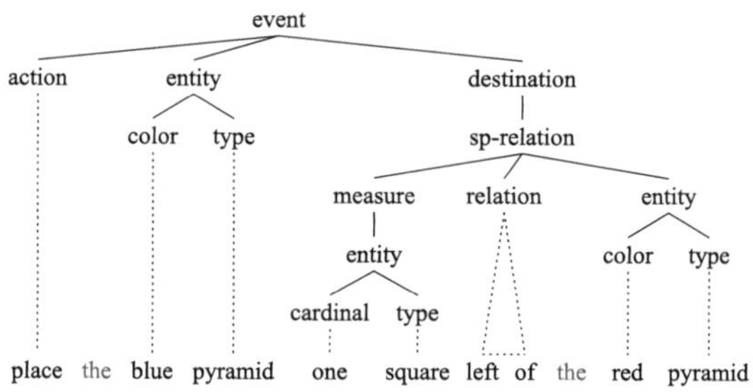

Fig.ure 5: A quantitative relation with a landmark.

RCL distinguishes between *relations* which relate entities and *indicators*, which are attributes of entities (such as 'left' in 'the left cube'). For the task, participants are asked to map NL sentences to well-formed RCL by identifying spatial relations and indicators, then parsing higher-level entities and events. Finally, a well-formed RCL tree with an event (or sequence of events) at top-level is given the simulator for execution.

4 Evaluation Metrics

Out of the 3,400 sentences annotated for the task, 2,500 sentences were provided to participants for system training. During evaluation, trained systems were presented with 909 previously unseen sentences and asked to generate corresponding RCL statements, with access to the spatial planner for additional context. To keep the evaluation process as simple as possible, each parser's output for a sentence was scored as correct if it exactly matched the expected RCL statement in the treebank. Participants were asked to calculate two metrics, *P* and *NP*, which are the proportion of exact matches with and without using the spatial planner respectively:

$$P = \frac{\#\ matches\ with\ planning}{\#\ sentences}$$

$$NP = \frac{\#\ matches\ without\ planning}{\#\ sentences}$$

System	Authors	Statistical?	Strategy	P	NP	NP - P
UW-MRS	Packard	Hybrid	Rule-based ERG + Berkeley parser	92.50	90.50	-2.00
AT&T Labs	Stoyanchev et al.	Statistical	Statistical maximum entropy parser	87.35	60.84	-26.51
RoBox	Evang and Bos	Statistical	CCG parser + structured perceptron	86.80	79.21	-7.59
Shrdlite	Ljunglöf	Rule-based	Hand crafted domain-specific grammar	86.10	51.50	-34.60
KUL-Eval	Mattelaer et al.	Statistical	CCG parser	71.29	57.76	-13.53
UWM	Kate	Statistical	KRISP parser	N/A	45.98	N/A

Table 3: System results for supervised semantic parsing of the Robot Commands Treebank (P = parsing with integrated spatial planning, NP = parsing without integrated spatial planning, NP - P = drop in performance without integrated spatial planning, N/A = performance not available).

These metrics contrast with measures for partially correct parsed structures, such as Parseval (Black et al., 1991) or the leaf-ancestor metric (Sampson and Babarczy, 2003). The rationale for using a strict match is that in the integrated system, a command will only be executed if it is completely understood, as both the spatial planner and the simulator require well-formed RCL.

5 Systems and Results

Six teams participated in the shared task using a variety of strategies (Table 3). The last measure in the table gives the performance drop without spatial context. The value *NP - P* = -2 for the best performing system suggests this as an upper bound for the task. The different values of this measure indicate the sensitivity to (or possibly reliance on) context to guide the parsing process. In the remainder of this section we compare the approaches and results of the six systems.

UW-MRS: Packard (2014) achieved the best score for parsing both with and without spatial context, at 92.5% and 90.5%, respectively, using a hybrid system that combines a rule-based grammar with the Berkeley parser (Petrov et al., 2006). The rule-based component uses the English Resource Grammar, a broad coverage handwritten HPSG grammar for English. The ERG produces a ranked list of Minimal Recursion Semantics (MRS) structures that encode predicate argument relations (Copestake et al., 2005). Approximately 80 rules were then used to convert MRS to RCL. The highest ranked result that is validated by the spatial planner was selected as the output of the rule-based system. Using this approach, Packard reports scores of *P* = 82.4% and *NP* = 80.3% for parsing the evaluation data.

To further boost performance, the Berkeley parser was used for back-off. To train the parser, the RCL treebank was converted to phrase structure by removing non-aligned nodes and inserting additional nodes to ensure one-to-one alignment with words in NL sentences. Performance of the Berkeley parser alone was *NP* = 81.5% (no *P*-measure was available as spatial planning was not integrated).

To combine components, the ERG was used initially, with fall back to the Berkeley parser when no contextually compatible RCL statement was produced. The hybrid approach improved accuracy considerably, with *P* = 92.5% and *NP* = 90.5%. Interestingly, Packard also performs precision and recall analysis, and reports that the rule-based component had higher precision, while the statistical component had higher recall, with the combined system outperforming each separate component in both precision and recall.

AT&T Labs Research: The system by Stoyanchev et al. (2014) scored second best for contextual parsing and third best for parsing without using the spatial planner (*P* = 87.35% and *NP* = 60.84%). In contrast to Packard's UW-MRS submission, the AT&T system is a combination of three statistical models for tagging, parsing and reference resolution. During the tagging phase, a two-stage sequence tagger first assigns a part-of-speech tag to each word in a sentence, followed by an RCL feature-value pair such as *(type: cube)* or *(color: blue)*, with unaligned words tagged as 'O'. For parsing, a constituency parser was trained using non-lexical RCL trees. Finally, anaphoric references were resolved using a maximum entropy feature model. When combined, the three components generate a list of weighted RCL trees, which are filtered by the spatial planner. Without integrated planning, the most-probable parse tree is selected.

In their evaluation, Stoyanchev et al. report accuracy scores for the separate phases as well as for the combined system. For the tagger, they report an accuracy score of 95.2%, using the standard split of 2,500 sentences for training and 909 for evaluation. To separately measure the joint accuracy of the parser together with reference resolution, gold-standard tags were used resulting in a performance of $P = 94.83\%$ and $NP = 67.55\%$. However, using predicted tags, the system's final performance dropped to $P = 87.35\%$ and $NP = 60.84\%$. To measure the effect of less supervision, the models were additionally trained on only 500 sentences. In this scenario, the tagging model degraded significantly, while the parsing and reference resolution models performed nearly as well.

RoBox: Using Combinatory Categorial Grammar (CCG) as a semantic parsing framework has been previously shown to be suitable for translating NL into logical form. Inspired by previous work using a CCG parser in combination with a structured perceptron (Zettlemoyer and Collins, 2007), RoBox (Evang and Bos, 2014) was the best performing CCG system in the shared task scoring $P = 86.8\%$ and $NP = 79.21\%$.

Using a similar approach to UW-MRS for its statistical component, RCL trees were interpreted as phrase-structure and converted to CCG derivations for training. During decoding, RCL statements were generated directly by the CCG parser. However, in contrast to the approach used by the AT&T system, RoBox interfaces with the planner during parsing instead of performing spatial validation a post-processing step. This enables early resolution of attachment ambiguity and helps constrain the search space. However, the planner is only used to validate *entity* elements, so that *event* and *sequence* elements were not validated. As a further difference to the AT&T system, anaphora resolution was not performed using a statistical model. Instead, multiple RCL trees were generated with different candidate anaphoric references, which were filtered out contextually using the spatial planner.

RoBox suffered only a 7.59% absolute drop in performance without using spatial planning, second only to UW-MRS at 2%. Evang and Bos perform error analysis on RoBox and report that most errors relate to ellipsis, the ambiguous word *one*, anaphora or attachment ambiguity. They suggest that the system could be improved with better feature selection or by integrating the CCG parser more closely with the spatial planner.

Shrdlite: The Shrdlite system by Ljunglöf (2014), inspired by the Classic SHRDLU system by Winograd (1972), is a purely rule-based system that was shown to be effective for the task. Scoring $P = 86.1\%$ and $NP = 51.5\%$, Shrdlite ranked fourth for parsing with integrated planning, and fifth without using spatial context. However, it suffered the largest absolute drop in performance without planning (34.6 points), indicating that integration with the planner is essential for the system's reported accuracy.

Shrdlite uses a hand-written compact unification grammar for the fragment of English appearing in the training data. The grammar is small, consisting of only 25 grammatical rules and 60 lexical rules implemented as a recursive-descent parser in Prolog. The lexicon consists of 150 words (and multi-word expressions) divided into 23 lexical categories, based on the RCL preterminal nodes found in the treebank. In a post-processing phase, the resulting parse trees are normalized to ensure that they are well-formed by using a small set of supplementary rules.

However, the grammar is highly ambiguous resulting in multiple parses for a given input sentence. These are filtered by the spatial planner. If multiple parse trees were found to be compatible with spatial context (or when not using the planner), the tree with the smallest number of nodes was selected as the parser's final output. Additionally, because both the training and evaluation data were collected via crowdsourcing, sentences occasionally contain spelling errors, which were intentionally included in the task. To handle misspelt words, Shrdlite uses Levenshtein edit distance with a penalty to reparse sentences when the parser initially fails to produce any analysis.

KUL-Eval: The CCG system by Mattelaer et al. (2014) uses a different approach to the RoBox system described previously. KUL-Eval scored $P = 71.29\%$ and $NP = 57.76\%$ in comparison to the RoBox scores of $P = 86.8\%$ and $NP = 79.21\%$.

During training, the RCL treebank was converted to λ-expressions. This process is fully reversible, so that no information in an RCL tree is lost during conversion. In contrast to RoBox, but in common with the AT&T parser, KUL-Eval performs spatial validation as a post-processing step and does not integrate the planner directly into the parsing process. A probabilistic CCG is used for parsing, so that multiple λ-expressions are returned (each with an associated confidence measure) that are translated into RCL. Finally, in the validation step, the spatial planner is used to discard RCL statements that are incompatible with spatial context and the remaining most-probable parse is returned as the system's output.

Mattelaer et al. note that in several cases the parser produced partially correct statements but that these outputs did not contribute to the final score, given the strictly matching measures used for the *P* and *NP* metrics. However, well-formed RCL statements are required by the spatial planner and robotic simulator for the integrated system to robustly execute the specified NL command. Partially correct structures included statements which almost matched the expected RCL tree with the exception of incorrect feature-values, or the addition or deletion of nodes. The most common errors were feature-values with incorrect entity types (such as 'edge' and 'region') and mismatched spatial relations (such as confusing 'above' and 'within' and confusing 'right', 'left' and 'front').

UWM: The UWM system submitted by Kate (2014) uses an existing semantic parser, KRISP, for the shared task. KRISP (Kernel-based Robust Interpretation for Semantic Parsing) is a trainable semantic parser (Kate and Mooney, 2006) that uses Support Vector Machines (SVMs) as the machine learning method with a string subsequence kernel. As well as training data consisting of RCL paired with NL commands, KRISP required a context-free grammar for RCL, which was hand-written for UWM. During training, *id* nodes were removed from the RCL trees. These were recovered after parsing in a post-processing phase to resolve anaphora by matching to the nearest preceding antecedent.

In contrast to other systems submitted for the task, UWM does not interface with the spatial planner and parses purely non-contextually. Because the planner was not used, the system's accuracy was negatively impacted by simple issues that may have been easily resolved using spatial context. For example, in RCL, the verb 'place' can map to either *drop* or *move* actions, depending on whether or not a block is held in the gripper in the corresponding spatial scene. Without using spatial context, it is hard to distinguish between these cases during parsing.

The system scored a non-contextual measure of *NP* = 45.98%, with Kate reporting a 51.18% best F-measure (at 72.67% precision and 39.49% recall). No *P*-measure was reported as the spatial planner was not used. Due to memory constraints when training the SVM classifiers, only 1,500 out of 2,500 possible sentences were used from the treebank to build the parsing model. However, it may be possible to increasing the size of training data in future work through sampling.

6 Discussion

The six systems evaluated for the task employed a variety of semantic parsing strategies. With the exception of one submission, all systems interfaced with the spatial planner, either in a post-processing phase, or directly during parsing to enable early disambiguation and to help constrain the search space. An open question that remains following the task is how applicable these methods would be to other domains. Systems that relied heavily on the planner to guide the parsing process could only be adapted to domains for a which a planner could conceivably exist. For example, nearly all robotic tasks such as such as navigation, object manipulation and task execution involve aspects of planning. NL question-answering interfaces to databases or knowledge stores are also good candidates for this approach, since parsing NL questions into a semantic representation within the context of a database schema or an ontology could be guided by a query planner.

However, approaches with a more attractive *NP* - *P* measure (such as UW-MRS and RoBox) are arguably more easily generalized to other domains, as they are less reliant on a planner. Additionally, the usual arguments for rule-based systems verses supervised statistical systems apply to any discussion on domain adaptation: rule-based systems require human manual effort, while supervised statistical systems required annotated data for the new domain.

In comparing the best two statistical systems (AT&T and RoBox) it is interesting to note that these performed similarly with integrated planning (*P* = 87.35% and 86.80%, respectively), but differed considerably without planning (*NP* = 60.84% and 79.21%). As these two systems employed different parsers (a constituency parser and a CCG parser), it is difficult to perform a direct comparison to understand why the AT&T system is more reliant on spatial context. It would also be interesting to understand, in further work, why the two CCG-based systems differed considerably in their *P* and *NP* scores.

It is also surprising that the best performing system, UW-MRS, suffered only a 2% drop in performance without using the planner, demonstrating clearly that in the majority of sentences in the evaluation data, spatial context is not actually required to perform semantic parsing. Although as shown by the *NP* - *P* scores, spatial context can dramatically boost performance of certain approaches for the task when used.

7 Conclusion and Future Work

This paper described a new task for SemEval: Supervised Semantic Parsing of Robotic Spatial Commands. Despite its novel nature, the task attracted high-quality submissions from six teams, using a variety of semantic parsing strategies.

It is hoped that this task will reappear at SemEval. Several lessons were learnt from this first version of the shared task which can be used to improve the task in future. One issue which several participants noted was the way in which the treebank was split into training and evaluation datasets. Out of the 3,409 sentences in the treebank, the first 2,500 sequential sentences were chosen for training. Because this data was not randomized, certain syntactic structures were only found during evaluation and were not present in the training data. Although this may have affected results, all participants evaluated their systems against the same datasets. Based on participant feedback, in addition to reporting *P* and *NP*-measures, it would also be illuminating to include a metric such as Parseval F1-scores to measure partial accuracy. An improved version of the task could also feature a better dataset by expanding the treebank, not only in terms of size but also in terms of linguistic structure. Many commands captured in the annotation game are not yet represented in RCL due to linguistic phenomena such as negation and conditional statements.

Looking forward, a more promising approach to improving the spatial planner could be probabilistic planning, so that semantic parsers could interface with probabilistic facts with confidence measures. This approach is particularly suitable for robotics, where sensors often supply noisy signals about the robot's environment.

Acknowledgements

The author would like to thank the numerous volunteer annotators who helped develop the dataset used for the task using crowdsourcing, by participating in the online game-with-a-purpose.

References

Yoav Artzi and Luke Zettlemoyer. 2011. Bootstrapping Semantic Parsers from Conversations. In *Proceedings of the Conference on Empirical Methods in Natural Language Processing*, EMNLP (pp. 421–432).

Jonathan Berant and Percy Liang. 2014. Semantic parsing via paraphrasing. In *Proceedings of the Conference of the Association for Computational Linguistics*, ACL (pp. 1415–1425).

Ezra Black, Steven Abney, Dan Flickinger, Claudia Gdaniec, et al. 1991. A Procedure for Quantitatively Comparing the Syntactic Coverage of English Grammars. In *Proceedings of the DARPA Speech and Natural Language Workshop* (pp. 306-311). San Mateo, California.

Ann Copestake, et al. 2005. Minimal Recursion Semantics: An Introduction. *Research on Language and Computation*, 3(2) (pp. 281-332).

Bob Coyne, Owen Rambow, et al. 2010. Frame Semantics in Text-to-Scene Generation. *Knowledge-Based and Intelligent Information and Engineering Systems* (pp. 375-384). Springer, Berlin.

Hubert Dreyfus and Stuart Dreyfus. 2009. Why Computers May Never Think Like *People. Readings in the Philosophy of Technology*.

Kais Dukes. 2009. LOGICON: A System for Extracting Semantic Structure using Partial Parsing. In *International Conference on Recent Advances in Natural Language Processing*, RANLP (pp. 18-22). Borovets, Bulgaria.

Kais Dukes. 2013a. Semantic Annotation of Robotic Spatial Commands. In *Proceedings of the Language and Technology Conference*, LTC.

Kais Dukes. 2013b. Train Robots: A Dataset for Natural Language Human-Robot Spatial Interaction through Verbal Commands. In *International Conference on Social Robotics. Embodied Communication of Goals and Intentions Workshop*.

Kais Dukes. 2014. Contextual Semantic Parsing using Crowdsourced Spatial Descriptions. *Computation and Language*, arXiv:1405.0145 [cs.CL]

Myroslava Dzikovska 2004. A Practical Semantic Representation For Natural Language Parsing. *PhD Thesis*. University of Rochester.

Kilian Evang and Johan Bos. 2014. RoBox: CCG with Structured Perceptron for Supervised Semantic Parsing of Robotic Spatial Commands. In *Proceedings of the International Workshop on Semantic Evaluation*, SemEval.

Charles Fillmore and Collin Baker. 2001. Frame semantics for Text Understanding. In *Proceedings of WordNet and Other Lexical Resources Workshop*.

Rohit Kate and Ray Mooney. 2006. Using String Kernels for Learning Semantic Parsers. In *Proceedings of the International Conference on Computational Linguistics and Annual Meeting of the Association for Computational Linguistics,* COLING-ACL (pp. 913–920).

Rohit Kate and Raymond Mooney. 2010. Joint Entity and Relation Extraction using Card-Pyramid Parsing. In *Proceedings of the Conference on Computational Natural Language Learning*, CoNLL (pp. 203-212).

Rohit Kate, Yuk Wah Wong and Raymond Mooney. 2005. Learning to Transform Natural to Formal Languages. In *Proceedings of the National Conference on Artificial Intelligence* (pp. 1062-1068).

Rohit Kate. 2014. UWM: Applying an Existing Trainable Semantic Parser to Parse Robotic Spatial Commands. In *Proceedings of the International Workshop on Semantic Evaluation*, SemEval.

Joohyun Kim and Raymond Mooney. 2012. Unsupervised PCFG Induction for Grounded Language Learning with Highly Ambiguous Supervision. In *Proceedings of the Joint Conference on Empirical Methods in Natural Language Processing and Computational Natural Language Learning*, EMNLP-CoNLL (pp. 433-444).

Jayant Krishnamurthy and Tom Mitchell. 2012. Weakly Supervised Training of Semantic Parsers. In *Proceedings of the Joint Conference on Empirical Methods in Natural Language Processing and Computational Natural Language Learning*, EMNLP-CoNLL.

Gregory Kuhlmann et al. 2004. Guiding a Reinforcement Learner with Natural Language Advice: Initial Results in RoboCup Soccer. In *Proceedings of the AAAI Workshop on Supervisory Control of Learning and Adaptive Systems*.

Tom Kwiatkowski, Eunsol Choi, Yoav Artzi and Luke Zettlemoyer. 2013. Scaling Semantic Parsers with On-the-fly Ontology Matching. In *Proceedings of the Conference on Empirical Methods in Natural Language Processing*, EMNLP.

Peter Ljunglöf. 2014. Shrdlite: Semantic Parsing using a Handmade Grammar. In *Proceedings of the International Workshop on Semantic Evaluation*, SemEval.

Willem Mattelaer, Mathias Verbeke and Davide Nitti. 2014. KUL-Eval: A Combinatory Categorial Grammar Approach for Improving Semantic Parsing of Robot Commands using Spatial Context. In *Proceedings of the International Workshop on Semantic Evaluation*, SemEval.

Ruslan Mitkov. 1999. Anaphora Resolution: The State of the Art. *Technical Report*. University of Wolverhampton.

Woodley Packard. 2014. UW-MRS: Leveraging a Deep Grammar for Robotic Spatial Commands. In *Proceedings of the International Workshop on Semantic Evaluation*, SemEval.

Slav Petrov, et al. 2006. Learning Accurate, Compact, and Interpretable Tree Annotation. *In Proceedings of the International Conference on Computational Linguistics and the Annual Meeting of the Association for Computational Linguistics*, COLING-ACL (pp. 433-440).

Hoifung Poon. 2013. Grounded Unsupervised Semantic Parsing. In *Proceedings of the Conference of the Association for Computational Linguistics*, ACL (pp. 466-477).

Geoffrey Sampson and Anna Babarczy. 2003. A Test of the Leaf-Ancestor Metric for Parse Accuracy. *Natural Language Engineering*, 9.4 (pp. 365-380).

Svetlana Stoyanchev, et al. 2014. AT&T Labs Research: Tag&Parse Approach to Semantic Parsing of Robot Spatial Commands. In *Proceedings of the International Workshop on Semantic Evaluation*, SemEval.

Lappoon Tang and Raymond Mooney. 2001. Using Multiple Clause Constructors in Inductive Logic Programming for Semantic Parsing. *Machine Learning*, ECML.

Stefanie Tellax, et al. 2011. Approaching the Symbol Grounding Problem with Probabilistic Graphical Models. *AI Magazine*, 32:4 (pp. 64-76).

Naushad UzZaman and James Allen. 2010. TRIPS and TRIOS System for TempEval-2. In *Proceedings of the International Workshop on Semantic Evaluation*, SemEval (pp. 276-283).

Terry Winograd. 1972. Understanding Natural Language. *Cognitive Psychology*, 3:1 (pp. 1-191).

Luke Zettlemoyer and Michael Collins. 2007. Online Learning of Relaxed CCG Grammars for Parsing to Logical Form. In *Proceedings of the Joint Conference on Empirical Methods in Natural Language Processing and Computational Natural Language Learning*, EMNLP-CoNLL (pp. 878-887).

SemEval-2014 Task 7: Analysis of Clinical Text

Sameer Pradhan[1], **Noémie Elhadad**[2], **Wendy Chapman**[3], **Suresh Manandhar**[4] **and Guergana Savova**[1]

[1]Harvard University, Boston, MA, [2]Columbia University, New York, NY
[3]University of Utah, Salt Lake City, UT, [4]University of York, York, UK

{sameer.pradhan,guergana.savova}@childrens.harvard.edu, noemie.elhadad@columbia.edu, wendy.chapman@utah.edu, suresh@cs.york.ac.uk

Abstract

This paper describes the SemEval-2014, Task 7 on the Analysis of Clinical Text and presents the evaluation results. It focused on two subtasks: (i) identification (Task A) and (ii) normalization (Task B) of diseases and disorders in clinical reports as annotated in the Shared Annotated Resources (ShARe)[1] corpus. This task was a follow-up to the ShARe/CLEF eHealth 2013 shared task, subtasks 1a and 1b,[2] but using a larger test set. A total of 21 teams competed in Task A, and 18 of those also participated in Task B. For Task A, the best system had a strict F_1-score of 81.3, with a precision of 84.3 and recall of 78.6. For Task B, the same group had the best strict accuracy of 74.1. The organizers have made the text corpora, annotations, and evaluation tools available for future research and development at the shared task website.[3]

1 Introduction

A large amount of very useful information—both for medical researchers and patients—is present in the form of unstructured text within the clinical notes and discharge summaries that form a patient's medical history. Adapting and extending natural language processing (NLP) techniques to mine this information can open doors to better, novel, clinical studies on one hand, and help patients understand the contents of their clinical records on the other. Organization of this shared task helps establish state-of-the-art benchmarks and paves the way for further explorations. It tackles two important sub-problems in NLP—named entity recognition and word sense disambiguation. Neither of these problems are new to NLP. Research in general-domain NLP goes back to about two decades. For an overview of the development in the field through roughly 2009, we refer the refer to Nadeau and Sekine (2007). NLP has also penetrated the field of bimedical informatics and has been particularly focused on biomedical literature for over the past decade. Advances in that sub-field has also been documented in surveys such as one by Leaman and Gonzalez (2008). Word sense disambiguation also has a long history in the general NLP domain (Navigli, 2009). In spite of word sense annotations in the biomedical literature, recent work by Savova et al. (2008) highlights the importance of annotating them in clinical notes. This is true for many other clinical and linguistic phenomena as the various characteristics of the clinical narrative present a unique challenge to NLP. Recently various initiatives have led to annotated corpora for clinical NLP research. Probably the first comprehensive annotation performed on a clinical corpora was by Roberts et al. (2009), but unfortunately that corpus is not publicly available owing to privacy regulations. The i2b2 initiative[4] challenges have focused on such topics as concept recognition (Uzuner et al., 2011), coreference resolution (Uzuner et al., 2012), temporal relations (Sun et al., 2013) and their datasets are available to the community. More recently, the Shared Annotated Resources (ShARe)[1] project has created a corpus annotated with disease/disorder mentions in clinical notes as well as normalized them to a concept unique identifier (CUI) within the SNOMED-CT subset of the Unified Medical Language System[5]

[1]http://share.healthnlp.org

[2]https://sites.google.com/site/shareclefehealth/evaluation

[3]http://alt.qcri.org/semeval2014/task7/

[4]http://www.i2b2.org

[5]https://uts.nlm.nih.gov/home.html

Proceedings of the 8th International Workshop on Semantic Evaluation (SemEval 2014), pages 54–62, Dublin, Ireland, August 23-24, 2014.

	Train	Development	Test
Notes	199	99	133
Words	94K	88K	153K
Disorder mentions	5,816	5,351	7,998
CUI-less mentions	1,639 (28%)	1,750 (32%)	1,930 (24%)
CUI-ied mentions	4,117 (72%)	3,601 (67%)	6,068 (76%)
Contiguous mentions	5,165 (89%)	4,912 (92%)	7,374 (92%)
Discontiguous mentions	651 (11%)	439 (8%)	6,24 (8%)

Table 1: Distribution of data in terms of notes and disorder mentions across the training, development and test sets. The disorders are further split according to two criteria – whether they map to a CUI or whether they are contiguous.

(UMLS) (Campbell et al., 1998). The task of normalization is a combination of word/phrase sense disambiguation and semantic similarity where a phrase is mapped to a unique concept in an ontology (based on the description of that concept in the ontology) after disambiguating potential ambiguous surface words, or phrases. This is especially true with abbreviations and acronyms which are much more common in clinical text (Moon et al., 2012). The SemEval-2014 task 7 was one of nine shared tasks organized at the SemEval-2014. It was designed as a follow up to the shared tasks organized during the ShARe/CLEF eHealth 2013 evaluation (Suominen et al., 2013; Pradhan et al., 2013; Pradhan et al., 2014). Like the previous shared task, we relied on the ShARe corpus, but with more data for training and a new test set. Furthermore, in this task, we provided the options to participants to utilize a large corpus of unlabeled clinical notes. The rest of the paper is organized as follows. Section 2 describes the characteristics of the data used in the task. Section 3 describes the tasks in more detail. Section 4 explains the evaluation criteria for the two tasks. Section 5 lists the participants of the task. Section 6 discusses the results on this task and also compares them with the ShARe/CLEF eHealth 2013 results, and Section 7 concludes.

2 Data

The ShARe corpus comprises annotations over de-identified clinical reports from a US intensive care department (version 2.5 of the MIMIC II database [6]) (Saeed et al., 2002). It consists of discharge summaries, electrocardiogram, echocardiogram, and radiology reports. Access to data was carried out following MIMIC user agreement requirements for access to de-identified medical data. Hence, all participants were required to register for the evaluation, obtain a US human subjects training certificate[7], create an account to the password-protected MIMIC site, specify the purpose of data usage, accept the data use agreement, and get their account approved. The annotation focus was on disorder mentions, their various attributes and normalizations to an UMLS CUI. As such, there were two parts to the annotation: identifying a span of text as a disorder mention and normalizing (or mapping) the span to a UMLS CUI. The UMLS represents over 130 lexicons/thesauri with terms from a variety of languages and integrates resources used world-wide in clinical care, public health, and epidemiology. A disorder mention was defined as any span of text which can be mapped to a concept in SNOMED-CT and which belongs to the Disorder semantic group[8]. It also provided a semantic network in which every concept is represented by its CUI and is semantically typed (Bodenreider and McCray, 2003). A concept was in the Disorder semantic group if it belonged to one of the following UMLS semantic types: Congenital Abnormality; Acquired Abnormality; Injury or Poisoning; Pathologic Function; Disease or Syndrome; Mental or Behavioral Dysfunction; Cell or Molecular Dysfunction; Experimental Model of Disease; Anatomical Abnormality; Neoplastic Process; and Signs and Symptoms. The Finding semantic type was left out as it is very noisy and our pilot study showed lower annotation agreement on it. Following are the salient aspects of the guidelines used to

[6] http://mimic.physionet.org – Multiparameter Intelligent Monitoring in Intensive Care

[7] The course was available free of charge on the Internet, for example, via the CITI Collaborative Institutional Training Initiative at https://www.citiprogram.org/Default.asp or, the US National Institutes of Health (NIH) at http://phrp.nihtraining.com/users.

[8] Note that this definition of Disorder semantic group did not include the Findings semantic type, and as such differed from the one of UMLS Semantic Groups, available at http://semanticnetwork.nlm.nih.gov/SemGroups

annotate the data.

- Annotations represent the most specific disorder span. For example, *small bowel obstruction* is preferred over *bowel obstruction*.
- A disorder mention is a concept in the SNOMED-CT portion of the Disorder semantic group.
- Negation and temporal modifiers are not considered part of the disorder mention span.
- All disorder mentions are annotated—even the ones related to a person other than the patient and including acronyms and abbreviations.
- Mentions of disorders that are coreferential/anaphoric are also annotated.

Following are a few examples of disorder mentions from the data.

Patient found to have *lower extremity DVT.* (E1)

In example (E1), lower extremity DVT is marked as the disorder. It corresponds to CUI C0340708 (preferred term: Deep vein thrombosis of lower limb). The span DVT can be mapped to CUI C0149871 (preferred term: Deep Vein Thrombosis), but this mapping would be incorrect because it is part of a more specific disorder in the sentence, namely lower extremity DVT.

A *tumor* was found in the left *ovary*. (E2)

In example (E2), *tumor ... ovary* is annotated as a discontiguous disorder mention. This is the best method of capturing the exact disorder mention in clinical notes and its novelty is in the fact that either such phenomena have not been seen frequently enough in the general domain to gather particular attention, or the lack of a manually curated general domain ontology parallel to the UMLS.

Patient admitted with *low blood pressure*. (E3)

There are some disorders that do not have a representation to a CUI as part of the SNOMED CT within the UMLS. However, if they were deemed important by the annotators then they were annotated as CUI-less mentions. In example (E3), *low blood pressure* is a finding and is normalized as a CUI-less disorder. We constructed the annotation guidelines to require that the disorder be a reasonable synonym of the lexical description of a SNOMED-CT disorder. There are a few instances where the disorders are abbreviated or shortened in the clinical note. One example is w/r/r, which is an abbreviation for concepts wheezing (CUI C0043144), rales (CUI C0034642), and ronchi (CUI C0035508). This abbreviation is also sometimes written as r/w/r and r/r/w. Another is *gsw* for *gunshot wound* and *tachy* for *tachycardia*. More details on the annotation scheme is detailed in the guidelines[9] and in a forthcoming manuscript. The annotations covered about 336K words. Table 1 shows the quantity of the data and the split across the training, development and test sets as well as in terms of the number of notes and the number of words.

2.1 Annotation Quality

Each note in the training and development set was annotated by two professional coders trained for this task, followed by an open adjudication step. By the time we reached annotating the test data, the annotators were quite familiar with the annotation and so, in order to save time, we decided to perform a single annotation pass using a senior annotator. This was followed by a correction pass by the same annotator using a checklist of frequent annotation issues faced earlier. Table 2 shows the inter-annotator agreement (IAA) statistics for the adjudicated data. For the disorders we measure the agreement in terms of the F_1-score as traditional agreement measures such as Cohen's kappa and Krippendorf's alpha are not applicable for measuring agreement for entity mention annotation. We computed agreements between the two annotators as well as between each annotator and the final adjudicated gold standard. The latter is to give a sense of the fraction of corrections made in the process of adjudication. The strict criterion considers two mentions correct if they agree in terms of the class and the exact string, whereas the relaxed criteria considers overlapping strings of the

[9] http://goo.gl/vU8KdW

	Disorder		CUI	
	Relaxed F_1	Strict F_1	Relaxed Acc.	Strict Acc.
A1-A2	90.9	76.9	77.6	84.6
A1-GS	96.8	93.2	95.4	97.3
A2-GS	93.7	82.6	80.6	86.3

Table 2: Inter-annotator (A1 and A2) and gold standard (GS) agreement as F_1-score for the Disorder mentions and their normalization to the UMLS CUI.

Institution	User ID	Team ID
University of Pisa, Italy	attardi	UniPI
University of Lisbon, Portugal	francisco	ULisboa
University of Wisconsin, Milwaukee, USA	ghiasvand	UWM
University of Colorado, Boulder, USA	gung	CLEAR
University of Guadalajara, Mexico	herrera	UG
Taipei Medical University, Taiwan	hjdai	TMU
University of Turku, Finland	kaewphan	UTU
University of Szeged, Hungary	katona	SZTE-NLP
Queensland University of Queensland, Australia	kholghi	QUT_AEHRC
KU Leuven, Belgium	kolomiyets	KUL
Universidade de Aveiro, Portugal	nunes	BioinformaticsUA
University of the Basque Country, Spain	oronoz	IxaMed
IBM, India	parikh	ThinkMiners
easy data intelligence, India	pathak	ezDI
RelAgent Tech Pvt. Ltd., India	ramanan	RelAgent
Universidad Nacional de Colombia, Colombia	riveros	MindLab-UNAL
IIT Patna, India	sikdar	IITP
University of North Texas, USA	solomon	UNT
University of Illinois at Urbana Champaign, USA	upadhya	CogComp
The University of Texas Health Science Center at Houston, USA	wu	UTH_CCB
East China Normal University, China	yi	ECNU

Table 3: Participant organization and the respective User IDs and Team IDs.

same class as correct. The reason for checking the class is as follows. Although we only use the disorder mention in this task, the corpus has been annotated with some other UMLS types as well and therefore there are instances where a different UMLS type is assigned to the same character span in the text by the second annotator. If exact boundaries are not taken into account then the IAA agreement score is in the mid-90s. For the task of normalization to CUIs, we used accuracy to assess agreement. For the relaxed criterion, all overlapping disorder spans with the same CUI were considered correct. For the strict criterion, only disorder spans with identical spans and the same CUI were considered correct.

3 Task Description

The participants were evaluated on the following two tasks:

- **Task A** – Identification of the character spans of disorder mentions.
- **Task B** – Normalizing disorder mentions to SNOMED-CT subset of UMLS CUIs.

For Task A, participants were instructed to develop a system that predicts the spans for disorder mentions. For Tasks B, participants were instructed to develop a system that predicts the UMLS CUI within the SNOMED-CT vocabulary. The input to Task B were the disorder mention predictions from Task A. Task B was optional. System outputs adhered to the annotation format. Each participant was allowed to submit up to three runs. The entire set of unlabeled MIMIC clinical notes (excluding the test notes) were made available to the participants for potential unsupervised approaches to enhance the performance of their systems. They were allowed to use additional annotations in their systems, but this counted towards the total allowable runs; systems that used annotations outside of those provided were evaluated separately. The evaluation for all tasks was conducted using the blind, withheld test data. The participants were provided a training set containing clinical text as well as pre-annotated spans and named entities for disorders (Tasks A and B).

4 Evaluation Criteria

The following evaluation criteria were used:

- **Task A** – The system performance was evaluated against the gold standard using the F_1-score of the Precision and Recall values. There were two variations: (i) Strict; and (ii) Relaxed. The formulae for computing these metrics are mentioned below.

$$Precision = P = \frac{D_{tp}}{D_{tp} + D_{fp}} \quad (1)$$

$$Recall = R = \frac{D_{tp}}{D_{tp} + D_{fn}} \quad (2)$$

Where, D_{tp} = Number of true positives disorder mentions; D_{fp} = Number of false positives disorder mentions; D_{fn} = Number of false negative disorder mentions. In the strict case, a span was counted as correct if it was identical to the gold standard span, whereas

Team ID	User ID	Run	Task A Strict P (%)	Task A Strict R (%)	Task A Strict F_1 (%)	Task A Relaxed P (%)	Task A Relaxed R (%)	Task A Relaxed F_1 (%)	Data
UTH_CCB	wu	0	84.3	78.6	81.3	93.6	86.6	90.0	T+D
UTH_CCB	wu	1	80.8	80.5	80.6	91.6	90.7	91.1	T+D
UTU	kaewphan	1	76.5	76.7	76.6	88.6	89.9	89.3	T+D
UWM	ghiasvand	0	78.7	72.6	75.5	91.1	85.6	88.3	T+D
UTH_CCB	wu	2	68.0	84.9	75.5	83.8	93.5	88.4	T+D
UTU	kaewphan	0	77.3	72.4	74.8	90.1	85.6	87.8	T
IxaMed	oronoz	1	68.1	78.6	73.0	87.2	89.0	88.1	T+D
UWM	ghiasvand	0	77.5	67.9	72.4	90.9	81.2	85.8	T
RelAgent	ramanan	0	74.1	70.1	72.0	89.5	84.0	86.7	T+D
IxaMed	oronoz	0	72.9	70.1	71.5	88.5	80.8	84.5	T+D
ezDI	pathak	1	75.0	68.2	71.4	91.5	82.7	86.9	T
CLEAR	gung	0	80.7	63.6	71.2	92.0	72.3	81.0	T
ezDI	pathak	0	75.0	67.7	71.2	91.4	81.9	86.4	T
ULisboa	francisco	0	75.3	66.3	70.5	91.4	81.5	86.2	T
ULisboa	francisco	1	75.2	66.0	70.3	90.9	80.6	85.5	T
ULisboa	francisco	2	75.2	66.0	70.3	90.9	80.6	85.5	T
BioinformaticsUA	nunes	0	81.3	60.5	69.4	92.9	69.3	79.4	T+D
ThinkMiners	parikh	0	73.4	65.0	68.9	89.2	80.2	84.4	T
ThinkMiners	parikh	1	74.9	61.7	67.7	90.7	75.8	82.6	T
ECNU	yi	0	75.4	61.1	67.5	89.8	72.2	80.0	T+D
UniPI	attardi	2	71.2	60.1	65.2	89.7	76.6	82.6	T+D
UNT	solomon	0	64.7	62.8	63.8	81.5	79.9	80.7	T+D
UniPI	attardi	1	65.9	61.2	63.5	90.2	77.5	83.4	T+D
BioinformaticsUA	nunes	2	75.3	53.8	62.8	86.5	62.1	72.3	T+D
BioinformaticsUA	nunes	1	60.0	62.1	61.0	69.8	72.3	71.0	T+D
UniPI	attardi	0	53.9	68.4	60.2	77.8	88.5	82.8	T+D
CogComp	upadhya	1	63.9	52.9	57.9	82.3	68.3	74.6	T+D
CogComp	upadhya	2	64.1	52.0	57.4	82.9	67.5	74.4	T+D
CogComp	upadhya	0	63.6	51.5	56.9	81.9	66.5	73.4	T+D
TMU	hjdai	0	52.4	57.6	54.9	91.4	76.5	83.3	T+D
MindLab-UNAL	riveros	2	56.1	53.4	54.7	76.9	67.7	72.0	T
MindLab-UNAL	riveros	1	57.8	51.5	54.5	77.7	65.4	71.0	T
TMU	hjdai	1	62.2	42.9	50.8	89.9	65.2	75.6	T+D
IITP	sikdar	0	50.0	47.9	48.9	81.5	79.7	80.6	T+D
IITP	sikdar	1	47.3	45.8	46.5	78.9	77.6	78.2	T+D
IITP	sikdar	2	45.0	48.1	46.5	76.9	82.6	79.6	T+D
MindLab-UNAL	riveros	0	32.1	56.5	40.9	43.9	72.5	54.7	T
SZTE-NLP	katona	1	54.7	25.2	34.5	88.4	40.1	55.1	T
SZTE-NLP	katona	2	54.7	25.2	34.5	88.4	40.1	55.1	T
QUT_AEHRC	kholghi	0	38.7	29.8	33.7	90.6	70.9	79.5	T+D
SZTE-NLP	katona	0	57.1	20.5	30.2	91.8	32.5	48.0	T
KUL	kolomiyets	0	65.5	17.8	28.0	72.1	19.6	30.8	P
UG	herrera	0	11.4	23.4	15.3	25.9	49.0	33.9	P

Table 4: Performance on *test* data for participating systems on Task A – Identification of disorder mentions.

Team ID	User ID	Run	Task A Strict P (%)	Task A Strict R (%)	Task A Strict F_1 (%)	Task A Relaxed P (%)	Task A Relaxed R (%)	Task A Relaxed F_1 (%)	Data
hjdai	TMU	1	0.687	0.922	0.787	0.952	1.000	0.975	T
wu	UTH_CCB	0	0.877	0.710	0.785	0.962	0.789	0.867	T
wu	UTH_CCB	1	0.828	0.747	0.785	0.941	0.853	0.895	T
Best ShARe/CLEF-2013 performance			**0.800**	**0.706**	**0.750**	**0.925**	**0.827**	**0.873**	T
ghiasvand	UWM	0	0.827	0.675	0.743	0.958	0.799	0.871	T
pathak	ezDI	0	0.813	0.670	0.734	0.954	0.800	0.870	T
pathak	ezDI	1	0.809	0.667	0.732	0.954	0.801	0.871	T
wu	UTH_CCB	2	0.657	0.790	0.717	0.806	0.893	0.847	T
francisco	ULisboa	1	0.803	0.646	0.716	0.954	0.781	0.858	T
francisco	ULisboa	2	0.803	0.646	0.716	0.954	0.781	0.858	T
francisco	ULisboa	0	0.796	0.642	0.711	0.959	0.793	0.868	T
oronoz	IxaMed	0	0.766	0.650	0.703	0.936	0.752	0.834	T
oronoz	IxaMed	1	0.660	0.721	0.689	0.899	0.842	0.870	T
hjdai	TMU	0	0.667	0.414	0.511	0.912	0.591	0.717	T
sikdar	IITP	0	0.525	0.430	0.473	0.862	0.726	0.788	T
sikdar	IITP	2	0.467	0.440	0.453	0.812	0.775	0.793	T
sikdar	IITP	1	0.493	0.410	0.448	0.828	0.706	0.762	T

Table 5: Performance on *development* data for participating systems on Task A – Identification of disorder mentions.

in the relaxed case, a span overlapping with the gold standard span was also considered correct.

- **Task B** – Accuracy was used as the performance measure for Task 1b. It was defined as follows:

$$Accuracy_{strict} = \frac{D_{tp} \cap N_{correct}}{T_g} \quad (3)$$

$$Accuracy_{relaxed} = \frac{D_{tp} \cap N_{correct}}{D_{tp}} \quad (4)$$

Where, D_{tp} = Number of true positive disorder mentions with identical spans as in the gold standard; $N_{correct}$ = Number of correctly normalized disorder mentions; and T_g = Total number of disorder mentions in the gold standard. For Task B, the systems were only evaluated on annotations they identified in Task A. Relaxed accuracy only measured the ability to normalize correct spans. Therefore, it was possible to obtain very high values for this measure by simply dropping any mention with a low confidence span.

5 Participants

A total of 21 participants from across the world participated in Task A and out of them 18 also participated in Task B. Unfortunately, although interested, the ThinkMiners team (Parikh et al., 2014) could not participate in Task B owing to some UMLS licensing issues. The participating organizations along with the contact user's User ID and their chosen Team ID are mentioned in Table 3. Eight teams submitted three runs, six submitted two runs and seven submitted just one run. Out of these, only 13 submitted system description papers. We based our analysis on those system descriptions.

6 System Results

Tables 4 and 6 show the performance of the systems on Tasks A and B. None of the systems used any additional annotated data so we did not have to compare them separately. Both tables mention performance of all the different runs that the systems submitted. Given the many variables, we deliberately left the decision on how many and how to define these runs to the individual participant. They used various different ways to differentiate their runs. Some, for example, UTU (Kaewphan et al., 2014), did it based on the composition of training data, i.e., whether they used just the training data or both the training and the development data for training the final system, which highlighted the fact that adding development data to training bumped the F_1-score on Task A by about 2 percent points. Some participants, however, did not make use of the development data in training their systems. This was partially due to the fact that we had not explicitly mentioned in the task description that participants were allowed to use the development data for training their final models. In order to be fair, we allowed some users an opportunity to submit runs post evaluation where they used the exact same system that they used for evaluation but used the development data as well. We added a column to the results tables showing whether the participant used only the training data (T) or both training and development data (T+D) for training their system. It can be seen that even though the addition of development data helps, there are still systems that perform in the lower percentile who have used both training and development data for training, indicating that both the features and the machine learning classifier contribute to the models. A novel aspect of the SemEval-2014 shared task that differentiates it from the ShARE/CLEF task—other than the fact that it used more data and a new test set—is the fact that SemEval-2014 allowed the use of a much larger set of unlabeled MIMIC notes to inform the models. Surprisingly, only two of the systems (ULisboa (Leal et al., 2014) and UniPi (Attardi et al., 2014)) used the unlabeled MIMIC corpus to generalize the lexical features. Another team—UTH_CCB(Zhang et al., 2014)—used off-the-shelf Brown clusters[10] as opposed to training them on the unlabeled MIMIC II data. For Task B, the accuracy of a system using the *strict* metric was positively correlated with its recall on the disorder mentions that were input to it (i.e., recall for Task A), and did not get penalized for lower precision. Therefore one could essentially gain higher accuracy in Task B by tuning a system to provide the highest mention recall in Task A potentially at the cost of precision and the overall F_1-score and using those mentions as input for Task B. This can be seen from the fact that the run 2 for UTH_CCB (Zhang et al., 2014) system with the lowest F_1-score has

[10] Personal conversation with the participants as it was not very clear in the system description paper.

Team ID	User ID	Run	Task B Strict Acc. (%)	Task B Relaxed Acc. (%)	Data
UTH_CCB	wu	2	74.1	87.3	T+D
UTH_CCB	wu	1	70.8	88.0	T+D
UTH_CCB	wu	0	69.4	88.3	T+D
UWM	ghiasvand	0	66.0	90.9	T+D
RelAgent	ramanan	0	63.9	91.2	T+D
UWM	ghiasvand	0	61.7	90.8	T
IxaMed	oronoz	0	60.4	86.2	T+D
UTU	kaewphan	1	60.1	78.3	T+D
ezDI	pathak	1	59.9	87.8	T
ezDI	pathak	0	59.2	87.4	T
UTU	kaewphan	0	57.7	79.7	T
BioinformaticsUA	nunes	1	53.1	85.5	T+D
BioinformaticsUA	nunes	0	52.7	87.0	T+D
CLEAR	gung	0	52.5	82.5	T
TMU	hjdai	0	48.9	84.9	T+D
UNT	solomon	0	47.0	74.8	T+D
UniPI	attardi	0	46.7	68.3	T+D
BioinformaticsUA	nunes	2	46.3	86.1	T+D
MindLab-UNAL	riveros	2	46.1	86.3	T
IxaMed	oronoz	1	43.9	55.8	T+D
MindLab-UNAL	riveros	0	43.5	77.1	T
UniPI	attardi	1	42.8	69.9	T+D
UniPI	attardi	2	41.7	69.3	T+D
MindLab-UNAL	riveros	1	41.1	79.7	T
ULisboa	francisco	2	40.5	61.5	T
ULisboa	francisco	1	40.4	61.2	T
ULisboa	francisco	0	40.2	60.6	T
ECNU	yi	0	36.4	59.5	T+D
TMU	hjdai	1	35.8	83.4	T+D
IITP	sikdar	0	33.3	69.6	T+D
IITP	sikdar	2	33.2	69.1	T+D
IITP	sikdar	1	31.9	69.6	T+D
CogComp	upadhya	1	25.3	47.9	T+D
CogComp	upadhya	2	24.8	47.7	T+D
CogComp	upadhya	0	24.4	47.3	T+D
KUL	kolomiyets	0	16.5	92.8	P
UG	herrera	0	12.5	53.4	P

Table 6: Performance on *test* data for participating systems on Task B – Normalization of disorder mentions to UMLS (SNOMED-CT subset) CUIs.

Team ID	User ID	Run	Task B Strict Acc. (%)	Task B Relaxed Acc. (%)	Data
TMU	hjdai	0	0.716	0.777	T
TMU	hjdai	1	0.716	0.777	T
UTH_CCB	wu	2	0.713	0.903	T
UTH_CCB	wu	1	0.680	0.910	T
UTH_CCB	wu	0	0.647	0.910	T
UWM	ghiasvand	0	0.623	0.923	T
ezDI	pathak	0	0.603	0.900	T
ezDI	pathak	1	0.600	0.899	T
Best ShARe/CLEF-2013 performance			**0.589**	**0.895**	T
IxaMed	oronoz	0	0.556	0.855	T
IxaMed	oronoz	1	0.421	0.584	T
ULisboa	francisco	2	0.388	0.601	T
ULisboa	francisco	1	0.385	0.596	T
ULisboa	francisco	0	0.377	0.588	T
IITP	sikdar	2	0.318	0.724	T
IITP	sikdar	0	0.312	0.725	T
IITP	sikdar	1	0.299	0.730	T

Table 7: Performance on *development* data for some participating systems on Task B – Normalization of disorder mentions to UMLS (SNOMED-CT subset) CUIs.

the best accuracy for Task B and vice-versa for run 0 with run 1 in between the two. In order to fairly compare the performance between two systems one would have to provide perfect mentions as input to Task B. One of the systems—UWM Ghiasvand and Kate (2014)—did run some ablation experiments using gold standard mentions as input to Task B and obtained a best performance of 89.5F_1-score (Table 5 of Ghiasvand and Kate (2014)) as opposed to 62.3 F_1-score (Table 7) in the more realistic setting which is a huge difference. In the upcoming SemEval-2014 where this same evaluation is going to carried out under Task 14, we plan to perform supplementary evaluation where gold disorder mentions would be input to the system while attempting Task B. An interesting outcome of planning a follow-on evaluation to the ShARe/CLEF eHealth 2013 task was that we could, and did, use the test data from the ShARe/CLEF eHealth 2013 task as the development set for this evaluation. After the main evaluation we asked participants to provide the system performance on the development set using the same number and run convention that they submitted for the main evaluation. These results are presented in Tables 5 and 7. We have inserted the best performing system score from the ShARe/CLEF eHealth 2013 task in these tables. For Task A, referring to Tables 4 and 5, there is a boost of 3.7 absolute percent points for the F_1-score over the same task (Task 1a) in the ShARe/CLEF eHealth 2013. For Task B, referring to Tables 6 and 7, there is a boost of 13.7 percent points for the F_1-score over the same task (Task 1b) in the ShARe/CLEF eHealth 2013 evaluation. The participants used various approaches for tackling the tasks, ranging from purely rule-based/unsupervised (RelAgent (Ramanan and Nathan, 2014), (Matos et al., 2014), KUL[11]) to a hybrid of rules and machine learning classifiers. The top performing systems typically used the latter. Various versions of the IOB formulation were used for tagging the disorder mentions. None of the standard variations on the IOB formulation were explicitly designed or used to handle discontiguous mentions. Some systems used novel variations on this approach. Probably the simplest variation was applied by the UWM team (Ghiasvand and Kate, 2014). In this formulation the following labeled sequence "the/O left/B atrium/I is/O moderately/O

[11]Personal communication with participant.

dilated/I" can be used to represent the discontiguous mention *left atrium...dilated*, and can be constructed as such from the output of the classification. The most complex variation was the one used by the UTH_CCB team (Zhang et al., 2014) where they used the following set of tags—B, I, O, DB, DI, HB, HI. This variation encodes discontiguous mentions by adding four more tags to the I, O and B tags. These are variations of the B and I tags with either a D or a H prefix. The prefix H indicates that the word or word sequence is the shared head, and the prefix D indicates otherwise. Another intermediate approach used by the ULisboa team (Leal et al., 2014) with the tagset—S, B, I, O, E and N. Here, S represents the single token entity to be recognized, E represents the end of an entity (which is part of one of the prior IOB variations) and an N tag to identify non-contiguous mentions. They don't provide an explicit example usage of this tag set in their paper. Yet another variation was used by the SZTE-NLP team (Katona and Farkas, 2014). This used tags B, I, L, O and U. Here, L is used for the last token similar to E earlier, and U is used for a unit-token mention, similar to S earlier. We believe that the only approach that can distinguish between discontiguous disorders that share the same head word/phrase is the one used by the UTH_CCB team (Zhang et al., 2014). The participants used various machine learning classifiers such as MaxEnt, SVM, CRF in combination with rich syntactic and semantic features to capture the disorder mentions. As mentioned earlier, a few participants used the available unlabeled data and also off-the-shelf clusters to better generalize features. The use of vector space models such as cosine similarities as well as continuous distributed word vector representations was useful in the normalization task. They also availed of tools such as MetaMap and cTakes to generate features as well as candidate CUIs during normalizations.

7 Conclusion

We have created a reference standard with high inter-annotator agreement and evaluated systems on the task of identification and normalization of diseases and disorders appearing in clinical reports. The results have demonstrated that an NLP system can complete this task with reasonably high accuracy. We plan to annotate another evaluation using the same data as part of the in the SemEval-2015, Task 14[12] adding another task of template filling where the systems will identify and normalize ten attributes the identified disease/disorder mentions.

Acknowledgments

We greatly appreciate the hard work and feedback of our program committee members and annotators David Harris, Jennifer Green and Glenn Zaramba. Danielle Mowery, Sumithra Velupillai and Brett South for helping prepare the manuscript by summarizing the approaches used by various systems. This shared task was partially supported by Shared Annotated Resources (ShARe) project NIH 5R01GM090187 and Temporal Histories of Your Medical Events (THYME) project (NIH R01LM010090 and U54LM008748).

References

Giuseppe Attardi, Vitoria Cozza, and Daniele Sartiano. 2014. UniPi: Recognition of mentions of disorders in clinical text. In *Proceedings of the International Workshop on Semantic Evaluations*, Dublin, Ireland, August.

Olivier Bodenreider and Alexa McCray. 2003. Exploring semantic groups through visual approaches. *Journal of Biomedical Informatics*, 36:414–432.

Keith E. Campbell, Diane E. Oliver, and Edward H. Shortliffe. 1998. The Unified Medical Language System: Towards a collaborative approach for solving terminologic problems. *J Am Med Inform Assoc*, 5(1):12–16.

Omid Ghiasvand and Rohit J. Kate. 2014. UWM: Disorder mention extraction from clinical text using crfs and normalization using learned edit distance patterns. In *Proceedings of the International Workshop on Semantic Evaluations*, Dublin, Ireland, August.

Suwisa Kaewphan, Kai Hakaka1, and Filip Ginter. 2014. UTU: Disease mention recognition and normalization with crfs and vector space representations. In *Proceedings of the International Workshop on Semantic Evaluations*, Dublin, Ireland, August.

Melinda Katona and Richárd Farkas. 2014. SZTE-NLP: Clinical text analysis with named entity recognition. In *Proceedings of the International Workshop on Semantic Evaluations*, Dublin, Ireland, August.

André Leal, Diogo Gonçalves, Bruno Martins, and Francisco M. Couto. 2014. ULisboa: Identification and classification of medical concepts. In *Proceedings of the International Workshop on Semantic Evaluations*, Dublin, Ireland, August.

[12] http://alt.qcri.org/semeval2015/task14

Robert Leaman and Graciela Gonzalez. 2008. Banner: an executable survey of advances in biomedical named entity recognition. In *Pacific Symposium on Biocomputing*, volume 13, pages 652–663.

Sérgio Matos, Tiago Nunes, and José Luís Oliveira. 2014. BioinformaticsUA: Concept recognition in clinical narratives using a modular and highly efficient text processing framework. In *Proceedings of the International Workshop on Semantic Evaluations*, Dublin, Ireland, August.

Sungrim Moon, Serguei Pakhomov, and Genevieve B Melton. 2012. Automated disambiguation of acronyms and abbreviations in clinical texts: Window and training size considerations. In *AMIA Annu Symp Proc*, pages 1310–1319.

David Nadeau and Satoshi Sekine. 2007. A survey of named entity recognition and classification. *Lingvisticae Investigationes*, 30(1):3–26.

Roberto Navigli. 2009. Word sense disambiguation. *ACM Computing Surveys*, 41(2):1–69, February.

Ankur Parikh, Avinesh PVS, Joy Mustafi, Lalit Agarwalla, and Ashish Mungi. 2014. ThinkMiners: SemEval-2014 task 7: Analysis of clinical text. In *Proceedings of the International Workshop on Semantic Evaluations*, Dublin, Ireland, August.

Sameer Pradhan, Noémie Elhadad, Brett South, David Martinez, Lee Christensen, Amy Vogel, Hanna Suominen, Wendy W. Chapman, and Guergana Savova. 2013. Task 1: ShARe/CLEF eHealth Evaluation Lab 2013. In *Working Notes of CLEF eHealth Evaluation Labs*.

Sameer Pradhan, Noémie Elhadad, Brett South, David Martinez, Lee Christensen, Amy Vogel, Hanna Suominen, Wendy W. Chapman, and Guergana Savova. 2014. Evaluating the state of the art in disorder recognition and normalization of the clinical narrative. In *Journal of the American Medical Informatics Association (to appear)*.

S. V. Ramanan and P. Senthil Nathan. 2014. RelAgent: Entity detection and normalization for diseases in clinical records: a linguistically driven approach. In *Proceedings of the International Workshop on Semantic Evaluations*, Dublin, Ireland, August.

Angus Roberts, Robert Gaizauskas, Mark Hepple, George Demetriou, Yikun Guo, Ian Roberts, and Andrea Setzer. 2009. Building a semantically annotated corpus of clinical texts. *J Biomed Inform*, 42(5):950–66.

Mohammed Saeed, C. Lieu, G. Raber, and R.G. Mark. 2002. MIMIC II: a massive temporal ICU patient database to support research in intelligent patient monitoring. *Comput Cardiol*, 29.

Guergana K. Savova, A. R. Coden, I. L. Sominsky, R. Johnson, P. V. Ogren, P. C. de Groen, and C. G. Chute. 2008. Word sense disambiguation across two domains: Biomedical literature and clinical notes. *J Biomed Inform*, 41(6):1088–1100, December.

Weiyi Sun, Anna Rumshisky, and Özlem Uzuner. 2013. Evaluating temporal relations in clinical text: 2012 i2b2 Challenge. *Journal of the American Medical Informatics Association*, 20(5):806–13.

Hanna Suominen, Sanna Salanterä, Sumithra Velupillai, Wendy W. Chapman, Guergana Savova, Noemie Elhadad, Sameer Pradhan, Brett R. South, Danielle L. Mowery, Gareth J. F. Jones, Johannes Leveling, Liadh Kelly, Lorraine Goeuriot, David Martinez, and Guido Zuccon. 2013. Overview of the ShARe/CLEF eHealth evaluation lab 2013. In *Working Notes of CLEF eHealth Evaluation Labs*.

Özlem Uzuner, Brett R South, Shuying Shen, and Scott L DuVall. 2011. 2010 i2b2/VA challenge on concepts, assertions, and relations in clinical text. *Journal of the American Medical Informatics Association*, 18(5):552–556.

Özlem Uzuner, Andreea Bodnari, Shuying Shen, Tyler Forbush, John Pestian, and Brett R South. 2012. Evaluating the state of the art in coreference resolution for electronic medical records. *Journal of American Medical Informatics Association*, 19(5):786–791, September.

Yaoyun Zhang, Jingqi Wang, Buzhou Tang, Yonghui Wu, Min Jiang, Yukun Chen, and Hua Xu. 2014. UTH_CCB: A report for SemEval 2014 task 7 analysis of clinical text. In *Proceedings of the International Workshop on Semantic Evaluations*, Dublin, Ireland, August.

SemEval 2014 Task 8: Broad-Coverage Semantic Dependency Parsing

Stephan Oepen[♣♠], Marco Kuhlmann[♡], Yusuke Miyao[◇], Daniel Zeman[○], Dan Flickinger[•], Jan Hajič[○], Angelina Ivanova[♣], and Yi Zhang[⋆]

[♣] University of Oslo, Department of Informatics

[♠] Potsdam University, Department of Linguistics

[♡] Linköping University, Department of Computer and Information Science

[◇] National Institute of Informatics, Tokyo

[○] Charles University in Prague, Faculty of Mathematics and Physics, Institute of Formal and Applied Linguistics

[•] Stanford University, Center for the Study of Language and Information

[⋆] Nuance Communications Aachen GmbH

sdp-organizers@emmtee.net

Abstract

Task 8 at SemEval 2014 defines *Broad-Coverage Semantic Dependency Parsing* (SDP) as the problem of recovering sentence-internal predicate–argument relationships for *all content words*, i.e. the semantic structure constituting the relational core of sentence meaning. In this task description, we position the problem in comparison to other sub-tasks in computational language analysis, introduce the semantic dependency target representations used, reflect on high-level commonalities and differences between these representations, and summarize the task setup, participating systems, and main results.

1 Background and Motivation

Syntactic dependency parsing has seen great advances in the past decade, in part owing to relatively broad consensus on target representations, and in part reflecting the successful execution of a series of shared tasks at the annual Conference for Natural Language Learning (CoNLL; Buchholz & Marsi, 2006; Nivre et al., 2007; inter alios). From this very active research area accurate and efficient syntactic parsers have developed for a wide range of natural languages. However, the predominant data structure in dependency parsing to date are *trees*, in the formal sense that every node in the dependency graph is reachable from a distinguished root node by exactly one directed path.

Unfortunately, tree-oriented parsers are ill-suited for producing meaning representations, i.e. moving from the analysis of grammatical structure to sentence semantics. Even if syntactic parsing arguably can be limited to tree structures, this is not the case in semantic analysis, where a node will often be the argument of multiple predicates (i.e. have more than one incoming arc), and it will often be desirable to leave nodes corresponding to semantically vacuous word classes unattached (with no incoming arcs).

Thus, Task 8 at SemEval 2014, *Broad-Coverage Semantic Dependency Parsing* (SDP 2014),[1] seeks to stimulate the dependency parsing community to move towards more general graph processing, to thus enable a more direct analysis of *Who did What to Whom?* For English, there exist several independent annotations of sentence meaning over the venerable Wall Street Journal (WSJ) text of the Penn Treebank (PTB; Marcus et al., 1993). These resources constitute parallel semantic annotations over the same common text, but to date they have not been related to each other and, in fact, have hardly been applied for training and testing of data-driven parsers. In this task, we have used three different such target representations for bi-lexical semantic dependencies, as demonstrated in Figure 1 below for the WSJ sentence:

(1) A similar technique is almost impossible to apply to other crops, such as cotton, soybeans, and rice.

Semantically, *technique* arguably is dependent on the determiner (the quantificational locus), the modifier *similar*, and the predicate *apply*. Conversely, the predicative copula, infinitival *to*, and the vac-

[1] See http://alt.qcri.org/semeval2014/task8/ for further technical details, information on how to obtain the data, and official results.

Proceedings of the 8th International Workshop on Semantic Evaluation (SemEval 2014), pages 63–72, Dublin, Ireland, August 23-24, 2014.

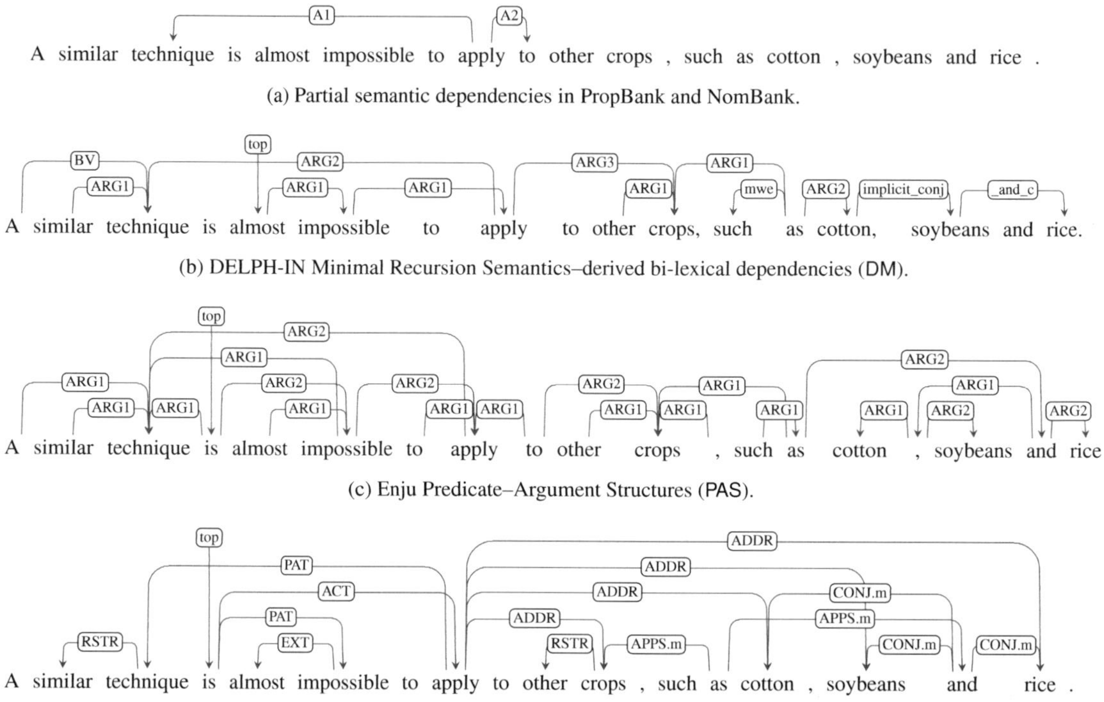

(a) Partial semantic dependencies in PropBank and NomBank.

(b) DELPH-IN Minimal Recursion Semantics–derived bi-lexical dependencies (DM).

(c) Enju Predicate–Argument Structures (PAS).

(d) Parts of the tectogrammatical layer of the Prague Czech-English Dependency Treebank (PCEDT).

Figure 1: Sample semantic dependency graphs for Example (1).

uous preposition marking the deep object of *apply* can be argued to not have a semantic contribution of their own. Besides calling for node reentrancies and partial connectivity, semantic dependency graphs may also exhibit higher degrees of non-projectivity than is typical of syntactic dependency trees.

In addition to its relation to syntactic dependency parsing, the task also has some overlap with Semantic Role Labeling (SRL; Gildea & Jurafsky, 2002). In much previous work, however, target representations typically draw on resources like PropBank and NomBank (Palmer et al., 2005; Meyers et al., 2004), which are limited to argument identification and labeling for verbal and nominal predicates. A plethora of semantic phenomena—for example negation and other scopal embedding, comparatives, possessives, various types of modification, and even conjunction—typically remain unanalyzed in SRL. Thus, its target representations are partial to a degree that can prohibit semantic downstream processing, for example inference-based techniques. In contrast, we require parsers to identify all semantic dependencies, i.e. compute a representation that integrates all content words in one structure. Another difference to common interpretations of SRL is that the SDP 2014 task definition does not encompass predicate disambiguation, a design decision in part owed to our goal to focus on parsing-oriented, i.e. structural, analysis, and in part to lacking consensus on sense inventories for all content words.

Finally, a third closely related area of much current interest is often dubbed 'semantic parsing', which Kate and Wong (2010) define as "the task of mapping natural language sentences into complete formal meaning representations which a computer can execute for some domain-specific application." In contrast to most work in this tradition, our SDP target representations aim to be task- and domain-independent, though at least part of this generality comes at the expense of 'completeness' in the above sense; i.e. there are aspects of sentence meaning that arguably remain implicit.

2 Target Representations

We use three distinct target representations for semantic dependencies. As is evident in our running example (Figure 1), showing what are called the DM, PAS, and PCEDT semantic dependencies, there are contentful differences among these annotations, and there is of course not one obvious (or even objective) truth. In the following paragraphs, we provide some background on the 'pedigree' and linguistic characterization of these representations.

DM: DELPH-IN MRS-Derived Bi-Lexical Dependencies These semantic dependency graphs originate in a manual re-annotation of Sections 00–21 of the WSJ Corpus with syntactico-semantic analyses derived from the LinGO English Resource Grammar (ERG; Flickinger, 2000). Among other layers of linguistic annotation, this resource—dubbed DeepBank by Flickinger et al. (2012)—includes underspecified logical-form meaning representations in the framework of Minimal Recursion Semantics (MRS; Copestake et al., 2005). Our DM target representations are derived through a two-step 'lossy' conversion of MRSs, first to variable-free Elementary Dependency Structures (EDS; Oepen & Lønning, 2006), then to 'pure' bi-lexical form—projecting some construction semantics onto word-to-word dependencies (Ivanova et al., 2012). In preparing our gold-standard DM graphs from DeepBank, the same conversion pipeline was used as in the system submission of Miyao et al. (2014). For this target representation, top nodes designate the highest-scoping (non-quantifier) predicate in the graph, e.g. the (scopal) degree adverb *almost* in Figure 1.[2]

PAS: Enju Predicate-Argument Structures The Enju parsing system is an HPSG-based parser for English.[3] The grammar and the disambiguation model of this parser are derived from the Enju HPSG treebank, which is automatically converted from the phrase structure and predicate–argument structure annotations of the PTB. The PAS data set is extracted from the WSJ portion of the Enju HPSG treebank. While the Enju treebank is annotated with full HPSG-style structures, only its predicate–argument structures are converted into the SDP data format for use in this task. Top nodes in this representation denote semantic heads. Again, the system description of Miyao et al. (2014) provides more technical detail on the conversion.

PCEDT: Prague Tectogrammatical Bi-Lexical Dependencies The Prague Czech-English Dependency Treebank (PCEDT; Hajič et al., 2012)[4] is a set of parallel dependency trees over the WSJ texts from the PTB, and their Czech translations. Similarly to other treebanks in the Prague family, there are two layers of syntactic annotation: *analytical* (a-trees) and *tectogrammatical* (t-trees). PCEDT bi-lexical dependencies in this task have been extracted from the t-trees. The specifics of the PCEDT representations are best observed in the procedure that converts the original PCEDT data to the SDP data format; see Miyao et al. (2014). Top nodes are derived from t-tree roots; i.e. they mostly correspond to main verbs. In case of coordinate clauses, there are multiple top nodes per sentence.

id	*form*	*lemma*	*pos*	*top*	*pred*	*arg1*	*arg2*
#20200002							
1	Ms.	Ms.	NNP	−	+	_	_
2	Haag	Haag	NNP	−	−	compound	ARG1
3	plays	play	VBZ	+	+	_	_
4	Elianti	Elianti	NNP	−	−	_	ARG2
5	.	.	.	−	−	_	_

Table 1: Tabular SDP data format (showing DM).

3 Graph Representation

The SDP target representations can be characterized as labeled, directed graphs. Formally, a *semantic dependency graph* for a sentence $x = x_1, \ldots, x_n$ is a structure $G = (V, E, \ell_V, \ell_E)$ where $V = \{1, \ldots, n\}$ is a set of *nodes* (which are in one-to-one correspondence with the tokens of the sentence); $E \subseteq V \times V$ is a set of *edges*; and ℓ_V and ℓ_E are mappings that assign *labels* (from some finite alphabet) to nodes and edges, respectively. More specifically for this task, the label $\ell_V(i)$ of a node i is a tuple consisting of four components: its word form, lemma, part of speech, and a Boolean flag indicating whether the corresponding token represents a *top* predicate for the specific sentence. The label $\ell_E(i \to j)$ of an edge $i \to j$ is a semantic relation that holds between i and j. The exact definition of what constitutes a top node and what semantic relations are available differs among our three target representations, but note that top nodes can have incoming edges.

All data provided for the task uses a column-based file format (dubbed the *SDP data format*) similar to the one of the 2009 CoNLL Shared Task (Hajič et al., 2009). As in that task, we assume gold-standard sentence and token segmentation. For ease of reference, each sentence is prefixed by a line with just a unique identifier, using the scheme *2SSDDIII*, with a constant leading 2, two-digit *section* code, two-digit *document* code (within each

[2] Note, however, that non-scopal adverbs act as mere intersective modifiers, e.g. *loudly* is a predicate in DM, but the main verb provides the top node in structures like *Abrams sang loudly*.

[3] See `http://kmcs.nii.ac.jp/enju/`.

[4] See `http://ufal.mff.cuni.cz/pcedt2.0/`.

section), and three-digit *item* number (within each document). For example, identifier `20200002` denotes the second sentence in the first file of PTB Section 02, the classic *Ms. Haag plays Elianti.* The annotation of this sentence is shown in Table 1.

With one exception, our fields (i.e. columns in the tab-separated matrix) are a subset of the CoNLL 2009 inventory: (1) `id`, (2) `form`, (3) `lemma`, and (4) `pos` characterize the current token, with token identifiers starting from 1 within each sentence. Besides the lemma and part-of-speech information, in the closed track of our task, there is no explicit analysis of syntax. Across the three target representations in the task, fields (1) and (2) are aligned and uniform, i.e. all representations annotate exactly the same text. On the other hand, fields (3) and (4) are representation-specific, i.e. there are different conventions for lemmatization, and part-of-speech assignments can vary (but all representations use the same PTB inventory of PoS tags).

The bi-lexical semantic dependency graph over tokens is represented by two or more columns starting with the obligatory, binary-valued fields (5) `top` and (6) `pred`. A positive value in the `top` column indicates that the node corresponding to this token is a *top* node (see Section 2 below). The `pred` column is a simplification of the corresponding field in earlier tasks, indicating whether or not this token represents a predicate, i.e. a node with outgoing dependency edges. With these minor differences to the CoNLL tradition, our file format can represent general, directed graphs, with designated top nodes. For example, there can be singleton nodes not connected to other parts of the graph, and in principle there can be multiple tops, or a non-predicate top node.

To designate predicate–argument relations, there are as many additional columns as there are predicates in the graph (i.e. tokens marked + in the `pred` column); these additional columns are called (7) `arg1`, (8) `arg2`, etc. These colums contain argument roles relative to the i-th predicate, i.e. a non-empty value in column `arg1` indicates that the current token is an argument of the (linearly) first predicate in the sentence. In this format, graph reentrancies will lead to a token receiving argument roles for multiple predicates (i.e. non-empty $\texttt{arg}_i$ values in the same row). All tokens of the same sentence must always have all argument columns filled in, even on non-predicate words; in other words, all lines making up one block of tokens will have the same number n of fields, but n can differ across sentences, depending on the count of graph nodes.

		DM	PAS	PCEDT
(1)	**# labels**	51	42	68
(2)	**% singletons**	22.62	4.49	35.79
(3)	**# edge density**	0.96	1.02	0.99
(4)	**$\%_g$ trees**	2.35	1.30	56.58
(5)	**$\%_g$ projective**	3.05	1.71	53.29
(6)	**$\%_g$ fragmented**	6.71	0.23	0.56
(7)	**$\%_n$ reentrancies**	27.35	29.40	9.27
(8)	**$\%_g$ topless**	0.28	0.02	0.00
(9)	**# top nodes**	0.9972	0.9998	1.1237
(10)	**$\%_n$ non-top roots**	44.71	55.92	4.36

Table 2: Contrastive high-level graph statistics.

4 Data Sets

All three target representations are annotations of the same text, Sections 00–21 of the WSJ Corpus. For this task, we have synchronized these resources at the sentence and tokenization levels and excluded from the SDP 2014 training and testing data any sentences for which (a) one or more of the treebanks lacked a gold-standard analysis; (b) a one-to-one alignment of tokens could not be established across all three representations; or (c) at least one of the graphs was cyclic. Of the 43,746 sentences in these 22 first sections of WSJ text, DeepBank lacks analyses for close to 15%, and the Enju Treebank has gaps for a little more than four percent. Some 500 sentences show tokenization mismatches, most owing to DeepBank correcting PTB idiosyncrasies like ⟨`G.m.b`, `H.`⟩, ⟨`S.p`, `A.`⟩, and ⟨`U.S.`, `.`⟩, and introducing a few new ones (Fares et al., 2013). Finally, 232 of the graphs obtained through the above conversions were cyclic. In total, we were left with 34,004 sentences (or 745,543 tokens) as training data (Sections 00–20), and 1348 testing sentences (29,808 tokens), from Section 21.

Quantitative Comparison As a first attempt at contrasting our three target representations, Table 2 shows some high-level statistics of the graphs comprising the training data.[5] In terms of distinctions

[5]These statistics are obtained using the 'official' SDP toolkit. We refer to nodes that have neither incoming nor outgoing edges and are not marked as top nodes as *singletons*; these nodes are ignored in subsequent statistics, e.g. when determining the proportion of edges per node (3) or the percentages of rooted trees (4) and fragmented graphs (6). The notation '$\%_n$' denotes (non-singleton) node percentages, and '$\%_g$' percentages over all graphs. We consider a *root* node any (non-singleton) node that has no incoming edges; *reentrant* nodes have at least two incoming edges. Following Sagae and Tsujii (2008), we consider a graph *projective* when there are no crossing edges (in a left-to-right rendering of nodes) and no roots are 'covered', i.e. for any root j there is no edge $i \rightarrow k$

	Directed			Undirected		
	DM	PAS	PCEDT	DM	PAS	PCEDT
DM	–	.6425	.2612	–	.6719	.5675
PAS	.6688	–	.2963	.6993	–	.5490
PCEDT	.2636	.2963	–	.5743	.5630	–

Table 3: Pairwise F_1 similarities, including punctuation (upper right diagonals) or not (lower left).

drawn in dependency labels (1), there are clear differences between the representations, with PCEDT appearing linguistically most fine-grained, and PAS showing the smallest label inventory. Unattached singleton nodes (2) in our setup correspond to tokens analyzed as semantically vacuous, which (as seen in Figure 1) include most punctuation marks in PCEDT and DM, but not PAS. Furthermore, PCEDT (unlike the other two) analyzes some high-frequency determiners as semantically vacuous. Conversely, PAS on average has more edges per (non-singleton) nodes than the other two (3), which likely reflects its approach to the analysis of functional words (see below).

Judging from both the percentage of actual trees (4), the proportions of projective graphs (5), and the proportions of reentrant nodes (7), PCEDT is much more 'tree-oriented' than the other two, which at least in part reflects its approach to the analysis of modifiers and determiners (again, see below). We view the small percentages of graphs without at least one top node (8) and of graphs with at least two non-singleton components that are not interconnected (6) as tentative indicators of general well-formedness. Intuitively, there should always be a 'top' predicate, and the whole graph should 'hang together'. Only DM exhibits non-trivial (if small) degrees of topless and fragmented graphs, and these may indicate imperfections in the DeepBank annotations or room for improvement in the conversion from full MRSs to bi-lexical dependencies, but possibly also exceptions to our intuitions about semantic dependency graphs.

Finally, in Table 3 we seek to quantify pairwise structural similarity between the three representations in terms of unlabeled dependency F_1 (dubbed UF in Section 5 below). We provide four variants of this metric, (a) taking into account the directionality of edges or not and (b) including edges involving punctuation marks or not. On this view, DM and PAS are structurally much closer to each other than either of the two is to PCEDT, even more so when discarding punctuation. While relaxing the comparison to ignore edge directionality also increases similarity scores for this pair, the effect is much more pronounced when comparing either to PCEDT. This suggests that directionality of semantic dependencies is a major source of diversion between DM and PAS on the one hand, and PCEDT on the other hand.

Linguistic Comparison Among other aspects, Ivanova et al. (2012) categorize a range of syntactic and semantic dependency annotation schemes according to the role that functional elements take. In Figure 1 and the discussion of Table 2 above, we already observed that PAS differs from the other representations in integrating into the graph auxiliaries, the infinitival marker, the case-marking preposition introducing the argument of *apply* (*to*), and most punctuation marks;[6] while these (and other functional elements, e.g. complementizers) are analyzed as semantically vacuous in DM and PCEDT, they function as predicates in PAS, though do not always serve as 'local' top nodes (i.e. the semantic head of the corresponding sub-graph): For example, the infinitival marker in Figure 1 takes the verb as its argument, but the 'upstairs' predicate *impossible* links directly to the verb, rather than to the infinitival marker as an intermediate.

At the same time, DM and PAS pattern alike in their approach to modifiers, e.g. attributive adjectives, adverbs, and prepositional phrases. Unlike in PCEDT (or common syntactic dependency schemes), these are analyzed as semantic predicates and, thus, contribute to higher degrees of node reentrancy and non-top (structural) roots. Roughly the same holds for determiners, but here our PCEDT projection of Prague tectogrammatical trees onto bi-lexical dependencies leaves 'vanilla' articles (like *a* and *the*) as singleton nodes.

The analysis of coordination is distinct in the three representations, as also evident in Figure 1. By design, DM opts for what is often called the Mel'čukian analysis of coordinate structures (Mel'čuk, 1988), with a chain of dependencies rooted at the first conjunct (which is thus considered the head, 'standing in' for the structure at large); in the DM approach, coordinating conjunctions are not integrated with the graph but rather contribute different types of dependencies. In PAS, the final coordinating conjunction is the head of the

such that $i < j < k$.

[6] In all formats, punctuation marks like dashes, colons, and sometimes commas can be contentful, i.e. at times occur as both predicates, arguments, and top nodes.

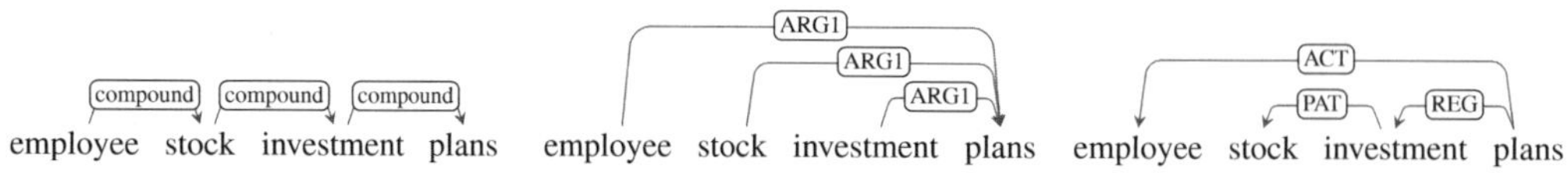

Figure 2: Analysis of nominal compounding in DM, PAS, and PCEDT, respectively .

structure and each coordinating conjunction (or intervening punctuation mark that acts like one) is a two-place predicate, taking left and right conjuncts as its arguments. Conversely, in PCEDT the last coordinating conjunction takes all conjuncts as its arguments (in case there is no overt conjunction, a punctuation mark is used instead); additional conjunctions or punctuation marks are not connected to the graph.[7]

A linguistic difference between our representations that highlights variable granularities of analysis and, relatedly, diverging views on the scope of the problem can be observed in Figure 2. Much noun phrase–internal structure is not made explicit in the PTB, and the Enju Treebank from which our PAS representation derives predates the bracketing work of Vadas and Curran (2007). In the four-way nominal compounding example of Figure 2, thus, PAS arrives at a strictly left-branching tree, and there is no attempt at interpreting semantic roles among the members of the compound either; PCEDT, on the other hand, annotates both the *actual* compound-internal bracketing and the assignment of roles, e.g. making *stock* the `PAT`(ient) of *investment*. In this spirit, the PCEDT annotations could be directly paraphrased along the lines of *plans by employees for investment in stocks*. In a middle position between the other two, DM disambiguates the bracketing but, by design, merely assigns an underspecified, construction-specific dependency type; its `compound` dependency, then, is to be interpreted as the most general type of dependency that can hold between the elements of this construction (i.e. to a first approximation either an argument role or a relation parallel to a preposition, as in the above paraphrase). The DM and PCEDT annotations of this specific example happen to diverge in their bracketing decisions, where the DM analysis corresponds to *[...] investments in stock for employees*, i.e. grouping the concept *employee stock* (in contrast to 'common stock').

Without context and expert knowledge, these decisions are hard to call, and indeed there has been much previous work seeking to identify and annotate the relations that hold between members of a nominal compound (see Nakov, 2013, for a recent overview). To what degree the bracketing and role disambiguation in this example are determined by the linguistic signal (rather than by context and world knowledge, say) can be debated, and thus the observed differences among our representations in this example relate to the classic contrast between 'sentence' (or 'conventional') meaning, on the one hand, and 'speaker' (or 'occasion') meaning, on the other hand (Quine, 1960; Grice, 1968). In turn, we acknowledge different plausible points of view about which level of semantic representation should be the target representation for data-driven *parsing* (i.e. structural analysis guided by the grammatical system), and which refinements like the above could be construed as part of a subsequent task of *interpretation*.

5 Task Setup

Training data for the task, providing all columns in the file format sketched in Section 3 above, together with a first version of the SDP toolkit—including graph input, basic statistics, and scoring—were released to candidate participants in early December 2013. In mid-January, a minor update to the training data and optional syntactic 'companion' analyses (see below) were provided, and in early February the description and evaluation of a simple baseline system (using tree approximations and the parser of Bohnet, 2010). Towards the end of March, an input-only version of the test data was released, with just columns (1) to (4) pre-filled; participants then had one week to run their systems on these inputs, fill in columns (5), (6), and upwards, and submit their results (from up to two different runs) for scoring. Upon completion of the testing phase, we have shared the gold-standard test data, official scores, and system results for all submissions with participants and are currently preparing all data for general release through the Linguistic Data Consortium.

[7]As detailed by Miyao et al. (2014), individual conjuncts can be (and usually are) arguments of other predicates, whereas the topmost conjunction only has incoming edges in nested coordinate structures. Similarly, a 'shared' modifier of the coordinate structure as a whole would take as its argument the local top node of the coordination in DM or PAS (i.e. the first conjunct or final conjunction, respectively), whereas it would depend as an argument on all conjuncts in PCEDT.

		DM				PAS				PCEDT			
	$\overline{\text{LF}}$	LP	LR	LF	LM	LP	LR	LF	LM	LP	LR	LF	LM
Peking	85.91	90.27	88.54	89.40	26.71	93.44	90.69	92.04	38.13	78.75	73.96	76.28	11.05
Priberam	85.24	88.82	87.35	88.08	22.40	91.95	89.92	90.93	32.64	78.80	74.70	76.70	09.42
Copenhagen-Malmö	80.77	84.78	84.04	84.41	20.33	87.69	88.37	88.03	10.16	71.15	68.65	69.88	08.01
Potsdam	77.34	79.36	79.34	79.35	07.57	88.15	81.60	84.75	06.53	69.68	66.25	67.92	05.19
Alpage	76.76	79.42	77.24	78.32	09.72	85.65	82.71	84.16	17.95	70.53	65.28	67.81	06.82
Linköping	72.20	78.54	78.05	78.29	06.08	76.16	75.55	75.85	01.19	60.66	64.35	62.45	04.01

		DM				PAS				PCEDT			
	$\overline{\text{LF}}$	LP	LR	LF	LM	LP	LR	LF	LM	LP	LR	LF	LM
Priberam	86.27	90.23	88.11	89.16	26.85	92.56	90.97	91.76	37.83	80.14	75.79	77.90	10.68
CMU	82.42	84.46	83.48	83.97	08.75	90.78	88.51	89.63	26.04	76.81	70.72	73.64	07.12
Turku	80.49	80.94	82.14	81.53	08.23	87.33	87.76	87.54	17.21	72.42	72.37	72.40	06.82
Potsdam	78.60	81.32	80.91	81.11	09.05	89.41	82.61	85.88	07.49	70.35	67.33	68.80	05.42
Alpage	78.54	83.46	79.55	81.46	10.76	87.23	82.82	84.97	15.43	70.98	67.51	69.20	06.60
In-House	75.89	92.58	92.34	92.46	48.07	92.09	92.02	92.06	43.84	40.89	45.67	43.15	00.30

Table 4: Results of the closed (top) and open tracks (bottom). For each system, the second column ($\overline{\text{LF}}$) indicates the averaged LF score across all target representations), which was used to rank the systems.

Evaluation Systems participating in the task were evaluated based on the accuracy with which they can produce semantic dependency graphs for previously unseen text, measured relative to the gold-standard testing data. The key measures for this evaluation were labeled and unlabeled precision and recall with respect to predicted dependencies (predicate–role–argument triples) and labeled and unlabeled exact match with respect to complete graphs. In both contexts, identification of the top node(s) of a graph was considered as the identification of additional, 'virtual' dependencies from an artificial root node (at position 0). Below we abbreviate these metrics as (a) labeled precision, recall, and F_1: LP, LR, LF; (b) unlabeled precision, recall, and F_1: UP, UR, UF; and (c) labeled and unlabeled exact match: LM, UM.

The 'official' ranking of participating systems, in both the closed and the open tracks, is determined based on the arithmetic mean of the labeled dependency F_1 scores (i.e. the geometric mean of labeled precision and labeled recall) on the three target representations (DM, PAS, and PCEDT). Thus, to be considered for the final ranking, a system had to submit semantic dependencies for all three target representations.

Closed vs. Open Tracks The task was subdivided into a *closed* track and an *open* track, where systems in the closed track could only be trained on the gold-standard semantic dependencies distributed for the task. Systems in the open track, on the other hand, could use additional resources, such as a syntactic parser, for example—provided that they make sure to not use any tools or resources that encompass knowledge of the gold-standard syntactic or semantic analyses of the SDP 2014 test data, i.e. were directly or indirectly trained or otherwise derived from WSJ Section 21.

This restriction implies that typical off-the-shelf syntactic parsers had to be re-trained, as many data-driven parsers for English include this section of the PTB in their default training data. To simplify participation in the open track, the organizers prepared ready-to-use 'companion' syntactic analyses, sentence- and token-aligned to the SDP data, in two formats, viz. PTB-style phrase structure trees obtained from the parser of Petrov et al. (2006) and Stanford Basic syntactic dependencies (de Marneffe et al., 2006) produced by the parser of Bohnet and Nivre (2012).

6 Submissions and Results

From 36 teams who had registered for the task, test runs were submitted for nine systems. Each team submitted one or two test runs per track. In total, there were ten runs submitted to the closed track and nine runs to the open track. Three teams submitted to both the closed and the open track. The main results are summarized and ranked in Table 4. The ranking is based on the average LF score across all three target representations, which is given in the $\overline{\text{LF}}$ column. In cases where a team submitted two runs to a track, only the highest-ranked score is included in the table.

Team	Track	Approach	Resources
Linköping	C	extension of Eisner's algorithm for DAGs, edge-factored structured perceptron	—
Potsdam	C & O	graph-to-tree transformation, Mate	companion
Priberam	C & O	model with second-order features, decoding with dual decomposition, MIRA	companion
Turku	O	cascade of SVM classifiers (dependency recognition, label classification, top recognition)	companion, syntactic n-grams, word2vec
Alpage	C & O	transition-based parsing for DAGs, logistic regression, structured perceptron	companion, Brown clusters
Peking	C	transition-based parsing for DAGs, graph-to-tree transformation, parser ensemble	—
CMU	O	edge classification by logistic regression, edge-factored structured SVM	companion
Copenhagen-Malmö	C	graph-to-tree transformation, Mate	—
In-House	O	existing parsers developed by the organizers	grammars

Table 5: Overview of submitted systems, high-level approaches, and additional resources used (if any).

In the closed track, the average LF scores across target representations range from 85.91 to 72.20. Comparing the results for different target representations, the average LF scores across systems are 85.96 for PAS, 82.97 for DM, and 70.17 for PCEDT. The scores for labeled exact match show a much larger variation across both target representations and systems.[8]

In the open track, we see very similar trends. The average LF scores across target representations range from 86.27 to 75.89 and the corresponding scores across systems are 88.64 for PAS, 84.95 for DM, and 67.52 for PCEDT. While these scores are consistently higher than in the closed track, the differences are small. In fact, for each of the three teams that submitted to both tracks (Alpage, Potsdam, and Priberam) improvements due to the use of additional resources in the open track do not exceed two points LF.

7 Overview of Approaches

Table 5 shows a summary of the systems that submitted final results. Most of the systems took a strategy to use some algorithm to process (restricted types of) graph structures, and apply machine learning like structured perceptrons. The methods for processing graph structures are classified into three types. One is to transform graphs into trees in the preprocessing stage, and apply conventional dependency parsing systems (e.g. Mate; Bohnet, 2010) to the converted trees. Some systems simply output the result of dependency parsing (which means they inherently lose some dependencies), while the others apply post-processing to recover non-tree structures. The second strategy is to use a parsing algorithm that can directly generate graph structures (in the spirit of Sagae & Tsujii, 2008; Titov et al., 2009). In many cases such algorithms generate restricted types of graph structures, but these restrictions appear feasible for our target representations. The last approach is more machine learning–oriented; they apply classifiers or scoring methods (e.g. edge-factored scores), and find the highest-scoring structures by some decoding method.

It is difficult to tell which approach is the best; actually, the top three systems in the closed and open tracks selected very different approaches. A possible conclusion is that exploiting existing systems or techniques for dependency parsing was successful; for example, Peking built an ensemble of existing transition-based and graph-based dependency parsers, and Priberam extended an existing dependency parser. As we indicated in the task description, a novel feature of this task is that we have to compute graph structures, and cannot assume well-known properties like projectivity and lack of reentrancies. However, many of the participants found that our representations are mostly tree-like, and this fact motivated them to apply methods that have been well studied in the field of syntactic dependency parsing.

Finally, we observe that three teams participated in both the closed and open tracks, and all of them reported that adding external resources improved accuracy by a little more than one point. Systems with (only) open submissions extensively use syntactic features (e.g. dependency paths) from external resources, and they are shown effective even

[8]Please see the task web page at the address indicated above for full labeled and unlabeled scores.

with simple machine learning models. Pre-existing, tree-oriented dependency parsers are relatively effective, especially when combined with graph-to-tree transformation. Comparing across our three target representations, system scores show a tendency PAS > DM > PCEDT, which can be taken as a tentative indicator of relative levels of 'parsability'. As suggested in Section 4, this variation most likely correlates at least in part with diverging design decisions, e.g. the inclusion of relatively local and deterministic dependencies involving function words in PAS, or the decision to annotate contextually determined speaker meaning (rather than 'mere' sentence meaning) in at least some constructions in PCEDT.

8 Conclusions and Outlook

We have described the motivation, design, and outcomes of the SDP 2014 task on semantic dependency parsing, i.e. retrieving bi-lexical predicate–argument relations between all content words within an English sentence. We have converted to a common format three existing annotations (DM, PAS, and PCEDT) over the same text and have put this to use for the first time in training and testing data-driven semantic dependency parsers. Building on strong community interest already to date and our belief that graph-oriented dependency parsing will further gain importance in the years to come, we are preparing a similar (slightly modified) task for SemEval 2015. Candidate modifications and extensions will include cross-domain testing and evaluation at the level of 'complete' predications (in contrast to more lenient per-dependency F_1 used this year). As optional new sub-tasks, we plan on offering cross-linguistic variation and predicate (i.e. semantic frame) disambiguation for at least some of the target representations. To further probe the role of syntax in the recovery of semantic dependency relations, we will make available to participants a wider selection of syntactic analyses, as well as add a third (idealized) 'gold' track, where syntactic dependencies are provided directly from available syntactic annotations of the underlying treebanks.

Acknowledgements

We are grateful to Željko Agić and Bernd Bohnet for consultation and assistance in preparing our baseline and companion parses, to the Linguistic Data Consortium (LDC) for support in distributing the SDP data to participants, as well as to Emily M. Bender and two anonymous reviewers for feedback on this manuscript. Data preparation was supported through access to the ABEL high-performance computing facilities at the University of Oslo, and we acknowledge the Scientific Computing staff at UiO, the Norwegian Metacenter for Computational Science, and the Norwegian tax payers. Part of this work has been supported by the infrastructural funding by the Ministry of Education, Youth and Sports of the Czech Republic (CEP ID LM2010013).

References

Bohnet, B. (2010). Top accuracy and fast dependency parsing is not a contradiction. In *Proceedings of the 23rd International Conference on Computational Linguistics* (p. 89 – 97). Beijing, China.

Bohnet, B., & Nivre, J. (2012). A transition-based system for joint part-of-speech tagging and labeled non-projective dependency parsing. In *Proceedings of the 2012 Joint Conference on Empirical Methods in Natural Language Processing and Conference on Natural Language Learning* (p. 1455 – 1465). Jeju Island, Korea.

Buchholz, S., & Marsi, E. (2006). CoNLL-X shared task on multilingual dependency parsing. In *Proceedings of the 10th Conference on Natural Language Learning* (p. 149 – 164). New York, NY, USA.

Copestake, A., Flickinger, D., Pollard, C., & Sag, I. A. (2005). Minimal Recursion Semantics. An introduction. *Research on Language and Computation, 3*(4), 281 – 332.

de Marneffe, M.-C., MacCartney, B., & Manning, C. D. (2006). Generating typed dependency parses from phrase structure parses. In *Proceedings of the 5th International Conference on Language Resources and Evaluation* (p. 449 – 454). Genoa, Italy.

Fares, M., Oepen, S., & Zhang, Y. (2013). Machine learning for high-quality tokenization. Replicating variable tokenization schemes. In *Computational linguistics and intelligent text processing* (p. 231 – 244). Springer.

Flickinger, D. (2000). On building a more efficient grammar by exploiting types. *Natural Language Engineering, 6 (1)*, 15 – 28.

Flickinger, D., Zhang, Y., & Kordoni, V. (2012). DeepBank. A dynamically annotated treebank of the Wall Street Journal. In *Proceedings of the 11th International Workshop on Treebanks and Linguistic Theories* (p. 85 – 96). Lisbon, Portugal: Edições Colibri.

Gildea, D., & Jurafsky, D. (2002). Automatic labeling of semantic roles. *Computational Linguistics, 28*,

245 – 288.

Grice, H. P. (1968). Utterer's meaning, sentence-meaning, and word-meaning. *Foundations of Language*, *4*(3), 225 – 242.

Hajič, J., Ciaramita, M., Johansson, R., Kawahara, D., Martí, M. A., Màrquez, L., ... Zhang, Y. (2009). The CoNLL-2009 Shared Task. syntactic and semantic dependencies in multiple languages. In *Proceedings of the 13th Conference on Natural Language Learning* (p. 1 – 18). Boulder, CO, USA.

Hajič, J., Hajičová, E., Panevová, J., Sgall, P., Bojar, O., Cinková, S., ... Žabokrtský, Z. (2012). Announcing Prague Czech-English Dependency Treebank 2.0. In *Proceedings of the 8th International Conference on Language Resources and Evaluation* (p. 3153 – 3160). Istanbul, Turkey.

Ivanova, A., Oepen, S., Øvrelid, L., & Flickinger, D. (2012). Who did what to whom? A contrastive study of syntacto-semantic dependencies. In *Proceedings of the Sixth Linguistic Annotation Workshop* (p. 2 – 11). Jeju, Republic of Korea.

Kate, R. J., & Wong, Y. W. (2010). Semantic parsing. The task, the state of the art and the future. In *Tutorial abstracts of the 20th Meeting of the Association for Computational Linguistics* (p. 6). Uppsala, Sweden.

Marcus, M., Santorini, B., & Marcinkiewicz, M. A. (1993). Building a large annotated corpora of English: The Penn Treebank. *Computational Linguistics*, *19*, 313 – 330.

Mel'čuk, I. (1988). *Dependency syntax. Theory and practice*. Albany, NY, USA: SUNY Press.

Meyers, A., Reeves, R., Macleod, C., Szekely, R., Zielinska, V., Young, B., & Grishman, R. (2004). Annotating noun argument structure for NomBank. In *Proceedings of the 4th International Conference on Language Resources and Evaluation* (p. 803 – 806). Lisbon, Portugal.

Miyao, Y., Oepen, S., & Zeman, D. (2014). In-house: An ensemble of pre-existing off-the-shelf parsers. In *Proceedings of the 8th International Workshop on Semantic Evaluation*. Dublin, Ireland.

Nakov, P. (2013). On the interpretation of noun compounds: Syntax, semantics, and entailment. *Natural Language Engineering*, *19*(3), 291 – 330.

Nivre, J., Hall, J., Kübler, S., McDonald, R., Nilsson, J., Riedel, S., & Yuret, D. (2007). The CoNLL 2007 shared task on dependency parsing. In *Proceedings of the 2007 Joint Conference on Empirical Methods in Natural Language Processing and Conference on Natural Language Learning* (p. 915 – 932). Prague, Czech Republic.

Oepen, S., & Lønning, J. T. (2006). Discriminant-based MRS banking. In *Proceedings of the 5th International Conference on Language Resources and Evaluation* (p. 1250 – 1255). Genoa, Italy.

Palmer, M., Gildea, D., & Kingsbury, P. (2005). The Proposition Bank. A corpus annotated with semantic roles. *Computational Linguistics*, *31*(1), 71 – 106.

Petrov, S., Barrett, L., Thibaux, R., & Klein, D. (2006). Learning accurate, compact, and interpretable tree annotation. In *Proceedings of the 21st International Conference on Computational Linguistics and the 44th Meeting of the Association for Computational Linguistics* (p. 433 – 440). Sydney, Australia.

Quine, W. V. O. (1960). *Word and object*. Cambridge, MA, USA: MIT press.

Sagae, K., & Tsujii, J. (2008). Shift-reduce dependency DAG parsing. In *Proceedings of the 22nd International Conference on Computational Linguistics* (p. 753 – 760). Manchester, UK.

Titov, I., Henderson, J., Merlo, P., & Musillo, G. (2009). Online graph planarisation for synchronous parsing of semantic and syntactic dependencies. In *Proceedings of the 21st International Joint Conference on Artifical Intelligence* (p. 1562 – 1567).

Vadas, D., & Curran, J. (2007). Adding Noun Phrase Structure to the Penn Treebank. In *Proceedings of the 45th Meeting of the Association for Computational Linguistics* (p. 240 – 247). Prague, Czech Republic.

SemEval-2014 Task 9: Sentiment Analysis in Twitter

Sara Rosenthal
Columbia University
sara@cs.columbia.edu

Alan Ritter
Carnegie Mellon University
rittera@cs.cmu.edu

Preslav Nakov
Qatar Computing Research Institute
pnakov@qf.org.qa

Veselin Stoyanov
Johns Hopkins University
ves@cs.jhu.edu

Abstract

We describe the *Sentiment Analysis in Twitter* task, ran as part of SemEval-2014. It is a continuation of the last year's task that ran successfully as part of SemEval-2013. As in 2013, this was the most popular SemEval task; a total of 46 teams contributed 27 submissions for subtask A (21 teams) and 50 submissions for subtask B (44 teams). This year, we introduced three new test sets: (*i*) regular tweets, (*ii*) sarcastic tweets, and (*iii*) LiveJournal sentences. We further tested on (*iv*) 2013 tweets, and (*v*) 2013 SMS messages. The highest F1-score on (*i*) was achieved by *NRC-Canada* at 86.63 for subtask A and by TeamX at 70.96 for subtask B.

1 Introduction

In the past decade, new forms of communication have emerged and have become ubiquitous through social media. Microblogs (e.g., Twitter), Weblogs (e.g., LiveJournal) and cell phone messages (SMS) are often used to share opinions and sentiments about the surrounding world, and the availability of social content generated on sites such as Twitter creates new opportunities to automatically study public opinion.

Working with these informal text genres presents new challenges for natural language processing beyond those encountered when working with more traditional text genres such as newswire. The language in social media is very informal, with creative spelling and punctuation, misspellings, slang, new words, URLs, and genre-specific terminology and abbreviations, e.g., RT for re-tweet and #hashtags[1].

Moreover, tweets and SMS messages are short: a sentence or a headline rather than a document.

How to handle such challenges so as to automatically mine and understand people's opinions and sentiments has only recently been the subject of research (Jansen et al., 2009; Barbosa and Feng, 2010; Bifet et al., 2011; Davidov et al., 2010; O'Connor et al., 2010; Pak and Paroubek, 2010; Tumasjan et al., 2010; Kouloumpis et al., 2011).

Several corpora with detailed opinion and sentiment annotation have been made freely available, e.g., the MPQA newswire corpus (Wiebe et al., 2005), the movie reviews corpus (Pang et al., 2002), or the restaurant and laptop reviews corpora that are part of this year's SemEval Task 4 (Pontiki et al., 2014). These corpora have proved very valuable as resources for learning about the language of sentiment in general, but they do not focus on tweets. While some Twitter sentiment datasets were created prior to SemEval-2013, they were either small and proprietary, such as the i-sieve corpus (Kouloumpis et al., 2011) or focused solely on message-level sentiment.

Thus, the primary goal of our SemEval task is to promote research that will lead to better understanding of how sentiment is conveyed in Social Media. Toward that goal, we created the SemEval Tweet corpus as part of our inaugural Sentiment Analysis in Twitter Task, SemEval-2013 Task 2 (Nakov et al., 2013). It contains tweets and SMS messages with sentiment expressions annotated with contextual phrase-level and message-level polarity. This year, we extended the corpus by adding new tweets and LiveJournal sentences.

Another interesting phenomenon that has been studied in Twitter is the use of the #sarcasm hashtag to indicate that a tweet should not be taken literally (González-Ibáñez et al., 2011; Liebrecht et al., 2013). In fact, sarcasm indicates that the message polarity should be flipped. With this in mind, this year, we also evaluate on sarcastic tweets.

[1]Hashtags are a type of tagging for Twitter messages.

Proceedings of the 8th International Workshop on Semantic Evaluation (SemEval 2014), pages 73–80,
Dublin, Ireland, August 23-24, 2014.

In the remainder of this paper, we first describe the task, the dataset creation process and the evaluation methodology. We then summarize the characteristics of the approaches taken by the participating systems, and we discuss their scores.

2 Task Description

As SemEval-2013 Task 2, we included two subtasks: an expression-level subtask and a message-level subtask. Participants could choose to participate in either or both. Below we provide short descriptions of the objectives of these two subtasks.

Subtask A: Contextual Polarity Disambiguation Given a message containing a marked instance of a word or a phrase, determine whether that instance is positive, negative or neutral in that context. The instance boundaries were provided: this was a classification task, not an entity recognition task.

Subtask B: Message Polarity Classification Given a message, decide whether it is of positive, negative, or neutral sentiment. For messages conveying both positive and negative sentiment, the stronger one is to be chosen.

Each participating team was allowed to submit results for two different systems per subtask: one constrained, and one unconstrained. A constrained system could only use the provided data for training, but it could also use other resources such as lexicons obtained elsewhere. An unconstrained system could use any additional data as part of the training process; this could be done in a supervised, semi-supervised, or unsupervised fashion.

Note that constrained/unconstrained refers to the data used to train a classifier. For example, if other data (excluding the test data) was used to develop a sentiment lexicon, and the lexicon was used to generate features, the system would still be constrained. However, if other data (excluding the test data) was used to develop a sentiment lexicon, and this lexicon was used to automatically label additional Tweet/SMS messages and then used with the original data to train the classifier, then such a system would be considered unconstrained.

3 Datasets

In this section, we describe the process of collecting and annotating the 2014 testing tweets, including the sarcastic ones, and LiveJournal sentences.

Corpus	Positive	Negative	Objective / Neutral
Twitter2013-train	5,895	3,131	471
Twitter2013-dev	648	430	57
Twitter2013-test	2,734	1,541	160
SMS2013-test	1,071	1,104	159
Twitter2014-test	1,807	578	88
Twitter2014-sarcasm	82	37	5
LiveJournal2014-test	660	511	144

Table 1: Dataset statistics for Subtask A.

3.1 Datasets Used

For training and development, we released the Twitter train/dev/test datasets from SemEval-2013 task 2, as well as the SMS test set, which uses messages from the NUS SMS corpus (Chen and Kan, 2013), which we annotated for sentiment in 2013.

We further added a new 2014 Twitter test set, as well as a small set of tweets that contained the #sarcasm hashtag to determine how sarcasm affects the tweet polarity. Finally, we included sentences from LiveJournal in order to determine how systems trained on Twitter perform on other sources. The statistics for each dataset and for each subtask are shown in Tables 1 and 2.

Corpus	Positive	Negative	Objective / Neutral
Twitter2013-train	3,662	1,466	4,600
Twitter2013-dev	575	340	739
Twitter2013-test	1,572	601	1,640
SMS2013-test	492	394	1,207
Twitter2014-test	982	202	669
Twitter2014-sarcasm	33	40	13
LiveJournal2014-test	427	304	411

Table 2: Dataset statistics for Subtask B.

3.2 Annotation

We annotated the new tweets as in 2013: by identifying tweets from popular topics that contain sentiment-bearing words by using SentiWordNet (Baccianella et al., 2010) as a filter. We altered the annotation task for the sarcastic tweets, displaying them to the Mechanical Turk annotators without the #sarcasm hashtag; the Turkers had to determine whether the tweet is sarcastic on their own. Moreover, we asked Turkers to indicate the degree of sarcasm as (a) definitely sarcastic, (b) probably sarcastic, and (c) not sarcastic.

As in 2013, we combined the annotations using intersection, where a word had to appear in 2/3 of the annotations to be accepted. An annotated example from each source is shown in Table 3.

Source	Example	Polarity
Twitter	Why would you [still]- wear shorts when it's this cold?! I [love]+ how Britain see's a bit of sun and they're [like 'OOOH]+ LET'S STRIP!'	positive
SMS	[Sorry]- I think tonight [cannot]- and I [not feeling well]- after my rest.	negative
LiveJournal	[Cool]+ posts , dude ; very [colorful]+ , and [artsy]+ .	positive
Twitter Sarcasm	[Thanks]+ manager for putting me on the schedule for Sunday	negative

Table 3: Example of polarity for each source of messages. The target phrases are marked in [. . .], and are followed by their polarity; the sentence-level polarity is shown in the last column.

3.3 Tweets Delivery

We did not deliver the annotated tweets to the participants directly; instead, we released annotation indexes, a list of corresponding Twitter IDs, and a download script that extracts the corresponding tweets via the Twitter API.[2] We provided the tweets in this manner in order to ensure that Twitter's terms of service are not violated. Unfortunately, due to this restriction, the task participants had access to different number of training tweets depending on when they did the downloading. This varied between a minimum of 5,215 tweets and the full set of 10,882 tweets. On average the teams were able to collect close to 9,000 tweets; for teams that did not participate in 2013, this was about 8,500. The difference in training data size did not seem to have had a major impact. In fact, the top two teams in subtask B (coooolll and TeamX) trained on less than 8,500 tweets.

4 Scoring

The participating systems were required to perform a three-way classification for both subtasks. A particular marked phrase (for subtask A) or an entire message (for subtask B) was to be classified as *positive*, *negative* or *objective/neutral*. We scored the systems by computing a score for predicting positive/negative phrases/messages. For instance, to compute positive precision, p_{pos}, we find the number of phrases/messages that a system correctly predicted to be positive, and we divide that number by the total number it predicted to be positive. To compute positive recall, r_{pos}, we find the number of phrases/messages correctly predicted to be positive and we divide that number by the total number of positives in the gold standard. We then calculate F1-score for the positive class as follows $F_{pos} = \frac{2(p_{pos}+r_{pos})}{p_{pos}*r_{pos}}$. We carry out a similar computation for F_{neg}, for the negative phrases/messages. The overall score is then $F = (F_{pos} + F_{neg})/2$.

[2]https://dev.twitter.com

We used the two test sets from 2013 and the three from 2014, which we combined into one test set and we shuffled to make it hard to guess which set a sentence came from. This guaranteed that participants would submit predictions for all five test sets. It also allowed us to test how well systems trained on standard tweets generalize to sarcastic tweets and to LiveJournal sentences, without the participants putting extra efforts into this. The participants were also not informed about the source the extra test sets come from.

We provided the participants with a scorer that outputs the overall score F and a confusion matrix for each of the five test sets.

5 Participants and Results

The results are shown in Tables 4 and 5, and the team affiliations are shown in Table 6. Tables 4 and 5 contain results on the two progress test sets (tweets and SMS messages), which are the official test sets from the 2013 edition of the task, and on the three new official 2014 testsets (tweets, tweets with sarcasm, and LiveJournal). The tables further show macro- and micro-averaged results over the 2014 datasets. There is an index for each result showing the relative rank of that result within the respective column. The participating systems are ranked by their score on the Twitter-2014 testset, which is the official ranking for the task; all remaining rankings are secondary.

As we mentioned above, the participants were not told that the 2013 test sets would be included in the big 2014 test set, so that they do not overtune their systems on them. However, the 2013 test sets were made available for development, but it was explicitly forbidden to use them for training. Still, some participants did not notice this restriction, which resulted in their unusually high scores on Twitter2013-test; we did our best to identify all such cases, and we asked the authors to submit corrected runs. The tables mark such resubmissions accordingly.

Most of the submissions were constrained, with just a few unconstrained: 7 out of 27 for subtask A, and 8 out of 50 for subtask B. In any case, the best systems were constrained. Some teams participated with both a constrained and an unconstrained system, but the unconstrained system was not always better than the constrained one: sometimes it was worse, sometimes it performed the same. Thus, we decided to produce a single ranking, including both constrained and unconstrained systems, where we mark the latter accordingly.

5.1 Subtask A

Table 4 shows the results for subtask A, which attracted 27 submissions from 21 teams. There were seven unconstrained submissions: five teams submitted both a constrained and an unconstrained run, and two teams submitted an unconstrained run only. The best systems were constrained. All participating systems outperformed the majority class baseline by a sizable margin.

5.2 Subtask B

The results for subtask B are shown in Table 5. The subtask attracted 50 submissions from 44 teams. There were eight unconstrained submissions: six teams submitted both a constrained and an unconstrained run, and two teams submitted an unconstrained run only. As for subtask A, the best systems were constrained. Again, all participating systems outperformed the majority class baseline; however, some systems were very close to it.

6 Discussion

Overall, we observed similar trends as in SemEval-2013 Task 2. Almost all systems used supervised learning. Most systems were constrained, including the best ones in all categories. As in 2013, we observed several cases of a team submitting a constrained and an unconstrained run and the constrained run performing better.

It is unclear why unconstrained systems did not outperform constrained ones. It could be because participants did not use enough external data or because the data they used was too different from Twitter or from our annotation method. Or it could be due to our definition of *unconstrained*, which labels as unconstrained systems that use additional tweets directly, but considers unconstrained those that use additional tweets to build sentiment lexicons and then use these lexicons.

As in 2013, the most popular classifiers were SVM, MaxEnt, and Naive Bayes. Moreover, two submissions used deep learning, *coooolll* (Harbin Institute of Technology) and *ThinkPositive* (IBM Research, Brazil), which were ranked second and tenth on subtask B, respectively.

The features used were quite varied, including word-based (e.g., word and character n-grams, word shapes, and lemmata), syntactic, and Twitter-specific such as emoticons and abbreviations. The participants still relied heavily on lexicons of opinion words, the most popular ones being the same as in 2013: MPQA, SentiWordNet and Bing Liu's opinion lexicon. Popular this year was also the NRC lexicon (Mohammad et al., 2013), created by the best-performing team in 2013, which is top-performing this year as well.

Preprocessing of tweets was still a popular technique. In addition to standard NLP steps such as tokenization, stemming, lemmatization, stopword removal and POS tagging, most teams applied some kind of Twitter-specific processing such as substitution/removal of URLs, substitution of emoticons, word normalization, abbreviation lookup, and punctuation removal. Finally, several of the teams used Twitter-tuned NLP tools such as part of speech and named entity taggers (Gimpel et al., 2011; Ritter et al., 2011).

The similarity of preprocessing techniques, NLP tools, classifiers and features used in 2013 and this year is probably partially due to many teams participating in both years. As Table 6 shows, 18 out of the 46 teams are returning teams.

Comparing the results on the progress Twitter test in 2013 and 2014, we can see that *NRC-Canada*, the 2013 winner for subtask A, have now improved their F1 score from 88.93 to 90.14, which is the 2014 best score. The best score on the Progress SMS in 2014 of 89.31 belongs to *ECNU*; this is a big jump compared to their 2013 score of 76.69, but it is less compared to the 2013 best of 88.37 achieved by *GU-MLT-LT*. For subtask B, on the Twitter progress testset, the 2013 winner *NRC-Canada* improves their 2013 result from 69.02 to 70.75, which is the second best in 2014; the winner in 2014, *TeamX*, achieves 72.12. On the SMS progress test, the 2013 winner *NRC-Canada* improves its F1 score from 68.46 to 70.28. Overall, we see consistent improvements on the progress testset for both subtasks: 0-1 and 2-3 points absolute for subtasks A and B, respectively.

#	System	Uncon-strain.?	2013: Progress Tweet	2013: Progress SMS	2014: Official Tweet	2014: Official Tweet sarcasm	2014: Official LiveJournal	2014: Average Macro	2014: Average Micro
1	NRC-Canada		90.14_{1}	88.03_{4}	86.63_{1}	77.13_{5}	85.49_{2}	83.08_{2}	85.61_{1}
2	SentiKLUE		90.11_{2}	85.16_{8}	84.83_{2}	79.32_{3}	85.61_{1}	83.25_{1}	85.15_{2}
3	CMUQ-Hybrid*		88.94_{4}	87.98_{5}	84.40_{3}	76.99_{6}	84.21_{3}	81.87_{3}	84.05_{3}
4	CMU-Qatar*		89.85_{3}	88.08_{3}	83.45_{4}	78.07_{4}	83.89_{5}	81.80_{4}	83.56_{4}
5	ECNU	✓	87.29_{6}	89.26_{2}	82.93_{5}	73.71_{8}	81.69_{7}	79.44_{7}	81.85_{6}
6	ECNU		87.28_{7}	89.31_{1}	82.67_{6}	73.71_{9}	81.67_{8}	79.35_{8}	81.75_{7}
7	Think_Positive	✓	88.06_{5}	87.65_{6}	82.05_{7}	76.74_{7}	80.90_{12}	79.90_{6}	81.15_{9}
8	Kea*		84.83_{10}	84.14_{10}	81.22_{8}	65.94_{17}	81.16_{11}	76.11_{13}	80.70_{10}
9	Lt_3		86.28_{8}	85.26_{7}	81.02_{9}	70.76_{13}	80.44_{13}	77.41_{11}	80.33_{13}
10	senti.ue		84.05_{11}	78.72_{16}	80.54_{10}	82.75_{1}	81.90_{6}	81.73_{5}	81.47_{8}
11	LyS		85.69_{9}	81.44_{12}	79.92_{11}	71.67_{10}	83.95_{4}	78.51_{10}	82.21_{5}
12	UKPDIPF		80.45_{15}	79.05_{14}	79.67_{12}	65.63_{18}	81.42_{9}	75.57_{14}	80.33_{11}
13	UKPDIPF	✓	80.45_{16}	79.05_{15}	79.67_{13}	65.63_{19}	81.42_{10}	75.57_{15}	80.33_{12}
14	TJP		81.13_{14}	84.41_{9}	79.30_{14}	71.20_{12}	78.27_{15}	76.26_{12}	78.39_{15}
15	SAP-RI		80.32_{17}	80.26_{13}	77.26_{15}	70.64_{14}	77.68_{18}	75.19_{17}	77.32_{16}
16	senti.ue*	✓	83.80_{12}	82.93_{11}	77.07_{16}	80.02_{2}	79.70_{14}	78.93_{9}	78.83_{14}
17	SAIL		78.47_{18}	74.46_{20}	76.89_{17}	65.56_{20}	70.62_{22}	71.02_{21}	72.57_{21}
18	columbia_nlp◇		81.50_{13}	74.55_{19}	76.54_{18}	61.76_{22}	78.19_{16}	72.16_{19}	77.11_{18}
19	IIT-Patna		76.54_{20}	75.99_{18}	76.43_{19}	71.43_{11}	77.99_{17}	75.28_{16}	77.26_{17}
20	Citius	✓	76.59_{19}	69.31_{21}	75.21_{20}	68.40_{15}	75.82_{20}	73.14_{18}	75.38_{19}
21	Citius		74.71_{21}	61.44_{25}	73.03_{21}	65.18_{21}	71.64_{21}	69.95_{22}	71.90_{22}
22	IITPatna		70.91_{23}	77.04_{17}	72.25_{22}	66.32_{16}	76.03_{19}	71.53_{20}	74.45_{20}
23	SU-sentilab		74.34_{22}	62.58_{24}	68.26_{23}	53.31_{25}	69.53_{23}	63.70_{24}	68.59_{23}
24	Univ. Warwick*		62.25_{26}	60.12_{26}	67.28_{24}	58.08_{24}	64.89_{25}	63.42_{25}	65.48_{25}
25	Univ. Warwick*	✓	64.91_{25}	63.01_{23}	67.17_{25}	60.59_{23}	67.46_{24}	65.07_{23}	67.14_{24}
26	DAEDALUS		67.42_{24}	63.92_{22}	60.98_{26}	45.27_{27}	61.01_{26}	55.75_{26}	60.50_{26}
27	DAEDALUS	✓	61.95_{27}	55.97_{27}	58.11_{27}	49.19_{26}	58.65_{27}	55.32_{27}	58.17_{27}
	Majority baseline		38.1	31.5	42.2	39.8	33.4		

Table 4: **Results for subtask A.** The * indicates system resubmissions (because they initially trained on Twitter2013-test), and the ◇ indicates a system that includes a task co-organizer as a team member. The systems are sorted by their score on the Twitter2014 test dataset; the rankings on the individual datasets are indicated with a subscript. The last two columns show macro- and micro-averaged results across the three 2014 test datasets.

Finally, note that for both subtasks, the best systems on the Twitter-2014 dataset are those that performed best on the 2013 progress Twitter dataset: *NRC-Canada* for subtask A, and *TeamX* (Fuji Xerox Co., Ltd.) for subtask B.

It is interesting to note that the best results for Twitter2014-test are lower than those for Twitter2013-test for both subtask A (86.63 vs. 90.14) and subtask B (70.96 vs 72.12). This is so despite the baselines for Twitter2014-test being higher than those for Twitter2013-test: 42.2 vs. 38.1 for subtask A, and 34.6 vs. 29.2 for subtask B. Most likely, having access to Twitter2013-test at development time, teams have overfitted on it. It could be also the case that some of the sentiment dictionaries that were built in 2013 have become somewhat outdated by 2014.

Finally, note that while some teams such as *NRC-Canada* performed well across all test sets, other such as *TeamX*, which used a weighting scheme tuned specifically for class imbalances in tweets, were only strong on Twitter datasets.

7 Conclusion

We have described the data, the experimental setup and the results for SemEval-2014 Task 9. As in 2013, our task was the most popular one at SemEval-2014, attracting 46 participating teams: 21 in subtask A (27 submissions) and 44 in subtask B (50 submissions).

We introduced three new test sets for 2014: an in-domain Twitter dataset, an out-of-domain LiveJournal test set, and a dataset of tweets containing sarcastic content. While the performance on the LiveJournal test set was mostly comparable to the in-domain Twitter test set, for most teams there was a sharp drop in performance for sarcastic tweets, highlighting better handling of sarcastic language as one important direction for future work in Twitter sentiment analysis.

We plan to run the task again in 2015 with the inclusion of a new sub-evaluation on detecting sarcasm with the goal of stimulating research in this area; we further plan to add one more test domain.

#	System	Uncon-strain.?	2013: Progress Tweet	SMS	2014: Official Tweet	Tweet sarcasm	Live-Journal	2014: Average Macro	Micro
1	TeamX		72.12_{1}	57.36_{26}	70.96_{1}	56.50_{3}	69.44_{15}	65.63_{3}	69.99_{5}
2	coooolll		70.40_{3}	67.68_{2}	70.14_{2}	46.66_{24}	72.90_{5}	63.23_{12}	70.51_{2}
3	RTRGO		69.10_{5}	67.51_{3}	69.95_{3}	47.09_{23}	72.20_{6}	63.08_{13}	70.15_{3}
4	NRC-Canada		70.75_{2}	70.28_{1}	69.85_{4}	58.16_{1}	74.84_{1}	67.62_{1}	71.37_{1}
5	TUGAS		65.64_{13}	62.77_{11}	69.00_{5}	52.87_{12}	69.79_{13}	63.89_{6}	68.84_{8}
6	CISUC_KIS*		67.56_{8}	65.90_{6}	67.95_{6}	55.49_{5}	74.46_{2}	65.97_{2}	70.02_{4}
7	SAIL		66.80_{11}	56.98_{28}	67.77_{7}	57.26_{2}	69.34_{17}	64.79_{4}	68.06_{10}
8	SWISS-CHOCOLATE		64.81_{18}	66.43_{5}	67.54_{8}	49.46_{16}	73.25_{4}	63.42_{10}	69.15_{6}
9	Synalp-Empathic		63.65_{23}	62.54_{12}	67.43_{9}	51.06_{15}	71.75_{9}	63.41_{11}	68.57_{9}
10	Think_Positive	✓	68.15_{7}	63.20_{9}	67.04_{10}	47.85_{21}	66.96_{24}	60.62_{18}	66.47_{15}
11	SentiKLUE		69.06_{6}	67.40_{4}	67.02_{11}	43.36_{30}	73.99_{3}	61.46_{14}	68.94_{7}
12	JOINT_FORCES	✓	66.61_{12}	62.20_{13}	66.79_{12}	45.40_{26}	70.02_{12}	60.74_{17}	67.39_{12}
13	AMI_ERIC		70.09_{4}	60.29_{20}	66.55_{13}	48.19_{20}	65.32_{26}	60.02_{21}	65.58_{20}
14	AUEB		63.92_{21}	64.32_{8}	66.38_{14}	56.16_{4}	70.75_{11}	64.43_{5}	67.71_{11}
15	CMU-Qatar*		65.11_{17}	62.95_{10}	65.53_{15}	40.52_{38}	65.63_{25}	57.23_{27}	64.87_{24}
16	Lt_3		65.56_{14}	64.78_{7}	65.47_{16}	47.76_{22}	68.56_{20}	60.60_{19}	66.12_{17}
17	columbia_nlp◇		64.60_{19}	59.84_{21}	65.42_{17}	40.02_{40}	68.79_{19}	58.08_{25}	65.96_{19}
18	LyS		66.92_{10}	60.45_{19}	64.92_{18}	42.40_{33}	69.79_{14}	59.04_{22}	66.10_{18}
19	NILC_USP		65.39_{15}	61.35_{16}	63.94_{19}	42.06_{34}	69.02_{18}	58.34_{24}	65.21_{21}
20	senti.ue		67.34_{9}	59.34_{23}	63.81_{20}	55.31_{6}	71.39_{10}	63.50_{7}	66.38_{16}
21	UKPDIPF		60.65_{29}	60.56_{17}	63.77_{21}	54.59_{7}	71.92_{7}	63.43_{8}	66.53_{13}
22	UKPDIPF	✓	60.65_{30}	60.56_{18}	63.77_{22}	54.59_{8}	71.92_{8}	63.43_{9}	66.53_{14}
23	SU-FMI*◇		60.96_{28}	61.67_{15}	63.62_{23}	48.34_{19}	68.24_{21}	60.07_{20}	64.91_{23}
24	ECNU		62.31_{27}	59.75_{22}	63.17_{24}	51.43_{14}	69.44_{16}	61.35_{15}	65.17_{22}
25	ECNU	✓	63.72_{22}	56.73_{29}	63.04_{25}	49.33_{17}	64.08_{31}	58.82_{23}	63.04_{27}
26	Rapanakis		58.52_{32}	54.02_{35}	63.01_{26}	44.69_{27}	59.71_{37}	55.80_{31}	61.28_{32}
27	Citius	✓	63.25_{24}	58.28_{24}	62.94_{27}	46.13_{25}	64.54_{29}	57.87_{26}	63.06_{26}
28	CMUQ-Hybrid*		63.22_{25}	61.75_{14}	62.71_{28}	40.95_{37}	65.14_{27}	56.27_{30}	63.00_{28}
29	Citius		62.53_{26}	57.69_{25}	61.92_{29}	41.00_{36}	62.40_{33}	55.11_{33}	61.51_{31}
30	KUNLPLab		58.12_{33}	55.89_{31}	61.72_{30}	44.60_{28}	63.77_{32}	56.70_{29}	62.00_{29}
31	senti.ue*	✓	65.21_{16}	56.16_{30}	61.47_{31}	54.09_{9}	68.08_{22}	61.21_{16}	63.71_{25}
32	UPV-ELiRF		63.97_{20}	55.36_{33}	59.33_{32}	37.46_{42}	64.11_{30}	53.63_{37}	60.49_{33}
33	USP_Biocom		58.05_{34}	53.57_{36}	59.21_{33}	43.56_{29}	67.80_{23}	56.86_{28}	61.96_{30}
34	DAEDALUS	✓	58.94_{31}	54.96_{34}	57.64_{34}	35.26_{44}	60.99_{35}	51.30_{39}	58.26_{35}
35	IIT-Patna		52.58_{40}	51.96_{37}	57.25_{35}	41.33_{35}	60.39_{36}	52.99_{38}	57.97_{36}
36	DejaVu		57.43_{36}	55.57_{32}	57.02_{36}	42.46_{32}	64.69_{28}	54.72_{34}	59.46_{34}
37	GPLSI		57.49_{35}	46.63_{42}	56.06_{37}	53.90_{10}	57.32_{41}	55.76_{32}	56.47_{37}
38	BUAP		56.85_{37}	44.27_{44}	55.76_{38}	51.52_{13}	53.94_{44}	53.74_{36}	54.97_{39}
39	SAP-RI		50.18_{44}	49.00_{41}	55.47_{39}	48.64_{18}	57.86_{40}	53.99_{35}	56.17_{38}
40	UMCC_DLSI_Sem		51.96_{41}	50.01_{38}	55.40_{40}	42.76_{31}	53.12_{45}	50.43_{40}	54.20_{42}
41	IBM_EG		54.51_{38}	46.62_{43}	52.26_{41}	34.14_{46}	59.24_{38}	48.55_{43}	54.34_{41}
42	Alberta		53.85_{39}	49.05_{40}	52.06_{42}	40.40_{39}	52.38_{46}	48.28_{44}	51.85_{44}
43	lsis_lif		46.38_{46}	38.56_{47}	52.02_{43}	34.64_{45}	61.09_{34}	49.25_{41}	54.90_{40}
44	SU-sentilab		50.17_{45}	49.60_{39}	49.52_{44}	31.49_{47}	55.11_{42}	45.37_{47}	51.09_{45}
45	SINAI		50.59_{42}	57.34_{27}	49.50_{45}	31.15_{49}	58.33_{39}	46.33_{46}	52.26_{43}
46	IITPatna		50.32_{43}	40.56_{46}	48.22_{46}	36.73_{43}	54.68_{43}	46.54_{45}	50.29_{46}
47	Univ. Warwick		39.17_{48}	29.50_{49}	45.56_{47}	39.77_{41}	39.60_{49}	41.64_{48}	43.19_{48}
48	UMCC_DLSI_Graph		43.24_{47}	36.66_{48}	45.49_{48}	53.15_{11}	47.81_{47}	48.82_{42}	46.56_{47}
49	Univ. Warwick	✓	34.23_{50}	24.63_{50}	45.11_{49}	31.40_{48}	29.34_{50}	35.28_{49}	38.88_{49}
50	DAEDALUS		36.57_{49}	40.86_{45}	33.03_{50}	28.96_{50}	40.83_{48}	34.27_{50}	35.81_{50}
	Majority baseline		29.2	19.0	34.6	27.7	27.2		

Table 5: **Results for subtask B.** The * indicates system resubmissions (because they initially trained on Twitter2013-test), and the ◇ indicates a system that includes a task co-organizer as a team member. The systems are sorted by their score on the Twitter2014 test dataset; the rankings on the individual datasets are indicated with a subscript. The last two columns show macro- and micro-averaged results across the three 2014 test datasets.

In the 2015 edition of the task, we might also remove the constrained/unconstrained distinction.

Finally, as there are multiple opinions about a topic in Twitter, we would like to focus on detecting the sentiment trend towards a topic.

Acknowledgements

We would like to thank Kathleen McKeown and Smaranda Muresan for funding the 2014 Twitter test sets. We also thank the anonymous reviewers.

Subtasks	Team	Affiliation	2013?
B	Alberta	University of Alberta	
B	AMI_ERIC	AMI Software R&D and Université de Lyon (ERIC LYON 2)	yes
B	AUEB	Athens University of Economics and Business	yes
B	BUAP	Benemérita Universidad Autónoma de Puebla	
B	CISUC_KIS	University of Coimbra	
A, B	Citius	University of Santiago de Compostela	
A, B	CMU-Qatar	Carnegie Mellon University, Qatar	
A, B	CMUQ-Hybrid	Carnegie Mellon University, Qatar (different from the above)	
A, B	columbia_nlp	Columbia University	yes
B	cooolll	Harbin Institute of Technology	
A, B	DAEDALUS	Daedalus	
B	DejaVu	Indian Institute of Technology, Kanpur	
A, B	ECNU	East China Normal University	yes
B	GPLSI	University of Alicante	
B	IBM_EG	IBM Egypt	
A, B	IITPatna	Indian Institute of Technology, Patna	
A, B	IIT-Patna	Indian Institute of Technology, Patna (different from the above)	
B	JOINT_FORCES	Zurich University of Applied Sciences	
A	Kea	York University, Toronto	yes
B	KUNLPLab	Koç University	
B	lsis_lif	Aix-Marseille University	yes
A, B	Lt_3	Ghent University	
A, B	LyS	Universidade da Coruña	
B	NILC_USP	University of São Paulo	yes
A, B	NRC-Canada	National Research Council Canada	yes
B	Rapanakis	Stamatis Rapanakis	
B	RTRGO	Retresco GmbH and University of Gothenburg	yes
A, B	SAIL	Signal Analysis and Interpretation Laboratory	yes
A, B	SAP-RI	SAP Research and Innovation	
A, B	senti.ue	Universidade de Évora	yes
A, B	SentiKLUE	Friedrich-Alexander-Universität Erlangen-Nürnberg	yes
B	SINAI	University of Jaén	yes
B	SU-FMI	Sofia University	
A, B	SU-sentilab	Sabanci University	yes
B	SWISS-CHOCOLATE	ETH Zurich	
B	Synalp-Empathic	University of Lorraine	
B	TeamX	Fuji Xerox Co., Ltd.	
A, B	Think_Positive	IBM Research, Brazil	
A	TJP	University of Northumbria at Newcastle Upon Tyne	yes
B	TUGAS	Instituto de Engenharia de Sistemas e Computadores, Investigação e Desenvolvimento em Lisboa	yes
A, B	UKPDIPF	Ubiquitous Knowledge Processing Lab	
B	UMCC_DLSI_Graph	Universidad de Matanzas and Univarsidad de Alicante	yes
B	UMCC_DLSI_Sem	Universidad de Matanzas and Univarsidad de Alicante (different from above)	yes
A, B	Univ. Warwick	University of Warwick	
B	UPV-ELiRF	Universitat Politècnica de València	
B	USP_Biocom	University of São Paulo and Federal University of São Carlos	

Table 6: Participating teams, their affiliations, subtasks they have taken part in, and an indication about whether the team participated in SemEval-2013 Task 2.

References

Stefano Baccianella, Andrea Esuli, and Fabrizio Sebastiani. 2010. SentiWordNet 3.0: An enhanced lexical resource for sentiment analysis and opinion mining. In *Proceedings of the Seventh International Conference on Language Resources and Evaluation*, LREC '10, Valletta, Malta.

Luciano Barbosa and Junlan Feng. 2010. Robust sentiment detection on Twitter from biased and noisy data. In *Proceedings of the 23rd International Conference on Computational Linguistics: Posters*, COLING '10, pages 36–44, Beijing, China.

Albert Bifet, Geoffrey Holmes, Bernhard Pfahringer, and Ricard Gavaldà. 2011. Detecting sentiment change in Twitter streaming data. *Journal of Machine Learning Research, Proceedings Track*, 17:5–11.

Tao Chen and Min-Yen Kan. 2013. Creating a live, public short message service corpus: the NUS SMS corpus. *Language Resources and Evaluation*, 47(2):299–335.

Dmitry Davidov, Oren Tsur, and Ari Rappoport. 2010. Semi-supervised recognition of sarcasm in Twitter and Amazon. In *Proceedings of the Fourteenth Conference on Computational Natural Language Learning*, CoNLL '10, pages 107–116, Uppsala, Sweden.

Kevin Gimpel, Nathan Schneider, Brendan O'Connor, Dipanjan Das, Daniel Mills, Jacob Eisenstein, Michael Heilman, Dani Yogatama, Jeffrey Flanigan, and Noah A. Smith. 2011. Part-of-speech tagging for Twitter: Annotation, features, and experiments. In *Proceedings of the 49th Annual Meeting of the Association for Computational Linguistics: Human Language Technologies*, ACL-HLT '11, pages 42–47, Portland, Oregon, USA.

Roberto González-Ibáñez, Smaranda Muresan, and Nina Wacholder. 2011. Identifying sarcasm in Twitter: a closer look. In *Proceedings of the 49th Annual Meeting of the Association for Computational Linguistics: Human Language Technologies - Short Papers*, ACL-HLT '11, pages 581–586, Portland, Oregon, USA.

Bernard Jansen, Mimi Zhang, Kate Sobel, and Abdur Chowdury. 2009. Twitter power: Tweets as electronic word of mouth. *J. Am. Soc. Inf. Sci. Technol.*, 60(11):2169–2188.

Efthymios Kouloumpis, Theresa Wilson, and Johanna Moore. 2011. Twitter sentiment analysis: The good the bad and the OMG! In *Proceedings of the Fifth International Conference on Weblogs and Social Media*, ICWSM '11, Barcelona, Catalonia, Spain.

Christine Liebrecht, Florian Kunneman, and Antal Van den Bosch. 2013. The perfect solution for detecting sarcasm in tweets #not. In *Proceedings of the 4th Workshop on Computational Approaches to Subjectivity, Sentiment and Social Media Analysis*, pages 29–37, Atlanta, Georgia, USA.

Saif Mohammad, Svetlana Kiritchenko, and Xiaodan Zhu. 2013. NRC-Canada: Building the state-of-the-art in sentiment analysis of tweets. In *Proceedings of the Seventh international workshop on Semantic Evaluation Exercises*, SemEval-2013, pages 321–327, Atlanta, Georgia, USA.

Preslav Nakov, Sara Rosenthal, Zornitsa Kozareva, Veselin Stoyanov, Alan Ritter, and Theresa Wilson. 2013. SemEval-2013 task 2: Sentiment analysis in Twitter. In *Second Joint Conference on Lexical and Computational Semantics (*SEM), Volume 2: Proceedings of the Seventh International Workshop on Semantic Evaluation*, SemEval '13, pages 312–320, Atlanta, Georgia, USA.

Brendan O'Connor, Ramnath Balasubramanyan, Bryan Routledge, and Noah Smith. 2010. From tweets to polls: Linking text sentiment to public opinion time series. In *Proceedings of the Fourth International Conference on Weblogs and Social Media*, ICWSM '10, Washington, DC, USA.

Alexander Pak and Patrick Paroubek. 2010. Twitter based system: Using Twitter for disambiguating sentiment ambiguous adjectives. In *Proceedings of the 5th International Workshop on Semantic Evaluation*, SemEval '10, pages 436–439, Uppsala, Sweden.

Bo Pang, Lillian Lee, and Shivakumar Vaithyanathan. 2002. Thumbs up?: Sentiment classification using machine learning techniques. In *Proceedings of the Conference on Empirical Methods in Natural Language Processing - Volume 10*, EMNLP '02, pages 79–86.

Maria Pontiki, Harris Papageorgiou, Dimitrios Galanis, Ion Androutsopoulos, John Pavlopoulos, and Suresh Manandhar. 2014. SemEval-2014 task 4: Aspect based sentiment analysis. In *Proceedings of the 8th International Workshop on Semantic Evaluation*, SemEval '14, Dublin, Ireland.

Alan Ritter, Sam Clark, Mausam, and Oren Etzioni. 2011. Named entity recognition in tweets: An experimental study. In *Proceedings of the Conference on Empirical Methods in Natural Language Processing*, EMNLP '11, pages 1524–1534, Edinburgh, Scotland, UK.

Andranik Tumasjan, Timm Sprenger, Philipp Sandner, and Isabell Welpe. 2010. Predicting elections with Twitter: What 140 characters reveal about political sentiment. In *Proceedings of the Fourth International Conference on Weblogs and Social Media*, ICWSM '10, Washington, DC, USA.

Janyce Wiebe, Theresa Wilson, and Claire Cardie. 2005. Annotating expressions of opinions and emotions in language. *Language Resources and Evaluation*, 39(2-3):165–210.

SemEval-2014 Task 10: Multilingual Semantic Textual Similarity

Eneko Agirre[a], **Carmen Banea**[b*], **Claire Cardie**[c], **Daniel Cer**[d], **Mona Diab**[e*]
Aitor Gonzalez-Agirre[a], **Weiwei Guo**[f], **Rada Mihalcea**[b], **German Rigau**[a], **Janyce Wiebe**[g]

[a]University of the Basque Country, Basque Country, Spain
[b]University of Michigan, Ann Arbor, MI
[c]Cornell University, Ithaca, NY
[d]Google Inc., Mountain View, CA
[e]George Washington University, Washington, DC
[f]Columbia University, New York, NY
[g]University of Pittsburgh, Pittsburgh, PA

Abstract

In Semantic Textual Similarity, systems rate the degree of semantic equivalence between two text snippets. This year, the participants were challenged with new data sets for English, as well as the introduction of Spanish, as a new language in which to assess semantic similarity. For the English subtask, we exposed the systems to a diversity of testing scenarios, by preparing additional OntoNotes-WordNet sense mappings and news headlines, as well as introducing new genres, including image descriptions, DEFT discussion forums, DEFT newswire, and tweet-newswire headline mappings. For Spanish, since, to our knowledge, this is the first time that official evaluations are conducted, we used well-formed text, by featuring sentences extracted from encyclopedic content and newswire. The annotations for both tasks leveraged crowdsourcing. The Spanish subtask engaged 9 teams participating with 22 system runs, and the English subtask attracted 15 teams with 38 system runs.

1 Introduction and motivation

Given two snippets of text, Semantic Textual Similarity (STS) captures the notion that some texts are more similar than others, measuring their degree of semantic equivalence. Textual similarity can range from complete unrelatedness to exact semantic equivalence, and a graded similarity intuitively captures the notion of intermediate shades of similarity, as pairs of text may differ from some minor nuanced aspects of meaning, to relatively important semantic differences, to sharing only some details, or to simply being related to the same topic (cf. Section 2).

One of the goals of the STS task is to create a unified framework for combining several semantic components that otherwise have historically tended to be evaluated independently and without characterization of impact on NLP applications. By providing such a framework, STS allows for an extrinsic evaluation of these modules. Moreover, such an STS framework itself could in turn be evaluated intrinsically and extrinsically as a grey/black box within various NLP applications such as Machine Translation (MT), Summarization, Generation, Question Answering (QA), etc.

STS is related to both Textual Entailment (TE) and Paraphrasing, but differs in a number of ways and it is more directly applicable to a number of NLP tasks. STS is different from TE inasmuch as it assumes bidirectional graded equivalence between the pair of textual snippets. In the case of TE the equivalence is directional, e.g. a car is a vehicle, but a vehicle is not necessarily a car. STS also differs from both TE and Paraphrasing (in as far as both tasks have been defined to date in the literature) in that, rather than being a binary yes/no decision (e.g. *a vehicle is not a car*), we define STS to be a graded similarity notion (e.g. *a vehicle* and *a car* are more similar than *a wave* and *a car*). A quantifiable graded bidirectional notion of textual similarity is useful for a myriad of NLP tasks such as MT evaluation, information extraction, question answering, summarization, etc.

In 2012 we held the first pilot task at SemEval 2012, as part of the *SEM 2012 conference, with great success: 35 teams participated with 88 system runs (Agirre et al., 2012). In addition, we held

*carmennb@umich.edu, mtdiab@gwu.edu

Proceedings of the 8th International Workshop on Semantic Evaluation (SemEval 2014), pages 81–91, Dublin, Ireland, August 23-24, 2014.

year	dataset	pairs	source
2012	MSRpar	1500	newswire
2012	MSRvid	1500	videos
2012	OnWN	750	glosses
2012	SMTnews	750	MT eval.
2012	SMTeuroparl	750	MT eval.
2013	HDL	750	newswire
2013	FNWN	189	glosses
2013	OnWN	561	glosses
2013	SMT	750	MT eval.
2014	HDL	750	newswire headlines
2014	OnWN	750	glosses
2014	Deft-forum	450	forum posts
2014	Deft-news	300	news summary
2014	Images	750	image descriptions
2014	Tweet-news	750	tweet-news pairs

Table 2: English subtask: Summary of train (2012 and 2013) and test (2014) datasets.

a DARPA sponsored workshop at Columbia University.[1] In 2013, STS was selected as the official Shared Task of the *SEM 2013 conference, with two subtasks: The Core task, which is similar to the 2012 task; and a Pilot task on Typed-similarity between semi-structured records. The Core task attracted 34 participants with 89 runs, and the Typed-similarity task attracted 6 teams with 14 runs.

For STS 2014 we defined two subtasks: English and Spanish. For the English subtask we provided five test datasets: two datasets that extend already released genres (the OntoNotes-WordNet sense mappings and news headlines) and three new genres: image descriptions, DEFT discussion forum data and newswire, as well as tweet-newswire headline mappings. Participants could use all datasets released in 2012 and 2013 as training data. The Spanish subtask introduced two diverse datasets on different genres, namely encyclopedic descriptions extracted from the Spanish Wikipedia and contemporary Spanish newswire. For the Spanish subtask, the participants had access to a limited amount of labeled data, consisting of 65 sentence pairs, which they could use for training.

2 Task Description

2.1 English Subtask

The English dataset comprises pairs of news headlines (HDL), pairs of glosses (OnWN), image descriptions (Images), DEFT-related discussion forums (Deft-forum) and news (Deft-news), and tweet comments and newswire headline mappings (Tweets).

For **HDL**, we used naturally occurring news headlines gathered by the Europe Media Monitor (EMM) engine (Best et al., 2005) from several different news sources. EMM clusters together related news. Our goal was to generate a balanced data set across the different similarity ranges, hence we built two sets of headline pairs: (i) a set where the pairs come from the same EMM cluster, (ii) and another set where the headlines come from a different EMM cluster, then we computed the string similarity between those pairs. Accordingly, we sampled 375 headline pairs of headlines that occur in the same EMM cluster, aiming for pairs equally distributed between minimal and maximal similarity using simple string similarity. We sampled other 375 pairs from the different EMM cluster in the same manner.

For **OnWN**, we used the sense definition pairs of OntoNotes (Hovy et al., 2006) and WordNet (Fellbaum, 1998). Different from previous tasks, the two definition sentences in a pair belong to different senses. We sampled 750 pairs based on a string similarity ranging from 0.5 to 1.

The **Images** data set is a subset of the PASCAL VOC-2008 data set (Rashtchian et al., 2010), which consists of 1,000 images and has been used by a number of image description systems. It was also sampled from string similarity values between 0.6 and 1.

Deft-forum and **Deft-news** are from DEFT data.[2] Deft-forum contains the forum post sentences, and Deft-news are news summaries. We selected 450 pairs for Deft-forum and 300 pairs for Deft-news. They are sampled evenly from string similarities falling in the interval 0.6 to 1.

The **Tweets** data set contains tweet-news pairs selected from the corpus released in (Guo et al., 2013), where each pair contains a sentence that pertains to the news title, while the other one represents a Twitter comment on that particular news. They are evenly sampled from string similarity values between 0.5 and 1.

Table 1 shows the explanations and values associated with each score between 5 and 0. As in prior years, we used Amazon Mechanical Turk (AMT)[3] to crowdsource the annotation of the English pairs.[4] Annotators are presented with the

[1] `http://www.cs.columbia.edu/~weiwei/workshop/`

[2] LDC2013E19, LDC2012E54

[3] `www.mturk.com`

[4] For STS 2013, we used CrowdFlower as a front-end to

Score	English	Spanish
5/4	*The two sentences are completely equivalent, as they mean the same thing.*	
	The bird is bathing in the sink. Birdie is washing itself in the water basin.	El pájaro se esta bañando en el lavabo. El pájaro se está lavando en el aguamanil.
4	*The two sentences are mostly equivalent, but some unimportant details differ.*	
	In May 2010, the troops attempted to invade Kabul. The US army invaded Kabul on May 7th last year, 2010.	
3	*The two sentences are roughly equivalent, but some important information differs/missing.*	
	John said he is considered a witness but not a suspect. "He is not a suspect anymore." John said.	John dijo que él es considerado como testigo, y no como sospechoso. "Él ya no es un sospechoso," John dijo.
2	*The two sentences are not equivalent, but share some details.*	
	They flew out of the nest in groups. They flew into the nest together.	Ellos volaron del nido en grupos. Volaron hacia el nido juntos.
1	*The two sentences are not equivalent, but are on the same topic.*	
	The woman is playing the violin. The young lady enjoys listening to the guitar.	La mujer está tocando el violín. La joven disfruta escuchar la guitarra.
0	*The two sentences are completely dissimilar.*	
	John went horse back riding at dawn with a whole group of friends. Sunrise at dawn is a magnificent view to take in if you wake up early enough for it.	Al amanecer, Juan se fue a montar a caballo con un grupo de amigos. La salida del sol al amanecer es una magnífica vista que puede presenciar si usted se despierta lo suficientemente temprano para verla.

Table 1: Similarity scores with explanations and examples for the English and Spanish subtasks, where the sentences in Spanish are translations of the English ones.
A similarity score of 5 in English is mirrored by a maximum score of 4 in Spanish; the definitions pertaining to scores 3 and 4 in English were collapsed under a score of 3 in Spanish, with the definition "The two sentences are mostly equivalent, but some details differ."

detailed instructions provided in Figure 1, and are asked to label each STS sentence pair on our six point scale, selecting from a dropdown box. Five sentence pairs are presented to each annotator at once, per human intelligence task (HIT), at a payrate of $0.20; we collect five separate annotations per sentence pair. Annotators were only eligible to work on the task if they had the Mechanical Turk Master Qualification. This is a special qualification conferred by AMT (using a priority statistical model) to annotators who consistently maintain a very high level of quality across a variety of tasks from numerous requesters). Access to these skilled workers entails a 20% surcharge.

To monitor the quality of the annotations, we use the gold dataset of 105 pairs that were manually annotated by the task organizers during STS 2013. We include one of these gold pairs in each set of five sentence pairs, where the gold pairs are indistinguishable from the rest. Unlike when we ran on CrowdFlower for STS 2013, the gold pairs are not used for training purposes, nor are workers automatically banned from the task if they make too many mistakes on annotating them. Rather, the gold pairs are only used to help in identifying and removing the data associated with poorly performing annotators. With few exceptions, 90% of the answers from each individual annotator fall within +/-1 of the answers selected by the organizers for

Amazon Mechanical Turk, since it provides numerous useful tools to assist in running a successful annotation project using crowdsourcing, such as support for hidden 'golden' questions that can be used both to train annotators and to automatically stop people who repeatedly make mistakes from contributing to the task. However, in 2013, CrowdFlower dropped Amazon Mechanical Turk as an annotation source. When we tried running pairs for STS 2014 on CrowdFlower using the same templates that were successfully used for the 2013 task, we found that we obtained significantly degraded annotation quality, with an average Pearson (AMT provider vs. rest of AMT providers) of only 22.8%. In contrast, when we ran the task for 2014 on AMT, we obtained a one-vs-rest annotation of 73.6%.

Compare the Meaning of Two Statements (v.2.5)

Instructions Hide

Two statements can mean the same thing even if they use very different words and phrases. Conversely, two statements that are superficially very similar in their word choice, phrasing and overall composition can have very different meanings.

Your job is to compare two statements and decide the type of relationship that holds between their underlying meanings or messages (i.e., what they say about or refer to in the world).

To do this task successfully, **picture** what is being described and contrast **exactly** what is conveyed by one statement versus what is being conveyed by the other.

Do the statements refer to the exact same person, action, event, idea or thing? Or, are they similar but differ according to either large or small details?

Tips:

- Be **precise** in your assignments and **try to avoid overusing any one of the category labels** (e.g., don't just label most of the pairs as "mostly equivalent" or "roughly equivalent").
- Be careful of **subtle differences** between the pairs that have an important impact on what is being said or described.
- Ignore grammatical errors and awkward wordings within the statements as long as they do not obscure what a statement is suppose to convey.

Figure 1: Annotation instructions for English subtask.

the gold dataset.

The distribution of scores obtained from the AMT providers in the Deft-forum, Deft-news, OnWN and tweet-news datasets is roughly uniform across the different grades of similarity, although the scores are slightly higher for tweet-news. Compared to the other data sets, the scores for OnWN, were more bimodal, ranging between 4.6 to 5 and 0 to 0.4, when compared to middle values (2.6-3.4).

In order to assess the annotation quality, we measure the correlation of each annotator with the average of the rest of the annotators, and then average the results. This approach to estimate the quality is identical to the method used for evaluations (see Section 3), and it can thus be considered as the upper bound of the systems. The inter-tagger correlation for each English dataset is as follows:

- HDL: 79.4%
- OnWN: 67.2%
- Deft-forum: 58.6%
- Deft-news: 70.7%
- Images: 83.6%
- Tweets-news: 74.4%

The correlation figures are generally high (over 70%), with the exception of the OnWN and Deft datasets, which score 67.2% and 58.6%, respectively. The reason for the low inter-tagger correlation on OnWN compared to the higher correlations in previous years is that we only used unmapped sense definitions, i.e., the two sentences in a pair belong to two different senses. For the Deft-forum dataset, we found that similarity values tend to be lower than in the other datasets, and more annotation disagreements happen in these low similarity values.

2.2 Spanish Subtask

The Spanish subtask follows a setup similar to the English subtask, except that the similarity scores were adapted to fit a range from 0 to 4 (see Table 1). We thought that the distinction between a score of 3 and 4 for the English task will pose more difficulty for us in conveying into Spanish, as the sole difference between the two lies in how the annotators perceive the importance of additional details or missing information with respect to the core semantic interpretation of the pair. As this aspect entails a subjective judgement, and since it is the first time that a Spanish STS evaluation is organized, we casted the annotation guidelines into straightforward and unambiguous instructions, and thus opted to use a similarity range from 0 to 4.

Prior to the evaluation window, we released 65 Spanish sentence pairs for trial / training. In order to evaluate system performance under different scenarios, we developed two test datasets, one extracted from the Spanish Wikipedia[5] (December 2013 dump) and one from contemporary news articles collected from media in Spanish (February 2014).

2.2.1 Spanish Wikipedia

The Wikipedia dump was processed using the Parse::MediaWikiDump Perl library. We removed all titles, html tags, wiki tags and hyperlinks (keeping only the surface forms). Each article was split into paragraphs, where the first paragraph was considered to be the article's abstract, while the remaining ones were deemed to be its content. Each of these were split into sentences using the Perl library Uplug::PreProcess::SentDetect, and only the sentences longer than eight words were used. We iteratively computed the lexical similarity[6] between every sentence in the abstract and every sentence in the content, and retained those pairs whose sentence length ratio was higher than 0.5, and their similarity scored over 0.35.

The final set of sentence pairs was split into five bins, and their scores normalized to range from 0 to 1. The more interesting and difficult pairs were found, perhaps not surprisingly, in bins 0 and 1, where synonyms/short paraphrases where more frequent. An example extracted from those bins, where the text in italics highlights the differences between the two sentences:

- "America*" es el* segund*o continente* más grande del planeta, *después* de Asia.
  "America" is the second largest continent in the world, following Asia.
- America *corresponde a la* segund*a masa de tierra* más grande del planeta, *luego* de Asia.
  America is the second largest land mass on the planet, after Asia.

The Spanish verb "*Es*" maps to (En:[7] is), "*corresponde a*" (En: corresponds to), the phrase "*el segundo continente*" (En: the second continent) is equivalent to "*la segunda masa de tierra*" (the second land mass), and "*despues*" (En: following) to "*luego*" (En: after). Despite the difference in vocabulary choice, the two sentences are paraphrases of each other.

From the candidate pairs, we manually selected 324 sentence pairs, in order to ensure a diverse and challenging set. This set was annotated in two ways, first by two graduate students in Computer Science who are native speakers of Spanish, and second by using AMT.

The AMT framework was set up to contain seven sentence pairs per HIT, where six of them were part of the test dataset, while one was used for control. AMT providers were eligible to complete a task if they had more than 500 accepted HITs, with 90%+ acceptance rate.[8] We paid $0.30 per HIT, and each HIT was annotated by five AMT providers. We sought to ensure that only Spanish speaking annotators would complete the HITs by providing all the information related to the task (its title, abstract, description, guidelines and examples), as well as the control pair in Spanish only. The participants were instructed to label the pairs on a scale from 0 to 4 (see Table 1). Each sentence pair was followed by a comment text box, which the AMT providers used to provide the topic of the sentences, corrections, etc.

The two students achieved a Pearson correlation of 0.6974 on the Wikipedia dataset. To see how their judgement compares to the crowd wisdom, we averaged the AMT scores for each pair, and computed their correlation with our annotators, obtaining 0.824 and 0.742, respectively. Surprisingly enough, both these correlation values are higher than the correlation among the annotators themselves. When averaging the annotator scores and comparing them with the AMT providers' average score per pair, the correlation becomes 0.8546, indicating that the task is well defined, and that the annotations contributed by the AMT providers are of satisfactory quality. Given these scores, the gold standard was annotated using the average AMT provider judgement per pair.

2.2.2 Spanish News

The second Spanish dataset was extracted from news articles published in Spanish language media from around the world in February 2014. The hyperlinks to the articles were obtained by parsing the "International" page of Spanish Google News,[9] which aggregates or clusters in real time articles describing a particular event from a diverse pool of news sites, where each grouping

[5] `es.wikipedia.org`

[6] Algorithm based on the Linux *diff* command (Algorithm::Diff Perl module).

[7] "En" stands for English.

[8] Initially, Amazon had automatically upgraded our annotation task to require Master level providers (as those participating in the English annotations), yet after approximately 4 days, no HIT had been completed.

[9] `news.google.es`

is labeled with the title of one of the predominant articles. By leveraging these clusters of links pointing to the sites where the articles were originally published, we are able to gather raw text that has a high probability of containing semantically similar sentences. We encountered several difficulties while mining the articles, ranging from each article having its own formatting depending on the source site, to advertisements, cookie requirements, to encoding for Spanish diacritics. We used the *lynx text-based browser*,[10] which was able to standardize the raw articles to a degree. The output of the browser was processed using a rule based approach taking into account continuous text span length, ratio of symbols and numbers to the text, etc., in order to determine when a paragraph is part of the article content. After that, a second pass over the predictions corrected mislabeled paragraphs if they were preceded and followed by paragraphs identified as content. All the content pertaining to articles on the same event was joined, sentence split, and *diff* pairwise similarities were computed. The set of candidate sentences followed the same requirements as for the Wikipedia dataset, namely length ratio higher than 0.5 and similarity score over 0.35. From these, we manually extracted 480 sentence pairs which were deemed to pose a challenge to an automated system.

Due to the high correlations obtained between the AMT providers' scores and the annotators' scores on Wikipedia, the news dataset was only annotated using AMT, following exactly the same task setup as for Wikipedia.

3 Evaluation

Evaluation of STS is still an open issue. STS experiments have traditionally used Pearson product-moment correlation between the system scores and the GS scores, or, alternatively, Spearman rank order correlation. In addition, we also need a method to aggregate the results from each dataset into an overall score. The analysis performed in (Agirre and Amigó, In prep) shows that Pearson and averaging across datasets are the best suited combination in general. In particular, Pearson is more informative than Spearman, in that Spearman only takes the rank differences into account, while Pearson does account for value differences as well. The study also showed that other alternatives need to be considered, depending on the requirements of the target application.

We leave application-dependent evaluations for future work, and focus on average Pearson correlation. When averaging, we weight each individual correlation by the size of the dataset. In order to compute statistical significance among system results, we use a one-tailed parametric test based on Fisher's z-transformation (Press et al., 2002, equation 14.5.10). In addition, English subtask participants could provide an optional confidence measure between 0 and 100 for each of their predictions. Team RTM-DCU is the only one who has provided these, and the evaluation of their runs using weighted Pearson (Pozzi et al., 2012) is listed at the end of Table 3.

Participants[11] could take part in the shared task with a maximum of 3 system runs per subtask.

3.1 English Subtask

In order to provide a simple word overlap baseline (Baseline-tokencos), we tokenize the input sentences splitting on white spaces, and then represent each sentence as a vector in the multidimensional token space. Each dimension has 1 if the token is present in the sentence, 0 otherwise. Vector similarity is computed using the cosine similarity metric.

We also run the freely available system, TakeLab (Šarić et al., 2012), which yielded state of the art performance in STS 2012 and strong results out-of-the-box in 2013.[12]

15 teams participated in the English subtask, submitting 38 system runs. One team submitted the results past the deadline, as explicitly marked in Table 3. After the submission deadline expired, the organizers published the gold standard and participant submissions on the task website, in order to ensure a transparent evaluation process.

Table 3 shows the results of the English subtask, with runs listed in alphabetical order. The correlation in each dataset is given, followed

[10] `lynx.browser.org`

[11] **Participating teams**: Bielefeld_SC (McCrae et al., 2013), BUAP (Vilariño et al., 2014), DLS@CU (Sultan et al., 2014b), FBK-TR (Vo et al., 2014), IBM_EG (no information), LIPN (Buscaldi et al., 2014), Meerkat_Mafia (Kashyap et al., 2014), NTNU (Lynum et al., 2014), RTM-DCU (Biçici and Way, 2014), SemantiKLUE (Proisi et al., 2014), StanfordNLP (Socher et al., 2014), TeamZ (Gupta, 2014), UMCC_DLSI_SemSim (Chavez et al., 2014), UNAL-NLP (Jimenez et al., 2014), UNED (Martinez-Romo et al., 2011), UoW (Rios, 2014).

[12] Code is available at `http://ixa2.si.ehu.es/stswiki`

Run Name	deft forum	deft news	Headl	images	OnWN	tweet news	Weighted mean	Rank
Baseline-tokencos	0.353	0.596	0.510	0.513	0.406	0.654	0.507	-
TakeLab	0.333	0.716	0.720	0.742	0.793	0.650	0.678	-
Bielefeld_SC-run1	0.211	0.432	0.321	0.368	0.367	0.415	0.354	32
Bielefeld_SC-run2	0.211	0.431	0.311	0.356	0.361	0.409	0.347	33
BUAP-EN-run1	0.456	0.686	0.689	0.697	0.654	0.771	0.671	19
DLS@CU-run1	0.483	0.766	0.765	0.821	0.723	0.764	0.734	7
DLS@CU-run2	0.483	0.766	0.765	0.821	0.859	0.764	0.761	1
FBK-TR-run1	0.322	0.523	0.547	0.601	0.661	0.462	0.535	25
FBK-TR-run2	0.167	0.421	0.485	0.521	0.572	0.359	0.441	28
FBK-TR-run3	0.305	0.405	0.471	0.489	0.551	0.438	0.459	27
IBM_EG-run1	0.474	0.743	0.737	0.801	0.760	0.730	0.722	8
IBM_EG-run2	0.464	0.641	0.710	0.747	0.732	0.696	0.684	15
LIPN-run1	0.454	0.640	0.653	0.809	-	0.551	0.508	26
LIPN-run2	0.084	-	-	-	-	-	0.010	35
Meerkat_Mafia-Hulk	0.449	0.785	0.757	0.790	0.787	0.757	0.735	6
Meerkat_Mafia-pairingWords	0.471	0.763	0.760	0.801	0.875	0.779	0.761	2
Meerkat_Mafia-SuperSaiyan	0.492	0.771	0.767	0.768	0.802	0.765	0.741	5
NTNU-run1	0.437	0.714	0.722	0.800	0.835	0.411	0.663	20
NTNU-run2	0.508	0.766	0.753	0.813	0.777	0.792	0.749	4
NTNU-run3	0.531	0.781	0.784	0.834	0.850	0.675	0.755	3
SemantiKLUE-run1	0.337	0.608	0.728	0.783	0.848	0.632	0.687	14
SemantiKLUE-run2	0.349	0.643	0.733	0.773	0.855	0.640	0.694	13
StanfordNLP-run1	0.319	0.635	0.636	0.758	0.627	0.669	0.627	22
StanfordNLP-run2	0.304	0.679	0.621	0.715	0.625	0.636	0.610	24
StanfordNLP-run3	0.342	0.650	0.602	0.754	0.609	0.638	0.614	23
UMCC_DLSI_SemSim-run1	0.475	0.662	0.632	0.742	0.813	0.675	0.682	16
UMCC_DLSI_SemSim-run2	0.469	0.662	0.625	0.739	0.814	0.654	0.676	18
UMCC_DLSI_SemSim-run3	0.283	0.385	0.267	0.436	0.603	0.278	0.381	30
UNAL-NLP-run1	0.504	0.721	0.762	0.807	0.782	0.614	0.711	12
UNAL-NLP-run2	0.383	0.730	0.765	0.771	0.827	0.403	0.657	21
UNAL-NLP-run3	0.461	0.722	0.761	0.778	0.843	0.658	0.721	9
UNED-run22_p_np	0.104	0.315	0.037	0.324	0.509	0.490	0.310	34
UNED-runS5K_10_np	0.118	0.506	0.057	0.498	0.488	0.579	0.379	31
UNED-runS5K_3_np	0.094	0.564	0.018	0.607	0.577	0.670	0.431	29
UoW-run1	0.342	0.751	0.754	0.776	0.799	0.737	0.714	11
UoW-run2	0.342	0.587	0.754	0.788	0.799	0.628	0.682	17
UoW-run3	0.342	0.763	0.754	0.788	0.799	0.753	0.721	10
†RTM-DCU-run1	0.434	0.697	0.620	0.699	0.806	0.688	0.671	
†RTM-DCU-run2	0.397	0.681	0.613	0.666	0.799	0.669	0.651	
†RTM-DCU-run3	0.308	0.556	0.630	0.647	0.800	0.553	0.608	
†RTM-DCU-run1	0.418	0.685	0.622	0.698	0.833	0.687	0.673	
†RTM-DCU-run2	0.383	0.674	0.609	0.663	0.826	0.669	0.653	
†RTM-DCU-run3	0.273	0.553	0.633	0.644	0.825	0.568	0.611	

Table 3: English evaluation results. Results at the top correspond to out-of-the-box systems. Results at the bottom correspond to results using the confidence score.
Notes: "-" for not submitted, "†" for post-deadline submission.

by the mean correlation (the official measure), and the rank of the run. The highest correlations are for OnWN (87.5%, by Meerkat_Mafia) and images (83.4%, by NTNU), followed by Tweets (79.2%, by NTNU), HEADL (78.4%, by NTNU) and deft news and forums (78.1% and 53.1%, respectively, by NTNU). Compared to the inter-annotator agreement correlation, the ranking among datasets is very similar, with the exception of OnWN, as it gets the best score but has very low agreement. One possible reason is that the participants used previously available data. The results of the best 4 top system runs are significantly different (p-value < 0.05) from the 5th top scoring system run and below. The top 4 systems did not show statistical significant variation among them.

Only three runs (cf. lower rows in Table 3) included non-uniform confidence scores, barely affecting their ranking.

Interestingly, the two top performing systems on the English STS sub-task are both unsupervised. DLS@CU (Sultan et al., 2014b) presents an unsupervised algorithm which predicts the STS score based on the proportion of word alignments in the two sentences. Two related words are aligned depending on how similar the two words are, and also on how similar the contexts of the words are in the respective sentences (Sultan et al., 2014a). Meerkat_Mafia_pairingWords (Kashyap et al., 2014) also follows a fully unsupervised approach. The authors train LSA on an English corpus of three billion words using a sliding window approach, resulting in a vocabulary size of 29,000 words associated with 300 dimensions. They account for named entities and out-of-vocabulary words by leveraging external resources such as DBpedia[13] and Wordnik.[14] In Spanish, the system equivalent to this run ranked second following a cross-lingual approach, by applying the English system to the translated version of the dataset (see 3.2).

The Table also shows the results of TakeLab, which was trained with all datasets from previous years. TakeLab would rank 18th, ten absolute points below the best system, a smaller difference than in 2013.

3.2 Spanish Subtask

The Spanish subtask attracted 9 teams with 22 participating systems, out of which 16 were supervised and 6 unsupervised. The participants were from both Spanish (Colombia, Cuba, Mexico, Spain), and non-Spanish speaking countries (two teams from France, Germany, Ireland, UK, US). The evaluation results appear in Table 4.

The top ranking system is the 2nd run of UMCC_DLSI_SemSim (Chavez et al., 2014), which achieves a weighted correlation of 0.807. It entails a cross-lingual approach, as it leverages a SVM-based English framework, by mapping the Spanish words to their English equivalent using the most common sense in WordNet 3.0. The classifier uses a combination of features, such as those derived from traditional knowledge-based ((Leacock and Chodorow, 1998; Wu and Palmer, 1994; Lin, 1998), and others) and corpus-based metrics (LSA (Landauer et al., 1997)), paired with lexical features (such as Dice-Similarity, Euclidean-distance, etc.). It is trained on a cumulative English STS dataset comprising train and test data released as part of tasks in SemEval2012 (Agirre et al., 2012) and *Sem 2013 (Agirre et al., 2013), as well as training data available from tasks 1 and 10 in SemEval 2014. Interestingly enough, run 2 of the system performs better than run 1, despite the fact that it uses half the features, and focuses on string based similarity measures only. This difference between runs is noticed on the Wikipedia dataset only, and it amounts to 4% Pearson correlation. While the system had a robust performance on the Spanish subtask, for English, its overall rank was 16, 18, and 33, respectively.

Coming in close at only 0.3% difference, is Meerkat-Mafia PairingAvg (run 2) (Kashyap et al., 2014), which also follows a cross-lingual approach, by applying the system the team developed for the English subtask to the translated version of the datasets (see 3.1). The interesting aspect of their work is that in their first submission (run 1), they only consider the similarity resulting from the sentence pair translation through the Google Translate service.[15] In the second run, they expand each sentence to 20 possible combinations by accounting for the multiple translation meanings of a given word, and considering the average similarity of all resulting pairs. While the first run achieves a weighted correlation of 73.8%,

[13] dbpedia.org

[14] wordnick.com

[15] translate.google.com

Run Name	System type	Wikipedia	News	Weighted mean	Rank
Bielefeld-SC-run1	unsupervised*	0.263	0.554	0.437	22
Bielefeld-SC-run2	unsupervised*	0.265	0.555	0.438	21
BUAP-run1	supervised	0.550	0.679	0.627	17
BUAP-run2	unsupervised	0.640	0.764	0.714	14
RTM-DCU-run1	supervised	0.422	0.700	0.588	18
RTM-DCU-run2	supervised	0.369	0.625	0.522	20
RTM-DCU-run3	supervised	0.424	0.641	0.554	19
LIPN-run1	supervised	0.652	0.826	0.756	11
LIPN-run2	supervised	0.716	0.832	0.785	6
LIPN-run3	supervised	0.716	0.809	0.771	10
Meerkat-Mafia-run1	unsupervised	0.668	0.785	0.738	13
Meerkat-Mafia-run2	unsupervised	0.743	**0.845**	0.804	2
Meerkat-Mafia-run3	supervised	0.738	0.822	0.788	5
TeamZ-run1	supervised	0.610	0.717	0.674	15
TeamZ-run2	supervised	0.604	0.710	0.667	16
UMCC-DLSI-run1	supervised	0.741	0.825	0.791	4
UMCC-DLSI-run2	supervised	0.7802	0.825	**0.807**	1
UNAL-NLP-run1	weakly supervised	**0.7803**	0.815	0.801	3
UNAL-NLP-run2	supervised	0.757	0.783	0.772	9
UNAL-NLP-run3	supervised	0.689	0.796	0.753	12
UoW-run1	supervised	0.748	0.800	0.779	7
UoW-run2	supervised	0.748	0.800	0.779	8

Table 4: Spanish evaluation results in terms of Pearson correlation.

the second one performs significantly better at 80.4%, indicating that the additional context may also include multiple instances of accurate translations, hence significantly impacting the overall similarity score. In English, the system equivalent to run 2 in Spanish, namely Meerkat Mafia-pairingWords, achieves a competitive ranked performance across all six datasets, ranking second, at an order of 10^{-4} distance from the top system. This supports the claim that, despite its unsupervised nature, the system is quite versatile and highly competitive with the top performing supervised frameworks, and that it may achieve an even higher performance in Spanish if accurate sentence translations were provided.

Overall, most systems were cross-lingual, relying on different translation approaches, such as 1) translating the test data into English (as the two systems above), and then exporting the score obtained for the English sentences back to Spanish, or 2) performing automatic translation of the English training data, and learning a classifier directly in Spanish. (Buscaldi et al., 2014) supplemented their training dataset with human annotations conducted in Spanish, using definition pairs extracted from a Spanish dictionary. A different angle was explored by (Rios, 2014), who proposed a multilingual framework using transfer learning across English and Spanish by training on traditional lexical, knowledge-based and corpus-based features. The semantic similarity task was approached from a monolingual perspective as well (Gupta, 2014), by focusing on Spanish resources, such as the trial data we released as part of the subtask, and the Spanish WordNet;[16] these were leveraged using meta-learning over variations of overlap-based metrics. Following the same line, (Biçici and Way, 2014) pursued language independent methods, who avoided relying on task or domain specific information through the usage of referential translation machines. This approach models textual semantic similarity as a decision in terms of translation quality between two datasets (in our case Spanish STS trial and test data) given relevant examples from an in-language reference corpus.

In comparison to the correlations obtained in the English subtask, where the highest weighted mean was 76.1%, for Spanish, we obtained 80.7%, probably due to the more formal nature of the datasets, since Wikipedia and news articles employ mostly well formed and grammatically correct sentences, and we selected all snippets to be longer than 8 words. The overall correlation scores obtained for English were hurt by the deft-forum data, which scored significantly lower (at a maximum correlation of 50.8%), when compared to all the other datasets whose correlation was higher than 70%. The OnWN data was most similar to our test sets, and it attained a maximum of 85.9%.

[16] grial.uab.es/descarregues.php

4 Conclusion

This year's STS task comprised a multilingual flair, by introducing Spanish datasets alongside the English ones. In English, the datasets sought to expose the participating teams to more diverse scenarios compared to the previous years, by introducing image descriptions, forum and newswire genre, and tweet-newswire headline mappings. For Spanish, two datasets were developed consisting of encyclopedic and newswire text acquired from Spanish sources. Overall, the English subtask attracted 15 teams (with 38 system variations), while the Spanish subtask had 9 teams (with 22 system runs). Most teams from the Spanish subtask have also submitted runs for the English evaluations.

Acknowledgments

The authors are grateful to Verónica Pérez-Rosas and Vanessa Loza for their help with the annotations for the Spanish subtask. This material is based in part upon work supported by National Science Foundation CAREER award #1361274 and IIS award #1018613, by DARPA-BAA-12-47 DEFT grant #12475008, and by MINECO CHIST-ERA READERS and SKATER projects (PCIN-2013-002-C02-01, TIN2012-38584-C06-02). Aitor Gonzalez Agirre is supported by a doctoral grant from MINECO. Any opinions, findings, and conclusions or recommendations expressed in this material are those of the authors and do not necessarily reflect the views of the National Science Foundation or the Defense Advanced Research Projects Agency.

References

Eneko Agirre and Enrique Amigó. In prep. Exploring evaluation measures for semantic textual similarity. In *Unpublished manuscript*.

Eneko Agirre, Daniel Cer, Mona Diab, and Aitor Gonzalez-Agirre. 2012. Semeval-2012 task 6: A pilot on semantic textual similarity. In **SEM 2012: The First Joint Conference on Lexical and Computational Semantics – Volume 1: Proceedings of the main conference and the shared task, and Volume 2: Proceedings of the Sixth International Workshop on Semantic Evaluation (SemEval 2012)*, pages 385–393, Montréal, Canada, 7-8 June.

Eneko Agirre, Daniel Cer, Mona Diab, Aitor Gonzalez-Agirre, and Weiwei Guo. 2013. *SEM 2013 Shared Task: Semantic textual similarity, including a pilot on typed-similarity. In *The Second Joint Conference on Lexical and Computational Semantics (*SEM 2013)*, pages 32–43.

Clive Best, Erik van der Goot, Ken Blackler, Tefilo Garcia, and David Horby. 2005. Europe media monitor - system description. In *EUR Report 22173-En*, Ispra, Italy.

Ergun Biçici and Andy Way. 2014. RTM-DCU: Referential translation machines for semantic similarity. In *Proceedings of the 8th International Workshop on Semantic Evaluation (SemEval-2014)*, Dublin, Ireland.

Davide Buscaldi, Jorge J. Garcia Flores, Joseph Le Roux, Nadi Tomeh, and Belem Priego Sanchez. 2014. LIPN: Introducing a new geographical context similarity measure and a statistical similarity measure based on the Bhattacharyya coefficient. In *Proceedings of the 8th International Workshop on Semantic Evaluation (SemEval-2014)*, Dublin, Ireland.

Alexander Chavez, Hector Davila, Yoan Gutierrez, Antonio Fernandez-Orquin, Andrés Montoyo, and Rafael Munoz. 2014. UMCC_DLSI_SemSim: Multilingual system for measuring semantic textual similarity. In *Proceedings of the 8th International Workshop on Semantic Evaluation (SemEval-2014)*, Dublin, Ireland.

Christiane Fellbaum. 1998. *WordNet - An electronic lexical database*. MIT Press.

Weiwei Guo, Hao Li, Heng Ji, and Mona Diab. 2013. Linking tweets to news: A framework to enrich online short text data in social media. In *Proceedings of the 51th Annual Meeting of the Association for Computational Linguistics*, pages 239–249.

Anubhav Gupta. 2014. TeamZ: Measuring semantic textual similarity for Spanish using an overlap-based approach. In *Proceedings of the 8th International Workshop on Semantic Evaluation (SemEval-2014)*, Dublin, Ireland.

Eduard Hovy, Mitchell Marcus, Martha Palmer, Lance Ramshaw, and Ralph Weischedel. 2006. OntoNotes: The 90% solution. In *Proceedings of the Human Language Technology Conference of the North American Chapter of the ACL*, pages 57–60.

Sergio Jimenez, George Dueñas, Julia Baquero, and Alexander Gelbukh. 2014. UNAL-NLP: Combining soft cardinality features for semantic textual similarity, relatedness and entailment. In *Proceedings of the 8th International Workshop on Semantic Evaluation (SemEval-2014)*, Dublin, Ireland.

Abhay Kashyap, Lushan Han, Roberto Yus, Jennifer Sleeman, Taneeya Satyapanich, Sunil Gandhi, and Tim Finin. 2014. Meerkat Mafia: Multilingual and cross-level semantic textual similarity systems. In *Proceedings of the 8th International Workshop on*

Semantic Evaluation (SemEval-2014), Dublin, Ireland.

Thomas K. Landauer, Darrell Laham, Bob Rehder, and M. E. Schreiner. 1997. How well can passage meaning be derived without using word order? A comparison of latent semantic analysis and humans. *Cognitive Science*.

Claudia Leacock and Martin Chodorow. 1998. Combining local context and WordNet similarity for word sense identification. In *WordNet: An Electronic Lexical Database*, pages 305–332.

Dekang Lin. 1998. An information-theoretic definition of similarity. In *Proceedings of the Fifteenth International Conference on Machine Learning*, pages 296–304, Madison, Wisconsin.

André Lynum, Partha Pakray, Björn Gambäck, and Sergio Jimenez. 2014. NTNU: Measuring semantic similarity with sublexical feature representations and soft cardinality. In *Proceedings of the 8th International Workshop on Semantic Evaluation (SemEval-2014)*, Dublin, Ireland.

Juan Martinez-Romo, Lourdes Araujo, Javier Borge-Holthoefer, Alex Arenas, José A. Capitán, and José A. Cuesta. 2011. Disentangling categorical relationships through a graph of co-occurrences. *Phys. Rev. E*, 84:046108, Oct.

John P. McCrae, Philipp Cimiano, and Roman Klinger. 2013. Orthonormal explicit topic analysis for cross-lingual document matching. In *Proceedings of the 2013 Conference on Empirical Methods in Natural Language Processing*, pages 1732–1740, Seattle, Washington, USA.

Francesco Pozzi, Tiziana Di Matteo, and Tomaso Aste. 2012. Exponential smoothing weighted correlations. *The European Physical Journal B*, 85(6).

William H. Press, Saul A. Teukolsky, William T. Vetterling, and Brian P. Flannery. 2002. *Numerical recipes: The art of scientific computing V 2.10 with Linux or single-screen license*. Cambridge University Press.

Thomas Proisi, Stefan Evert, Paul Greiner, and Besim Kabashi. 2014. SemantiKLUE: Robust semantic similarity at multiple levels using maximum weight matching. In *Proceedings of the 8th International Workshop on Semantic Evaluation (SemEval-2014)*, Dublin, Ireland.

Cyrus Rashtchian, Peter Young, Micah Hodosh, and Julia Hockenmaier. 2010. Collecting image annotations using Amazon's Mechanical Turk. In *Proceedings of the NAACL HLT 2010 Workshop on Creating Speech and Language Data with Amazon's Mechanical Turk*, CSLDAMT '10, pages 139–147, Stroudsburg, PA, USA.

Miguel Rios. 2014. UoW: Multi-task learning Gaussian process for semantic textual similarity. In *Proceedings of the 8th International Workshop on Semantic Evaluation (SemEval-2014)*, Dublin, Ireland.

Richard Socher, Andrej Karpathy, Quoc V. Le, Christopher D. Manning, and Andrew Y. Ng. 2014. Grounded compositional semantics for finding and describing images with sentences. *Transactions of the Association for Computational Linguistics*, pages 207–218.

Md Arafat Sultan, Steven Bethard, and Tamara Sumner. 2014a. Back to basics for monolingual alignment: Exploiting word similarity and contextual evidence. *Transactions of the Association for Computational Linguistics*, 2:219–230.

Md Arafat Sultan, Steven Bethard, and Tamara Sumner. 2014b. DLS@CU: Sentence similarity from word aligment. In *Proceedings of the 8th International Workshop on Semantic Evaluation (SemEval-2014)*, Dublin, Ireland.

Darnes Vilariño, David Pinto, Saúl León, Mireya Tovar, and Beatriz Beltrán. 2014. BUAP: Evaluating features for multilingual and cross-level semantic textual similarity. In *Proceedings of the 8th International Workshop on Semantic Evaluation (SemEval-2014)*, Dublin, Ireland.

Ngoc Phuoc An Vo, Tommaso Caselli, and Octavian Popescu. 2014. FBK-TR: Applying SVM with multiple linguistic features for cross-level semantic similarity. In *Proceedings of the 8th International Workshop on Semantic Evaluation (SemEval-2014)*, Dublin, Ireland.

Frane Šarić, Goran Glavaš, Mladen Karan, Jan Šnajder, and Bojana Dalbelo Bašić. 2012. Takelab: Systems for measuring semantic text similarity. In *Proceedings of the Sixth International Workshop on Semantic Evaluation (SemEval 2012)*, pages 441–448, Montréal, Canada, 7-8 June.

Zhibiao Wu and Martha Palmer. 1994. Verbs semantics and lexical selection. In *Proceedings of the 32nd annual meeting on Association for Computational Linguistics*, pages 133–138, Las Cruces, New Mexico.

AI-KU: Using Co-Occurrence Modeling for Semantic Similarity

Osman Başkaya
Artificial Intelligence Laboratory
Koç University, Istanbul, Turkey
obaskaya@ku.edu.tr

Abstract

In this paper, we describe our unsupervised method submitted to the Cross-Level Semantic Similarity task in Semeval 2014 that computes semantic similarity between two different sized text fragments. Our method models each text fragment by using the co-occurrence statistics of either occurred words or their substitutes. The co-occurrence modeling step provides dense, low-dimensional embedding for each fragment which allows us to calculate semantic similarity using various similarity metrics. Although our current model avoids the syntactic information, we achieved promising results and outperformed all baselines.

1 Introduction

Semantic similarity is a measure that specifies the similarity of one text's meaning to another's. Semantic similarity plays an important role in various Natural Language Processing (NLP) tasks such as textual entailment (Berant et al., 2012), summarization (Lin and Hovy, 2003), question answering (Surdeanu et al., 2011), text classification (Sebastiani, 2002), word sense disambiguation (Schütze, 1998) and information retrieval (Park et al., 2005).

There are three main approaches to computing the semantic similarity between two text fragments. The first approach uses Vector Space Models (see Turney & Pantel (2010) for an overview) where each text is represented as a bag-of-word model. The similarity between two text fragments can then be computed with various metrics such as cosine similarity. Sparseness in the input nature is the key problem for these models. Therefore, later works such as Latent Semantic Indexing (**?**) and Topic Models (Blei et al., 2003) overcome sparsity problems via reducing the dimensionality of the model by introducing latent variables. The second approach blends various lexical and syntactic features and attacks the problem through machine learning models. The third approach is based on word-to-word similarity alignment (Pilehvar et al., 2013; Islam and Inkpen, 2008).

The Cross-Level Semantic Similarity (CLSS) task in SemEval 2014[1] (Jurgens et al., 2014) provides an evaluation framework to assess similarity methods for texts in different volumes (i.e., lexical levels). Unlike previous SemEval and *SEM tasks that were interested in comparing texts with similar volume, this task consists of four subtasks (paragraph2sentence, sentence2phrase, phrase2word and word2sense) that investigate the performance of systems based on pairs of texts of different sizes. A system should report the similarity score of a given pair, ranging from 4 (two items have very similar meanings and the most important ideas, concepts, or actions in the larger text are represented in the smaller text) to 0 (two items do not mean the same thing and are not on the same topic).

In this paper, we describe our two unsupervised systems that are based on co-occurrence statistics of words. The only difference between the systems is the input they use. The first system uses the words directly (after lemmatization, stop-word removal and excluding the non-alphanumeric characters) in text while the second system utilizes the most likely substitutes consulted by a 4-gram language model for each observed word position (i.e., context). Note that we participated two subtasks which are paragraph2sentence and sentence2phrase.

The remainder of the paper proceeds as follows. Section 2 explains the preprocessing part, the difference between the systems, co-occurrence modeling, and how we calculate the similarity between

[1] http://alt.qcri.org/semeval2014/task3/

Proceedings of the 8th International Workshop on Semantic Evaluation (SemEval 2014), pages 92–96,
Dublin, Ireland, August 23-24, 2014.

Type-ID	Lemma
Sent-33	choose
Sent-33	buy
Sent-33	gift
Sent-33	card
Sent-33	hard
Sent-33	decision

Table 1: Instance id-word pairs for a given sentence.

two texts after co-occurrence modeling has been done. Section 3 discusses the results of our systems and compares them to other participants'. Section 4 discusses the findings and concludes with plans for future work.

2 Algorithm

This section explains preprocessing steps of the data and the details of our two systems[2]. Both systems rely on the co-occurrence statistics. The slight difference between the two is that the first one uses the words that occur in the given text fragment (e.g., paragraph, sentence), whereas the latter employs co-occurrence statistics on 100 substitute samples for each word within the given text fragment.

2.1 Data Preprocessing

Two AI-KU systems can be distinguished by their inputs. One uses the raw input words, whereas the other uses words' likely substitutes according to a language model.

AI-KU$_1$: This system uses the words that were in the text. All words are transformed into lower-case equivalents. Lemmatization[3] and stop-word removal were performed, and non-alphanumeric characters were excluded. Table 1 displays the pairs for the following sentence which is an instance from paragraph2sentence test set:

> "Choosing what to buy with a $35 gift card is a hard decision."

Note that the input that we used to model co-occurrence statistics consists of all such pairs for each fragment in a given subtask.

[2]The code to replicate our work can be found at `https://github.com/osmanbaskaya/semeval14-task3`.

[3]Lemmatization is carried out with Stanford CoreNLP and transforms a word into its canonical or base form.

AI-KU$_2$: Previously, the utilization of high probability substitutes and their co-occurrence statistics achieved notable performance on Word Sense Induction (WSI) (Baskaya et al., 2013) and Part-of-Speech Induction (Yatbaz et al., 2012) problems. AI-KU$_2$ represents each context of a word by finding the most likely 100 substitutes suggested by the 4-gram language model we built from ukWaC[4] (Ferraresi et al., 2008), a 2-billion word web-gathered corpus. Since S-CODE algorithm works with discrete input, for each context we sample 100 substitute words with replacement using their probabilities. Table 2 illustrates the context and substitutes of each context using a bigram language model. No lemmatization, stop-word removal and lower-case transformation were performed.

2.2 Co-Occurrence Modeling

This subsection will explain the unsupervised method we employed to model co-occurrence statistics: the Co-occurrence data Embedding (CODE) method (Globerson et al., 2007) and its spherical extension (S-CODE) proposed by Maron et al. (2010). Unlike in our WSI work, where we ended up with an embedding for each word in the co-occurrence modeling step in this task, we model each text unit such as a paragraph, a sentence or a phrase, to obtain embeddings for each instance.

Input data for S-CODE algorithm consist of instance-id and each word in the text unit for the first system (Table 1 illustrates the pairs for only one text fragment) instance-ids and 100 substitute samples of each word in text for the second system. In the initial step, S-CODE puts all instance-ids and words (or substitutes, depending on the system) randomly on an n-dimensional sphere. If two different instances have the same word or substitute, then these two instances attract one another — otherwise they repel each other. When S-CODE converges, instances that have similar words or substitutes will be closely located or else, they will be distant from each other.

AI-KU$_1$: According to the training set performances for various n (i.e., number of dimensions for S-CODE algorithm), we picked 100 for both tasks.

AI-KU$_2$: We picked n to be 200 and 100 for paragraph2sentence and sentence2phrase subtasks, respectively.

[4]Available here: http://wacky.sslmit.unibo.it

Word	Context	Substitutes
the	<s> ___ dog	The (0.12), A (0.11), If (0.02), As (0.07), Stray (0.001),..., w_n (0.02)
dog	the ___	cat (0.007), dog (0.005), animal (0.002), wolve (0.001), ..., w_n (0.01)
bites	dog ___ .	runs (0.14), bites (0.13), catches (0.04), barks (0.001), ..., w_n (0.01)

Table 2: Contexts and substitute distributions when a bigram language model is used. w and n denote an arbitrary word in the vocabulary and the vocabulary size, respectively.

	System	Pearson	Spearman
Paragraph-2-Sentence	$AI\text{-}KU_1$	0.671	0.676
	$AI\text{-}KU_2$	0.542	0.531
	LCS	0.499	0.602
	lch	0.584	0.596
	lin	0.568	0.562
	JI	0.613	0.644

Table 3: Paragraph-2-Sentence subtask scores for the training data. Subscripts in AI-KU systems specify the run number.

	System	Pearson	Spearman
Sentence-2-Phrase	$AI\text{-}KU_1$	0.607	0.568
	$AI\text{-}KU_2$	0.620	0.579
	LCS	0.500	0.582
	lch	0.484	0.491
	lin	0.492	0.470
	JI	0.465	0.465

Table 4: Sentence2phrase subtask scores for the training data.

Since this step is unsupervised, we tried to enrich the data with ukWaC, however, enrichment with ukWaC did not work well on the training data. To this end, proposed scores were obtained using only the training and the test data provided by organizers.

2.3 Similarity Calculation

When the S-CODE converges, there is an n-dimensional embedding for each textual level (e.g., paragraph, sentence, phrase) instance. We can use a similarity metric to calculate the similarity between these embeddings. For this task, systems should report only the similarity between two specific cross level instances. Note that we used cosine similarity to calculate similarity between two textual units. This similarity is the eventual similarity for two instances; no further processing (e.g., scaling) has been done.

In this task, two correlation metrics were used to evaluate the systems: Pearson correlation and Spearman's rank correlation. Pearson correlation tests the degree of similarity between the system's similarity ratings and the gold standard ratings. Spearman's rank correlation measures the degree of similarity between two rankings; similarity ratings provided by a system and the gold standard ratings.

3 Evaluation Results

Tables 3 and 4 show the scores for Paragraph-2-Sentence and Sentence-2-Phrase subtasks on the training data, respectively. These tables contain the best individual scores for the performance metrics, Normalized Longest Common Substring (LCS) baseline, which was given by task organizers, and three additional baselines: lin (Lin, 1998), lch (Leacock and Chodorow, 1998), and the Jaccard Index (JI) baseline. lin uses the information content (Resnik, 1995) of the least common subsumer of concepts A and B. Information content (IC) indicates the specificity of a concept; the least common subsumer of a concept A and B is the most specific concept from which A and B are inherited. lin similarity[5] returns the difference between two times of the IC of the least common subsumer of A and B, and the sum of IC of both concepts. On the other hand, lch is a score denoting how similar two concepts are, calculated by using the shortest path that connects the concept and the maximum depth of the taxonomy in which the concepts occur[6] (please see Pedersen et al. (2004) for further details of these measures). These two baselines were calculated as follows. First, using the Stan-

[5]lin similarity $= 2 * IC(lcs)/(IC(A) + IC(B))$ where lcs indicates the least common subsumer of concepts A and B.

[6]The exact formulation is $-log(L/2d)$ where L is the shortest path length and d is the taxonomy depth.

	System	Pearson	Spearman
Paragraph-2-Sentence	Best	0.837	0.821
	2nd Best	0.834	0.820
	3rd Best	0.826	0.817
	AI-KU_1	0.732	0.727
	AI-KU_2	0.698	0.700
	LCS	0.527	0.613
	lch	0.629	0.627
	lin	0.612	0.601
	JI	0.640	0.687

Table 5: Paragraph-2-Sentence subtask scores for the test data. *Best* indicates the best correlation score for the subtask. LCS stands for Normalized Longest Common Substring. Subscripts in AI-KU systems specify the run number.

ford Part-of-Speech Tagger (Toutanova and Manning, 2000) we tagged words across all textual levels. After tagging, we found the synsets of each word matched with its part-of-speech using WordNet 3.0 (Miller and Fellbaum, 1998). For each synset of a word in the shorter textual unit (e.g., sentence is shorter than paragraph), we calculated the lin/lch measure of each synset of all words in the longer textual unit and picked the highest score. When we found the scores for all words, we calculated the mean to find out the similarity between one pair in the test set. Finally, Jaccard Index baseline was used to simply calculate the number of words in common (intersection) with two cross textual levels, normalized by the total number of words (union). Table 5 and 6 demonstrate the AI-KU runs on the test data. Next, we present our results pertaining to the test data.

Paragraph2Sentence: Both systems outperformed all the baselines for both metrics. The best score for this subtask was .837 and our systems achieved .732 and .698 on Pearson and did similar on Spearman metric. These scores are promising since our current unsupervised systems are based on bag-of-words approach — they do not utilize any syntactic information.

Sentence2Phrase: In this subtask, AI-KU systems outperformed all baselines with the exception of the AI-KU_2 system which performed slightly worse than LCS on Spearman metric. Performances of systems and baselines were lower than Paragraph2Sentence subtask, since smaller textual units (such as phrases) make the problem more difficult.

	System	Pearson	Spearman
Sentence-2-Phrase	Best	0.777	0.642
	2nd Best	0.771	0.760
	3rd Best	0.760	0.757
	AI-KU_1	0.680	0.646
	AI-KU_2	0.617	0.612
	LCS	0.562	0.626
	lch	0.526	0.544
	lin	0.501	0.498
	JI	0.540	0.555

Table 6: Sentence2phrase subtask scores for the test data.

4 Conclusion

In this work, we introduced two unsupervised systems that utilize co-occurrence statistics and represent textual units as dense, low dimensional embeddings. Although current systems are based on bag-of-word approach and discard the syntactic information, they achieved promising results in both paragraph2sentence and sentence2phrase subtasks. For future work, we will extend our algorithm by adding syntactic information (e.g, dependency parsing output) into the co-occurrence modeling step.

References

Osman Baskaya, Enis Sert, Volkan Cirik, and Deniz Yuret. 2013. AI-KU: Using substitute vectors and co-occurrence modeling for word sense induction and disambiguation. In *Proceedings of the Second Joint Conference on Lexical and Computational Semantics (*SEM), Volume 2: Seventh International Workshop on Semantic Evaluation (SemEval 2013)*, pages 300–306.

Jonathan Berant, Ido Dagan, and Jacob Goldberger. 2012. Learning entailment relations by global graph structure optimization. *Computational Linguistics*, 38(1):73–111.

David M. Blei, Andrew Y. Ng, and Michael I. Jordan. 2003. Latent dirichlet allocation. *The Journal of Machine Learning Research*, 3:993–1022.

Adriano Ferraresi, Eros Zanchetta, Marco Baroni, and Silvia Bernardini. 2008. Introducing and evaluating ukwac, a very large web-derived corpus of english. In *In Proceedings of the 4th Web as Corpus Workshop (WAC-4)*.

Amir Globerson, Gal Chechik, Fernando Pereira, and Naftali Tishby. 2007. Euclidean embedding of co-occurrence data. *Journal of Machine Learning Research*, 8(10).

Aminul Islam and Diana Inkpen. 2008. Semantic text similarity using corpus-based word similarity and string similarity. *ACM Transactions on Knowledge Discovery from Data (TKDD)*, 2(2):10.

David Jurgens, Mohammed Taher Pilehvar, and Roberto Navigli. 2014. Semeval-2014 task 3: Cross-level semantic similarity. In *Proceedings of the 8th International Workshop on Semantic Evaluation (SemEval-2014). August 23-24, 2014, Dublin, Ireland.*

Claudia Leacock and Martin Chodorow. 1998. Combining local context and wordnet similarity for word sense identification. *WordNet: An electronic lexical database*, 49(2):265–283.

Chin-Yew Lin and Eduard Hovy. 2003. Automatic evaluation of summaries using n-gram co-occurrence statistics. In *Proceedings of the 2003 Conference of the North American Chapter of the Association for Computational Linguistics on Human Language Technology-Volume 1*, pages 71–78.

Dekang Lin. 1998. An information-theoretic definition of similarity. In *ICML*, volume 98, pages 296–304.

Yariv Maron, Michael Lamar, and Elie Bienenstock. 2010. Sphere Embedding: An Application to Part-of-Speech Induction. In J Lafferty, C K I Williams, J Shawe-Taylor, R S Zemel, and A Culotta, editors, *Advances in Neural Information Processing Systems 23*, pages 1567–1575.

George Miller and Christiane Fellbaum. 1998. Wordnet: An electronic lexical database.

Eui-Kyu Park, Dong-Yul Ra, and Myung-Gil Jang. 2005. Techniques for improving web retrieval effectiveness. *Information processing & management*, 41(5):1207–1223.

Ted Pedersen, Siddharth Patwardhan, and Jason Michelizzi. 2004. Wordnet:: Similarity: measuring the relatedness of concepts. In *Demonstration Papers at HLT-NAACL 2004*, pages 38–41.

Mohammad Taher Pilehvar, David Jurgens, and Roberto Navigli. 2013. Align, disambiguate and walk: A unified approach for measuring semantic similarity. In *Proceedings of the 51st Annual Meeting of the Association for Computational Linguistics (ACL 2013).*

Philip Resnik. 1995. Using information content to evaluate semantic similarity in a taxonomy. *arXiv preprint cmp-lg/9511007.*

Hinrich Schütze. 1998. Automatic word sense discrimination. *Computational Linguistics*, 24(1):97–123.

Fabrizio Sebastiani. 2002. Machine learning in automated text categorization. *ACM computing surveys (CSUR)*, 34(1):1–47.

Mihai Surdeanu, Massimiliano Ciaramita, and Hugo Zaragoza. 2011. Learning to rank answers to non-factoid questions from web collections. *Computational Linguistics*, 37(2):351–383.

Kristina Toutanova and Christopher D Manning. 2000. Enriching the knowledge sources used in a maximum entropy part-of-speech tagger. In *Proceedings of the 2000 Joint SIGDAT conference on Empirical methods in natural language processing and very large corpora: held in conjunction with the 38th Annual Meeting of the Association for Computational Linguistics-Volume 13*, pages 63–70.

Peter D. Turney and Patrick Pantel. 2010. From Frequency to Meaning: Vector Space Models of Semantics. *Journal of Artificial Intelligence Research*, 37:141–188.

Mehmet Ali Yatbaz, Enis Sert, and Deniz Yuret. 2012. Learning syntactic categories using paradigmatic representations of word context. In *Proceedings of the 2012 Joint Conference on Empirical Methods in Natural Language Processing and Computational Natural Language Learning*, pages 940–951.

Alpage: Transition-based Semantic Graph Parsing with Syntactic Features

Corentin Ribeyre[⋆ ◦] **Eric Villemonte de la Clergerie**[⋆] **Djamé Seddah**[⋆ ⋄]
[⋆]Alpage, INRIA
[◦]Univ Paris Diderot, Sorbonne Paris Cité
[⋄] Université Paris Sorbonne
firstname.lastname@inria.fr

Abstract

This paper describes the systems deployed by the ALPAGE team to participate to the *SemEval-2014 Task on Broad-Coverage Semantic Dependency Parsing*. We developed two transition-based dependency parsers with extended sets of actions to handle non-planar acyclic graphs. For the open track, we worked over two orthogonal axes – lexical and syntactic – in order to provide our models with lexical and syntactic features such as word clusters, lemmas and tree fragments of different types.

1 Introduction

In recent years, we have seen the emergence of semantic parsing, relying on various techniques ranging from graph grammars (Chiang et al., 2013) to transitions-based dependency parsers (Sagae and Tsujii, 2008). Assuming that obtaining predicate argument structures is a necessary goal to move from syntax to accurate surface semantics, the question of the representation of such structures arises. Regardless of the annotation scheme that should be used, one of the main issues of semantic representation is the construction of graph structures, that are inherently harder to generate than the classical tree structures.

In that aspect, the shared task's proposal (Oepen et al., 2014), to evaluate different syntactic-semantic schemes (Ivanova et al., 2012; Hajic et al., 2006; Miyao and Tsujii, 2004) could not arrive at a more timely moment when state-of-the-art surface syntactic parsers regularly reach, or cross, a 90% labeled dependency recovery plateau for a wide range of languages (Nivre et al., 2007a; Seddah et al., 2013).

The two systems we present both extend transition-based parsers in order to be able to generate acyclic dependency graphs. The first one follows the standard greedy search mechanism of (Nivre et al., 2007b), while the second one follows a slightly more global search strategy (Huang and Sagae, 2010; Goldberg et al., 2013) by relying on dynamic programming techniques. In addition to building graphs directly, the main originality of our work lies in the use of different kinds of syntactic features, showing that using syntax for pure deep semantic parsing improves global performance by more than two points.

Although not state-of-the-art, our systems perform very honorably compared with other single systems in this shared task and pave quite an interesting way for further work. In the remainder of this paper, we present the parsers and their extensions for building graphs; we then present our syntactic features and discuss our results.

2 Systems Description

Shift-reduce transition-based parsers essentially rely on *configurations* formed of a stack and a buffer, with stack transitions used to go from a configuration to the next one, until reaching a final configuration. Following Kübler et al. (2009), we define a configuration by $c = (\sigma, \beta, A)$ where σ denotes a stack of words w_i, β a buffer of words, and A a set of dependency arcs of the form (w_i, r, w_j), with w_i the head, w_j the dependent, and r a label in some set R.

However, despite their overall similarities, transition-based systems may differ on many aspects, such as the exact definition of the configurations, the set of transitions extracted from the configurations, the way the search space is explored (at parsing and training time), the set of features, the way the transition weights are learned and ap-

Proceedings of the 8th International Workshop on Semantic Evaluation (SemEval 2014), pages 97–103, Dublin, Ireland, August 23-24, 2014.

$(\sigma, w_i\|\beta, A)$	$\vdash$	$(\sigma\|w_i, \beta, A)$	(shift)	BOTH
$(\sigma\|w_j\|w_i, \beta, A)$	$\vdash$	$(\sigma\|w_i, \beta, A \cup (w_i, r, w_j))$	(left-reduce)	S&T PARSER
$(\sigma\|w_j\|w_i, \beta, A)$	$\vdash$	$(\sigma\|w_j, \beta, A \cup (w_j, r, w_i))$	(right-reduce)	S&T PARSER
$(\sigma\|w_j\|w_i, \beta, A)$	$\vdash$	$(\sigma\|w_j\|w_i, \beta, A \cup (w_i, r, w_j))$	(left-attach)	BOTH
$(\sigma\|w_j\|w_i, \beta, A)$	$\vdash$	$(\sigma\|w_j, w_i\|\beta, A \cup (w_j, r, w_i)$	(right-attach)	BOTH
$(\sigma\|w_i, \beta, A)$	$\vdash$	(σ, β, A)	(pop0)	BOTH
$(\sigma\|w_j\|w_i, \beta, A)$	$\vdash$	$(\sigma\|w_i, \beta, A)$	(pop1)	DYALOG-SR
$(\sigma\|w_j\|w_i, \beta, A)$	$\vdash$	$(\sigma\|w_i\|w_j, \beta, A)$	(swap)	DYALOG-SR

Figure 1: An extended set of transitions for building dependency graphs.

plied, etc.

For various reasons, we started our experiments with two rather different transition-based parsers, which have finally converged on several aspects. In particular, the main convergence concerns the set of transitions needed to parse the three proposed annotation schemes. To be able to attach zero, one, or more heads to a word, it is necessary to clearly dissociate the addition of a dependency from the reduction of a word (i.e. its removal from the stack). Following Sagae and Tsujii (2008), as shown in Figure 1, beside the usual shift and reduce transitions of the *arc-standard* strategy, we introduced the new left and right attach actions for adding new dependencies (while keeping the dependent on the stack) and two reduce `pop0` and `pop1` actions to remove a word from the stack after attachement of its dependents. All transitions adding an edge should also satisfy the condition that the new edge does not create a cycle or multiple edges between the same pair of nodes. It is worth noting that the pop actions may also be used to remove words with no heads.

2.1 Sagae & Tsujii's DAG Parser

Our first parsing system is a partial rewrite, with several extensions, of the Sagae and Tsujii (2008) DAG parser (henceforth S&T PARSER). We modified it to handle dependency graphs, in particular non-governed words using `pop0` transitions. This new transition removes the topmost stack element when all its dependents have been attached (through attach or reduce transitions). Thus, we can handle partially connected graphs, since a word can be discarded when it has no incoming arc.

We used two different learning algorithms: (i) the averaged perceptron because of its good balance between training time and performance (Daume, 2006), (ii) the logistic regression model (maximum entropy (Ratnaparkhi, 1997)). For the latter, we used the truncated gradient optimization (Langford et al., 2009), implemented in Classias (Okazaki, 2009), in order to estimate the parameters. These algorithms have been used interchangeably to test their performance in terms of F-score. But the difference was negligeable in general.

2.2 DYALOG-SR

Our second parsing system is DYALOG-SR (Villemonte De La Clergerie, 2013), which has been developed to participate to the SPMRL'13 shared task. Coded on top of tabular logic programming system DYALOG, it implements a transition-based parser relying on dynamic programming techniques, beams, and an averaged structured perceptron, following ideas from (Huang and Sagae, 2010; Goldberg et al., 2013).

It was initially designed to follow an *arc-standard* parsing strategy, relying on shift and left/right reduce transitions. To deal with dependency graphs and non governed words, we first added the two `attach` transitions and the `pop0` transition. But because there exist some overlap between the reduce and attach transitions leading to some spurious ambiguities, we finally decided to remove the left/right reduce transitions and to complete with the `pop1` transition. In order to handle some cases of non-projectivty with minimal modifications of the system, we also added a `swap` transition. The parsing strategy is now closer to the *arc-eager* one, with an oracle suggesting to attach as soon as possible.

2.3 Tree Approximations

In order to stack several dependency parsers, we needed to transform our graphs into trees. We report here the algorithms we used.

The first one uses a simple strategy. For nodes with multiple incoming edges, we keep the longest incoming edge. Singleton nodes (with no head) are attached with a `_void_`-labeled edge (by decreasing priority) to the immediately adjacent

Word_{σ_1}	Lemma_{σ_1}	POS_{σ_1}
$\text{leftPOS}_{\sigma_1}$	$\text{rightPOS}_{\sigma_1}$	$\text{leftLabel}_{\sigma_1}$
$\text{rightLabel}_{\sigma_1}$	Word_{σ_2}	Lemma_{σ_2}
POS_{σ_2}	$\text{leftPOS}_{\sigma_2}$	$\text{rightPOS}_{\sigma_2}$
$\text{leftLabel}_{\sigma_2}$	$\text{rightLabel}_{\sigma_2}$	Word_{σ_3}
POS_{σ_3}	Word_{β_1}	Lemma_{β_1}
POS_{β_1}	Word_{β_2}	Lemma_{β_2}
POS_{β_2}	POS_{β_3}	$a\ d_{12}\ d'_{11}$

Table 1: Baseline features for S&T PARSER.

node N, or the virtual root node (token 0). This strategy already improves over the baseline, provided by the task organisers, on the PCEDT by 5 points.

The second algorithm tries to preserve more edges: when it is possible, the deletion of a reentrant edge is replaced by reversing its direction and changing its label l into $<l$. We do this for nodes with no incoming edges by reversing the longest edge only if this action does not create cycles. The number of labels increases, but many more edges are kept, leading to better results on DM and PAS corpora.

3 Feature Engineering

3.1 Closed Track

For S&T PARSER we define Word_{β_i} (resp. Lemma_{β_i} and POS_{β_i}) as the word (resp. lemma and part-of-speech) at position i in the queue. The same goes for σ_i, which is the position i in the stack. Let $d_{i,j}$ be the distance between Word_{σ_i} and Word_{σ_j}. We also define $d'_{i,j}$, the distance between Word_{β_i} and Word_{σ_j}. In addition, we define $\text{leftPOS}_{\sigma_i}$ (resp. $\text{leftLabel}_{\sigma_i}$) the part-of-speech (resp. the label if any) of the word immediately at the left handside of σ_i, and the same goes for $\text{rightPOS}_{\sigma_i}$ (resp. $\text{rightLabel}_{\sigma_i}$). Finally, a is the previous predicted action by the parser. Table 1 reports our baseline features.

For DYALOG-SR we have the following *lexical features* `lex`, `lemma`, `cat`, and morphosyntactic `mstag`. They apply to next unread word (`*I`, say `lemmaI`), the three next lookahead words (`*I2` to `*I4`), and (when present) to the 3 stack elements (`*0` to `*2`), their two leftmost and rightmost children (*before* `b[01]*[012]` and *after* `a[01]*[012]`). We have *dependency features* such as the labels of the two leftmost and rightmost edges (`[ab][01]label[012]`), the left and right *valency* (number of dependency, `[ab]v[012]`) and *domains* (set of dependency labels, `[ab]d[012]`). Finally, we have 3 (discretized) *distance features* between the next word and the stack elements (`delta[01]`) and between the two topmost stack elements (`delta01`). Most feature values are atomic (either numerical or symbolic), but they can also be (recursively) a list of values, for instance for the `mstag` and *domain* features. For dealing with graphs, features were added about the incoming edges to the 3 topmost stack elements, similar to valency (`ngov`[012]) and domain (`gov[012]`). For the PCEDT scheme, because of the high number of dependency labels, the 30 most unfrequent ones were replaced by a generic label when used as feature value.

Besides, for the PCEDT and DM corpora, static and dynamic guiding features have been tried for DYALOG-SR, provided by MATE (Bohnet, 2010) (trained on versions of these corpora projected to trees, using a 10-fold cross validation). The two static features `mate_label` and `mate_distance` are attached to each token h, indicating the label and the relative distance to its governor d (if any). At runtime, dynamic features are also added relative to the current configuration: if a semantic dependency (h, l, d) has been predicted by MATE, and the topmost 2 stack elements are either (h, d) or (d, h), a feature suggesting a left or right attachment for l is added.

We did the same for S&T PARSER, except that we used a simple but efficient hack: instead of keeping the labels predicted by our parser, we replaced them by MATE predictions whenever it was possible.

3.2 Open Track

For this track, we combined the previously described features (but the MATE-related ones) with various lexical and syntactic features, our intuition being that syntax and semantic are interdependent, and that syntactic features should therefore help semantic parsing. In particular, we have considered the following bits of information.

Unsupervized Brown clusters To reduce lexical sparsity, we extracted 1,000 clusters from the BNC (Leech, 1992) preprocessed following Wagner et al. (2007). We extended them with capitalization, digit features and 3 letters suffix signatures, leading to a vocabulary size reduced by half.

Constituent tree fragments They were part of the companion data provided by the organizers.

They consist of fragments of the syntactic trees and can be used either as enhanced parts of speech or as features.

Spinal elementary trees A full set of parses was reconstructed from the tree fragments. Then we extracted a *spine grammar* (Seddah, 2010), using the head percolation table of the Bikel (2002) parser, slightly modified to avoid determiners to be marked as head in some configurations.

Predicted MATE dependencies Also provided in the companion data, they consist in the parses built by the MATE parsers, trained on the Stanford dependency version of the PTB. We combined the labels with a distance $\delta = t - h$ where t is the token number and h the head number.

Constituent head paths Inspired by Björkelund et al. (2013), we used the MATE dependencies to extract the shortest path between a token and its lexical head and included the path length (in terms of traversed nodes) as feature.

	Tree frag.	MATE labels+δ	Spines trees	Head Paths
Train	648	1305	637	27,670
Dev	272	742	265	3,320
Test	273	731	268	2,389

Table 2: Syntactic features statistics.

4 Results and Discussion

We present here the results on section 21 (test set)[1] for both systems. We report in Table 3, the different runs we submitted for the final evaluation of the shared task. We also report improvements between the two tracks.

Both systems show relatively close F-measures, with correct results on every corpus. If we compare the results more precisely, we observe that in general, DYALOG-SR tends to behave better for the unlabeled metrics. Its main weakness is on MRS scheme, for both tracks.[2]

On the other hand, it is worth noting that syntactic features greatly improve semantic parsing. In fact, we report in Figure 2(a) the improvement of the five most frequent labels and, in Figure 2(b), the five best improved labels with a frequency over 0.5% in the training set, which represent 95% of the edges in the DM Corpus. As we can see, syntactic information allow the systems to perform better on coordination structures and to reduce ambiguity between modifiers and verbal arguments (such as the *ARG3* label).

We observed the same behaviour on the PAS corpus, which contains also predicate-argument structures. For PCEDT, the results show that syntactic features give only small improvements, but the corpus is harder because of a large set of labels and is closer to syntactic structures than the two others.

Of course, we only scratched the surface with our experiments and we plan to further investigate the impact of syntactic information during semantic parsing. We especially plan to explore the deep parsing of French, thanks to the recent release of the Deep Sequoia Treebank (Candito et al., 2014).

5 Conclusion

In this paper, we presented our results on the task 8 of the *SemEval-2014 Task on Broad-Coverage Semantic Dependency Parsing*. Even though the results do not reach state-of-the-art, they compare favorably with other single systems and show that syntactic features can be efficiently used for semantic parsing.

In future work, we will continue to investigate this idea, by combining with more complex systems and more efficient machine learning techniques, we are convinced that we can come closer to state of the art results. and that syntax is the key for better semantic parsing.

Acknowledgments

We warmly thank Kenji Sagae for making his parser's code available and kindly answering our questions.

References

Anne Abeillé, Lionel Clément, and François Toussenel. 2003. Building a Treebank for French. In *Treebanks*

[1] Dev set results are available online at http://goo.gl/w3XcpW.

[2] The main and still unexplained problem of DYALOG-SR was that using larger beams has no impact, and often a negative one, when using the attach and pop transitions. Except for PAS and PCEDT where a beam of size 4 worked best for the open track, all other results were obtained for beams of size 1. This situation is in total contradiction with the large impact of beam previously observed for the arc standard strategy during the SPMRL'13 shared task and during experiments led on the French TreeBank (Abeillé et al., 2003) (FTB). Late experiments on the FTB using the attach and pop actions (but delaying attachments as long as possible) has confirmed a problem with beams, even if less visible. We are still investigating why the use of the attach transitions and/or of the pop transitions seems to be incompatible with beams.

Closed track			Open track				
PCEDT	LF	UF	PCEDT	LF		UF	
PEKING - BEST	76.28	89.19	PRIBERAM - BEST	77.90		89.03	
S&T PARSER b5	67.83	80.86	S&T PARSER b5	69.20	+1.37	82.68	+1.86
DYALOG-SR b1	67.81	81.23	DYALOG-SR b4	69.58	+1.77	84.80	+3.77
DM (MRS)			DM (MRS)				
PEKING - BEST	89.40	90.82	PRIBERAM - BEST	89.16		90.32	
S&T PARSER b5	78.44	80.88	S&T PARSER b5	81.46	+3.02	83.68	+2.80
DYALOG-SR b1	78.32	81.85	DYALOG-SR b1	79.71	+1.39	81.97	+0.12
PAS (ENJU)			PAS (ENJU)				
PEKING - BEST	92.04	93.13	PRIBERAM - BEST	91.76		92.81	
S&T PARSER b5	82.44	84.41	S&T PARSER b5	84.97	+2.53	86.64	+2.23
DYALOG-SR b1	84.16	86.09	DYALOG-SR b4	85.58	+1.42	86.98	+0.87

Table 3: Results on section 21 (test) of the PTB for closed and open track.

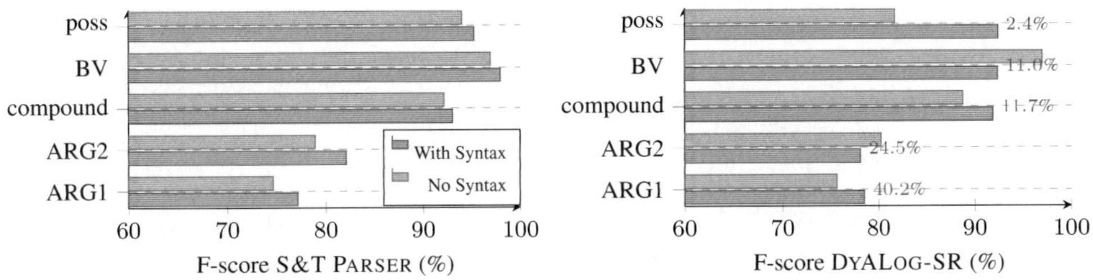

(a) the 5 most frequent labels

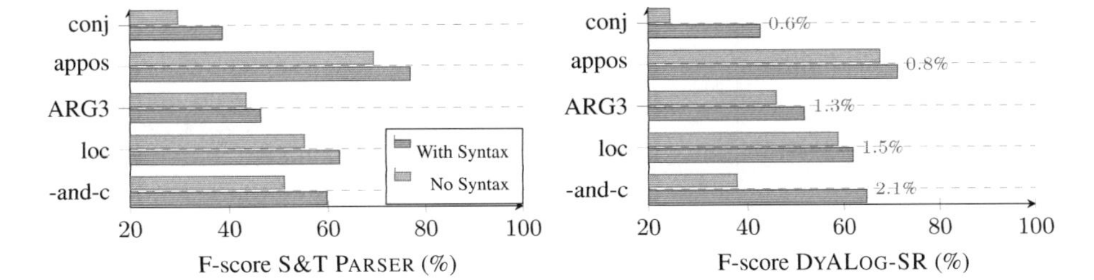

(b) the 5 best improved labels (edges frequency above 0.5 % in the training set)

Figure 2: Improvement with syntactic features for DM (test) corpus.
(numbers indicate edge frequency in training set)

: *Building and Using Parsed Corpora*, pages 165–188. Springer.

Daniel M. Bikel. 2002. Design of a multi-lingual, parallel-processing statistical parsing engine. In *Proceedings of the second international conference on Human Language Technology Research*, pages 178–182. Morgan Kaufmann Publishers Inc. San Francisco, CA, USA.

Anders Björkelund, Ozlem Cetinoglu, Richárd Farkas, Thomas Mueller, and Wolfgang Seeker. 2013. (re)ranking meets morphosyntax: State-of-the-art results from the SPMRL 2013 shared task. In *Proceedings of the Fourth Workshop on Statistical Parsing of Morphologically-Rich Languages*, pages 135–145, Seattle, Washington, USA, October.

Bernd Bohnet. 2010. Very high accuracy and fast dependency parsing is not a contradiction. In *Proceedings of the 23rd International Conference on Computational Linguistics*, COLING '10, pages 89–97, Stroudsburg, PA, USA.

Marie Candito, Guy Perrier, Bruno Guillaume, Corentin Ribeyre, Karën Fort, Djamé Seddah, and Éric De La Clergerie. 2014. Deep Syntax Annotation of the Sequoia French Treebank. In *International Conference on Language Resources and Evaluation (LREC)*, Reykjavik, Islande, May.

David Chiang, Jacob Andreas, Daniel Bauer, Karl Moritz Hermann, Bevan Jones, and Kevin Knight. 2013. Parsing graphs with hyperedge replacement grammars. In *Proceedings of the 51st Meeting of the ACL*.

Harold Charles Daume. 2006. *Practical structured learning techniques for natural language processing*. Ph.D. thesis, University of Southern California.

Yoav Goldberg, Kai Zhao, and Liang Huang. 2013. Efficient implementation of beam-search incremental parsers. In *Proceedings of the 51st Annual Meeting of the Association for Computational Linguistics (ACL)*, Sophia, Bulgaria, August.

Jan Hajic, Jarmila Panevová, Eva Hajicová, Petr Sgall, Petr Pajas, Jan Štepánek, Jiří Havelka, Marie Mikulová, Zdenek Zabokrtskỳ, and Magda Ševcıková Razımová. 2006. Prague dependency treebank 2.0. *CD-ROM, Linguistic Data Consortium, LDC Catalog No.: LDC2006T01, Philadelphia*, 98.

Liang Huang and Kenji Sagae. 2010. Dynamic programming for linear-time incremental parsing. In *Proceedings of the 48th Annual Meeting of the Association for Computational Linguistics*, pages 1077–1086. Association for Computational Linguistics.

Angelina Ivanova, Stephan Oepen, Lilja Øvrelid, and Dan Flickinger. 2012. Who did what to whom?: A contrastive study of syntacto-semantic dependencies. In *Proceedings of the sixth linguistic annotation workshop*, pages 2–11.

Sandra Kübler, Ryan McDonald, and Joakim Nivre. 2009. *Dependency Parsing*. Morgan and Claypool Publishers.

John Langford, Lihong Li, and Tong Zhang. 2009. Sparse online learning via truncated gradient. *Journal of Machine Learning Research*, 10(777-801):65.

Geoffrey Leech. 1992. 100 million words of English: the British National Corpus. *Language Research*, 28(1):1–13.

Yusuke Miyao and Jun'ichi Tsujii. 2004. Deep Linguistic Analysis for the Accurate Identification of Predicate-Argument Relations. In *Proceedings of the 18th International Conference on Computational Linguistics (COLING 2004)*, pages 1392–1397, Geneva, Switzerland.

Joakim Nivre, Johan Hall, Sandra Kübler, Ryan McDonald, Jens Nilsson, Sebastian Riedel, and Deniz Yuret. 2007a. The CoNLL 2007 shared task on dependency parsing. In *Proceedings of the CoNLL Shared Task Session of EMNLP-CoNLL 2007*, pages 915–932, Prague, Czech Republic, June.

Joakim Nivre, Johan Hall, Jens Nilsson, Atanas Chanev, Gülşen Eryiğit, Sandra Kübler, Svetoslav Marinov, and Erwin Marsi. 2007b. MaltParser: A language-independent system for data-driven dependency parsing. *Natural Language Engineering*, 13(2):95–135.

Stephan Oepen, Marco Kuhlmann, Yusuke Miyao, Daniel Zeman, Dan Flickinger, Jan Hajič, Angelina Ivanova, and Yi Zhang. 2014. SemEval 2014 Task 8: Broad-coverage semantic dependency parsing. In *Proceedings of the 8th International Workshop on Semantic Evaluation*, Dublin, Ireland.

Naoaki Okazaki. 2009. Classias: A collection of machine learning algorithms for classification.

Adwait Ratnaparkhi. 1997. A simple introduction to maximum entropy models for natural language processing. *IRCS Technical Reports Series*, page 81.

Kenji Sagae and Jun'ichi Tsujii. 2008. Shift-reduce dependency DAG parsing. In *Proceedings of the 22nd International Conference on Computational Linguistics (Coling 2008)*, pages 753–760, Manchester, UK, August. Coling 2008 Organizing Committee.

Djamé Seddah, Reut Tsarfaty, Sandra Kübler, Marie Candito, Jinho D. Choi, Richárd Farkas, Jennifer Foster, Iakes Goenaga, Koldo Gojenola Galletebeitia, Yoav Goldberg, Spence Green, Nizar Habash, Marco Kuhlmann, Wolfgang Maier, Joakim Nivre, Adam Przepiórkowski, Ryan Roth, Wolfgang Seeker, Yannick Versley, Veronika Vincze, Marcin Woliński, Alina Wróblewska, and Éric Villemonte De La Clergerie. 2013. Overview of the SPMRL 2013 shared task: A cross-framework evaluation of parsing morphologically rich languages. In *Proceedings of the Fourth Workshop on Statistical Parsing of Morphologically-Rich Languages*, pages 146–182, Seattle, Washington, USA, October.

Djamé Seddah. 2010. Exploring the spinal-stig model for parsing french. In *Proceedings of the Seventh conference on International Language Resources and Evaluation (LREC'10)*, Valletta, Malta, may. European Language Resources Association (ELRA).

Éric Villemonte De La Clergerie. 2013. Exploring beam-based shift-reduce dependency parsing with DyALog: Results from the SPMRL 2013 shared task. In *4th Workshop on Statistical Parsing of Morphologically Rich Languages (SPMRL'2013)*, Seattle, États-Unis.

Joachim Wagner, Djamé Seddah, Jennifer Foster, and Josef Van Genabith. 2007. C-structures and F-structures for the British National Corpus. In *Proceedings of the Twelfth International Lexical Functional Grammar Conference*. Citeseer.

ASAP: Automatic Semantic Alignment for Phrases

Ana O. Alves
CISUC - University of Coimbra
and Polytechnic Institute of Coimbra
Portugal
ana@dei.uc.pt

Adriana Ferrugento
Mariana Lourenço
Filipe Rodrigues
CISUC - University of Coimbra
Portugal
{aferr,mrlouren}@student.dei.uc.pt
fmpr@dei.uc.pt

Abstract

In this paper we describe the ASAP system (***A**utomatic **S**emantic **A**lignment for **P**hrases*)[1] which participated on the Task 1 at the SemEval-2014 contest (Marelli et al., 2014a). Our assumption is that STS (Semantic Text Similarity) follows a function considering lexical, syntactic, semantic and distributional features. We demonstrate the learning process of this function without any deep preprocessing achieving an acceptable correlation.

1 Introduction

Evaluation of compositional semantic models on full sentences through semantic relatedness and textual entailment, title of this task on SemEval, aims to collect systems and approaches able to predict the difference of meaning between phrases and sentences based on their included words (Baroni and Zamparelli, 2010; Grefenstette and Sadrzadeh, 2011; Mitchell and Lapata, 2010; Socher et al., 2012).

Our contribution is in the use of complementary features in order to learn the function STS, a part of this challenge. Rather than specifying rules, constraints and lexicons manually, we advocate a system for automatically acquiring linguistic knowledge using machine learning (ML) methods. For this we apply some preprocessing techniques over the training set in order to find different types of features. Related to the semantic aspect, we make use of known semantic relatedness and similarity measures on WordNet, in this case, applied to see the relatedness/similarity between phrases from sentences.

Considering the problem of modeling a text corpus to find short descriptions of documents, we aim an efficient processing of large collections while preserving the essential statistical relationships that are useful for, in this case, similarity judgment. Therefore we also apply topic modeling in order to get topic distribution over each sentence set. These features are then used to feed an ensemble algorithm to learn the STS function.

2 Background

2.1 WordNet

WordNet (Miller, 1995) is a computational lexicon of English created and maintained at Princeton University. It encodes concepts in terms of sets of synonyms (called synsets). A synset can be seen as a set of word senses all expressing the same meaning. Each word sense uniquely identifies a single synset. For instance, $car\#n\#1$ uses the notation followed by WordNet and subscript $word\#p\#n$ where p denotes the part-of-speech tag and n the word's sense identifier, respectively. In this case, the corresponding synset $car\#n\#1$, $auto\#n\#1$, $automobile\#n\#1$, $machine\#n\#6$, $motorcar\#n\#1$ is uniquely determined. As words are not always so ambiguous, a word $w\#p$ is said to be *monosemous* when it can convey only one meaning. Alternatively, $w\#p$ is *polysemous* if it can convey more meanings each one represented by a sense number *s* in $w\#p\#s$. For each synset, WordNet provides the following information: A gloss, that is, a textual definition of the synset; Semantic relations, which connect pairs of synsets. In this context we focus our attention on the Hypernym/Hyponym relation which refers to inheritance between nouns, also known as an *is-a*, or *kind-of* relation and their respective inverses. Y is a hypernym of X if every X is a (kind of) Y (motor_vehicle#n#1 is a hypernym of car#n#1 and, conversely, car#n#1 is

[1]This work was supported by the Crowds project-PTDC/EIA-EIA/115014/2009

Proceedings of the 8th International Workshop on Semantic Evaluation (SemEval 2014), pages 104–108,
Dublin, Ireland, August 23-24, 2014.

a hyponym of vehicle#n#1).

2.2 Semantic similarity

There are mainly two approaches to semantic similarity. First approach is making use of a large corpus and gathering statistical data from this corpus to estimate a score of semantic similarity. Second approach makes use of the relations and the entries of a thesaurus (Lesk, 1986), which is generally a hand-crafted lexical database such as WordNet (Banerjee and Pedersen, 2003). Hybrid approaches combines both methods (Jiang and Conrath, 1997). **Semantic similarity** can be seen as a different measure from **semantic relatedness** since the former compute the proximity between concepts in a given concept hierarchy (e.g. $car\#n\#1$ is similar to $motorcycle\#n$); while the later the common use of both concepts together (e.g. $car\#n\#1$ is related to $tire\#n$).

The Lesk algorithm (Lesk, 1986) uses dictionary definitions (glosses) to disambiguate a polysemous word in a sentence context. The major objective of his idea is to count the number of words that are shared between two glosses, but, sometimes, dictionary glosses are often quite brief, and may not include sufficient vocabulary to identify related sense. In this sense, Banerjee and Pedersen (Banerjee and Pedersen, 2003) adapted this algorithm to use WordNet as the dictionary for the word definitions and extended this metric to use the rich network of relationships between concepts present in WordNet.

The Jiang and Conrath similarity measure (Jiang and Conrath, 1997) computes the information shared between two concepts. The shared information is determined by Information content of the most specific subsume of the two concepts in the hierarchy. Furthermore this measure combines the distance between this subsuming concept and the other two concepts, counting the edge-based distance from them in the WordNet Hypernym/Hyponym hierarchy.

2.3 Topic Modeling

Topic models are based upon the idea that documents are mixtures of topics, where a topic is a probability distribution over words. A topic model is a generative model for documents: it specifies a simple probabilistic procedure by which documents can be generated. To make a new document, one chooses a distribution over topics. Then, for each word in that document, one chooses a topic at random according to this distribution, and draws a word from that topic.

Latent Dirichilet allocation (LDA) is a generative probabilistic topic model of a corpus (Blei et al., 2003). The basic idea is that documents are represented as random mixtures over latent topics, where each topic is characterized by a distribution over words. This process does not make any assumptions about the order of words as they appear in documents. The only information relevant to the model is the number of times words are produced. This is known as the bag-of-words assumption. The main variables of interest in the model are the topic-word distributions Φ and the topic distributions θ for each document.

3 Proposed Approach

Our approach to STS is mainly founded on the idea of learning a regression function that computes that similarity using other variable/features as components. Before obtaining those features, sentences are preprocessed trough known state-of-the-art Natural Language techniques. The resulting preprocessed sentences are then lexically, syntactically and semantically decomposed in order to obtain different partial similarities. These partial similarities are the features used in the supervised learning. These specific stages in our system are explained in detail in the following sections.

3.1 Natural Language Preprocessing

Before computing partial similarities considering different properties of sentences, we need to apply some known Natural Language techniques. For this purpose, we chose OpenNLP[2] as an open-source tool suite which contains a variety of Java-based NLP components. Our focus is here on three core NLP components: tokenization, POS tagging and chunking. Besides the fact OpenNLP also offers a stemmer for English we adopted other implementation self-contained in the specific framework for Topic Modeling (detailed in section 3.3).

OpenNLP is a homogeneous package based on a single machine learning approach, maximum entropy (ME) (Berger et al., 1996). Each OpenNLP tool requires an ME model that contains statistics about the components default features combining diverse contextual information. OpenNLP offers the possibility of both create component or use pre-built models create for different languages.

[2]http://opennlp.sourceforge.net

On one side, components can be trained and customizable models are built for the language and/or domain in study. On the other, the availability of pre-trained models allows the immediate application of such tools on a new problem. We followed the second approach since the sentences are of common-sense and not about a specific domain and are in English[3].

3.2 Feature Engineering

Features, sometimes called attributes, encode information from raw data that allows machine learning algorithms estimate an unknown value. We focus on, what we call, *light* features since they are completely automatic and unsupervised computed, non-requiring a specific labeled dataset for this phase. Each feature is computed as a partial similarity metric, which will later feed the posterior regression analysis. This process is fully automatized, being all features extracted using a pipeline from OpenNLP and other tools that will be introduced in the specific stage where they are used. For convenience and an easier identification in the later machine learning process, we set for each feature an id in the form $f\#n, n \in \{1..65\}$.

3.2.1 Lexical Features

Some basic similarity metrics are used as features related exclusively with word forms. In this set we include: number of negative words[4] for each sentence ($f1$ and $f2$ respectively), and the absolute value of the difference of these counts ($f3 = |f1 - f2|$); the absolute value of the difference of overlapping words for each sentence pair ($f4..7$)[5].

3.2.2 Syntactic Features

OpenNLP tokenization, POS (Part-of-Speech) tagging[6] and text chunking applied on a pipeline fashion allows the identification of (NPs) Noun Phrases, VPs (Verbal Phrases) and (Prepositional Phrases) in sentences. Heuristically, these NPs are further identified as subjects if they are in the beginning of sentences. This kind of shallow parser will be useful to identify the syntactic structure of sentences. Considering only this property, different features were computed as the absolute value of the difference of the number of NPs ($f8$), VPs ($f9$) and PPs($f10$) for each sentence pair.

3.2.3 Semantic Features

WordNet::Similarity (Pedersen et al., 2004) is a freely available software package for measuring the semantic similarity or relatedness between a pair of concepts (or word senses). At this stage we have for each sentence the subject identified as the first NP beginning a sentence.

This NP can be composed of a simple or compound noun, in a root form (lemma) or in a inflected form (plural) (e.g. *electrics* or *economic electric cars*). WorNet::Similarity package also contains a lemmatizer, in the module WordNet::QueryData, which compare a inflected word form and return all WordNet entries which can be the root form of this word. This search is made in all four morphological categories in WordNet (Adjectives, Adverbs, Nouns and Verbs), except when indicated the POS in the end of the queried word, the lemmatizer only see in that specific category (e.g. $flies\#n$ returns $flies\#n, fly\#n$, while $flies$ returns more entries: $flies\#n, fly\#n, fly\#v$). Therefore, a lemmatized is successively applied over the Subjects found for each pair of sentences. The compound subjects are reduced from left to right until a head noun been found as a valid WordNet entry (e.g. the subject $economicelectriccars$ is reduced until the valid entry $electriccar$ which is present on WordNet).

After all the subjects been found and a valid WordNet entry has been matched semantic similarity ($f11$) (Jiang and Conrath, 1997) and semantic relatedness ($f12$) (Lesk, 1986) is computed for each sentence pair. In the case where pair $word\#n$ has multiple senses, the one that maximizes partial similarity is selected.

3.3 Distributional Features

The distribution of topics over documents (in our case, sentences) may contribute to model Distributional Semantic in texts since in the way that the model is defined, there is no notion of mutual exclusivity that restricts words to be part of one topic only. This allows topic models to cap-

[3]OpenNLP offers, for the vast majority of components, at least one pre-trained model for this language.

[4]The Snowball stop word list(Porter, 2001) was used and those words expressing negation were identified (such as: never, not, neither, no, nobody, aren't, isn't, don't, doesn't, hasn't, hadn't, haven't)

[5]Thanks to the SemEval organizers in making available the python script which computes baselines compute_overlap_baseline.py which was applied using different setting for stop word removal, from 0 to 3.

[6]As alternative models are available, the Maxent model with tag dictionary was used on this component. Available at http://opennlp.sourceforge.net/models-1.5/en-pos-maxent.bin

ture polysemy, where the same word has multiple meanings. In this sense we can see topics as natural word sense contexts where words appear in different topics with distinct senses.

Gensim (Řehůřek and Sojka, 2010) is a machine learning framework for Topic Modeling which includes several preprocessing techniques such as stop-word removal and TF-IDF. TF-IDF is a standard statistical method that combines the frequency of a term in a particular document with its inverse document frequency in general use (Salton and Buckley, 1988). This score is high for rare terms that appear frequently in a document and are therefore more likely to be significant. In a pragmatic view, $tf\text{-}idf_{t,d}$ assigns to term t a weight in document d that is: highest when t occurs many times within a small number of documents; lower when the term occurs fewer times in a document, or occurs in many documents; lowest when the term occurs in virtually all documents.

Gensim computes a distribution of 25 topics over sentences not and using TF-IDF ($f13...37$ and $f38...63$). Each feature is the absolute value of the difference of topic$_i$ (i.e. $topic[i] = |topic[i]_{s1} - topic[i]_{s2}|$). Euclidean distance over the difference of topic distribution between sentence pairs in each case (without and with TF-IDF) was also considered as a feature ($f64$ and $f65$).

3.4 Supervised Learning

WEKA(Hall et al., 2009) is a large collection of state-of-the-art machine learning algorithms written in Java. WEKA contains tools for classification, regression, classifier ensemble, and others. Considering the developer version 3.7.11[7] we used the following experiment setup considering the 65 features previously computed for both sentence dataset (train and test) (Marelli et al., 2014b).

One of four approaches is commonly adopted for building classifier ensembles each one focusing a different level of action. Approach A concerns the different ways of combining the results from the classifiers, but there is no evidence that this strategy is better than using different models (Approach B). At feature level (Approach C) different feature subsets can be used for the classifiers, either if they use the same classification model or not. Finally, the data sets can be modified so that each classifier in the ensemble is trained on its own data set (Approach D).

[7]http://www.cs.waikato.ac.nz/ml/weka/downloading.html

Different methods for generating and combining models exist, like *Stacking* (Seewald, 2002) (Approach B). These combined models share sometimes however the disadvantage of being difficult to analyse, once they can comprise dozens of individual classifiers. Stacking is used to combine different types of classifiers and it demands the use of another learner algorithm to predict which of the models would be the most reliable for each case. This combination is done using a meta-learner, another learner scheme that combines the output of the base learners. The base learners are generally called level-0 models, and the meta-learner is a level-1 model. The predictions of the base learners are input to the meta-learner.

In WEKA, there is a meta classifier called "Stacking".We use this stacking ensemble combining two level-0 models: a K-Nearest Neighbour classifier ($K = 1$) (Aha et al., 1991); and a Linear Regression model without any attribute selection method ($-S1$) and the ridge parameter by default ($1.0\exp{-8}$). The meta-classifier was M5P which implements base routines for generating M5 Model trees and rules (Quinlan, 1992; Wang and Witten, 1997).

4 Conclusions and Future Work

Our contribution is in the use of complementary features in order to learn the function of STS, a part of the challenge of building Compositional Distributional Semantic Models. For this we applied some preprocessing tasks over the sentence set in order to find lexical, syntactic, semantic and distributional features. On the semantic aspect, we made use of known semantic relatedness and similarity measures on WordNet, in this case, applied to see the relatedness/similarity between phrases from sentences. We also applied topic modeling in order to get topic distributions over set of sentences. These features were then used to feed an ensemble learning algorithm in order to learn the STS function. This was achieved with a Pearson's r of 0.62780. One direction to follow is to find where the ensemble is failing and try to complement the feature set with more semantic features. Indeed, we plan to explore different topic distribution varying number of topics in order to maximize the log likelihood. Also we would like to select the most relevant feature from this set. We are motivated after this first participation in continuing to improve the system here proposed.

References

David W. Aha, Dennis Kibler, and Marc K. Albert. 1991. Instance-based learning algorithms. *Mach. Learn.*, 6(1):37–66.

Satanjeev Banerjee and Ted Pedersen. 2003. Extended gloss overlaps as a measure of semantic relatedness. In *Proceedings of the 18th International Joint Conference on Artificial Intelligence (IJCAI'03)*, pages 805–810, CA, USA.

Marco Baroni and Roberto Zamparelli. 2010. Nouns are vectors, adjectives are matrices: Representing adjective-noun constructions in semantic space. In *Proceedings of the 2010 Conference on Empirical Methods in Natural Language Processing (EMNLP'10)*, pages 1183–1193, PA, USA.

Adam L. Berger, Vincent J. Della Pietra, and Stephen A. Della Pietra. 1996. A maximum entropy approach to natural language processing. *Comput. Linguist.*, 22(1):39–71.

David M. Blei, Andrew Y. Ng, and Michael I. Jordan. 2003. Latent dirichlet allocation. *Journal of Machine Learning Research*, 3:993–1022.

Edward Grefenstette and Mehrnoosh Sadrzadeh. 2011. Experimental support for a categorical compositional distributional model of meaning. In *Proceedings of the Conference on Empirical Methods in Natural Language Processing (EMNLP '11)*, pages 1394–1404, PA, USA.

Mark Hall, Eibe Frank, Geoffrey Holmes, Bernhard Pfahringer, Peter Reutemann, and Ian H. Witten. 2009. The weka data mining software: An update. *SIGKDD Explor. Newsl.*, 11(1):10–18.

Jay J. Jiang and David W. Conrath. 1997. Semantic similarity based on corpus statistics and lexical taxonomy. In *Proc. of the Int'l. Conf. on Research in Computational Linguistics*, pages 19–33.

Michael Lesk. 1986. Automatic sense disambiguation using machine readable dictionaries: How to tell a pine cone from an ice cream cone. In *Proceedings of the 5th Annual International Conference on Systems Documentation (SIGDOC '86)*, pages 24–26, NY, USA.

Marco Marelli, Luisa Bentivogli, Marco Baroni, Raffaella Bernardi, Stefano Menini, and Roberto Zamparelli. 2014a. Semeval-2014 task 1: Evaluation of compositional distributional semantic models on full sentences through semantic relatedness and textual entailment. SemEval-2014.

Marco Marelli, Stefano Menini, Marco Baroni, Luisa Bentivogli, Raffaella Bernardi, and Robertomode Zamparelli. 2014b. A sick cure for the evaluation of compositional distributional semantic models. In *Proceedings of LREC 2014*.

George A. Miller. 1995. Wordnet: A lexical database for english. *COMMUNICATIONS OF THE ACM*, 38:39–41.

Jeff Mitchell and Mirella Lapata. 2010. Composition in distributional models of semantics. *Cognitive Science*, 34(8):1388–1439.

Ted Pedersen, Siddharth Patwardhan, and Jason Michelizzi. 2004. Wordnet::similarity: Measuring the relatedness of concepts. In *Demonstration Papers at HLT-NAACL 2004*, HLT-NAACL–Demonstrations '04, pages 38–41, PA, USA.

Martin F. Porter. 2001. Snowball: A language for stemming algorithms. Published online.

Ross J. Quinlan. 1992. Learning with continuous classes. In *5th Australian Joint Conference on Artificial Intelligence*, pages 343–348, Singapore.

Radim Řehůřek and Petr Sojka. 2010. Software Framework for Topic Modelling with Large Corpora. In *Proceedings of the Workshop on New Challenges for NLP Frameworks (LREC 2010)*, pages 45–50, Valletta, Malta.

Gerard Salton and Christopher Buckley. 1988. Term-weighting approaches in automatic text retrieval. *Inf. Process. Manage.*, 24(5):513–523.

Alexander K. Seewald. 2002. How to make stacking better and faster while also taking care of an unknown weakness. In C. Sammut and A. Hoffmann, editors, *Nineteenth International Conference on Machine Learning*, pages 554–561.

Richard Socher, Brody Huval, Christopher D. Manning, and Andrew Y. Ng. 2012. Semantic compositionality through recursive matrix-vector spaces. In *Proceedings of the 2012 Joint Conference on Empirical Methods in Natural Language Processing and Computational Natural Language Learning (EMNLP-CoNLL '12)*, pages 1201–1211, PA, USA.

Yong Wang and Ian H. Witten. 1997. Induction of model trees for predicting continuous classes. In *Poster papers of the 9th European Conference on Machine Learning*.

AT&T: The Tag&Parse Approach to Semantic Parsing of Robot Spatial Commands

Svetlana Stoyanchev, Hyuckchul Jung, John Chen, Srinivas Bangalore
AT&T Labs Research
1 AT&T Way Bedminster NJ 07921
{sveta,hjung,jchen,srini}@research.att.com

Abstract

The *Tag&Parse* approach to semantic parsing first assigns semantic tags to each word in a sentence and then parses the tag sequence into a semantic tree. We use statistical approach for tagging, parsing, and reference resolution stages. Each stage produces multiple hypotheses which are re-ranked using spatial validation. We evaluate the *Tag&Parse* approach on a corpus of Robotic Spatial Commands as part of the SemEval Task6 exercise. Our system accuracy is 87.35% and 60.84% with and without spatial validation.

1 Introduction

In this paper we describe a system participating in the SemEval2014 Task-6 on Supervised Semantic Parsing of Robotic Spatial Commands. It produces a semantic parse of natural language commands addressed to a robot arm designed to move objects on a grid surface. Each command directs a robot to change position of an object given a current configuration. A command uniquely identifies an object and its destination, for example *"Move the turquoise pyramid above the yellow cube"*. System output is a Robot Control Language (RCL) parse (see Figure 1) which is processed by the robot arm simulator. The Robot Spatial Commands dataset (Dukes, 2013) is used for training and testing.

Our system uses a *Tag&Parse* approach which separates semantic tagging and semantic parsing stages. It has four components: 1) semantic tagging, 2) parsing, 3) reference resolution, and 4) spatial validation. The first three are trained using LLAMA (Haffner, 2006), a supervised machine learning toolkit, on the RCL-parsed sentences.

For semantic tagging, we train a maximum entropy sequence tagger for assigning a semantic label and value to each word in a sentence, such as *type_cube* or *color_blue*. For parsing, we train a constituency parser on non-lexical RCL semantic trees. For reference resolution, we train a maximum entropy model that identifies entities for *reference* tags found by previous components. All of these components can generate multiple hypotheses. Spatial validation re-ranks these hypotheses by validating them against the input spatial configuration. The top hypothesis after re-ranking is returned by the system.

Separating tagging and parsing stages has several advantages. A tagging stage allows the system flexibility to abstract from possible grammatical or spelling errors in a command. It assigns a semantic category to each word in a sentence. Words not contributing to the semantic meaning are assigned 'O' label by the tagger and are ignored in the further processing. Words that are misspelled can potentially receive a correct tag when a word similarity feature is used in building a tagging model. This will be especially important when processing output of spoken commands that may contain recognition errors.

The remainder of the paper is organized thusly. In Section 2 we describe each of the components used in our system. In Section 3 we describe the results reported for SemEval2014 and evaluation of each system component. We summarize our findings and present future work in Section 4.

2 System

2.1 Sequence Tagging

A sequence tagging approach is used for conditional inference of tags given a word sequence. It is used for many natural language tasks, such as part of speech (POS) and named entity tagging (Toutanova and others, 2003; Carreras et al., 2003). We train a sequence tagger for assign-

Proceedings of the 8th International Workshop on Semantic Evaluation (SemEval 2014), pages 109–113, Dublin, Ireland, August 23-24, 2014.

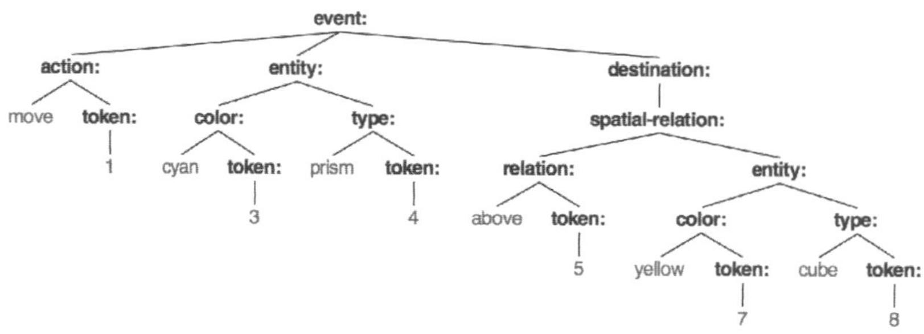

Figure 1: RCL tree for a sentence *Move the turquoise pyramid above the yellow cube.*

Word	index	tag	label
Move	1	action	move
the	2	O	-
turquoise	3	color	cyan
pyramid	4	type	prism
above	5	relation	above
the	6	O	-
yellow	7	color	yellow
cube	8	type	cube

Table 1: Tagging labels for a sentence *Move the turquoise pyramid above the yellow cube.*

ing a combined semantic tag and label (such as *type_cube*) to each word in a command. The tags used for training are extracted from the leaf-level nodes of the RCL trees. Table 2 shows tags and labels for a sample sentence *"Move the turquoise pyramid above the yellow cube"* extracted from the RCL parse tree (see Figure 1). In some cases, a label is the same as a word (yellow, cube) while in other cases, it differs (turquoise - cyan, pyramid - prism).

We train a sequence tagger using LLAMA maximum entropy (maxent) classification (Haffner, 2006) to predict the combined semantic tag and label of each word. Neighboring words, immediately neighboring semantic tags, and POS tags are used as features, where the POS tagger is another sequence tagging model trained on the Penn Treebank (Marcus et al., 1993). We also experimented with a tagger that assigns tags and labels in separate sequence tagging models, but it performed poorly.

2.2 Parsing

We use a constituency parser for building RCL trees. The input to the parser is a sequence of tags assigned by a sequence tagger, such as *"action color type relation color type"* for the example in Figure 1.

The parser generates multiple RCL parse tree hypotheses sorted in the order of their likelihood. The likelihood of a tree T given a sequence of tags T is determined using a probabilistic context free grammar (PCFG) G:

$$P(T|S) = \prod_{r \in T} P_G(r) \qquad (1)$$

The n-best parses are obtained using the CKY algorithm, recording the n-best hyperedge backpointers per constituent along the lines of (Huang and Chiang, 2005). G was obtained and P_G was estimated from a corpus of non-lexical RCL trees generated by removing all nodes descendant from the tag nodes (action, color, etc.). Parses may contain empty nodes not corresponding to any tag in the input sequence. These are hypothesized by the parser at positions in between input tags and inserted as edges according to the PCFG, which has probabilistic rules for generating empty nodes.

2.3 Reference Resolution

Reference resolution identifies the most probable antecedent for each anaphor within a text (Hirschman and Chinchor, 1997). It applies when multiple candidates antecedents are present. For example, in a sentence *"Pick up the red cube standing on a grey cube and place it on top of the yellow one"*, the anaphor *it* has two candidate antecedents corresponding to entity segments *the red cube* and *a grey cube*. In our system, anaphor and antecedents are represented by *reference tags* occurring in one sentence. A reference tag is either assigned by a sequence tagger to one of the words (e.g. to a pronoun) or is inserted into a tree by the parser (e.g. ellipsis). We train a binary maxent model for this task using LLAMA. The input is a pair consisting of an anaphor and a candidate antecedent, along with their features.

Features that are used include the preceding and following words as well as the tags/labels of both the anaphor and candidate antecedent. The reference resolution component selects the antecedent for which the model returns the highest score.

2.4 Spatial Validation

SemEval2014 Task6 provided a spatial planner which takes an RCL command as an input and determines if that command is executable in the given spatial context. At each step described in 2.1~2.3, due to the statistical nature of our approach, multiple hypotheses can be easily computed with different confidence values. We used the spatial planner to validate the final output RCL commands from the three steps by checking if the RCLs are executable or not. We generate multiple tagger output hypotheses. For each tagger output hypothesis, we generate multiple parser output hypotheses. For each parser output hypothesis, we generate multiple reference resolution output hypotheses. The resulting output hypotheses are ranked in the order of confidence scores with the highest tagging output scores ranked first, followed by the parsing output scores, and, finally, reference resolution output scores. The system returns the result of the top scored command that is valid according to the spatial validator.

In many applications, there can be a tool or method to validate tag/parse/reference outputs fully or partially. Note that in our system the validation is performed after all output is generated. Tightly coupled validation, such as checking validity of a tagged entity or a parse constituent, could help in computing hypotheses at each step (e.g., feature values based on possible entities or actions) and it remains as future work.

3 Results

In this section, we present evaluation results on the three subsets of the data summarized in Table 3. In the TEST2500 data set, the models are trained on the initial 2500 sentences of the Robot Commands Treebank and evaluated on the last 909 sentences (this corresponds to the data split of the SemEval task). In TEST500 data set, the models are trained on the initial 500 sentences of the training set and evaluated on the last 909 test sentences. We report these results to analyze the models' performance on a reduced training size. In DEV2500 data set, models are trained on 90% of the initial 2500 sentences and evaluated on 10% of the 2500 sentences using a random data split. We observe that sentence length and standard deviation of test sentences in the TEST2500 data set is higher than on the training sentences while in the DEV2500 data set training and test sentence length and standard deviation are comparable.

#	Dataset	Avg # hyp	Accuracy
1	TEST2500 1-best	1	86.0%
2	TEST2500 max-5	3.34	95.2%
3	TEST500 1-best	1	67.9%
4	TEST500 max-5	4.25	83.8%
5	DEV2500 1-best	1	90.8%
6	DEV2500 max-5	2.9	98.0%

Table 3: Tagger accuracy for 1-best and maximum of 5-best hypotheses (max-5).

3.1 Semantic Tagging

Table 3 presents sentence accuracy of the semantic tagging stage. Tagging accuracy is evaluated on 1-best and on max-5 best tagger outputs. In the max-5 setting the number of hypotheses generated by the tagger varies for each input with the average numbers reported in Table 3. Tagging accuracy on TEST2500 using 1-best is 86.0%. Considering max-5 best tagging sequences, the accuracy is 95.2%. On the TEST500 data set tagging accuracy is 67.9% and 83.8% on 1-best and max-5 best sequences respectively, approximately 8% points lower than on TEST2500 data set. On the DEV2500 data set tagging accuracy is 90.8% and 98.0% on 1-best and max-5 best sequences, 4.8% and 2.8% points higher than on the TEST2500 data set. The higher performance on DEV2500 in comparison to the TEST2500 can be explained by the higher complexity of the test sentences in comparison to the training sentences in the TEST2500 data set.

3.2 RCL Parsing

Parsing was evaluated using the EVALB scoring metric (Collins, 1997). Its 1-best F-measure accuracy on gold standard TEST2500 and DEV2500 semantic tag sequences was 96.17% and 95.20%, respectively. On TEST500, its accuracy remained 95.20%. On TEST2500 with system provided input sequences, its accuracy was 94.79% for 869 out of 909 sentences that were tagged correctly.

3.3 System Accuracy

Table 4 presents string accuracy of automatically generated RCL parse trees on each data set. The

Name	Train #sent	Train Sent. len. (stdev)	Test #sent	Test Sent. Len. (stdev)
TEST2500	2500	13.44 (5.50)	909	13.96 (5.59)
TEST500	500	14.62(5.66)	909	13.96 (5.59)
DEV2500	2250	13.43 (5.53)	250	13.57 (5.27)

Table 2: Number of sentences, average length and standard deviation of the data sets.

results are obtained by comparing system output RCL parse string with the reference RCL parse string. For each data set, we ran the system with and without spatial validation. We ran RCL parser and reference resolution on automatically assigned semantic tags (Auto) and oracle tagging (Orcl). We observed that some tag labels can be verified systematically and corrected them with simple rules: e.g., change "front" to "forward" because relation specification in (Dukes, 2013) doesn't have "front" even though annotations included cases with "front" as relation.

The system performance on TEST2500 data set using automatically assigned tags and no spatial validation is 60.84%. In this mode, the system uses 1-best parser and 1-best tagger output. With spatial validation, which allows the system to re-rank parser and tagger hypotheses, the performance increases by 27% points to 87.35%. This indicates that the parser and the tagger component often produce a correct output which is not ranked first. Using oracle tags without / with spatial validation on TEST2500 data set the system accuracy is 67.55% / 94.83%, 7% points above the accuracy using predicted tags.

The system performance on TEST500 data set using automatically assigned tags with / without spatial validation is 48.95% / 74.92%, approximately 12% points below the performance on TEST2500 (Row 1). Using oracle tags without / with spatial validation the performance on TEST500 data set is 63.89% / 94.94%. The performance without spatial validation is only 4% below TEST2500, while with spatial validation the performance on TEST2500 and TEST500 is the same. These results indicate that most performance degradation on a smaller data set is due to the semantic tagger.

The system performance on DEV2500 data set using automatically assigned tags without / with spatial validation is 68.0% / 96.80% (Row 5), 8% points above the performance on TEST2500 (Row 1). With oracle tags, the performance is 69.60% / 98.0%, which is 2-3% points above TEST2500 (Row 2). These results indicate that most performance improvement on a better balanced data set

#	Dataset	Tag	Accuracy without / with spatial validation
1	TEST2500	Auto	60.84 / 87.35
2	TEST2500	Orcl	67.55 / 94.83
3	TEST500	Auto	48.95 / 74.92
4	TEST500	Orcl	63.89 / 94.94
5	DEV2500	Auto	68.00 / 96.80
6	DEV2500	Orcl	69.60 / 98.00

Table 4: System accuracy with and without spatial validation using automatically assigned tags and oracle tags (OT).

DEV2500 is due to better semantic tagging.

4 Summary and Future Work

In this paper, we present the results of semantic processing for natural language robot commands using *Tag&Parse* approach. The system first tags the input sentence and then applies non-lexical parsing to the tag sequence. Reference resolution is applied to the resulting parse trees. We compare the results of the models trained on the data sets of size 500 (TEST500) and 2500 (TEST2500) sentences. We observe that sequence tagging model degrades significantly on a smaller data set. Parsing and reference resolution models, on the other hand, perform nearly as well on both training sizes. We compare the results of the models trained on more (DEV2500) and less (TEST2500) homogeneous training/testing data sets. We observe that a semantic tagging model is more sensitive to the difference between training and test set than parsing model degrading significantly a less homogeneous data set. Our results show that 1) both tagging and parsing models will benefit from an improved re-ranking, and 2) our parsing model is robust to a data size reduction while tagging model requires a larger training data set.

In future work we plan to explore how *Tag&Parse* approach will generalize in other domains. In particular, we are interested in using a combination of domain-specific tagging models and generic semantic parsing (Das et al., 2010) for processing spoken commands in a dialogue system.

References

Xavier Carreras, Lluís Màrquez, and Lluís Padró. 2003. A Simple Named Entity Extractor Using AdaBoost. In *Proceedings of the CoNLL*, pages 152–157, Edmonton, Canada.

Michael Collins. 1997. Three Generative Lexicalized Models for Statistical Parsing. In *Proceedings of the 35th Annual Meeting of the ACL*, pages 16–23.

Dipanjan Das, Nathan Schneider, Desai Chen, and Noah A. Smith. 2010. Probabilistic Frame-Semantic Parsing. In *HLT-NAACL*, pages 948–956.

Kais Dukes. 2013. Semantic Annotation of Robotic Spatial Commands. In *Language and Technology Conference (LTC)*.

Patrick Haffner. 2006. Scaling large margin classifiers for spoken language understanding. *Speech Communication*, 48(3-4):239–261.

Lynette Hirschman and Nancy Chinchor. 1997. MUC-7 Coreference Task Definition. In *Proceedings of the Message Understanding Conference (MUC-7)*. Science Applications International Corporation.

Liang Huang and David Chiang. 2005. Better K-best Parsing. In *Proceedings of the Ninth International Workshop on Parsing Technology*, Parsing '05, pages 53–64, Stroudsburg, PA, USA.

Mitchell Marcus, Beatrice Santorini, and Mary Ann Marcinkiewicz. 1993. Building a Large Annotated Corpus of English: The Penn Treebank. *Computational Linguistics*, 19(2):313–330.

Kristina Toutanova, Dan Klein, Christopher D. Manning, and Yoram Singer. 2003. Feature-Rich Part-of-Speech Tagging with a Cyclic Dependency Network. In *Proceedings of the 2003 Conference of the NAACL on Human Language Technology - Volume 1*, pages 173–180.

AUEB: Two Stage Sentiment Analysis of Social Network Messages

Rafael Michael Karampatsis, John Pavlopoulos and **Prodromos Malakasiotis**
mpatsis13@gmail.com, annis@aueb.gr, rulller@aueb.gr
Department of Informatics
Athens University of Economics and Business
Patission 76, GR-104 34 Athens, Greece

Abstract

This paper describes the system submitted for the Sentiment Analysis in Twitter Task of SEMEVAL 2014 and specifically the Message Polarity Classification subtask. We used a 2–stage pipeline approach employing a linear SVM classifier at each stage and several features including morphological features, POS tags based features and lexicon based features.

1 Introduction

Recently, Twitter has gained significant popularity among the social network services. Lots of users often use Twitter to express feelings or opinions about a variety of subjects. Analysing this kind of content can lead to useful information for fields, such as personalized marketing or social profiling. However such a task is not trivial, because the language used in Twitter is often informal presenting new challenges to text analysis.

In this paper we focus on sentiment analysis, the field of study that analyzes people's sentiment and opinions from written language (Liu, 2012). Given some text (e.g., tweet), sentiment analysis systems return a sentiment label, which most often is positive, negative, or neutral. This classification can be performed directly or in two stages; in the first stage the system examines whether the text carries sentiment and in the second stage, the system decides for the sentiment's polarity (i.e., positive or negative).[1] This decomposition is based on the assumption that subjectivity detection and sentiment polarity detection are different problems. We choose to follow the 2–stage approach, because it allows us to focus on each of the two problems separately (e.g., features, tuning, etc.). In the following we will describe the system with which we participated in the Message Polarity Classification subtask of Sentiment Analysis in Twitter (Task 9) of SEMEVAL 2014 (Rosenthal et al., 2014). Specifically Section 2 describes the data provided by the organizers of the task. Sections 3 and 4 present our system and its performance respectively. Finally, Section 5 concludes and provides hints for future work.

[1] For instance a 2–stage approach is better suited to systems that focus on subjectivity detection; e.g., aspect based sentiment analysis systems which extract aspect terms only from evaluative texts.

2 Data

At first, we describe the data used for this year's task. For system tuning the organizers released the training and development data of SEMEVAL 2013 Task 2 (Wilson et al., 2013). Both these sets are allowed to be used for training. The organizers also provided the test data of the same Task to be used for development only. As argued in (Malakasiotis et al., 2013) these data suffer from class imbalance. Concerning the test data, they contained 8987 messages broken down in the following 5 datasets:

- LJ_{14}: 2000 sentences from LIVEJOURNAL.
- SMS_{13}: SMS test data from last year.
- TW_{13}: Twitter test data from last year.
- TW_{14}: 2000 new tweets.
- $TWSARC_{14}$: 100 tweets containing sarcasm.

The details of the test data were made available to the participants only after the end of the Task. Recall that SMS_{13} and TW_{13} were also provided as development data. In this way the organizers were able to check, i) the progress of the systems since last year's task, and ii) the generalization capability of the participating systems.

Proceedings of the 8th International Workshop on Semantic Evaluation (SemEval 2014), pages 114–118,
Dublin, Ireland, August 23-24, 2014.

3 System Overview

The main objective of our system is to detect whether a message M expresses positive, negative or no sentiment. To achieve that we follow a 2–stage approach. During the first stage we detect whether M expresses sentiment ("subjective") or not; this process is called subjectivity detection. In the second stage we classify the "subjective" messages of the first stage as "positive" or "negative". Both stages utilize a Support Vector Machine (SVM (Vapnik, 1998)) classifier with linear kernel.[2] Similar approaches have also been proposed in (Pang and Lee, 2004; Wilson et al., 2005; Barbosa and Feng, 2010; Malakasiotis et al., 2013). Finally, we note that the 2–stage approach, in datasets such the one here (Malakasiotis et al., 2013), alleviates the class imbalance problem.

3.1 Data preprocessing

A very essential part of our system is data preprocessing. At first, each message M is passed through a twitter specific tokenizer and part-of-speech (POS) tagger (Owoputi et al., 2013) to obtain the tokens and the corresponding POS tags, which are necessary for some sets of features.[3] We then use a dictionary to replace any slang with the actual text.[4] We also normalize the text of each message by combining a trie data structure (De La Briandais, 1959) with an English dictionary.[5] In more detail, we replace every token of M not in the dictionary with the most similar word of the dictionary. Finally, we obtain POS tags of all the new tokens.

3.2 Sentiment lexicons

Another key attribute of our system is the use of sentiment lexicons. We have used the following:

- HL (Hu and Liu, 2004).
- SENTIWORDNET (Baccianella et al., 2010).
- SENTIWORDNET lexicon with POS tags (Baccianella et al., 2010).
- AFINN (Nielsen, 2011).
- MPQA (Wilson et al., 2005).
- NRC Emotion lexicon (Mohammad and Turney, 2013).
- NRC S140 lexicon (Mohammad et al., 2013).
- NRC Hashtag lexicon (Mohammad et al., 2013).
- The three lexicons created from the training data in (Malakasiotis et al., 2013).

Note that concerning the MPQA Lexicon we applied preprocessing similar to Malakasiotis et al. (2013) to obtain the following sub–lexicons:

S_+ : Contains strong subjective expressions with positive prior polarity.

S_- : Contains strong subjective expressions with negative prior polarity.

$S_\pm$: Contains strong subjective expressions with either positive or negative prior polarity.

S_0 : Contains strong subjective expressions with neutral prior polarity.

W_+ : Contains weak subjective expressions with positive prior polarity.

W_- : Contains weak subjective expressions with negative prior polarity.

$W_\pm$: Contains weak subjective expressions with either positive or negative prior polarity.

W_0 : Contains weak subjective expressions with neutral prior polarity.

3.3 Feature engineering

Our system employs several types of features based on morphological attributes of the messages, POS tags, and lexicons of section 3.2.[6]

3.3.1 Morphological features

- The existence of elongated tokens (e.g., "baaad").
- The number of elongated tokens.
- The existence of date references.
- The existence of time references.

[2] We used the LIBLINEAR distribution (Fan et al., 2008)

[3] Tokens could be words, emoticons, hashtags, etc. No lemmatization or stemming has been applied

[4] See http://www.noslang.com/dictionary/.

[5] We used the OPENOFFICE dictionary

[6] All the features are normalized to $[-1, 1]$

- The number of tokens that contain only upper case letters.
- The number of tokens that contain both upper and lower case letters.
- The number of tokens that start with an upper case letter.
- The number of exclamation marks.
- The number of question marks.
- The sum of exclamation and question marks.
- The number of tokens containing only exclamation marks.
- The number of tokens containing only question marks.
- The number of tokens containing only exclamation or question marks.
- The number of tokens containing only ellipsis (...).
- The existence of a subjective (i.e., positive or negative) emoticon at the message's end.
- The existence of an ellipsis and a link at the message's end.
- The existence of an exclamation mark at the message's end.
- The existence of a question mark at the message's end.
- The existence of a question or an exclamation mark at the message's end.
- The existence of slang.

3.3.2 POS based features

- The number of adjectives.
- The number of adverbs.
- The number of interjections.
- The number of verbs.
- The number of nouns.
- The number of proper nouns.
- The number of urls.
- The number of subjective emoticons.[7]
- The number of positive emoticons.[8]
- The number of negative emoticons.[9]
- The average, maximum and minimum F_1 scores of the message's POS bigrams for the subjective and the neutral classes.[10]
- The average, maximum and minimum F_1 scores of the message's POS bigrams for the positive and the negative classes.[11]

For a bigram b and a class c, F_1 is calculated as:

$$F_1(b,c) = \frac{2 \cdot Pre(b,c) \cdot Rec(b,c)}{Pre(b,c) + Rec(b,c)} \quad (1)$$

where:

$$Pre(b,c) = \frac{\#\text{messages of } c \text{ containing } b}{\#\text{messages containing } b} \quad (2)$$

$$Rec(b,c) = \frac{\#\text{messages of } c \text{ containing } b}{\#\text{messages of } c} \quad (3)$$

3.3.3 Sentiment lexicon based features

For each lexicon we use seven different features based on the scores provided by the lexicon for each word present in the message.[12]

- Sum of scores.
- Maximum of scores.
- Minimum of scores.
- Average of scores.
- The count of words with scores.
- The score of the last word of the message that appears in the lexicon.
- The score of the last word of the message.

[7]This feature is used only for subjectivity detection.
[8]This feature is used only for polarity detection.
[9]This feature is used only for polarity detection.
[10]This feature is used only for subjectivity detection.
[11]This feature is used only for polarity detection.
[12]If a word does not appear in the lexicon it is assigned with a score of 0 and it is not considered in the calculation of the average, maximum, minimum and count scores. Also, we have removed from SENTIWORDNET any instances having positive and negative scores that sum to zero. Moreover, the MPQA lexicon does not provide scores, so, for each word in the lexicon we assume a score equal to 1.

We also created features based on the Pre and F_1 scores of MPQA and the train data generated lexicons in a similar manner to that described in (Malakasiotis et al., 2013), with the difference that the features are stage dependent. Thus, for subjectivity detection we use the subjective and neutral classes and for polarity detection we use the positive and negative classes to compute the scores.

3.3.4 Miscellaneous features

Negation. Negation not only is a good subjectivity indicator but it also may change the polarity of a message. We therefore add 7 more features, one indicating the existence of negation, and the remaining six indicating the existence of negation that precedes words from lexicons $S_{\pm}$, S_{+}, S_{-}, $W_{\pm}$, W_{+} and W_{-}.[13] Each feature is used in the appropriate stage.[14] We have not implement this type of feature for other lexicons but it might be a good addition to the system.

Carnegie Mellon University's Twitter clusters. Owoputi et al. (2013) released a dataset of 938 clusters containing words coming from tweets. Words of the same clusters share similar attributes. We try to exploit this observation by adding 938 features, each of which indicates if a message's token appears or not in the corresponding attributes.

3.4 Feature Selection

To allow our model to better scale on unseen data we have performed feature selection. More specifically, we first merged training and development data of SEMEVAL 2013 Task 2. Then, we ranked the features with respect to their information gain (Quinlan, 1986) on this dataset. To obtain the best set of features we started with a set containing the top 50 features and we kept adding batches of 50 features until we have added all of them. At each step we evaluated the corresponding feature set on the TW_{13} and SMS_{13} datasets and chose the feature set with the best performance. This resulted in a system which used the top 900 features for Stage 1 and the top 1150 features for Stage 2.

[13]We use a list of words with negation. We assume that a token precedes a word if it is in a distance of at most 5 tokens.

[14]The features concerning $S_{\pm}$ and $W_{\pm}$ are used in subjectivity detection and the remaining four in polarity detection.

Test Set	AUEB	Median	Best
LJ_{14}	70.75	65.48	74.84
SMS_{13}	64.32	57.53	70.28
TW_{13}	63.92	62.88	72.12
TW_{14}	66.38	63.03	70.96
$TWSARC_{14}$	56.16	45.77	58.16
AVG_{all}	64.31	56.56	68.78
AVG_{14}	64.43	57.97	67.62

Table 1: $F_1(\pm)$ scores per dataset.

Test Set	Ranking
LJ_{14}	9/50
SMS_{13}	8/50
TW_{13}	21/50
TW_{14}	14/50
$TWSARC_{14}$	4/50
AVG_{all}	6/50
AVG_{14}	5/50

Table 2: Rankings of our system.

4 Experimental Results

The official measure of the Task is the average F_1 score of the positive and negative classes ($F_1(\pm)$). Table 1 illustrates the $F_1(\pm)$ score per evaluation dataset achieved by our system along with the median and best $F_1(\pm)$. In the same table AVG_{all} corresponds to the average $F_1(\pm)$ across the five datasets while AVG_{14} corresponds to the average $F_1(\pm)$ across LJ_{14}, TW_{14} and $TWSARC_{14}$. We observe that in all cases our results are above the median. Table 2 illustrates the ranking of our system according to $F_1(\pm)$. Our system ranked 6th according to AVG_{all} and 5th according to AVG_{14} among the 50 participating systems. Note that our best results were achieved on the new test sets (LJ_{14}, TW_{14}, $TWSARC_{14}$) meaning that our system has a good generalization ability.

5 Conclusion and future work

In this paper we presented our approach for the Message Polarity Classification subtask of the Sentiment Analysis in Twitter Task of SEMEVAL 2014. We proposed a 2–stage pipeline approach, which first detects sentiment and then decides about its polarity. The results indicate that our system handles well the class imbalance problem and has a good generalization ability. A possible explanation is that we do not use bag-of-words features which often suffer from over–fitting. Nevertheless, there is still some room for improvement. A promising direction would be to improve the 1st stage (subjectivity detection) either by adding more data or by adding more features, mostly because the performance of stage 1 greatly affects that of stage 2. Finally, the addition of more data for the negative class on stage 2 might be a good improvement because it would further reduce the class imbalance of the training data for this stage.

References

Stefano Baccianella, Andrea Esuli, and Fabrizio Sebastiani. 2010. Sentiwordnet 3.0: An enhanced lexical resource for sentiment analysis and opinion mining. In Nicoletta Calzolari (Conference Chair), Khalid Choukri, Bente Maegaard, Joseph Mariani, Jan Odijk, Stelios Piperidis, Mike Rosner, and Daniel Tapias, editors, *Proceedings of the Seventh International Conference on Language Resources and Evaluation (LREC'10)*, Valletta, Malta, may.

Luciano Barbosa and Junlan Feng. 2010. Robust sentiment detection on twitter from biased and noisy data. In *Proceedings of the 23rd International Conference on Computational Linguistics: Posters*, COLING '10, pages 36–44, Beijing, China.

Rene De La Briandais. 1959. File searching using variable length keys. In *Papers Presented at the the March 3-5, 1959, Western Joint Computer Conference*, IRE-AIEE-ACM '59 (Western), pages 295–298, New York, NY, USA.

Rong-En Fan, Kai-Wei Chang, Cho-Jui Hsieh, Xiang-Rui Wang, and Chih-Jen Lin. 2008. Liblinear: A library for large linear classification. *The Journal of Machine Learning Research*, 9:1871–1874.

Minqing Hu and Bing Liu. 2004. Mining and summarizing customer reviews. In *Proceedings of the Tenth ACM SIGKDD International Conference on Knowledge Discovery and Data Mining*, KDD '04, pages 168–177, New York, NY, USA.

Bing Liu. 2012. Sentiment analysis and opinion mining. *Synthesis Lectures on Human Language Technologies*, 5(1):1–167.

Prodromos Malakasiotis, Rafael Michael Karampatsis, Konstantina Makrynioti, and John Pavlopoulos. 2013. nlp.cs.aueb.gr: Two stage sentiment analysis. In *Second Joint Conference on Lexical and Computational Semantics (*SEM), Volume 2: Proceedings of the Seventh International Workshop on Semantic Evaluation (SemEval 2013)*, pages 562–567, Atlanta, Georgia, June.

Saif Mohammad and Peter Turney. 2013. Crowdsourcing a word-emotion association lexicon. 29(3):436–465.

Saif Mohammad, Svetlana Kiritchenko, and Xiaodan Zhu. 2013. Nrc-canada: Building the state-of-the-art in sentiment analysis of tweets. In *Proceedings of the Seventh International Workshop on Semantic Evaluation (SemEval 2013)*, Atlanta, Georgia, USA, June.

Finn Årup Nielsen. 2011. A new anew: evaluation of a word list for sentiment analysis in microblogs. In Matthew Rowe, Milan Stankovic, Aba-Sah Dadzie, and Mariann Hardey, editors, *Proceedings of the ESWC2011 Workshop on 'Making Sense of Microposts': Big things come in small packages*, volume 718 of *CEUR Workshop Proceedings*, pages 93–98, May.

Olutobi Owoputi, Brendan OConnor, Chris Dyer, Kevin Gimpel, Nathan Schneider, and Noah A Smith. 2013. Improved part-of-speech tagging for online conversational text with word clusters. In *Proceedings of NAACL.*

Bo Pang and Lillian Lee. 2004. A sentimental education: sentiment analysis using subjectivity summarization based on minimum cuts. In *Proceedings of the 42nd Annual Meeting on Association for Computational Linguistics*, ACL '04, Barcelona, Spain.

Ross Quinlan. 1986. Induction of decision trees. *Mach. Learn.*, 1(1):81–106, March.

Sara Rosenthal, Preslav Nakov, Alan Ritter, and Veselin Stoyanov. 2014. SemEval-2014 Task 9: Sentiment Analysis in Twitter. In Preslav Nakov and Torsten Zesch, editors, *Proceedings of the 8th International Workshop on Semantic Evaluation*, SemEval '14, Dublin, Ireland.

Vladimir Vapnik. 1998. *Statistical learning theory.*

Theresa Wilson, Janyce Wiebe, and Paul Hoffmann. 2005. Recognizing contextual polarity in phrase-level sentiment analysis. In *Proceedings of the conference on Human Language Technology and Empirical Methods in Natural Language Processing*, pages 347–354.

Theresa Wilson, Zornitsa Kozareva, Preslav Nakov, Sara Rosenthal, Veselin Stoyanov, and Alan Ritter. 2013. SemEval-2013 task 2: Sentiment analysis in twitter. In *Proceedings of the International Workshop on Semantic Evaluation*, SemEval '13, June.

Bielefeld SC: Orthonormal Topic Modelling for Grammar Induction

John P. McCrae
CITEC, Bielefeld University
Inspiration 1
Bielefeld, Germany
jmccrae@cit-ec.uni-bielefeld.de

Philipp Cimiano
CITEC, Bielefeld University
Inspiration 1
Bielefeld, Germany
cimiano@cit-ec.uni-bielefeld.de

Abstract

In this paper, we consider the application of topic modelling to the task of inducting grammar rules. In particular, we look at the use of a recently developed method called orthonormal explicit topic analysis, which combines explicit and latent models of semantics. Although, it remains unclear how topic model may be applied to the case of grammar induction, we show that it is not impossible and that this may allow the capture of subtle semantic distinctions that are not captured by other methods.

1 Introduction

Grammar induction is the task of inducing high-level rules for application of grammars in spoken dialogue systems. In practice, we can extract relevant rules and the task of grammar induction reduces to finding similar rules between two strings. As these strings are not necessarily similar in surface form, what we really wish to calculate is the semantic similarity between these strings. As such, we could think of applying a semantic analysis method. As such we attempt to apply topic modelling, that is methods such as Latent Dirichlet Allocation (Blei et al., 2003), Latent Semantic Analysis (Deerwester et al., 1990) or Explicit Semantic Analysis (Gabrilovich and Markovitch, 2007). In particular we build on the recent work to unify latent and explicit methods by means of orthonormal explicit topics.

In topic modelling the key choice is the document space that will act as the corpus and hence topic space. The standard choice is to regard all articles from a background document collection – Wikipedia articles are a typical choice – as the topic space. However, it is crucial to ensure that these topics cover the semantic space evenly and completely. Following McCrae et al. (McCrae et al., 2013) we remap the semantic space defined by the topics in such a manner that it is orthonormal. In this way, each document is mapped to a topic that is distinct from all other topics.

The structure of the paper is as follows: we describe our method in three parts, first the method in section 2, followed by approximation method in section 3, the normalization methods in section 4 and finally the application to grammar induction in section 5, we finish with some conclusions in section 6.

2 Orthonormal explicit topic analysis

ONETA (McCrae et al., 2013, Orthonormal explicit topic analysis) follows Explicit Semantic Analysis in the sense that it assumes the availability of a background document collection $B = \{b_1, b_2, ..., b_N\}$ consisting of textual representations. The mapping into the explicit topic space is defined by a language-specific function Φ that maps documents into $\mathbb{R}^N$ such that the jth value in the vector is given by some *association measure* $\phi_j(d)$ for each background document b_j. Typical choices for this association measure ϕ are the sum of the TF-IDF scores or an information retrieval relevance scoring function such as BM-25 (Sorg and Cimiano, 2010).

For the case of TF-IDF, the value of the j-th element of the topic vector is given by:

$$\phi_j(d) = \overrightarrow{\text{tf-idf}}(b_j)^{\text{T}}\ \overrightarrow{\text{tf-idf}}(d)$$

Thus, the mapping function can be represented as the product of a TF-IDF vector of document d multiplied by a word-by-document ($W \times N$) TF-IDF matrix, which we denote as a $\mathbf{X}$:[1]

[1] ^{T} denotes the matrix transpose as usual

Proceedings of the 8th International Workshop on Semantic Evaluation (SemEval 2014), pages 119–122,
Dublin, Ireland, August 23-24, 2014.

$$\Phi(d) = \begin{pmatrix} \overrightarrow{\text{tf-idf}}(b_1)^{\mathrm{T}} \\ \vdots \\ \overrightarrow{\text{tf-idf}}(b_N)^{\mathrm{T}} \end{pmatrix} \overrightarrow{\text{tf-idf}}(d) = \mathbf{X}^{\mathrm{T}} \cdot \overrightarrow{\text{tf-idf}}(d)$$

For simplicity, we shall assume from this point on that all vectors are already converted to a TF-IDF or similar numeric vector form.

In order to compute the similarity between two documents d_i and d_j, typically the cosine-function (or the normalized dot product) between the vectors $\Phi(d_i)$ and $\Phi(d_j)$ is computed as follows:

$$\text{sim}(d_i, d_j) = \cos(\Phi(d_i), \Phi(d_j)) = \frac{\Phi(d_i)^{\mathrm{T}}\Phi(d_j)}{||\Phi(d_i)||||\Phi(d_j)||}$$

$$\text{sim}(d_i, d_j) = \cos(\mathbf{X}^{\mathrm{T}} d_i, \mathbf{X}^{\mathrm{T}} d_j) = \frac{d_i^{\mathrm{T}}\mathbf{X}\mathbf{X}^{\mathrm{T}} d_j}{||\mathbf{X}^{\mathrm{T}} d_i||||\mathbf{X}^{\mathrm{T}} d_j||}$$

The key challenge with topic modelling is choosing a good background document collection $B = \{b_1, ..., b_N\}$. A simple minimal criterion for a good background document collection is that each document in this collection should be maximally similar to itself and less similar to any other document:

$$\forall i \neq j \;\; 1 = \text{sim}(b_j, b_j) > \text{sim}(b_i, b_j) \geq 0$$

As shown in McCrae et al. (2013), this property is satisfied by the following projection:

$$\Phi_{\text{ONETA}}(d) = (\mathbf{X}^{\mathrm{T}}\mathbf{X})^{-1}\mathbf{X}^{\mathrm{T}} d$$

And hence the similarity between two documents can be calculated as:

$$\text{sim}(d_i, d_j) = \cos(\Phi_{\text{ONETA}}(d_i), \Phi_{\text{ONETA}}(d_j))$$

3 Approximations

ONETA relies on the computation of a matrix inverse, which has a complexity that, using current practical algorithms, is approximately cubic and as such the time spent calculating the inverse can grow very quickly.

We notice that $\mathbf{X}$ is typically very sparse and moreover some rows of $\mathbf{X}$ have significantly fewer non-zeroes than others (these rows are for terms with low frequency). Thus, if we take the first N_1 columns (documents) in $\mathbf{X}$, it is possible to rearrange the rows of $\mathbf{X}$ with the result that there is some W_1 such that rows with index greater than W_1 have only zeroes in the columns up to N_1. In other words, we take a subset of N_1 documents and enumerate the words in such a way that the terms occurring in the first N_1 documents are enumerated $1, \ldots, W_1$. Let $N_2 = N - N_1$, $W_2 = W - W_1$. The result of this row permutation does not affect the value of $\mathbf{X}^{\mathrm{T}}\mathbf{X}$ and we can write the matrix $\mathbf{X}$ as:

$$\mathbf{X} = \begin{pmatrix} \mathbf{A} & \mathbf{B} \\ \mathbf{0} & \mathbf{C} \end{pmatrix}$$

where $\mathbf{A}$ is a $W_1 \times N_1$ matrix representing term frequencies in the first N_1 documents, $\mathbf{B}$ is a $W_1 \times N_2$ matrix containing term frequencies in the remaining documents for terms that are also found in the first N_1 documents, and $\mathbf{C}$ is a $W_2 \times N_2$ containing the frequency of all terms not found in the first N_1 documents.

Application of the well-known divide-and-conquer formula (Bernstein, 2005, p. 159) for matrix inversion yields the following easily verifiable matrix identity, given that we can find $\mathbf{C}'$ such that $\mathbf{C}'\mathbf{C} = \mathbf{I}$.

$$\begin{pmatrix} (\mathbf{A}^{\mathrm{T}}\mathbf{A})^{-1}\mathbf{A}^{\mathrm{T}} & -(\mathbf{A}^{\mathrm{T}}\mathbf{A})^{-1}\mathbf{A}^{\mathrm{T}}\mathbf{B}\mathbf{C}' \\ \mathbf{0} & \mathbf{C}' \end{pmatrix} \begin{pmatrix} \mathbf{A} & \mathbf{B} \\ \mathbf{0} & \mathbf{C} \end{pmatrix} = \mathbf{I} \quad (1)$$

The inverse $\mathbf{C}'$ is approximated by the *Jacobi Preconditioner*, $\mathbf{J}$, of $\mathbf{C}^{\mathrm{T}}\mathbf{C}$:

$$\begin{aligned} \mathbf{C}' &\simeq \mathbf{J}\mathbf{C}^{\mathrm{T}} \quad (2) \\ &= \begin{pmatrix} ||c_1||^{-2} & & 0 \\ & \ddots & \\ 0 & & ||c_{N_2}||^{-2} \end{pmatrix} \mathbf{C}^{\mathrm{T}} \end{aligned}$$

4 Normalization

A key factor in the effectiveness of topic-based methods is the appropriate normalization of the elements of the document matrix $\mathbf{X}$. This is even more relevant for orthonormal topics as the matrix inversion procedure can be very sensitive to small changes in the matrix. In this context, we consider two forms of normalization, term and document normalization, which can also be considered as row/column normalizations of $\mathbf{X}$.

A straightforward approach to normalization is to normalize each column of $\mathbf{X}$ to obtain a matrix as follows:

$$\mathbf{X}' = \left(\frac{x_1}{||x_1||} \cdots \frac{x_N}{||x_N||} \right)$$

If we calculate $\mathbf{X}'^{\mathrm{T}}\mathbf{X}' = \mathbf{Y}$ then we get that the (i, j)-th element of $\mathbf{Y}$ is:

$$y_{ij} = \frac{x_i^{\mathrm{T}} x_j}{||x_i|| ||x_j||}$$

Thus, the diagonal of $\mathbf{Y}$ consists of ones only and due to the Cauchy-Schwarz inequality we have that $|y_{ij}| \leq 1$, with the result that the matrix $\mathbf{Y}$ is already close to $\mathbf{I}$. Formally, we can use this to state a bound on $||\mathbf{X}'^{\mathrm{T}}\mathbf{X}' - \mathbf{I}||_{\mathcal{F}}$, but in practice it means that the orthonormalizing matrix has more small or zero values. Previous experiments have indicated that in general term normalization such as TF-IDF is not as effective as using the direct term frequency in ONETA, so we do not apply term normalization.

5 Application to grammar induction

The application to grammar induction is simply carried out by taking the rules and creating a single ground instance. That is if we have a rule of the form

`LEAVING FROM <CITY>`

We would replace the instance of `<CITY>` with a known terminal for this rule, e.g.,

leaving from Berlin

This reduces the task to that of string similarity which can be processed by means of any string similarity function, for example such as the ONETA function described above. As such the procedure is as follows:

1. Ground the input grammar rule to an English string d
2. Ground each candidate matching rule to an English string d_i
3. Calculate for each d_i, the similarity $\mathrm{sim}_{\mathrm{ONETA}}(d, d_i)$
4. Add the rule to the grammar class with the highest similarity

This approach has the obvious drawback that it removes all information about the valence of the rule, however the effect of this loss of information remains unclear.

For application, we used 20,000 Wikipedia articles, filtered to contain only those of over 100 words, giving us a corpus of 15.6 million tokens. We applied ONETA using document normalization but no term normalization and the value $N_1 = 5000$. These parameters were chosen based on the best results in previous experiments.

6 Conclusions

The results show that such a naive approach is not directly applicable to the case of grammar induction, however we believe that it is possible that the subtle semantic similarities captured by topic modelling may yet prove useful for grammar induction. However it is clear from the presented results that the use of a topic model alone does not suffice to solve this task. We notice that from the data many of the distinctions rely on antonyms and stop words, especially distinctions such as 'to'/'from', which are not captured by a topic model as topic models generally ignore stop words, and generally consider antonyms to be in the same topic, as they frequently occur together in text. The question of when semantic similarity such as provided by topic modelling is applicable remains an open question.

References

Dennis S Bernstein. 2005. *Matrix mathematics, 2nd Edition*. Princeton University Press Princeton.

David M Blei, Andrew Y Ng, and Michael I Jordan. 2003. Latent Dirichlet Allocation. *Journal of Machine Learning Research*, 3:993–1022.

Scott C. Deerwester, Susan T Dumais, Thomas K. Landauer, George W. Furnas, and Richard A. Harshman. 1990. Indexing by latent semantic analysis. *JASIS*, 41(6):391–407.

Evgeniy Gabrilovich and Shaul Markovitch. 2007. Computing semantic relatedness using Wikipedia-based explicit semantic analysis. In *Proceedings of the 20th International Joint Conference on Artificial Intelligence*, volume 6, page 12.

John P. McCrae, Philipp Cimiano, and Roman Klinger. 2013. Orthonormal explicit topic analysis for cross-lingual document matching. In *Proceedings of the 2013 Conference on Empirical Methods in Natural Language Processing*, pages 1732–1740.

Philipp Sorg and Philipp Cimiano. 2010. An experimental comparison of explicit semantic analysis implementations for cross-language retrieval. In *Natural Language Processing and Information Systems*, pages 36–48. Springer.

Biocom_Usp: Tweet Sentiment Analysis with Adaptive Boosting Ensemble

Nádia F. F. Silva, Eduardo R. Hruschka
University of São Paulo, USP
São Carlos, SP, Brazil
nadia, erh@icmc.usp.br

Estevam Rafael Hruschka Jr.
Department of Computer Science
Federal University of Sao Carlos.
São Carlos, SP, Brazil
estevam@dc.ufscar.br

Abstract

We describe our approach for the *SemEval-2014 task 9: Sentiment Analysis in Twitter*. We make use of an ensemble learning method for sentiment classification of tweets that relies on varied features such as feature hashing, part-of-speech, and lexical features. Our system was evaluated in the Twitter message-level task.

1 Introduction

The sentiment analysis is a field of study that investigates feelings present in texts. This field of study has become important, especially due to the internet growth, the content generated by its users, and the emergence of the social networks. In the social networks such as Twitter people post their opinions in a colloquial and compact language, and it is becoming a large dataset, which can be used as a source of information for various automatic tools of sentiment inference. There is an enormous interest in sentiment analysis of Twitter messages, known as *tweets*, with applications in several segments, such as (i) directing *marketing* campaigns, extracting consumer reviews of services and products (Jansen et al., 2009); (ii) identifying manifestations of *bullying* (Xu et al., 2012); (iii) predicting to forecast box-office revenues for movies (Asur and Huberman, 2010); and (iv) predicting acceptance or rejection of presidential candidates (Diakopoulos and Shamma, 2010; O'Connor et al., 2010).

One of the problems encountered by researchers in tweet sentiment analysis is the scarcity of *public datasets*. Although Twitter sentiment datasets have already been created, they are either small — such as Obama-McCain Debate corpus (Shamma et al., 2009) and Health Care Reform corpus (Speriosu et al., 2011) or big and proprietary such as in (Lin and Kolcz, 2012). Others rely on noisy labels obtained from emoticons and hashtags (Go et al., 2009). The *SemEval-2014 task 9: Sentiment Analysis in Twitter* (Nakov et al., 2013) provides a public dataset to be used to compare the accuracy of different approaches.

In this paper, we propose to analyse tweet sentiment with the use of Adaptive Boosting (Freund and Schapire, 1997), making use of the well-known Multinomial Classifier. Boosting is an approach to machine learning that is based on the idea of creating a highly accurate prediction rule by combining many relatively weak and inaccurate rules. The AdaBoost algorithm (Freund and Schapire, 1997) was the first practical boosting algorithm, and remains one of the most widely used and studied, with applications in numerous fields. Therefore, it has potential to be very useful for tweet sentiment analysis, as we address in this paper.

2 Related Work

Classifier ensembles for tweet sentiment analysis have been underexplored in the literature — a few exceptions are (Lin and Kolcz, 2012; Clark and Wicentwoski, 2013; Rodriguez et al., 2013; Hassan et al., 2013).

Lin and Kolcz (2012) used logistic regression classifiers learned from hashed byte 4-grams as features – The feature extractor considers the tweet as a raw byte array. It moves a four-byte sliding window along the array,

Proceedings of the 8th International Workshop on Semantic Evaluation (SemEval 2014), pages 123–128,
Dublin, Ireland, August 23-24, 2014.

and hashes the contents of the bytes, the value of which was taken as the feature id. Here the 4-grams refers to four characters (and not to four words). They made no attempt to perform any linguistic processing, not even word tokenization. For each of the (proprietary) datasets, they experimented with ensembles of different sizes. The ensembles were formed by different models, obtained from different training sets, but with the same learning algorithm (logistic regression). Their results show that the ensembles lead to more accurate classifiers.

Rodrígues et al. (2013) and Clark et al. (2013) proposed the use of classifier ensembles at the expression-level, which is related to *Contextual Polarity Disambiguation*. In this perspective, the sentiment label (positive, negative, or neutral) is applied to a specific phrase or word within the tweet and does not necessarily match the sentiment of the entire tweet.

Finally, another type of ensemble framework has been recently proposed by Hassan et al. (2013), who deal with class imbalance, sparsity, and representational issues. The authors propose to enrich the corpus using multiple additional datasets related to the task of sentiment classification. Differently from previous works, the authors use a combination of unigrams and bigrams of simple words, part-of-speech, and semantic features.

None of the previous works used AdaBoost (Freund and Schapire, 1996). Also, lexicons and/or part-of-speech in combination with feature hashing, like in (Lin and Kolcz, 2012) have not been addressed in the literature.

3 AdaBoost Ensemble

Boosting is a relatively young, yet extremely powerful, machine learning technique. The main idea behind boosting algorithms is to combine multiple weak learners – classification algorithms that perform only slightly better than random guessing – into a powerful composite classifier. Our focus is on the well known AdaBoost algorithm (Freund and Schapire, 1997) based on Multinomial Naive Bayes as base classifiers (Figure 1).

AdaBoost and its variants have been applied to diverse domains with great success, owing to their solid theoretical foundation, accurate prediction, and great simplicity (Freund and Schapire, 1997). For example, Viola and Jones (2001) used AdaBoost to face detection, Hao and Luo (2006) dealt with image segmentation, recognition of handwritten digits, and outdoor scene classification problems. In (Bloehdorn and Hotho, 2004) text classification is explored.

Figure 1: AdaBoost Approach

4 Feature Engineering

The most commonly used text representation method adopted in the literature is known as Bag of Words (BOW) technique, where a document is considered as a BOW, and is represented by a feature vector containing all the words appearing in the corpus. In spite of BOW being simple and very effective in text classification, a large amount of information from the original document is not considered, word order is ruptured, and syntactic structures are broken. Therefore, sophisticated feature extraction methods with a deeper understanding of the documents are required for sentiment classification tasks. Instead of using only BOW, alternative ways to represent text, including Part of Speech (PoS) based features, feature hashing, and lexicons have been addressed in the literature.

We implemented an ensemble of classifiers that receive as input data a combination of three features sets: i) *lexicon features* that captures the semantic aspect of a tweet; ii) *feature hashing* that captures the surface-form as abbreviations, slang terms from this type of social network, elongated words (for example, *loveeeee*), sentences with words without a space between them (for instance, *Ilovveapple!*), and so on; iii) and a *specific syntactic features* for tweets. Technical details of each feature set are provided in the sequel.

Lexicon Features

We use the sentimental lexicon provided by (Thelwall et al., 2010) and (Hu and Liu, 2004). The former is known as SentiStrength and provides: an emotion vocabulary, an emoticons list (with positive, negative, and neutral icons), a negation list, and a booster word list. We use the negative list in cases where the next term in a sentence is an opinion word (either positive or negative). In such cases we have polarity inversion. For example, in the sentence "The house is *not beautiful*", the negative word "*not*" invert the polarity of the opinion word *beautiful*. The booster word list is composed by adverbs that suggest more or less emphasis in the sentiment. For example, in the sentence "He was *incredibly rude*." the term "*incredibly*" is an adverb that lay emphasis on the opinion word "*rude*". Besides using SentiStrength, we use the lexicon approach proposed by (Hu and Liu, 2004). In their approach, a list of words and associations with positive and negative sentiments has been provided that are very useful for sentiment analysis.

These two lexicons were used to build the first feature set according to Table 1, where it is presented an example of tweet representation for the $tweet_1$: "The soccer team didn't play extremely bad last Wednesday." The word "bad" exists in the lexicon list of (Hu and Liu, 2004), and it is a negative word. The word "bad" also exists in the negation list provided by (Thelwall et al., 2010). The term "didn't" is a negative word according to SentiStrength (Thelwall et al., 2010) and there is a polarity inversion of the opinion words ahead. Finally, the term "extremely" belongs the booster word list and this word suggests more emphasis to the opinion words existing ahead.

	positive	negative	neutral	class
$tweet_1$	3	0	0	positive

Table 1: Representing Twitter messages with lexicons.

Feature hashing

Feature hashing has been introduced for text classification in (Shi et al., 2009), (Weinberger et al., 2009), (Forman and Kirshenbaum, 2008), (Langford et al., 2007), (Caragea et al., 2011). In the context of tweet classification, feature hashing offers an approach to reducing the number of features provided as input to a learning algorithm. The original high-dimensional space is "reduced" by *hashing* the features into a lower-dimensional space, i.e., mapping features to hash keys. Thus, multiple features can be mapped to the same hash key, thereby "aggregating" their counts.

We used the MurmurHash3 function (SMHasher, 2010), that is a non-cryptographic hash function suitable for general hash-based lookup tables. It has been used for many purposes, and a recent approach that has emerged is its use for feature hashing or hashing trick. Instead of building and storing an explicit traditional bag-of-words with n-grams, the feature hashing uses a hash function to reduce the dimensionality of the output space and the length of this space (features) is explicitly fixed in advance. For this paper, we used this code (in Python):

Code Listing 1: Murmurhash:

```
from sklearn.utils.murmurhash
import murmurhash3_bytes_u32

for w in "i loveee apple".split():
  print("{0} => {1}".format(
    w,murmurhash3_bytes_u32(w,0)%2**10))
```

The dimensionality is $2 * *10$, i.e 2^{10} features. In this code the output is a hash code for each word "w" in the phrase "i loveee apple", i.e. i => 43, *loveee* => 381 and *apple* => 144. Table 2 shows an example of feature hashing representation.

	1	2	3	4	···	1024	class
$tweet_1$	0	0	1	1	···	0	positive
$tweet_2$	0	1	0	3	···	0	negative
$tweet_3$	2	0	0	0	···	0	positive
⋮	⋮	⋮	⋮	⋮	...	⋮	⋮
$tweet_n$	0	0	2	1	···	0	neutral

Table 2: Representing Twitter messages with feature hashing.

Specific syntactic (PoS) features

We used the Part of Speech (PoS) tagged for tweets with the Twitter NLP tool (Gimpel et al., 2011). It encompasses 25 tags including Nominal, Nominal plus Verbal, Other open-class words like adjectives, adverbs and interjection, Twitter specific tags such as hashtags, mention, discourse marker, just to name a few. Table 3 shows an example of syntactic features representation.

	tag_1	tag_2	tag_3	tag_4	$\cdots$	tag_{25}	class
$tweet_1$	0	0	3	1	$\cdots$	0	positive
$tweet_2$	0	2	0	1	$\cdots$	0	negative
$tweet_3$	1	0	0	0	$\cdots$	0	positive
$\vdots$	$\vdots$	$\vdots$	$\vdots$	$\vdots$	$\ldots$	$\vdots$	$\vdots$
$tweet_n$	0	0	1	1	$\cdots$	0	neutral

Table 3: Representing Twitter messages with syntactic features.

A combination of lexicons, feature hashing, and part-of-speech is used to train the ensemble classifiers, thereby resulting in 1024 features from feature hashing, 3 features from lexicons, and 25 features from PoS.

5 Experimental Setup and Results

We conducted experiments by using the WEKA platform[1]. Table 4 shows the class distributions in training, development, and testing sets. Table 5 presents the results for positive and negative classes with the classifiers used in training set, and Table 6 shows the computed results by SemEval organizers in the test sets.

Training Set				
Set	Positive	Negative	Neutral	Total
Train	3,640 (37%)	1,458 (15%)	4,586 (48%)	9,684
Development Set				
Set	Positive	Negative	Neutral	Total
Dev	575 (35%)	340(20%)	739 (45%)	1,654
Testing Sets				
Set	Positive	Negative	Neutral	Total
LiveJournal	427 (37%)	304 (27%)	411 (36%)	1,142
SMS2013	492 (23%)	394(19%)	1,207 (58%)	2,093
Twitter2013	1,572 (41%)	601 (16%)	1,640 (43%)	3,813
Twitter2014	982 (53%)	202 (11%)	669 (36%)	1,853
Twitter2014Sar	33 (38%)	40 (47%)	13 (15%)	86

Table 4: Class distributions in the training set (Train), development set (Dev) and testing set (Test).

6 Concluding Remarks

From our results, we conclude that the use of AdaBoost provides good performance in the sentiment analysis (message-level subtask). In the cross-validation process, Multinomial Naive Bayes (MNB) has shown better results than Support Vector Machines (SVM) as a component for AdaBoost. However, we feel

[1]http://www.cs.waikato.ac.nz/ml/weka/

Set	Algorithm	F-Measure Positive	F-Measure Negative	Average
Train	MNB	63.40	49.40	56.40
Train	SVM	64.00	44.50	54.20
Train	AdaBoost w/ SVM	62.50	44.50	53.50
Train	**AdaBoost w/ MNB**	**65.10**	**49.60**	**57.35**

Table 5: Results from 10-fold cross validation in the training set with default parameters of Weka. MNB and SVM stand for Multinomial Naive Bayes and Support Vector Machine, respectively.

Scoring LiveJournal2014			
class	precision	recall	F-measure
positive	69.79	64.92	67.27
negative	76.64	61.64	68.33
neutral	51.82	69.84	59.50
overall score : 67.80			
Scoring SMS2013			
positive	61.99	46.78	53.32
negative	72.34	42.86	53.82
neutral	53.85	83.76	65.56
overall score : 53.57			
Scoring Twitter2013			
positive	68.07	66.13	67.08
negative	48.09	50.00	49.02
neutral	67.20	68.15	67.67
overall score : 58.05			
Scoring Twitter2014			
positive	65.17	70.48	67.72
negative	53.47	48.21	50.70
neutral	59.94	55.62	57.70
overall score : 59.21			
Scoring Twitter2014Sarcasm			
positive	63.64	44.68	52.50
negative	22.50	75.00,	34.62
neutral	76.92	37.04	50.00
overall score : 43.56			

Table 6: Results in the test sets — AdaBoost plus Multinomial Naive Bayes, which was the best algorithm in cross validation.

that further investigations are necessary before making strong claims about this result.

Overall, the SemEval Tasks have make evident the usual challenges when mining opinions from Social Media channels: noisy text, irregular grammar and orthography, highly specific lingo, and others. Moreover, temporal dependencies can affect the performance if the training and test data have been gathered at different.

Acknowledgements

The authors would like to thank the Research Agencies CAPES, FAPESP, and CNPq for their financial support.

References

Sitaram Asur and Bernardo A. Huberman. 2010. Predicting the future with social media. In *Proceedings of the 2010 International Conference on*

Web Intelligence and Intelligent Agent Technology - Volume 01, WI-IAT '10, pages 492–499, Washington, DC, USA. IEEE Computer Society.

Stephan Bloehdorn and Andreas Hotho. 2004. Text classification by boosting weak learners based on terms and concepts. In *Proceedings of the Fourth IEEE International Conference on Data Mining*, pages 331–334. IEEE Computer Society Press, November.

Cornelia Caragea, Adrian Silvescu, and Prasenjit Mitra. 2011. Protein sequence classification using feature hashing. In Fang-Xiang Wu, Mohammed Javeed Zaki, Shinichi Morishita, Yi Pan, Stephen Wong, Anastasia Christianson, and Xiaohua Hu, editors, *BIBM*, pages 538–543. IEEE.

Sam Clark and Rich Wicentwoski. 2013. Swatcs: Combining simple classifiers with estimated accuracy. In *Second Joint Conference on Lexical and Computational Semantics (*SEM), Volume 2: Proceedings of the Seventh International Workshop on Semantic Evaluation (SemEval 2013)*, pages 425–429, Atlanta, Georgia, USA, June.

Nicholas A. Diakopoulos and David A. Shamma. 2010. Characterizing debate performance via aggregated twitter sentiment. In *Proceedings of the SIGCHI Conference on Human Factors in Computing Systems*, CHI '10, pages 1195–1198, New York, NY, USA. ACM.

George Forman and Evan Kirshenbaum. 2008. Extremely fast text feature extraction for classification and indexing. In *CIKM '08: Proceeding of the 17th ACM conference on Information and knowledge management*, pages 1221–1230, New York, NY, USA. ACM.

Yoav Freund and Robert E. Schapire. 1996. Experiments with a new boosting algorithm. In *Thirteenth International Conference on Machine Learning*, pages 148–156, San Francisco. Morgan Kaufmann.

Yoav Freund and Robert E Schapire. 1997. A decision-theoretic generalization of on-line learning and an application to boosting. *Journal of Computer and System Sciences*, 55(1):119 – 139.

Kevin Gimpel, Nathan Schneider, Brendan O'Connor, Dipanjan Das, Daniel Mills, Jacob Eisenstein, Michael Heilman, Dani Yogatama, Jeffrey Flanigan, and Noah A. Smith. 2011. Part-of-speech tagging for twitter: Annotation, features, and experiments. In *Proceedings of the 49th Annual Meeting of the Association for Computational Linguistics – Short Papers - Volume 2*, HLT '11, pages 42–47, Stroudsburg, PA, USA.

Alec Go, Richa Bhayani, and Lei Huang. 2009. Twitter sentiment classification using distant supervision. *Processing*, pages 1–6.

Wei Hao and Jiebo Luo. 2006. Generalized Multiclass AdaBoost and Its Applications to Multimedia Classification. In *Computer Vision and Pattern Recognition Workshop, 2006. CVPRW '06. Conference on*, page 113, Washington, DC, USA, June. IEEE.

Ammar Hassan, Ahmed Abbasi, and Daniel Zeng. 2013. Twitter sentiment analysis: A bootstrap ensemble framework. In *SocialCom*, pages 357–364. IEEE.

Minqing Hu and Bing Liu. 2004. Mining and summarizing customer reviews. In *Proceedings of the tenth ACM SIGKDD international conference on Knowledge discovery and data mining*, KDD '04, pages 168–177, New York, NY, USA. ACM.

Bernard J. Jansen, Mimi Zhang, Kate Sobel, and Abdur Chowdury. 2009. Twitter power: Tweets as electronic word of mouth. *J. Am. Soc. Inf. Sci. Technol.*, 60(11):2169–2188, nov.

John Langford, Alex Strehl, and Lihong Li. 2007. Vowpal wabbit online learning project. `http://mloss.org/software/view/53/`.

Jimmy Lin and Alek Kolcz. 2012. Large-scale machine learning at twitter. In *Proceedings of the 2012 ACM SIGMOD International Conference on Management of Data*, SIGMOD '12, pages 793–804, New York, NY, USA. ACM.

Preslav Nakov, Sara Rosenthal, Zornitsa Kozareva, Veselin Stoyanov, Alan Ritter, and Theresa Wilson. 2013. Semeval-2013 task 2: Sentiment analysis in twitter. In *Second Joint Conference on Lexical and Computational Semantics (*SEM), Volume 2: Proceedings of the Seventh International Workshop on Semantic Evaluation (SemEval 2013)*, pages 312–320, Atlanta, Georgia, USA, June.

Brendan O'Connor, Ramnath Balasubramanyan, Bryan R. Routledge, and Noah A. Smith. 2010. From tweets to polls: Linking text sentiment to public opinion time series. In *ICWSM'10*, pages 1–1.

Penagos Carlos Rodriguez, Jordi Atserias, Joan Codina-Filba, David Garcıa-Narbona, Jens Grivolla, Patrik Lambert, and Roser Saurı. 2013. Fbm: Combining lexicon-based ml and heuristics for social media polarities. In *Proceedings of SemEval-2013 – International Workshop on Semantic Evaluation Co-located with *Sem and NAACL*, Atlanta, Georgia. Url date at 2013-10-10.

David A. Shamma, Lyndon Kennedy, and Elizabeth F. Churchill. 2009. Tweet the debates: Understanding community annotation of uncollected sources. In *In WSM ?09: Proceedings of the international workshop on Workshop on Social.*

Qinfeng Shi, James Petterson, Gideon Dror, John Langford, Alex Smola, and S.V.N. Vishwanathan. 2009. Hash kernels for structured data. *J. Mach. Learn. Res.*, 10:2615–2637.

SMHasher. 2010. The murmurhash family of hash functions.

Michael Speriosu, Nikita Sudan, Sid Upadhyay, and Jason Baldridge. 2011. Twitter polarity classification with label propagation over lexical links and the follower graph. In *Proceedings of the First Workshop on Unsupervised Learning in NLP*, pages 53–63, Stroudsburg, PA, USA.

Mike Thelwall, Kevan Buckley, Georgios Paltoglou, Di Cai, and Arvid Kappas. 2010. Sentiment in short strength detection informal text. *J. Am. Soc. Inf. Sci. Technol.*, 61(12):2544–2558, December.

Paul Viola and Michael Jones. 2001. Robust real-time object detection. In *International Journal of Computer Vision*.

Kilian Q. Weinberger, Anirban Dasgupta, John Langford, Alexander J. Smola, and Josh Attenberg. 2009. Feature hashing for large scale multitask learning. In Andrea Pohoreckyj Danyluk, L Bottou, and Michael L. Littman, editors, *ICML*, volume 382 of *ACM International Conference Proceeding Series*, page 140. ACM.

Jun-Ming Xu, Kwang-Sung Jun, Xiaojin Zhu, and Amy Bellmore. 2012. Learning from bullying traces in social media. In *HLT-NAACL*, pages 656–666.

Gap in pagination due to formatting issues.

Pages 129-134

BioinformaticsUA: Concept Recognition in Clinical Narratives Using a Modular and Highly Efficient Text Processing Framework

Sérgio Matos
DETI/IEETA
University of Aveiro
3810-193 Aveiro, Portugal
aleixomatos@ua.pt

Tiago Nunes
DETI/IEETA
University of Aveiro
3810-193 Aveiro, Portugal
tiago.nunes@ua.pt

José Luís Oliveira
DETI/IEETA
University of Aveiro
3810-193 Aveiro, Portugal
jlo@ua.pt

Abstract

Clinical texts, such as discharge summaries or test reports, contain a valuable amount of information that, if efficiently and effectively mined, could be used to infer new knowledge, possibly leading to better diagnosis and therapeutics. With this in mind, the SemEval-2014 Analysis of Clinical Text task aimed at assessing and improving current methods for identification and normalization of concepts occurring in clinical narrative. This paper describes our approach in this task, which was based on a fully modular architecture for text mining. We followed a pure dictionary-based approach, after performing error analysis to refine our dictionaries.

We obtained an F-measure of 69.4% in the entity recognition task, achieving the second best precision over all submitted runs (81.3%), with above average recall (60.5%). In the normalization task, we achieved a strict accuracy of 53.1% and a relaxed accuracy of 87.0%.

1 Introduction

Named entity recognition (NER) is an information extraction task where the aim is to identify mentions of specific types of entities in text. This task has been one of the main focus in the biomedical text mining research field, specially when applied to the scientific literature. Such efforts have led to the development of various tools for the recognition of diverse entities, including species names, genes and proteins, chemicals and drugs, anatomical concepts and diseases. These tools use methods based on dictionaries, rules, and machine learning, or a combination of those depending on the specificities and requirements of each concept type (Campos et al., 2013b). After identifying entities occurring in texts, it is also relevant to disambiguate those entities and associate each occurrence to a specific concept, using an univocal identifier from a reference database such as Uniprot[1] for proteins, or OMIM[2] for genetic disorders. This is usually performed by matching the identified entities against a knowledge-base, possibly evaluating the textual context in which the entity occurred to identify the best matching concept.

The SemEval-2014 Analysis of Clinical Text task aimed at the identification and normalization of concepts in clinical narrative. Two subtasks were defined, where Task A was focused on the recognition of entities belonging to the 'disorders' semantic group of the Unified Medical Language System (UMLS), and Task B was focused on normalization of these entities to a specific UMLS Concept Unique Identifier (CUI). Specifically, the task definition required that concepts should only be normalized to CUIs that could be mapped to the SNOMED CT[3] terminology.

In this paper, we present a dictionary-based approach for the recognition of these concepts, supported by a modular text analysis and annotation pipeline.

2 Methods

2.1 Data

The task made use of the ShARe corpus (Pradhan et al., 2013), which contains manually annotated clinical notes from the MIMIC II database[4] (Saeed et al., 2011). The corpus contains 298 documents,

[1] http://www.uniprot.org/
[2] http://www.omim.org/
[3] http://www.ihtsdo.org/snomed-ct/
[4] http://mimic.physionet.org/database.html

Proceedings of the 8th International Workshop on Semantic Evaluation (SemEval 2014), pages 135–139,
Dublin, Ireland, August 23-24, 2014.

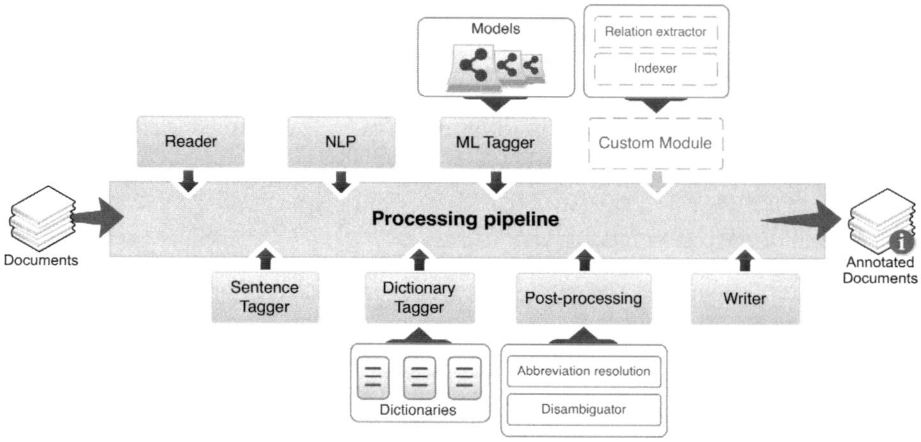

Figure 1: Neji's processing pipeline used for annotating the documents. Boxes with dotted lines indicate optional processing modules. Machine-learning models were not used.

with a total of 11156 annotations of disorder mentions. These annotations include a UMLS concept identifier when such normalization was possible according to the annotation guidelines.

Besides this manually annotated corpus, a larger unannotated data set was also made available to task participants, in order to allow the application of unsupervised methods.

2.2 Processing Pipeline

We used Neji, an open source framework for biomedical concept recognition based on an automated processing pipeline that supports the combined application of machine learning and dictionary-based approaches (Campos et al., 2013a). Apart from offering a flexible framework for developing different text mining systems, Neji includes various built-in methods, from text loading and pre-processing, to natural language parsing and entity tagging, all optimized for processing biomedical text. Namely, it includes a sentence splitting module adapted from the Lingpipe library[5] and a customized version of GDep (Sagae and Tsujii, 2007) for tokenization, part-of-speech tagging, and other natural language processing tasks. Figure 1 shows the complete Neji text processing pipeline, illustrating its module based architecture built on top of a common data structure. The dictionary module performs exact, case-insensitive matching using Deterministic Finite Automatons (DFAs), allowing very efficient processing of documents and matching against dozens of dictionaries containing millions of terms.

Neji has been validated against different biomedical literature corpora, using specifically created machine learning models and dictionaries. Regarding the recognition of disorder concepts, Neji achieved an F-measure of 68% on exact mathing and 83% on approximate matching against the NCBI disease corpus, using a pure dictionary-based approach (Doğan and Lu, 2012).

2.3 Dictionaries

Following the task description and the corpus annotation guidelines, we compiled dictionaries for the following UMLS semantic types, using the 2012AB version of the UMLS Metathesaurus:

- Congenital Abnormality
- Acquired Abnormality
- Injury or Poisoning
- Pathologic Function
- Disease or Syndrome
- Mental or Behavioral Dysfunction
- Cell or Molecular Dysfunction
- Anatomical Abnormality
- Neoplastic Process
- Signs and Symptoms

Additionally, although the semantic type 'Findings' was not considered as part of the 'Disorders' group, we created a customized dictionary including only those concepts of this semantic type that occurred as an annotation in the training data. If

[5] http://alias-i.com/lingpipe/index.html

a synonym of a given concept was present in the training data annotations, we added all the synonyms of that concept to this dictionary. This allowed including some concepts that occur very frequently (e.g. 'fever'), while filtering out many concepts of this semantic type that are not relevant for this task. In total, these dictionaries contain almost 1.5 million terms, of which 525 thousand (36%) were distinct terms, for nearly 293 thousand distinct concept identifiers.

Refining the dictionaries

In order to expand the dictionaries, we preprocessed the UMLS terms to find certain patterns indicating acronyms. For example, if a term such as 'Miocardial infarction (MI)' or 'Miocardial infarction - MI' appeared as a synonym for a given UMLS concept, we checked if the acronym (in this example, 'MI') was also a synonym for that concept, and added it to a separate dictionary if this was not the case. This resulted in the addition of 10430 terms, for which only 1459 (14%) were distinct, for 2086 concepts. These numbers reflect the expected ambiguity in the acronyms, which represents one of the main challenges in the annotation of clinical texts.

Furthermore, in order to improve the baseline results obtained with the initial dictionaries, we performed error analysis to identify frequent errors in the automatic annotations. Using the manual annotations as reference, we counted the number of times a term was correctly annotated in the documents (true positives) and compared it to the number of times that same term caused an annotation to be incorrectly added (a false positive). We then defined an exclusion list containing 817 terms for which the ratio of these two counts was 0.25 or less.

Following the same approach, we created a second exclusion list by comparing the number of FNs to the number of FPs, and selecting those terms for which this ratio was lower than 0.5. This resulted in an exclusion list containing 623 terms.

We also processed the unannotated data set, in order to identify frequently occurring terms that could be removed from the dictionaries to avoid large numbers of false positives. This dataset includes over 92 thousand documents, which were processed in around 23 minutes (an average of 67 documents per second) and produced almost 4 million annotations. Examples of terms from our dictionaries that occur very frequently in this data set are: 'sinus rhythm', which occurred almost 35 thousand times across all documents, and 'past medical history', 'allergies' and 'abnormalities', all occurring more than 15 thousand times. In fact, most of the highly frequent terms belonged to the 'Findings' semantic type. Although this analysis gave some insights regarding the content of the data, its results were not directly used to refine the dictionaries, since the filtering steps described above led to better overall results.

2.4 Concept Normalization

According to the task description, only those UMLS concepts that could be mapped to a SNOMED CT identifier should be considered in the normalization step, while all other entities should be added to the results without a concept identifier. We followed a straightforward normalization strategy, by assigning the corresponding UMLS CUIs to each identified entity, during the dictionary-matching phase. We then filtered out any CUIs that did not have a SNOMED CT mapping in the UMLS data. In the cases when multiple idenfiers were still left, we naively selected the first one, according the dictionary ordering defined above, followed in the end by the filtered 'Findings' dictionary and the additional acronyms dictionary.

3 Results and Discussion

3.1 Evaluation Metrics

The common evaluation metrics were used to evaluate the entity recognition task, namely $Precision = TP/(TP + FP)$ and $Recall = TP/(TP+FN)$, where TP, FP and FN are respectively the number of true positive, false positive, and false negative annotations, and $Fmeasure = 2 \times Precision \times Recall/(Precision + Recall)$, the harmonic mean of precision and recall. Additionally, the performance was evaluated considering both strict and relaxed, or overlap, matching of the gold standard annotations.

For the normalization task, the metric used to evaluate performance was accuracy. Again, two matching methods were considered: strict accuracy was defined as the ratio between the number of correct identifiers assigned to the predicted entities, and the total number of entities manually annotated in the corpus; while relaxed accuracy measured the ratio between the number of correct

	Task A						Task B	
	Strict			Relaxed			Strict	Relaxed
Run	P	R	F	P	R	F	Acc	Acc
Best	0,843	0,786	0,813	0,936	0,866	0,900	0,741	0,873
Average	0,648	0,574	0,599	0,842	0,731	0,770	0,461	0,753
0	**0,813**	**0,605**	**0,694**	**0,929**	**0,693**	**0,794**	0,527	**0,870**
1	0,600	0,621	0,610	0,698	0,723	0,710	**0,531**	0,855
2	0,753	0,538	0,628	0,865	0,621	0,723	0,463	0,861

Table 1: Official results on the test dataset. The best results for each task and matching strategy are identified in bold. The best run from all participating teams as well as the overall average are shown for comparison.

identifiers and the number of entities correctly predicted by the system.

3.2 Test Results

We submitted three runs of annotations for the documents in the test set, as described below:

- Run 0: Resulting annotations were filtered using the first exclusion list (817 terms, TP/FP ratio 0.25 or lower). The extra acronyms dictionary was not used, and matches up to 3 characters long were filtered out, except if they were 3 characters long and appeared as uppercase in the original text.

- Run 1: The extra acronyms dictionary was included. The same exclusion list as in Run 0 was used, but short annotations were not removed.

- Run 2: The extra acronyms dictionary was included. The second exclusion list was used, and short annotations were not removed.

Table 1 shows the official results obtained on the test set for each submitted run.

Overall, the best results were obtained with the more stringent dictionaries and filtering, leading to a precision of 81.3% and and F-measure of 69.4%. This results was achieved without the use of the additional acronyms list, and also by removing short annotations. This filtering does not discard annotations with three characters if they appeared in uppercase in the original text, as this more clearly indicates the use of an acronym. Preliminary evaluation on the training data showed that this choice had a small, but positive contribution to the overall results.

We achieved the second-best precision results with this first run, considering both strict and relaxed matching. Although this level of precision was not associated to a total loss in recall, we were only able to identify 70% of the disorder entities, even when considering relaxed matching. To overcome this limitation, we will evaluate the combined use of dictionaries and machine-learning models, taking advantage of the Neji framework. Another possible limitation has to do with the recognition and disambiguation of acronyms, which we will also evaluate further.

Regarding the normalization results (Task B), we achieved the 12th and 10th best overall results, considering strict and relaxed accuracies respectively, corresponding to the 7th and 6th best team. For relaxed matching, our results are 5,8% lower than the best team, which is a positive result given the naïve approach taken. These performances may be improved as a result of enhancements in the entity recognition step, and by applying a better normalization strategy.

4 Conclusions

We present results for the recognition and normalization of disorder mentions in clinical texts, using a dictionary-based approach . The dictionaries were iteratively filtered following error-analysis, in order to better tailor the dictionaries according to the task annotation guidelines. In the end, a precision of 81.3% was achieved, for a recall of 60.5% and a F-measure of 69.4%. The use of a machine-learning based approach and a better acronym resolution method are being studied with the aim of improving the recall rate.

In the normalization task, using the refined dictionaries directly, we achieved a strict accuracy of 53.1% and a relaxed accuracy of 87.0%. Strict normalization results, as given by the metric defined for this task, are dependent on the entity recognition recall rate, and are expected to follow improvements that may be achieved in that step.

Acknowledgements

This work was supported by National Funds through FCT - Foundation for Science and Technology, in the context of the project PEst-OE/EEI/UI0127/2014. S. Matos is funded by FCT under the FCT Investigator programme.

References

David Campos, Sérgio Matos, and José Luís Oliveira. 2013a. A modular framework for biomedical concept recognition. *BMC Bioinformatics*, 14:281.

David Campos, Sérgio Matos, and José Luís Oliveira, 2013b. *Current Methodologies for Biomedical Named Entity Recognition*, pages 839–868. John Wiley & Sons, Inc., Hoboken, New Jersey.

Rezarta Islamaj Doğan and Zhiyong Lu. 2012. An improved corpus of disease mentions in PubMed citations. In *Proceedings of BioNLP'12*, pages 91–99, Stroudsburg, PA, USA, June.

Sameer Pradhan, Noemie Elhadad, Brett South, David Martinez, Lee Christensen, Amy Vogel, Hanna Suominen, Wendy Chapman, and Guergana Savova. 2013. Task 1: ShARe/CLEF eHealth Evaluation Lab 2013. *Online Working Notes of the CLEF 2013 Evaluation Labs and Workshop*.

Mohammed Saeed, Mauricio Villarroel, Andrew Reisner, Gari Clifford, Li-Wei Lehman, George Moody, Thomas Heldt, Tin Kyaw, Benjamin Moody, and Roger Mark. 2011. Multiparameter Intelligent Monitoring in Intensive Care II (MIMIC-II): a public-access intensive care unit database. *Critical Care Medicine*, 39(5):952.

Kenji Sagae and Jun'ichi Tsujii. 2007. Dependency parsing and domain adaptation with LR models and parser ensembles. In *Joint Conference on Empirical Methods in Natural Language Processing and Computational Natural Language Learning*, pages 1044–1050, Prague, Czech Republic.

Blinov: Distributed Representations of Words for Aspect-Based Sentiment Analysis at SemEval 2014

Pavel Blinov, Eugeny Kotelnikov
Vyatka State Humanities University
{blinoff.pavel, kotelnikov.ev}@gmail.com

Abstract

The article describes our system submitted to the SemEval-2014 task on Aspect-Based Sentiment Analysis. The methods based on distributed representations of words for the aspect term extraction and aspect term polarity detection tasks are presented. The methods for the aspect category detection and category polarity detection tasks are presented as well. Well-known skip-gram model for constructing the distributed representations is briefly described. The results of our methods are shown in comparison with the baseline and the best result.

1 Introduction

The sentiment analysis became an important Natural Language Processing (NLP) task in the recent few years. As many NLP tasks it's a challenging one. The sentiment analysis can be very helpful for some practical applications. For example, it allows to study the users' opinions about a product automatically.

Many research has been devoted to the general sentiment analysis (Pang et al., 2002), (Amine et al., 2013), (Blinov et al., 2013) or analysis of individual sentences (Yu and Hatzivassiloglou, 2003), (Kim and Hovy, 2004), (Wiebe and Riloff, 2005). Soon it became clear that the sentiment analysis on the level of a whole text or even sentences is too coarse. General sentiment analysis by its design is not capable to perform the detailed analysis of an expressed opinion. For example, it cannot correctly detect the opinion in the sentence "*Great food but the service was dreadful!*". The sentence carries opposite opinions on two facets of a restaurant. Therefore the more detailed version of the sentiment analysis is needed. Such a version is called the aspect-based sentiment analysis and it works on the level of the significant aspects of the target entity (Liu, 2012).

The aspect-based sentiment analysis includes two main subtasks: the aspect term extraction and its polarity detection (Liu, 2012). In this article we describe the methods which address both subtasks. The methods are based on the distributed representations of words. Such word representations (or word embeddings) are useful in many NLP task, e.g. (Turian et al., 2009), (Al-Rfou' et al., 2013), (Turney, 2013).

The remainder of the article is as follows: section two gives the overview of the data; the third section shortly describes the distributed representations of words. The methods of the aspect term extraction and polarity detection are presented in the fourth and the fifth sections respectively. The conclusions are given in the sixth section.

2 The Data

The organisers provided the train data for restaurant and laptop domains. But as it will be clear further our methods are heavily dependent on unlabelled text data. So we additionally collected the user reviews about restaurants from *tripadviser.com* and about laptops from *amazon.com*. General statistics of the data are shown in Table 1.

Proceedings of the 8th International Workshop on Semantic Evaluation (SemEval 2014), pages 140–144,
Dublin, Ireland, August 23-24, 2014.

Table 1: The amount of reviews.

Domain	The amount of reviews
Restaurants	652 055
Laptops	109 550

For all the data we performed tokenization, stemming and morphological analysis using the FreeLing library (Padró and Stanilovsky, 2012).

3 Distributed Representations of Words

In this section we'll try to give the high level idea of the distributed representations of words. The more technical details can be found in (Mikolov et al., 2013).

It is closely related with a new promising direction in machine learning called the deep learning. The core idea of the unsupervised deep learning algorithms is to find automatically the "good" set of features to represent the target object (text, image, audio signal, etc.). The object represented by the vector of real numbers is called *the distributed representation* (Rumelhart et al., 1986). We used the skip-gram model (Mikolov et al., 2013) implemented in Gensim toolkit (Řehůřek and Sojka, 2010).

In general the learning procedure is as follows. All the texts of the corpus are stuck together in a single sequence of sentences. On the basis of the corpus the lexicon is constructed. Next, the dimensionality of the vectors is chosen (we used 300 in our experiments). The greater number of dimensions allows to capture more language regularities but leads to more computational complexity of the learning. Each word from the lexicon is associated with the real numbers vector of the selected dimensionality. Originally all the vectors are randomly initialized. During the learning procedure the algorithm "slides" with the fixed size window (it's algorithm parameter that was retained by default – 5 words) along the words of the sequence and calculates the probability (1) of context words appearance within the window based on its central word under review (or more precisely, its vector representation) (Mikolov et al., 2013).

$$p(w_O \mid w_I) = \frac{\exp({v'_{w_O}}^T v_{w_I})}{\sum_{w=1}^{W} \exp({v'_w}^T v_w)}, \quad (1)$$

where v_w and v'_w are the input and output vector representations of w; w_I and w_O are the current and predicted words, W – the number of words in vocabulary.

The ultimate goal of the described process is to get such "good" vectors for each word, which allow to predict its probable context. All such vectors together form the vector space where semantically similar words are grouped.

4 Aspect Term Extraction Method

We apply the same method for the aspect term extraction task (Pontiki et al., 2014) for both domains. The method consists of two steps: the candidate selection and the term extraction.

4.1 Candidate Selection

First of all we collect some statistics about the terms in the train collection. We analysed two facets of the aspect terms: the number of words and their morphological structure. The information about the number of words in a term is shown in Table 2.

Table 2: The statistics for the number of words in a term.

	Domain	
Aspect term	Restaurant, %	Laptop, %
One-word	72.13	55.66
Two-word	19.05	32.87
Greater	8.82	11.47

On the basis of that we've decided to process only single and two-word aspect terms. From the single terms we treat only singular (NN, e.g. *staff, rice, texture, processor, ram, insult*) and plural nouns (NNS, e.g. *perks, bagels, times, dvds, buttons, pictures*) as possible candidates, because they largely predominate among the one-word terms. All conjunctions of the form NN_NN (e.g. *sea_bass, lotus_leaf, chicken_dish, battery_life, virus_protection, customer_disservice*) and NN_NNS (e.g. *sushi_places, menu_choices, seafood_lovers, usb_devices, recovery_discs, software_works*) were candidates for the two-word terms also because they are most common in two-word aspect terms.

4.2 Term Extraction

The second step for the aspect term identification is the term extraction. As has already been told the space (see Section 3) specifies the word groups. Therefore the measure of similarity between the words (vectors) can be defined. For NLP tasks it is often the cosine similarity measure. The similarity between two vectors $\vec{a} = (a_1,...,a_n)$ and $\vec{b} = (b_1,...,b_n)$ is given by (Manning et al., 2008):

$$\cos(\theta) = \frac{\sum_{i=1}^{n} a_i b_i}{\sqrt{\sum_{i=1}^{n} a_i^2} \cdot \sqrt{\sum_{i=1}^{n} b_i^2}}, \quad (2)$$

where θ – the angle between the vectors, n – the dimensionality of the space.

In case of the restaurant domain the category and aspect terms are specified. For each category the seed of the aspect terms can be automatically selected: if only one category is assigned for a train sentence then all its terms belong to it. Within each set the average similarity between the terms (the threshold category) can be found.

For the new candidate the average similarities with the category's seeds are calculated. If it is greater than the threshold of any category than the candidate is marked as an aspect term.

Also we've additionally applied some rules:

- Join consecutive terms in a single term.
- Join neutral adjective ahead the term (see Section 5.2 for clarification about the neutral adjective).
- Join fragments matching the pattern: <an aspect term> of <an aspect term>.

In case of the laptop domain there are no specified categories so we treated all terms as the terms belonging to one general category. And the same procedure with candidates was performed.

4.3 Category Detection

For the restaurant domain there was also the aspect category detection task (Pontiki et al., 2014).

Since each word is represented by a vector, each sentence can be cast to a single point as the average of its vectors. Further average point for each category can be found by means of the sentence points. Then for an unseen sentence the average point of its word vectors is calculated. The category is selected by calculating the distances between all category points and a new point and by choosing the minimum distance.

4.4 Results

The aspect term extraction and the aspect category detection tasks were evaluated with Precision, Recall and F-measure (Pontiki et al., 2014). The F-measure was a primary metric for these tasks so we present only it.

The result of our method ranked 19 out of 28 submissions (constrained and unconstrained) for the aspect term extraction task for the laptop domain and 17 out of 29 for the restaurant domain. For the category detection task (restaurant domain) the method ranked 9 out of 21.

Table 3 shows the results of our method (**Bold**) for aspect term extraction task in comparison with the baseline (Pontiki et al., 2014) and the best result. Analogically the results for the aspect category detection task are presented in Table 4.

Table 3: Aspect term extraction results (F-measure).

	Laptop	**Restaurant**
Best	0.7455	0.8401
Blinov	**0.5207**	**0.7121**
Baseline	0.3564	0.4715

Table 4: Aspect category detection results (F-measure).

	Restaurant
Best	0.8858
Blinov	**0.7527**
Baseline	0.6389

5 Polarity Detection Method

Our polarity detection method also exploits the vector space (from Section 3) because the emotional similarity between words can be traced in it. As with the aspect term extraction method we follow two-stage approach: the candidate selection and the polarity detection.

5.1 Candidate Selection

All adjectives and verbs are considered as the polarity term candidates. The amplifiers and the negations have an important role in the process of result polarity forming. In our method we took into account only negations because it strongly affects the word polarity. We've joined into one unit all text fragments that match the following pattern: not + <JJ | VB>.

5.2 Term Polarity Detection

At first we manually collected the small etalon sets of positive and negative words for each domain. Every set contained 15 words that clearly identify the sentiment. For example, for the positive polarity there were words such as: great, fast, attentive, yummy, etc. and for the negative polarity there were words like: terrible, ugly, not_work, offensive, etc.

By measuring the average similarity for a candidate to the positive and the negative seed words we decided whether it is positive (+1) or negative (–1). Also we set up a neutral threshold and a candidate's polarity was treated as neutral (0) if it didn't exceed the threshold.

For each term (within the window of 6 words) we were looking for its closest polarity term candidate and sum up their polarities. For the final decision about the term's polarity there were some conditions:

- **If** sum > 0 **then** *positive*.
- **If** sum < 0 **then** *negative*.
- **If** sum == 0 **and** all polarity terms are neutral **then** *neutral* **else** *conflict*.

5.3 Category Polarity Detection

By analogy with the category detection method, using the train collection, we calculate the average polarity points for each category, i.e. there were 5×4 such points (5 categories and 4 values of polarity). Then a sentence was cast to a point as the average of all its word-vectors. And closest polarity points for the specified categories defined the polarity.

5.4 Results

The results of our method (**Bold**) for the polarity detection tasks are around the baseline results for the Accuracy measure (Tables 5, 6).

Table 5: Aspect term polarity detection results (Accuracy).

	Laptop	Restaurant
Best	0.7049	0.8095
Blinov	**0.5229**	**0.6358**
Baseline	0.5107	0.6428

Table 6: Category polarity detection results (Accuracy).

	Restaurant
Best	0.8293
Blinov	**0.6566**
Baseline	0.6566

However the test data is skewed to the positive class and for that case the Accuracy is a poor indicator. Because of that we also show macro F-measure results for our and baseline methods (Tables 7, 8).

Table 7: Aspect term polarity detection results (F-measure).

	Laptop	Restaurant
Blinov	**0.3738**	**0.4334**
Baseline	0.2567	0.2989

Table 8: Category polarity detection results (F-measure).

	Restaurant
Blinov	**0.5051**
Baseline	0.3597

From that we can conclude that our method of the polarity detection more delicately deals with the minor represented classes than the baseline method.

6 Conclusion

In the article we presented the methods for two main subtasks for aspect-based sentiment analysis: the aspect term extraction and the polarity detection. The methods are based on the distributed representation of words and the notion of similarities between the words.

For the aspect term extraction and category detection tasks we get satisfied results which are consistent with our cross-validation metrics. Unfortunately for the polarity detection tasks the result of our method by official metrics are low. But we showed that the proposed method is not so bad and is capable to deal with the skewed data better than the baseline method.

Acknowledgments

We would like to thank the organizers and the reviewers for their efforts.

Reference

Abdelmalek Amine, Reda Mohamed Hamou and Michel Simonet. 2013. Detecting Opinions in Tweets. *International Journal of Data Mining and Emerging Technologies*, 3(1):23–32.

Christopher Manning, Prabhakar Raghavan and Hinrich Schütze. 2008. Introduction to Information Retrieval. *Cambridge University Press*, New York, NY, USA.

Bo Pang, Lillian Lee and Shivakumar Vaithyanathan. 2002. Thumbs up?: sentiment classification using machine learning techniques. In *Proceedings of the Conference on Empirical Methods in Natural Language Processing*, pages 79–86.

Bing Liu. 2012. Sentiment Analysis and Opinion Mining. *Synthesis Lectures on Human Language Technologies*.

Pavel Blinov, Maria Klekovkina, Eugeny Kotelnikov and Oleg Pestov. 2013. Research of lexical approach and machine learning methods for sentiment analysis. *Computational Linguistics and Intellectual Technologies*, 2(12):48–58.

Janyce Wiebe and Ellen Riloff. 2005. Creating subjective and objective sentence classifiers from unannotated texts. In *Proceedings of the 6th International Conference on Computational Linguistics and Intelligent Text Processing*, pages 486–497.

Joseph Turian, Lev Ratinov, Yoshua Bengio and Dan Roth. 2009. A preliminary evaluation of word representations for named-entity recognition. In *Proceedings of NIPS Workshop on Grammar Induction, Representation of Language and Language Learning*.

Tomas Mikolov, Ilya Sutskever, Kai Chen, Greg Corrado and Jeffrey Dean. 2013. Distributed Representations of Words and Phrases and their Compositionality. In *Proceedings of NIPS*, pages 3111–3119.

Lluís Padró and Evgeny Stanilovsky. 2012. FreeLing 3.0: Towards Wider Multilinguality. In *Proceedings of the Language Resources and Evaluation Conference*, LREC 2012, pages 2473–2479.

Soo-Min Kim and Eduard Hovy. 2004. Determining the sentiment of opinions. In *Proceedings of the 20th International Conference on Computational Linguistics*, COLING-2004.

Maria Pontiki, Dimitrios Galanis, John Pavlopoulos, Harris Papageorgiou, Ion Androutsopoulos and Suresh Manandhar. 2014. SemEval-2014 Task 4: Aspect Based Sentiment Analysis. In *Proceedings of the 8th International Workshop on Semantic Evaluation*, SemEval 2014, Dublin, Ireland.

Peter Turney. 2013. Distributional semantics beyond words: Supervised learning of analogy and paraphrase. *Transactions of the Association for Computational Linguistics*, 1:353-366.

Radim Řehůřek and Petr Sojka. 2010. Software Framework for Topic Modelling with Large Corpora. In *Proceedings of the LREC 2010 Workshop on New Challenges for NLP Frameworks*, pages 46–50.

Rami Al-Rfou', Bryan Perozzi, Steven Skiena. 2013. Polyglot: Distributed Word Representations for Multilingual NLP. In *Proceedings of Conference on Computational Natural Language Learning*, CoNLL'2013.

David Rumelhart, Geoffrey Hintont, Ronald Williams. 1986. Learning representations by back-propagating errors. *Nature*.

Hong Yu and Vasileios Hatzivassiloglou. 2003. Towards answering opinion questions: Separating facts from opinions and identifying the polarity of opinion sentences. In *Proceedings of the 2003 Conference on Empirical Methods in Natural Language Processing*, pages 129–136.

BUAP: Evaluating Compositional Distributional Semantic Models on Full Sentences through Semantic Relatedness and Textual Entailment

Saúl León, Darnes Vilariño, David Pinto, Mireya Tovar, Beatriz Beltrán
Benemérita Universidad Autónoma de Puebla
Faculty of Computer Science
14 Sur y Av. San Claudio, CU
Puebla, Puebla, México
{saul.leon,darnes,dpinto,mtovar,bbeltran}@cs.buap.mx

Abstract

The results obtained by the BUAP team at Task 1 of SemEval 2014 are presented in this paper. The run submitted is a supervised version based on two classification models: 1) We used logistic regression for determining the semantic relatedness between a pair of sentences, and 2) We employed support vector machines for identifying textual entailment degree between the two sentences. The behaviour for the second subtask (textual entailment) obtained much better performance than the one evaluated at the first subtask (relatedness), ranking our approach in the 7th position of 18 teams that participated at the competition.

1 Introduction

The Compositional Distributional Semantic Models (CDSM) applied to sentences aim to approximate the meaning of those sentences with vectors summarizing their patterns of co-occurrence in corpora. In the Task 1 of SemEval 2014, the organizers aimed to evaluate the performance of this kind of models through the following two tasks: semantic relatedness and textual entailment. Semantic relatedness captures the degree of semantic similarity, in this case, between a pair of sentences, whereas textual entailment allows to determine the entailment relation holding between two sentences.

This document is a description paper, therefore, we focus the rest of it on the features and models we used for carrying out the experiments. A complete description of the task and the dataset used are given in Marelli et al. (2014a) and in Marelli et al. (2014b), respectively.

The remaining of this paper is structured as follows. In Section 2 we describe the general model we used for comparing two sentences and the set of the features used for constructing the vectorial representation for each sentence. Section 3 shows how we integrate the features calculated in a single vector which fed a supervised classifier aiming to construct a classication model that solves the two aforementioned problems: semantic relatedness and textual entailment. In the same section we show the obtained results. Finally, in Section 4 we present our findings.

2 Description of the Distributional Semantic Model Used

Given a sentence $S = w_1 w_2 \cdots w_{|S|}$, with w_i a sentence word, we have calculated different correlated terms ($t_{i,j}$) or a numeric vector (V_i) for each word w_i as follows:

1. $\{t_{i,j} | relation(t_{i,j}, w_i)\}$ such as "relation" is one the following dependency relations: "object", "subject" or "property".

2. $\{t_{i,j} | t_{i,j} = c_k \cdots c_{k+n}\}$ with $n = 2, \cdots, 5$, and $c_k \in w_i$; these tokens are also known as n-grams of length n.

3. $\{t_{i,j} | t_{i,j} = c_k \cdots c_{k+((n-1)*r)}\}$ with $n =$

Proceedings of the 8th International Workshop on Semantic Evaluation (SemEval 2014), pages 145–148,
Dublin, Ireland, August 23-24, 2014.

$2, \cdots, 5$, $r = 2, \cdots, 5$, and $c_k \in w_i$; these tokens are also known as $skip$-grams of length n.

4. V_i is obtained by applying the Latent Semantic Analysis (LSA) algorithm implemented in the R software environment for statistical computing and graphics. V_i is basically a vector of values that represent relation of the word w_i with it context, calculated by using a corpus constructed by us, by integrating information from Europarl, Project-Gutenberg and Open Office Thesaurus.

3 A Classification Model for Semantic Relatedness and Textual Entailment based on DSM

Once each sentence has been represented by means of a vectorial representation of patterns, we constructed a single vector, $\overrightarrow{u}$, for each pair of sentences with the aim of capturing the semantic relatedness on the basis of a training corpus.

The entries of this representation vector are calculated by obtaining the semantic similarity between each pair of sentences, using each of the DSM shown in the previous section. In order to calculate each entry, we have found the maximum similarity between each word of the first sentence with respect to the second sentence and, thereafter, we have added all these values, thus, $\overrightarrow{u} = \{f_1, \cdots, f_9\}$.

Given a pair of sentences $S_1 = w_{1,1}w_{2,1} \cdots w_{|S_1|,1}$ and $S_2 = w_{1,2}w_{2,2} \cdots w_{|S_2|,2}$, such as each $w_{i,k}$ is represented according to the correlated terms or numeric vectors established at Section 2, the entry f_i of $\overrightarrow{u}$ is calculated as: $f_l = \sum_{i=1}^{|S_1|} max\{sim(w_{i,1}, w_{j,2})\}$, with $j = 1, \cdots, |S_2|$.

The specific similarity measure ($sim()$) and the correlated term or numeric vector used for each f_l is described as follows:

1. $f_1 : w_{i,k}$ is the "object" of w_i (as defined in 2), and $sim()$ is the maximum similarity obtained by using the following six WordNet similarity metrics offered by NLTK: Leacock & Chodorow (Leacock and Chodorow, 1998), Lesk (Lesk, 1986), Wu & Palmer (Wu and Palmer, 1994), Resnik (Resnik, 1995), Lin (Lin, 1998), and Jiang & Conrath[1] (Jiang and Conrath, 1997).

2. $f_2 : w_{i,k}$ is the "subject" of w_i, and $sim()$ is the maximum similarity obtained by using the same six WordNet similarity metrics.

3. $f_3 : w_{i,k}$ is the "property" of w_i, and $sim()$ is the maximum similarity obtained by using the same six WordNet similarity metrics.

4. $f_4 : w_{i,k}$ is an n-gram containing w_i, and $sim()$ is the cosine similarity measure.

5. $f_5 : w_{i,k}$ is an $skip$-gram containing w_i, and $sim()$ is the cosine similarity measure.

6. $f_6 : w_{i,k}$ is numeric vector obtained with LSA, and $sim()$ is the Rada Mihalcea semantic similarity measure (Mihalcea et al., 2006).

7. $f_7 : w_{i,k}$ is numeric vector obtained with LSA, and $sim()$ is the cosine similarity measure.

8. $f_8 : w_{i,k}$ is numeric vector obtained with LSA, and $sim()$ is the euclidean distance.

9. $f_9 : w_{i,k}$ is numeric vector obtained with LSA, and $sim()$ is the Chebyshev distance.

All these 9 features were introduced to a logistic regression classifier in order to obtain a classification model which allows us to determine the value of relatedness between a new pair of sentences[2]. Here, we use as supervised class, the value of relatedness given to each pair of sentences on the training corpus.

The obtained results for the relatedness subtask are given in Table 1. In columns 2, 3 and 5, a large value signals a more efficient system, but a large MSE (column 4) means a less efficient system. As can be seen, our run obtained the rank 12 of 17, with values slightly below the overall average.

3.1 Textual Entailment

In order to calculate the textual entailment judgment, we have enriched the vectorial representation previously mentioned with synonyms, antonyms and cue-

[1]Natural Language Toolkit of Python; http://www.nltk.org/

[2]We have employed the Weka tool with the default settings for this purpose

Table 1: Results obtained at the substask "Relatedness" of the Semeval 2014 Task 1

TEAM ID	PEARSON	SPEARMAN	MSE	Rank
ECNU_run1	0.82795	0.76892	0.32504	1
StanfordNLP_run5	0.82723	0.75594	0.32300	2
The_Meaning_Factory_run1	0.82680	0.77219	0.32237	3
UNAL-NLP_run1	0.80432	0.74582	0.35933	4
Illinois-LH_run1	0.79925	0.75378	0.36915	5
CECL_ALL_run1	0.78044	0.73166	0.39819	6
SemantiKLUE_run1	0.78019	0.73598	0.40347	7
CNGL_run1	0.76391	0.68769	0.42906	8
UTexas_run1	0.71455	0.67444	0.49900	9
UoW_run1	0.71116	0.67870	0.51137	10
FBK-TR_run3	0.70892	0.64430	0.59135	11
BUAP_run1	**0.69698**	**0.64524**	**0.52774**	**12**
UANLPCourse_run2	0.69327	0.60269	0.54225	13
UQeResearch_run1	0.64185	0.62565	0.82252	14
ASAP_run1	0.62780	0.59709	0.66208	15
Yamraj_run1	0.53471	0.53561	2.66520	16
asjai_run5	0.47952	0.46128	1.10372	17
overall average	0.71876	0.67159	0.63852	8-9
Our difference against the overall average	-2%	-3%	11%	-

words ("no", "not", "nobody" and "none") for detecting negation at the sentences[3]. Thus, if some of these new features exist on the training pair of sentences, we add a boolean value of 1, otherwise we set the feature to zero.

This new set of vectors is introduced to a support vector machine classifier[4], using as class the textual entailment judgment given on the training corpus.

The obtained results for the textual entailment subtask are given in Table 2. Our run obtained the rank 7 of 18, with values above the overall average. We consider that this improvement over the relatedness task was a result of using other features that are quite important for semantic relatedness, such as lexical relations (synonyms and antonyms), and the consideration of the negation phenomenon in the sentences.

4 Conclusions

This paper describes the use of compositional distributional semantic models for solving the problems of semantic relatedness and textual entailment. We proposed different features and measures for that purpose. The obtained results show a competitive approach that may be further improved by considering more lexical relations or other type of semantic similarity measures.

In general, we obtained the 7th place in the official ranking list from a total of 18 teams that participated at the textual entailment subtask. The result at the semantic relatedness subtask could be improved if we were considered to add the new features taken into consideration at the textual entailment subtask, an idea that we will implement in the future.

[3]Synonyms were extracted from WordNet, whereas the antonyms were collected from Wikipedia.

[4]Again, we have employed the weka tool with the default settings for this purpose.

References

Jay J. Jiang and David W. Conrath. Semantic similarity based on corpus statistics and lexical taxonomy. In *Proc of 10th International Conference on Research in Computational Linguistics, ROCLING'97*, pages 19–33, 1997.

Claudia Leacock and Martin Chodorow. Combining local context and wordnet similarity for word sense identification. In Christiane Fellfaum, editor, *MIT Press*, pages 265–283, 1998.

Table 2: Results obtained at the substask "Textual Entailment" of the Semeval 2014 Task 1

TEAM ID	ACCURACY	Rank
Illinois-LH_run1	84.575	1
ECNU_run1	83.641	2
UNAL-NLP_run1	83.053	3
SemantiKLUE_run1	82.322	4
The_Meaning_Factory_run1	81.591	5
CECL_ALL_run1	79.988	6
BUAP_run1	**79.663**	**7**
UoW_run1	78.526	8
CDT_run1	77.106	9
UIO-Lien_run1	77.004	10
FBK-TR_run3	75.401	11
StanfordNLP_run5	74.488	12
UTexas_run1	73.229	13
Yamraj_run1	70.753	14
asjai_run5	69.758	15
haLF_run2	69.413	16
CNGL_run1	67.201	17
UANLPCourse_run2	48.731	18
Overall average	75.358	11-12
Our difference against the overall average	4.31%	-

Michael Lesk. Automatic sense disambiguation using machine readable dictionaries: How to tell a pine cone from an ice cream cone. In *Proceedings of the 5th Annual International Conference on Systems Documentation*, pages 24–26. ACM, 1986.

Dekang Lin. An information-theoretic definition of similarity. In *Proceedings of the Fifteenth International Conference on Machine Learning*, ICML '98, pages 296–304, San Francisco, CA, USA, 1998. Morgan Kaufmann Publishers Inc.

Marco Marelli, Luisa Bentivogli, Marco Baroni, Raffaella Bernardi, Stefano Menini, and Roberto Zamparelli. Semeval-2014 task 1: Evaluation of compositional distributional semantic models on full sentences through semantic relatedness and textual entailment. In *Proceedings of the 8th International Workshop on Semantic Evaluation (SemEval-2014)*, Dublin, Ireland, 2014a.

Marco Marelli, Stefano Menini, Marco Baroni, Luisa Bentivogli, Raffaella Bernardi, and Roberto Zamparelli. A sick cure for the evaluation of compositional distributional semantic models. In *Proceedings of LREC 2014*, Reykjavik, Iceland, 2014b.

Rada Mihalcea, Courtney Corley, and Carlo Strapparava. Corpus-based and knowledge-based measures of text semantic similarity. In *Proceedings of the 21st National Conference on Artificial Intelligence*, pages 775–780, 2006.

Philip Resnik. Using information content to evaluate semantic similarity in a taxonomy. In *Proceedings of the 14th International Joint Conference on Artificial Intelligence*, IJCAI'95, pages 448–453, San Francisco, CA, USA, 1995.

Zhibiao Wu and Martha Stone Palmer. Verb semantics and lexical selection. In *Proceedings of the 32nd Annual Meeting of the Association for Computational Linguistics*, pages 133–138, 1994.

BUAP: Evaluating Features for Multilingual and Cross-Level Semantic Textual Similarity

Darnes Vilariño, David Pinto, Saúl León, Mireya Tovar,Beatriz Beltrán
Benemérita Universidad Autónoma de Puebla
Faculty of Computer Science
14 Sur y Av. San Claudio, CU
Puebla, Puebla, México
{darnes,dpinto,saul.leon,mtovar,bbeltran}@cs.buap.mx

Abstract

In this paper we present the evaluation of different features for multiligual and cross-level semantic textual similarity. Three different types of features were used: lexical, knowledge-based and corpus-based. The results obtained at the Semeval competition rank our approaches above the average of the rest of the teams highlighting the usefulness of the features presented in this paper.

1 Introduction

Semantic textual similarity aims to capture whether the meaning of two texts are similar. This concept is somehow different from the textual similarity definition itself, because in the latter we are only interested in measuring the number of lexical components that the two texts share. Therefore, textual similarity can range from exact semantic equivalence to a complete unrelatedness pair of texts.

Finding the semantic similarity between a pair of texts has become a big challenge for specialists in Natural Language Processing (NLP), because it has applications in some NLP task such as machine translation, automatic construction of summaries, authorship attribution, machine reading comprehension, information retrieval, among others, which usually need a manner to calculate degrees of similarity between two given texts.

Semantic textual similarity can be calculated using texts of different sizes, for example between, a paragraph and a sentence, or a sentence and a phrase, or a phrase and a word, or even a word and a sense. When we consider this difference, we say the task is called "Cross-Level Semantic Similarity", but when this distinction is not considered, then we call the task just as "Semantic Textual Similarity".

In this paper, we evaluate different features for determining those that obtain the best performances for calculating both, cross-level semantic similarity and multilingual semantic textual similarity.

The remaining of this paper is structured as follows. Section 2 presents the features used in both experiments. Section 3 shows the manner we used the features for determining the degree of semantic textual similarity. Section 4, on the other hand, shows the experiments we have carried out for determining cross-level semantic similarity. Finally, in Section 5 the conclusions and findings are given.

2 Description of Features

In this section we describe the different features used for evaluation semantic textual similarity. Basically, we have used three different types of features: lexical, knowledge-based and corpus-based. The first one, counts the frequency of ocurrence of lexical features which include n-grams of characters, *skip*-grams[1], words and some lexical relationships such as synonymy or hypernymy. Additionally, we have used two other features: the Jaccard coefficient between the two text, expanding each term with a set of

[1] They are also known as disperse n-grams because they consider to "skip" a certain number of characters.

Proceedings of the 8th International Workshop on Semantic Evaluation (SemEval 2014), pages 149–153, Dublin, Ireland, August 23-24, 2014.

synonyms taken from WordReference Carrillo et al. (2012), and the cosine between the two texts represented each by a bag of character n-grams and $skip$-grams. In this case, we did not applied any word sense disambiguation system before expanding with synonyms, a procedure that may be performed in a further work.

The second set of features considers the following six word similarity metrics offered by NLTK: Leacock & Chodorow (Leacock and Chodorow, 1998), Lesk (Lesk, 1986), Wu & Palmer (Wu and Palmer, 1994), Resnik (Resnik, 1995), Lin (Lin, 1998), and Jiang & Conrath[2] (Jiang and Conrath, 1997). In this case, we determine the similarity between two texts as the maximum possible pair of words similarity. The third set of features considers two corpus-based measures, both based on Rada Mihalcea's textual semantic similarity (Mihalcea et al., 2006). The first one uses Pointwise Mutual Information (PMI) (Turney, 2001) for calculating the similarity between pairs of words, whereas the second one uses Latent Semantic Analysis (LSA) (Landauer et al., 1998) (implemented in the R software environment for statistical computing) for that purpose. In particular, the PMI and LSA values were obtained using a corpus built on the basis of Europarl, Project-Gutenberg and Open Office Thesaurus. A summary of these features can be seen in Table 1.

3 Multilingual Semantic Textual Similarity

This task aims to find the semantic textual similarity between two texts written in the same language. Two different languages were considered: English and Spanish. The degree of semantic similarity ranges from 0 to 5; the bigger this value, the best semantic match between the two texts. For the experiments we have used the training datasets provided at 2012, 2013 and 2014 Semeval competitions. These datasets are completely described at the task description papers of these Semeval editions Agirre et al. (2013, 2014).

In order to calculate the semantic textual similarity for the English language, we have used all the features mentioned at Section 2. We have constructed a single vector for each pair of texts of the training corpus, thus resulting 6,627 vectors in total. The resulting set of vectors fed a supervised classifier, in particular, a logistic regression model[3]. This approach has been named as *BUAP-EN-run1*. The most representative results obtained at the competition for the English language can be seen in Table 2. As can be seen, we outperformed the average result in all the cases, except on the case that the *OnWN* corpus was used.

In order to calculate the semantic textual similarity for the Spanish language, we have submitted two runs, the first one is a supervised approach which constructs a regression model, similar that the one constructed for the English language, but considering only the following features: character n-grams, character $skip$-grams, and the cosine similarity of bag of character n-grams and $skip$-grams. This approach was named *BUAP-run1*. Given that the number of Spanish samples was so small, we decided to investigate the behaviour of training with English and testing with Spanish language. It is quite interesting that this approach obtained a relevant ranking (17 from 22 runs), even if the type of features used were naïve.

The second approach submitted for determining the semantic textual similarity for the Spanish language is an unsupervised one. It uses the same features of the supervised approach for Spanish, but these features were used to create a representation vector for each text (independently), so that we may be able to calculate the similarity by means of the cosine measure between the two vectors. The approach was named *BUAP-run2*.

The most representative results obtained at the competition for the Spanish language can be seen in Table 3. There we can see that our unsupervised approach slightly outperformed the overall average, but the supervised approach was below the overall average, a fact that is expected since we have trained using the English corpus and testing with the Spanish language. Despite this, it is quite interesting that the result obtained with this supervised approach is not so bad.

Due to space constraints, we did not reported the complete set of results of the competition, however, these results can be seen at the task 10 description

[2]Natural Language Toolkit of Python; http://www.nltk.org/

[3]We used the version of the logistic classifier implemented in the the Weka toolkit

Table 1: Features used for calculating semantic textual similarity

Feature	Type
n-grams of characters ($n = 2, \cdots, 5$)	Lexical
$skip$-grams of characters ($skip = 2, \cdots, 5$)	Lexical
Number of words shared	Lexical
Number of synonyms shared	Lexical
Number of hypernyms shared	Lexical
Jaccard coefficient with synonyms expansion	Lexical
Cosine of bag of character n-grams and $skip$-grams	Lexical
Leacock & Chodorow's word similarity	Knowledge-based
Lesk's word similarity	Knowledge-based
Wu & Palmer's word similarity	Knowledge-based
Resnik's word similarity	Knowledge-based
Lin's word similarity	Knowledge-based
Jiang & Conrath's word similarity	Knowledge-based
Rada Mihalcea's metric using PMI	Corpus-based
Rada Mihalcea's metric using LSA	Corpus-based

Table 2: Results obtained at the Task 10 of the Semeval competition for the English language

Team Name	deft-forum	deft-news	headlines	images	OnWN	tweet-news	Weighted mean	Rank
DLS@CU-run2	0.4828	0.7657	0.7646	0.8214	0.8589	0.7639	0.7610	1
Meerkat_Mafia-pairingWords	0.4711	0.7628	0.7597	0.8013	0.8745	0.7793	0.7605	2
NTNU-run3	0.5305	0.7813	0.7837	0.8343	0.8502	0.6755	0.7549	3
BUAP-EN-run1	**0.4557**	**0.6855**	**0.6888**	**0.6966**	**0.6539**	**0.7706**	**0.6715**	**19**
Overall average	0.3607	0.6198	0.5885	0.6760	0.6786	0.6001	0.6015	27-28
Bielefeld_SC-run2	0.2108	0.4307	0.3112	0.3558	0.3607	0.4087	0.3470	36
UNED-run22_p_np	0.1043	0.3148	0.0374	0.3243	0.5086	0.4898	0.3097	37
LIPN-run2	0.0843	-	-	-	-	-	0.0101	38
Our difference against the average	9%	7%	10%	2%	-2%	17%	7%	-

Table 3: Results obtained at the Task 10 of the Semeval competition for the Spanish language (NOTE: The * symbol denotes a system that used Wikipedia to build its model for the Wikipedia test dataset)

Team Name	System type	Wikipedia	News	Weighted correlation	Rank
UMCC_DLSI-run2	supervised	0.7802	0.8254	0.8072	1
Meerkat_Mafia-run2	unsupervised	0.7431	0.8454	0.8042	2
UNAL-NLP-run1	weakly supervised	0.7804	0.8154	0.8013	3
BUAP-run2	**unsupervised**	**0.6396**	**0.7637**	**0.7137**	**14**
Overall average	-	0.6193	0.7504	0.6976	14-15
BUAP-run1	**supervised**	**0.5504**	**0.6785**	**0.6269**	**17**
RTM-DCU-run2	supervised	0.3689	0.6253	0.5219	20
Bielefeld_SC-run2	unsupervised*	0.2646	0.5546	0.4377	21
Bielefeld_SC-run1	unsupervised*	0.2632	0.5545	0.4371	22
Difference between our run1 and the overall average	-	-7%	-7%	-7%	-
Difference between our run2 and the overall average	-	2%	1%	2%	-

paper (Agirre et al., 2014) of Semeval 2014.

4 Cross-Level Semantic Similarity

This task aims to find semantic similarity between a pair of texts of different length written in English language, actually each text belong to a different level of representation of language (paragraph, sentence, phrase, word, and sense). Thus, the pair of levels that were required to be compared in order to determine their semantic similarity were: paragraph-to-sentence, sentence-to-phrase, phrase-to-word, and word-to-sense.

The task cross level similarity judgments are based on five rating levels which goes from 0 to

4. The first (0) implies that the two items do not mean the same thing and are not on the same topic, whereas the last one (4) implies that the two items have very similar meanings and the most important ideas, concepts, or actions in the larger text are represented in the smaller text. The remaining rating levels imply something in the middle.

For word-to-sense comparison, a sense is paired with a word and the perceived meaning of the word is modulated by virtue of the comparison with the paired sense's definition. For the experiments presented at the competition, a corpus of 2,000 pairs of texts were provided for training and other 2,000 pairs for testing. This dataset considered 500 pairs for each type of level of semantic similarity. The complete description of this task together with the dataset employed is given in the task description paper Jurgens et al. (2014).

We submitted two supervised approaches, to this task employing all the features presented at Section 2. The first approach simply constructs a single vector for each pair of training texts using the aforementioned features. These vectors are introduced in Weka for constructing a classification model based on logistic regression. This approach was named *BUAP-run1*.

We have observed that when comparing texts of different length, there may be a high discrepancy between those texts because a very small length in the texts may difficult the process of determining the semantic similarity. Therefore, we have proposed to expand small text with the aim of having more term useful in the process of calculating the degree of semantic similarity. In particular, we have expanded words for the phrase-to-word and word-to-sense cases. The expansion has been done as follows. When we calculated the similarity between phrases and words, we expanded the word component with those related terms obtained by means of the Related-Tags Service of Flickr. When we calculated the semantic similarity between words and senses, we expanded the word component with their WordNet Synsets (none word sense disambiguation method was employed). This second approach was named *BUAP-run2*.

The most representative results for the cross-level semantic similarity task (which include our results) are shown in Table 4. There we can see that the features obtained a good performance when we computed the semantic similarity between paragraphs and sentences, and when we calculated the similiraty between sentences to phrases. Actually, both runs obtained exactly the same result, because the main difference between these two runs is that the second one expands the word/sense using the Related Tags of Flickr. However, the set of expansion words did not work properly, in particular when calculating the semantic similarity between phrases and words. We consider that this behaviour is due to the domain of the expansion set do not match with the domain of the dataset to be evaluated. In the case of expanding words for calculating the similarity between words and senses, we obtained a slightly better performance, but again, this values are not sufficient to highly outperform the overall average. As future work we consider to implement a self-expansion technique for obtaining a set of related terms by means of the same training corpus. This technique has proved to be useful when the expansion process is needed in restricted domains Pinto et al. (2011).

5 Conclusions

This paper presents the results obtained by the BUAP team at the Task 3 and 10 of SemEval 2014. In both task we have used a set of similar features, due to the aim of these two task are quite similar: determining semantic similarity. Some special modifications has been done according to each task in order to tackle some issues like the language or the text length.

In general, the features evaluated performed well over the two approaches, however, some issues arise that let us know that we need to tune the approaches presented here. For example, a better expansion set is required in the case of the Task 3, and a great number of samples for the spanish samples of Task 10 will be required.

References

Eneko Agirre, Daniel Cer, Mona Diab, Aitor Gonzalez-Agirre, and Weiwei Guo. *sem 2013 shared task: Semantic textual similarity. In *2nd Joint Conference on Lexical and Computational*

Table 4: Results obtained at Task 3 of Semeval 2014

Team	System	Paragraph-to-Sentence	Sentence-to-Phrase	Phrase-to-Word	Word-to-Sense	Rank
SimCompass	run1	0.811	0.742	0.415	0.356	1
ECNU	run1	0.834	0.771	0.315	0.269	2
UNAL-NLP	run2	0.837	0.738	0.274	0.256	3
BUAP	**run1**	**0.805**	**0.714**	**0.162**	**0.201**	**9**
BUAP	**run2**	**0.805**	**0.714**	**0.142**	**0.194**	**10**
Overall average	-	0.728	0.651	0.198	0.192	11-12
Our run1 - Overall average		8%	6%	-4%	1%	-
Our run2 - Overall average		8%	6%	-6%	0%	-

*Semantics (*SEM)*, pages 32–43, Atlanta, Georgia, USA, 2013.

Eneko Agirre, Carmen Banea, Claire Cardie, Daniel Cer, Mona Diab, Aitor Gonzalez-Agirre, Weiwei Guo, Rada Mihalcea, German Rigau, and Janyce Wiebe. Semeval-2014 task 10: Multilingual semantic textual similarity. In *Proceedings of the 8th International Workshop on Semantic Evaluation (SemEval-2014)*, Dublin, Ireland, 2014.

Maya Carrillo, Darnes Vilariño, David Pinto, Mireya Tovar, Saul León, and Esteban Castillo. Fcc: Three approaches for semantic textual similarity. In *Proceedings of the 1st Joint Conference on Lexical and Computational Semantics (SemEval 2012)*, pages 631–634, Montréal, Canada, 2012.

Jay J. Jiang and David W. Conrath. Semantic similarity based on corpus statistics and lexical taxonomy. In *Proc of 10th International Conference on Research in Computational Linguistics, ROCLING'97*, pages 19–33, 1997.

David Jurgens, Mohammad Taher Pilehvar, and Roberto Navigli. Semeval-2014 task 3: Cross-level semantic similarity. In *Proceedings of the 8th International Workshop on Semantic Evaluation (SemEval-2014)*, Dublin, Ireland, 2014.

Thomas K. Landauer, Peter W. Foltz, and Darrell Laham. An Introduction to Latent Semantic Analysis. *Discourse Processes*, (25):259–284, 1998.

Claudia Leacock and Martin Chodorow. Combining local context and wordnet similarity for word sense identification. In Christiane Fellbaum, editor, *MIT Press*, pages 265–283, 1998.

Michael Lesk. Automatic sense disambiguation using machine readable dictionaries: How to tell a pine cone from an ice cream cone. In *Proceedings of the 5th Annual International Conference on Systems Documentation*, pages 24–26. ACM, 1986.

Dekang Lin. An information-theoretic definition of similarity. In *Proceedings of the Fifteenth International Conference on Machine Learning*, ICML '98, pages 296–304, San Francisco, CA, USA, 1998. Morgan Kaufmann Publishers Inc.

Rada Mihalcea, Courtney Corley, and Carlo Strapparava. Corpus-based and knowledge-based measures of text semantic similarity. In *Proceedings of the 21st National Conference on Artificial Intelligence*, pages 775–780, 2006.

David Pinto, Paolo Rosso, and Héctor Jiménez-Salazar. A self-enriching methodology for clustering narrow domain short texts. *Computer Journal*, 54(7):1148–1165, 2011.

Philip Resnik. Using information content to evaluate semantic similarity in a taxonomy. In *Proceedings of the 14th International Joint Conference on Artificial Intelligence*, IJCAI'95, pages 448–453, San Francisco, CA, USA, 1995.

Peter D. Turney. Mining the web for synonyms: Pmi-ir versus lsa on toefl. In *Proceedings of the 12th European Conference on Machine Learning*, pages 491–502. Springer-Verlag, 2001.

Zhibiao Wu and Martha Stone Palmer. Verb semantics and lexical selection. In *Proceedings of the 32nd Annual Meeting of the Association for Computational Linguistics*, pages 133–138, 1994.

BUAP: Polarity Classification of Short Texts

David Pinto[1], **Darnes Vilariño**[1], **Saul León**[1], **Miguel Jasso**[1,2], **Cupertino Lucero**[2]
[1] Benemérita Universidad Autónoma de Puebla
14 Sur y Av. San Claudio, CU, 72570
Puebla, Puebla, México
{dpinto,darnes,saul.leon}@cs.buap.mx
[2] Universidad Tecnológica de Izúcar de Matamoros
Prolongación Reforma 168, Santiago Mihuacan, 74420
Izúcar de Matamoros, Puebla, México
migueljhdz18@yahoo.com.mx, cuper_lucero@hotmail.com

Abstract

We report the results we obtained at the subtask B (Message Polarity Classification) of SemEval 2014 Task 9. The features used for representing the messages were basically trigrams of characters, trigrams of PoS and a number of words selected by means of a graph mining tool. Our approach performed slightly below the overall average, except when a corpus of tweets with sarcasm was evaluated, in which we performed quite well obtaining around 6% above the overall average.

1 Introduction

Analyzing polarity in texts is an important task that may have various applications in real life. There exist plenty of tasks that may be benefited of computational procedures that automatically allow to detect if the author intention has been to express himself as a positive, negative, neutral or objective manner. Let us consider, for instance, when a public figure (such as a politician, celebrity, or business leader) would like to investigate its reputation in public media. Another example would be to calculate the reputation of a public or private institution. In any case, the construction of methods for determining the polarity of messages at Internet would help to investigate their reputation.

In this paper, we present the results we obtained when we carried out experiments for the subtask B of Semeval 2014 Task 9, which was named "Message Polarity Classification", and was defined as follow: "Given a message, decide whether the message is of positive, negative, or neutral sentiment. For messages conveying both a positive and negative sentiment, whichever is the stronger sentiment should be chosen".

The remaining of this paper is structured as follows. In Section 2 we present some related work found at the literature with respect to the identification of emotions in short texts such as twitter. Section 3 presents the description of the features and classification model used in our experiments. The results obtained together with a discussion of these results are given in Section 4. Finally, the conclusions are given in Section 5.

2 Related Work

There exist a number of works in literature associated to the automatic identification of emotions in Twitter, mainly due to the massification of this social network around the world and the easy manner we can access to the Tweets from API's provided by Twitter itself. Some of these works have focused on the contribution of some particular features, such as Part of Speech (PoS) tags, emoticons, etc. on the aforementioned task. In Agarwal et al. (2011), for example, the a priori likelihood of each PoS is calculated. They use up to 100 additional features that include emoticons and a dictionary of positive and negative words. They have reported a 60% of accuracy in the task. On the other hand, in Mukherjee and Bhattacharyya (2012), a strategy based on discursive relations, such as conectiveness and con-

Proceedings of the 8th International Workshop on Semantic Evaluation (SemEval 2014), pages 154–159,
Dublin, Ireland, August 23-24, 2014.

ditionals, with low number of lexical resources is proposed. These relations are integrated in classical models of representation like bag of words with the aim of improving the accuracy values obtained in the process of classification. The influence of semantic operators such as modals and negations are analyzed, in particular, the degree in which they affect the emotion present in a given paragraph or sentence.

One of the major advances obtained in the task of sentiment analysis has been done in the framework of the SemEval competition. In 2013, several teams have participated with different approaches Becker et al. (2013); Han et al. (2013); Chawla et al. (2013); Balahur and Turchi (2013); Balage Filho and Pardo (2013); Moreira et al. (2013); Reckman et al. (2013); Tiantian et al. (2013); Marchand et al. (2013); Clark and Wicentwoski (2013); Hamdan et al. (2013); Martínez-Cámara et al. (2013); Levallois (2013). Most of these works have contributed in the mentioned task by proposing methods, techniques for representing and classifying documents towards the automatic classification of sentiment in Tweets.

3 Description of the Presented Approach

We have employed a supervised approach based on machine learning in which we construct a classification model using the following general features obtained from the training corpus.

1. Character trigrams
2. PoS tags trigrams
3. Significant Tweet words obtained by using a graph mining tool known as SubDue

The description of how we calculated each feature in order to construct a representation vector for each message is given as follows.

The probability of each character trigram given the polarity class, $P(trigram|class)$, was calculated in the training corpus. Thereafter, we assigned a normalized probability to each sentence polarity by combining the probability of each character trigram of the sentence, i.e., $\sum_{i=1}^{|message|} log\left[P(trigram_i|class)\right]$. Since we have four classes ("positive","negative","neutral" and "objective"), we have obtained four features for the final vectorial representation of the message.

We then calculated other four features by performing a similar calculation than the previous one, but in this case, using the PoS tags of the message. For this purpose, we used the Twitter NLP and Part-of-Speech Tagging tool provided by the Carnegie Mellon University (Owoputi et al., 2013). Since the PoS tag given by this tool is basically a character, then the same procedure can be applied.

We performed preliminary experiments by using these eight features on a trial corpus, and we observed that the results may be improved by selecting significant words that may not be discovered by the statistical techniques used until now. So, we decided to make use of techniques based on graph mining for attempting to find those significant words. In order to find them, we constructed a graph representation for each message class ("positive","negative","neutral" and "objective"), using the training corpus. The manner we constructed those graphs is shown as follows.

Formally, given a graph $G = (V, E, L, f)$ with V being the non-empty set of vertices, $E \subseteq V \times V$ the edges, L the tag set, and $f : E \rightarrow L$, a function that assigns a tag to a pair of associated vertices. This graph-based representation attempt to capture the sequence among the sentence words, so as the sequence among their PoS tags with the aim of feeding a graph mining tool which may extract relevant features that may be further used for representing the texts. Thus, the set V is constructed from the different words and PoS of the target document.

In order to demonstrate the way we construct the graph for each short text, consider the following message: "ooh i love you for posting this :-)". The associated graph representation to this message is shown in Figure 1.

Once each paragraph is represented by means of a graph, we apply a data mining algorithm in order to find subgraphs from which we will be able to find the significant words which will be, in our case, basically, the nodes of these subgraphs. Subdue is a data mining tool widely used in structured domains. This tool has been used for discovering structured patterns in texts represented by means of graphs Olmos et al. (2005). Subdue uses an evaluation model named "Minimum encoding", a tech-

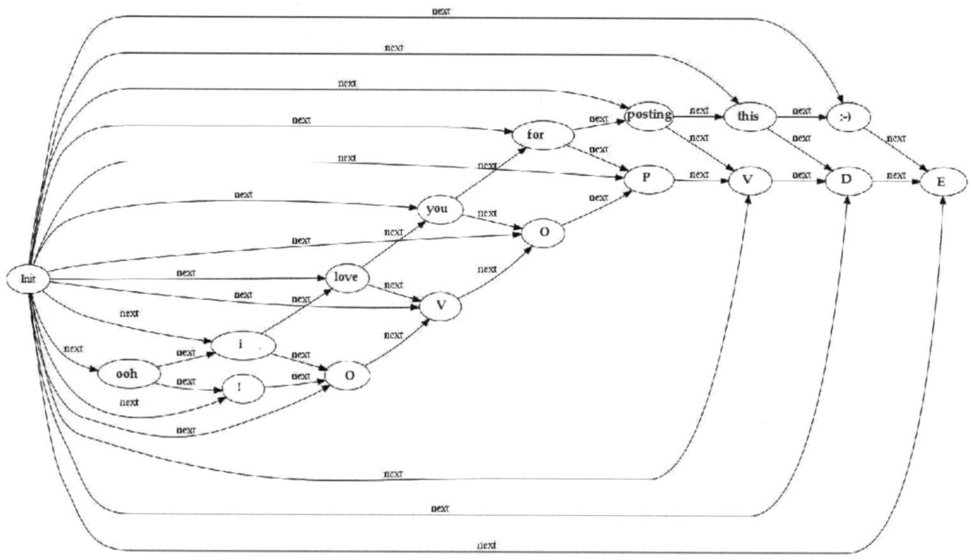

Figure 1: Graph based message representation with words and their corresponding PoS tags

nique derived from the minimum description length principle Rissanen (1989), in which t he best graph sub-structures are chosen. The best subgraphs are those that minimize the number of bits that represent the graph. In this case, the number of bits is calculated consi dering the size of the graph adjancency matrix. Thus, the best substructure is the one that minimizes $I(S) + I(G|S)$, where $I(S)$ is the number of bits required to describe the sub structure S, and $I(G|S)$ is the number of bits required to describe graph G after it has been compacted by the substructure S.

By applying this procedure we obtained 597 signicant negative words, 445 positive words, 616 objective words and 925 positive words. For the final representation vector we compiled the union of these words, obtaining 1915 significant words. Therefore, the total number of features for each message was 1,923.

We have used the training corpus provided at the competition (Rosenthal et al., 2014), however, we removed all those messsages tagged as the class "objective-OR-neutral", because all these messages introduced noise to the classification process. In total, we constructed 5,217 vectors of message representation which fed a support vector machine classifier. We have used the SVM implementation of the WEKA tool with default parameters for our experiments (Hall et al., 2009). The obtained results are shown in the next section.

4 Experimental Results

The test corpus was made up short texts (messages) categorized as: "LiveJournal2014", "SMS2013", "Twitter2013", "Twitter2014" and "Twitter2014Sarcasm". A complete description of the training and test datasets can be found at the task description paper (Rosenthal et al., 2014).

In Table 1 we can see the results obtained at the competition. Our approach performed in almost all the cases slightly below to the overall average, except when we processed the corpus of Twitter with Sarcasm characteristics. We consider that two main problems were the cause of this result: 1) The corpus was very unbalanced and our approaches for alleviating this problem were not sufficient, and 2) From our particular point of view, there were a high difference between the vocabulary of the training and the test corpus, thus, leading the classification model to fail.

Table 1: Results obtained at the substask B of the Semeval 2014 Task 9

System	LiveJournal2014	SMS2013	Twitter2013	Twitter2014	Twitter2014Sarcasm	Average
NRC-Canada-B	74.84	70.28	70.75	69.85	58.16	68.78
CISUC_KIS-B-late	74.46	65.90	67.56	67.95	55.49	66.27
coooolll-B	72.90	67.68	70.40	70.14	46.66	65.56
TeamX-B	69.44	57.36	72.12	70.96	56.50	65.28
RTRGO-B	72.20	67.51	69.10	69.95	47.09	65.17
AUEB-B	70.75	64.32	63.92	66.38	56.16	64.31
SWISS-CHOCOLATE-B	73.25	66.43	64.81	67.54	49.46	64.30
SentiKLUE-B	73.99	67.40	69.06	67.02	43.36	64.17
TUGAS-B	69.79	62.77	65.64	69.00	52.87	64.01
SAIL-B	69.34	56.98	66.80	67.77	57.26	63.63
senti.ue-B	71.39	59.34	67.34	63.81	55.31	63.44
Synalp-Empathic-B	71.75	62.54	63.65	67.43	51.06	63.29
Lt_3-B	68.56	64.78	65.56	65.47	47.76	62.43
UKPDIPF-B	71.92	60.56	60.65	63.77	54.59	62.30
AMI_ERIC-B	65.32	60.29	70.09	66.55	48.19	62.09
ECNU-B	69.44	59.75	62.31	63.17	51.43	61.22
LyS-B	69.79	60.45	66.92	64.92	42.40	60.90
SU-FMI-B-late	68.24	61.67	60.96	63.62	48.34	60.57
NILC_USP-B-twitter	69.02	61.35	65.39	63.94	42.06	60.35
CMU-Qatar-B-late	65.63	62.95	65.11	65.53	40.52	59.95
columbia_nlp-B	68.79	59.84	64.60	65.42	40.02	59.73
CMUQ-Hybrid-B-late	65.14	61.75	63.22	62.71	40.95	58.75
Citius-B	62.40	57.69	62.53	61.92	41.00	57.11
KUNLPLab-B	63.77	55.89	58.12	61.72	44.60	56.82
USP_Biocom-B	67.80	53.57	58.05	59.21	43.56	56.44
UPV-ELiRF-B	64.11	55.36	63.97	59.33	37.46	56.05
Rapanakis-B	59.71	54.02	58.52	63.01	44.69	55.99
DejaVu-B	64.69	55.57	57.43	57.02	42.46	55.43
GPLSI-B	57.32	46.63	57.49	56.06	53.90	54.28
Indian_Inst_of_Tech-Patna-B	60.39	51.96	52.58	57.25	41.33	52.70
BUAP-B	**53.94**	**44.27**	**56.85**	**55.76**	**51.52**	**52.47**
SAP-RI-B	57.86	49.00	50.18	55.47	48.64	52.23
UMCC_DLSI_Sem	53.12	50.01	51.96	55.40	42.76	50.65
Alberta-B	52.38	49.05	53.85	52.06	40.40	49.55
SINAI-B	58.33	57.34	50.59	49.50	31.15	49.38
IBM_EG-B	59.24	46.62	54.51	52.26	34.14	49.35
SU-sentilab-B-tweet	55.11	49.60	50.17	49.52	31.49	47.18
Isis_lif-B	61.09	38.56	46.38	52.02	34.64	46.54
IITPatna-B	54.68	40.56	50.32	48.22	36.73	46.10
UMCC_DLSI_Graph-B	47.81	36.66	43.24	45.49	53.15	45.27
University-of-Warwick-B	39.60	29.50	39.17	45.56	39.77	38.72
DAEDALUS-B	40.83	40.86	36.57	33.03	28.96	36.05
Overall average	63.81	55.82	59.72	60.30	45.43	57.02

5 Conclusions

We have presented an approach for detecting message polarity using basically three kind of features: character trigrams, PoS tags trigrams and significant words obtained by means of a graph mining tool. The obtained results show that these features were not sufficient for detecting the correct polarity of a given message with high precision. We consider that the unbalanced characteristic and the fact the vocabulary changed significantly from the training to the test corpus influenced the results we obtained at the competition. However, a deep analysis we plan to do to the datasets evaluated will allow us in the future to find more accurate features for the message polarity detection task.

References

Apoorv Agarwal, Boyi Xie, Ilia Vovsha, Owen Rambow, and Rebecca Passonneau. Sentiment analysis of twitter data. In *Proceedings of the Workshop on Language in Social Media (LSM 2011)*, pages 30–38, Portland, Oregon, June 2011.

Pedro Balage Filho and Thiago Pardo. Nilc_usp: A hybrid system for sentiment analysis in twitter messages. In *Second Joint Conference on Lexical and Computational Semantics (*SEM), Volume 2:*

Proceedings of the Seventh International Workshop on Semantic Evaluation (SemEval 2013), pages 568–572, Atlanta, Georgia, USA, June 2013.

Alexandra Balahur and Marco Turchi. Improving sentiment analysis in twitter using multilingual machine translated data. In *Proceedings of the International Conference Recent Advances in Natural Language Processing RANLP 2013*, pages 49–55, Hissar, Bulgaria, September 2013. INCOMA Ltd. Shoumen, BULGARIA.

Lee Becker, George Erhart, David Skiba, and Valentine Matula. Avaya: Sentiment analysis on twitter with self-training and polarity lexicon expansion. In *Second Joint Conference on Lexical and Computational Semantics (*SEM), Volume 2: Proceedings of the Seventh International Workshop on Semantic Evaluation (SemEval 2013)*, pages 333–340, Atlanta, Georgia, USA, June 2013.

Karan Chawla, Ankit Ramteke, and Pushpak Bhattacharyya. Iitb-sentiment-analysts: Participation in sentiment analysis in twitter semeval 2013 task. In *Second Joint Conference on Lexical and Computational Semantics (*SEM), Volume 2: Proceedings of the Seventh International Workshop on Semantic Evaluation (SemEval 2013)*, pages 495–500, Atlanta, Georgia, USA, June 2013.

Sam Clark and Rich Wicentwoski. Swatcs: Combining simple classifiers with estimated accuracy. In *Second Joint Conference on Lexical and Computational Semantics (*SEM), Volume 2: Proceedings of the Seventh International Workshop on Semantic Evaluation (SemEval 2013)*, pages 425–429, Atlanta, Georgia, USA, June 2013.

Mark Hall, Eibe Frank, Geoffrey Holmes, Bernhard Pfahringer, Peter Reutemann, and Ian H. Witten. The weka data mining software: an update. *SIGKDD Explor. Newsl.*, 11(1):10–18, November 2009. ISSN 1931-0145.

Hussam Hamdan, Frederic Béchet, and Patrice Bellot. Experiments with dbpedia, wordnet and sentiwordnet as resources for sentiment analysis in micro-blogging. In *Second Joint Conference on Lexical and Computational Semantics (*SEM), Volume 2: Proceedings of the Seventh International Workshop on Semantic Evaluation (SemEval 2013)*, pages 455–459, Atlanta, Georgia, USA, June 2013.

Qi Han, Junfei Guo, and Hinrich Schuetze. Codex: Combining an svm classifier and character n-gram language models for sentiment analysis on twitter text. In *Second Joint Conference on Lexical and Computational Semantics (*SEM), Volume 2: Proceedings of the Seventh International Workshop on Semantic Evaluation (SemEval 2013)*, pages 520–524, Atlanta, Georgia, USA, June 2013.

Clement Levallois. Umigon: sentiment analysis for tweets based on terms lists and heuristics. In *Second Joint Conference on Lexical and Computational Semantics (*SEM), Volume 2: Proceedings of the Seventh International Workshop on Semantic Evaluation (SemEval 2013)*, pages 414–417, Atlanta, Georgia, USA, June 2013.

Morgane Marchand, Alexandru Ginsca, Romaric Besançon, and Olivier Mesnard. [lvic-limsi]: Using syntactic features and multi-polarity words for sentiment analysis in twitter. In *Second Joint Conference on Lexical and Computational Semantics (*SEM), Volume 2: Proceedings of the Seventh International Workshop on Semantic Evaluation (SemEval 2013)*, pages 418–424, Atlanta, Georgia, USA, June 2013.

Eugenio Martínez-Cámara, Arturo Montejo-Ráez, M. Teresa Martín-Valdivia, and L. Alfonso Ureña López. Sinai: Machine learning and emotion of the crowd for sentiment analysis in microblogs. In *Second Joint Conference on Lexical and Computational Semantics (*SEM), Volume 2: Proceedings of the Seventh International Workshop on Semantic Evaluation (SemEval 2013)*, pages 402–407, Atlanta, Georgia, USA, June 2013.

Silvio Moreira, João Filgueiras, Bruno Martins, Francisco Couto, and Mário J. Silva. Reaction: A naive machine learning approach for sentiment classification. In *Second Joint Conference on Lexical and Computational Semantics (*SEM), Volume 2: Proceedings of the Seventh International Workshop on Semantic Evaluation (SemEval 2013)*, pages 490–494, Atlanta, Georgia, USA, June 2013.

Subhabrata Mukherjee and Pushpak Bhattacharyya.

Sentiment analysis in Twitter with lightweight discourse analysis. In *Proceedings of COLING 2012*, pages 1847–1864, Mumbai, India, December 2012. The COLING 2012 Organizing Committee.

Ivan Olmos, Jesus A. Gonzalez, and Mauricio Osorio. Subgraph isomorphism detection using a code based representation. In *FLAIRS Conference*, pages 474–479, 2005.

Olutobi Owoputi, Brendan O'Connor, Chris Dyer, Kevin Gimpel, Nathan Schneider, and Noah A Smith. Improved part-of-speech tagging for online conversational text with word clusters. In *Proceedings of NAACL-HLT*, pages 380–390, 2013.

Hilke Reckman, Cheyanne Baird, Jean Crawford, Richard Crowell, Linnea Micciulla, Saratendu Sethi, and Fruzsina Veress. teragram: Rule-based detection of sentiment phrases using sas sentiment analysis. In *Second Joint Conference on Lexical and Computational Semantics (*SEM), Volume 2: Proceedings of the Seventh International Workshop on Semantic Evaluation (SemEval 2013)*, pages 513–519, Atlanta, Georgia, USA, June 2013.

Jorma Rissanen. *Stochastic Complexity in Statistical Inquiry Theory*. World Scientific Publishing Co., Inc., River Edge, NJ, USA, 1989. ISBN 981020311X.

Sara Rosenthal, Preslav Nakov, Alan Ritter, and Veselin Stoyanov. Semeval-2014 task 9: Sentiment analysis in twitter. In *Proceedings of the 8th International Workshop on Semantic Evaluation (SemEval-2014)*, Dublin, Ireland, 2014.

Zhu Tiantian, Zhang Fangxi, and Man Lan. Ecnucs: A surface information based system description of sentiment analysis in twitter in the semeval-2013 (task 2). In *Second Joint Conference on Lexical and Computational Semantics (*SEM), Volume 2: Proceedings of the Seventh International Workshop on Semantic Evaluation (SemEval 2013)*, pages 408–413, Atlanta, Georgia, USA, June 2013.

CECL: a New Baseline and a Non-Compositional Approach for the Sick Benchmark

Yves Bestgen
Centre for English Corpus Linguistics
Université catholique de Louvain
yves.bestgen@uclouvain.be

Abstract

This paper describes the two procedures for determining the semantic similarities between sentences submitted for the SemEval 2014 Task 1. MeanMaxSim, an unsupervised procedure, is proposed as a new baseline to assess the efficiency gain provided by compositional models. It outperforms a number of other baselines by a wide margin. Compared to the word-overlap baseline, it has the advantage of taking into account the distributional similarity between words that are also involved in compositional models. The second procedure aims at building a predictive model using as predictors MeanMaxSim and (transformed) lexical features describing the differences between each sentence of a pair. It finished sixth out of 17 teams in the textual similarity sub-task and sixth out of 19 in the textual entailment sub-task.

1 Introduction

The SemEval-2014 Task 1 (Marelli et al., 2014a) was designed to allow a rigorous evaluation of compositional distributional semantic models (CDSMs). CDSMs aim to represent the meaning of phrases and sentences by composing the distributional representations of the words they contain (Baroni et al., 2013; Bestgen and Cabiaux, 2002; Erk and Pado, 2008; Grefenstette, 2013; Kintsch, 2001; Mitchell and Lapata, 2010); they are thus an extension of Distributional Semantic Models (DSMs), which approximate the meaning of words with vectors summarizing their patterns of co-occurrence in a corpus (Baroni and Lenci, 2010; Bestgen et al., 2006; Kintsch, 1998; Landauer and Dumais, 1997). The dataset for this task, called SICK (*Sentences Involving Compositional Knowledge*), consists of almost 10,000 English sentence pairs annotated for relatedness in meaning and entailment relation by ten annotators (Marelli et al., 2014b).

The rationale behind this dataset is that "understanding when two sentences have close meanings or entail each other crucially requires a compositional semantics step" (Marelli et al., 2014b), and thus that annotators judge the similarity between the two sentences of a pair by first building a mental representation of the meaning of each sentence and then comparing these two representations. However, another option was available to the annotators. They could have paid attention only to the differences between the sentences, and assessed the significance of these differences. Such an approach could have been favored by the dataset built on the basis of a thousand sentences modified by a limited number of (often) very specific transformations, producing sentence pairs that might seem quite repetitive. An analysis conducted during the training phase of the challenge brought some support for this hypothesis. The analysis focused on pairs of sentences in which the only difference between the two sentences was the replacement of one content word by another, as in *A man is singing to a girl* vs. *A man is singing to a woman*, but also in *A man is sitting in a field* vs. *A man is running in a field*. The material was divided into two parts, 3500 sentence pairs in the training set and the remaining 1500 in the test set. First, the average similarity score for each pair of interchanged words was calculated on the training set (e.g., in this sample, there were 16 sentence pairs in which *woman* and *man* were interchanged, and their mean similarity score was 3.6). Then, these mean scores were used as the similarity scores of the sentence pairs of the test sample

Proceedings of the 8th International Workshop on Semantic Evaluation (SemEval 2014), pages 160–165,
Dublin, Ireland, August 23-24, 2014.

in which the same words were interchanged. The correlation between the actual scores and the predicted score was 0.83 (N=92), a value that can be considered as very high, given the restrictions on the range in which the predicted similarity scores vary (min=3.5 and max=5.0; Howell, 2008, pp. 272-273). It is important to note that this observation does not prove that the participants have not built a compositional representation, especially as it only deals with a very specific type of transformation. It nevertheless suggests that analyzing only the differences between the sentences of a pair could allow the similarity between them to be effectively estimated.

Following these observations, I opted to try to determine the degree of efficacy that can be achieved by two non-compositional approaches. The first approach, totally unsupervised, is proposed as a new baseline to evaluate the efficacy gains brought by compositional systems. The second, a supervised approach, aims to capitalize on the properties of the SICK benchmark. While these approaches have been developed specifically for the semantic relatedness sub-task, the second has also been applied to the textual entailment sub-task. This paper describes the two proposed approaches, their implementation in the context of SemEval 2014 Task 1, and the results obtained.

2 Proposed Approaches

2.1 A New Baseline for CDSM

An evident baseline in the field of CDSM is based on the proportion of common words in two sentences after the removal (or retaining) of stop words (Cheung and Penn, 2012). Its main weakness is that it does not take into account the semantic similarities between the words that are combined in the CDSM models. It follows that a compositional approach may seem significantly better than this baseline, even if it is not compositionality that matters but only the distributional part. At first glance, this problem can be circumvented by using as baseline a simple compositional model like the additive model. The analyses below show that this model is much less effective for the SILK dataset than the distributional baseline proposed here.

MeanMaxSim, the proposed baseline, is an extension of the classic measure based on the proportion of common words, taking advantage of the distributional similarity but not of compositionality. It corresponds to the mean, calculated using all the words of the two sentences, of the maximum semantic similarity between each word in a sentence and all the words of the other sentence. More formaly, given two sentences $a = (a_1, .., a_n)$ and $b = (b_1, ..b_m)$,

$$MMS = \frac{(\sum_i \max_j sim(a_i,b_j) + \sum_j \max_i sim(a_i,b_j))}{n+m}$$

In this study, the cosine between the word distributional representations was used as the measure of semantic similarity, but other measures may be used. The common words of the two sentences have an important impact on MeanMaxSim, since their similarity with themselves is equal to the maximum similarity possible. Their impact would be much lower if the average similarity between a word and all the words in the other sentence were employed instead of the maximum similarity. Several variants of this measure can be used, for example not taking into account every instance where a word is repeated in a sentence or not allowing any single word to be the "most similar" to several other words.

2.2 A Non-Compositional Approach Based on the Differences Between the Sentences

The main limitation of the first approach in the context of this challenge is that it is completely unsupervised and therefore does not take advantage of the training set provided by the task organizers. The second approach addresses this limitation. It aims to build a predictive model, using as predictors MeanMaxSim but also lexical features describing the differences between each sentence of a pair. For the extraction of these features, each pair of sentences of the whole dataset (training and testing sets) is analyzed to identify all the lemmas that are not present with the same frequency in both sentences. Each of these differences is encoded as a feature whose value corresponds to the unsigned frequency difference. This step leads to a two-way contingency table with sentence pairs as rows and lexical features as columns. Correspondence Analysis (Blasius and Greenacre, 1994; Lebart et al., 2000), a statistical procedure available in many off-the-shelf software like R (Nenadic and Greenacre, 2006), is then used to decompose this table into orthogonal dimensions ordered according to the corresponding part of associations between rows and columns they explain. Each row receives a coordinate on these dimensions and these coordinates are used as predictors of the relatedness scores of the sentence pairs. In this way, not only are the frequencies of lexical features transformed into continuous predictors, but these predictors also take into account the redundancy between the lexical features. Finally, a predictive model is built on the basis of the training set by means of multiple linear regression with stepwise selection of the best predictors. For the textual entailment sub-task, the same procedure was used except that the linear regression was replaced by a linear discriminant analysis.

3 Implementation Details

This section describes the steps and additional resources used to implement the proposed approaches for the SICK challenge.

3.1 Preprocessing of the Dataset

All sentences were tokenized and lemmatized by the Stanford Parser (de Marneffe et al., 2006; Toutanova et al., 2003).

3.2 Distributional Semantics

Latent Semantic Analysis (LSA), a classical DSM (Deerwester et al., 1991; Landauer et al., 1998), was used to gather the semantic similarity between words from corpora. The starting point of the analysis is a lexical table containing the frequencies of every word in each of the text segments included in the corpus. This table is submitted to a singular value decomposition, which extracts the most significant orthogonal dimensions. In this semantic space, the meaning of a word is represented by a vector and the semantic similarity between two words is estimated by the cosine between their corresponding vectors.

Three corpora were used to estimate these similarities. The first one, the TASA corpus, is composed of excerpts, with an approximate average length of 250 words, obtained by a random sampling of texts that American students read (Landauer et al., 1998). The version to which T.K. Landauer (Institute of Cognitive Science, University of Colorado, Boulder) provided access contains approximately 12 million words.

The second corpus, the BNC (British National Corpus; Aston and Burnard, 1998) is composed of approximately 100 million words and covers many different genres. As the documents included in this corpus can be of up to 45,000 words, they were divided into segments of 250 words, the last segment of a text being deleted if it contained fewer than 250 words.

The third corpus (WIKI, approximately 600 million words after preprocessing) is derived from the Wikipedia Foundation database, downloaded in April 2011. It was built using WikiExtractor.py by A. Fuschetto. As for the BNC, the texts were cut into 250-word segments, and any segment of fewer than 250 words was deleted.

All these corpora were lemmatized by means of the TreeTagger (Schmid, 1994). In addition, a series of functional words were removed as well as all the words whose total frequency in the corpus was lower than 10. The resulting (log-entropy weighted) matrices of co-occurrences were submitted to a singular value decomposition (SVD-PACKC, Berry et al., 1993) and the first 300 eigenvectors were retained.

3.3 Unsupervised Approach Details

Before estimating the semantic similarity between a pair of sentences using MeanMaxSim, words (in their lemmatized forms) considered as stop words were filtered out. This stop word list (n=82), was built specifically for the occasion on the basis of the list of the most frequent words in the training dataset.

3.4 Supervised Approach Details

To identify words not present with the same frequency in both sentences, all the lemmas (including those belonging to the stop word list) were taken into account. The optimization of the parameters of the predictive model was performed using a three-fold cross-validation procedure, with two thirds of the 5000 sentence pairs for training and the remaining third for testing. The values tested by means of an exhaustive search were:

- Minimum threshold frequency of the lexical features in the complete dataset: from 10 to 70 by step of 10.
- Number of dimensions retained from the CA: from 10 to the total number of dimensions available by step of 10.
- P-value threshold to enter or remove predictors from the model: 0.01 and from 0.05 to 0.45 by step of 0.05.

This cross-validation procedure was repeated five times, each time changing the random distribution of sentence pairs in the samples. The final values of the three parameters were selected on the basis of the average correlation calculated over all replications. For the relatedness sub-task, the selected values were a minimum threshold frequency of 40, 140 dimensions and a p-value of 0.20. For the entailment sub-task, they were a minimum threshold frequency of 60, 100 dimensions and a p-value of 0.25.

4 Results

4.1 Semantic Relatedness Sub-Task

The main measure of performance selected by the task organizers was the Pearson correlation, calculated on the test set (4927 sentence pairs), between the mean values of similarity according to the annotators and the values predicted by the automatic procedures.

Unsupervised Approach: MeanMaxSim. Table 1 shows the results obtained by MeanMaxSim, based on the three corpora, and by three other baselines:

- WO: The word-overlap baseline proposed by the organizers of the task, computed as the number of distinct tokens in both sentences divided by the number of distinct tokens in the longer sentence, optimizing the number of the most frequent words stripped off the sentences on the test set.
- SWL: The word-overlap baseline computed as in WO but using lemmas instead of words and the stop words list.
- ADD: The simple additive compositional model, in which each sentence is represented by the sum of the vectors of the lemmas that compose it (stripping off stop words and using the best performing corpus) and the similarity is the cosine between these two vectors (Bestgen et al., 2010; Guevara, 2011) .

MeanMaxSim	r	Baseline	r
TASA	0.696	WO	0.627
BNC	0.698	SWL	0.613
WIKI	0.696	ADD	0.500

Table 1: Pearson's correlation for MeanMaxSim and several other baselines on the test set.

MeanMaxSim produces almost identical results regardless of the corpus used. The lack of difference between the three corpora was unexpected. It could be related to the type of vocabulary used in the SICK materials, seemingly mostly frequent and concrete words whose use could be relatively similar in the three corpora. MeanMaxSim performance is clearly superior to all other baselines; among these, the additive model is the worst. This result is important because it shows that this compositional model is not, for the SICK benchmark, the most interesting baseline to assess compositional approaches. In the context of the best performance of the other teams, MeanMaxSim is (hopefully) well below the most effective procedures, which reached correlations above 0.80.

Supervised Approach. The supervised approach resulted in a correlation of 0.78044, a value well above all baselines reported above. This correlation ranked the procedure sixth out of 17, tied with another team (0.78019). The three best teams scored significantly higher, with correlations between 0.826 and 0.828.

4.2 Textual Entailment Sub-Task

Only the supervised approach was used for this sub-task. The proposed procedure achieved an accuracy of 79.998%, which ranks it sixth again, but out of 19 teams, still at a respectable distance from the best performance (84.575%).

5 Conclusion

The main contribution of this research seems to be the proposal of MeanMaxSim as baseline for evaluating CDSM. It outperforms a number of other baselines by a wide margin and is very easy to calculate. Compared to the word-overlap baseline, it has the advantage of taking into account the distributional similarity between words that are also involved in compositional models. The supervised approach proposed achieved an acceptable result (sixth out of 17) and it could easily be improved, for example by replacing standard linear regression by a procedure less sensitive to the risk of overfit due to the large number of predictors such as Partial Least Squares regression (Guevara, 2011). However, since this approach is not compositional and its efficacy (compared to others) is limited, it is not obvious that trying to improve it would be very useful.

Acknowledgements

Yves Bestgen is Research Associate of the Belgian Fund for Scientific Research (F.R.S-FNRS).

References

Aston Guy, and Burnard Lou (1998). *The BNC Handbook: Exploring the British National Corpus with SARA*. Edinburgh: Edinburgh University Press.

Baroni, Marco, and Lenci Alessandro (2010) Distributional memory: A general framework for corpus-based semantics, *Computational Linguistics*, 36, 673-721.

Baroni, Marco, Bernardi, Raffaella, and Zamparelli, Roberto (2013). Frege in space: a program for compositional distributional semantics. In Annie Zaenen, Bonnie Webber and Martha Palmer. *Linguistic Issues in Language Technologies* (LiLT), CSLI Publications.

Berry, Michael, Do, Theresa, O'Brien, Gavin, Krishna, Vijay, and Varadhan, Sowmini (1993). Svdpackc: Version 1.0 user's guide, Technical Report Number CS-93-194, University of Tennessee, Knoxville, TN.

Bestgen, Yves, and Cabiaux, Anne-Franoise (2002). L'analyse sémantique latente et l'identification des métaphores. In *Actes de la 9me Conférence annuelle sur le traitement automatique des langues naturelles* (pp. 331-337). Nancy : INRIA.

Bestgen, Yves, Degand, Liesbeth, and Spooren, Wilbert (2006). Towards automatic determination of the semantics of connectives in large newspaper corpora. *Discourse Processes*, 41, 175-193.

Bestgen, Yves, Lories, Guy, and Thewissen, Jennifer (2010). Using latent semantic analysis to measure coherence in essays by foreign language learners? In Sergio Bolasco, Isabella Chiari and Luca Giuliano (Eds.), *Proceedings of 10th International Conference on Statistical Analysis of Textual Data*, 385-395. Roma: LED.

Blasius, Jorg, and Greenacre, Michael (1994). Computation of Correspondence Analysis. In Michael Greenacre and Jorg Blasius (eds.), *Correspondence Analysis in the Social Sciences*, pp. 53-75. Academic Press, London.

Cheung, Jackie, and Penn, Gerald (2012). Evaluating distributional models of semantics for syntactically invariant inference. In *Conference of the European Chapter of the Association for Computational Linguistics*, 33-43, Avignon, France.

de Marneffe, Marie-Catherine, MacCartney, Bill, and Manning, Christopher (2006). Generating Typed Dependency Parses from Phrase Structure Parses. In *Proceedings of the 5th Edition of the Language Resources and Evaluation Conference*. Genoa, Italy.

Deerwester, Scott, Dumais, Susan, Furnas, George, Landauer, Thomas and Harshman, Richard (1990). Indexing by latent semantic analysis. *Journal of the American Society for Information Science*, 41, 391-407.

Erk, Katrin, and Pado, Sebastian (2008). A structured vector space model for word meaning in context. In *Proceedings of the 2008 Conference on Empirical Methods in Natural Language Processing*, 897-906, Honolulu, Hawaii.

Grefenstette, Edward (2013). *Category-theoretic quantitative compositional distributional models of natural language semantics*. PhD Thesis, University of Oxford, UK.

Guevara, Emiliano (2011). Computing semantic compositionality in distributional semantics. In *Proceedings of the Ninth International Conference on Computational Semantics*, 135-144, Oxford, UK.

Howell, David (2008). *Méthodes statistiques en sciences humaines*. Bruxelles, Belgique: De Boeck Université.

Kintsch, Walter (1998). *Comprehension: A Paradigme for Cognition*. New York: Cambridge University Press.

Kintsch, Walter (2001). Predication. *Cognitive Science*, 25(2), 173-202.

Landauer, Thomas, and Dumais, Susan, (1997). A solution to Plato's problem: The latent semantic analysis theory of acquisition, induction and representation of knowledge. *Psychological Review*, 104(2), 211-240.

Landauer, Thomas, Foltz, Peter, and Laham, Darrell (1998). An introduction to latent semantic analysis, *Discourse Processes*, 25, 259-284.

Lebart, Ludovic, Piron Marie, et Morineau Alain (2000). *Statistique exploratoire multidimensionnelle* (3e édition), Paris: Dunod.

Marelli, Marco, Bentivogli, Luisa, Baroni, Marco, Bernardi, Raffaella, Menini, Stefano, and Zamparelli, Roberto (2014a). Semeval-2014 task 1: Evaluation of compositional distributional semantic models on full sentences through semantic relatedness and textual entailment. In *Proceedings of SemEval-2014: Semantic Evaluation Exercises*. Dublin, Ireland.

Marelli, Marco, Menini, Stefano, Baroni, Marco, Bentivogli, Luisa, Bernardi, Raffaella, and Zamparelli, Roberto (2014b). A SICK cure for the evaluation of compositional distributional semantic models. In *Proceedings of the 9th Edition of the Language Resources and Evaluation Conference*, Reykjavik, Iceland.

Mitchell, Jeff, and Lapata, Mirella (2010). Composition in distributional models of semantics. *Cognitive Science*, 34, 1388-1429.

Nenadic, Oleg, and Greenacre, Michael (2007). Correspondence analysis in R, with two- and three-dimensional graphics: the CA package, *Journal of Statistical Software*, 20(3), 1-13.

Schmid, Helmut (1994). Probabilistic part-of-speech tagging using decision trees. In *Proceedings of the 1994 International Conference on New Methods in Language Processing*, 44-49, Manchester, UK.

Toutanova, Kristina, Klein, Dan, Manning, Christopher, and Singer, Yoram (2003). Feature-rich part-of-speech tagging with a cyclic dependency network. In *Proceddings of the Human Language Technology Conference of the North American Chapter of the Association for Computational Linguistic 2003*, 252-259, Edmonton, Canada.

CISUC-KIS: Tackling Message Polarity Classification with a Large and Diverse set of Features

João Leal, Sara Pinto, Ana Bento, Hugo Gonçalo Oliveira, Paulo Gomes
CISUC, Department of Informatics Engineering
University of Coimbra
Portugal
{jleal,sarap,arbc}@student.dei.uc.pt, {hroliv,pgomes}@dei.uc.pt

Abstract

This paper presents the approach of the CISUC-KIS team to the SemEval 2014 task on Sentiment Analysis in Twitter, more precisely subtask B - Message Polarity Classification. We followed a machine learning approach where a SVM classifier was trained from a large and diverse set of features that included lexical, syntactic, sentiment and semantic-based aspects. This led to very interesting results which, in different datasets, put us always in the top-7 scores, including second position in the LiveJournal2014 dataset.

1 Introduction

Everyday people transmit their opinion in social networks and microblogging services. Identifying the sentiment transmitted in all those shared messages is of great utility for recognizing trends and supporting decision making, key in areas such as social marketing. Sentiment Analysis deals with the computational treatment of sentiments in natural language text, often normalized to positive or negative polarities. It is a very challenging task, not only for machines, but also for humans.

SemEval 2014 is a semantic evaluation of Natural Language Processing (NLP) that comprises several tasks. This paper describes our approach to the Sentiment Analysis in Twitter task, which comprises two subtasks: (A) Contextual Polarity Disambiguation; and (B) Message Polarity Classification. We ended up addressing only task B, which is more sentence oriented, as it targets the polarity of the full messages and not individual words in those messages.

We tackled this task with a machine learning-based approach, in which we first collect several features from the analysis of the given text at several levels. The collected features are then used to learn a sentiment classification model, which can be done with different algorithms. Features were collected from several different resources, including: sentiment lexicons, dictionaries and available APIs for this task. Moreover, since microblogging text has particular characteristics that increase the difficulty of NLP, we gave special focus on text pre-processing. Regarding the tested features, they went from low-level ones, such as punctuation and emoticons, to more high-level, including topics extracted using topic modelling techniques, as well features from sentiment lexicons, some structured on plain words and others based on WordNet, and thus structured on word senses. Using the latter, we even explored word sense disambiguation. We tested several learning algorithms with all these features, but Support Vector Machines (SVM) led to the best results, so it was used for the final evaluation.

In all our runs, a model was learned from tweets, and no SMS were used for training. The model's performance was assessed with the F-Score of positive and negative classes, with 10-fold cross validation. In the official evaluation, we achieved very interesting scores, namely: 74.46% for the LiveJournal2014 (2nd place), 65.9% for the SMS2013 (7th), 67.56% for the Twitter2013 (7th), 67.95% for the Twitter2014 (4th) and 55.49% for the Twitter2014Sarcasm (4th) datasets, which ranked us always among the top-7 participations.

The next section describes the external resources exploited. Section 3 presents our approach with more detail, and is followed by section 4, where the experimental results are described. Section 5 concludes with a brief balance and the main lessons learned from our participation.

Proceedings of the 8th International Workshop on Semantic Evaluation (SemEval 2014), pages 166–170,
Dublin, Ireland, August 23-24, 2014.

2 External resources

We have used several external resources, including not only several sentiment lexicons, but also dictionaries that helped normalizing the text of the tweets, as well as available APIs that already classify the sentiment transmitted by a piece of text.

2.1 Sentiment Lexicons

We used several public handcrafted or semi-automatically created sentiment lexicons, where English words have assigned polarity values. Those included lexicons structured in plain words, namely Bing Liu's Opinion Lexicon (Hu and Liu, 2004) ($\approx$2,000 positive and 4,800 negative words), the AFINN list (Nielsen, 2011) ($\approx$2,500 words with polarities between 5 and -5, 900 positive and 1,600 negative), the NRCEmoticon Lexicon (Mohammad and Turney, 2010) ($\approx$14,000 words, their polarity, $\approx$2,300 positive, $\approx$3,300 negative, and eight basic emotions), MPQA Subjectivity Lexicon (Wilson et al., 2005) ($\approx$2,700 positive and $\approx$4,900 negative words), Sentiment140 Lexicon (Mohammad et al., 2013) ($\approx$62,000 unigrams, $\approx$677,000 bigrams; $\approx$480,000 pairs), NRC Hashtag Lexicon (Mohammad et al., 2013) ($\approx$54,000 unigrams; $\approx$316,000 bigrams; $\approx$308,000 pairs) and labMT 1.0 (Dodds et al., 2011) ($\approx$10,000 words).

We also used two resources with polarities assigned automatically to a subset of Princeton WordNet (Fellbaum, 1998) synsets, namely SentiWordNet 3.0 (Baccianella et al., 2010) ($\approx$117,000 synsets with graded positive and negatives strengths between 0 and 1), and Q-WordNet (Agerri and García-Serrano, 2010) ($\approx$7,400 positive and $\approx$8,100 negative senses).

2.2 Dictionaries

These included handcrafted dictionaries with the most common abbreviations, acronyms, emoticons and web slang used on the Internet and their meaning. Also, a list of regular expressions with elongated words like *'loool'* and *'loloolll'*, which can be normalized to *'lol'*, and a set of idiomatic expressions and their corresponding polarity.

2.3 APIs

Three public APIs were used, namely Sentiment140 (Go et al., 2009), SentimentAnalyzer[1] and SentiStrength (Thelwall et al., 2012). All of a them classify a given text snippet as positive or negative. Sentiment140 returns a value which can be 0 (negative polarity), 2 (neutral), and 4 (positive). SentimentAnalyzer returns -1 (negative) or 1 (positive), and SentiStrength a strength value between 1 and 5 (positive) or -1 and -5 (negative).

[1] `http://sentimentanalyzer.appspot.com/`

3 Approach

Our approach consisted of extracting lexical, syntactic, semantic and sentiment information from the tweets and using it in the form of features, for learning a sentiment classifier that would detect polarity in messages. This is a popular approach for these types of tasks, followed by other systems, including the winner of SemEval 2013 (Mohammad et al., 2013), where a variety of surface-form, semantic, and sentiment features was used. Our set of features is similar for the base classifier are similar, except that we included additional features that take advantage of word disambiguation to get the polarity of target word senses.

3.1 Features

Among the collected features, some were related to the content of the tweets and others were obtained from the sentiment lexicons.

3.1.1 Content Features

The tweets were tokenized and part-of-speech (POS) tagged with the CMU ARK Twitter NLP Tool (Gimpel et al., 2011) and Stanford CoreNLP (Toutanova and Manning, 2000). Each tweet was represented as a feature vector containing the following group of features: (i) emoticons (presence or absence, sum of all positive and negative polarities associated with each, polarity of the last emoticon of each tweet); (ii) length (total length of the tweet, average length per word, number of words per tweet); (iii) elongated words (number of all the words containing a repeated character more than two times); (iv) hashtags (total number of hashtags); (v) topic modelling (id of the corresponding topic); (vi) capital letters (number of words in which all letters are capitalized); (vii) negation (number of words that reverse polarity to a negative context, such as 'no' or 'never'); (viii) punctuation (number of punctuation sequences with only exclamation points, question marks or both, ASCII code of the most common punctuation and of the last punctuation in every tweet); (ix) dashes and asterisks (number of words surrounded by dashes or asterisks, such as '*yay*' or '-me-'); (x) POS (number of nouns, adjectives, adverbs, verbs and interjections).

3.1.2 Lexicon Features

A wide range of features were created using the lexicons. For each tweet and for each lexicon the following set of features were generated: (i) total number of positive and negative opinion words; (ii) sum of all positive/negative polarity values in the tweet; (iii) the highest positive/negative polarity value in the tweet; and (iv) the polarity value of the last polarity word. Those features were collected for: unigrams, bigrams and pairs (only on the NRC Hashtag Lexicon and Sentiment140), nouns, adjectives, verbs, interjections, hashtags, all caps tokens (e.g 'GO AWAY'), elongated words, asterisks and dashes tokens.

Different approaches were followed to get the polarity of each word from the wordnets. From SentiWordNet, we computed combined scores of all senses, with decreasing weights for lower ranked senses, as well as the scores of the first sense only, both considering: (i) positive and negative; (ii) just positive; (iii) just negative scores. Moreover, we performed word sense disambiguation using the full WordNet 3.0 to get the previous scores for the selected sense. For this purpose, we applied the Lesk Algorithm adapted to wordnets (Banerjee and Pedersen, 2002), using all the tweet's content words as the word context, and the synset words, gloss words and words in related synsets as the synset's context. Given that SentiWordNet is aligned to WordNet 3.0, after selecting the most adequate sense of the word, we could get its polarity scores. From Q-WordNet, similar scores were computed but, since it doesn't use a graded strength and only classifies word senses as positive or negative, there were just positive or just negative scores.

3.2 Classifier

In our final approach we used a SVM (Fan et al., 2008) which is an effective solution in high dimensional spaces and proved to be the best learning algorithm for this task. We tested various kernels (e.g. PolyKernel, RBF) and their parameters with cross validation on the training data. Given the results, we confirmed that the RBF kernel, computed according to equation 1, is most effective with a $C = 4$ and a $\gamma = 0.0003$.

$$K(x^i, x^j) = \Phi(x^i)^T\Phi(x^j) = exp(-\gamma||x^i - x^j||^2) \quad (1)$$

Considering we are working on a multi-class classification problem, we implemented the "one-against-one" approach (Knerr et al., 1990) where $\#classes * (\#classes - 1)/2$ classifiers are constructed and each one trains data from classes. Due to the non-scale invariant nature of SVM algorithms, we've scaled our data on each attribute to have $\mu = 0$ and $\sigma = 1$ and took caution against class unbalance.

4 Experiments

For training the SVM classifier, we used a set of 9,634 tweets with a known polarity and also 1,281 tweets as development test to grid search the best parameters. No SMS messages were used as training or as development test. For the scorer function, we used a macro-averaged F-Score of positive and negative classes – the one made available and used by the task organizers.

4.1 Some Results

The results obtained by the system were 70.41% on the training set (using 10-Folds) and 71.03% on the development set, after train on the training set. When tested against the training set, after train in the same set, we get a score of 84.32%, which could indicate a case of underfitting. Though, our classifier generalized well, given that we got a 74.46% official score on LiveJournal2014, second in that category. On the other hand, our experiments with decision trees showed that they couldn't generalize so well, although they achieved scores of >99 on the training set. In the SMS category, our system would benefit from a specific data set in the training phase. Yet, it still managed to reach 7th place in that category. In the sarcasm category our submission ranked 4th, with a score of 58.16%, 2.69% below the best rank. On the Twitter2014 dataset, we scored 67.95% (4th), which is slightly below our prediction based on development tests. A possible explanation is that we might have over-fitted the classifier parameters when grid searching.

4.2 Features Relevance

In order to get some insights on the most relevant group of features, we did a series of experiments where each group of features were removed for the classification, then tested against the original score. We concluded that the lexicon related features contribute highly to the performance of our system, including the set of features with n-grams and POS. Clusters, sport score, asterisks and elongated words provide little gains but, on the other hand, emoticons and hashtags showed some importance and provided enough new information for the system to learn. The API information is largely captured by some of our features and that makes it much less discriminating than what they would be on their own, but still worth using for the small gain. We also observed that it is best to create a diversified set of lexicon features with extra very specific targeted features, such as punctuation, instead of focusing on using a specific lexicon alone. Even though they usually overlap in information and may perform worse individually than a hand-refined single dictionary approach, they complement each other and that results in larger gains.

4.3 Selected Parameters

For the parameter values, we did a grid search using the development set as a test. We also found that large values of C (25) and small γ values (0.0001) performed worse than smaller values of C (4) with a slightly higher γ (0.0003) when using the development set but not when using the training set under K-Folds. For the official evaluation, we opted for the best-performing results on the development set. Using intermediate values accomplished worse results in either case.

5 Concluding Remarks

We have described the work developed for the subtask B of SemEval 2014 Sentiment Analysis in Twitter task. We followed a machine learning approach, with a diversified set of features, which tend to complemented each other. Some of the main takeaways are that the most important features are the lexicon related ones, including the n-grams and POS tags. Due to time constraints, we could not take strong conclusions on the impact of the word sense disambiguation related features alone. As those are probably the most differentiating features of our classifier, this is something we wish to target in the future.

To conclude, we have achieved very interesting results in terms of overall classification. Considering that this was our first participation in such an evaluation, we make a very positive balance. And of course, we are looking forward for upcoming editions of this task.

Acknowledgement

This work was supported by the iCIS project (CENTRO-07-ST24-FEDER-002003), co-financed by QREN, in the scope of the Mais Centro Program and European Union's FEDER.

References

Rodrigo Agerri and Ana García-Serrano. 2010. Q-wordnet: Extracting polarity from WordNet senses. In *Proceedings of the 7th International Conference on Language Resources and Evaluation*, LREC 2010, pages 2300–2305, La Valletta, Malta. ELRA.

Stefano Baccianella, Andrea Esuli, and Fabrizio Sebastiani. 2010. SentiWordNet 3.0: An enhanced lexical resource for sentiment analysis and opinion mining. In *Proceedings of the 7th International Conference on Language Resources and Evaluation*, LREC 2010, pages 2200–2204, Valletta, Malta. ELRA.

Satanjeev Banerjee and Ted Pedersen. 2002. An adapted Lesk algorithm for word sense disambiguation using WordNet. In *Proceedings of the 3rd International Conference on Computational Linguistics and Intelligent Text Processing (CICLing 2002)*, volume 2276 of *LNCS*, pages 136–145, London, UK. Springer.

Peter Sheridan Dodds, Kameron Decker Harris, Isabel M. Kloumann, Catherine A. Bliss, and Christopher M. Danforth. 2011. Temporal patterns of happiness and information in a global social network: Hedonometrics and Twitter. *PLoS ONE*, 6(12), December.

Rong-En Fan, Kai-Wei Chang, Cho-Jui Hsieh, Xiang-Rui Wang, and Chih-Jen Lin. 2008. Liblinear: A library for large linear classification. *Journal of Machine Learning Research*, 9:1871–1874, June.

Christiane Fellbaum, editor. 1998. *WordNet: An Electronic Lexical Database (Language, Speech, and Communication)*. The MIT Press.

Kevin Gimpel, Nathan Schneider, Brendan O'Connor, Dipanjan Das, Daniel Mills, Jacob Eisenstein, Michael Heilman, Dani Yogatama, Jeffrey Flanigan, and Noah A Smith. 2011. Part-of-speech tagging for Twitter: Annotation, features, and experiments. In *Proceedings of the 49th Annual Meeting of the Association for Computational Linguistics: Human Language Technologies: short papers-Volume 2*, ACL 2011, pages 42–47. ACL Press.

Alec Go, Richa Bhayani, and Lei Huang. 2009. Twitter sentiment classification using distant supervision. Technical report, Stanford University.

Minqing Hu and Bing Liu. 2004. Mining and summarizing customer reviews. In *Proceedings of the 10th ACM SIGKDD International Conference on Knowledge Discovery and Data Mining*, KDD 2004, pages 168–177.

Stefan Knerr, Léon Personnaz, and Gérard Dreyfus. 1990. Single-layer learning revisited: a stepwise procedure for building and training neural network. In *Proceedings of the NATO Advanced Research Workshop on Neurocomputing, Algorithms, Architectures and Applications*, Nato ASI, Computer and Systems Sciences, pages 41–50. Springer.

Saif M. Mohammad and Peter D. Turney. 2010. Emotions evoked by common words and phrases: Using Mechanical Turk to create an emotion lexicon. In *Proceedings of the NAACL HLT 2010 Workshop on Computational Approaches to Analysis and Generation of Emotion in Text*, CAAGET '10, pages 26–34, Los Angeles, CA. ACL Press.

Saif Mohammad, Svetlana Kiritchenko, and Xiaodan Zhu. 2013. NRC-Canada: Building the state-of-the-art in sentiment analysis of tweets. In *2nd Joint Conference on Lexical and Computational Semantics (*SEM), Volume 2: Proceedings of the Seventh International Workshop on Semantic Evaluation*, SemEval 2013, pages 321–327, Atlanta, Georgia, USA, June. ACL Press.

Finn Årup Nielsen. 2011. A new anew: Evaluation of a word list for sentiment analysis in microblogs. In *Proceedings of the ESWC2011 Workshop on 'Making Sense of Microposts': Big things come in small packages*, pages 93–98, May.

Mike Thelwall, Kevan Buckley, and Georgios Paltoglou. 2012. Sentiment strength detection for the social web. *Journal of the American Society for Information Science and Technology*, 63(1):163–173, January.

Kristina Toutanova and Christopher D Manning. 2000. Enriching the knowledge sources used in a maximum entropy part-of-speech tagger. In *Proceedings of the 2000 Joint SIGDAT conference on Empirical methods in natural language processing and very large corpora*, EMNLP 2000, pages 63–70. ACL Press.

Theresa Wilson, Janyce Wiebe, and Paul Hoffmann. 2005. Recognizing contextual polarity in phrase-level sentiment analysis. In *Proceedings of the Conference on Human Language Technology and Empirical Methods in Natural Language Processing*, HLT '05, pages 347–354, Vancouver, British Columbia, Canada. ACL Press.

Citius: A Naive-Bayes Strategy for Sentiment Analysis on English Tweets*

Pablo Gamallo
CITIUS
Univ. de Santiago de Compostela
pablo.gamallo@usc.es

Marcos Garcia
Cilenis Language Technology, S.L.
marcos.garcia@cilenis.com

Abstract

This article describes a strategy based on a naive-bayes classifier for detecting the polarity of English tweets. The experiments have shown that the best performance is achieved by using a binary classifier between just two sharp polarity categories: positive and negative. In addition, in order to detect tweets with and without polarity, the system makes use of a very basic rule that searchs for polarity words within the analysed tweets/texts. When the classifier is provided with a polarity lexicon and multiwords it achieves 63% F-score.

1 Introduction

Sentiment Analysis consists in finding the opinion (e.g. positive, negative, or neutral) from text documents such as movie reviews or product reviews. Opinions about movies, products, etc. can be found in web blogs, social networks, discussion forums, and so on. Companies can improve their products and services on the basis of the reviews and comments of their costumers. Recently, many works have stressed the microblogging service Twitter. As Twitter can be seen as a large source of short texts (tweets) containing user opinions, most of these works make sentiment analysis by identifying user attitudes and opinions toward a particular topic or product (Go et al., 2009). The task of making sentiment analysis from tweets is a hard challenge. On the one hand, as in any sentiment analysis framework, we have to deal with human subjectivity. Even humans often disagree on the categorization of the positive or negative sentiment that is supposed to be expressed on a given text (Villena-Román et al., 2013). On the other hand, tweets are too short text to be linguistically analyzed, and it makes the task of finding relevant information (e.g. opinions) much harder.

The SemEval-2014 task "Sentiment Analysis in Twitter" is an evaluation competition that includes a specific task directly related to sentiment analyisis. In particular, subtask B, called "Message Polarity Classification", consists in classifying whether a given message is of positive, negative, or neutral sentiment. For messages conveying both a positive and negative sentiment, the stronger sentiment should be chosen. The results of our system in this task are situated in the average out of 51 evaluated systems.

In this article, we describe the learning strategies we developed so as to perform this task, all of them based on bayesian classification.

2 Naive Bayes Classifier

Most of the algorithms for sentiment analysis are based on a classifier trained using a collection of annotated text data. Before training, data is preprocessed so as to extract the main features. Some classification methods have been proposed: Naive Bayes, Support Vector Machines, K-Nearest Neighbors, etc. However, and according to (Go et al., 2009), it is not clear which of these classification strategies is the more appropriate to perform sentiment analysis.

We decided to use a classification strategy based on Naive Bayes (NB) because it is a simple and intuitive method whose performance is similar to other approaches. NB combines efficiency (optimal time performance) with reasonable accuracy. The main theoretical drawback of NB methods is that it assumes conditional independence among the linguistic features. If the main features are the tokens extracted from texts, it is evident that they

*This work has been supported by the projects: HPC-PLN: Ref:EM13/041 (Program *Emergentes*, Xunta de Galicia), Celtic: Ref:2012-CE138 and Plastic: Ref:2013-CE298 (Program Feder-Innterconecta)

Proceedings of the 8th International Workshop on Semantic Evaluation (SemEval 2014), pages 171–175,
Dublin, Ireland, August 23-24, 2014.

cannot be considered as independent, since words co-occuring in a text are somehow linked by different types of syntactic and semantic dependencies. However, even if NB produces an oversimplified model, its classification decisions are surprinsingly accurate (Manning et al., 2008).

2.1 Strategy

Two different naive bayes classifiers have been built, according to two different strategies:

Baseline This is a naive bayes classifier that learns from the original training corpus how to classify the three categories found in the corpus: Positive, Negative, and Neutral. So, no modification has been introduced in the training corpus.

Binary The second classifier was trained on a simplified training corpus and makes use of a polarity lexicon. The corpus was simplified since only positive and negative tweets were considered. Neutral tweets were not taken into account. As a result, a basic binary (or boolean) classifier which only identifies both Positive and Negative tweets was trained. In order to detect tweets without polarity (or Neutral), the following basic rule is used: if the tweet contains at least one word that is also found in the polarity lexicon, then the tweet has some degree of polarity. Othewise, the tweet has no polarity at all and is classified as Neutral. The binary classifier is actually suited to specify the basic polarity between positive and negative, reaching a precision of more than 80% in a corpus with just these two categories.

3 Preprocessing

As we will describe in the next section, the main features of the model are lemmas extracted using lemmatization. Given that the language of microblogging requires a special treatment, we propose a pre-processing task to correct and normalize the tweets before lemmatizing them.

The main preprocessing tasks we considered are the following:

- removing urls, references to usernames, and hashtags
- reduction of replicated characters (e.g. *loooveeee* → *love*)
- identifying emoticons and interjections and replacing them with polarity or sentiment expressions (e.g. :-) → *good*)

4 Features

The features considered by the classifier are lemmas, multiwords, polarity lexicons, and valence shifters.

4.1 Lemmas (UL)

To characterise the main features underlying the classifier, we make use of unigrams of lemmas instead of tokens to minimize the problems derived from the sparse distribution of words. Moreover, only lemmas belonging to lexical categories are selected as features, namely nouns, verbs, adjectives, and adverbs. So, grammatical words, such as determiners, conjunctions, and prepositions are removed from the model.

To configure the feature representation, the frequency of each selected lemma in a tweet is stored.

4.2 Multiwords (MW)

There is no agreement on which is the best option for sentiment analysis (unigrams, bigrams, ...). In (Pak and Paroubek, 2010), the best performance is achieved with bigrams, while (Go et al., 2009) show that the better results are reached with unigrams. An alternative option is to make use of a selected set of n-grams (or multiwords) identified by means of regular patterns of PoS tags. Multiword expressions identified by means of PoS tags patterns can be conceived as linguistically motivated terms, since most of them are pairs of words linked by syntactic dependencies.

So, in addition to unigrams of lemmas, we also consider multiwords extracted by an algorithm based on patterns of PoS tags. In particular, we used the following set of patterns:

- NOUN-ADJ
- NOUN-NOUN
- ADJ-NOUN
- NOUN-PRP-NOUN
- VERB-NOUN
- VERB-PRP-NOUN

The instances of bigrams and trigrams extracted with these patterns ared added to the unigrams to build the language model. Multiword extraction was performed using our tool *GaleXtra*[1], released under GPL license and described in (Mario Barcala and Eva Domínguez and Pablo Gamallo and Marisol López and Eduardo Moscoso and Guillermo Rojo and Paula Santalla and Susana Sotelo, 2007).

4.3 Polarity Lexicon (LEX)

We have built a polarity lexicon with both *Positive* and *Negative* entries from different sources:

- AFINN-111[2] contains $2,477$ word forms, which were lemmatized and converted into $1,520$, positive and negative lemmas.

- Hedonometer[3] contains about $10,000$ frequent words extracted from tweets which were classified as expressing some degree of hapiness (Dodds et al., 2011). We selected the 300 most positive lemmas from the initial list.

- Hu&Liu list (Liu et al., 2005) contains over $6,800$ words out of which 5 positive and negative lemmas were selected $5,695$.

- Sentiwordnet-3.0 (Baccianella et al., 2010) contains more than $100,000$ entries. We selected a subset of $6,600$ positive and negative lemmas with the highest polarity values.

- Finally, we have built a polarity lexicon with $10,850$ entries by merging the previous ones.

The final polarity lexicon is used in two different ways: on the one hand, it is used to identify neutral tweets, since a tweet is considered as being neutral if it does not contain any lemma appearing in the polarity lexicon. On the other hand, we have built artificial tweets as follows: each entry of the lexicon is converted into an artificial tweet with just one lemma inheriting the polarity (positive or negative) from the lexicon. The frequency of the word in each new tweet is the average frequency of lemmas in the training corpus. These artificial tweets will be taken into account for training the classifiers.

4.4 Valence Shifters (VS)

We take into account negative words that can shift the polarity of specific lemmas in a tweet. In the presented work, we will make use of only those valence shifters that reverse the sentiment of words, namely *negations*. The strategy to identify the scope of negations relies on the PoS tags of the negative word as well as of those words appearing to its right in the sequence. The algorithm is as follows:

Whenever a negative word is found, its PoS tag is considered and, according to its syntactic properties, we search for a polarity word (noun, verb, or adjective) within a window of 2 words after the negation. If a polarity word is found and is syntactically linked to the negative word, then its polarity is reversed. For instance, if the negation word is the adverb "not", the system only reverses the polarity of verbs or adjectives appearing to its right. Nouns are not syntactically linked to this adverb. By contrast, if the negation is the determiner "no" or "none", only the polarity of nouns can be reversed. Our strategy to deal with negation scope is not so basic as those described in (Yang, 2008) and (Anta et al., 2013), which are just based on a rigid window after the negation word: 1 and 3 words, respectively.

5 Experiments and Evaluation

5.1 Training corpus

In our preliminary experiments we have used the training dataset of tweets provided by SemEval-2014 organization (tweeti-b.dist.tsv). This set contains $6,408$ tweets, which were tagged with the following polarity values: Positive, Negative, Neutral, Objective, and Neutral-or-Objective. In order to fill the requirements of the task, we transformed Neutral, Objective, and Natural-or-Objective into a single tag: Neutral. In addition, we also used a selection of annotated tweets (namely $5,050$ positive and negative ones), which were compiled from an external source (Narr et al., 2012). Using the terminology provided by the organizers of SemEval-2014, we call "constrained" the systems trained with only the dataset provided by the organization and "unconstrained" the systems trained with both datasets.

5.2 Evaluated classifiers

We have implemented and evaluated several classifiers by making use of the two strategies de-

[1] http://gramatica.usc.es/\~gamallo/gale-extra/index.htm
[2] http://arxiv.org/abs/1103.2903
[3] http://www.hedonometer.org/

scribed in section 2, combined with the features defined in 4. We also distinguished those classifiers trained with only tweeti-b.dist.tsv (constrained systems) from those trained with both internal and external datasets (unconstrained). As a result, we implemented the following classifiers:

CONSTRAINED-BASELINE: This system was implemented on the basis of the "Baseline" strategy and the following two features: unigrams of lemmas (UL) and valence shifters (VS).

CONSTRAINED-BASELINE-LEX: This system was implemented on the basis of the "Baseline" strategy and the following three features: unigrams of lemmas (UL), polarity lexicon (LEX), and valence shifters (VS).

CONSTRAINED-BINARY-LEX: This system was implemented on the basis of the "Baseline" strategy and the following three features: unigrams of lemmas (UL), polarity lexicon (LEX), and valence shifters (VS).

CONSTRAINED-BINARY-LEX-MW: This system was implemented on the basis of the "Binary" strategy and the following features: unigrams of lemmas (UL), multiwords (MW), polarity lexicon (LEX), and valence shifters (VS).

UNCONSTRAINED-BINARY-LEX: This system was implemented on the basis of the "Binary" strategy and the following features: unigrams of lemmas (UL), polarity lexicon (LEX), and valence shifters (VS).

UNCONSTRAINED-BINARY-LEX-MW: This system was implemented on the basis of the "Binary" strategy and the following features: unigrams of lemmas (UL), multiwords (MW), polarity lexicon (LEX), and valence shifters (VS).

All the classifers have been implemented with Perl language. They rely on the naive-bayes algorithm and incorporate the preprocessing tasks defined in section 3.

5.3 Evaluation

To evaluate the classification performance of these classifiers, we used as test corpus another dataset provided by the organization: tweeti-b.devel.tsv. The results are shown in table 1, where the names of the evaluated systems are in the first column and F-Score in the second one.

System	F-score
CONSTR-BASE	.49
CONSTR-BASE-LEX	.56
CONSTR-BIN-LEX	.57
CONSTR-BIN-LEX-MW	**.61**
UNCONSTR-BIN-LEX	.58
UNCONSTR-BIN-LEX-MW	**.63**

Table 1: Results of our six systems

The results show that there is an improvement in performance when the classifiers are implemented with the Binary strategy, when they use a polarity lexicon, and when multiwords are considered as features. The two systems submmited to Semeval competition were those obtained the best scores: CONSTR-BIN-LEX-MW and UNCONSTR-BIN-LEX-MW. The scores obtained by these two systems in the competition are very similar to those obtained in the experiments depicted in Table 1. More precisely, in the Tweets2014 test corpus, the constrained system reached 0.62 F-score while the unconstrained version achieved 0.63. Our best system was ranked as 26th from 53 systems. A Spanish version of this system (Gamallo et al., 2013) also participated in the TASS-2013 competition (Villena-Román et al., 2013), where it was ranked as the 3th best system out of 13 participants.

6 Conclusions

We have presented a family of naive-bayes classifiers for detecting the polarity of English tweets. The experiments have shown that the best performance is achieved by using a binary classifier trained to detect just two categories: positive and negative. In order to detect tweets with and without polarity we used a very basic strategy based on searching for polarity lemmas within the text/tweet. If the tweet does not contain at least one lemma also found in an external polarity lexicon, then the tweet has not any polarity and, thereby, is tagged with the Neutral value. The use of both a polarity lexicon and multiwords also improves the results in a significant way. Our system is being used by Cilenis S.L, a company specialised in natural language technology, and being applied to four languages: English, Spanish, Portuguese, and Galician.

References

Antonio Fernández Anta, Luis Núñez Chiroque, Philippe Morere, and Agustín Santos. 2013. Sentiment Analysis and Topic Detection of Spanish Tweets: A Comparative Study of NLP Techniques. *Procesamiento del Lenguaje Natural*, 50:45–52.

Stefano Baccianella, Andrea Esuli, and Fabrizio Sebastiani. 2010. SentiWordNet 3.0: An Enhanced Lexical Resource for Sentiment Analysis and Opinion Mining. In *Human Language Technology Conference - North American chapter of the Association for Computational Linguistics*, pages 2200–2204.

Peter Sheridan Dodds, Kameron Decker Harris, Isabel M. Kloumann, Catherine A. Bliss, and Christopher M. Danforth. 2011. Temporal patterns of happiness and information in a global social network: Hedonometrics and Twitter. *PLoS ONE*, 6(12):e26752.

Pablo Gamallo, Marcos Garcia, and Santiago Fernández-Lanza. 2013. TASS: A Naive-Bayes strategy for sentiment analysis on Spanish tweets. In *Workshop on Sentiment Analysis at SEPLN (TASS2013)*, pages 126–132, Madrid, Spain.

Alec Go, Richa Bhayani, and Lei Huang. 2009. Twitter sentiment classification using distant supervision. In *CS224N Technical report*. Standford.

Bing Liu, Minqing Hu, and Junsheng Cheng. 2005. Opinion observer: Analyzing and comparing opinions on the web. In *14th International World Wide Web conference (WWW-2005)*, pages 342–351, New York, NY, USA.

Chris Manning, Prabhakar Raghadvan, and Hinrich Schütze. 2008. *Introduction to Information Retrieval*. Cambridge University Press, Cambridge, MA, USA.

Mario Barcala and Eva Domínguez and Pablo Gamallo and Marisol López and Eduardo Moscoso and Guillermo Rojo and Paula Santalla and Susana Sotelo. 2007. A Corpus and Lexical Resources for Multi-word Terminology Extraction in the Field of Economy. In *3rd Language & Technology Conference (LeTC'2007)*, pages 355–359, Poznan, Poland.

Sascha Narr, Michael Hulfenhaus, and Sahin Albayrak. 2012. Language-Independent Twitter Sentiment Analysis. In *Knowledge Discovery and Machine Learning (KDML), LWA*, pages 12–14, Dortmund, Germany.

Alexander Pak and Patrick Paroubek. 2010. Twitter as a Corpus for Sentiment Analysis and Opinion Mining. In *LREC-2010*, Valletta, Malta.

Julio Villena-Román, Sara Lana, Eugeinio Martínez-Cámara, and Juan Carlos González-Cristóbal. 2013. TASS - Workshop on Sentiment Analysis at SEPLN. *Procesamiento del Lenguaje Natural*, 50:37–44.

Kiduk Yang. 2008. WIDIT in TREC 2008 blog track: Leveraging Multiple Sources of Opinion Evidence. In *The Seventeenth Text Retrieval Conference (TREC-2008)*, Gaithersburg, Maryland, USA.

CMU: Arc-Factored, Discriminative Semantic Dependency Parsing

Sam Thomson Brendan O'Connor Jeffrey Flanigan David Bamman
Jesse Dodge Swabha Swayamdipta Nathan Schneider Chris Dyer Noah A. Smith
Language Technologies Institute
Carnegie Mellon University
Pittsburgh, PA 15213, USA
{sthomson,brenocon,jflanigan,dbamman,jessed,
swabha,nschneid,cdyer,nasmith}@cs.cmu.edu

Abstract

We present an arc-factored statistical model for semantic dependency parsing, as defined by the SemEval 2014 Shared Task 8 on Broad-Coverage Semantic Dependency Parsing. Our entry in the open track placed second in the competition.

1 Introduction

The task of broad coverage semantic dependency parsing aims to provide a shallow semantic analysis of text not limited to a specific domain. As distinct from deeper semantic analysis (e.g., parsing to a full lambda-calculus logical form), shallow semantic parsing captures relationships between pairs of words or concepts in a sentence, and has wide application for information extraction, knowledge base population, and question answering (among others).

We present here two systems that produce semantic dependency parses in the three formalisms of the SemEval 2014 Shared Task 8 on Broad-Coverage Semantic Dependency Parsing (Oepen et al., 2014). These systems generate parses by extracting features for each potential dependency arc and learning a statistical model to discriminate between good arcs and bad; the first treats each labeled edge decision as an independent multiclass logistic regression (§3.2.1), while the second predicts arcs as part of a graph-based structured support vector machine (§3.2.2). Common to both models is a rich set of features on arcs, described in §3.2.3. We include a discussion of features found to have no discernable effect, or negative effect, during development (§4).

Our system placed second in the open track of the Broad-Coverage Semantic Dependency Parsing task (in which output from syntactic parsers and other outside resources *can* be used). We present our results in §5.

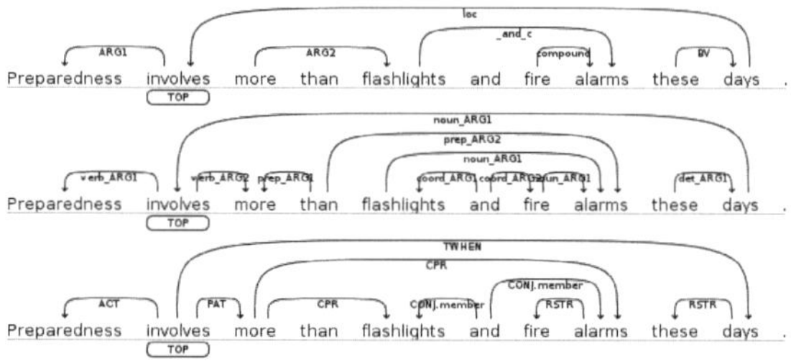

Figure 1: Example annotations for DM (top), PAS (middle), and PCEDT (bottom).

2 Formalisms

The Shared Task 8 dataset consists of annotations of the WSJ Corpus in three different semantic dependency formalisms. DM is derived from LinGO English Resource Grammar (ERG) annotations in DeepBank (Flickinger et al., 2012). PAS is derived from the Enju HPSG treebank using the conversion rules of Miyao et al. (2004). PCEDT is derived from the tectogrammatical layer of the Prague Czech-English Dependency Treebank (Hajič, 1998). See Figure 1 for an example.

The three formalisms come from very different linguistic theories, but all are represented as labeled directed graphs, with words as vertices, and all have "top" annotations, corresponding roughly to the semantic focus of the sentence. (A "top" need not be a root of the graph.) This allows us to use the same machinery (§3) for training and testing statistical models for the three formalisms.

3 Models

We treat the problem as a three-stage pipeline. The first stage prunes words by predicting whether they have any incoming or outgoing edges at all (§3.1); if a word does not, then it is not considered for any attachments in later stages. The second stage

Proceedings of the 8th International Workshop on Semantic Evaluation (SemEval 2014), pages 176–180,
Dublin, Ireland, August 23-24, 2014.

predicts where edges are present, and their labels (§3.2). The third stage predicts whether a predicate word is a *top* or not (§3.3). Formalisms sometimes annotate more than one "top" per sentence, but we found that we achieve the best performance on all formalisms by predicting only the one best-scoring "top" under the model.

3.1 Singleton Classification

For each formalism, we train a classifier to recognize *singletons*, nodes that have no parents or children. (For example, punctuation tokens are often singletons.) This makes the system faster without affecting accuracy. For singleton prediction, we use a token-level logistic regression classifier, with features including the word, its lemma, and its part-of-speech tag. If the classifier predicts a probability of 99% or higher the token is pruned; this removes around 10% of tokens. (The classifier performs differently on different formalisms; on PAS it has perfect accuracy, while on DM and PCEDT accuracy is in the mid-90's.)

3.2 Edge Prediction

In the second stage of the pipeline, we predict the set of labeled directed edges in the graph. We use the same set of edge-factored features (§3.2.3) in two alternative models: an edge-independent multiclass logistic regression model (LOGISTICEDGE, §3.2.1); and a structured SVM (Taskar et al., 2003; Tsochantaridis et al., 2004) that enforces a *determinism* constraint for certain labels, which allows each word to have at most one outgoing edge with that label (SVMEDGE, §3.2.2). For each formalism, we trained both models with varying features enabled and hyperparameter settings and submitted the configuration that produced the best labeled F_1 on the development set. For DM and PCEDT, this was LOGISTICEDGE; for PAS, this was SVMEDGE. We report results only for the submitted configurations, with different features enabled. Due to time constraints, full hyperparameter sweeps and comparable feature sweeps were not possible.

3.2.1 LOGISTICEDGE Parser

The LOGISTICEDGE model considers only token index pairs (i, j) where $|i - j| \leq 10$, $i \neq j$, and both t_i and t_j have been predicted to be non-singletons by the first stage. Although this prunes some gold edges, among the formalisms, 95%–97% of all gold edges are between tokens of distance 10 or less. Both directions $i \rightarrow j$ and $j \rightarrow i$ are considered between every pair.

Let L be the set of $K + 1$ possible output labels: the formalism's original K edge labels, plus the additional label NOEDGE, which indicates that no edge exists from i to j. The model treats every pair of token indices (i, j) as an independent multiclass logistic regression over output space L. Let x be an input sentence. For candidate parent index i, child index j, and edge label ℓ, we extract a feature vector $\boldsymbol{f}(x, i, j, \ell)$, where ℓ is conjoined with every feature described in §3.2.3. The multiclass logistic regression model defines a distribution over L, parametrized by weights $\boldsymbol{\phi}$:

$$P(\ell \mid \boldsymbol{\phi}, x, i, j) = \frac{\exp\{\boldsymbol{\phi} \cdot \boldsymbol{f}(x, i, j, \ell)\}}{\sum_{\ell' \in L} \exp\{\boldsymbol{\phi} \cdot \boldsymbol{f}(x, i, j, \ell')\}}.$$

$\boldsymbol{\phi}$ is learned by minimizing total negative log-likelihood of the above (with weighting; see below), plus ℓ_2 regularization. AdaGrad (Duchi et al., 2011) is used for optimization. This seemed to optimize faster than L-BFGS (Liu and Nocedal, 1989), at least for earlier iterations, though we did no systematic comparison. Stochastic gradient steps are applied one at a time from individual examples, and a gradient step for the regularizer is applied once per epoch.

The output labels have a class imbalance; in all three formalisms, there are many more NOEDGE examples than true edge examples. We improved F_1 performance by downweighting NOEDGE examples through a weighted log-likelihood objective, $\sum_{i,j} \sum_{\ell} w_\ell \log P(\ell \mid \boldsymbol{\phi}, x, i, j)$, with $w_{\text{NOEDGE}} = 0.3$ (selected on development set) and $w_\ell = 1$ otherwise.

Decoding: To predict a graph structure at test-time for a new sentence, the most likely edge label is predicted for every candidate (i, j) pair of unpruned tokens. If an edge is predicted for both directions for a single (i, j) pair, only the edge with the higher score is chosen. (There are no such bidirectional edges in the training data.) This post-processing actually did not improve accuracy on DM or PCEDT; it did improve PAS by ≈0.2% absolute F_1, but we did not submit LOGISTICEDGE for PAS.

3.2.2 SVMEDGE Parser

In the SVMEDGE model, we use a structured SVM with a determinism constraint. This constraint ensures that each word token has at most one outgoing edge for each label in a set of deterministic labels L_d. For example, in DM a predicate never has more than one child with edge label "ARG1." L_d was chosen to be the set of edges that were $> 99.9\%$ deterministic in the training data.[1]

Consider the fully dense graph of all edges between all words predicted as not singletons by the singleton classifier §3.1 (in all directions with all possible labels). Unlike LOGISTICEDGE, the label set L does not include an explicit NOEDGE label. If $\boldsymbol{\psi}$ denotes the model weights, and $\boldsymbol{f}$ denotes the features, then an edge from i to j with label ℓ in the dense graph has a weight $c(i, j, \ell)$ assigned to it using the linear scoring function $c(i, j, \ell) = \boldsymbol{\psi} \cdot \boldsymbol{f}(x, i, j, \ell)$.

Decoding: For each node and each label ℓ, if $\ell \in L_d$, the decoder adds the highest scoring outgoing edge, if its weight is positive. For $\ell \notin L_d$, every outgoing edge with positive weight is added. This procedure is guaranteed to find the highest scoring subgraph (largest sum of edge weights) of the dense graph subject to the determinism constraints. Its runtime is $O(n^2)$.

The model weights are trained using the structured SVM loss. If x is a sentence and y is a graph over that sentence, let the features be denoted $\boldsymbol{f}(x, y) = \sum_{(i,j,\ell)\in y} \boldsymbol{f}(x, i, j, \ell)$. The SVM loss for each training example (x_i, y_i) is:

$$-\boldsymbol{\psi}^\top \boldsymbol{f}(x_i, y_i) + \max_y \boldsymbol{\psi}^\top \boldsymbol{f}(x_i, y) + cost(y, y_i)$$

where $cost(y, y_i) = \alpha|y \setminus y_i| + \beta|y_i \setminus y|$. α and β trade off between precision and recall for the edges (Gimpel and Smith, 2010). The loss is minimized with AdaGrad using early-stopping on a development set.

3.2.3 Edge Features

Table 1 describes the features we used for predicting edges. These features were computed over an edge e with parent token s at index i and child token t at index j. Unless otherwise stated, each feature template listed has an indicator feature that fires for each value it can take on. For the submitted results, LOGISTICEDGE uses all features except Dependency Path v2, POS Path, and Distance Thresholds, and SVMEDGE uses all features except Dependency Path v1. This was due to SVMEDGE being faster to train than LOGISTICEDGE when including POS Path features, and due to time constraints for the submission we were unable to retrain LOGISTICEDGE with these features.

Tokens: The tokens s and t themselves.
Lemmas: Lemmas of s and t.
POS tags: Part of speech tags of s and t.
Linear Order: Fires if $i < j$.
Linear Distance: $i - j$.
Dependency Path v1 (LOGISTICEDGE only): The concatenation of all POS tags, arc labels and up/down directions on the path in the syntactic dependency tree from s to t. Conjoined with s, with t, and without either.
Dependency Path v2 (SVMEDGE only): Same as Dependency Path v1, but with the lemma of s or t instead of the word, and substituting the token for any "IN" POS tag.
Up/Down Dependency Path: The sequence of upward and downward moves needed to get from s to t in the syntactic dependency tree.
Up/Down/Left/Right Dependency Path: The unlabeled path through the syntactic dependency tree from s to t, annotated with whether each step through the tree was up or down, and whether it was to the right or left in the sentence.
Is Parent: Fires if s is the parent of t in the syntactic dependency parse.
Dependency Path Length: Distance between s and t in the syntactic dependency parse.
POS Context: Concatenated POS tags of tokens at $i-1$, i, $i+1$, $j-1$, j, and $j+1$. Concatenated POS tags of tokens at $i-1$, i, $j-1$, and j. Concatenated POS tags of tokens at i, $i+1$, j, and $j+1$.
Subcategorization Sequence: The sequence of dependency arc labels out of s, ordered by the index of the child. Distinguish left children from right children. If t is a direct child of s, distinguish its arc label with a "+". Conjoin this sequence with the POS tag of s.
Subcategorization Sequence with POS: As above, but add the POS tag of each child to its arc label.
POS Path (SVMEDGE only): Concatenated POS tags between and including i and j. Conjoined with head lemma, with dependent lemma, and without either.
Distance Thresholds (SVMEDGE only): Fires for every integer between 1 and $\lfloor \log(|i-j|+1)/\log(1.39) \rfloor$ inclusive.

Table 1: Features used in edge prediction

3.2.4 Feature Hashing

The biggest memory usage was in the map from feature names to integer indices during feature extraction. For experimental expedience, we implemented multitask feature hashing (Weinberger et al., 2009), which hashes feature names to indices, under the theory that errors due to collisions tend to cancel. No drop in accuracy was observed.

3.3 Top Prediction

We trained a separate token-level binary logistic regression model to classify whether a token's node had the "top" attribute or not. At decoding time, all predicted predicates (i.e., nodes where there is at

[1] By this we mean that of the nodes that have at least one outgoing ℓ edge, 99.9% of them have only one outgoing ℓ edge. For DM, $L_d = L \setminus \{$"_and_c," "_or_c," "_then_c," "loc," "mwe," "subord"$\}$; for PAS, $L_d = L$; and for PCEDT, $L_d = \{$"DPHR," "INTF," "VOCAT"$\}$.

least one outbound edge) are possible candidates to be "top"; the classifier probabilities are evaluated, and the highest-scoring node is chosen to be "top." This is suboptimal, since some graphs have multiple tops (in PCEDT this is more common); but selection rules based on probability thresholds gave worse F_1 performance on the dev set. For a given token t at index i, the top classifier's features included t's POS tag, i, those two conjoined, and the depth of t in the syntactic dependency tree.

4 Negative Results

We followed a forward-selection process during feature engineering. For each potential feature, we tested the current feature set versus the current feature set plus the new potential feature. If the new feature did not improve performance, we did not add it. We list in table 2 some of the features which we tested but did not improve performance.

In order to save time, we ran these feature selection experiments on a subsample of the training data, for a reduced number of iterations. These results thus have a strong caveat that the experiments were not exhaustive. It may be that some of these features could help under more careful study.

Word vectors: Features derived from 64-dimensional vectors from (Faruqui and Dyer, 2014), including the concatenation, difference, inner product, and element-wise multiplication of the two vectors associated with a parent-child edge. We also trained a Random Forest on the word vectors using Liaw and Wiener's (2002) *R* implementation. The predicted labels were then used as features in LOGISTICEDGE.
Brown clusters Features derived from Brown clusters (Brown et al., 1992) trained on a large corpus of web data. Parent, child, and conjoined parent-child edge features from cluster prefixes of length 2, 4, 6, 8, 10, and 12. Conjunctions of those features with the POS tags of the parent and child tokens.
Active/passive: Active/passive voice feature (as in Johansson and Nugues (2008)) conjoined with both the Linear Distance features and the Subcategorization Sequence features. Voice information may already be captured by features from the Stanford dependency–style parses, which include passivization information in arc labels such as *nsubjpass* and *auxpass* (de Marneffe and Manning, 2008).
Connectivity constraint: Enforcing that the graph is connected (ignoring singletons), similar to Flanigan et al. (2014). Almost all semantic dependency graphs in the training data are connected (ignoring singletons), but we found that enforcing this constraint significantly hurt precision.
Tree constraint: Enforces that the graph is a tree. Unsurprisingly, we found that enforcing a tree constraint hurt performance.

Table 2: Features and constraints giving negative results.

	LP	LR	LF	LM
DM	0.8446	0.8348	0.8397	0.0875
PAS	0.9078	0.8851	0.8963	0.2604
PCEDT	0.7681	0.7072	0.7364	0.0712
Average	0.8402	0.8090	0.8241	0.1397

Table 3: Labeled precision (LP), recall (LR), F_1 (LF), and whole-sentence match (LM) on the held-out test data.

5 Experimental Setup

We participated in the Open Track, and used the syntactic dependency parses supplied by the organizers. Feature engineering was performed on a development set (§20), training on §§00–19. We evaluate labeled precision (LP), labeled recall (LR), labeled F_1 (LF), and labeled whole-sentence match (LM) on the held-out test data using the evaluation script provided by the organizers. LF was averaged over the formalisms to determine the winning system. Table 3 shows our scores.

6 Conclusion and Future Work

We found that feature-rich discriminative models perform well at the task of mapping from sentences to semantic dependency parses. While our final approach is fairly standard for work in parsing, we note here additional features and constraints which did not appear to help (contrary to expectation). There are a number of clear extensions to this work that could improve performance. While an edge-factored model allows for efficient inference, there is much to be gained from **higher-order features** (McDonald and Pereira, 2006; Martins et al., 2013). The amount of information shared between the three formalisms suggests that a **multi-task learning** (Evgeniou and Pontil, 2004) framework could lead to gains. And finally, there is additional structure in the formalisms which could be exploited (such as the deterministic processes by which an original PCEDT tree annotation was converted into a graph); formulating more subtle **graph constraints** to capture this a priori knowledge could lead to improved performance. We leave such explorations to future work.

Acknowledgements

We are grateful to Manaal Faruqui for his help in word vector experiments, and to reviewers for helpful comments. The research reported in this paper was sponsored by the U.S. Army Research Laboratory and the U. S. Army Research Office under contract/grant number W911NF-10-1-0533, DARPA grant FA8750-12-2-0342 funded under the DEFT program, U.S. NSF grants IIS-1251131 and IIS-1054319, and Google's support of the Reading is Believing project at CMU.

References

Peter F. Brown, Peter V. deSouza, Robert L. Mercer, Vincent J. Della Pietra, and Jenifer C. Lai. 1992. Class-based n-gram models of natural language. *Computational Linguistics*, 18(4):467–479.

Marie-Catherine de Marneffe and Christopher D. Manning. 2008. The Stanford typed dependencies representation. In *Coling 2008: Proc. of the Workshop on Cross-Framework and Cross-Domain Parser Evaluation*, pages 1–8. Manchester, UK.

John Duchi, Elad Hazan, and Yoram Singer. 2011. Adaptive subgradient methods for online learning and stochastic optimization. *Journal of Machine Learning Research*, 12:2121–2159.

Theodoros Evgeniou and Massimiliano Pontil. 2004. Regularized multitask learning. In *Proc. of KDD*, pages 109–117. Seattle, WA, USA.

Manaal Faruqui and Chris Dyer. 2014. Improving vector space word representations using multilingual correlation. In *Proc. of EACL*, pages 462–471. Gothenburg, Sweden.

Jeffrey Flanigan, Sam Thomson, Jaime Carbonell, Chris Dyer, and Noah A. Smith. 2014. A discriminative graph-based parser for the Abstract Meaning Representation. In *Proc. of ACL*, pages 1426–1436. Baltimore, MD, USA.

Dan Flickinger, Yi Zhang, and Valia Kordoni. 2012. DeepBank: a dynamically annotated treebank of the Wall Street Journal. In *Proc. of the Eleventh International Workshop on Treebanks and Linguistic Theories*, pages 85–96. Lisbon, Portugal.

Kevin Gimpel and Noah A. Smith. 2010. Softmax-margin training for structured log-linear models. Technical Report CMU-LTI-10-008, Carnegie Mellon University. URL `http://lti.cs.cmu.edu/sites/default/files/research/reports/2010/cmulti10008.pdf`.

Jan Hajič. 1998. Building a syntactically annotated corpus: the Prague Dependency Treebank. In Eva Hajičová, editor, *Issues of Valency and Meaning. Studies in Honour of Jarmila Panevová*, pages 106–132. Prague Karolinum, Charles University Press, Prague.

Richard Johansson and Pierre Nugues. 2008. Dependency-based semantic role labeling of PropBank. In *Proc. of EMNLP*, pages 69–78. Honolulu, HI, USA.

Andy Liaw and Matthew Wiener. 2002. Classification and regression by randomForest. *R News*, 2(3):18–22. URL `http://cran.r-project.org/web/packages/randomForest/`.

Dong C. Liu and Jorge Nocedal. 1989. On the limited memory BFGS method for large scale optimization. *Mathematical Programming*, 45(3):503–528.

André F. T. Martins, Miguel Almeida, and Noah A. Smith. 2013. Turning on the turbo: Fast third-order non-projective turbo parsers. In *Proc. of ACL*, pages 617–622. Sofia, Bulgaria.

Ryan McDonald and Fernando Pereira. 2006. Online learning of approximate dependency parsing algorithms. In *Proc. of EACL*, pages 81–88. Trento, Italy.

Yusuke Miyao, Takashi Ninomiya, and Jun'ichi Tsujii. 2004. Corpus-oriented grammar development for acquiring a head-driven phrase structure grammar from the Penn Treebank. In *Proc. of IJCNLP*, pages 684–693. Hainan Island, China.

Stephan Oepen, Marco Kuhlmann, Yusuke Miyao, Daniel Zeman, Dan Flickinger, Jan Hajič, Angelina Ivanova, and Yi Zhang. 2014. SemEval 2014 Task 8: Broad-coverage semantic dependency parsing. In *Proc. of SemEval*. Dublin, Ireland.

Ben Taskar, Carlos Guestrin, and Daphne Koller. 2003. Max-margin Markov networks. In *Proc. of NIPS*, pages 25–32. Vancouver, British Columbia, Canada.

Ioannis Tsochantaridis, Thomas Hofmann, Thorsten Joachims, and Yasemin Altun. 2004. Support vector machine learning for interdependent and structured output spaces. In *Proc. of ICML*, pages 104–111. Banff, Alberta, Canada.

Kilian Weinberger, Anirban Dasgupta, John Langford, Alex Smola, and Josh Attenberg. 2009. Feature hashing for large scale multitask learning. In *Proc. of ICML*, pages 1113–1120. Montreal, Quebec, Canada.

CMUQ-Hybrid: Sentiment Classification By Feature Engineering and Parameter Tuning

Kamla Al-Mannai[1], **Hanan Alshikhabobakr**[2],
Sabih Bin Wasi[2], **Rukhsar Neyaz**[2], **Houda Bouamor**[2], **Behrang Mohit**[2]
Texas A&M University in Qatar[1], Carnegie Mellon University in Qatar [2]
almannaika@hotmail.com[1]
{halshikh, sabih, rukhsar, hbouamor, behrang}@cmu.edu

Abstract

This paper describes the system we submitted to the SemEval-2014 shared task on sentiment analysis in Twitter. Our system is a hybrid combination of two system developed for a course project at CMU-Qatar. We use an SVM classifier and couple a set of features from one system with feature and parameter optimization framework from the second system. Most of the tuning and feature selection efforts were originally aimed at task-A of the shared task. We achieve an F-score of 84.4% for task-A and 62.71% for task-B and the systems are ranked 3rd and 29th respectively.

1 Introduction

With the proliferation of Web2.0, people increasingly express and share their opinion through social media. For instance, microblogging websites such as Twitter[1] are becoming a very popular communication tool. An analysis of this platform reveals a large amount of community messages expressing their opinions and sentiments on different topics and aspects of life. This makes Twitter a valuable source of subjective and opinionated text that could be used in several NLP research works on sentiment analysis. Many approaches for detecting subjectivity and determining polarity of opinions in Twitter have been proposed (Pang and Lee, 2008; Davidov et al., 2010; Pak and Paroubek, 2010; Tang et al., 2014). For instance, the Twitter sentiment analysis shared task (Nakov et al., 2013) is an interesting testbed to develop and evaluate sentiment analysis systems on social media text. Participants are asked to implement a system capable of determining whether a given tweet expresses **positive**, **negative** or **neutral** sentiment. In this paper, we describe the CMUQ-Hybrid system we developed to participate in the two subtasks of SemEval 2014 Task 9 (Rosenthal et al., 2014). Our system uses an SVM classifier with a rich set of features and a parameter optimization framework.

2 Data Preprocessing

Working with tweets presents several challenges for NLP, different from those encountered when dealing with more traditional texts, such as newswire data. Tweet messages usually contain different kinds of orthographic and typographical errors such as the use of special and decorative characters, letter duplication used generally for emphasis, word duplication, creative spelling and punctuation, URLs, #hashtags as well as the use of slangs and special abbreviations. Hence, before building our classifier, we start with a preprocessing step on the data, in order to normalize it. All letters are converted to lower case and all words are reduced to their root form using the WordNet Lemmatizer in NLTK[2] (Bird et al., 2009). We kept only some punctuation marks: periods, commas, semi-colons, and question and exclamation marks. The excluded characters were identified to be performance boosters using the best-first branch and bound technique described in Section 3.

3 Feature Extraction

Out of a wide variety of features, we selected the most effective features using the *best-first branch and bound method* (Neapolitan, 2014), a search tree technique for solving optimization problems. We used this technique to determine which punctuation marks to keep in the preprocessing step and

[1]http://twitter.com

[2]http://www.nltk.org/api/nltk.stem.html

Proceedings of the 8th International Workshop on Semantic Evaluation (SemEval 2014), pages 181–185,
Dublin, Ireland, August 23-24, 2014.

in selecting features as well. In the feature selection step, the root node is represented by a bag of words feature, referred as textual tokens.

At each level of the tree, we consider a set of different features, and iteratively we carry out the following steps: we process the current feature by generating its successors, which are all the other features. Then, we rank features according to the f-score and we only process the best feature and prune the rest. We pass all the current pruned features as successors to the next level of the tree. The process iterates until all partial solutions in the tree are processed or terminated. The selected features are the following:

Sentiment lexicons : we used the Bing Liu Lexicon (Hu and Liu, 2004), the MPQA Subjectivity Lexicon (Wilson et al., 2005), and NRC Hashtag Sentiment Lexicon (Mohammad et al., 2013). We count the number of words in each class, resulting in three features: (a) positive words count, (b) negative words count and (c) neutral words count.

Negative presence: presence of negative words in a term/tweet using a list of negative words. The list used is built from the Bing Liu Lexicon (Hu and Liu, 2004).

Textual tokens: the target term/tweet is segmented into tokens based on space. Token identity features are created and assigned the value of 1.

Overall polarity score: we determine the polarity scores of words in a target term/tweet using the Sentiment140 Lexicon (Mohammad et al., 2013) and the SentiWordNet lexicon (Baccianella et al., 2010). The overall score is computed by adding up all word scores.

Level of association: indicates whether the overall polarity score of a term is greater than 0.2 or not. The threshold value was optimized on the development set.

Sentiment frequency: indicates the most frequent word sentiment in the tweet. We determine the sentiment of words using an automatically generated lexicon. The lexicon comprises 3,247 words and their sentiments. Words were obtained from the provided training set for task-A and sentiments were generated using our expression-level classifier.

We used slightly different features for Task-A and Task-B. The features extracted for each task are summarized in Table 1.

Feature	Task A	Task B
Positive words count	✓	
Negative words count	✓	
Neutral words count		✓
Negative presence	✓	✓
Textual tokens	✓	✓
Overall polarity score	✓	✓
Level of association	✓	
Sentiment frequency		✓

Table 1: Feature summary for each task.

4 Modeling Kernel Functions

Initially we experimented with both logistic regression and the Support Vector Machine (SVM) (Fan et al., 2008), using the Stochastic Gradient Descent (SGD) algorithm for parameter optimization. In our development experiments, SVM outperformed and became our single classifier. We used the LIBSVM package (Chang and Lin, 2011) to train and test our classifier.

An SVM kernel function and associated parameters were optimized for best F-score on the development set. In order to avoid the model overfitting the data, we select the optimal parameter value only if there are smooth gaps between the near neighbors of the corresponded F-score. Otherwise, the search will continue to the second optimal value.

In machine learning, the difference between the number of training samples, m, and the number of features, n, is crucial in the selection process of SVM kernel functions. The Gaussian kernel is suggested when m is slightly larger than n. Otherwise, the linear kernel is recommended. In Task-B, the $n : m$ ratio was $1 : 3$ indicating a large difference between the two numbers. Whereas in Task-A, a ratio of $5 : 2$ indicated a small difference between the two numbers. We selected the theoretical types, after conducting an experimental verification to identify the best kernel function according to the f-score.

We used a radical basis function kernel for the expression-level task and the value of its gamma parameter was adjusted to 0.319. Whereas, we used a linear function kernel for the message-level task and the value of its cost parameter was adjusted to 0.053.

5 Experiments and Results

In this section, we describe the data and the several experiments we conducted for both tasks. We train and evaluate our classifier with the training, development and testing datasets provided for the SemEval 2014 shared task. A short summary of the data distribution is shown in Table 2.

Dataset	Postive	Negative	Neutral
Task-A:			
Train (9,451)	62%	33%	5%
Dev (1,135)	57%	38%	5%
Test (10,681)	60%	35%	5%
Task-B:			
Train (9,684)	38%	15%	47%
Dev (1,654)	35%	21%	44%
Test (5,754)	45%	15%	40%

Table 2: Datasets distribution percentage per class.

Our test dataset is composed of five different sets: The test dataset is composed of five different sets: *Twitter2013* a set of tweets collected for the SemEval2013 test set, *Twitter2014*, tweets collected for this years version, *LiveJournal2014* consisting of formal tweets, *SMS2013*, a collection of sms messages, *TwitterSarcasm*, a collection of sarcastic tweets.

5.1 Task-A

For this task, we train our classifier on 10,586 terms (9,451 terms in the training set and 1,135 in the development set), tune it on 4,435 terms, and evaluate it using 10,681 terms. The average F-score of the positive and negative classes for each dataset is given in the first part of Table 3. The best F-score value of 88.94 is achieved on the Twitter2013.

We conducted an ablation study illustrated in the second part of Table 3 shows that all the selected features contribute well in our system performance. Other than the *textual tokens* feature, which refers to a bag of preprocessed tokens, the study highlights the role of the *term polarity score* feature: -4.20 in the F-score, when this feature is not considered on the TwitterSarcasm dataset.

Another study conducted is a feature correlation analysis, in which we grouped features with similar intuitions. Namely the two features *negative presence* and *negative words count* are grouped as "negative features", and the features *positive words count* and *negative words count* are grouped as "words count". We show in Table 4 the effect on f-score after removing each group from the features set. Also we show the f-score after removing each individual feature within the group. This helps us see whether features within a group are redundant or not. For the Twitter2014 dataset, we notice that excluding one of the features in any of the two groups leads to a significant drop, in comparison to the total drop by its group. The uncorrelated contributions of features within the same group indicate that features are not redundant to each other and that they are indeed capturing different information. However, in the case of the TwitterSarcasm dataset, we observe that the *negative presence* feature is not only not contributing to the system performance but also adding noise to the feature space, specifically, to the *negative words count* feature.

5.2 Task-B

For this task, we trained our classifier on 11,338 tweets (9,684 terms in the training set and 1,654 in the development set), tuned it on 3,813 tweets, and evaluated it using 8,987 tweets. Results for different feature configurations are reported in Table 5.

It is important to note that if we exclude the *textual tokens feature*, all datasets benefit the most from the *polarity score* feature. It is interesting to note that the bag of words, referred to as *textual tokens*, is not helping in one of the datasets, the TwitterSarcasm set. For all datasets, performance could be improved by removing different features.

In Table 5, we observe that the *Negative presence* feature decreases the F-score on the TwitterSarcasm dataset. This could be explained by the fact that negative words do not usually appear in a negative implication in sarcastic messages. For example, this tweet: *Such a fun Saturday catching up on hw.* which has a negative sentiment, is classified positive because of the absence of negative words. Table 5 shows that the *textual tokens* feature increases the classifier's performance up to +21.07 for some datasets. However, using a large number of features in comparison to the number of training samples could increase data sparseness and lower the classifier's performance.

We conducted a post-competition experiment to examine the relationship between the number of features and the number of training samples. We

	Twitter2014	TwitterSarcasm	LiveJournal2014	Twitter2013	SMS2013
F-score	84.40	76.99	84.21	88.94	87.98
Negative presence	-0.45	0.00	-0.45	-0.23	+0.30
Positive words count	-0.52	-1.37	-0.11	-0.02	+0.38
Negative words count	-0.50	-2.20	**-0.61**	-0.47	-1.66
Polarity score	**-1.83**	**-4.20**	-0.23	**-2.14**	**-3.00**
Level of association	-0.18	0.00	-0.18	-0.07	+0.57
Textual tokens	-8.74	-2.40	-3.02	-4.37	-6.06

Table 3: Task-A feature ablation study. F-scores calculated on each set along with the effect when removing one feature at a time.

	Twitter2014	TwitterSarcasm	LiveJournal2014	Twitter2013	SMS2013
F-score	84.40	76.99	84.21	88.94	87.98
Negative features	-1.53	-0.84	-3.05	-1.88	-0.67
Negative presence	-0.45	0.00	-0.45	-0.23	+0.3
Negative words count	-0.50	-2.20	-0.61	-0.47	-1.66
Words count	-1.07	-2.2	-0.79	-0.62	-2.01
Positive words count	-0.52	-1.37	-0.11	-0.02	+0.38
Negative words count	-0.50	-2.20	-0.61	-0.47	-1.66

Table 4: Task-A features correlation analysis. We grouped features with similar intuitions and we calculated F-scores on each set along with the effect when removing one feature at a time.

fixed the size of our training dataset. Then, we compared the performance of our classifier using only the bag of tokens feature, in two different sizes. In the first experiment, we included all tokens collected from all tweets. In the second, we only considered the top 20 ranked tokens from each tweet. Tokens were ranked according to the difference between their highest level of association into one of the sentiments and the sum of the rest. The level of associations for tokens were determined using the Sentiment140 and SentiWordNet lexicons. The threshold number of tokens was identified empirically for best performance. We found that the classifier's performance has been improved by 2 f-score points when the size of tokens bag is smaller. The experiment indicates that the contribution of the *bag of words feature* can be increased by reducing the size of vocabulary list.

6 Error Analysis

Our efforts are mostly tuned towards task-A, hence our inspection and analysis is focused on task-A. The error rate calculated per sentiment class: positive, negative and neutral are 6.8%, 14.9% and 93.8%, respectively. The highest error rate in the neutral class, 93.8%, is mainly due to the few neutral examples in the training data (only 5% of the data). Hence the system could not learn from such a small set of neutral class examples.

In the case of negative class error rate, 14.9%, most of which were classified as positive. An example of such classification: *I knew it was **too good to be true** OTL*. Since our system highly relies on lexicon, hence looking at lexicon assigned polarity to the phrase *too good to be true* which is positive, happens because the positive words *good* and *true* has dominating positive polarity.

Lastly for the positive error rate, which is relatively lower, 6%, most of which were classified negative instead of positive. An example of such classification: *Looks like we're getting the heaviest snowfall in five years tomorrow. Awesome. I'll **never get tired** of winter*. Although the phrase carries a positive sentiment, the individual negative words of the phrase *never* and *tired* again dominates over the phrase.

7 Conclusion

We described our systems for Twitter Sentiment Analysis shared task. We participated in both tasks, but were mostly focused on task-A. Our hybrid system was assembled by integrating a rich set of lexical features into a framework of feature selection and parameter tuning, The *polarity*

	Twitter2014	TwitterSarcasm	LiveJournal2014	Twitter2013	SMS2013
F-score	62.71	40.95	65.14	63.22	61.75
Negative presence	-1.65	+1.26	-3.37	-3.66	-0.95
Neutral words count	+0.05	0.00	-0.72	-0.57	-0.54
Polarity score	**-4.03**	**-6.92**	**-3.82**	**-3.83**	**-4.84**
Sentiment frequency	+0.10	0.00	+0.18	-0.12	-0.05
textual tokens	-17.91	+6.5	-21.07	-19.97	-15.8

Table 5: Task B feature ablation study. F-scores calculated on each set along with the effect when removing one feature at a time.

score feature was the most important feature for our model in both tasks. The F-score results were consistent across all datasets, except the Twitter-Sarcasm dataset. It indicates that feature selection and parameter tuning steps were effective in generalizing the model to unseen data.

Acknowledgment

We would like to thank Kemal Oflazer and also the shared task organizers for their support throughout this work.

References

Stefano Baccianella, Andrea Esuli, and Fabrizio Sebastiani. 2010. SentiWordNet 3.0: An Enhanced Lexical Resource for Sentiment Analysis and Opinion Mining. In *Proceedings of the Seventh conference on International Language Resources and Evaluation (LREC'10)*, pages 2200–2204, Valletta, Malta.

Steven Bird, Ewan Klein, and Edward Loper. 2009. *Natural Language Processing with Python*. O'Reilly Media, Inc.

Chih-Chung Chang and Chih-Jen Lin. 2011. LIBSVM: A Library for Support Vector Machines. *ACM Transactions on Intelligent Systems and Technology*, 2:27:1–27:27.

Dmitry Davidov, Oren Tsur, and Ari Rappoport. 2010. Enhanced sentiment learning using twitter hashtags and smileys. In *Proceedings of the 23rd International Conference on Computational Linguistics: Posters*, pages 241–249, Uppsala, Sweden.

Rong-En Fan, Kai-Wei Chang, Cho-Jui Hsieh, Xiang-Rui Wang, and Chih-Jen Lin. 2008. Liblinear: A library for large linear classification. *The Journal of Machine Learning Research*, 9:1871–1874.

Minqing Hu and Bing Liu. 2004. Mining and Summarizing Customer Reviews. In *Proceedings of the Tenth ACM SIGKDD International Conference on Knowledge Discovery and Data Mining*, pages 168–177, Seattle, WA, USA.

Saif Mohammad, Svetlana Kiritchenko, and Xiaodan Zhu. 2013. NRC-Canada: Building the State-of-the-Art in Sentiment Analysis of Tweets. In *Second Joint Conference on Lexical and Computational Semantics (*SEM), Volume 2: Proceedings of the Seventh International Workshop on Semantic Evaluation (SemEval 2013)*, pages 321–327, Atlanta, Georgia, USA.

Preslav Nakov, Sara Rosenthal, Zornitsa Kozareva, Veselin Stoyanov, Alan Ritter, and Theresa Wilson. 2013. SemEval-2013 Task 2: Sentiment Analysis in Twitter. In *Second Joint Conference on Lexical and Computational Semantics (*SEM), Volume 2: Proceedings of the Seventh International Workshop on Semantic Evaluation (SemEval 2013)*, pages 312–320, Atlanta, Georgia, USA.

Richard E. Neapolitan, 2014. *Foundations of Algorithms*, pages 257–262. Jones & Bartlett Learning.

Alexander Pak and Patrick Paroubek. 2010. Twitter Based System: Using Twitter for Disambiguating Sentiment Ambiguous Adjectives. In *Proceedings of the 5th International Workshop on Semantic Evaluation*, pages 436–439, Uppsala, Sweden.

Bo Pang and Lillian Lee, 2008. *Opinion Mining and Sentiment Analysis*, volume 2, pages 1–135. Now Publishers Inc.

Sara Rosenthal, Preslav Nakov, Alan Ritter, and Veselin Stoyanov. 2014. SemEval-2014 Task 9: Sentiment Analysis in Twitter. In *Proceedings of the Eighth International Workshop on Semantic Evaluation (SemEval'14)*, Dublin, Ireland.

Duyu Tang, Furu Wei, Nan Yang, Ming Zhou, Ting Liu, and Bing Qin. 2014. Learning Sentiment-Specific Word Embedding for Twitter Sentiment Classification. In *Proceedings of the 52nd Annual Meeting of the Association for Computational Linguistics*, pages 1555–1565, Baltimore, Maryland.

Theresa Wilson, Janyce Wiebe, and Paul Hoffmann. 2005. Recognizing Contextual Polarity in Phrase-level Sentiment Analysis. In *Proceedings of the Human Language Technology Conference and Conference on Empirical Methods in Natural Language Processing*, pages 347–354, Vancouver, B.C., Canada.

CMUQ@Qatar:Using Rich Lexical Features for Sentiment Analysis on Twitter

Sabih Bin Wasi, Rukhsar Neyaz, Houda Bouamor, Behrang Mohit
Carnegie Mellon University in Qatar
{sabih, rukhsar, hbouamor, behrang}@cmu.edu

Abstract

In this paper, we describe our system for the Sentiment Analysis of Twitter shared task in SemEval 2014. Our system uses an SVM classifier along with rich set of lexical features to detect the sentiment of a phrase within a tweet (Task-A) and also the sentiment of the whole tweet (Task-B). We start from the lexical features that were used in the 2013 shared tasks, we enhance the underlying lexicon and also introduce new features. We focus our feature engineering effort mainly on Task-A. Moreover, we adapt our initial framework and introduce new features for Task-B. Our system reaches weighted score of 87.11% in Task-A and 64.52% in Task-B. This places us in the 4th rank in the Task-A and 15th in the Task-B.

1 Introduction

With more than 500 million tweets sent per day, containing opinions and messages, Twitter[1] has become a gold-mine for organizations to monitor their brand reputation. As more and more users post about products and services they use, Twitter becomes a valuable source of people's opinions and sentiments: what people can think about a product or a service, how positive they can be about it or what would people prefer the product to be like. Such data can be efficiently used for marketing. However, with the increasing amount of tweets posted on a daily basis, it is challenging and expensive to manually analyze them and locate the meaningful ones. There has been a body of recent work to automatically learn the public sentiments from tweets using natural language processing techniques (Pang and Lee, 2008; Jansen et al., 2009; Pak and Paroubek, 2010; Tang et al., 2014). However, the task of sentiment analysis of tweets in their free format is harder than that of any well-structured document. Tweet messages usually contain different kinds of orthographic errors such as the use of special and decorative characters, letter or word duplication, extra punctuation, as well as the use of special abbreviations.

In this paper, we present our machine learning based system for sentiment analysis of Twitter shared task in SemEval 2014. Our system takes as input an arbitrary tweet and assigns it to one of the following classes that best reflects its sentiment: positive, negative or neutral. While positive and negative tweets are subjective, neutral class encompasses not only objective tweets but also subjective tweets that does not contain any "polar" emotion. Our classifier was developed as an undergrad course project but later pursued as a research topic. Our training, development and testing experiments were performed on data sets published in SemEval 2013 (Nakov et al., 2013). Motivated with its performance, we participated in SemEval 2014 Task 9 (Rosenthal et al., 2014). Our approach includes an extensive usage of off-the-shelf resources that have been developed for conducting NLP on social media text. Our original aim was enhancement of the task-A. Moreover, we adapted our framework and introduced new features for task-B and participated in both shared tasks. We reached an F-score of 83.3% in Task-A and an F-score of 65.57% in Task-B. That placed us in the 4th rank in the task-A and 15th rank in the task-B.

Our approach includes an extensive usage of off-the-shelf resources that have been developed for conducting NLP on social media text. That includes the Twitter Tokenizer and also the Twitter POS tagger, several sentiment analysis lexica

[1] http://twitter.com

Proceedings of the 8th International Workshop on Semantic Evaluation (SemEval 2014), pages 186–191,
Dublin, Ireland, August 23-24, 2014.

and finally our own enhanced resources for special handling of Twitter-specific text. Our original aim in introducing and evaluating many of the features was enhancement of the task-A. Moreover, we adapted our framework and introduced new features for task-B and participated in both shared tasks. We reached an F-score of 83.3% in Task-A and an F-score of 65.57% in Task-B. That placed us in the 4th rank in the task-A and 15th rank in the task-B.

2 System Overview

We participate in tasks A and B. We use three-way classification framework in which we design and use a rich feature representation of the Twitter text. In order to process the tweets, we start with a pre-processing step, followed by feature extraction and classifier training.

2.1 Data Pre-processing

Before the tweet is fed to the system, it goes through pre-processing phase that breaks tweet string into words (tokenization), attaches more information to each word (POS tagging), and other treatments.

Tokenization: We use CMU ARK Tokenizer (Owoputi et al., 2013) to tokenize each tweet. This tokenizer is developed to tokenize not only space-separated text but also tokens that need to be analyzed separately.

POS tagging: We use CMU ARK POS Tagger (Owoputi et al., 2013) to assign POS tags to the different tokens. In addition to the grammatical tags, this tagger assigns also twitter-specific tags like @ mentions, hash tags, etc. This information is used later for feature extraction.

Other processing: In order to normalize the different tokens and convert them into a correct English, we find acronyms in the text and add their expanded forms at the end of the list. We decide to keep both the acronym and the new word to ensure that if the token without its expansion was the word the user meant, then we are not losing any information by getting its acronym. We extend the NetLingo[2] top 50 Internet acronym list to add some missing acronyms. In order to reduce inflectional forms of a word to a common base form we use WordNetlemmatizer in NLTK (Bird et al., 2009)[3]. This could be useful for the feature extraction, to get as much matches as possible between the train and test data (e.g., for bag-of-words feature).

[2]http://www.netlingo.com/top50/popular-text-terms.php

Tweet	"This is so awesome @henry:D! #excited"
Bag of Words	"This":1, "is":1, "so":1, "awesome":1, "@henry":1, ":D":1, "!,":1, #excited":1
POS features	numHashTags:1, numAdverb:1, numAdjective:1
Polarity features	positiveWords:1, negWords:0, avgScore: -0.113
Task-B specific features	numCapsWords:0, numEmoticons:1, numUrls:0

Table 1: Set of Features demonstrated on a sample tweet for Task-B.

2.2 Feature Extraction

Assigning a sentiment to a single word, phrase or a full tweet message requires a rich set of features. For this, we adopt a forward selection approach (Ladha and Deepa, 2011) to select the features that characterize to the best the different sentiments and help distinguishing them. In this approach, we incrementally add the features one by one and test whether this boosts the development results. We heavily rely on a binary feature representation (Heinly et al., 2012) to ensure the efficiency and robustness of our classifier. The different features used are illustrated in the example given in Table 1.

Bag-of-words feature: indicates whether a given token is present in the phrase.

Morpho-syntactic feature: we use the POS and twitter-specific tags extracted for each token. We count the number of adjectives, adverbs and hashtags present in the focused part of the tweet message (entire tweet or phrase). We tried adding other POS based features (e.g., number of possessive pronouns, etc.), but only the aforementioned tags increased the result figures for both tasks.

Polarity-based features: we use freely available sentiment resources to explicitly define the polarity at a token-level. We define three feature categories, based on the lexicon used:

[3]http://www.nltk.org/api/nltk.stem.html

	Task-A			Task-B		
	Dev	Train	Test	Dev	Train	Test
Positive	57.09 %	62.06%	59.49%	34.76%	37.59%	39.01%
Negative	37.89%	33.01%	35.31%	20.56%	15.06%	17.15%
Neutral	5.02%	4.93%	5.21%	44.68%	47.36%	43.84%
All	1,135	9,451	10,681	1,654	9,684	8,987

Table 2: Class size distribution for all the three sets for both Task-A and Task-B.

- *Subjectivity:* number of words mapped to "positive" from the MPQA Subjectivity lexicon (Wilson et al., 2005).

- *Hybrid Lexicon:* We combine the Sentiment140 lexicon (Mohammad et al., 2013) with the Bing Liu's bag of positive and negative words (Hu and Liu, 2004) to create a dictionary in which each token is assigned a sentiment.

- *Token weight:* we use the SentiWordNet lexicon (Baccianella et al., 2010) to define this feature. SentiWordNet contains positive, negative and objective scores between 0 and 1 for all senses in WordNet. Based on this sense level annotation, we first map each token to its weight in this lexicon and then the sum of all these weights was used as the tweet weight.

Furthermore, in order to take into account the presence of negative words, which modify the polarity of the context within which they are invoked, we reverse the polarity score of adjectives or adverbs that come within 1-2 token distance after a negative word.

Task specific features: In addition to the features described above, we also define some task-specific ones. For example, we indicate the number of capital letters in the phrase as a feature in Task-A. This could help in this task, since we are focusing on short text. For Task-B we indicate instead the number of capital words. This relies on the intuition that polarized tweets would carry more (sometimes all) capital words than the neutral or objective ones. We also added the number of emoticons and number of URL links as features for Task-B. Here, the goal is to segregate fact-containing objective tweets from emotion-containing subjective tweets.

2.3 Classifier

We use a Support Vector Machine (SVM) classifier (Chang and Lin, 2011) to which we provide the rich set of features described in the previous section. We use a linear kernel and tune its parameter C separately for the two tasks. Task-A system was bound tight to the development set with C=0.18 whereas in Task-B the system was given freedom by setting C=0.55. These values were optimized during the development using a brute-force mechanism.

	Task-A	Task-B
LiveJournal 2014	83.89	65.63
SMS 2013	88.08	62.95
Twitter 2013	89.85	65.11
Twitter 2014	83.45	65.53
Sarcasm	78.07	40.52
Weighted average	**87.11**	**64.52**

Table 3: F1 measures and final results of the system for Task-A and Task-B for all the data sets including the weighted average of the sets.

3 Experiments and Results

In this section, we explain details of the data and the general settings for the different experiments we conducted. We train and evaluate our classifier for both tasks with the training, development and testing datasets provided for the SemEval 2014 shared task. The size of the three datasets we use as well as their class distributions are illustrated in Table 2 . It is important to note that the total dataset size for training and development set (10,586) is about the same as test set making the learning considerably challenging for correct predictions. **Positive** instances covered more than half of each dataset for Task-A while **Neutral** were the most popular class for Task-B. The class distribution of training set is the same as the test set.

	Task-A	Task-B
all features	87.11	64.52
all-preprocessing	80.79(-6.32)	59.20(-5.32)
all-ARK tokenization	83.69(-3.42)	60.61(-3.91)
all-other treatments	85.06(-2.05)	62.19(-2.33)
only BOW	81.69(-5.42)	57.85(-6.67)
all-bow	82.05(-5.06)	52.04(-12.48)
all-pos	86.92(-0.19)	64.31(-0.21)
all-polarity based features	81.80(-5.31)	57.95(-6.57)
all-SVM tuning	80.82(-6.29)	21.41(-43.11)
all-SVM c=0.01	84.20(-2.91)	59.87(-4.65)
all-SVM c=selected	87.11(0.00)	64.52(0.00)
all-SVM c=1	86.39(-0.72)	62.51(-2.01)

Table 4: F-scores obtained on the test sets with the specific feature removed.

The test dataset is composed of five different sets: *Twitter2013* a set of tweets collected for the SemEval2013 test set, *Twitter2014*, tweets collected for this years version, *LiveJournal2014* consisting of formal tweets, *SMS2013*, a collection of sms messages,*TwitterSarcasm*, a collection of sarcastic tweets. The results of our system are shown in Table 3. The top five rows shows the results by the SemEval scorer for all the data sets used by them. This scorer took the average of F1-score of only positive and negative classes. The last row shows the weighted average score of all the scores for Task A and B from the different data sets.

Our scores for Task-A and Task-B were 83.45 and 65.53 respectively for Twitter 2014.

Our system performed better on Twitter and SMS test sets from 2013. This was reasonable since we tuned our system on these datasets. On the other hand, the system performed worst on sarcasm test set. This drop is extremely evident in Task-B where the results were dropped by 25%. To analyze the effects of each step of our system, we experimented with our system using different configurations. The results are shown in Table 4 and our analysis is described in the following subsections. The results were scored by SemEval 2014 scorer and we took the weighted average of all data sets to accurately reflect the performance of our system.

We show the polarities values assigned to each token of a tweet by our classifier, in Table 5.

Tokens	POS Tags	Sentiments	Polarity
This	O	Neutral	-0.194
Is	V	Neutral	-0.115
So	R	Neutral	-0.253
Awesome	A	Positive	2.351
@Henry	@	-	-
#excited	#	Positive	1.84

Table 5: Polarity assigned using our classifier to each word of a Tweet message.

3.1 Preprocessing Effects

We compared the effects of basic tokenization (based on white space) against the richer ARK Twitter tokenizer. The scores dropped by 3.42% and 3.91% for Task-A and Task-B, respectively. Other preprocessing enhancements like lemmatization and acronym additions also gave our system performance a boost. Again, the effects were more visible for Task-B than for Task-A. Overall, the system performance was boosted by 6.32% for Task-A and 5.32% for Task-B. Considering the overall score for Task-B, this is a significant change.

3.2 Feature Engineering Effects

To analyze the effect of feature extraction process, we ran our system with different kind of features disabled - one at a time. For Task-A, unigram model and polarity based features were equally important. For Task-B, bag of words feature easily outperformed the effects of any other feature. However, polarity based features were second important class of features for our system. These suggest that if more accurate, exhaustive and social media representative lexicons are made, it would help both tasks significantly. POS based features were not directly influential in our system. However, these tags helped us find better matches in lexicons where words are further identified with their POS tag.

3.3 Classifier Tuning

We also analyzed the significance of SVM tuning to our system. Without setting any parameter to SVMutil library (Chang and Lin, 2011), we noticed a drop of 6.29% to scores of Task-A and a significant drop of 43.11% to scores of Task-B. Since the library use poly kernel by default, the results were drastically worse for Task-B due to large feature set. We also compared the performance with SVM kernel set to C=1. In this restricted setting, the results were slightly lower than the result obtained for our final system.

4 Discussion

During this work, we found that two improvements to our system would have yielded better scores. The first would be lexicons: Since the lexicons like Sentiment140 Lexicon are automatically generated, we found that they contain some noise. As we noticed a drop of that our results were critically dependent on these lexicons, this noise would have resulted in incorrect predictions. Hence, more accurate and larger lexicons are required for better classification, especially for the tweet-level task. Unlike SentiWordNet these lexicons should contain more informal words that are common in social media. Additionally, as we can see our system was not able to confidently predict sarcasm tweets on both expression and message level, special attention is required to analyze the nature of sarcasm on Twitter and build a feature set that can capture the true sentiment of the tweet.

5 Conclusion

We demonstrated our classification system that could predict sentiment of an input tweet. Our system performed more accurately in expression-level prediction than on entire tweet-level prediction. Our system relied heavily on bag-of-words feature and polarity based features which in turn relied on correct part-of-speech tagging and third-party lexicons. With this system, we ranked 4th in SemEval 2014 expression-level prediction task and 15th in tweet-level prediction task.

Acknowledgment

We would like to thank Kemal Oflazer and the shared task organizers for their support throughout this work.

References

Stefano Baccianella, Andrea Esuli, and Fabrizio Sebastiani. 2010. SentiWordNet 3.0: An Enhanced Lexical Resource for Sentiment Analysis and Opinion Mining. In *Proceedings of the Seventh conference on International Language Resources and Evaluation (LREC'10)*, pages 2200–2204, Valletta, Malta.

Steven Bird, Ewan Klein, and Edward Loper. 2009. *Natural Language Processing with Python*. O'Reilly Media, Inc.

Chih-Chung Chang and Chih-Jen Lin. 2011. LIBSVM: A Library for Support Vector Machines. *ACM Transactions on Intelligent Systems and Technology*, 2:27:1–27:27.

Jared Heinly, Enrique Dunn, and Jan-Michael Frahm. 2012. Comparative Evaluation of Binary Features. In *Proceedings of the 12th European Conference on Computer Vision*, pages 759–773, Firenze, Italy.

Minqing Hu and Bing Liu. 2004. Mining and Summarizing Customer Reviews. In *Proceedings of the Tenth ACM SIGKDD International Conference on Knowledge Discovery and Data Mining*, pages 168–177, Seattle, WA, USA.

Bernard J Jansen, Mimi Zhang, Kate Sobel, and Abdur Chowdury. 2009. Twitter Power: Tweets as Electronic Word of Mouth. *Journal of the American society for information science and technology*, 60(11):2169–2188.

L. Ladha and T. Deepa. 2011. Feature Selection Methods and Algorithms. *International Journal on Computer Science and Engineering (IJCSE)*, 3:1787–1797.

Saif Mohammad, Svetlana Kiritchenko, and Xiaodan Zhu. 2013. NRC-Canada: Building the State-of-the-Art in Sentiment Analysis of Tweets. In *Second Joint Conference on Lexical and Computational Semantics (*SEM), Volume 2: Proceedings of the Seventh International Workshop on Semantic Evaluation (SemEval 2013)*, pages 321–327, Atlanta, Georgia, USA.

Preslav Nakov, Sara Rosenthal, Zornitsa Kozareva, Veselin Stoyanov, Alan Ritter, and Theresa Wilson. 2013. SemEval-2013 Task 2: Sentiment Analysis in Twitter. In *Second Joint Conference on Lexical and Computational Semantics (*SEM), Volume 2: Proceedings of the Seventh International Workshop on Semantic Evaluation (SemEval 2013)*, pages 312–320, Atlanta, Georgia, USA.

Olutobi Owoputi, Brendan O'Connor, Chris Dyer, Kevin Gimpel, Nathan Schneider, and Noah A. Smith. 2013. Improved Part-of-Speech Tagging for Online Conversational Text with Word Clusters. In *Proceedings of the 2013 Conference of the North American Chapter of the Association for Computational Linguistics: Human Language Technologies*, pages 380–390, Atlanta, Georgia.

Alexander Pak and Patrick Paroubek. 2010. Twitter as a Corpus for Sentiment Analysis and Opinion Mining. In *Proceedings of the Seventh conference on International Language Resources and Evaluation (LREC'10)*, pages 1320–1326, Valletta, Malta.

Bo Pang and Lillian Lee. 2008. *Opinion Mining and Sentiment Analysis*, volume 2. Now Publishers Inc.

Sara Rosenthal, Preslav Nakov, Alan Ritter, and Veselin Stoyanov. 2014. SemEval-2014 Task 9: Sentiment Analysis in Twitter. In *Proceedings of the Eighth International Workshop on Semantic Evaluation (SemEval'14)*, Dublin, Ireland.

Duyu Tang, Furu Wei, Nan Yang, Ming Zhou, Ting Liu, and Bing Qin. 2014. Learning Sentiment-Specific Word Embedding for Twitter Sentiment Classification. In *Proceedings of the 52nd Annual Meeting of the Association for Computational Linguistics*, pages 1555–1565, Baltimore, Maryland.

Theresa Wilson, Janyce Wiebe, and Paul Hoffmann. 2005. Recognizing Contextual Polarity in Phrase-level Sentiment Analysis. In *Proceedings of the conference on human language technology and empirical methods in natural language processing*, pages 347–354.

CNRC-TMT: Second Language Writing Assistant System Description

Cyril Goutte **Michel Simard** **Marine Carpuat**
National Research Council Canada
Multilingual Text Processing
1200 Montreal Road, Ottawa, Ontario K1A 0R6, Canada
FirstName.LastName@nrc.ca

Abstract

We describe the system entered by the National Research Council Canada in the SemEval-2014 L2 writing assistant task. Our system relies on a standard Phrase-Based Statistical Machine Translation trained on generic, publicly available data. Translations are produced by taking the already translated part of the sentence as fixed context. We show that translation systems can address the L2 writing assistant task, reaching out-of-five word-based accuracy above 80 percent for 3 out of 4 language pairs. We also present a brief analysis of remaining errors.

1 Introduction

The Semeval L2 writing assistant task simulates the situation of an L2 language learner trying to translate a L1 fragment in a L2 context. This is clearly motivated by a L2 language learning scenario.

However, a very similar scenario can be encountered in Computer-Aided Translation. Translation memories retrieve from a large corpus of already translated documents the source segments that best match a new sentence to be translated. If an exact source match is found, the corresponding target translation can be expected to be suitable with little or no post-editing. However, when only approximate matches are found, post-editing will typically be required to adapt the target side of the partially matching source segment to the source sentence under consideration. It is possible to automate this process: standard string matching algorithms and word alignment techniques can be used to locate the parts of the source segment that do not match the sentence to translate, and from there the parts of the target segment that need to be modified (Biçici and Dymetman, 2008; Simard and Isabelle, 2009; Koehn and Senellart, 2010). The task of translating a L1 fragment in L2 context therefore has much broader application than language learning. This motivation also provides a clear link of this task to the Machine Translation setting. There are also connections to the code-switching and mixed language translation problems (Fung et al., 1999).

In our work, we therefore investigate the use of a standard Phrase-Based Statistical Machine Translation (SMT) system to translate L1 fragments in L2 context. In the next section, we describe the SMT system that we used in our submission. We then describe the corpora used to train the SMT engine (Section 3), and our results on the trial and test data, as well as a short error analysis (Section 4).

section

2 System Description

The core Machine Translation engine used for all our submissions is Portage (Larkin et al., 2010), the NRC's phrase-based SMT system. Given a suitably trained SMT system, the Task 5 input is processed as follows. For each sentence with an L1 fragment to translate, the already translated parts are set as left and right context. The L1 fragment in L2 context is sent to the decoder. The output is a full sentence translation that ensures 1) that the context is left untouched, and 2) that the L1 fragment is translated in a way that fits with the L2 context.

We now describe the key components of the MT system (language, translation and reordering models), as well as the decoding and parameter tuning.

Translation Models We use a single static phrase table including phrase pairs extracted from the symmetrized HMM word-alignment learned

Proceedings of the 8th International Workshop on Semantic Evaluation (SemEval 2014), pages 192–197,
Dublin, Ireland, August 23-24, 2014.

on the entire training data. The phrase table contains four features per phrase pair: lexical estimates of the forward and backward probabilities obtained either by relative frequencies or using the method of Zens and Ney (2004). These estimates are derived by summing counts over all possible alignments. This yields four corresponding parameters in the log-linear model.

Reordering Models We use standard reordering models: a distance-based distortion feature, as well as a lexicalized distortion model (Tillmann, 2004; Koehn et al., 2005). For each phrase pair, the orientation counts required for the lexicalized distortion model are computed using HMM word-alignment on the full training corpora. We estimate lexicalized probabilities for monotone, swap, and discontinuous ordering with respect to the previous and following target phrase. This results in a total of 6 feature values per phrase pair, in addition to the distance-based distortion feature, hence seven parameters to tune in the log-linear model.

Language Models When translating L1 fragments in L2 context, the L2 language model (LM) is particularly important as it is the only component of the SMT system that scores how well the translation of the L1 fragment fits in the existing L2 context. We test two different LM configurations. The first of these (*run1*) uses a single static LM: a standard 4-gram, estimated using Kneser-Ney smoothing (Kneser and Ney, 1995) on the target side of the bilingual corpora used for training the translation models. In the second configuration (*run2*), in order to further adapt the translations to the test domain, a smaller LM trained on the L2 contexts of the test data is combined to the training corpus LM in a linear mixture model (Foster and Kuhn, 2007). The linear mixture weights are estimated on the L2 context of each test set in a cross-validation fashion.

Decoding Algorithm and Parameter Tuning Decoding uses the cube-pruning algorithm (Huang and Chiang, 2007) with a 7-word distortion limit. Log-linear parameter tuning is performed using a lattice-based batch version of MIRA (Cherry and Foster, 2012).

3 Data

SMT systems require large amounts of data to estimate model parameters. In addition, translation performance largely depends on having in-domain data to train on. As we had no information on the domain of the test data for Task 5, we chose to rely on general purpose publicly available data. Our main corpus is Europarl (Koehn, 2005), which is available for all 4 language pairs of the evaluation. As Europarl covers parliamentary proceedings, we added some news and commentary (henceforth "News") data provided for the 2013 workshop on Machine Translation shared task (Bojar et al., 2013) for language pairs other than nl-en. In all cases, we extracted from the corpus a tuning ("dev") set of around 2000 sentence pairs. Statistics for the training data are given in Table 1.

		Europarl	News	Total
en-de	train	1904k	177k	2081k
	dev	-	2000	2000
en-es	train	1959k	174k	2133k
	dev	-	2000	2000
fr-en	train	2002k	157k	2158k
	dev	-	2000	2000
nl-en	train	1974k	-	1974k
	dev	1984	-	1984

Table 1: Number of training segments for each language pair.

The trial and test data each consist of 500 sentences with L1 fragments in L2 context provided by the organizers. As the trial data came from Europarl, we filtered our training corpora in order to remove close matches and avoid training on the trial data (Table 1 takes this into account).

All translation systems were trained on lowercased data, and predictions were recased using a standard (LM-based) truecasing approach.

4 Experimental Results

4.1 Results on Trial and Simulated Data

Our first evaluation was performed on the trial data provided by the Task 5 organizers. Each example was translated in context by two systems:

run1: Baseline, non-adapted system (marked **1** below);

run2: Linear LM mixture adaptation, using a context LM (marked **2** below).

Table 2 shows that our *run1* system already yields high performance on the trial data, while

	W@1	F@1	W@5	F@5	+BLEU
en-de1	78.1	77.0	95.6	94.8	12.4
en-de2	79.8	79.0	95.8	95.0	12.6
en-es1	81.8	80.2	97.7	97.2	12.1
en-es2	84.3	83.2	97.7	97.2	12.5
fr-en1	84.4	83.6	97.1	96.4	11.8
fr-en2	85.9	85.0	97.4	96.6	12.0
nl-en1	83.3	82.0	97.0	96.4	11.8
nl-en2	86.7	86.2	97.5	97.0	12.1

Table 2: Trial data performance, from official evaluation script: (W)ord and (F)ragment accuracy at (1) and (5)-best and BLEU score gain.

	W@1	F@1	W@5	F@5	+BLEU
en-de1	48.0	46.4	70.8	68.7	4.26
en-de2	52.3	50.6	71.0	68.9	4.63
en-es1	47.6	45.2	68.0	65.8	4.12
en-es2	50.0	47.9	67.8	65.5	4.34
fr-en1	50.1	49.2	73.6	71.8	5.18
fr-en2	51.1	49.5	73.1	71.2	5.19

Table 3: News data performance (cf Tab. 2).

adapting the language model on the L2 contexts in *run2* provides a clear gain in the top-1 results. That improvement all but disappears when taking into account the best out of five translations (except maybe for nl-en). The BLEU scores[1] are very high (97-98) and the word error rates (not reported) are around 1%, suggesting that the system output almost matches the references. This is no doubt due to the proximity between the trial data and the MT training corpus. Both are fully or mainly drawn from Europarl material.

In order to get a less optimistic estimate of performance, we automatically constructed a number of test examples from the WMT News Commentary development test sets. The L1 source segments and their L2 reference translations were word aligned in both directions using the GIZA++ implementation of IBM4 (Och and Ney, 2003) and the grow-diag-final-and combination heuristic (Koehn et al., 2005). Test instances were created by substituting some L2 fragments with their word-aligned L1 source within L2 reference segments. Since the goal was to select examples that were more ambiguous and harder to translate than the trial data, a subset of interesting L1 phrases was randomly selected among phrases that occured at least 4 times in the training corpus and have a high entropy in the baseline phrase-table. We selected roughly 1000 L1 phrases per language pair. For each occurrence p_1 of these L1 phrases in the news development sets, we identify the shortest L2 phrase p_2 that is consistently aligned with p_1.[2] A new mixed language test example is constructed by replacing p_2 with p_1 in L2 context.

Results on that simulated data are given in Table 3. Performance is markedly lower than on the trial data. This is due in part to the fact that the News data is not as close to the training material as the official trial set, and in part to the fact that this automatically extracted data contains imperfect alignments with an unknown (but sizeable) amount of "noise". However, it still appears *run2* consistently provides several points of increase in performance for the top-1 results, over the baseline *run1*. Performance on the 5-best is either unaffected or lower, and the gain in BLEU is much lower than in Table 2 although the resulting BLEU is around 96%.

4.2 Test Results

Official test results provided by the organizers are presented in Table 4. While these results are clearly above what we obtained on the synthetic news data, they fall well below the performance observed on the trial data. This is not unexpected as the trial data is unrealistically close to the training material, while the automatically extracted news data is noisy. What we did not expect, however, is the mediocre performance of LM adaptation (*run2*): while consistently better than *run1* on both trial and news, it is consistently worse on the official test data. This may be due to the fact that test sentences were drawn from different sources[3] such that it does not constitute a homogeneous domain on which we can easily adapt a language model.

For German and Spanish, and to a lesser extent

[1] +BLEU in Tables 2-4 is the difference between our system's output and the sentence with untranslated L1 fragment.

[2] As usual in phrase-based MT, two phrases are said to be consistently aligned, if there is at least one link between their words and no external links.

[3] According to the task description, the test set is based on "language learning exercises with gaps and cloze-tests, as well as learner corpora with annotated errors".

	W@1	F@1	W@5	F@5	+BLEU
en-de1	71.7	65.7	86.8	83.4	16.6
en-de2	70.2	64.5	86.5	82.8	16.4
en-es1	74.5	66.7	88.7	84.3	17.0
en-es2	73.5	65.1	88.4	83.7	17.5
fr-en1	69.4	55.6	83.9	73.9	10.2
fr-en2	68.6	53.3	83.4	73.1	9.9
nl-en1	61.0	45.0	72.3	60.6	5.03
nl-en2	60.9	44.4	72.1	60.2	5.02

Table 4: Test data performance, from official evaluation results (cf. Table 2).

	OOV's	failed align
en-de	0.002	0.058
en-es	0.010	0.068
fr-en	0.026	0.139
nl-en	0.123	0.261

Table 5: Test data error analysis: *OOV's* is the proportion of all test fragments containing out-of-vocabulary tokens; *failed align* is the proportion of fragments which our system cannot align to any of the reference translations by forced decoding.

for French and Dutch, the BLEU and Word Error Rate (WER) gains are much higher on the test than on the trial data, although the resulting BLEU are around 86-92%. This results from the fact that the amount of L1 material to translate relative to the L2 context was significantly higher on the test data than it was on the trial data (e.g. 17% of words on en-es test versus 7% on trial).

4.3 Error Analysis

On the French and, especially, on the Dutch data, our systems suffer from a high rate of out-of-vocabulary (OOV) source words in the L1 fragments, i.e. words that simply did not appear in our training data (see Table 5). In the case of Dutch, OOV's impose a hard ceiling of 88% on fragment-level accuracy. These problems could possibly be alleviated by using more training data, and incorporating language-specific mechanisms to handle morphology and compounding into the systems.

We also evaluate the proportion of reference target fragments that can not be reached by *forced decoding* (Table 5). Note that to produce trial and test translations, we use standard decoding to predict a translation that maximizes model score given the input. Once we have the reference translation, we use *forced decoding* to try to produce the exact reference given the source fragment and our translation model. In some situations, the correct translations are simply not reachable by our systems, either because some target word has not been observed in training, some part of the correspondence between source and target fragments has not been observed, or the system's word alignment mechanism is unable to account for this correspondence, in whole or in part. Table 5 shows that this happens between 6% ans 26% of cases, which gives a better upper bound on the fragment-level accuracy that our system may achieve. Again, many of these problems could be solved by using more training data.

Freq	Type
77	Incorrect L2 sense chosen
75	Incorrect or mangled syntax
26	Incomplete reference
20	Non-idiomatic translation
13	Out-of-vocab. word in fragment
6	Problematic source fragment
3	Casing error
220	Total

Table 6: Analysis of the types of error on 220 French-English test sentences.

To better understand the behavior of our systems, we manually reviewed 220 sentences where our baseline French-English system did not exactly match any of the references. We annotated several types of errors (Table 6). The most frequent source of errors is incorrect sense (35%), i.e. the system produced a translation of the fragment that may be correct in some setting, but is not the correct sense in that context. Those are presumably the errors of interest in a sense disambiguation setting. A close second (34%) were errors involving incorrect syntax in the fragment translation, which points to limitations of the Statistical MT approach, or to a limited language model.

The last third combines several sources of errors. Most notable in this category are *non-idiomatic translations*, where the system's output was both syntactically correct and understandable, but clearly not fluent (e.g. "take a siesta" for "have a nap"); We also identified a number of cases where we felt that either the source segment was incorrect (eg “je vais évanouir” instead of “je vais m’évanouir”), or the references were incomplete. Table 7 gives a few examples.

5 Conclusion

We described the systems used for the submissions of the National Research Council Canada to the L2 writing assistant task. We framed the problem as a machine translation task, and used standard statistical machine translation systems trained on publicly available corpora for translating L1 fragments in their L2 context. This approach leverages the strengths of phrase-based statistical machine translation, and therefore performs particularly well when the test examples are close to the training domain. Conversely, it suffers from the inherent weaknesses of phrase-based models, including their inability to generalize beyond seen vocabulary, as well as sense and syntax errors. Overall, we showed that machine translation systems can be used to address the L2 writing assistant task with a high level of accuracy, reaching out-of-five word-based accuracy above 80 percent for 3 out of 4 language pairs.

References

Ergun Biçici and Marc Dymetman. 2008. Dynamic Translation Memory: Using Statistical Machine Translation to Improve Translation Memory Fuzzy Matches. In *Computational Linguistics and Intelligent Text Processing*, pages 454–465. Springer.

Ondřej Bojar, Christian Buck, Chris Callison-Burch, Christian Federmann, Barry Haddow, Philipp Koehn, Christof Monz, Matt Post, Radu Soricut, and Lucia Specia. 2013. Findings of the 2013 Workshop on Statistical Machine Translation. In *Proceedings of the Eighth Workshop on Statistical Machine Translation*, pages 1–44, Sofia, Bulgaria, August.

Colin Cherry and George Foster. 2012. Batch Tuning Strategies for Statistical Machine Translation. In *Proceedings of the 2012 Conference of the North American Chapter of the Association for Computational Linguistics: Human Language Technologies*, pages 427–436, Montréal, Canada, June.

George Foster and Roland Kuhn. 2007. Mixture-model adaptation for SMT. In *Proceedings of the Second Workshop on Statistical Machine Translation*, pages 128–135, Prague, Czech Republic, June.

Pascale Fung, Xiaohu Liu, and Chi Shun Cheung. 1999. Mixed Language Query Disambiguation. In *Proceedings of ACL’99*, pages 333–340, Maryland, June.

Liang Huang and David Chiang. 2007. Forest Rescoring: Faster Decoding with Integrated Language Models. In *Proceedings of the 45th Annual Meeting of the Association of Computational Linguistics*, pages 144–151, Prague, Czech Republic, June.

Reinhard Kneser and Hermann Ney. 1995. Improved Backing-off for M-gram Language Modeling. In *Acoustics, Speech, and Signal Processing, 1995. ICASSP-95., 1995 International Conference on*, volume 1, pages 181–184. IEEE.

Philipp Koehn and Jean Senellart. 2010. Convergence of Translation Memory and Statistical Machine Translation. In *Proceedings of AMTA Workshop on MT Research and the Translation Industry*, pages 21–31.

Philipp Koehn, Amittai Axelrod, Alexandra Birch Mayne, Chris Callison-Burch, Miles Osborne, and David Talbot. 2005. Edinburgh System Description for the 2005 IWSLT Speech Translation Evaluation. In *Proceedings of IWSLT-2005*, pages 68–75, Pittsburgh, PA.

Philipp Koehn. 2005. Europarl: A Parallel Corpus for Statistical Machine Translation. In *Machine Translation Summit X*, pages 79–86, Phuket, Thailand, September.

Samuel Larkin, Boxing Chen, George Foster, Ullrich Germann, Éric Joanis, J. Howard Johnson, and Roland Kuhn. 2010. Lessons from NRC’s Portage System at WMT 2010. In *5th Workshop on Statistical Machine Translation*, pages 127–132.

Franz Josef Och and Hermann Ney. 2003. A Systematic Comparison of Various Statistical Alignment Models. *Computational Linguistics*, 29(1):19–52.

Michel Simard and Pierre Isabelle. 2009. Phrase-based Machine Translation in a Computer-assisted Translation Environment. *Proceedings of the Twelfth Machine Translation Summit (MT Summit XII)*, pages 120–127.

Christoph Tillmann. 2004. A Unigram Orientation Model for Statistical Machine Translation. In Daniel Marcu Susan Dumais and Salim Roukos, editors, *HLT-NAACL 2004: Short Papers*, pages 101–104, Boston, Massachusetts, USA, May 2 - May 7.

Richard Zens and Hermann Ney. 2004. Improvements in Phrase-Based Statistical Machine Translation. In Daniel Marcu Susan Dumais and Salim Roukos, editors, *HLT-NAACL 2004: Main Proceedings*, pages 257–264, Boston, Massachusetts, USA, May 2 - May 7.

Incorrect L2 sense:		
In:	My dog usually barks **au facteur** - but look at that , for once , he is being friendly . . .	
Out:	My dog usually barks **to the factor** - but look at that , for once , he is being friendly . . .	
Ref:	My dog usually barks **at the postman** - but look at that , for once , he is being friendly . . .	
In:	Grapes **ne poussent pas** in northern climates , unless one keeps them in a hot-house .	
Out:	Grapes **do not push** in northern climates , unless one keeps them in a hot-house .	
Ref:	Grapes **do not grow** in northern climates , unless one keeps them in a hot-house .	
Missing reference?		
In:	Twenty-two other people **ont été blessées** in the explosion .	
Out:	Twenty-two other people **were injured** in the explosion .	
Ref:	Twenty-two other people **have been wounded** in the explosion .	
Non-idiomatic translation:		
In:	After patiently stalking its prey , the lion makes a **rapide comme l' éclair** charge for the kill .	
Out:	After patiently stalking its prey , the lion makes a **rapid as flash** charge for the kill .	
Ref:	After patiently stalking its prey , the lion makes a **lightning-fast** charge for the kill .	
Problem with input:		
In:	every time I do n't eat for a while and my blood sugar gets low I feel like **je vais évanouir** .	
Out:	every time I do n't eat for a while and my blood sugar gets low I feel like **I will evaporate** .	
Ref:	every time I do n't eat for a while and my blood sugar gets low I feel like **I 'm going to faint** .	

Table 7: Examples errors on French-English.

Columbia_NLP: Sentiment Detection of Sentences and Subjective Phrases in Social Media

Sara Rosenthal
Dept. of Computer Science
Columbia University
New York, NY 10027, USA
sara@cs.columbia.edu

Apoorv Agarwal
Dept. of Computer Science
Columbia University
New York, NY 10027, USA
apoorv@cs.columbia.edu

Kathleen McKeown
Dept. of Computer Science
Columbia University
New York, NY 10027, USA
kathy@cs.columbia.edu

Abstract

We present two supervised sentiment detection systems which were used to compete in SemEval-2014 Task 9: Sentiment Analysis in Twitter. The first system (Rosenthal and McKeown, 2013) classifies the polarity of subjective phrases as positive, negative, or neutral. It is tailored towards online genres, specifically Twitter, through the inclusion of dictionaries developed to capture vocabulary used in online conversations (e.g., slang and emoticons) as well as stylistic features common to social media. The second system (Agarwal et al., 2011) classifies entire tweets as positive, negative, or neutral. It too includes dictionaries and stylistic features developed for social media, several of which are distinctive from those in the first system. We use both systems to participate in Subtasks A and B of SemEval-2014 Task 9: Sentiment Analysis in Twitter. We participated for the first time in Subtask B: Message-Level Sentiment Detection by combining the two systems to achieve improved results compared to either system alone.

1 Introduction

In this paper we describe two prior sentiment detection algorithms for social media. Both systems (Rosenthal and McKeown, 2013; Agarwal et al., 2011) classify the polarity of sentence phrases and tweets as positive, negative, or neutral. These algorithms were used to participate in the the expression level task (Subtask A) and message level task (Subtask B) of the SemEval-2014 Task 9: Sentiment Analysis in Twitter (Rosenthal et al., 2014) which one of the authors helped organize.

We first show improved results compared to our participation in the prior year in the expression-level task (Subtask A) by incorporating a new dictionary and new features into the system. Our focus this year was on Subtask B which we participated in for the first time. We integrated two systems to achieve improved results compared to either system alone. Our analysis shows that the first system performs better on recall while the second system performs better on precision. We used confidence metrics outputted by the systems to determine which answer should be used. This resulted in a slight improvement in the Twitter dataset compared to either system alone. In this rest of this paper, we discuss related work, the methods for each system, and experiments and results for each subtask using the data provided by Semeval-2014 Task 9: Sentiment Analysis in Twitter (Rosenthal et al., 2014).

2 Related Work

Several recent papers have explored sentiment analysis in Twitter. Go et al (2009) and Pak and Paroubek (2010) classify the sentiment of tweets containing emoticons using n-grams and POS. Barbosa and Feng (2010) detect sentiment using a polarity dictionary that includes web vocabulary and tweet-specific social media features. Bermingham and Smeaton (2010) compare polarity detection in twitter to blogs and movie reviews using lexical features.

Finally, there is a large amount of related work

Proceedings of the 8th International Workshop on Semantic Evaluation (SemEval 2014), pages 198–202,
Dublin, Ireland, August 23-24, 2014.

through the participants of Semeval 2013 Task 2, and Semeval 2014 Task9: Sentiment Analysis in Twitter (Nakov et al., 2013; Rosenthal et al., 2014). A full list of teams and results can be found in the task description papers.

3 Phrased-Based Sentiment Detection

We developed a phrase based sentiment detection system geared towards Social Media by augmenting the state of the art system developed by Agarwal et al. (2009) to include additional dictionaries such as Wiktionary and new features such as word lengthening (e.g. helllllloooo) and emoticons (e.g. :)) (Rosenthal and McKeown, 2013). We initially evaluated our system through our participation in the first Sentiment Analysis in Twitter task (Nakov et al., 2013). We have improved our system this year by adding a new dictionary and additional features.

3.1 Lexicons

We assign a prior polarity score to each word by using the scores provided by the Dictionary of Affect in Language (DAL) (Whissel, 1989) augmented with WordNet (Fellbaum, 1998) to improve coverage. We additionally augment it with Wiktionary, emoticon, and acronym dictionaries to improve coverage in social media (Rosenthal and McKeown, 2013). The DAL covers 50.1% of the vocabulary, 16.5% are proper nouns which we exclude due to their lack of polarity. WordNet covers 8.7% of the vocabulary and Wiktionary covers 12.5% of the vocabulary. Finally, 3.6% of the vocabulary are emoticons, acronyms, word lengthening, and forms of punctuation. 8.6% of the vocabulary is not covered which means we find a prior polarity for 96.4% of the vocabulary. In addition to these dictionaries we also use SentiWordNet (Baccianella et al., 2010) as a new distinct feature that is used in addition to the prior polarity computed from the DAL scores.

3.2 Method

We include POS tags and the top n-gram features as described in prior work (Agarwal et al., 2009; Rosenthal and McKeown, 2013). The DAL and other dictionaries are used along with a negation state machine (Agarwal et al., 2009) to determine the polarity for each word in the sentence. We include all the features described in the original system (Agarwal et al., 2009) such as the DAL scores, polar chunk n-grams, and count of syntactic chunks with their prior polarity based on the chunks position. Finally, we include several lexical-stylistic features that can occur in all datasets. We divide these features into two groups, **general**: ones that are common across online and traditional genres (e.g. exclamation points), and **social media**: one that are far more common in online genres (e.g. emoticons). The features are described in further detail in the precursor to this work (Rosenthal and McKeown, 2013). Feature selection was performed using chi-square in Weka (Hall et al., 2009).

In addition we introduce some new features that were not used in the prior year. SentiWordNet (Baccianella et al., 2010) is a sentiment dictionary built upon WordNet that contains scores for each word where scores > 0 indicate the word is positive and scores < 0 indicate the word is negative. We sum the scores for each word in the phrase and use this as a single polarity feature. We found that this feature alone gave us a 2% improvement over our best results from last year. We also include some other minor features: tweet and phrase length and the position of the phrase within the tweet.

Data Set	Majority	2013	2014
Twitter Dev	38.14	77.6	81.5
Twitter Test	42.22	N/A	76.54
Twitter Sarcasm	39.81	N/A	61.76
SMS	31.45	73.3	74.55
LiveJournal	33.42	N/A	78.19

Table 1: A comparison between the 2013 and 2014 results for Subtask A using the SemEval Twitter training corpus. All results exceed the majority baseline of the positive class significantly.

3.3 Experiments and Results

We ran all of our experiments in Weka (Hall et al., 2009) using Logistic Regression. We also experimented with other learning methods (e.g. SVM and Naive Bayes) but found that Logistic Regression worked the same or better than other methods. All results are shown using the average F-measure of the positive and negative class. The results are compared against the majority baseline of the positive class. We do not use neutral/objective as the majority class because it is not included in the average F-score in the Semeval task.

The full results in the participation of SemEval 2014: Sentiment Analysis in Twitter, Subtask A, are shown in Table 1. Our system outperforms the majority baseline significantly in all classes. Our submitted system was trained using 3-way classification (positive/negative/polarity). It included all the dictionaries from prior years and the top 100 n-grams with feature selection. In addition, it included SentiWordNet and the other new features added in 2014 which provided a 4% increase compared to our best results during the prior year (77.6% to 81.5%) and a rank of 10/20 amongst the constrained systems which used no external data. Our results on the new test set is 76.54% for a rank of 14/20. We do not do well in detecting the polarity of phrases in sarcastic tweets. This is consistent with the other teams as sarcastic tweets tend to have their polarity flipped. The improvements to our system provided a 1% boost in the SMS data with a rank of 15/20. Finally, in the LiveJournal dataset we had an F-Score of 78.19% for a rank of 12/20.

4 Message-Level Sentiment Detection

Our message-level system combines two prior systems to achieve improved results. The first system inputs an entire tweet as a "phrase" to the phrase-level sentiment detection system described in Section 3. The second system is described below.

4.1 Lexicons

The second system (Agarwal et al., 2011) makes use of two dictionaries distinctive from the other system: 1) an emoticon dictionary and 2) an acronym dictionary. The emoticon dictionary was prepared by hand-labeling 170 emoticons listed on Wikipedia.[1] For example, :) is labeled as positive whereas :=(is labeled as negative. Each emoticon is assigned a label from the following set of labels: Extremely-positive, Extremely-negative, Positive, Negative, and Neutral. We compile an acronym dictionary from an on-line resource.[2] The dictionary has translations for 5,184 acronyms. For example, lol is translated to laughing out loud.

4.2 Prior Polarity Scoring

A number of our features are based on prior polarity of words. As in the phrase-based system we too build off of prior work (Agarwal et al., 2009) by using the DAL and augmenting it with WordNet. However, we do not follow the earlier method but use it as motivation. We consider words with with a polarity score (using the pleasantness metric from the DAL) of less than 0.5 as negative, higher than 0.8 as positive and the rest as neutral. If a word is not directly found in the dictionary, we retrieve all synonyms from Wordnet. We then look for each of the synonyms in the DAL. If any synonym is found in the DAL, we assign the original word the same pleasantness score as its synonym. If none of the synonyms is present in the DAL, the word is not associated with any prior polarity. For the given data we directly found the prior polarity of 50.1% of the words. We find the polarity of another 8.7% of the words by using WordNet. So we find prior polarity of about 58.7% of English language words.

4.3 Features

We propose a set of 50 features. We calculate these features for the whole tweet and for the last one-third of the tweet. In total, we get 100 additional features. Our features may be divided into three broad categories: ones that are primarily counts of various features and therefore the value of the feature is a natural number $\in \mathbf{N}$. Second, we include features whose value is a real number $\in \mathbf{R}$. These are primarily features that capture the score retrieved from DAL. The third category is features whose values are boolean $\in \mathbf{B}$. These are bag of words, presence of exclamation marks and capitalized text. Each of these broad categories is divided into two subcategories: Polar features and Non-polar features. We refer to a feature as polar if we calculate its prior polarity either by looking it up in DAL (extended through WordNet) or in the emoticon dictionary. All other features which are not associated with any prior polarity fall in the Non-polar category. Each of the Polar and Non-polar features is further subdivided into two categories: POS and Other. POS refers to features that capture statistics about parts-of-speech of words and Other refers to all other types of features.

A more detailed explanation of the system can be found in Agarwal et al (2011).

4.4 Combined System

Our analysis showed that the first system performs better on recall while the second system performs better on precision. We also found that there were 785 tweets in the development set where one system got it correct and the other one got it incorrect. This leaves room for a significant improvement

[1] http://en.wikipedia.org/wiki/List of emoticons

[2] http://www.noslang.com/

Experiment	Twitter			SMS	LiveJournal
	Dev	Test	Sarcasm		
Majority	29.19	34.64	27.73	19.03	27.21
Phrase-Based System	62.09	64.74	40.75	56.86	62.22
Tweet-Level System	62.4	63.73	42.41	60.54	69.44
Combined System	64.6	65.42	40.02	59.84	68.79

Table 2: A comparison between the different systems using the Twitter training corpus provided by the SemEval task for Subtask B. All results exceed the majority baseline of the positive class significantly.

compared to using each system independently. We combined the two systems for the evaluation by using the confidence provided by the phrase-based system. If the phrase-based system was $< 70\%$ confident we use the message-level system.

4.5 Experiments and Results

This task was evaluated on the Twitter dataset provided by Semeval-2013 Task 2, Subtask B. All results are shown using the average F-measure of the positive and negative class. The full results in the participation of SemEval 2014: Sentiment Analysis in Twitter, Subtask B, are shown in Table 2. All the results outperform the majority baseline of the more prominent positive polarity class significantly. The combined system outperforms the individual systems for the Twitter development and test set. It does not outperform the sarcasm test set, but this may be due to the small size; it contains only 100 tweets. The Tweet-Level system outperforms the phrase-based and combined system for the LiveJournal and SMS test sets. A closer look at the results indicated that the phrase-based system has particular difficulty with the short sentences which are more common in SMS and LiveJournal. For example, the average number of characters in a tweet is 120 whereas it is 95.6 in SMS messages (Nakov et al., 2013). Short sentences are harder because there are fewer polarity words which causes the phrase-based system to incorrectly pick neutral. In addition, short sentences are harder because the BOW feature space, which is huge and already sparse, becomes sparser and individual features start to over-fit. Part of this problem is handled by using Senti-features so the space will be less sparse.

Our ranking in the Twitter 2013 and SMS 2013 development data is 18/50 and 20/50 respectively. Our rank in the Twitter 2014 test set is 15/50 and our rank in the LiveJournal test set is 19/50. Based on our rankings it is clear that our systems are geared more towards Twitter than other social media. Finally our ranking in the Sarcasm test set is 41/50. Although this ranking is quite low, it is in fact encouraging. It indicates that the sarcasm has switched the polarity of the tweet. In the future we would like to include a system (e.g. (González-Ibáñez et al., 2011)) that can detect whether the tweet is sarcastic.

5 Discussion and Future Work

We participated in Semeval-2014 Task 9: Sentiment Analysis in Twitter Subtasks A and B. In Subtask A, we show that adding additional features related to location and using SentiWordNet gives us improvement compared to our prior system. In Subtask B, we show that combining two systems achieves slight improvements over using either system alone. Combining the two system achieves greater coverage as the systems use different emoticon and acronym dictionaries and the phrase-based system uses Wiktionary. The message-level system is geared toward entire tweets whereas the phrase-based is geared toward phrases (even though, in this case we consider the entire tweet to be a "phrase"). This is reflective in several features, such as the position of the target phrase and the syntactic chunk scores in the phrase based system and the features related to the last third of the tweet in the message-level system. In the future, we'd like to perform an error analysis to determine the source of our errors and specific examples of the kind of differences found in the two systems. Finally, we have found that at times the scores of the DAL do not line up with polarity in social media. Therefore, we would like to explore including more sentiment dictionaries instead of, or in addition to, the DAL.

6 Acknowledgements

This research was funded by the DARPA DEFT Program. All statements of fact, opinion or conclusions contained herein are those of the authors and should not be construed as representing the official views, policies, or positions of the Department of Defense, or the U.S. Government.

References

Apoorv Agarwal, Fadi Biadsy, and Kathleen R. Mckeown. 2009. Contextual phrase-level polarity analysis using lexical affect scoring and syntactic n-grams. In *Proceedings of the 12th Conference of the European Chapter of the Association for Computational Linguistics*, EACL '09, pages 24–32, Stroudsburg, PA, USA. Association for Computational Linguistics.

Apoorv Agarwal, Boyi Xie, Ilia Vovsha, Owen Rambow, and Rebecca Passonneau. 2011. Sentiment analysis of twitter data. In *Proceedings of the Workshop on Language in Social Media (LSM 2011)*, pages 30–38, Portland, Oregon, June. Association for Computational Linguistics.

Stefano Baccianella, Andrea Esuli, and Fabrizio Sebastiani. 2010. Sentiwordnet 3.0: An enhanced lexical resource for sentiment analysis and opinion mining. In Nicoletta Calzolari (Conference Chair), Khalid Choukri, Bente Maegaard, Joseph Mariani, Jan Odijk, Stelios Piperidis, Mike Rosner, and Daniel Tapias, editors, *Proceedings of the Seventh International Conference on Language Resources and Evaluation (LREC'10)*, Valletta, Malta, may. European Language Resources Association (ELRA).

Luciano Barbosa and Junlan Feng. 2010. Robust sentiment detection on twitter from biased and noisy data. In *COLING (Posters)*, pages 36–44.

Adam Bermingham and Alan F. Smeaton. 2010. Classifying sentiment in microblogs: is brevity an advantage? In Jimmy Huang, Nick Koudas, Gareth J. F. Jones, Xindong Wu, Kevyn Collins-Thompson, and Aijun An, editors, *CIKM*, pages 1833–1836. ACM.

Christiane Fellbaum, editor. 1998. *WordNet An Electronic Lexical Database*. The MIT Press, Cambridge, MA ; London, May.

Alec Go, Richa Bhayani, and Lei Huang. 2009. Twitter sentiment classification using distant supervision. *Processing*, pages 1–6.

Roberto González-Ibáñez, Smaranda Muresan, and Nina Wacholder. 2011. Identifying sarcasm in twitter: A closer look. In *Proceedings of the 49th Annual Meeting of the Association for Computational Linguistics: Human Language Technologies: Short Papers - Volume 2*, HLT '11, pages 581–586, Stroudsburg, PA, USA. Association for Computational Linguistics.

Mark Hall, Eibe Frank, Geoffrey Holmes, Bernhard Pfahringer, Peter Reutemann, and Ian H. Witten. 2009. The weka data mining software: an update. *SIGKDD Explor. Newsl.*, 11(1):10–18, November.

Preslav Nakov, Sara Rosenthal, Zornitsa Kozareva, Veselin Stoyanov, Alan Ritter, and Theresa Wilson. 2013. Semeval-2013 task 2: Sentiment analysis in twitter. In *Second Joint Conference on Lexical and Computational Semantics (*SEM), Volume 2: Proceedings of the Seventh International Workshop on Semantic Evaluation (SemEval 2013)*, pages 312–320, Atlanta, Georgia, USA, June. Association for Computational Linguistics.

Alexander Pak and Patrick Paroubek. 2010. Twitter as a corpus for sentiment analysis and opinion mining. In Nicoletta Calzolari (Conference Chair), Khalid Choukri, Bente Maegaard, Joseph Mariani, Jan Odijk, Stelios Piperidis, Mike Rosner, and Daniel Tapias, editors, *Proceedings of the Seventh International Conference on Language Resources and Evaluation (LREC'10)*, Valletta, Malta, may. European Language Resources Association (ELRA).

Sara Rosenthal and Kathleen McKeown. 2013. Columbia nlp: Sentiment detection of subjective phrases in social media. In *Second Joint Conference on Lexical and Computational Semantics (*SEM), Volume 2: Proceedings of the Seventh International Workshop on Semantic Evaluation (SemEval 2013)*, pages 478–482, Atlanta, Georgia, USA, June. Association for Computational Linguistics.

Sara Rosenthal, Preslav Nakov, Alan Ritter, and Veselin Stoyanov. 2014. Semeval-2014 task 9: Sentiment analysis in twitter. In *Proceedings of the 8th International Workshop on Semantic Evaluation (SemEval 2014)*, Dublin, Ireland, August. The COLING 2014 Organizing Committee.

C. M. Whissel. 1989. The dictionary of affect in language. In *R. Plutchik and H. Kellerman, editors, Emotion: theory research and experience*, volume 4, London. Acad. Press.

COMMIT-P1WP3: A Co-occurrence Based Approach to Aspect-Level Sentiment Analysis

Kim Schouten[1,2] **Flavius Frasincar**[1] **Franciska de Jong**[2]
schouten@ese.eur.nl frasincar@ese.eur.nl fdejong@ese.eur.nl
[1]Econometric Institute, Erasmus University Rotterdam, The Netherlands
[2]Erasmus Studio, Erasmus University Rotterdam, The Netherlands

Abstract

In this paper, the crucial ingredients for our submission to SemEval-2014 Task 4 "Aspect Level Sentiment Analysis" are discussed. We present a simple aspect detection algorithm, a co-occurrence based method for category detection and a dictionary based sentiment classification algorithm. The dictionary for the latter is based on co-occurrences as well. The failure analysis and related work section focus mainly on the category detection method as it is most distinctive for our work.

1 Introduction

In recent years, sentiment analysis has taken flight and is now actively used, on the Web and beyond (Liu, 2012). To provide users of sentiment tools with more detailed and useful information, a number of innovations have been introduced, and among others a switch from document-level sentiment analysis towards fine-grained, aspect-level sentiment analysis can be seen (Feldman, 2013). In line with the many challenges associated with this, SemEval-2014 Task 4 "Aspect Level Sentiment Analysis" (Pontiki et al., 2014) is split into four sub-tasks: Aspect Detection, Aspect Sentiment Classification, Category Detection, and Category Sentiment Classification.

The main focus of this paper is on the category detection algorithm we developed, but a method for aspect detection and a sentiment classification algorithm (both for aspects and categories) are also included. The aspect detection algorithm will be presented first, followed by the category detection algorithm and the sentiment classification method. Next, the benchmark results for all algorithms are presented, plus a discussion and failure analysis of the category detection method. Finally, conclusions are drawn and some suggestions for future work are presented.

2 Related Work

Because the focus of this paper lies on the category detection method, only for that method a short snippet of related work is given. That algorithm, being an adapted version of Schouten and Frasincar (2014), is inspired by the work of Zhang and Zhu (2013) and Hai et al (2011). In these works, a co-occurrence matrix is created between words in the sentence and aspects in order to find implicit aspects (i.e., aspects that are not literally mentioned, as opposed to the explicit aspects used in this task).

While implicit aspects are similar to aspect categories to some extent, these methods do not work when a fixed, limited set of possible aspect categories is used that is, most importantly, not a subset of the set of aspects. The above methods could never, for instance, identify the 'anecdotes/miscellaneous' category, as this word never appears as an aspect in the data set. This is the main reason why we have chosen to count the co-occurrences between words and the annotated aspect categories.

3 Aspect Detection Method

In the work reported here, the aspect detection method plays the role of a baseline method rather than a full-fledged algorithm. In its most basic form, it annotates all noun phrases as aspects. However, by using the training set to count how often each word appears within an aspect, a simple probability can be computed representing the chance that this word is an aspect word or not. This probability is used to filter the set of noun phrases, such that only noun phrases remain that

Proceedings of the 8th International Workshop on Semantic Evaluation (SemEval 2014), pages 203–207, Dublin, Ireland, August 23-24, 2014.

have at least one word for which the aspect probability ≥ 0.05 and for those noun phrases, all leading words in the noun phrase with a probability below 0.05 are removed. This will remove words like determiners from the initial noun phrase, as those are not included in the aspect term. Because this filtering is strict, the result is a typical high precision, low recall algorithm for aspect detection.

4 Category Detection Method

To find the aspect categories, the co-occurrence based algorithm from Schouten and Frasincar (2014) is used and improved upon. The central construct in this algorithm is a co-occurrence matrix that captures the frequency of the co-occurrences between words (i.e., the lemmas of the words) in the sentence and the annotated aspect category. This gives a mapping from words to aspect categories. When processing an unlabelled sentence, a score is computed for each aspect category as shown in Eq. 1.

$$score_{a_i} = \frac{1}{v} \sum_{j=1}^{v} \frac{c_{i,j}}{o_j}, \tag{1}$$

where v is the number of words in the sentence, a_i is the ith aspect category in the list of possible aspect categories for which the $score$ is computed, j represents the jth word in the sentence, $c_{i,j}$ is the co-occurrence frequency of aspect category i and lemma j in the data set, and o_j is the frequency of lemma j in the data set.

Whereas in Schouten and Frasincar (2014), the highest scoring category was chosen on the condition that its score exceeded a threshold, our method is now able to choose more than one aspect category per sentence. This is done by training a separate threshold for each of the five aspect categories using all training data. When the score for some aspect category is higher than its associated threshold (i.e., $score_{a_i} > threshold_{a_i}$), the sentence is annotated as having that aspect category.

Since we assume the five threshold values to be independent of each other, a simple linear search is performed separately for all five of them to find the optimal threshold value by optimizing F_1 (cf. Sec. 6). As a default option, the fifth category ('anecdotes/miscellaneous') is associated to any sentence for which none of the five categories exceeded their threshold. The trained threshold values for the five categories are:

ambience	price	food	service	misc
0.042	0.024	0.211	0.071	0.143

The pseudocode for the creation of the co-occurrence matrix can be found in Algorithm 1, and Algorithm 2 describes the process of annotating a sentence with aspect categories.

Algorithm 1 Aspect category detection training.

```
Initialize set of word lemmas with frequencies O
Initialize set of aspect categories A
Initialize co-occurrence matrix C
for sentence s ∈ training data do
    for word w ∈ s do
        O(w) = O(w) + 1
    end for
    for aspect category a ∈ s do
        add a to A
        for word w ∈ s do
            C(w, a) = C(w, a) + 1
        end for
    end for
end for
for aspect category a in A do
    threshold_a=0
    bestF_1 = 0
    for t = 0 to 1 step 0.001 do
        Execute Algorithm 2 on training data
        Compute F_1
        if F_1 > bestF_1 then threshold_a = t
        end if
    end for
end for
```

5 Sentiment Classification Method

For sentiment classification, a method is developed that first creates a sentiment lexicon based on the aspect sentiment annotation. That lexicon is then consequently used to determine the sentiment of both aspects and categories that have no sentiment annotation. The intuition behind this method is that a lexicon should cover domain-specific words and expressions in order to be effective. To avoid creating such a sentiment lexicon manually, the aspect sentiment annotations are leveraged to create one automatically. The idea is that words that often appear close to positive or

Algorithm 2 Aspect category detection execution.

```
for sentence s ∈ test data do
    for aspect category a ∈ A do
        score = 0
        for word w ∈ s do
            if O(w) > 0 then
                score = score + C(w, a)/O(w)
            end if
        end for
        score = score/ length(s)
        if score > threshold_a then
            Assign aspect category a to s
        end if
    end for
    if s has no assigned aspect categories then
        Assign 'anecdotes/miscellaneous' to s
    end if
end for
```

negative aspects are likely to have the same polarity. Since sentiment is also carried by expressions, rather than single words only, the constructed sentiment lexicon has entries for encountered unigrams, bigrams, and trigrams. In each sentence, the distance between each n-gram and each aspect is computed and the sentiment of the aspect, discounted by the computed distance, is added to the sentiment value of the n-gram, as shown in Eq. 2.

$$sentiment_g = \frac{1}{freq_g} \cdot \sum_{s \in S_g} p \cdot t_{order(g)} \cdot \sum_{a \in A_s} \frac{polarity_a}{(distance_{g,a})^m}, \quad (2)$$

where g is the n-gram (i.e., word unigram, bigram, or trigram), $freq_g$ is the frequency of n-gram g in the data set, s is a sentence in S_g, which is the set of sentences that contain n-gram g, p is a parameter to correct for the overall positivity of the data set, t is a parameter that corrects for the relative influence of the type of n-gram (i.e., different values are used for t_1, t_2, and t_3), a is an aspect in A_s, which is the set of aspects in sentence s, $polarity_a$ is 1 when aspect a is positive and -1 when a is negative, and m is a parameter that determines how strong the discounting by the distance should be. The distance computed is the shortest word distance between the aspect and the n-gram (i.e., both an n-gram and an aspect can consist of multiple words, in which case the closest two are used to compute the distance). Note that essentially, dictionary creation is based on how often an n-gram co-occurs with positive or negative aspects. In our submitted run on the restaurant data, we set $t_{order(g)}$ to 1, 5, and 4 for unigrams, bigrams, and trigrams, respectively, and $p = 2$ and for the laptop data we set $t_{order(g)}$ to 1, 0, and 3 for the n-grams and $p = 1$. In both cases, m was kept at 1. These values were determined by manual experimentation.

To compute the sentiment of an aspect, the sentiment value of each n-gram is divided by the distance between that n-gram and the aspect, computed in a similar fashion as in the above formula) and summed up, as shown in Eq. 3.

$$sentiment_{a,s_a} = \sum_{g \in s_a} \frac{sentiment_g}{(\min distance_{g,a})^m}, \quad (3)$$

where, in addition to the definitions in the previous equation, g is an n-gram in s_a, which is the sentence in which aspect a occurs. Note that for each occurrence of a term, its sentiment value is added to the total score. If the result is above zero, the class will be 'positive', and if the result is below zero, the class will be 'negative'. In the rare event of the sentiment score being exactly zero, the 'neutral' class is assigned.

For category sentiment classification, the formula of Eq. 3 remains the same, except that the distance term $\min distance_{g,a}^m$ is set to 1, since aspect categories pertain to the whole sentence instead of having specific offsets.

6 Evaluation

All three algorithms presented above were evaluated through a submission in the SemEval-2014 Task 4 "Aspect Level Sentiment Analysis". Two data sets have been used, one consisting of sentences from restaurant reviews, the other consisting of sentences from laptop reviews. Both sets have been annotated with aspects and aspect sentiment, but only the restaurant set is also annotated with aspect categories and their associated sentiment class. Both data sets are split into a training set of roughly 3000 sentences and a test set of 800 sentences.

All sentences in the data set have been preprocessed by a tokenizer, a Part-of-Speech tagger, and a lemmatizer. These tasks were performed by

Table 1: Official results for both algorithms.

aspect detection (subtask 1)			
	precision	recall	F_1
laptop	0.836	0.148	0.252
restaurant	0.909	0.388	0.544
category detection (subtask 3)			
	precision	recall	F_1
restaurant	0.633	0.558	0.593
aspect sentiment classification (subtask 2)			
laptop	accuracy	0.570	
restaurant	accuracy	0.660	
category sentiment classification (subtask 4)			
restaurant	accuracy	0.677	

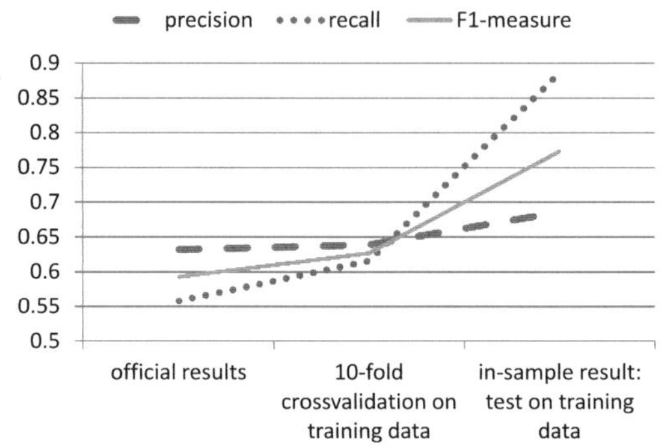

Figure 1: Performance measure of category detection on different parts of data.

the Stanford CoreNLP framework[1]. Furthermore, the OpenNLP[2] chunker was used to provide basic phrase chunking in order to retrieve noun phrases for instance.

The official scores, as computed by the task organizers are shown in Table 1. Note that the sentiment classification algorithm is used for subtasks 2 and 4, so two scores are reported, and that subtasks 3 and 4 can only be performed with the restaurant data set.

As the performance of the category detection method was lower than anticipated, a failure analysis has been performed. This led to the observation that overfitting is one of major factors in explaining the lower performance . This is shown in Figure 1, in which one can easily notice the great difference in in-sample performance, and the performance on unseen data. Notice that by using 10-fold cross-validation, better results are achieved than on the official test set. This indicates that there are factors other than overfitting that influence the performance.

Interestingly, especially recall is influenced by the overfitting problem: precision is almost the same for the 10-fold cross-validation and even with the in-sample performance it increases only a little bit. To gain more insight into the difference in recall, a graph showing the relative contribution to false negatives of the five categories is shown in Figure 2. For completeness, the same graph but for false positives is also shown, together with the frequency distribution of the categories in both training and test set.

Immediately visible is the effect of defaulting to the 'anecdotes/miscellaneous' when no category is assigned to that sentence: many false positives are generated by this rule, but there are almost no false negatives for this category. Note that without this default, F_1-measure would drop by roughly 3 percentage points.

Also notable is the difference between the in-sample bar and the official results bar: two categories, namely 'anecdotes/miscellaneous' and 'food' show large differences in contribution to false positives and false negatives. The algorithm finds fewer 'food' categories in the test set, than in the training set, while for 'anecdotes/miscellaneous', the reverse is the case. This can at least be partly explained by the change in data statistics: in the training set, 33% of the annotated categories are 'food' and 30% are 'anecdotes/miscellaneous', whereas in the test set, these numbers are 40% and 22%, respectively. With much more sentences having the 'food' category, false positives will be lower but false negatives will be higher. For 'anecdotes/miscellaneous', the reverse is true: with less sentences in the test set having this category, false positives will by higher, but false negatives will be lower, a change reinforced by 'anecdotes/miscellaneous' being the default.

Two factors remain that might have negatively impacted the performance of the algorithm. The first is that in the restaurant set, many words appear only once (e.g., dishes, ingredients), and when words do not appear in the training set, no co-occurrence with any category can be recorded. This primarily affects recall. The second is that the category thresholds, while working well on the training set, do not seem to generalize well to the

[1]http://nlp.stanford.edu/software/corenlp.shtml

[2]https://opennlp.apache.org/

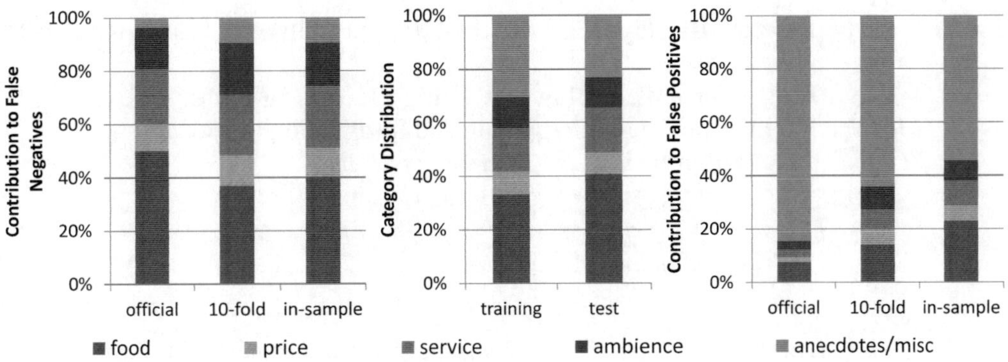

Figure 2: The frequency distribution of each category and its relative contribution to the total number of false negatives (left graph) and false positives (right graph). The middle graph shows the change in the distribution of categories in the training and test set.

test set. Testing the algorithm with one threshold for all five categories, while showing a sharply decreased in-sample performance, yields an out-of-sample F_1-measure that is only slightly lower than F_1-measure with different thresholds.

7 Conclusion

In this paper the main ingredients for our submission to SemEval-2014 Task 4 "Aspect Level Sentiment Analysis" are discussed: a simple aspect detection method, a co-occurrence based method for category detection, and a dictionary based sentiment classification algorithm. Since the category detection algorithm did not perform as expected, a failure analysis has been performed, while for the others this was less necessary as they performed roughly as expected.

The failure analysis provides several starting points for future research. First, it would be interesting to determine the exact nature of the dependency between category performance and category frequency, as discussed above, and to remove this dependency, since it is not guaranteed in real-life scenarios that the frequency distribution of the training set is the same as the set of instances an algorithm will encounter when in use. Furthermore, training five separate category threshold, while good for performance in general, also aggravates the problem of overfitting. Hence, improving the generalization of the algorithm, and the thresholds in particular, is important. Last, a method to deal with very low frequency words could prove useful as well.

Acknowledgment

The authors are partially supported by the Dutch national program COMMIT.

References

Ronen Feldman. 2013. Techniques and Applications for Sentiment Analysis. *Communications of the ACM*, 56(4):82–89.

Zhen Hai, Kuiyu Chang, and J. Kim. 2011. Implicit Feature Identification via Co-occurrence Association Rule Mining. In *Proceedings of the 12th International Conference on Computational Linguistics and Intelligent Text processing (CICLing 2011)*, volume 6608, pages 393–404. Springer.

Bing Liu. 2012. *Sentiment Analysis and Opinion Mining*, volume 16 of *Synthesis Lectures on Human Language Technologies*. Morgan & Claypool.

Maria Pontiki, Dimitrios Galanis, John Pavlopoulos, Harris Papageorgiou, Ion Androutsopoulos, and Suresh Manandhar. 2014. SemEval-2014 Task 4: Aspect Based Sentiment Analysis. In *Proceedings of the International Workshop on Semantic Evaluation (SemEval 2014)*.

Kim Schouten and Flavius Frasincar. 2014. Finding Implicit Features in Consumer Reviews for Sentiment Analysis. In *Proceedings of the 14th International Conference on Web Engineering (ICWE 2014)*, pages 130–144. Springer.

Yu Zhang and Weixiang Zhu. 2013. Extracting Implicit Features in Online Customer Reviews for Opinion Mining. In *Proceedings of the 22nd International Conference on World Wide Web Companion (WWW 2013 Companion)*, pages 103–104. International World Wide Web Conferences Steering Committee.

Coooolll: A Deep Learning System for Twitter Sentiment Classification*

Duyu Tang[†], **Furu Wei**[‡], **Bing Qin**[†], **Ting Liu**[†], **Ming Zhou**[‡]
[†]Research Center for Social Computing and Information Retrieval
Harbin Institute of Technology, China
[‡]Microsoft Research, Beijing, China
{dytang, qinb, tliu}@ir.hit.edu.cn
{fuwei, mingzhou}@microsoft.com

Abstract

In this paper, we develop a deep learning system for message-level Twitter sentiment classification. Among the 45 submitted systems including the SemEval 2013 participants, our system (**Coooolll**) is ranked 2nd on the Twitter2014 test set of SemEval 2014 Task 9. Coooolll is built in a supervised learning framework by concatenating the sentiment-specific word embedding (**SSWE**) features with the state-of-the-art hand-crafted features. We develop a neural network with hybrid loss function [1] to learn SSWE, which encodes the sentiment information of tweets in the continuous representation of words. To obtain large-scale training corpora, we train SSWE from 10M tweets collected by positive and negative emoticons, without any manual annotation. Our system can be easily re-implemented with the publicly available sentiment-specific word embedding.

1 Introduction

Twitter sentiment classification aims to classify the sentiment polarity of a tweet as positive, negative or neutral (Jiang et al., 2011; Hu et al., 2013; Dong et al., 2014). The majority of existing approaches follow Pang et al. (2002) and employ machine learning algorithms to build classifiers from tweets with manually annotated sentiment polarity. Under this direction, most studies focus on designing effective features to obtain better classification performance (Pang and Lee, 2008; Liu, 2012; Feldman, 2013). For example, Mohammad et al. (2013) implement diverse sentiment lexicons and a variety of hand-crafted features. To leverage massive tweets containing positive and negative emoticons for automatically feature learning, Tang et al. (2014) propose to learn sentiment-specific word embedding and Kalchbrenner et al. (2014) model sentence representation with Dynamic Convolutional Neural Network.

In this paper, we develop a deep learning system for Twitter sentiment classification. Firstly, we learn sentiment-specific word embedding (**SSWE**) (Tang et al., 2014), which encodes the sentiment information of text into the continuous representation of words (Mikolov et al., 2013; Sun et al., 2014). Afterwards, we concatenate the SSWE features with the state-of-the-art hand-crafted features (Mohammad et al., 2013), and build the sentiment classifier with the benchmark dataset from SemEval 2013 (Nakov et al., 2013). To learn SSWE, we develop a tailored neural network, which incorporates the supervision from sentiment polarity of tweets in the hybrid loss function. We learn SSWE from tweets, leveraging massive tweets with emoticons as distant-supervised corpora without any manual annotations.

We evaluate the deep learning system on the test set of Twitter Sentiment Analysis Track in SemEval 2014 [2]. Our system (**Coooolll**) is ranked 2nd on the Twitter2014 test set, along with the SemEval 2013 participants owning larger training data than us. The performance of only using SSWE as features is comparable to the state-of-the-art hand-crafted features (detailed in Table 3), which verifies the effectiveness of the sentiment-specific word embedding. We release the sentiment-specific word embedding learned

* This work was partly done when the first author was visiting Microsoft Research.

[1] This is one of the three sentiment-specific word embedding learning algorithms proposed in Tang et al. (2014).

[2] http://alt.qcri.org/semeval2014/task9/

Proceedings of the 8th International Workshop on Semantic Evaluation (SemEval 2014), pages 208–212,
Dublin, Ireland, August 23-24, 2014.

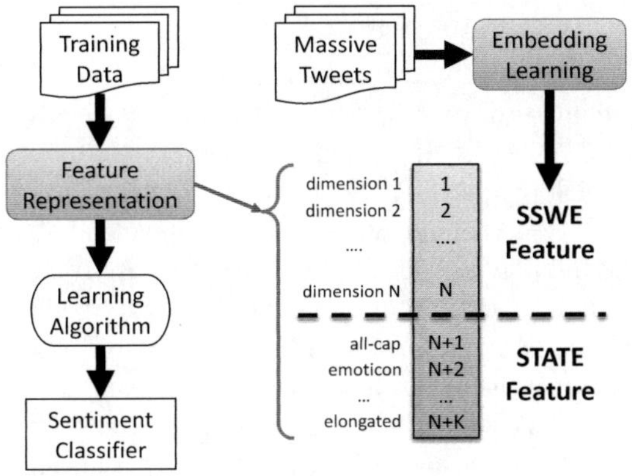

Figure 1: Our deep learning system (Coooolll) for Twitter sentiment classification.

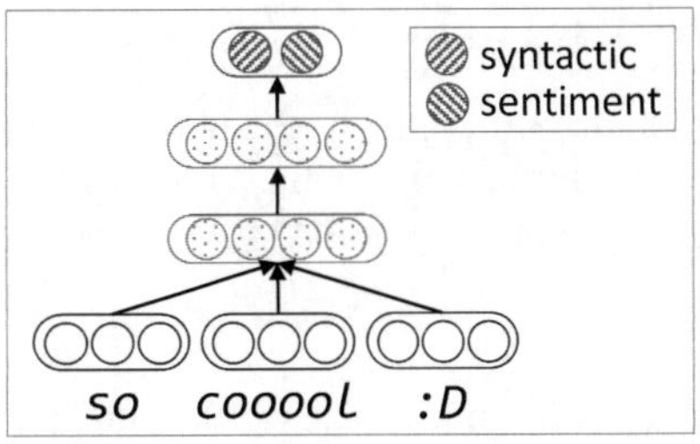

Figure 2: Our neural network (SSWE_u) for learning sentiment-specific word embedding.

from 10 million tweets, which can be easily used to re-implement our system and adopted off-the-shell in other sentiment analysis tasks.

2 A Deep Learning System

In this section, we present the details of our deep learning system for Twitter sentiment classification. As illustrated in Figure 1, Coooolll is a supervised learning method that builds the sentiment classifier from tweets with manually annotated sentiment polarity. In our system, the feature representation of tweet is composed of two parts, the sentiment-specific word embedding features (SSWE features) and the state-of-the-art hand-crafted features (STATE features). In the following parts, we introduce the SSWE features and STATE features, respectively.

2.1 SSWE Features

In this part, we first describe the neural network for learning sentiment-specific word embedding. Then, we generate the SSWE features of a tweet from the embedding of words it contains.

Our neural network is an extension of the traditional C&W model (Collobert et al., 2011), as illustrated in Figure 2. Unlike C&W model that learns word embedding by only modeling syntactic contexts of words, we develop **SSWE_u**, which captures the sentiment information of sentences as well as the syntactic contexts of words. Given an original (or corrupted) ngram and the sentiment polarity of a sentence as the input, SSWE_u predicts a two-dimensional vector for each input ngram. The two scalars ($\boldsymbol{f}_0^u$, $\boldsymbol{f}_1^u$) stand for language model score and sentiment score of the input ngram, respectively. The training objectives of SSWE_u are that (1) the original ngram should obtain a higher language model score $\boldsymbol{f}_0^u(t)$ than the corrupted ngram $\boldsymbol{f}_0^u(t^r)$, and (2) the sentiment score of original ngram $\boldsymbol{f}_1^u(t)$ should be more consistent with the gold polarity annotation of sentence than corrupted ngram $\boldsymbol{f}_1^u(t^r)$. The loss function of SSWE_u is the linear combination of two hinge losses,

$$\begin{aligned} loss_u(t, t^r) &= \alpha \cdot loss_{cw}(t, t^r) + \\ &\quad (1-\alpha) \cdot loss_{us}(t, t^r) \end{aligned} \tag{1}$$

where where t is the original ngram, t^r is the corrupted ngram which is generated from t with middle word replaced by a randomly selected one, $loss_{cw}(t, t^r)$ is the syntactic loss as given in Equation 2, $loss_{us}(t, t^r)$ is the sentiment loss as described in Equation 3. The hyper-parameter α weighs the two parts.

$$loss_{cw}(t, t^r) = max(0, 1 - f^{cw}(t) + f^{cw}(t^r)) \tag{2}$$

$$\begin{aligned} loss_{us}(t, t^r) = max(0, 1 - \delta_s(t)\boldsymbol{f}_1^u(t) \\ + \delta_s(t)\boldsymbol{f}_1^u(t^r)\ ) \end{aligned} \tag{3}$$

where $\delta_s(t)$ is an indicator function reflecting the sentiment polarity of a sentence, whose value is 1 if the sentiment polarity of tweet t is positive and -1 if t's polarity is negative. We train sentiment-specific word embedding from 10M tweets collected with positive and negative emoticons (Hu et al., 2013). The details of training phase are described in Tang et al. (2014).

After finish learning SSWE, we explore min, $average$ and max convolutional layers (Collobert et al., 2011; Socher et al., 2011; Mitchell and Lapata, 2010), to obtain the tweet representation. The result is the concatenation of vectors derived from different convolutional layers.

2.2 STATE Features

We re-implement the state-of-the-art hand-crafted features (Mohammad et al., 2013) for Twitter sentiment classification. The STATE features are described below.

- *All-Caps*. The number of words with all characters in upper case.
- *Emoticons*. We use the presence of positive (or negative) emoticons and whether the last unit of a segmentation is emoticon [3].
- *Elongated Units*. The number of elongated words (with one character repeated more than two times), such as *gooood*.
- *Sentiment Lexicon*. We utilize several sentiment lexicons [4] to generate features. We explore the number of sentiment words, the score of last sentiment words, the total sentiment score and the maximal sentiment score for each lexicon.
- *Negation*. The number of individual negations [5] within a tweet.
- *Punctuation*. The number of contiguous sequences of dot, question mark and exclamation mark.
- *Cluster*. The presence of words from each of the 1,000 clusters from the Twitter NLP tool (Gimpel et al., 2011).
- *Ngrams*. The presence of word ngrams (1-4) and character ngrams (3-5).

3 Experiments

We evaluate our deep learning system by applying it for Twitter sentiment classification within a supervised learning framework. We conduct experiments on both positive/negative/neutral and positive/negative classification of tweets.

[3]We use the positive and negative emoticons from SentiStrength, available at http://sentistrength.wlv.ac.uk/.

[4]*HL* (Hu and Liu, 2004), *MPQA* (Wilson et al., 2005), *NRC_Emotion* (Mohammad and Turney, 2013), *NRC_Hashtag* and *Sentiment140Lexicon* (Mohammad et al., 2013).

[5]http://sentiment.christopherpotts.net/lingstruc.html

3.1 Dataset and Setting

We train the Twitter sentiment classifier on the benchmark dataset in SemEval 2013 (Nakov et al., 2013). The training and development sets were completely in full to task participants of SemEval 2013. However, we were unable to download all the training and development sets because some tweets were deleted or not available due to modified authorization status. The distribution of our dataset is given in Table 1. We train sentiment classifiers with LibLinear (Fan et al., 2008) on the training set and dev set, and tune parameter $-c$, $-wi$ of SVM on the test set of SemEval 2013. In both experiment settings, the evaluation metric is the macro-F1 of positive and negative classes (Nakov et al., 2013).

	Positive	Negative	Neutral	Total
Train	2,642	994	3,436	7,072
Dev	408	219	493	1,120
Test	1,570	601	1,639	3,810

Table 1: Statistics of our SemEval 2013 Twitter sentiment classification dataset.

The test sets of SemEval 2014 is directly provided to the participants, which is composed of five parts. The statistic of test sets in SemEval 2014 is given in Table 2.

	Positive	Negative	Neutral	Total
T1	427	304	411	1,142
T2	492	394	1,207	2,093
T3	1,572	601	1,640	3,813
T4	982	202	669	1,939
T5	33	40	13	86

Table 2: Statistics of SemEval 2014 Twitter sentiment classification test set. T1 is LiveJournal2014, T2 is SMS2013, T3 is Twitter2013, T4 is Twitter2014, T5 is Twitter2014Sarcasm.

3.2 Results and Analysis

The experiment results of different methods on positive/negative/neutral and positive/negative Twitter sentiment classification are listed in Table 3. The meanings of T1$\sim$T5 in each column are described in Table 2. *SSWE* means the approach that only utilizes the sentiment-specific word embedding as features for Twitter sentiment classification. In *STATE*, we only utilize the existing features (Mohammad et al., 2013) for building the

Method	Positive/Negative/Neutral					Positive/Negative				
	T1	T2	**T3**	**T4**	T5	T1	T2	**T3**	**T4**	T5
SSWE	70.49	64.29	68.69	66.86	50.00	84.51	85.19	85.06	86.14	62.02
Coooolll	72.90	67.68	**70.40**	**70.14**	46.66	86.46	85.32	**86.01**	**87.61**	56.55
STATE	71.48	65.43	66.18	67.07	44.89	83.96	82.82	84.39	86.16	58.27
W2V	55.19	52.98	52.33	50.58	49.63	68.87	71.89	74.50	71.52	61.60
Top	74.84	70.28	72.12	70.96	58.16	- -	- -	- -	- -	- -
Average	63.52	55.63	59.78	60.41	45.44	- -	- -	- -	- -	- -

Table 3: Macro-F1 of positive and negative classes in positive/negative/neutral and positive/negative Twitter sentiment classification on the test sets (T1-T5, detailed in Table 2) of SemEval 2014. The performances of Coooolll on the Twitter-relevant test sets are **bold**.

sentiment classifier. In *Coooolll*, we use the concatenation of SSWE features and STATE features. In *W2V*, we only use the word embedding learned from word2vec[6] as features. *Top* and *Average* are the top and average performance of the 45 teams of SemEval 2014, including the SemEval 2013 participants who owns larger training data.

On positive/negative/neutral classification of tweets as listed in Table 3 (**left** table), we find that the learned sentiment-specific word embedding features (*SSWE*) performs comparable with the state-of-the-art hand-crafted features (*STATE*), especially on the Twitter-relevant test sets (**T3** and **T4**) [7]. After feature combination, *Coooolll* yields 4.22% and 3.07% improvement by macro-F1 on T3 and T4,which verifies the effectiveness of SSWE by learning discriminate features from massive data for Twitter sentiment classification. From the 45 teams, *Coooolll* gets the Rank **5/2/3/2** on T1-T4 respectively, along with the SemEval 2013 participants owning larger training data. We also comparing *SSWE* with the context-based word embedding (*W2V*), which don't capture the sentiment supervision of tweets. We find that *W2V* is not effective enough for Twitter sentiment classification as there is a big gap between *W2V* and *SSWE* on T1-T4. The reason is that *W2V* does not capture the sentiment information of text, which is crucial for sentiment analysis tasks and effectively leveraged for learning the sentiment-specific word embedding.

We also conduct experiments on the positive/negative classification of tweets. The reason is that the sentiment-specific word embedding is learned from the positive/negative supervision of tweets through emoticons, which is tailored for positive/negative classification of tweets. From Table 3 (**right** table), we find that the performance of positive/negative Twitter classification is consistent with the performance of 3-class classification. *SSWE* performs comparable to *STATE* on T3 and T4, and yields better performance (1.62% and 1.45% improvements on T3 and T4, respectively) through feature combination. *SSWE* outperforms *W2V* by large margins (more than 10%) on T3 and T4, which further verifies the effectiveness of sentiment-specific word embedding.

4 Conclusion

We develop a deep learning system (**Coooolll**) for message-level Twitter sentiment classification in this paper. The feature representation of Coooolll is composed of two parts, a state-of-the-art hand-crafted features and the sentiment-specific word embedding (**SSWE**) features. The SSWE is learned from 10M tweets collected by positive and negative emoticons, without any manual annotation. The effectiveness of *Coooolll* has been verified in both positive/negative/neutral and positive/negative classification of tweets. Among 45 systems of SemEval 2014 Task 9 subtask(b), *Coooolll* yields Rank 2 on the Twitter2014 test set, along with the SemEval 2013 participants owning larger training data.

Acknowledgments

We thank Li Dong for helpful discussions. This work was partly supported by National Natural Science Foundation of China (No.61133012, No.61273321, No.61300113).

[6]We utilize the Skip-gram model. The embedding is trained from the 10M tweets collected by positive and negative emoticons, as same as the training data of SSWE.

[7]The result of *STATE* on T3 is different from the results reported in Mohammad et al. (2013) and Tang et al. (2014) because we have different training data with the former and different *-wi* of SVM with the latter.

References

Ronan Collobert, Jason Weston, Léon Bottou, Michael Karlen, Koray Kavukcuoglu, and Pavel Kuksa. 2011. Natural language processing (almost) from scratch. *Journal of Machine Learning Research*, 12:2493–2537.

Li Dong, Furu Wei, Chuanqi Tan, Duyu Tang, Ming Zhou, and Ke Xu. 2014. Adaptive recursive neural network for target-dependent twitter sentiment classification. In *Proceedings of the 52nd Annual Meeting of the Association for Computational Linguistics*, pages 49–54.

Rong-En Fan, Kai-Wei Chang, Cho-Jui Hsieh, Xiang-Rui Wang, and Chih-Jen Lin. 2008. Liblinear: A library for large linear classification. *The Journal of Machine Learning Research*, 9:1871–1874.

Ronen Feldman. 2013. Techniques and applications for sentiment analysis. *Communications of the ACM*, 56(4):82–89.

Kevin Gimpel, Nathan Schneider, Brendan O'Connor, Dipanjan Das, Daniel Mills, Jacob Eisenstein, Michael Heilman, Dani Yogatama, Jeffrey Flanigan, and Noah A. Smith. 2011. Part-of-speech tagging for twitter: Annotation, features, and experiments. In *Proceedings of the Annual Meeting of the Association for Computational Linguistics*, pages 42–47.

Ming Hu and Bing Liu. 2004. Mining and summarizing customer reviews. In *Proceedings of the tenth ACM SIGKDD Conference on Knowledge Discovery and Data Mining*, pages 168–177.

Xia Hu, Jiliang Tang, Huiji Gao, and Huan Liu. 2013. Unsupervised sentiment analysis with emotional signals. In *Proceedings of the International World Wide Web Conference*, pages 607–618.

Long Jiang, Mo Yu, Ming Zhou, Xiaohua Liu, and Tiejun Zhao. 2011. Target-dependent twitter sentiment classification. *The Proceeding of Annual Meeting of the Association for Computational Linguistics*, 1:151–160.

Nal Kalchbrenner, Edward Grefenstette, and Phil Blunsom. 2014. A convolutional neural network for modelling sentences. In *Proceedings of the 52nd Annual Meeting of the Association for Computational Linguistics*, pages 655–665.

Bing Liu. 2012. Sentiment analysis and opinion mining. *Synthesis Lectures on Human Language Technologies*, 5(1):1–167.

Tomas Mikolov, Kai Chen, Greg Corrado, and Jeffrey Dean. 2013. Efficient estimation of word representations in vector space. *arXiv preprint arXiv:1301.3781*.

Jeff Mitchell and Mirella Lapata. 2010. Composition in distributional models of semantics. *Cognitive Science*, 34(8):1388–1429.

Saif M Mohammad and Peter D Turney. 2013. Crowdsourcing a word–emotion association lexicon. *Computational Intelligence*, 29(3):436–465.

Saif M Mohammad, Svetlana Kiritchenko, and Xiaodan Zhu. 2013. Nrc-canada: Building the state-of-the-art in sentiment analysis of tweets. *Proceedings of the International Workshop on Semantic Evaluation*, pages 321–327.

Preslav Nakov, Sara Rosenthal, Zornitsa Kozareva, Veselin Stoyanov, Alan Ritter, and Theresa Wilson. 2013. Semeval-2013 task 2: Sentiment analysis in twitter. In *Proceedings of the International Workshop on Semantic Evaluation*, volume 13, pages 312–320.

Bo Pang and Lillian Lee. 2008. Opinion mining and sentiment analysis. *Foundations and trends in information retrieval*, 2(1-2):1–135.

Bo Pang, Lillian Lee, and Shivakumar Vaithyanathan. 2002. Thumbs up?: sentiment classification using machine learning techniques. In *Proceedings of the Conference on Empirical Methods in Natural Language Processing*, pages 79–86.

Richard Socher, Eric H Huang, Jeffrey Pennington, Andrew Y Ng, and Christopher D Manning. 2011. Dynamic pooling and unfolding recursive autoencoders for paraphrase detection. *The Conference on Neural Information Processing Systems*, 24:801–809.

Yaming Sun, Lei Lin, Duyu Tang, Nan Yang, Zhenzhou Ji, and Xiaolong Wang. 2014. Radical-enhanced chinese character embedding. *arXiv preprint arXiv:1404.4714*.

Duyu Tang, Furu Wei, Nan Yang, Ming Zhou, Ting Liu, and Bing Qin. 2014. Learning sentiment-specific word embedding for twitter sentiment classification. In *Proceedings of the 52nd Annual Meeting of the Association for Computational Linguistics*, pages 1555–1565.

Theresa Wilson, Janyce Wiebe, and Paul Hoffmann. 2005. Recognizing contextual polarity in phrase-level sentiment analysis. In *Proceedings of the Conference on Empirical Methods in Natural Language Processing*, pages 347–354.

Copenhagen-Malmö: Tree Approximations of Semantic Parsing Problems

Natalie Schluter[†], Jakob Elming, Sigrid Klerke, Héctor Martínez Alonso, Dirk Hovy Barbara Plank, Anders Johannsen, and Anders Søgaard

[†]Dpt. of Computer Science
Malmö University
natalie.schluter@mah.se

Center for Language Technology
University of Copenhagen
{zmk867,skl,alonso}@hum.ku.dk
{dirk,bplank}@cst.dk,
{ajohannsen,soegaard}@hum.ku.dk

Abstract

In this shared task paper for SemEval-2014 Task 8, we show that most semantic structures can be approximated by trees through a series of almost bijective graph transformations. We transform input graphs, apply off-the-shelf methods from syntactic parsing on the resulting trees, and retrieve output graphs. Using tree approximations, we obtain good results across three semantic formalisms, with a 15.9% error reduction over a state-of-the-art semantic role labeling system on development data. Our system came in 3/6 in the shared task closed track.

1 Introduction

Semantic analyses often go beyond tree-structured representations, assigning multiple semantic heads to nodes, some semantic formalisms even tolerating directed cycles.[1] At the same time, syntactic parsing is a mature field with efficient, highly optimised decoding and learning algorithms for tree-structured representations. We present tree approximation algorithms that in combination with a state-of-the-art syntactic parser achieve competitive performance in semantic digraph parsing.

We investigate two kinds of tree approximation algorithms that we will refer to as *pruning* algorithms and *packing* algorithms. Our pruning algorithms simply remove and reverse edges until the graph is a tree; edge reversals are then undone as a postprocessing step. Our packing algorithms, on the other hand, carry out two bijective graph transformations to pack structural information into new edge labels, making it possible to reconstruct most of the structural complexity as a postprocessing step. Specifically, we present a packing algorithm that consists of two fully bijective graph transformations, in addition to a further transformation that incurs only a small information loss.

We carry out experiments across three semantic annotations of the Wall Street Journal section of the Penn Treebank (Marcus et al., 1993), corresponding to simplified versions of the semantic formalisms minimal recursion semantics (MRS) (Copestake et al., 2005), Enju-style predicate-argument structures (Miyao and Tsujii, 2003), and Prague-style tectogrammar semantics (Böhmová et al., 2003). We show that pruning and packing algorithms lead to state-of-the-art performance across these semantic formalisms using an off-the-shelf syntactic dependency parser.

2 Related work

Sagae and Tsujii (2008) present a pruning algorithm in their paper on transition-based parsing of directed acyclic graphs (DAGs), which discards the edges of longest span entering nodes. They apply the dependency parser described in Sagae and Tsujii (2007) to the tree representations. We note that this algorithm is not sufficient to produce trees in our case, where the input graphs are not necessarily acyclic. It does correspond roughly to our LONGEST-EDGE baseline, which removes the longest edge in cycles, in addition to flow reversal.

Sagae and Tsujii (2008) also present a shift-reduce automaton approach to parsing DAGs. In their paper, they report a labeled F1-score of 88.7% on the PAS dataset (see Section 3), while we obtain 89.1%, however the results are thus not directly comparable due to different data splits.[2]

[1]For example, HPSG predicate-argument structures (Pollard and Sag, 1994).

[2]We obtained code to run this as a baseline, but were unable to, due to memory leaks, caused by subsets of our data, and on the subsets of data that actually parsed, recall was very

Proceedings of the 8th International Workshop on Semantic Evaluation (SemEval 2014), pages 213–217,
Dublin, Ireland, August 23-24, 2014.

The shared task organizers of the Broad-coverage Semantic Dependency Parsing task at SemEval-2014[3] also presented a pruning-based baseline system. They eliminate re-entrancies in the graph by removing dependencies to nodes with multiple incoming edges. Of these edges, they again keep the shortest. They incorporate all singleton nodes by attaching nodes to the immediately following node or to a virtual root - in case the singleton is sentence-final. Finally, they integrate fragments by subordinating remaining nodes with in-degree 0 to the root node. They apply the parser described in Bohnet (2010), also used below, to the resulting trees. This system obtained a labeled F1-score of 54.7% on the PAS dataset. The performance of their pruning algorithm was also considerably lower than our algorithms on the other datasets considered below.

3 Tree approximations

This section describes two approaches to approximating graphs by trees, namely pruning and packing. Pruning optimizes the number of "good" edges in trees (Section 3.1), while packing transforms graphs into trees by means of a pipeline of operations which are 99.6% reversible (see Figure 1); that is, almost no information from the original graphs is lost in the trees (Section 3.2).

Under both approaches, we first introduce artificial root nodes to the graphs and append them to the word list. Graphs may initially be disconnected. We connect all weakly connected components as follows. We first identify a most important node in each weakly connected component, which we will refer to as the *root*. This root is taken to be the first node with the "top" feature from the data, if one exists. If none exists, then the node with highest degree is chosen as the "root". (Note that the "root" of each non-singleton connected component is marked as a "top" node in the inverse transformation.) The root of each non-singleton weakly connected component is attached as a dependent of the artificial root node with a special new label for the corresponding edge. Also, each disconnected node is attached as a dependent of the node to the right of it, with a distinct special new label. It is these connected graphs that we take to be the input in the following two subsections describing our graph pruning and packing algorithms.

3.1 Graph pruning

Our PRUNING algorithm removes a small number of edges in the semantic graphs to be able to represent them as trees. The average edge counts from the training data (see Section 4.1) indicate that the potential edge loss in pruning is relatively small (5.7% in the worst case). In this approach, two transformations on the connected semantic graphs are carried out: pruning and flow reversal.

Pruning. The input digraph may contain underlying *undirected* cycles. We break these cycles by iteratively removing the longest edge from the node with the fewest predecessors (lowest depth) in the digraph. The resulting underlying undirected graph is a tree.

Depth-first flow reversal. We then carry out depth-first traversal of the resulting underlying undirected tree, reversing the direction of edges from the leaves upwards, as needed, until reaching the root. Any reversed edge's label is given a special prefix, so that this reversal can be undone in a post-processing step.

Following the above two transformations, we train our parsers on the transformed semantic annotations and output graphs such as the one in Figure 1a.

3.2 Graph packing

Our PACKING algorithm consists of a pipeline of four graph transformations. The two major transformations are for coordination and generalised long-distance dependencies, being both parallel path inducing constructions. The transformations are both linguistically and topologically inspired by the f-structure annotated c-structures in Lexical Functional Grammar and f-structure parsing via off-the-shelf dependency parsers (Schluter and Van Genabith, 2009). We further ensure the defining tree property that every node is connected by a unique path from the root, by carrying out flow reversal when necessary. Finally remaining parallel paths are broken according to an heuristic on path locality.

Coordination. In some semantic representations of coordination, individual conjunct nodes may all dominate a same argument, or be dominated by a same head. In both these cases, parallel paths are generated. The same structures may

low, suggesting that maybe the decoding algorithm was tuned to a specific planarization of the complex graphs.

[3]http://alt.qcri.org/semeval2014/task8/

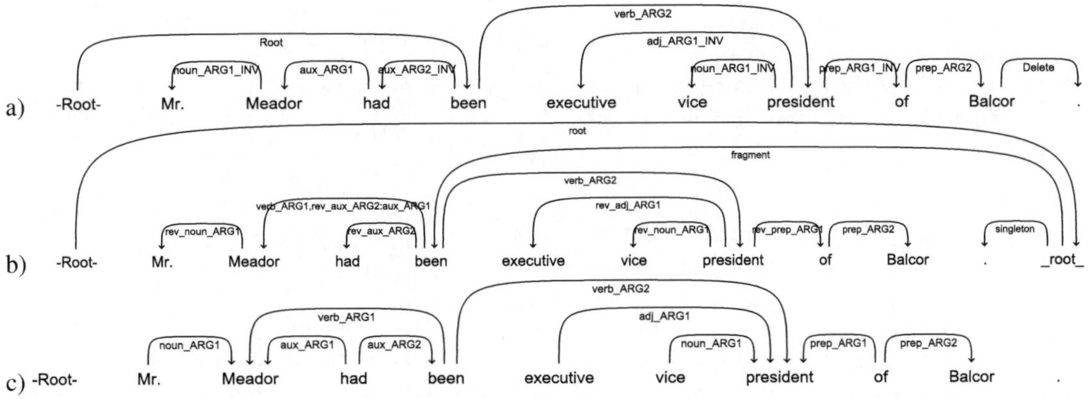

Figure 1: Example of pruned (top), packed (middle), and original (bottom) semantic graph. (Sentence 22002004 from the PAS dataset.)

be represented if the head or arguments are "factored out". To do this, we remove all edges from conjuncts towards a same argument (resp. from a shared head to each conjunct), and introduce a new edge from the root of the coordination subtree towards this argument (resp. from a shared head to the root of the coordination subtree). The new edges receive a special prefix to facilitate applying the inverse transformation.

Breadth-first flow reversal. Unlike our pruning algorithm, there is not yet any clear distinct path from the root to the all nodes (as there are not leaves yet). After carrying out the coordination transformation, we carry out a breadth-first search on the graph to direct flow away from the root, and again, reversed edges' labels are given a special prefix. As we do this, we test resulting nodes to see if there are any parallel paths leading to them. If so, these paths may be transformed immediately according to the following transformation.

Generalized long-distance dependencies. Long-distance dependencies are represented in f-structure annotated c-structures by path equations. This gives a tree representation of parallel paths, at least one of which is exactly one edge long. Given two parallel paths p_1 and p_2 in the graph, where $p_1 = (v_1, l, v_n)$ and $p_2 = (v_1, l_1, v_2), (v_2, l_2, v_3), \ldots, (v_{n-1}, l_{n-1}, v_n)$, we remove the last edge of p_2 and augment p_1's label with the representation $l_1 : l_2 : \cdots : l_{n-1}$ of p_2. p_1 becomes $(v_1, l \texttt{ and } l_1 : l_2 : \cdots : l_{n-1}, v_n)$, indicating that v_n is also the child (with dependency label l_{n-1}) of the node found by travelling (from v_1) down an l_1 labelled edge, followed by an l_2 labelled edge, and so on until the child of the l_{n-2} labelled edge is found.

Maximum average locality heuristic. Following these transformations, there may still be parallel paths in the graph: those not parallel to a single edge. We remove "worst" re-entrant edges using the simple heuristic that the path with the lowest average edge span should be conserved entirely. These removed edges clearly cannot be recovered after transformation.

Our parsers are trained on the output graphs of these four transformations such as the one in Figure 1b. We observe the main difference between PRUNING and PACKING: coordination and long-distance dependencies. For example, PACKING keeps the edge between the conjunction and the first conjunct, which is pruned away in PRUNING. Such a difference provides a partial explanation for the lower recall of PRUNING vis-à-vis PACKING (see Section 4.5).

4 Experiments

4.1 Data

The three datasets are semantic annotations of the WSJ section of the Penn Treebank of English. The average sentence length, which is also the average number of dependency edges in the tree approximations that we use to induce our semantic parsers, is 22.93. The three semantic formalisms are slightly richer, and the average number of edges in the PAS-annotated treebank is 24.32. For DM, the average number of edges is 23.77, and for DM it is 23.33. While the pruning-based approaches thus suffers from a modest information loss, throwing out 5.7% of the edges in the worst case, this is not the case for packing. The reversibility of the packed representations is given by the score upper bound in the last row in Table 1. We use the dataset splits of the SemEval 2014 shared task.

4.2 Model

For both our pruning and packing models, we use the Mate parser (Bohnet, 2010)[4] with default parameters to learn our parsing models. The Mate parser is trained on the output of the transformation pipeline on Sections 00-19 of the three semantically annotated WSJ datasets. Some models use Brown clusters generated from Sections 00-19 only. This does not solve OOV problems, but allows of slightly better generalisation across distributionally similar words in the training data.

4.3 Baselines

We use the SemEval 2014 shared task baseline (SIMPLE-PRUNE; see Section 2), as well as the LONGEST-EDGE baseline, also mentioned above. The latter is our strongest baseline system. It is very similar to PRUNING, in doing both edge pruning and flow reversal, but the pruning step only removes the longest edge rather than considering node depth. Our third baseline is the Mate semantic role labeling learner (SRL-DEP) (Björkelund et al., 2009), which uses predicted syntactic parses as input; for this, we use the syntactic parses made available in the SemEval 2014 shared task for replicability.

Approach	**Cl**	DM	PAS	PCEDT	*Av*
Systems					
PRUNING	NO	86.6	88.8	72.7	82.7
	YES	**86.9**	**89.1**	72.5	**82.8**
PACKING	NO	85.8	88.7	71.8	82.1
	YES	86.1	88.7	**72.9**	82.6
Baselines					
SIMPLE-PRUNE		54.7	50.9	67.8	57.8
LONGEST-EDGE		83.8	88.9	66.1	79.6
SRL-DEP		79.5	82.4	70.1	77.4
Upper bound					
PACKING		*99.9*	*99.5*	*99.5*	*99.6*

Table 1: Labelled F1-score results on development data, with and without use of Brown clusters (**Cl**).

4.4 Results

The results are presented in Tables 1 through 3, where the system evaluations for the SemEval task are marked with asterisks in Table 2. We note that all our approaches do considerably better than our three baselines. The error reduction of our best system over the SRL system across all three formalisms is 24.2%, and the error reduction over the more competitive pruning baseline LONGEST-EDGE is 15.9%. As mentioned in Section 2, these results seem to promise better performance than current DAG parsing models. Note from the results in Table 2 that, as expected, PRUNING leads to higher precision than PACKING at the expense of recall.

[4]https://code.google.com/p/mate-tools/

Approach	metric	DM	PAS	PCEDT	*Av*
Systems					
PACKING	PREC	84.8	87.7	71.2	81.2
(W/ TOP)	REC	84.0	88.4	68.6	80.3
	F1	**84.4**	**88.0**	**69.9**	**80.8***
	PREC	85.4	87.9	70.8	81.4
(W/O TOP)	REC	84.6	88.6	68.8	80.7
	F1	**85.0**	**88.3**	**69.9**	**81.1**
PRUNING	PREC	87.2	91.3	72.8	83.8
(W/ TOP)	REC	80.2	81.3	62.8	74.8
	F1	**83.6**	**86.0**	**67.4**	**79.0***
	PREC	87.2	91.3	72.8	83.8
(W/O TOP)	REC	85.1	85.1	68.0	79.4
	F1	**86.2**	**88.1**	**70.3**	**81.5**

Table 2: Labelled results on test data, with and without evaluation of top nodes. The scores with asterisks correspond to the output evaluated in the SemEval task.

Approach	metric	DM	PAS	PCEDT	*Av*
Systems					
PACKING	PREC	86.8	89.1	84.8	86.9
(W/ TOP)	REC	86.0	89.8	81.8	85.9
	F1	**86.4**	**89.4**	**83.2**	**86.3**
	PREC	87.5	89.4	85.4	87.4
(W/O TOP)	REC	86.7	90.1	83.0	86.6
	F1	**87.1**	**89.7**	**84.2**	**87.0**
PRUNING	PREC	89.2	92.6	88.2	90.0
(W/ TOP)	REC	82.0	82.5	76.1	80.2
	F1	**85.4**	**87.3**	**81.7**	**84.8**
	PREC	89.2	92.6	88.2	90.0
(W/O TOP)	REC	87.1	86.3	82.4	85.3
	F1	**88.1**	**89.3**	**85.2**	**87.5**

Table 3: Unlabelled results on test data, with and without evaluation of top nodes.

4.5 Error Analysis

We observe that pruning leads to high precision, while our packing algorithm gives us much better recall. This is not surprising, since our packed representations introduce new labels, making it harder to generalize at training time. On the other hand, pruning approaches suffer in recall, simply because edges are thrown away in preprocessing the data.

5 Conclusions

In this paper, we experimented with using tree approximation algorithms to reduce semantic structures to trees and use off-the-shelf structured prediction techniques to train semantic parsers. Our approximation algorithms include both pruning and packing algorithms, i.e., algorithms that try to reduce graphs to trees optimally, as well as algorithms that pack information about graphs into trees from which we later recover the richer structures. Using these tree approximation algorithms, we obtain 15.9% error reductions over a state-of-the-art SRL system.

References

Anders Björkelund, Love Hafdell, and Pierre Nugues. 2009. Multilingual semantic role labeling. In *Proc. of CoNLL: Shared Task*, pages 43–48, Boulder, CO, USA.

Alena Böhmová, Jan Hajič, Eva Hajičová, and Barbora Hladká. 2003. The Prague Dependency Treebank: A three-level annotation scenario. In Anne Abeillé, editor, *Treebanks: Building and Using Syntactically Annotated Corpora*, pages 103–127. Kluwer, Netherlands.

Bernd Bohnet. 2010. Top accuracy and fast dependency parsing is not a contradiction. In *Proc. of COLING*, pages 89–97, Beijing, China.

Ann Copestake, Dan Flickinger, Carl Pollard, and Ivan Sag. 2005. Minimal recursion semantics. *Research on Language and Computation*, 3:281–332.

Mitchell Marcus, Mary Marcinkiewicz, and Beatrice Santorini. 1993. Building a large annotated corpus of English: the Penn Treebank. *Computational Linguistics*, 19(2):313–330.

Yusuke Miyao and Jun'ichi Tsujii. 2003. Probabilistic modeling of argument structures including nonlocal dependencies. In *Proc. of RANLP*, pages 79–85, Borovets, Bulgaria.

Carl Pollard and Ivan Sag. 1994. *Head-driven phrase structure grammar*. University of Chicago Press.

Kenji Sagae and Jun'ichi Tsujii. 2007. Dependency parsing and domain adaptation with LR models and parser ensembles. In *Proc. of CoNLL Shared task session of EMNLP-CoNLL*, pages 1044–1050, Prague, Czech Republic.

Kenji Sagae and Jun'ichi Tsujii. 2008. Shift-reduce dependency DAG parsing. In *Proc. of COLING*, pages 753–760, Manchester, UK.

Natalie Schluter and Josef Van Genabith. 2009. Dependency parsing resources for French. In *Proc. of NODALIDA*, pages 166–173, Odense, Denmark.

DAEDALUS at SemEval-2014 Task 9: Comparing Approaches for Sentiment Analysis in Twitter

Julio Villena-Román
Daedalus, S.A.
jvillena@daedalus.es

Janine García-Morera
Daedalus, S.A.
jgarcia@daedalus.es

José Carlos González-Cristóbal
Universidad Politécnica de Madrid
josecarlos.gonzalez@upm.es

Abstract

This paper describes our participation at SemEval-2014 sentiment analysis task, in both contextual and message polarity classification. Our idea was to compare two different techniques for sentiment analysis. First, a machine learning classifier specifically built for the task using the provided training corpus. On the other hand, a lexicon-based approach using natural language processing techniques, developed for a generic sentiment analysis task with no adaptation to the provided training corpus. Results, though far from the best runs, prove that the generic model is more robust as it achieves a more balanced evaluation for message polarity along the different test sets.

1 Introduction

SemEval[1] is an international competitive evaluation workshop on semantic related tasks. Among the ten different tasks that have been proposed in 2014, Task 9 at SemEval-2014[2] focuses on sentiment analysis in Twitter.

Sentiment analysis could be described as the application of natural language processing and text analytics to identify and extract subjective information from texts. Given a message in English, the objective is to determine if the text expresses a positive, negative or neutral sentiment in that context.

It is a major technological challenge and the task is so hard that even humans often disagree on the sentiment of a given text, as issues that one individual may find acceptable or relevant may not be the same to others, along with multilingual aspects and different cultural factors.

The task defines two subtasks, where the difference is that whereas the output in subtask B must be the message polarity classification, i.e., the global polarity of the whole message, subtask A is focused on contextual polarity disambiguation, i.e., the message contains a marked instance of a word or phrase and the expected output must be the polarity of that specific instance within the whole message.

Daedalus (2014) is a leading provider of language-based solutions in Spain, and long-time participants in different research conferences and evaluation workshops such as CLEF (2014) and NTCIR (2014), in many different tasks including sentiment analysis (Villena-Román et al., 2008; Villena-Román et al., 2012).

This paper describes our participation in both contextual (subtask A) and message (subtask B) polarity classification. The main idea behind our participation is to compare two different techniques for sentiment analysis: a machine learning approach using the provided corpus to train a model specifically adapted to that scenario against a lexicon-based approach using advanced natural language processing techniques for capturing the meaning of the text, developed prior to the task and obviously without using the provided corpus.

Our point of view is that although machine learning classifiers generally achieve better results in competitive evaluations that provide a training corpus, when these same models are applied to a different scenario, the precision and recall metrics are drastically reduced, thus affecting to the perception and confidence of stakeholders in sentiment analysis technologies.

Our different approaches, experiments and results achieved are presented and discussed in the following sections.

[1] http://alt.qcri.org/semeval2014/

[2] http://alt.qcri.org/semeval2014/task9/

Proceedings of the 8th International Workshop on Semantic Evaluation (SemEval 2014), pages 218–222,
Dublin, Ireland, August 23-24, 2014.

2 Constrained Runs: Machine Learning Classifier

The first approach is a simple quite naive machine learning classifier trained exclusively with the provided training corpus. This is the approach adopted for constrained runs in both subtask A and B.

First, based on the Vector Space Model (Salton et al., 1975), the text of each tweet is converted into a term vector where terms are assumed to represent the semantic content of the message. Textalytics parsing API (Textalytics, 2014a) offered through a REST-based web service is used to get the lemma of each word and filter part-of-speech categories: currently nouns, verbs, adjectives and adverbs are selected as terms. A weighted term vector based on the classical TF-IDF is used. Both the training and the test set are preprocessed in this same way.

After this preprocessing, a classifier trained on the training corpus is used to classify the test corpus. Many different supervised learning algorithms where evaluated with 10-fold cross validation, using Weka (Hall et al., 2009). We finally selected Multinomial Naive Bayes algorithm, training three different binary classifiers: positive/not_positive, negative/not_negative and neutral/not_neutral. To select the final global message polarity, a simple rule-based decision is made:

```
if positive and not_negative and
  not_neutral then positive
else if negative and not_positive and
  not_neutral then negative
else neutral
```

This is directly the output for subtask B. For subtask A, this same global polarity is assigned to each text fragment, i.e., subtask A and B are treated in the same way.

3 Unconstrained Runs: Lexicon-Based Model

Our second approach, used in the unconstrained runs in both subtasks, is based on 1) the information provided by a semantic model that includes rules and resources (polarity units, modifiers, stopwords) annotated for sentiment analysis, 2) a detailed morphosyntactic analysis of the tweet to lemmatize and split the text into segments, useful to control the scope of semantic units and perform a fine-grained detection of negation in clauses, and 3) the use of an aggregation algorithm to calculate the global polarity value of the text based on the local polarity values of the different segments, including an outlier detection.

We consider this approach to be unconstrained because the lexicon in the semantic model (which would be valid itself for a constrained run) has been generated, tested and validated using additional training data.

All this functionality is encapsulated and provided by our Textalytics API for multilingual sentiment analysis (Textalytics, 2014b) in several languages, including English. Apart from the text itself, a required input parameter is the semantic model to use in the sentiment evaluation. This semantic model defines the domain of the text (the analysis scenario) and is mainly based on an extensive set of dictionaries and rules that incorporate both the well-known "domain-independent" polarity values (for instance, in general, in all contexts, *good* is positive and *awful* is negative) and also the specificities of each analysis scenario (for instance, an *increase* in the *interest rate* is probably positive for financial companies but negative for the rest).

First the local polarity of the different clauses in the text (segments) is identified based on the sentence syntactic tree and then the relation among them is evaluated in order to obtain a global polarity value for the whole given text. The detailed process may be shortly described as follows:

1. **Segment detection**. The text is parsed and split into segments, based on the presence of punctuation marks and capitalization of words.

2. **Linguistic processing**: each segment is tokenized (considering multiword units) and then each token is analyzed to extract its lemma(s). In addition, a morphosyntactic analysis divides the segment into proposition or clauses and builds the sentence syntactic tree. This division is useful, as described later, for detecting the negation and analyzing the effect of modifiers on the polarity values.

3. **Detection of negation**. The next step is to iterate over every token of each segment to tag whether the token is affected by negation or not. If a given token is affected by negation, the eventual polarity level is reversed (turns from positive to negative and the other round). For this purpose, the semantic model includes a

list of negation units, such as the obvious negation particles (adverbs) such as *not* (and contracted forms), *neither* and also expressions such as *against*, *far from*, *no room for*, etc.

4. **Detection of modifiers**. Some special units do not assign a specific polarity value but operate as modifiers of this value, incrementing or decrementing it. These units included in the semantic model can be assigned a + (positive), ++ (strong positive), - (negative) or -- (strong negative) value. For instance, if *good* is positive (P), *very good* is be strong positive (P+), thus *very* would be a positive modifier (+). Other examples are *additional*, *a lot*, *completely* (positive) or *descend*, *almost* (negative).

5. **Polarity tagging**. The next step is to detect polarity units in the segments. The semantic model assigns one of the following values, ranging from the most positive to the most negative: P++, P+, P, P-, P--, N--, N-, N, N+ and N++. Moreover, these units can include a context filter, i.e., one or several words or expressions that must appear or not in the segment so that the unit is considered in the sentiment analysis. The final value for each token is calculated from the polarity value of the unit in the semantic model, adding or subtracting the polarity value of the modifier (if thresholds are fulfilled) and considering the negation (again, if thresholds are fulfilled).

6. **Segment scoring.** To calculate the overall polarity of each segment, an aggregation algorithm is applied to the set of polarity values detected in the segment. The average of polarity values is calculated and assigned as the score of the segment, ranging from -1 (strong negative) to +1 (strong positive). In addition to this numeric score, discrete nominal values are also assigned (N+, N, NEU, P, P+). When there are no polarity units, the segment is assigned with a polarity value of NONE. The aggregation algorithm performs an outlier filtering to try to reduce the effect of wrong detections, based on a threshold over the standard deviation from the average.

7. **Global text scoring**. The same aggregation algorithm is applied to the local polarity values of each segment to calculate the global polarity value of the text, represented by an average value (both numeric and nominal values).

Although unconstrained runs were allowed to use the training corpus for improving the model, we were interested on not doing so, as we pointed out in the introduction, to compare the robustness of both models.

For the purpose of both subtasks, the provided output was adapted so that P+ and P were grouped into positive and similarly N+ and N into negative. In subtask B, the global polarity was directly used as the output, whereas in subtask A, the polarity assigned to each text fragment was the polarity value of the segment in which this text fragment is located. As compared to the constrained task, this allows a more fine-grained assignment of polarity and, expectedly, achieve a better evaluation.

Although we had different models available, some developed for specific domains such as the financial, telecommunications and tourism domains, for this task, a general-purpose model for English was used. This model was initially based on the linguistic resources provided by General Inquirer[3] in English. Some information about the model is shown in Table 1.

Unit Type		Count
Negation (NEG)		31
Modifiers (MOD)		117
	--	3
	-	16
	+	75
	++	23
Polarity (POL)		4 606
	N++	81
	N+	297
	N	2 222
	N-	221
	N--	13
	P--	6
	P-	82
	P	1 340
	P+	316
	P++	28
Stopwords (SW)		59
Macros		19
TOTAL UNITS		4 832

Table 1. English semantic model.

[3] http://www.wjh.harvard.edu/~inquirer

4 Results

We submitted two runs, constrained and unconstrained, for each subtask, so four runs in all. As defined by the organization, the evaluation metric was the average F-measure (averaged F-positive and F-negative, ignoring F-neutral). Separate rankings for several test dataset were also produced for comparing different scenarios.

Results achieved for runs in subtask A are shown in Table 2.

Run	A	B	C	D	E	Avg
DAEDALUS-A-constrained	61.0	63.9	**67.4**	61.0	45.3	59.7
DAEDALUS-A-unconstrained	58.7	56.0	**62.0**	58.1	49.2	56.7
Average	77.1	77.4	**80.0**	76.8	68.3	75.9
NRC-Canada-A-constrained (best run)	85.5	88.0	**90.1**	86.6	77.1	85.5

A=LiveJournal 2014, B=SMS 2013, C=Twitter 2013
D=Twitter 2014, E=Twitter 2014 Sarcasm

Table 2. Results for subtask A.

We did not specifically the contextual polarity classification in subtask A, so results are not good. The machine learning classifier achieved a slightly better result on average for all test corpus than the lexicon-based model, as expected, about a 5% improvement. As compared to other participants, we rank the second-to-last group (19 out of 20) and our best experiment is 27% below the average, and 43% below the best run.

The best test set for our experiments is the Twitter 2013 corpus, as it is the most similar to the training corpus. If Twitter 2014 Sarcasm corpus is removed from the evaluation, which clearly is the most difficult set for all runs, the constrained run is only 22% below the average and 38% below the best run, so a relative improvement against the others.

Run	A	B	C	D	E	Avg
DAEDALUS-B-constrained	40.8	**40.9**	36.6	33.0	29.0	36.1
DAEDALUS-B-unconstrained	**61.0**	55.0	59.0	57.6	35.2	53.6
Average	**63.5**	55.6	59.8	60.4	45.4	57.0
TeamX-B-constrained (best run)	69.4	57.4	**72.1**	71.0	56.5	65.3

A=LiveJournal 2014, B=SMS 2013, C=Twitter 2013
D=Twitter 2014, E=Twitter 2014 Sarcasm

Table 3. Results for subtask B.

On the other hand, results achieved for runs in subtask B are shown in Table 3. The subtask was a bit more difficult than the first one, and results are in general worse than in the first subtask, as more difficult aspects arise in the global polarity assignment, such as the appearance of coordinated or subordinated clauses or a higher impact of negation.

We think that the specific consideration of these issues is the main reason why in this case our best run is the lexicon-based model, with an improvement of 48 % over the constrained run.

Also results are more robust as they are more consistent for the different test sets. The best results are achieved for the LiveJournal 2014 corpus, which presumably contains longer texts with more formal writing corpus, so benefiting with the use of the advanced linguistic preprocessing.

Comparing to other participants, we rank 29 out of 42 groups, and our best experiment is just 6% below the average, and 22% below the best run. If, again, the worst set, the Twitter 2014 Sarcasm corpus, is removed from the evaluation, our unconstrained run is around the average (2% below), and, a bit surprisingly, the best group changes to the one that submitted the best run in subtask A, and our experiment is just 23% below (comparing to 38% below in subtask A).

5 Conclusions and Future Work

Our main conclusion after our first participation in SemEval is that, although results are not good compared to the best ranked participants, our lexicon-based model, externally developed for a generic sentiment analysis task, without any adaptation to the provided training corpus, and currently in production, is robust and achieves a balanced evaluation result for message polarity along the different test corpus analyzed. Despite of the difficulty of the task, results are valuable and validate the fact that this technology is ready to be included into an automated workflow process for social media mining.

Due to lack of time, no error analysis has been carried out yet by studying the confusion matrix for the different categories, which is left as short-term future work. We expect to get a better understanding of the miss classifications of our system and find a way to solve the issues that may arise. Probably there is still much to do in both the enlargement of the semantic resources and also the improvement of the linguistic processing (specially building the sentence syntactic tree) in a general domain for a non-formal writing style.

Acknowledgements

This work has been supported by several Spanish R&D projects: *Ciudad2020: Hacia un nuevo modelo de ciudad inteligente sostenible* (INNPRONTA IPT-20111006), MA2VICMR: *Improving the Access, Analysis and Visibility of Multilingual and Multimedia Information in Web* (S2009/TIC-1542) and MULTIMEDICA: *Multilingual Information Extraction in Health Domain and Application to Scientific and Informative Documents* (TIN2010-20644-C03-01).

References

CLEF. 2014. CLEF Initiative (Conference and Labs of the Evaluation Forum). http://www.clef-initiative.eu/

NTCIR. 2014. NII Testbeds and Community for Information Access Research. http://research.nii.ac.jp/ntcir/

Julio Villena-Román, Sara Lana-Serrano and José C. González-Cristóbal. 2008. MIRACLE at NTCIR-7 MOAT: First Experiments on Multilingual Opinion Analysis. 7th NTCIR Workshop Meeting. Evaluation of Information Access Technologies: Information Retrieval, Question Answering and Cross-Lingual Information Access. Tokyo, Japan, December 2008.

Julio Villena-Román, Sara Lana-Serrano, Cristina Moreno-García, Janine García-Morera, José Carlos González-Cristóbal. 2012. DAEDALUS at RepLab 2012: Polarity Classification and Filtering on Twitter Data. CLEF 2012 Labs and Workshop Notebook Papers. Rome, Italy, September 2012.

Daedalus. 2014. http://www.daedalus.es/

G. Salton, A. Wong, and C. S. Yang. 1975. A vector space model for automatic indexing, Communications of the ACM, v.18 n.11, p.613-620, Nov. 1975.

Textalytics. 2014. Meaning as a service. http://textalytics.com/home.

Textalytics Parser API. 2014. Lemmatization, PoS and Parsing v1.2. http://textalytics.com/core/parser-info

Textalytics Sentiment API. 2014. Sentiment Analysis v1.1. http://textalytics.com/core/sentiment-info

M. Hall, E. Frank, G. Holmes, B. Pfahringer, P. Reutemann, and I.H. Witten. 2009. The WEKA Data Mining Software: An Update. SIGKDD Explorations, Volume 11, Issue 1.

DCU: Aspect-based Polarity Classification for SemEval Task 4

Joachim Wagner, Piyush Arora, Santiago Cortes, Utsab Barman
Dasha Bogdanova, Jennifer Foster and Lamia Tounsi
CNGL Centre for Global Intelligent Content
National Centre for Language Technology
School of Computing
Dublin City University
Dublin, Ireland
{jwagner,parora,scortes,ubarman}@computing.dcu.ie
{dbogdanova,jfoster,ltounsi}@computing.dcu.ie

Abstract

We describe the work carried out by DCU on the Aspect Based Sentiment Analysis task at SemEval 2014. Our team submitted one constrained run for the restaurant domain and one for the laptop domain for sub-task B (aspect term polarity prediction), ranking highest out of 36 systems on the restaurant test set and joint highest out of 32 systems on the laptop test set.

1 Introduction

This paper describes DCU's participation in the Aspect Term Polarity sub-task of the Aspect Based Sentiment Analysis task at SemEval 2014, which focuses on predicting the sentiment polarity of aspect terms for a restaurant and a laptop dataset. Given, for example, the sentence *I have had so many problems with the computer* and the aspect term *the computer*, the task is to predict whether the sentiment expressed towards the aspect term is *positive*, *negative*, *neutral* or *conflict*.

Our polarity classification system uses supervised machine learning with support vector machines (SVM) (Boser et al., 1992) to classify an aspect term into one of the four classes. The features we employ are word n-grams (with n ranging from 1 to 5) in a window around the aspect term, as well as features derived from scores assigned by a sentiment lexicon. Furthermore, to reduce data sparsity, we experiment with replacing sentiment-bearing words in our n-gram feature set with their polarity scores according to the lexicon and/or their part-of-speech tag.

The paper is organised as follows: in Section 2, we describe the sentiment lexicons used in this work and detail the process by which they are combined, filtered and extended; in Section 3, we describe our baseline method, a heuristic approach which makes use of the sentiment lexicon, followed by our machine learning method which incorporates the rule-based method as features in addition to word n-gram features; in Section 4, we present the results of both methods on the training and test data, and perform an error analysis on the test set; in Section 5, we compare our approach to previous research in sentiment classification; Section 6 discusses efficiency of our system and ongoing work to improve its speed; finally, in Section 7, we conclude and provide suggestions as to how this research could be fruitfully extended.

2 Sentiment Lexicons

The following four lexicons are employed:

1. **MPQA**[1] (Wilson et al., 2005) classifies a word or a stem and its part of speech tag into positive, negative, both or neutral with a strong or weak subjectivity.
2. **SentiWordNet**[2] (Baccianella et al., 2010) specifies the positive, negative and objective scores of a synset and its part of speech tag.
3. **General Inquirer**[3] indicates whether a word expresses positive or negative sentiment.
4. **Bing Liu's Opinion Lexicon**[4] (Hu and Liu,

[1] http://mpqa.cs.pitt.edu/lexicons/subj_lexicon/

[2] http://sentiwordnet.isti.cnr.it/

[3] http://www.wjh.harvard.edu/~inquirer/inqtabs.txt

[4] http://www.cs.uic.edu/~liub/FBS/sentiment-analysis.html#lexicon

Proceedings of the 8th International Workshop on Semantic Evaluation (SemEval 2014), pages 223–229,
Dublin, Ireland, August 23-24, 2014.

2004) indicates whether a word expresses positive or negative sentiment.

2.1 Lexicon Combination

Since the four lexicons differ in their level of detail and in how they present information, it is necessary, when combining them, to consolidate the information and present it in a uniform manner. Our combination strategy assigns a sentiment score to a word as follows:

- **MPQA:** 1 for strong positive subjectivity, -1 for strong negative subjectivity, 0.5 for weak positive subjectivity, -0.5 for weak negative subjectivity, and 0 otherwise
- **SentiWordNet:** The positive score if the positive score is greater than the negative and objective scores, the negative score if the negative score is greater than the positive and the objective scores, and 0 otherwise
- **General Inquirer and Bing Liu's Opinion Lexicon:** 1 for positive and -1 for negative

The above four scores are summed to arrive at a final score between -4 and 4 for a word.[5]

2.2 Lexicon Filtering

Initial experiments with our sentiment lexicon and the training data led us to believe that there were many irrelevant entries that, although capable of conveying sentiment in some other context, were not contributing to the sentiment of aspect terms in the two domains of the task. Therefore, these words are manually filtered from the lexicon. Examples of deleted words are *just*, *clearly*, *indirectly*, *really* and *back*.

2.3 Adding Domain-Specific Words

A manual inspection of the training data revealed words missing from the merged sentiment lexicon but which do express sentiment in these domains. Examples are *mouthwatering*, *watery* and *better-configured*. We add these to the lexicon with a score of either 1 or -1 (depending on their polarity in the training data). We also add words (e.g. *zesty, acrid*) from an online list of culinary terms.[6]

[5]We also tried to vote over the four lexicon scores but this did not improve over summing.

[6]`http://world-food-and-wine.com/describing-food`

2.4 Handling Variation

In order to ensure that all inflected forms of a word are covered, we lemmatise the words in the training data using the IMS TreeTagger (Schmid, 1994) and we construct new possibilities using a suffix list. To correct misspelled words, we consider the corrected form of a misspelled word to be the form with the highest frequency in a reference corpus[7] among all the forms within an edit distance of 1 and 2 from the misspelled word (Norvig, 2012). Multi-word expressions of the form *x-y* are added with the polarity of *xy* or *x*, as in *laid-back/laidback* and *well-shaped/well*. Expressions *x y*, are added with the polarity of *x-y*, as in *so so/so-so*.

3 Methodology

We first build a rule-based system which classifies the polarity of an aspect term based solely on the scores assigned by the sentiment lexicon. We then explore different ways of converting the rule-based system into features which can then be combined with bag-of-n-gram features in a supervised machine learning set-up.

3.1 Rule-Based Approach

In order to predict the polarity of an aspect term, we sum the polarity scores of all the words in the surrounding sentence according to our sentiment lexicon. Since not all the sentiment words occurring in a sentence influence the polarity of the aspect term to the same extent, it is important to weight the score of each sentiment word by its distance to the aspect term. Therefore, for each word in the sentence which is found in our lexicon we take the score from the lexicon and divide it by its distance to the aspect term. The distance is calculated using the sum of the following three distance functions:

- **Token Distance**: This function calculates the difference in the position of the sentiment word and the aspect term by counting the tokens between them.

[7]The reference corpus consists of about a million words retrieved from several public domain books from Project Gutenberg (`http://www.gutenberg.org/`), lists of most frequent words from Wiktionary (`http://en.wiktionary.org/wiki/Wiktionary:Frequency_lists`) and the British National Corpus (`http://www.kilgarriff.co.uk/bnc-readme.html`) and two thousand laptop reviews crawled from CNET (`http://www.cnet.com/`).

- **Discourse Chunk Distance**: This function counts the discourse chunks that must be crossed in order to get from the sentiment word to the aspect term. If the sentiment word and the aspect term are in the same discourse chunk, then the distance is zero. We use the discourse segmenter described in (Tofiloski et al., 2009).
- **Dependency Path Distance**: This function calculates the shortest path between the sentiment word and the aspect term in a syntactic dependency graph for the sentence, produced by parsing the sentence with a PCFG-LA parser (Attia et al., 2010) trained on consumer review data (Le Roux et al., 2012)[8], and converting the resulting phrase-structure tree into a dependency graph using the Stanford converter (de Marneffe and Manning, 2008) (version 3.3.1).

Since our lexicon also contains multi-word expressions such as *finger licking*, we also look up bigrams and trigrams from the input sentence in our lexicon. Negation is handled by reversing the polarity of sentiment words that appear within a window of three words of the following negators: *not*, *n't*, *no* and *never*.

For each aspect term, we use the distance-weighted sum of the polarity scores to predict one of the three classes *positive*, *negative* and *neutral*.[9] After experimenting with various thresholds we settled on the following simple strategy: if the polarity score for an aspect term is greater than zero then it is classified as positive, if the score is less than zero, then it is classified as negative, otherwise it is classified as neutral.

3.2 Machine Learning Approach

We train a four-way SVM classifier for each domain (laptop and restaurant), using Weka's SMO implementation (Platt, 1998; Hall et al., 2009).[10]

[8]To facilitate parsing, the data was normalised using the process described in (Le Roux et al., 2012) with minor modifications, e. g. treatment of non-breakable space characters, abbreviations and emoticons. The normalised version of the data was used for all experiments.

[9]We also experimented with classifying aspect terms as *conflict* when the individual scores for positive and negative sentiment were both relatively high. However, this proved unsuccessful.

[10]We also experimented with logistic regression, random forests, k-nearest neighbour, naive Bayes and multi-layer perceptron in Weka, but did not match performance of an SVM trained with default parameters.

Transf.	n	c	n-gram	Freq.
-L—	2	2	cord with	1
AL—	2	2	<aspect> with	56
ALS–	1	4	<negu080>	595
ALSR-	1	4	<negu080>	502
AL—	2	4	and skip	1
ALSR-	2	4	and <negu080>	25
ALSRP	1	4	<negu080>/vb	308

Table 1: 7 of the 2,640 bag-of-n-gram features extracted for the aspect term *cord* from the laptop training sentence *I charge it at night and skip taking the cord with me because of the good battery life*. The last column shows the frequency of the feature in the training data. Transformations: A=aspect, L=lowercase, S=score, R=restricted to certain POS, P=POS annotation

Our system submission uses bag-of-n-gram features and features derived from the rule-based approach. Decisions about parameters are made in 5-fold cross-validation on the training data provided for the task.

3.2.1 Bag-of-N-gram Features

We extract features encoding the presence of specific lower-cased n-grams (L) ($n = 1, ..., 5$) in the context of the aspect term to be classified (c words to the left and c words to the right with $c = 1, ..., 5, \text{inf}$) for 10 combinations of transformations: replacement of the aspect term with <ASPECT> (A), replacement of sentiment words with a discretised score (S), restriction (R) of the sentiment word replacement to certain parts-of-speech, and annotation of the discretised score with the POS (P) of the sentiment word. An example is shown in Table 1.

3.2.2 Adding Rule-Based Score Features

We explore two approaches for incorporating information from the rule-based approach (Section 3.1) into our SVM classifier. The first approach is to encode polarity scores directly as the following four features:

1. distance-weighted sum of scores of positive words in the sentence
2. distance-weighted sum of scores of negative words in the sentence
3. number of positive words in the sentence

4. number of negative words in the sentence

The second approach is less direct: for each domain, we train J48 decision trees with minimum leaf size 60 using the four rule-based features described above. We then use the decision rules and the conjunctions leading from the root node to each leaf node to binarise the above four basic score features, producing 122 features. Furthermore, we add normalised absolute values, rank of values and interval indicators, producing 48 features.

3.2.3 Submitted Runs

We eliminate features that have redundant value columns for the training data, and we apply frequency thresholds (13, 18, 25 and 35) to further reduce the number of features. We perform a grid-search to optimise the parameters C and γ of the SVM RBF kernel. We choose the system to submit based on average cross-validation accuracy. We experiment with combinations of the three feature sets described above. We choose the binarised features over the raw rule-based scores because cross-validation results are inferior for the rule-based scores in initial experiments with feature frequency threshold 35: 70.26 vs. 71.36 for laptop and 72.06 vs. 72.15 for restaurant. Therefore, we decide to focus on systems with binarised score features for lower feature frequency thresholds, which are more CPU-intensive to train. For both domains, the system we end up submitting is a combination of the n-gram features and the binarised features with parameters $C = 3.981$, $\gamma = 0.003311$ for the laptop data, $C = 1.445$, $\gamma = 0.003311$ for the restaurant data, and a frequency threshold of 13.

4 Results and Analysis

Table 2 shows the training and test accuracy of the task baseline system (Pontiki et al., 2014), a majority baseline classifying everything as positive, our rule-based system and our submitted system. The restaurant domain has a higher accuracy than the laptop domain for all systems, the SVM system outperforms the rule-based system on both domains, and the test accuracy is higher than the training accuracy for all systems in the restaurant domain.

We observe that the majority of our systems' errors fall into the following categories:

Dataset	System	Training	Test
Laptop	Baseline	—	51.1%
Laptop	All positive	41.9%	52.1%
Laptop	Rule-based	65.4%	67.7%
Laptop	SVM	72.3%	70.5%
Restaurant	Baseline	—	64.3%
Restaurant	All positive	58.6%	64.2%
Restaurant	Rule-based	69.5%	77.8%
Restaurant	SVM	72.7%	81.0%

Table 2: Accuracy of the task baseline system, a system classifying everything as positive, our rule-based system and our submitted SVM-based system on train (5-fold cross-validation) and test sets

- **Sentiment not expressed explicitly:** The sentiment cannot be inferred from local lexical and syntactic information, e. g. *The sushi is cut in blocks bigger than my cell phone.*
- **Non-obvious expression of negation:** For example, *The Management was less than accomodating [sic].* The rule-based approach does not capture such cases and there are not enough similar training examples for the SVM to learn to correctly classify them.
- **Conflict cases:** The training data contains too few examples of conflict sentences for the system to learn to detect them.[11]

For the restaurant domain, there are more than fifty cases where the rule-based approach fails to detect sentiment, but the machine learning approach classifies it correctly. Most of these cases contain no sentiment lexicon words, thus the rule-based system marks them as being neutral. However, the machine learning system was able to figure out the correct polarity. Examples of such cases include *Try the rose roll (not on menu)* and *The gnocchi literally melts in your mouth!*. Furthermore, in the laptop domain, a number of the errors made by the rule-based system arise from the ambiguous nature of some lexicon words. For example, the sentence *Only 2 usb ports ... seems kind of ... limited* is misclassified because the word *kind* is considered to be positive.

There are a few cases where the rule-based system outperforms the machine learning one. It happens when a sentence contains a rare word with strong polarity, e. g. the word *heavenly* in *The*

[11]We only classify one test instance as *conflict*.

chocolate raspberry cake is heavenly - not too sweet, but full of flavor.

5 Related Work

The use of supervised machine learning with bag-of-word or bag-of-n-gram feature sets has been a standard approach to the problem of sentiment polarity classification since the seminal work by Pang et al. (2002) on movie review polarity prediction. Heuristic methods which rely on a lexicon of sentiment words have also been widespread and much of the research in this area has been devoted to the unsupervised induction of good quality sentiment indicators (see, for example, Hatzivassiloglou and McKeown (1997) and Turney (2002), and Liu (2010) for an overview). The integration of sentiment lexicon scores as features in supervised machine learning to supplement standard bag-of-n-gram features has also been employed before (see, for example, Bakliwal et al. (2013)). The replacement of training/test words with scores/labels from sentiment lexicons has also been used by Baccianella et al. (2009), who supplement n-grams such as *horrible location* with generalised expressions such as `NEGATIVE` *location*. Linguistic features which capture generalisations at the level of syntax (Matsumoto et al., 2005), semantics (Johansson and Moschitti, 2010) and discourse (Lazaridou et al., 2013) have also been widely applied. In using binarised features derived from the nodes of a decision tree, we are following our recent work which uses the same technique in a different task: quality estimation for machine translation (Rubino et al., 2012; Rubino et al., 2013).

The main novelty in our system lies not in the individual techniques but rather in they way they are combined and integrated. For example, our combination of token/chunk/dependency path distance used to weight the relationship between a sentiment word and the aspect term has – to the best of our knowledge – not been applied before.

6 Efficiency

Building a system for a shared task, we focus solely on the accuracy of the system in all our decisions. For example, we parse all training and test data multiple times using different grammars to increase sentence coverage from 99.87% to 100%.

To offer a more practical system, we work on implementing a simplified, fully automated system that is more efficient. So far, we replaced time-consuming parsing with POS tagging. The system accepts as input and generates as output valid SemEval ABSA XML documents.[12] After extracting the text and the aspect terms from the input, the text is normalised using the process described in Footnote 8. The feature extraction is performed as described in Section 3 with the following modifications:

- The POS information used by the n-gram feature extractor is obtained using the IMS TreeTagger (Schmid, 1994) instead of using the PCFG-LA parser (Attia et al., 2010).
- The distance used by the rule-based approach is the token distance only, instead of a combination of three distance functions.

The sentiment lexicon and the classification models used are described in Sections 2 and 3 respectively.

The test sets containing 800 sentences are POS tagged in less than half a second each. Surprisingly, accuracy of aspect term polarity prediction increases to 71.4% (from 70.5% for the submitted system) on the laptop test set, using the same SVM parameters as for the submitted system. However, we see a degradation to 78.8% (from 81.0% for the submitted system) for the restaurant test set. This is an encouraging result as the SVM parameters are not yet fully optimised for the slightly different information and as the remaining modifications to be implemented should not change accuracy any further.

The next bottleneck that needs to be addressed before the system can be used in applications requiring quick responses is the current implementation of the n-gram feature extractor: It enumerates all n-grams (for all context window sizes and n-gram transformations) only to then intersect these features with the list of selected features. For the shared task, this made sense as we initially need all features to make our selection of features, and as we only need to run the feature extractor a few times. For a practical system that has to process new test sets frequently, however, it will be more efficient to check for each selected feature whether the respective event occurs in the input.

[12] We validate documents using the XML schema definition provided on the shared task website.

7 Conclusion

We have described our aspect term polarity prediction system, which employs supervised machine learning using a combination of n-grams and sentiment lexicon features. Although our submitted system performs very well, it is interesting to note that our rule-based system is not that far behind. This suggests that a state-of-the-art system can be build without machine learning and that careful design of the other system components is important. However, the very good performance of our machine-learning-based system also suggests that word n-gram features do provide useful information that is missed by a sentiment lexicon alone, and that it is always worthwhile to perform careful parameter tuning to eke out as much as possible from such an approach.

Future work should investigate how much each system component contributes to the overall performance, e. g. lexicon combination, lemmatisation, spelling correction, other normalisations, negation handling, distance function and n-gram feature transformations. There is also room for improvements in most of these components, e. g. our handling of complex negations. Detection of conflicts also needs more attention. Features indicating the presence of trigger words for negation and conflicts that are currently used only internally in the rule-based component could be added to the SVM feature set. It would also be interesting to see how the compositional approach described by Socher et al. (2013) handles these difficult cases. The score features could be easily augmented by breaking down scores by the four employed lexicons. This way, the SVM can choose to combine the information from these scores differently than just summing them, allowing it to learn more complex relations. Lexicon filtering and addition of domain-specific entries could be automated to reduce the time needed to adjust to a new domain. Finally, machine learning methods that can efficiently handle large feature sets such as logistic regression should be tried with the full feature set (not applying frequency thresholds).

Acknowledgements

This research is supported by the Science Foundation Ireland (Grant 12/CE/I2267) as part of CNGL (www.cngl.ie) at Dublin City University. The authors wish to acknowledge the DJEI/DES/SFI/HEA Irish Centre for High-End Computing (ICHEC) for the provision of computational facilities and support. We are grateful to Qun Liu and Josef van Genabith for their helpful comments.

References

Mohammed Attia, Jennifer Foster, Deirdre Hogan, Joseph Le Roux, Lamia Tounsi, and Josef van Genabith. 2010. Handling unknown words in statistical latent-variable parsing models for arabic, english and french. In *Proceedings of the NAACL HLT 2010 First Workshop on Statistical Parsing of Morphologically-Rich Languages*, pages 67–75.

Stefano Baccianella, Andrea Esuli, and Fabrizio Sebastiani. 2009. Multi-facet rating of product reviews. In *Proceedings of ECIR*, pages 461–472.

Stefano Baccianella, Andrea Esuli, and Fabrizio Sebastiani. 2010. SentiWordNet 3.0: An Enhanced Lexical Resource for Sentiment Analysis and Opinion Mining. In *Proceedings of the Seventh Conference on International Language Resources and Evaluation (LREC'10)*.

Akshat Bakliwal, Jennifer Foster, Jennifer van der Puil, Ron O'Brien, Lamia Tounsi, and Mark Hughes. 2013. Sentiment analysis of political tweets: Towards an accurate classifier. In *Proceedings of the NAACL Workshop on Language Analysis in Social Media*, pages 49–58.

Bernhard E. Boser, Isabelle M. Guyon, and Vladimir N. Vapnik. 1992. A training algorithm for optimal margin classifiers. In *Proceedings of the Fifth Annual Workshop on Computational Learning Theory*, pages 144–152.

Marie-Catherine de Marneffe and Christopher D. Manning. 2008. The stanford typed dependencies representation. In *COLING 2008 Workshop on Cross-framework and Cross-domain Parser Evaluation.*, pages 1–8.

Mark Hall, Eibe Frank, Geoffrey Holmes, Bernhard Pfahringer, Peter Reutemann, and Ian H. Witten. 2009. The WEKA data mining software: an update. *ACM SIGKDD Explorations Newsletter*, 11(1):10–18.

Vasileios Hatzivassiloglou and Kathleen R. McKeown. 1997. Predicting the semantic orientation of adjectives. In *Proceedings of the 35th Annual Meeting of the ACL and the 8th Conference of the European Chapter of the ACL*, pages 174–181.

Minqing Hu and Bing Liu. 2004. Mining and summarizing customer reviews. In *Proceedings of the Tenth ACM SIGKDD International Conference on Knowledge Discovery and Data Mining*, KDD '04, pages 168–177.

Richard Johansson and Alessandro Moschitti. 2010. Syntactic and semantic structure for opinion expression detection. In *Proceedings of the Fourteenth Conference on Computational Natural Language Learning*, pages 67–76.

Angeliki Lazaridou, Ivan Titov, and Caroline Sporleder. 2013. A bayesian model for joint unsupervised induction of sentiment, aspect and discourse representations. In *Proceedings of the 51th Annual Meeting of the Association for Computational Linguistics*, pages 1630–1639.

Joseph Le Roux, Jennifer Foster, Joachim Wagner, Rasul Samad Zadeh Kaljahi, and Anton Bryl. 2012. DCU-Paris13 systems for the SANCL 2012 shared task. Notes of the First Workshop on Syntactic Analysis of Non-Canonical Language (SANCL).

Bing Liu. 2010. Sentiment analysis and subjectivity. In *Handbook of Natural Language Processing*.

Shotaro Matsumoto, Hiroya Takamura, and Manubu Okumura, 2005. *Advances in Knowledge Discovery and Data Mining*, volume 3518 of *Lecture Notes in Computer Science*, chapter Sentiment Classification Using Word Sub-sequences and Dependency Subtrees, pages 301–311.

Peter Norvig. 2012. How to write a spelling corrector. `http://norvig.com/spell-correct.html`. [Online; accessed 2014-03-19].

Po Pang, Lillian Lee, and Shivakumar Vaithyanathan. 2002. Thumbs up?: sentiment classification using machine learning techniques. In *Proceedings of EMNLP*, pages 79–86.

John C. Platt. 1998. Fast training of support vector machines using sequential minimal optimization. In B. Schoelkopf, C. Burges, and A. Smola, editors, *Advances in Kernel Methods - Support Vector Learning*, pages 185–208.

Maria Pontiki, Dimitrios Galanis, John Pavlopoulos, Harris Papageorgiou, Ion Androutsopoulos, and Suresh Manandhar. 2014. Semeval-2014 task 4: Aspect based sentiment analysis. In *Proceedings of the International Workshop on Semantic Evaluation (SemEval)*.

Raphael Rubino, Jennifer Foster, Joachim Wagner, Johann Roturier, Rasul Samad Zadeh Kaljahi, and Fred Hollowood. 2012. Dcu-symantec submission for the wmt 2012 quality estimation task. In *Proceedings of the Seventh Workshop on Statistical Machine Translation*, pages 138–144.

Raphael Rubino, Joachim Wagner, Jennifer Foster, Johann Roturier, Rasoul Samad Zadeh Kaljahi, and Fred Hollowood. 2013. DCU-Symantec at the WMT 2013 quality estimation shared task. In *Proceedings of the Eighth Workshop on Statistical Machine Translation*, pages 392–397.

Helmut Schmid. 1994. Probabilistic part-of-speech tagging using decision trees. In *Proceedings of the International Conference on New Methods in Language Processing*, pages 44–49.

Richard Socher, Alex Perelygin, Jean Y. Wu, Jason Chuang, Christopher D. Manning, Andrew Y. Ng, and Christopher Potts. 2013. Recursive deep models for semantic compositionality over a sentiment treebank. In *Proceedings of EMNLP*, pages 1631–1642.

Milan Tofiloski, Julian Brooke, and Maite Taboada. 2009. A syntactic and lexical-based discourse segmenter. In *Proceedings of the ACL-IJCNLP 2009 Conference Short Papers*, ACLShort '09, pages 77–80.

Peter Turney. 2002. Thumbs up or thumbs down? semantic orientation applied to unsupervised classification of reviews. In *Proceedings of the ACL*, pages 417–424.

Theresa Wilson, Janyce Wiebe, and Paul Hoffmann. 2005. Recognizing contextual polarity in phrase-level sentiment analysis. In *Proceedings of the Conference on Human Language Technology and Empirical Methods in Natural Language Processing*, HLT '05, pages 347–354.

DIT: Summarisation and Semantic Expansion in Evaluating Semantic Similarity

Magdalena Kacmajor
IBM Technology Campus
Dublin Software Lab
Ireland
magdalena.kacmajor@ie.ibm.com

John D. Kelleher
Applied Intelligence Research Centre
Dublin Institute of Technology
Ireland
john.d.kelleher@dit.ie

Abstract

This paper describes an approach to implementing a tool for evaluating semantic similarity. We investigated the potential benefits of (1) using text summarisation to narrow down the comparison to the most important concepts in both texts, and (2) leveraging WordNet information to increase usefulness of cosine comparisons of short texts. In our experiments, text summarisation using a graph-based algorithm did not prove to be helpful. Semantic and lexical expansion based upon word relationships defined in WordNet increased the agreement of cosine similarity values with human similarity judgements.

1 Introduction

This paper describes a system that addresses the problem of assessing semantic similarity between two different-sized texts. The system has been applied to SemEval-2014 Task 3, Cross-Level Semantic Similarity (Jurgens et al, 2014). The application is limited to a single comparison type, that is, paragraph to sentence.

The general approach taken can be characterised as text summarisation followed by a process of semantic expansion and finally similarity computation using cosine similarity.

The rationale for applying summarisation is to focus the comparison on the most important elements of the text by selecting key words to be used in the similarity comparison. This summarisation approach is based on the assumption that if summary of a paragraph is similar to the summary sentence paired with the paragraph in the task dataset, then the original paragraph and sentence pair must have been similar and so should receive a high similarity rating.

The subsequent semantic expansion is intended to counteract the problem arising from the small size of both compared text units. The similarity metric used by the system is essentially a function of word overlap. However, because both the paragraphs and sentences being compared are relatively short, the probability of a word overlap - even between semantically similar texts - is quite small. Therefore prior to estimating the similarity between the texts we extend the word vectors created by the summarisation process with the synonyms and other words semantically and lexically related to the words occurring in the text.

By using cosine similarity measure, we normalize the lengths of word vectors representing different-sized documents (paragraphs and sentences).

The rest of the paper is organized as follows: section 2 describes the components of the system in more detail; section 3 describes parameters used in the experiments we conducted and presents our results; and section 4 provides concluding remarks.

2 System Description

2.1 Overview

There are four main stages in the system processing pipeline: (1) text pre-processing; (2) summarisation; (3) semantic expansion; (4) computing the similarity scores. In the following sections we describe each of these stages in turn.

2.2 Pre-processing

Paragraphs and sentences are tokenized and annotated using Stanford CoreNLP[1]. The annotations include part-of-speech (POS), lemmatisation, dependency parse and coreference resolution. Then

[1]http://nlp.stanford.edu/software/corenlp.shtml

Proceedings of the 8th International Workshop on Semantic Evaluation (SemEval 2014), pages 230–234,
Dublin, Ireland, August 23-24, 2014.

the following processes are applied: (a) **Token selection**, the system ignores tokens with POS other than nouns, adjectives and verbs (in our experiments we tested various combinations of these three categories); (b) **Token merging**, the criteria for merging can be more restrictive (same word form) or less restrictive – based on same lemma, or even same lemma ignoring POS; (c) **Stopword removal**, we apply a customized stopword list to exclude verbs that have very general meaning.

In this way, each text unit is processed to produce a filtered set of tokens which at the next step can be directly transformed into nodes in the graph representation of the text. Dependency and coreference annotations will be used for defining edges in the graph.

2.3 Summarisation system

Summarisation has been implemented using TextRank (Mihalcea and Tarau, 2004), an iterative graph-based ranking algorithm derived from PageRank (Brin and Page, 1998).

The ranking is based on the following principle: when node *i* links to node *j*, a vote is cast that increases the rank of node *j*. The strength of the vote depends on the importance (rank) of the casting node, thus the algorithm is run iteratively until the ranks stop changing beyond a given threshold, or until a specified limit of iterations is reached.

To apply this algorithm to paragraphs and sentences, our system builds a graph representation for each of these text units, with nodes representing the tokens selected and merged at the preceding stage. The nodes are connected by co-occurrence (Mihalcea and Tarau, 2004), dependency and/or coreference relations. Next, a unweighted or weighted version of the ranking algorithm is iterated until convergence.

For each test unit, the output of the summariser is a list of words sorted by rank. Depending on the experimental setup, the summariser forwards on all processed words, or only a subset of top-ranked words.

2.4 Lexico-semantic expansion

For each word returned from the summariser, we retrieve all (or a predetermined number of) synsets that have this word as a member. For each retrieved synset, we also identify synsets related through semantic and lexical relations. Finally, using all these synsets we create the synonym group for a word that includes all the members of these synsets.

If a word has many different senses, then the synonym group grows large, and the chances that the sense of a given member of this large group will match the sense of the original word are shrinking. To account for this fact, each member of the synonym group is assigned a weight using Equation 1. This weight is simply 1 divided by the count of the number of words in the synonym group.

$$synweight = \frac{1}{\#SynonymGroup} \quad (1)$$

At the end of this process for each document we have the set of words that occurred in the document, and each of these words has a synonym group associated with it. All of the members of the synonym groups have a weight value.

2.5 Similarity comparison

Cosine similarity is used to compute the similarity for each paragraph-sentence pair. For this calculation each text (paragraph or sentence) is represented by a bag-of-words vector containing all the words derived from the text together with their synonym groups.

The bag-of-words can be binary or frequency based, with the counts optionally modified by the word ranks. The counts for words retrieved from WordNet are weighted with *synweights*, which means that they are usually represented by very small numbers. However, if a match is found between a WordNet word and a word observed in the document, the weight of both is adjusted according to semantic match rules. These rules have been established empirically, and are presented in section 3.3.1.

The cosine values for each paragraph-sentence pair are not subject to any further processing.

3 Experiments

3.1 Dataset

All experiments were carried out on training dataset provided by SemEval-2014 Task 3 for paragraph to sentence comparisons.

3.2 Parameters

For each stage in the pipeline, there is a set of parameters whose values influence the final results. Each set of parameters will be discussed next.

3.2.1 Pre-processing parameters

The parameters used for pre-processing determine the type and number of nodes included in the graph:

- **POS**: Parts-of-speech that are allowed into the graph, e.g. only nouns and verbs, or nouns, verbs and adjectives.
- **Merging criteria**: The principle by which we decide whether two tokens should be represented by the same node in the graph.
- **Excluded verbs**: The contents of the stop-word list.

3.2.2 Summarisation parameters

These parameters control the structure of the graph and the results yielded by TextRank algorithm. The types of nodes in the graph are already decided at the pre-processing stage.

- **Relation type**: In order to link the nodes (words) in the graph representation of a document, we use co-occurrence relations (Mihalcea and Tarau, 2004), dependency relations and coreference relations. The two latter are defined based on the Stanford CoreNLP annotations, whereas a co-occurrence edge is created when two words appear in the text within a word span of a specified length. The co-occurrence relation comes with two additional parameters:
  - **Window size**: Maximum number of words constituting the span.
  - **Window application**: The window can be applied before or after filtering away tokens of unwanted POS, i.e. we can require either the co-occurrence within the original text or in the filtered text.
- **Graph type**: A document can be represented as an unweighted or weighted graph. In the second case we use a weighted version of TextRank algorithm (Mihalcea and Tarau, 2004) in which the strength of a vote depends both on the rank of the casting node and on the weight of the link producing the vote.
  - **Edge weights**: In general, the weight of an edge between any two nodes depends on the number of identified relations, but we also experimented with assigning different weights depending on the relation type.
- **Normalisation**: This parameter refers to normalising word ranks computed for the longer and the shorter text unit.
- **Word limit**: The maximum number of top-ranked words included in vector representation of the longer text. May be equal to the number of words in the shorter of the two compared texts, or fixed at some arbitrary value.

3.2.3 Semantic extension parameters

The following factors regulate the impact of additional words retrieved from WordNet:

- **Synset limit**: The maximum number of synsets (word senses) retrieved from WordNet per each word. Can be controlled by word ranks returned from the summariser.
- **Synonym limit**: The maximum number of synonyms (per synset) added to vector representation of the document. Can be controlled by word ranks.
- **WordNet relations**: The types of semantic and lexical relations used to acquire additional synsets.

3.2.4 Similarity comparison parameters

- **Bag-of-words model**: The type of bag-of-word used for cosine comparisons.
- **Semantic match weights**: The rules for adjusting weights of WordNet words that match observed words from the other vector.

3.3 Results

The above parameters in various combinations were applied in an extensive series of experiments. Contrary to our expectations, the results indicate that the summariser has either no impact or has a negative effect. Table 1 presents the set of parameters that seem to have impact, and the values that resulted in best scores, as calculated by SemEval Task 3 evaluation tool against the training dataset.

3.3.1 Discussion

In the course of experiments we consistently observed higher performance when all words from both compared documents were included, as opposed to selecting top-ranked words from the longer document. Furthermore, less restrictive criteria for merging tended to give better results.

Parameter	Value
Word limit	no limit
POS	JJ, NN, V
Merging criteria	lemma, ignore POS
Custom stopword list	yes
Synset limit	15
Synonym limit	no limit
WordNet relations	similar to, pertainym, hypernym
Bag-of-words model	binary

Table 1: Parameter values yielding the best scores.

We noticed clear improvement after extending word vectors with synonyms and related words. WordNet relations that contributed most are *similar to*, *hypernym* (ISA relation), *pertainym* (relational adjective) and *derivationally related form*. The results obtained before and after applying summarisation and lexico-semantic expansion (while keeping other parameters fixed at values reported in Table 1) are shown in Table 2.

Word ranks \ Expansion	No	Yes
Ignored	0.728	**0.755**
Used to select top-rank words	0.690	0.716
Used to control synset limit	N/A	0.752
Used to weight vector counts	0.694	N/A

Table 2: The effects of applying text summarisation and lexico-semantic expansion.

Table 3 summarises the most efficient rules for adjusting weights in word vectors when a match has been found between an observed word from one vector and a WordNet word in the other vector. The rules are as follows: (1) If the match is between an observed word from the paragraph vector and a WordNet word from the sentence vector, the weight of both is set to 0.25; (2) If the match is between an observed word from the sentence vector and the WordNet word from the paragraph vector, the weight of both is set to 0.75; (3) If the match is between two WordNet words, one from the paragraph and one from the sentence, the weight of both is set to whichever *synweight* is higher; (4) If the match is between two observed words, the weight of both is set to 1.

We received slightly better results after setting a limit on the number of included word senses, and

Paragr. \ Sent.	Obs. word	WordNet word
Observed word	1.0	0.25
WordNet word	0.75	max(synweight)

Table 3: Optimal weights for semantic match.

after ignoring a few verbs with particularly broad meaning.

3.3.2 Break-down into categories

Pearson correlation between gold standard and the submitted results was 0.785. Table 4 shows the correlations within each category, both for the test set and the train set. The results are very consistent across datasets, except for *Reviews* which scored much lower with the test data. The overall result was lower with the training data because of higher number of examples in *Metaphoric* category, where the performance of our system was extremely poor.

Category	Test data	Train data
newswire	0.907	0.926
cqa	0.778	0.779
metaphoric	0.099	-0.16
scientific	0.856	-
travel	0.880	0.887
review	0.752	0.884
overall	0.785	0.755

Table 4: Break-down of the results.

4 Conclusions

We described our approach, parameters used in the system, and the results of experiments. Text summarisation didn't prove to be helpful. One possible explanation of the neutral or negative effect of summarisation is the small size of the texts units: with the limited number of words available for comparison, any procedure reducing this already scarce set may be disadvantageous.

The results benefited from adding synonyms and semantically and lexically related words. Lemmatisation and merging same-lemma words regardless the POS, as well as ignoring very general verbs seem to be helpful.

The best performance has been observed in *Newswire* category. Finally, given that the similarity metric used by the system is essentially a function of word overlap between the two texts, it is not surprising that the system struggled with metaphorically related texts.

References

Sergey Brin and Lawrence Page. 1998. The Anatomy of Large-Scale Hypertextual Web Search Engine. In *Computer Networks and ISDN Systems*, 30(1-7):107–117.

Christiane Fellbaum. 1998. WordNet: An Electronic Lexical Database. Cambridge, MA: MIT Press.

David Jurgens, Mohammad Taher Pilehvar, and Roberto Navigli. 2014. SemEval-2014 Task 3: Cross-Level Semantic Similarity. In *Proceedings of the 8th International Workshop on Semantic Evaluation (SemEval-2014)*. August 23-24, 2014, Dublin, Ireland.

Rada Mihalcea and Paul Tarau. 2004. TextRank: Bringing Order into Texts. In *Proceedings of EMNLP 2004*:404–411, Barcelona, Spain.

George A. Miller. 1995. WordNet: A Lexical Database for English. *Communications of the ACM*, Vol. 38, No. 11:39–41.

DLIREC: Aspect Term Extraction and Term Polarity Classification System

Zhiqiang Toh
Institute for Infocomm Research
1 Fusionopolis Way
Singapore 138632
ztoh@i2r.a-star.edu.sg

Wenting Wang
magicwwt@gmail.com

Abstract

This paper describes our system used in the Aspect Based Sentiment Analysis Task 4 at the SemEval-2014. Our system consists of two components to address two of the subtasks respectively: a Conditional Random Field (CRF) based classifier for Aspect Term Extraction (ATE) and a linear classifier for Aspect Term Polarity Classification (ATP). For the ATE subtask, we implement a variety of lexicon, syntactic and semantic features, as well as cluster features induced from unlabeled data. Our system achieves state-of-the-art performances in ATE, ranking 1st (among 28 submissions) and 2rd (among 27 submissions) for the restaurant and laptop domain respectively.

1 Introduction

Sentiment analysis on document and sentence level no longer fulfills user's needs of getting more accurate and precise information. By performing sentiment analysis at the aspect level, we can help users gain more insights on the sentiments of the various aspects of the target entity. Task 4 of SemEval-2014 provides a good platform for (1) aspect term extraction and (2) aspect term polarity classification.

For the first subtask, we follow the approach of Jakob and Gurevych (2010) by modeling term extraction as a sequential labeling task. Specifically, we leverage on semantic and syntactic resources to extract a variety of features and use CRF as the learning algorithm. For the second subtask, we simply treat it as a multi-class classification problem where a linear classifier is learned to predict the polarity class. Our system achieves good performances for the first subtask in both domains, ranking 1st for the restaurant domain, and 2nd for the laptop domain.

The remainder of this paper is structured as follows: In Section 2, we describe our ATE system in detail, including experiments and result analysis. Section 3 describes the general approach of our ATP system. Finally, Section 4 summarizes our work.

2 Aspect Term Extraction

This subtask is to identify the aspects of given target entities in the restaurant and laptop domains. Many aspect terms in the laptop domain contains digits or special characters such as "17 inch screen" and "screen/video resolution"; while in the restaurant domain, aspects in the sentences are specific for a type of restaurants such as "pizza" for Italian restaurants and "sushi" for Japanese restaurants.

We model ATE as a sequential labeling task and extract features to be used for CRF training. Besides the common features used in traditional Named Entity Recognition (NER) systems, we also utilize extensive external resources to build various name lists and word clusters.

2.1 Preprocessing

Following the traditional BIO scheme used in sequential labeling, we assign a label for each word in the sentence, where "B-TERM" indicates the start of an aspect term, "I-TERM" indicates the continuation of an aspect term, and "O" indicates not an aspect term.

All sentences are tokenized and parsed using the Stanford Parser[1]. The parsing information is used

[1] http://nlp.stanford.edu/software/lex-parser.shtml

Proceedings of the 8th International Workshop on Semantic Evaluation (SemEval 2014), pages 235–240,
Dublin, Ireland, August 23-24, 2014.

to extract various syntactic features (e.g. POS, head word, dependency relation) described in the next section.

2.2 General (or Closed) Features

In this section, we describe the features commonly used in traditional NER systems. Such features can easily be extracted from the training set or with the help of publicly available NLP tools (e.g. Stanford Parser, NLTK, etc).

2.2.1 Word

The string of the current token and its lowercase format are used as features. To capture more context information, we also extract the previous and next word strings (in original format) as additional word features.

2.2.2 POS

The part-of-speech (POS) tag of the current token is used as a feature. Since aspect terms are often nouns, the POS tag provides useful information about the lexical category of the word, especially for unseen words in the test sentences.

2.2.3 Head Word

This feature represents the head word of the current token. If the current token does not have a head word, the value "null" is used.

2.2.4 Head Word POS

This feature represents the POS of the head word of the current token. If the current token does not have a head word, the value "null" is used.

2.2.5 Dependency Relation

From the dependency parse, we identify the dependency relations of the current token. We extract two different sets of strings: one set contains the relation strings (e.g. "amod", "nsubj") where the current token is the governor (i.e. head) of the relation, the other set contains the relation strings where the current token is the dependent of the relation. For each set, we only keep certain relations: "amod", "nsubj" and "dep" for the first set and "nsubj", "dobj" and "dep" for the second set. Each set of strings is used as a feature value for the current token, resulting in two separate features.

2.2.6 Name List

Name lists (or gazetteers) have proven to be useful in the task of NER (Ratinov and Roth, 2009). We create a name list feature that uses the name lists for membership testing.

For each domain, we extract two high precision name lists from the training set. For the first list, we collect and keep those aspect terms whose frequency counts are greater than c_1. Since an aspect term can be multi-word, we also extract a second list to consider the counts of individual words. All words whose frequency counts greater than c_2 are collected. For each word, the probability of it being annotated as an aspect word in the training set is calculated. Only those words whose probability value is greater than t is kept in the second list. The specified values of c_1, c_2 and t for each domain are determined using 5-fold cross validation.

2.3 Open/External Sources Generated Features

This section describes additional features we use that require external resources and/or complex processings.

2.3.1 WordNet Taxonomy

This feature represents the set of syntactic categories (e.g "noun.food") of the current token as organized in WordNet lexicographer files (Miller, 1995). We only consider noun synsets of the token when determining the syntactic categories.

2.3.2 Word Cluster

Turian et al. (2010) used unsupervised word representations as extra word features to improve the accuracy of both NER and chunking. We followed their approach by inducing Brown clusters and K-means clusters from in-domain unlabeled data.

We used the review text from two sources of unlabeled dataset: the Multi-Domain Sentiment Dataset that contains Amazon product reviews (Blitzer et al., 2007)[2], and the Yelp Phoenix Academic Dataset that contains user reviews[3].

We induce 1000 Brown clusters for each dataset[4]. For each word in the training/testing set, its corresponding binary (prefix) string is used as the feature value.

We experiment with different prefix lengths and use the best settings using 5-fold cross validation.

[2] We used the unprocessed.tar.gz archive found at `http://www.cs.jhu.edu/~mdredze/datasets/sentiment/`

[3] `http://www.yelp.com/dataset_challenge/`

[4] Brown clustering are induced using the implementation by Percy Liang found at `https://github.com/percyliang/brown-cluster/`.

For the laptop domain, we create a Brown cluster feature from Amazon Brown clusters, using prefix length of 5. For the restaurant domain, we created three Brown cluster features: two from Yelp Brown clusters, using prefix lengths of 4 and 8, and the last one from Amazon Brown clusters, using prefix length of 10.

K-means clusters are induced using the `word2vec` tool (Mikolov et al., 2013)[5]. Similar to Brown cluster feature, the cluster id of each word is used as the feature value.

When running the `word2vec` tool, we specially tune the values for word vector size (size), cluster size (classes) and sub-sampling threshold (sample) for optimum 5-fold cross validation performances. We create one K-means cluster feature for the laptop domain from Amazon K-means clusters (size = 100, classes = 400, sample = 0.0001), and two K-means cluster features for the restaurant domain, one from Yelp K-means clusters (size = 200, classes = 300, sample = 0.001), and the other from Amazon K-means clusters (size = 1000, classes = 300, sample = 0.0001).

2.3.3 Name List Generated using Double Propagation

We implement the Double Propagation (DP) algorithm described in Qiu et al. (2011) to identify possible aspect terms in a semi-supervised way. The terms identified are stored in a list which is used as another name list feature.

Our implementation follow the Logic Programming approach described in Liu et al. (2013)[6]. We write our rules in Prolog and use SWI-Prolog[7] as the solver.

We use the seed opinion lexicon provided by Hu and Liu (2004) for both domain[8]. In addition, for the restaurant domain, we augment the opinion lexicon with addition seed opinion words by using the 75 restaurant seed words listed in Sauper and Barzilay (2013). To increase the coverage, we expand this list of 75 words by including related words (e.g. antonym, similar to) in WordNet. The final expanded list contains 551 words.

Besides the seed opinion words, we also use the last word of each aspect term in the training set as a seed aspect word.

The propagation rules we use are modifications of the rules presented in Liu et al. (2013). A total of 11 rules and 13 rules are used for the laptop and restaurant domain respectively. An example of a Prolog rule concerning the extraction of aspect words is stated below:

```
aspect(A) :-
  relation(nsubj, O, A),
  relation(cop, O, _),
  pos(A, P),
  is_noun(P),
  opinion(O).
```

For example, given the sentence "The rice is amazing.", and "amazing" is a known opinion word, we can extract "rice" as a possible aspect word using the rule.

All our rules can only identify individual words as possible aspect terms. To consider a phrase as a possible aspect term, we extend the left boundary of the identified span to include any consective noun words right before the identified word.

2.4 Algorithms and Evaluation

We use the CRFsuite tool (Okazaki, 2007) to train our CRF model. We use the default settings, except for the negative state features (`-p feature.possible_states=1`).

Feature	F1
Word	0.6641
+ Name List	0.7106
+ POS	0.7237
+ Head Word	0.7280
+ DP Name List	0.7298
+ Word Cluster	0.7430
+ Head Word POS	0.7437
+ Dependency Relation	0.7521

Table 1: 5-fold cross-validation performances on the laptop domain. Each row uses all features added in the previous rows.

2.5 Preliminary Results on Training Set

Table 1 and Table 2 show the 5-fold cross-validation performances after adding each feature group for the laptop and restaurant domain respectively. Most features are included in the optimum feature set for both domains, except for WordNet Taxonomy feature (only used in the restaurant domain) and Dependency Relation feature (only used in the laptop domain).

[5]`https://code.google.com/p/word2vec/`
[6]We did not implement incorrect aspect pruning.
[7]`http://www.swi-prolog.org/`
[8]We ignore the polarity of the opinion word.

	laptop			restaurant		
System	**Precision**	**Recall**	**F1**	**Precision**	**Recall**	**F1**
DLIREC constrained	0.7931	0.6330	0.7041 (C)	0.8404	0.7337	0.7834 (C)
DLIREC unconstrained	0.8190	**0.6713**	0.7378 (U)	0.8535	**0.8272**	**0.8401** (U)
Baseline	0.4432	0.2982	0.3565 (C)	0.5255	0.4277	0.4716 (C)
Ranked 1st	**0.8480**	0.6651	**0.7455** (C)	0.8535	**0.8272**	**0.8401** (U)
Ranked 2nd	0.8190	**0.6713**	0.7378 (U)	**0.8625**	0.8183	0.8398 (C)
Ranked 3rd	0.7931	0.6330	0.7041 (C)	0.8441	0.7637	0.8019 (C)

Table 3: Results of the Aspect Term Extraction subtask. We also indicate whether the system is constrained (C) or unconstrained (U).

Feature	**F1**
Word	0.7541
+ Name List	0.7808
+ POS	0.7951
+ Head Word	0.7962
+ DP Name List	0.8036
+ Word Cluster	0.8224
+ WordNet Taxonomy	0.8252
+ Head Word POS	0.8274

Table 2: 5-fold cross-validation performances on the restaurant domain. Each row uses all features added in the previous rows.

For each domain, we make submissions in both constrained and unconstrained settings. The constrained submission only uses the Word and Name List features, while all features listed in Table 1 and Table 2 are used in the unconstrained submission for the respective domain.

2.6 Results on Test Set

Using the optimum feature set described in Section 2.5, we train separate models for each domain and evaluate them against the SemEval-2014 Task 4 test set[9]. Table 3 presents the official results of our submissions. We also include the official baseline results and the results of the top three participating systems for comparison (Pontiki et al., 2014).

As shown from the table, our system performed well for both domains. For the laptop domain, our system is ranked 2nd and 3rd (among 27 submissions) for the unconstrained and constrained setting respectively. For the restaurant domain, our system is ranked 1st and 9th (among 28 submissions) for the unconstrained and constrained setting respectively.

Our unconstrained submissions for both domains outperformed our constrained submissions, due to a significantly better recall. This indicates the use of additional external resources (e.g. unlabeled data) can improve the extraction performance.

2.7 Further Analysis of Feature Engineering

Table 4 shows the F1 loss on the test set resulting from training with each group of feature removed. We also include the F1 loss when all features are used.

Feature	**laptop**	**restaurant**
Word	0.0260	0.0241
Name List	0.0090	0.0054
POS	-0.0059	-0.0052
Head Word	0.0072	0.0038
DP Name List	0.0049	0.0064
Word Cluster	0.0061	0.0185
WordNet Taxonomy	-	-0.0018
Head Word POS	-0.0040	-0.0011
Dependency Relation	-0.0105	-
All features	-0.0132	0.0014

Table 4: Feature ablation study on the test set. The quantity is the F1 loss resulted from the removal of a single feature group. The last row indicates the F1 loss when all features are used.

Our ablation study showed that a few of our features are helpful in varying degrees on both domains: Word, Name List, Head Word, DP Name List and Word Cluster. However, the use of the rest of the features individually has a negative impact. In particular, we are surprised that the POS and Dependency Relation features are detrimental to the performances, even though our 5-fold

[9] We train each model using only single-domain data.

cross validation experiments suggested otherwise. Another observation we make is that the WordNet Taxonomy feature is actually useful for the laptop test set: including this feature would have improved our laptop unconstrained performance from 0.7378 F1 to 0.7510 F1 (+0.0132), which is better than the top system performance. We also note that our restaurant performance on the test set can potentially be improved from 0.8401 F1 to 0.8454 F1 (+0.0052) if we originally omit the POS feature.

Overall, we see that all the features we proposed are potentially beneficial to the task. However, more thorough feature selection experiments should be conducted to prevent overfitting and to identify the settings (e.g. domain) in which each feature may be useful.

3 Aspect Term Polarity

In this section, we describe a baseline classifier for ATP, where we treat the problem as a multi-class classification problem.

To correctly identify the polarity of an aspect term, it is crucial to know which words within the sentence indicate its sentiment. A general lexicon or WordNet is not sufficient. Thus, we attempt to build the aspect lexicon based on other information such as POS (Sauper and Barzilay, 2013). For example, sentiment words are more likely to be adjectives.

3.1 Features

3.1.1 Aspect Word

This is to model the idea that certain aspects tend to have a particular polarity most of the time. We compute the most frequent polarity of each aspect in the training set. For each aspect instance, the feature corresponding to its most frequent polarity is set to 1.

3.1.2 General Sentiment Word Lexicon

One sentence may express opinions on multiple aspect terms. According to our observations, words surrounding the aspect term tend to be associated with it. Based on the best settings obtained from 5-fold cross validation, we set a window size of 12 words and consider words with the following POS: JJ*, RB*, VB*, DT and NN*[10].

Some sentiment words are consistent across aspects. For example, "great" for positive and "terrible" for negative. On the other hand, some sentiment words are quite distinct between aspects. In certain cases, they may have opposite sentiment meanings for different aspects (Kim et al., 2013). For example, "fast" is positive when describing boot up speed but negative when describing battery life. Therefore, a general sentiment word lexicon is created from the training set.

If a general sentiment word occurs in the surrounding context of the aspect instance, the feature value for the matched sentiment word is 1. Since the training set does not contain every possible sentiment expression, we use synonyms and antonyms in RiTa WordNet[11] to expand the general sentiment word lexicon. The expanded lexicon contains 2419 words for the laptop domain and 4262 words for the restaurant domain.

3.1.3 Aspect-Sentiment Word Pair

Besides general sentiment word lexicon, we also build aspect-sentiment word pair lexicon from the training set. This lexicon contains 9073 word pairs for the laptop domain and 22171 word pairs for the restaurant domain. If an aspect-sentiment word occurs in the surrounding context of the aspect instance, the feature value for the matched aspect-sentiment word pair is 1.

3.2 Experiments and Results

We use LIBLINEAR[12] to train our logistic regression classifier using default settings.

	laptop	restaurant
5-fold cross validation	0.6322	0.6704
DLIREC unconstrained	0.3654	0.4233

Table 5: Accuracy of the Aspect Term Polarity subtask.

Table 5 shows the classification accuracy of our baseline system on the training and test set for each domain. The performance drops a lot in the test set as we use very simple approaches to generate the lexicons. This may cause overfitting on the training set. We also observe that in the test set of both domains, more than half of the instances are positive. In the future, we can explore on using more sophisticated ways to build more effective features and to better model data skewness.

[10]NN* is only used in the restaurant domain.

[11]http://www.rednoise.org/rita/wordnet/

[12]http://www.csie.ntu.edu.tw/~cjlin/liblinear/

4 Conclusion

For ATE subtask, we leverage on the vast amount of external resources to create additional effective features, which contribute significantly to the improvement of our system. For the unconstrained setting, our system is ranked 1st (among 28 submissions) and 2rd (among 27 submissions) for the restaurant and laptop domain respectively. For ATP subtask, we implement a simple baseline system.

Our current work focus on implementing a separate term extraction system for each domain. In future, we hope to investigate on domain adaptation methods across different domains. In addition, we will also address the feature sparseness problem in our ATP baseline system.

Acknowledgements

This research work is supported by a research project under Baidu-I^{2}R Research Centre.

References

John Blitzer, Mark Dredze, and Fernando Pereira. 2007. Biographies, Bollywood, Boom-boxes and Blenders: Domain Adaptation for Sentiment Classification. In *Proceedings of the 45th Annual Meeting of the Association of Computational Linguistics*, pages 440–447, Prague, Czech Republic, June.

Minqing Hu and Bing Liu. 2004. Mining and Summarizing Customer Reviews. In *Proceedings of the Tenth ACM SIGKDD International Conference on Knowledge Discovery and Data Mining*, KDD '04, pages 168–177, New York, NY, USA.

Niklas Jakob and Iryna Gurevych. 2010. Extracting Opinion Targets in a Single and Cross-Domain Setting with Conditional Random Fields. In *Proceedings of the 2010 Conference on Empirical Methods in Natural Language Processing*, pages 1035–1045, Cambridge, MA, October.

Suin Kim, Jianwen Zhang, Zheng Chen, Alice Oh, and Shixia Liu. 2013. A Hierarchical Aspect-Sentiment Model for Online Reviews. In *AAAI Conference on Artificial Intelligence*.

Qian Liu, Zhiqiang Gao, Bing Liu, and Yuanlin Zhang. 2013. A Logic Programming Approach to Aspect Extraction in Opinion Mining. In *Web Intelligence (WI) and Intelligent Agent Technologies (IAT), 2013 IEEE/WIC/ACM International Joint Conferences on*, volume 1, pages 276–283, Nov.

Tomas Mikolov, Wen-tau Yih, and Geoffrey Zweig. 2013. Linguistic Regularities in Continuous Space Word Representations. In *Proceedings of the 2013 Conference of the North American Chapter of the Association for Computational Linguistics: Human Language Technologies*, pages 746–751, Atlanta, Georgia, June.

George A. Miller. 1995. WordNet: A Lexical Database for English. *Commun. ACM*, 38(11):39–41, November.

Naoaki Okazaki. 2007. CRFsuite: a fast implementation of Conditional Random Fields (CRFs).

Maria Pontiki, Dimitrios Galanis, John Pavlopoulos, Harris Papageorgiou, Ion Androutsopoulos, and Suresh Manandhar. 2014. SemEval-2014 Task 4: Aspect Based Sentiment Analysis. In *Proceedings of the 8th International Workshop on Semantic Evaluation (SemEval 2014)*, Dublin, Ireland.

Guang Qiu, Bing Liu, Jiajun Bu, and Chun Chen. 2011. Opinion Word Expansion and Target Extraction through Double Propagation. *Computational Linguistics*, 37(1):9–27.

Lev Ratinov and Dan Roth. 2009. Design Challenges and Misconceptions in Named Entity Recognition. In *Proceedings of the Thirteenth Conference on Computational Natural Language Learning (CoNLL-2009)*, pages 147–155, Boulder, Colorado, June.

Christina Sauper and Regina Barzilay. 2013. Automatic Aggregation by Joint Modeling of Aspects and Values. *J. Artif. Int. Res.*, 46(1):89–127, January.

Joseph Turian, Lev-Arie Ratinov, and Yoshua Bengio. 2010. Word Representations: A Simple and General Method for Semi-Supervised Learning. In *Proceedings of the 48th Annual Meeting of the Association for Computational Linguistics*, pages 384–394, Uppsala, Sweden, July.

DLS@CU: Sentence Similarity from Word Alignment

Md Arafat Sultan[†], **Steven Bethard**[‡], **Tamara Sumner**[†]
[†]Institute of Cognitive Science and Department of Computer Science
University of Colorado Boulder
[‡]Department of Computer and Information Sciences
University of Alabama at Birmingham
arafat.sultan@colorado.edu, bethard@cis.uab.edu, sumner@colorado.edu

Abstract

We present an algorithm for computing the semantic similarity between two sentences. It adopts the hypothesis that semantic similarity is a monotonically increasing function of the degree to which (1) the two sentences contain similar semantic units, and (2) such units occur in similar semantic contexts. With a simplistic operationalization of the notion of semantic units with individual words, we experimentally show that this hypothesis can lead to state-of-the-art results for sentence-level semantic similarity. At the SemEval 2014 STS task (task 10), our system demonstrated the best performance (measured by correlation with human annotations) among 38 system runs.

1 Introduction

Semantic textual similarity (STS), in the context of short text fragments, has drawn considerable attention in recent times. Its application spans a multitude of areas, including natural language processing, information retrieval and digital learning. Examples of tasks that benefit from STS include text summarization, machine translation, question answering, short answer scoring, and so on.

The annual series of SemEval STS tasks (Agirre et al., 2012; Agirre et al., 2013; Agirre et al., 2014) is an important platform where STS systems are evaluated on common data and evaluation criteria. In this article, we describe an STS system which participated and outperformed all other systems at SemEval 2014.

The algorithm is a straightforward application of the monolingual word aligner presented in (Sultan et al., 2014). This aligner aligns related words in two sentences based on the following properties of the words:

1. They are semantically similar.
2. They occur in similar semantic contexts in the respective sentences.

The output of the word aligner for a sentence pair can be used to predict the pair's semantic similarity by taking the proportion of their aligned content words. Intuitively, the more semantic components in the sentences we can meaningfully align, the higher their semantic similarity should be. In experiments on STS 2013 data reported by Sultan et al. (2014), this approach was found highly effective. We also adopt this hypothesis of semantic compositionality for STS 2014.

We implement an STS algorithm that is only slightly different from the algorithm in (Sultan et al., 2014). The approach remains equally successful on STS 2014 data.

2 Background

We focus on two relevant topics in this section: the state of the art of STS research, and the word aligner presented in (Sultan et al., 2014).

2.1 Semantic Textual Similarity

Since the inception of textual similarity research for short text, perhaps with the studies reported by Mihalcea et al. (2006) and Li et al. (2006), the topic has spawned significant research interest. The majority of systems have been reported as part of the SemEval 2012 and *SEM 2013 STS tasks (Agirre et al., 2012; Agirre et al., 2013). Here we confine our discussion to systems that participated in these tasks.

With designated training data for several test sets, supervised systems were the most successful in STS 2012 (Bär et al., 2012; Šarić et al., 2012;

Proceedings of the 8th International Workshop on Semantic Evaluation (SemEval 2014), pages 241–246,
Dublin, Ireland, August 23-24, 2014.

Jimenez et al., 2012). Such systems typically apply a regression algorithm on a large number of STS features (e.g., string similarity, syntactic similarity and word or phrase-level semantic similarity) to generate a final similarity score. This approach continued to do well in 2013 (Han et al., 2013; Wu et al., 2013; Shareghi and Bergler, 2013) even without domain-specific training data, but the best results were demonstrated by an unsupervised system (Han et al., 2013). This has important implications for STS since extraction of each feature adds to the latency of a supervised system. STS systems are typically important in the context of a larger system rather than on their own, so high latency is an obvious drawback for such systems.

We present an STS system that has simplicity, high accuracy and speed as its design goals, can be deployed without any supervision, operates in a linguistically principled manner with purely semantic sentence properties, and was the top system at SemEval STS 2014.

2.2 The Sultan et al. (2014) Aligner

The word aligner presented in (Sultan et al., 2014) has been used unchanged in this work and plays a central role in our STS algorithm. We give only an overview here; for the full details, see the original article.

We will denote the sentences being aligned (and are subsequently input to the STS algorithm) as $S^{(1)}$ and $S^{(2)}$. We describe only content word alignment here; stop words are not used in our STS computation.

The aligner first identifies word pairs $w_i^{(1)} \in S^{(1)}$ and $w_j^{(2)} \in S^{(2)}$ such that:

1. $w_i^{(1)}$ and $w_j^{(2)}$ have non-zero semantic similarity, sim_{Wij}. The calculation of sim_{Wij} is described in Section 2.2.1.
2. The semantic contexts of $w_i^{(1)}$ and $w_j^{(2)}$ have some similarity, sim_{Cij}. We define the semantic context of a word w in a sentence S as a set of words in S, and the semantic context of the word pair $(w_i^{(1)}, w_j^{(2)})$, denoted by $context_{ij}$, as the Cartesian product of the context of $w_i^{(1)}$ in $S^{(1)}$ and the context of $w_j^{(2)}$ in $S^{(2)}$. We define several types of context (i.e., several selections of words) and describe the corresponding calculations of sim_{Cij} in Section 2.2.2.
3. There are no competing pairs scoring higher than $(w_i^{(1)}, w_j^{(2)})$ under $f(sim_W, sim_C) = 0.9 \times sim_W + 0.1 \times sim_C$. That is, there are no pairs $(w_k^{(1)}, w_j^{(2)})$ such that $f(sim_{Wkj}, sim_{Ckj}) > f(sim_{Wij}, sim_{Cij})$, and there are no pairs $(w_i^{(1)}, w_l^{(2)})$ such that $f(sim_{Wil}, sim_{Cil}) > f(sim_{Wij}, sim_{Cij})$. The weights 0.9 and 0.1 were derived empirically via a grid search in the range $[0, 1]$ (with a step size of 0.1) to maximize alignment performance on the training set of the (Brockett, 2007) alignment corpus. This set contains 800 human-aligned sentence pairs collected from a textual entailment corpus (Bar-Haim et al., 2006).

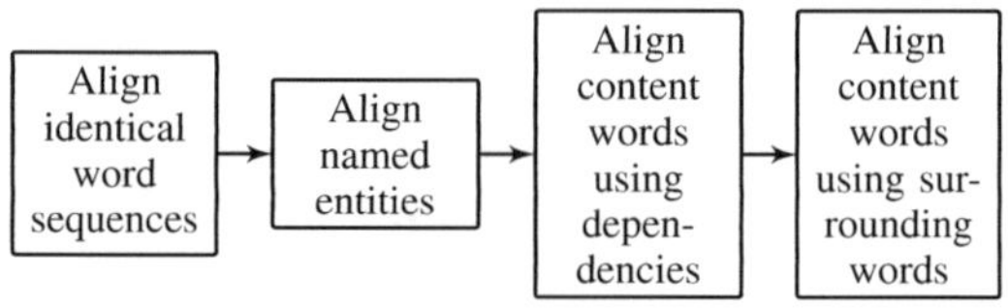

Figure 1: The alignment pipeline.

The aligner then performs one-to-one word alignments in decreasing order of the f value.

This alignment process is applied in four steps as shown in Figure 1; each step applies the above process to a particular type of context: identical words, dependencies and surrounding content words. Additionally, named entities are aligned in a separate step (details in Section 2.2.2).

Words that are aligned by an earlier module of the pipeline are not allowed to be re-aligned by downstream modules.

2.2.1 Word Similarity

Word similarity (sim_W) is computed as follows:

1. If the two words or their lemmas are identical, then $sim_W = 1$.
2. If the two words are present as a pair in the lexical XXXL corpus of the Paraphrase Database[1] (PPDB) (Ganitkevitch et al., 2013), then $sim_W = 0.9$.[2] For this step, PPDB was augmented with lemmatized forms of the already existing word pairs.[3]

[1] PPDB is a large database of lexical, phrasal and syntactic paraphrases.

[2] Again, the value 0.9 was derived empirically via a grid search in [0, 1] (step size = 0.1) to maximize alignment performance on the (Brockett, 2007) training data.

[3] The Python NLTK WordNetLemmatizer was used to lemmatize the original PPDB words.

3. For any other word pair, $sim_W = 0$.

2.2.2 Contextual Similarity

Contextual similarity (sim_C) for a word pair $(w_i^{(1)}, w_j^{(2)})$ is computed as the sum of the word similarities for each pair of words in the context of $(w_i^{(1)}, w_j^{(2)})$. That is:

$$sim_{Cij} = \sum_{(w_k^{(1)}, w_l^{(2)}) \in context_{ij}} sim_{Wkl}$$

Each of the stages in Figure 1 employs a specific type of context.

Identical Word Sequences. Contextual similarity for identical word sequences (a word sequence W which is present in both $S^{(1)}$ and $S^{(2)}$ and contains at least one content word) defines the context by pairing up each word in the instance of W in $S^{(1)}$ with its occurrence in the instance of W in $S^{(2)}$. All such sequences with length ≥ 2 are aligned; longer sequences are aligned before shorter ones. This simple step was found to be of very high precision in (Sultan et al., 2014) and reduces the overall computational cost of alignment.

Named Entities. Named entities are a special case in the alignment pipeline. Even though the context for a named entity is defined in the same way as it is defined for any other content word (as described below), named entities are aligned in a separate step before other content words because they have special properties such as coreferring mentions of different lengths (e.g. Smith and John Smith, BBC and British Broadcasting Corporation). The head word of the named entity is used in dependency calculations.

Dependencies. Dependency-based contextual similarity defines the context for the pair $(w_i^{(1)}, w_j^{(2)})$ using the syntactic dependencies of $w_i^{(1)}$ and $w_j^{(2)}$. The context is the set of all word pairs $(w_k^{(1)}, w_l^{(2)})$ such that:

- $w_k^{(1)}$ is a dependency of $w_i^{(1)}$,
- $w_l^{(2)}$ is a dependency of $w_j^{(2)}$,
- $w_i^{(1)}$ and $w_j^{(2)}$ have the same lexical category,
- $w_k^{(1)}$ and $w_l^{(2)}$ have the same lexical category, and,
- The two dependencies are either identical or semantically "equivalent" according to the equivalence table provided by Sultan et al. (2014). We explain semantic equivalence of dependencies using an example below.

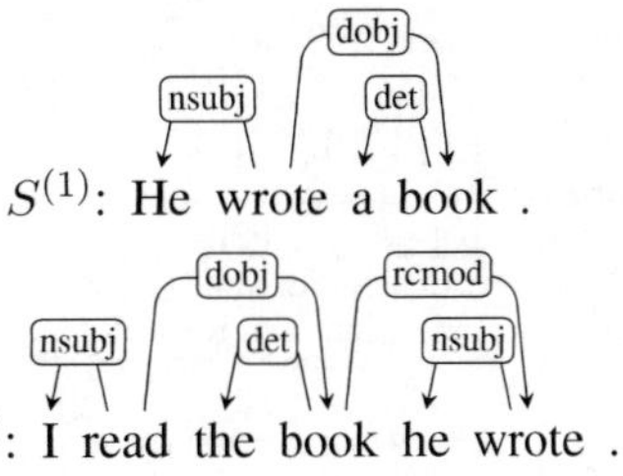

Figure 2: Example of dependency equivalence.

Equivalence of Dependency Structures. Consider $S^{(1)}$ and $S^{(2)}$ in Figure 2. Note that $w_2^{(1)} = w_6^{(2)}$ = 'wrote' and $w_4^{(1)} = w_4^{(2)}$ = 'book' in this pair. Now, each of the two following typed dependencies: $dobj(w_2^{(1)}, w_4^{(1)})$ in $S^{(1)}$ and $rcmod(w_4^{(2)}, w_6^{(2)})$ in $S^{(2)}$, represents the relation "thing that was written" between the verb 'wrote' and its argument 'book'. Thus, to summarize, an instance of contextual evidence for a possible alignment between the pair $(w_2^{(1)}, w_6^{(2)})$ ('wrote') lies in the pair $(w_4^{(1)}, w_4^{(2)})$ ('book') and the equivalence of the two dependency types *dobj* and *rcmod*.

The equivalence table of Sultan et al. (2014) is a list of all such possible equivalences among different dependency types (given that $w_i^{(1)}$ has the same lexical category as $w_j^{(2)}$ and $w_k^{(1)}$ has the same lexical category as $w_l^{(2)}$).

If there are no word pairs with identical or equivalent dependencies as defined above, i.e. if $sim_{Cij} = 0$, then $w_i^{(1)}$ and $w_j^{(2)}$ will not be aligned by this module.

Surrounding Content Words. Surrounding-word-based contextual similarity defines the context of a word in a sentence as a fixed window of 3 words to its left and 3 words to its right. Only content words in the window are considered. (As explained in the beginning of this section, the context of the pair $(w_i^{(1)}, w_j^{(2)})$ is then the Cartesian product of the context of $w_i^{(1)}$ in $S^{(1)}$ and $w_j^{(2)}$ in $S^{(2)}$.) Note that $w_i^{(1)}$ and $w_j^{(2)}$ can be of different lexical categories here.

A content word can often be surrounded by stop words which provide almost no information about its semantic context. The chosen window size is assumed, on average, to effectively make

Data Set	Source of Text	# of Pairs
deft-forum	discussion forums	450
deft-news	news articles	300
headlines	news headlines	750
images	image descriptions	750
OnWN	word sense definitions	750
tweet-news	news articles and tweets	750

Table 1: Test sets for SemEval STS 2014.

sufficient contextual information available while avoiding the inclusion of contextually unrelated words. But further experiments are necessary to determine the best span in the context of alignment.

Unlike dependency-based alignment, even if there are no similar words in the context, i.e. if $sim_{Cij} = 0$, $w_i^{(1)}$ may still be aligned to $w_j^{(2)}$ if $sim_{Wij} > 0$ and no alignments for $w_i^{(1)}$ or $w_j^{(2)}$ have been found by earlier stages of the pipeline.

2.2.3 The Alignment Sequence

The rationale behind the specific sequence of alignment steps (Figure 1) was explained in (Sultan et al., 2014): (1) Identical word sequence alignment was found to be the step with the highest precision in experiments on the (Brockett, 2007) training data, (2) It is convenient to align named entities before other content words to enable alignment of entity mentions of different lengths, (3) Dependency-based evidence was observed to be more reliable (i.e. of higher precision) than textual evidence on the (Brockett, 2007) training data.

3 Method

Our STS score is a function of the proportions of aligned content words in the two input sentences.

The proportion of content words in $S^{(1)}$ that are aligned to some word in $S^{(2)}$ is:

$$prop_{Al}^{(1)} = \frac{|\{i : [\exists j : (i,j) \in Al] \text{ and } w_i^{(1)} \in C\}|}{|\{i : w_i^{(1)} \in C\}|}$$

where C is the set of all content words in English and Al are the predicted word alignments. A word alignment is a pair of indices (i, j) indicating that word $w_i^{(1)}$ is aligned to $w_j^{(2)}$. The proportion of aligned content words in $S^{(2)}$, $prop_{Al}^{(2)}$, can be computed in a similar way.

We posit that a simple yet sensible way to obtain an STS estimate for $S^{(1)}$ and $S^{(2)}$ is to take a mean of $prop_{Al}^{(1)}$ and $prop_{Al}^{(2)}$. Our two submitted runs use the harmonic mean:

$$sim(S^{(1)}, S^{(2)}) = \frac{2 \times prop_{Al}^{(1)} \times prop_{Al}^{(2)}}{prop_{Al}^{(1)} + prop_{Al}^{(2)}}$$

It is a more conservative estimate than the arithmetic mean, and penalizes sentence pairs with a large disparity between the values of $prop_{Al}^{(1)}$ and $prop_{Al}^{(2)}$. Experiments on STS 2012 and 2013 data revealed the harmonic mean of the two proportions to be a better STS estimate than the arithmetic mean.

Data Set	Run 1	Run 2
deft-forum	0.4828	0.4828
deft-news	0.7657	0.7657
headlines	0.7646	0.7646
images	0.8214	0.8214
OnWN	0.7227	0.8589
tweet-news	0.7639	0.7639
Weighted Mean	0.7337	0.7610

Table 2: Results of evaluation on SemEval STS 2014 data. Each value on columns 2 and 3 is the correlation between system output and human annotations for the corresponding data set. The last row shows the value of the final evaluation metric.

4 Data

STS systems at SemEval 2014 were evaluated on six data sets. Each test set consists of a number of sentence pairs; each pair has a human-assigned similarity score in the range [0, 5] which increases with similarity. Every score is the mean of five scores crowdsourced using the Amazon Mechanical Turk. The sentences were collected from a variety of sources. In Table 1, we provide a brief description of each test set.

5 Evaluation

We submitted the results of two system runs at SemEval 2014 based on the idea presented in Section 3. The two runs were identical, except for the fact that for the *OnWN* test set, we specified the following words as additional stop words during run 2 (but not during run 1): *something*, *someone*, *somebody*, *act*, *activity*, *some*, *state*.[4] For both

[4] *OnWN* has many sentence pairs where each sentence is of the form "the act/activity/state of verb+ing something/somebody". The selected words act merely as fillers in such pairs and consequently do not typically contribute to the similarity scores.

Data Set	Run 1	Run 2
FNWN	0.4686	0.4686
headlines	0.7797	0.7797
OnWN	0.6083	0.8197
SMT	0.3837	0.3837
Weighted Mean	0.5788	0.6315

Table 3: Results of evaluation on *SEM STS 2013 data.

runs, the *tweet-news* sentences were preprocessed by separating the hashtag from the word for each hashtagged word.

Table 2 shows the performance of each run. Rows 1 through 6 show the Pearson correlation coefficients between the system scores and human annotations for all test sets. The last row shows the value of the final evaluation metric, which is a weighted sum of all correlations in rows 1–6. The weight assigned to a data set is proportional to its number of pairs. Our run 1 ranked 7th and run 2 ranked 1st among 38 submitted system runs.

An important implication of these results is the fact that knowledge of domain-specific stop words can be beneficial for an STS system. Even though we imparted this knowledge to our system during run 2 via a manually constructed set of additional stop words, simple measures like TF-IDF can be used to automate the process.

5.1 Performance on STS 2012 and 2013 Data

We applied our algorithm on the 2012 and 2013 STS test sets to examine its general utility. Note that the STS 2013 setup was similar to STS 2014 with no domain-dependent training data, whereas several of the 2012 test sets had designated training data.

Over all the 2013 test sets, our two runs demonstrated weighted correlations of 0.5788 (rank: 4) and 0.6315 (rank: 1), respectively. Table 3 shows performances on individual test sets. (Descriptions of the test sets can be found in (Agirre et al., 2013).) Again, run 2 outperformed run 1 on *OnWN* by a large margin.

On the 2012 test sets, however, the performance was worse (relative to other systems), with respective weighted correlations of 0.6476 (rank: 8) and 0.6423 (rank: 9). Table 4 shows performances on individual test sets. (Descriptions of the test sets can be found in (Agirre et al., 2012).)

This performance drop seems to be an obvious consequence of the fact that our algorithm was not trained on domain-specific data: on STS 2013

Data Set	Run 1	Run 2
MSRpar	0.6413	0.6413
MSRvid	0.8200	0.8200
OnWN	0.7227	0.7004
SMTeuroparl	0.4267	0.4267
SMTnews	0.4486	0.4486
Weighted Mean	0.6476	0.6423

Table 4: Results of evaluation on SemEval STS 2012 data.

data, the top two STS 2012 systems, with respective weighted correlations of 0.5652 and 0.5221 (Agirre et al., 2013), were outperformed by our system by a large margin.

In contrast to the other two years, our run 1 outperformed run 2 on the 2012 *OnWN* test set by a very small margin. A closer inspection revealed that the previously mentioned sentence structure "the act/activity/state of verb+ing something/somebody" is much less common in this set, and as a result, our additional stop words tend to play more salient semantic roles in this set than in the other two *OnWN* sets (i.e. they act relatively more as content words than stop words). The drop in correlation with human annotations is a consequence of this role reversal. This result again shows the importance of a proper selection of stop words for STS and also points to the challenges associated with making such a selection.

6 Conclusions and Future Work

We show that alignment of related words in two sentences, if carried out in a principled and accurate manner, can yield state-of-the-art results for sentence-level semantic similarity. Our system has the desired quality of being both accurate and fast. Evaluation on test data from different STS years demonstrates its general applicability as well.

The idea of STS from alignment is worth investigating with larger semantic units (i.e. phrases) in the two sentences. Another possible research direction is to investigate whether the alignment proportions observed for the two sentences can be used as features to improve performance in a supervised setup (even though this scenario is arguably less common in practice because of unavailability of domain or situation-specific training data).

Acknowledgments

This material is based in part upon work supported by the National Science Foundation under Grant

Numbers EHR/0835393 and EHR/0835381. Any opinions, findings, and conclusions or recommendations expressed in this material are those of the author(s) and do not necessarily reflect the views of the National Science Foundation.

References

Eneko Agirre, Daniel Cer, Mona Diab, and Aitor Gonzalez-Agirre. 2012. SemEval-2012 task 6: A pilot on semantic textual similarity. In *Proceedings of the First Joint Conference on Lexical and Computational Semantics, Volume 2: Proceedings of the Sixth International Workshop on Semantic Evaluation*, SemEval '12, pages 385-393, Montreal, Canada.

Eneko Agirre, Daniel Cer, Mona Diab, Aitor Gonzalez-Agirre, and Weiwei Guo. 2013. *SEM 2013 shared task: Semantic Textual Similarity. In *Proceedings of the Second Joint Conference on Lexical and Computational Semantics*, *SEM '13, pages 32-43, Atlanta, Georgia, USA.

Eneko Agirre, Carmen Banea, Claire Cardie, Daniel Cer, Mona Diab, Aitor Gonzalez-Agirre, Weiwei Guo, Rada Mihalcea, German Rigau, and Janyce Wiebe. 2014. SemEval-2014 Task 10: Multilingual semantic textual similarity. In *Proceedings of the 8th International Workshop on Semantic Evaluation*, SemEval '14, Dublin, Ireland.

Roy Bar-Haim, Ido Dagan, Bill Dolan, Lisa Ferro, Danilo Giampiccolo, Bernardo Magnini, and Idan Szpektor. 2006. The Second PASCAL Recognising Textual Entailment Challenge. In *Proceedings of the Second PASCAL Challenges Workshop on Recognising Textual Entailment*, Venice, Italy.

Daniel Bär, Chris Biemann, Iryna Gurevych, and Torsten Zesch. 2012. UKP: computing semantic textual similarity by combining multiple content similarity measures. In *Proceedings of the 6th International Workshop on Semantic Evaluation, held in conjunction with the 1st Joint Conference on Lexical and Computational Semantics*, SemEval '12, pages 435-440, Montreal, Canada.

Chris Brockett. 2007. Aligning the RTE 2006 Corpus. Technical Report MSR-TR-2007-77, Microsoft Research.

Juri Ganitkevitch, Benjamin Van Durme, and Chris Callison-Burch. 2013. PPDB: The Paraphrase Database. In *Proceedings of the 2013 Conference of the North American Chapter of the Association for Computational Linguistics*, NAACL-HLT '13, pages 758-764, Atlanta, Georgia, USA.

Lushan Han, Abhay Kashyap, Tim Finin, James Mayfield, and Jonathan Weese. 2013. UMBC EBIQUITY-CORE: Semantic Textual Similarity Systems. In *Proceedings of the Second Joint Conference on Lexical and Computational Semantics*, *SEM '13, pages 44-52, Atlanta, Georgia, USA.

Sergio Jimenez, Claudia Becerra, and Alexander Gelbukh. 2012. Soft Cardinality: a parameterized similarity function for text comparison. In *Proceedings of the 6th International Workshop on Semantic Evaluation, held in conjunction with the 1st Joint Conference on Lexical and Computational Semantics*, SemEval '12, pages 449-453, Montreal, Canada.

Yuhua Li, David Mclean, Zuhair A. Bandar, James D. O'Shea, and Keeley Crockett. 2006. Sentence similarity based on semantic nets and corpus statistics. *IEEE Transactions on Knowledge and Data Engineering, vol.18, no.8.* 1138-1150.

Rada Mihalcea, Courtney Corley, and Carlo Strapparava. 2006. Corpus-based and knowledge-based measures of text semantic similarity. In *Proceedings of the 21st national conference on Artificial intelligence*, AAAI '06, pages 775-780, Boston, Massachusetts, USA.

Frane Šarić, Goran Glavaš, Mladen Karan, Jan Šnajder, and Bojana Dalbelo Bašić. 2012. TakeLab: systems for measuring semantic text similarity. In *Proceedings of the 6th International Workshop on Semantic Evaluation, held in conjunction with the 1st Joint Conference on Lexical and Computational Semantics*, SemEval '12, pages 441-448, Montreal, Canada.

Ehsan Shareghi and Sabine Bergler. 2013. CLaC-CORE: Exhaustive Feature Combination for Measuring Textual Similarity. In *Proceedings of the Second Joint Conference on Lexical and Computational Semantics*, *SEM '13, pages 202-206, Atlanta, Georgia, USA.

Md Arafat Sultan, Steven Bethard, and Tamara Sumner. 2014. Back to Basics for Monolingual Alignment: Exploiting Word Similarity and Contextual Evidence. *Transactions of the Association for Computational Linguistics*, 2 (May), pages 219-230.

Stephen Wu, Dongqing Zhu, Ben Carterette, and Hongfang Liu. 2013. MayoClinicNLP-CORE: Semantic representations for textual similarity. In *Proceedings of the Second Joint Conference on Lexical and Computational Semantics*, *SEM '13, pages 148-154, Atlanta, Georgia, USA.

Duluth : Measuring Cross–Level Semantic Similarity with First and Second–Order Dictionary Overlaps

Ted Pedersen
Department of Computer Science
University of Minnesota
Duluth, MN 55812
tpederse@d.umn.edu

Abstract

This paper describes the Duluth systems that participated in the Cross–Level Semantic Similarity task of SemEval–2014. These three systems were all unsupervised and relied on a dictionary melded together from various sources, and used first–order (Lesk) and second–order (Vector) overlaps to measure similarity. The first–order overlaps fared well according to Spearman's correlation (top 5) but less so relative to Pearson's. Most systems performed at comparable levels for both Spearman's and Pearson's measure, which suggests the Duluth approach is potentially unique among the participating systems.

1 Introduction

Cross–Level Semantic Similarity (CLSS) is a novel variation on the problem of semantic similarity. As traditionally formulated, pairs of words, pairs of phrases, or pairs of sentences are scored for similarity. However, the CLSS shared task (Jurgens et al., 2014) included 4 subtasks where pairs of different granularity were measured for semantic similarity. These included : word-2-sense (w2s), phrase-2-word (p2w), sentence-2-phrase (s2p), and paragraph-2-sentence (g2s). In addition to different levels of granularity, these pairs included slang, jargon and other examples of non–standard English.

We were drawn to this task because of our long–standing interest in semantic similarity. We have pursued approaches ranging from those that rely on structured knowledge sources like WordNet (e.g., WordNet::Similarity) (Pedersen et al., 2004) to those that use distributional information found in raw text (e.g., SenseClusters) (Purandare and Pedersen, 2004). Our approach in this shared task is a bit of both, but relies on using definitions for each item in a pair so that similarity can be measured using first or second–order overlaps.

A first–order approach finds direct matches between the words in a pair of definitions. In a second–order approach each word in a definition is replaced by a vector of the words it co–occurs with, and then the vectors for all the words in a definition are averaged together to represent the definition. Then, similarity can be measured by finding the cosine between pairs of these vectors. We decided on a definition based approach since it had the potential to normalize the differences in granularity of the pairs.

The main difficulty in comparing definitions is that they can be very brief or may not even exist at all. This is why we combined various different kinds of resources to arrive at our dictionary. While we achieved near total coverage of words and senses, phrases were sparsely covered, and sentences and paragraphs had no coverage. In those cases we used the text of the phrase, sentence or paragraph to serve as its own definition.

The Duluth systems were implemented using the UMLS::Similarity package (McInnes et al., 2009) (version 1.35)[1], which includes support for user–defined dictionaries, first–order Lesk methods, and second–order Vector methods. As a result the Duluth systems required minimal implementation, so once a dictionary was ready experiments could begin immediately.

This paper is organized as follows. First, the first–order Lesk and second–order Vector measures are described. Then we discuss the details of the three Duluth systems that participated in this task. Finally, we review the task results and consider future directions for this problem and our system.

[1] http://umls-similarity.sourceforge.net

Proceedings of the 8th International Workshop on Semantic Evaluation (SemEval 2014), pages 247–251, Dublin, Ireland, August 23-24, 2014.

2 Measures

The Duluth systems use first–order Lesk methods (Duluth1 and Duluth3) and second–order Vector methods (Duluth2). These require that definitions be available for both items in a pair, with the caveat that we use the term *definition* somewhat loosely to mean both traditional dictionary definitions as well as various proxies when those are not available.

2.1 First–order Overlaps : Lesk

The Lesk measure (Lesk, 1986) was originally a method of word sense disambiguation that measured the overlap among the definitions of the possible senses of an ambiguous word with those of surrounding words (Lesk, 1986). The senses which have the largest number of overlaps are presumed to be the correct or intended senses for the given context. A modified approach compares the glosses of an ambiguous word with the surrounding context (Kilgarriff and Rosenzweig, 2000). These are both first–order methods where definitions are directly compared with each other, or with the surrounding context.

In the Duluth systems, we measure overlaps by summing the number of words shared between definitions. Sequences of words that match are weighted more heavily and contribute the square of their length, while individual matching words just count as one. For example, given the definitions *a small noisy collie* and *a small noisy border collie* the stop word *a* would not be matched, and then *small noisy* would match (and be given a score of 4) and then *collie* would also match (receiving a score of 1). So, the total Lesk score would be 5. The scores of the Duluth systems were normalized by dividing by the maximum Lesk score for any pair in a subtask. This moves the scores to a 0–1 scale, where 1.00 means the definitions are exactly the same, and where 0 means they share no words.

One of the main drawbacks of the original Lesk method is that glosses tend to be very short. Various methods have been proposed to overcome this. For example, (Banerjee and Pedersen, 2003) introduced the Extended Gloss Overlap measure which creates super–glosses by augmenting the glosses of the senses to be measured with the glosses of semantically related senses (which are connected via relation links in WordNet). This adaptation of the Lesk measure was first implemented in WordNet::Similarity (Pedersen et al., 2004) and then later in UMLS::Similarity (McInnes et al., 2009). It has been applied to both word sense disambiguation and semantic similarity, and generally found to improve on original Lesk (Banerjee, 2002; Banerjee and Pedersen, 2002; Patwardhan et al., 2003; McInnes and Pedersen, 2013). However, the Duluth systems do not build super–glosses in this way since many of the items in the pairs are not found in WordNet. However, definitions are expanded in a simpler way, by merging together various different resources to increase both coverage and the length of definitions.

2.2 Second–order Overlaps : Vector

The main limitation of first–order Lesk approaches is that if terminology differs from one definition to another, then meaningful matches may not be found. For example, consider the definitions *a small noisy collie* and *a dog that barks a lot*. A first–order overlap approach would find no similarity (other than the stop word *a*) between these definitions.

In cases like this some form of term expansion could improve the chances of matching. Synonym expansion is a well–known possibility, although in the Duluth systems we opted to expand words with their co–occurrence vectors. This follows from an approach to word sense discrimination developed by (Schütze, 1998). Once words are expanded then all the vectors in a definition are averaged together and this averaged vector becomes the representation of the definition. This idea was first implemented in WordNet::Similarity (Pedersen et al., 2004) and then later in UMLS::Similarity (McInnes et al., 2009), and has been applied to word sense disambiguation and semantic similarity (Patwardhan, 2003; Patwardhan and Pedersen, 2006; Liu et al., 2012).

The co–occurrences for the words in the definitions can come from any corpus of text. Once a co–occurrence matrix is constructed, then each word in each definition is replaced by its vector from that matrix. If no such vector is found the word is removed from the definition. Then, all the vectors representing a definition are averaged together, and this vector is used to measure against other vectors created in the same way. The scores returned by the Vector measure are between 0 and 1 (inclusive) where 1.00 means exactly the same and 0 means no similarity.

3 Duluth Systems

There were three Duluth systems. Duluth1 and Duluth3 use first–order Lesk, and Duluth2 uses second–order Vector. Duluth3 was an ensemble made up of Duluth1 and a close variant of it (Duluth1a, where the only difference was the stop list employed).

Duluth1 and Duluth2 use the NSP stoplist[2] which includes approximately 390 words and comes from the SMART stoplist. Duluth1a treated any word with 4 or fewer characters as a stop word. Stemming was performed by all Duluth systems using the Porter algorithm as implemented in the Lingua::Stem::en Perl module.

Before processing, all of the similarity pairs and the dictionary entries were converted to lower case and any non alpha-numeric characters were replaced with spaces. Also, any stop listed words were removed.

3.1 Dictionary Creation

The key step for all the Duluth systems is the creation of the dictionary. We elected to treat senses as word forms, and so our dictionary did not make sense distinctions (and would include all the senses of a word or phrase in its entry).

Since the words and phrases used in some pairs are slang or non–standard English, traditional lexical resources like WordNet do not provide adequate coverage. However, WordNet provides a good foundation for coverage of standard English, so we began by extracting the glosses from WordNet v3.0 using the WordNet::QueryData Perl module.

Wiktionary is a crowd sourced lexical resource that includes more slang and jargon, so we also extracted entries from it using the Wiktionary::Parser Perl module. In hopes of increasing our coverage of phrases in particular, we looked up words and phrases in Wikipedia using the WWW::Wikipedia Perl module and used the first paragraph of an entry (up to the first heading) as a definition. Finally, we also used the `dict` program in Linux which we configured to use the following resources : the Collaborative International Dictionary of English v.0.48 (gcide), Moby Thesaurus II by Grady Ward, 1.0 (moby-thes), V.E.R.A. – Virtual Entity of Relevant Acronyms (June 2006) (vera), the Jargon File (version 4.4.7, 29 Dec 2003) (argon), the Free On-line Dictionary of Computing (26 July 2010) (foldoc), and the CIA World Factbook 2002 (world02).

The most obvious question that arises about these resources is how much coverage they provide for the pairs in the task. Based on experiments on the trial data, we found that none of the resources individually provided satisfactory coverage, but if they were all combined then coverage was reasonably good (although still not complete). In the test data, it turned out there were only 20 items in the w2s subtask for which we did not have a dictionary entry (out of 1000). However, for p2w (phrase-2-word) there were 407 items not included in the dictionary (most of which were phrases). In the s2p (sentence-2-phrase) subtask there were only 15 phrases which had definitions, so for this subtask and also for g2s (paragraph-2-sentence) the items themselves were the definitions for essentially all the pairs.

Also of interest might be the total size of the dictionaries created. The number of tokens in g2s (paragraph-2-sentence) was 46,252, and in s2p (sentence-2-phrase) it was 12,361. This is simply the token count for the pairs included in each subtask. However, the dictionaries were much larger for p2w (phrase-2-word), where the token count was 262,876, and for w2s (word-2-sense) where it was 499,767.

3.2 Co–occurrence Matrix for Vector

In the Duluth systems, the co–occurrence matrix comes from treating the WordNet glosses as a corpus. Any pair of words that occur together in a WordNet gloss are considered a co–occurrence.

There are 117,659 glosses, made up of 1,460,921 words. This resulted in a matrix of 90,516 rows and 99,493 columns, representing 708,152 unique bigrams. The matrix is not symmetric since the co–occurrences are bigrams, so *dog house* is treated differently than *house dog*.

The WordNet glosses were extracted from version 3.0 using the glossExtract Perl program[3].

4 Results

Results for the CLSS task were ranked both by Pearson's and Spearman's Correlation coefficients. Duluth system results are shown in Tables 1 and 2. These tables also include the results of

[2]http://cpansearch.perl.org/src/TPEDERSE/Text-NSP-1.27/bin/utils/stoplist-nsp.regex

[3]http://www.d.umn.edu/~tpederse/Code/glossExtract-v0.03.tar.gz

Table 1: Spearman's Results

	g2s	s2p	p2w	w2s	rank (of 38)
Top	.801	.728	.424	.343	1
Duluth3	.725	.660	.399	.327	3
Duluth1	.726	.658	.385	.316	5
Duluth2	.553	.473	.235	.231	21
Baseline	.613	.626	.162	.128	

Table 2: Pearson's Results

	g2s	s2p	p2w	w2s	rank (of 38)
Top	.811	.742	.415	.355	1
Duluth2	.501	.450	.241	.224	23
Duluth1	.458	.440	.075	.076	30
Duluth3	.455	.426	.075	.080	31
Baseline	.527	.562	.165	.110	

the top ranked system (which was the same system according to both measures) and results from a baseline system that measures the Least Common Substring between the terms in a pair, except in the w2s subtask, where it measured the LCS between the associated WordNet glosses.

Table 1 shows that the Duluth3 system offers a slight improvement upon Duluth1. Recall that Duluth3 is an ensemble that includes Duluth1 and its minor variant Duluth1a. Both of these are first–order methods, and significantly outperform the second–order method Duluth2.

However, Table 2 tells a completely different story. There the second–order system Duluth2 performs better, although overall rankings suffer according to Pearson's measure. It is also very apparent that the ranks between Pearson's and Spearman's for Duluth1 and Duluth3 differ significantly (from 3 to 30 and 5 to 31). This is very atypical, and most systems maintained approximately the same rankings between the two correlation measures. Note that Duluth2 behaves in this way, where the relative ranking is 21 and 23.

Table 3 shows the number of pairs in each subtask which returned a score of 0. This could be due to missing definitions, or no matches occurring between the definitions. Interestingly Duluth2 has a much smaller number of 0 valued scores, which shows the second–order method provides greater coverage due to its more flexible notion of matching. However, despite much higher numbers of

Table 3: Number of Pairs with Score of 0

	g2s	s2p	p2w	w2s
Duluth1	107	197	211	23
Duluth2	9	101	40	15
Duluth3	101	196	205	23

0s, Duluth1 and Duluth3 perform much better with Spearman's rank correlation coefficient. This suggests that there is a kind of precision–recall tradeoff between these systems, where Duluth2 has higher recall and Duluth1 and Duluth3 have higher precision.

5 Future Directions

The relatively good performance of the first–order Duluth systems (at least with respect to rank correlation) shows again the important role of lexical resources. Our first–order method was not appreciably more complex than the baseline method, yet it performed significantly better (especially for the p2w and w2s tasks). This is no doubt due to the more extensive dictionary that we employed.

That said, our approach to building the dictionary was relatively crude, and could be substantially improved. For example, we could be more selective in the content we add to the entries for words or phrases. We could also do more than simply use the sentences and paragraphs as their own definitions. For example, we could replace words or phrases in sentences and paragraphs with their definitions, and then carry out first or second–order matching.

Second–order matching did not perform as well as we had hoped. We believe this is due to the somewhat noisy nature of the dictionaries we constructed, and expanding those definitions by replacing words with vectors created even more noise. We believe that a more refined approach to creating dictionaries would certainly improve these results, as would a more selective method of combining the co–occurrence vectors (rather than simply averaging them).

Acknowledgments

The Duluth systems relied heavily on the freely available software package UMLS::Similarity. We are grateful to Bridget McInnes and Ying Liu for their work in developing this package, and in particular for the `--dict` functionality.

References

Satanjeev Banerjee and Ted Pedersen. 2002. An adapted Lesk algorithm for word sense disambiguation using WordNet. In *Proceedings of the Third International Conference on Intelligent Text Processing and Computational Linguistics*, pages 136–145, Mexico City, February.

Satanjeev Banerjee and Ted Pedersen. 2003. Extended gloss overlaps as a measure of semantic relatedness. In *Proceedings of the Eighteenth International Joint Conference on Artificial Intelligence*, pages 805–810, Acapulco, August.

Satanjeev Banerjee. 2002. Adapting the Lesk algorithm for word sense disambiguation to WordNet. Master's thesis, University of Minnesota, Duluth, December.

David Jurgens, Mohammad Taher Pilehvar, and Roberto Navigli. 2014. Semeval-2014 task 3: Cross–level semantic similarity. In *Proceedings of the 8th International Workshop on Semantic Evaluation (SemEval 2014)*, Dublin, August.

Adam Kilgarriff and Joseph Rosenzweig. 2000. Special issue on SENSEVAL: Framework and results for english SENSEVAL. *Computers and the Humanities*, 34(1–2):15–48.

Michael Lesk. 1986. Automatic sense disambiguation using machine readable dictionaries: how to tell a pine cone from an ice cream cone. In *Proceedings of the 5th annual international conference on Systems documentation*, pages 24–26. ACM Press.

Ying Liu, Bridget McInnes, Ted Pedersen, Genevieve Melton-Meaux, and Serguei Pakhomov. 2012. Semantic relatedness study using second–order co–occurrence vectors computed from biomedical corpora, UMLS, and WordNet. In *Proceedings of the 2nd ACM SIGHIT International Health Informatics Symposium*, pages 363–371, Miami, FL.

Bridget McInnes and Ted Pedersen. 2013. Evaluating measures of semantic similarity and relatedness to disambiguate terms in biomedical text. *Journal of Biomedical Informatics*, 46:1116–1124.

Bridget McInnes, Ted Pedersen, and Serguei Pakhomov. 2009. UMLS-Interface and UMLS-Similarity : Open source software for measuring paths and semantic similarity. In *Proceedings of the Annual Symposium of the American Medical Informatics Association*, pages 431–435, San Francisco.

Siddharth Patwardhan and Ted Pedersen. 2006. Using WordNet-based Context Vectors to Estimate the Semantic Relatedness of Concepts. In *Proceedings of the EACL 2006 Workshop on Making Sense of Sense: Bringing Computational Linguistics and Psycholinguistics Together*, pages 1–8, Trento, Italy, April.

Siddharth Patwardhan, Satanjeev Banerjee, and Ted Pedersen. 2003. Using measures of semantic relatedness for word sense disambiguation. In *Proceedings of the Fourth International Conference on Intelligent Text Processing and Computational Linguistics*, pages 241–257, Mexico City, February.

Siddharth Patwardhan. 2003. Incorporating dictionary and corpus information into a context vector measure of semantic relatedness. Master's thesis, University of Minnesota, Duluth, August.

Ted Pedersen, Siddharth Patwardhan, and Jason Michelizzi. 2004. Wordnet::Similarity - Measuring the relatedness of concepts. In *Proceedings of Fifth Annual Meeting of the North American Chapter of the Association for Computational Linguistics*, pages 38–41, Boston, MA.

Amruta Purandare and Ted Pedersen. 2004. Word sense discrimination by clustering contexts in vector and similarity spaces. In *Proceedings of the Conference on Computational Natural Language Learning*, pages 41–48, Boston, MA.

Hinrich Schütze. 1998. Automatic word sense discrimination. *Computational Linguistics*, 24(1):97–123.

ECNU: A Combination Method and Multiple Features for Aspect Extraction and Sentiment Polarity Classification

Fangxi Zhang, Zhihua Zhang, Man Lan*
Department of Computer Science and Technology
East China Normal University
51111201041,51131201039@ecnu.cn; mlan@cs.ecnu.edu.cn*

Abstract

This paper reports our submissions to the four subtasks of Aspect Based Sentiment Analysis (ABSA) task (i.e., task 4) in SemEval 2014 including aspect term extraction and aspect sentiment polarity classification (Aspect-level tasks), aspect category detection and aspect category sentiment polarity classification (Category-level tasks). For aspect term extraction, we present three methods, i.e., noun phrase (NP) extraction, Named Entity Recognition (NER) and a combination of NP and NER method. For aspect sentiment classification, we extracted several features, i.e., topic features, sentiment lexicon features, and adopted a Maximum Entropy classifier. Our submissions rank above average.

1 Introduction

Recently, sentiment analysis has attracted a lot of attention from researchers. Most previous work attempted to detect overall sentiment polarity on a text span, such as document, paragraph and sentence. Since sentiments expressed in text always adhere to objects, it is much meaningful to identify the sentiment target and its orientation, which helps user gain precise sentiment insights on specific sentiment target.

The aspect based sentiment analysis (ABSA) task (Task 4) (Pontiki et al., 2014) in SemEval 2014 is to extract aspect terms, determine its semantic category, and then to detect the sentiment orientation of the extracted aspect terms and its category. Specifically, it consists of 4 subtasks. The aspect term extraction (ATE) aims to extract the aspect terms from the sentences in two given domains (laptop and restaurant). The aspect category detection (ACD) is to identify the semantic category of aspects in a predefined set of aspect categories (e.g., food, price). The aspect term polarity (ATP) classification is to determine whether the sentiment polarity of each aspect is positive, negative, neutral or conflict (i.e., both positive and negative). The aspect category polarity (ACP) classification is to determine the sentiment polarity of each aspect category. We participated in these four subtasks.

Generally, there are three methods to extract aspect terms: unsupervised learning method based on word frequency ((Ku et al., 2006), (Long et al., 2010)), supervised machine learning method (Kovelamudi et al., 2011) and semi-supervised learning method (Mukherjee and Liu, 2012) where only several user interested category seeds are given and used to extract more categorize aspect terms. Since sentiments always adhere to entities, several researchers worked on polarity classification of entity. For example, (Godbole et al., 2007) proposed a system that assigned scores representing positive or negative opinion to each distinct entity in the corpus. (Kim et al., 2013) presented a hierarchical aspect sentiment model to classify the polarity of aspect terms from unlabeled online reviews. Moreover, some sentiment lexicons, such as SentiWordNet (Baccianella et al., 2010) and MPQA Subjectivity Lexicon (Wilson et al., 2009), have been used to generate sentiment score features (Zhu et al., 2013).

The rest of this paper is organized as follows. From Section 2 to Section 5, we describe our approaches to the Aspect Term Extraction task, the Aspect Category detection task, the Aspect Term Polarity task and the Aspect Category Polarity task respectively. Section 6 provides the conclusion.

Proceedings of the 8th International Workshop on Semantic Evaluation (SemEval 2014), pages 252–258,
Dublin, Ireland, August 23-24, 2014.

2 Aspect Term Extraction System

For aspect terms extraction task, we first adopted two methods: a noun phrase (NP) based method and a Named Entity Recognition (NER) based method. In our preliminary experiments, we found that the NP-based method generates many noisy terms resulting in high recall and low precision, and the NER-based method performs inverse results. In order to overcome their drawbacks and make use of their advantages, we proposed a third method which combines the two methods by using the results of NP-based method as an additional name list feature to the NER system.

2.1 Preprocessing

We used Stanford Parser Tools[1] for POS tagging and for parsing while the Natural Language Toolkit[2] was used for removing stop words and lemmatization.

2.2 NP-based Method

(Liu, 2012) showed that the majority of aspect terms are noun phrases. Moreover, through the observation of the training set, we found that more than half of the aspects are pure noun phrases or nested noun phrases. So we considered these two types of noun phrases as aspect terms and adopted a rule-based noun phrases extraction system to perform aspect term extraction. This extraction is performed on parsed sentences. For example, from parsed sentence:

"(CC but)
(S
(NP (NN iwork))
(VP (VBZ is)
(ADJP (JJ cheap))
(PP (VBN compared)
(PP (TO to)
(NP (NN office))))))"

iwork and *office* with NN tag are extracted as aspect terms. However, to make a more precise extraction, we first removed white lines from parsed sentences. Then we performed extraction only using three continuous lines. Since the NPs we extracted contain much noise which only appear in NPs rather than in gold aspect terms list, we built a *stopwords* list containing these noisy terms especially the numeric expressions. Table 1 shows the set of manually built rules used for NP extraction.

[1]http://nlp.stanford.edu/software/lex-parser.shtml
[2]http://www.nltk.org/

Based on the experimental results on training data, we found the NP-based method achieves high recall and low precision as shown in Table 2. This indicates that we extracted plenty of NPs which consist of a large proportion of aspect terms and much noise such as irrelevant NPs and overlapping phrases. Thus the NP-based method alone has not produced good results.

2.3 NER-based Method

We also cast aspect term extraction task as a traditional NER task (Liu, 2012). We adopted the commonly used BIO tag format to represent the aspect terms in the given annotated training data (Toh et al., 2012), where *B* indicates the beginning of an aspect term, *I* indicates the inside of an aspect term and *O* indicates the outside of an aspect term. For example, given *"the battery life is excellent"*, where *battery life* is annotated as aspect term, we tagged the three words *the*, *is* and *excellent* as *O*, *battery* as *B* and *life* as *I*.

We adopted several widely used features for the NER-based aspect term extraction system.

Word features: current word (*word_0*), previous word (*word_-1*) and next word (*word_1*) are used as word features.

POS feature: the POS tag of current word (*POS_0*), the POS tags of two words around current word (*POS_-2, POS_-1, POS_1, POS_2*), and the combinations of contextual POS tags (*POS_-1/POS_0, POS_0/POS_1, POS_-1/POS_0/POS_1*) are included as POS features.

Word_shape: a tag sequence of characters in current word is recorded, i.e., the lowercase letter tagged as *a*, and the uppercase letter tagged as *A*.

Chunk: We extracted this feature from the POS tag sequence, which is defined as follows: the shortest phrase based on POS taggers, i.e., *"(VP (VBD took) (NP (NN way)) (ADVP (RB too) (RB long))"*, *took* labeled as *O*, *way* labeled as *B-NP*, *too* labeled as *B-ADVP*, *long* labeled as *I-ADVP*.

We implemented a CRF++ [3] based NER system with the above feature types.

2.4 Combination of NP and NER Method

Based on our preliminary experiments, we considered to combine the above two methods. To do so, we adopted the results of the NP system as additional name lists feature for the NER system. Through the observation on the results of the

[3]http://crfpp.googlecode.com/svn/trunk/doc/index.html

if (NP in line_1)	then select line_1 as candidate
if (NP in line_1 and PP in line_2 and NP in line_3)	then select line_1 + line_2 + line_3 as candidate
else if (VB in line_1 and NN in line_2)	then select line_1 + line_2 as candidate
else if (NP in line_1 and NP in line_2)	then select line_1 + line_2 as candidate
else if (NP in line_1 and CC in line_2 and NN in line_3)	then select line_3 as candidate
else if (JJ in line_1 and NN in line_2)	then select line_2 as candidate
if (current term in candidate existing in stopwords)	then remove current term
if (CD start candidate)	then remove CD
if (DT or PRP start candidate)	then remove DT or PRP
if (JJR in candidate)	then remove JJR
if (Punctuation in candidate)	then remove Punctuation

Table 1: The rules in NP-based method.

method	Laptop			Restaurant		
	Precision(%)	Recall(%)	F-score(%)	Precision(%)	Recall(%)	F-score(%)
NP-based	44.35	**74.43**	55.59	45.99	70.50	56.17
NER-based	70.46	48.27	57.29	80.87	68.24	74.02
Combination	**72.79**	55.11	**62.73**	**82.31**	**70.62**	**76.02**

Table 2: The F-scores of three methods on training data.

NP-based method and the NER-based method, we built two types of name lists for our combination method as follows:

Gold Namelist: containing the gold aspect terms and the intersection between the results of the NP-based method and the NER-based method.

Stop Namelist: the words in original sentences but not in gold aspect terms set or not in NPs set we extracted before.

Table 3 shows the results of feature selection for the combination method on training data. The best performance was obtained by using all features. Thus, our final submission system adopted the combination method with all features.

Feature	Dataset	
	Laptop	Restaurant
word:		
+word_0	40.35	58.58
+word_1	54.78	72.23
POS:		
+POS_0	55.81	71.11
+POS_1	57.07	74.02
+POS_2	57.18	73.24
+POS_0/POS_1	51.85	70.58
chunk:		
+chunk_0	56.74	73.45
word_shape:		
+word_shape_0	57.29	74.02
name_list:		
+Gold Namelist	62.66	75.39
+Stop Namelist	**62.73**	**76.02**

Table 3: The F-scores of combination method of subtask 1 on training data based on 2 cross-validation

Table 2 shows the results of the above three systems on training data. Comparing with other two methods, we easily find that the combination method outperforms the other two systems in terms of precision, recall and F values on both domains.

2.5 Result and Discussion

In constrained run, we submitted the results using the method in combination of NP and NER. Specifically, we adopted all features and the name lists listed in Table 3 and the CRF++ tool for the NER system. Table 4 lists the results of our final system and the top two systems officially released by organizers. On both domains, our system ranks above the average under constrained model, which proves the effectiveness of the combination method by using NP extraction and NER.

From Table 2 and Table 4 we find that the results on restaurant data are much better than those on laptop data. Based on our further observation on training data, the possible reason is that the number of numeric descriptions in laptop dataset is much larger than those in restaurant dataset and the aspect terms containing numeric description are quite difficult to be extracted.

Dataset	DLIREC	NRC-Canada	Our result
laptop	70.41	68.57	65.88
restaurant	78.34	80.19	78.24

Table 4: The F-scores (%) of our system and the top two systems of subtask 1 on test dataset.

3 Aspect Category Classification System

Aspect category classification task tries to assign each aspect one or more semantic category labels. Thus, we regarded this task as a multi-class classification problem. Following (Rennie, 2001), we built a binary model for each category, where bag-of-words is used as features.

3.1 Features

We adopted the bag-of-words schema to represent features as follows. Since not all training instances have annotated aspect terms, we extracted only annotated aspect terms from sentence if the sentence contains annotated aspect terms, or extracted all words from sentence which does not contain any annotated aspect terms as features, which results in 5200 word features in total.

3.2 Classification Algorithm

We adopted the maximum entropy algorithm implemented in Mallet toolkit (McCallum, 2002) to build a binary classifier for each category. All parameters are set as defaults. This subtask only provides restaurant data and there are five predefined categories (i.e., food, price, service, ambience and anecdotes/miscellaneous), thus we build five binary classifiers in total.

3.3 Results and Discussions

Table 5 lists the precision, recall and F-score of our final system along with the top two systems released by the organizers.

	Precision(%)	Recall(%)	F-score(%)
our system	65.26	69.46	67.30
rank 1 system	91.04	86.24	88.58
rank 2 system	83.23	81.37	82.29

Table 5: The results of our system and the top two systems of subtask 3 on the test data.

From Table 5, we find that there are quite a large room to improve our system. One main reason is that our system only uses simple features (i.e., bag-of-words) and these simple features may have poor discriminating power. Another possible reason may be that in training data there are at least half sentences without annotated aspect terms. In this case, when we used all words in the sentences as features, it may bring much noise. In future work, we consider to generate more effective features from external resources to indicate the relationships between aspects and categories to improve our system.

4 Aspect Term Sentiment Polarity Classification System

Once we extract aspect terms, this task aims at classifying the sentiment orientation of the annotated aspect terms. To address this task, we firstly extracted three types of features: sentiment lexicon based features, topic model based features and other features. Then two machine learning algorithms, i.e., SVM and MaxEnt, were used to conduct classification models.

4.1 Features

4.1.1 Sentiment Lexicon (SL) Features

We observed that the sentiment orientation of an aspect term is usually revealed by the surrounding terms. So in this feature we took four words before and four words after the current aspect term and then calculated their respective positive,negative and neutral scores. During the calculation we reversed the sentiment orientation of the term if a negation occurs before it. We manually built a negative list: {*no, nor, not, neither, none, nobody, nothing, hardly, seldom*}. Eight sentiment lexicons are used: Bing Liu opinion lexicon[4], General Inquirer lexicon[5], IMDB[6], MPQA[7], SentiWordNet[8], NRC emotion lexicon[9], NRC Hashtag Sentiment Lexicon[10] and NRC Sentiment140 Lexicon[11]. With regard to the synonym selection of SentiWordNet, we selected the first term in the synset as our lexicon. If the eight words surrounding the aspect term do not exist in the eight corresponding sentiment lexicons, we set their three sentiment scores as 0. Then we got 24 sentiment values for each word (3 polarities * 8 lexicons) and summed up the values of eight words for each sentiment polarity (i.e., positive, negative and neural). Finally we got 24 sentiment lexicon features for each aspect.

[4]http://www.cs.uic.edu/~liub/FBS/sentiment-analysis.html#lexicon

[5]http://www.wjh.harvard.edu/~inquirer/homecat.htm

[6]http://anthology.aclweb.org//S/S13/S13-2.pdf#page=444

[7]http://mpqa.cs.pitt.edu/

[8]http://sentiwordnet.isti.cnr.it/

[9]http://mailman.uib.no/public/corpora/2012-June/015643.html

[10]http://www.umiacs.umd.edu/~saif/WebDocs/NRC-Hashtag-Sentiment-Lexicon-v0.1.zip

[11]http://sentiwordnet.isti.cnr.it/

feature	F-pos(%)		F-neg(%)		F-neu(%)		Acc(%)	
	MaxEnt	SVM	MaxEnt	SVM	MaxEnt	SVM	MaxEnt	SVM
SL	72.50± 1.91	70.99± 5.91	65.10± 1.99	65.66± 3.48	25.54± 5.68	24.02± 9.28	62.28± 2.59	61.61± 4.68
+Other	72.92± 2.12	72.70± 1.44	65.93± 3.89	65.09± 3.67	31.14± 5.77	34.00± 7.31	62.88± 3.22	62.54± 3.17
+Topic	**73.14± 1.02**	72.21± 1.44	**65.55± 5.43**	65.58± 3.45	**34.34± 10.55**	12.16± 4.96	**63.00± 4.34**	61.74± 3.10

Table 6: The results of our system in subtask 2 on laptop training data based on 5-fold cross validation.

features	F-pos(%)		F-neg(%)		F-neu(%)		Acc(%)	
	MaxEnt	SVM	MaxEnt	SVM	MaxEnt	SVM	MaxEnt	SVM
SL	79.78± 1.37	79.85± 1.35	49.37± 3.54	47.96± 4.52	26.02± 3.62	31.67± 2.84	65.61± 2.59	65.45± 1.98
+Other	80.48± 2.18	79.09± 1.42	53.17± 2.70	50.51± 3.34	29.25± 3.60	33.13± 6.89	66.80± 2.33	65.21± 2.35
+Topic	**80.71± 1.71**	77.94± 1.34	**52.61± 2.52**	46.65± 3.17	**34.51± 3.35**	3.40± 2.79	**67.18± 2.52**	64.72± 1.48

Table 7: The results of our system in subtask 2 on restaurant training data based on 5-fold cross validation.

4.1.2 Topic Features

In this section we considered to use the bag-of-topics feature to replace the traditional bag-of-words feature since the bag-of-words feature are very sparse in the data set. To construct the clusters of topics, we used the LDA[12] based topic model to estimate the K topics (in our experiment, we set K to 50) from training data. Then we inferred the topic distribution from training and test data respectively as topic features.

4.1.3 Other Features

Besides, we also proposed the following other features in order to capture more useful information from the short texts.

Aspect distance This feature records the number of words from the current aspect to the next aspect in the same sentence. If the current aspect term is the last term in the sentence, this value is calculated as the negative number of words from the current aspect to the former aspect. If only one aspect term exists in a sentence, then the value is set to zero.

Number of aspects This feature describes the number of aspect terms in the current sentence.

Negation flag feature We set this feature as 1 if a negation word occurs in the current sentence, otherwise -1.

Number of negations This feature is the number of negation words in the current sentence.

4.2 Classification Algorithms

The maximum entropy and SVM which are implemented in Mallet toolkit (McCallum, 2002) and LibSVM (Chang and Lin, 2011) respectively are used to construct the classification model from training data. Due to the limit of time, all parameters are set as defaults.

[12]http://www.cs.princeton.edu/ blei/lda-c/

4.3 Results and Discussions

4.3.1 Results on Training Data

To compare the performance of different features and different algorithms, we performed a 5-fold cross validation on training data of two domains. Table 6 and Table 7 show the results of two domains in terms of F-scores and accuracy with mean and standard deviation. The best results are shown in bold.

From above two tables, we found that (1) MaxEnt performed better than SVM on both datasets and all feature types, and (2) using all features achieved the best results. Moreover, the F-pos result was the highest in both datasets and the possible reason is that the majority of training instances are positive sentiment. We also found that in restaurant dataset, F-neg (52.61%) was much smaller than F-pos (80.17%). However, in laptop dataset, they performed comparable results. The possible reason is that the number of negative instances (805) is much smaller than the number of positive instances (2164) in restaurant dataset, while the distribution is nearly even in laptop dataset. So for restaurant data, we also conducted another controlled experiment which doubled the amount of negative instances of restaurant dataset. Table 8 shows the preliminary experimental results on the doubled negative training data. It illustrates that the F-neg increases a little but the overall accuracy without any improvement even slightly decreases after doubling the negative instances. This result is beyond our expectation but no further deep analysis has been done so far.

Strategy	F-pos(%)	F-neg(%)	F-neu(%)	Acc(%)
Double	80.28	**55.11**	19.22	65.48
No double	**80.71**	52.61	**34.51**	**67.18**

Table 8: The results of controlled experiment on restaurant dataset (MaxEnt).

4.3.2 Results on Test Data

Based on above results on training data, our final system used all provided training data for both domains. The MaxEnt algorithm is used for our final system. Table 9 shows our results alone with the top two systems results released by organizers.

Our final results ranked the 12th on the laptop dataset and the 14th on the restaurant dataset. On one hand, the accuracy in restaurant dataset is higher than laptop dataset for the possible reason that the data size of restaurant dataset is much bigger than that of laptop dataset. On the other hand, our results ranked middle in both datasets. Since we utilized eight contextual words around aspect to extract features and it may bring some noise.

Dataset	laptop	restaurant
our system	61.16	70.72
rank 1 system	70.49	80.95
rank 2 system	66.97	80.16

Table 9: The Accuracy (%) of our system and the top two systems on test dataset in subtask 2.

5 Aspect Category Sentiment Polarity System

The aspect category sentiment polarity classification task is also only applicable to restaurant domain. For this task, we adopted the bag-of-sentiment_words representation, extracted sentiment features and used the supervised machine learning algorithms to determine the sentiment orientation of each category.

5.1 Features

To extract features, we firstly used eight sentiment lexicons mentioned in Section 4.1.1 to build a big sentiment words dictionary. Then we extracted all aspect words and all sentiment words in training set as features. In the training and test data, we used the sentiment polarity score of sentiment word and the presence or absence of each aspect term as their feature values.

5.2 Classification Algorithms

The MaxEnt algorithm implemented in Mallet (McCallum, 2002) with default parameters is used to build a polarity classifier.

5.3 Experiment and Results

We used all features and the maximum entropy algorithm to conduct our final system. Table 10 lists the final results of our submitted system along with top two systems.

As shown in Table 10, the accuracy of our system is 0.63 while the best result is 0.83. The main reason is that the features we used are quite simple. For the future work, more sufficient features are examined to help classification.

6 Conclusion

In this work we proposed a combination of NP and NER method and multiple features for aspect extraction. And we also used multiple features including eight sentiment lexicons for aspect and category sentiment classification. Our final systems rank above average in the four subtasks. In future work, we would expect to improve the recall of aspect terms extraction by extending name lists using external data and seek other effective features such as discourse relation, syntactic structure to improve the classification accuracy.

Systems	our system	rank 1 system	rank 2 system
Acc(%)	63.41	82.93	78.15

Table 10: The accuracy of our system and the top two systems of subtask 4 on test dataset

Acknowledgements

The authors would like to thank the organizers and reviewers for this interesting task and their helpful suggestions and comments. This research is supported by grants from National Natural Science Foundation of China (No.60903093) and Shanghai Knowledge Service Platform Project (No. ZF1213).

References

Stefano Baccianella, Andrea Esuli, and Fabrizio Sebastiani. 2010. Sentiwordnet 3.0: An enhanced lexical resource for sentiment analysis and opinion mining. In *LREC*, volume 10, pages 2200–2204.

Chih-Chung Chang and Chih-Jen Lin. 2011. LIBSVM: A library for support vector machines. *ACM Transactions on Intelligent Systems and Technology*, 2:27:1–27:27. Software available at `http://www.csie.ntu.edu.tw/~cjlin/libsvm`.

Namrata Godbole, Manja Srinivasaiah, and Steven Skiena. 2007. Large-scale sentiment analysis for news and blogs. *ICWSM*, 7.

Suin Kim, Jianwen Zhang, Zheng Chen, Alice Oh, and Shixia Liu. 2013. A hierarchical aspect-sentiment model for online reviews. In *Proceedings of AAAI*.

Sudheer Kovelamudi, Sethu Ramalingam, Arpit Sood, and Vasudeva Varma. 2011. Domain independent model for product attribute extraction from user reviews using wikipedia. In *IJCNLP*, pages 1408–1412.

Lun-Wei Ku, Yu-Ting Liang, and Hsin-Hsi Chen. 2006. Opinion extraction, summarization and tracking in news and blog corpora. In *AAAI Spring Symposium: Computational Approaches to Analyzing Weblogs*, volume 100107.

Bing Liu. 2012. Sentiment analysis and opinion mining. *Synthesis Lectures on Human Language Technologies*, 5(1):1–167.

Chong Long, Jie Zhang, and Xiaoyan Zhut. 2010. A review selection approach for accurate feature rating estimation. In *Proceedings of the 23rd International Conference on Computational Linguistics: Posters*, pages 766–774. Association for Computational Linguistics.

Andrew Kachites McCallum. 2002. Mallet: A machine learning for language toolkit. http://mallet.cs.umass.edu.

Arjun Mukherjee and Bing Liu. 2012. Aspect extraction through semi-supervised modeling. In *Proceedings of the 50th Annual Meeting of the Association for Computational Linguistics: Long Papers-Volume 1*, pages 339–348. Association for Computational Linguistics.

Maria Pontiki, Dimitrios Galanis, John Pavlopoulos, Haris Papageorgiou, Ion Androutsopoulos, and Suresh Manandhar. 2014. Semeval-2014 task 4: Aspect based sentiment analysis. in proceedings of the 8th international workshop on semantic evaluation (semeval 2014). *Dublin, Ireland*.

Jason DM Rennie. 2001. *Improving multi-class text classification with naive Bayes*. Ph.D. thesis, Massachusetts Institute of Technology.

Zhiqiang Toh, Wenting Wang, Man Lan, and Xiaoli Li. 2012. An ner-based product identification and lucene-based product linking approach to cprod1 challenge: Description of submission system to cprod1 challenge. In *Data Mining Workshops (ICDMW), 2012 IEEE 12th International Conference on*, pages 869–871. IEEE.

Theresa Wilson, Janyce Wiebe, and Paul Hoffmann. 2009. Recognizing contextual polarity: An exploration of features for phrase-level sentiment analysis. *Computational linguistics*, 35(3):399–433.

Tian Tian Zhu, Fang Xi Zhang, and Man Lan. 2013. Ecnucs: A surface information based system description of sentiment analysis in twitter in the semeval-2013 (task 2). *Atlanta, Georgia, USA*, page 408.

ECNU: Expression- and Message-level Sentiment Orientation Classification in Twitter Using Multiple Effective Features

Jiang Zhao[†], **Man Lan**[*], **Tian Tian Zhu**[†]
Department of Computer Science and Technology
East China Normal University
[†]51121201042,51111201046@ecnu.cn; [*]mlan@cs.ecnu.edu.cn

Abstract

Microblogging websites (such as Twitter, Facebook) are rich sources of data for opinion mining and sentiment analysis. In this paper, we describe our approaches used for sentiment analysis in twitter (task 9) organized in SemEval 2014. This task tries to determine whether the sentiment orientations conveyed by the whole tweets or pieces of tweets are positive, negative or neutral. To solve this problem, we extracted several simple and basic features considering the following aspects: surface text, syntax, sentiment score and twitter characteristic. Then we exploited these features to build a classifier using SVM algorithm. Despite the simplicity of features, our systems rank above the average.

1 Introduction

Microblogging services such as Twitter[1], Facebook[2] today play an important role in expressing opinions on a variety of topics, discussing current issues or sharing one's feelings about different objects in our daily life (Agarwal and Sabharwal, 2012). Therefore, Twitter (and other platforms) has become a valuable source of users' sentiments and opinions and with the continuous and rapid growth of the number of tweets, analyzing the sentiments expressed in twitter has attracted more and more researchers and communities, for example, the sentiment analysis task in twitter was held in SemEval 2013 (Nakov et al., 2013). It will benefit lots of real applications such as simultaneously businesses, media outlets, and help investors to discover product trends, identify customer preferences and categorize users by analyzing these tweets (Becker et al., 2013).

The task of sentiment analysis in twitter in SemEval 2014 (Sara et al., 2014) aims to classify whether a tweet's sentiment is positive, negative or neutral at expression level or message level. The expression-level subtask (i.e., subtask A) is to determine the sentiment of a marked instance of a word or phrase in the context of a given message, while the message-level subtask (i.e., subtask B) aims to determine the sentiment of a whole message. Previous work (Nakov et al., 2013) showed that message-level sentiment classification is more difficult than that of expression-level (i.e., 0.690 vs 0.889 in terms of F-measure) since a message may be composed of inconsistent sentiments.

To date, lots of approaches have been proposed for conventional blogging sentiment analysis and a very broad overview is presented in (Pang and Lee, 2008). Inspired by that, many features used in microblogging mining are adopted from traditional blogging sentiment analysis task. For example, n-grams at the character or word level, part-of-speech tags, negations, sentiment lexicons were used in most of current work (Agarwal et al., 2011; Barbosa and Feng, 2010; Zhu et al., 2013; Mohammad et al., 2013; Kökciyan et al., 2013). They found that n-grams are still effective in spite of the short length nature of microblogging and the distributions of different POS tags in tweets with different polarities are highly different (Pak and Paroubek, 2010). Compared with formal blog texts, tweets often contain many informal writings including slangs, emoticons, cre-

[1]http://twitter.com

[2]http://facebook.com/

Proceedings of the 8th International Workshop on Semantic Evaluation (SemEval 2014), pages 259–264, Dublin, Ireland, August 23-24, 2014.

ative spellings, abbreviations and special marks (i.e., mentions @ and hashtags #), and thus many twitter-specific features are proposed to characterize this phenomena. For example, features record the number of emoticons, elongated words and hashtags were used in (Mohammad et al., 2013; Zhu et al., 2013; Kökciyan et al., 2013). In this work, we adopted many features from previous work and then these features were fed to SVM to perform classification.

The remainder of this paper is organized as follows. Section 2 describes our systems including preprocessing, feature representations, data sets, etc. Results of two subtasks and discussions are reported in Section 3. Finally, we conclude this paper in Section 4.

2 Our Systems

We extracted eight types of features and the first six types were used in subtask A and all features were used in subtask B. Then, several classification algorithms were examined on the development data set and the algorithm with the best performance was chosen in our final submitted systems.

2.1 Preprocessing

In order to remedy as many informal texts as possible, we recovered the elongated words to their normal forms, e.g., "*goooooood*" to "*good*" and collected about five thousand slangs or abbreviations from Internet to convert each slang to its complete form, e.g., "*1dering*" to "*wondering*", "*2g2b4g*" to "*to good to be forgotten*". Then these preprocessed texts were used to extract non twitter-specific features (i.e., POS, lexicon, *n*-grams, word cluster and indicator feature).

2.2 Feature Representations

2.2.1 POS Features

(Pak and Paroubek, 2010) found that POS tags help to identify the sentiments of tweets and they pointed out that objective tweets often contain more nouns than subjective tweets and subjective tweets may carry more adjectives and adverbs than objective tweets. Therefore, we used Stanford POS Tagger[3] and recorded the number of four different tags for each tweet: noun (the corresponding POS tags are "NN", "NNP", "NNS" and "NNPS"), verb (the corresponding POS tags are "VB", "VBD", "VBG", "VBN", "VBP" and "VBZ"), adjective (the corresponding POS tags are "JJ", "JJR" and "JJS") and adverb (the corresponding POS tags are "RB", "RBR" and "RBS"). Then we normalized them by the length of given instance or message.

[3]http://nlp.stanford.edu/software/tagger.shtml

2.2.2 Sentiment Lexicon-based Features

Sentiment lexicons are widely used to calculate the sentiment scores of phrases or messages in previous work (Nakov et al., 2013; Mohammad et al., 2013) and they are proved to be very helpful to detect the sentiment orientation. Given a phrase or message, we calculated the following six feature values: (1) the ratio of positive words to all words, i.e., the number of positive words divided by the number of total words; (2) the ratio of negative words to all words; (3) the ratio of objective words to all words; (4) the ratio of positive sentiment score to the total score (i.e., the sum of the positive and negative score); (5) the ratio of negative sentiment score to the total score; (6) the ratio of positive score to negative score, if the negative score is zero, which means this phrase or message has a very strong positive sentiment orientation, we set ten times of positive score as its value.

During the calculation, we also considered the effects of negation words since they may reverse the sentiment orientation in most cases. To do so, we defined the negation context as a snippet of a tweet that starts with a negation word and ends with punctuation marks. If a non-negation word is in a negation context and also in the sentiment lexicon, we reverse its polarity. For example, the word "bad" in phrase "not bad" originally has a negative score of 0.625, after reversal, this phrase has a positive score of 0.625. A manually made list containing 29 negation words (e.g., *no*, *hardly*, *never*, etc) was used in our experiment.

Four sentiment lexicons were used to decide whether a word is subjective or objective and obtain its sentiment score.

MPQA (Wilson et al., 2009). This subjectivity lexicon contains about 8000 subjective words and each word has two types of sentiment strength: strong subjective and weak subjective, and four kinds of sentiment polarities: positive, negative, both (positive and negative) and neutral. We used this lexicon to determine whether a word is positive, negative or objective and assign a value of 0.5 or 1 if it is weak or strong subjective (i.e., positive or negative) respectively.

SentiWordNet(SWN) (Baccianella et al., 2010). This sentiment lexicon contains about 117 thousand items and each item corresponds to a synset of WordNet. Three sentiment scores: positivity, negativity, objectivity are provided and the sum of these three scores is always 1, for example, *living*#a#3, positivity: 0.5, negativity: 0.125, objectivity: 0.375. In experiment we used the most common sense of a word.

NRC (Mohammad et al., 2013). Mohammad et al. collected two sets of tweets and each tweet contains the seed hashtags or emoticons and then they labeled the sentiment orientation for each tweet according to its hashtags or emoticons. They used pointwise mutual information (PMI) to calculate the sentiment score for each word and obtained two sentiment lexicons (i.e., hashtag lexicon and emoticon lexicon).

IMDB. We generated an unigram lexicon by ourselves from a large movie review data set from IMDB website (Maas et al., 2011) which contains 25,000 positive and 25,000 negative movie reviews by calculating their PMI scores.

2.2.3 Word *n*-Gram

Words in themselves in tweets usually carry out the original sentiment orientation, so we consider word *n*-grams as one feature. We removed URLs, mentions, hashtags, stopwords from tweet and then all words were stemmed using the nltk[4] toolkit. For subtask A, only unigram was used and we used word frequency as feature values. For subtask B, both unigram and bigram were used. Besides, weighted unigram was also used where we replaced word frequency with their sentiment scores using the hashtag lexicon and emoticon lexicon in NRC.

2.2.4 Twitter-specific Features

Punctuation Generally, punctuation may express users' sentiment in a certain extent. Therefore we recorded the frequency of the following four types of punctuation: exclamation (!), question (?), double (") and single marks ('). In addition, we also recorded the number of contiguous sequences of exclamation marks, question marks, and both of them which appeared at the end of a phrase or message.

Emoticon Emoticons are widely used to directly express the sentiment of users and thus we counted the number of positive emoticons, negative emoticons and the sum of positive and negative emoticons. To identify the polarities of emoticons, we collected 36 positive emoticons and 33 negative emoticons from the Internet.

Hashtag A hashtag is a short phrase that concatenates more than one words together without white spaces and users usually use hashtags to label the subject topic of a tweet, e.g., *#toobad*, *#ihateschool*, *#NewGlee*. Since a hashtag may contain a strong sentiment orientation, we first used the Viterbi algorithm (Berardi et al., 2011) to split hashtags and then calculated the sentiment scores of hashtags using the hashtag and emoticon lexicon in NRC.

2.2.5 Word Cluster

Apart from *n*-gram, we presented another word representations based on word clusters to explore shallow semantic meanings and reduced the sparsity of the word space. 1000 word clusters provided by CMU pos-tagging tool[5] were used to represent tweet contents. For each tweet we recorded the number of words from each cluster, resulting in 1000 features.

2.2.6 Indicator Features

We observed that the polarity of a message sometimes is revealed by some special individual positive or negative words in a certain degree. However the sentiment lexicon based features where a synthetical sentiment score of a message is calculated may hide this information. Therefore, we directly used several individual sentiment scores as features. Specifically, we created the following sixteen features for each message where the hashtag and emoticon lexicons were used to obtain sentiment scores: the sentiment scores of the first and last sentiment-bearing words, the three highest and lowest sentiment scores.

2.3 Data sets and Evaluation Metric

The organizers provide tweet ids and a script for all participants to collect data. Table 1 shows the statistics of the data set used in our experiments. To examine the generalization of models trained on tweets, the test data provided by the organizers consists of instances from different domains for both subtasks. Specifically, five corpora are included: LiveJournal(2014) is a collection of comments from LiveJournal blogs, SMS2013 is a SMS

[4] http://nltk.org/

[5] http://www.ark.cs.cmu.edu/TweetNLP/

data set directly from last year, Twitter2013 is a twitter data set directly from last year, Twitter2014 is a new twitter data set and Twitter2014Sarcasm is a collection of tweets that contain sarcasm. Notice that the data set SMS2013 and Twitter2013 were also used as our development set. Form Table 1, we find that (1) the class distributions of test data sets almost agree with training data sets for both subtasks, (2) the percentages of class *neutral* in two subtasks are significantly different (4.7% vs 45.5%), which reflects that a sentence which is composed of different sentiment expressions may act neutrality, (3) Twitter2014Sarcasm data set is very small. According to the guideline, we did not use any development data for training in the evaluation period.

data set	Positive	Negative	Neutral	Total
subtask A:				
train	3,609(61%)	2,023(34%)	265(5%)	5,897
dev	2,734(62%)	1,541(35%)	160(3%)	4,435
test				
LiveJournal	660(50%)	511(39%)	144(11%)	1,315
SMS2013	1,071(46%)	1,104(47%)	159(7%)	2,334
Twitter2013	2,734(62%)	1,541(35%)	160(3%)	4,435
Twitter2014	1,807(73%)	578(23%)	88(4%)	2,473
Twitter2014S	82(66%)	37(30%)	5(4%)	124
all	6,354(59%)	3,771(35%)	556(6%)	10,681
subtask B:				
train	3,069(36%)	1,313(15%)	4,089(49%)	8,471
dev	1,572(41%)	601(16%)	1,640(43%)	3,813
test				
LiveJournal	427(37%)	304(27%)	411(36%)	1,142
SMS2013	492(24%)	394(19%)	1,207(57%)	2,093
Twitter2013	1,572(41%)	601(16%)	1,640(43%)	3,813
Twitter2014	982(53%)	202(11%)	669(36%)	1,853
Twitter2014S	33(38%)	40(47%)	13(15%)	86
all	3,506(39%)	1,541(17%)	3,940(44%)	8,987

Table 1: Statistics of data sets in training (train), development (dev), test (test) set. Twitter2014S stands for Twitter2014Sarcasm.

We used macro-averaged F-measure of positive and negative classes (without neutral since it is margin in training data) to evaluate the performance of our systems and the averaged F-measure of five corpora was used to rank the final results.

2.4 Submitted System Configurations

For each subtask, each team can submit two runs: (1) *constrained*: only the provided data set can be used for training and no additional annotated data is allowed for training, however other resources such as lexicons are allowed; (2) *unconstrained*: any additional data can be used for training. We explored several classification algorithms on the development set and configured our final systems as follows. For constrained system, we used SVM and logistic regression algorithm implemented in scikit-learn toolkit (Pedregosa et al., 2011) to address two subtasks respectively and used self-training strategy to conduct unconstrained system. Self-training is a semi-supervised learning method where a classifier is first trained with a small amount of labeled data and then we repeat the following procedure: the most confident predictions by the current classifier are added to training pool and then the classifier is retrained(Zhu, 2005). The parameters in constrained models and the growth size k and iteration number T in self-training are listed in Table 2 according to the results of preliminary experiments.

task	constrained	unconstrained
subtask A	SVM, kernel=*rbf*, c=500	k=100, T=40
subtask B	LogisticRegression, c=1	k=90, T=40

Table 2: System configurations for the constrained and unconstrained runs in two subtasks.

3 Results and Discussion

3.1 Results

We submitted four systems as described above and their final results are shown in Table 3, as well as the top-ranked systems released by the organizers. From the table, we observe the following findings.

Firstly, we find that the results of message-level polarity classification are much worse than the results of expression-level polarity disambiguation (82.93 vs 61.22) on both constrained and unconstrained systems, which is consistent with the previous work (Nakov et al., 2013). The low performance of message-level task may result from two possible reasons: (1) a message may contain mixed sentiments and (2) the strength of sentiments is different. In contrast, the texts in expression-level task are usually short and contain a single sentiment orientation, which leads to better performance.

Secondly, whether on constrained or unconstrained systems, the performance on Twitter2014Sarcasm data set is much worse than the performance on the other four data sets. This is because that sarcasm often expresses the opposite meaning of what it seems to say, that means the actual sentiment orientation of a word is opposite to its original orientation. Moreover, even for our human it is a challenge to identify whether it is a sarcasm or not.

Thirdly, the results on LiveJournal and SMS are comparable to the results on Twitter2013 and Twitter2014 in both subtasks, which indicates that online comments and SMS share some common characteristics with tweets (e.g., emoticons and punctuation). Therefore, in case of lack of labeled online comments or SMS data, we can use the existing tweets as training data instead.

Fourthly, our unconstrained systems exploit the test data of year 2014 in training stage and perform a worse result in subtask B. We speculate that the failure of using self-training on message-level data set is because that the performance of initial classifier was low and thus in the following iterations more and more noisy instances were selected to add the training pool, which eventually resulted in a final weak classifier.

In summary, we adopted some simple and basic features to classify the polarities of expressions and messages and they were promising. For subtask A, our systems rank 5th out of 19 submissions under the constrained setting and rank 2nd out of 6 submissions under the unconstrained setting. For subtask B, our systems rank 16th out of 42 submissions under the constrained setting and rank 5th out of 8 submissions under the unconstrained setting.

3.2 Feature Combination Experiments

To explore the effectiveness of different feature types, we conducted a series of feature combination experiments using the constrained setting as shown in Table 2 for both subtasks. For each time we repeated to add one feature type to current feature set and then selected the best one until all the feature types were processed. Table 4 shows the results of different feature combinations and the best results are shown in bold font.

From Table 4, we find that (1) MPQA, *n*-gram and Word_cluster are the most effective feature types to identify the polarities; (2) The POS tags make margin contribution to improve the performance since Stanford parser is designed for formal texts and in the future we may use specific parser instead; (3) The lexicon IMDB extracted from movie reviews has negative effects to classify twitter data, which indicates that there exist differences in the way of expressing sentiments between these two domains; (4) Twitter-specific features, i.e., hashtag and emoticon, are not as effective as expected. This is because they are sparse in the data sets. In subtask A with 16578 instances, only 292 instances (1.76%) have hashtags and 419 instances (2.52%) have emoticons. In subtask B with 17458 messages, more instances have hashtags (16.72%) and emoticons (26.70%). (5) For subtask A MPQA, *n*-gram, NRC and punctuation features achieve the best performance and for subtask B the best performance is achieved by using almost all features.

In summary, we find that *n*-gram and some lexicons such as MPQA are the most effective while twitter-specific features (i.e., hashtag and emoticon) are not as discriminating as expected and the main reason for this is that they are sparse in the data sets.

Feature	Subtask A	Feature	Subtask B
MPQA	77.49	Word_cluster	53.50
.+*n*-gram	80.08(2.59)	.+MPQA	58.35(4.85)
.+NRC	82.42(2.34)	.+W1Gram	60.22(1.87)
.+Pun.	**83.83**(1.41)	.+Pun.	60.99(0.77)
.+POS	83.83(0)	.+Indicator	61.38(0.39)
.+Emoticon	83.49(-0.34)	.+SWN	61.51(0.13)
.+Hashtag	83.54(0.05)	.+Hashtag	61.54(0.03)
.+IMDB	83.51(-0.03)	.+*n*-gram	61.56(0.02)
.+SWN	82.92(-0.59)	.+Emoticon	61.69(0.13)
-	-	.+POS	**61.71**(0.02)
-	-	.+IMDB	61.11(-0.6)
-	-	.+NRC	61.23(0.12)

Table 4: The results of feature combination experiments. The numbers in the brackets are the performance increments compared with the previous results. ".+" means to add current feature to the previous feature set.

4 Conclusion

In this paper we used several basic feature types to identify the sentiment polarity at expression level or message level and these feature types include *n*-gram, sentiment lexicon and twitter-specific features, etc. Although they are simple, our systems are still promising and rank above average (e.g., rank 5th out of 19 and 16th out of 42 in subtask A and B respectively under the constrained setting). For the future work, we would like to analyze the distributions of different sentiments in sentences.

Acknowledgments

This research is supported by grants from National Natural Science Foundation of China (No.60903093) and Shanghai Knowledge Service Platform Project (No. ZF1213).

References

Apoorv Agarwal and Jasneet Sabharwal. 2012. End-to-end sentiment analysis of twitter data. In *Pro-*

Systems	LiveJournal	SMS2013	Twitter2013	Twitter2014	Twitter2014S	Average
A-constrained (expression-level)	81.67	89.31	87.28	82.67	73.71	82.93
A-unconstrained	81.69	89.26	87.29	82.93	73.71	82.98
NRC-Canada-A-constrained*	85.49	88.03	90.14	86.63	77.13	85.48
Think_Positive-A-unconstrained*	80.90	87.65	88.06	82.05	76.74	83.08
B-constrained(message-level)	69.44	59.75	62.31	63.17	51.43	61.22
B-unconstrained	64.08	56.73	63.72	63.04	49.33	59.38
NRC-Canada-B-constrained*	74.84	70.28	70.75	69.85	58.16	68.78
Think_Positive-B-unconstrained*	66.96	63.20	68.15	67.04	47.85	62.64

Table 3: Performance of our systems and the top-ranked systems (marked with asterisk).

ceedings of the Workshop on Information Extraction and Entity Analytics on Social Media Data, pages 39–44, Mumbai, India, December. The COLING 2012 Organizing Committee.

Apoorv Agarwal, Boyi Xie, Ilia Vovsha, Owen Rambow, and Rebecca Passonneau. 2011. Sentiment analysis of twitter data. In *Proceedings of the Workshop on Languages in Social Media*, LSM '11, pages 30–38. Association for Computational Linguistics.

Stefano Baccianella, Andrea Esuli, and Fabrizio Sebastiani. 2010. Sentiwordnet 3.0: An enhanced lexical resource for sentiment analysis and opinion mining. In *LREC*, volume 10, pages 2200–2204.

Luciano Barbosa and Junlan Feng. 2010. Robust sentiment detection on twitter from biased and noisy data. In *Proceedings of the 23rd International Conference on Computational Linguistics: Posters*, pages 36–44. Association for Computational Linguistics.

Lee Becker, George Erhart, David Skiba, and Valentine Matula. 2013. Avaya: Sentiment analysis on twitter with self-training and polarity lexicon expansion. In *Proceedings of the Seventh International Workshop on Semantic Evaluation (SemEval 2013)*, pages 333–340. Association for Computational Linguistics, June.

Giacomo Berardi, Andrea Esuli, Diego Marcheggiani, and Fabrizio Sebastiani. 2011. Isti@ trec microblog track 2011: Exploring the use of hashtag segmentation and text quality ranking. In *TREC*.

Nadin Kökciyan, Arda Çelebi, Arzucan Özgür, and Suzan Üsküdarli. 2013. Bounce: Sentiment classification in twitter using rich feature sets. In *Proceedings of the Seventh International Workshop on Semantic Evaluation (SemEval 2013)*, pages 554–561. Association for Computational Linguistics, June.

Andrew L Maas, Raymond E Daly, Peter T Pham, Dan Huang, Andrew Y Ng, and Christopher Potts. 2011. Learning word vectors for sentiment analysis. In *Proceedings of the 49th Annual Meeting of the Association for Computational Linguistics: Human Language Technologies-Volume 1*, pages 142–150. Association for Computational Linguistics.

Saif Mohammad, Svetlana Kiritchenko, and Xiaodan Zhu. 2013. Nrc-canada: Building the state-of-the-art in sentiment analysis of tweets. In *Proceedings of the Seventh International Workshop on Semantic Evaluation (SemEval 2013)*, pages 321–327. Association for Computational Linguistics, June.

Preslav Nakov, Sara Rosenthal, Zornitsa Kozareva, Veselin Stoyanov, Alan Ritter, and Theresa Wilson. 2013. Semeval-2013 task 2: Sentiment analysis in twitter. In *Proceedings of the Seventh International Workshop on Semantic Evaluation (SemEval 2013)*, pages 312–320. Association for Computational Linguistics, June.

Alexander Pak and Patrick Paroubek. 2010. Twitter as a corpus for sentiment analysis and opinion mining. In *Proceedings of the International Conference on Language Resources and Evaluation, LREC*.

Bo Pang and Lillian Lee. 2008. Opinion mining and sentiment analysis. *Foundations and trends in information retrieval*, 2(1-2):1–135.

Fabian Pedregosa, Gaël. Varoquaux, Alexandre Gramfort, Vincent Michel, Bertrand Thirion, Olivier Grisel, Mathieu Blondel, Peter Prettenhofer, Ron Weiss, Vincent Dubourg, Jake Vanderplas, Alexandre Passos, David Cournapeau, Matthieu Brucher, Matthieu Perrot, and Édouard Duchesnay. 2011. Scikit-learn: Machine learning in Python. *Journal of Machine Learning Research*, 12:2825–2830.

Rosenthal Sara, Ritter Alan, Veselin Stoyanov, and Nakov Preslav. 2014. Semeval-2014 task 9: Sentiment analysis in twitter. In *Proceedings of the Eighth International Workshop on Semantic Evaluation (SemEval'14)*. Association for Computational Linguistics, August.

Theresa Wilson, Janyce Wiebe, and Paul Hoffmann. 2009. Recognizing contextual polarity: An exploration of features for phrase-level sentiment analysis. *Computational linguistics*, pages 399–433.

Tian Tian Zhu, Fang Xi Zhang, and Man Lan. 2013. Ecnucs: A surface information based system description of sentiment analysis in twitter in the semeval-2013 (task 2). In *Proceedings of the Seventh International Workshop on Semantic Evaluation (SemEval 2013)*, page 408.

Xiaojin Zhu. 2005. Semi-supervised learning literature survey. Technical Report 1530, Computer Sciences, University of Wisconsin-Madison.

ECNU: Leveraging on Ensemble of Heterogeneous Features and Information Enrichment for Cross Level Semantic Similarity Estimation

Tian Tian Zhu
Department of Computer Science and Technology
East China Normal University
51111201046@ecnu.cn

Man Lan*
Department of Computer Science and Technology
East China Normal University
mlan@cs.ecnu.edu.cn*

Abstract

This paper reports our submissions to the Cross Level Semantic Similarity (CLSS) task in SemEval 2014. We submitted one Random Forest regression system on each cross level text pair, i.e., Paragraph to Sentence (P-S), Sentence to Phrase (S-Ph), Phrase to Word (Ph-W) and Word to Sense (W-Se). For text pairs on P-S level and S-Ph level, we consider them as sentences and extract heterogeneous types of similarity features, i.e., string features, knowledge based features, corpus based features, syntactic features, machine translation based features, multi-level text features, etc. For text pairs on Ph-W level and W-Se level, due to lack of information, most of these features are not applicable or available. To overcome this problem, we propose several information enrichment methods using WordNet synonym and definition. Our systems rank the 2nd out of 18 teams both on Pearson correlation (official rank) and Spearman rank correlation. Specifically, our systems take the second place on P-S level, S-Ph level and Ph-W level and the 4th place on W-Se level in terms of Pearson correlation.

1 Introduction

Semantic similarity is an essential component of many applications in Natural Language Processing (NLP). Previous works often focus on text semantic similarity on the same level, i.e., paragraph to paragraph or sentence to sentence, and many effective text semantic measurements have been proposed (Islam and Inkpen, 2008), (Bär et al., 2012), (Heilman and Madnani, 2012). However, in many real world cases, the two texts may not always be on the same level. The Cross Level Semantic Similarity (CLSS) task in SemEval 2014 provides a universal platform to measure the degree of semantic equivalence between two texts across different levels. For each text pair on four cross levels, i.e., Paragraph to Sentence (P-S), Sentence to Phrase (S-Ph), Phrase to Word (Ph-W) and Word to Sense (W-Se), participants are required to return a similarity score which ranges from 0 (no relation) to 4 (semantic equivalence). We participate in all the four cross levels and take the second place out of all 18 teams both on Pearson correlation (official) and Spearman correlation ranks.

In this work, we present a supervised regression system for each cross level separately. For P-S level and S-Ph level, we regard the paragraph of P-S as a long sentence, and the phrase of S-Ph as a short sentence. Then we use various types of text similarity features including string features, knowledge based features, corpus based features, syntactic features, machine translation based features, multi-level text features and so on, to capture the semantic similarity between two texts. Some of these features are borrowed from our previous system in the Semantic Textual Similarity (STS) task in *SEM Shared Task 2013 (Zhu and Lan, 2013). Others followed the previous work in (Šaric et al., 2012) and (Pilehvar et al., 2013). For Ph-W level and W-Se level, since the text pairs lack contextual information, for example, word or sense alone no longer shares the property of sentence, most features used in P-S level and S-Ph level are not applicable or available. To overcome the problem of insufficient information in word and sense level, we propose several information enrichment methods to extend information with the aid of WordNet (Miller, 1995), which significantly improved the system performance.

The rest of this paper is organized as follows.

Proceedings of the 8th International Workshop on Semantic Evaluation (SemEval 2014), pages 265–270, Dublin, Ireland, August 23-24, 2014.

Section 2 describes the similarity features used on four cross levels in detail. Section 3 presents experiments and the results of four cross levels on training data and test data. Conclusions and future work are given in Section 4.

2 Text Similarity Measurements

To estimate the semantic similarity on P-S level and S-Ph level, we treat the text pairs on both levels as traditional semantic similarity computation on sentence level and adopt 7 types of features, i.e., string features, knowledge based features, corpus based features, syntactic features, machine translation based features, multi-level text features and other features. All of them are borrowed from previous work due to their superior performance reported. For Ph-W level and W-Se level, since word and sense alone cannot be treated as sentence, we propose an information enrichment method to extend original text with the help of WordNet. Once the word or sense is enriched with its synonym and its definition description, we can thus adopt the previous features as well.

2.1 Preprocessing

For P-S level and S-Ph level, we perform text preprocessing before we extract semantic similarity features. Firstly, the Stanford parser[1] is used for sentence tokenization and parsing. Specifically, the tokens *n't* and *'m* are replaced with *not* and *am*. Secondly, the Stanford POS Tagger[2] is used for POS tagging. Thirdly, we use Natural Language Toolkit[3] for WordNet based Lemmatization, which lemmatizes the word to its nearest base form that appears in WordNet, for example, was is lemmatized as is rather than *be*.

2.2 Features on P-S Level and S-Ph Level

We treat all text pairs of P-S level and S-Ph level as sentences and then extract 7 types of similarity features as below. Totally we get 52 similarity features. Generally, these similarity features are represented as numerical values.

String features. Intuitively, if two texts share more strings, they are considered to be more semantic similar. We extract 13 string based features in consideration of the common sequence shared by two texts. We chose the Longest Common Sequence (LCS) feature (Zhu and Lan, 2013), the N-gram Overlap feature (n=1,2,3) and the Weighted Word Overlap feature (Šaric et al., 2012). All these features are computed from original text and from the processed text after lemmatization as well. Besides, we also computed the N-gram Overlap on character level, named Character N-gram (n=2,3,4).

Knowledge based features. Knowledge based similarity estimation relies on the semantic network of words. In this work we used the knowledge based features in our previous work (Zhu and Lan, 2013), which include four word similarity metrics based on WordNet: ***Path*** similarity (Banea et al., 2012), ***WUP*** similarity (Wu and Palmer, 1994), ***LCH*** similarity (Leacock and Chodorow, 1998) and ***Lin*** similarity (Lin, 1998). Then two strategies, i.e., the best alignment strategy and the aggregation strategy, are employed to propagate the word similarity to the text similarity. Totally we get 8 knowledge based features.

Corpus based features. Latent Semantic Analysis (LSA) (Landauer et al., 1997) is a widely used corpus based measure when evaluating text similarity. In this work we use the Vector Space Sentence Similarity proposed by (Šaric et al., 2012), which represents each sentence as a single distributional vector by summing up the LSA vector of each word in the sentence. Two corpora are used to compute the LSA vector of words: New York Times Annotated Corpus (NYT) and Wikipedia. Besides, in consideration of different weights for different words, they also calculated the weighted LSA vector for each word. In addition, we use the Co-occurrence Retrieval Model (CRM) feature from our previous work (Zhu and Lan, 2013) as another corpus-based feature. The CRM is calculated based on a notion of substitutability, that is, the more appropriate it is to substitute word w_1 in place of word w_2 in a suitable natural language task, the more semantically similar they are. At last, 6 corpus based features are extracted.

Syntactic features. Dependency relations of sentences often contain semantic information. In this work we follow two syntactic dependency similarity features presented in our previous work (Zhu and Lan, 2013), i.e., Simple Dependency Overlap and Special Dependency Overlap. The Simple Dependency Overlap measures all dependency relations while the Special Dependency Overlap fea-

[1] http://nlp.stanford.edu/software/lex-parser.shtml
[2] http://nlp.stanford.edu/software/tagger.shtml
[3] http://nltk.org/

ture only focuses on the primary roles extracted from several special dependency relations, i.e., subject, object and predict.

Machine Translation based features. Machine translation (MT) evaluation metrics are designed to assess whether the output of a MT system is semantically equivalent to a set of reference translations. This type of feature has been proved to be effective in our previous work (Zhu and Lan, 2013). As a result, we extend the original 6 lexical level MT metrics to 10 metrics, i.e., *WER, TER, PER, BLEU, NIST, ROUGE-L, GTM-1,GTM-2, GTM-3* and *METEOR-ex*. All these metrics are calculated using the Asiya Open Toolkit for Automatic Machine Translation (Meta-) Evaluation[4].

Multi-level text Features. (Pilehvar et al., 2013) presented a unified approach to semantic similarity at multiple levels from word senses to text documents through the semantic signature representation of texts (e.g., sense, word or sentence). Given initial nodes (senses), they performed random walks on semantic network like WordNet, then the resulting frequency distribution over all nodes in WordNet served as semantic signature of the text. By doing so the similarity of two texts can be computed as the similarity of two semantic signatures. In this work, we borrowed their semantic signature method and adopted 3 similarity measures to estimate two semantic signatures, i.e., Cosine similarity, Weighted Overlap and Top-k Jaccard (k=250, 500).

Other Features. Besides, other simple surface features from texts, such as numbers, symbols and length of texts, are extracted. Following (Šaric et al., 2012) we adopt relative length difference, relative information content difference, numbers overlap, case match and stocks match.

2.3 Features on Ph-W Level

For Ph-W level, since word and phrase no longer share the property of sentence, most features used for sentence similarity estimation are not applicable for this level. Therefore, we adopt the following features as the basic feature set for Ph-W level.

String features. This type contains two features. The first is a boolean feature which records whether the word appears in the phrase. The second is the Weighted Word Overlap feature mentioned in Section 2.2.

Knowledge based features. As described in Section 2.2, we compute the averaged score and the maximal score between word and phrase using the four word similarity measures based on WordNet, i.e., ***Path***, ***WUP***, ***LCH*** and ***Lin***.

Corpus based features. We adopt the Vector Space Similarity described in Section 2.2. Specifically, for word the single distributional vector is the LSA vector of itself.

Multi-level text Features. As described in Section 2.2, since the semantic signatures are proposed for various kinds of texts (e.g., sense, word or sentence), they serve as one basic feature.

Obviously, the above features extracted from the phrase-word pair is significantly less than the features used in P-S level and S-Ph level. This is because the information contained in phrase-word pair is much less than that in sentences and paragraphs. To overcome this information insufficient problem, we propose an information enrichment method based on WordNet to extend the initial word in Ph-W level as below.

Word Expansion with Definition. For the word part in Ph-W level, we extract its definition in terms of its most common concept in WordNet and then replace the initial word with this definition. This gives a much richer set of initial single word. Since a word may have many senses, not all of this word definition expansion are correct. But we show below empirically that using this expanded set improves performance. By doing so we treat the phrase and the definition of the original word as two sentences, and thus, all features described in Section 2.2 are calculated.

2.4 Features on W-Se Level

For W-Se level, the information that a word and a sense carry is less than other levels. Hence, the basic features that can be extracted from the original word-sense pair are even less than Ph-W level. Therefore the basic features we use for W-Se level are as follows.

String features. Two boolean string features are used. One records whether the word-sense pair shares the same POS tag and another records whether the word-sense pair share the same word.

Knowledge based features. As described in Section 2.2, four knowledge-based word similarity measures based on WordNet are calculated.

Multi-level text Features. The multi-level text features are the same as Ph-W level.

In consideration of the lack of contextual infor-

[4]http://nlp.lsi.upc.edu/asiya/

mation between word-sense pair, we also propose three information enrichment methods in order to generate more effective information for word and sense with the aid of WordNet.

Word Expansion with Synonyms. For the word part in W-Se level, we extract its synonyms with the help of WordNet, then update the values of above basic features if its synonyms achieve higher feature value than the original word itself.

Sense Expansion with Definition. For the sense in W-Se level, we directly use its definition in WordNet to enrich its information. By doing so the similarity estimation of W-Se level can be converted to that of word-phrase level, therefore we use all basic features for Ph-W level described in Section2.3.

Word-Sense Expansion with Definition. Unlike the above two expansion methods which focus only on one part of W-Se level, the third method is to enrich information for word and sense together by using their definitions in WordNet. As before we extract the word definition in terms of its most common concept in WordNet and then replace the initial word with this definition. Then we use all features in Section 2.2.

3 Experiment and Results

We adopt supervised regression model for each cross level. In order to compare the performance of different regression algorithms, we perform 5-fold cross validation on training data for each cross level. We used several regression algorithms including Support Vector Regression (SVR) with 3 different kernels (i.e., linear, polynomial and rbf), Random Forest, Stochastic Gradient Descent (SGD) and Decision Tree implemented in the scikit-learn toolkit (Pedregosa et al., 2011). The system performance is evaluated in Pearson correlation (r) (official measure) and Spearman's rank correlation (ρ).

3.1 Results on Training Data

Table 1 and Table 2 show the averaged performance of different regression algorithms in terms of Pearson correlation (r) and Spearman's rank correlation (ρ) on the training data of P-S level and S-Ph level using 5-fold cross validation, where the standard deviation is given in brackets. The results show that Random Forest performs the best both on P-S level and S-Ph level whether in (r) or (ρ). We also find that the results of P-S level are better than that of S-Ph level, and the reason may be that paragraph and sentence pair contain more information than the sentence and phrase pair.

Regression Algorithm	r (%)	ρ (%)
SVR, ker=rbf	80.70 (±1.47)	79.90 (±1.66)
SVR, ker=poly	73.78 (±1.57)	74.41 (±1.89)
SVR, ker=linear	80.43 (±1.13)	79.46 (±1.51)
Random Forest	**80.92** (±1.40)	**80.20** (±2.00)
SGD	77.61 (±0.76)	77.14 (±1.49)
Decision Tree	73.23 (±2.14)	71.84 (±2.55)

Table 1: Results of different algorithms using 5-fold cross validation on training data of P-S level

Regression Algorithm	r (%)	ρ (%)
SVR, ker=rbf	66.14 (±5.14)	65.76 (±5.93)
SVR, ker=poly	58.93 (±2.29)	63.62 (±4.15)
SVR, ker=linear	66.78 (±4.51)	66.34 (±4.90)
Random Forest	**73.18** (±5.23)	**70.30** (±5.51)
SGD	63.18 (±3.61)	64.80 (±4.21)
Decision Tree	67.66 (±6.76)	66.03 (±6.64)

Table 2: Results of different algorithms using 5-fold cross validation on training data of S-Ph level

Table 3 shows the results of different regression algorithms and different feature sets in terms of r and ρ on the training data of Ph-W level using 5-fold cross validation, where the basic features are denoted as Feature Set A and their combination with word definition expansion features are denoted as Feature Set B. The results show that almost all algorithms performance have been improved by using word definition expansion feature except Decision Tree. This proves the effectiveness of the information enrichment method we proposed in this level. Besides, Random Forest achieves the best performance again with r=44% and ρ=41%. However, in comparison with P-S level and S-Ph level, all scores in Table 3 drop a lot even with information enrichment method. The possible reason may be two: the reduction of information on Ph-W level and our information enrichment method brings in a certain noise as well.

For W-Se level, in order to examine the performance of different information enrichment methods, we perform experiments on 4 different feature sets from A to D, where feature set A contains the basic features, feature set B, C and D add one information enrichment method based on former feature set. Table 4 and 5 present the r and ρ results of 4 feature sets using different regression algorithms. From Table 4 and 5 we see that most correlation scores are below 40% and

Regression Algorithm	r (%)		ρ (%)	
	Feature Set A[1]	Feature Set B[2]	Feature Set A	Feature Set B
SVR, ker=rbf	34.67 (±4.34)	42.62 (±6.36)	33.26 (±4.24)	40.87 (±6.24)
SVR, ker=poly	19.00 (±4.26)	24.06 (±5.55)	21.13 (±4.86)	28.35 (±6.11)
SVR, ker=linear	34.87 (±4.65)	41.91 (±2.05)	35.42 (±5.05)	42.69 (±0.55)
Random Forest	43.17 (±7.72)	**44.00** (±6.88)	40.34 (±5.71)	**41.80** (±6.76)
SGD	26.20 (±3.37)	38.69 (±4.60)	23.55 (±5.01)	38.00 (±2.64)
Decision Tree	39.22 (±7.54)	32.22 (±12.74)	38.90 (±6.03)	31.64 (±10.47)

[1] Feature Set A = basic feature set
[2] Feature Set B = Feature Set A + Word Definition Expansion Features

Table 3: Results of different algorithms using 5-fold cross validation on training data of Ph-W level

the performance of W-Se level is the worst among all these four levels. This illustrates that the less information the texts contain, the worse performance the model achieves. Again the Random Forest algorithm performs the best among all algorithms. Again almost all information enrichment features perform better than Feature set A. This illustrates that these information enrichment methods do help to improve performance. When we observe the three information enrichment methods, we find that feature set C performs the best. In comparison with feature set C, feature set B only used word synonyms to expand information and this expansion is quite limited. Feature set D performs better than B but still worse than C. The reason may be that when we extend sense with its definition, the definition is accurate and exactly represents the meaning of sense. However since a word often contains more than one concepts, and when we use the definition of the most common concept to extend word, such extension may not be correct and the generated information may contain more noise and/or change the original meaning of word.

3.2 Results on Test Data

According to the experiments on training data, we select Random Forest as the final regression algorithm. The number of trees in Random Forest n is optimized to 50 and the rest parameters are set to be default. All features in Section 2.2 are used on P-S level, S-Ph level and Ph-W level. For W-Se level, we take all features except word-sense definition expansion feature which has been shown to impair the system performance. For each level, all training examples are used to learn the corresponding regression model. According to the official results released by organizers, Table 6 and Table 7 list the top 3 systems in terms of r (official) and ρ. Our final systems rank the second both in terms of r and ρ and also achieve the second place on P-S level, S-Ph level and Ph-W level, as well as the 4th place on W-Se level in terms of official Pearson correlation.

Team	P-S	S-Ph	Ph-W	W-Se	r Rank
SimCompass	0.811	0.742	0.415	0.356	1
ECNU	0.834	0.771	0.315	0.269	2
UNAL-NLP	0.837	0.738	0.274	0.256	3

Table 6: Pearson Correlation (official) on test data

Team	P-S	S-Ph	Ph-W	W-Se	ρ Rank
SimCompass	0.801	0.728	0.424	0.344	1
ECNU	0.821	0.757	0.306	0.263	2
UNAL-NLP	0.820	0.710	0.249	0.236	6

Table 7: Spearman Correlation on test data

4 Conclusion

We build a supervised Random Forest regression model for each cross level. For P-S and S-Ph level, we adopt the ensemble of heterogeneous similarity features, i.e., string features, knowledge based features, corpus based features, syntactic features, machine translation based features, multi-level text features and other features to capture the semantic similarity between two texts with distinctively different lengths. For Ph-W and W-Se level, we propose information enrichment methods to lengthen original texts in order to generate more semantic features, which has been proved to be effective. Our submitted final systems rank the 2nd out of 18 teams both on Pearson Rank (official rank) and Spearman Rank, and also rank the second place on P-S level, S-Ph level and Ph-W level, as well as the 4th place on W-Se level in terms of Pearson correlation. In future work we will focus on information enrichment methods which bring in more accurate information and less noises.

Acknowledgments

This research is supported by grants from National Natural Science Foundation of China

Regression Algorithm	Feature Set A[1]	Feature Set B[2]	Feature Set C[3]	Feature Set D[4]
SVR, ker=rbf	29.85 (±7.29)	34.49 (±5.55)	36.80 (±6.46)	22.19 (±6.49)
SVR, ker=poly	24.62 (±3.63)	29.27 (±3.53)	26.55 (±1.27)	25.89 (±5.63)
SVR, ker=linear	29.58 (±5.88)	34.87 (±3.97)	35.96 (±1.75)	34.57 (±3.75)
Random Forest	22.87 (±5.59)	33.97 (±1.78)	**40.43** (±3.00)	37.54 (±3.20)
SGD	26.32 (±7.31)	27.36 (±6.44)	32.50 (±6.02)	18.00 (±6.13)
Decision Tree	23.40 (±5.65)	26.33 (±3.86)	33.64 (±6.97)	31.86 (±3.95)

[1] Feature Set A = basic feature set
[2] Feature Set B = Feature Set A + Synonym Expansion
[3] Feature Set C = Feature Set B + Sense Definition Expansion Features
[4] Feature Set D = Feature Set C + Word-Sense Definition Expansion Features

Table 4: Results of different algorithms using 5-fold CV on training data of W-Se level (r (%))

Regression Algorithm	Feature Set A	Feature Set B	Feature Set C	Feature Set D
SVR, ker=rbf	28.41 (±8.99)	29.61 (±6.23)	34.18 (±6.36)	22.90 (±6.78)
SVR, ker=poly	23.05 (±7.53)	22.47 (±4.47)	21.63 (±4.37)	25.37 (±7.25)
SVR, ker=linear	27.29 (±7.02)	31.79 (±4.00)	34.75 (±3.55)	34.19 (±3.06)
Random Forest	19.66 (±6.75)	31.98 (±3.21)	**38.57** (±3.60)	37.56 (±3.15)
SGD	24.12 (±7.98)	24.62 (±6.36)	29.27 (±5.86)	23.05 (±11.23)
Decision Tree	22.30 (±5.25)	25.09 (±3.64)	31.99 (±7.81)	30.51 (±5.27)

Table 5: Results of different algorithms using 5-fold CV on training data of W-Se level (ρ (%))

(No.60903093) and Shanghai Knowledge Service Platform Project (No. ZF1213).

References

Carmen Banea, Samer Hassan, Michael Mohler, and Rada Mihalcea. 2012. Unt: A supervised synergistic approach to semantic text similarity. pages 635–642. First Joint Conference on Lexical and Computational Semantics (*SEM).

Daniel Bär, Chris Biemann, Iryna Gurevych, and Torsten Zesch. 2012. Ukp: Computing semantic textual similarity by combining multiple content similarity measures. pages 435–440. First Joint Conference on Lexical and Computational Semantics (*SEM).

Michael Heilman and Nitin Madnani. 2012. Ets: Discriminative edit models for paraphrase scoring. pages 529–535. First Joint Conference on Lexical and Computational Semantics (*SEM).

Aminul Islam and Diana Inkpen. 2008. Semantic text similarity using corpus-based word similarity and string similarity. *ACM Transactions on Knowledge Discovery from Data (TKDD)*, 2(2):10.

Thomas K Landauer, Darrell Laham, Bob Rehder, and Missy E Schreiner. 1997. How well can passage meaning be derived without using word order? a comparison of latent semantic analysis and humans. In *Proceedings of the 19th annual meeting of the Cognitive Science Society*, pages 412–417.

Claudia Leacock and Martin Chodorow. 1998. Combining local context and wordnet similarity for word sense identification. *WordNet: An electronic lexical database*, 49(2):265–283.

Dekang Lin. 1998. An information-theoretic definition of similarity. In *Proceedings of the 15th international conference on Machine Learning*, volume 1, pages 296–304. San Francisco.

George A Miller. 1995. Wordnet: a lexical database for english. *Communications of the ACM*, 38(11):39–41.

Fabian Pedregosa, Gaël. Varoquaux, Alexandre Gramfort, Vincent Michel, Bertrand Thirion, Olivier Grisel, Mathieu Blondel, Peter Prettenhofer, Ron Weiss, Vincent Dubourg, Jake Vanderplas, Alexandre Passos, David Cournapeau, Matthieu Brucher, Matthieu Perrot, and Édouard Duchesnay. 2011. Scikit-learn: Machine learning in Python. *Journal of Machine Learning Research*, 12:2825–2830.

Mohammad Taher Pilehvar, David Jurgens, and Roberto Navigli. 2013. Align, disambiguate and walk: A unified approach for measuring semantic similarity. In *Proceedings of the 51st Annual Meeting of the Association for Computational Linguistics (ACL 2013)*.

Frane Šaric, Goran Glavaš, Mladen Karan, Jan Šnajder, and Bojana Dalbelo Bašic. 2012. Takelab: Systems for measuring semantic text similarity. pages 441–448. First Joint Conference on Lexical and Computational Semantics (*SEM).

Zhibiao Wu and Martha Palmer. 1994. Verbs semantics and lexical selection. In *Proceedings of the 32nd annual meeting on Association for Computational Linguistics*, pages 133–138. Association for Computational Linguistics.

Tian Tian Zhu and Man Lan. 2013. Ecnucs: Measuring short text semantic equivalence using multiple similarity measurements. *Atlanta, Georgia, USA*, page 124.

ECNU: One Stone Two Birds: Ensemble of Heterogenous Measures for Semantic Relatedness and Textual Entailment

Jiang Zhao, Tian Tian Zhu, Man Lan*
Department of Computer Science and Technology
East China Normal University
51121201042,51111201046@ecnu.cn; mlan@cs.ecnu.edu.cn*

Abstract

This paper presents our approach to semantic relatedness and textual entailment subtasks organized as task 1 in SemEval 2014. Specifically, we address two questions: (1) Can we solve these two subtasks together? (2) Are features proposed for textual entailment task still effective for semantic relatedness task? To address them, we extracted seven types of features including text difference measures proposed in entailment judgement subtask, as well as common text similarity measures used in both subtasks. Then we exploited the same feature set to solve the both subtasks by considering them as a regression and a classification task respectively and performed a study of influence of different features. We achieved the first and the second rank for relatedness and entailment task respectively.

1 Introduction

Distributional Semantic Models (DSMs)(surveyed in (Turney et al., 2010)) exploit the co-occurrences of other words with the word being modeled to compute the semantic meaning of the word under the distributional hypothesis: "similar words share similar contexts" (Harris, 1954). Despite their success, DSMs are severely limited to model the semantic of long phrases or sentences since they ignore grammatical structures and logical words. Compositional Distributional Semantic Models (CDSMs)(Zanzotto et al., 2010; Socher et al., 2012) extend DSMs to sentence level to capture the *compositionality* in the semantic vector space, which has seen a rapidly growing interest in recent years. Although several CDSMs have been proposed, benchmarks are lagging behind. Previous work (Grefenstette and Sadrzadeh, 2011; Socher et al., 2012) performed experiments on their own datasets or on the same datasets which are limited to a few hundred instances of very short sentences with a fixed structure.

To provide a benchmark so as to compare different CDSMs, the sentences involving compositional knowledge task in SemEval 2014 (Marelli et al., 2014) develops a large dataset which is full of lexical, syntactic and semantic phenomena. It consists of two subtasks: semantic relatedness task, which measures the degree of semantic relatedness of a sentence pair by assigning a relatedness score ranging from 1 (completely unrelated) to 5 (very related); and textual entailment (TE) task, which determines whether one of the following three relationships holds between two given sentences A and B: (1) *entailment*: the meaning of B can be inferred from A; (2) *contradiction*: A contradicts B; (3) *neutral*: the truth of B cannot be inferred on the basis of A.

Semantic textual similarity (STS) (Lintean and Rus, 2012) and semantic relatedness are closely related and interchangeably used in many literatures except that the concept of semantic similarity is more specific than semantic relatedness and the latter includes concepts as antonymy and meronymy. In this paper we regard the semantic relatedness task as a STS task. Besides, regardless of the original intention of this task, we adopted the mainstream machine learning methods instead of CDSMs to solve these two tasks by extracting heterogenous features.

Proceedings of the 8th International Workshop on Semantic Evaluation (SemEval 2014), pages 271–277,
Dublin, Ireland, August 23-24, 2014.

Like semantic relatedness, TE task (surveyed in (Androutsopoulos and Malakasiotis, 2009)) is also closely related to STS task since in TE task lots of similarity measures at different levels are exploited to boost classification. For example, (Malakasiotis and Androutsopoulos, 2007) used ten string similarity measures such as cosine similarity at the word and the character level. Therefore, the first fundamental question arises, i.e., "Can we solve both of these two tasks together?" At the same time, since high similarity does not mean entailment holds, the TE task also utilizes other features besides similarity measures. For example, in our previous work (Zhao et al., 2014) text difference features were proposed and proved to be effective. Therefore, the second question surfaces here, i.e., "Are features proposed for TE task still effective for STS task?" To answer the first question, we extracted seven types of features including text similarity and text difference and then fed them to classifiers and regressors to solve TE and STS task respectively. Regarding the second question, we conducted a series of experiments to study the performance of different features for these two tasks.

The rest of the paper is organized as follows. Section 2 briefly describes the related work on STS and TE tasks. Section 3 presents our systems including features, learning methods, etc. Section 4 shows the experimental results on training data and Section 5 reports the results of our submitted systems on test data and gives a detailed analysis. Finally, Section 6 concludes this paper with future work.

2 Related Work

Existing work on STS can be divided into 4 categories according to the similarity measures used (Gomaa and Fahmy, 2013): (1) string-based method (Bär et al., 2012; Malakasiotis and Androutsopoulos, 2007) which calculates similarities using surface strings at either character level or word level; (2) corpus-based method (Li et al., 2006) which measures word or sentence similarities using the information gained from large corpora, including Latent Semantic Analysis (LSA), pointwise mutual information (PMI), etc. (3) knowledge-based method (Mihalcea et al., 2006) which estimates similarities with the aid of external resources, such as WordNet[1]; (4) hybrid method (Zhu and Lan, 2013; Croce et al., 2013) which integrates multiple similarity measures and adopts supervised machine learning algorithms to learn the different contributions of different features.

The approaches to the task of TE can be roughly divided into two groups: (1) logic inference method (Bos and Markert, 2005) where automatic reasoning tools are used to check the logical representations derived from sentences and (2) machine learning method (Zhao et al., 2013; Gomaa and Fahmy, 2013) where a supervised model is built using a variety of similarity scores.

Unlike previous work which separately addressed these two closely related tasks by using simple feature types, in this paper we endeavor to simultaneously solve these two tasks by using heterogenous features.

3 Our Systems

We consider the two tasks as one by exploiting the same set of features but using different learning methods, i.e., classification and regression. Seven types of features are extracted and most of them are based on our previous work on TE (Zhao et al., 2014) and STS (Zhu and Lan, 2013). Many learning algorithms and parameters are examined and the final submitted systems are configured according to the preliminary results on training data.

3.1 Preprocessing

Three text preprocessing operations were performed before we extracted features, which included: (1) we converted the contractions to their formal writings, for example, *doesn't* is rewritten as *does not*. (2) the WordNet-based Lemmatizer implemented in Natural Language Toolkit[2] was used to lemmatize all words to their nearest base forms in WordNet, for example, *was* is lemmatized to *be*. (3) we replaced a word from one sentence with another word from the other sentence if the two words share the same meaning, where WordNet was used to look up synonyms. No word sense disambiguation was performed and all synsets for a particular lemma were considered.

3.2 Feature Representations

3.2.1 Length Features (len)

Given two sentences A and B, this feature type records the length information using the follow-

[1]http://wordnet.princeton.edu/

[2]http://nltk.org/

ing eight measure functions:
$|A|, |B|, |A-B|, |B-A|, |A \cup B|, |A \cap B|, \frac{(|A|-|B|)}{|B|}, \frac{(|B|-|A|)}{|A|}$ where $|A|$ stands for the number of non-repeated words in sentence A, $|A-B|$ means the number of unmatched words found in A but not in B, $|A \cup B|$ stands for the set size of non-repeated words found in either A or B and $|A \cap B|$ means the set size of shared words found in both A and B.

Moreover, in consideration of different types of words make different contributions to text similarity, we also recorded the number of words in set $A-B$ and $B-A$ whose POS tags are noun, verb, adjective and adverb respectively. We used Stanford POS Tagger[3] for POS tagging. Finally, we collected a total of sixteen features.

3.2.2 Surface Text Similarity (st)

As shown in Table 1, we adopted six commonly used functions to calculate the similarity between sentence A and B based on their surface forms, where $\overrightarrow{x}$ and $\overrightarrow{y}$ are vectorial representations of sentences A and B in $tf * idf$ schema.

Measure	Definition
Jaccard	$S_{jacc} = \|A \cap B\|/\|A \cup B\|$
Dice	$S_{dice} = 2 * \|A \cap B\|/(\|A\| + \|B\|)$
Overlap	$S_{over} = \|A \cap B\|/\|A\|$ and $\|A \cap B\|/\|B\|$
Cosine	$S_{cos} = \overrightarrow{x} \cdot \overrightarrow{y}/(\| \overrightarrow{x} \| \cdot \| \overrightarrow{y} \|)$
Manhattan	$M(\overrightarrow{x}, \overrightarrow{y}) = \sum_{i=1}^{n} \|x_i - y_i\|$
Euclidean	$E(\overrightarrow{x}, \overrightarrow{y}) = \sqrt{\sum_{i=1}^{n} (x_i - y_i)^2}$

Table 1: Surface text similarity measures and their definitions used in our experiments.

We also used three statistical correlation coefficients (i.e., Pearson, Spearmanr, Kendalltau) to measure similarity by regarding the vectorial representations as different variables. Thus we got ten features at last.

3.2.3 Semantic Similarity (ss)

The above surface text similarity features only consider the surface words rather than their actual meanings in sentences. In order to build the semantic representations of sentences, we used a latent model to capture the contextual meanings of words. Specifically, we adopted the weighted textual matrix factorization (WTMF) (Guo and Diab, 2012) to model the semantics of sentences due to its reported good ability to model short texts. This model first factorizes the original term-sentence matrix X into two matrices such that $X_{i,j} \approx P_{*,i}^T . Q_{*,j}$, where $P_{*,i}$ is a latent semantic vector profile for word w_i and $Q_{*,j}$ is a vector profile that represents the sentence s_j. Then we employed the new representations of sentences, i.e., Q, to calculate the semantic similarity between sentences using Cosine, Manhattan, Euclidean, Pearson, Spearmanr, Kendalltau measures respectively, which results in six features.

3.2.4 Grammatical Relationship (gr)

The grammatical relationship feature measures the semantic similarity between two sentences at the grammar level and this feature type was also explored in our previous work (Zhao et al., 2013; Zhu and Lan, 2013). We used Stanford Parser[4] to acquire the dependency information from sentences and the grammatical information are represented in the form of relation unit, e.g. *nsubj*(example, this), where *nsubj* stands for a dependency relationship between *example* and *this*. We obtained a sequence of relation units for each sentence and then used them to estimate similarity by adopting eight measure functions described in Section 3.2.1, resulting in eight features.

3.2.5 Text Difference Measures (td)

There are two types of text difference measures. The first feature type is specially designed for the *contradiction* entailment relationship, which is based on the following observation: there exist antonyms between two sentences or the negation status is not consistent (i.e., one sentence has a negation word while the other does not have) if *contradiction* holds. Therefore we examined each sentence pair and set this feature as 1 if at least one of these conditions is met, otherwise -1. WordNet was used to look up antonyms and a negation list with 28 words was used.

The second feature type is extracted from two word sets $A-B$ and $B-A$ as follows: we first calculated the similarities between every word from $A-B$ and every word from $B-A$, then took the maximum, minimum and average value of them as features. In our experiments, four WordNet-based similarity measures (i.e., *path, lch, wup, jcn* (Gomaa and Fahmy, 2013)) were used to calculate the similarity between two words.

Totally, we got 13 text difference features.

[3]http://nlp.stanford.edu/software/tagger.shtml

[4]http://nlp.stanford.edu/software/lex-parser.shtml

3.2.6 String Features (str)

This set of features is taken from our previous work (Zhu and Lan, 2013) due to its superior performance.

Longest common sequence (LCS) We computed the LCS similarity on the original and lemmatized sentences. It was calculated by finding the maximum length of a common contiguous subsequence of two strings and then dividing it by the smaller length of two strings to eliminate the impacts of length imbalance.

Jaccard similarity using *n*-grams We obtained *n*-grams at three different levels, i.e., the original word level, the lemmatized word level and the character level. Then these *n*-grams were used for calculating Jaccard similarity defined in Table 1. In our experiments, $n = \{1, 2, 3\}$ were used for the word level and $n = \{2, 3, 4\}$ were used for the character level.

Weighted word overlap (WWO) Since not all words are equally important, the traditional Overlap similarity may not be always reasonable. Thus we used the information content of word w to estimate the importance of word w as follows:

$$ic(w) = \ln \frac{\sum_{w' \in C} freq(w')}{freq(w)}$$

where C is the set of words in the corpus and $freq(w)$ is the frequency of the word w in the corpus. To compute $ic(w)$, we used the Web 1T 5-gram Corpus [5]. Then the WWO similarity of two sentence s_1 and s_2 was calculated as follows:

$$Sim_{wwo}(s_1, s_2) = \frac{\sum_{w \in s_1 \cap s_2} ic(w)}{\sum_{w' \in s_2} ic(w')}$$

Due to its asymmetry, we used the harmonic mean of $Sim_{wwo}(s_1, s_2)$ and $Sim_{wwo}(s_2, s_1)$ as the final WWO similarity. The WWO similarity is calculated on the original and lemmatized strings respectively.

Finally, we got two LCS features, nine Jaccard *n*-gram features and two WWO features.

3.2.7 Corpus-based Features (cps)

Two types of corpus-based feature are also borrowed from our previous work (Zhu and Lan, 2013), i.e., vector space sentence similarity and co-occurrence retrieval model (CRM), which results in six features.

[5] https://catalog.ldc.upenn.edu/LDC2006T13

Co-occurrence retrieval model (CRM) The CRM word similarity is calculated as follows:

$$Sim_{CRM}(w_1, w_2) = \frac{2 * |c(w_1) \cap c(w_2)|}{|c(w_1)| + |c(w_2)|}$$

where $c(w)$ is the set of words that co-occur with word w. We used the 5-gram part of the Web 1T 5-gram Corpus to obtain $c(w)$. We only considered the word w with $|c(w)| > T$ and then took the top 200 co-occurring words ranked by the co-occurrence frequency as its $c(w)$. In our experiment, we set $T = \{50, 200\}$. To propagate the similarity from words to sentences, we adopted the best alignment strategy used in (Banea et al., 2012) to align two sentences.

Vector space sentence similarity This feature set is taken from (Šarić et al., 2012), which is based on distributional vectors of words. First we performed latent semantic analysis (LSA) over two corpora, i.e., the New York Times Annotated Corpus (NYT) (Sandhaus, 2008) and Wikipedia, to estimate the distributions of words. Then we used two strategies to convert the distributional meanings of words to sentence level: (i) simply summing up the distributional vector of each word w in the sentence, (ii) using the information content $ic(w)$ to weigh the LSA vector of each word w and summing them up. Then we used cosine similarity to measure the similarity of two sentences.

3.3 Learning Algorithms

We explored several classification algorithms to classify entailment relationships and regression algorithms to predict similarity scores using the above 72 features after performing max-min standardization procedure by scaling them to [-1,1]. Five supervised learning methods were explored: Support Vector Machine (SVM) which makes the decisions according to the hyperplanes, Random Forest (RF) which constructs a multitude of decision trees at training time and selects the mode of the classes output by individual trees, Gradient Boosting (GB) that produces a prediction model in the form of an ensemble of weak prediction models, *k*-nearest neighbors (*k*NN) that decides the class labels with the aid of the classes of *k* nearest neighbors, and Stochastic Gradient Descent (SGD) which uses SGD technique to minimize loss functions. These supervised learning methods are implemented in scikit-learn toolkit (Pedregosa et al., 2011). Besides, we also used a semi-supervised learning strategy for both tasks in order to make full use of unlabeled test data. Specifically, the co-training algorithm was used to address TE task according to (Zhao et al., 2014). Its strategy is to train two classifiers with two data views and to add the top confident predicted instances by one classifier to expand the training set of another classifier and then to re-train the two classifiers on the expanded training sets. For STS task, we utilized CoReg algorithm (Zhou and Li, 2005) which uses two *k*NN regressors to perform co-training paradigm.

3.4 Evaluation Measures

In order to evaluate the performance of different algorithms, we adopted the official evaluation measures, i.e., *Pearson* correlation coefficient for STS task and *accuracy* for TE task.

4 Experiments on Training Data

To make a reasonable comparison between different algorithms, we performed 5-fold cross validation on training data with 5000 sentence pairs. The parameters tuned in different algorithms are listed below: the trade-off parameter *c* in SVM, the number of trees *n* in RF, the number of boosting stages *n* in GB, the number of nearest neighbors *k* in *k*NN and the number of passes over the training data *n* in SGD. The rest parameters are set to be default.

Algorithm	STS task		TE task	
	Pearson	para.	*Accuracy*	para.
SVM	.807±.058	c=10	83.46±2.09	c=100
RF	.805±.052	*n*=40	83.16±2.64	*n*=30
GB	.806±.055	*n*=210	83.22±2.48	*n*=140
kNN	.797±.062	*k*=25	82.54±2.45	*k*=17
SGD	.765±.064	*n*=29	78.88±1.99	*n*=15

Table 2: The 5-fold cross validation results on training data with mean and standard deviation for each algorithm.

Table 2 reports the experimental results of 5-fold cross validation with mean and standard deviation and the optimal parameters on training data. The results of semi-supervised learning methods are not listed because only a few parameters are tried due to the limit of time. From this table we see that SVM, RF and GB perform comparable results to each other.

5 Results on Test Data

5.1 Submitted System Configurations

According to the above preliminary experimental results, we configured five final systems for each task. Table 3 presents the classification and regression algorithms with their parameters used in the five systems for each task.

System	STS task	TE task
1	SVR, *c*=10	SVC, *c*=100
2	GB, *n*=210	GB, *n*=140
3	RF, *n*=40	RF, *n*=30
4	CoReg, *k*=13	co-training, *k*=40
5	majority voting	majority voting

Table 3: Five system configurations for test data for two tasks.

Among them, System 1 acts as our primary and baseline system that employs SVM algorithm and as comparison System 2 and System 3 exploit GB and RF algorithm respectively. Unlike supervised settings in the aforementioned systems, System 4 employs a semi-supervised learning strategy to make use of unlabeled test data. For CoReg, the number of iteration and the number of nearest neighbors are set as 100 and 13 respectively, and for each iteration in co-training, the number of confident predictions is set as 40. To further improve performance, System 5 combines the results of 5 different algorithms (i.e. MaxEnt, SVM, *k*NN, GB, RF) through majority voting. We used the averaged values of the outputs from different regressors as final similarity scores for semantic similarity measurement task and chose the major class label for entailment judgement task.

5.2 Results and Discussion

Table 4 lists the final results officially released by the organizers in terms of *Pearson* and *accuracy*. The best performance among these five systems is shown in bold font. All participants can submit a maximum of five runs for each task and only one primary system is involved in official ranking. The lower part of Table 4 presents the top 3 results and the results with $*$ are achieved by our systems.

System	STS task	TE task(%)
1	0.8279	83.641
2	0.8389	**84.128**
3	**0.8414**	83.945
4	0.8210	81.165
5	0.8349	83.986
rank 1st	0.8279*	84.575
rank 2nd	0.8272	83.641*
rank 3rd	0.8268	83.053

Table 4: The results of our five systems for two tasks and the officially top-ranked systems.

From this table, we found that (1) System 3 (using GB algorithm) and System 2 (using RF algorithm) achieve the best performance among three supervised systems in STS and TE task respectively. However, there is no significant difference among these systems. (2) Surprisingly, the semi-supervised system (i.e., System 4) that employs the co-training strategy to make use of test data performs the worst, which is beyond our expectation. Based on our further observation in TE task, the possible reason is that a lot of misclassified examples are added into the training pool in the initial iteration, which results in worse models built in the subsequent iterations. And we speculate that the weak learner *k*NN employed in CoReg may lead to poor performance as well. (3) The majority voting strategy fails to boost the performance since GB and RF algorithm obtain the best performance among these algorithms. (4) Our systems obtain very good results on both STS and TE task, i.e., we rank 1st out of 17 participants in STS task and rank 2nd out of 18 participants in TE task according to the results of primary systems and as shown in Table 4 our primary system (i.e., System 1) do not achieve the best performance.

In a nutshell, our systems rank first and second in STS and TE task respectively. Therefore the answer to the first question raised in Section 1 is *yes*. For two tasks, i.e., STS and TE, which are very closely related but slightly different, we can use the same features to solve them together.

5.3 Feature Combination Experiments

To answer the second question and explore the influences of different feature types, we performed a series of experiments under the best system setting. Table 5 shows the results of different feature combinations where for each time we selected and added one best feature type. From this table, we find that for STS the most effective feature is *cps* and for TE task is *td*. Almost all feature types have positive effects on performance. Specifically, *td* alone achieves 81.063% in TE task which is quite close to the best performance (84.128%) and *cps* alone achieves 0.7544 in STS task. Moreover, the *td* feature proposed for TE task is quite effective in STS task as well, which suggests that text semantic difference measures are also crucial when measuring sentence similarity.

Therefore the answer to the second question is *yes*. It is clear that the features proposed for TE are also effective for STS and heterogenous features yield better performance than a single feature type.

len	st	ss	gr	td	str	cps	result
						+	0.7544 (STS)
				+		+	0.8057(+5.13)
		+		+		+	0.8280(+2.23)
		+	+	+		+	0.8365(+0.85)
	+	+	+	+		+	0.8426(+0.61)
	+	+	+	+	+	+	**0.8432**(+0.06)
+	+	+	+	+	+	+	0.8429(-0.03)
				+			81.063 (TE)
	+			+			82.484(+1.421)
	+			+	+		82.992(+0.508)
	+			+	+	+	83.844(+0.852)
	+		+	+	+	+	83.925(+0.081)
	+	+	+	+	+	+	84.067(+0.142)
+	+	+	+	+	+	+	**84.128**(+0.061)

Table 5: Results of feature combinations, the numbers in the brackets are the performance increments compared with the previous results.

6 Conclusion

We set up five state-of-the-art systems and each system employs different classifiers or regressors using the same feature set. Our submitted systems rank the 1st out of 17 teams in STS task with the best performance of 0.8414 in terms of *Pearson* coefficient and rank the 2nd out of 18 teams in TE task with 84.128% in terms of *accuracy*. This result indicates that (1) we can use the same feature set to solve these two tasks together, (2) the features proposed for TE task are also effective for STS task and (3) heterogenous features outperform a single feature. For future work, we may explore the underlying relationships between these two tasks to boost their performance by each other.

Acknowledgments

This research is supported by grants from National Natural Science Foundation of China (No.60903093) and Shanghai Knowledge Service Platform Project (No. ZF1213).

References

Ion Androutsopoulos and Prodromos Malakasiotis. 2009. A survey of paraphrasing and textual entailment methods. *arXiv preprint arXiv:0912.3747*.

Carmen Banea, Samer Hassan, Michael Mohler, and Rada Mihalcea. 2012. Unt:a supervised synergistic approach to semantictext similarity. In *First Joint Conference on Lexical and Computational Semantics (*SEM*.

Daniel Bär, Chris Biemann, Iryna Gurevych, and Torsten Zesch. 2012. Ukp: Computing semantic textual similarity by combining multiple content similarity measures. In *Proceedings of the First Joint Conference on Lexical and Computational Semantics*, pages 435–440. Association for Computational Linguistics.

Johan Bos and Katja Markert. 2005. Recognising textual entailment with logical inference. In *Proceedings of the conference on Human Language Technology and Empirical Methods in Natural Language Processing*, pages 628–635. Association for Computational Linguistics.

Danilo Croce, Valerio Storch, and Roberto Basili. 2013. Unitor-core typed: Combining text similarity and semantic filters through sv regression. In *Proceedings of the 2nd Joint Conference on Lexical and Computational Semantics*, page 59.

Wael H Gomaa and Aly A Fahmy. 2013. A survey of text similarity approaches. *International Journal of Computer Applications*, 68(13):13–18.

Edward Grefenstette and Mehrnoosh Sadrzadeh. 2011. Experimental support for a categorical compositional distributional model of meaning. In *Proceedings of the Conference on Empirical Methods in Natural Language Processing*, pages 1394–1404. Association for Computational Linguistics.

Weiwei Guo and Mona Diab. 2012. Modeling sentences in the latent space. In *Proceedings of the 50th Annual Meeting of the Association for Computational Linguistics*.

Zellig S Harris. 1954. Distributional structure. *The Philosophy of Linguistics*,.

Yuhua Li, David McLean, Zuhair A Bandar, James D O'shea, and Keeley Crockett. 2006. Sentence similarity based on semantic nets and corpus statistics. *Knowledge and Data Engineering, IEEE Transactions on*, 18(8):1138–1150.

Mihai C. Lintean and Vasile Rus. 2012. Measuring semantic similarity in short texts through greedy pairing and word semantics. In *FLAIRS Conference*. AAAI Press.

Prodromos Malakasiotis and Ion Androutsopoulos. 2007. Learning textual entailment using svms and string similarity measures. In *Proceedings of the ACL-PASCAL Workshop on Textual Entailment and Paraphrasing*, pages 42–47. Association for Computational Linguistics.

M. Marelli, L. Bentivogli, M. Baroni, R. Bernardi, S. Menini, and R. Zamparelli. 2014. Semeval-2014 task 1: Evaluation of compositional distributional semantic models on full sentences through semantic relatedness and textual entailment. In *Proceedings of SemEval 2014: International Workshop on Semantic Evaluation*.

Rada Mihalcea, Courtney Corley, and Carlo Strapparava. 2006. Corpus-based and knowledge-based measures of text semantic similarity. In *AAAI*, volume 6, pages 775–780.

Fabian Pedregosa, Gaël. Varoquaux, Alexandre Gramfort, Vincent Michel, Bertrand Thirion, Olivier Grisel, Mathieu Blondel, Peter Prettenhofer, Ron Weiss, Vincent Dubourg, Jake Vanderplas, Alexandre Passos, David Cournapeau, Matthieu Brucher, Matthieu Perrot, and Édouard Duchesnay. 2011. Scikit-learn: Machine learning in Python. *Journal of Machine Learning Research*, 12:2825–2830.

Evan Sandhaus. 2008. The new york times annotated corpus ldc2008t19. *Philadelphia: Linguistic Data Consortium*.

Socher, Richard, Huval Brody, Manning Christopher, and Ng Andrew. 2012. Semantic compositionality through recursive matrix-vector spaces. In *Proceedings of EMNLP*, Jeju Island, Korea.

Peter D Turney, Patrick Pantel, et al. 2010. From frequency to meaning: Vector space models of semantics. *Journal of artificial intelligence research*, 37(1):141–188.

Frane Šarić, Goran Glavaš, Mladen Karan, Jan Šnajder, and Bojana Dalbelo Bašić. 2012. Takelab: Systems for measuring semantic text similarity. In *Proceedings of the First Joint Conference on Lexical and Computational Semantics*, pages 441–448, Stroudsburg, PA, USA. Association for Computational Linguistics.

Fabio Massimo Zanzotto, Ioannis Korkontzelos, Francesca Fallucchi, and Suresh Manandhar. 2010. Estimating linear models for compositional distributional semantics. In *Proceedings of the 23rd International Conference on Computational Linguistics*, pages 1263–1271. Association for Computational Linguistics.

Jiang Zhao, Man Lan, and Zheng-Yu Niu. 2013. Ecnucs: Recognizing cross-lingual textual entailment using multiple text similarity and text difference measures. In *Proceedings of the Seventh International Workshop on Semantic Evaluation (SemEval 2013)*, pages 118–123, Atlanta, Georgia, USA, June. Association for Computational Linguistics.

Jiang Zhao, Man Lan, Zheng-Yu Niu, and Donghong Ji. 2014. Recognizing cross-lingual textual entailment with co-training using similarity and difference views. In *The 2014 International Joint Conference on Neural Networks (IJCNN2014)*. IEEE.

Zhi-Hua Zhou and Ming Li. 2005. Semi-supervised regression with co-training. In *IJCAI*, pages 908–916.

Tian Tian Zhu and Man Lan. 2013. Ecnucs: Measuring short text semantic equivalence using multiple similarity measurements. In *Proceedings of the 2nd Joint Conference on Lexical and Computational Semantics*, page 124.

ezDI: A Hybrid CRF and SVM based Model for Detecting and Encoding Disorder Mentions in Clinical Notes

Parth Pathak, Pinal Patel, Vishal Panchal, Narayan Choudhary, Amrish Patel, Gautam Joshi
ezDI, LLC.
{parth.p,pinal.p,vishal.p,narayan.c,amrish.p,gautam.j}@ezdi.us

Abstract

This paper describes the system used in Task-7 (Analysis of Clinical Text) of SemEval-2014 for detecting disorder mentions and associating them with their related CUI of UMLS[1]. For Task-A, a CRF based sequencing algorithm was used to find different medical entities and a binary SVM classifier was used to find relationship between entities. For Task-B, a dictionary look-up algorithm on a customized UMLS-2012 dictionary was used to find relative CUI for a given disorder mention. The system achieved F-score of 0.714 for Task A & accuracy of 0.599 for Task B when trained only on training data set, and it achieved F-score of 0.755 for Task A & accuracy of 0.646 for Task B when trained on both training as well as development data set. Our system was placed 3rd for both task A and B.

1 Introduction

A clinical document contains plethora of information regarding patient's medical condition in unstructured format. So a sophisticated NLP system built specifically for clinical domain can be very useful in many different clinical applications. In recent years, clinical NLP has gained a lot of significance in research community because it contains challenging tasks such as medical entity recognition, abbreviation disambiguation, interconceptual relationship detection, anaphora resolution, and text summarization. Clinical NLP has also gained a significant attraction among the health care industry because it promises to deliver applications like computer assisted coding, automated data abstraction, core/quality measure monitoring, fraud detection, revenue loss prevention system, clinical document improvement system and so on.

Task-7 of SemEval-2014 was in continuation of the 2013 ShaRe/CLEF Task-1 (Sameer Pradhan, et al., 2013). This task was about finding disorder mentions from the clinical text and associating them with their related CUIs (concept unique identifiers) as given in the UMLS (Unified Medical Language System). UMLS is the largest available medical knowledge resource. It contains 2,885,877 different CUIs having 6,497,937 different medical terms from over 100 different medical vocabularies. Finding accurate CUIs from free clinical text can be very helpful in many healthcare applications. Our aim for participating in this task was to explore new techniques of finding CUIs from clinical document.

Over the last few years many different Clinical NLP systems like cTAKES (Savova, Guergana K., et al., 2010), MetaMap (A. Aronson, 2001), MedLEE (C. Friedman et al., 1994) have been developed to extract medical concepts from a clinical document. Most of these systems focus on rule based, medical knowledge driven dictionary look-up approaches. In very recent past, a few attempts have been made to use supervised or semi-supervised learning models. In 2009, Yefang Wang (Wang et al., 2009) used cascading classifiers on manually annotated data which fetched F-score of 0.832. In 2010, i2b2 shared task challenge focused on finding test, treatment and problem mentions from clinical document.

In 2013, ShARe/CLEF task focused on finding disorder mentions from clinical document and assigning relevant CUI code to it. In both i2b2 task and ShaRe/CLEF task most of the systems used either supervised or semi-supervised learning ap-

[1] http://www.nlm.nih.gov/research/umls/

Proceedings of the 8th International Workshop on Semantic Evaluation (SemEval 2014), pages 278–283,
Dublin, Ireland, August 23-24, 2014.

proaches.

In this paper we have proposed a hybrid supervised learning approach based on CRF and SVM to find out disorder mentions from clinical documents and a dictionary look-up approach on a customized UMLS meta-thesaurus to find corresponding CUI.

2 Data

The SemEval-2014 corpus comprises of de-identified plain text from MIMIC[2] version 2.5 database. A disorder mention was defined as any span of text which can be mapped to a concept in UMLS and which belongs to the Disorder semantic group. There were 431 notes extracted from intensive care unit having various clinical report types (like radiology, discharge summary, echocardiogram and ECG), out of which 99 notes were used in development data set, 199 notes were used in training data set and 133 notes were used in testing data set.

Preliminary analysis on this data showed that number of sentences in training documents were comparatively smaller than the development or test data set (Table 1). Number of disorder mentions were also significantly lower in training data set than in development data set (Table 1).

Type	Dev	Train	Test
Docuemnts	99	199	133
Sentence	9860	10485	17368
Token	102k	113k	177k
Avg token/sen	10.42	10.79	10.24
Cont. entity	4912	5,165	7,186
Disjoint Entity	439	651	4588
Avg Ent/Doc	54.05	29.22	57.47
Distinct CUI	1007	938	NA

Table 1: Numerical analysis on data.

3 System Design

Analysis of Task-A showed that disorder mentions also contain other UMLS semantic types like findings, anatomical sites and modifiers (Table 2). So we divided the task of finding disorder mention in to two subtasks. First a CRF based sequencing model was used to find different disorder mentions, modifiers, anatomical sites and findings. Then a binary SVM classifier was used to check if relationship exists between a disorder and other types of entities or not.

Example	Disorder	Findings	Anatomy	Modifier
There is persistent **left lower lobe opacity** presumably **atelectasis**.	✓	✓	✗	✗
He had substernal **chest pain**, sharp but without **radiation**.	✓	✓	✗	✗
Patientt also developed some **erythema** around the **stoma** site on hospital day two.	✓	✗	✓	✗
The tricuspid valve **leaflets** are mildly **thickened**.	✗	✓	✓	✗
Please call,if you find **swelling** in the **wound**.	✓	✓	✗	✗
She also notes new sharp **pain** in **left shoulder blade**/back area.	✓	✗	✓	✗
An echocardiogram demonstrated mild **left** and **right atrial dilatation**	✓	✗	✗	✓

Table 2: Entity Types co-relation and examples

For Task-B, we have used a simple dictionary look up algorithm on a customized UMLS dictionary. A preliminary analysis of UMLS entities in general show that a single disorder mention may consist of various types of linguistic phrases. It is not necesarry that the system to detect these entities as a single phrase. The entities and their relations may also occur in disjoint phrases as well. Our analysis of the disorder entities inside UMLS reveals that out of a total 278,859 disorders (based on SNOMED-CT library), 96,069 are such that can be broken down into more than one phrase, which is roughly 1/3 of total number of disorders in the UMLS.

3.1 System Workflow

The Work-flow of the system is as follow:

[2]http://mimic.physionet.org/database/releases/70-version-25.html

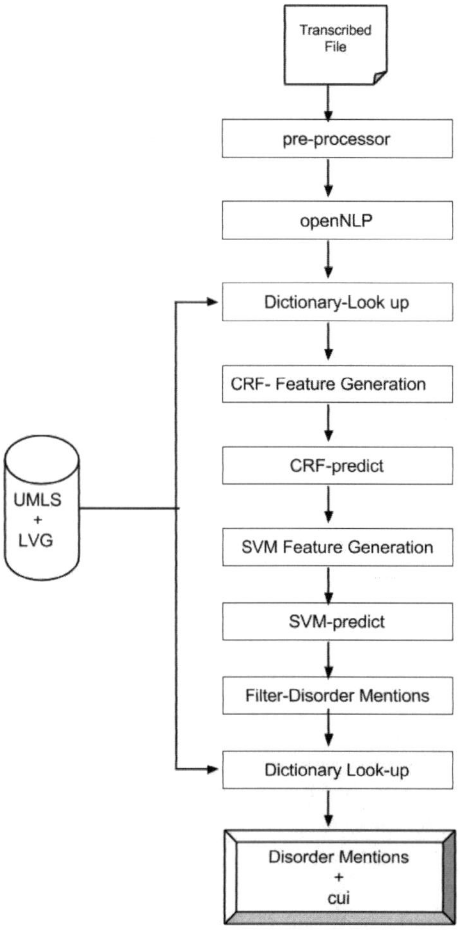

Figure 1: System Workflow

3.1.1 Pre-processing

All the clinical documents used in this task were de-identified. So information related to hospital name, patient demographics, physician names/signatures, dates, places, and certain lab-data were converted into predefined patterns. These patterns were hindering the flow of natural language. As a result of it, we were unable to get accurate results for PoS tagging and chunking of the sentences. So we replaced all of these de-identified patterns with some text that appear more as natural language. There were also some headers and footers associated with all the documents, which were actually irrelevant to this task. Therefore all headers and footers were also removed at the pre-processing level.

3.1.2 openNLP

We have used openNLP[3] to perform basic NLP tasks like sentence detection, tokenizing, PoS tagging, chunking, parsing and stemming.

3.1.3 Dictionary Lookup

UMLS 2012AA dictionary with Lexical Variant Generator (LVG)[4] was used to perform dictionary lookup task. Even though the task was only about finding disorder mentions, we also identified entities like procedures, finding, lab data, medicine, anatomical site and medical devices to be used as features in our CRF model. This was helpful in decreasing the number of false positive. UMLS TUI (Type Unique Identifier) used for different entity type is described in Table 3. A rule-based approach on the output of the OpenNLP syntactic parser was used to detect possible modifiers for disorder mentions.

Type	Tui list
Disorder	T046,T047,T048,T049,T050,T191, T037,T019,T184
Anatomical Sites	T017,T021,T023,T024,T025,T026, T029,T030
Procedures	T059,T060,T061
Medicines	T200,T120,T110
Lab Data	T196,T119
Modifiers	Customized Dictionary
Findings	T033,T034,T041,T084,T032,T201, T053,T054

Table 3: Entity Types and their related TUI list from UMLS

3.1.4 CRF Feature Generation

The feature sets were divided into three categories.

1) Clinical Features

i) Section Headers: A clinical note is often divided into relevant segments called Section Headers. These section headers provide very useful information at the discourse level. Same section header can have multiple variants. For example History of Present Illness can also be written as HPI, HPIS, Brief History etc. We have created a dictionary of more than 550 different section headers and classified them into more than 40 hierarchical categories. But using only section header dictionary for classification can fetch many false

[3]https://opennlp.apache.org/

[4]http://lexsrv2.nlm.nih.gov/

positives. Section header always appears in a predefined similar sequences. So to remove these false positives, we have used a Hidden Markov Model(HMM) (Parth Pathak, et al, 2013). For this task, we have used unigram section header id as a feature for all the tokens in CRF.

ii) Dictionary Lookup: A binary feature was used for all the different entity types detected from UMLS dictionary from last pipeline.

iii) Abbreviations: Abbreviations Disambiguation is one of the most challenging tasks in clinical NLP. The primary reason for the same is a lack of dictionary which contains most of the valid list of abbreviations. For this task, we have used LRABR as base dictionary to find out all the possible abbreviations and on top of that, a binary SVM classifier was used to check if the given abbreviation has medical sense or not.

2) Textual Feature:

Snowball stemmer[5] was used to find out stem value of all the word tokens. Prefix and suffix of length 2 to 5 were also used as features. Different orthographic features like whole word capital, first char capital, numeric values, dates, words containing hyphen or slash, medical units (mg/gram/ltr etc.) were used as features.

3) Syntactic Features:

Different linguistic features like PoS tags and chunks for each token were used. We have also used head of the noun phrase as one of the feature which can be very helpful in detecting the type of an entity.

3.1.5 CRF toolkit

All the annotated data was converted into BIO sequencing format. CRF++[6] toolkit was used to train and predict the model.

3.1.6 SVM

SVM was used to check whether a relationship exists between two entities or not. For this purpose all the tokens between these two entities, their part of speech tags and chunks were used as features. Rules based on output of a syntactic parser were also used as a binary feature. Some orthographic features like all letter capital, contains colon (:), contains semi colon (;), were also used as features. LibSVM[7] was used to train as well as predict the model.

3.1.7 Dictionary Look-up for CUI detection

For a better mapping of the entities detected by NLP inside the given input text, we found it to be a better approach to divide the UMLS entities into various phrases. This was done semi-automatically by splitting the strings based on function words such as prepositions, particles and non-nominal word classes such as verbs, adjectives and adverbs. While most of the disorder entities in UMLS can be contained into a single noun phrase (NP) there are also quite a few that contain multiple NPs related with prepositional phrases (PPs), verb phrases (VPs) and adjectival phrases (ADJPs).

This task gave us a modified version of the UMLS disorder entities along with their CUIs. The following table (Table 4) gives a snapshot of what this customized UMLS dictionary looked like.

CUI	Text	P1	P2	P3
C001 3132	Dribbling from mouth	Dribbling	from	mouth
C001 4591	Bleeding from nose	Bleeding	from	nose
C002 9163	Hemorr- hage from mouth	Hemo- rrhage	from	mouth
C039 2685	Chest pain at rest	Chest pain	at	rest
C026 9678	Fatigue during pregnancy	Fatigue	during	pregn ancy

Table 4: An example of the modified UMLS disorder entities split as per their linguistic phrase types

Our dictionary look-up algorithm used this customized UMLS dictionary as resource to find the entities and assign the right CUIs.

4 Results & Error Analysis

4.1 Evaluation Calculations

The evaluation measures for Task A are Precision, Recall and F-Meas, defined as:

$$\text{Precision} = \frac{TP}{FP+TP}$$

$$\text{Recall} = \frac{TP}{TP+FN}$$

[5] http://snowball.tartarus.org/

[6] http://crfpp.googlecode.com/

[7] http://www.csie.ntu.edu.tw/\~cjlin/libsvm/

F-measure = $\frac{2*Precision*Recall}{Precision+Recall}$

where
TP = Disorder mention span matches with gold standard
FP = Disorder mention span detected by the system was not present in the gold standard;
FN = Disorder mention span was present in the gold standard but system was not able detect it

In Task B, the Accuracy was defined as the number of pre-annotated spans with correctly generated code divided by the total number of pre-annotated spans.

Strict Accuracy = $\frac{Total\ correct\ CUIs}{Total\ annotation\ in\ gold\ standard}$

Relaxed Accuracy = $\frac{Total\ correct\ CUIs}{Total\ span\ detected\ by\ system}$

4.2 System Accuracy

The system results were calculated on two different runs. For the first evaluation, only training data was used for the training purpose while for the second evaluation, both the training as well as the development data sets were used for training purpose. The results for Task A and B are as follows:

	Precision	Recall	F-Meas
Strict (T)	0.750	0.682	0.714
Relaxed (T)	0.915	0.827	0.869
Strict (T+D)	0.770	0.740	0.755
Relaxed (T+D)	0.911	0.887	0.899

Table 5: Task-A Results

where T= Training Data set
D= Development Data set

4.3 Error Analysis

Error Analysis on training data revealed that for Task-A our system got poor results in detecting non-contiguous disjoint entities. Our system also performed very poorly in identifying abbreviations and misspelled entities. We also observed that the accuracy of the part of speech tagger and the chunker also contributes a lot towards the final outcome. For Task-B, we got many false positives. Many CUIs which we identified from the UMLS were not actually annotated.

	Accuracy
Strict (T)	0.599
Relaxed (T)	0.878
Strict (T+D)	0.643
Relaxed (T+D)	0.868

Table 6: Task-B Results

5 Conclusion

In this paper we have proposed a CRF and SVM based hybrid approach to find Disorder mentions from a given clinical text and a novel dictionary look-up approach for discovering CUIs from UMLS meta-thesaurus. Our system did produce competitive results and was third best among the participants of this task. In future, we would like to explore semi-supervised learning approaches to take advantage of large amount of available unannotated free clinical text.

References

Savova, Guergana K., James J. Masanz, Philip V. Ogren, Jiaping Zheng, Sunghwan Sohn, Karin C. Kipper-Schuler, and Christopher G. Chute. 2010. *Mayo clinical Text Analysis and Knowledge Extraction System (cTAKES): architecture, component evaluation and applications.* Journal of the American Medical Informatics Association 17, no. 5 (2010): 507-513.

Friedman C, Alderson PO, Austin JH, Cimino JJ, Johnson SB. 1994. *A general natural-language text processor for clinical radiology.* J Am Med Inform Assoc 1994 Mar-Apr;1(2):16174. [PubMed:7719797]

Aronson, Alan R. 2001. *Effective mapping of biomedical text to the UMLS Metathesaurus: the MetaMap program.* In Proceedings of the AMIA Symposium, p. 17. American Medical Informatics Association, 2001.

Wang, Yefeng, and Jon Patrick. 2009. *Cascading classifiers for named entity recognition in clinical notes.* In Proceedings of the workshop on biomedical information extraction, pp. 42-49. Association for Computational Linguistics, 2009.

Suominen, Hanna, Sanna Salanter, Sumithra Velupillai, Wendy W. Chapman, Guergana Savova, Noemie Elhadad, Sameer Pradhan 2013 *Overview of the ShARe/CLEF eHealth evaluation lab 2013.* In Information Access Evaluation. Multilinguality, Multimodality, and Visualization, pp. 212-231. Springer Berlin Heidelberg, 2013.

. ""

Parth Pathak, Raxit Goswami, Gautam Joshi, Pinal Patel, and Amrish Patel. 2013 *CRF-based Clinical Named Entity Recognition using clinical Features*

FBK-TR: Applying SVM with Multiple Linguistic Features for Cross-Level Semantic Similarity

Ngoc Phuoc An Vo
Fondazione Bruno Kessler
University of Trento
Trento, Italy
ngoc@fbk.eu

Tommaso Caselli
TrentoRISE
Trento, Italy
t.caselli@trentorise.eu

Octavian Popescu
Fondazione Bruno Kessler
Trento, Italy
popescu@fbk.eu

Abstract

Recently, the task of measuring semantic similarity between given texts has drawn much attention from the Natural Language Processing community. Especially, the task becomes more interesting when it comes to measuring the semantic similarity between different-sized texts, e.g paragraph-sentence, sentence-phrase, phrase-word, etc. In this paper, we, the FBK-TR team, describe our system participating in Task 3 "Cross-Level Semantic Similarity", at SemEval 2014. We also report the results obtained by our system, compared to the baseline and other participating systems in this task.

1 Introduction

Measuring semantic text similarity has become a hot trend in NLP as it can be applied to other tasks, e.g. Information Retrieval, Paraphrasing, Machine Translation Evaluation, Text Summarization, Question and Answering, and others. Several approaches proposed to measure the semantic similarity between given texts. The first approach is based on vector space models (VSMs) (Meadow, 1992). A VSM transforms given texts into "bag-of-words" and presents them as vectors. Then, it deploys different distance metrics to compute the closeness between vectors, which will return as the distance or similarity between given texts. The next well-known approach is using text-alignment. By assuming that two given texts are semantically similar, they could be aligned on word or phrase levels. The alignment quality can serve as a similarity measure. "It typically pairs words from the two texts by maximizing the summation of the word similarity of the resulting pairs" (Mihalcea et al., 2006). In contrast, the third approach uses machine learning techniques to learn models built from different lexical, semantic and syntactic features and then give predictions on degree of similarity between given texts (Šarić et al., 2012).

At SemEval 2014, the Task 3 "Cross-Level Semantic Similarity" (Jurgens et al., 2014) is to evaluate the semantic similarity across different sizes of texts, in particular, a larger-sized text is compared to a smaller-sized one. The task consists of four types of semantic similarity comparison: paragraph to sentence, sentence to phrase, phrase to word, and word to sense. The degree of similarity ranges from 0 (different meanings) to 4 (similar meanings). For evaluation, systems were evaluated, first, within comparison type and second, across all comparison types. Two methods are used to evaluate between system outputs and gold standard (human annotation), which are Pearson correlation and Spearman's rank correlation (rho).

The FBK-TR team participated in this task with three different runs. In this paper, we present a clear and comprehensive description of our system which obtained competitive results. Our main approach is using machine learning technique to learn models from different lexical and semantic features from train corpora to make prediction on the test corpora. We used support vector machine (SVM) regression model to solve the task.

The remainder of the paper is organized as follows. Section 2 presents the system overview. Sections 3, 4 and 5 describe the Semantic Word Similarity, String Similarity and other features, respectively. Section 6 discusses about SVM approach. Section 7 presents the experiment settings for each subtask. Finally, Sections 8 and 9 present the evaluation and conclusion.

Proceedings of the 8th International Workshop on Semantic Evaluation (SemEval 2014), pages 284–288, Dublin, Ireland, August 23-24, 2014.

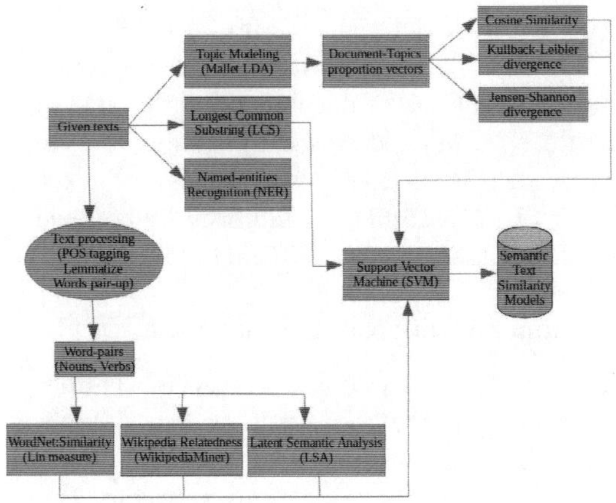

Figure 1: System Overview.

2 System Overview

Our system was built on different linguistic features as shown in Figure 1. By constructing a pipeline system, each linguistic feature can be used independently or together with others to measure the semantic similarity of given texts as well as to evaluate the significance of each feature to the accuracy of system's predictions. On top of this, the system is expandable and scalable for adopting more useful features aiming for improving the accuracy.

3 Semantic Word Similarity Measures

At the lexical level, we built a simple, yet effective Semantic Word Similarity model consisting of three components: WordNet similarity, Wikipedia relatedness and Latent Semantic Analysis (LSA). These components played important and complimentary roles to each other.

3.1 Data Processing

We used the TreeTagger tool (Schmid, 1994) to extract Part-of-Speech (POS) from each given text, then tokenize and lemmatize it. On the basis of the POS tags, we only picked lemmas of content words (Nouns and Verbs) from the given texts and then paired them up regarding to similar POS tags.

3.2 WordNet Similarity and Levenshtein Distance

WordNet (Fellbaum, 1999) is a lexical database for the English language in which words are grouped into sets of synonyms (namely synsets, each expressing a distinct concept) to provide short, general definitions, and record the various semantic relations between synsets. We used Perdersen's package WordNet:Similarity (Pedersen et al., 2004) to obtain similarity scores for the lexical items covered in WordNet. Similarity scores have been computed by means of the Lin measure (Lin, 1998). The Lin measure is built on Resnik's measure of similarity (Resnik, 1995):

$$Sim_{lin} = \frac{2 * IC(LCS)}{IC(concept_1) + IC(concept_2)} \quad (1)$$

where *IC(LCS)* is the information content *(IC)* of the least common subsumer *(LCS)* of two concepts.

To overcome the limit in coverage of WordNet, we applied the Levenshtein distance (Levenshtein, 1966). The distance between two words is defined by the minimum number of operations (insertions, deletions and substitutions) needed to transform one word into the other.

3.3 Wikipedia Relatedness

Wikipedia Miner (Milne and Witten, 2013) is a Java-based package developed for extracting semantic information from Wikipedia. Through our experiments, we observed that Wikipedia relatedness plays an important role for providing extra information to measure the semantic similarity between words. We used the package Wikipedia Miner from University of Waikato (New Zealand) to extract additional relatedness scores between words.

3.4 Latent Semantic Analysis (LSA)

We also took advantage from corpus-based approaches to measure the semantic similarity between words by using Latent Semantic Analysis (LSA) technique (Landauer et al., 1998). LSA assumes that similar and/or related words in terms of meaning will occur in similar text contexts. In general, a LSA matrix is built from a large corpus. Rows in the matrix represent unique words and columns represent paragraphs or documents. The content of the matrix corresponds to the word count per paragraph/document. Matrix size is then reduced by means of Single Value Decomposition (SVD) technique. Once the matrix has been obtained, similarity and/or relatedness between the words is computed by means of cosine values (scaled between 0 and 1) for each word vector in the matrix. Values close to 1 are assumed to be very similar/related, otherwise dissimilar. We trained our LSA model on the British National Corpus (BNC) [1] and Wikipedia [2] corpora.

4 String Similarity Measures

The Longest Common Substring (LCS) is the longest string in common between two or more strings. Two given texts are considered similar if they are overlapping/covering each other (e.g sentence 1 covers a part of sentence 2, or otherwise). We implemented a simple algorithm to extract the LCS between two given texts. Then we divided the LCS length by the product of normalized lengths of two given texts and used it as a feature.

4.1 Analysis Before and After LCS

After extracting the LCS between two given texts, we also considered the similarity for the parts before and after the LCS. The similarity between the text portions before and after the LSC has been obtained by means of the Lin measure and the Levenshtein distance.

5 Other Features

To take into account other levels of analysis for semantic similarity between texts, we extended our features by means of topic modeling and Named Entities.

5.1 Topic Modeling (Latent Dirichlet Allocation - LDA)

Topic modeling is a generative model of documents which allows to discover topics embedded in a document collection and their balance in each document. If two given texts are expressing the same topic, they should be considered highly similar. We applied topic modeling, particularly, Latent Dirichlet allocation (LDA) (Blei et al., 2003) to predict the topics expressed by given texts.

The MALLET topic model package (McCallum, 2002) is a Java-based tool used for inferring hidden "topics" in new document collections using trained models. We used Mallet topic modeling tool to build different models using BNC and Wikipedia corpora.

We noticed that, in LDA, the number of topics plays an important role to fine grained predictions. Hence, we built different models for different numbers of topics, from minimum 20 topics to maximum 500 topics (20, 50, 100, 150, 200, 250, 300, 350, 400, 450 and 500). From the proportion vectors (distribution of documents over topics) of given texts, we applied three different measures to compute the distance between each pair of texts, which are Cosine similarity, Kullback-Leibler and Jensen-Shannon divergences (Gella et al., 2013).

5.2 Named-Entity Recognition (NER)

NER aims at identifying and classifying entities in a text with respect to a predefined set of categories such as person names, organizations, locations, time expressions, quantities, monetary values, percentages, etc. By exploring the training set, we observed that there are lot of texts in this task containing named entities. We deployed the Stanford Named Entity Recognizer tool (Finkel et al., 2005) to extract the similar and overlapping named entities between two given texts. Then we divided the number of similar/overlapping named entities by the sum length of two given texts.

6 Support Vector Machines (SVMs)

Support vector machine (SVM) (Cortes and Vapnik, 1995) is a type of supervised learning approaches. We used the LibSVM package (Chang and Lin, 2011) to learn models from the different linguistic features described above. However, in SVM the problem of finding optimal kernel parameters is critical and important for the learning process. Hence, we used practical advice (Hsu et al., 2003) for data scaling and a grid-search process for finding the optimal parameters (C and gamma) for building models. We trained the SVM models in a regression framework.

7 Experiment Settings

For subtasks paragraph-to-sentence and sentence-to-phrase, since the length between two units is completely different, we decided, first to apply topic model to identify if two given texts are expressing a same topic. Furthermore, named entities play an important role in these subtasks. However, as there are many named entities which are not English words and cannot be identified by the NER tool, we developed a program to detect and identify common words occurring in both given texts. Then we continued to extract other lexical and semantic features to measure the similarity between the two texts.

[1] http://www.natcorp.ox.ac.uk

[2] http://en.wikipedia.org/wiki/Wikipedia:Database_download

Team	Para2Sent (Pearson)	Para2Sent (Spearman)
UNAL-NLP, run2 (ranked 1st)	**0.837**	0.820
ECNU, run1(ranked 1st)	0.834	**0.821**
FBK-TR, run2	0.77	0.775
FBK-TR, run3	0.759	0.770
FBK-TR, run1	0.751	0.759
Baseline (LCS)	0.527	0.613

Table 1: Results for paragraph-to-sentence.

Team	Sent2Phr (Pearson)	Sent2Phr (Spearman)
Meerkat_Mafia, SuperSaiyan (ranked 1st)	0.777	0.760
FBK-TR, run3	0.702	0.695
FBK-TR, run1	0.685	0.681
FBK-TR, run2	0.648	0.642
Baseline (LCS)	0.562	0.626

Table 2: Results for sentence-to-phrase.

For the subtask word-to-sense, we used the Semantic Word Similarity model which consists of three components: WordNet similarity, Wikipedia relatedness and LSA similarity (described in section 3). For phrase-to-word, we extracted all glosses of the given word, then computed the similarity between the given phrase and each extracted gloss. Finally, we selected the highest similarity score for result.

8 Evaluations

As a result, we report our performance in the four subtasks as follows.

8.1 Subtasks: Paragraph-to-Sentence and Sentence-to-Phrase

The evaluation results using Pearson and Spearman correlations show the difference between our system and best system in these two subtasks in the Tables 1 and 2.

Team	Para2Sent	Sent2Phr	Phr2Word	Word2Sens	Sum
SimCompass (ranked 1st)	0.811	0.742	0.415	0.356	2.324
FBK-TR	0.759	0.702	0.305	0.155	1.95
Baseline	0.527	0.562	0.165	0.109	1.363

Table 3: Overall result using Pearson.

Team	Para2Sent	Sent2Phr	Phr2Word	Word2Sens	Sum
SimCompass (ranked 1st)	0.801	0.728	0.424	0.344	2.297
FBK-TR	0.770	0.695	0.298	0.150	1.913
Baseline	0.613	0.626	0.162	0.130	1.528

Table 4: Overall result using Spearman.

8.2 Subtasks: Phrase-to-Word and Word-to-Sense

Even though we did not submit the results as they looked very low, we report the scores for the phrase-to-word and word-to-sense subtasks. In the phrase-to-word subtask, we obtained a Pearson score of 0.305 and Spearman value of 0.298. As for the word-to-sense subtask, we scored 0.155 for Pearson and 0.150 for Spearman.

Overall, with the submitted results for two subtasks described in Section 8.1, our system's runs ranked 20th, 21st and 22nd among 38 participating systems. However, by taking into account the un-submitted results for the two other subtasks, our best run obtained 1.95 (Pearson correlation) and 1.913 (Spearman correlation), which can be ranked in the top 10 among 38 systems (figures are reported in Table 3 and 4).

9 Conclusions and Future Work

In this paper, we describe our system participating in the Task 3, at SemEval 2014. We present a compact system using machine learning approach (particularly, SVMs) to learn models from a set of lexical and semantic features to predict the degree of similarity between different-sized texts. Although we only submitted the results for two out of four subtasks, we obtained competitive results among the other participants. For future work, we are planning to increase the number of topics in LDA, as more fine-grained topics should allow predicting better similarity scores. Finally, we will investigate more on the use of syntactic features.

References

David M Blei, Andrew Y Ng, and Michael I Jordan. 2003. Latent Dirichlet Allocation. *The Journal of Machine Learning research*, 3:993–1022.

Chih-Chung Chang and Chih-Jen Lin. 2011. LIBSVM: A Library for Support Vector Machines. *ACM Transactions on Intelligent Systems and Technology (TIST)*, 2(3):27.

Corinna Cortes and Vladimir Vapnik. 1995. Support-

Vector Networks. *Machine learning*, 20(3):273–297.

Christiane Fellbaum. 1999. *WordNet*. Wiley Online Library.

Jenny Rose Finkel, Trond Grenager, and Christopher Manning. 2005. Incorporating Non-local Information into Information Extraction Systems by Gibbs Sampling. In *Proceedings of the 43rd Annual Meeting on Association for Computational Linguistics*, pages 363–370.

Spandana Gella, Bahar Salehi, Marco Lui, Karl Grieser, Paul Cook, and Timothy Baldwin. 2013. Unimelb_nlp-core: Integrating predictions from multiple domains and feature sets for estimating semantic textual similarity. *Atlanta, Georgia, USA*, page 207.

Chih-Wei Hsu, Chih-Chung Chang, Chih-Jen Lin, et al. 2003. A Practical Guide to Support Vector Classification.

David Jurgens, Mohammad Taher Pilehvar, and Roberto Navigli. 2014. Semeval-2014 Task 3: Cross-Level Semantic Similarity. In *Proceedings of the 8th International Workshop on Semantic Evaluation (SemEval-2014) August 23-24, 2014, Dublin, Ireland*.

Thomas K Landauer, Peter W Foltz, and Darrell Laham. 1998. An Introduction to Latent Semantic Analysis. *Discourse processes*, 25(2-3):259–284.

Vladimir I Levenshtein. 1966. Binary Codes Capable of Correcting Deletions, Insertions and Reversals. In *Soviet physics doklady*, volume 10, page 707.

Dekang Lin. 1998. An Information-Theoretic Definition of Similarity. In *ICML*, volume 98, pages 296–304.

Andrew Kachites McCallum. 2002. Mallet: A Machine Learning for Language Toolkit.

Charles T Meadow. 1992. *Text Information Retrieval Systems*. Academic Press, Inc., Orlando, FL, USA.

Rada Mihalcea, Courtney Corley, and Carlo Strapparava. 2006. Corpus-based and Knowledge-based Measures of Text Semantic Similarity. In *AAAI*, volume 6, pages 775–780.

David Milne and Ian H Witten. 2013. An Open-Source Toolkit for Mining Wikipedia. *Artificial Intelligence*, 194:222–239.

Ted Pedersen, Siddharth Patwardhan, and Jason Michelizzi. 2004. Wordnet::similarity - Measuring the Relatedness of Concepts. In *Demonstration Papers at HLT-NAACL 2004*, pages 38–41.

Philip Resnik. 1995. Using Information Content to Evaluate Semantic Similarity in a Taxonomy. *arXiv preprint cmp-lg/9511007*.

Frane Šarić, Goran Glavaš, Mladen Karan, Jan Šnajder, and Bojana Dalbelo Bašić. 2012. Takelab: Systems for Measuring Semantic Text Similarity. In *Proceedings of the First Joint Conference on Lexical and Computational Semantics-Volume 1: Proceedings of the main conference and the shared task, and Volume 2: Proceedings of the Sixth International Workshop on Semantic Evaluation*, pages 441–448.

Helmut Schmid. 1994. Probabilistic Part-of-Speech Tagging Using Decision Trees. In *Proceedings of international conference on new methods in language processing*, volume 12, pages 44–49. Manchester, UK.

FBK-TR: SVM for Semantic Relatedness and Corpus Patterns for RTE

Ngoc Phuoc An Vo
Fondazione Bruno Kessler
University of Trento
Trento, Italy
ngoc@fbk.eu

Octavian Popescu
Fondazione Bruno Kessler
Trento, Italy
popescu@fbk.eu

Tommaso Caselli
TrentoRISE
Trento, Italy
t.caselli@trentorise.eu

Abstract

This paper reports the description and scores of our system, FBK-TR, which participated at the SemEval 2014 task #1 "Evaluation of Compositional Distributional Semantic Models on Full Sentences through Semantic Relatedness and Entailment". The system consists of two parts: one for computing semantic relatedness, based on SVM, and the other for identifying the entailment values on the basis of both semantic relatedness scores and entailment patterns based on verb-specific semantic frames. The system ranked 11th on both tasks with competitive results.

1 Introduction

In the Natural Language Processing community, meaning related tasks have gained an increasing popularity. These tasks focus, in general, on a couple of short pieces of text, like pair of sentences, and the systems are required to infer a certain meaning relationship that exists between these texts. Two of the most popular meaning related tasks are the identification of Semantic Text Similarity (STS) and Recognizing Textual Entailment (RTE). The STS tasks require to identify the degree of similarity (or relatedness) that exists between two text fragments (sentences, paragraphs, ...), where similarity is a broad concept and its value is normally obtained by averaging the opinion of several annotators. The RTE task requires the identification of a directional relation between a pair of text fragments, namely a text (T) and a hypothesis (H). The relation (T $\rightarrow$ H) holds whenever the truth of H follows from T.

At SemEval 2014, the Task #1 "Evaluation of Compositional Distributional Semantic Models on Full Sentences through Semantic Relatedness and Entailment" (Marelli et al., 2014a) primarily aimed at evaluating Compositional Distributional Semantic Models (CDSMs) of meaning over two subtasks, namely semantic relatedness and textual entailment (ENTAILMENT, CONTRADICTION and NEUTRAL), over pairs of sentences (Marelli et al., 2014b). Concerning the relatedness subtask, the system outputs are evaluated against gold standard ratings in two ways, using Pearson correlation and Spearman's rank correlation (rho). The Pearson correlation is used for evaluating and ranking the participating systems. Similarly, for the textual entailment subtask, system outputs are evaluated against a gold standard rating with respect to accuracy.

Our team, FBK-TR, participated in both subtasks with five different runs. In this paper, we present a comprehensive description of our system which obtained competitive results in both tasks and which is not based on CDSMs. Our approach for the relatedness task is based on machine learning techniques to learn models from different lexical and semantic features from the train corpus and then to make prediction on the test corpus. Particularly, we used support vector machine (SVM) (Chang and Lin, 2011), regression model to solve this subtask. On the other hand, the textual entailment task uses a methodology mainly based on corpus patterns automatically extracted from annotated text corpora.

The remainder of the paper is organized as follows: Section 2 presents the SVM system for semantic relatedness. Section 3 describes the methodology used for extracting patterns and computing the textual entailment values. Finally, Section 4 discusses about the evaluations and Section 5 presents conclusions and future work.

Proceedings of the 8th International Workshop on Semantic Evaluation (SemEval 2014), pages 289–293,
Dublin, Ireland, August 23-24, 2014.

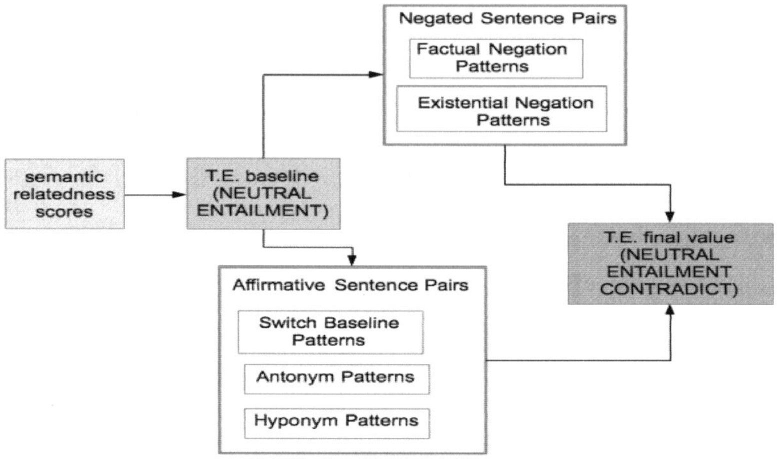

Figure 1: Schema of the system for computing entailment.

2 System Overview for Semantic Relatedness Subtask

Concerning the Semantic Relatedness subtask our SVM system is built on different linguistic features, ranging from relatedness at the lexical level (WordNet based measures, Wikipedia relatedness and Latent Semantic Analysis), to sentence level, including topic modeling based on Latent Dirichlet allocation (LDA) and string similarity (Longest Common Substring).

2.1 Lexical Features

At the lexical level, we built a simple, yet effective Semantic Word Relatedness model, which consists of 3 components: WordNet similarity (based on the Lin measure as implemented in Pedersen package `WordNet:Similarity` (Pedersen et al., 2004), Wikipedia relatedness (as provided by the Wikipedia Miner package (Milne and Witten, 2013)), and Latent Semantic Analysis (Landauer et al., 1998), with a model trained on the British National Corpus (BNC) [1] and Wikipedia. At this level of analysis, we concentrated only on the best matched (lemma) pairs of content words, i.e. Noun-Noun, Verb-Verb, extracted from each sentence pair. The content words have been automatically extracted by means of part-of-speech tagging (TreeTagger (Schmid, 1994)) and lemmatization.

For words which are not present in WordNet, the relatedness score has been obtained by means of the Levenshtein distance (Levenshtein, 1966).

[1] http://www.natcorp.ox.ac.uk

2.2 Topic Modeling

We have applied topic modeling based on Latent Dirichlet allocation (LDA) (Blei et al., 2003) as implemented in the MALLET package (McCallum, 2002). The topic model was developed using the BNC and Wikipedia (with the numbers of topics varying from 20 to 500 topics). From the proportion vectors (distribution of documents over topics) of the given texts, we apply 3 different measures (Cosine similarity, Kullback-Leibler and Jensen-Shannon divergences) to compute the distances between each pair of sentences.

2.3 String Similarity: Longest Common Substring

As for the string level, two given sentences are considered similar/related if they are overlapping/covering each other (e.g sentence 1 covers a part of sentence 2, or otherwise). Hence, we considered the text overlapping between two given texts as a feature for our system. The extraction of the features at the string level was computed in two steps: first, we obtained Longest Common Substring between two given sentences. After this, we also considered measuring the similarity for the parts before and after the LCS between two given texts, by means of the Lin measure and the Levenshtein distance.

3 System Overview for RTE Subtask

The system for the identification of the entailment values is illustrated in Figure 1. Entailment values are computed starting from a baseline (only ENTAILMENT and NEUTRAL values) which relies on the output (i.e. scores) of the semantic relatedness system. After this step, two groups of entailment patterns are applied whether the surface form of a sentence pair is affirmative (i.e. absence of negation words) or negative. Each type of pattern provides in output an associated entailment value which corresponds to the final value assigned by the system.

The entailment patterns are based on verb-specific semantic frames that include both syntactic and semantic information. Hence, we have explicit access to the information that individual words have and to the process of combining them in bigger units, namely phrases, which carry out meanings. The patterns have two properties: i.) the senses of the words inside the pattern are stable, they do not change whatever context is added to the left, right or inside the phrase matching the pattern, and ii.) the replacement of a word with another word belonging to a certain class changes the senses of the words. Patterns with these properties are called Sense Discriminative Patterns (SDPs). It has been noted (Popescu et al., 2011) that we can associate to a phrase that is matched by an SDP a set of phrases for which an entailment relationship is decidable showing that there is a direct relationship between SDPs and entailment .

SDP patterns have been obtained from large parsed corpora. To maximize the accuracy of the corpus we have chosen sentences containing at maximum two finite verbs from BNC and Annotated English Gigaword. We parsed this corpus with the Stanford parser, discarding the sentences from the Annotated English Gigaword which have a different parsing. Each words is replaced with their possible SUMO attributes (Niles and Pease, 2003). Only the following Stanford dependencies are retained as valid *[n, nsub]sbj, [d,i,p]obj, prep, [x,c]comp*. We considered only the most frequent occurrences of such patterns for each verb. To cluster into a single SDP pattern, all patterns that are sense auto-determinative, we used the OntoNotes (Hovy et al., 2006) and CPA (Hanks, 2008) lexica. Inside each cluster, we searched for the most general hypernyms for each syntactic slot such that there are no common patterns between clusters (Popescu, 2013). However, the patterns thus obtained are not sufficient enough for the task. Some expressions may be the paraphrasis a word in the context of an SDP. To extract this information, we considered all the pairs in training that are in an ENTAILMENT relationship, with a high relatedness score (4 to 5), and we extracted the parts that are different for each grammatical slot. In this way, we compiled a list of quasi synonym phrases that can be replaced inside an SDP without affecting the replacement. This is the only component that depends on the training corpus. Figure 2 describes the algorithm for computing entailment on the basis of the SDPs. The following subsections illustrate the identification of entailment relation for affirmative sentences and negated sentences.

Algorithm Entailment via SDPs

Require: Parsed pairs of phrases
Require: Synonymy repository
Require: Hyponym, Hypernym repository
Require: NegativeWordsList
Require: *DepSet* dependency set
Ensure: {ENTAILMENT, CONTRADICTION, NEUTRAL}

```
Consider the SDP for phrase_1 and phrase_2
flNeg ← 0;
if phrase_1 xor phrase_2 contain words ∈ NegativeWordsList then
    generate EA sets
    flNeg ← 1;
end if
match ← 1
while match do
    consider each syntactic position in SDPs
    if word_1 and word_2 ∉ repositories then
        match ← -1
    end if
end while
if match == 1 then
    if flNeg == 1 then
        return CONTRADICTION
    end if
    return ENTAILMENT
end if
return NEUTRAL
```

Figure 2: Algorithm for computing entailment.

3.1 Entailment on Affirmative Sentences

Affirmative sentences use three types of entailment patterns. The switch baseline and hyponym patterns works in this way: If two sentences are matched by the same SDP, and the difference between them is that the second one contains a hypernym on the same syntactic position, then the first one is entailed by the second (i.e. ENTAILMENT). If the two SDPs are such that the difference between them is that the second contains a word which is not synonym, hypernym or hyponym on the same syntactic position, then there is no entailment between the two phrases (i.e. NEUTRAL). The entailment direction is from the sentence that contains the hyponym toward the other sentence. The antonym patterns check if the two SDPs are the same, with the only difference being in the verb of the second sentence being an antonym of the verb in the first sentence (i.e. CONTRADICTION).

3.2 Entailment on Negative Sentences

As for negated sentences, we distinguish between existential negative phrases (i.e. *there is no* or *there are no*) and factual negative ones (presence of a negative polarity word). An assumption related to each SDP is that it entails the existence of any of the component of the pattern which can be expressed by means of dedicated phrases. A SDP of the kind "*[Human] beat [Animal]*", entails both phrases, namely *there is a [Human]* and *there is a [Animal].* We call this set of associated existential phrases, Existential Assumptions (EAs). This type of existential entailment obtained through the usage of SDP has a direct consequence for handling the ENTAILMENT, CONTRADICTION and NEUTRAL types of entailment when one of the phrases is negated. If the first phrase belongs to the EA of the second one, then the first phrase is entailed by the second phrase; if the first phrase is an existential negation of a phrase belonging to the EA set of the second phrase, meaning that it contains the string *there is/are no*, then the first one is a contradiction of the second phrase; if neither the first phrase, nor its negation belong to the EA set of the second phrase, then the two sentences are neutral with respect to the entailment. The general rule described in 3.1 applies to these types of phrases as well: replacing a word on the same syntactic slot inside a phrase that is matched by a SDP leads to a CONTRADICTION type of entailment, if the replacement is a hypernym of the original word. Similarly, the approach can be applied to factual negative phrases. The scope of negation is considered to be the extension of the SDP and thus the negative set of EAs.

4 Evaluation and Ranking

Table 1 illustrates the results for Pearson and Spearman correlations for the relatedness subtask on the test set. Table 2 reports the Accuracy values for the entailment subtask on the test set.

Concerning the relatedness results our systems ranked 11th out of 17 participating systems. Best score of our system is reported in Table 1. One of the main reason for the relatively low results of the systems for this subtask concerns the fact that it is designed for a general-level of texts (i.e. compositionality is not taken into account).

Team	**Pearson**	**Spearman**
ECNU_run1 (ranked 1st)	0.82795	0.76892
FBK-TR_run3	0.70892	0.64430

Table 1: Results for semantic relatedness subtask.

Team	**Accuracy**
Illinois-LH_run1 (ranked 1st)	84.575
FBK-TR_run3	75.401
∗FBK-TR_baseline	64.080
∗FBK-TR_new	**85.082**

Table 2: Results for entailment subtask.

As for the entailment subtask, our system ranked 11th out of 18 participating systems. The submitted results of the system are illustrated in Table 2 and are compared against the best system, our baseline system (∗FBK-TR_baseline) as described in Figure 1, and a new version of the participating system after fixing some bugs in the submitted version due to the processing of the parser's output (∗FBK-TR_new). The new version of the system scores in the top provides a new state of the art result, with an improvement of 10 points with respect to our submitted system.

5 Conclusion and Future Work

This paper reports the description of our system, FBK-TR, which implements a general SVM semantic relatedness system based on distributional features (LSA, LDA), knowledge-based related features (WordNet and Wikipedia) and string overlap (LCS). On top of that, we added structural information at both semantic and syntactic level by using SDP patterns. The system reached competitive results in both subtasks. By correcting some bugs in the entailment scripts, we obtained an improvement over our submitted systems as well as for the best ranking system. We plan to improve and extend the relatedness system by means of compositional methods. Finally, the entailment system can be improved by taking into account additional linguistic evidences, such as the alternation between indefinite and definite determiners, noun modifiers and semantically empty heads.

References

David M Blei, Andrew Y Ng, and Michael I Jordan. 2003. Latent Dirichlet Allocation. *The Journal of Machine Learning research*, 3:993–1022.

Chih-Chung Chang and Chih-Jen Lin. 2011. LIBSVM: A Library for Support Vector Machines. *ACM Transactions on Intelligent Systems and Technology (TIST)*, 2(3):27.

Patrick Hanks. 2008. Mapping meaning onto use: a Pattern Dictionary of English Verbs. In *Proceedings of the AACL 2008*.

Eduard Hovy, Mitchell Marcus, Martha Palmer, Lance Ramshaw, and Ralph Weischedel. 2006. OntoNotes: The 90% Solution. In *Proceedings of the human language technology conference of the NAACL, Companion Volume: Short Papers*, pages 57–60.

Thomas K Landauer, Peter W Foltz, and Darrell Laham. 1998. An Introduction to Latent Semantic Analysis. *Discourse processes*, 25(2-3):259–284.

Vladimir I Levenshtein. 1966. Binary Codes Capable of Correcting Deletions, Insertions and Reversals. In *Soviet Physics Doklady*, volume 10, page 707.

M Marelli, L Bentivogli, M Baroni, R Bernardi, S Menini, and R Zamparelli. 2014a. Semeval-2014 Task 1: Evaluation of compositional distributional semantic models on full sentences through semantic relatedness and textual entailment. In *Proceedings of SemEval 2014: International Workshop on Semantic Evaluation, August 23-24, 2014, Dublin, Ireland.*

M Marelli, S Menini, M Baroni, L Bentivogli, R Bernardi, and R Zamparelli. 2014b. A SICK cure for the evaluation of compositional distributional semantic models. In *Proceedings of LREC 2014, Reykjavik (Iceland): ELRA.*

Andrew Kachites McCallum. 2002. MALLET: A Machine Learning for Language Toolkit.

David Milne and Ian H Witten. 2013. An Open-Source Toolkit for Mining Wikipedia. *Artificial Intelligence*, 194:222–239.

Ian Niles and Adam Pease. 2003. Mapping WordNet to the SUMO Ontology. In *Proceedings of the IEEE International Knowledge Engineering Conference*, pages 23–26.

Ted Pedersen, Patwardhan Siddharth, and Michelizzi Jason. 2004. Wordnet::Similarity: Measuring the Relatedness of Concepts. In *Proceedings of the HLT-NAACL 2004.*

Octavian Popescu, Elena Cabrio, and Bernardo Magnini. 2011. Textual Entailment Using Chain Clarifying Relationships. In *Proceedings of the IJCAI Workshop Learning by Reasoning and its Applications in Intelligent Question-Answering*.

Octavian Popescu. 2013. Learning Corpus Patterns Using Finite State Automata. In *Proceedings of the ICSC 2013.*

Helmut Schmid. 1994. Probabilistic Part-of-Sspeech Tagging Using Decision Trees. In *Proceedings of international conference on new methods in language processing*, volume 12, pages 44–49. Manchester, UK.

GPLSI: Supervised Sentiment Analysis in Twitter using Skipgrams

Javi Fernández, Yoan Gutiérrez, José M. Gómez, Patricio Martínez-Barco
Department of Software and Computing Systems
University of Alicante
{javifm,ygutierrez,jmgomez,patricio}@dlsi.ua.es

Abstract

In this paper we describe the system submitted for the *SemEval 2014 Task 9 (Sentiment Analysis in Twitter) Subtask B*. Our contribution consists of a supervised approach using machine learning techniques, which uses the terms in the dataset as features. In this work we do not employ any external knowledge and resources. The novelty of our approach lies in the use of words, ngrams and *skipgrams* (not-adjacent ngrams) as features, and how they are weighted.

1 Introduction

The Web 2.0 has become one of the most important sources of data to extract useful and heterogeneous knowledge from. Texts can provide *factual information*, such as descriptions and lists of features, and *opinion-based information*, which would include reviews, emotions, or feelings. This subjective information can be expressed through different textual genres, such as blogs, forums, social networks and microblogs.

An example of microblogging social network is Twitter[1], which has gained much popularity in the last years. This website enables its users to send and read text-based messages of up to 140 characters, known as *tweets*. This site can be a vast source of subjective information in real time; millions of users share opinions on different aspects of their everyday life. Extracting this subjective information has a great value for both general and expert users. However, it is difficult to exploit it accordingly, mainly because of the short length of the tweets, the informality, and the lack of context. *Sentiment Analysis* (SA) systems must be adapted to face the challenges of this new textual genre.

International competitions related to the assessment of SA systems in Twitter have taken place. Some of them include the *TASS* workshop in the *SEPLN* conference (Villena-Román et al., 2013), the *RepLab* workshop in the *CLEF* conference (Amigó et al., 2012), and the *Sentiment Analysis in Twitter* task (Task 2) in the last *SemEval* workshop (Nakov et al., 2013).

In this paper we describe the system submitted for the *SemEval 2014 Sentiment Analysis in Twitter* task (Task 9 Subtask B)[2] (Rosenthal et al., 2014). This task consists of performing an automatic sentiment analysis to determine whether a message expresses a *positive*, *negative*, or *neutral* sentiment. The organisers of this task provide three datasets: *training*, *development training*, and *development test*. The participants can use the *training* and *development training* datasets to train and validate their models, but the *development test* dataset can only be used for validation. The size and distribution of polarities of these datasets is shown in Table 1. Once their systems are ready, the participants must classify each text in the *official test* corpus and send the results to the organisers, who will perform the official evaluation.

Polarity	**Train**	**Dev Train**	**Dev Test**
Positive	2,148	362	1,572
Neutral	2,915	448	1,640
Negative	836	187	601
Total	5,899	997	3,813

Table 1: Dataset distribution in number of tweets.

The goal of the present work is to create a reliable polarity classifier, built only from a training set without any external knowledge and resources.

[1] http://twitter.com

[2] http://alt.qcri.org/semeval2014/

Proceedings of the 8th International Workshop on Semantic Evaluation (SemEval 2014), pages 294–299,
Dublin, Ireland, August 23-24, 2014.

Our contribution consists of a supervised approach using machine learning techniques, which uses the terms in the dataset as features. The novelty of our approach lies in the feature generation and weighting, using not only *single words* and *ngrams* as features but also *skipgrams*. This approach is described in detail in Section 3. Subsequently, in Section 4 we show the assessment of our model in the competition. Finally, the conclusions and future work are presented in Section 5. The following Section 2 shows some relevant background related to this work.

2 Related Work

The goal of *Sentiment analysis* (SA) is to identify the opinions expressed in text and classify texts accordingly (Dadvar et al., 2011). Two main approaches can be followed (Annett and Kondrak, 2008; Liu, 2010; Taboada et al., 2011): *lexical* approaches (unsupervised SA) and *machine learning* approaches (supervised SA). Lexical approaches focus on building dictionaries and lexicons of labelled words. This labeling gives a score for each word, that indicates how strong is the relation between that word and each polarity. The most common way to classify a text using these scores is by adding the positive values and subtracting the negative values of the terms in that text. If the total score is positive, that text is classified as positive, otherwise it is classified as negative. These dictionaries can be created manually (Stone et al., 1966) or automatically (Turney, 2002). Examples of lexicons are *WordNet Affect* (Strapparava and Valitutti, 2004), *SentiWordNet* (Esuli and Sebastiani, 2006), *MicroWNOP* (Cerini et al., 2007) or *JRC Tonality* (Balahur et al., 2009). However, it is very difficult to collect and maintain a universal sentiment lexicon because different words may be used in different domains (Qiu et al., 2009) and some words are domain dependent (Turney, 2002).

The second approach uses machine learning techniques. These techniques require the previous creation of a corpus containing a set of classified texts to train a classifier, which can then be applied to classify a set of unclassified texts. The majority of the researches employ *Support Vector Machines* (Mullen and Collier, 2004; Prabowo et al., 2009; Wilson et al., 2005) or *Naïve Bayes* (Pang and Lee, 2004; Wiebe et al., 2005; Tan et al., 2009) classifiers because they usually obtain the best results. In this approach, texts are represented as vectors of features, and depending on the features used the system can reach better results (bag-of-words and lexeme-based features are the more commonly used (Pang and Lee, 2008)). These classifiers perform very well in the domain that they are trained on, but their performance drops when the same classifier is used in a different domain (Pang and Lee, 2008; Tan et al., 2009).

The problem of the *domain dependence* is common to both approaches. When the lexicons and classifiers generated are used in a domain different from the one they were built for, they use to perform worse (Turney, 2002; Pang and Lee, 2008; Qiu et al., 2009; Tan et al., 2009). Creating a domain-specific lexicon or classifier means making a manual effort. Although some studies try to overcome this problem by generating the lexicons *automatically* (Turney, 2002), learning from *unannotated* texts (Wiebe et al., 2005) or using *hybrid* approaches (Andreevskaia and Bergler, 2008; Bollen et al., 2011; Zhang and Ye, 2008), a minimal intervention from experts in the domain is needed. In this study we use the machine learning approach due to the promising results obtained in previous works (Boldrini et al., 2009; Fernández et al., 2011; Fernández et al., 2013).

3 Methodology

Our contribution consists of a supervised approach using machine learning techniques, which uses the terms in the dataset as features. In summary, our approach starts making a basic normalisation of each tweet in the dataset (see Section 3.1). Next, these texts are tokenised to extract their terms, and these terms are combined to create *skipgrams* (see Section 3.2). Finally, these skipgrams are employed as features for a supervised machine learning algorithm (see Section 3.3).

3.1 Basic normalisation

We perform a very basic normalisation, as we do not want to lose the potential subjective information given by the not normalised original text. Each tweet in the dataset is normalised following these steps:

1. **Lower case conversion**. All the characters in the tweet text are converted to lower case.

2. **Character repetition removal**. If the same character is repeated more than 3 times, the rest of repetitions are removed, so we can

still recognize if a word had repeated characters. For example, the words *gooood* and *gooooood* would be normalised to *goood*, but the word *good* would remain the same. We assume the ambiguity of some words like the one in the example, which can refer to the words *good* and *god*.

3. **Usernames and hashtags substitution**. We do not consider usernames and hashtags as they are not usually the words that represent a subjective sentence, they use to be the *topic* of the tweet. They are not removed completely but they are replaced by the strings `USERNAME` and `HASHTAG`.

So excited to go to #Alicante tomorrow with the best friend everrrrr @John!!!!

↓

so excited to go to #alicante tomorrow with the best friend everrrrr @john!!!!

↓

so excited to go to #alicante tomorrow with the best friend everrr @john!!!

↓

so excited to go to HASHTAG tomorrow with the best friend everrr USERNAME!!!

Figure 1: Example of normalisation process.

3.2 Tokenisation

Once we have normalised the texts, we extract all their terms. In this work, we consider a term as a group of adjacent characters of the same type (letters, numbers or punctuation symbols). For example, the text *want2go!!* would be tokenised to the terms *want*, *2*, *go*, and *!!*. Note that we employ all the terms extracted, not filtering any of them.

Finally, we obtain the *skipgrams* of the terms in the text. Skipgrams are a technique largely used in the field of speech processing, whereby n-grams are formed (bigrams, trigrams, etc.) but in addition to allowing adjacent sequences of words, it also allows tokens to be *skipped* (Guthrie et al., 2006). More specifically, in a *k-skip-n-gram*, *n* determines the maximum number of terms, and *k* the maximum number of skips allowed. In this way skipgrams are new terms that retain part of the sequentiality of the terms, but in a more flexible way than ngrams. Note that a ngram can be described as a skipgram where $k = 0$. An example is shown in Figure 2.

Normalised tweet

so excited to go to HASHTAG tomorrow with the best friend everrr USERNAME!!!

↓

Single terms

(so) (excited) (to) (go) (to) (HASHTAG) (with) (the) (best) (friend) (everrr) (USERNAME) (!!!)

↓

Skipgrams ($n = 2, k = 1$)

(so) (so excited) (so to) (excited) (excited to) (excited go) (to) (to go) (to to) (go) (go to) (go HASHTAG) (to) (to HASHTAG) (to with) (HASHTAG) (HASHTAG with) (HASHTAG the) (with) (with the) (with best) (the) (the best) (the friend) (best) (best friend) (best everrr) (friend) (friend everrr) (friend USERNAME) (everrr) (everrr USERNAME) (everrr !!!) (USERNAME) (USERNAME !!!)

Figure 2: Example of tokenisation process.

3.3 Supervised Learning

To build our model we employed *Support Vector Machines* (SVM) as the supervised machine learning algorithm, as it has been proved to be effective on text categorisation tasks and robust on large feature spaces (Sebastiani, 2002; Mohammad et al., 2013). More specifically, we used the *Weka*[3] (Hall et al., 2009) *LibSVM* (Chang and Lin, 2011) implementation with the default parameters (*linear kernel*, $C = 1$, $\epsilon = 0.1$).

The skipgrams extracted in the previous step are employed as features for the SVM. The weight of each feature in each text will be calculated depending on the skipgram it represents, using the formula in Equation 1.

$$w(s,t) = \frac{terms(s)}{terms(s) + skips(s,t)} \qquad (1)$$

Where $w(s,t)$ represents the weight of the skipgram s in the text t, $terms$ is a function that returns the number of terms in skipgram s, and $skips$ is a function that returns the number of skips of the skipgram s in the text t. This formula gives more importance to the skipgrams with a lower number of skips. In the example of the Figure 2, the skipgram *best friend* would have a weight of $2/(2+0) = 1$, while skipgram *best everrr* would have a weight of $2/(2+1) = 0.66$.

[3] `http://www.cs.waikato.ac.nz/ml/weka/`

	Parameters	P	R	F1	Score
Baseline		0.630	0.604	0.580	0.447
Words	$n = 1$	0.611	0.612	0.604	0.530
Ngrams	$n = 2$	0.617	0.620	0.618	0.557
	$n = 3$	0.620	0.621	0.621	0.564
	$n = 4$	0.620	0.621	0.620	0.565
	$n = max$	0.621	0.622	0.621	0.566
Skipgrams	$n = 2, k = 1$	0.623	**0.625**	0.624	0.571
	$n = 2, k = 2$	0.626	0.624	**0.626**	0.572
	$n = 2, k = max$	0.627	0.624	0.625	**0.575**
	$n = 3, k = 1$	0.620	0.616	0.617	0.566
	$n = 3, k = 2$	0.625	0.614	0.618	0.564
	$n = 3, k = max$	**0.636**	0.588	0.599	0.544

Table 2: Experiments performed and scores obtained.

4 Evaluation

We performed a series of experiments employing both the *training* corpus and the *development training* corpus to create our model, and the *development test* corpus to validate it. We used as baseline the system presented to the workshop *TASS 2012* (Fernández et al., 2013), which also uses skipgrams and scores them depending on their density but, instead of using the skipgrams as features of a machine learning model, the polarity of each text is determined by a combination of the scores of its skipgrams.

The results of our experiments are shown in Table 2. In this table we show the *weighted precision* (**P**), the *weighted recall* (**R**), the *weighted F-score* (**F1**) and the *score* obtained using the scorer tool provided by the workshop organisers (**Score**). The notation $n = max$ indicates there was no limit with the number of terms, and $k = max$ indicates there was no restriction with the number of skips. As we can see, the presented approach outperforms the baseline proposed and the best results are obtained using skipgrams, specifically when $n = 2$ and $k = max$. These are the parameters of the system submitted to the competition.

Our main observation is that incrementing the number of terms increases the precision of the system. A possible explanation for this might be that ngrams/skipgrams with a greater number of words are more specific and representative of a given polarity. In addition, using skipgrams insted of ngrams also improves the precision. However, no significant differences were found between experiments with a different number of skips.

In Table 3 we can see the official results obtained in the SemEval 2014 competition. The best rank was obtained in the experiments with the *Twitter 2014 Sarcasm* dataset.

Dataset	Rank	Score
Live Journal	34	0.573
SMS 2013	35	0.466
Twitter 2013	28	0.575
Twitter 2014	30	0.561
Twitter 2014 Sarcasm	8	0.539

Table 3: Official SemEval 2014 Subtask B results.

5 Conclusions

In this paper we described the system submitted for the *SemEval 2014 Task 9 (Sentiment Analysis in Twitter)*. It consists of a supervised approach using machine learning techniques, without employing any external knowledge and resources. The novelty of our approach lies in the feature generation and weighting, using not only single words and *ngrams* as features but also *skipgrams*. In the experiments performed we showed that employing skipgrams instead of single words or ngrams improves the results for these datasets. This fact suggests that our approach is promising and encourages us to continue with our research.

As future work, we plan to find new methods to combine the weights of the skipgrams, evaluate our approaches on different corpora and different domains (in order to check their robustness), and start adding external knowledge and resources.

Acknowledgements

This research work has been partially funded by the *University of Alicante*, *Generalitat Valenciana*, *Spanish Government* and the *European Commission* through the projects, "Tratamiento inteligente de la información para la ayuda a la toma de decisiones" (GRE12-44), *ATTOS* (TIN2012-38536-C03-03), *LEGOLANG* (TIN2012-31224), *SAM* (FP7-611312), *FIRST* (FP7-287607) and *ACOMP*/2013/067.

References

Enrique Amigó, Adolfo Corujo, Julio Gonzalo, Edgar Meij, and Maarten de Rijke. 2012. Overview of RepLab 2012: Evaluating Online Reputation Management Systems. In *Conference and Labs of the Evaluation Forum (CLEF 2012)*.

Alina Andreevskaia and Sabine Bergler. 2008. When Specialists and Generalists Work Together: Overcoming Domain Dependence in Sentiment Tagging. In *Proceedings of the 46th Annual Meeting of the Association for Computational Linguistics on Human Language Technologies (ACL HLT 2008)*, pages 290–298.

Michelle Annett and Grzegorz Kondrak. 2008. A Comparison of Sentiment Analysis Techniques: Polarizing Movie Blogs. In *Proceedings of the 21st Canadian Conference on Artificial Intelligence (CCAI 2008)*, pages 25–35.

Alexandra Balahur, Ralf Steinberger, Erik Van Der Goot, Bruno Pouliquen, and Mijail Kabadjov. 2009. Opinion Mining on Newspaper Quotations. In *2009 IEEE/WIC/ACM International Joint Conference on Web Intelligence and Intelligent Agent Technology*, pages 523–526.

Ester Boldrini, Javier Fernández Martínez, José Manuel Gómez Soriano, Patricio Martínez Barco, et al. 2009. Machine learning techniques for automatic opinion detection in non-traditional textual genres.

Johan Bollen, Alberto Pepe, and Huina Mao. 2011. Modeling Public Mood and Emotion: Twitter Sentiment and Socio-Economic Phenomena. In *Fifth International AAAI Conference on Weblogs and Social Media (ICWSM 2011)*.

Sabrina Cerini, Valentina Compagnoni, Alice Demontis, Maicol Formentelli, and G Gandini. 2007. Micro-WNOp: A Gold Standard for the Evaluation of Automatically Compiled Lexical Resources for Opinion Mining. *Language resources and linguistic theory: Typology, second language acquisition, English linguistics*, pages 200–210.

Chih-chung Chang and Chih-jen Lin. 2011. LIBSVM : A Library for Support Vector Machines. *ACM Transactions on Intelligent Systems and Technology (TIST)*, 2:1–39.

Maral Dadvar, Claudia Hauff, and FMG De Jong. 2011. Scope of Negation Detection in Sentiment Analysis. In *Proceedings of the Dutch-Belgian Information Retrieval Workshop (DIR 2011)*, pages 16–20.

Andrea Esuli and Fabrizio Sebastiani. 2006. Sentiwordnet: A Publicly Available Lexical Resource for Opinion Mining. In *Proceedings of LREC*, volume 6, pages 417–422.

Javi Fernández, Ester Boldrini, José M. Gómez, and Patricio Martínez-Barco. 2011. Evaluating EmotiBlog Robustness for Sentiment Analysis Tasks. In *Natural Language Processing and Information Systems*, pages 290–294.

Javi Fernández, Yoan Gutiérrez, José M. Gómez, Patricio Martínez-Barco, Andrés Montoyo, and Rafael Muñoz. 2013. Sentiment Analysis of Spanish Tweets Using a Ranking Algorithm and Skipgrams. In *XXIX Congreso de la Sociedad Española de Procesamiento de Lenguaje Natural (SEPLN 2013)*, pages 133–142.

David Guthrie, Ben Allison, Wei Liu, Louise Guthrie, and Yorick Wilks. 2006. A Closer Look at Skip-gram Modelling. In *5th international Conference on Language Resources and Evaluation (LREC 2006)*, pages 1–4.

Mark Hall, Eibe Frank, Geoffrey Holmes, Bernhard Pfahringer, Peter Reutemann, and Ian H Witten. 2009. The WEKA Data Mining Software: an Update. *ACM SIGKDD Explorations Newsletter*, 11(1):10–18.

Bing Liu. 2010. Sentiment Analysis and Subjectivity. In *Handbook of Natural Language Processing*, pages 1–38.

Saif M. Mohammad, Svetlana Kiritchenko, and Xiaodan Zhu. 2013. NRC-Canada: Building the State-of-the-Art in Sentiment Analysis of Tweets. In *Proceedings of the International Workshop on Semantic Evaluation (SemEval-2013)*.

Tony Mullen and Nigel Collier. 2004. Sentiment Analysis using Support Vector Machines with Diverse Information Sources. In *Proceedings of the 2004 Conference on Empirical Methods in Natural Language Processing (EMNLP 2004)*, pages 412–418.

Preslav Nakov, Sara Rosenthal, Alan Ritter, and Theresa Wilson. 2013. SemEval-2013 Task 2: Sentiment Analysis in Twitter. In *Proceedings of the International Workshop on Semantic Evaluation (SemEval-2013)*, volume 2, pages 312–320.

Bo Pang and Lillian Lee. 2004. A Sentimental Education: Sentiment Analysis Using Subjectivity Summarization Based on Minimum Cuts. In *Proceedings of the 42nd annual meeting on Association for Computational Linguistics (ACL 2004)*, page 271.

Bo Pang and Lillian Lee. 2008. Opinion Mining and Sentiment Analysis. *Foundations and Trends in Information Retrieval*, 2(1–2):1–135.

Rudy Prabowo, Mike Thelwall, and Wulfruna Street. 2009. Sentiment Analysis: A Combined Approach. *Journal of Informetrics*, 3:143–157.

Guang Qiu, Bing Liu, Jiajun Bu, and Chun Chen. 2009. Expanding Domain Sentiment Lexicon through Double Propagation. In *Proceedings of the 21st international Joint Conference on Artificial Intelligence (IJCAI 2009)*, pages 1199–1204.

Sara Rosenthal, Preslav Nakov, Alan Ritter, and Veselin Stoyanov. 2014. SemEval-2014 Task 9: Sentiment Analysis in Twitter. In *Proceedings of the International Workshop on Semantic Evaluation (SemEval-2014)*.

Fabrizio Sebastiani. 2002. Machine Learning in Automated Text Categorization. *ACM Computing Surveys (CSUR)*, 34(1):1–47, March.

Philip J. Stone, Dexter C. Dunphy, and Marshall S. Smith. 1966. The General Inquirer: A Computer Approach to Content Analysis.

Carlo Strapparava and Alessandro Valitutti. 2004. WordNet Affect: an Affective Extension of WordNet. In *LREC*, volume 4, pages 1083–1086.

Maite Taboada, Julian Brooke, Milan Tofiloski, Kimberly Voll, and Manfred Stede. 2011. Lexicon-based methods for sentiment analysis. *Computational Linguistics*, 37(2):267–307.

Songbo Tan, Xueqi Cheng, Yuefen Wang, and Hongbo Xu. 2009. Adapting Naive Bayes to Domain Adaptation for Sentiment Analysis. *Advances in Information Retrieval*, pages 337–349.

Peter D. Turney. 2002. Thumbs Up or Thumbs Down? Semantic Orientation Applied to Unsupervised Classification of Reviews. In *Proceedings of the 40th Annual Meeting of the Association for Computational Linguistics (ACL 2002)*, pages 417–424.

Julio Villena-Román, Eugenio Martínez-Cámara, Sara Lana-Serrano, and José Carlos González-Cristóbal. 2013. TASS - Workshop on Sentiment Analysis at SEPLN. *Procesamiento del Lenguaje Natural*, 50:37–44.

Janyce Wiebe, Theresa Wilson, and Claire Cardie. 2005. Annotating Expressions of Opinions and Emotions in Language. *Language resources and evaluation*, 39(2-3):165–210.

Theresa Wilson, Paul Hoffmann, Swapna Somasundaran, Jason Kessler, Janyce Wiebe, Yejin Choi, Claire Cardie, Ellen Riloff, and Siddharth Patwardhan. 2005. OpinionFinder: A System for Subjectivity Analysis. In *Proceedings of HLT/EMNLP on Interactive Demonstrations*, pages 34–35.

Min Zhang and Xingyao Ye. 2008. A Generation Model to Unify Topic Relevance and Lexicon-based Sentiment for Opinion Retrieval. In *Proceedings of the 31st annual international ACM SIGIR Conference on Research and Development in Information Retrieval (SIGIR 2008)*, pages 411–418, New York, New York, USA. ACM Press.

haLF: Comparing a Pure CDSM Approach with a Standard Machine Learning System for RTE

Lorenzo Ferrone
University of Rome "Tor Vergata"
Via del Politecnico 1
00133 Roma, Italy
lorenzo.ferrone@gmail.com

Fabio Massimo Zanzotto
University of Rome "Tor Vergata"
Via del Politecnico 1
00133 Roma, Italy
fabio.massimo.zanzotto@uniroma2.it

Abstract

In this paper, we describe our submission to the Shared Task #1. We tried to follow the underlying idea of the task, that is, evaluating the gap of full-fledged recognizing textual entailment systems with respect to compositional distributional semantic models (CDSMs) applied to this task. We thus submitted two runs: 1) a system obtained with a machine learning approach based on the feature spaces of rules with variables and 2) a system completely based on a CDSM that mixes structural and syntactic information by using distributed tree kernels. Our analysis shows that, under the same conditions, the fully CDSM system is still far from being competitive with more complex methods.

1 Introduction

Recognizing Textual Entailment is a largely explored problem (Dagan et al., 2013). Past challenges (Dagan et al., 2006; Bar-Haim et al., 2006; Giampiccolo et al., 2007) explored methods and models applied in complex and natural texts. In this context, machine learning solutions show interesting results. The Shared Task #1 of SemEval instead wants to explore systems in a more controlled textual environment where the phenomena to model are clearer. The aim of the Shared Task is to study how RTE systems built upon compositional distributional semantic models behave with respect to the above tradition. We tried to capture this underlying idea of the task.

In this paper, we describe our submission to the Shared Task #1. We tried to follow the underlying idea of the task, that is, evaluating the gap of full-fledged recognizing textual entailment systems with respect to compositional distributional semantic models (CDSMs) applied to this task. We thus submitted two runs: 1) a system obtained with a machine learning approach based on the feature spaces of rules with variables (Zanzotto et al., 2009) and 2) a system completely based on a CDSM that mixes structural and syntactic information by using distributed tree kernels (Zanzotto and Dell'Arciprete, 2012). Our analysis shows that, under the same conditions, the fully CDSM system is still far from being competitive with more complete methods.

The rest of the paper is organized as follows. Section 2 describes the full-fledged recognizing textual entailment system that is used for comparison. Section 3 introduces a novel compositional distributional semantic model, namely, the distributed smoothed tree kernels, and the way this model is applied to the task of RTE. Section 4 describes the results in the challenge and it draws some preliminary conclusions.

2 A Standard full-fledged Machine Learning Approach for RTE

For now on, the task of recognizing textual entailment (RTE) is defined as the task to decide if a pair $p = (a, b)$ like:

("Two children are lying in the snow and are making snow angels", "Two angels are making snow on the lying children")

is in entailment, in contradiction, or neutral. As in the tradition of applied machine learn-

Proceedings of the 8th International Workshop on Semantic Evaluation (SemEval 2014), pages 300–304,
Dublin, Ireland, August 23-24, 2014.

ing models, the task is framed as a multi-classification problem. The difficulty is to determine the best feature space on which to train the classifier.

A full-fledged RTE systems based on machine learning that has to deal with natural occurring text is generally based on:

- some within-pair features that model the similarity between the sentence a and the sentence b
- some features representing more complex information of the pair (a, b) such as rules with variables that fire (Zanzotto and Moschitti, 2006)

In the following, we describe the within-pair feature and the syntactic rules with variable features used in the full-fledged RTE system.

As the second space of features is generally huge, the full feature space is generally used in kernel machines where the final kernel between two instances $p_1 = (a_1, b_1)$ and $p_2 = (a_2, b_2)$ is:

$$K(p_1, p_2) = FR(p_1, p_2) + \\ + (WTS(a_1, b_1) \cdot WTS(a_2, b_2) + 1)^2$$

where FR counts how many rules are in common between p_1 and p_2 and WTS computes a lexical similarity between a and b. In the following sections we describe the nature of WTS and of FR

2.1 Weighted Token Similarity (WTS)

This similarity model was first defined bt Corley and Mihalcea (2005) and since then has been used by many RTE systems. The model extends a classical bag-of-word model to a Weighted-Bag-of-Word (WBOW) by measuring similarity between the two sentences of the pair at the semantic level, instead of the lexical level.

For example, consider the pair: "Oscars forgot Farrah Fawcett", "Farrah Fawcett snubbed at Academy Awards". This pair is redundant, and, hence, should be assigned a very high similarity. Yet, a bag-of-word model would assign a low score, since many words are not shared across the two sentences. WBOW fixes this problem by matching 'Oscar'-'Academy Awards' and 'forgot'-'snubbed' at the semantic level. To provide these matches, WBOW relies on specific word similarity measures over WordNet (Miller, 1995), that allow synonymy and hyperonymy matches: in our experiments we specifically use Jiang&Conrath similarity (Jiang and Conrath, 1997).

2.2 Rules with Variables as Features

The above model alone is not sufficient to capture all interesting entailment features as the relation of entailment is not only related to the notion of similarity between a and b. In the tradition of RTE, an interesting feature space is the one where each feature represents a rule with variables, i.e. a first order rule that is activated by the pairs if the variables are unified. This feature space has been introduced in (Zanzotto and Moschitti, 2006) and shown to improve over the one above. Each feature $\langle fr_1, fr_2 \rangle$ is a pair of syntactic tree fragments augmented with variables. The feature is active for a pair (t_1, t_2) if the syntactic interpretations of t_1 and t_2 can be unified with $< fr_1, fr_2 >$. For example, consider the following feature:

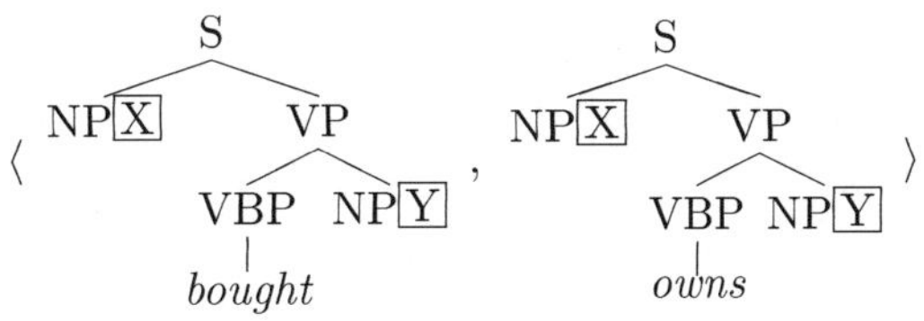

This feature is active for the pair ("*GM bought Opel*","*GM owns Opel*"), with the variable unification X = "*GM*" and Y = "*Opel*". On the contrary, this feature is not active for the pair ("*GM bought Opel*","*Opel owns GM*") as there is no possibility of unifying the two variables.

$FR(p_1, p_2)$ is a kernel function that counts the number of common rules with variables between p_1 and p_2. Efficient algorithms for the computation of the related kernel functions can be found in (Moschitti and Zanzotto, 2007; Zanzotto and Dell'Arciprete, 2009; Zanzotto et al., 2011).

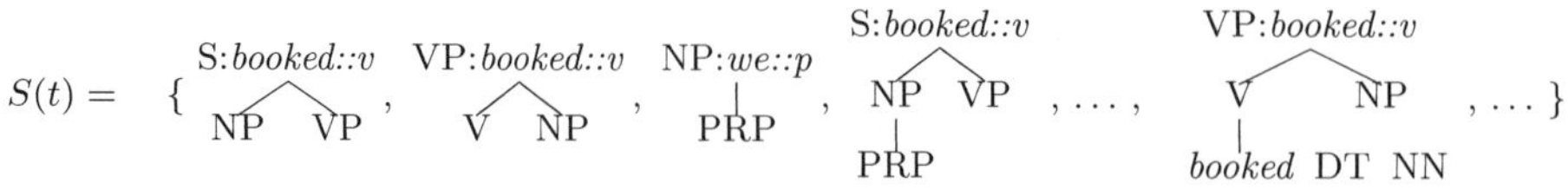

Figure 1: Subtrees of the tree t in Figure 2 (a non-exhaustive list.)

3 Distributed Smoothed Tree Kernel: a Compositional Distributional Semantic Model for RTE

The above full-fledged RTE system, although it may use distributional semantics, is not a model that applies a compositional distributional semantic model as it does not explicitly transform sentences in vectors, matrices, or tensors that represent their meaning.

We here propose a model that can be considered a compositional distributional semantic model as it transforms sentences into matrices that are then used by the learner as feature vectors. Our model is called *Distributed Smoothed Tree Kernel* (Ferrone and Zanzotto, 2014) as it mixes the distributed trees (Zanzotto and Dell'Arciprete, 2012) representing syntactic information with distributional semantic vectors representing semantic information. The computation of the final matrix for each sentence is done compositionally.

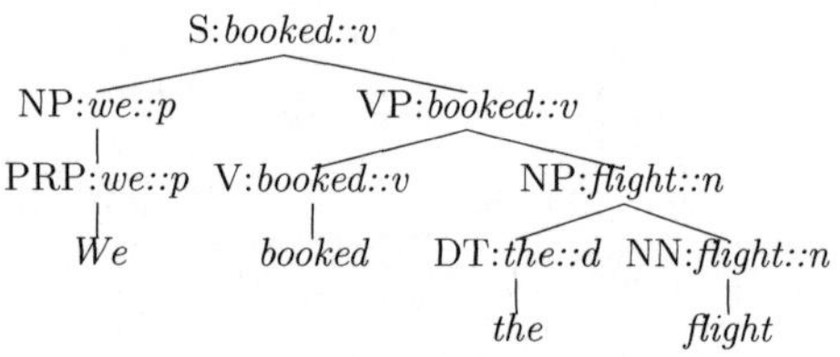

Figure 2: A lexicalized tree.

3.1 Notation

Before describing the *distributed smoothed trees* (DST) we introduce a formal way to denote constituency-based *lexicalized parse trees*, as DSTs exploit this kind of data structures. *Lexicalized trees* are denoted with the letter t and $N(t)$ denotes the set of non terminal nodes of tree t. Each non-terminal node $n \in N(t)$ has a label l_n composed of two parts $l_n = (s_n, w_n)$: s_n is the syntactic label, while w_n is the semantic headword of the tree headed by n, along with its part-of-speech tag. Terminal nodes of trees are treated differently, these nodes represent only words w_n without any additional information, and their labels thus only consist of the word itself (see Fig. 2). The structure of a DST is represented as follows: Given a tree t, $\mathsf{h}(t)$ is its root node and $\mathsf{s}(t)$ is the tree formed from t but considering only the syntactic structure (that is, only the s_n part of the labels), $c_i(n)$ denotes i-th child of a node n. As usual for constituency-based parse trees, pre-terminal nodes are nodes that have a single terminal node as child.

Finally, we use $\vec{w_n} \in \mathbb{R}^k$ to denote the *distributional* vector for word w_n, whereas $\mathbf{T}$ represents the matrix of a tree t encoding structure and distributional meaning.

3.2 The Method in a Glance

We describe here the approach in a few sentences. In line with tree kernels over structures (Collins and Duffy, 2002), we introduce the set $S(t)$ of the subtrees t_i of a given lexicalized tree t. A subtree t_i is in the set $S(t)$ if $\mathsf{s}(t_i)$ is a subtree of $\mathsf{s}(t)$ and, if n is a node in t_i, all the siblings of n in t are in t_i. For each node of t_i we only consider its syntactic label s_n, except for the head $\mathsf{h}(t_i)$ for which we also consider its semantic component w_n (see Fig. 1). The functions DSTs we define compute the following:

$$DST(t) = \mathbf{T} = \sum_{t_i \in S(t)} \mathbf{T}_i$$

where $\mathbf{T}_i$ is the matrix associated to each subtree t_i. The similarity between two text fragments a and b represented as lexicalized trees t^a and t^b can be computed using the Frobenius product between the two matrices $\mathbf{T}^a$ and $\mathbf{T}^b$, that is:

$$\langle \mathbf{T}^a, \mathbf{T}^b \rangle_F = \sum_{\substack{t_i^a \in S(t^a) \\ t_j^b \in S(t^b)}} \langle \mathbf{T}_i^a, \mathbf{T}_j^b \rangle_F \qquad (1)$$

We want to obtain that the product $\langle \mathbf{T}_i^a, \mathbf{T}_j^b \rangle_F$ approximates the dot product between the distributional vectors of the head words ($\langle \mathbf{T}_i^a, \mathbf{T}_j^b \rangle_F \approx \langle \overrightarrow{\mathsf{h}(t_i^a)}, \overrightarrow{\mathsf{h}(t_j^b)} \rangle$) whenever the syntactic structure of the subtrees is the same (that is $\mathsf{s}(t_i^a) = \mathsf{s}(t_j^b)$), and $\langle \mathbf{T}_i^a, \mathbf{T}_j^b \rangle_F \approx 0$ otherwise. This property is expressed as:

$$\langle \mathbf{T}_i^a, \mathbf{T}_j^b \rangle_F \approx \delta(\mathsf{s}(t_i^a), \mathsf{s}(t_j^b)) \cdot \langle \overrightarrow{\mathsf{h}(t_i^a)}, \overrightarrow{\mathsf{h}(t_j^b)} \rangle \quad (2)$$

To obtain the above property, we define

$$\mathbf{T}_i = \overrightarrow{\mathsf{s}(t_i)} \overrightarrow{w_{\mathsf{h}(t_i)}}^\top$$

where $\overrightarrow{\mathsf{s}(t_i)}$ are distributed tree fragment (Zanzotto and Dell'Arciprete, 2012) for the subtree t and $\overrightarrow{w_{\mathsf{h}(t_i)}}$ is the distributional vector of the head of the subtree t. Distributed tree fragments have the property that $\overrightarrow{\mathsf{s}(t_i)}\overrightarrow{\mathsf{s}(t_j)} \approx \delta(t_i, t_j)$. Thus, given the important property of the outer product that applies in the Frobenius product: $\langle \vec{a}\vec{w}^\top, \vec{b}\vec{v}^\top \rangle_F = \langle \vec{a}, \vec{b} \rangle \cdot \langle \vec{w}, \vec{v} \rangle$. we have that Equation 2 is satisfied as:

$$\begin{aligned} \langle \mathbf{T}_i, \mathbf{T}_j \rangle_F &= \langle \overrightarrow{\mathsf{s}(t_i)}, \overrightarrow{\mathsf{s}(t_j)} \rangle \cdot \langle \overrightarrow{w_{\mathsf{h}(t_i)}}, \overrightarrow{w_{\mathsf{h}(t_j)}} \rangle \\ &\approx \delta(\mathsf{s}(t_i), \mathsf{s}(t_j)) \cdot \langle \overrightarrow{w_{\mathsf{h}(t_i)}}, \overrightarrow{w_{\mathsf{h}(t_j)}} \rangle \end{aligned}$$

It is possible to show that the overall compositional distributional model $DST(t)$ can be obtained with a recursive algorithm that exploit vectors of the nodes of the tree.

The compositional distributional model is then used in the same learning machine used for the traditional RTE system with the following kernel function:

$$\begin{aligned} &K(p_1, p_2) = \\ &\langle DST(a_1), DST(a_2) \rangle + \langle DST(b_1), DST(b_2) \rangle + \\ &+(WTS(a_1, b_1) \cdot WTS(a_2, b_2) + 1)^2 \end{aligned}$$

4 Results and Conclusions

For the submission we used the java version of LIBSVM (Chang and Lin, 2011). Distributional vectors are derived with DISSECT (Dinu et al., 2013) from a corpus obtained by the concatenation of ukWaC (wacky.sslmit.unibo.it), a mid-2009 dump of the English Wikipedia (en.wikipedia.org) and the British National Corpus (www.natcorp.ox.ac.uk), for a total of about 2.8 billion words. The raw co-occurrences count vectors were transformed into positive Pointwise Mutual Information scores and reduced to 300 dimensions by Singular Value Decomposition. This setup was picked without tuning, as we found it effective in previous, unrelated experiments.

Model	Accuracy (3-ways)
DST	69.42
full-fledged RTE System	75.66
Max	84.57
Min	48.73
Average	75.35

Table 1: Accuracies of the two systems on the test set, together with the maximum, minimum and average score for the challenge.

We parsed the sentence with the Stanford Parser (Klein and Manning, 2003) and extracted the heads for use in the lexicalized trees with Collins' rules (Collins, 2003).

Table 1 reports our results on the textual entailment classification task, together with the maximum, minimum and average score for the challenge. The first observation is that the full-fledged RTE system is still definitely better than our CDSM system. We believe that the main reason is that the DST cannot encode variables which is an important aspect to capture when dealing with textual entailment recognition. This is particularly true for this dataset as it focuses on word ordering and on specific and recurrent entailment rules. Our full-fledged system scored among the first 10 systems, slightly above the overall average score, but our pure CDSM system is instead ranked within the last 3. We think that a more in-depth comparison with other fully CDSM systems will give us a better insight on our model and will also assess more realistically the quality of our system.

References

Roy Bar-Haim, Ido Dagan, Bill Dolan, Lisa Ferro, Danilo Giampiccolo, Bernardo Magnini, and Idan Szpektor. 2006. The second pascal recognising textual entailment challenge. In *Proceedings of the Second PASCAL Challenges Work-*

shop on Recognising Textual Entailment. Venice, Italy.

Chih-Chung Chang and Chih-Jen Lin. 2011. LIBSVM: A library for support vector machines. *ACM Transactions on Intelligent Systems and Technology*, 2:27:1–27:27. Software available at `http://www.csie.ntu.edu.tw/~cjlin/libsvm`.

Michael Collins and Nigel Duffy. 2002. New ranking algorithms for parsing and tagging: Kernels over discrete structures, and the voted perceptron. In *Proceedings of ACL02*.

Michael Collins. 2003. Head-driven statistical models for natural language parsing. *Comput. Linguist.*, 29(4):589–637.

Courtney Corley and Rada Mihalcea. 2005. Measuring the semantic similarity of texts. In *Proc. of the ACL Workshop on Empirical Modeling of Semantic Equivalence and Entailment*, pages 13–18. Association for Computational Linguistics, Ann Arbor, Michigan, June.

Ido Dagan, Oren Glickman, and Bernardo Magnini. 2006. The pascal recognising textual entailment challenge. In Quionero-Candela et al., editor, *LNAI 3944: MLCW 2005*, pages 177–190. Springer-Verlag, Milan, Italy.

Ido Dagan, Dan Roth, Mark Sammons, and Fabio Massimo Zanzotto. 2013. *Recognizing Textual Entailment: Models and Applications.* Synthesis Lectures on Human Language Technologies. Morgan & Claypool Publishers.

Georgiana Dinu, Nghia The Pham, and Marco Baroni. 2013. DISSECT: DIStributional SEmantics Composition Toolkit. In *Proceedings of ACL (System Demonstrations)*, pages 31–36, Sofia, Bulgaria.

Lorenzo Ferrone and Fabio Massimo Zanzotto. 2014. Towards syntax-aware compositional distributional semantic models. In *Proceedings of Coling 2014*. COLING, Dublin, Ireland, Aug 23–Aug 29.

Danilo Giampiccolo, Bernardo Magnini, Ido Dagan, and Bill Dolan. 2007. The third pascal recognizing textual entailment challenge. In *Proceedings of the ACL-PASCAL Workshop on Textual Entailment and Paraphrasing*, pages 1–9. Association for Computational Linguistics, Prague, June.

Jay J. Jiang and David W. Conrath. 1997. Semantic similarity based on corpus statistics and lexical taxonomy. In *Proc. of the 10th ROCLING*, pages 132–139. Tapei, Taiwan.

Dan Klein and Christopher D. Manning. 2003. Accurate unlexicalized parsing. In *Proceedings of the 41st Annual Meeting on Association for Computational Linguistics - Volume 1*, ACL '03, pages 423–430, Stroudsburg, PA, USA. Association for Computational Linguistics.

George A. Miller. 1995. WordNet: A lexical database for English. *Communications of the ACM*, 38(11):39–41, November.

Alessandro Moschitti and Fabio Massimo Zanzotto. 2007. Fast and effective kernels for relational learning from texts. In *Proceedings of the International Conference of Machine Learning (ICML)*. Corvallis, Oregon.

Fabio Massimo Zanzotto and Lorenzo Dell'Arciprete. 2009. Efficient kernels for sentence pair classification. In *Conference on Empirical Methods on Natural Language Processing*, pages 91–100, 6-7 August.

F.M. Zanzotto and L. Dell'Arciprete. 2012. Distributed tree kernels. In *Proceedings of International Conference on Machine Learning*, pages 193–200.

Fabio Massimo Zanzotto and Alessandro Moschitti. 2006. Automatic learning of textual entailments with cross-pair similarities. In *Proceedings of the 21st Coling and 44th ACL*, pages 401–408. Sydney, Australia, July.

Fabio Massimo Zanzotto, Marco Pennacchiotti, and Alessandro Moschitti. 2009. A machine learning approach to textual entailment recognition. *NATURAL LANGUAGE ENGINEERING*, 15-04:551–582.

Fabio Massimo Zanzotto, Lorenzo Dell'Arciprete, and Alessandro Moschitti. 2011. Efficient graph kernels for textual entailment recognition. *Fundamenta Informaticae*, 107(2-3):199 – 222.

HulTech: A General Purpose System for Cross-Level Semantic Similarity based on Anchor Web Counts

Jose G. Moreno **Rumen Moraliyski** **Asma Berrezoug** **Gaël Dias**
Normandie University
UNICAEN, GREYC CNRS
F-14032 Caen, France
firstname.lastname@unicaen.fr

Abstract

This paper describes the HULTECH team participation in Task 3 of SemEval-2014. Four different subtasks are provided to the participants, who are asked to determine the semantic similarity of cross-level test pairs: paragraph-to-sentence, sentence-to-phrase, phrase-to-word and word-to-sense. Our system adopts a unified strategy (general purpose system) to calculate similarity across all subtasks based on word Web frequencies. For that purpose, we define ClueWeb InfoSimba, a cross-level similarity corpus-based metric. Results show that our strategy overcomes the proposed baselines and achieves adequate to moderate results when compared to other systems.

1 Introduction

Similarity between text documents is considered a challenging task. Recently, many works concentrate on the study of semantic similarity for multi-level text documents (Pilehvar et al., 2013), but skipping the cross-level similarity task. In the later, the underlying idea is that text similarity can be considered between pairs of text documents at different granularities levels: paragraph, sentence, phrase or word. One obvious particularity of this task is that text pairs may not share the same characteristics of size, context or structure, i.e., the granularity level.

In task 3 of SemEval-2014, two different strategies have been proposed to solve this issue. On the one hand, participants may propose a combination of individual systems, each one solving a particular subtask. On the other hand, a general purpose system may be proposed, which deals with all the subtasks following the exact same strategy.

In this paper, we describe a language-independent corpus-based general purpose system, which relies on a huge freely available Web collection called Anchor-ClueWeb12 (Hiemstra and Hauff, 2010). In particular, we calculate ClueWeb InfoSimba[1] a cross-level semantic similarity based on word-word frequencies. Indeed, these frequencies are captured by the use of a collocation metric called SCP[2] (Silva et al., 1999), which has similar properties as the well studied PMI-IR (Turney, 2001) but does not over-evaluate rare events.

Our system outputs a normalized (between 0 and 1) similarity value between two pieces of texts. However, the subtasks proposed in task 3 of SemEval-2014 include a different scoring scale between 0 and 4. To solve this issue, we applied linear, polynomial and exponential regressions as three different runs. Results show that our strategy overcomes the proposed baselines and achieves adequate to moderate results when compared to other systems.

2 System Description

Our system is based on a reduced version of the ClueWeb12 dataset called Anchor ClueWeb12 and an informative attributional similarity measure called InfoSimba (Dias et al., 2007) adapted to this dataset.

2.1 Anchor ClueWeb12 Dataset

The Anchor ClueWeb12 dataset contains 0.5 billion Web pages, which cover about 64% of the total number of Web pages in ClueWeb12. The particularity of Anchor ClueWeb12 is that each Web page is represented by the anchor texts of the links pointing to it in ClueWeb12. Web pages are indexed not on their content but on their references. As such, the size of the index is drastically reduced and the overall results are consistent with full text indexing as discussed in (Hiemstra and Hauff, 2010).

For development purposes, this dataset was indexed in Solr 4.4 on a desktop computer using a batch indexing script. Particularly, each compressed part file of the Anchor ClueWeb12 was uncompressed, preprocessed and indexed in a sequential way using the features of incremental indexing offered by Solr (Smiley and Pugh, 2009).

2.2 InfoSimba

In (Dias et al., 2007), the authors proposed the hypothesis that two texts are similar if they share related (eventually different) constituents. So, their concept of simi-

[1] It is a Web version of InfoSimba (Dias et al., 2007).

[2] Symmetric Conditional Probability.

Proceedings of the 8th International Workshop on Semantic Evaluation (SemEval 2014), pages 305–308,
Dublin, Ireland, August 23-24, 2014.

larity is not any more based on the exact match of constituents but relies on related constituents (e.g. words). For example, it is clear that the following text pieces extracted from the sentence-to-phrase subtask are related[3] although they do not share any word.

1. *he is a nose-picker*

2. *an uncouth young man*

The InfoSimba similarity measure models this phenomenon evaluating individual similarities between all possible words pairs. Indeed, each piece of text is represented by the vector of its words. So, given two pieces of texts X_i and X_j, their similarity is defined in Equation 1 where $SCP(.,.)$ is the Symmetric Conditional Probability association measure proposed in (Silva et al., 1999) and defined in Equation 2.

$$IS(X_i, X_j) = \frac{1}{pq}\sum_{k=1}^{p}\sum_{l=1}^{q} SCP(w_{ik}, w_{jl}). \quad (1)$$

$$SCP(w_{ik}, w_{jl}) = \frac{P(w_{ik}, w_{jl})^2}{P(w_{ik}) \times P(w_{jl})}. \quad (2)$$

Following the previous example, the InfoSimba value between the two vectors $X_1 = \{\text{"}he\text{"}, \text{"}is\text{"}, \text{"}a\text{"}, \text{"}nose\text{-}picker\text{"}\}$ and $X_2 = \{\text{"}an\text{"}, \text{"}uncouth\text{"}, \text{"}young\text{"}, \text{"}man\text{"}\}$ is an average weight formed by all possible words pairs associations as illustrated in Figure 1. Note that each vertex is a word of a X_l vector and each edge is weighted by the $SCP(.,.)$ value of the connected words. In particular, each w_{ij} corresponds to the word at the jth position in vector X_i, $P(.,.)$ is the joint probability of two words appearing in the same document, $P(.)$ is the marginal probability of any word appearing in a document and p (resp. q) is the size of the vector X_i (resp. X_j).

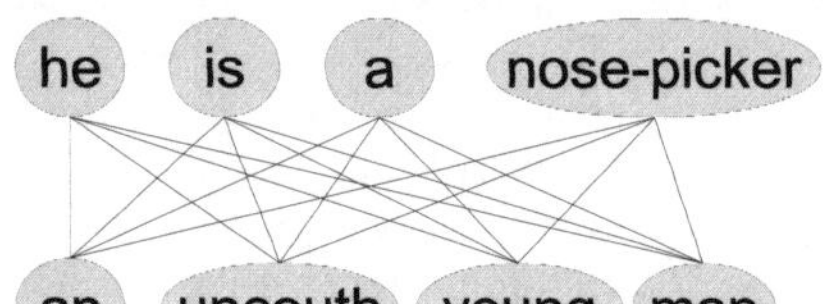

Figure 1: Pairs of words evaluated when InfoSimba is calculated.

In the case of task 3 of SemEval-2014, each text pair is represented by two word vectors for which a modified version of InfoSimba, ClueWeb InfoSimba, is computed.

[3]The score of this pair (#85) in the training set is the maximum value 4.

2.3 ClueWeb InfoSimba

The final similarity metric, called ClueWeb InfoSimba ($CWIS$), between two pieces of texts is defined in Equation 3, where $hits(w)$ returns the number of documents retrieved by Solr over Anchor ClueWeb12 for the query w and $hits(w_a \wedge w_b)$ is the number of documents retrieved when both words are present simultaneously. In this case, SCP is modified into SCP-IR similarly as PMI is to PMI-IR, i.e., using hits counts instead of probability values (see Equation 4).

$$CWIS(X_i, X_j) = \frac{1}{pq}\sum_{k=1}^{p}\sum_{l=1}^{q} SCP-IR(w_{ik}, w_{jl}). \quad (3)$$

$$SCP-IR(w_{ik}, w_{jl}) = \frac{hits(w_{ik} \wedge w_{jl})^2}{hits(w_{ik}).hits(w_{jl})}. \quad (4)$$

2.4 System Input

The task 3 of SemEval-2014 consists of (1) paragraph-to-sentence, (2) sentence-to-phrase, (3) phrase-to-word and (4) word-to-sense subtasks. Before submitting the pieces of texts to our system, we first performed simple stop-words removal with the NLTK toolkit (Bird et al., 2009). Note that in the case of the word-to-sense subtask, the similarity is performed over the word itself and the gloss of the corresponding sense[4].

2.5 Output Values Transformations

The $CWIS(.,.)$ similarity metric returns a value between 0 and 1. However, the subtasks suppose that each pair must be attributed a score between 0 and 4. As such, an adequate scale transformation must be performed. For that purpose, we proposed linear, polynomial and exponential regressions and submitted three different runs, one for each regression[5]. Note that the regressions have been tuned on the training dataset using the respective R regression functions with default parameters:

- $lm(y \sim x)$,
- $lm(y \sim x + I(x^2) + I(x^3))$,
- $lm(log(y + \epsilon) \sim x)$,

where ϵ[6] is a small value included to avoid undefined log values. The regression results on the test datasets are presented in Figure 2.

[4]Glosses are obtained from WordNet using the sense id provided for the task by the organizers.

[5]In the case of linear and exponential, these are monothetic functions therefore ranking-based evaluation metrics give the same score before and after this step.

[6]In our experiments, this value was set to 0.001.

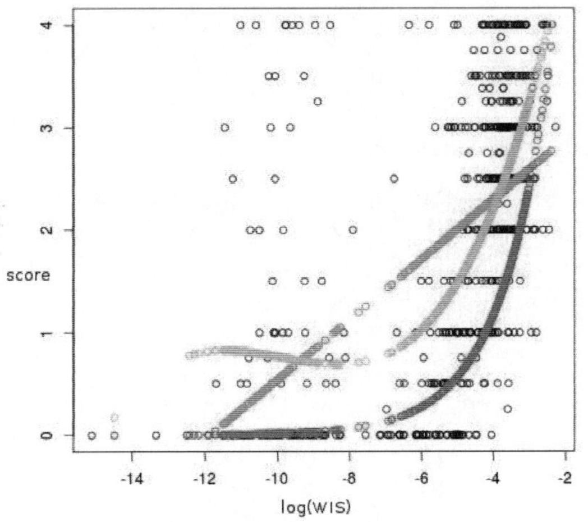

Figure 2: Linear, polynomial and exponential predictions for the test dataset of the paragraph-to-sentence subtask (colored dots). Black dots correspond to the obtained ClueWeb InfoSimba value versus the manually assigned score in the training dataset.

3 Evaluation and Results

For evaluation purposes, two metrics have been selected by the organizers: Pearson correlation (Pearson, 1895) and Spearman's rank correlation (Hollander and Wolfe, 1973). Detailed information about the evaluation setup can be found in the task discussion paper (Jurgens et al., 2014).

All results are given in Tables 1 and 2 for each run. Note that the baseline metric is calculated for the longest common string (LCS) and that each regression has been tuned on the training dataset for each one of the four tasks.

First, in almost all cases, the results outperform the baseline. Second, performances show that with a certain amount of information (longer pieces of texts), interesting results can be obtained. However, when the size decreases, the performance diminishes and extra information is certainly needed to better capture the semantics between two pieces of text. Third, the polynomial regression provides better results for the Pearson correlation evaluation, while for the Rho test, linear and polynomial regressions get the lead. Note that this situation depends on the data distribution and cannot be seen as a conclusive remark. However, it is certainly an important subject of study for our unsupervised methodology.

Another key point is that training examples were used only for evaluation purposes[7]. In the case of Spearman's rank correlation, the linear and exponential transformations obviously show exact same values (See Table 2).

[7] For Pearson correlation, valid interval was fixed to [0,4].

4 Conclusions

In this paper, we proposed a general purpose system to deal with cross-level text similarity. The aim of our research was to push as far as possible the limits of language-independent corpus-based solutions in a general context of text similarity. We were also concerned with reproducibility and as such we exclusively used publicly available datasets and tools[8]. The results clearly show the limits of a simple solution based on word statistics. Nevertheless, the framework can easily be empowered with the straightforward introduction of more competitive resources.

Acknowledgement

The authors would like to thank the University of Mostaganem (Algeria) for providing an internship to Asma Berrezoug at the Normandie University.

References

Steven Bird, Ewan Klein, and Edward Loper. 2009. *Natural Language Processing with Python*. O'Reilly Media, Inc., 1st edition.

Gaël Dias, Elsa Alves, and José Gabriel Pereira Lopes. 2007. Topic segmentation algorithms for text summarization and passage retrieval: An exhaustive evaluation. In *Proceedings of AAAI*, pages 1334–1339.

Djoerd Hiemstra and Claudia Hauff. 2010. Mirex: Mapreduce information retrieval experiments. In *CTIT Technical Report TR-CTIT-10-15, Centre for Telematics and Information Technology, University of Twente*, pages 1–8.

Myles Hollander and Douglas A. Wolfe. 1973. *Nonparametric Statistical Methods*. John Wiley and Sons, New York.

David Jurgens, Mohammad Taher Pilehvar, and Roberto Navigli. 2014. Task 3: Cross-level semantic similarity. In *Proceedings of SemEval-2014*.

Karl Pearson. 1895. Note on regression and inheritance in the case of two parents. *Proceedings of the Royal Society of London*, 58(347-352):240–242.

Mohammad Taher Pilehvar, David Jurgens, and Roberto Navigli. 2013. Align, disambiguate and walk: A unified approach for measuring semantic similarity. In *Proceedings of ACL*, pages 1341–1351.

Joaquim Ferreira da Silva, Gaël Dias, Sylvie Guilloré, and José Gabriel Pereira Lopes. 1999. Using localmaxs algorithm for the extraction of contiguous and

[8] Scripts to Index the Anchor ClueWeb12 Dataset are available under request.

Method	Paragraph2Sentence	Sentence2Phrase	Phrase2Word	Word2Sense
Linear (run 3)	0.669	0.671	0.232	0.137
Polynomial (run 1)	0.693	0.665	0.254	0.150
Exponential (run 2)	0.667	0.633	0.180	0.169
Baseline (LCS)	0.527	0.562	0.165	0.109

Table 1: Overall results for the Pearson correlation.

Method	Paragraph2Sentence	Sentence2Phrase	Phrase2Word	Word2Sense
Linear (run 3)	0.688	0.633	0.260	0.124
Polynomial (run 1)	0.666	0.633	0.260	0.126
Exponential (run 2)	0.688	0.633	0.260	0.124
Baseline (LCS)	0.613	0.626	0.162	0.130

Table 2: Overall results for the Spearman's rank correlation.

non-contiguous multiword lexical units. In *Proceedings of EPIA*, pages 113–132.

David Smiley and Eric Pugh. 2009. *Solr 1.4 Enterprise Search Server.* Packt Publishing.

Peter Turney. 2001. Mining the web for synonyms: Pmi-ir versus lsa on toefl. In *Proceedings of ECML*, pages 491–502.

IHS R&D Belarus: Cross-domain Extraction of Product Features using Conditional Random Fields

Maryna Chernyshevich
IHS Inc. / IHS Global Belarus
131 Starovilenskaya St.
220123, Minsk, Belarus
Marina.Chernyshevich@ihs.com

Abstract

This paper describes the aspect extraction system submitted by IHS R&D Belarus team at the SemEval-2014 shared task related to Aspect-Based Sentiment Analysis. Our system is based on IHS Goldfire linguistic processor and uses a rich set of lexical, syntactic and statistical features in CRF model. We participated in two domain-specific tasks – restaurants and laptops – with the same system trained on a mixed corpus of reviews. Among submissions of constrained systems from 28 teams, our submission was ranked first in laptop domain and fourth in restaurant domain for the subtask A devoted to aspect extraction.

1 Introduction

With a rapid growth of the blogs, forums, review sites and social networks, more and more people express their personal views about products on the Internet in form of reviews, ratings, or recommendations. This is a great source of data used by many researchers and commercial applications that are focused on the sentiment analysis to determine customer opinions.

Sentiment analysis can be done on document, sentence, and phrase level (Jagtap, V. S., Karishma Pawar, 2013). Earlier works were focused mainly on the document (Turney, 2002; Pang, Lee and Vaithyanathan, 2002) and the sentence level (Kim and Hovy, 2004). However, this information can be insufficient for customers who are seeking opinions on specific product features (aspects) such as design, battery life, or screen. This fine-grained classification is a topic of aspect-based sentiment analysis (Moghaddam and Ester, 2012).

Traditional approaches to aspect extraction are based on frequently used nouns and noun phrases (Popescu and Etzioni, 2005; Blair-Goldensohn et al., 2008), exploiting opinions (Zhuang et al., 2006; Kobayashi, 2006), and supervised learning (Mukherjee and Liu, 2012).

In this paper, we describe a system (IHS_RD_Belarus in official results) developed to participate in the international shared task organized by the Conference on Semantic Evaluation Exercises (SemEval-2014) and focused on the phrase-level sentiment classification, namely aspect extraction (Pontiki et al., 2014). An *aspect term* means particular feature of a product or service used in opinion-bearing sentences (`My phone has amazing screen`), as well as in neutral sentences (`The screen brightness automatically adjusts`).

The organizers of SemEval-2014 task have provided a dataset of customer reviews with annotated aspects of the target entities from two domains: restaurants (3041 sentences) and laptops (3045 sentences). The results were evaluated separately in each domain. Table 1 shows the distribution of the provided data for each domain dataset, training and testing set, with number of sentences and aspects.

	Laptops	Restaurants
Training		
Sentences	3045	3041
Aspects	2358	3693
Testing		
Sentences	800	800
Aspects	654	1134

Table 1. Distribution of the provided data.

Many studies showed that sentiment analysis is very sensitive to the source domain (training corpus domain) and performs poorly on data from other domain (Jakob and Gurevych, 2010). This restriction limits the applicability of in-

Proceedings of the 8th International Workshop on Semantic Evaluation (SemEval 2014), pages 309–313,
Dublin, Ireland, August 23-24, 2014.

domain models to a wide domain diversity of reviews. One of the common approaches to develop a cross-domain system is training on a mixture of labeled data from different domains (Aue and Gamon, 2005). Cross-domain approach has the advantage of better portability, but it suffers from lower accuracy compared to in-domain aspect extraction. Our cross-domain system is trained on mixed training data, and the same model was used unchanged for classification of both domain-specific test datasets.

2 System Description

Aspect extraction may be considered as a sequence labeling task because the product aspects occur at a sequence in a sentence (Liu, 2014). One of the state-of-the-art methods used for sequence labeling is Conditional Random Fields (CRF) (Lafferty, 2001). This method takes as an input a sequence of tokens, calculates the probabilities of the various possible labelings and chooses the one with the maximum probability.

We decided to deviate from Inside-Outside-Begin (IOB) scheme used by Jakob and Gurevych (Jakob and Gurevych, 2010) and Li (Li et al., 2010) and introduced the following labels: **FA** for the attribute word preceding head word of a noun group; **FH** for the head word of a noun group; **FPA** for attribute word after head word of a noun group (`Microsoft Office 2003`), and **O** for other non-aspect tokens. The following is an example of our suggested tagging: `I`/**O** `want`/**O** `to`/**O** `unplug`/**O** `the`/**O** *`external`*/**FA** *`keyboard`*/**FH**.

Our experiments showed that the words used in aspect terms are easier to recognize when they are always tagged with the same tags. For example, let's consider the tagging of the word "camera" in the following cases: "camera" and "compact camera". We propose the **FH** tag for both examples, while the IOB scheme assumes the **FB** tag for the first example and the **FI** tag for the second.

2.1 Pre-processing

To facilitate feature generation for supervised CRF learning, sentences were pre-processed with IHS Goldfire linguistic processor that performs the following operations: slang and misspelling correction (*"excelent"* → *"excellent"*, *"amazin"* → *"amazing"*, *"wouldnt"* → *"wouldn't"*), part-of-speech tagging, parsing, noun phrase extraction, semantic role labeling within expanded Subject-Action-Object (eSAO) relations (Todhunter et al., 2013), named entity recognition, labeling for predictive question-answering including rule-based sentiment analysis (Todhunter et al., 2014).

In addition, we designed some simple rules to detect entity boundaries that take precedence over CRF labeling. For example, in the sentence "`I run Final Cut Pro 7 and a few other applications`", our boundary detector recognizes "`Final Cut Pro 7`" as an entity represented by a single token (Tkachenko and Simanovsky, 2012).

2.2 Features

Below we will describe the features used in CRF model to represent the current token, two previous and two next tokens.

Word features:

- *Token feature* represents a base form of a token (word or entity) normalized by case folding. The vocabulary of terms is pretty compact within one domain, so this feature can have considerable impact on terms extraction performance.
- *Part of speech feature* represents the part-of-speech tag of the current token with slight generalization, for example, the NNS tag (plural noun) is mapped to NN (singular noun).
- *Named entity feature* labels named entities, e.g., people, organizations, locations, etc.
- *Semantic category* denotes the presence of the token in manually crafted domain-independent word-lists – sets of words having a common semantic meaning – such as parameter (characteristics of object, e.g., "durability"), process (e.g., "charging"), sentiment-bearing word (e.g., "problem"), person (e.g., "sister"), doer of an action (someone or something that performs an action, e.g., "organizer"), temporal word (date- or time-related words, e.g., "Monday"), nationality, word of reasoning (e.g., "decision", "reason"), etc.
- *Semantic orientation (SO) score of token* represents a low, mean or high SO score as separate feature values (the thresholds were determined experimentally). The SO of a word indicates the strength of its association with positive and negative reviews. We calculated SO of each word *w* using Pointwise Mutual Information (PMI) measures as

$$SO(w) = PMI(w, pr) - PMI(w, nr),$$

where PMI is the amount of information that we acquire about the presence of the word in positive *pr* or negative reviews *nr* (Turney, 2002). For the calculation of SO score, we used rated reviews from Epinions.com, Amazon.com and TripAdvisor.com. To make corpus more precise, we included only 5-star reviews in our positive corpus, and 1-star reviews in our negative corpus.

- *Frequency of token occurrence* is represented by five values ranging from very frequent to very rare words with an experimentally determined threshold. The frequency was obtained by dividing the number of reviews containing the token by the total number of reviews. The reason of using this as a feature is that people usually comment on the same product aspects and the vocabulary that they use usually converges (Liu, 2012).
- *Opinion target feature* is a binary feature that indicates whether a token is a part of an item which opinions are expressed on and comes from the rule-based sentiment analysis integrated in the predictive question-answering component of the IHS Goldfire linguistic processor. Opinion target can be a product feature as well as a product itself.

Noun phrase features:

- *Role of a token in a noun phrase*: head word or attribute word.
- *Noun phrase introduction feature* marks all tokens of noun phrase beginning with possessive pronoun, demonstrative pronoun, definite or indefinite article.
- *Number of attributes* with SO score higher than the experimentally chosen threshold. This feature labels all words in a noun group. Our research showed that people often use sentiment-bearing adjectives to describe an aspect, e.g., "`My phone has a great camera`".
- *List feature* was added to designate the availability of list indicators ("and" or comma) in the noun group, e.g., "`The leather carrying case, keyboard and mouse arrived in two days`".
- *Leaves-up feature* denotes the number of of-phrases in a noun phrase before the token under consideration. For example, the token "battery" has one preceding of-phrase in the phrase "durability of battery".
- *Leaves-down feature* denotes the number of of-phrases in a noun phrase after the token under consideration.

SAO features:

- *Semantic label feature* represents the role of the token in eSAO relation: subject, action, adjective, object, preposition, indirect object or adverb.
- *SAO feature* labels all words presented in an eSAO relation. We used a set of eSAO patterns to determine basic relations between words. To form a SAO pattern, each non-empty component of an eSAO relation was mapped to an abstract value, e.g., proper noun phrases to "PNP", common noun phrases to "CNP", predicates are left in their canonical form. For example, the sentence "`The restaurant Tal offers authentic chongqing hotpot.`" is represented by the SAO pattern "PNP offer CNP". All words from eSAO are marked with the same SAO feature.

2.3 Results and Experiments

Our CRF model was trained on the mixed set of 6086 sentences with annotated aspect terms (3045 from the laptop domain and 3041 from the restaurant domain). The same model was applied unchanged to the test dataset from laptop domain (800 sentences) and restaurant domain (800 sentences). We evaluated our system using 5-fold cross-validation: in each of the five iterations of the cross-validation, we used 80% of the provided training data for learning, and 20% for testing.

	laptops	restaurants
training set	0.707	0.7784
development set	0.7214	0.7865
test set	0.7455	0.7962
baseline	0.3564	0.4715

Table 2. Performance on different datasets (F_1-score).

The Table 2 shows the model performance (F_1-score) obtained on the training set (using 5-fold cross validation), on the development set (we used a part of the training set as development set), on the final test set and the baseline provided by the task organizers.

To evaluate the individual contribution of different feature sets, we performed ablation experiment, presented in Table 3. This test involves removing one of the following feature sets at a time: current token and its POS tag (TOK), combinations with two previous and two next tokens and their POS tags (CONT), named entity (NE), semantic category (SC), semantic orientation (SO), word frequency (WF), opinion target (OT), noun phrase related features (NP_F), and SAO pattern and semantic label (SAO_F). Some features complement each other, so that despite small individual contribution, a cumulative improvement is generally achieved by using them in a set.

	Dev set		Test set	
	lap	rest	lap	rest
overall	**0.7214**	**0.7865**	**0.7455**	**0.7962**
-TOK	0.6642 (-7.9%)	0.7244 (-7.9%)	0.692 (-7.2%)	0.7445 (-6.4%)
-CONT	0.7101 (-1.6%)	0.77 (-2.1%)	0.7323 (-1.8%)	0.7811 (-1.9%)
-SC	0.6982 (-3.3%)	0.7854 (-0.1%)	0.7048 (-5.8%)	0.7864 (-1.2%)
-SO	0.709 (-1.7%)	0.7815 (-0.6%)	0.7442 (-0.2%)	0.7937 (-0.3%)
-OT	0.7026 (-2.6%)	0.7812 (-0.7%)	0.7381 (-1%)	0.7973 (0.1%)
-NP_F	0.717 (-0.6%)	0.777 (-1.2%)	0.7303 (-2%)	0.7801 (-2%)
-WF	0.716 (-0.8%)	0.788 (0.2%)	0.7399 (-0.7%)	0.7937 (-0.3%)
-SAO_F	0.7198 (-0.2%)	0.7854 (-0.1%)	0.7297 (-2.1%)	0.7981 (0.2%)
-NE	0.7191 (-0.3%)	0.7836 (-0.4%)	0.7444 (-0.1%)	0.7961 (0)

Table 3. Ablation experiment (F_1-score).

The importance of a feature set is measured by F_1-score on development and testing datasets for both domains separately.

Feature sets are listed in descending order of their impact on overall performance. The analysis shows that the most important feature set is the combination of Token and POS features. Other features contribute to the performance to a smaller degree.

As can be seen, the relative influence of features on F_1-score is similar on test and development sets, showing that our model effectively overcomes the overfitting problem.

We conducted several experiments on the training data to prove the domain portability of our CRF model. The results are shown in Table 4. As can be seen, the training on single-domain data improves the performance of in-domain classification by about 2%, but lowers the performance of cross-domain classification by about 40%. The training on the mixed dataset demonstrates acceptable accuracy on both domain-specific test sets.

Training dataset	Results on laptops dataset	Results on restaurants dataset
laptops	0.7667	0.3778
restaurants	0.2961	0.8223
mixed	0.7455	0.7962

Table 4. Results of classification with different training datasets (F_1-score).

2.4 Error Analysis and Further Work

The error analysis showed three main error types: not recognized, excessively recognized and partially recognized aspect terms (head word is recognized correctly, e.g., "`separate RAM memory`" instead of "`RAM memory`"). While first types are recall and precision errors respectively, partial aspect extraction yields both recall and precision errors. A summary of the errors on test dataset is presented in Table 5.

	laptops	restaurants
not recognized	68%	58%
partially recognized	18%	30%
excessively recognized	14%	12%

Table 5. Error types distribution.

From Table 5, we can see that a major source of errors is related to not recognized aspect terms. In the future, we would like to experiment with additional techniques to overcome recall problem, e.g., using dictionaries or concept taxonomies and employ skip-chain CRF, proposed by Li et al. (2010). Further improvements can also be made by tuning parameters of CRF learning.

To verify the cross-domain portability of the system, we are going to test it on a third domain test dataset without including additional instances in the training corpus, as proposed by Aue and Gamon (2005).

3 Conclusion

In this paper, we have presented a CRF-based learning technique applied to the aspect extraction task. We implemented rich set of lexical, syntactic and statistical features and showed that our approach has good domain portability and performance ranked first out of 28 participating teams in the laptop domain and fourth in restaurant domain.

References

Anthony Aue and Michael Gamon. 2005. Customizing sentiment classifiers to new domains: a case study. In *Proceedings of Recent Advances in Natural Language Processing*, RANLP-2005.

Sasha Blair-Goldensohn, Kerry Hannan, Ryan McDonald, Tyler Neylon, George A. Reis, and Jeff Reynar. 2008. Building a sentiment summarizer for local service reviews. In *Proceedings of WWW-2008 workshop on NLP in the Information Explosion Era.*

V. S. Jagtap and Karishma Pawar. 2012. Analysis of different approaches to Sentence-Level Sentiment Classification. *International Journal of Scientific Engineering and Technology, Volume 2, Issue 3.*

Niklas Jakob and Iryna Gurevych. 2010. Extracting opinion targets in a single- and cross-domain setting with conditional random fields. In *Proceedings of the 2010 Conference on Empirical Methods in Natural Language Processing,* EMNLP'10.

Soo-Min Kim and Eduard Hovy. 2004. Determining the sentiment of opinions. In *Proceedings of Interntional Conference on Computational Linguistics*, COLING'04.

Nozomi Kobayashi, Ryu Iida, Kentaro Inui, and Yuji Matsumoto. 2006. Opinion mining on the Web by extracting subject-attribute-value relations. In *Proceedings of AAAI-CAAW '06.*

John Lafferty, Andrew McCallum, and Fernando Pereira. 2001. Conditional Random Fields: Probabilistic Models for Segmenting and Labeling Sequence Data. In *Proceedings of the Eighteenth International Conference on Machine Learning,* ICML'01.

Fangtao Li, Chao Han, Minlie Huang, Xiaoyan Zhu, Ying-Ju Xia, Shu Zhang, and Hao Yu. 2010. Structure-aware review mining and summarization. In *Proceedings of the 23rd International Conference on Computational Linguistics*, COLING'10.

Bing Liu. 2012. Sentiment Analysis and Opinion Mining.

Samaneh Moghaddam and Martin Ester. 2012. Aspect-based opinion mining from online reviews. Tutorial at SIGIR Conference.

Arjun Mukherjee and Bing Liu. 2012. Aspect Extraction through Semi-Supervised Modeling. In *Proceedings of 50th Anunal Meeting of Association for Computational Linguistics,* ACL'12.

Bo Pang, Lillian Lee, and Shivakumar Vaithyanathan. 2002. Thumbs up?: sentiment classification using machine learning techniques. In *Proceedings of Conference on Empirical Methods in Natural Language Processing,* EMNLP'02.

Ana-Maria Popescu and Oren Etzioni. 2005. Extracting product features and opinions from reviews. In *Proceedings of Conference on Empirical Methods in Natural Language Processing*, EMNLP'05.

Lawrence R. Rabiner. 1989. A tutorial on hidden Markov models and selected applications in speech recognition. In *Proceedings of the IEEE*, 77(2): p. 257-286.

Maksim Tkachenko and Andrey Simanovsky. 2012. Named Entity Recognition: Exploring Features. In *Proceedings of* KONVENS'12.

James Todhunter, Igor Sovpel and Dzianis Pastanohau. System and method for automatic semantic labeling of natural language texts. *U.S. Patent 8 583 422, November 12, 2013.*

James Todhunter, Igor Sovpel and Dzianis Pastanohau. Question-answering system and method based on semantic labeling of text documents and user questions. *U.S. Patent 8 666 730, September 16, 2014.*

Peter D. Turney. 2002. Thumbs up or thumbs down?: semantic orientation applied to unsupervised classification of reviews. In *Proceedings of Annual Meeting of the Association for Computational Linguistics,* ACL'02.

Theresa Wilson, Janyce Wiebe, and Paul Hoffmann. 2005. Recognizing contextual polarity in phrase-level sentiment analysis. In *Proceedings of the Human Language Technology Conference and the Conference on Empirical Methods in Natural Language Processing*, HLT/EMNLP'05.

Lei Zhang and Bing Liu. 2014. Aspect and Entity Extraction for Opinion Mining. Data Mining and Knowledge Discovery for Big Data.

Li Zhuang, Feng Jing, and Xiaoyan Zhu. 2006. Movie review mining and summarization. In *Proceedings of ACM International Conference on Information and Knowledge Management*, CIKM'06.

Maria Pontiki, Dimitrios Galanis, John Pavlopoulos, Haris Papageorgiou, Ion Androutsopoulos, and Suresh Manandhar. 2014. SemEval-2014 Task 4: Aspect Based Sentiment Analysis. In *Proceedings of the 8th International Workshop on Semantic Evaluation* (SemEval 2014), Dublin, Ireland.

IITP: A Supervised Approach for Disorder Mention Detection and Disambiguation

Utpal Kumar Sikdar, Asif Ekbal and Sriparna Saha
Department of Computer Science and Engineering
Indian Institute of Technology Patna, India
{utpal.sikdar,asif,sriparna}@iitp.ac.in

Abstract

In this paper we briefly describe our supervised machine learning approach for disorder mention detection system that we submitted as part of our participation in the SemEval-2014 Shared task. The main goal of this task is to build a system that automatically identifies mentions of clinical conditions from the clinical texts. The main challenge lies due in the fact that the same mention of concept may be represented in many surface forms. We develop the system based on the supervised machine learning algorithms, namely Conditional Random Field and Support Vector Machine. One appealing characteristics of our system is that most of the features for learning are extracted automatically from the given training or test datasets without using deep domain specific resources and/or tools. We submitted three runs, and best performing system is based on Conditional Random Field. For task A, it shows the precision, recall and F-measure values of 50.00%, 47.90% and 48.90%, respectively under the strict matching criterion. When the matching criterion is relaxed, it shows the precision, recall and F-measure of 81.50%, 79.70% and 80.60%, respectively. For task B, we obtain the accuracies of 33.30% and 69.60% for the relaxed and strict matches, respectively.

1 Introduction

The SemEval-2014 Shared Task 7 is concerned with the analysis of clinical texts, particularly for disorder mention detection and disambiguation. The purpose of this task is to enhance current research in Natural Language Processing (NLP) methods used in the clinical domain. The task is a continuation of the CLEF/eHealth ShARe 2013 Shared Task. In particular there were two specific tasks, *viz.* (i). **Task A:** To identify disorder mentions from biomedicine domain and (ii) **Task B:** To classify each mention with respect to the Unified Medical Language System (UMLS) Concept Unique Identifier (CUI). The task is challenging in the sense that the same mention of concept may be represented in many surface forms and mention may appear in the different parts of texts. Some systems (Cogley et al., 2013; Zuccon et al., 2013; Tang et al., 2013; Cogley et al., 2013) are available for disorder mention detection. Looking at the challenges and resources available at our hand we planned to adapt our existing system (Sikdar et al., 2013) for disorder mention detection. The original architecture was conceptualized as part of our participation in the BioCreative-IV Track-2 Shared Task on Chemical Compound and Drug Name Recognition. Although our submitted system for SemEval-14 shared task is in line with BioCreative-IV[1], it has many different features and characteristics.

We develop three systems (e.g. **Model-1**: sikdar.run-0, **Model-2**: sikdar.run-1 and **Model-3**: sikdar.run-2) based on the popular supervised machine learning algorithms, namely Conditional Random Field (CRF) (Lafferty et al., 2001) and Support Vector Machine (SVM) (Cortes and Vapnik, 1995; Joachims, 1999). The models were developed by varying the features and feature templates. A baseline model is constructed by using the UMLS MetaMap[2] tool. During testing we merge the development set with the training set. Evaluation results on test data with the benchmark set up show the F-measure values of

[1]www.biocreative.org/tasks/biocreative-iv/chemdner/
[2]http://mmtx.nlm.nih.gov/

Proceedings of the 8th International Workshop on Semantic Evaluation (SemEval 2014), pages 314–318,
Dublin, Ireland, August 23-24, 2014.

48.90%, 46.50% and 46.50%, respectively under the strict criterion. Under relaxed matching criterion the models show the F-measure values of 80.60%, 78.20% and 79.60%, respectively. Our submission for Task-B is simple in nature where we consider only those mentions that are also predicted in the baseline model, i.e. only the common CUIs are considered. It shows the accuracies of 33.30%, 31.90% and 33.20%, respectively under strict matching criterion; and 69.60%, 69.60% and 69.10%, respectively under the relaxed matching criterion.

2 Method

Our method for disorder mention detection from clinical text is based on the supervised machine learning algorithms, namely CRF and SVM. The key focus was to develop a system that could be easily adapted to other domains and applications. We submitted three runs defined as below:
Model-1:sikdar.run-0: This is based on CRF, and makes use of the features as mentioned below.
Model-2:sikdar.run-1: This model is built by training a SVM classifier with the same set of features as CRF.
Model-3:sikdar.run-2: This model is constructed by defining a heuristics that looks at the outputs of both the models. For given instance, if one of the models predicts it to belong to the category of candidate disorder mention then this is given more priority in assigning the class. We observed performance improvement on the development set with this heuristic.

We identify and implement different features, mostly without using any deep domain knowledge or domain-specific external resources and/or tools. The features that are used to train the classifiers are briefly described below:

- **Context words:** Surrounding words carry effective information to identify disorder mention. In our case we consider the previous three and next three words as the features.
- **MetaMap match:** MetaMap is a widely used tool that maps biomedical mention to the UMLS CUI[3]. In UMLS, there are 11 semantic types denoting disorders. These are *Congenital Abnormality*, *Acquired Abnormality*, *Injury or Poisoning*, *Pathologic Function*, *Disease or Syndrome*, *Mental or Behavioral Dysfunction*, *Cell or Molecular Dysfunction*, *Experimental Model of Disease*, *Anatomical Abnormality*, *Neoplastic Process* and *Signs and Symptoms*. The training set is passed through the MetaMap, and then we prepare a list of mentions that belong to the UMLS semantic types. A feature is thereafter defined that takes a value of 1 if the current token appears in the list; otherwise the value becomes 0.
- **Part-of-Speech (PoS) Information:** In this work, we use PoS information of the current token as the feature. PoS information was extracted from the GENIA tagger[4] V2.0.2, which is a freely available resource.
- **Root words:** Stems or root words, which are extracted form GENIA tagger V2.0.2, are used as the feature.
- **Chunk information:** We use GENIA tagger V2.0.2 to extract the chunk information. It helps to identify the boundaries of disorder mentions.
- **Initial capital:** The feature is set to true if the first character of the current token is a capital letter.
- **All capital:** The feature is set to true if all the letters of the current token are capitalized.
- **Stop words:** A feature is defined that is set to one if the current token appears in the list of stop words.
- **Word normalization:** Word shapes refer to the mapping of each word to their equivalence classes. Each capitalized character of the word is replaced by 'A', small characters are replaced by 'a' and digits are replaced by '0'.
- **Word suffix and prefix:** These features indicate the fixed-length character sequences (here 4) stripped either from the end (suffix) or beginning positions of words. This is useful in the sense that disorder mentions share some common sub-strings.

[3]http://www.nlm.nih.gov/research/umls/

[4]http://www-tsujii.is.s.u-tokyo.ac.jp/GENIA/tagger

- **Unknown word:** This feature is implemented depending upon whether the current token was found during training or not. For the training set this has been set randomly.

- **Word length:** If the length of a token is more than a predefined threshold (here 5) then it is most likely a disorder mention. This feature is defined with the observation that very short words are most probably not disorder mentions.

- **Alpha digit:** If the current token contains digit character(s), then the feature is set to true otherwise false.

- **Informative words**: This feature is developed from the training dataset. The words or the sequence of words that precede and follow the disorder mentions could be useful for mention detection. The most frequently occurring words that appear within the context of $w_{i-2}^{i+2} = w_{i-2} \ldots w_{i+2}$ of w_i are extracted from the training data. Two different lists are prepared, one for the informative words that precede the mentions and the other contains the informative words that follow the mentions. Thereafter we define two features that fire for the words of these lists.

- **Disorder mention prefix and suffix**: We extract most frequently occurring prefixes and suffixes of length 2 from the disorder mentions present in the training data. We prepare two lists containing the prefix and suffix sub-sequences (of length two) that appear at least 10 times in the training set. We define two features that go on/off depending upon whether the current word contains any subsequence present in the lists.

- **Dynamic information**: The feature is extracted from the output label(s) of the previous token(s). The feature value is determined at run time.

3 Experimental Results

3.1 Datasets

In SemEval-2014 Shared task 7, three types of data were provided- training, development and test. Training data contains four different types of notes- discharge, ecg, echo and radiology. Development data consists of notes of three different domains, *viz.* discharge, echo and radiology. But the test set contains only the discharge notes. For a given document, the start and end indices are mentioned for the disorder mentions. There are 199, 99 and 133 documents in the training, development and test set, respectively.

3.2 Results and Analysis

We use a regular expression based simple pattern (e.g. dot and space) matching techniques for the sentence splitting and tokenization. We use C^{++} based CRF^{++} package[5] for CRF experiments. We set the default values of the following parameters (a). the hyper-parameter of CRF. With larger value, CRF tends to overfit to the given training data; (b). parameter which sets the cut-off threshold for the features (default value is 1). CRF uses only those features, having more than the cut-off threshold in the given training data.

In case of SVM we used YamCha[6] toolkit along with TinySVM[7]. We use the polynomial kernel function of degree two. In order to denote the boundaries of a multi-word disorder mention properly we use the standard BIO encoding scheme, where B, I and O represent the beginning, intermediate and outside, respectively, for a multi-word token. Please note that the mentions are not continuous, i.e. they could appear at the various positions of the text. For example, in the sentence *The left atrium is moderately dilated*, there is a single mention *left atrium dilated.* Its BIO format is represented in Table 1.

Token	Tag
The	O
left	B-Men
atrium	I-Men
is	O
moderately	O
dilated	I-Men
.	O

Table 1: An example of BIO representation.

Experiments are conducted on the benchmark setup as provided by the competition organizer. At first we train our system using the training set and evaluate using the development set in order to de-

[5]http://crfpp.sourceforge.net

[6]http://chasen-org/ taku/software/yamcha/

[7]http://chasen.org/ taku/software/TinySVM/

System	Strict			Relaxed		
	P	R	F	P	R	F
Baseline	19.9	29.0	23.6	44.9	63.0	52.4
Model-1	52.5	43.0	47.3	86.2	72.6	78.8
Model-2	49.3	41.0	44.8	82.8	70.6	76.2
Model-3	46.7	44.0	45.3	81.2	77.5	79.3

Table 2: Results on development set for Task A.

System	Strict	Relaxed
	Accuracy	Accuracy
Baseline	24.6	85.1
Model-1	31.2	72.5
Model-2	29.9	73.0
Model-3	31.8	72.4

Table 3: Results on development set for Task B.

termine the best configuration. We define a baseline model by passing the development set to the UMLS MetaMap tool. Its results along with the baseline model are reported in Table 2 for Task A. Evaluation shows that our proposed system performs reasonably better compared to the baseline model. It is also to be noted that Model-1 performs better compared to the other two submitted models for the strict matching, but for relaxed evaluation, Model-3 performs better than Model-1 and Model-2. Under strict matching criterion, Model-1 achieves 2.7% and 5.0% increments in precision over the second and third models, respectively. For relaxed matching, Model-3 achieves 4.9% and 6.9% increments in recall over the first and second models, respectively. Results on the development set for Task-B are reported in Table 3. Please note that although our system performs better than the baseline in terms of strict matching, it does not show better accuracy under relaxed matching criterion. This is because our system for Task-B is developed by considering only those mentions that lie in the intersection of baseline and CRF models. As a result many mentions are missed. During final submissions we merged development sets with the respective training sets, and perform evaluation on the test sets. We report our results on the test sets in Table 4 and Table 5 for Task-A and Task-B, respectively.

We carefully analyze the results and find that most of the errors encountered because of the discontiguous mentions. Different components of a mention may be mapped to the different concepts. In our system we treat two mentions as a single unit if they have some shared tokens. For example, the sentence "She also notes new sharp pain in left shoulder blade/back area" contains two different mentions, *viz.*"pain shoulder blade" and "pain back". Here shared word of these two mentions is "pain", but we consider these two mentions as a single unit such as "pain shoulder blade back". This contributes largely to the errors that our system faces for the first task. For the second task, we miss a number of mentions, and this can be captured if we directly match the system identified mentions to the entire UMLS database.

System	Strict			Relaxed		
	P	R	F	P	R	F
Model-1	50.0	47.9	48.9	81.5	79.7	80.6
Model-2	47.3	45.8	46.5	78.9	77.6	78.2
Model-3	45.0	48.1	46.5	76.9	82.6	79.6

Table 4: Evaluation results on test set for Task A.

System	Strict	Relaxed
	Accuracy	Accuracy
Model-1	33.3	69.6
Model-2	31.9	69.6
Model-3	33.2	69.1

Table 5: Results of Task B for the test set.

4 Conclusion

In this paper we report on our works as part of our participation in the SemEval-2014 shared task related to clinical text mining. We submitted three runs for both the tasks, *viz.* disorder mention detection and disambiguation. Our submitted runs for the first task are based on CRF and SVM. We make use of a set of features that are not very domain-specific. The system developed for the second task is very simple and is based on UMLS Meta Map tool.

There are many avenues for future research: identification of more features for the first task; use of some domain-specific resources and/or tools for the first task; use of entire UMLS thesaurus for mapping the disorder mentions; use of some machine learning techniques for disambiguation. We also plan to investigate how systematic feature selection, ensemble learning and machine learning optimization have impact on disorder mention detection and disambiguation.

References

James Cogley, Nicola Stokes, and Joe Carthy. 2013. Medical Disorder Recognition with Structural Support Vector Machines. *In Proceedings of CLEF*.

Corinna Cortes and Vladimir Vapnik. 1995. Support Vector Networks. *Machine Learning*, 20:273–297.

Thorsten Joachims, 1999. *Making Large Scale SVM Learning Practical*, pages 169–184. MIT Press, Cambridge, MA, USA.

John Lafferty, Andrew McCallum, and Fernando C. N. Pereira. 2001. Conditional Random Fields: Probabilistic Models for Segmenting and Labeling Sequence Data. In *ICML*, pages 282–289.

Utpal Kumar Sikdar, Asif Ekbal, and Sriparna Saha. 2013. Domain-independent Model for Chemical Compound and Drug Name Recognition. *Proceedings of the Fourth BioCreative Challenge Evaluation Workshop*, vol. 2:158–161.

Buzhou Tang, Yonghui Wu, M. Jiang, J. C. Denny, and Hua Xu. 2013. Recognizing and Encoding Disorder Concepts in Clinical Text using Machine Learning and Vector Space Model. *In Proceedings of CLEF*.

Guido Zuccon, A. Holloway, B. Koopman, and A. Nguyen. 2013. Identify Disorders in Health Records using Conditional Random Fields and Metamap. *In Proceedings of CLEF*.

IITP:Supervised Machine Learning for Aspect based Sentiment Analysis

Deepak Kumar Gupta
Indian Institute of Technology Patna
Patna, India
deepak.mtmc13@iitp.ac.in

Asif Ekbal
Indian Institute of Technology Patna
Patna, India
asif@iitp.ac.in

Abstract

The shared task on *Aspect based Sentiment Analysis* primarily focuses on mining relevant information from the thousands of online reviews available for a popular product or service. In this paper we report our works on aspect term extraction and sentiment classification with respect to our participation in the SemEval-2014 shared task. The aspect term extraction method is based on supervised learning algorithm, where we use different classifiers, and finally combine their outputs using a majority voting technique. For sentiment classification we use Random Forest classifier. Our system for aspect term extraction shows the F-scores of 72.13% and 62.84% for the restaurants and laptops reviews, respectively. Due to some technical problems our submission on sentiment classification was not evaluated. However we evaluate the submitted system with the same evaluation metrics, and it shows the accuracies of 67.37% and 67.07% for the restaurants and laptops reviews, respectively.

1 Introduction

Nowadays user review is one of the means to drive the sales of products or services. There is a growing trend among the customers who look at the online reviews of products or services before taking a final decision. In sentiment analysis and opinion mining, aspect extraction aims to extract entity aspects or features on which opinions have been expressed (Hu and Liu, 2004; Liu, 2012). An aspect is an attribute or component of the product that has been commented on in a review. For example:*"Dell Laptop has very good battery life and click pads"*. Here aspect terms are *battery life* and *click pads*. Sentiment analysis is the task of identifying the polarity (*positive, negative* or *neutral*) of review. Aspect terms can influence sentiment polarity within a single domain. As an example, for the restaurant domain *cheap* is usually positive with respect to *food*, but it denotes a negative polarity when discussing the decor or ambiance (Brody and Elhadad, 2010).

A key task of aspect based sentiment analysis is to extract aspects of entities and determine the sentiment corresponding to aspect terms that have been commented in review document. In recent times there has been huge interest to identify aspects and sentiments simultaneously. The method proposed in (Hu and Liu, 2004) is based on information extraction (IE) approach that identifies frequently occurring noun phrases using association mining. Some other works include the methods, *viz* those that define aspect terms using a manually specified subset of the Wikipedia category (Fahrni and Klenner, 2008) hierarchy, unsupervised clustering technique (Popescu and Etzionir, 2005) and semantically motivated technique (Turney, 2002) etc. Our proposed approach for aspect term extraction is based on supervised machine learning, where we build many models based on different classifiers, and finally combine their outputs using majority voting. Before combining, the output of each classifier is post-processed with a set of heuristics. Each of these classifiers is trained with a moderate set of features, which are generated without using any domain-specific knowledge and/or resources. Our submitted system for the second task is based on Random Forest (Breiman, 2001).

Proceedings of the 8th International Workshop on Semantic Evaluation (SemEval 2014), pages 319–323,
Dublin, Ireland, August 23-24, 2014.

2 Tasks

The SemEval-2014 shared task on Aspect based Sentiment Analysis [1] focuses on identifying the aspects of a given target entities and the sentiment expressed towards each aspect. A benchmark setup was provided with the datasets consisting of customer reviews with human-annotated annotations of the aspects and their polarity information. There were four subtasks, and we participated in the first two of them. These are defined as follows:

Subtask-1: The first task is related to aspect term extraction. Given a set of sentences with pre-identified entities, identify the aspect terms present in the sentence and return a list containing all the distinct aspect terms.

Substask-2: The second task addresses the aspect term polarity. For a given set of aspect terms within a sentence, determine whether the polarity of each aspect term is positive, negative, neutral or conflict (i.e. both positive and negative).

3 Methods

3.1 Pre-processing

Each review is in the XML form. At first we extract the reviews along with their identifiers. Each review is tokenized using the Stanford parser [2] and Part-of-Speech tagged using the Stanford PoS tagger [3]. At the various levels we need the chunk-level information. We extract these information using the OpenNLP chunker available at [4].

3.2 Aspect Term Extraction

The approach we adopted for aspect term extraction is based on the supervised machine learning algorithm. An aspect can be expressed by a noun, adjective, verb or adverb. But the recent research in (Liu, 2007) shows that 60-70% of the aspect terms are explicit nouns. The aspect terms could also consist of multiword entities such as *"battery life"* and *"spicy tuna rolls"* etc. As the classification algorithms we make use of Sequential minimal optimization (SMO), Multiclass classifier, Random forest and Random tree. For faster computation of Support Vector Machine, SMO (Platt, 1998) was proposed. Random tree (Breiman, 2001) is basically a decision tree, and in general used as a weak learner to be included in some ensemble learning method. Multiclass classifier is a meta learner based on binary SMO. This has been converted to multiclass classifier using the pairwise method. In order to reduce the errors caused by the incorrect boundary identification we define a set of heuristics, and apply on each output. At the end these models are combined together using a simple majority voting.

We implement the following set of features for aspect terms extraction.

- **Local context:** Local contexts that span the preceding and following few tokens of the current word are used as the features. Here we use the previous two and next two tokens as the features.

- **Part-of-Speech information:** Part-of-Speech(PoS)information plays an important role in identifying the aspect terms. We use the PoS information of the current token as the feature.

- **Chunk Information:** Chunk information helps in identifying the boundaries of aspect terms. This is particularly more helpful to recognize multiword aspect terms.

- **Root word:** Roots of the surface forms are used as the features. We use the Porter Stemmer algorithm [5] to extract the root forms.

- **Stop word:** We use the list of stop words available at [6]. A feature is defined that takes the value equal to 1 or 0 depending upon whether it appears in the training/test set or not.

- **Length:** Length of token plays an important role in identifying the aspect terms. We assume an entity as the candidate aspect term if its length exceeds a predefined threshold value equal to five.

- **Prefix and Suffix**: Prefix and suffix of fixed length character sequences are stripped from each token and used as the features of classifier. Here we use the prefixes and suffixes of length upto three characters as the features.

[1] http://alt.qcri.org/semeval2014/task4/

[2] http://nlp.stanford.edu/software/lexparser.shtml

[3] http://nlp.stanford.edu/software/tagger.shtml

[4] http://opennlp.sourceforge.net/models-1.5/

[5] http://tartarus.org/martin/PorterStemmer/java.txt

[6] http://ir.dcs.gla.ac.uk/resources/linguistic_utils/stop_words

- **Frequent aspect term**: We extract the the aspect terms from the training data, and prepare a list by considering the most frequently occurring terms. We consider an aspect term to be frequent if it appears at least five times in the training data. A feature is then defined that fires if and only if the current token appears in this list.

The output of each classifiers is post-processed with a set of hand-crafted rules, defined as below:
Rule 1: If the PoS tag of the target token is noun, chunk tag is *I-NP* (denoting the intermediate token of a noun phrase) and the observed class of the previous token is *O* (other than aspect terms) then the current token should be assigned the class *B-Aspect* (denotes the beginning of an aspect term).
Rule 2: If the current token has PoS tag noun, chunk tag *I-NP* and the observed class of the immediately preceding token is *B-Aspect* then the current token should be assigned the class *I-Aspect* (denoting the intermediate token).

3.3 Polarity Identification

Polarity classification of aspect terms is the classical problem in sentiment analysis. The task is to classify the sentiments or opinions into semantic classes such as *positive*, *negative*, and *neutral*. We develop a Random Forest classifier for this task. In this particular task one more class *conflict* is introduced. It is assigned if the sentiment can either be positive or negative. For classification we make use of some of the features such as local context, PoS, Chunk, prefix and suffix etc., as defined in the previous Subsection. Some other problem-specific features that we implement for sentiment classification are defined as below:

- **MPQA feature**: We make use of MPQA subjectivity lexicon (Wiebe and Mihalcea, 2006) that contains sentiment bearing words as feature in our classifier. This list was prepared semi-automatically from the corpora of MPQA[7] and Movie Review dataset[8]. A feature is defined that takes the values as follows: 1 for positive; -1 for negative; 0 for neutral and 2 for those words that do not appear in the list.

- **Function words**: A list of function words is compiled from the web[9]. A binary-valued feature is defined that fires for those words that appear in this list.

4 Experiments and Analysis

We use the datasets and the evaluation scripts as provided by the SemEval-2014 shared task organizer.

4.1 Datasets

The datasets comprise of the domains of restaurants and laptop reviews. The training sets consist of 3,044 and 3,045 reviews. There are 3,699 and 2,358 aspect terms, respectively. The test set contains 800 reviews for each domain. There are 1,134 and 654 test instances in the respective domains.

4.2 Results and Analysis

At first we develop several machine learning models based on the different classification algorithms. All these classifiers were trained using the same set of features as mentioned in Section 3. We use the default implementations of these classifiers in Weka[10]. We post-process the outputs of all the models using some heuristics. Finally, all these classifiers are combined together using majority voting. It is to be noted that we determine the best configuration by carrying out different experiments on the development set, which is constructed by taking a part of the training set, and finally blind evaluation is performed on the respective test set. We use the evaluation script provided with the SemEval-2014 shared task. The training sets contain multiword aspect terms, and so we use the standard BIO notation[11] for proper boundary marking.

Experiments show the precision, recall and F-score values 77.97%, 72.13% and 74.94%, respectively for the restaurant dataset. This is approximately 10 points below compared to the best system. But it shows the increments of 4.16 and 27.79 points over the average and baseline models, respectively. For the laptop dataset we obtain the precision, recall and F-score values of 70.74%, 62.84% and 66.55%, respectively. This is 8 points below the best one and 10.35 points

[7] http://cs.pitt.edu/mpqa/
[8] http://cs.cornell.edu/People/pabo/movie-review-data/

[9] http://www2.fs.u-bunkyo.ac.jp/ gilner/wordlists.html
[10] www.cs.waikato.ac.nz/ml/weka/
[11] B, I and O denote the beginning, intermediate and outside tokens

Model	precision	recall	F-score
Random Tree	65.21	59.63	62.29
Random Forest	70.93	62.69	66.55
SMO	71.18	64.22	67.52
Multiclass	73.44	68.50	70.88
Ensemble	77.97	72.13	74.94
Best system	85.35	82.71	84.01
Average	76.74	67.26	70.78
Baseline	-	-	47.15

Table 1: Result of Task-A for restaurants dataset with different classifiers (in %).

Model	precision	recall	F-score
Random Tree	56.52	56.17	56.34
Random Forest	58.38	58.02	58.19
SMO	63.62	63.22	63.39
Multiclass	65.30	64.90	65.09
Ensemble	70.74	62.84	66.55
Best system	84.80	66.51	74.55
Average	68.97	50.45	56.20
Baseline	-	-	35.64

Table 2: Results of aspect term extraction for laptops dataset with different classifiers (in %).

above the average system. Compared to the baseline it achieves more than 20 point increment. Detailed evaluation results for all the classifiers are reported in Table 1 and Table 2 for restaurant and laptop datasets, respectively. Results show that multiclass classifier achieves the highest performance with precision, recall and F-score values of 73.44%, 68.50% and 70.88%, respectively for the restaurant dataset. The same model shows the highest performance with precision, recall and F-score values of 65.30%, 64.90% and 65.09%, respectively for the laptop dataset. Because of majority ensemble we observe increments of 4.06% and 1.46% F-score points over the best individual model, respectively.

We also perform error analysis to understand the possible sources of errors. We show only the confusion matrix for Task-A in Table 3. It shows that in most cases I-ASP is misclassified as B-ASP. System also suffers because of the misclassification of aspect terms to others.

Experiments for classification are reported in Table 4. Evaluation shows that the system achieves the accuracies of 67.37% and 67.07% for

	B-ASP	I-ASP	Other
B-ASP	853	15	269
I-ASP	114	213	142
Other	123	35	11431

Table 3: Confusion matrix for Task-A on restaurants dataset.

Datasets	#Aspect Terms	#Correct Identification	Accuracy (in %)
Restaurants	1134	764	67.37
Laptops	654	438	67.07

Table 4: Results of aspect terms polarity (in %).

the restaurants and laptops datasets, respectively. Please note that our system for the second task was not officially evaluated because of the technical problems of the submitted zipped folder. However we evaluated the same system with the official evaluation script, and it shows the accuracies as reported in Table 4. We observe that the classifier performs reasonably well for the positive and negative classes, and suffers most for the conflict classes. This may be due to the number of instances present in the respective training set. Results show that our system achieves much lower classification accuracy (13.58 points below) compared to the best system for the restaurant datasets. However, for the laptop datasets the classification accuracy is quite encouraging (just 3.42 points below the best system). It is also to be noted that our classifier achieves quite comparable performance for both the datasets. Therefore it is more general and not biased to any particular domain.

5 Conclusion

In this paper we report our works on aspect term extraction and sentiment classification as part of our participation in the SemEval-2014 shared task. For aspect term extraction we develop an ensemble system. Our aspect term classification model is based on Random Forest classifier. Runs for both of our systems were constrained in nature, i.e. we did not make use of any external resources. Evaluation on the shared task dataset shows encouraging results that need further investigation.

Our analysis suggests that there are many ways to improve the performance of the system. In future we will identify more features to improve the performance of each of the tasks.

References

Leo Breiman. 2001. Random forests. 45(1):5–32.

S. Brody and N. Elhadad. 2010. An unsupervised aspect-sentiment model for online reviews. In *Proceedings of NAACL*, pages 804–812, Los Angeles, CA.

Angela Fahrni and Manfred Klenner. 2008. Old wine or warm beer: Target-specic sentiment analysis of adjectives. In *Symsposium on Affective Language in Human and Machine*, pages 60–63. The Society for the Study of Artificial Intelligence and Simulation of Behavior (AISB).

M. Hu and B. Liu. 2004. Mining and summarizing customer reviews. In *Proceedings of the 10th KDD*, pages 168–177, Seattle, WAs.

B. Liu. 2007. *Exploring Hyperlinks, Contents, and Usage Data*. Springer.

Bing Liu. 2012. *Sentiment Analysis and Opinion Mining*. Synthesis Lectures on Human Language Technologies. Morgan & Claypool Publishers.

John C. Platt. 1998. Sequential minimal optimization: A fast algorithm for training support vector machines. Technical report, ADVANCES IN KERNEL METHODS - SUPPORT VECTOR LEARNING.

Ana-Maria Popescu and Oren Etzionir. 2005. Extracting product features and opinions from reviews. In *Proceedings of the Conference on HLT/EMNLP*, pages 339–346.

P. D. Turney. 2002. Thumbs up or thumbs down?: Semantic orientation applied to unsupervised classification of reviews. In *Proceedings of the 40th ACL*, pages 417–424.

Janyce Wiebe and Rada Mihalcea. 2006. Word sense and subjectivity. In *Proceedings of the COLING/ACL*, pages 065–1072, Australia.

IIT Patna: Supervised Approach for Sentiment Analysis in Twitter

Raja Selvarajan and Asif Ekbal
Department of Computer Science and Engineering
Indian Institute of Technology Patna, India
{raja.cs10,asif}@iitp.ac.in

Abstract

In this paper we report our works for SemEval-2014 Sentiment Analysis in Twitter evaluation challenge. This is the first time we attempt for this task, and our submissions are based on supervised machine learning algorithm. We use Support Vector Machine for both the tasks, *viz. contextual polarity disambiguation* and *message polarity classification*. We identify and implement a small set of features for each the tasks, and did not make use of any external resources and/or tools. The systems are tuned on the development sets and finally blind evaluation is performed on the respective test set, which consists of the datasets of five different domains. Our submission for the first task shows the F-score values of 76.3%, 77.04%, 70.91%, 72.25% and 66.32% for LiveJournal2014, SMS2013, Twitter2013, Twitter2014 and Twitter2014Sarcasm datasets, respectively. The system developed for the second task yields the F-score values of 54.68%, 40.56%, 50.32%, 48.22% and 36.73%, respectively for the five different test datasets.

1 Introduction

During the past few years, the communications in the forms of microblogging and text messaging have emerged and become ubiquitous. Opinions and sentiments about the surrounding worlds are widely expressed through the mediums of Twitter messages (Tweets) and Cell phone messages (SMS). The availability of social content generated on sites such as Twitter creates new opportunities to automatically study public opinion. Dealing with these informal text genres presents new challenges for data mining and language processing techniques beyond those encountered when working with more traditional text genres such as newswire. Tweets and SMS messages are short in length, usually a sentence or a headline rather than a document. These texts are very informal in nature and contains creative spellings and punctuation symbols (Nakov et al., 2013). Text also contains lots of misspellings, slang, out-of-vocabulary words, URLs, and genre-specific terminology and abbreviations, e.g., RT for reTweet and #hashtags. The kind of these specific features pose great challenges for building various lexical and syntactic resources and/or tools, which are required for efficient processing of texts. These aspects also introduce complexities to build the state-of-the-art data mining systems. In recent times, there has been a huge interest to mine and understand the opinions and sentiments that people are communicating in social media (Barbosa and Feng, 2010; Bifet et al., 2011; Pak and Paroubek, 2010; Kouloumpis et al., 2011). Recent studies show the interests in sentiment analysis of Tweets across a variety of domains such as commerce (Jansen et al., 2009), health (Chew and Eysenbach, 2010; Salathe and Khandelwal, 2011) and disaster management (Mandel et al., 2012).

Another aspect of social media data, such as twitter messages, is that they include rich information about the individuals involved in the communication. For e.g., twitter maintains information about who follows whom. ReTweets (reshares of a Tweet) and tags inside of Tweets provide discourse information (Nakov et al., 2013). Efficient modelling of such information is crucial in the sense that it provides a mean to empirically study the social interactions where opinion is conveyed.

Several corpora with detailed opinion and sentiment annotation have been made freely available,

Proceedings of the 8th International Workshop on Semantic Evaluation (SemEval 2014), pages 324–328,
Dublin, Ireland, August 23-24, 2014.

e.g., the MPQA corpus (Barbosa and Feng, 2005) of newswire text; i-sieve (Kouloumpis et al., 2011) and TASS corpus2 (Villena-Roman et al., 2013) for Twitter sentiment. These resources were either in non-social media or they were small and proprietary. They further focused on message-level sentiment. The SemEval-2013 shared task (Nakov et al., 2013) on sentiment analysis in Twitter releases SemEval Tweet corpus, which contains Tweets and SMS messages with sentiment expressions annotated with contextual phrase-level polarity as well as an overall message-level polarity. Among the 44 submissions, the highest-performing system (Mohammad et al., 2013) made use of Support Vector Machine (SVM) classifier. It obtained the F-scores of 69.02% in the message-level task and 88.93% in the term-level task. Variety of features were implemented based on surface-forms, semantics, and sentiment features. They generated two large wordsentiment association lexicons, one from Tweets with sentiment-word hashtags, and one from Tweets with emoticons. They showed that in message-level task, the lexicon-based features gained 5 F-score points over all the others.

SemEval-14 shared task [1] on sentiment analysis in Twitter is a continuing effort to promote the research in this direction. Similar to the previous year's evaluation campaigns two primary tasks were addressed in this year challenge. The first task (i.e. Subtask A) deals with *contextual polarity disambiguation* and the second task (i.e. Subtask B) was about *message polarity classification*. For Subtask A, for a given message containing a marked instance of a word or phrase, the goal is to determine whether that instance is positive, negative or neutral in that context. In Subtask B, for a given message, the task is to classify whether the message is of positive, negative, or neutral sentiment. For messages that convey both positive and negative sentiments, the stronger one should be chosen.

In this paper we report on our submissions as part of our first-time participation in this kind of task (i.e. sentiment classification). We develop the systems based on supervised machine learning algorithm, namely Support Vector Machine (SVM) (Joachims, 1999; Vapnik, 1995). We identify and implement a very small set of features that do not make use of any external resources and/or tools. For each task the system is tuned on the development data, and finally blind evaluation is performed on the test data.

[1]http://alt.qcri.org/semeval2014/task9/

2 Methods

We develop two systems, one for contextual polarity disambiguation and the other for message polarity classification. Each of the systems is based on supervised machine learning algorithm, namely SVM. Support vector machines (Joachims, 1999; Vapnik, 1995) have been shown to be highly effective at traditional text categorization, generally outperforming many other classifiers such as naive Bayes (Joachims, 1999; Vapnik, 1995). They are large-margin, rather than probabilistic, classifiers. For solving the two-class problem, the basic idea behind the training procedure is to find a hyperplane, represented by vector $\vec{w}$, that not only separates the document vectors in one class from those in the other, but for which the separation, or margin, is as large as possible. This search corresponds to a constrained optimization problem; letting c_j in 1,-1 (corresponding to positive and negative classes, respectively) be the correct class of the document d_j, the solution could be written as:
$\vec{w} := \sum_j a_j cj \vec{d_j}, \quad a_j >= 0$
where, the a_j's are obtained by solving a dual optimization problem. Those $\vec{d_j}$ such that a_j is greater than zero are called support vectors, since they are the only document vectors contributing to $\vec{w}$. Classification of test instances consists simply of determining which side of $\vec{w}$'s hyperplane they fall on.

2.1 Preprocessing

We pre-process Tweet to normalize it by replacing all "URLs" to "http://url" and all user-ids to "@usr", and this is performed by the regular expression based simple pattern matching techniques. We remove punctuation markers from the start and end positions of Tweets. For e.g., 'the day is beautiful!' is converted to 'the day is beautiful'. Multiple whitespaces are replaced with single whitespace. Stop-words are removed from each review.

2.2 Features

In this work we use same set of features for both the tasks. Each Tweet is represented as a vector consisting of the following features:

1. **Local contexts**: We extract the unigrams and bigrams from the training and test datasets.

A feature is defined that checks the occurrences of these n-grams in a particular Tweet or phrase.

2. **Upper case**: This feature is binary valued with a value set to 1 if all the characters of a phrase or Tweet are capitalized, and 0 otherwise. This indicates that the target message or context contains either positive or negative sentiment.

3. **Elongated words**: The feature checks whether a word contains a character that repeats more than twice. This indicates the presence of a positive sentiment word in the surrounding. This was defined in lines with the one reported in (Mohammad et al., 2013).

4. **Hash tags**: This feature checks the number of hash tags in the Tweet. The value of this feature is set equal to the absolute number of features.

5. **Repeated characters**: This feature checks whether the word(s) have at least three consecutive repeated characters (e.g., happppppppy, hurrrrrey etc.). In such cases, the words are normalized to contain only upto two repeated characters. This helps to capture the words having similar structures.

6. **Negated contexts**: A negated word can affect the polarity of the target word. A negated segment is defined as a sequence of tokens that starts with a negation word (e..g, no, couldn't etc.) and ends with a punctuation marks (e.g.,,,,, :, ;, !, ?). All the words following the negation word are suffixed with NEGATIVE, and the polarity features are also converted with NEGATIVE in line with (Mohammad et al., 2013).

3 Experimental Results and Analysis

The SemEval-2014 shared task datasets are based on SemEval-2013 competition datasets. It covers a range of topics, including a mixture of entities, products and events. Keywords and Twitter hashtags were used to identify messages relevant to the selected topic. The selected test sets were taken from the five different domains. We perform experiment with the python based NLTK toolki[2]. We

[2]http://www.nltk.org/

Class	precision	recall	F-score
Positive	72.02	90.45	80.19
Negative	76.86	53.70	63.23
Neutral	7.69	22.22	3.45
Average	52.19	55.46	53.77

Table 1: Results on development set for Task-A (%).

Class	precision	recall	F-score
Positive	49.92	63.75	55.99
Negative	42.59	31.94	36.51
Neutral	59.54	53.49	56.35
Average	50.68	49.73	66.39

Table 2: Results on development set for Task-B (in %).

carried out experiments with the different classifiers. However we report the results of SVM as it produced the highest accuracy with respect to this particular feature set. We use the default parameters of SVM as implemented in this toolkit. We submitted two runs, one for each task. Both of our submissions were constrained in nature, i.e. we did not make use of any additional resources and/or tools to build our systems.

We perform several experiments using the development set. Best results are reported in Table 1 and Table 2 for Task-A and Task-B, respectively. Evaluation shows that for message polarity disambiguation we obtain the average precision, recall and F-score values of 52.19%, 55.46% and 53.77%, respectively. For message polarity classification we obtain the precision, recall and F-Score values of 50.68%, 49.73% and 66.39%, respectively. It is evident from the evaluation that the first task suffers most due to the problems in classifying the tweets having neutral sentiments, whereas the second task faces difficulties in classifying the negative sentiments. We report the confusion matrices in Table 3 and Table 4 for the first

gs\pred	positive	negative	neutral
positive	502	50	3
negative	160	196	9
neutral	35	9	1

Table 3: Confusion matrix for A. Here, gs: Gold standard; pred: Predicted class.

gs\pred	positive	negative	neutral
positive	313	43	135
negative	102	92	94
neutral	212	81	337

Table 4: Confusion matrix for B. Here, gs: Gold standard; pred: Predicted class.

and second development sets, respectively. Error analysis suggests that most miss-classifications are because of the less number of neutral instances compared to the positive and negative instances in Task-A. For the Task-B training set, the number of instances of positive and neutral sentiments are very low compared to the negative sentiment.

After tuning the systems on the development sets, we perform blind evaluation on the test datasets. Evaluation results on the test sets are reported in Table 5 for both the tasks. The evaluation is carried out based on the evaluation scripts as provided by the organizers. For message polarity disambiguation we obtain the highest F-score of 77.04% for the SMS data type in Task-A. The system shows the F-scores of 76.03%, 70.91%, 72.25% and 66.35% for LiveJournal2014, Twitter2013, Twitter2014 and Twitter2014sarcasm, respectively. For the second task the system attains the highest F-score value of 54.68% for the LiveJournal2014 dataset. For the other datasets, the system shows the F-scores of 40.56%, 50.32%, 48.22% and 36.73% for the SMS2013, Twitter2013 and Twitter2014Sarcasm, respectively. We followed a simple approach that needs fine-tuning in many places. Currently our systems lack behind the best reported systems by margins of approximately 11-18% F-scores for Task-A, and 19-30% F-scores for Task-B.

4 Conclusion

In this paper we report our works as part of our participation to the SemEval-14 shared task on sentiment analysis for Twitter data. Our systems were developed based on SVM. We use a small set of features, and did not make use of any external resources and/or tools in any of the tasks. Each of the systems is tuned on the development set, and blind evaluation is performed on the test set. Evaluation shows that our system achieves the F-score values in the ranges of 66-76% for Task-A and 36-55% for Task-B.

It is to be noted that this is our first participation, and there are many ways to improve the performance of the models. Firstly we would like to identify more features in order to improve the accuracies. We also plan to come up with proper sets of features for the two task. Efficient feature selection techniques will be implemented to identify the most effective feature set for each of the tasks. We would like to apply evolutionary optimization techniques to optimize the different issues of machine learning algorithm.

Task	Test-set	Average F-score
A	LiveJournal2014	76.03
	SMS2013	77.04
	Twitter2013	70.91
	Twitter2014	72.25
	Twitter2014Sarcasm	66.35
B	LiveJournal2014	54.68
	SMS2013	40.56
	Twitter2013	50.32
	Twitter2014	48.22
	Twitter2014Sarcasm	36.73

Table 5: Results on the test set.

References

Luciano Barbosa and Junlan Feng. 2005. Robust Sentiment Detection on Twitter from Biased and Noisy Data. 39:2-3.

Luciano Barbosa and Junlan Feng. 2010. Robust Sentiment Detection on Twitter from Biased and Noisy Data. In *Proceedings of the 23rd International Conference on Computational Linguistics (COLING)*, Beijing, China.

Albert Bifet, Geoffrey Holmes, Bernhard Pfahringer, and Ricard Gavald'a. 2011. Detecting Sentiment Change in Twitter Streaming Data. *Journal of Machine Learning Research - Proceedings Track*, 17:5–11.

Cynthia Chew and Gunther Eysenbach. 2010. Pandemics in the Age of Twitter: Content Analysis of Tweets during the 2009 H1N1 Outbreak. *PLoS ONE*, 5(11):e14118+.

Bernard J. Jansen, Mimi Zhang, Kate Sobel, and Abdur Chowdury. 2009. Twitter Power: Tweets as Electronic Word of Mouth. *Journal of the American Society for Information Science and Technology*, 60(11):2169–2188.

Thorsten Joachims, 1999. *Making Large Scale SVM Learning Practical*, pages 169–184. MIT Press, Cambridge, MA, USA.

Efthymios Kouloumpis, Theresa Wilson, and Johanna Moore. 2011. Twitter Sentiment Analysis: The Good the Bad and the OMG! In *Proceedings of the Fifth International Conference on Weblogs and Social Media, ICWSM*, pages 538–541, Barcelona, Spain.

Benjamin Mandel, Aron Culotta, John Boulahanis, Danielle Stark, Bonnie Lewis, and Jeremy Rodrigue. 2012. A Demographic Analysis of Online Sentiment during Hurricane Irene. In *Proceedings of the Second Workshop on Language in Social Media, LSM 12*, Stroudsburg.

Saif M. Mohammad, Svetlana Kiritchenko, and Xiaodan Zhu. 2013. NRC-Canada: Building the State-of-the-Art in Sentiment Analysis of Tweets. In *Proceedings of Second Joint Conference on Lexical and Computational Semantics (*SEM), Volume 2: Seventh International Workshop on Semantic Evaluation (SemEval 2013)*, pages 321–327, Atlanta, Georgia.

Preslav Nakov, Sara Rosenthal, Zornitsa Kozareva, Veselin Stoyanov, Alan Ritter, and Theresa Wilson. 2013. Semeval-2013 task 2: Sentiment Analysis in Twitter. In *Second Joint Conference on Lexical and Computational Semantics (*SEM), Volume 2: Proceedings of the Seventh International Workshop on Semantic Evaluation (SemEval 2013)*, pages 312–320, Atlanta, Georgia, USA, June.

Alexander Pak and Patrick Paroubek. 2010. Twitter Based System: Using Twitter for Disambiguating Sentiment Ambiguous Adjectives. In *Proceedings of the 5th International Workshop on Semantic Evaluation, SemEval 10*, Los Angeles,USA.

Marcel Salathe and Shashank Khandelwal. 2011. Assessing Vaccination Sentiments with Online Social Media: Implications for Infectious Disease Dynamics and Control. *PLoS Computational Biology*, 7(10):e14118+.

Vladimir N. Vapnik. 1995. *The Nature of Statistical Learning Theory*. Springer-Verlag New York, Inc., New York, NY, USA.

Julio Villena-Roman, Sara Lana-Serrano, Eugenio Martnez-Camara, Jose Carlos Gonzalez, and Cristobal. 2013. Tass - Workshop on Sentiment Analysis at SEPLN. In *Proceedings of Procesamiento del Lenguaje Natural*, pages 50:37–44.

Illinois-LH: A Denotational and Distributional Approach to Semantics

Alice Lai and Julia Hockenmaier
Department of Computer Science
University of Illinois at Urbana-Champaign
{aylai2, juliahmr}@illinois.edu

Abstract

This paper describes and analyzes our SemEval 2014 Task 1 system. Its features are based on distributional and denotational similarities; word alignment; negation; and hypernym/hyponym, synonym, and antonym relations.

1 Task Description

SemEval 2014 Task 1 (Marelli et al., 2014a) evaluates system predictions of semantic relatedness (SR) and textual entailment (TE) relations on sentence pairs from the SICK dataset (Marelli et al., 2014b). The dataset is intended to test compositional knowledge without requiring the world knowledge that is often required for paraphrase classification or Recognizing Textual Entailment tasks. SR scores range from 1 to 5. TE relations are 'entailment,' 'contradiction,' and 'neutral.'

Our system uses features that depend on the amount of word overlap and alignment between the two sentences, the presence of negation, and the semantic similarities of the words and substrings that are not shared across the two sentences. We use simple distributional similarities as well as the recently proposed *denotational* similarities of Young et al. (2014), which are intended as more precise metrics for tasks that require entailment. Both similarity types are estimated on Young et al.'s corpus, which contains 31,783 images of everyday scenes, each paired with five descriptive captions.

2 Our System

Our system combines different sources of semantic similarity to predict semantic relatedness and textual entailment. We use distributional similarity features, denotational similarity features, and alignment features based on shallow syntactic structure.

2.1 Preprocessing

We lemmatize all sentences with the Stanford CoreNLP system[1] and extract syntactic chunks with the Illinois Chunker (Punyakanok and Roth, 2001). Like Young et al. (2014), we use the Malt parser (Nivre et al., 2006) to identify 5 sets of constituents for each sentence: subject NPs, verbs, VPs, direct object NPs, and other NPs.

For stopwords, we use the NLTK English stopword list of 127 high-frequency words. We remove negation words (*no*, *not*, and *nor*) from the stopword list since their presence is informative for this dataset and task.

2.2 Distributional Similarities

After stopword removal and lemmatization, we compute vectors for tokens that appear at least 10 times in Young et al. (2014)'s image description corpus. In the vector space, each dimension corresponds to one of the 1000 most frequent lemmas (contexts). The jth entry of the vector of w_i is the positive normalized pointwise mutual information (pnPMI) between target w_i and context w_j:

$$\text{pnPMI}(w_i, w_j) = \max\left(0, \frac{\log\left(\frac{P(w_i,w_j)}{P(w_i)P(w_j)}\right)}{-\log\left(P\left(w_i, w_j\right)\right)}\right)$$

We define $P(w_i)$ as the fraction of images with at least one caption containing w_i, and $P(w_i, w_j)$ as the fraction of images whose captions contain both w_i and w_j. Following recent work that extends distributional similarities to phrases and sentences (Mitchell and Lapata, 2010; Baroni and Zamparelli, 2010; Grefenstette and Sadrzadeh,

[1] http://nlp.stanford.edu/software/corenlp.shtml

Proceedings of the 8th International Workshop on Semantic Evaluation (SemEval 2014), pages 329–334, Dublin, Ireland, August 23-24, 2014.

Features	Description	# of features
Negation	True if either sentence contains explicit negation; False otherwise	1
Word overlap	Ratio of overlapping word types to total word types in s_1 and s_2	1
Denotational constituent similarity	Positive normalized PMI of constituent nodes in the denotation graph	30
Distributional constituent similarity	Cosine similarity of vector representations of constituent phrases	30
Alignment	Ratio of number of aligned words to length of s_1 and s_2; max, min, average unaligned chunk length; number of unaligned chunks	23
Unaligned matching	Ratio of number of matched chunks to unaligned chunks; max, min, average matched chunk similarity; number of crossings in matching	31
Chunk alignment	Number of chunks; number of unaligned chunk labels; ratio of unaligned chunk labels to number of chunks; number of matched labels; ratio of matched to unmatched chunk labels	17
Synonym	Number of matched synonym pairs (w_1, w_2)	1
Hypernym	Number of matched hypernym pairs (w_1, w_2), number of matched hypernym pairs (w_2, w_1)	2
Antonym	Number of matched antonym pairs (w_1, w_2)	1

Table 1: Summary of features.

2011; Socher et al., 2012), we define a phrase vector p to be the pointwise multiplication product of the vectors of the words in the phrase:

$$p = w_1 \odot ... \odot w_n$$

where $\odot$ is the multiplication of corresponding vector components, i.e. $p_i = u_i \cdot v_i$.

2.3 Denotational Similarities

In Young et al. (2014), we introduce *denotational* similarities, which we argue provide a more precise metric for semantic inferences. We use an image-caption corpus to define the *(visual) denotation* of a phrase as the set of images it describes, and construct a *denotation graph*, i.e. a subsumption hierarchy (lattice) of phrases paired with their denotations. For example, the denotation of the node *man* is the set of images in the corpus that contain a man, and the denotation of the node *person is rock climbing* is the set of images that depict a person rock climbing. We define the (symmetric) denotational similarity of two phrases as the pnPMI between their corresponding sets of images. We associate each constituent in the SICK dataset with a node in the denotation graph, but new nodes that are unique to the SICK data have no quantifiable similarity to other nodes in the graph.

2.4 Features

Table 1 summarizes our features. Since TE is a directional task and SR is symmetric, we express features that depend on sentence order twice: 1) f_1 are the features of s_1 and f_2 are the features of s_2, 2) f_1 are the features of the longer sentence and f_2 are the features of the shorter sentence. These directional features are specified in the following feature descriptions.

Negation In this dataset, contradictory sentence pairs are often marked by explicit negation, e.g. s_1 = *"The man is stirring the sauce for the chicken"* and s_2 = *"The man is not stirring the sauce for the chicken."* A binary feature is set to 1 if either sentence contains *not*, *no*, or *nobody*, and set to 0 otherwise.

Word Overlap We compute $\frac{|W_1 \cap W_2|}{|W_1 \cup W_2|}$ on lemmatized sentences without stopwords where W_i is the set of word types that appear in s_i. Training a MaxEnt or log-linear model using this feature achieves better performance than the word overlap baseline provided by the task organizers.

Denotational Constituent Similarity Denotational similarity captures entailment-like relations between events. For example, *sit* and *eat lunch* have a high pnPMI, which follows our intuition that a person who is *eating lunch* is likely to be *sitting*. We use the same denotational constituent features that Young et al. (2014) use for a textual similarity task. C are original nodes, C^{anc} are parent and grandparent nodes, and sim(C_a, C_b) is the maximum pnPMI of any pair of nodes $a \in C_a$, $b \in C_b$.

C-C features compare constituents of the same type. These features express how often we expect corresponding constituents to describe the same situation. For example, s_1 = *"Girls are doing backbends and playing outdoors"* and s_2 = *"Chil-*

dren are doing backbends" have subject nodes $\{$*girl*$\}$ and $\{$*child*$\}$. *Girls* are sometimes described as *children*, so sim(*girl, child*) $= 0.498$. In addition, *child* is a parent node of *girl*, so max(sim(*anc(girl), child*)) $= 1$. There are 15 C-C features: $\text{sim}(C_1, C_2)$, $\max(\text{sim}(C_1, C_2^{anc}), \text{sim}(C_1^{anc}, C_2))$, $\text{sim}(C_1^{anc}, C_2^{anc})$ for each constituent type.

C-all features compare different constituent types. These features express how often we expect any pair of constituents to describe the same scene. For example, s_1 = *"Two teams are competing in a football match"* and s_2 = *"A player is throwing a football"* are topically related sentences. Comparing constituents of different types like *player* and *compete* or *player* and *football match* gives us more information about the similarity of the sentences. There are 15 C-all features: the maximum, minimum, and sum of $\text{sim}(C_1^t, C_2)$ and $\text{sim}(C_1, C_2^t)$ for each constituent type.

Distributional Constituent Similarity Distributional vector-based similarity may alleviate the sparsity of the denotation graph. For example, for subject NP C-C features, we have non-zero distributional similarity for 87% of instances in the trial data, but non-zero denotational similarity for only 56% of the same instances. The *football* and *team* nodes may have no common images in the denotation graph, but we still have distributional vectors for *football* and for *team*. The 30 distributional similarity features are the same as the denotational similarity features except $\text{sim}(a, b)$ is the cosine similarity between constituent phrase vectors.

Alignment Since contradictory and entailing sentences have limited syntactic variation in this dataset, aligning sentences can help to predict semantic relatedness and textual entailment. We use the Needleman-Wunsch algorithm (1970) to compute an alignment based on exact word matches between two lemmatized sentences. The similarity between two lemmas is 1.0 if the words are identical and 0.0 otherwise, and we do not penalize gaps. This gives us the longest subsequence of matching lemmas.

The alignment algorithm results in a sentence pair alignment and 2 unaligned chunk sets defined by syntactic chunks. For example, s_1 = *"A brown and white dog is running through the tall grass"* and s_2 = *"A brown and white dog is moving through the wild grass"* are mostly aligned, with the remaining chunks u_1 = {[*VP run*], [*NP tall*]} and u_2 = {[*VP move*], [*NP wild*]}.

There are 23 alignment features. Directional features per sentence are the number of words (2 features), the number of aligned words (2 features), and the ratio between those counts (2 features). These features are expressed twice, once according to the sentence order in the dataset and once ordered by longer sentence before shorter sentence, for a total of 12 directional features. Non-directional features are the maximum, minimum, and average unaligned chunk length for each sentence and for both sentences combined (9 features), and the number of unaligned chunks in each sentence (2 features).

Unaligned Chunk Matching We want to know the similarity of the remaining unaligned chunks because when two sentences have a high overlap, their differences are very informative. For example, in the case that two sentences are identical except for a single word in each sentence, if we know that the two words are synonymous, then we should predict that the two sentences are highly similar. However, if the two words are antonyms, the sentences are likely to be contradictory.

We use phrase vector similarity to compute the most likely matches between unaligned chunks. We repeat the matching process twice: for simple matching, any 2 chunks with non-zero phrase similarity can be matched across sentences, while for strict matching, chunks can match only if they have the same type, e.g. *NP* or *VP*. This gives us two sets of features.

For s_1 = *"A brown and white dog is running through the tall grass"* and s_2 = *"A brown and white dog is moving through the wild grass,"* the unaligned chunks are u_1 = {[*VP run*], [*NP tall*]} and u_2 = {[*VP move*], [*NP wild*]}. For strict matching, the only valid matches are [*VP run*]–[*VP move*] and [*NP tall*]–[*NP wild*]. For simple matching, [*NP tall*] could also match [*VP move*] instead and [*VP run*] could match [*NP wild*].

There are a total of 31 unaligned chunk matching features. Directional features per sentence include the number of unaligned chunks (2 features) and the ratio of the number of matched chunks to the total number of chunks (2 features). These features are expressed twice, once according to the sentence order in the dataset and once ordered by longer sentence before shorter sentence, for a total of 8 directional features. Non-directional features per sentence pair include the maximum, minimum, and average similarity of the matched chunks (3 features); the maximum, minimum, and average length of the matched chunks (3 features); and the number of matched chunks (1 feature). We extract these 15 features for both simple matching and strict matching. In addition, we also count the number of crossings that result from matching the unaligned chunks in place (1 feature). This penalizes matched sets that contain many crossings or long-distance matches.

Chunk Label Alignment and Matching Since similar sentences in this dataset often have similar syntax, we compare their chunk label sequences, e.g. [NP *A brown and white dog*] [VP *is running*] [PP *through*] [NP *the tall grass*] becomes *NP VP PP NP*. We compute 17 features based on aligning and matching these chunk label sequences. Directional features are the total number of labels in the sequence (2 features), the number of unaligned labels (2 features), the ratio of the number of unaligned labels to the total number of labels (2 features), and the ratio of the number of matched labels to the number of unaligned labels (2 features). These features are expressed twice, once according to the sentence order in the dataset and once ordered by longer sentence before shorter sentence, for a total of 16 directional features. We also count the number of matched labels for the sentence pair (1 feature).

Synonyms and Hypernyms We count the number of synonyms and hypernyms in the matched chunks for each sentence pair. Synonyms are words that share a WordNet synset, and hypernyms are words that have a hypernym relation in WordNet. There are two hypernym features because hypernymy is directional: num_hyp_1 is the number of words in s_1 that have a hypernym in s_2, while num_hyp_2 is the number of words in s_2 that have a hypernym in s_1. For example, s_1 = *"A woman is cutting a **lemon**"* and s_2 = *"A woman is cutting a **fruit**"* have $num\_hyp_1 = 1$. For synonyms, num_syn is the number of word pairs in s_1 and s_2 that are synonyms. For example, s_1 = *"A brown and white dog is **running** through the tall grass"* and s_2 = *"A brown and white dog is **moving** through the wild grass"* have $num\_syn = 1$.

Antonyms When we match unaligned chunks, the highest similarity pair are sometimes antonyms, e.g. s_1 = *"Some people are on a **crowded** street"* and s_2 = *"Some people are on an **empty** street."* In other cases, they are terms that we think of as mutually exclusive, e.g. *man* and *woman*. In both cases, the sentences are unlikely to be in an entailing relationship. Since resources like WordNet will fail to identify the mutually exclusive pairs that are common in this dataset, e.g. *bike* and *car* or *piano* and *guitar*, we use the training data to build a list of these pairs. We identify the matched chunks that occur in contradictory or neutral sentences but not entailed sentences. We exclude synonyms and hypernyms and apply a frequency filter of $n = 2$. Commonly matched chunks in neutral or contradictory sentences include *sit–stand*, *boy–girl*, and *cat–dog*. These are terms with different and often mutually exclusive meanings. Commonly matched chunks in entailed sentences include *man–person*, and *lady–woman*. These are terms that could easily be used to describe the same situation. However, *cut–slice* is a common pair in both neutral and entailed sentences and we do not want to count it as an antonym pair. Therefore, we consider frequent pairs that occur in contradictory or neutral but not entailed sentences to be antonyms.

The feature num_ant is the number of matched antonyms in a sentence pair. We identify an antonym if c_a and c_b are on the antonym list or occur in one of these patterns: *X–not X*, *X–no X*, *X–no* ***head-noun****(X)* (e.g. *blue hat–no hat*), *X–no* ***hypernym****(X)* (e.g. *poodle–no dog*), *X–no* ***synonym****(X)* (e.g. *kid–no child*). For each antonym pair, we set the similarity score of that match to 0.0.

For example, $num\_ant = 1$ for s_1 = *"A **small** white dog is running across a lawn"* and s_2 = *"A **big** white dog is running across a lawn."* In addition, $num\_ant = 1$ for s_1 = *"A **woman** is leaning on the ledge of a balcony"* and s_2 = *"A **man** is leaning on the ledge of a balcony."*

2.5 Models

For the SR task, we implement a log-linear regression model using Weka (Hall et al., 2009). Specif-

	Accuracy	Pearson ρ
Chance baseline	33.3	–
Majority baseline	56.7	–
Probability baseline	41.8	–
Overlap baseline	56.2	0.627
Submitted system	**84.5**	**0.799**

Table 2: TE and SR results on test data.

Model	Accuracy	Pearson ρ
Overlap baseline	56.8	0.646
Negation	61.0	0.093
Word overlap	65.0	0.694
(+Vector composition)	66.4	0.697
+Denotational similarity	74.4	0.751
+Distributional similarity	71.8	0.756
+Den +Dist	77.0	0.782
+Alignment	70.4	0.697
+Unaligned chunk matching	75.8	0.719
+Align +Match	75.2	0.728
+Synonyms	65.2	0.696
+Hypernyms	66.8	0.716
+Antonyms	71.0	0.704
All features	**84.2**	**0.802**

Table 3: TE and SR results on trial data.

ically, under Weka's default settings, we train a ridge regression model with regularization parameter $\alpha = 1 \times 10^{-8}$. For the TE task, we use a MaxEnt model implemented with MALLET (McCallum, 2002). The MaxEnt model is optimized with L-BFGS, using the default settings. Both models use the same set of features.

3 Results

Our submitted system was trained on the full training and trial data (5000 sentences). Table 2 shows our results on the test data. We substantially outperform all baselines.

3.1 Feature Ablation

We train models on the training data and test on the trial data. Models marked with + include our word overlap feature. We also examine a single compositional feature (vector composition): the cosine similarity of two sentence vectors. A sentence vector is the pointwise multiplication product of component word vectors.

Table 3 compares performance on both tasks. For TE, unaligned chunk matching outperforms other features. Denotational constituent similarity also does well. For SR, distributional and denotational features have the highest correlation with gold scores. Combining them further improves performance.

	% Accuracy		
Model	N	E	C
Overlap baseline	77.3	44.8	0.0
Negation	85.4	0.0	**86.4**
Word overlap	82.9	63.8	0.0
(+Vector composition)	84.7	64.5	0.0
+Denotational similarity	83.6	67.3	52.7
+Distributional similarity	86.5	60.4	37.8
+Den +Dist	85.4	68.7	60.8
+Alignment	87.9	50.6	41.8
+Unaligned chunk matching	**90.4**	66.6	37.8
+Align +Match	88.6	61.8	50.0
+Synonyms	82.2	65.2	0.0
+Hypernyms	84.0	68.0	0.0
+Antonyms	83.6	82.6	0.0
All features	86.5	**83.3**	77.0

Table 4: TE accuracy on trial data by entailment type (Neutral, Entailment, Contradiction).

Table 4 shows TE accuracy of each model by entailment label. On contradictions, the negation model has 86.0% accuracy while our final system has only 77.0% accuracy. However, the negation model cannot identify entailment. Its performance is due to the high proportion of contradictions that can be identified by explicit negation.

We expected antonyms to improve classification of contradictions, but the antonym feature actually has the highest accuracy of any feature on entailed sentences. The dataset contains few contradictions, and most involve explicit negation, not antonyms. The antonym feature indicates that when two sentences have high word overlap and no antonyms, one is likely to entail the other. Neutral sentences often contain word pairs that are mutually exclusive, so the antonym feature distinguishes between neutral and entailed sentences.

4 Conclusion

Our system combines multiple similarity metrics to predict semantic relatedness and textual entailment. A binary negation feature and similarity comparisons based on chunking do very well, as do denotational constituent similarity features. In the future, we would like to focus on multiword paraphrases and prepositional phrases, which our current system has trouble analyzing.

Acknowledgements

We gratefully acknowledge support of the National Science Foundation under grants 1053856 and 1205627, as well as an NSF Graduate Research Fellowship to Alice Lai.

References

Marco Baroni and Roberto Zamparelli. 2010. Nouns are vectors, adjectives are matrices: Representing adjective-noun constructions in semantic space. In *Proceedings of the 2010 Conference on Empirical Methods in Natural Language Processing*, pages 1183–1193, Cambridge, MA, October.

Edward Grefenstette and Mehrnoosh Sadrzadeh. 2011. Experimental support for a categorical compositional distributional model of meaning. In *Proceedings of the 2011 Conference on Empirical Methods in Natural Language Processing*, pages 1394–1404, Edinburgh, Scotland, UK., July.

Mark Hall, Eibe Frank, Geoffrey Holmes, Bernhard Pfahringer, Peter Reutemann, and Ian H. Witten. 2009. The WEKA data mining software: An update. *SIGKDD Explorations*, 11(1):10–18.

Marco Marelli, Luisa Bentivogli, Marco Baroni, Raffaela Bernardi, Stefano Menini, and Roberto Zamparelli. 2014a. SemEval-2014 task 1: Evaluation of compositional distributional semantic models on full sentences through semantic relatedness and textual entailment. In *Proceedings of SemEval 2014: International Workshop on Semantic Evaluation*.

Marco Marelli, Stefano Menini, Marco Baroni, Luisa Bentivogli, Raffaela Bernardi, and Roberto Zamparelli. 2014b. A SICK cure for the evaluation of compositional distributional semantic models. In *Proceedings of LREC*.

Andrew Kachites McCallum. 2002. Mallet: A machine learning for language toolkit. http://mallet.cs.umass.edu.

Jeff Mitchell and Mirella Lapata. 2010. Composition in distributional models of semantics. *Cognitive Science*, 34(8):1388–1429.

Joakim Nivre, Johan Hall, and Jens Nilsson. 2006. Maltparser: A data-driven parser-generator for dependency parsing. In *Proceedings of LREC*, volume 6, pages 2216–2219.

Vasin Punyakanok and Dan Roth. 2001. The use of classifiers in sequential inference. In *NIPS*, pages 995–1001. MIT Press.

Richard Socher, Brody Huval, Christopher D. Manning, and Andrew Y. Ng. 2012. Semantic compositionality through recursive matrix-vector spaces. In *Proceedings of the 2012 Joint Conference on Empirical Methods in Natural Language Processing and Computational Natural Language Learning*, pages 1201–1211, Jeju Island, Korea, July.

Peter Young, Alice Lai, Micah Hodosh, and Julia Hockenmaier. 2014. From image descriptions to visual denotations: New similarity metrics for semantic inference over event descriptions. *Transactions of the Association for Computational Linguistics*, 2:67–78.

In-House: An Ensemble of Pre-Existing Off-the-Shelf Parsers

Yusuke Miyao♣, Stephan Oepen♠♡, and Daniel Zeman◊

♣ National Institute of Informatics, Tokyo

♠ University of Oslo, Department of Informatics

♡ Potsdam University, Department of Linguistics

◊ Charles University in Prague, Faculty of Mathematics and Physics, Institute of Formal and Applied Linguistics

yusuke@nii.ac.jp, oe@ifi.uio.no, zeman@ufal.mff.cuni.cz

Abstract

This submission to the *open* track of Task 8 at SemEval 2014 seeks to connect the Task to pre-existing, 'in-house' parsing systems for the same types of target semantic dependency graphs.

1 Background and Motivation

The three target representations for Task 8 at SemEval 2014, *Broad-Coverage Semantic Dependency Parsing* (SDP; Oepen et al., 2014), are rooted in language engineering efforts that have been under continuous development for at least the past decade. The gold-standard semantic dependency graphs used for training and testing in the Task result from largely manual annotation, in part re-purposing and adapting resources like the Penn Treebank (PTB; Marcus et al., 1993), PropBank (Palmer et al., 2005), and others. But the groups who prepared the SDP target data have also worked in parallel on automated parsing systems for these representations.

Thus, for each of the target representations, there is a pre-existing parser, often developed in parallel to the creation of the target dependency graphs, viz. (a) for the DM representation, the parser of the hand-engineered LinGO English Resource Grammar (ERG; Flickinger, 2000); (b) for PAS, the Enju parsing system (Miyao, 2006), with its probabilistic HPSG acquired through linguistic projection of the PTB; and (c) for PCEDT, the scenario for English analysis within the Treex framework (Popel and Žabokrtský, 2010), combining data-driven dependency parsing with hand-engineered tectogrammatical conversion. At least for DM and PAS, these parsers have been extensively engineered and applied successfully in a variety of applications, hence represent relevant points of comparison. Through this 'in-house' submission (of our 'own' parsers to our 'own' task), we hope to facilitate the comparison of different approaches submitted to the Task with this pre-existing line of parser engineering.

2 DM: The English Resource Grammar

Semantic dependency graphs in the DM target representation, *DELPH-IN MRS-Derived Bi-Lexical Dependencies*, stem from a two-step 'reduction' (simplification) of the underspecified logical-form meaning representations output natively by the ERG parser, which implements the linguistic framework of Head-Driven Phrase Structure Grammar (HPSG; Pollard and Sag, 1994). Gold-standard DM training and test data for the Task were derived from the manually annotated DeepBank Treebank (Flickinger et al., 2012), which pairs Sections 00–21 of the venerable PTB Wall Street Journal (WSJ) Corpus with complete ERG-compatible HPSG syntactico-semantic analyses. DeepBank as well as the ERG rely on Minimal Recursion Semantics (MRS; Copestake et al., 2005) for meaning representation, such that the exact same post-processing steps could be applied to the parser outputs as were used in originally reducing the gold-standard MRSs from DeepBank into the SDP bi-lexical semantic dependency graphs.

Parsing Setup The ERG parsing system is a hybrid, combining (a) the hand-built, broad-coverage ERG with (b) an efficient chart parser for unification grammars and (c) a conditional probability distribution over candidate analyses. The parser most commonly used with the ERG, called PET (Callmeier, 2002),[1] constructs a complete,

[1]The SDP test data was parsed using the 1212 release of the ERG, using PET and converter versions from what

Proceedings of the 8th International Workshop on Semantic Evaluation (SemEval 2014), pages 335–340, Dublin, Ireland, August 23-24, 2014.

subsumption-based parse forest of partial HPSG derivations (Oepen and Carroll, 2000), and then extracts from the forest n-best lists (in globally correct rank order) of complete analyses according to a discriminative parse ranking model (Zhang et al., 2007). For our experiments, we trained the parse ranker on Sections 00–20 of DeepBank and otherwise used the default, non-pruning development configuration, which is optimized for accuracy. In this setup, ERG parsing on average takes close to ten seconds per sentence.

Post-Parsing Conversion After parsing, MRSs are reduced to DM bi-lexical semantic dependencies in two steps. First, Oepen and Lønning (2006) define a conversion to variable-free *Elementary Dependency Structures* (EDS), which (a) maps each predication in the MRS logical-form meaning representation to a node in a dependency graph and (b) transforms argument relations represented by shared logical variables into directed dependency links between graph nodes. This first step of the conversion is 'mildly' lossy, in that some scope-related information is discarded; the EDS graph, however, will contain the same number of nodes and the same set of argument dependencies as there are predications and semantic role assignments in the original MRS. In particular, the EDS may still reflect non-lexical semantic predications introduced by grammatical constructions like covert quantifiers, nominalization, compounding, or implicit conjunction.[2]

Second, in another conversion step that is not information-preserving, the EDS graphs are further reduced into strictly bi-lexical form, i.e. a set of directed, binary dependency relations holding exclusively between lexical units. This conversion is defined by Ivanova et al. (2012) and seeks to (a) project some aspects of construction semantics onto word-to-word dependencies (for example introducing specific dependency types for compounding or implicit conjunction) and (b) relate the linguistically informed ERG-internal tokenization to the conventions of the PTB.[3] Seeing as both conversion steps are by design lossy, DM semantic dependency graphs present a true subset of the information encoded in the full, original MRS.

3 PAS: The Enju Parsing System

Enju *Predicate–Argument Structures* (PAS) are derived from the automatic HPSG-style annotation of the PTB, which was primarily used for the development of the Enju parsing system[4] (Miyao, 2006). A notable feature of this parser is that the grammar is not developed by hand; instead, the Enju HPSG-style treebank is first developed, and the grammar (or, more precisely, the vast majority of lexical entries) is automatically extracted from the treebank (Miyao et al., 2004). In this 'projection' step, PTB annotations such as empty categories and coindexation are used for deriving the semantic representations that correspond to HPSG derivations. Its probabilistic model for disambiguation is also trained using this treebank (Miyao and Tsujii, 2008).[5]

The PAS data set is an extraction of predicate–argument structures from the Enju HPSG treebank. The Enju parser outputs results in 'ready-to-use' formats like phrase structure trees and predicate–argument structures, as full HPSG analyses are not friendly to users who are not familiar with the HPSG theory. The gold-standard PAS target data in the Task was developed using this function; the conversion program from full HPSG analyses to predicate–argument structures was applied to the Enju Treebank.

Predicate–argument structures (PAS) represent word-to-word semantic dependencies, such as semantic subject and object. Each dependency type is represented with two elements: the type of the predicate, such as verb and adjective, and the argument label, such as `ARG1` and `ARG2`.[6]

is called the LOGON SVN trunk as of January 2014; see `http://moin.delph-in.net/LogonTop` for detail.

[2]Conversely, semantically vacuous parts of the original input (e.g. infinitival particles, complementizers, relative pronouns, argument-marking prepositions, auxiliaries, and most punctuation marks) were not represented in the MRS in the first place, hence have no bearing on the conversion.

[3]Adaptations of tokenization encompass splitting 'multiword' ERG tokens (like *such as* or *ad hoc*), as well as 'hiding' ERG token boundaries at hyphens or slashes (e.g. *77-year-old*), which the PTB does not split.

[4]See `http://kmcs.nii.ac.jp/enju/`.

[5]Abstractly similar to the ERG, the annotations of the Enju treebank instantiate the linguistic theory of HPSG. However, the two resources have been developed independently and implementation details are quite different. The most significant difference is that the Enju HPSG treebank is developed by linguistic projection of PTB annotations, and the Enju parser derived from the treebank; conversely, the ERG was predominantly manually crafted, and it was later applied in the DeepBank re-annotation of the WSJ Corpus.

[6]Full details of the predicate–argument structures in the Enju HPSG Treebank, are available in two documents linked from the Enju web site (see above), viz. the Enju *Output Specification Manual* and the *XML Format Documentation*.

Parsing Setup Basically we used the publicly available package of the Enju parser 'as is' (see the above web site). We did not change default parsing parameters (beam width, etc.) and features. However, the release version of the Enju parser is trained with the HPSG treebank corresponding to the Penn Treebank WSJ Sections 2–21, which includes the test set of the Task (Section 21). Therefore, we re-trained the Enju parser using Sections 0–20, and used this re-trained parser in preparing the PAS semantic dependency graphs in this ensemble submission.

Post-Parsing Conversion The dependency format of the Enju parser is almost equivalent to what is provided as the PAS data set in this shared task. Therefore, the post-parsing conversion for the PAS data involves only formatting, viz. (a) format conversion into the tabular file format of the Task; and (b) insertion of dummy relations for punctuation tokens ignored in the output of Enju.[7]

4 PCEDT: The Treex Parsing Scenario

The *Prague Czech-English Dependency Treebank* (PCEDT; Hajič et al., 2012)[8] is a set of parallel dependency trees over the same WSJ texts from the Penn Treebank, and their Czech translations. Similarly to other treebanks in the Prague family, there are two layers of syntactic annotation: *analytical* (a-trees) and *tectogrammatical* (t-trees). Unlike for the other two representations used in the Task, for PCEDT there is no pre-existing parsing system designed to deliver the full scale of annotations of the SDP gold-standard data. The closest available match is a parsing scenario implemented in the Treex natural language processing framework.

Parsing Setup Treex[9] (Popel and Žabokrtský, 2010) is a modular, open-source framework originally developed for transfer-based machine translation. It can accomplish any NLP-related task by sequentially applying to the same piece of data various *blocks* of code. Blocks operate on a common data structure and are chained in *scenarios*.

Some early experiments with scenarios for tectogrammatical analysis of English were described by Klimeš (2007). It is of interest that they report an F_1 score of assigning *functors* (dependency labels in PCEDT terminology) of 70.3%; however, their results are not directly comparable to ours.

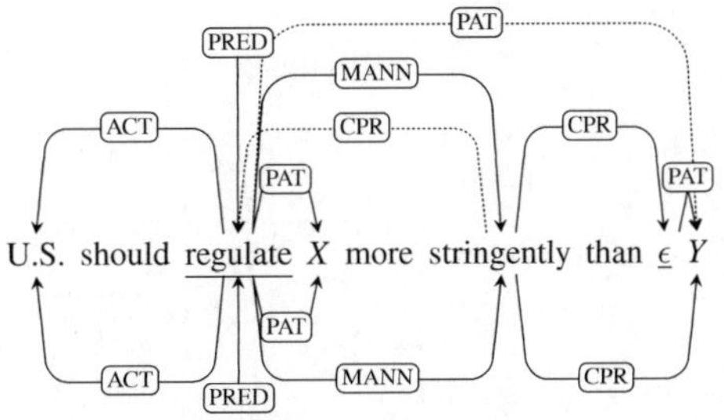

Figure 1: PCEDT asserts two copies of the token *regulate* (shown here as 'regulate' and 'ϵ', underlined). Projecting t-nodes onto the original tokens, required by the SDP data format, means that the ϵ node will be merged with *regulate*. The edges going to and from ϵ will now lead to and from *regulate* (see the dotted arcs), which results in a cycle. To get rid of the cycle, we skip ϵ and connect directly its children, as shown in the final SDP graph below the sentence.

Due to the modular nature of Treex, there are various conceivable scenarios to get the t-tree of a sentence. We use the default scenario that consists of 48 blocks: two initial blocks (reading the input), one final block (writing the output), two `A2N` blocks (named entity recognition), twelve `W2A` blocks (dependency parsing at the analytical layer) and 31 `A2T` and `T2T` blocks (creating the t-tree based on the a-tree).

Most blocks are highly specialized in one particular subtask (e.g. there is a block just to make sure that quotation marks are attached to the root of the quoted subtree). A few blocks are responsible for the bulk of the work. The a-tree is constructed by a block that contains the MST Parser (McDonald et al., 2005), trained on the CoNLL 2007 English data (Nivre et al., 2007), i.e. Sections 2–11 of the PTB, converted to dependencies. The annotation style of CoNLL 2007 differs from PCEDT 2.0, and thus the unlabeled attachment score of the analytical parser is only 66%.

Obviously one could expect better results if we retrained the MST Parser directly on the PCEDT a-trees, and on the whole training data. The only reason why we did not do so was lack of time. Our results thus really demonstrate what is available 'off-the-shelf'; on the other hand, the PCEDT component of our ensemble fails to set any 'upper bound' of output quality, as it definitely is not bet-

[7] The Enju parser ignores tokens tagged as '.', while the PAS representation includes them with dummy relations; thus, missing periods are inserted in post-processing by comparison to the original PTB token sequence.

[8] See `http://ufal.mff.cuni.cz/pcedt2.0/`.

[9] See `http://ufal.mff.cuni.cz/treex/`.

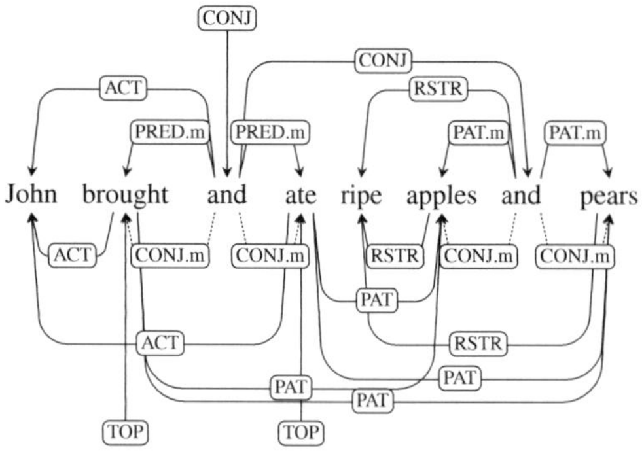

Figure 2: Coordination in PCEDT t-tree (above) and in the corresponding SDP graph (below).

ter informed than the other systems participating in the Task.

Functor assignment is done heuristically, based on POS tags and function words. The primary focus of the scenario was on functors that could help machine translation, thus it only generated 25 different labels (of the total set of 65 labels in the SDP gold-standard data)[10] and left about 12% of all nodes without functors. Precision peaks at 78% for ACT(or) relations, while the most frequent error type (besides labelless dependencies) is a falsely proposed RSTR(iction) relation. Both ACT and RSTR are among the most frequent dependency types in PCEDT.

Post-Parsing Conversion Once the t-tree has been constructed, it is converted to the PCEDT target representation of the Task, using the same conversion code that was used to prepare the gold-standard SDP data.[11]

SDP graphs are defined over surface tokens but the set of nodes of a t-tree need not correspond one-to-one to the set of tokens. For example, there are no t-nodes for punctuation and function words (except in coordination); these tokens are rendered as semantically vacuous in SDP, i.e. they do not participate in edges. On the other hand, t-trees can contain *generated nodes*, which represent elided words and do not correspond to any surface token. Most generated nodes are leaves and, thus, can simply be omitted from the SDP graphs. Other generated nodes are *copies* of normal nodes and they are linked to the same token to which the source node is mapped. As a result, one token can appear at several different positions in the tree; if we project these occurrences into one node, the graph will contain cycles. We decided to remove all generated nodes causing cycles. Their children are attached to their parents and inherit the functor of the generated node (Figure 1). The conversion procedure also removes cycles caused by more fine-grained tokenization of the t-layer.

Furthermore, t-trees use technical edges to capture paratactic constructions where the relations are not 'true' dependencies. The conversion procedure extracts true dependency relations: Each conjunct is linked to the parent or to a shared child of the coordination. In addition, there are also links from the conjunction to the conjuncts and they are labeled CONJ.m(ember). These links preserve the paratactic structure (which can even be nested) and the type of coordination. See Figure 2 for an example.

	DM		PAS		PCEDT	
	LF	LM	LF	LM	LF	LM
Priberam	.8916	.2685	.9176	.3783	.7790	.1068
In-House	.9246	.4807	.9206	.4384	.4315	.0030
	UF	UM	UF	UM	UF	UM
Priberam	.9032	.2990	.9281	.3924	.8903	.3071
In-House	.9349	.5230	.9317	.4429	.6919	.0148

Table 1: End-to-end 'in-house' parsing results.

5 Results and Reflections

Seeing as our 'in-house' parsers are not directly trained on the semantic dependency graphs provided for the Task, but rather are built from additional linguistic resources, we submitted results from the parsing pipelines sketched in Sections 2 to 4 above to the *open* SDP track. Table 1 summarizes parser performance in terms of labeled and unlabeled F_1 (LF and UF)[12] and full-sentence exact match (LM and UM), comparing to the best-performing submission (dubbed Priberam; Martins and Almeida, 2014) to this track. Judging by the official SDP evaluation metric, average labeled F_1 over the three representations, our ensemble ranked last among six participating

[10]The system was able to output the following functors (ordered in the descending order of their frequency in the system output): RSTR, PAT, ACT, CONJ.member, APP, MANN, LOC, TWHEN, DISJ.member, BEN, RHEM, PREC, ACMP, MEANS, ADVS.member, CPR, EXT, DIR3, CAUS, COND, TSIN, REG, DIR2, CNCS, and TTILL.

[11]In the SDP context, the target representation derived from the PCEDT is called by the same name as the original treebank; but note that the PCEDT semantic dependency graphs only encode a subset of the information annotated at the tectogrammatical layer of the full treebank.

[12]Our ensemble members exhibit comparatively small differences in recall vs. precision.

teams; in terms of unlabeled average F_1, the 'in-house' submission achieved the fourth rank.

As explained in the task description (Oepen et al., 2014), parts of the WSJ Corpus were excluded from the SDP training and testing data because of gaps in the DeepBank and Enju treebanks, and to exclude cyclic dependency graphs, which can sometimes arise in the DM and PCEDT conversions. For these reasons, one has to allow for the possibility that the testing data is positively biased towards our ensemble members.[13] But even with this caveat, it seems fair to observe that the ERG and Enju parsers both are very competitive for the DM and PAS target representations, respectively, specifically so when judged in exact match scores. A possible explanation for these results lies in the depth of grammatical information available to these parsers, where DM or PAS semantic dependency graphs are merely a simplified view on the complete underlying HPSG analyses. These parsers have performed well in earlier contrastive evaluation too (Miyao et al., 2007; Bender et al., 2011; Ivanova et al., 2013; inter alios).

Results for the Treex English parsing scenario, on the other hand, show that this ensemble member is not fine-tuned for the PCEDT target representation; due to the reasons mentioned above, its performance even falls behind the shared task baseline. As is evident from the comparison of labeled vs. unlabeled F_1 scores, (a) the PCEDT parser is comparatively stronger at recovering semantic dependency *structure* than at assigning *labels*, and (b) about the same appears to be the case for the best-performing Priberam system (on this target representation).

Acknowledgements

Data preparation and large-scale parsing in the DM target representation was supported through access to the ABEL high-performance computing facilities at the University of Oslo, and we acknowledge the Scientific Computing staff at UiO, the Norwegian Metacenter for Computational Science, and the Norwegian tax payers. This project has been supported by the infrastructural funding by the Ministry of Education, Youth and Sports of the Czech Republic (CEP ID LM2010013).

[13]There is no specific evidence that the WSJ sentences excluded in the Task for technical issues in either of the underlying treebanks or conversion procedures would be comparatively much easier to parse for other submissions than for the members of our 'in-house' ensemble, but unlike other systems these parsers 'had a vote' in the selection of the data, particularly so for the DM and PAS target representations.

References

Bender, E. M., Flickinger, D., Oepen, S., and Zhang, Y. (2011). Parser evaluation over local and non-local deep dependencies in a large corpus. In *Proceedings of the 2011 Conference on Empirical Methods in Natural Language Processing* (p. 397 – 408). Edinburgh, Scotland, UK.

Callmeier, U. (2002). Preprocessing and encoding techniques in PET. In S. Oepen, D. Flickinger, J. Tsujii, and H. Uszkoreit (Eds.), *Collaborative language engineering. A case study in efficient grammar-based processing* (p. 127 – 140). Stanford, CA: CSLI Publications.

Copestake, A., Flickinger, D., Pollard, C., and Sag, I. A. (2005). Minimal Recursion Semantics. An introduction. *Research on Language and Computation*, *3*(4), 281 – 332.

Flickinger, D. (2000). On building a more efficient grammar by exploiting types. *Natural Language Engineering, 6 (1)*, 15 – 28.

Flickinger, D., Zhang, Y., and Kordoni, V. (2012). DeepBank. A dynamically annotated treebank of the Wall Street Journal. In *Proceedings of the 11th International Workshop on Treebanks and Linguistic Theories* (p. 85 – 96). Lisbon, Portugal: Edições Colibri.

Hajič, J., Hajičová, E., Panevová, J., Sgall, P., Bojar, O., Cinková, S., ... Žabokrtský, Z. (2012). Announcing Prague Czech-English Dependency Treebank 2.0. In *Proceedings of the 8th International Conference on Language Resources and Evaluation* (p. 3153 – 3160). Istanbul, Turkey.

Ivanova, A., Oepen, S., Dridan, R., Flickinger, D., and Øvrelid, L. (2013). On different approaches to syntactic analysis into bi-lexical dependencies. An empirical comparison of direct, PCFG-based, and HPSG-based parsers. In *Proceedings of the 13th International Conference on Parsing Technologies* (p. 63 – 72). Nara, Japan.

Ivanova, A., Oepen, S., Øvrelid, L., and Flickinger, D. (2012). Who did what to whom?

A contrastive study of syntacto-semantic dependencies. In *Proceedings of the Sixth Linguistic Annotation Workshop* (p. 2 – 11). Jeju, Republic of Korea.

Klimeš, V. (2007). Transformation-based tectogrammatical dependency analysis of English. In V. Matoušek and P. Mautner (Eds.), *Text, speech and dialogue 2007, LNAI 4629* (p. 15 – 22). Berlin / Heidelberg, Germany: Springer.

Marcus, M., Santorini, B., and Marcinkiewicz, M. A. (1993). Building a large annotated corpora of English: The Penn Treebank. *Computational Linguistics*, *19*, 313 – 330.

Martins, A. F. T., and Almeida, M. S. C. (2014). Priberam. A turbo semantic parser with second order features. In *Proceedings of the 8th International Workshop on Semantic Evaluation.* Dublin, Ireland.

McDonald, R., Pereira, F., Ribarov, K., and Hajič, J. (2005). Non-projective dependency parsing using spanning tree algorithms. In *Proceedings of the Human Language Technology Conference and Conference on Empirical Methods in Natural Language Processing* (p. 523 – 530). Vancouver, British Columbia, Canada.

Miyao, Y. (2006). *From linguistic theory to syntactic analysis. Corpus-oriented grammar development and feature forest model.* Doctoral Dissertation, University of Tokyo, Tokyo, Japan.

Miyao, Y., Ninomiya, T., and Tsujii, J. (2004). Corpus-oriented grammar development for acquiring a Head-Driven Phrase Structure Grammar from the Penn Treebank. In *Proceedings of the 1st International Joint Conference on Natural Language Processing* (p. 684 – 693).

Miyao, Y., Sagae, K., and Tsujii, J. (2007). Towards framework-independent evaluation of deep linguistic parsers. In *Proceedings of the 2007 Workshop on Grammar Engineering across Frameworks* (p. 238 – 258). Palo Alto, California.

Miyao, Y., and Tsujii, J. (2008). Feature forest models for probabilistic HPSG parsing. *Computational Linguistics*, *34*(1), 35 – 80.

Nivre, J., Hall, J., Kübler, S., McDonald, R., Nilsson, J., Riedel, S., and Yuret, D. (2007). The CoNLL 2007 shared task on dependency parsing. In *Proceedings of the 2007 Joint Conference on Empirical Methods in Natural Language Processing and Conference on Natural Language Learning* (p. 915 – 932). Prague, Czech Republic.

Oepen, S., and Carroll, J. (2000). Ambiguity packing in constraint-based parsing. Practical results. In *Proceedings of the 1st Meeting of the North American Chapter of the Association for Computational Linguistics* (p. 162 – 169). Seattle, WA, USA.

Oepen, S., Kuhlmann, M., Miyao, Y., Zeman, D., Flickinger, D., Hajič, J., ... Zhang, Y. (2014). SemEval 2014 Task 8. Broad-coverage semantic dependency parsing. In *Proceedings of the 8th International Workshop on Semantic Evaluation.* Dublin, Ireland.

Oepen, S., and Lønning, J. T. (2006). Discriminant-based MRS banking. In *Proceedings of the 5th International Conference on Language Resources and Evaluation* (p. 1250 – 1255). Genoa, Italy.

Palmer, M., Gildea, D., and Kingsbury, P. (2005). The Proposition Bank. A corpus annotated with semantic roles. *Computational Linguistics*, *31*(1), 71 – 106.

Pollard, C., and Sag, I. A. (1994). *Head-Driven Phrase Structure Grammar.* Chicago, USA: The University of Chicago Press.

Popel, M., and Žabokrtský, Z. (2010). TectoMT. Modular NLP framework. *Advances in Natural Language Processing*, 293 – 304.

Zhang, Y., Oepen, S., and Carroll, J. (2007). Efficiency in unification-based n-best parsing. In *Proceedings of the 10th International Conference on Parsing Technologies* (p. 48 – 59). Prague, Czech Republic.

Indian_Institute_of_Technology-Patna: Sentiment Analysis in Twitter

Vikram Singh, Arif Md. Khan and Asif Ekbal
Indian Institute of Technology Patna
Patna, India
(vikram.mtcs13,arif.mtmc13,asif)@iitp.ac.in

Abstract

This paper is an overview of the system submitted to the SemEval-2014 shared task on sentiment analysis in twitter. For the very first time we participated in both the tasks, *viz contextual polarity disambiguation* and *message polarity classification*. Our approach is supervised in nature and we use sequential minimal optimization classifier. We implement the features for sentiment analysis without using deep domain-specific resources and/or tools. Experiments within the benchmark setup of SemEval-14 shows the F-scores of 77.99%, 75.99%, 76.54 %, 76.43% and 71.43% for LiveJournal2014, SMS2013, Twitter2013, Twitter2014 and Twitter2014Sarcasm, respectively for Subtask A. For Subtask B we obtain the F-scores of 60.39%, 51.96%, 52.58%, 57.25%, 41.33% for five different test sets, respectively.

1 Introduction

In current era microblogging is an efficient way of communication where people can communicate without physical presence of receiver(s). Twitter is the medium where people post real time messages to discuss on the different topics, and express their sentiments. The texts used in twitter are generally informal and unstructured in nature. Tweets and SMS messages are very short in length, usually a sentence or a headline rather than a document. These texts are very informal in nature and contains creative spellings and punctuation symbols. Text also contains lots of misspellings, slang, out-of-vocabulary words, URLs, and genre-specific terminology and abbreviations, e.g., RT for re-Tweet and #hashtags. Such kinds of structures introduce difficulties in building various lexical and syntactic resources and/or tools, which are required for efficient processing of texts. Finding relevant information from these posts poses big challenges to the researchers compared to the traditional text genres such as newswire.

In recent times, there has been a huge interest to mine and understand the opinions and sentiments that people are communicating in social media (Barbosa and Feng, 2010; Bifet et al., ; Pak and Paroubek, 2010; Kouloumpis et al., 2011). There is a tremendous interest in sentiment analysis of Tweets across a variety of domains such as commerce (Jansen et al., 2009), health (Chew and Eysenbach, 2010; Salathe and Khandelwal, 2011) and disaster management (Verma et al., 2011; Mandel et al., 2012). Agarwal et al.(Agarwal et al., 2011) used tree kernel decision tree that made use of the features such as Part-of-Speech (PoS) information, lexicon-based features and several other features. They acquired 11,875 manually annotated Twitter data (Tweets) from a commercial source, and reported an accuracy of 75.39%. Semantics has also been used as the feature to improve the performance of sentiment analysis (Saif et al., 2012). For each extracted entity (e.g. iPhone) from Tweets, they added its semantic concept (e.g. Apple product) as an additional feature. Thereafter they devised a method to measure the correlation of the representative concept with negative/positive sentiment, and applied this approach to predict sentiment for three different Twitter datasets. They showed that semantic features produce better recall and F-score when classifying negative sentiment, and better precision with lower recall and F-score in positive sentiment classification. The benchmark corpus were made available with the SemEval-2013 shared task (Nakov et al., 2013) on

Proceedings of the 8th International Workshop on Semantic Evaluation (SemEval 2014), pages 341–345, Dublin, Ireland, August 23-24, 2014.

sentiment analysis in twitter. The datasets used are from the domains of Tweets and SMS messages. The datasets were labelled with contextual phrase-level polarity and overall message-level polarity. Among the 44 submissions, the support vector machine based system proposed in (Mohammad et al., 2013) achieved the highest F-scores of 69.02% for Task A, i.e. the message-level polarity and and 88.93% for Task B, i.e. term-level polarity.

The issues addressed in SemEval-13 are further extended in SemEval-14 shared task [1]. The same two tasks, *viz.* Subtask A and Subtask B denoting *contextual polarity disambiguation* and *message polarity classification*. The goal of Subtask A is to determine, for a given message containing a marked instance of a word or phrase, whether that instance is positive, negative or neutral in that context. Given a message, the task is to classify it with its entirety whether it is positive, negative, or neutral sentiment. For messages that convey both positive and negative sentiments, the stronger one should be chosen. In this paper we report on our submitted systems for both the tasks. Our evaluation for the first task shows the F-scores of 77.99%, 75.99%, 76.54%, 76.43% and 71.43% for LiveJournal2014, SMS2013, Twitter2013, Twitter2014 and Twitter2014Sarcasm, respectively for Subtask A. For Subtask B we obtain the F-scores of 60.39%, 51.96%, 52.58%, 57.25%, 41.33% for five different test sets, respectively.

2 Methods

In this section we describe preprocessing steps, features and our methods for sentiment classification

2.1 Preprocessing of Data

The data has to be pre-processed before being used for actual machine learning training. Each Tweet is processed to extract only those relevant parts that are useful for sentiment classification. For example, stop words are removed; symbols and punctuation markers are filtered out; URLs are replaced by the word URL etc. Each Tweet is then passed through the ARK tagger developed by CMU [2] for tokenization and Part-of-Speech (PoS) tagging.

[1]http://alt.qcri.org/semeval2014/task9/

[2]http://www.ark.cs.cmu.edu/TweetNLP/

2.2 Approach

Our approach is based on supervised machine learning. We explored different models such as naive Bayes, decision tree and support vector machine. Based on the results obtained on the development sets we finally select SVM for both the tasks. We also carried out a number of experiments with the various feature combinations. Once the model is fixed with certain feature combinations, these are finally used for blind evaluation on the test sets for both the tasks. We submit two runs, one for each task. Both of our submissions were constrained in nature, i.e. we did not make use of any additional resources and/or tools to build our systems. We adapt a supervised machine learning algorithm, namely Support Vector Machine (Joachims, 1999; Vapnik, 1995). We use its sequential minimal optimization version for faster training[3]. We use the same set of features for both the tasks. Development sets are used to identify the best feature combinations for both the tasks. Default parameters as implemented in Weka are used for the SVM experiments.

2.3 Features

Like any other classification algorithm, features play an important role for sentiment classification. For the very first time we participated in this kind of task, and therefore had to spend quite long time in conceptualization and implementation of the features. We focused on implementing the features without using any domain-dependent resources and/or tools. Brief descriptions of the features that we use are presented below:

- **Bag-of-words**: Bag-of-words in the expression or in the entire Tweet is used as the feature(s).

- **SentiWordNet feature**: This feature is defined based on the scores assigned to each word of a Tweet using the SentiWordNet[4]. A feature vector of length three is defined. The scores of all words of the phrase or Tweet is summed over and normalized in the scale of 3. We define the following three thresholds: if the score is less than 0.5 then it is treated to be a negative polarity; for the score above 0.8, it is assumed to contain positive sentiment;

[3]http://research.microsoft.com/en-us/um/people/jplatt/smo-book.pdf

[4]sentiwordnet.isti.cnr.it/

and the polarity is considered to be neutral for all the other words. Depending upon the score the corresponding bit of the feature vector is set.

- **Stop_word**: If a Tweet/phrase is having more number of stop words then it most likely contains neutral sentiment. We obtain the stop words from the Wikipedia[5]. We assume that a particular Tweet or phrase most likely bears a neutral sentiment if 20% of its words belong to the category of stop words.

- **All_Cap_Words**: This feature is defined to count the number of capitalized words in an entire Tweet/phrase. More the number of capitalized words, more the chances of being positive or negative sentiment bearing units. While counting, the words preceded by # are not considered. We include this with the assumption that the texts written in capitalized letters express the sentiment strongly.

- **Init_Cap**: The words starting with capitalized letter contribute more towards classifying it.

- **Percent_Cap**: This feature is based on the percentage of capitalized characters in a Tweet/phrase. If this is more than 75%, then most likely it is not of neutral type.

- **Psmiley (+ve Smiley)**: Generally people use smileys to represent their emotions. A smiley present in a Tweet/phrase directly represents its sentiment. A feature is defined that takes the value equal to the number of positive smileys. We make use of the list available at this page[6].

- **Nsmiley (-ve Smiley)**: The value of this feature is set to the number of negative smileys present in the Tweet. This list was also obtained from the web[7].

- **NumberPostive words**: This feature takes the value equal to the number of positive words present in the Tweet/phrase. We search the adjective words present in the Tweet in the SentiWordNet to determine whether it bears positive sentiment.

- **NumberNegative words**: This feature takes the value equal to the number of negative words present in the Tweet/phrase. The words are again looked at the SentiWordNet to determine its polarity.

- **NumberNeutral words**: This feature determines the number of neutral words present in the Tweet or phrase. This information is obtained by looking the adjective words in the SentiWordNet.

- **Repeating_char**: It has been seen that people express strong emotion by typing a character many times in a Tweet. For example, happpppppppy, hurrrrrey etc. This feature checks whether the word(s) have at least three consecutive repeated characters.

- **LenTweet**: Length of the Tweet is used as the feature. The value of this feature is set equal to the number of words present in the Tweet/phrase.

- **Numhash**: The value of this feature is set equal to the number of hashtags present in the Tweet.

3 Experiments and Analysis

SemEval-2014 shared task is a continuation of the SemEval-2013 shared task. In 2014 shared task, datasets from different domains were incorporated with a wide range of topics, including a mixture of entities, products and events. Messages relevant to the topics are selected based on the keywords and twitter hashtags.

The training set of Task-A has 4,914 positive, 2,592 negative and 384 neutral class instances. The Task-B training set contains 3,057 positive, 1,200 negative and 3,941 neutral sentiments. Developments sets contain 555, 45 and 365 positive, negative and neutral sentiments, respectively for the first task; and 493, 288 and 632 positive, negative and neutral sentiments, respectively for the second task. The selected test sets were taken mainly from the following domains:
LiveJournal2014: 2000 sentences from LiveJournal blogs;
SMS2013: SMS test from last year-used as a progress test for comparison;
Twitter2013: Twitter test data from last year-used as a progress test for comparison;
Twitter2014: A new Twitter test data of 2000

[5]http://en.wikipedia.org/wiki/Stop_words
[6]http://en.wikipedia.org/wiki/List_of_emoticons
[7]http://en.wikipedia.org/wiki/List_of_emoticons

Model	Avg. F-score
Model-1	75.75
Model-2	72.69
Model-3	75.45
Model-4	75.77

Table 1: Results for Task-A on development set(in %).

Tweets;
Twitter2014Sarcasm: 100 Tweets that are known to contain sarcasm.

We build different models by varying the features as follows:

1. **Model-1**: This model is constructed by considering the features, "Repeating_char", "Numhash", "LenTweet", "Percent_Cap", "Init_Cap", "All_Cap", "Bag-of-words", "Nsmiley", "Psmiley", "SentiWordNet" and "Stop_Words".

2. **Model-2**: This model is constructed by the features "Repeating_char", "Percent_Cap", "Numhash", "LenTweet", "Init_Cap", "All_Cap", "Bag-of-words", "SentiWordNet" and "Stop_Words".

3. **Model-3**: This model is built by considering the features "Repeating_char", "Bag-of-words", "SentiWordNet", "Nsmiley" and "Psmiley".

4. **Model-4**: The model incorporates the features "Repeating_char", "Bag-of-words", "SentiWordNet", "Nsmiley", "Psmiley", "Stop_Words", "Numhash", "LenTweet", "Init_Cap" and "All_Cap".

Results on the development set for Task-A are reported in Table 1 that shows the highest performance in Model-4 with the average F-score value of 75.77%. Thereafter we use this particular feature combination for training SVM, and to report the results. Detailed results are reported in Table 2 for both the tasks. It shows 77.99%, 75.99%, 76.54 %, 76.43% and 71.43% F-scores for the LiveJournal2014, SMS2013, Twitter2013, Twitter2014 and Twitter2014Sarcasm, respectively for Subtask A. For Subtask B we obtain the F-scores of 60.39%, 51.96%, 52.58%, 57.25% and 41.33% for the five different test sets, respectively. A closer investigation to the evaluation results reveals that most of the errors are due to the confusions between positive vs. neutral and negative vs. neutral classes.

Comparisons with the best system(s) submitted in this shared task show that we are behind approximately in the range of 6-14% F-score measures for all the domains for Task-A. Results that we obtain in Task-B need more attention as these fall much shorter compared to the best one (in the the range of 14-18%).

Features used	**Classifier**	**Result(Task A)**	**Result(Task B)**
SWN +ve		LiveJournal2014	LiveJournal2014
SWN -ve		77.99	60.39
SWN neutral		SMS2013	SMS2013
#Stop_Words		75.99	51.96
#All_Cap_Words		Twitter2013	Twitter2013
#Numhash		76.54	52.58
Len_Tweet		Twitter2014	Twitter2014
#Init_Cap_Words		76.43	57.25
%_Init_Cap	SVM	T2014S	T2014S
#+ve_Smiley		71.43	41.33
#-ve_Smiley			
#+ve_Words			
#-ve_Words			
#Neutral_Words			
#Bag_of_words			
Rep_character			

Table 2: Result on test sets for Task-A and Task-B.

4 Conclusion

In this paper we report our works as part of our participation to the SemEval-14 shared task on sentiment analysis for twitter data. Our systems were based on supervised classification, where we fixed SVM to report the test results after conducting several experiments with different classifiers on the development data. We implement a set of features that are applied for both the tasks. Our runs are constrained in nature, i.e. we did not make use of any external resources and/or tools. Our results are quite promising that need further investigation. A closer analysis to the results suggest that most of the errors are due to the confusions between positive vs. neutral and negative vs. neutral classes.

This is our first participation, and within the short period of time we developed the systems with reasonable accuracies. There are still many ways to improve the performance. Possible immediate future extension will be to investigate and implement more features, specific to the task.

References

Agarwal, Boyi Xie, Ilia Vovsha, Owen Rambow, and Rebecca Passonneau. 2011. Sentiment Analysis of Twitter Data. *ACL Workshop on Languages in Social Media LSM-2011*, pages 30–38.

Luciano Barbosa and Junlan Feng. 2010. Robust Sentiment Detection on Twitter from Biased and Noisy Data. In *Proceedings of the 23rd International Conference on Computational Linguistics (COLING)*, Beijing, China.

Albert Bifet, Geoffrey Holmes, Bernhard Pfahringer, and Ricard Gavald'a. Detecting Sentiment Change in Twitter Streaming Data. *Journal of Machine Learning Research - Proceedings Track*, 17.

Cynthia Chew and Gunther Eysenbach. 2010. Pandemics in the Age of Twitter: Content Analysis of Tweets during the 2009 H1N1 Outbreak. *PLoS ONE*, 5(11):e14118+.

Bernard J. Jansen, Mimi Zhang, Kate Sobel, and Abdur Chowdury. 2009. Twitter Power: Tweets as Electronic Word of Mouth. *Journal of the American Society for Information Science and Technology*, 60(11):2169–2188.

Thorsten Joachims, 1999. *Making Large Scale SVM Learning Practical*, pages 169–184. MIT Press, Cambridge, MA, USA.

Efthymios Kouloumpis, Theresa Wilson, and Johanna Moore. 2011. Twitter Sentiment Analysis: The Good the Bad and the OMG! In *Proceedings of the Fifth International Conference on Weblogs and Social Media, ICWSM*, pages 538–541, Barcelona, Spain.

Benjamin Mandel, Aron Culotta, John Boulahanis, Danielle Stark, Bonnie Lewis, and Jeremy Rodrigue. 2012. A Demographic Analysis of Online Sentiment during Hurricane Irene. In *Proceedings of the Second Workshop on Language in Social Media, LSM 12*, Stroudsburg.

Saif M. Mohammad, Svetlana Kiritchenko, and Xiaodan Zhu. 2013. NRC-Canada: Building the State-of-the-art in Sentiment Analysis of Tweets. In *Proceedings of Second Joint Conference on Lexical and Computational Semantics (*SEM), Volume 2: Seventh International Workshop on Semantic Evaluation (SemEval 2013)*, pages 321–327, Atlanta, Georgia.

Preslav Nakov, Sara Rosenthal, Zornitsa Kozareva, Veselin Stoyanov, Alan Ritter, and Theresa Wilson. 2013. Semeval-2013 Task 2: Sentiment Analysis in Twitter. In *Second Joint Conference on Lexical and Computational Semantics (*SEM), Volume 2: Proceedings of the Seventh International Workshop on Semantic Evaluation (SemEval 2013)*, pages 312–320, Atlanta, Georgia, USA.

Alexander Pak and Patrick Paroubek. 2010. Twitter based System: Using Twitter for Disambiguating Sentiment Ambiguous Adjectives. In *Proceedings of the 5th International Workshop on Semantic Evaluation, SemEval 10*, pages 436–439, Los Angeles,USA.

Hassan Saif, Yulan He, and Harith Alani. 2012. Semantic Sentiment Analysis of Twitter. In *ISWC'12 Proceedings of the 11th International Conference on the Semantic Web - Volume Part I*, pages 508–524.

Marcel Salathe and Shashank Khandelwal. 2011. Assessing Vaccination Sentiments with Online Social Media: Implications for Infectious Disease Dynamics and Control. *PLoS Computational Biology*, 7(10):e14118+.

Vladimir N. Vapnik. 1995. *The Nature of Statistical Learning Theory*. Springer-Verlag New York, Inc., New York, NY, USA.

Sudha Verma, Sarah Vieweg, William Corvey, Leysia Palen, James Martin, Martha Palmer, Aaron Schram, and Kenneth Anderson. 2011. Natural Language Processing to the Rescue? Extracting Situational Awareness Tweets during Mass Emergency. In *Proceedings of the AAAI Conference on Weblogs and Social Media*, Velingrad.

INSIGHT_Galway: Syntactic and Lexical Features for Aspect Based Sentiment Analysis

Sapna Negi
Insight Centre for Data Analytics
National University of Ireland
Galway

Paul Buitelaar
Insight Centre for Data Analytics
National University of Ireland
Galway

{sapna.negi, paul.buitelaar}@insight-centre.org

Abstract

This work analyses various syntactic and lexical features for sentence level aspect based sentiment analysis. The task focuses on detection of a writer's sentiment towards an aspect which is explicitly mentioned in a sentence. The target sentiment polarities are positive, negative, conflict and neutral. We use a supervised learning approach, evaluate various features and report accuracies which are much higher than the provided baselines. Best features include unigrams, clauses, dependency relations and SentiWordNet polarity scores.

1 Introduction

The term *aspect* refers to the features or aspects of a product, service or topic being discussed in a text. The task of detection of sentiment towards these aspects involves two major processing steps, identifying the aspects in the text and identifying the sentiments towards these aspects. Our work describes a submitted system in the *Aspect Based Sentiment Analysis* task of SemEval 2014 (Pontiki et al., 2014). The task was further divided into 4 subtasks; our work corresponds to the subtask 2, called *Aspect Term Polarity Detection*. We predict the polarity of sentiments expressed towards the aspect terms which are already annotated in a sentence. The target polarity types are *positive, negative, neutral and conflict*.

We employ a statistical classifier and experiment with various syntactic and lexical features. Selected features for the submitted system include words which hold certain dependency relations with the aspect terms, clause in which the aspect term appears, unigrams, and sum of lexicon based sentiment polarities of the words in the clause.

2 Related Work

Pang et al. (2002) proved that unigrams and bigrams, adjectives and part of speech tags are important features for a machine learning based sentiment classifier. Later, verbs and adjectives were also identified as important features (Chesley, 2006). Meena and Prabhakar (2007) performed sentence level sentiment analysis using rules based on clauses of a sentence. However, in our case we cannot simply consider the adjectives and verbs as features, since they might relate to different aspects. For example, in the sentence 'The pizza is the best if you like thin crusted pizza.', sentiment towards 'pizza' is positive because of the adjective 'best'; however for the term 'thin crusted pizza', 'like' would be the sentiment verb. Therefore, only those adjectives and verbs which relate to the target aspect, can be considered as the indicator of their polarity. Wilson et al. (2009) showed that the words which share certain dependency relations with aspect terms, tend to indicate the sentiments expressed towards those terms.

Saif et al. (2012) showed the co-relation between topic and sentiment polarity in tweets, and asserted that majority of people tend to express similar sentiments towards same topics, especially in the case of positive sentiments. The baseline approach for this task (Pontiki et al., 2014) also associates polarity with aspect terms. Therefore, we also consider aspect term as a potential feature.

Our approach for this task is based on our observation of the data, with a provenance of the above mentioned findings.

3 Approach

We employ a statistical classifier which trains on the provided training datasets.

Proceedings of the 8th International Workshop on Semantic Evaluation (SemEval 2014), pages 346–350, Dublin, Ireland, August 23-24, 2014.

Datasets: Training datasets comprise of 3000 sentences from laptop and restaurant reviews. Training sentences were tagged with the target aspect term and the corresponding polarity, where more than one aspect term can be tagged in a sentence.

3.1 Feature Sets

We divide the candidate features into four feature sets.

1. **Non-contextual:** These features comprise of training vocabulary. They do not target aspect based sentiments, but the overall sentiment of the sentence. There might be cases where the aspect based sentiment is same as the overall sentiment of the sentence. The feature set comprises of three feature types, unigrams, bigrams, adjectives and verbs of the sentence.

2. **Lexicon Non-Contextual:** These features are the Sentiwordnet_v3.0 polarity scores (Andrea Baccianella and Sebastiani, 2010) of the words obtained from the best non-contextual feature type. This feature set would include two numerical features, positive polarity score and negative polarity score of the best non-contextual feature types. Best non-contextual feature type is decided by comparing the classification accuracies of individual feature types, with cross validation on the training data (Table 1). We evaluated two algorithms to obtain the positive and negative polarities of words using SentiWordNet. Later, we would provide details of these algorithms.

3. **Contextual:** These features target aspect based sentiments. Feature types comprise of the clause in which an aspect term appears, the adjective and verbs of this clause, aspect term itself, and the words which hold certain dependency relations with aspect term. We only considered the Stanford parser dependencies 'nn', 'amod', and 'nsubj'. The dependency relations were chosen on the basis of best classification accuracy in a cross validation trial, where the only features were the words holding different dependency relations with the aspect term. However, we only list the accuracy from the best performing dependency relations in the Tables 1, 3. By the feature type *clause*, we mean the unigrams contained in a clause.

4. **Lexicon Contextual:** Similar to Lexicon Non-Contextual features, these are the numeric values obtained from SentiWordNet polarity scores of the best performing contextual feature type.

Polarity Calculation using SentiWordNet: WordNet (Fellbaum, 1998) is a lexical database for the English language. It assigns each listed word the senses to which it may belong, where each unique sense is represented by a synset id. SentiWordNet is built on the top of WordNet, where a pair of positive and negative polarity score is assigned to each sense of a word. SentiWordnet entry for each word comprises of all the possible parts of speech in which the word could appear, all the senses corresponding to each part of speech, and a pair of polarity scores associated with each sense [1]. The magnitude of positive and negative polarity scores for each sense ranges from 0 to 1.

In order to automatically obtain the polarity scores corresponding to the desired sense of a word, word sense disambiguation is required to be performed. We did not perform sense disambiguation, and picked the polarity scores simply on the basis of word and part of speech matching. This gives more than one candidate senses, and thus more than one pair of polarity scores for each word. We evaluated the following 2 methods to assign single values of sentiment polarity scores to each word.

1. **Default:** The SentiWordnet website [2] provides a basic algorithm to assign sentiwordnet based polarities to a word. SentiWordnet assigns a rank to each sense of a word, where most commonly appearing sense is ranked as 1. The default algorithm first calculates an overall polarity (Positive score - Negative score), for each sense of a word. It then calculates a weighted sum of the overall polarity scores of all the senses of a word, where the weights are the ranks of senses. This sum is considered as a single value polarity score of a word, which can be a positive or negative number.

[1] http://sentiwordnet.isti.cnr.it/search.php?q=good
[2] http://sentiwordnet.isti.cnr.it

2. **Our algorithm:** We do not obtain an overall polarity score for each word, but we obtain a pair of aggregated negative and positive score for each word. Aggregate positive score is obtained by taking the average of the positive scores of each sense of the word, and same goes for the aggregate negative score.

One reason for keeping the positive and negative scores separate in our algorithm is that the task also involves sentiment classes *conflict* and *neutral*. Using only the overall polarity score results in a loss of information in the case of very low negativity and positivity (neutral sentiments), or high but comparable negativity and positivity (conflicting sentiments). Also, our algorithm produced better results when used with an SVM classifier, with features as unigrams and their polarity scores.

3.2 Classifier Model

Our system is built on the state of the art LibSVM classifier (EL-Manzalawy and Honavar, 2005). We used Weka 3.7.10 toolkit (Hall et al., 2009) for our experiments. The parameters [3] of the SVM classifier are tuned to the values which give best results with unigrams. Table 2 provides the tuned parameters, rest of the parameters are set at default values.

Pre-processing: We perform stemming using Weka's implementation of Snowball stemmer, convert strings to lower case and filter out stopwords. We use a customised list of stopwords, based on our observations of the data. The customised list is created using the stopword list of Weka, with certain words removed. For example, negators like 'not', 'didn't' etc. are important for negative sentiments, for example 'I can barely use any usb devices because they will not stay properly connected'. Words like 'but', 'however' are prominent in conflicting sentiments, for example 'No backlit keyboard, but not an issue for me'. Tables 1, 3 show the difference in results on using filtered stopword list, compared against no stopword removal, and original stopword list.

G	R	C	E	Z
0.10	1.0	2	1.0	normalise

Table 2: Parameter Settings for SVM Classifier.

[3] http://weka.sourceforge.net/doc.stable/weka/classifiers/functions/LibSVM.html

3.3 Feature Evaluation

We evaluated our features using 8-fold cross validation on the training data. We evaluated each feature by using it as the only feature for the classifier (Tables 1, 3). We performed experiments on different combinations of features, but we only present the best performing combination of features in the last row of the tables. The baseline approach (Pontiki et al., 2014) provided by the organisers, produced an accuracy of 47% for laptop and 57% for restaurant, by splitting the training data.

Metrics include, F score for each class, and overall classification accuracy. F score ranges from 0-1, and overall accuracy range from 0-100.

4 Submission and Results

Submission involved the prediction of sentiment polarity towards the already tagged aspect terms in two test datasets. There were 800 sentences in each test dataset. The laptop test dataset was obtained by dividing the original laptop data into training and test. However, restaurant test dataset and training dataset come from different sources. We trained our classifier using the provided training dataset and the highlighted features (last row) in the Tables 1, 3. In order to evaluate the submission, gold standard datasets corresponding to each test dataset were later released, and submission's accuracy was compared against it.

Results: The system performance was evaluated and ranked on the basis of overall accuracy of sentiment prediction. We were ranked as 20/32 for the laptop domain, and 16/34 for the restaurant domain. The task organisers reported that 8 polarity predictions for laptop data, and 34 for restaurant data were missing from our submission. We later debugged our system, and obtained the actual accuracy which our system is capable of producing with the given test data. The results are summarised in Table 4.

5 Observations and Analysis

We hypothesize that aspect terms should serve as features when training data and test data come from same source, which means that they relate to the same brand, product, service etc. This is because aspect terms change with data, for example names of dishes would change with different restaurants even if the domain is same. In our case, the laptop test data was obtained from the

Feature Set	Features	Positive	Negative	Conflict	Neutral	Accuracy
non-contextual	unigrams,bigrams	0.827	0.590	0.210	0.422	70.699
	unigrams	0.830	0.584	0.154	0.413	70.962
	adjectives,verbs	0.704	0.412	0.000	0.257	63.465
	adjectives	0.623	0.430	0.000	0.000	56.410
non-contextual + lexicon	unigrams, unigram polarity scores	0.833	0.596	0.154	0.414	71.300
contextual	clause	0.823	0.571	0.117	0.0.456	71.170
	adjective, verbs within clause	0.784	0.472	0.000	0.257	66. 465
	aspects	0.734	0.154	0.000	0.264	59.442
	dependencies	0.751	0.235	0.000	0.061	61.257
contextual + lexicon	clause, clause polarity score	0.735	0.000	0.000	0.000	58.101
combined	**unigrams, clause, dependencies, clause polarity score, filtered stopword list**	0.837	0.610	0.162	0.418	71.960
	used original stopword	0.825	0.587	0.078	0.371	70.830
	no stopwords used	0.830	0.610	0.151	0.435	72.000

Table 1: Feature Analysis for Restaurant Reviews.

Feature Set	Features	Positive	Negative	Conflict	Neutral	Accuracy
Non-Contextual	unigrams,bigrams	0.827	0.590	0.210	0.422	70.699
	unigrams	0.781	0.747	0.110	0.484	71.202
	adjectives,verbs	0.569	0.620	0.000	0.164	54.516
	adjectives	0.521	0.613	0.000	0.090	51.230
non-contextual + lexicon	unigrams, unigram polarity scores	0.783	0.754	0.179	0.529	71.850
Contextual	Clause	0.823	0.571	0.117	0.0.456	71.170
	adjective, verbs within clause	0.569	0.620	0.000	0.164	54.510
	aspects	0.602	0.259	0.000	0.050	45.240
	dependencies	0.590	0.078	0.000	0.000	42.480
contextual + lexicon	clause, clause polarity score	0.750	0.705	0.000	0.407	67.230
combined	**unigrams, clause, dependencies, clause polarity score, filtered stopword list**	0.786	0.752	0.100	0.498	71.600
	weka stopword list	0.780	0.744	0.113	0.442	70.590
	no stopwords	0.782	0.758	0.154	0.530	72.170

Table 3: Feature Analysis for Laptop Reviews.

same dataset which was used to prepare training data, while restaurant was from a different source. We observed that, although aspect terms produced better results with cross validation, it did not happen in the case of test data. The restaurant test data produced better accuracy without aspect term features, while laptop test data produced better accuracy with aspect term features. We submitted our systems without using aspect terms as features. If aspect terms were used as features, the laptop test data would have been classified with an accuracy of 60.8 %. Another interesting observation is, unigrams produce better results on their own, as compared to adjectives and verbs. Dependency and clauses also seem to be very important features, since they produce an accuracy of above 60% on their own. We also observed that some stopwords are important features for this task, and complete removal of stopwords lowers the classification accuracy.

Domain	Baseline	Best System	Submitted System	Debugged System
laptop	51.07	70.48	57.03	59.15
restaurant	64.28	80.95	70.70	71.44

Table 4: Results on Gold Standard Data.

6 Conclusion

We presented an analysis and evaluation of syntactic and lexical features for performing sentence level aspect based sentiment analysis. Our features depend on part of speech tagging and dependency parsing, and therefore the accuracy might vary with different parsers. Although our system did not produce the highest accuracy for the task, it is capable of achieving accuracies much above the baselines. Therefore, the proposed features can be worth testing on different datasets and can be used in combination with other features.

Acknowledgement

This work has been funded by the European project EUROSENTIMENT under grant no. 296277, and the Science Foundation Ireland under Grant Number SFI/12/RC/2289 (Insight Center).

References

Stefano Esuli Andrea Baccianella and Fabrizio Sebastiani. 2010. Sentiwordnet 3.0: An enhanced lexical resource for sentiment analysis and opinion mining. In *Proceedings of the Seventh conference on International Language Resources and Evaluation*

(LREC'10). European Language Resources Association (ELRA).

Paula Chesley. 2006. Using verbs and adjectives to automatically classify blog sentiment. In *In Proceedings of AAAI-CAAW-06, the Spring Symposia on Computational Approaches*, pages 27–29.

Yasser EL-Manzalawy and Vasant Honavar, 2005. *WLSVM: Integrating LibSVM into Weka Environment*.

Christiane Fellbaum, editor. 1998. *WordNet An Electronic Lexical Database*. The MIT Press.

Mark Hall, Eibe Frank, Geoffrey Holmes, Bernhard Pfahringer, Peter Reutemann, and Ian H. Witten. 2009. The weka data mining software, an update. *SIGKDD Explorations*, 11:10–18.

Arun Meena and Prabhakar T.V. 2007. Sentence level sentiment analysis in the presence of conjuncts using linguistic analysis. In *ECIR*, volume 4425 of *Lecture Notes in Computer Science*. Springer.

Bo Pang, Lillian Lee, and Shivakumar Vaithyanathan. 2002. Thumbs up?: sentiment classification using machine learning techniques. In *Proceedings of the ACL-02 conference on Empirical methods in natural language processing - Volume 10*, EMNLP '02, pages 79–86, Stroudsburg, PA, USA. Association for Computational Linguistics.

Maria Pontiki, Dimitrios Galanis, John Pavlopoulos, Harris Papageorgiou, Ion Androutsopoulos, and Suresh Manandhar. 2014. Semeval-2014 task 4: Aspect based sentiment analysis. In *Proceedings of the International Workshop on Semantic Evaluation, SemEval 2014*, Dublin, Ireland.

Hassan Saif, Yulan He, and Harith Alani. 2012. Semantic sentiment analysis of twitter. In *International Semantic Web Conference (1)*, volume 7649 of *Lecture Notes in Computer Science*, pages 508–524. Springer.

Wilson Theresa, Janyce Wiebe, and Paul Hoffmann. 2009. Recognizing contextual polarity: An exploration of features for phrase-level sentiment analysis. *Computational Linguistics*, pages 399–433.

iTac: Aspect Based Sentiment Analysis using Sentiment Trees and Dictionaries

Fritjof Bornebusch[1], Glaucia Cancino[1], Melanie Diepenbeck[1], Rolf Drechsler[1,2],
Smith Djomkam[1], Alvine Nzeungang Fanseu[1], Maryam Jalali[1], Marc Michael[1], Jamal Mohsen[1],
Max Nitze[1], Christina Plump[1], Mathias Soeken[1,2], Fred Tchambo[1], Toni[1], Henning Ziegler[1]

[1] Faculty of Mathematics and Computer Science, University of Bremen, Germany
[2] Cyber-Physical Systems, DFKI GmbH, Bremen, Germany
itac@cs.uni-bremen.de

Abstract

This paper describes our approach for the fourth task of the *SemEval 2014 challenge: Aspect Based Sentiment Analysis*. Our system is designed to solve all four subtasks: (i) identifying aspect terms, (ii) determining the polarity of an aspect term, (iii) detecting aspect categories, and (iv) determining the polarity of a predefined aspect category. Our system is based on the Stanford sentiment tree.

1 Introduction

Online reviewing, rating, and recommendation have become quite popular nowadays. Based on online reviews and rating, people may decide whether to buy a certain product or visit a certain place (restaurant, shop, etc.). Due to the increasing number of reviews, an automatic system is needed that can evaluate these reviews as positive, negative, or neutral.

In this paper, we propose a system for the fourth task of the SemEval 2014 challenge (*Aspect Based Sentiment Analysis*). The target is to identify aspects of given target entities and to determine the sentiment that is expressed towards each aspect in terms of a polarity. The problem has been divided into four different subtasks: (i) extracting aspects from a given sentence, (ii) determining the polarity of each aspect, (iii) matching suitable aspect categories and (iv) identifying the polarity of these categories.

2 Related Work

There are several different approaches to perform sentiment analysis on a given sentence. References Turney (2002) and Pang et al. (2002) started to classify a given sentence to be either *positive* or *negative*. Dave et al. (2003) continued to include the *neutral* semantic orientation to his work. These approaches perform sentiment analysis on a whole sentence and use phrases such as adjectives and adverbs to get a polarity. They collect all these phrases and determine their polarity (e.g. positive, neutral, or negative). Hence, it differs from our work that performs sentiment analysis based on each aspect term.

Another approach by Snyder and Barzilay (2007) tries to perform aspect based sentiment analysis, which performs sentiment analysis for various aspects for a given restaurant. Our work differs from their approach and is more closely related to Hu and Liu (2004). Individual parts of the sentence are classified separately since different parts can express different polarities. But the authors only consider product features instead of aspect terms. Aspect terms can be product features but they can also include conditions such as *ambience* that influences an opinion which have not been addressed in Hu and Liu (2004).

3 Preliminaries

Our system is based on *Natural Language Processing (NLP)* libraries such as the *Stanford CoreNLP*.[1] The system is heavily based on the Stanford sentiment tree.

3.1 Stanford sentiment tree

The *sentiment treebank* introduced by Socher et al. (2013) was developed at the University of Stanford to predict the sentiment of movie reviews. It contains approximately 12,000 sentiment annotated parse trees of movie reviews. The sentiment prediction can determine five sentiment classes (very negative, negative, neutral, positive, very positive) using a recursive neural tensor network trained on

[1] *http://nlp.stanford.edu/software/corenlp.shtml*

Proceedings of the 8th International Workshop on Semantic Evaluation (SemEval 2014), pages 351–355,
Dublin, Ireland, August 23-24, 2014.

Table 1: Removed word categories with examples.

Category	Example
person	husband, wife, mother, boyfriend
time	date, year, month, Monday-Sunday
location	NYC, Manhattan, street, Avenue
misstagged	everything, something, none, some, any

Table 2: Rule-satisfication for example.

Rule	Result			
found nouns	wife	drives	battery	life
frequent noun?	✓	✓	✓	✓
non-forbidden?	x	✓	✓	✓
terms		drives	battery life	
gold terms		hard drives	battery life	

Table 3: Results for term extraction.

Domain	Precision	Recall	F-measure
Laptop	0.23	0.25	0.24
Restaurant	0.37	0.40	0.38

the sentiment treebank. We aggregate the sentiment classes into three classes (negative, neutral, positive).

4 Implementation

Our system is divided into four subsystems that are described separately in the following section. Although described separately, some subtasks depend on each other (e.g. Aspect Category Extraction and Aspect Category Polarity).

4.1 Aspect term extraction

The aim of this subtask is to find aspect terms that are discussed in a given sentence. Our approach follows an idea presented by Hu and Liu (2004). A word in a given sentence is considered to be an aspect term if it satisfies the following three conditions.

C1.1 It is tagged as a noun (tagged with NN, NNS, NNP, or NNPS).

C1.2 It is one of the 20% most common nouns of all given sentences.

C1.3 It does not belong to a forbidden word category (listed in Table 1).

Following this extraction, adjacent aspect terms are combined to multi-word aspect terms.

Example 1 *"My wife bought it and was very happy, especially with the hard drives and battery life." The result of the rule application is shown in Table 2. When multi-word aspect terms are considered,* battery *and* life *are combined to a single term. The row indicated by* terms *shows the extracted aspect terms of the sentence. In the last row* gold terms *are compared to actual aspect terms given by the training data.*

The results of our system are shown in Table 3. These results could be improved by using typed dependencies. The use of the *adjectival modifier (amod)* and the *noun compound modifier (nn)* relations can help to improve finding multi-word aspect terms.

4.2 Aspect term polarity

After extracting the aspect term from the sentence the next task is to predict its polarity. For this task we are using the Stanford sentiment tree.

The sentiment tree is designed to predict the sentiment of a whole sentence. Because the sentiment tree contains polarities for every node of the parse tree it is reasonable to use it for aspect sentiment prediction.

Our algorithm examines the sentiment tree nodes to predict the polarity of an aspect. The following outlines the basic steps for aspect sentiment prediction.

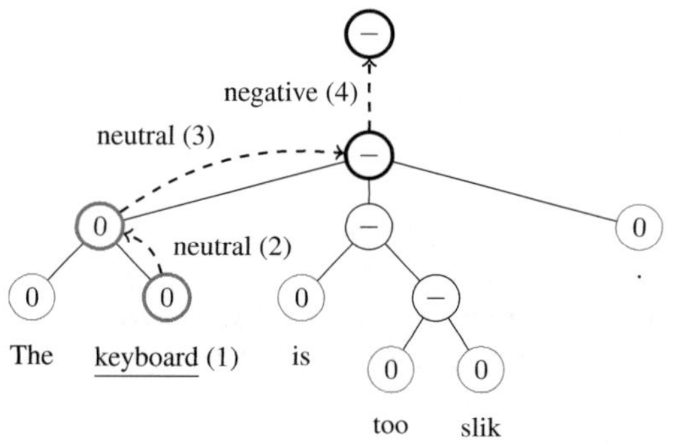

Figure 1: Example of the sentiment tree algorithm for the sentence "The keyboard is too slik.".

1. Create the sentiment tree for the sentence and fetch the node of the aspect term stem.
2. Traverse the tree from that node up to the root. The first non-neutral polarity on the path from the node to the root node is chosen.
3. If the algorithm reaches the root node without finding a non-neutral polarity, the aspect term is predicted as neutral.

Table 4: Results for term polarity.

Domain	Prec.	Rec.	F-measure	Accuracy
Laptop				0.52
- negative	0.31	0.79	0.45	
- neutral	0.33	0.09	0.15	
- positive	0.79	0.65	0.72	
Restaurant				0.62
- negative	0.35	0.78	0.48	
- neutral	0.25	0.05	0.08	
- positive	0.83	0.75	0.79	

Example 2 *Figure 1 illustrates the algorithm for the sentence "The keyboard is too slik.". The aspect term* keyboard *is underlined. The algorithm starts at the keyboard node (denoted with 1) and examines the parent node (2). Since the parent node has a neutral polarity, the root node needs to be examined (3). Due to the negative polarity of the root node, the aspect term keyboard is negative (4).*

The results of the algorithm with the test data set are shown in Table 4. We got quite good results for negative and positive aspect terms. But there are problems to predict neutral aspect terms, due to the fact that the sentiment tree rarely predicts neutral polarities. Overall our accuracy is nearly 10 percent points above the ABSA baselines.

4.3 Aspect category detection

This section describes the approach for the third subtask that identifies aspect categories discussed in a given sentence, using a predefined set of aspect categories, such as *food, service, ambience, price*, and *anecdotes/miscellaneous* as a neutral category. Our approach is twofold, depending on whether the sentence contains aspect terms or not.

Sentences with aspect terms. We illustrate our approach with the following example sentence.

Example 3 *Consider the sentence "Even though it is good seafood, the prices are too high." with the predefined aspects terms* seafood *and* price.

1. If the aspect term is a category, it can be directly assigned as a category. In this example the category *price* is present and will be assigned.

2. Dishes are very challenging to detect as an aspect term. For that problem we added a list of dishes scraped from Wikipedia to detect them. If a noun is not part of the list we search DuckDuckGo[2] for the description of that noun and check whether it is a dish. If it is a dish, then the category food is assigned.

3. For unassigned aspect terms, the similarity between aspect terms and all categories will be calculated. For this purpose, *RiTa.WordNet similarity* has been used. If the path length is smaller than 0.4 (with the help of the training data we experimentally determined the best comparison value) the aspect term is assigned to the category. In our example *seafood* is similar to *food* and therefore the category is *food*.

4. If no aspect category could be found, the category is *anecdotes/miscellaneous*.

[2]https://duckduckgo.com

Table 5: Result for category extraction.

Domain	Precision	Recall	F-measure
Restaurant	0.63	0.52	0.59

Sentences without aspect term. The third step from the previous approach is executed for all nouns in the sentence. But the threshold is decreased to 0.19 to reduce the number of recognized categories. If no similarity falls below the threshold, the category is *anecdotes/miscellaneous*.

The results of the third subtask are presented in Table 5. Although the presented results are moderately good, there exist some issues worth to be considered here: Using WordNet (Miller, 1995), it is only possible to find the similarity between two concepts and not a group of concepts. For example *Japanese Tapas* with *food* would not work. Furthermore, WordNet only recognizes the similarity between words of the same part of speech, it means many possible relations between verbs and nouns, and also adjectives and nouns are missing. Also, we were not able to calculate the similarity between a term and the default category.

4.4 Category polarity

This section describes the last subtask which aims to find the polarity of an aspect category for a given sentence. For the given aspect category which can be *food*, *service*, *ambience*, *price*, or *anecdotes/miscellaneous*, the task is to find its polarity. This subtask is applied only for the topic *restaurant*. The second and third subtask must have been solved since their evaluations are required to classify which aspect term belongs to which aspect category. In the third subtask all aspect terms are grouped in categories and in the second one the aspect terms are set with their polarities, which we use to calculate how many times a specific polarity is chosen under the same aspect category. Then we can assign a polarity to a specific aspect category. In order to find the polarities of an aspect category we carefully analyzed the training data and defined a set of rules to find all possible cases. We will discuss these rules in the following.

R4.1 If the aspect term polarities of the same category are equal, then their polarity is tagged as the category polarity.

Example 4 *"Prices are higher to dine in and their chicken tikka marsala is quite good." The found aspect terms in this sentence are* Prices *which is* negative *and* chicken tikka marsala *which is* positive. *Both aspect terms belong to different categories. The category* food *(chicken tikka marsala) is* positive *and the category* price *(Prices) is* negative.

R4.2 If one of the aspects of a specified category is neutral, it has no influence on the polarity of a category, as long as at least one other polarity exists. The polarities of all other aspect terms will determine the polarity of a specific category.

Example 5 *"Our server checked on us maybe twice during the entire meal." In this sentence the following aspect terms are found:* server *as* negative *and* meal *as* neutral. *Both aspect terms belong to the same category* service, *so the category* service *has the value* negative.

R4.3 If the aspect term polarities under a same category are both *positive* and *negative*, then the category polarity is tagged as *conflict*.

Example 6 *As an example consider the sentence: "The sweet lassi was excellent as was the lamb chettinad and the garlic naan but the rasamalai was forgettable." Here four aspect terms were found:* sweet lassi, lamb chettinad, *and* garlic naan *with* positive *polarities but* rasamalai *has a* negative *polarity. This results in a* conflict *polarity for the category* food.

R4.4 If the found category was annotated as *anecdotes/miscellaneous* but no aspect term was found in the second subtask, then we use the sentiment tree. It generates a specific polarity for the entire sentence which we define as the category's polarity.

Example 7 *The sentence: "A guaranteed delight!" has no aspect term. Using the sentiment tree the polarity for the category* anecdotes/miscellaneous *is* positive.

Table 6: Results for category polarity.

Domain	Prec.	Rec.	F-measure	Accuracy
Restaurant				0.63
- conflict	0.08	0.10	0.09	
- negative	0.45	0.73	0.56	
- neutral	0.24	0.17	0.20	
- positive	0.86	0.70	0.77	

We applied our approach on the training data. The results are shown in Table 6. We achieved an F-measure of 0.85 for the *positive* polarity. Our accuracy is 0.56 which is not a good achievement in comparison to other submissions in this subtask. The possible reason for this result could be that the first subtask also did not reach good accuracy measures.

5 Conclusion & future works

This paper describes our system to solve the individual subtasks by using the Stanford CoreNLP, RiTa.WordNet (Guerini et al., 2013) and a food database developed by ourselves. These libraries offer methods to classify sentences and determine the polarities.

Through the usage of the library based methods, it is not possible to take effect to the result. At this point other libraries such as NLTK[3] could help to increase it. They offer the possibility to train several classifiers with own data. But the classifier are not domain independent, because they need to be trained with sentences that belong to a specific domain, e.g. laptop or restaurant, in order to get the right polarity.

Our approach is more domain independent, because we do not need any domain to calculate the right polarities. That's why we can use our tool to process sentences of any domain, without further changing the algorithms.

In the future, we expect progress towards the following directions. First, we want to improve the identification of aspect terms which consist of more than two consecutive nouns. Second, we want to identify aspect terms which are not available as a part of the sentence. Finally, improvements to determine polarity of sentences with unclear context (i.e. the absence of adjectives).

[3] *http://www.nltk.org/*

References

Kushal Dave, Steve Lawrence, and David M. Pennock. 2003. Mining the peanut gallery: Opinion extraction and semantic classification of product reviews. In *WWW*, pages 519–528.

Marco Guerini, Lorenzo Gatti, and Marco Turchi. 2013. Sentiment analysis: How to derive prior polarities from SentiWordNet. In *EMNLP*, pages 1259–1269.

Minqing Hu and Bing Liu. 2004. Mining and summarizing customer reviews. In *KDD*, pages 168–177.

George A. Miller. 1995. WordNet: A lexical database for english. *Commun. ACM*, 38(11):39–41.

Bo Pang, Lillian Lee, and Shivakumar Vaithyanathan. 2002. Thumbs up? sentiment classification using machine learning techniques. In *EMNLP*, pages 79–86.

Benjamin Snyder and Regina Barzilay. 2007. Multiple aspect ranking using the Good Grief algorithm. In *HLT-NAACL*, pages 300–307.

Richard Socher, Alex Perelygin, Jean Y. Wu, Jason Chuang, Christopher D. Manning, Andrew Y. Ng, and Christopher Potts. 2013. Recursive deep models for semantic compositionality over a Sentiment Treebank. In *EMNLP*, pages 1631–1642.

Peter D. Turney. 2002. Thumbs up or thumbs down?: Semantic orientation applied to unsupervised classification of reviews. In *ACL*, pages 417–424.

IUCL: Combining Information Sources for SemEval Task 5

Alex Rudnick, Levi King, Can Liu, Markus Dickinson, Sandra Kübler
Indiana University
Bloomington, IN, USA
{alexr,leviking,liucan,md7,skuebler}@indiana.edu

Abstract

We describe the Indiana University system for SemEval Task 5, the L2 writing assistant task, as well as some extensions to the system that were completed after the main evaluation. Our team submitted translations for all four language pairs in the evaluation, yielding the top scores for English-German. The system is based on combining several information sources to arrive at a final L2 translation for a given L1 text fragment, incorporating phrase tables extracted from bitexts, an L2 language model, a multilingual dictionary, and dependency-based collocational models derived from large samples of target-language text.

1 Introduction

In the L2 writing assistant task, we must translate an L1 fragment in the midst of an existing, nearly complete, L2 sentence. With the presence of this rich target-language context, the task is rather different from a standard machine translation setting, and our goal with our design was to make effective use of the L2 context, exploiting collocational relationships between tokens anywhere in the L2 context and the proposed fragment translations.

Our system proceeds in several stages: (1) looking up or constructing candidate translations for the L1 fragment, (2) scoring candidate translations via a language model of the L2, (3) scoring candidate translations with a dependency-driven word similarity measure (Lin, 1998) (which we call *SIM*), and (4) combining the previous scores in a log-linear model to arrive at a final n-best list. Step 1 models transfer knowledge between the L1 and L2; step 2 models facts about the L2 syntax, *i.e.*, which translations fit well into the local context; step 3 models collocational and semantic tendencies of the L2; and step 4 gives different weights to each of the three sources of information. Although we did not finish step 3 in time for the official results, we discuss it here, as it represents the most novel aspect of the system – namely, steps towards the exploitation of the rich L2 context. In general, our approach is language-independent, with accuracy varying due to the size of data sources and quality of input technology (*e.g.*, syntactic parse accuracy). More features could easily be added to the log-linear model, and further explorations of ways to make use of target-language knowledge could be promising.

2 Data Sources

The data sources serve two major purposes for our system: For L2 candidate generation, we use Europarl and BabelNet; and for candidate ranking based on L2 context, we use Wikipedia and the Google Books Syntactic N-grams.

Europarl The Europarl Parallel Corpus (Europarl, v7) (Koehn, 2005) is a corpus of proceedings of the European Parliament, containing 21 European languages with sentence alignments. From this corpus, we build phrase tables for English-Spanish, English-German, French-English, Dutch-English.

BabelNet In the cases where the constructed phrase tables do not contain a translation for a source phrase, we need to back off to smaller phrases and find candidate translations for these components. To better handle sparsity, we extend look-up using the multilingual dictionary BabelNet, v2.0 (Navigli and Ponzetto, 2012) as a way to find translation candidates.

Proceedings of the 8th International Workshop on Semantic Evaluation (SemEval 2014), pages 356–360,
Dublin, Ireland, August 23-24, 2014.

Wikipedia For German and Spanish, we use recent Wikipedia dumps, which were converted to plain text with the Wikipedia Extractor tool.[1] To save time during parsing, sentences longer than 25 words are removed. The remaining sentences are POS-tagged and dependency parsed using Mate Parser with its pre-trained models (Bohnet, 2010; Bohnet and Kuhn, 2012; Seeker and Kuhn, 2013). To keep our English Wikipedia dataset to a manageable size, we choose an older (2006), smaller dump. Long sentences are removed, and the remaining sentences are POS-tagged and dependency parsed using the pre-trained Stanford Parser (Klein and Manning, 2003; de Marneffe et al., 2006). The resulting sizes of the datasets are (roughly): German: 389M words, 28M sentences; Spanish: 147M words, 12M sentences; English: 253M words, 15M sentences. Dependencies extracted from these parsed datasets serve as training for the SIM system described in section 3.3.

Google Books Syntactic N-grams For English, we also obtained dependency relationships for our word similarity statistics using the arcs dataset of the Google Books Syntactic N-Grams (Goldberg and Orwant, 2013), which has 919M items, each of which is a small "syntactic n-gram", a term Goldberg and Orwant use to describe short dependency chains, each of which may contain several tokens. This data set does not contain the actual parses of books from the Google Books corpus, but counts of these dependency chains. We converted the longer chains into their component $(head, dependent, label)$ triples and then collated these triples into counts, also for use in the SIM system.

3 System Design

As previously mentioned, at run-time, our system decomposes the fragment translation task into two parts: generating many possible candidate translations, then scoring and ranking them in the target-language context.

3.1 Constructing Candidate Translations

As a starting point, we use phrase tables constructed in typical SMT fashion, built with the training scripts packaged with Moses (Koehn et al., 2007). These scripts preprocess the bitext, estimate word alignments with GIZA++ (Och and Ney, 2000) and then extract phrases with the `grow-diag-final-and` heuristic.

At translation time, we look for the given source-language phrase in the phrase table, and if it is found, we take all translations of that phrase as our candidates.

When translating a phrase that is not found in the phrase table, we try to construct a "synthetic phrase" out of the available components. This is done by listing, combinatorially, all ways to decompose the L1 phrase into sub-phrases of at least one token long. Then for each decomposition of the input phrase, such that all of its components can be found in the phrase table, we generate a translation by concatenating their target-language sides. This approach naively assumes that generating valid L2 text requires no reordering of the components. Also, since there are 2^{n-1} possible ways to split an n-token phrase into sub-sequences (*i.e.*, each token is either the first token in a new sub-sequence, or it is not), we perform some heuristic pruning at this step, taking only the first 100 decompositions, preferring those built from longer phrase-table entries. Every phrase in the phrase table, including these synthetic phrases, has both a "direct" and "inverse" probability score; for synthetic phrases, we estimate these scores by taking the product of the corresponding probabilities for the individual components.

In the case that an individual word cannot be found in the phrase table, the system attempts to look up the word in BabelNet, estimating the probabilities as uniformly distributed over the available BabelNet entries. Thus, synthetic phrase table entries can be constructed by combining phrases found in the training data and words available in BabelNet.

For the evaluation, in cases where an L1 phrase contained words that were neither in our training data nor BabelNet (and thus were simply out-of-vocabulary for our system), we took the first translation for that phrase, without regard to context, from Google Translate, through the semi-automated Google Docs interface. This approach is not particularly scalable or reproducible, but simulates what a user might do in such a situation.

3.2 Scoring Candidate Translations via a L2 Language Model

To model how well a phrase fits into the L2 context, we score candidates with an n-gram lan-

[1] `http://medialab.di.unipi.it/wiki/Wikipedia_Extractor`

guage model (LM) trained on a large sample of target-language text. Constructing and querying a large language model is potentially computationally expensive, so here we use the KenLM Language Model Toolkit and its Python interface (Heafield, 2011). Here our models were trained on the Wikipedia text mentioned previously (without filtering long sentences), with KenLM set to 5-grams and the default settings.

3.3 Scoring Candidate Translations via Dependency-Based Word Similarity

The candidate ranking based on the n-gram language model – while quite useful – is based on very shallow information. We can also rank the candidate phrases based on how well each of the components fits into the L2 context using syntactic information. In this case, the fitness is measured in terms of dependency-based word similarity computed from dependency triples consisting of the the head, the dependent, and the dependency label. We slightly adapted the word similarity measure by Lin (1998):

$$SIM(w_1, w_2) = \frac{2 * c(h, d, l)}{c(h, -, l) + c(-, d, l)} \quad (1)$$

where $h = w_1$ and $d = w_2$ and $c(h, d, l)$ is the frequency with which a particular $(head, dependent, label)$ dependency triple occurs in the L2 corpus. $c(h, -, l)$ is the frequency with which a word occurs as a head in a dependency labeled l with any dependent. $c(-, d, l)$ is the frequency with which a word occurs as a dependent in a dependency labeled l with any head. In the measure by Lin (1998), the numerator is defined as the information of all dependency features that w_1 and w_2 share, computed as the negative sum of the log probability of each dependency feature. Similarly, the denominator is computed as the sum of information of dependency features for w_1 and w_2.

To compute the fitness of a word w_i for its context, we consider a set D of all words that are directly dependency-related to w_i. The fitness of w_i is thus computed as:

$$FIT(w_i) = \frac{\sum_{w_j}^{D} SIM(w_i, w_j)}{|D|} \quad (2)$$

The fitness of a phrase is the average word similarity over all its components. For example, the fitness of the phrase "eat with chopsticks" would be computed as:

$$FIT(\text{eat with chopsticks}) = \frac{FIT(\text{eat}) + FIT(\text{with}) + FIT(\text{chopsticks})}{3} \quad (3)$$

Since we consider the heads and dependents of a target phrase component, these may be situated inside or outside the phrase. Both cases are included in our calculation, thus enabling us to consider a broader, syntactically determined local context of the phrase. By basing the calculation on a single word's head and dependents, we attempt to avoid data sparseness issues that we might get from rare n-gram contexts.

Back-Off Lexical-based dependency triples suffer from data sparsity, so in addition to computing the lexical fitness of a phrase, we also calculate the POS fitness. For example, the POS fitness of "eat with chopsticks" would be computed as follows:

$$FIT(\text{eat/VBG with/IN chopsticks/NNS}) = \frac{FIT(\text{VBG}) + FIT(\text{IN}) + FIT(\text{NNS})}{3} \quad (4)$$

Storing and Caching The large vocabulary and huge number of combinations of our $(head, dependent, label)$ triples poses an efficiency problem when querying the dependency-based word similarity values. Thus, we stored the dependency triples in a database with a Python programming interface (SQLite3) and built database indices on the frequent query types. However, for frequently searched dependency triples, re-querying the database is still inefficient. Thus, we built a query cache to store the recently-queried triples. Using the database and cache significantly speeds up our system.

This database only stores dependency triples and their corresponding counts; the dependency-based similarity value is calculated as needed, for each particular context. Then, these FIT scores are combined with the scores from the phrase table and language model, using weights tuned by MERT.

system	acc	wordacc	oofacc	oofwordacc
run2	0.665	0.722	0.806	0.857
SIM	0.647	0.706	0.800	0.852
nb	0.657	0.717	0.834	0.868

Figure 1: Scores on the test set for English-German; here next-best is CNRC-run1.

system	acc	wordacc	oofacc	oofwordacc
run2	0.633	0.72	0.781	0.847
SIM	0.359	0.482	0.462	0.607
best	0.755	0.827	0.920	0.944

Figure 2: Scores on the test set for English-Spanish; here best is UEdin-run2.

system	acc	wordacc	oofacc	oofwordacc
run2	0.545	0.682	0.691	0.800
SIM	0.549	0.687	0.693	0.800
best	0.733	0.824	0.905	0.938

Figure 3: Scores on the test set for French-English; here best is UEdin-run1.

system	acc	wordacc	oofacc	oofwordacc
run2	0.544	0.679	0.634	0.753
SIM	0.540	0.676	0.635	0.753
best	0.575	0.692	0.733	0.811

Figure 4: Scores on the test set for Dutch-English; here best is UEdin-run1.

3.4 Tuning Weights with MERT

In order to rank the various candidate translations, we must combine the different sources of information in some way. Here we use a familiar log-linear model, taking the log of each score – the direct and inverse translation probabilities, the LM probability, and the surface and POS SIM scores – and producing a weighted sum. Since the original scores are either probabilities or probability-like (in the range $[0, 1]$), their logs are negative numbers, and at translation time we return the translation (or n-best) with the highest (least negative) score.

This leaves us with the question of how to set the weights for the log-linear model; in this work, we use the ZMERT package (Zaidan, 2009), which implements the MERT optimization algorithm (Och, 2003), iteratively tuning the feature weights by repeatedly requesting n-best lists from the system. We used ZMERT with its default settings, optimizing our system's BLEU scores on the provided development set. We chose, for convenience, BLEU as a stand-in for the word-level accuracy score, as BLEU scores are maximized when the system output matches the reference translations.

4 Experiments

In figures 1-4, we show the scores on this year's test set for running the two variations of our system: *run2*, the version without the SIM extensions, which we submitted for the evaluation, and *SIM*, with the extensions enabled. For comparison, we also include the best (or for English-German, next-best) submitted system. We see here that the use of the SIM features did not improve the performance of the base system, and in the case of English-Spanish caused significant degradation, which is as of yet unexplained, though we suspect difficulties parsing the Spanish test set, as for all of the other language pairs, the effects of adding SIM features were small.

5 Conclusion

We have described our entry for the initial running of the "L2 Writing Assistant" task and explained some possible extensions to our base log-linear model system.

In developing the SIM extensions, we faced some interesting software engineering challenges, and we can now produce large databases of dependency relationship counts for various languages. Unfortunately, these extensions have not yet led to improvements in performance on this particular task. The databases themselves seem at least intuitively promising, capturing interesting information about common usage patterns of the target language. Finding a good way to make use of this information may involve computing some measure that we have not yet considered, or perhaps the insights captured by SIM are covered effectively by the language model.

We look forward to future developments around this task and associated applications in helping language learners communicate effectively.

References

Bernd Bohnet and Jonas Kuhn. 2012. The best of both worlds – A graph-based completion model for transition-based parsers. In *Proceedings of the 13th Conference of the European Chapter of the Association for Computational Linguistics (EACL)*, pages 77–87, Avignon, France.

Bernd Bohnet. 2010. Top accuracy and fast dependency parsing is not a contradiction. In *Proceedings of the 23rd International Conference on Computational Linguistics (COLING)*, pages 89–97, Beijing, China.

Marie-Catherine de Marneffe, Bill MacCartney, and Christopher Manning. 2006. Generating typed dependency parses from phrase structure parses. In *Proceedings of LREC-06*, Genoa, Italy.

Yoav Goldberg and Jon Orwant. 2013. A dataset of syntactic-ngrams over time from a very large corpus of English books. In *Second Joint Conference on Lexical and Computational Semantics (*SEM)*, pages 241–247, Atlanta, GA.

Kenneth Heafield. 2011. KenLM: faster and smaller language model queries. In *Proceedings of the EMNLP 2011 Sixth Workshop on Statistical Machine Translation*, pages 187–197, Edinburgh, Scotland, United Kingdom, July.

Dan Klein and Christopher Manning. 2003. Accurate unlexicalized parsing. In *Proceedings of ACL-2003*, pages 423–430, Sapporo, Japan.

Philipp Koehn, Hieu Hoang, Alexandra Birch, Chris Callison-Burch, Marcello Federico, Nicola Bertoldi, Brooke Cowan, Wade Shen, Christine Moran, Richard Zens, Chris Dyer, Ondrej Bojar, Alexandra Constantin, and Evan Herbst. 2007. Moses: Open source toolkit for statistical machine translation. In *Proceedings of the 45th Annual Meeting of the Association for Computational Linguistics Companion Volume Proceedings of the Demo and Poster Sessions*, Prague, Czech Republic.

Philipp Koehn. 2005. Europarl: A parallel corpus for statistical machine translation. In *MT Summit*.

Dekang Lin. 1998. An information-theoretic definition of similarity. In *International Conference on Machine Learning (ICML)*, volume 98, pages 296–304.

Roberto Navigli and Simone Paolo Ponzetto. 2012. BabelNet: The automatic construction, evaluation and application of a wide-coverage multilingual semantic network. *Artificial Intelligence*, 193:217–250.

Franz Josef Och and Hermann Ney. 2000. Improved statistical alignment models. In *Proceedings of the 38th Annual Meeting of the Association for Computational Linguistics (ACL)*, pages 440–447, Hong Kong.

Franz Josef Och. 2003. Minimum error rate training in statistical machine translation. In *Proceedings of the 41st Annual Meeting of the Association for Computational Linguistics*, pages 160–167, Sapporo, Japan, July.

Wolfgang Seeker and Jonas Kuhn. 2013. Morphological and syntactic case in statistical dependency parsing. *Computational Linguistics*, 39(1):23–55.

Omar F. Zaidan. 2009. Z-MERT: A fully configurable open source tool for minimum error rate training of machine translation systems. *The Prague Bulletin of Mathematical Linguistics*, 91:79–88.

IxaMed: Applying Freeling and a Perceptron Sequential Tagger at the Shared Task on Analyzing Clinical Texts

Koldo Gojenola, Maite Oronoz, Alicia Pérez, Arantza Casillas

IXA Taldea (UPV-EHU)
maite.oronoz@ehu.es
http://ixa.si.ehu.es

Abstract

This paper presents the results of the *IxaMed* team at the SemEval-2014 Shared Task 7 on Analyzing Clinical Texts. We have developed three different systems based on: a) exact match, b) a general-purpose morphosyntactic analyzer enriched with the SNOMED CT terminology content, and c) a perceptron sequential tagger based on a Global Linear Model. The three individual systems result in similar f-score while they vary in their precision and recall. We have also tried direct combinations of the individual systems, obtaining considerable improvements in performance.

1 Introduction

This paper presents the results of the *IxaMed* team. The task is focused on the identification (Task A) and normalization (Task B) of diseases and disorders in clinical reports.

We have developed three different systems based on: a) exact match, b) a general-purpose morphosyntactic analyzer enriched with the SNOMED CT terminology content, and c) a perceptron sequential tagger based on a Global Linear Model. The first system can be seen as a baseline that can be compared with other approaches, while the other two represent two alternative approaches based on knowledge organized in dictionaries/ontologies and machine learning, respectively. We also tried direct combinations of the individual systems, obtaining considerable improvements in performance.

These approaches are representative of different solutions that have been proposed in the literature (Pradhan et al., 2013), which can be broadly classified in the following types:

- *Knowledge-based.* This approach makes use of large-scale dictionaries and ontologies, that are sometimes integrated in general tools adapted to the clinical domain, as MetaMap (Aronson and Lang, 2010) and cTAKES (Xia et al., 2013).
- *Rule-based.* For example, in (Wang and Akella, 2013) the authors show the use of a rule-based approach on the output of MetaMap.
- *Statistical techniques.* These systems take a training set as input and apply different variants of machine learning, such as sequential taggers based on hidden Markov models (HMMs) or conditional random fields (CRFs) (Zuccon et al., 2013; Bodnari et al., 2013; Gung, 2013; Hervas et al., 2013; Leaman et al., 2013).
- *Combinations.* These approaches try to take the advantages of different system types, using methods such as voting or metaclassifiers (Liu et al., 2013).

In the rest of the paper, we will first introduce the different systems that we have developed in section 2, presenting the main results in section 3, and ending with the main conclusions.

2 System Description

The task of detecting diseases and their corresponding concept unique identifiers (CUI) has been faced using three methods that are described in the following subsections.

2.1 Exact Match

The system based on Exact Match (EM) simply obtained a list of terms and their corresponding

Proceedings of the 8th International Workshop on Semantic Evaluation (SemEval 2014), pages 361–365,
Dublin, Ireland, August 23-24, 2014.

CUI identifier from the training set and marked any appearance of those terms in the evaluation set. This simple method was improved with some additional extensions:

- *Improving precision*. In order to reduce the number of false positives (FP), we applied first the EM system to the training set itself. This process helped to measure FPs, for example, *blood* gave 184 FPs and 2 true positives (TPs). For the sake of not hurting the recall, we allowed the system to detect only those terms where $TP > FP$, that is, "blood" would not be classified as disorder.

- *Treatment of discontinuous terms*. For these terms, our system performed a soft-matching comparison allowing a limited variation for the text comprised between the term elements (for example "***right atrium*** *is mildly/moderately* ***dilated***"). These patterns were tuned manually.

2.2 Adapting Freeling to the Medical Domain

Freeling is an open-source multilingual language processing library providing a wide range of analyzers for several languages (Padró et al., 2010), Spanish and English among others. We had already adapted Freeling to the medical domain in Spanish (Oronoz et al., 2013), so we used our previous experience to adapt the English version to the same domain. For the sake of clarity, we will refer to this system as FreeMed henceforth.

The linguistic resources (lexica, grammars,...) in Freeling can be modified, so we took advantage of this flexibility extending two standard Freeling dictionaries: a basic dictionary of terms consisting of a unique word, and a multiword-term dictionary. Both of them were enriched with a dictionary of medical abbreviations[1] and with the Systematized Nomenclature of Medicine Clinical Terms (SNOMED CT) version dated 31st of July of 2013. In addition to the changes in the lexica, we added regular expressions in the tokenizer to recognize medical terms as *"Alzheimer's disease"* as a unique term.

In our approach, the system distinguishes between morphology and syntax on one side and semantics on the other side. First, on the morphosyntactic processing, our system only categorizes word-forms using their basic part-of-speech (POS) categories. Next, the semantic distinctions are applied (the identification of the term as substance, disorder, procedure,...). Following this approach, whenever the specific term on the new domain (biomedicine in this case) was already in Freeling's standard dictionaries, the specific entries will not be added to the lexicon. Instead, medical meanings are added in a later semantic tagging stage. For example: the widely used term *"fever"*, as common noun, was not added to the lexicon but its semantic class is given in a second stage. Only very specific terms not appearing in the lexica as, for instance, *"diskospondylitis"* were inserted. This solution helps to avoid an explosion of ambiguity in the morphosyntactic analysis and, besides, it enables a clear separation between morphosyntax and semantics.

In figure 1 the results of both levels of analysis, morphosyntactic and semantic, are shown. The linguistic and medical information of medical texts is stored in the Kyoto Annotation Format or KAF (Bosma et al., 2009) that is based in the eXtended Markup Language (XML). In this example the term *aneurysm* is analyzed as NN (meaning noun) and it is semantically categorized as *morphological abnormality* and *disorder*.

SNOMED CT is part of the Metathesaurus, one of the elements of the Unified Medical Language System (UMLS). We used the Metathesaurus vocabulary database to extract the mapping between SNOMED CT's concept identifiers and their corresponding UMLS's concept unique identifier (CUI). All the medical terms appearing in SNOMED CT and analyzed with FreeMed are tagged with both identifiers. For instance, the term *aneurysm* in figure 1 has the *85659009* SNOMED CT identifier when the term is classified in the *morphological abnormality* content hierarchy and the *432119003* identifier as *disorder*. Both are linked to the same concept identifier, *C0002940*, in UMLS. This mapping has been used for Task B, whenever the CUI is the same in all the analysis of the same term.

All the terms from all the 19 content hierarchies of SNOMED CT were tagged with semantic information in the provided texts.

The training corpus was linguistically analyzed and its format was changed from XML to the format specified at the shared task. After a manual inspection of the results and the Gold Standard, some selection of terms was performed:

[1] http://www.jdmd.com/abbreviations-glossary.asp

```
<term tid="t241" lemma="aneurysm" pos="NN">
 <extRefs>
  <extRef resource="SCT_20130731" reference="85659009"
    reftype="morphologic_abnormality" >
   <extRef resource="UMLS-2010AB" reference="C0002940"/ >
  </extRef>
  <extRef resource="SCT_20130731" reference="432119003"
    reftype="disorder" >
   <extRef resource="UMLS-2010AB" reference="C0002940"/>
  </extRef>
 </extRefs>
</term>
```

Figure 1: Analysis with augmented information.

- *Selection and combination of semantic classes.* All the terms from the *disorder* semantic class (for example *"Hypothyroidism"*) and from the *finding* class (for instance *"headache"*) are chosen, as well as some tag combinations (see figure 1). After analyzing the train corpus we decided to join into a unique term a *body structure* immediately followed by a *disorder/finding*. In this way, we identify terms as *"MCA aneurysm"* that are composed of the *MCA* abbreviation (meaning *"middle cerebral artery"*) and the inmediately following *"aneurysm"* disorder.

- *Filtering.* Not all the terms from the mentioned SNOMED CT hierarchies are identified as disorders in the Gold Standard. Some terms are discarded following these criteria: i) findings describing personal situations (e.g. *"alcoholic"*), ii) findings describing current situations (e.g. *"awake"*), iii) findings with words indicating a negation or normal situation (e.g. *"stable blood pressure"*) and iv) too general terms (e.g. *"problems"*).

The medical terms indicating disorders that are linked to more than one CUI identifier, were tagged as *CUI-less*. That is, we did not perform any CUI disambiguation.

In subsequent iterations and after analyzing our misses, new terms and term variations (Hina et al., 2013) are added to the lexica in Freeling with the restriction that, at least, one synonym should appear in SNOMED CT. Thus, equivalent forms were created for all the terms indicating a *cancer*, a *tumor*, a *syndrome*, or a specific *disease*. For instance, variants for the term *"cancer of colon"* and with the same SNOMED CT concept identifier (number 363406005) are created with the forms *"colon cancer"*, *"cancer of the colon"* and *"cancer in colon"*. Some abbreviation variations found in the Gold Standard are added in the lexica too, following the same criteria.

2.3 Perceptron Sequential Tagger

This system uses a Global Linear Model (GLM), a sequential tagger using the perceptron algorithm (Collins, 2002), that relies on Viterbi decoding of training examples combined with simple additive updates. The algorithm is competitive to other options such as maximum-entropy taggers or CRFs.

The original textual files are firstly processed by FreeMed, and then the tagger uses all the available information to assign tags to the text. Each token contains information about the word form, lemma, part of speech, and SNOMED CT category.

Our GLM system only deals with Task A, and it will not tackle the problem of concept normalization, due to time constraints. In this respect, for Task B the GLM system will simply return the first SNOMED CT category given by FreeMed. This does not mean that GLM and FreeMed will give the same result for Task B, as the GLM system first categorizes each element as a disease, and it gives a CUI only when that element is identified.

2.4 Combinations

The previous subsections presented three different approaches to the problem that obtain comparable scores (see table 1). In the area of automatic tagging, there are several works that combine disparate systems, usually getting good results. For this reason, we tried the simplest approach of merging the outputs of the three individual systems into a single file.

3 Results

Table 1 presents the results of the individual and combined systems on the development set. Looking at the individual systems on Task A, we can see that all of them obtain a similar f-score, although there are important differences in terms of precision and recall. Contrary to our initial intuition, the FreeMed system, based on dictionaries and ontologies, gives the best precision and the lowest recall. In principle, having SNOMED CT as a base, we could expect that the coverage would be more complete (attaining the highest recall). However, the results show that there is a gap between the writing of the standard SNOMED CT terms and the terms written by doctors in their notes. On the other hand, the sequential tagger gives the best re-

System	Task A Strict Precision	Task A Strict Recall	Task A Strict F-Score	Task A Relaxed Precision	Task A Relaxed Recall	Task A Relaxed F-Score	Task B Strict Accuracy	Task B Relaxed Accuracy
INDIVIDUAL SYSTEMS								
Exact Match (EM)	0.804	0.505	0.620	**0.958**	0.604	0.740	**0.479**	**0.948**
FreeMed	**0.822**	0.501	0.622	0.947	0.578	0.718	0.240	0.479
GLM	0.715	**0.570**	**0.634**	0.908	**0.735**	**0.813**	0.298	0.522
COMBINATIONS								
FreeMed + EM	**0.766**	0.652	**0.704**	**0.936**	0.754	0.835	**0.556**	0.855
FreeMed + GLM	0.689	0.668	0.678	0.903	0.790	0.843	0.345	0.518
EM + GLM	0.680	0.679	0.679	0.907	0.819	0.861	0.398	**0.598**
FreeMed + EM + GLM	0.659	**0.724**	0.690	0.899	**0.845**	**0.871**	0.421	0.584

Table 1: Results of the different systems on the development set.

System	Task A Strict Precision	Task A Strict Recall	Task A Strict F-Score	Task A Relaxed Precision	Task A Relaxed Recall	Task A Relaxed F-Score	Task B Strict Accuracy	Task B Relaxed Accuracy
FreeMed + EM	**0.729**	0.701	0.715	**0.885**	0.808	0.845	**0.604**	**0.862**
FreeMed + EM + GLM	0.681	**0.786**	**0.730**	0.872	**0.890**	**0.881**	0.439	0.558
Best system	**0.843**	**0.786**	**0.813**	**0.936**	**0.866**	**0.900**	**0.741**	**0.873**

Table 2: Results on the test set.

call. Since the tagger uses both contextual words and prefixes and suffixes as features for learning, this method has proven helpful for the recognition of terms that do not appear in the training data (see the difference with the EM approach).

Looking at the different combinations in table 1, we see that two approaches work best, either combining FreeMed and EM, or combining the three individual systems. The inclusion of GLM results in the best coverage, but at the expense of precision. On the other hand, combining FreeMed and EM gives a better precision but lower coverage. As pointed out by Collins (2002), the results of the perceptron tagger are competitive with respect to other statistical approaches such as CRFs (Zuccon et al., 2013; Bodnari et al., 2013; Gung, 2013; Hervas et al., 2013; Leaman et al., 2013).

Regarding Task B, we can see that the EM system is by far the most accurate, while FreeMed is well below its a priori potential. The reason of this low result is mainly due to the high ambiguity found on the output of the SNOMED CT tagger, as many terms are associated with more than one CUI and, consequently, are left untagged. This problem deserves future work on automatic semantic disambiguation. On the combinations, FreeMed and EM together give the best result. However, as we told before, the GLM system was only trained for Task A, so it is not surprising to see that its results deteriorate the accuracy in Task B.

We chose these best two combinations for the evaluation on the test set (using training and development for experimentation or training), which are presented in table 2. Here we can see that results on the development also hold on the test set.

Given the unsophisticated approach to combine the systems, we can figure out more elaborated solutions, such as majority or weighted voting, or even more, the definition of a machine learning classifier to select the best system for every proposed term. These ideas are left for future work.

4 Conclusions

We have presented the IxaMed approach, composed of three systems that are based on exact match, linguistic and knowledge repositories, and a statistical tagger, respectively. The results of individual systems are comparable, with differences in precision and recall. We also tested a simple combination of the systems, which proved to give significant improvements over each individual system. The results are competitive, although still far from the winning system.

For future work, we plan to further improve the individual systems. Besides, we hope that the experimentation with new combination approaches will offer room for improvement.

Acknowledgements

This work was partially supported by the European Commission (325099 and SEP-210087649), the Spanish Ministry of Science and Innovation (TIN2012-38584-C06-02) and the Industry of the Basque Government (IT344-10).

References

Alan R Aronson and Francois-Michel Lang. 2010. An overview of MetaMap: historical perspective and recent advances. *Journal of the American Medical Informatics Association (JAMIA)*, 17:229–236.

Andreea Bodnari, Louise Deleger, Thomas Lavergne, Aurelie Neveol, and Pierre Zweigenbaum. 2013. A Supervised Named-Entity Extraction System for Medical Text. In *Online Working Notes of the CLEF 2013 Evaluation Labs and Workshop*, September.

Wauter Bosma, Piek Vossen, Aitor Soroa, German Rigau, Maurizio Tesconi, Andrea Marchetti, Monica Monachini, and Carlo Aliprandi. 2009. KAF: a Generic Semantic Annotation Format. In *Proceedings of the 5th International Conference on Generative Approaches to the Lexicon GL*, pages 17–19, Septembre.

Michael Collins. 2002. Discriminative Training Methods for Hidden Markov Models: Theory and Experiments with Perceptron Algorithms. In *Proceedings of the 2002 Conference on Empirical Methods in Natural Language Processing*, pages 1–8. Association for Computational Linguistics, July.

James Gung. 2013. Using Relations for Identification and Normalization of Disorders: Team CLEAR in the ShARe/CLEF 2013 eHealth Evaluation Lab. In *Online Working Notes of the CLEF 2013 Evaluation Labs and Workshop*, September.

Lucia Hervas, Victor Martinez, Irene Sanchez, and Alberto Diaz. 2013. UCM at CLEF eHealth 2013 Shared Task1. In *Online Working Notes of the CLEF 2013 Evaluation Labs and Workshop*, September.

Saman Hina, Eric Atwell, and Owen Johnson. 2013. SnoMedTagger: A semantic tagger for medical narratives. In *Conference on Intelligent Text Processing and Computational Linguistics (CICLING)*.

Robert Leaman, Ritu Khare, and Zhiyong Lu. 2013. NCBI at 2013 ShARe/CLEF eHealth Shared Task: Disorder Normalization in Clinical Notes with Dnorm. In *Online Working Notes of the CLEF 2013 Evaluation Labs and Workshop*, September.

Hongfang Liu, Kavishwar Wagholikar, Siddhartha Jonnalagadda, and Sunghwan Sohn. 2013. Integrated cTAKES for Concept Mention Detection and Normalization. In *Online Working Notes of the CLEF 2013 Evaluation Labs and Workshop*, September.

Maite Oronoz, Arantza Casillas, Koldo Gojenola, and Alicia Perez. 2013. Automatic Annotation of Medical Records in Spanish with Disease, Drug and Substance Names. In *Lecture Notes in Computer Science, 8259. Progress in Pattern Recognition, ImageAnalysis, ComputerVision, and Applications 18th Iberoamerican Congress, CIARP 2013, Havana, Cuba*, November 20-23.

Lluis Padró, Samuel Reese, Eneko Agirre, and Aitor Soroa. 2010. Semantic Services in Freeling 2.1: WordNet and UKB. In *Global Wordnet Conference*, Mumbai, India.

Sameer Pradhan, Noemie Elhadad, Brett R. South, David Martinez, Lee Christensen, Amy Vogel, Hanna Suominen, Wendy W. Chapman, and Guergana Savova. 2013. Task 1: ShARe/CLEF eHealth Evaluation Lab 2013. In *Online Working Notes of the CLEF 2013 Evaluation Labs and Workshop*, September.

Chunye Wang and Ramakrishna Akella. 2013. UCSCs System for CLEF eHealth 2013 Task 1. In *Online Working Notes of the CLEF 2013 Evaluation Labs and Workshop*, September.

Yunqing Xia, Xiaoshi Zhong, Peng Liu, Cheng Tan, Sen Na, Qinan Hu, and Yaohai Huang. 2013. Combining MetaMap and cTAKES in Disorder Recognition: THCIB at CLEF eHealth Lab 2013 Task 1. In *Online Working Notes of the CLEF 2013 Evaluation Labs and Workshop*, September.

Guido Zuccon, Alexander Holloway, Bevan Koopman, and Anthony Nguyen. 2013. Identify Disorders in Health Records using Conditional Random Fields and Metamap AEHRC at ShARe/CLEF 2013 eHealth Evaluation Lab Task 1. In *Online Working Notes of the CLEF 2013 Evaluation Labs and Workshop*, September.

JOINT_FORCES: Unite Competing Sentiment Classifiers with Random Forest

Oliver Dürr, Fatih Uzdilli, and Mark Cieliebak
Zurich University of Applied Sciences
Winterthur, Switzerland
{dueo, uzdi, ciel}@zhaw.ch

Abstract

In this paper, we describe how we created a meta-classifier to detect the message-level sentiment of tweets. We participated in SemEval-2014 Task 9B by combining the results of several existing classifiers using a random forest. The results of 5 other teams from the competition as well as from 7 general-purpose commercial classifiers were used to train the algorithm. This way, we were able to get a boost of up to 3.24 F_1 score points.

1 Introduction

The interest in sentiment analysis grows as publicly available text content grows. As one of the most used social media platforms, Twitter provides its users a unique way of expressing themselves. Thus, sentiment analysis of tweets has become a hot research topic among academia and industry.

In this paper, we describe our approach of combining multiple sentiment classifiers into a meta-classifier. The introduced system participated in SemEval-2014 Task 9: "Sentiment Analysis in Twitter, Subtask–B Message Polarity Classification" (Rosenthal et al., 2014). The goal was to classify a tweet on the message level using the three classes positive, negative, and neutral. The performance is measured using the macro-averaged F_1 score of the positive and negative classes which is simply named "F_1 score" throughout the paper. An almost identical task was already run in 2013 (Nakov et al., 2013).

The tweets for training and development were only provided as tweet ids. A fraction (10-15%) of the tweets was no longer available on twitter, which makes the results of the competition not fully comparable. For testing, in addition to last year's data (tweets and SMS) new tweets and data from a surprise domain (LiveJournal) were provided. An overview of the provided data is shown in Table 1.

Using additional manually labelled data for training the algorithm was not allowed for a "constrained" submission. Submissions using additional data for training were marked as "unconstrained".

Dataset	Total	Pos	Neg	Neu
Training (Tweets)	8224	3058	1210	3956
Dev (Tweets)	1417	494	286	637
Test: Twitter2013	3813	1572	601	1640
Test: SMS2013	2093	492	394	1207
Test: Twitter2014	1853	982	202	669
Test: Twitter'14Sarcasm	86	33	40	13
Test: LiveJournal2014	1142	427	304	411

Table 1: Number of Documents we were able to download for Training, Development and Testing.

Our System. The results of 5 other teams from the competition as well as from 7 general-purpose commercial classifiers were used to train our algorithm. Scientific subsystems were s_gez (Gezici et al., 2013), s_jag (Jaggi et al., 2014), s_mar (Marchand et al., 2013), s_fil (Filho and Pardo, 2013), s_gun (Günther and Furrer, 2013). They are all "constrained" and machine learning-based, some with hybrid rule-based approaches. Commercial subsystems were provided by

Proceedings of the 8th International Workshop on Semantic Evaluation (SemEval 2014), pages 366–369, Dublin, Ireland, August 23-24, 2014.

Lymbix (c_lym), MLAnalyzer[1] (c_mla), Semantria (c_sem), Sentigem (c_snt), Syttle (c_sky), Text-Processing.com (c_txp), and Webknox (c_web). Subsystems c_txp and c_web are machine learning-based, c_sky is rule-based, and m_mla is a mix (other tools unknown). All subsystems were designed to handle tweets and further text types.

Our submission included a subset of all classifiers including unconstrained ones, leading to an unconstrained submission. The 2014 winning team obtained an F_1 score of 70.96 on the Twitter2014 test set. Our approach was ranked on the 12th place out of the 50 participating submissions, with an F_1 score of 66.79. Our further rankings were 12th on the LiveJournal data, 12th on the SMS data, 12th on Twitter-2013, and 26th on Twitter Sarcasm.

Improvement. Although our meta-classifier did not reach a top position in the competition, we were able to beat even the best single subsystem it was based on for almost all test sets (except sarcasm). In previous research we showed that same behaviour on different systems and data sets (Cieliebak et al., 2014). This shows that also other systems from the competition, even best ones, probably can be improved using our approach.

2 Approach

Meta-Classifier. A meta-classifier is an approach to predict a classification given the individual results of other classifiers by combining them. A robust classifier, which can naturally handle categorical input such as sentiments by design, is the random forest classifier (Breiman, 2001). The algorithm uses the outputs of individual classifiers as features and the labels on the training data as input for training. Afterwards, in the test phase, the random forest makes predictions using the outputs of the same individual classifiers. We use the random forest implementation of the R-package "randomForest" and treat the three votes (negative, neutral, positive) as categorical input.

Training Data. To build a meta-classifier, first, one has to train all the subsystems with a dataset. Second, the meta-classifier has to be trained based on the output of the subsystems with a different dataset than the one used for training the subsystems. We decided to take the natural split of the data provided by the organizers (see Table 1). For the scientific subsystems we used the Training set to train on; for training the random forest classifier we used the Dev set. The commercial systems were used "as-is", in particular, we did not train them on any of the provided data sets. Table 2 shows the performance of the individual subsystems on the different data sets.

ID	**Dev**	**SMS2013**	**Twitter2013**	**Twitter2014**	**Sarcasm2014**	**LiveJournal2014**
s_gez	32.22	31.23	30.77	28.57	**51.57**	50.83
s_jag	61.47	56.17	60.21	62.73	44.26	63.91
s_mar	28.95	22.94	26.68	22.86	31.01	24.47
s_fil	52.88	49.94	55.61	55.08	38.22	56.41
s_gun	**63.93**	**61.51**	**65.33**	**65.09**	48.80	**68.91**
c_lym	48.38	44.40	48.68	54.17	34.87	58.71
c_mla	49.79	46.41	50.17	47.74	43.16	59.02
c_sma	55.89	52.26	56.15	53.51	49.33	56.53
c_sky	56.30	52.04	54.67	56.28	40.60	54.61
c_txp	43.69	46.47	41.15	44.00	**59.74**	56.57
c_web	47.44	41.64	45.21	48.83	45.25	53.45
c_snt	**56.86**	**58.42**	**62.17**	**58.35**	36.08	**65.74**

Table 2: F_1 scores of the individual systems. Bold shows the best commercial or scientific system per data set; grey cells indicates the overall maximum.

3 Experiments

There exist three obvious selections of subsystems for our meta-classifier: all subsystems, only scientific subsystems, and only commercial subsystems (called All_Subsystems, All_Scientific, and All_Commercial, respectively). Table 3 shows performance of these selections of subsystems on the data sets. For comparison, the table shows also the performance of the overall best individual subsystem in the first row. It turns out that All_Subsystems is almost always better than the best individual subsystem, while the other two meta-classifiers are inferior.

Testing All Subsets. We performed a systematic evaluation on how the performance depends on the choice of a particular selection of individual subsystems. This resembles feature selection, which is a common task in machine learning, and

[1] mashape.com/mlanalyzer/ml-analyzer

	Dev (OOB)	SMS2013	Twitter2013	Twitter2014	Twitter2014 Sarcasm	LiveJournal2014
Best Individual	*63.93*	*61.51*	*65.33*	*65.09*	*48.80*	*68.91*
All_Subsystems	63.54	**64.22**	67.03	67.70	**46.37**	71.11
All_Scientific	64.52	60.42	64.54	64.99	43.35	67.86
All_Commercial	62.11	58.34	60.70	63.86	44.85	65.57
Max_OOB_Subset	**68.27**	63.02	**67.49**	**68.33**	45.40	**71.43**
Our Submission	65.00	62.20	66.61	66.79	45.40	70.02

Table 3: Performance (in F1 score) of meta-classifiers with different subsystems. The subset used in our submission is composed of s_gez, s_jag, s_mar, s_fil, s_gun, c_sma, c_sky, c_snt. "Max_OOB_Subset" is composed of s_jag, s_mar, s_gun, c_lym, c_sma, c_sky, c_txp. Bold shows best result per data set. The first row shows results of the best individual subsystem.

As a general trend we see that the performance increases with the number of classifiers; however, there exist certain subsets which perform better than using all available classifiers.

Best Subset Selection. In Figure 1, we marked for each number of subsystems the highest OOB-F_1-Score on the Dev set by a diamond. In addition, the subset with the overall highest OOB-F_1-Score, consisting of 7 classifiers, is displayed as a filled diamond.

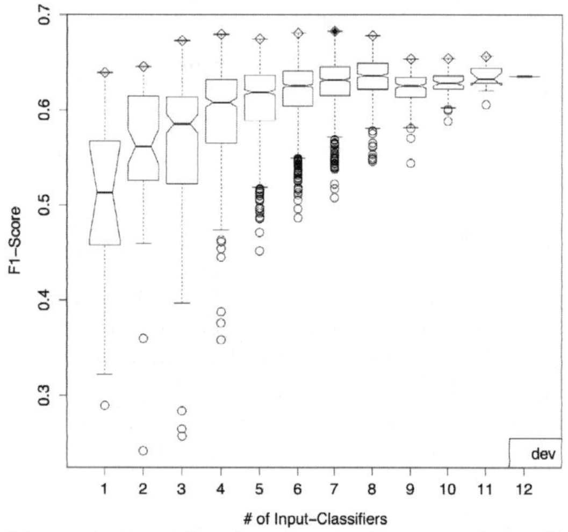

Figure 1: Box Plot showing the F_1 scores (out-of-bag) for all subsets on the Dev set. Diamonds mark the best combination of classifiers for the corresponding number.

We also evaluated the performance of these "best" subsets on other unseen test data. In Figure 2, we show the results of the test set Twitter2014. The scores for the very subsets marked in Figure 1 are displayed in the same way here.

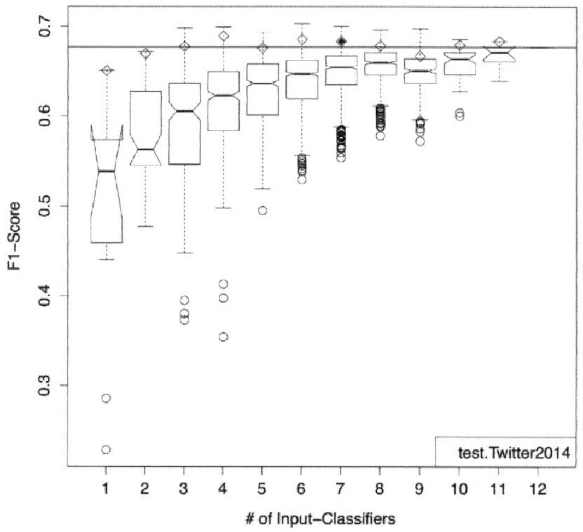

Figure 2: F_1 scores of all subsets on the Twitter2014 test set.

For comparison, we marked the performance of the system with all classifiers by a straight line. We find that all subsets that are "best" on the Dev set perform very well on the Twitter2014 set. In fact, some even beat the system with all classifiers. Similar behaviour can be observed for Twitter2013 and LiveJournal2014 (data not shown), while All_Subsets yields significantly superior results on SMS2013 (see Figure 3). No conclusive observation is possible for Sarcasm2014 (data not shown).

To elucidate on the question whether to use a subset with the highest OOB-F_1 on the Dev set (called Max_OOB_Subset) or to use all available classifiers, we show in Table 3 the performance of these systems on all test sets in rows 2 and 5, respectively. Since All_Systems is in 2 out of 5 cases the best classifier, and "Max_OOB_Subset" in 3 out of 5 cases, a decisive answer cannot be drawn. However, we find that All_Systems generalizes better to foreign types of data, while Max_OOB_Subset performs well on similar data (in this case, tweets).

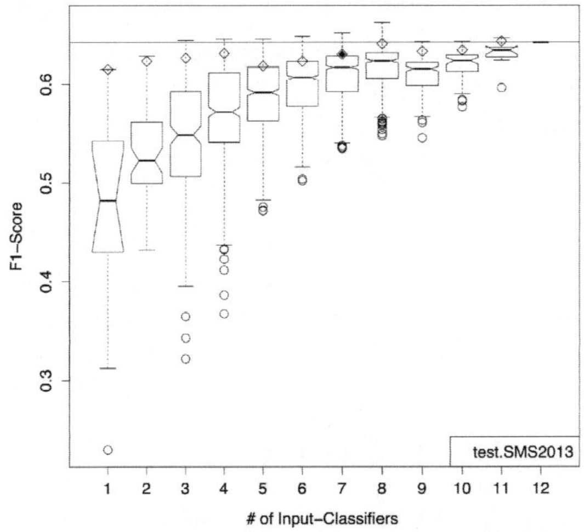

Figure 3: F_1 score of all subsets on the SMS2013 test set.

4 Conclusion

We have shown that a meta-classifier approach using random forest can beat the performance of the individual sentiment classifiers it is based on. Typically, the more subsystems are used, the better the performance. However, there exist selections of only few subsystems that perform comparable to using all subsystems. In fact, a good selection strategy is to select the subset which has maximum out-of-bag F_1 score on the training data. This subset performs slightly better than All_Systems on similar data sets, and only slightly worse on new types of data. Advantage of this subset is that it requires less classifiers (7 instead of 12 in our case), which reduces the cost (runtime or license fees) of the meta-classifier.

5 Acknowledgements

We would like to thank all system providers for giving us the opportunity to use their systems for this evaluation, and especially Tobias Günther and Martin Jaggi for carefully reading the manuscript.

References

Leo Breiman. 2001. Random Forests. Machine Learning 45(1), 5-32.

Mark Cieliebak, Oliver Dürr, Fatih Uzdilli. 2014. Meta-Classifiers Easily Improve Commercial Sentiment Detection Tools. In *Proceedings of the 9th edition of the Language Resources and Evaluation Conference* (LREC), pages 3100-3104, May 26-31, 2014, Reykjavik, Iceland.

Pedro P. Balage Filho, Thiago A. S. Pardo. 2013. NILC USP: A Hybrid System for Sentiment Analysis in Twitter Messages. In *Proceedings of the International Workshop on Semantic Evaluation* (SemEval-2013), pages 568-572, June 14-15, 2013, Atlanta, Georgia, USA.

Gizem Gezici, Rahim Dehkharghani, Berrin Yanikoglu, Dilek Tapucu, Yucel Saygin. 2013. SU-Sentilab: A Classification System for Sentiment Analysis in Twitter. In *Proceedings of the International Workshop on Semantic Evaluation* (SemEval-2013), pages 471-477, June 14-15, 2013, Atlanta, Georgia, USA.

Tobias Günther, Lenz Furrer. 2013. GU-MLT-LT: Sentiment Analysis of Short Messages using Linguistic Features and Stochastic Gradient Descent. In *Proceedings of the International Workshop on Semantic Evaluation* (SemEval-2013), pages 328-332, June 14-15, 2013, Atlanta, Georgia, USA.

Martin Jaggi, Fatih Uzdilli, and Mark Cieliebak. 2014. Swiss-Chocolate: Sentiment Detection using Sparse SVMs and Part-Of-Speech n-Grams. In *Proceedings of the International Workshop on Semantic Evaluation* (SemEval-2014), August 23-24, 2014, Dublin, Ireland.

Morgane Marchand, Alexandru Ginsca, Romaric Besançon, Olivier Mesnard. 2013. [LVIC-LIMSI]: Using Syntactic Features and Multi-polarity Words for Sentiment Analysis in Twitter. In *Proceedings of the International Workshop on Semantic Evaluation* (SemEval-2013), pages 418-424, June 14-15, 2013, Atlanta, Georgia, USA.

Sara Rosenthal, Preslav Nakov, Alan Ritter, and Veselin Stoyanov. 2014. SemEval-2014 Task 9: Sentiment Analysis in Twitter. In *Proceedings of the International Workshop on Semantic Evaluation* (SemEval-2014), August 23-24, 2014, Dublin, Ireland.

Preslav Nakov, Sara Rosenthal, Zornitsa Kozareva, Veselin Stoyanov, Alan Ritter, Theresa Wilson. 2013. SemEval-2013 Task 2: Sentiment Analysis in Twitter. In *Proceedings of the International Workshop on Semantic Evaluation* (SemEval-2013), pages 312-320, June 14-15, 2013, Atlanta, Georgia, USA.

JU_CSE: A Conditional Random Field (CRF) Based Approach to Aspect Based Sentiment Analysis

Braja Gopal Patra, Soumik Mandal, Dipankar Das and Sivaji Bandyopadhyay
Department of Computer Science & Engineering,
Jadavpur University, Kolkata, India
brajagopal.cse@gmail.com, mandal.soumik@gmail.com,
dipankar.dipnil2005@gmail.com, sivaji_cse_ju@yahoo.com

Abstract

The fast upswing of online reviews and their sentiments on the Web became very useful information to the people. Thus, the opinion/sentiment mining has been adopted as a subject of increasingly research interest in the recent years. Being a participant in the Shared Task Challenge, we have developed a Conditional Random Field based system to accomplish the Aspect Based Sentiment Analysis task. The *aspect term* in a sentence is defined as the target entity. The present system identifies *aspect term*, *aspect categories* and their sentiments from the *Laptop* and *Restaurants* review datasets provided by the organizers.

1 Introduction

In recent times, the research activities in the areas of Opinion Mining/Sentiment Analysis in natural language texts and other media are gaining ground under the umbrella of subjectivity analysis and affect computing[1]. The reason may be the huge amount of available text data in Social Web in the forms of news, reviews, blogs, chat and twitter etc. Majority of research efforts are being carried out for the identification of *positive* or *negative* polarity from the textual contents like sentence, paragraph, or text span regardless of the entities (e.g., *laptops*, *restaurants*) and their aspects (e.g., *battery*, *screen*; *food*, *service*).

Aspect is a multinomial distribution over words that represent a more specific topic in reviews (Jo and Oh, 2011). For example, in case of *Laptop* reviews, "*touchpad*" is considered an aspect. Similarly, given a predefined entity, an *aspect term* describes a specific aspect of that entity (e.g., for the entity "*restaurant*", "*wine*" can be an *aspect term*). *Aspect term* can be appeared as a single word (e.g., "*menu*") or multiple words ("*side dish*").

It is observed that for a particular entity, one or more number of *aspect terms* can be grouped into a single category (e.g., *aspect terms* "*drinks*", "*main course*" belongs to the same category, "*food*").

The main goal of the Aspect Based Sentiment Analysis (ABSA) (Pontiki et al., 2014) task is to identify the *aspect terms* and their categories from the given target entities as well as to identify the sentiments expressed towards each of the *aspect terms*. The datasets provided by the shared task organizers consist of customer reviews with human-annotations.

We have participated in all of the four tasks. A combination of Conditional Random Field (CRF) based machine learning algorithm and rule based techniques has been adopted for identifying the *aspect term*, *aspect category* and their sentiments. We have used several features like Part of Speech (POS), Stanford dependency relations[2], WordNet information, and sentiment lexicon (SentiWordNet[3]) to accomplish these tasks.

The rest of the paper is organized in the following manner. Section 2 provides the details of previous works. Section 3 provides an elaborative description of the data used in the task. Features used in these experiments are described in Section 4. The detailed setup of experimentation and analysis of the results are described in Sec-

[1] http://www.saaip.org/

[2] http://nlp.stanford.edu/software/lex-parser.shtml

[3] http://sentiwordnet.isti.cnr.it/

Proceedings of the 8th International Workshop on Semantic Evaluation (SemEval 2014), pages 370–374,
Dublin, Ireland, August 23-24, 2014.

tion 5. Finally, conclusions and future directions are presented.

2 Related Work

It has been observed that most of the previous works on aspect detection were based on information extraction, to find the most frequent noun phrases (Hu and Liu, 2004). This approach is generally useful in finding aspects which are strongly associated with a single noun. But, one principal disadvantage of this approach is that it cannot detect the *aspect terms* which are of low frequency and noun phrases (e.g., different names of *dishes* like *Biryani, Dosa* and *Uttapam* etc. for the *aspect category*, "*food*"). The proposed work of such problem involves semantic hierarchy, rule-based or combination of both (Popescu and Etzioni 2005). More recent approaches of aspect detection are based on topic modelling, that use Latent Dirichlet Allocation (LDA) (Brody and Elhadad, 2010). But, the standard Latent Dirichlet Allocation (LDA) is not exactly suitable for the task of aspect detection due to their inherent nature of capturing global topics in the data, rather than finding local aspects related to the predefined entity. This approach was further modified in Sentence-LDA (SLDA) and Aspect and Sentiment Unification Model (ASUM) (Jo and Oh, 2011). Similarly, the identification of focussed text spans for opinion topics and targets were identified in (Das and Bandyopadhyay, 2010).

Snyder and Barzilay (2007) addressed the problem of identifying categories for multiple related *aspect terms* appeared in the text. For instance, in a restaurant review, such categories may include *food*, *ambience* and *service* etc. In our task, we call them as *aspect* or *review categories*. The authors implemented the Good Grief decoding algorithm on a corpus collected on restaurant review[4], which outperforms over the famous PRank algorithm (Crammer and Singer, 2001).

Ganu et al., (2009) have classified the restaurant reviews collected from *City search New York*[5] into six categories namely *Food, Service, Price, Ambience, Anecdotes, and Miscellaneous*. Sentiment associated with each category has also been identified and both the experiments were carried out using *Support Vector Machine* classifiers. Finally, they implemented the regression based model containing MATLAB regression function (*mvregress*) to give rating (1 to 5) to each review.

To determine the sentiment or polarity of the *aspect term* and *aspect category*, we need a prior sentiment annotated lexicon. Several works have been conducted on building emotional corpora in different English languages such as SentiWordNet (Baccianella et al., 2010), WordNet Affect (Strapparava and Valitutti, 2004) (Patra et al., 2013) etc. Among all these publicly available sentiment lexicons, SentiWordNet is one of the well-known and widely used ones (number of citations is higher than other resources[6]) that has been utilized in several applications such as sentiment analysis, opinion mining and emotion analysis.

Several works have been performed on the automated opinion detection or polarity identification from reviews (Yu and Hatzivassiloglou, 2003; Hu and Liu, 2004). Yu and Hatzivassiloglou (2003) has focused on characterizing opinions and facts in a generic manner, without examining who the opinion holder is or what the opinion is about. Then, they have identified the polarity or sentiment of the fact using Naive Bayes classifier. Hu and Liu, (2004) has summarized the customer review and then identified the sentiment of that review. They have achieved promising accuracy in case of identifying polarity of the reviews.

3 Data

The sentences collected from the customer reviews of *Restaurants* and *Laptops* are used in these tasks. The training data of *Restaurant* reviews contains 3041 English sentences annotated with *aspect terms* and *aspect categories* along with their *polarity*. The training data of *Laptop* reviews contains 3045 sentences annotated with *aspect terms* along with their *polarity*. The test data contains 800 sentences from each of the review sets.

An example extracted from the corpus is as follows:

But the staff was so horrible to us.

Here, "*staff*" is the *aspect term* and its polarity is "*negative*". The *aspect category* is "*service*" and *polarity* of the *aspect category* is also "*negative*".

---

[4] http://people.csail.mit.edu/bsnyder/naacl07/

[5] http://www.citysearch.com/guide/newyork-ny-metro

[6] http://citeseerx.ist.psu.edu/index

4 Feature Analysis

In general, the feature selection always plays an important role in any machine learning framework and depends upon the data set used for the experiments. Based on a preliminary investigation of the dataset, we have identified some of the following features. Different combinations of the features have also been used to get the best results from the classification task.

Parts-of-Speech (POS): the *aspect terms* are basically represented by the noun phrases. On the other hand, the POS tag plays an important role in *aspect term* identification (Hu and Liu, 2004; Brody and Elhadad, 2010). Thus, we have used the *Stanford CoreNLP*[7] tool to parse each of the review sentences to find out the part-of-speech tag of each word and included them as a feature in all of our experiments.

POS Frequency: We have observed that the *aspect terms* surrounded by a noun or adjective are also denoted as *aspect terms*. Therefore, we have utilized this information in our system. For example, in the phrase "*external_JJ mouse_NN*". Here the word "*mouse*" is an object and *aspect term*. The word "*external*" is also tagged as *aspect term*.

Before be verb: We have observed that the nouns occur before the "*be*" verbs denote the *aspect terms* in most of the cases. e.g. "*The hard disk is noisy*". Here "*hark disk*" is an *aspect term* and is followed by the "*be*" verb "is".

Inanimate words: In case of the *Restaurant and Laptop* reviews, we observed that many of the inanimate nouns occur as *aspect terms*. We have used the hyponym tree of *RiTa.WordNet*[8] to identify the inanimate words. For example, in the following sentence, the words *food, kitchen* and *menu* are inanimate nouns occurred as *aspect terms*.

"The food is uniformly exceptional, with a very capable kitchen which will proudly whip up whatever you feel like eating, whether it's on the menu or not."

Dependency Relation for finding Object: We have identified the object based dependency relations from parsed sentences, as we have observed that the words occupied in such relations are represented as *aspect terms* in many cases. "*dobj*", "*obj*" and "*xobj*" are considered as the probable candidate relations for identifying the *aspect terms*. Here, the *Stanford Parser*[9] has been used to get the dependency relations.

Ontology Information (Liu, 2012)***:*** We have counted the *aspect terms* in the training data. The *aspect terms* occurred more than five times in the corpus are considered during our experiments. At first, we have tested this ontology information on the development set and observed that the *aspect terms* with frequency five or more also give better results in the test set.

Sentiment Words: We have used the sentiment words as a feature for the sentiment identification tasks (Liu, 2012; Brody and Elhadad, 2010). Words are identified as *positive*, *negative* or *neutral* using SentiWordNet[10].

WordNet Information: The *RiTa.WordNet* package has been used to extract different properties of the words.

For *aspect category* identification, we have matched the hypernym tree of each word with the four categories (*service, price, food*, and *ambience*). If the hypernym tree does not contain any of such words, we check the next level hypernym tree of the words derived from hypernym of previous word. We have checked up to the second degree hypernym tree. We also searched hypernym tree of the synset of each word.

Number of Sentence: It has been found that many reviews contain more than one sentence. Therefore, we have included the number of sentence as a feature based on the output of *Stanford Parser*. We have split the output of *Stanford Parser* by the mark, "*(S*".

In case of our experiments, the stop words are excluded. Total of 329 stop words was prepared manually.

5 Experimentation and Result Analysis

We have used the CRF++ 0.58[11], an open source tool for implementing the machine learning framework for our experiments. CRF is well known for sequence labeling tasks (Lafferty et al., 2001). Similarly, in the present task, the *aspect terms* use the context information and are represented in sequences. Many of the *aspect terms* are multiword expressions such as "*hard disk*". We have created different templates for different subtasks to capture all the relations between different sequence related features.

[7]http://nlp.stanford.edu/software/corenlp.shtml
[8]www.rednoise.org/rita/reference/RiWordNet.html
[9]http://nlp.stanford.edu/software/lex-parser.shtml
[10]http://sentiwordnet.isti.cnr.it/
[11]http://crfpp.googlecode.com/svn/trunk/doc/index.htm

a. Classification of Aspect Term

Features used in case of identifying aspect terms are *POS, POS Frequency, Before be verb, Inanimate word, objects of the sentence, ontology information*. We have used several rules to identify these features. Then, we have used the CRF++ to identify the *aspect terms*. Some post processing techniques are also used in order to get better accuracy. The present system identifies only single word *aspect terms*. But it is found in the training data that many *aspect terms* consist of multiple words. Therefore, if there is a stop word in between two system identified aspect words, the stop word is also considered as a part of the *aspect term*. We have joined the aspect words along with the stop words to form a single but multiword *aspect terms*.

Precisions, Recalls and F-scores are recorded for our system in Table 1. The maximum F-scores achieved in the aspect term identification task for *Laptop* and *Restaurant* are 0.7455012 and 0.84012544, respectively. Our system performs better on *Restaurant* reviews than *Laptop* reviews.

	Laptop	**Restaurant**
Precision	0.4938838	0.6481481
Recall	0.7442396	0.8184855
F-score	0.59375	0.72342515

Table 1: JU_CSE system result for *aspect term* identification.

b. Classification of Aspect Category

Features used in this experiment are *POS, Dependency relations for object* and a few semantic relations of *WordNet*. In this subtask, we have also used *aspect term* knowledge as a feature. We identified the POS of the words using *Stanford CoreNLP* tool and used the words which are not listed in our stop-word list. The objects are identified from the dependency relations. The hpernym trees of these words are searched up to second degree to find four *aspect categories* (*service, price, food*, and *ambience*). If we don't find these four categories in the hypernym tree, we increase the frequency of *anecdotes/ miscellaneous* category. Frequency counts of these matched words are listed as a feature. The accuracy of the system for *aspect categories* in the *Restaurant* reviews are shown in Table 2.

Maximum F-score achieved in this *aspect category* identification is 0.8857715. The main problem faced in this task was to assign the *anecdotes/ miscellaneous* category to the respective reviews. There are many cases in which the *anecdotes/miscellaneous* categories occurred with other categories. In these cases, our system fails to identify the *anecdotes/miscellaneous* category.

Restaurant		
Precision	**Recall**	**F-score**
0.7307317	0.68029064	0.7046096

Table 2: JU_CSE system result for *aspect category* identification.

We have also observed that every review has at least one category. If any word of the review does not belong to any of the four categories, we assign these reviews with *anecdotes/ miscellaneous* category at the time of post processing.

c. Classification of Sentiment of Aspect term and category

Features used in these experiments are *POS, Positive, Negative* and *Neutral* words and number of sentences. Some reviews with multiple sentences contain different sentiments associated with different *aspect terms*. This observation also leads to *conflict* sentiment. Therefore, we have also included the *aspect term* and *aspect category* information during sentiment identification. The accuracy of the system is given in the Table 3.

Accuracy →	**Aspect Term Sentiment**	**Aspect Category Sentiment**
Laptop	0.5321101	NaN
Restaurant	0.65547705	0.6409756

Table 3: JU_CSE system result for *aspect term* and category sentiment identification.

Our system performs moderate in case of sentiment identification. Mainly, the system was biased towards the *positive* tags. It is found that the number of *positive* tags in the training data was more as compared to others. We have observed that a *conflict* tag occurs when an *aspect term* was present as both *positive* and *negative*. As the present system identifies the sentiment based on word level only, it was unable to detect the conflict tags. The feature, *number of sentences* fails to identify the *conflict* tags. Therefore, we need to find more suitable features for our system to improve the accuracy.

6 Conclusion

In this paper, we have presented a CRF based system for identifying the *aspect terms*, *aspect categories* and their sentiments. We believe that this problem will become increasingly important for common people. This task will not only be useful to common shoppers, but also crucial to product manufacturers and restaurateurs.

Overall accuracies of our system were moderate. In future, we will include more suitable features to improve accuracy of our system. We also intend to explore different machine learning algorithms for these tasks in future.

Reference

Benjamin Snyder and Regina Barzilay. 2007. Multiple Aspect Ranking Using the Good Grief Algorithm. In Proceedings of the *Human Language Technologies: The Annual Conference of the North American Chapter of the Association for Computational Linguistics (NAACL-HLT 2007)*, pp. 300-307.

Bing Liu. 2012. Sentiment Analysis and Opinion Mining. *Synthesis Lectures on Human Language Technologies* 5, no. 1 (2012): 1-167.

Braja G. Patra, Hiroya Takamura, Dipankar Das, Manabu Okumura, and Sivaji Bandyopadhyay. 2013. Construction of Emotional Lexicon Using Potts Model. In Proceedings of the *6th International Joint Conference on Natural Language Processing (IJCNLP-2013)*, Nagoya, Japan, pp. 674–679.

Carlo Strapparava, and Alessandro Valitutti. 2004. WordNet Affect: an Affective Extension of WordNet. In *LREC*, vol. 4, pp. 1083-1086.

Dipankar Das and Sivaji Bandyopadhyay. 2010. Extracting emotion topics from blog sentences: use of voting from multi-engine supervised classifiers. In Proceedings of the *2nd international workshop on Search and mining user-generated contents*, pp. 119-126.

Ganu Gayatree, Noemie Elhadad, and Amelie Marian. 2009. Beyond the stars: Improving rating predictions using review text content. In Proceedings of the *12th International Workshop on the Web and Databases*, Providence, Rhode Island.

Hong Yu and Vasileios Hatzivassiloglou. 2003. Towards answering opinion questions: Separating facts from opinions and identifying the polarity of opinion sentences. In Proceedings of the *Conference on Empirical Methods in Natural Language Processing (EMNLP-2013)*, pp. 129-136.

Koby Crammer and Yoram Singer. 2001. Pranking with ranking. In *NIPS*, vol. 14, pp. 641-647.

John Lafferty, Andrew McCallum, Fernando C.N. Pereira. 2001. Conditional Random Fields: Probabilistic Models for Segmenting and Labeling Sequence Data. In Proceedings of the *18th International Conference on Machine Learning (ICML 2001)*, pp. 282-289.

Minqing Hu and Bing Liu. 2004. Mining and summarizing customer reviews. In Proceedings of the *10th ACM SIGKDD International Conference on Knowledge Discovery and Data Mining*, pp. 168-177.

Ana-Maria Popescu and Oren Etzioni. 2005. Extracting product features and opinions from reviews. In proceedings of the *Human Language Technology Conference: Conference on Empirical Methods in Natural Language Processing (HLT-EMNLP)*. Morristown, NJ, USA, pp. 339–346.

Samaneh Moghaddam and Martin Ester. 2010. Opinion digger: an unsupervised opinion miner from unstructured product reviews. In Proceedings of the *19th ACM international conference on Information and knowledge management*, pp. 1825-1828.

Samuel Brody and Noemie Elhadad. 2010. An unsupervised aspect-sentiment model for online reviews. In Proceedings of the *Human Language Technologies: The 2010 Annual Conference of the North American Chapter of the Association for Computational Linguistics (HLT-NAACL)*.

Soo-Min Kim and Eduard Hovy. 2006. Extracting opinions, opinion holders, and topics expressed in online news media text. In Proceedings of the *Workshop on Sentiment and Subjectivity in Text,* pp. 1-8.

Stefano Baccianella, Andrea Esuli, and Fabrizio Sebastiani. 2010. SentiWordNet 3.0: An Enhanced Lexical Resource for Sentiment Analysis and Opinion Mining. In *LREC*, vol. 10, pp. 2200-2204.

Yohan Jo and Alice H. Oh. 2011. Aspect and sentiment unification model for online review analysis. In Proceedings of the *fourth ACM international conference on Web search and data mining*.

Zhongwu Zhai, Bing Liu, Hua Xu, and Peifa Jia. 2011. Clustering product features for opinion mining. In Proceedings of the *fourth ACM international conference on Web search and data mining*, pp. 347-354.

Maria Pontiki, Dimitrios Galanis, John Pavlopoulos, Haris Papageorgiou, Ion Androutsopoulos, and Suresh Manandhar. 2014. SemEval-2014 Task 4: Aspect Based Sentiment Analysis. In Proceedings of the 8th International Workshop on Semantic Evaluation (SemEval 2014), Dublin, Ireland.

JU-Evora: A Graph Based Cross-Level Semantic Similarity Analysis using Discourse Information

Swarnendu Ghosh
Dept. of Computer Science and Engineering
Jadavpur University, Kolkata, India
swarbir@gmail.com

Nibaran Das
Dept. of Computer Science and Engineering
Jadavpur University, Kolkata, India
nibaran@ieee.org

Teresa Gonçalves
Dept. of Informática
University of Évora, Évora, Portugal
tcg@evora.pt

Paulo Quaresma
Dept. of Informática
University of Évora, Évora, Portugal
pq@evora.pt

Abstract

Text Analytics using semantic information is the latest trend of research due to its potential to represent better the texts content compared with the bag-of-words approaches. On the contrary, representation of semantics through graphs has several advantages over the traditional representation of feature vector. Therefore, error tolerant graph matching techniques can be used for text comparison. Nevertheless, not many methodologies exist in the literature which expresses semantic representations through graphs. The present system is designed to deal with cross level semantic similarity analysis as proposed in the SemEval-2014 : Semantic Evaluation, International Workshop on Semantic Evaluation, Dublin, Ireland.

1 Introduction

Text Analytics has been the focus of much research work in the last years. State of the art approaches typically represent documents as vectors (bag-of-words) and use a machine learning algorithm, such as k-NN or SVM, to create a model and to compare and classify new documents. However, and in spite of being able to obtain good results, these approaches fail to represent the semantic content of the documents, losing much information and limiting the tasks that can be implemented over the document representation structures. To overcome these shortcomings some research has been done aiming to use and evaluate more complex knowledge representation structures. In this paper, a new approach which integrates a deep linguistic analysis of the documents with graph-based classification algorithms and metrics has been proposed.

2 Overview of the Task

This task provides an evaluation for semantic similarity across different sizes of text, which we refer to as lexical levels. Specifically, this task encompasses four semantic similarity comparisons:

- paragraph to sentence(P2S),
- sentence to phrase(S2Ph),
- phrase to word(Ph2W), and
- word to sense(W2S).

Task participants were provided with pairs of each comparison type and asked to rate the pair according to the semantic similarity of the smaller item to the larger item. As an example, given a sentence and a paragraph, a system would assess how similar is the meaning of the sentence to the meaning of the paragraph. Ideally, a high-similarity sentence would reflect overall meaning of the paragraph. The participants were expected to assign a score between [0,4] to each pairs of sentences, where 0 shows no similarity in concept while 4 shows complete similarity in concept.

3 Theoretical Concepts

3.1 Discourse Representation Structures

Extraction and representation of the information conveyed by texts can be performed through several approaches, starting from statistical analysis to deep linguistic techniques. In this paper

Proceedings of the 8th International Workshop on Semantic Evaluation (SemEval 2014), pages 375–379,
Dublin, Ireland, August 23-24, 2014.

we will use a deep linguistic processing sequence: lexical, syntactic, and semantic analysis.

One of the most prominent research work on semantic analysis is the Discourse Representation Theory (DRT)(Kamp & Reyle, 1993). In DRT, we aim to associate sentences with expressions in a logical language, which indicate their meaning. In DRT, each sentence is viewed as an update of an existing context, having as result a new context.

DRT provides a very powerful platform for the representation of semantic structures of documents including complex relations like implications, propositions and negations. It is also able to separately analyse almost all kinds of events and find out their agent and patient.

The main component of DRT is the Discourse Representation Structure (DRS These expressions have two main parts: a) a set of referents, which refer to entities present in the context and b) a set of conditions, which are the relations that exist between the entities. An example of a DRS representation for the sentence "He throws a ball." is shown below.

```
[
    x1, x2, x3:
    male(x1),
    ball(x2),
    throw(x3),
    event(x3),
    agent(x3,x1),
    patient(x3, x2)
]
```

3.2 GML Structure

Graph Modelling Language (GML)(Himsolt & Passau, 1996) is a simple and efficient way to represent weighted directed graphs. A GML file is basically a 7-bit ASCII file, and, as such, can be easily read, parsed, and written. Several open source applications [1] are available that enable viewing and editing GML files.

Graphs are represented by the keys viz. graph, node and edge. The basic structure is modelled with the node's id and the edge's source and target at-tributes. The id attributes assign numbers to nodes, which are then referenced by source and target. Weights can be represented by the label attribute.

[1]http://en.wikipedia.org/wiki/Graph_Modelling_Language

3.3 Similarity Metrics for Graphs

It has already been mentioned that the objective of the present work is to generate similarity scores among documents of different lexical levels using an approach which integrates a deep linguistic analysis of the documents with graph-based classification algorithms and metrics. Here, five different distance metrics taken from (Bunke, 2010) are utilized for this purpose. They are popularly used in object recognition task, but for text similarity measure they have not yet been used.

For two graphs G_1 and G_2, if $d(G_1, G_2)$ is the dissimilarity/similarity measure, then this measure would be a distance if d has the following properties:

1. $d(G_1, G_2) = 0$, iff $G_1 = G_2$
2. $d(G_1, G_2) = g(G_2, G_1)$
3. $d(G_1, G_2) + d(G_2, G_3) \geq d(G_1, G_3)$

The measures used in the present work follow the above rules and the corresponding equations are

$$d_{mcs}(G_1, G_2) = 1 - \frac{|mcs(G_1, G_2)|}{max(|G_1|, |G_2|)} \quad \text{...(1)}$$

$$d_{wgu}(G_1, G_2) = 1 - \frac{|mcs(G_1, G_2)|}{|G_1| + |G_2| - |mcs(G_1, G_2)|} \quad \text{...(2)}$$

$$d_{ugu}(G_1, G_2) = |G_1| + |G_2| - 2 * |mcs(G_1, G_2)| \quad \text{...(3)}$$

$$d_{MMCS}(G_1, G_2) = |MCS(G_1, G_2)| - |mcs(G_1, G_2)| \quad \text{...(4)}$$

$$d_{MMCSN}(G_1, G_2) = 1 - \frac{|mcs(G_1, G_2)|}{|MCS(G_1, G_2)|} \quad \text{...(5)}$$

In the equations $mcs(G_1, G_2)$ and $MCS(G_1, G_2)$ denote maximal common subgraph and minimum common super graphs of two graphs G_1 and G_2. Theoretically $mcs(G_1, G_2)$ is the largest graph in terms of edges that is isomorphic to a subgraph of G_1 and G_2. The $mcs(G_1, G_2)$ has been formally defined in a work of Horst Bunke (Bunke, Foggia, Guidobaldi, Sansone, & Vento, 2002). As stated earlier, it is a NP complete problem and actually, the method of finding the $mcs()$ is a brute force method which finds all the subgraphs of both the graphs and select the maximum graph which is common to both. To make the program computationally faster, the program is modified to an approximate version of $mcs(G_1, G_2)$ on the fact that the vertices which exhibit greater similarity in their local structures among the two graphs have a greater probability of inclusion in the $mcs()$. The two pass approach used in the present work to form the approximate $mcs(G_1, G_2)$ is as follows:

- All the node pairs (one from each graph) are ranked according the number of matching self-loops.
- The *mcs* is built by including each node pair (starting with the one with the highest number of matching self-loops) and considering it as a common node; and then include the rest of the edges (i.e. non-self-loop edges) which occur in the same fashion in both the graphs.

In this way it ensures that the approximation version exhibits most of the properties of a *mcs*, while keeping the complexity in a polynomial time.

The minimum common supergraph (MCS)(Angelova & Weikum, 2006) is formed using the union of two graphs, i.e. $MCS(G_1, G_2) = G_1 \cup G_2$.

The distance metrics of Equations 1-3 were used directly without any modifications; the ones of Equations 3-4 were divided by $(|G_1| + |G_2|)$ and $|MCS(G_1, G_2) + mcs(G_1, G_2)|$ respectively to make them normalized, keeping the value of distance metrics within the range $[0, 1]$.

It is worthy to note that label matching that is performed during the above mentioned step may not necessarily be exact matching. Rather in this case we have used the WordNet to find an approximate conceptual similarity between two labels. For our experiment we have used the Wu and Palmer's conceptual similarity (Wu & Palmer, 1994).

$If\ L = lso(c_1, c_2)$, where c_1 and c_2 are a pair of concepts corresponding to two words and $lso(c_1, c_2)$ means the lowest super ordinate then,

$$sim_{WP}(c_1, c_2) = \frac{2 \times depth(L)}{len(c_1, L) + len(c_2, L) + 2 \times depth(L)}$$

3.4 Tools Used

In order to process texts C&C/Boxer (Bos, 2008; Curran, Clark, & Bos, 2007) a well-known open source tool available as a plugin to Natural Language Toolkit (NLTK) is used. The tool consists of a combinatory categorical grammar (CCG) (Curran et al., 2007) parser and outputs the semantic representations using discourse representation structures (DRS) of Discourse Representation Theory (DRT) (Kamp & Reyle, 1993).

4 System Description

The method described in the present work, is mainly divided into three major components. The first is the creation of the DRS of the semantic interpretation of the text. The second is the construction of graphs in GML from the obtained DRS using some predefined rules. The third one is the classification phase where the different graph distances are assessed using a k-NN classifier (Zhang, Li, Sun, & Nadee, 2013).

The algorithm semantic evaluation of text content may be described as follows.

- **NLTK Module** : For each pair of text, to

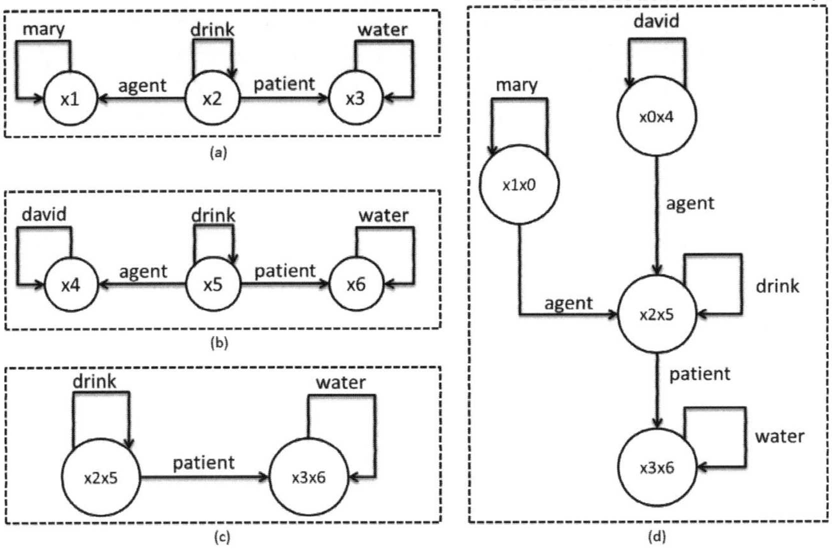

Figure 1: Graphical overview of mcs and MCS: (a), (b) graph representation of sentences meaning "Mary drinks water" and "David drinks water " respectively, (c) maximum common subgraph, (d) minimum common supergraph.

compare their similarity measure we need to find their DRS using the C&C/Boxer toolkit. The toolkit first uses the C&C Parser to find the combinatorial categorical grammar(CCG) of the text. Next the Boxer Module uses the CCG to find the discourse representation structures.

- **Graph building module** : In general Boxer represents a sentence through some discourse referents and conditions based on the semantic interpretation of the sentence. In the graph, the referent is represented by vertex after resolving the equity among different referents of the DRS; and a condition is represented by an edge value between two referents. The condition of a single referent is represented as a self-loop of the referent (source and destination referents are same). Special relationships such as proposition, implication etc. are treated as edge values between two referents; Agent and patient are also treated as conditions of discourse, hence represented by the edge values of two referents.
- **Calculating Similarity Index** : It has already been mentioned that the different distance metrics (see Equations 1-5) calculated based on the mcs() and MCS(). The values of mcs() and MCS() are represented by the number of similar edges. Thus, ten different distances are calculated based on Equations 1-5.
- **Learning** : We obtained 5 similarity scores for each pair of texts. Our task requires us to assign a score between 0-4 for each pair of text. Hence using the gold standard a K-NN Classifier have been trained to find the output score for a test sample. The value of K has been empirically adjusted using the cross validation technique to find the optimal value.

Our method works smoothly for the first two lexical levels. But for the last two levels i.e. phrase to word and word to sense it is not possible to find out DRS for a single word. Hence we have used the WordNet(Fellbaum, 1998) to extract the definition of the word in question and calculate its DRS and proceed with the method. When a word has multiple definitions, all the definitions are fused to a single sentence after conjugating them with the conjunction 'or'.

5 Results and Discussions

The JU-Evora system performed fairly in the SemEval Competition 2014. All the correlation scores are not as good as the Baseline(LCS) scores, however it provides a better Pearson correlation score in case of Paragraph to Sentence. The other scores, though not higher, are in the vicinity of the baseline. All the scores are shown below in Table 1.

PEARSON'S CORRELATION				
	P2S	**S2Ph**	**Ph2W**	**W2S**
JU-Evora	0.536	0.442	0.090	0.091
Baseline (LCS)	0.527	0.562	0.165	0.109
SPEARMAN CORRELATION				
JU-Evora	0.533	0.440	0.096	0.075
Baseline (LCS)	0.613	0.626	0.162	0.130

Table 1: Performance of JU-Evora system with respect to Baseline.

6 Conclusion

In this paper a new approach has been proposed to the text comparison task which integrates a deep linguistic analysis of the documents with a graph-based comparison algorithm. In the linguistic analysis, discourse representation structures (DRS) are used to represent text semantic content and, afterwards, these structures are transformed into graphs. We have evaluated existent graph distance metrics and proposed some modifications, more adequate to calculate graph distances between graph-drs structures. Finally, we integrated graph-drs structures and the proposed graph distance metrics into a k-NN classifier for calculating the similarity between two documents. Future works in this area would be concentrated on the use of external knowledge sources to make the system more robust.

References

Angelova, Ralitsa, & Weikum,Gerhard. (2006). Graph-based Text Classification: Learn from Your Neighbors. In *Proceedings of the 29th Annual International ACM SIGIR Conference on Research and Development in Information Retrieval* (pp. 485–492). New York, NY, USA: ACM.

Bos, Johan (2008). Wide-Coverage Semantic Analysis with Boxer. In J. Bos & R. Delmonte

(Eds.), *Semantics in Text Processing. STEP 2008 Conference Proceedings* (pp. 277–286). College Publications.

Bunke, Horst (2010). *Graph Classification and Clustering Based on Vector Space Embedding* (Vol. Volume 77, pp. 15–34). WORLD SCIENTIFIC. doi:doi:10.1142/9789814304726_0002

Bunke, Horst, Foggia, Pasquale, Guidobaldi, Corrado, Sansone, Carlo, & Vento, Mario (2002). A Comparison of Algorithms for Maximum Common Subgraph on Randomly Connected Graphs. In T. Caelli, A. Amin, R. W. Duin, D. Ridder, & M. Kamel (Eds.), *Structural, Syntactic, and Statistical Pattern Recognition SE - 12* (Vol. 2396, pp. 123–132). Springer Berlin Heidelberg.

Curran, James, Clark, Stephen, & Bos, Johan (2007). Linguistically Motivated Large-Scale NLP with C&C and Boxer. In *Proceedings of the 45th Annual Meeting of the Association for Computational Linguistics Companion Volume Proceedings of the Demo and Poster Sessions* (pp. 33–36). Prague, Czech Republic: Association for Computational Linguistics.

Fellbaum, Christiane (1998). *WordNet: An Electronic Lexical Database. British Journal Of Hospital Medicine London England 2005* (Vol. 71, p. 423).

Himsolt, Michael, & Passau, Universität (1996). GML : A portable Graph File Format. *Syntax*, 1–11.

Kamp, Hans, & Reyle, Uwe (1993). *From discourse to logic: Introduction to model theoretic semantics of natural language, formal logic and discourse representation theory.*

Wu, Zhibiao, & Palmer, Martha (1994). Verb semantics and lexical selection. *In 32nd Annual Meeting of the Association for Computational Linguistics,*, *32*, 133–138.

Zhang, Libiao, Li, Yuefeng, Sun, Chao, & Nadee, Winai (2013). Rough Set Based Approach to Text Classification. *Web Intelligence (WI) and Intelligent Agent Technologies (IAT), 2013 IEEE/WIC/ACM International Joint Conferences on.*

Kea: Sentiment Analysis of Phrases Within Short Texts

Ameeta Agrawal, Aijun An
Department of Computer Science and Engineering
York University, Toronto, Canada M3J 1P3
{ameeta, aan}@cse.yorku.ca

Abstract

Sentiment Analysis has become an increasingly important research topic. This paper describes our approach to building a system for the Sentiment Analysis in Twitter task of the SemEval-2014 evaluation. The goal is to classify a phrase within a short piece of text as positive, negative or neutral. In the evaluation, classifiers trained on Twitter data are tested on data from other domains such as SMS, blogs as well as sarcasm. The results indicate that apart from sarcasm, classifiers built for sentiment analysis of phrases from tweets can be generalized to other short text domains quite effectively. However, in cross-domain experiments, SMS data is found to generalize even better than Twitter data.

1 Introduction

In recent years, new forms of communication such as microblogging and text messaging have become quite popular. While there is no limit to the range of information conveyed by tweets and short texts, people often use these messages to share their sentiments. Working with these informal text genres presents challenges for natural language processing beyond those typically encountered when working with more traditional text genres. Tweets and short texts are shorter, the language is very informal, with creative spelling and punctuation, misspellings, slang, new words, URLs, and genre-specific terminology such as, RT for "re-tweet" and #hashtags for tagging (Rosenthal et al., 2014).

Although several systems have tackled the task of analyzing sentiment from entire tweets, the task of analyzing sentiments of phrases (a word or more) within a tweet has remained largely unexplored. This paper describes the details of our system that participated in the subtask A of Semeval-2014 Task 9: Sentiment Analysis in Twitter (Rosenthal et al., 2014). The goal of this task is to determine whether a phrase within a message is positive, negative or neutral in that context. Here, a *message* indicates any short informal piece of text such as a tweet, SMS data, or a sentence from Live Journal blog, which is a social networking service where Internet users keep an online diary. A *phrase* could be a word or a few consecutive words within a message.

The novelty of this task lies in the fact that a model built using only Twitter data is used to classify instances from other short text domains such as SMS and Live Journal. Moreover, a short test corpus of sarcastic tweets is also used to test the performance of the sentiment classifier.

The main contributions of this paper include a) developing a sentiment analysis classifer for phrases; b) training on Twitter data and testing on other domains such as SMS and Live Journal data to see how well the classifier generalizes to different types of text, and c) testing on sarcastic tweets.

2 Related Work

Sentiment analysis from Twitter data has attracted much attention from the research community in the past few years (Asiaee T. et al., 2012; Go et al., 2009; Pang et al., 2002; Pang and Lee, 2004; Wilson et al., 2005). However, most of these approaches classify entire tweets by their overall sentiment (positive, negative, or neutral).

The task at hand is to classify the sentiment of a phrase within a short message. The challenges of classifying contextual polarity of phrases has been previously explored by first determining whether the phrase is neutral or polar, and then disambiguating the polarity of the polar phrases (Wilson et al., 2005). Another approach entails using

Proceedings of the 8th International Workshop on Semantic Evaluation (SemEval 2014), pages 380–384, Dublin, Ireland, August 23-24, 2014.

manually developed patterns (Nasukawa and Yi, 2003). Both these techniques, however, experimented with general web pages and online reviews but not Twitter data.

Previously, a few systems that participated in Semeval-2013: Sentiment Analysis in Twitter task (Wilson et al., 2013; Mohammad et al., 2013; Gunther and Furrer, 2013) tackled the problem of sentiment analysis of phrases by training on data that exclusively came from tweets and tested on a corpus made up of tweets and SMS data. This time though, the task is to see how well a system trained on tweets will perform on not only SMS data, but also blog sentences from Live Journal, as well as *sarcastic* tweets.

3 Task Setup

Formally, given a message containing a phrase (one or more words), the task is to determine whether that phrase is positive, negative or neutral in that context. We were able to download 8880 tweets (7910 for training, and 970 for development) from the corpus made available by the task organizers, where each tweet includes a phrase marked as positive, negative or neutral. Keywords and hashtags were used to identify and collect messages, which were then annotated using Amazon Mechanical Turk. This task setup is further described in the task description paper (Rosenthal et al., 2014).

The evaluation consists of Twitter data as well as surprise genres such as SMS, Live Journal and Twitter Sarcasm. The purpose of hidden test genres was to see how well a system trained on tweets will perform on previously unseen domains.

4 System Description

This section describes the system components.

4.1 Supervised Machine Learning

During development time, we experimented with various supervised machine learning classifiers, but the final model was trained using Support Vector Machines (SVM) with a linear kernel as it outperformed all other classifiers. The c value was empirically selected and set to 1.

4.2 Features

For all tweets, the *URL* links and *@username* mentions are replaced by "URL" and "username" placeholders, respectively. The following features were included in the final model:

- Prior polarities: Previous research (Agrawal and An, 2013; Mohammad et al., 2013) has shown prior polarities of words to be one of the most important features in contextual sentiment analysis of phrases. So, for one of the features, the sum of the sentiscores of all the terms in the phrase was computed from SentiWordNet (Esuli and Sebastiani, 2006). For another feature, the prior polarity of the phrase was estimated by averaging the positive/negative strength of all its terms by looking them up in the Subjectivity Clues database (Wilson et al., 2005).

- Emoticons: An emoticon lexicon containing frequent positive and negative emoticons, as well as some of their misspellings that are generally found in tweets, was created manually[1]. The prior positive and negative emoticon features contain the counts of all positive and negative emoticons in the phrase.

- Lengths: Counts of the total number of words in the phrase, the average number of characters in the phrase, and the total number of words in the message were included.

- Punctuation: Whether the phrase contains punctuation such as '?', '!', '...', etc.

- Clusters: Word cluster IDs were obtained for each term via unsupervised Brown clustering of tweets (Owoputi et al., 2013). For example, words such as *anyone*, *anybody*, *any1*, *ne1* and *anyonee* are all represented by cluster path *0111011110*. This allows grouping multiple (mis)spellings of a word together, which would otherwise be unique unigrams.

- Unigrams: Each phrase consists of one or more words, with the average number of words in a phrase being 2. We used only unigrams as bigrams were found to reduce the accuracy on the development set.

5 Experiments and Discussion

The task organizers made available a test data set composed of 10681 instances. Table 1 describes

[1]http://goo.gl/fh6Pjr

Test sets (# instances)	Sentiment	Example Phrase to be classified (in bold)
Twitter (6908)	positive	No school at the Cuse till Wednesday **#hyped**
	negative	i know it's in january, but i **can't wait** for Winter Jam !
	neutral	Bye bye Kyiv! See you in December **:-***
SMS (2334)	positive	later on **wanna** catch a movie?
	negative	U had ur dinner already? She just **wont believe** wat i said, haiz..
	neutral	Im free on sat ... **Ok** we watch together lor
LiveJournal (1315)	positive	And Tess you are going to **prom** too on the same day as us as well
	negative	Does not seem likely that there would be any **confusion** .
	neutral	if i am **ever** king i will make it up to you .
TwitterSarcasm (124)	positive	@ImagineMore **CHEER up.** It's Monday after all. #mondayblues
	negative	I may or may not be getting sick...perfect. **#idontwantit**
	neutral	@Ken_Rosenthal mistakes? **C'mon Kenny!! ;)**

Table 1: Test corpus details.

the breakdown of the various types of text, with example phrases that are to be classified.

As expected, Live Journal has a slightly more formal sentence structure with properly spelt words, whereas Twitter and SMS data include more creative spellings. Clearly, the sarcasm category includes messages with two contradictory sentiments in close proximity. The challenge of this task lies precisely in the fact that one classifier trained on Twitter data should be able to generalize reasonably well on different types of text.

5.1 Task Results

We participated in the *constrained* version of the task which meant working with only the provided Twitter training data without any additional annotated messages. The macro-average F1-scores of the positive and negative classes, which were the evaluation criteria for the task, of our system (trained on Twitter training data and tested on Twitter test, SMS and Live Journal blog data) are presented in Table 2.

There are two interesting observations here: firstly, even though the classifier was trained solely on tweets, it performs equally well on SMS and Live Journal data; and secondly, the sarcasm category has the poorest overall performance, unsurprisingly. This suggests that cross-domain sentiment classification of phrases in short texts is a feasible option. However, sarcasm seems to be a subtle sentiment and calls for exploring features that capture not only semantic but also syntactic nuances. The low recall of the negative sarcastic instances could be due to the fact that 30% of the negative phrases are hashtags (e.g., #don'tjudge, #smartmove, #killmenow, #sadlife, #runninglate, #asthmaticproblems, #idontwantit), that require term-splitting.

Further analysis reveals that generally the positive class has better F1-scores than the negative class across all domains, except for the SMS data. One possible reason for this could be the fact that, while in all data sets (Twitter train, Twitter test, Sarcasm test) the ratio of positive to negative instances is nearly 2:1, the SMS test set is the only one with class distribution different from the training set (with less positive instances than negative). The extremely low F1-score for the neutral class is perhaps also due to the skewed class distribution, where in all data sets, the neutral instances only make up about 4 to 9% of the data.

The positive class also has a better recall than the negative class across all domains, which suggests that the system is able to identify most of the positive test instances, perhaps due to the bigger proportion of positive training instances as well as positive words in the polarity lexicons. One simple way of improving the recall of the negative class could be by increasing the number of negative instances in the training set. In fact, in a preliminary experiment with an increased number of negative instances (resampled using SMOTE (Chawla et al., 2002)), the macro-average F1-score of the SMS data set improved by 0.5 points and that of the Sarcasm set by almost 2 points. However, there was no notable improvement in the Twitter and Live Journal test sets.

We also ran some ablation experiments on the test corpus after the submission to observe the influence of individual features on the classification

	POS.			NEG.			NEU.			AVG.
	P	R	F	P	R	F	P	R	F	
Twitter	87.6	89.7	**88.6**	82.4	76.2	79.2	23.3	28.2	25.5	**83.90**
SMS	75.9	89.9	82.3	89.8	82.4	**86.0**	32.7	10.7	16.1	**84.14**
LiveJournal	76.1	87.3	**81.3**	81.8	80.2	81.0	42.1	16.7	23.9	**81.16**
Sarcasm	77.0	93.9	**84.6**	72.2	35.1	47.3	16.7	20.0	18.2	**65.94**

Table 2: Macro-average F1-scores. P, R and F represent precision, recall and F1-score, respectively.

process. Table 3 reports the macro-average F1-scores of the experiments. The "all features*" scores here are different from those submitted as the four test corpora were tested individually here as opposed to all instances mixed into one data set. The row "- prior polarities" indicates a feature set that *excludes* the prior polarities feature, and its effect on the F1-score. MCB is the Majority Class Baseline, whereas unigrams uses only the phrase unigrams, with no additional features.

	Twitter	SMS	Jour.	Sarc.
MCB	39.65	31.45	33.40	39.80
unigrams	81.85	82.15	79.95	74.85
all features*	**86.20**	**87.80**	**81.90**	**78.05**
- prior polarity	***-1.8***	-0.1	-0.05	-1.95
- lengths	-0.3	0	***-0.20***	-1.3
- punctuation	-0.45	-0.45	+0.10	***-2.95***
- emoticon lex	-0.15	0	+0.05	0
- word clusters	-0.15	***-1.25***	+0.05	-0.25

Table 3: Ablation tests: Trained on Twitter only.

A few observations from the feature ablation study include:

- The prior polarities and lengths seem to be two of the most distinguishing features for Twitter and Twitter Sarcasm, whereas for SMS data, the word clusters are quite useful.
- While for Twitter Sarcasm, punctuation seems to be the most important feature, it has the opposite effect on the Live Journal blog data. This may be because the punctuation features learned from Twitter data do not translate that well to blog data due to their dissimilar writing styles.
- Even though the classifier was trained on Twitter data, it has quite a strong performance on the SMS data, which is rather unsurprising in retrospect as both genres have similar character limits, which leads to creative spellings and slang.
- While using all the features leads to almost 5 F1-score points improvement over unigrams baseline in Twitter, SMS and Sarcasm data sets, they increase only 2 F1-score points in Live Journal blog data set, suggesting that this feature set is only marginally suited for blog instances. This prompted us to explore the hypothesis: how well do SMS and Live Journal data generalize to other domains, discussed in the following section.

5.2 Cross-domain Experiments

In this section, we test how well the classifiers trained on one type of text classify other types of text. In table 4, for example, the *last row* shows the results of a model trained on Journal data (1000 instances) and tested on Twitter, SMS and Sarcasm test sets, and 10-fold cross-validated on Journal data. Since this experiment measures the generalizability of different data sets, we randomly selected 500 positive and 500 negative instances for each data set, in order to minimize the influence of the size of the training data set on the classification process. Note that this experiment does not include the neutral class. As expected, the best results on the test sets are obtained when using cross-validation (except on Twitter set). However, the model built using SMS data has the best or the second-best result overall, which suggests that out of the three types of text, it is the SMS data that generalize the best.

	Test		
	Twitter	**SMS**	**Journal**
Twitter (1000)	76.4 (cv)	80.2	78.1
SMS (1000)	**76.8**	87.1 (cv)	**79.4**
Journal (1000)	73.8	82.8	85.3 (cv)

Table 4: Cross-domain training and tests.

6 Conclusion

This paper presents the details of our system that participated in the subtask A of SemEval:2014: Sentiment Analysis in Twitter. An SVM classifier was trained on a feature set consisting of prior polarities, word clusters and various Twitter-specific features. Our experiments indicate that prior polarities are one of the most important features in the sentiment analysis of phrases from short texts. Furthermore, a classifier trained on just tweets can generalize considerably well to other texts such as SMS and blog sentences, but not to sarcasm, which calls for more research. Lastly, SMS data generalizes to other texts better than Twitter data.

Acknowledgements

We would like to thank the organizers of this task for their effort and the reviewers for their useful feedback. This research is funded in part by the Centre for Information Visualization and Data Driven Design (CIV/DDD) established by the Ontario Research Fund.

References

Ameeta Agrawal and Aijun An. 2013. Kea: Expression-level sentiment analysis from Twitter data. In *Proceedings of the Seventh International Workshop on Semantic Evaluation*, SemEval '13, June.

Amir Asiaee T., Mariano Tepper, Arindam Banerjee, and Guillermo Sapiro. 2012. If you are happy and you know it... tweet. In *Proceedings of the 21st ACM International Conference on Information and Knowledge Management*, CIKM '12, pages 1602–1606, New York, NY, USA. ACM.

Nitesh V. Chawla, Kevin W. Bowyer, Lawrence O. Hall, and W. Philip Kegelmeyer. 2002. SMOTE: Synthetic minority over-sampling technique. *Journal of Artificial Intelligence Research*, 16(1):321–357, June.

Andrea Esuli and Fabrizio Sebastiani. 2006. Sentiwordnet: A publicly available lexical resource for opinion mining. In *Proceedings of the 5th Conference on Language Resources and Evaluation*, pages 417–422.

Alec Go, Richa Bhayani, and Lei Huang. 2009. Twitter sentiment classification using distant supervision. *CS224N Project Report, Stanford*, pages 1–6.

Tobias Gunther and Lenz Furrer. 2013. Gu-mlt-lt: Sentiment analysis of short messages using linguistic features and stochastic gradient descent. In *Proceedings of the Seventh International Workshop on Semantic Evaluation*, SemEval '13, June.

Saif M. Mohammad, Svetlana Kiritchenko, and Xiaodan Zhu. 2013. NRC-Canada: Building the state-of-the-art in sentiment analysis of tweets. In *Proceedings of the seventh international workshop on Semantic Evaluation Exercises (SemEval-2013)*, Atlanta, Georgia, USA, June.

Tetsuya Nasukawa and Jeonghee Yi. 2003. Sentiment analysis: capturing favorability using natural language processing. In *Proceedings of the 2nd international conference on Knowledge capture*, K-CAP '03, pages 70–77, New York, NY, USA. ACM.

Olutobi Owoputi, Brendan O?Connor, Chris Dyer, Kevin Gimpel, Nathan Schneider, and Noah A Smith. 2013. Improved part-of-speech tagging for online conversational text with word clusters. In *Proceedings of NAACL-HLT*, pages 380–390.

Bo Pang and Lillian Lee. 2004. A sentimental education: sentiment analysis using summarization based on minimum cuts. In *Proceedings of the 42nd Annual Meeting on Association for Computational Linguistics*, ACL '04, Stroudsburg, PA, USA.

Bo Pang, Lillian Lee, and Shivakumar Vaithyanathan. 2002. Thumbs up?: sentiment classification using machine learning techniques. In *Proceedings of the ACL-02 conference on Empirical methods in natural language processing - Volume 10*, EMNLP '02, pages 79–86, Stroudsburg, PA, USA.

Sara Rosenthal, Preslav Nakov, Alan Ritter, and Veselin Stoyanov. 2014. Semeval-2013 task 9: Sentiment analysis in twitter. In *Proceedings of the International Workshop on Semantic Evaluation (SemEval-2014)*, August.

Theresa Wilson, Janyce Wiebe, and Paul Hoffmann. 2005. Recognizing contextual polarity in phrase-level sentiment analysis. In *Proceedings of the conference on Human Language Technology and Empirical Methods in Natural Language Processing*, HLT '05, pages 347–354, Stroudsburg, PA, USA.

Theresa Wilson, Zornitsa Kozareva, Preslav Nakov, Sara Rosenthal, Veselin Stoyanov, and Alan Ritter. 2013. Semeval-2013 task 2: Sentiment analysis in twitter. In *Proceedings of the International Workshop on Semantic Evaluation (SemEval-2013)*, June.

KUL-Eval: A Combinatory Categorial Grammar Approach for Improving Semantic Parsing of Robot Commands using Spatial Context

Willem Mattelaer, Mathias Verbeke and Davide Nitti
Department of Computer Science, KU Leuven, Belgium
willem.mattelaer@gmail.com
mathias.verbeke@cs.kuleuven.be
davide.nitti@cs.kuleuven.be

Abstract

When executing commands, a robot has a certain level of contextual knowledge about the environment in which it operates. Taking this knowledge into account can be beneficial to disambiguate commands with multiple interpretations. We present an approach that uses combinatory categorial grammars for improving the semantic parsing of robot commands that takes into account the spatial context of the robot. The results indicate a clear improvement over non-contextual semantic parsing. This work was done in the context of the SemEval-2014 task on supervised semantic parsing of spatial robot commands.

1 Introduction

One of the long-standing goals of robotics is to build autonomous robots that are able to perform everyday tasks. Two important requirements to achieve this are an efficient way of communicating with the robot, and transforming these commands such that the robot is able to capture their meaning. Furthermore, this needs to be consistent with the context in which the robot is operating, i.e., the robot's *belief*.

Semantic parsing focuses on translating natural language (NL) into a formal representation that captures the meaning of the sentence. Most of the current semantic parsing approaches are non-contextual, i.e., they do not take into account the context in which the command sentence should be executed. This can lead to erroneous parses, most often due to ambiguity in the original sentence. Consider the following example sentence *"Move the pyramid on the blue cube on the gray cube"*. This sentence has two valid interpretations. Either the robot needs to move the pyramid that is currently standing on the blue cube and put it on the gray cube, or move the pyramid and place it on the blue cube that is standing on the gray cube.

Humans will decide on the correct interpretation by taking into account the context. For instance, by looking at Figure 1, it is clear that the second interpretation is not possible, because there is no blue cube on top of a gray cube. However, there is a pyramid on top of a blue cube, making the first interpretation possible. The goal of this paper is to improve on non-contextual semantic parsing by tailoring the context to guide the parser. In this way, part of the ambiguity that causes multiple interpretations can be resolved.

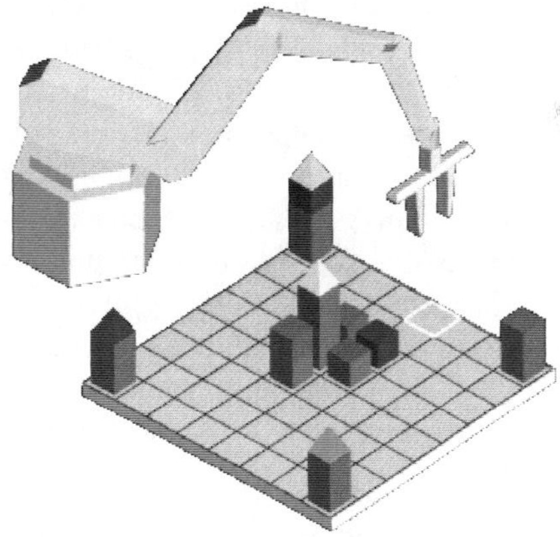

Figure 1: Possible situation (taken from (Dukes, 2013b)).

Our approach consists of two steps. First, non-contextual semantic parsing using combinatory categorial grammars (CCG) (Steedman, 1996; Steedman, 2000) is performed on the sentence. This returns multiple possible parses, each with an attached likelihood of correctness. Subsequently, each parse is checked against the current context. The parse with the highest score that is possible given the current context is returned.

Proceedings of the 8th International Workshop on Semantic Evaluation (SemEval 2014), pages 385–390, Dublin, Ireland, August 23-24, 2014.

This paper is organized as follows. In Section 2 we discuss related work, followed by a detailed description of our approach in Section 3. In Section 4, the approach is evaluated and compared to non-contextual parsing. Finally, in Section 5 we conclude and outline directions for future work.

The software is available from `https://github.com/wmattelaer/Thesis`.

2 Related Work

There is a significant body of previous work on learning semantic parsers. We will first review approaches that translate NL sentences into a formal representation without taking context into account, followed by related techniques that use the context to improve the parsing.

Our approach is inspired by the work of Kwiatkowski et al. (2010). The authors present a supervised CCG approach to parse queries to a geographical information database and a flight-booking system. This differs from the current setting in that the database querying does not require to take the context of the environment into account, as is the case when executing robot commands. SILT (Kate et al., 2005) uses transformation rules to translate the NL sentence to a query for the robot. This approach was extended to tailor support vector machines with string kernels (KRISP) (Kate and Mooney, 2006) and statistical machine learning (WASP) (Mooney, 2007). Also unsupervised approaches exist. Poon (2013) solves this lack of supervision by 1) inferring supervision using the target database, which constrains the search space, and 2) by using augmented dependency trees.

Artzi and Zettlemoyer (2013) study the use of grounded CCG semantic parsing using weak supervision for interpreting navigational robot commands. Their approach is similar to ours, but instead of postprocessing the results in a verification step, the context (or state) is added to the training data. Krishnamurthy and Kollar (2013) use CCGs as a foundation, but match it to the context using an evaluation function. This evaluation function scores a denotation, i.e., the set of entity referents for the entire sentence, given a logical form and a knowledge base, which is considered as the context.

3 Methodology

Our approach consists of two steps: a parse step and a verification step. Before these steps can be executed, a Combinatory Categorial Grammar needs to be trained. The training data for this grammar consists of typed λ-expressions (Carpenter, 1997) that are annotated with their corresponding NL sentences. As the input data for the SemEval-2014 task consists of Robot Control Language (RCL) expressions (Dukes, 2013a)[1], the data needs to be preprocessed first.

3.1 Preprocessing

During preprocessing, the RCL expressions are transformed into equivalent λ-expressions. In the λ-expressions, each entity is represented by a lambda term where the variable is a reference to the object. The properties of an entity are defined by a conjunction of literals with two arguments. The predicate details the property that is being defined. An example entity, a blue cube, can be represented as $\lambda x.color(x, blue), type(x, cube)$. A spatial relation between two entities is a literal with three arguments: the variable of the first entity, the type of relation and the second entity. The latter is given by its lambda term. This lambda term has to be wrapped in a definite determiner, det, that selects a single element from the set created by the lambda term (Artzi and Zettlemoyer, 2013). For example: the RCL expression

```
(entity:
    (type: prism)
    (spatial-relation:
        (relation: above)
        (entity:
            (color: blue)
            (type: cube))))
```

is transformed to the λ-calculus expression

$$\lambda x.type(x,prism), relation(x, above, det(\lambda y.color(y, blue), type(y, cube)))$$

Events are contained in one lambda term with one variable per event. There are three possible event predicates. The $action$ predicate defines the action by detailing the action type and the object entity. The $destination$ predicate will set the destination of the object[2]. Finally, the $sequence$ predicate is necessary to detail the order of the events.

[1]RCL is a linguistically-oriented formal language for controlling a robot arm, that represents entities, attributes, anaphora, ellipsis and qualitative spatial relations.

[2]Note that this event is not always necessary, e.g., in the case of a $take$ action, the robot will not release the object.

An example of this can be seen at the bottom of Figure 2.

Besides transforming the RCL expressions to λ-calculus, also the action types of the events are checked. If an event has an action of type $move$ or $drop$, it is changed to the combined $move$ & $drop$ action type. This change was introduced because the actual verbs that are used to instruct the robot to perform one of these two actions are often the same. To illustrate this, consider the following two sentences taken from the training data: *"place blue block on top of single red block"* and *"place green block on top of blue block"*. In the former, the intended action is a $drop$ action, while in the latter the action should be a $move$ action. During parsing, the correct action can be selected by looking at the context it has to be executed in. If the robot is currently grasping an object, the intended action is a $drop$ action, otherwise it is a $move$ action.

Furthermore, the anaphoric references are resolved in the natural language sentences. Anaphoric references are words that refer to one or more words mentioned earlier in the sentence. The sentences of the dataset are annotated with markers that capture the references in the sentence. The markers that are used are `[1]`, `(1)` and $\{$`1`$\}$ and are placed right after the word that is used for the reference. `[1]` is used to mark a word that is referred to by another word, whereas `(1)` is used to detail a word that refers to another word, e.g., *it*. Finally, $\{$`1`$\}$ marks a word that refers to the type of an earlier entity, e.g., *one*. The numbers in these markers can increase if there are different references in one sentence, but the sentences of this dataset do not contain different references. For instance, the sentence *Pick the blue block and place it above the gray one* is transformed to the sentence *Pick the blue block [1] and place it (1) above the gray one* $\{$*1*$\}$.

The anaphoric references are found using the coreference resolution system of *Stanford CoreNLP* (Recasens et al., 2013; Lee et al., 2013; Lee et al., 2011; Raghunathan et al., 2010). However, it is not capable of finding references that use *one*. This can be solved by letting the *one* always refer to the first entity of the sentence, because of the simplicity of the sentences.

3.2 Parsing

To parse the robot commands, a Probabilistic Combinatory Categorial Grammar (PCCG) (Kwiatkowski et al., 2010) is used. Regular CCGs consist out of two sets: a lexicon of lexical items and a set of operations. A lexical entry combines a word or phrase with its meaning. This meaning is represented by a category. A category captures the syntactic as well as the the semantic information of a word. A number of primitive symbols, a subset of the part-of-speech tags, are used to represent the syntax. These primitive symbols can be combined using specific operator symbols (/, \). The semantics are represented by a λ-expression. Some example lexical entries are:

blue $\vdash ADJ : \lambda x.color(x, blue)$
pyramid $\vdash N : \lambda x.type(x, prism)$
pick up $\vdash S/NP : \lambda y \lambda x.action(x, take, y)$

The operator symbols can now be used to determine how the categories can be combined using operations. The operations that are used by the CCG take one or two categories as input and return one category as output. These operations will simultaneously address syntax and semantics. The two most frequently used operations are the application operations, i.e., *forward* (>) and *backward* (<):

$$X/Y : f \quad Y : g \Rightarrow X : f(g) \quad (>)$$
$$Y : g \quad X\backslash Y : f \Rightarrow X : f(g) \quad (<)$$

The forward application takes as input a CCG category with syntax X/Y and λ-expression f followed by a category with syntax Y and λ-expression g and returns a CGG category with syntax X and λ-expression $f(g)$.

The operations will derive syntactic and semantic information, while keeping track of the word order that is encoded using the slash direction.

Another important operation deals with the definite determiner in the λ-expressions:

$$N : f \Rightarrow NP : det(f)$$

This operation takes a single noun (N) category as input and returns an noun phrase (NP) category where the original λ-expression is wrapped in a determiner. A complete parsing example is shown in Figure 2.

CCGs will usually have multiple possible parses for a sentence given a certain lexicon for which it

Take	the	pyramid
S/NP	N/N	N
$\lambda z \lambda y.action(y, take, z)$	$\lambda x.x$	$\lambda x.type(x, prism)$

$$\frac{\frac{N/N: \lambda x.x \quad N: \lambda x.type(x, prism)}{N: \lambda x.type(x, prism)}>}{NP: det(\lambda x.type(x, prism))}$$

$$\frac{S/NP: \lambda z \lambda y.action(y, take, z) \quad NP: det(\lambda x.type(x, prism))}{S: \lambda y.action(y, take, det(\lambda x.type(x, prism)))}>$$

Figure 2: A possible parse for the sentence "Take the pyramid".

is not possible to determine which of these is best. To alleviate this problem, PCCGs have been introduced (Kwiatkowski et al., 2010). PCCGs will return the most likely parse using a log-linear model that contains a parameter vector θ, estimated using stochastic gradient updates. The joint probability of a λ-calculus expression z and a parse y is given by $P(y, z|x; \theta, \Lambda)$, with Λ being the entire lexicon. The most likely λ-calculus expression z given a sentence x can then be found by:

$$f(x) = \arg\max_z P(z|x; \theta, \Lambda)$$

where the probability of z is equal to the sum of the probabilities of all parses that produce z:

$$P(z|x; \theta, \Lambda) = \sum_y P(y, z|x; \theta, \Lambda)$$

For training the PCCGs, the algorithm as described by Kwiatkowski et al. (2010) was used. It consists of two steps. In the first step the lexicon is expanded with new lexical items. The second step will update the parameters of the grammar using stochastic gradient updates (LeCun et al., 1998). All parameters are associated with a feature. The system uses *lexical features*: for each item in the lexicon a feature is added that fires when the item is used.

3.3 Verification

The parser will return multiple λ-expressions, each with an attached likelihood score. In the verification step, these resulting expressions are checked against the context. These λ-expressions are first transformed to RCL expressions[3]. Next, the entities are extracted from the RCL expressions and for each entity a corresponding object is searched using a spatial planner, provided by the task organizer. This spatial planner will, given an entity description in RCL, return the objects in the context that satisfy that description. RCL expressions with entities that have no corresponding object in the context are discarded. From the remaining RCL expressions the one with the highest likelihood is returned.

[3]Note that during pre- and postprocessing no information is lost, as the mapping between λ-calculus and RCL is a one-to-one function.

	Complete	Partial	Without context
Correct	71.29%	78.58%	57.76%
Wrong	11.66%	4.37%	27.72%
No result	17.05%	17.05%	14.52%

Table 1: Results.

4 Evaluation

The provided dataset for the task was crowd-sourced using Train Robots, an online game in which players were given before and after images of a scene and were asked to give the NL command that the robot had executed (Dukes, 2013a). Each scene is a formal description of a discrete 8x8x8 3D game board consisting of colored blocks. The entire dataset consists of 3409 annotated examples, and was split in a training and test set of 2500 and 909 sentences respectively.

The results are listed in Table 1. The first column ("Complete") contains the results when the resulting RCL expression is exactly the same as the ground-truth RCL expression. Next to the full matching scores, we also provide the scores for partial matching of the RCL expressions ("Partial"), based on the Parseval metric (Black et al., 1991). Each RCL expression is scored between 0 and 1 according to the resemblance with the expected expression. The tree representations of the RCL expressions are compared and the number of correct nodes in the actual expression are divided by the number of nodes in the tree of the expected expression to calculate the score. A node is correct if it is present at the same position in both trees and if all children are correct.

The last column ("Without context") contains the results when using the parser without the verification step. This can be considered a baseline.

It may be clear that the use of contextual parsing is advantageous when comparing the contextual with the non-contextual setting, with an increase of 13% in the number of correct results.

Error Analysis

When inspecting the wrong parses, it could be observed that the wrong results were usually minimally wrong. Either the value of a certain element

Expected	Actual	Occurrences
edge	region	17
above	within	15
right	left	8
left	front	7
within	above	6

Table 2: Wrong values.

was wrong, an unnecessary element was added to the expression or a required element was not present in the resulting expression. This is also clear when comparing the complete with the partial match results, from which it can be seen that 66 sentences were only partially incorrect. Some of the most commonly wrong values are listed in Table 2. A final common reason for a wrong parse was that a sequence of a *take* and a *drop* action is considered as a single *move* action. There are 6 occurrences of this final case of which 5 would result in the same end state.

One of the most common reasons that the parser returned no result for a sentence, is because one type of sentences was not present in the training set. Sentences of the form *"pick up red block. put it on grey block"* were completely absent from the training data, but did appear 34 times in the test set. Their structure is quite simple and should not present a problem, but the parser was only trained on sentences that combined the two actions with an "and" connective. This is a problem because the trained grammar is very dependent on the provided training data. Another difficult type of sentences are the ones that contain measures. Only 17 of these were parsed correctly, while 70 had no result and 3 were wrong.

Without considering the context, the combined *move* & *drop* action is not possible, since the context is required to decide afterwards which specific action has to be executed. 59 sentences (6.5%) were wrong because a wrong action was selected.

5 Conclusions and Future Work

In this paper we have presented an improved semantic parsing approach for robot commands by integrating spatial context. It consists of two steps. First, the sentence is parsed using a Probabilistic Combinatory Categorial Grammar. Next, the parses are checked against the context. The resulting parse is the one with the highest likelihood that is valid given the context. This approach was evaluated on the SemEval-2014 Task 6 dataset. The results indicate that integrating contextual knowledge is advantageous for parsing spatial robot commands.

In future work, we will perform an in-depth analysis of our system in comparison with the other participating systems. Furthermore, we will extend our approach to contexts that also contain probabilistic facts, in order to be able to handle noisy sensor data.

References

Yoav Artzi and Luke Zettlemoyer. 2013. Weakly supervised learning of semantic parsers for mapping instructions to actions. *Transactions of the ACL*, 1:49–62.

Ezra W. Black, Steven P. Abney, Daniel P. Flickenger, Claudia Gdaniec, Ralph Grishman, Philip Harrison, Donald Hindle, Robert J. P. Ingria, Frederick Jelinek, Judith L. Klavans, Mark Y. Liberman, Mitchell P. Marcus, Salim Roukos, Beatrice Santorini, and Tomek Strzalkowski. 1991. A procedure for quantitatively comparing the syntactic coverage of English grammars. In *HLT*. Morgan Kaufmann.

Bob Carpenter. 1997. *Type-Logical Semantics*. The MIT Press.

Kais Dukes. 2013a. Semantic Annotation of Robotic Spatial Commands. In *Language and Technology Conference*.

Kais Dukes. 2013b. Supervised semantic parsing of robotic spatial commands. `http://alt.qcri.org/semeval2014/task6/`.

Rohit J. Kate and Raymond J. Mooney. 2006. Using string-kernels for learning semantic parsers. In *Proceedings of the 21st International Conference on Computational Linguistics and the 44th Annual Meeting of the ACL*, ACL-44, pages 913–920, Stroudsburg, PA, USA. ACL.

Rohit J. Kate, Yuk Wah Wong, and Raymond J. Mooney. 2005. Learning to transform natural to formal languages. In *Proceedings of the 20th National Conference on Artificial Intelligence - Volume 3*, AAAI'05, pages 1062–1068. AAAI Press.

Jayant Krishnamurthy and Thomas Kollar. 2013. Jointly Learning to Parse and Perceive : Connecting Natural Language to the Physical World. In *Transactions of ACL*, volume 1, pages 193–206.

Tom Kwiatkowski, Luke Zettlemoyer, Sharon Goldwater, and Mark Steedman. 2010. Lexical generalization in ccg grammar induction for semantic parsing. In *Proceedings of the Conference on Empirical Methods in Natural Language Processing*, EMNLP '11, pages 1512–1523, Stroudsburg, PA, USA. ACL.

Yann LeCun, Léon Bottou, Yoshua Bengio, and Patrick Haffner. 1998. Gradient-based learning applied to document recognition. *Proceedings of the IEEE*, 86(11):2278–2324.

Heeyoung Lee, Yves Peirsman, Angel Chang, Nathanael Chambers, Mihai Surdeanu, and Dan Jurafsky. 2011. Stanford's multi-pass sieve coreference resolution system at the CoNLL-2011 shared task. In *Proceedings of the CoNLL-11 Shared Task.*

Heeyoung Lee, Angel Chang, Yves Peirsman, Nathanael Chambers, Mihai Surdeanu, and Dan Jurafsky. 2013. Deterministic coreference resolution based on entity-centric, precision-ranked rules. *Computational Linguistics*, 39(4).

Raymond J. Mooney. 2007. Learning for semantic parsing. In Alexander Gelbukh, editor, *Computational Linguistics and Intelligent Text Processing*, volume 4394 of *Lecture Notes in Computer Science*, pages 311–324. Springer Berlin Heidelberg.

Hoifung Poon. 2013. Grounded unsupervised semantic parsing. In *ACL (1)*, pages 933–943. ACL.

Karthik Raghunathan, Heeyoung Lee, Sudarshan Rangarajan, Nathanael Chambers, Mihai Surdeanu, Dan Jurafsky, and Christopher Manning. 2010. A multipass sieve for coreference resolution. EMNLP-2010, Boston, USA.

Marta Recasens, Marie-Catherine de Marneffe, and Christopher Potts. 2013. The life and death of discourse entities: Identifying singleton mentions. In *Proceedings of NAACL 2013*, pages 627–633. ACL.

Mark Steedman. 1996. *Surface structure and interpretation*. Linguistic inquiry monographs. The MIT Press, Cambridge, MA, USA.

Mark Steedman. 2000. *The Syntactic Process*. The MIT Press, Cambridge, MA, USA.

KUNLPLab:Sentiment Analysis on Twitter Data

Beakal Gizachew Assefa
Koc Unversity
bassefa13@ku.edu.tr

Abstract

This paper presents the system submitted by KUNLPLab for SemEval-2014 Task9 - Subtask B: Message Polarity on Twitter data. Lexicon features and bag-of-words features are mainly used to represent the datasets. We trained a logistic regression classifier and got an accuracy of 6% increase from the baseline feature representation. The effect of pre-processing on the classifier's accuracy is also discussed in this work.

1 Introduction

Microblogging sites has become a common way of reflecting peoples' opinion. Unlike the regular blogs, the size of a message on a microblogging site is relatively small. The need to automatically detect and summarize the sentiment of messages from users on a given topic or product has gained the interest of researchers.

The sentiment of a message can be negative, positive, or neutral. In the broader sense, automatically detecting the polarity of a message would help business firms easily detect customers' feedback on their product or services. Which in turn helps them improve their decision making by providing information of user preferences, product trend, and user categories.(Chew and Eysenbach, 2010; Salethe and Khandelwal,2011). Sentiment analysis is also used in other domains.(Mandel et al.,2012).

Twitter is one of the mostly widely used microblogging web site with over 200 million users send over 400 million tweets daily(September 2013). A peculiar characteristic of a Twitter data are as follow: emoticons are widely used, the maximum length of a tweet is 140 character, some words are abbreviated, or some are elongated by repeating letters of a word multiple times.

The organizers of the SemEval-2014 has provided a corpus of tweets and posted a task to automatically detect their respective sentiments.

Sub task B of Task 9: Sentiment Analysis on Twitter is describe as follows

Task B - Message Polarity Classification

"Given a message, classify whether the message is of positive, negative, or neutral sentiment. For messages conveying both a positive and negative sentiment, whichever is the stronger sentiment should be chosen."

This paper describes the system submitted by KUNLBLab for participation in SemEval-2014 Task 9 subtask B. Models were trained using the LIBLINEAR classification library (Fan et al., 2008). An accuracy of 66.11% is attained by the classifier by testing on the development set.

The remaining of the document is organized as follows: Section 2 presents a brief literature review on sentiment analysis on Twitter data. Section 3 discusses the system developed to solve the above task, characteristics of the dataset, prepressing on the dataset, and various feature representation. Section 4 illustrates the evaluation results. Section 5 presents conclusion and remarks.

2 Related Work

Sentiment analysis has been studied in Natural Language Processing. Different approaches have been implemented to automatically detect sentiment on texts (Pang et al., 2002; Pang and Lee, 2004; Wiebe and Riloff, 2005; Glance et al., 2005; Wilson et al., 2005).

There is also an active research on Sentiment analysis on Twitter data. (Go et al., 2009, Bermingham and Smeaton, 2010, and Pak and

Proceedings of the 8th International Workshop on Semantic Evaluation (SemEval 2014), pages 391–394,
Dublin, Ireland, August 23-24, 2014.

Paroubek 2010) consider tweets with good emoticons as positive examples and tweets with bad emoticons as negative examples for the training data, and built a classifier using unigrams and bigrams as features.

Barbosa and Feng (2010) classified the subjectivity of tweets based on traditional features with the inclusion of some witter specific clues such as retweets, hashtags, links, uppercase words, emoticons, and exclamation and question marks.

(Agarwal et al. 2011) introduced a POS-specific prior polarity features and used a tree kernel to obviate the need for tedious feature engineering.

3 System Description

3.1 Dataset

The organizer of SemEval-2014 have provided training and development sets. Table 1 bellow illustrates the characteristics of the dataset.

	Positive	Negative	Neutral
Train	3045	1,209	4004
Dev	575	340	739

Table 1. Dataset characteristics

3.2 Pre-processing

We employed two major pre-processing in the datasets. Converting terms to their correct representation, and stemming.

Mostly, in Twitter, words are not written in their correct/full form. For instance, love, loooove, looove convey the same meaning as the word love alone regardless of the extent of the emphasis intended to describe. Reducing this various representations of the same term to common word helps in better matching them even if they are written in different way. This is more problematic if our features are based on term matching and hence increase the number of unknown terms.

The second pre-processing we employed is stemming the terms in the dataset. In most cases, morphological variants of words have similar semantic interpretations and can be considered as equivalent. The advantage of stemming is two-fold. Primarily it reduces the number of OOVs (Out Of Vocabulary) terms. The second one is feature reduction.

3.3 Features

There are two main categories of features used in the development of this system. Bag-of-Words and sentiment lexicon features.

Bag-of-Words features takes a given input text and extracts the raw words as features independent of one another. One issue in using this feature is how to represent negations. In the texts "I *like the movie.* ", and "*I do not like the movie.*", the sentiment of the words in the two texts is opposite since the two statements are negations of one another. One way of representing the negated word is by appending the tag **_NOT** (Chen (2001) and Pang et al. (2002). The **_NOT** tag suffixes all words between the negation word and the first punctuation mark after the negation word. In the above example the second text is transformed to " *I do like_**NOT** the_**NOT** movie_**NOT***". In representation of the negations, we employ the above approach. Lee Becker et al. (2013) directly integrated the polarized word representation in their system. One disadvantage of this representation is the number of features doubles in worst case.

Sentiment lexicons are words, which have association with positive or negative sentiments. Unlike the Bag-Of-Words, instead of taking the raw word as a feature, every word has a score, which is a measure of how much positive or negative sentiment the lexicon has. In this work we use the NRC Hashtag Sentiment Lexicon, and Sentiment140 Lexicon (Mohammad 2013). Both list of lexicons are used in the SemEval 2013 by NRC-Canada team.

The ***NRCHashtag Sentiment Lexicon*** is based on the common practice that users use the # symbol to emphasis on a topic or a word. The hashtag lexicon was created from a collection of tweets that had a positive or a negative word hashtag such as #good, #excellent, #bad, and #terrible (Mohammad 2012). It was created from 775,310 tweets posted between April and December 2012 using a list of 78 positive and negative word hashtags. They have provided unigram, bigram, and trigram datasest. In this work however, we used the unigram features which contains 54,129 terms.

The ***Sentiment140*** is also a list of words with associations to positive an negative sentiments. It has the same format as the NRC Hashtag Sentiment Lexicon. However, it was created from the sentiment140 corpus of 1.6 million tweets, and emoticons were used as positive and negative labels (instead of hashtagged words).

In order to investigate the effect of the features listed above, we have used various combination of them. Table 2 shows 12 kinds of features used for the system we have developed.

The converted versions of the features are the ones where the enlongated words are shortened to their normal form and terms with less than 5 occurances in the training set are ignored.

Code	Features
F1	RawBag-Of-Word
F2	Bag-Of-WordStemmed
F3	ConvertedStemedBag-Of-Word
F4	Hashtag
F5	Sentiment140
F6	CombinedLexicons
F7	ConvertedHashtag
F8	ConvertedSentiment140
F9	ConvertedNegatedHashtag
F10	ConvertedNegatedSentiment140
F11	ConvertedStemmeLexicon
F12	AllCombined

Table 2. Code of features and their names

The description of the features is as follow, F1 is a raw Bag-Of-Word features in which terms with more than five frequency are taken as features. F2 takes the stem of the words whereas F3 applies both stemmig and shortening of elongeted words to the corpus then takes Bag-Of-Word features of the converted corpus.

F4 and F5 are sentiment lexcon features hashtag. F6 is a combined Sentiment140, and Hashtag features. F7 and F8 are applications of the sentiment lexicons after applying shortening and steming. Negative message representation is included in features F9 and F10. F11 is the combination of a preprocessed corpus by applicaiton of stemming and short represenation of elnogated terms, negative message representation, and extracting a combined sentiword140 and hash tag features.

Feature F12 is the combination of all the features. If a term after being preprocessed is found in one of the lexicon features, the lexicon polarity measure is taken as feature value.Otherwise; we resort to the Bag-Of-Word feature.

3.4 The classifier

For this task, we have used L2 regularized logistic regression and used the LIBLINEAR implementation (Rong-En Fan et al.).To estimate the hyper parameters, we applied a 10 fold cross validation on the training set. Liblinear implementation of a L2 regularized logistic regression takes a single cost C parameter. The value of the cost C parameter decides the weight between the L1 regularization term and L2 regularization term. If the value of C is less than one, it means the more weight it given to the L1 regularization term. On the other hand C values more than one gives more weight to the L2 regularizing term. The cost parameter C=1 gives the best result on the cross validation test. The same value is used to train our model.

4 Evaluation Results

As described in Table 2 of section 3.3, the major features used in this work are bag-of-word and sentiment lexicon features. In addition to the feature representation, pre-processing has been done on the datasets.

F1 is a baseline feature (raw Bag-Of-Word), with a total accuracy of 60.16. Simply converting the elongated terms to their normal form and applying stemming on the corpus increase the accuracy from 60.16 to 64.92 (**4.76%**).

	Positive	Negative	Neutral	Total
F1	<u>61.71</u>	<u>52.48</u>	<u>60.55</u>	<u>60.16</u>
F2`	61.71	51.43	61.18	60.36
F3	67.64	62.86	63.64	64.92
F4	66.67	52.94	60.10	61.65
F5	67.91	54.72	61.00	62.54
F6	64.86	55.24	61.47	61.94
F7	67.72	60.42	63.07	63.51
F8	70.29	58.93	63.02	64.17
F9	70.27	56.12	62.28	63.36
F10	71.73	59.29	62.86	64.65
F11	67.25	62.89	63.14	64.52
F12	**71.12**	**61.4**	**64.13**	**66.11**

Table 3. Results of the evaluation on the development set

F6 (the combined lexicon feature- sentiword140 and hashtag) yields an accuracy of 61.94. Applying conversion, negative representation and stemming raises the accuracy to 64.52 (**F11**)

Testset	MacroF1
LiveJournal2014	63.77
SMS2013	55.89
Twitter2013	58.12
Twitter2014	61.72
Twitter2014Sarcasm	44.60

Table 4. Evaluation result on test set

The accuracy of identifying negative sentiment is the least in all features. This shows that we need a better representation of negated messages.

A test dataset was also provided by the organizer of semEval-2014. Table 4 show the accuracy of the KUNPLab classifier.

Our model has performed poorly on the Twitter2014Sarcasm test set (44.60%). The performance of our classifier on LiveJournal2014 is similar to the development set test performance.

5 Conclusion

The performance of a classifier depends on feature representation, hyperparameter optimization and regularization. In this work, we mainly used bag-of-word features and sentiment lexicon features. We trained a L2 regularized logistic regression model. Two major features are used to represent the datasets; Bag-of-Word features and Lexical features. It has been shown that stemming the terms increases accuracy of the classifier in either case. The accuracy of the classifier on development set and training set is reported and has shown an increase of 6% in accuracy form the baseline with 95% confidence interval..The evaluation of our system on SemEval-2014 test data is also shown with an F measure of 44.60 to 63.77%.

6 Acknowledgement

I would like to acknowledge Ass.Prof. Dr. Deniz YURET for his advice, guidance, encouragement and inspiration to participate in SemEval-2014. I also like to thank Mohammad Khuram SALEEM, and Mohamad IRFAN for proof reading this document.

Reference

Cynthia Chew and Gunther Eysenbach. 2010. Pandemics in the Age of Twitter: Content Analysis of Tweets during the 2009 H1N1 Outbreak. PLoS ONE, 5(11):e14118+, November.

Marcel Salath´e and Shashank Khandelwal. 2011. Assessing vaccination sentiments with online social media: Implications for infectious disease dynamics and control. PLoS Computational Biology, 7(10).

Benjamin Mandel, Aron Culotta, John Boulahanis, Danielle Stark, Bonnie Lewis, and Jeremy Rodrigue. 2012. A demographic analysis of online sentiment during hurricane irene. In Proceedngs of the Second Workshop on Language in Social Media, LSM'12, pages 27–36, Stroudsburg, PA, USA. Association for Computational Linguistics.

Sanjiv Das and Mike Chen. 2001. Yahoo! for amazon: extracting market sentiment from stock message boards. In Proceedings of the 8th Asia Pacific Finance Association Annual Conference.

Lee Becker, George Erhart, David Skiba and Valentine Matula. 2013. AVAYA: Sentiment Analysis on Twitter with Self-Training and Polarity Lexicon Expansion. Seventh International Workshop on Semantic Evaluation (SemEval 2013)

Saif Mohammad. 2012. Emotional Tweets. In Proceedings of the First Joint Conference on Lexical and Computational Semantics (*SEM), pages 246–255, Montr´eal, Canada. Association for Computational Linguistics.

Bo Pang, Lillian Lee, and Shivakumar Vaithyanathan. 2002. Thumbs up? Sentiment Classification Using Machine Learning Techniques. In Proceedings of the Conference on Empirical Methods in Natural Language Processing (EMNLP 2002)

Mohammad, Saif and Kiritchenko, Svetlana and Zhu, Xiaodan 2013. NRC-Canada: Building the State-of-the-Art in Sentiment Analysis of Tweets Proceedings of the seventh international workshop on Semantic Evaluation Exercises (SemEval-2013).

Go, A., Bhayani, R., Huang, L.: Twitter sentiment classification using distant supervision. CS224N Project Report, Stanford (2009)

Barbosa, L., Feng, J.: Robust sentiment detection on Twitter from biased and noisy data. In: Proceedings of COLING. pp. 36–44 (2010)

Agarwal, A., Xie, B., Vovsha, I., Rambow, O., Passonneau, R.: Sentiment analysis of Twitter data. In: Proc. ACL 2011 Workshop on Languages in Social Media. pp. 30–38 (2011)

Adam Bermingham and Alan Smeaton. 2010. Classifying sentiment in microblogs: is brevity an advantage is brevity an advantage? ACM, pages 1833–1836.

Alexander Pak and Patrick Paroubek. 2010. Twitter as a corpus for sentiment analysis and opinion mining. Proceedings of LREC.

Glance, N., M. Hurst, K. Nigam, M. Siegler, R. Stock ton, and T. Tomokiyo. 2005. Deriving marketing intelligence from online discussion. In Proceedings of the eleventh ACM SIGKDD, pages 419–428. ACM.

Wiebe, J. and E. Riloff. 2005. Creating subjective and objective sentence classifiers from unannotated texts. Computational Linguistics and Intelligent Text Processing, pages 486–497.

R.-E. Fan, K.-W. Chang, C.-J. Hsieh, X.-R. Wang, and C.-J. Lin. LIBLINEAR: A Library for Large Linear Classification, Journal of Machine Learning Research 9(2008), 1871-1874

Linköping: Cubic-Time Graph Parsing with a Simple Scoring Scheme

Marco Kuhlmann
Dept. of Computer and Information Science
Linköping University, Sweden
marco.kuhlmann@liu.se

Abstract

We turn the Eisner algorithm for parsing to projective dependency trees into a cubic-time algorithm for parsing to a restricted class of directed graphs. To extend the algorithm into a data-driven parser, we combine it with an edge-factored feature model and online learning. We report and discuss results on the SemEval-2014 Task 8 data sets (Oepen et al., 2014).

1 Introduction

This paper describes the system that we submitted to the closed track of the SemEval-2014 Task on Broad-Coverage Semantic Dependency Parsing (Oepen et al., 2014).[1] However, the main contribution of the paper is not the system as such (which had the lowest score among all systems submitted to the task), but the general approach for which it is a proof of concept.

Graphs support natural representations of linguistic structure. For this reason, algorithms that can learn, process and transform graphs are of central importance to language technology. Yet, most of the algorithms that are used in natural language processing today focus on the restricted case of trees, and do so for a reason: Computation on general graphs is hard or even intractable, and efficient processing is possible only for restricted classes (cf. Courcelle and Engelfriet (2012)). The task then is to identify classes of graphs that are both expressive enough to cover the linguistic data, and restricted enough to facilitate efficient processing.

This paper shows that there are graphs that satisfy both of these desiderata. Our system is based on a new algorithm for parsing to a restricted class of directed graphs (Section 2). This class is restricted in so far as our algorithm runs in cubic time with respect to the length of the sentence; it thus has the same asymptotic complexity as parsing with context-free phrase structure grammars. The class of graphs defined by our algorithm is also expressive, in so far that it covers more than 98% of the SemEval data.

To demonstrate that our parsing algorithm can be turned into a practical system, we combine it with two techniques taken straight from the literature on data-driven syntactic dependency parsing:

- an edge-factored scoring model, as it has been used as the core of practical parsers since the seminal work of McDonald et al. (2005), and
- online learning using the structured perceptron, in the style of Collins (2002).

State-of-the-art parsers use considerably more advanced (and computationally more demanding) techniques, and therefore our system cannot be expected to deliver competitive results. (Its results on the SemEval data are reported in Section 4.) Instead, the main point of our contribution to the SemEval Task is to provide evidence that research on classes of graphs that balance linguistic coverage and parsing efficiency holds a lot of potential.

2 Parsing Algorithm

We start the description of our system with the description of our cubic-time parsing algorithm. The remaining components of our system will be described in Section 3.

[1] https://github.com/liu-nlp/gamma

Proceedings of the 8th International Workshop on Semantic Evaluation (SemEval 2014), pages 395–399,
Dublin, Ireland, August 23-24, 2014.

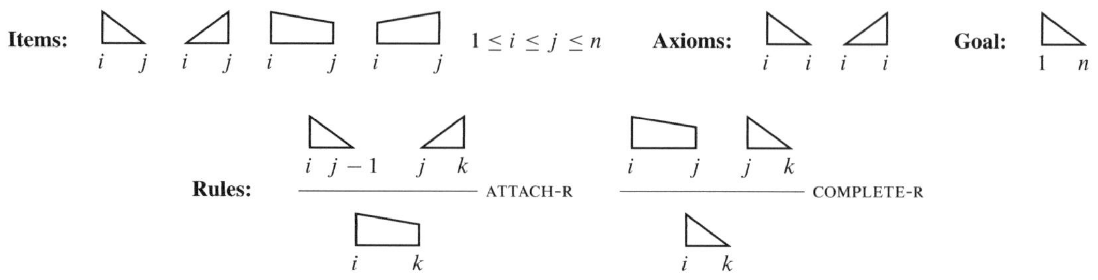

Figure 1: The Eisner algorithm for building the packed forest of all projective dependency trees with n nodes. Only the rightward versions of ATTACH and COMPLETE are shown here.

2.1 The Eisner Algorithm

We recall the algorithm for projective dependency parsing by Eisner and Satta (1999). The declarative specification of this algorithm in terms of a deduction system (Shieber et al., 1995) is given in Figure 1. The algorithm uses four types of items, ◺, ◿, ▭, and ▭, and two types of inference rules called ATTACH and COMPLETE. These rules can be interpreted as operations on graphs: An ATTACH rule *concatenates* two graphs and adds one of two possible edges—from the left endpoint of the first graph to the right endpoint of the second graph, or vice versa. Similarly, a COMPLETE rule *fuses* two graphs by unifying the right endpoint of the first with the left endpoint of the second. The algorithm by Eisner and Satta (1999) produces a compact representation of the set of all dependency graphs over the input sentence that can be built using these operations. This is exactly the set of projective dependency trees for the input sentence.

2.2 The Graph-Parsing Algorithm

To parse to dependency graphs rather than trees, we modify the Eisner algorithm as follows:

- We give up the distinction between ▭ and ▭. This distinction is essential for ensuring that the parser builds a tree. Since our goal is to parse to graphs, we do not need it.
- We allow ATTACH to add one, zero, or several edges. This modification makes it possible to parse graphs with reentrancies (several incoming edges) and isolated nodes.

To implement the first modification, we introduce a new type of items, ▭, that subsumes ▭ and ▭.

To implement the second modification, we parametrize the ATTACH rule by a set ω that specifies the edges that are added during the concatenation. We refer to the left and right endpoints of a graph as its *ports* and number the ports of the antecedents of the ATTACH rule left-to-right from 1 to 4. A set ω then takes the form

$$\omega \subseteq \big(\{1,2\} \times \{3,4\}\big) \cup \big(\{3,4\} \times \{1,2\}\big)\,.$$

The rule ATTACH_ω adds an edge $u \to v$ if and only if u and v are nodes corresponding to ports s and t, respectively, and $(s,t) \in \omega$. For example, the ATTACH rule in Figure 1 is specified by the set $\omega = \{(1,4)\}$: it adds one edge, from the left endpoint of the graph corresponding to the first antecedent to the right endpoint of the other graph.

The complete parsing algorithm is specified in Figure 2, where the rule CONC (for *concatenation*) corresponds to the two conflated ATTACH rules and FUSE corresponds to the two COMPLETE rules. Inspecting the specification, we find that the algorithm runs in time $O(mn^3)$ where n is the number of nodes and m is the number of concatenation rules. Note that, because each concatenation rule is determined by a set ω as defined above, each parser in our framework can use at most $2^8 = 256$ different CONC rules.[2]

3 Data-Driven Parsing

We now extend our parsing algorithm into a simple parser for data-driven parsing. We cast parsing as an optimization problem over a parametrized scoring function: Given a sentence x we compute

$$\hat{y} = \operatorname*{arg\,max}_{y \in \mathcal{Y}(x)} s(x,y) \qquad (1)$$

where $\mathcal{Y}(x)$ is the set of candidate graphs for x and the scoring function is decomposed as $s(x,y) = \theta \cdot f(x,y)$. The function f returns a high-dimensional feature vector that describes characteristic properties of the sentence–graph pair (x,y), and the vector θ assigns to each feature a weight.

[2]This is because a set ω specifies up to $2 \times 2 + 2 \times 2 = 8$ different concatenation operations.

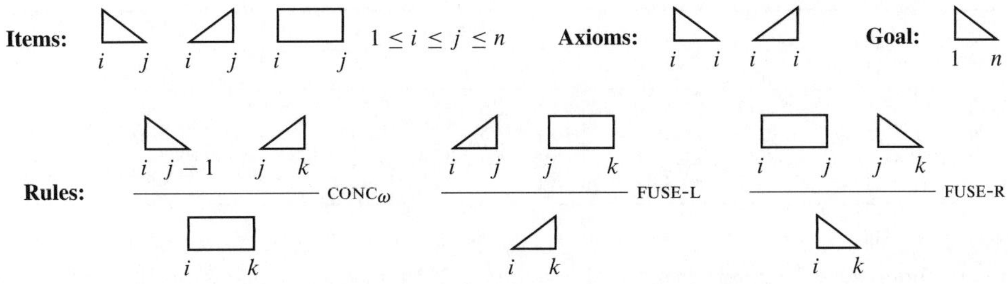

Figure 2: The parsing algorithm used in this paper. The concatenation rules (CONC) are parametrized with respect to an edge specification ω (see Section 2.2).

3.1 Candidate Graphs

Our set of candidate graphs is the set of all graphs that can be built using the operations of our parsing algorithm. The size of this set and hence the maximal coverage of our parser is determined by the set of CONC rules: The more different concatenation operations we use, the more graphs we can build. At the same time, increasing the number of operations also increases the runtime of our parser. This means that we need to find a good trade-off between coverage and parsing efficiency.

To obtain upper bounds on the coverage of our parser we compute, for each graph G in the SemEval test data, a graph $\tilde{G}$ that maximizes the set of edges that it has in common with G. This can be done using a Viterbi-style variant of our parsing algorithm that scores an item by the number of edges that it has in common with G. The results are reported in Table 1. As we can see, our approach has the potential to achieve more than 98% labelled recall (LR) on all three representation types used in the task. This figure is obtained for the full set of concatenation operations. For our submission we chose to optimize for parsing speed and used a parser with a reduced set of only three operations:

$$\omega_1 = \{(1,4)\}, \quad \omega_2 = \{(4,1)\}, \quad \omega_3 = \{\}.$$

These are the two operations that correspond to the ATTACH rules of the algorithm by Eisner and Satta (ω_1, ω_2), together with the operation that concatenates two graphs without adding any edges at all (ω_3). The latter is required to produce graphs where a node has no incoming edges. As can be seen in Table 1, the upper bounds for the reduced set of operations are still surprisingly high when measured in terms of LR: 95.70% for DM, 93.06% for PAS, and 93.51% for PCEDT. However, there is a significant loss when coverage is measured in terms of labelled exact match (LM).

	DM	PAS	PCEDT
full	98.25 / 75.74	98.13 / 69.81	98.19 / 83.23
reduced	95.70 / 52.15	93.06 / 23.66	93.51 / 54.75

Table 1: Upper bounds for recall (LR/LM) on the test data for two different sets of operations.

3.2 Scoring Function

We use the same features as in the first-order model implemented in the MSTParser system for syntactic dependency parsing (McDonald et al., 2005).[3] Under this model, the feature vector for a dependency graph is the sum of the feature vectors of its edges, which take into account atomic features such as the word forms and part-of-speech tags of the tokens connected by the edge, the length of the edge, the edge label, as well as combinations of those atomic features. To set the feature weights we use averaged perceptron training in the style of Collins (2002).

3.3 Top-Node Tagger

The final component in our system is a simple tagger that is used to annotate the output of our parser with information about *top nodes* (as defined in the task's data format). It is based on Matthew Honnibal's part-of-speech tagger[4] and uses features based on the word form and part-of-speech of the node to be tagged, as well as the labels of the edges incident to that node; these features were selected based on tagging accuracy with the recommended development train/dev-split. The tagger is a sequence model without global constraints; in particular, it does not enforce unique top nodes. Tagging accuracy on the final test set was 98.50% for DM, 99.21% for PAS, and 99.94% for PCEDT.

[3]http://sourceforge.net/projects/mstparser/
[4]http://honnibal.wordpress.com/

	DM			PAS			PCEDT		
	LP	LR	LF	LP	LR	LF	LP	LR	LF
Baseline	83.20%	40.73%	54.68%	88.34%	35.74%	50.89%	74.82%	62.08%	67.84%
Linköping	78.54%	78.05%	78.29%	76.16%	75.55%	75.85%	60.66%	64.35%	62.45%
Task average	84.21%	81.29%	82.69%	87.95%	83.57%	85.65%	72.17%	68.44%	70.21%
Peking	90.27%	88.54%	89.40%	93.44%	90.69%	92.04%	78.75%	73.96%	76.28%

Table 2: Labelled precision (LP), labelled recall (LR), and labelled F1 (LF) scores of our own system (Linköping) and three points of comparison on the SemEval-2014 Task 8 test data: baseline, task average, and the best-performing system from Peking University (Du et al., 2014).

4 Experiments

We report experimental results on the SemEval data sets (closed track). We trained one parser for each representation (DM, PAS, PCEDT). Averaged perceptron training can be parametrized by the number N of iterations over the training data; to determine the value of this parameter, for each representation type and each $1 \leq N \leq 10$ we trained a development system using the recommended development train/dev-split and selected that value of N which gave the highest accuracy on the held-out data. The selected values and the number of (binary) features in the resulting systems are reported in Table 3. Training took around 8 minutes per iteration on an iMac computer (Late 2013, 3,4 GHz Intel Core i5) with a 6 GB Java heap size.

4.1 Results

Table 2 reports the labelled precision (LP) and labelled recall (LR) of our system on the final test data. Compared to the tree-based baseline, our system has substantially lower precision (between 4.66 and 14.16 points) but substantially higher recall (between 2.27 and 39.81 points). Compared to the top-scoring system, our system is way behind in terms of both scores (11.11–16.19 points). The scores of our system are also substantially below the task average, which resulted in it being ranked last of all six systems participating in the closed track. Given these results, we have refrained from doing a detailed error analysis. It may be interesting to note, however, that our system is the only one in the task for which labelled F1 is higher on the DM data than on the PAS data.

	DM	PAS	PCEDT
# iterations	4	1	9
# features	7.3M	8.7M	8.1M

Table 3: Characteristics of the trained models.

4.2 Discussion

The comparatively low scores of our system do not come unexpected. Our parser uses a very simple scoring model and learning method, whereas even the baseline relies on a state-of-the-art syntactic dependency parser (Bohnet, 2010). Also, we did not do any feature engineering (on the parser), but just used the feature extraction procedure of MSTParser. Regarding both of these points, the potential for improving the system is apparent. Finally, our post-hoc prediction of top nodes is extremely simplistic. It would have been much more desirable to integrate this prediction into the parser, for example by adding virtual incoming dependencies to all top nodes. However, preliminary experiments showed that this particular strategy had a severely negative impact on coverage.

5 Conclusion

We have presented a new algorithm for parsing to a restricted class of digraphs and shown how to extend this algorithm into a system for data-driven dependency parsing. Our main goal was to show that it is possible to develop algorithms for direct parsing to directed graphs that are both efficient and achieve good coverage on practical data sets: Our algorithm runs in cubic time in the length of the sentence, and has more than 98% coverage on each of the three data sets.

Our future work will address both theoretical and practical issues. On the theoretical side, we feel that it is important to obtain a better understanding of the specific graph-structural properties that characterise the linguistic data. Our parser provides an operational definition of a class of graphs (those graphs that can be built by the parser); it would be more satisfying to obtain a declarative characterisation that does not depend on a specific algorithm. Such a characterisation would be interesting even for a restricted set of operations.

On the practical side, we would like to extend our approach into a more competitive system for semantic dependency parsing. In particular, we would like to use a more powerful scoring function (incorporating second- and third-order features) and a more predicative learning method (such as max-margin training).

Acknowledgements

We thank the two anonymous reviewers of this paper for their detailed and constructive comments.

References

Bernd Bohnet. 2010. Very high accuracy and fast dependency parsing is not a contradiction. In *Proceedings of the 23rd International Conference on Computational Linguistics (COLING)*, pages 89–97, Beijing, China.

Michael Collins. 2002. Discriminative training methods for Hidden Markov Models: Theory and experiments with perceptron algorithms. In *Proceedings of the Conference on Empirical Methods in Natural Language Processing (EMNLP)*, pages 1–8, Philadelphia, USA.

Bruno Courcelle and Joost Engelfriet. 2012. *Graph Structure and Monadic Second-Order Logic*, volume 138 of *Encyclopedia of Mathematics and its Applications*. Cambridge University Press.

Yantao Du, Fan Zhang, Weiwei Sun, and Xiaojun Wan. 2014. Peking: Profiling syntactic tree parsing techniques for semantic graph parsing. In *Proceedings of the Eighth International Workshop on Semantic Evaluation (SemEval 2014)*, Dublin, Republic of Ireland.

Jason Eisner and Giorgio Satta. 1999. Efficient parsing for bilexical context-free grammars and Head Automaton Grammars. In *Proceedings of the 37th Annual Meeting of the Association for Computational Linguistics (ACL)*, pages 457–464, College Park, MD, USA.

Ryan McDonald, Koby Crammer, and Fernando Pereira. 2005. Online large-margin training of dependency parsers. In *Proceedings of the 43rd Annual Meeting of the Association for Computational Linguistics (ACL)*, pages 91–98, Ann Arbor, USA.

Stephan Oepen, Marco Kuhlmann, Yusuke Miyao, Daniel Zeman, Dan Flickinger, Jan Hajič, Angelina Ivanova, and Yi Zhang. 2014. SemEval 2014 Task 8: Broad-coverage semantic dependency parsing. In *Proceedings of the Eighth International Workshop on Semantic Evaluation (SemEval 2014)*, Dublin, Republic of Ireland.

Stuart M. Shieber, Yves Schabes, and Fernando Pereira. 1995. Principles and implementation of deductive parsing. *Journal of Logic Programming*, 24(1–2):3–36.

LIPN: Introducing a new Geographical Context Similarity Measure and a Statistical Similarity Measure Based on the Bhattacharyya Coefficient

Davide Buscaldi, Jorge J. García Flores, Joseph Le Roux, Nadi Tomeh
Laboratoire d'Informatique de Paris Nord, CNRS (UMR 7030)
Université Paris 13, Sorbonne Paris Cité, Villetaneuse, France
{buscaldi,jgflores,joseph.le-roux,nadi.tomeh}@lipn.univ-paris13.fr

Belém Priego Sanchez
Laboratoire LDI (Lexique, Dictionnaires, Informatique)
Université Paris 13, Sorbonne Paris Cité, Villetaneuse, France
LKE, FCC, BUAP, San Manuel, Puebla, Mexico
belemps@gmail.com

Abstract

This paper describes the system used by the LIPN team in the task 10, Multilingual Semantic Textual Similarity, at SemEval 2014, in both the English and Spanish sub-tasks. The system uses a support vector regression model, combining different text similarity measures as features. With respect to our 2013 participation, we included a new feature to take into account the geographical context and a new semantic distance based on the Bhattacharyya distance calculated on co-occurrence distributions derived from the Spanish Google Books n-grams dataset.

1 Introduction

After our participation at SemEval 2013 with LIPN-CORE (Buscaldi et al., 2013) we found that geography has an important role in discriminating the semantic similarity of sentences (especially in the case of newswire). If two events happened in a different location, their semantic relatedness is usually low, no matter if the events are the same. Therefore, we worked on a similarity measure able to capture the similarity between the geographic contexts of two sentences. We tried also to reinforce the semantic similarity features by introducing a new measure that calculates word similarities on co-occurrence distributions extracted from Google Books bigrams. This measure was introduced only for the Spanish runs, due to time constraints. The regression model used to integrate the features was the ν-Support Vector Regression model (ν-SVR) (Schölkopf et al., 1999) implementation provided by LIBSVM (Chang and Lin, 2011), with a radial basis function kernel with the standard parameters ($\nu = 0.5$). We describe all the measures in Section 2; the results obtained by the system are detailed in Section 3.

2 Similarity Measures

In this section we describe the measures used as features in our system. The description of measures already used in our 2013 participation is less detailed than the description of the new ones. Additional details on the measures may be found in (Buscaldi et al., 2013). When POS tagging and NE recognition were required, we used the Stanford CoreNLP[1] for English and FreeLing[2] 3.1 for Spanish.

2.1 WordNet-based Conceptual Similarity

This measure has been introduced in order to measure similarities between concepts with respect to an ontology. The similarity is calculated as follows: first of all, words in sentences p and q are lemmatised and mapped to the related WordNet synsets. All noun synsets are put into the set of synsets associated to the sentence, C_p and C_q, respectively. If the synsets are in one of the other POS categories (verb, adjective, adverb) we look for their derivationally related forms in order to find a related noun synset: if there exists one, we put this synset in C_p (or C_q). No disambiguation process is carried out, so we take all possible meanings into account.

Given C_p and C_q as the sets of concepts contained in sentences p and q, respectively, with

[1] http://www-nlp.stanford.edu/software/corenlp.shtml
[2] http://nlp.lsi.upc.edu/freeling/

Proceedings of the 8th International Workshop on Semantic Evaluation (SemEval 2014), pages 400–405,
Dublin, Ireland, August 23-24, 2014.

$|C_p| \geq |C_q|$, the conceptual similarity between p and q is calculated as:

$$ss(p,q) = \frac{\sum_{c_1 \in C_p} \max_{c_2 \in C_q} s(c_1,c_2)}{|C_p|}$$

where $s(c_1,c_2)$ is a conceptual similarity measure. Concept similarity can be calculated in different ways. We used a variation of the Wu-Palmer formula (Wu and Palmer, 1994) named "ProxiGenea3", introduced by (Dudognon et al., 2010), which is inspired by the analogy between a family tree and the concept hierarchy in WordNet. The ProxiGenea3 measure is defined as:

$$s(c_1,c_2) = \frac{1}{1 + d(c_1) + d(c_2) - 2 \cdot d(c_0)}$$

where c_0 is the most specific concept that is present both in the synset path of c_1 and c_2 (that is, the Least Common Subsumer or LCS). The function returning the depth of a concept is noted with d.

2.2 IC-based Similarity

This measure has been proposed by (Mihalcea et al., 2006) as a corpus-based measure which uses Resnik's Information Content (IC) and the Jiang-Conrath (Jiang and Conrath, 1997) similarity metric. This measure is more precise than the one introduced in the previous subsection because it takes into account also the importance of concepts and not only their relative position in the hierarchy. We refer to (Buscaldi et al., 2013) and (Mihalcea et al., 2006) for a detailed description of the measure. The idf weights for the words were calculated using the Google Web 1T (Brants and Franz, 2006) frequency counts, while the IC values used are those calculated by Ted Pedersen (Pedersen et al., 2004) on the British National Corpus[3].

2.3 Syntactic Dependencies

This measure tries to capture the syntactic similarity between two sentences using dependencies. Previous experiments showed that converting constituents to dependencies still achieved best results on out-of-domain texts (Le Roux et al., 2012), so we decided to use a 2-step architecture to obtain syntactic dependencies. First we parsed pairs of sentences with the LORG parser[4]. Second we converted the resulting parse trees to Stanford dependencies[5].

Given the sets of parsed dependencies D_p and D_q, for sentence p and q, a dependency $d \in D_x$ is a triple (l,h,t) where l is the dependency label (for instance, *dobj* or *prep*), h the governor and t the dependant. The similarity measure between two syntactic dependencies $d_1 = (l_1,h_1,t_1)$ and $d_2 = (l_2,h_2,t_2)$ is the levenshtein distance between the labels l_1 and l_2 multiplied by the average of $idf_h * s_{WN}(h_1,h_2)$ and $idf_t * s_{WN}(t_1,t_2)$, where idf_h and idf_t are the inverse document frequencies calculated on Google Web 1T for the governors and the dependants (we retain the maximum for each pair), respectively, and s_{WN} is calculated using formula **??**. NOTE: This measure was used only in the English sub-task.

2.4 Information Retrieval-based Similarity

Let us consider two texts p and q, an IR system S and a document collection D indexed by S. This measure is based on the assumption that p and q are similar if the documents retrieved by S for the two texts, used as input queries, are ranked similarly.

Let be $L_p = \{d_{p_1}, \ldots, d_{p_K}\}$ and $L_q = \{d_{q_1}, \ldots, d_{q_K}\}$, $d_{x_i} \in D$ the sets of the top K documents retrieved by S for texts p and q, respectively. Let us define $s_p(d)$ and $s_q(d)$ the scores assigned by S to a document d for the query p and q, respectively. Then, the similarity score is calculated as:

$$sim_{IR}(p,q) = 1 - \frac{\sum_{d \in L_p \cap L_q} \frac{\sqrt{(s_p(d)-s_q(d))^2}}{\max(s_p(d),s_q(d))}}{|L_p \cap L_q|}$$

if $|L_p \cap L_q| \neq \emptyset$, 0 otherwise.

For the participation in the English sub-task we indexed a collection composed by the AQUAINT-2[6] and the English NTCIR-8[7] document collections, using the Lucene[8] 4.2 search engine with BM25 similarity. The Spanish index was created using the Spanish QA@CLEF 2005 (agencia EFE1994-95, El Mundo 1994-95) and multiUN

[3]http://www.d.umn.edu/ tpederse/similarity.html

[4]https://github.com/CNGLdlab/LORG-Release

[5]We used the default built-in converter provided with the Stanford Parser (2012-11-12 revision).

[6]http://www.nist.gov/tac/data/data_desc.html#AQUAINT-2

[7]http://metadata.berkeley.edu/NTCIR-GeoTime/ntcir-8-databases.php

[8]http://lucene.apache.org/core

(Eisele and Chen, 2010) collections. The K value was set to 70 after a study detailed in (Buscaldi, 2013).

2.5 N-gram Based Similarity

This measure tries to capture the fact that similar sentences have similar n-grams, even if they are not placed in the same positions. The measure is based on the Clustered Keywords Positional Distance (CKPD) model proposed in (Buscaldi et al., 2009) for the passage retrieval task.

The similarity between a text fragment p and another text fragment q is calculated as:

$$sim_{ngrams}(p,q) = \sum_{\forall x \in Q} \frac{h(x,P)}{\sum_{i=1}^{n} w_i d(x, x_{max})}$$

Where P is the set of the heaviest n-grams in p where all terms are also contained in q; Q is the set of all the possible n-grams in q, and n is the total number of terms in the longest sentence. The weights for each term w_i are calculated as $w_i = 1 - \frac{log(n_i)}{1+log(N)}$ where n_i is the frequency of term t_i in the Google Web 1T collection, and N is the frequency of the most frequent term in the Google Web 1T collection. The weight for each n-gram ($h(x,P)$), with $|P| = j$ is calculated as:

$$h(x,P) = \begin{cases} \sum_{k=1}^{j} w_k & \text{if } x \in P \\ 0 & \text{otherwise} \end{cases}$$

The function $d(x, x_{max})$ determines the minimum distance between a n-gram x and the heaviest one x_{max} as the number of words between them.

2.6 Geographical Context Similarity

We observed that in many sentences, especially those extracted from news corpora, the compatibility of the geographic context between the sentences is an important clue to determine if the sentences are related or not. This measure tries to measure if the two sentences refer to events that took place in the same geographical area. We built a database of geographically-related entities, using geo-WordNet (Buscaldi and Rosso, 2008) and expanding it with all the synsets that are related to a geographically grounded synset. This implies that also adjectives and verbs may be used as clues for the identification of the geographical context of a sentence. For instance, “Afghan” is associated to “Afghanistan”, “Sovietize” to “Soviet Union”, etc. The Named Entities of type PER (Person) are also used as clues: we use Yago[9] to check whether the NE corresponds to a famous leader or not, and in the affirmative case we include the related nation to the geographical context of the sentence. For instance, “Merkel” is mapped to “Germany”. Given G_p and G_q the sets of places found in sentences p and q, respectively, the geographical context similarity is calculated as follows:

$$sim_{geo}(p,q) = 1 - \log_K \left(1 + \frac{\sum_{x \in G_p} \min_{y \in G_q} d(x,y)}{\max(|G_p|, |G_q|)} \right)$$

Where $d(x,y)$ is the spherical distance in Km. between x and y, and K is a normalization factor set to 10000 Km. to obtain similarity values between 1 and 0.

2.7 2-grams “Spectral” Distance

This measure is used to calculate the semantic similarity of two words on the basis of their context, according to the distributional hypothesis. The measure exploits bi-grams in the Google Books n-gram collection[10] and is based on the distributional hypothesis, that is, “words that tend to appear in similar contexts are supposed to have similar meanings”. Given a word w, we calculate the probability of observing a word x knowing that it is preceded by w as $p(x|w) = p(w \cap x)/p(w) = c(\text{“}wx\text{”})/c(\text{“}w\text{”})$, where $c(\text{“}wx\text{”})$ is the number of bigrams “w x” observed in Google Books (counting all publication years) 2-grams and $c(\text{“}w\text{”})$ is the number of occurrences of w observed in Google Books 1-grams. We calculate also the probability of observing a word y knowing that it is followed by w as $p(y|w) = p(w \cap y)/p(w) = c(\text{“}yw\text{”})/c(\text{“}w\text{”})$. In such a way, we may obtain for a word w_i two probability distributions $D_p^{w_i}$ and $D_f^{w_i}$ that can be compared to the distributions obtained in the same way for another word w_j. Therefore, we calculate the distance of two words comparing the distribution probabilities built in this way, using the Bhattacharyya coefficient:

[9] http://www.mpi-inf.mpg.de/yago-naga/yago/
[10] https://books.google.com/ngrams/datasets

$$s_f(w_i, w_j) = -\log\left(\sum_{x\in X}\sqrt{D_f^{w_i}(x) * D_f^{w_j}(x)}\right)$$

$$s_p(w_i, w_j) = -\log\left(\sum_{x\in X}\sqrt{D_p^{w_i}(x) * D_p^{w_j}(x)}\right)$$

the resulting distance between w_i and w_j is calculated as the average between $s_f(w_i, w_j)$ and $s_p(w_i, w_j)$. All words in sentence p are compared to the words of sentence q using this similarity value. The words that are semantically closer are paired; if a word cannot be paired (average distance with any of the words in the other sentence > 10), then it is left unpaired. The value used as the final feature is the averaged sum of all distance scores.

2.8 Other Measures

In addition to the above text similarity measures, we used also the following common measures:

Cosine

Cosine distance calculated between $\mathbf{p} = (w_{p_1}, \ldots, w_{p_n})$ and $\mathbf{q} = (w_{q_1}, \ldots, w_{q_n})$, the vectors of $tf.idf$ weights associated to sentences p and q, with idf values calculated on Google Web 1T.

Edit Distance

This similarity measure is calculated using the Levenshtein distance on characters between the two sentences.

Named Entity Overlap

This is a per-class overlap measure (in this way, "France" as an Organization does not match "France" as a Location) calculated using the Dice coefficient between the sets of NEs found, respectively, in sentences p and q.

3 Results

3.1 Spanish

In order to train the Spanish model, we translated automatically all the sentences in the English SemEval 2012 and 2013 using Google Translate. We also built a corpus manually using definitions from the RAE[11] (Real Academia Española de la Lengua). The definitions were randomly extracted and paired at different similarity levels (taking into account the Dice coefficient calculated on the definitions bag-of-words). Three annotators gave independently their similarity judgments on these paired definitions. A total of 200 definitions were annotated for training. The official results for the Spanish task are shown in Table 1. In Figure 1 we show the results obtained by taking into account each individual feature as a measure of similarity between texts. These results show that the combination was always better than the single features (as expected), and the feature best able to capture semantic similarity alone was the cosine distance. In Table 2 we show the results of the ablation test, which shows that the features that most contributed to improve the results were the IR-based similarity for the news dataset and the cosine distance for the Wikipedia dataset. The worst feature was the NER overlap (not taking into account it would have allowed us to gain 2 places in the final rankings).

	Wikipedia	**News**	**Overall**
LIPN-run1	0.65194	0.82554	0.75558
LIPN-run2	**0.71647**	**0.8316**	**0.7852**
LIPN-run3	0.71618	0.80857	0.77134

Table 1: Spanish results (Official runs).

The differences between the three submitted runs are only in the training set used. `LIPN-run1` uses all the training data available together, `LIPN-run3` uses a training set composed by the translated news for the news dataset and the RAE training set for the Wikipedia dataset; finally, the best run `LIPN-run2` uses the same training sets of run3 together to build a single model.

3.2 English

Our participation in the English task was hampered by some technical problems which did not allow us to complete the parsing of the tweet data in time. As a consequence of this and some errors in the scripts launched to finalize the experiments, the submitted results were incomplete and we were able to detect the problem only after the submission. We show in Table 3 the official results of run1 with the addition of the results on the OnWN dataset calculated after the participation to the task.

[11] http://www.rae.es/

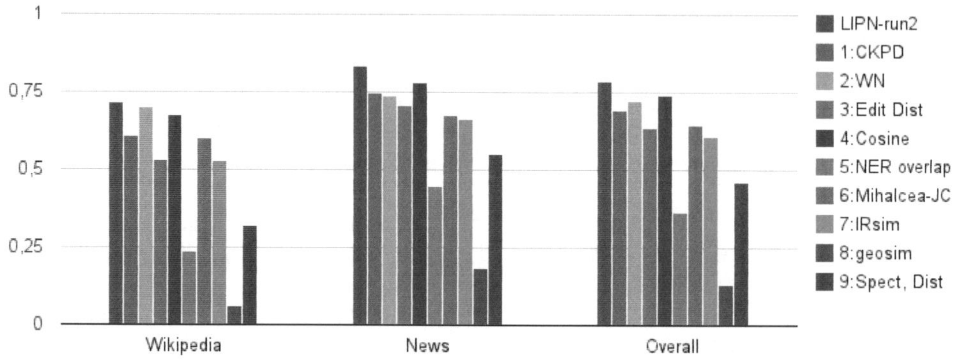

Figure 1: Spanish task: results taking into account the individual features as semantic similarity measures.

Ablated feature	**Wikipedia**	**News**	**Overall**	**diff**
LIPN-run2 (none)	0.7165	0.8316	0.7852	0.00%
1:CKPD	0.7216	0.8318	0.7874	0.22%
2:WN	0.7066	0.8277	0.7789	−0.63%
3:Edit Dist	0.708	0.8242	0.7774	−0.78%
4:Cosine	**0.6849**	0.8235	0.7677	**−1.75%**
5:NER overlap	**0.7338**	**0.8341**	0.7937	**0.85%**
6:Mihalcea-JC	0.7103	0.8301	0.7818	−0.34%
7:IRsim	0.7161	**0.8026**	0.7677	**−1.74%**
8:geosim	0.7185	0.8325	0.7865	0.14%
9:Spect. Dist	0.7243	0.8311	0.7880	0.28%

Table 2: Spanish task: ablation test.

Dataset	**Correlation**
Complete (official + OnWN)	0.6687
Complete (only official)	0.5083
deft-forum	0.4544
deft-news	0.6402
headlines	0.6527
images	0.8094
OnWN (unofficial)	0.8039
tweet-news	0.5507

Table 3: English results (Official run + unofficial OnWN).

4 Conclusions and Future Work

The introduced measures were studied on the Spanish subtask, observing a limited contribution from geographic context similarity and spectral distance. The IR-based measure introduced in 2013 proved to be an important feature for newswire-based datasets as in the 2013 English task, even when trained on a training set derived from automatic translation, which include many errors. Our participation in the English subtask was inconclusive due to the technical faults experienced to produce our results. We will nevertheless take into account the lessons learned in this participation for future ones.

Acknowledgements

Part of this work has been carried out with the support of LabEx-EFL (Empirical Foundation of Linguistics) strand 5 (computational semantic analysis). We are also grateful to CoNACyT (Consejo NAcional de Ciencia y Tecnologia) for support to this work.

References

Thorsten Brants and Alex Franz. 2006. Web 1t 5-gram corpus version 1.1.

Davide Buscaldi and Paolo Rosso. 2008. Geo-WordNet: Automatic Georeferencing of WordNet. In *Proceedings of the International Conference on Language Resources and Evaluation, LREC 2008*, Marrakech, Morocco.

Davide Buscaldi, Paolo Rosso, José Manuel Gómez, and Emilio Sanchis. 2009. Answering questions with an n-gram based passage retrieval engine. *Journal of Intelligent Information Systems (JIIS)*, 34(2):113–134.

Davide Buscaldi, Joseph Le Roux, Jorge J. Garcia Flores, and Adrian Popescu. 2013. Lipn-core: Semantic text similarity using n-grams, wordnet, syntactic analysis, esa and information retrieval based features. In *Second Joint Conference on Lexical and Computational Semantics (*SEM), Volume 1: Proceedings of the Main Conference and the Shared Task: Semantic Textual Similarity*, pages 162–168, Atlanta, Georgia, USA, June. Association for Computational Linguistics.

Davide Buscaldi. 2013. Une mesure de similarité sémantique basée sur la recherche d'information. In *5ème Atelier Recherche d'Information SEmantique - RISE 2013*, pages 81–91, Lille, France, July.

Chih-Chung Chang and Chih-Jen Lin. 2011. LIBSVM: A library for support vector machines. *ACM Transactions on Intelligent Systems and Technology*, 2:27:1–27:27. Software available at `http://www.csie.ntu.edu.tw/~cjlin/libsvm`.

Damien Dudognon, Gilles Hubert, and Bachelin Jhonn Victorino Ralalason. 2010. Proxigénéa : Une mesure de similarité conceptuelle. In *Proceedings of the Colloque Veille Stratégique Scientifique et Technologique (VSST 2010)*.

Andreas Eisele and Yu Chen. 2010. Multiun: A multilingual corpus from united nation documents. In Daniel Tapias, Mike Rosner, Stelios Piperidis, Jan Odjik, Joseph Mariani, Bente Maegaard, Khalid Choukri, and Nicoletta Calzolari (Conference Chair), editors, *Proceedings of the Seventh conference on International Language Resources and Evaluation*, pages 2868–2872. European Language Resources Association (ELRA), 5.

J.J. Jiang and D.W. Conrath. 1997. Semantic similarity based on corpus statistics and lexical taxonomy. In *Proc. of the Int'l. Conf. on Research in Computational Linguistics*, pages 19–33.

Joseph Le Roux, Jennifer Foster, Joachim Wagner, Rasul Samad Zadeh Kaljahi, and Anton Bryl. 2012. DCU-Paris13 Systems for the SANCL 2012 Shared Task. In *The NAACL 2012 First Workshop on Syntactic Analysis of Non-Canonical Language (SANCL)*, pages 1–4, Montréal, Canada, June.

Rada Mihalcea, Courtney Corley, and Carlo Strapparava. 2006. Corpus-based and knowledge-based measures of text semantic similarity. In *Proceedings of the 21st national conference on Artificial intelligence - Volume 1*, AAAI'06, pages 775–780. AAAI Press.

Ted Pedersen, Siddharth Patwardhan, and Jason Michelizzi. 2004. Wordnet::similarity: measuring the relatedness of concepts. In *Demonstration Papers at HLT-NAACL 2004*, HLT-NAACL–Demonstrations '04, pages 38–41, Stroudsburg, PA, USA. Association for Computational Linguistics.

Bernhard Schölkopf, Peter Bartlett, Alex Smola, and Robert Williamson. 1999. Shrinking the tube: a new support vector regression algorithm. In *Proceedings of the 1998 conference on Advances in neural information processing systems II*, pages 330–336, Cambridge, MA, USA. MIT Press.

Zhibiao Wu and Martha Palmer. 1994. Verbs semantics and lexical selection. In *Proceedings of the 32nd annual meeting on Association for Computational Linguistics*, ACL '94, pages 133–138, Stroudsburg, PA, USA. Association for Computational Linguistics.

LT3: Sentiment Classification in User-Generated Content Using a Rich Feature Set

Cynthia Van Hee, Marjan Van de Kauter, Orphée De Clercq, Els Lefever and Véronique Hoste
LT[3], Language and Translation Technology Team
Department of Translation, Interpreting and Communication – Ghent University
Groot-Brittanniëlaan 45, 9000 Ghent, Belgium
Firstname.Lastname@UGent.be

Abstract

This paper describes our contribution to the SemEval-2014 Task 9 on sentiment analysis in Twitter. We participated in both strands of the task, viz. classification at message-level (subtask B), and polarity disambiguation of particular text spans within a message (subtask A). Our experiments with a variety of lexical and syntactic features show that our systems benefit from rich feature sets for sentiment analysis on user-generated content. Our systems ranked ninth among 27 and sixteenth among 50 submissions for task A and B respectively.

1 Introduction

Over the past few years, Web 2.0 applications such as microblogging services, social networking sites, and short messaging services have considerably increased the amount of user-generated content produced online. Millions of people rely on these services to send messages, share their views or gather information about others. Simultaneously, companies, marketeers and politicians are anxious to detect sentiment in UGC since these messages might contain valuable information about the public opinion. This explains why sentiment analysis has been a research area of great interest in the last few years (Wiebe et al., 2005; Wilson et al., 2005; Pang and Lee, 2008; Mohammad and Yang, 2011). Though first studies focussed more on product or movie reviews, we see that analyzing sentiment in UGC is currently becoming increasingly popular. The main difference between these two sources of information is that the former is rather long and contains quite formal language whereas the latter one is generally very brief and noisy and thus represents some different challenges (Maynard et al., 2012).

In this paper, we describe our contribution to the SemEval-2014 Task 9: Sentiment Analysis in Twitter (Rosenthal et al., 2014), which was a rerun of SemEval-2013 Task 2 (Nakov et al., 2013) and consisted of two subtasks:

- **Subtask A - Contextual Polarity Disambiguation:** *Given a message containing a marked instance of a word or phrase, determine whether that instance is positive, negative or neutral in that context.*

- **Subtask B - Message Polarity Classification:** *Given a message, classify whether the message is of positive, negative, or neutral sentiment. For messages conveying both a positive and negative sentiment, whichever is the stronger sentiment should be chosen.*

The datasets for training, development and testing were provided by the task organizers. The training datasets consisted of Twitter messages on a variety of topics. The test sets contained regular tweets (Twitter2013, Twitter2014), tweets labeled as sarcastic (TwitterSarcasm), SMS messages (SMS2013), and blog posts (LiveJournal2014). For both subtasks, the possible polarity labels were *positive*, *negative*, *neutral*, and *objective*. The datasets for subtask B contained an additional label, i.e. *objective-OR-neutral*. Table 1 presents an overview of all provided datasets. For each task and test dataset, two runs could be submitted: a constrained run using the provided training data only, and an unconstrained one using additional training data. For both tasks, we created a constrained model based on supervised learning, relying on additional lexicons and using the test datasets of SemEval-2013 as development data. Evaluation was based on averaged F-measure, considering averaged F-positive and F-negative.

Proceedings of the 8th International Workshop on Semantic Evaluation (SemEval 2014), pages 406–410,
Dublin, Ireland, August 23-24, 2014.

Dataset	Subtask A	Subtask B
Training		
Training data	26,928	9,684
Development data	1,135	1,654
Total training data	28,063	11,338
Dev-test (test SemEval-2013)		
Tweets	4,435	3,813
SMS messages	2,334	2,094
Test SemEval-2014		
Tweets + SMS messages + blog posts + sarcastic tweets	10,681	8,987

Table 1: Number of labeled instances contained by the training, development (test data SemEval-2013), and SemEval-2014 test sets.

2 System Description

Our main goal was to develop, for each polarity classification task, a classifier to label a message or an instance of that message as either positive, negative, or neutral. We ran several experiments to identify the most discriminative classifier features. This section gives an overview of the pipeline we developed and which features were implemented.

2.1 Linguistic Preprocessing

First, we performed manual cleaning on the datasets to replace non-UTF-8 characters, and we tokenized all messages using the Carnegie Mellon University Twitter Part-of-Speech Tagger (Gimpel et al., 2011). Subsequently, we Part-of-Speech tagged all instances using the CMU Twitter Part-of-Speech Tagger (Gimpel et al., 2011), and performed dependency parsing using a caseless parsing model of the Stanford parser (de Marneffe et al., 2006). Besides that, we also tagged all named entities using the Twitter NLP tools (Ritter et al., 2011) for Named Entity Recognition. As a final preprocessing step, we decided to combine the labels *neutral*, *objective* and *neutral-OR-objective*, thus recasting the task as a three-way classification task.

2.2 Feature Extraction

We implemented a number of lexical and syntactic features that represent every phrase (subtask A) or message (subtask B) within a feature vector:

N-gram features

- Word token n-gram features: a binary value for every token unigram, bigram, and trigram found in the training data.
- Character n-gram features: a binary value for every character trigram, and fourgram (within word tokens) found in the training data.
- Normalized n-gram features: n-grams that consisted of URLs and mentions or @-replies were replaced by *http://someurl* and by *@someuser*, respectively. We also normalized commonly used abbreviations [1] to their full written form (e.g. *h8* → *hate*).

Word shape features

- Character flooding: the number of word tokens with a character repeated more than two times (e.g. *sooooooo join*).
- Punctuation flooding: the number of contiguous sequences of exclamation/question marks (e.g. *GRADUATION?!?!*).
- Punctuation of the last token: a binary value indicating whether the last word token of a message contains a question/exclamation mark (e.g. *Going to Helsinki tomorrow or on the day after tomorrow, yay!*).
- The number of capitalized words (e.g. *SO EXCITED*).
- The number of hashtags (e.g. *#win*).

Lexicon features: As sentiment lexicons we consulted existing resources: AFINN (Nielsen, 2011), General Inquirer (Stone et al., 1966), MPQA (Wilson et al., 2005), NRC Emotion (Mohammad and Turney, 2010; Mohammad and Yang, 2011), Bing Liu (Hu and Liu, 2004), and Bounce (Kökciyan et al., 2013) – the latter three are Twitter-specific. Additionally, we created a list of emoticons extracted from the SemEval-2014 training data. Based on these resources, the following features were extracted:

- The number of positive, negative, and neutral lexicon words averaged over text length
- The overall polarity, which is the sum of the values of identified sentiment words

These features were extracted by 1) looking at all tokens in the instance, and 2) looking at hashtag tokens only (e.g. *win* from *#win*). We also considered negation cues by flipping the polarity

[1] These were extracted from an existing list of chat abbreviations (http://www.chatslang.com/terms/abbreviations).

sign of a sentiment word if it occurred in a negation relation (e.g. *@_2Shades_maybe 3rd team bro, he's* ***not better*** *than trey Burke from Michigan*). Negation relations were identified using the output of the dependency parser. In the example above, the positive polarity of the sentiment word *better* is flipped into negative since it occurs in a relation with *not*.

Syntactic features:

- Part-of-Speech – 25 tags, including Twitter-specific tags such as # (hashtags), @ (at-mentions), ~ (retweets), *U* (URLs or e-mail addresses), and *E* (emoticons): binary (tag occurs in the tweet or not), ternary (tag occurs zero, one, or two or more times), absolute (number of occurrences), and frequency (frequency of the tag).

- Dependency relations – four binary values for every dependency relation found in the training data. The first value indicates the presence of the lexicalized dependency relations in the test data. Additionally, as proposed by (Joshi and Penstein-Rosé, 2009), the dependency relation features are generalized in three ways: by backing off the head word to its PoS-tag, by backing off the modifier word to its PoS-tag, and by backing off both the head and modifier word.

Named entity features: This feature group consists of four features: binary (tweet contains NEs or not), absolute (number of NEs), absolute tokens (number of tokens that are part of an NE), and frequency tokens (frequency of NE tokens).

PMI features: PMI (pointwise mutual information) values indicating the association of a word with positive and negative sentiment. The higher the PMI value, the stronger the word-sentiment association. For each unigram and bigram in the training data, PMI values were extracted from the word-sentiment association lexicon created by NRC Canada (Mohammad et al., 2013). A second PMI feature was considered for each unigram based on the word-sentiment associations found in the SemEval-2014 training dataset. PMI values were calculated as follows:

$$PMI(w) = PMI(w, positive) - PMI(w, negative) \quad (1)$$

As the equation shows, the association score of a word with negative sentiment is subtracted from the word's association score with positive sentiment.

2.3 Optimizing the Classification Results

The core of our approach consisted in evaluating the aforementioned features and selecting those feature groups contributing most to the classification results. To this end, we trained an SVM classifier using the LIBSVM package (Chang and Lin, 2001) and created models for various feature combinations. A linear kernel and a cost value of 1 were chosen as parameter settings for all further experiments after cross-validation on the training data. Our experimental setup consisted of three steps: 1) training an SVM on the original training data provided by the task organizers (no development data was used), 2) generating a model, and 3) applying and evaluating the model on the development data (Twitter and SMS test data of SemEval-2013). We started our experiments with sentiment lexicon and n-gram features only, and gradually added other feature groups to identify the most contributive features. Tables 2 and 3 reveal the obtained F-scores for each step.

Features	Dev Twitter	Dev SMS
lexicons	0.6855	0.6402
n-grams	0.8482	0.8229
n-grams + lexicons	0.8628	0.8489
+ normalization n-grams	0.8632 (+ 0.0004)	0.8502 (+ 0.0013)
+ Part-of-Speech	0.8646 (+ 0.0014)	0.8582 (+ 0.0080)
+ negation	**0.8650** (+ 0.0004)	0.8654 (+ 0.0072)
+ word shape	0.8649 (- 0.0001)	0.8650 (- 0.0004)
+ named entity	0.8642 (- 0.0007)	**0.8660** (+ 0.0010)
+ dependency	0.8642 (=)	**0.8660** (=)
+ PMI	0.8610 (- 0.0032)	0.8654 (- 0.0006)

Table 2: F-scores obtained after adding other features for the Twitter and SMS development data (test data SemEval-2013) – subtask A.

Features	Dev Twitter	Dev SMS
lexicons	0.5342	0.5119
n-grams	0.5896	0.5628
n-grams + lexicons	0.6442	0.6040
+ normalization n-grams	0.6414 (- 0.0028)	0.6084 (+ 0.0044)
+ Part-of-Speech	0.6466 (+ 0.0052)	0.6333 (+ 0.0249)
+ negation	0.6542 (+ 0.0076)	0.6384 (+ 0.0051)
+ word shape	**0.6581** (+ 0.0039)	0.6394 (+ 0.0010)
+ named entity	0.6559 (- 0.0022)	0.6399 (+ 0.0005)
+ dependency	0.6467 (- 0.0092)	0.6430 (+ 0.0031)
+ PMI	0.6525 (+ 0.0058)	**0.6525** (+ 0.0095)

Table 3: F-scores obtained after adding other features for the Twitter and SMS development data (test data SemEval-2013) – subtask B.

As can be inferred from the tables, F-scores

	SMS2013	Twitter2013	LiveJournal2014	Twitter2014	Twitter2014 Sarcasm
Task A	85.26 (7/27)	86.28 (8/27)	80.44 (13/27)	81.02 (9/27)	70.76 (13/27)
Task B	64.78 (7/50)	65.56 (14/50)	68.56 (20/50)	65.47 (16/50)	47.76 (22/50)

Table 4: F-scores and rankings of our systems across the various data genres for subtask A (Contextual Polarity Disambiguation) and subtask B (Message Polarity Classification).

were already relatively high (~0.8559 for subtask A and ~0.6241 for subtask B) for the combined lexicon and n-gram features (on average 0.8559 for subtask A and 0.6241 for subtask B), which we therefore consider as a our baseline setup. Considering the results for both subtasks and data genres, we conclude that n-grams, sentiment lexicons, and PoS-tags were the most contributive feature groups, whereas named entity and dependency features did not improve the overall classification performance. However, using all feature groups (n-grams, lexicons, normalized n-grams, Part-of-Speech features, negation features, word shape features, named entity features, dependency features, and PMI features) improved the classification results (reaching an averaged F= 0.8632 for subtask A, and F= 0.6525 for subtask B) compared to classification based on lexicon (averaged F= 0.6629 for subtask A, and F= 0.5231 for subtask B) or n-gram features only (averaged F= 0.8356 for subtask A, and F= 0.5762 for subtask B). Based on these results, we conclude that using the full feature set for the classification of unseen data appears to be a promising approach, considering that it achieves good performance and that it would not tune the training model to a particular data genre.

For further optimization of the classification results, we performed feature selection in the feature groups by using a genetic algorithm approach which can explore different areas of the search space in parallel. In order to do so, we made use of the Gallop (Genetic Algorithms for Linguistic Learner Optimization) python package (Desmet et al., 2013). This enabled us to select the most contributive features from every feature group: n-gram features at token and character level, lexicon features from General Inquirer, Liu, AFINN, and Bounce, character flooding and token capitalization features, Part-of-Speech features (binary, ternary, and absolute), named entity features (binary, absolute tokens, and frequency tokens), and PMI features based on the NRC lexicon. None of the dependency relation features were selected.

3 Results

We submitted sentiment labels for the Contextual Polarity Disambiguation (subtask A) and for the Message Polarity Classification (subtask B). Our competition results are reported in Table 4. Rankings for each dataset are added between brackets. The results reveal that our systems achieved good performance in the polarity classification of unseen data across the various genres and tasks. Overall, we achieved our best classification performance on the Twitter2013 test set, obtaining an F-score of 86.28, while the best performance for this data genre is an F-score of 90.14. We saw a drop in performance on the Twitter2014 Sarcasm test set. This is consistent with most other teams as sarcastic language is hard to handle in sentiment analysis. Considering the rankings, we conclude that we performed particularly well on the SMS test dataset of SemEval-2013 for both subtasks, ranking seventh for this genre. Our systems ranked ninth among 27 submissions and sixteenth among 50 submissions for subtasks A and B respectively.

4 Conclusions and Future Work

Using a rich feature set proves to be beneficial for automatic sentiment analysis on user-generated content. Feature selection experiments revealed that features based on n-grams, sentiment lexicons, and PoS-tags were most contributive for both classification tasks, while dependency features did not contribute to overall classification performance. As future work it will be interesting to study the impact of normalization of the data on the classification performance.

Based on a shallow error analysis, we believe that including additional classification features may also be promising: modifiers other than negation cues (diminishers, increasers, modal verbs, etc.) that affect the polarity intensity, emoticon flooding, and pre- and suffixes that indicate emotion (*un-*, *dis-*, *-less*, etc.). Additionally, lemmatization and hashtag segmentation on the training data could also improve classification results.

References

Chih-Chung Chang and Chih-Jen Lin, 2001. *LIBSVM: a library for support vector machines.*

Marie-Catherine de Marneffe, Bill MacCartney, and Christopher D. Manning. 2006. Generating Typed Dependency Parses from Phrase Structure Parses. In *Proc. of LREC'06).*

Bart Desmet, Véronique Hoste, David Verstraeten, and Jan Verhasselt. 2013. Gallop Documentation. Technical Report LT3 13-03, University of Ghent.

Kevin Gimpel, Nathan Schneider, Brendan O'Connor, Dipanjan Das, Daniel Mills, Jacob Eisenstein, Michael Heilman, Dani Yogatama, Jeffrey Flanigan, and Noah A. Smith. 2011. Part-of-speech tagging for Twitter: Annotation, features, and experiments. In *Proceedings of the 49th Annual Meeting of the Association for Computational Linguistics: Human Language Technologies: Short Papers - Volume 2*, HLT '11, pages 42–47, Stroudsburg, PA, USA. Association for Computational Linguistics.

Minqing Hu and Bing Liu. 2004. Mining and summarizing customer reviews. In *Proceedings of the tenth ACM SIGKDD international conference on Knowledge discovery and data mining, KDD04*, pages 168–177, New York, NY. ACM.

Mahesh Joshi and Carolyn Penstein-Rosé. 2009. Generalizing dependency features for opinion mining. In *Proceedings of the ACL-IJCNLP 2009 Conference Short Papers*, ACLShort '09, pages 313–316, Stroudsburg, PA, USA. Association for Computational Linguistics.

Nadin Kökciyan, Arda Çelebi, Arzucan Özgür, and Suzan Üsküdarli. 2013. Bounce: Sentiment classification in Twitter using rich feature sets. In *Second Joint Conference on Lexical and Computational Semantics (*SEM), Volume 2: Proceedings of the Seventh International Workshop on Semantic Evaluation (SemEval 2013)*, pages 554–561, Atlanta, Georgia, USA. ACL.

Diane Maynard, Kalina Bontcheva, and Dominic Rout. 2012. Challenges in developing opinion mining tools for social media. In *Proc. of the LREC workshop NLP can u tag #usergeneratedcontent?!*

Saif Mohammad and Peter Turney. 2010. Emotions Evoked by Common Words and Phrases: Using Mechanical Turk to Create an Emotion Lexicon. In *Proceedings of the NAACL-HLT 2010 Workshop on Computational Approaches to Analysis and Generation of Emotion in Text*, LA, California.

Saif Mohammad and Tony Yang. 2011. Tracking Sentiment in Mail: How Genders Differ on Emotional Axes. In *Proceedings of the 2nd Workshop on Computational Approaches to Subjectivity and Sentiment Analysis (WASSA 2011)*, pages 70–79, Portland, Oregon. ACL.

Saif M. Mohammad, Svetlana Kiritchenko, and Xiaodan Zhu. 2013. Nrc-canada: Building the state-of-the-art in sentiment analysis of tweets. *CoRR*, abs/1308.6242.

Preslav Nakov, Sara Rosenthal, Zornitsa Kozareva, Veselin Stoyanov, Alan Ritter, and Theresa Wilson. 2013. Semeval-2013 task 2: Sentiment analysis in Twitter. In *Second Joint Conference on Lexical and Computational Semantics (*SEM), Volume 2: Proceedings of the Seventh International Workshop on Semantic Evaluation (SemEval 2013)*, pages 312–320, Atlanta, Georgia, USA, June. Association for Computational Linguistics.

Finn Nielsen. 2011. A new anew: Evaluation of a word list for sentiment analysis in microblogs. In *Proceedings of the ESWC2011 Workshop on Making Sense of Microposts: Big things come in small packages.*

Bo Pang and Lillian Lee. 2008. Opinion mining and sentiment analysis. *Found. Trends Inf. Retr.*, 2(1-2):1–135, January.

Alan Ritter, Sam Clark, Mausam, and Oren Etzioni. 2011. Named entity recognition in tweets: An experimental study. In *Proceedings of the Conference on Empirical Methods in Natural Language Processing*, EMNLP '11, pages 1524–1534, Stroudsburg, PA, USA. Association for Computational Linguistics.

Sara Rosenthal, Preslav Nakov, Alan Ritter, and Veselin Stoyanov. 2014. SemEval-2014 Task 9: Sentiment Analysis in Twitter. In Preslav Nakov and Torsten Zesch, editors, *Proceedings of the 8th International Workshop on Semantic Evaluation*, SemEval '14, Dublin, Ireland.

Philip J. Stone, Dexter C. Dunphy, Marshall S. Smith, and Daniel M. Ogilvie. 1966. The General Inquirer: A Computer Approach to Content Analysis. *MIT Press.*

Janyce Wiebe, Theresa Wilson, and Claire Cardie. 2005. Annotating expressions of opinions and emotions in language. *Computer Intelligence*, 39(2):165–210.

Theresa Wilson, Janyce Wiebe, and Paul Hoffmann. 2005. Recognizing contextual polarity in phrase-level sentiment analysis. In *Proceedings of the conference on Human Language Technology and Empirical Methods in Natural Language Processing, HLT05*, pages 347–354, Stroudsburg, PA. ACL.

LyS: Porting a Twitter Sentiment Analysis Approach from Spanish to English

David Vilares, Miguel Hermo, Miguel A. Alonso, Carlos Gómez-Rodríguez, Yerai Doval
Grupo LyS, Departamento de Computación, Facultade de Informática
Universidade da Coruña, Campus de A Coruña
15071 A Coruña, Spain
{david.vilares, miguel.hermo, miguel.alonso, carlos.gomez, yerai.doval}@udc.es

Abstract

This paper proposes an approach to solve message- and phrase-level polarity classification in Twitter, derived from an existing system designed for Spanish. As a first step, an *ad-hoc* preprocessing is performed. We then identify lexical, psychological and semantic features in order to capture different dimensions of the human language which are helpful to detect sentiment. These features are used to feed a supervised classifier after applying an information gain filter, to discriminate irrelevant features. The system is evaluated on the SemEval 2014 task 9: Sentiment Analysis in Twitter. Our approach worked competitively both in message- and phrase-level tasks. The results confirm the robustness of the approach, which performed well on different domains involving short informal texts.

1 Introduction

Millions of opinions, conversations or just trivia are published each day in Twitter by users of different cultures, countries and ages. This provides an effective way to poll how people praise, complain or discuss about virtually any topic. Comprehending and analysing all this information has become a new challenge for organisations and companies, which aim to find out a way to make quick and more effective decisions for their business. In particular, identifying the perception of the public with respect to an event, a service or an entity are some of their main goals in a short term. In this respect, *sentiment analysis*, and more specifically *polarity classification*, is playing an important role in order to automatically analyse subjective information in texts.

This paper describes our participation at SemEval 2014 task 9: Sentiment Analysis in Twitter. Specifically, two subtasks were presented: (A) contextual polarity disambiguation and (B) message polarity classification. The first subtask consists on determining the polarity of words or phrases extracted from short informal texts, the scope of extracts being provided by the SemEval organisation. Subtask B focusses on classifying the content of the whole message. In both cases, three possible sentiments are considered: *positive*, *negative* and *neutral* (which involves mixed and non-opinionated instances). Although the training set only contains tweets, the test set also includes short informal texts from other domains, in order to measure cross-domain portability. You can test the model for subtask B at miopia.grupolys.org.

2 SemEval 2014-Task 9: Sentiment Analysis in Twitter

Our contribution is a reduced version of a Spanish sentiment classification system (Vilares et al., 2013a; Vilares et al., 2013b) that participated in TASS 2013 (Villena-Román et al., 2014), achieving the 5th place on the global sentiment classification task and the 1st place on topic classification on tweets. In this section we describe how we have ported to English this system originally designed for Spanish. Tasks A and B are addressed from the same perspective, which is described below.

2.1 Preprocessing

We implement a naive preprocessing algorithm which seeks to normalise some of the most common ungrammatical elements. It is intended for Twitter, but many of the issues addressed would also be valid in other domains:

Proceedings of the 8th International Workshop on Semantic Evaluation (SemEval 2014), pages 411–415,
Dublin, Ireland, August 23-24, 2014.

- *Replacement of frequent abbreviations* The list of the most frequent ones was extracted from the training set, taking the Penn Treebank (Marcus et al., 1993) as our dictionary. A term is considered ungrammatical if it does not appear in our dictionary. We then carry out a manual review to distinguish between unknown words and abbreviations, providing a correction in the latter case. For example, *'c'mon'* becomes *'come on'* and *'Sat'* is replaced by *'Saturday'*.
- *Emoticon normalisation*: We employ the emoticon collection published in (Agarwal et al., 2011). Each emoticon is replaced with one of these five labels: strong positive (ESP), positive (EP), neutral (ENEU), negative (EN) or strong negative (ESN).
- *Laughs* : Multiple forms used in social media to reflect laughs (*e.g. 'hhahahha'*, *'HHEHEHEH'*) are preprocessed in a homogeneous way to obtain a pattern of the form *'hxhx'* where $x \in \{a, e, i, o, u\}$.
- *URL normalisation*: External links are replaced by the string *'url'*.
- *Hashtags ('#') and usernames ('@')*: If the hashtag appears at the end or beginning of the tweet, we remove the hashtag. Based on other participant approaches at SemEval 2013 (Nakov et al., 2013), we realized maybe this is not the best option, although we believe hashtags will not be useful in most of cases, since they refer to very specific events. Otherwise, only the '#' is removed, hypothesising the hashtag is used to emphasise a term (e.g. *'Matthew #Mcconaughey has won the Oscar'*).

2.2 Feature Extraction

Our approach only takes into account information extracted from the text, without considering any kind of meta-data. Extracted features combine lexical, psychological and semantic knowledge in order to build a linguistic model able to analyse tweets, but also other kinds of messages. These features can be divided into two types: *corpus-extracted features* and *lexicon-extracted features*. All of them take the total number of occurrences of the respective feature as the weighting factor to then feed the supervised classifier.

2.2.1 Corpus-extracted features

Given a corpus, we use it to extract the following set of features:

- *Word forms*: A model based on this type of features is our baseline. Each single word is considered as a feature in order to feed the supervised classifier. This often becomes a simple and acceptable start point which obtains a decent performance.
- *Part-of-speech (PoS) information*: some coarse-grained PoS-tags such as *adjective* or *adverb* are usually good indicators of subjective texts while some fine-grained PoS tags such as *third person personal pronoun* provide evidence of non-opinionated messages (Pak and Paroubek, 2010).

2.2.2 Lexicon-extracted features

We also consider information obtained from external lexicons in order to capture linguistic information that can not be extracted from a training corpus by means of bag-of-words and PoS-tag models. We rely on two manually-build lexicons:

- *Pennebaker et al. (2001) psychometric dictionaries*. Linguistic Inquiry and Word Count[1] (LIWC) is a software which includes a semantic dictionary to measure how people use different kinds of words over a wide number of texts. It categorises terms into *psychometric properties*, which correspond to different dimensions of the human language. The dictionary relates terms with psychological properties (*e.g. anger* or *anxiety*), but also with topics (*e.g. family*, *friends*, *religion*) or even morphological features (*e.g. future time*, *past time* or *exclamations*).
- *Hu and Liu (2004) opinion lexicon*. It is a collection of positive and negative words. Many of the occurrences are misspelled, since they often come from web environments.

2.2.3 Syntactic features

We also parsed the tweets using MaltParser (Nivre et al., 2007) in order to obtain dependency triplets of the form $(w_i,\ arc_{ij},\ w_j)$, where w_i is the head word w_j, the dependent one and arc_{ij} the existing syntactic relation between them. We tried to incorporate generalised dependency triplets (Joshi

[1]http://www.liwc.net/

and Penstein-Rosé, 2009), following an enriched perspective presented in Vilares et al. (2014). A generalisation consists on backing off the words to more abstracted terms. For example, a valid dependency triplet for the phrase *'awesome villain'* is *(villain, modifier, awesome)*, which could be generalised into *(anger, modifier, assent)* by means of psychometric properties. However, experimental results over the development corpus using these features decreased performance with respect to our best model, probably due to the small size of the training corpus, since dependency triplets tend to suffer from sparsity, so a larger training corpus is needed to exploit them in a proper way (Vilares et al., 2014).

2.3 Feature Selection

For a machine learning approach, sparsity could be an issue. In particular, due to the size of the corpus, many of the terms extracted from the training set only appear a few times in it. This makes it impossible to properly learn the polarity of many tokens. Thus, we carry out a filtering step before feeding our classifier. In particular, we rely on the information gain (IG) method to then rank the most relevant features. Information gain measures the relevance of an attribute with respect to a class. It takes values between 0 and 1, where a higher value implies a higher relevance. Table 1 shows the top five relevant features based on their information gain for our best model. The top features for task A were very similar. Our official runs only consider features with an IG greater than zero.

IG	Feature	Category
0.140	positive emotion	Pennebaker et al. (2001)
0.137	#positive-words	Hu and Liu (2004)
0.126	affect	Pennebaker et al. (2001)
0.089	#negative-words	Hu and Liu (2004)
0.083	negative emotion	Pennebaker et al. (2001)

Table 1: Most relevant features for task B. '#' must be read this table as 'the number of'and not as a hashtag.

2.4 Classifier

We have trained our runs with a SVM LibLINEAR classifier (Fan et al., 2008) taking the implementation provided in WEKA (Hall et al., 2009). The selection was motivated by the acceptable results that some of the participants in SemEval 2013, e.g. Becker et al. (2013), obtained using this implementation. We configured the multi-class support vector machine by Crammer and Singer (2002) as the SVMtype. Since the corpus was unbalanced, we tuned the weights for the classes using the development corpus: 1 for the *positive* class, 2 for *negative* and 0.5 for *neutral*. The rest of parameters were set to default values.

3 Experimental Results

The SemEval 2014 organisation provides a standard training corpus for both tasks A an B. For task A, each tweet is marked with a list of the words and phrases to analyse, and for each one its sentiment label is provided. In addition, a development corpus was released for tuning the system parameters. The training and the development corpus can be used jointly (*constrained runs*) to train models that are then evaluated over the test corpus.[2] Some participants used external annotated corpora (*unconstrained runs*) to build their models. With respect to the test corpus, it contains texts from tweets but also from LiveJournal texts, which we are abbreviating as LJ, and SMS messages.

Table 2 contains the statistics of the corpora we used. Sharing data is a violation of Twitter's terms of service, so we had to download them. Unfortunately, some of the tweets were no longer available for several reasons, e.g., user or a tweet does not exist anymore or the privacy settings of a user have changed. As a result, the size of our training and development corpora may be different from those of other participant's corpora.

Task	Set	Positive	Negative	Neutral
A	Train	4,917	2,591	385
	Dev	555	365	45
	Test	6,354	3,771	556
B	Train	3,063	1,202	3,935
	Dev	493	290	633
	Test	3,506	1,541	3,940

Table 2: SemEval 2014 corpus statistics.

3.1 Evaluation Metrics

F-measure is the official score to measure how systems behave on each class. In order to rank participants, the SemEval 2014 organisation proposed the averaged F-measure of positive and negative tweets.

[2]We followed this angle.

3.2 Performance on Sets

Tables 3 and 4 show performance on the test set of different combinations of the proposed features. Table 5 shows the performance of our run on task A. The results over the corresponding sets for task B are illustrated in Table 6. They are significant lower than in task A. This suggests that when a message involves more than one of two tokens, a lexical approach is not enough. Improving performance should involve taking into account context and linguistic phenomena that appear in sentences to build a model based on the composition of linguistic information.

Model	LJ	SMS	Twitter 2013	Twitter 2014	Twitter Sarcasm
WPLT (no IG)	82.21	**82.32**	84.82	**81.69**	71.19
WPL	83.55	81.04	84.85	80.64	68.79
WPLT*	**83.96**	81.46	**85.63**	79.93	71.98
WP	78.53	80.97	80.34	73.35	**74.18**
P	75.70	78.74	73.58	65.75	71.82
W	61.58	65.45	64.56	59.16	62.93
L	66.04	64.11	62.96	53.81	61.26
T	47.07	51.37	71.82	43.64	49.37

Table 3: Performance on the test set for task A. The model marked with a * was our official run. W stands for features obtained from a bag-of-words approach, L from Hu and Liu (2004), P from Pennebaker et al. (2001) and T for fine-grained PoS-tags. They can be combined, e.g., a model named WP use both words and psychometric properties.

Model	LJ	SMS	Twitter 2013	Twitter 2014	Twitter Sarcasm
WPLT*	69.79	60.45	**66.92**	**64.92**	42.40
WPL	**70.19**	**61.41**	66.71	64.51	45.72
WP	66.84	60.22	65.29	63.90	45.90
WPLT (no IG)	66.38	57.01	61.96	62.84	43.71
W	65.12	56.00	62.87	62.64	48.75
P	63.42	54.80	60.05	57.66	**54.20**
T	45.99	35.85	46.53	45.99	48.58
L	57.53	45.14	48.80	44.48	49.14

Table 4: Performance on the test set for task B.

4 Conclusions

This papers describes the participation of the LyS Research Group (`http://www.grupolys.org`) at the SemEval 2014 task 9: Sentiment Analysis in Twitter, with a system that attained competitive performance both in message and phrase-level tasks, as can be observed in Table 7. This system is a reduced version of a sentiment classification model for Spanish texts that performed well in the TASS 2013 (Villena et al., 2013). The official results show how our approach works competitively both on tasks A and B without needing large and automatically-built resources. The approach is based on a bag-of-words that includes word-forms and PoS-tags. We also extract psychometric and sentiment information from external lexicons. In order to reduce sparsity problems, we firstly apply an information gain filter to select only the most relevant features. Experiments on the development set showed a significant improvement on the same model with respect to skipping it on subtask B.

Test set	Positive	Negative	Neutral
DEV	86.30	81.60	4.30
TWITTER 2013 (full)	88.70	81.90	17.60
TWITTER 2013 (progress subset)	88.81	82.57	20.75
LJ	84.34	83.56	13.84
SMS	80.31	82.56	7.10
TWITTER 2014	89.02	70.82	4.44
TWITTER SARCASM	85.71	57.63	28.57

Table 5: Performance on different sets for our model on task A. The model evaluated on the development set was only built using the training set.

Test set	Positive	Negative	Neutral
DEV	69.80	60.40	66.70
TWITTER 2013 (full)	72.50	64.30	72.30
TWITTER 2013 (progress subset)	71.92	61.92	71.22
LJ	71.94	67.65	66.23
SMS	63.83	57.06	73.76
TWITTER 2014	74.26	55.58	66.76
TWITTER SARCASM	55.17	29.63	51.61

Table 6: Performance on different sets for our model on task B.

Test set	Task A	Task B
LiveJournal 2014	4 / 27	13 / 50
SMS 2013	12 / 27	19 / 50
Twitter 2013	9 / 27	10 / 50
Twitter 2014	11 / 27	18 / 50
Twitter 2014 Sarcasm	10 / 27	33 / 50

Table 7: Position of our submission on each corpus and task, according to results provided by the organization on April 22, 2014.

Acknowledgements

Research reported in this paper has been partially funded by Ministerio de Economía y Competitividad and FEDER (Grant TIN2010-18552-C03-02) and by Xunta de Galicia (Grant CN2012/008).

References

Apoorv Agarwal, Boyi Xie, Ilia Vovsha, Owen Rambow, and Rebecca Passonneau. 2011. Sentiment analysis of Twitter data. In *Proceedings of the Workshop on Languages in Social Media*, LSM '11, pages 30–38, Stroudsburg, PA, USA. ACL.

Lee Becker, George Erhart, David Skiba, and Valentine Matula. 2013. AVAYA: Sentiment Analysis on Twitter with Self-Training and Polarity Lexicon Expansion. *Atlanta, Georgia, USA*, page 333.

Koby Crammer and Yoram Singer. 2002. On the algorithmic implementation of multiclass kernel-based vector machines. *The Journal of Machine Learning Research*, 2:265–292.

Rong-En Fan, Kai-Wei Chang, Cho-Jui Hsieh, Xiang-Rui Wang, and Chih-Jen Lin. 2008. LIBLINEAR: A library for large linear classification. *The Journal of Machine Learning Research*, 9:1871–1874.

Mark Hall, Eibe Frank, Geoffrey Holmes, Bernhard Pfahringer, Peter Reutemann, and Ian H. Witten. 2009. The WEKA data mining software: an update. *SIGKDD Explorations*, 11(1):10–18, November.

Minqing Hu and Bing Liu. 2004. Mining and summarizing customer reviews. In *Proceedings of the tenth ACM SIGKDD international conference on Knowledge discovery and data mining*, pages 168–177. ACM.

Manesh Joshi and Carolyn Penstein-Rosé. 2009. Generalizing dependency features for opinion mining. In *Proceedings of the ACL-IJCNLP 2009 Conference Short Papers*, ACLShort '09, pages 313–316, Suntec, Singapore.

Mitchell P Marcus, Mary Ann Marcinkiewicz, and Beatrice Santorini. 1993. Building a large annotated corpus of english: The penn treebank. *Computational linguistics*, 19(2):313–330.

Preslav Nakov, Sara Rosenthal, Zornitsa Kozareva, Veselin Stoyanov, Alan Ritter, and Theresa Wilson. 2013. SemEval-2013 Task 2: Sentiment Analysis in Twitter. pages 312–320, June.

Joakim Nivre, Johan Hall, Jens Nilsson, Atanas Chanev, Gülsen Eryigit, Sandra Kübler, Svetoslav Marinov, and Erwin Marsi. 2007. Maltparser: A language-independent system for data-driven dependency parsing. *Natural Language Engineering*, 13(2):95–135.

A. Pak and P. Paroubek. 2010. Twitter as a Corpus for Sentiment Analysis and Opinion Mining. In *Proceedings of the Seventh conference on International Language Resources and Evaluation (LREC'10)*, pages 1320–1326, Valletta, Malta, May. European Language Resources Association (ELRA).

J.W. Pennebaker, M.E. Francis, and R.J. Booth. 2001. Linguistic inquiry and word count: LIWC 2001. *Mahway: Lawrence Erlbaum Associates*, 71.

David Vilares, Miguel A. Alonso, and Carlos Gómez-Rodríguez. 2013a. LyS at TASS 2013: Analysing Spanish tweets by means of dependency parsing, semantic-oriented lexicons and psychometric word-properties. In Alberto Díaz Esteban, Iñaki Alegría Loinaz, and Julio Villena Román, editors, *XXIX Congreso de la Sociedad Española de Procesamiento de Lenguaje Natural (SEPLN 2013). TASS 2013 - Workshop on Sentiment Analysis at SEPLN 2013*, pages 179–186, Madrid, Spain, September.

David Vilares, Miguel A. Alonso, and Carlos Gómez-Rodríguez. 2013b. Supervised polarity classification of Spanish tweets based on linguistic knowledge. In *DocEng'13. Proceedings of the 13th ACM Symposium on Document Engineering*, pages 169–172, Florence, Italy, September. ACM.

David Vilares, Miguel A. Alonso, and Carlos Gómez-Rodríguez. 2014. On the usefulness of lexical and syntactic processing in polarity classification of Twitter messages. *Journal of the Association for Information Science Science and Technology*, to appear.

Julio Villena-Román, Janine García-Morera, Cristina Moreno-García, Sara Lana-Serrano, and José Carlos González-Cristóbal. 2014. TASS 2013 — a second step in reputation analysis in Spanish. *Procesamiento del Lenguaje Natural*, 52:37–44, March.

Meerkat_Mafia: Multilingual and Cross-Level Semantic Textual Similarity Systems

Abhay Kashyap, Lushan Han, Roberto Yus, Jennifer Sleeman, Taneeya Satyapanich, Sunil Gandhi and Tim Finin
University of Maryland, Baltimore County
Baltimore, MD 21250 USA
{abhay1,lushan1,ryus,jsleem1,taneeya1,sunilga1,finin}@umbc.edu

Abstract

We describe UMBC's systems developed for the SemEval 2014 tasks on *Multilingual Semantic Textual Similarity (Task 10)* and *Cross-Level Semantic Similarity (Task 3)*. Our best submission in the Multilingual task ranked second in both English and Spanish subtasks using an unsupervised approach. Our best systems for Cross-Level task ranked second in Paragraph-Sentence and first in both Sentence-Phrase and Word-Sense subtask. The system ranked first for the Phrase-Word subtask but was not included in the official results due to a late submission.

1 Introduction

We describe the semantic text similarity systems we developed for two of the SemEval tasks for the 2014 International Workshop on Semantic Evaluation. We developed systems for task 3, Cross-Level Semantic Similarity (Jurgens et al., 2014), and task 10, Multilingual Semantic Textual Similarity (Agirre et al., 2014). A key component in all the systems was an enhanced version of the word similarity system used in our entry (Han et al., 2013b) in the 2013 SemEval Semantic Textual Similarity task.

Our best system in the Multilingual Semantic Textual Similarity task used an unsupervised approach and ranked second in both the English and Spanish subtasks. In the Cross-Level Semantic Similarity task we developed a number of new algorithms and used new linguistic data resources. In this task, our best systems ranked second in the Paragraph-Sentence task, first in the Sentence-Phrase task and first in the Word-Sense task. The system ranked first for the Phrase-Word task but was not included in the official results due to a late submission.

The remainder of the paper proceeds as follows. Section 2 describes our word similarity model and it's wrapper to deal with named entities and out of vocabulary words. Sections 3 and 4 describe how we extended the word similarity model for the specific tasks. Section 5 presents the results we achieved on these tasks along with instances where the system failed. Section 6 highlights our future plans for improving the system.

2 Semantic Word Similarity Model

2.1 LSA Word Similarity Model

Our word similarity model is a revised version of the one we used in the 2013 *SEM semantic text similarity task. This was in turn derived from a system developed for the Graph of Relations project (UMBC, 2013b). For SemEval, we wanted a measure that considered a word's semantics but not its lexical category, e.g., the verb "marry" should be semantically similar to the noun "wife". An online demonstration of a similar model developed for the GOR project is available (UMBC, 2013a), but it lacks some of this version's features.

LSA-based word similarity. LSA Word Similarity relies on the distributional hypothesis that words occurring in the same context tend to have similar meanings (Harris, 1968). LSA relies on the fact that words that are semantically similar (e.g., cat and feline or nurse and doctor) are more likely to occur near one another in text. Thus evidence for word similarity can be computed from a statistical analysis of a large text corpus.

We extracted raw word co-occurrence statistics from a portion of the 2007 crawl of the Web corpus from the Stanford WebBase project (Stanford, 2001). We processed the collection to remove some undesirable elements (text duplica-

Proceedings of the 8th International Workshop on Semantic Evaluation (SemEval 2014), pages 416–423,
Dublin, Ireland, August 23-24, 2014.

Word pair	±4 model	±1 model
1 doctor_NN, physician_NN	0.775	0.726
2 car_NN, vehicle_NN	0.748	0.802
3 person_NN, car_NN	0.038	0.024
4 car_NN, country_NN	0.000	0.016
5 person_NN, country_NN	0.031	0.069
6 child_NN, marry_VB	0.098	0.000
7 wife_NN, marry_VB	0.548	0.274
8 author_NN, write_VB	0.364	0.128
9 doctor_NN, hospital_NN	0.473	0.347
10 car_NN, driver_NN	0.497	0.281

Table 1: Examples from the LSA similarity model.

tions, truncated text, non-English text and strange characters) and produced a three billion word corpus of high quality English, which is available online (Han and Finin, 2013).

We performed POS tagging and lemmatization on the corpus using the Stanford POS tagger (Toutanova et al., 2000). Word/term co-occurrences were counted in a moving window of a fixed size that scans the entire corpus. We generated two co-occurrence models using window sizes ± 1 and ± 4 because we observed different natures of the models. ± 1 window produces a context similar to the dependency context used in (Lin, 1998). It provides a more precise context but is only good for comparing words within the same POS. This is because words of different POS are typically surrounded by words in different syntactic forms. In contrast, a context window of ± 4 words allows us to compute semantic similarity between words with different POS.

Examples from our LSA similarity model are given in Table 1. Pairs 1 to 6 illustrate that the measure has a good property of differentiating similar words from non-similar words. Examples 7 and 8 show that the ± 4 model can detect semantically similar words even with different POS while the ± 1 model yields poor results. The pairs in 9 and 10 show that highly related, but not substitutable, words may have a strong similarity and that the ± 1 model is better at detecting them.

Our word co-occurrence models were based on a predefined vocabulary of more than 22,000 common English words and noun phrases. We also added to it more than 2,000 verb phrases extracted from WordNet. The final dimensions of our word co-occurrence matrices are 29,000 $\times$ 29,000 when words are POS tagged. Our vocabulary includes only open-class words, i.e., nouns, verbs, adjectives and adverbs. There are no proper nouns in the vocabulary with the only exception of country names.

Singular Value Decomposition (SVD) has been found to be effective in improving word similarity measures (Landauer and Dumais, 1997). SVD is typically applied to a *word by document* matrix, yielding the familiar LSA technique. In our case, we apply it to our *word by word* matrix (Burgess et al., 1998). Before performing SVD, we transform the raw word co-occurrence count f_{ij} to its log frequency $log(f_{ij}+1)$. We select the 300 largest singular values and reduce the 29K word vectors to 300 dimensions. The LSA similarity between two words is defined as the cosine similarity of their corresponding word vectors after the SVD transformation. See (Han et al., 2013b; Lushan Han, 2014) for examples and more information on the LSA model.

Statistical word similarity measures have limitations. Related words can have similarity scores as high as what similar words get, e.g., "doctor" and "hospital". Word similarity is typically low for synonyms that have many word senses since information about different senses are mashed together (Han et al., 2013a). To address these issues, we augment the similarity between two words using knowledge from WordNet, for example, increasing the score if they are in the same WordNet synset or if one is a direct or two link hypernym of the other. See (Han et al., 2013b) for further details.

2.2 Word Similarity Wrapper

Our word similarity model is restricted to the vocabulary size which only comprises open class words. For words outside of the vocabulary, we can only rely on their lexical features and determine equivalence (which we score as 0 or 1, since a continuous scale makes little sense in this scenario). An analysis of the previous STS datasets show that out-of-vocabulary words account for about $25-45\%$ of the total words. Datasets like MSRpar and headlines lie on the higher end of this spectrum due to the high volume of proper nouns.

In the previous version, we computed a character bigram overlap score given by

$$characterBigramScore = \frac{|A \cap B|}{|A \cup B|}$$

where A and B are the set of bigrams from the first and second word respectively. We compare this against a preset threshold (0.8) to determine equivalence. While this is reasonable for named entities, it is not the best approach for other classes.

Named Entities. The wrapper is extended to handle all classes of named entities that are included in Stanford CoreNLP (Finkel et al., 2005). We use heuristic rules to compute the similarity between two numbers or two dates. To handle named entity mentions of people, locations and organizations, we supplement our character bigram overlap method with the DBpedia Lookup service (Mendes et al., 2011). For each entity mention, we select the DBpedia entity with the most inlinks, which serves as a good estimate of popularity or significance (Syed et al., 2010). If the two named entity mentions map to identical DBpedia entities, we lower our character bigram overlap threshold to 0.6.

OOV words. As mentioned earlier, when dealing with out-of-vocabulary words, we only have its lexical features. A straightforward approach is to simply get more context for the word. Since our vocabulary is limited, we need to use external dictionaries to find the word. For our system, we use Wordnik (Davidson, 2013), which is a compilation of several dictionaries including The American Heritage Dictionary, Wikitionary and WordNet. Wordnik provides a REST API to access several attributes for a given word such as it's definitions, examples, related words etc. For out of vocabulary words, we simply retrieve the word pair's top definitions and supply it to our existing STS system (UMBC, 2013a) to compute its similarity. As a fallback, in case the word is absent even in Wordnik, we resort to our character bigram overlap measure.

3 Multilingual Semantic Text Similarity

3.1 English STS

For the 2014 STS-English subtask we submitted three runs. They all used a simple term alignment strategy to compute sentence similarities. The first run was an unsupervised approach that used the basic word-similarity model for term alignment. The next two used a supervised approach to combine the scores from the first run with alignment scores using the enhanced word-similarity wrapper. The two runs differed in their training.

Align and Penalize Approach. The *pairingWord* run was produced by the same Align-and-Penalize system (Han et al., 2013b) that we used in the 2013 STS task with only minor changes. The biggest change is that we included a small list of disjoint concepts (Han et al., 2013b) that are used in the penalization phase, such as $\{$*piano*, *violin*$\}$ and $\{$*dog*, *cat*$\}$. The disjoint concepts were manually collected from the MSRvid dataset provided by the 2012 STS task because we still lack a reliable general method to automatically produce them. The list only contains 23 pairs, which can be downloaded at (dis, 2014).

We also slightly adjusted our stopword list. We removed a few words that appear in the trial datasets of 2013 STS task (e.g., *frame*) but we did not add any new stopwords for this year's task. All the changes are small and we made them only in the hope that they can slightly improve our system.

Unlike machine learning methods that require manually selecting an appropriate trained model for a particular test dataset, our unsupervised Align-and-Penalize system is applied uniformly to all six test datasets in 2014 STS task, namely, deft-forum, deft-news, headlines, images, OnWN and tweet-news. It achieves the second best rank among all submitted runs.

Supervised Machine Learning. Our second and third runs used machine learning approaches similar to those we developed for the 2013 STS task but with significant changes in both pre-processing and the features extracted.

The most significant pre-processing change was the use of Stanford coreNLP (Finkel et al., 2005) tool for tokenization, part-of-speech tagging and identifying named entity mentions. For the *tweet-news* dataset we also removed the hashtag symbol ('#') prior to applying the Stanford tools. We use only open class words and named entity mentions and remove all other tokens.

We align tokens between two sentences based on the updated word similarity wrapper that was described in Section 2.2. We use information content from Google word frequencies for word weights similar to our approach last year. The alignment process is a many-to-one mapping similar to the Align and Penalize approach and two tokens are only aligned if their similarity is greater than 0.1. The sentence similarity score is then computed as the average of the scores of their aligned tokens. This score, along with the Align and Penalize approach score, are used as features to train support vector regression (SVR) models.

We use an epsilon SVR with a radial basis kernel function and use a grid search to get the optimal parameter values for cost, gamma and epsilon. We use datasets from the previous STS tasks as training data and the two submitted runs differ in the choice of their training data.

The first approach, named *Hulk*, is an attempt to use a generic model trained on a large data set. The SVR model uses a total of 3750 sentence pairs (1500 from MSRvid, 1500 from MSRpar and 750 from headlines) for training. Datasets like SMT were excluded due to poor quality.

The second approach, named *Super Saiyan*, is an attempt at domain specific training. For OnWN, we used 1361 sentence pairs from previous OnWN dataset. For Images, we used 1500 sentence pairs from MSRvid dataset. The others lacked any domain specific training data so we used a generic training dataset comprising 5111 sentence pairs from MSRvid, MSRpar, headlines and OnWN datasets.

3.2 Spanish STS

As a base-line for this task we first considered translating the Spanish sentences to English and running the same systems explained for the English Subtask (i.e., *pairingWord* and *Hulk*). The results obtained applying this approach to the provided training data gave a correlation of 0.777 so, we selected this approach (with some improvements) for the competition.

Translating the sentences. For the automatic translation of the sentences from Spanish to English we used the Google Translate API[1], a free, multilingual machine-translation product by Google. Google Translate presents very accurate translations for European languages by using statistical machine translation (Brown et al., 1990) where the translations are generated on the basis of statistical models derived from bilingual text corpora. In fact, Google used as part of this corpora 200 billion words from United Nations documents that are typically published in all six official UN languages, including English and Spanish.

In the experiments performed with the trial data we manually evaluated the quality of the translations (one of the authors is a native Spanish speaker). The overall translation was very accurate but some statistical anomalies, incorrect translations due to the abundance of a specific sense of a word in the training set, appeared.

> *I1: Las costas o costa de un mar, lago o extenso río es la tierra a lo largo del borde de estos.*
>
> T11: Costs or the cost of a sea, lake or wide river is the land along the edge of these.
>
> T12: Coasts or the coast of a sea, lake or wide river is the land along the edge of these.
>
> T13: Coasts or the coast of a sea, lake or wide river is the land along the border of these.
>
> ...

Figure 1: Three of the English translations for the Spanish sentence I1.

On one hand, some homonym words are wrongly translated. For example, the Spanish sentence *"Las* ***costas o costa*** *de un mar [...]"* was translated to *"**Costs or the cost** of a sea [...]"*. The Spanish word *costa* has two different senses: "coast" (the shore of a sea or ocean) and "'cost" (the property of having material worth). On the other hand, some words are translated preserving their semantics but with a slightly different meaning. For example, the Spanish sentence *"Un **cojín** es una funda de tela [...]"* was correctly translated to *"A **cushion** is a fabric cover [...]"*. However, the Spanish sentence *"Una almohada es un **cojín** en forma rectangular [...]"* was translated to *"A pillow is a rectangular **pad** [...]"*[2].

Dealing with statistical anomalies. The aforementioned problem of statistical machine translation caused a slightly adverse effect when computing the similarity of two English (translated from Spanish) sentences with the systems explained in Section 3.1. Therefore, we improved the direct translation approach by taking into account the different possible translations for each word in a Spanish sentence. For that, our system used the information provided by the Google Translate API, that is, all the possible translations for every word of the sentence along with a popularity value. For each Spanish sentence the system generates all its possible translations by combining the different possible translations of each word. For example, Figure 1 shows three of the English sentences generated for a given Spanish sentence from the trial data.

As a way of controlling the combinatorial explosion of this step, especially for long sentences, we limited the maximum number of generated

[1] `http://translate.google.com`

[2] Notice that both Spanish sentences used the term *cojín* that should be translated as *cushion* (the Spanish word for *pad* is *almohadilla*).

sentences for each Spanish sentence to 20 and we only selected words with a popularity greater than 65. We arrived at the popularity threshold through experimentation on every sentence in the trial data set. After this filtering, our input for the "news" and "wikipedia" tests went from 480 and 324 pairs of sentences to 5756 and 1776 pairs, respectively.

Given a pair of Spanish sentences, $I1$ and $I2$, and the set of possible translations generated by our system for each sentence, $T_{I1} = \{T_{11}, T_{12}, T_{13}, \ldots, T_{1n}\}$ and $T_{I2} = \{T_{21}, T_{22}, \ldots, T_{2m}\}$, we compute the similarity between them by using the following formula:

$$SimSPA(I1, I2) = \frac{\sum_{i=1}^{n}\sum_{j=1}^{m} SimENG(T_{1i}, T_{2j})}{n * m}$$

where $SimENG(x, y)$ computes the similarity of two English sentences using our existing STS system (Han et al., 2013b).

For the final competition we submitted three runs. The first (*Pairing* in Table 3) used the *pairingWord* system with the direct translation of the Spanish sentences to English. The second run (*PairingAvg* in Table 3) used the formula for $SimSPA(x, y)$ based on $SimENG(x, y)$ with the *pairingWord* system. Finally, the third one (*Hulk* in Table 3) used the *Hulk* system with the direct translation.

4 Cross Level Similarity

4.1 Sentence to Paragraph/Phrase

We used the three systems developed for the English sentence similarity subtask and described in Section 3.1 for both the sentence to paragraph and sentence to phrase subtasks, producing three runs. The model for *Hulk* remained the same (trained on 3750 sentence pairs from MSRvid, MSRpar and headlines dataset) but the *SuperSaiyan* system, which is the domain specific approach, used the given train and trial text pairs (about 530) for the respective subtasks as training to generate task specific models.

4.2 Phrase to Word

In our initial experiments, we directly computed the phrase-word pair similarity using our English STS. This yielded a very low correlation of 0.239 for the training set, primarily due to the absence of these phrases and words in our vocabulary. To address this issue, we used external sources to obtain more contextual information and extracted several features.

Dictionary features. We used Wordnik as a dictionary resource and retrieved definitions and usage examples for the word. We then used our English STS system to measure the similarity between these and the given phrase to extract two features.

Web search features. These features were based on the hypothesis that if a word and phrase have similar meanings, then a web search that combines the word and phrase should return similar documents when compared to a web search for each individually.

We implemented this idea by comparing results of three search queries: the word alone, the phrase alone, and the word and phrase together.

Using the Bing Search API (BIN, 2014), we retrieved the top five results for each search, indexed them with Lucene (Hatcher et al., 2004), and extracted term frequency vectors for each of the three search result document sets. For the phrase *'spill the beans'* and word *'confess'*, for example, we built a Lucene index for the set of documents retrieved by a Bing search for 'spill the beans', 'confess', and 'spill the beans confess'. We calculated the similarity of pairs of search result sets using the cosine similarity (1) of their term frequency vectors.

$$CosineSimilarity = \frac{\sum_{i=1}^{n} V1_i \times V2_i}{\sqrt{\sum_{i=1}^{n}(V1_i)^2} \times \sqrt{\sum_{i=1}^{n}(V2_i)^2}} \quad (1)$$

We calculated the mean and minimum similarity of pairs of results for the phrase and phrase+word searches. These features were extracted from the provided training set and used in conjunction with the dictionary features to train an SVM regression model to predict similarity scores.

We observed this method can be problematic when a word or phrase has multiple meanings. For example, *'spill the beans'* relates to *'confessing'* but it is also the name of a coffee shop and a soup shop. A mix of these pages do get returned by Bing and reduces the accuracy of our results. However, we found that this technique often strengthens evidence of similarity enough that it improves our overall accuracy when used in combination with our dictionary features.

Dante#n#1: an Italian poet famous for writing the Divine Comedy that describes a journey through Hell and purgatory and paradise guided by Virgil and his idealized Beatrice

writer#n#1: writes books or stories or articles or the like professionally for pay

generator#n#3: someone who originates or causes or initiates something, "he was the generator of several complaints"

author#v#1: be the author of, "She authored this play"

Figure 2: The WordNet sense for *Dante#n#1* and the three *author#n* senses.

4.3 Word to Sense

For this subtask, we used external resources to retrieve more contextual information. For a given word, we retrieved its synonym set from WordNet along with their corresponding definitions. We retrieved the WordNet definition for the word sense as well. For example, given a word-sense pair (*author#n, Dante#n#1*), we retrieved the synset of *author#n* (*writer.n.01, generator.n.03, author.v.01*) along with their WordNet definitions and the sense definition of *Dante#n#1*. Figure 2 shows the WordNet data for this example.

By pairing every combination of the word's synset and their corresponding definitions with the sense's surface form and definition, we created four features. For each feature, we used our English STS system to compare their semantic similarity and kept the maximum score as feature's value.

We found that about 10% of the training dataset's words fell outside of WordNet's vocabulary. Examples of missing words included many informal or "slang" words like *kegger*, *crackberry* and *post-season*. To address this, we used Wordnik to retrieve the word's top definition and computed its similarity with the sense. This reduced the out-of-vocabulary words to about 2% for the training data. Wordnik thus gave us two additional features: the maximum semantic similarity score of word-sense using Wordnik's additional definitions for all words and for just the out-of-vocabulary words. We used these features to train an SVM regression model with the provided training set to predict similarity scores.

Dataset	Pairing	Hulk	SuperSaiyan
deft-forum	0.4711 (9)	0.4495 (15)	0.4918 (4)
deft-news	0.7628 (8)	**0.7850 (1)**	0.7712 (3)
headlines	0.7597 (8)	0.7571 (9)	0.7666 (2)
images	0.8013 (7)	0.7896 (10)	0.7676 (18)
OnWN	**0.8745 (1)**	0.7872 (18)	0.8022 (12)
tweet-news	0.7793 (2)	0.7571 (7)	0.7651 (4)
Weighted Mean	**0.7605 (2)**	**0.7349 (6)**	**0.7410 (5)**

Table 2: Performance of our three systems on the six English test sets.

Dataset	Pairing	PairingAvg	Hulk
Wikipedia	0.6682 (12)	0.7431 (6)	0.7382 (8)
News	0.7852 (12)	**0.8454 (1)**	0.8225 (6)
Weighted Mean	**0.7380 (13)**	**0.8042 (2)**	**0.7885 (5)**

Table 3: Performance of our three systems on the two Spanish test sets.

5 Results

Multilingual Semantic Text Similarity. Table 2 shows the system performance for the English STS task. Our best performing system ranked second [3], behind first place by only 0.0005. It employs an unsupervised approach with no training data required. The supervised systems that handled named entity recognition and out-of-vocabulary words performed slightly better on datasets in the news domain but still suffered from noise due to diverse training datasets.

Table 3 shows the performance for the Spanish subtask. The best run achieved a weighted correlation of 0.804, behind first place by only 0.003. The *Hulk* system was similar to the *Pairing* run and used only one translation per sentence. The performance boost could be attributed to large number of named entities in the News and Wikipedia datasets.

Cross Level Similarity. Table 4 shows our performance in the Cross Level Similarity tasks. The Paragraph-Sentence and Sentence-Phrase yielded good results (ranked second and first respectively) with our English STS system because of sufficient amount of textual information. The correlation scores dropped as the granularity level of the text got finer.

The Phrase-Word run achieved a correlation of 0.457, the highest for the subtask. However, an incorrect file was submitted prior to the deadline

[3]An incorrect file for 'deft-forum' dataset was submitted. The correct version had a correlation of 0.4896 instead of 0.4710. This would have placed it at rank 1 overall.

				Wordnik		BingSim			Score		
ID	S1	S2	Baseline	Definitions	Example	Sim	Avg	Min	SVM	GS	Error
Idiomatic-212	spill the beans	confess	0	0	0	0.0282	0.1516	0.1266	0.5998	4.0	3.4002
Idiomatic-292	screw the pooch	mess up	0	0.04553	0.0176	0.0873	0.4238	0.0687	0.7185	4.0	3.2815
Idiomatic-273	on a shoogly peg	insecure	0	0.0793	0	0.0846	0.3115	0.1412	0.8830	4.0	3.1170
Slang-115	wacky tabaccy	cannabis	0	0	0	0.0639	0.4960	0.1201	0.5490	4.0	3.4510
Slang-26	pray to the porcelain god	vomiting	0	0	0	0.0934	0.5275	0.0999	0.6452	4.0	3.3548
Slang-79	rock and roll	commence	0	0.2068	0.0720	0.0467	0.5106	0.0560	0.8820	4.0	3.1180
Newswire-160	exercising rights under canon law	lawyer	0.0044	0.6864	0.0046	0.3642	0.4990	0.2402	3.5562	0.5	3.0562

Table 5: Examples where our algorithm performed poorly and the scores for individual features.

Dataset	Pairing	Hulk	SuperSaiyan	WordExpand
Para.-Sent.	0.794 (10)	0.826 (4)	0.834 (2)	
Sent.-Phrase	0.704 (14)	0.705 (13)	**0.777 (1)**	
Phrase-Word				**0.457 (1)**
Word-Sense				**0.389 (1)**

Table 4: Performance of our systems on the four Cross-Level Subtasks.

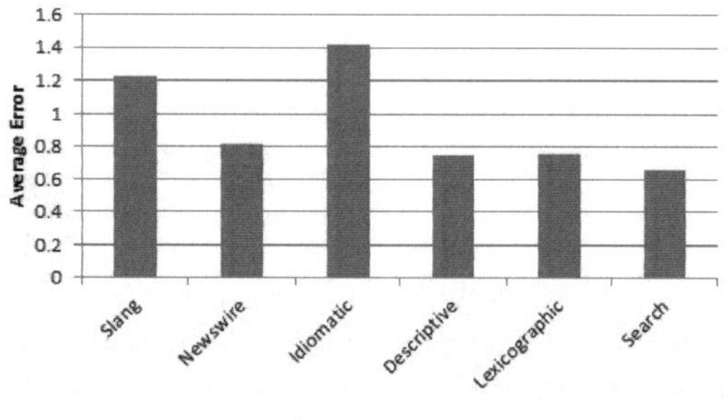

Figure 3: Average error with respect to category.

which meant that this was not included in the official results. Figure 3 shows the average error (measured as the average deviation from the gold standard) across different categories for phrase to word subtask. Our performance is slightly worse for slang and idiomatic categories when compared to others which is due to two reasons: (i) the semantics of idioms is not compositional, reducing the effectiveness of a distributional similarity measure and (ii) dictionary-based features often failed to find definitions and/or examples of idioms. Table 5 shows some of the words where our algorithm performed poorly and their scores for individual features.

The Word-Sense run ranked first in the subtask with a correlation score of 0.389. Table 6 shows some of the word-sense pairs where the system performed poorly. Our system only used Wordnik's top definition which was not always the right one to use to detect the similarity. For example, the first definition of *cheese#n* is "a solid food prepared from the pressed curd of milk" but there is a latter, less prominent one, which is

ID	word	sense key	sense number	predicted	gold
80	cheese#n	moolah%1:21:00::	moolah#n#1	0.78	4
377	bone#n	chalk%1:07:00::	chalk#n#2	1.52	4
441	wasteoid#n	drug user%1:18:00::	drug user#n#1	0.78	3

Table 6: Examples where our system performed poorly.

"money". A second problem is that some words, like *wasteoid#n*, were absent even in Wordnik.

Using additional online lexical resources to include more slangs and idioms, like the *Urban Dictionary* (Urb, 2014), could address these issues. However, care must be taken since the quality of some content is questionable. For example, the Urban Dictionary's first definition of "programmer" is "An organism capable of converting caffeine into code".

6 Conclusion

We described our submissions to the *Multilingual Semantic Textual Similarity (Task 10)* and *Cross-Level Semantic Similarity (Task 3)* tasks for the 2014 International Workshop on Semantic Evaluation. Our best runs ranked second in both English and Spanish subtasks for Task 10 while ranking first in Sentence-Phrase, Phrase-Word, Word-Sense tasks and second in Paragraph-Sentence subtasks for Task 3. Our success is attributed to a powerful word similarity model based on LSA word similarity and WordNet knowledge. We used new linguistic resources like Wordnik to improve our existing system for the Phrase-Word and Word-Sense tasks and plan to include other resources like "Urban dictionary" in the future.

Acknowledgements

This research was supported by awards 1228198, 1250627 and 0910838 from the U.S. National Science Foundation.

References

Eneko Agirre, Carmen Banea, Claire Cardie, Daniel Cer, Mona Diab, Aitor Gonzalez-Agirre, Weiwei Guo, Rada Mihalcea, German Rigau, and Janyce Wiebe. 2014. SemEval-2014 Task 10: Multilingual semantic textual similarity. In *Proceedings of the 8th International Workshop on Semantic Evaluation (SemEval-2014)*, Dublin, Ireland.

2014. BING search API. http://bing.com/developers-/s/APIBasics.html.

Peter F Brown, John Cocke, Stephen A Della Pietra, Vincent J Della Pietra, Fredrick Jelinek, John D Lafferty, Robert L Mercer, and Paul S Roossin. 1990. A statistical approach to machine translation. *Computational linguistics*, 16(2):79–85.

Curt Burgess, Kay Livesay, and Kevin Lund. 1998. Explorations in context space: Words, sentences, discourse. *Discourse Processes*, 25(2-3):211–257.

Sara Davidson. 2013. Wordnik. *The Charleston Advisor*, 15(2):54–58.

2014. Disjoint concept pairs. http://semanticweb-archive.cs.umbc.edu/disjointConcepts.txt.

Jenny Rose Finkel, Trond Grenager, and Christopher D. Manning. 2005. Incorporating non-local information into information extraction systems by gibbs sampling. In *43rd Annual Meeting of the ACL*, pages 363–370.

Lushan Han and Tim Finin. 2013. UMBC webbase corpus. http://ebiq.org/r/351.

Lushan Han, Tim Finin, Paul McNamee, Anupam Joshi, and Yelena Yesha. 2013a. Improving Word Similarity by Augmenting PMI with Estimates of Word Polysemy. *IEEE Trans. on Knowledge and Data Engineering*, 25(6):1307–1322.

Lushan Han, Abhay L. Kashyap, Tim Finin, James Mayfield, and Johnathan Weese. 2013b. UMBC_EBIQUITY-CORE: Semantic Textual Similarity Systems. In *2nd Joint Conf. on Lexical and Computational Semantics*. ACL, June.

Zellig Harris. 1968. *Mathematical Structures of Language*. Wiley, New York, USA.

Erik Hatcher, Otis Gospodnetic, and Michael McCandless. 2004. *Lucene in action*. Manning Publications Greenwich, CT.

David Jurgens, Mohammad Taher Pilehvar, and Roberto Navigli. 2014. SemEval-2014 Task 3: Cross-Level Semantic Similarity. In *Proceedings of the 8th International Workshop on Semantic Evaluation (SemEval-2014)*, Dublin, Ireland.

Thomas K Landauer and Susan T Dumais. 1997. A solution to plato's problem: The latent semantic analysis theory of acquisition, induction, and representation of knowledge. *Psychological review*, 104(2):211.

Dekang Lin. 1998. Automatic retrieval and clustering of similar words. In *Proc. 17th Int. Conf. on Computational Linguistics*, pages 768–774, Montreal, CN.

Lushan Han. 2014. *Schema Free Querying of Semantic Data*. Ph.D. thesis, University of Maryland, Baltimore County.

Pablo N Mendes, Max Jakob, Andrés García-Silva, and Christian Bizer. 2011. Dbpedia spotlight: shedding light on the web of documents. In *7th Int. Conf. on Semantic Systems*, pages 1–8. ACM.

Stanford. 2001. Stanford WebBase project. http://bit.ly/WebBase.

Zareen Syed, Tim Finin, Varish Mulwad, and Anupam Joshi. 2010. Exploiting a Web of Semantic Data for Interpreting Tables. In *Proceedings of the Second Web Science Conference*, April.

Kristina Toutanova, Dan Klein, Christopher Manning, William Morgan, Anna Rafferty, and Michel Galley. 2000. Stanford log-linear part-of-speech tagger. http://nlp.stanford.edu/software/tagger.shtml.

UMBC. 2013a. Semantic similarity demonstration. http://swoogle.umbc.edu/SimService/.

UMBC. 2013b. Umbc graph of relations project. http://ebiq.org/j/95.

2014. Urban dictionary. http://urbandictionary.com/.

MindLab-UNAL: Comparing Metamap and T-mapper for Medical Concept Extraction in SemEval 2014 Task 7

Alejandro Riveros, Maria De-Arteaga, Fabio A. González and **Sergio Jimenez**
Universidad Nacional de Colombia
Ciudad Universitaria
Bogotá, Colombia
[lariverosc,mdeg,fagonzalezo,sgjimenezv]@unal.edu.co

Henning Müller
Univ. of Applied Sciences
Western Switzerland, HES-SO
Sierre, Switzerland
henning.mueller@hevs.ch

Abstract

This paper describes our participation in task 7 of SemEval 2014, which focuses on analysis of clinical text. The task is divided into two parts: recognizing mentions of concepts that belong to the UMLS (Unified Medical Language System) semantic group *disorders*, and mapping each disorder to a unique UMLS CUI (Concept Unique Identifier), if possible. For identifying and mapping disorders belonging to the UMLS meta thesaurus, we explore two tools: Metamap and T-mapper. Additionally, a Named Entity Recognition system, based on a maximum entropy model, was implemented to identify other disorders.

1 Introduction

Clinical texts are unstructured data that, when processed properly, can be of great value. Extracting key information from these documents can make medical notes more suitable for automatic processing. It can also help diagnose patients, structure their medical histories and optimize other clinical procedures and research.

The task of identifying mentions to medical concepts in free text and mapping these mentions to a knowledge base was recently proposed in ShARe/CLEF eHealth Evaluation Lab 2013, attracting the attention of several research groups worldwide (Pradhan et al., 2013). The task 7 in SemEval 2014 (Pradhan et al., 2014) elaborates in that previous effort focusing on the recognition and normalization of named entity mentions belonging to the UMLS semantic group *disorders*.

The paper is organized as follows: in section 2 we briefly present the data, section 3 contains the description of the methods and tools used in our system. Later, on sections 4 and 5 we provide the details of the three submitted runs and expose the official results. Finally, sections 6 and 7 include discussions on variations that could be done to improve performance and conclusions to be drawn from our participation in the task.

2 Data Description

The training data for SemEval 2014 Task 7 consists of the ShARe (Shared Annotation Resource) corpus, which contains clinical notes from MIMIC II database (Multiparameter Intelligent Monitoring in Intensive Care). The data were manually annotated for disorder mentions, normalized to a UMLS Concept Unique Identifier when possible, and marked as CUI-less otherwise.

Four types of reports where found in the corpus: 61 discharge summaries, 54 ECG reports, 42 ECHO reports and 42 radiology reports, for a total of 199 training documents, each containing several disorder mentions.

3 Methods Used

3.1 Named-Entity Recognition

Using the Java libraries Apache OpenNLP[1] and Maxent[2], a maximum entropy model was implemented for Named Entity Recognition (NER). Two types of classifiers were built: the first one using the library's default configuration, and a second one including additional features. The default model includes the following attributes: target word, two words of context at the left of the target word, two words of context at the right of the target word, type of token for target word (capitalized word, number, hyphen, commas, etc.), and type of token for words in the context.

[1] http://opennlp.apache.org

[2] http://maxent.sourceforge.net/about.html

Proceedings of the 8th International Workshop on Semantic Evaluation (SemEval 2014), pages 424–427,
Dublin, Ireland, August 23-24, 2014.

For the enhanced model, we included n-grams at character level extracted from the target word, going from two to five characters.

OpenNLP uses the BIO tagging scheme, which marks each token as either beginning a chunk, continuing it, or not in a chunk, therefore, this model cannot identify discontinuous terms. Given this, we excluded discontinuous term annotations from the training data, and trained the model with the resulting corpus.

During the experiments, we also considered POS (Part of Speech) tags obtained with the OpenNLP library, POS tags obtained with the Stanford Java library and the number of characters in each token. However, we decided not to include any of these because accuracy decreased when using them.

3.2 Weirdness Measure

According to preliminary experiments, the chosen enhanced NER method exhibited low precision, i.e. a high number of false positives. To deal with this problem we calculated a measure for the specificity of a candidate named entity with respect to a specialized corpus, this quantity is based on the weirdness (Ahmad et al., 1999) of the candidate words. Having a general corpus C_g and a specialized corpus C_s, where w_g and w_s refer to the number of occurrences of a word w in each corpus and t_s and t_g to the total count of words in each corpus, the weirdness of a word is defined as follows:

$$Weirdness(w) = \frac{w_s}{t_s} / \frac{w_g}{t_g}$$

Those words that are common to any domain will very likely have a low weirdness score, while those with a high weirdness score indicate w is not used in the general corpus as much as in the specialized one, meaning it probably corresponds to specialized vocabulary.

Using around 1000 books from the Guttenberg Project as the general corpus, and the terms in UMLS as the specialized corpus, we applied the weirdness measure to those words that, according to the NER model, are disorders. By keeping only those with high weirdness measures, we prevent our system from tagging words that are not even medical vocabulary, thus reducing the amount of false positives.

3.3 Metamap

For identifying and mapping disorders included in the UMLS meta thesaurus to its corresponding CUI, we explored two tools. Both of them find candidates in the document and give the possible CUIs for each; in both cases, we selected the CUI that belongs to the UMLS semantic group *disorders*, as specified in the task description.

The first tool we explored is Metamap. For processing the documents, we use the following Metamap features: allow concept gap and word sense disambiguation.

After processing a document, the results were filtered, keeping only those tags that were mapped to a CUI that belongs to one of the following UMLS semantic types: *congenital abnormality, acquired abnormality, injury or poisoning, pathologic function, disease or syndrome, mental or behavioral dysfunction, cell or molecular dysfunction, experimental model of disease, anatomical abnormality, neoplastic process*, and *signs or symptoms*.

3.4 T-mapper

As an alternative to Metamap we experimented with T-mapper[3], an annotation tool developed at MindLab[4] that works in languages different than English and with any knowledge source (i.e. not only UMLS). The method implemented by T-mapper is inspired by the one in Metamap, with some modifications. The method works as follows:

1. Indexing and vocabulary generation: an inverted index and other data structures are built to perform fast lookups over the dictionary and the vocabulary list in C_g and C_s.
2. Sentence detection and tokenization: the input text is divided into sentences and then each sentence is divided into tokens using a whitespace as separator.
3. Spelling correction: to deal with noise and simple morphological variations, each token that does not match a word within the vocabulary is replaced by the most frequent word among the most similar words found above a threshold of 0.75. The similarity is computed using a normalized score based on the Levenshtein distance.

[3]https://github.com/lariverosc/tmapper
[4]http://mindlaboratory.org/

4. Candidate generation and scoring: a subset that contains all the terms that match at least one of the words in the sentence is generated, the terms contained in this set are called candidates. Once this subset is built, each of the candidate terms is scored using a simplified version of Metamap's scoring function (Aronson, 2001). In comparison, T-mapper's function uses only variation, coverage and cohesiveness as criteria, excluding centrality, since it is language dependant.

5. Candidate selection and disambiguation: the score computed in the previous step is used to choose the candidates that will be used as mappings. Ambiguity can occur because of two reasons: a tie in the scores or by overlapping over the sentence tokens. In the first case, the Lin's measure (Lin, 1998) is used as disambiguation criteria between the candidates and the previous detected concepts. In the second case, the most concrete term is chosen according to the UMLS hierarchy.

4 System Submissions

The team submitted three runs. The *run 0* was intended as a baseline; *run 1* used Metamap for UMLS concept mapping and *run 2* did this using T-mapper. Both *run 1* and *run 2* used the enhanced features for NER and applied the weirdness measure.

For *run 0*, the documents were processed with Metamap and those concepts mapped to a CUI belonging to one of the desired UMLS semantic types were chosen. Parallel to this, the document was tagged using the default NER model. Finally, results were merged, preferring Metamap mapping outputs in the cases where a concept was mapped by both tools (in an ideal scenario, all terms mapped by Metamap would have also been mapped by the NER model).

Run 1 differs from *run 0* in two steps of the process: the NER model included the enhanced features described previously and its output was filtered, keeping only those concepts whose weirdness measure exceeds 0.7. For multiword concepts the weirdness of each word was aggregated.

Finally, *run 2* was equal to *run 1*, with the difference that T-mapper was used to map concepts to the UMLS meta thesaurus.

Rank	Run	Strict P	Strict R	Strict F
1	*best*	0.843	0.786	0.813
31	2	0.561	0.534	0.547
32	1	0.578	0.515	0.545
37	0	0.321	0.565	0.409

Table 1: Official results for task A obtained by the best system and our runs (ranked by exact acc.)

Rank	Run	Strict Accuracy
1	*best*	0.741
19	2	0.461
21	0	0.435
24	1	0.411

Table 2: Official results for task B obtained by the best system and our runs (ranked by exact acc.)

5 Results

For both task A and B, *run 2* produced the best performance among our systems. In Table 1 the results of the three runs are presented, together with the information of the system with the best performance among all participating teams (labeled as *best*). The position in the ranking is from a total of 43 submitted systems. Table 2 shows analogous results for Task B, where 37 systems were submitted.

Even though the official ranking is based on the strict accuracy, which only considers a tag to be correct if it matches exactly both the first and last characters, a relaxed accuracy is also provided by the organizers. This second scoring measure considers a tag to be correct if it has an overlap with the actual one. Tables 3 and 4 show these results.

In both tables 1 and 3, P stands for Precision, R for Recall, and F for F-score. The ranking is based on the F-score.

6 Discussion

The system that gave the best results for both tasks was the one based on T-mapper. Certain features

Rank	Run	Relax P	Relax R	Relax F
1	*best*	0.916	0.907	0.911
35	2	0.769	0.677	0.720
37	1	0.777	0.654	0.710
40	0	0.439	0.725	0.547

Table 3: Official results for task A obtained by the best system and our runs (ranked by relaxed acc.)

Rank	Run	Relaxed Accuracy
1	*best*	0.928
11	2	0.863
19	0	0.797
21	1	0.771

Table 4: Official results for task B obtained by the best system and our runs (ranked by relaxed acc.)

of this tool make this finding particularly interesting: it works for any language and ontology, and it is considerably faster than Metamap. While Metamap took 581 minutes to tag 133 documents, T-mapper only required 96 minutes (133 is the number of documents in the test set).

One aspect that might have damaged the performance of our system is the fact that, unlike most of the teams, we did not use the development data for training. However, there are still a number of changes that could be made, which would very likely improve the accuracy of our system. First, the tokenizer used for the NER model and for T-mapper were too simple. Separation was done based on blank spaces, therefore slashes, certain punctuation marks and hyphens might not be treated properly.

In addition to this, the spell checker used by T-mapper also needs to be improved. Currently, it gives a ranked list of options for each word that should be replaced, and automatically chooses the first one in the ranking. However, the best match is often the second or third in the list. Changing the criteria used to choose the replacement, taking into account word sense disambiguation, would enhance the accuracy of T-mapper.

The weirdness measure is also something that should be reconsidered, since it would be interesting to use a metric that responds better to unseen terms. And in case this was still the chosen measure, other training corpora could work better, since an ontology might lack words that are currently used in a medical context but do not have a CUI, and it also fails to give a notion of which words are more frequently used than others. It is not easy, however, to replace UMLS as corpus, since it is not easy to compete with its size and richness.

Finally, the OpenNLP NER system does not recognize discontinuous terms. Therefore, no CUI-less term with a gap can currently be identified by the system. For this reason, the NER method should be changed to one that allows this type of mentions to be present in texts.

For Task B, it is very interesting to see the difference between the strict and relaxed evaluation rankings. We go from being in position 19 to being in position 11. This might be partially explained by some of the flaws previously mentioned; in particular, the weak tokenizer and the incapability to identify CUI-less terms with gaps.

7 Conclusion

We participated with three runs in the Semeval 2014 task for analysis of clinical texts. Even though the performance of our runs indicates they still need to be enhanced in order to be competitive in this specific task, the performance of the run based on T-mapper compared to that of the ones that use Metamap proves that T-mapper is a viable alternative for mapping concepts to clinical terminologies. Moreover, T-mapper should also be considered for cases in which Metamap cannot be used: languages other than English and terminologies other than UMLS.

References

Khurshid Ahmad, Lee Gillam, Lena Tostevin, et al. 1999. University of surrey participation in trec8: Weirdness indexing for logical document extrapolation and retrieval (wilder). In *TREC*.

Alan R Aronson. 2001. Effective mapping of biomedical text to the umls metathesaurus: the metamap program. In *Proceedings of the AMIA Symposium*, page 17. American Medical Informatics Association.

Dekang Lin. 1998. An information-theoretic definition of similarity. In *ICML*, volume 98, pages 296–304.

Sameer Pradhan, Noemie Elhadad, Brett R. South, David Martinez, Lee Chistensen, Amy Vogel, Hanna Suominen, Wendy W. Chapman, and Guergana Savova. 2013. Task 1: ShARe/CLEF eHealth evaluation lab 2013. In *Online Working Notes of the CLEF 2013 Evaluation Labs and Workshop*, Valencia, Spain, September.

Sameer Pradhan, Noemie Elhadad, Wendy W. Chapman, and Guergana Savova. 2014. Semeval-2014 task : Analysis of clinical text. In *Proceedings of the 8th International Workshop on Semantic Evaluation (SemEval-2014)*, Dublin, Ireland, August.

NILC_USP: An Improved Hybrid System for Sentiment Analysis in Twitter Messages

Pedro P. Balage Filho, Lucas Avanço, Thiago A. S. Pardo, Maria G. V. Nunes
Interinstitutional Center for Computational Linguistics (NILC)
Institute of Mathematical and Computer Sciences, University of São Paulo
São Carlos - SP, Brazil
{balage, taspardo, gracan}@icmc.usp.br avanco@usp.br

Abstract

This paper describes the NILC_USP system that participated in *SemEval-2014 Task 9: Sentiment Analysis in Twitter*, a re-run of the SemEval 2013 task under the same name. Our system is an improved version of the system that participated in the 2013 task. This system adopts a hybrid classification process that uses three classification approaches: rule-based, lexicon-based and machine learning. We suggest a pipeline architecture that extracts the best characteristics from each classifier. In this work, we want to verify how this hybrid approach would improve with better classifiers. The improved system achieved an F-score of 65.39% in the Twitter message-level subtask for 2013 dataset (+ 9.08% of improvement) and 63.94% for 2014 dataset.

1 Introduction

Twitter is an important platform of social communication. The analysis of the Twitter messages (tweets) offers a new possibility to understand social behavior. Understanding the sentiment contained in such messages showed to be very important to understand user behavior and also to assist market analysis (Java et al., 2007; Kwak et al., 2010).

Sentiment analysis, the area in charge of studying how sentiments and opinions are expressed in texts, is usually associated with text classification tasks. Sentiment classifiers are commonly categorized in two basic approaches: lexicon-based and machine learning approaches (Taboada et al., 2011). A lexicon-based classifier uses a lexicon to provide the polarity, or semantic orientation, of each word or phrase in the text. A machine learning classifier uses features (usually the vocabulary in the texts) obtained from labeled examples to classify the texts according to their polarity.

In this paper, we present a hybrid system for sentiment classification in Twitter messages. Our system combines the lexicon-based and machine learning approaches, as well as uses simple rules to aid in the process. Our system participated in *SemEval-2014 Task 9: Sentiment Analysis in Twitter* (Rosenthal et al., 2014), a re-run for the SemEval 2013 task under the same name (Nakov et al., 2013). The task goal was to determine the sentiment contained in tweets. The task included two sub-tasks: a expression-level classification (Task A) and a message-level classification (Task B). Our system participated only in Task B, where, for a given message, it should classify it as positive, negative, or neutral.

The system presented is an improved version of the system submitted for Semeval 2013. Our previous system had demonstrated that a hybrid approach could achieve good results (F-measure of 56.31%), even if we did not use the state-of-the-art algorithms for each approach (Balage Filho and Pardo, 2013). In this way, this work aims to verify how much this hybrid system could improve in relation to the previous one by including modifications on both lexicon-based and machine learning approaches.

Proceedings of the 8th International Workshop on Semantic Evaluation (SemEval 2014), pages 428–432, Dublin, Ireland, August 23-24, 2014.

2 Related work

The analysis of Tweets has gained lots of interest recently. One evidence is the expressive number of participants in the *SemEval-2013 Task 2: Sentiment Analysis in Twitter* (Nakov et al., 2013). There were a total of 149 submissions from 44 teams. The best performing system on twitter dataset for task B was reported by Mohammad et al. (2013) with an F-mesaure of 69.02%. Their system used a machine learning approach and a very rich feature set. They showed that the best results were achieved using a built-in positive and negative lexicon and a bag-of-words as features.

Other important system in Semeval 2013 was reported by Malandrakis et al. (2013). The authors presented a hybrid system for twitter sentiment analysis combining two approaches: a hierarchical model based on an affective lexicon and a language modeling approach. The system achieved an F-mesaure of 60.14%.

Most work in sentiment analysis uses either machine learning or lexicon-based techniques. However, few studies have shown promising results with the hybrid approach. König and Brill (2006) proposed a hybrid classifier that uses human reasoning over automatically discovered text patterns to complement machine learning. Prabowo and Thelwall (2009) evaluated the effectiveness of different classifiers. Their study showed that the use of multiple classifiers in a hybrid manner could improve the effectiveness of sentiment analysis.

3 System Architecture

Our system is described as a pipeline solution of four main processes: normalization, rule-based classification, lexicon-based classification and machine learning classification. This is the same architecture presented by our system in 2013.

This pipeline architecture works as a back-off model. In this model, each classifier tries to classify the tweets by using the underlying approach. If a certain degree of confidence is achieved, the classifier will provide the final sentiment class for the message. Otherwise, the next classifier will continue the classification task. The last possibility is the machine learning classifier, responsible to deliver the class when the previous two could not achieve the confidence level. We decided to use this back-off model instead of a voting system, for example, due to the high precision achieved for the rule-based and the lexicon-based classifiers.

The aim of this pipeline architecture is to improve the classification process. In Balage Filho and Pardo (2013), we have shown that this hybrid classification approach may outperform the individual approaches.

In the following subsections, we detail the components of our system. In the next section, we explain how the confidence level was determined.

3.1 Normalization and Rule-based Classifier

The normalization module is responsible for normalizing and tagging the texts. This module performs the following operations:

- Hashtags, urls and mentions are transformed into codes;
- Emoticons are grouped into representative categories (such as 'happy', 'sad', 'laugh') and are converted to particular codes;
- Part-of-speech tagging is performed by using the Ark-twitter NLP (Owoputi et al., 2013)

The rule-based classifier is designed to provide rules that better impact the precision than the recall. In our 2014 system, we decided to use the same rule-based classifier from the 2013 system. The rules in this classifier only verify the presence of emoticons in the text. Empirically, we evidenced that the use of emoticons indicates the actual polarity of the message. In this module, we consider the number of positive and negative emoticons found in the text to determine its classification.

3.2 Lexicon-based Classifier

The lexicon-based classifier is based on the idea that the polarity of a text can be given by the sum of the individual polarity values of each word or phrase present in the text. For this, a sentiment lexicon identifies polarity words and assigns polarity values to them (known as semantic orientations).

In the 2013 system, we had used SentiStrength lexicon (Thelwall et al., 2010). In 2014, we improved our lexicon-based classifier by using a larger sentiment lexicon. We used the sentiment lexicon provided by Opinion-Lexicon (Hu and Liu, 2004) and a list of sentiment hashtags provided by the NRC Hashtag Sentiment Lexicon (Mohammad et al., 2013). For dealing with negation, we used a handcrafted list of negative words.

In our algorithm, the semantic orientations of each individual word in the text are added up. In this approach, the algorithm searches for each word in the lexicon and only the words that were found are returned. We associate the value +1 to the positive words, and -1 to the negative words. If a polarity word is negated, its value is inverted. This lexicon-based classifier assumes the signal of the final score as the sentiment class (positive or negative) and the score zero as neutral.

3.3 Machine Learning Classifier

The machine learning classifier uses labeled examples to learn how to classify new instances. The features used for this 2014 system were completely changed from 2013 system. We inspired our machine learning module in the work reported by Mohammad et al. (2013). The features used by the classifier are:

1. unigrams, bigrams and trigrams
2. the presence of negation
3. the presence of three or more characters in the words
4. the sequence of three or more punctuation marks
5. the number of words with all letters in uppercase
6. the total number of each tag present in the text
7. the number of positive words computed by the lexicon-based method
8. the number of negative words computed by the lexicon-based method

We use a Linear Kernel SVM classifier provided by the python sckit-learn library with C=0.005[1].

4 Hybrid Approach and Tuning

The organization from *SemEval-2014 Task 9: Sentiment Analysis in Twitter* provided four datasets for the task: a training dataset (TrainSet) with 9675 messages directly retrieved from Twitter; a development dataset (DevSet), with 1654 messages; the testing dataset from 2013 run, which was not used; and the testing dataset for 2014 with 8987 messages. The 2014 testing dataset was composed of 5 different sources:

- Twitter2013: Twitter test data from 2013 run
- SMS2013: SMS test data from 2013 run
- Twitter2014: 2000 tweets
- LiveJournal2014: 2000 sentences from LiveJournal blogs
- Twitter2014Sarcasm: 100 tweets that contain sarcasm

As we said in the previous section, our system is a pipeline of classifiers where each classifier may assign a sentiment class if it achieves a particular confidence threshold score. This confidence score is a fixed value set for each system in order to have a decision boundary. This decision was made by inspecting the results obtained for the development set. Tables 1 and 2 shows how the rule-based and lexicon-based classifiers perform for the development dataset in terms of score. The score obtained by the rule-based classifier consists of the difference between the number of positive emoticons and the number of negative emoticons found in the messages. The score obtained by the lexicon-based classifier represents the total semantic orientation obtained by the algorithm by adding up the semantic orientation for their lexicon.

Inspecting Table 1, for the best threshold, we adjusted the rule-based classifier boundary to decide when the score is different from zero. For values greater than zero, the classifier will assign the positive class and, for values below zero, the classifier will assign the negative class. For values equal to zero, the classifier will call the lexicon-based classifier.

Table 1: Correlation between the rule-based classifier scores and the gold standard classes in the DevSet

Rule-based classifier score	Gold Standard Class		
	Negative	Neutral	Positive
-1	22	3	3
0	311	709	495
1	7	26	73
2	0	0	2
3 to 6	0	1	2

Inspecting Table 2, for the best threshold, we adjusted the lexicon-based classifier to assign the

[1] Available at http://scikit-learn.org/

positive class when the total score is greater than 1 and negative class when the total score is below -2. For any other values, the classifier will call the machine learning classifier.

Table 2: Correlation between the lexicon-based classifier score and the gold standard classes in the devset

Lexicon-based	Gold Standard Class		
classifier scores	Negative	Neutral	Positive
-7 to -4	2	0	0
-3	10	4	0
-2	48	18	7
-1	111	99	35
0	108	432	178
1	48	143	210
2	11	39	104
3 to 5	3	4	47

As the machine learning classifier is responsible for the final stage, we did not have to decide any threshold for this classifier. However, we empirically identified a bias toward the positive class (the negative class was barely chosen). In order to correct this problem, we setup the machine learning classifier to decide for the negative class whenever the SVM score for this class is bigger than -0.4. Next section shows the results achieved for the Semeval test dataset.

5 Results

Table 3 shows the results obtained by each individual classifier and by the hybrid classifier for the Twitter2014 messages in the testset. In the task, the systems were evaluated with the average F-score obtained for positive and negative classes.

Table 3: Average F-score (positive and negative) obtained by each classifier and the hybrid approach for the Twitter2014 testset

Classifier	Twitter2014 Testset
Rule-based	14.03
Lexicon-Based	47.55
Machine Learning	63.36
Hybrid Approach	**63.94**

Table 4 shows the improvement of the system over the 2013 run. Unlike last year, we notice that the performance of this hybrid system is very close to the performance of the machine-learning.

Table 4: Comparison of the average F-score (positive and negative) obtained by each classifier and the hybrid approach for the Twitter2013 testset for 2013 and 2014 versions

Classifier	2013 system	2014 system
Rule-based	14.37	13.31
Lexicon-Based	44.87	46.80
Machine Learning	49.99	63.75
Hybrid Approach	**56.31**	**65.39**

Table 5 shows the scores for each source in the testset. Last column shows our system rank among the 50 systems that participated in the competition. For the entire testing dataset, our algorithm had 503 (5%) examples classified by the rule-based classifier, 3204 (36%) by the lexicon-based classifier and 5280 (59%) by the machine learning classifier.

6 Conclusion

We described our improved hybrid classification system used for *Semeval-2014 Task 9: Sentiment Analysis in Twitter*. This work showed that this hybrid classifier can be improved as its modules are too. However, we noticed that, improving the lexicon and machine learning modules, the overall score tends towards the machine learning score.

The source code produced for the experiment is available at https://github.com/pedrobalage.

Acknowledgments

We would like to thank the organizers for their work in constructing the dataset and in the overseeing of the task. We also would like to thank FAPESP and SAMSUNG for supporting this work.

References

Pedro Balage Filho and Thiago Pardo. 2013. NILC_USP: A Hybrid System for Sentiment Analysis in Twitter Messages. In *Second Joint Conference on Lexical and Computational Semantics (*SEM), Volume 2: Proceedings of the Seventh International Workshop on Semantic Evaluation (SemEval 2013)*, pages 568–572, Atlanta, Georgia, USA, June. Association for Computational Linguistics.

Minqing Hu and Bing Liu. 2004. Mining and summarizing customer reviews. In *Proceedings of the Tenth ACM SIGKDD International Conference on Knowledge Discovery and Data Mining*, KDD '04, pages 168–177, New York, NY, USA. ACM.

Table 5: Results for Twitter TestSet

TestSet Source	Majority Baseline	Our Score	Best Result	Our Rank
Twitter2013	29.2	**65.39**	72.12	15th
SMS2013	19.0	**61.35**	70.28	16th
Twitter2014	34.6	**63.94**	70.96	19th
LiveJournal2014	27.2	**69.02**	74.84	18th
Twitter2014Sarcasm	27.7	**42.06**	58.16	34th

Akshay Java, Xiaodan Song, Tim Finin, and Belle Tseng. 2007. Why we twitter: understanding microblogging usage and communities. In *Proceedings of the 9th WebKDD and 1st SNA-KDD 2007 workshop on Web mining and social network analysis*, WebKDD/SNA-KDD '07, pages 56–65, New York, NY, USA. ACM.

Arnd Christian König and Eric Brill. 2006. Reducing the human overhead in text categorization. In *Proceedings of the 12th ACM SIGKDD international conference on Knowledge discovery and data mining*, KDD '06, pages 598–603, New York, NY, USA. ACM.

Haewoon Kwak, Changhyun Lee, Hosung Park, and Sue Moon. 2010. What is twitter, a social network or a news media? In *Proceedings of the 19th international conference on World wide web*, WWW '10, pages 591–600, New York, NY, USA. ACM.

Nikolaos Malandrakis, Abe Kazemzadeh, Alexandros Potamianos, and Shrikanth Narayanan. 2013. SAIL: A hybrid approach to sentiment analysis. In *Second Joint Conference on Lexical and Computational Semantics (*SEM), Volume 2: Proceedings of the Seventh International Workshop on Semantic Evaluation (SemEval 2013)*, pages 438–442, Atlanta, Georgia, USA, June. Association for Computational Linguistics.

Saif Mohammad, Svetlana Kiritchenko, and Xiaodan Zhu. 2013. NRC-Canada: Building the State-of-the-Art in Sentiment Analysis of Tweets. In *Second Joint Conference on Lexical and Computational Semantics (*SEM), Volume 2: Proceedings of the Seventh International Workshop on Semantic Evaluation (SemEval 2013)*, pages 321–327, Atlanta, Georgia, USA, June. Association for Computational Linguistics.

Preslav Nakov, Sara Rosenthal, Zornitsa Kozareva, Veselin Stoyanov, Alan Ritter, and Theresa Wilson. 2013. Semeval-2013 task 2: Sentiment analysis in twitter. In *Second Joint Conference on Lexical and Computational Semantics (*SEM), Volume 2: Proceedings of the Seventh International Workshop on Semantic Evaluation (SemEval 2013)*, pages 312–320, Atlanta, Georgia, USA, June. Association for Computational Linguistics.

Olutobi Owoputi, Brendan O'Connor, Chris Dyer, Kevin Gimpel, Nathan Schneider, and Noah A. Smith. 2013. Improved part-of-speech tagging for online conversational text with word clusters. In *Proceedings of the 2013 Conference of the North American Chapter of the Association for Computational Linguistics: Human Language Technologies*, pages 380–390, Atlanta, Georgia, June. Association for Computational Linguistics.

Rudy Prabowo and Mike Thelwall. 2009. Sentiment analysis: A combined approach. *Journal of Informetrics*, 3(2):143–157.

Sara Rosenthal, Preslav Nakov, Alan Ritter, and Veselin Stoyanov. 2014. SemEval-2014 Task 9: Sentiment Analysis in Twitter. In Preslav Nakov and Torsten Zesch, editors, *Proceedings of the 8th International Workshop on Semantic Evaluation*, SemEval '14, Dublin, Ireland.

Maite Taboada, Julian Brooke, Milan Tofiloski, Kimberly Voll, and Manfred Stede. 2011. Lexicon-Based Methods for Sentiment Analysis. *Computational Linguistics*, 37(2):267–307, June.

Mike Thelwall, Kevan Buckley, Georgios Paltoglou, Di Cai, and Arvid Kappas. 2010. Sentiment in short strength detection informal text. *Journal of the American Society for Information Science and Technology*, 61(12):2544–2558, December.

NILC_USP: Aspect Extraction using Semantic Labels

Pedro P. Balage Filho and **Thiago A. S. Pardo**
Interinstitutional Center for Computational Linguistics (NILC)
Institute of Mathematical and Computer Sciences, University of São Paulo
São Carlos - SP, Brazil
{balage, taspardo}@icmc.usp.br

Abstract

This paper details the system NILC_USP that participated in the Semeval 2014: Aspect Based Sentiment Analysis task. This system uses a Conditional Random Field (CRF) algorithm for extracting the aspects mentioned in the text. Our work added semantic labels into a basic feature set for measuring the efficiency of those for aspect extraction. We used the semantic roles and the highest verb frame as features for the machine learning. Overall, our results demonstrated that the system could not improve with the use of this semantic information, but its precision was increased.

1 Introduction

Sentiment analysis, or opinion mining, has gained lots of attention lately. The importance of this field of study is linked with the grown of information in the internet and the commercial attention it brought.

According to Liu et al. (2010), there are two kinds of information available in the internet: facts and opinions. Facts are objective statements about entities and events in the world. Opinions are subjective statements that reflect people's sentiments or perceptions about the entities and events. According to Liu, by that time, there was a lot of attention on the processing of facts but little work had been done on the processing of opinions.

Three levels of analysis for sentiment analysis are known (Liu, 2012): document level, sentence level and aspect level. The aspect-based sentiment analysis is the name of the research topic that aims to extract the sentiments about the aspects present in the text.

This work presents a system evaluated in the *SemEval Task4: Aspect Based Sentiment Analysis* shared task (Pontiki et al., 2014). Our system participated only in subtask 1: Aspect Term Extraction. In this subtask, given a text, the system should extract all aspects that are present. There were two different domains for this task: restaurants and laptops.

The goal of our system was to verify how semantic labels used in machine learning classification would improve the aspect extraction task. For this goal, we used two kinds of semantic labels: the semantic roles (Palmer et al., 2010) and the semantic frames (Baker et al., 1998).

Liu et al. (2012) categorizes the works for aspect extraction in four types, regarding the approach they follow, using: frequent terms, infrequent terms, machine learning, and topic modeling. This work uses a machine learning approach that consists in training a sequential labeling algorithm for aspect detection and extraction.

In what follows, we present some related work in Section 2. Section 3 and 4 introduce our system and report the achieved results. Some conclusions are presented in Section 5.

2 Related work

Jin and Hovy (2009) reported one the first works using sequential labeling for aspect extraction. In this work, the authors used a Lexicalized Hidden Markov Model to learn patterns to extract aspects and opinions. Jakob and Gurevych (2010) trained

Proceedings of the 8th International Workshop on Semantic Evaluation (SemEval 2014), pages 433–436,
Dublin, Ireland, August 23-24, 2014.

a Conditional Random Field for aspect extraction. In this work, the authors report the results for a single domain and a cross domain experiment. They show that even in other domains the method could be good.

Kim and Hovy (2006) explored the semantic structure of a sentence, anchored to an opinion bearing verb or adjective. Their method uses semantic role labeling as an intermediate step to label an opinion holder and topic using data from FrameNet.

Houen (2011) presented a system for opinion mining with semantic analysis. The author explores the use of the semantic frame-based analyzer FrameNet (Baker et al., 1998) for modeling features in a machine learning approach. The author found that the FrameNet information was not helpful in this classifier.

3 System Description

Our system uses a sequential labeling algorithm. In our work, we use the Conditional Random Field (Lafferty et al., 2001) algorithm provided by the CRF++ tool[1].

For training the sequential labeling algorithm, we give as input features for each word in the corpus. The algorithm will then learn how to classify those words. In our approach, the possible classes are: True, representing an aspect word; and False, representing the remaining words.

The goal of our system was to evaluate the performance of the semantic labels for the task. In order to model our system, we built a feature set consisting of 6 features.

1. the word
2. the part-of-speech
3. the chunk
4. the named-entity category
5. the semantic role label (SRL)
6. the most generic frame in FrameNet

The use of the first four features is consistent with the best approaches in aspect-based sentiment analysis. The last two features are the ones we are testing in our work.

In order to extract the features, we used two important tools: the Senna (Collobert et al., 2011), a semantic role labeling system, and the ARK SEMAFOR, a Semantic Analyzer of Frame Representations (Das et al., 2010).

[1] Available at http://crfpp.googlecode.com/

The Senna system uses a deep learning neural network (Collobert, 2011) to provide several predictions for natural language processing. The system output is represented in the CONLL format, the same used in CRF++.

Our first 5 features were directly provided by the Senna output. In these features, we decided to keep the IOBE information since the initial experiments showed the results were better with it than without.

Our fifth feature, the semantic role label, was retrieved from Senna as well. In the corresponding paper, they reported Senna could achieve a F1 of 75% for the SRL task.

The example below shows how the features were represented. In this example, we are only showing four features: the word, the part-of-speech, the chunk and the SRL. The classes are in the last column.

```
WORD     POS  CHUNK  SRL IS_ASPECT?
Great     JJ  B-NP   B-A0    False
laptop    NN  E-NP   E-A0    False
that     WDT  S-NP   S-R-A0  False
offers   VBZ  S-VP   S-V     False
many      JJ  B-NP   B-A1    False
great     JJ  I-NP   I-A1    False
features NNS  E-NP   E-A1    True
!          .  O      -       False
```

The last feature was retrieved by ARK SEMAFOR tool. ARK SEMAFOR uses a probabilistic frame-semantic parsing using the FrameNet resource. The ARK SEMAFOR output is the analysis of the frames present in the text for a given verb. As our feature set has only word related features, we decided to use the most upper level structure in the frame. In case of multiple verbs in the sentence, we used the structure for the verb that is closest to the word of interest.

The following example shows how the frames were added into the training model. We limit to show only the word, frame and the class. For training, we used the full training set with the six features plus the class.

```
WORD    FRAME               IS_ASPECT?
I       Shopping                 False
shopped Shopping                 False
around  Relational_quantity False
before  Relational_quantity False
```

```
buying  Relational_quantity False
.       O                   False
```

The organization from *SemEval-2014 Task 4: Aspect Based Sentiment Analysis* provided two domains for evaluation: restaurants and laptops. For each domain, the organization provided three datasets: a trainset, a devset and a testset.

We executed our algorithm with C parameter equal to 4.0. The experiment code is fully available at the weblink https://github.com/pedrobalage/

4 Results

Tables 1 and 2 show our system results for the restaurants and laptops domains respectively. In these tables, the results are discriminated by the feature sets that were used. The reader may see that a "+ Frame" system, for example, stands for all the features discriminated above (Word, POS, Chunk, NR, SRL) plus the Frame feature. The last line shows the results scored by our system in the SemEval shared task with all the features. We also show the results for the baseline system provided by the shared task (Pontiki et al., 2014).

Table 1: Results for restaurants domain

System	Precision	Recall	F1-mesaure
Baseline	52.54	42.76	47.15
Word + POS	83.76	68.69	75.48
+ Chunk	83.38	68.16	75.01
+ NE	83.45	68.07	74.98
+ SRL	82.79	67.46	74.34
+ Frame	**87.72**	**34.03**	**49.04**

Table 2: Results for laptops domain

System	Precision	Recall	F1-mesaure
Baseline	44.31	29.81	35.64
Word + POS	80.87	39.44	53.03
+ Chunk	78.83	39.29	52.44
+ NE	79.93	39.60	52.96
+ SRL	78.22	38.99	52.04
+ Frame	**83.62**	**14.83**	**25.19**

Comparing with the baseline, we may noticed that our submitted system (+Frame) outperformed the baseline for the restaurants domain but it did not outperformed the baseline for the laptops domain (considering F1 mesaure).

When we look in detail for the inclusion of features in our feature set, we may notice that, at every new feature, the precision goes up, but the recall goes down. We believe this is due to the behaviour of the conditional random field algorithm for compensating for a sparser feature set.

In general, the semantic labels (SRL and Frame) could not improve the results. However, if we are interested only on precision, these features are helpful. This may be the case in scenarios where a lot of information is available, as in the web, and we want to be sure about the retrieved information. Certainly, there is a conflict between precision and computational complexity, since the semantic features are more expensive to be achieved (in relation to the usual simpler features that may be used).

Despite of that, we judge to be necessary to conduct more experiments in order to better evaluate the impact of semantic labels in the aspect extraction task.

5 Conclusion

We presented an aspect extraction system built on a conditional random field algorithm. We used a rich feature set with the semantic roles and the FrameNet upper frames for each word. We have showed that the semantic labels may help to achieve a more precise classifier, but it did not help to improve the overall F-measure of the system.

Regarding the shared task, our system achieved the second best precision value among the competing systems, but the lowest recall value. Future work should investigate ways of also improving recall without penalty for the achieved precision.

Acknowledgments

We would like to thank the organizers for their work constructing the dataset and overseeing the task. We also would like to thank FAPESP for the financial support.

References

Collin F Baker, Charles J Fillmore, and John B Lowe. 1998. The berkeley framenet project. In *Proceedings of the 36th Annual Meeting of the Association for Computational Linguistics and 17th International Conference on Computational Linguistics-Volume 1*, pages 86–90. Association for Computational Linguistics.

Ronan Collobert, Jason Weston, Léon Bottou, Michael Karlen, Koray Kavukcuoglu, and Pavel Kuksa. 2011. Natural language processing (almost) from scratch. *The Journal of Machine Learning Research*, 12:2493–2537.

Ronan Collobert. 2011. Deep learning for efficient discriminative parsing. In Geoffrey J. Gordon and David B. Dunson, editors, *Proceedings of the Fourteenth International Conference on Artificial Intelligence and Statistics (AISTATS-11)*, volume 15, pages 224–232. Journal of Machine Learning Research - Workshop and Conference Proceedings.

Dipanjan Das, Nathan Schneider, Desai Chen, and Noah A Smith. 2010. Semafor 1.0: A probabilistic frame-semantic parser. Technical report, Language Technologies Institute, School of Computer Science, Carnegie Mellon University.

Søren Houen. 2011. *Opinion Mining with Semantic Analysis*. Ph.D. thesis, Department of Computer Science, University of Copenhagen.

Niklas Jakob and Iryna Gurevych. 2010. Extracting opinion targets in a single-and cross-domain setting with conditional random fields. In *Proceedings of the 2010 Conference on Empirical Methods in Natural Language Processing*, pages 1035–1045.

Wei Jin and Hung Hay Ho. 2009. A Novel Lexicalized HMM-based Learning Framework for Web Opinion Mining. In Léon Bottou and Michael Littman, editors, *Proceedings of International Conference on Machine Learning (ICML-2009)*, ICML '09, pages 1–8. ACM, ACM Press.

Soo-Min Kim and Eduard Hovy. 2006. Extracting opinions, opinion holders, and topics expressed in online news media text. In *Proceedings of the Workshop on Sentiment and Subjectivity in Text*, SST '06, pages 1–8, Stroudsburg, PA, USA. Association for Computational Linguistics.

John D. Lafferty, Andrew McCallum, and Fernando C. N. Pereira. 2001. Conditional random fields: Probabilistic models for segmenting and labeling sequence data. In *Proceedings of the Eighteenth International Conference on Machine Learning*, ICML '01, pages 282–289, San Francisco, CA, USA. Morgan Kaufmann Publishers Inc.

Bing Liu. 2010. Sentiment Analysis and Subjectivity. In N Indurkhya and F J Damerau, editors, *Handbook of Natural Language Processing*, number 1, chapter 28, pages 627–666. CRC Press, Taylor and Francis Group, Boca Raton.

Bing Liu. 2012. Sentiment Analysis and Opinion Mining. *Synthesis Lectures on Human Language Technologies*, 5(1):1–167.

Martha Palmer, Daniel Gildea, and Nianwen Xue. 2010. Semantic role labeling. *Synthesis Lectures on Human Language Technologies*, 3(1):1–103.

Maria Pontiki, Dimitrios Galanis, John Pavlopoulos, Haris Papageorgiou, Ion Androutsopoulos, and Suresh Manandhar. 2014. SemEval-2014 Task 4: Aspect Based Sentiment Analysis. In *Proceedings of the 8th International Workshop on Semantic Evaluation*, SemEval 2014, Dublin, Ireland.

NRC-Canada-2014: Detecting Aspects and Sentiment in Customer Reviews

Svetlana Kiritchenko, Xiaodan Zhu, Colin Cherry, and Saif M. Mohammad
National Research Council Canada
1200 Montreal Rd., Ottawa, ON, Canada
{Svetlana.Kiritchenko, Xiaodan.Zhu, Colin.Cherry, Saif.Mohammad}
@nrc-cnrc.gc.ca

Abstract

Reviews depict sentiments of customers towards various *aspects* of a product or service. Some of these aspects can be grouped into coarser *aspect categories*. SemEval-2014 had a shared task (Task 4) on aspect-level sentiment analysis, with over 30 teams participated. In this paper, we describe our submissions, which stood first in detecting aspect categories, first in detecting sentiment towards aspect categories, third in detecting aspect terms, and first and second in detecting sentiment towards aspect terms in the laptop and restaurant domains, respectively.

1 Introduction

Automatically identifying sentiment expressed in text has a number of applications, including tracking sentiment towards products, movies, politicians, etc.; improving customer relation models; and detecting happiness and well-being. In many applications, it is important to associate sentiment with a particular entity or an aspect of an entity. For example, in reviews, customers might express different sentiment towards various aspects of a product or service they have availed. Consider:

The lasagna was great, but the service was a bit slow.

The review is for a restaurant, and we can gather from it that the customer has a positive sentiment towards the lasagna they serve, but a negative sentiment towards the service.

The SemEval-2014 Task 4 (Aspect Based Sentiment Analysis) is a shared task where given a customer review, automatic systems are to determine *aspect terms, aspect categories*, and sentiment towards these aspect terms and categories. An aspect term is defined to be an explicit mention of a feature or component of the target product or service. The example sentence above has the aspect term *lasagna*. Similar aspect terms can be grouped into aspect categories. For example, *lasagna* and other food items can be grouped into the aspect category of 'food'. In Task 4, customer reviews are provided for two domains: restaurants and laptops. A fixed set of five aspect categories is defined for the restaurant domain: food, service, price, ambiance, and anecdotes. Automatic systems are to determine if any of those aspect categories are described in a review. The example sentence above describes the aspect categories of food (positive sentiment) and service (negative sentiment). For the laptop reviews, there is no aspect category detection subtask. Further details of the task and data can be found in the task description paper (Pontiki et al., 2014).

Restaurants				Laptops	
Term	T-Sent.	Cat.	C-Sent.	Term	T-Sent.
3	2	1	1	3	1

Table 1: Rank obtained by NRC-Canada in various subtasks of SemEval-2014 Task 4.

We present an in-house sequence tagger to detect aspect terms and supervised classifiers to detect aspect categories, sentiment towards aspect terms, and sentiment towards aspect categories. A summary of the ranks obtained by our submissions to the shared task is provided in Table 1.

2 Lexical Resources

2.1 Unlabeled Reviews Corpora

Apart from the training data provided for Task 4, we compiled large corpora of reviews for restaurants and laptops that were not labeled for aspect terms, aspect categories, or sentiment. We generated lexicons from these corpora and used them as a source of additional features in our machine learning systems.

Proceedings of the 8th International Workshop on Semantic Evaluation (SemEval 2014), pages 437–442, Dublin, Ireland, August 23-24, 2014.

Yelp restaurant reviews corpus: The Yelp Phoenix Academic Dataset[1] contains customer reviews posted on the Yelp website. The businesses for which the reviews are posted are classified into over 500 categories. Further, many of the businesses are assigned multiple business categories. We identified all food-related business categories (58 categories) that were grouped along with the category 'restaurant' and extracted all customer reviews for these categories. We will refer to this corpus of 183,935 reviews as the *Yelp restaurant reviews corpus*.

Amazon laptop reviews corpus: McAuley and Leskovec (2013) collected reviews posted on Amazon.com from June 1995 to March 2013. A subset of this corpus is marked as reviews for electronic products. We extracted from this subset all reviews that mention either *laptop* or *notebook*. We will refer to this collection of 124,712 reviews as the *Amazon laptop reviews corpus*.

Both the Yelp and the Amazon reviews have one to five star ratings associated with each review. We treated the one- and two-star reviews as negative reviews, and the four- and five-star reviews as positive reviews.

2.2 Lexicons

Sentiment Lexicons: From the Yelp restaurant reviews corpus, we automatically created an in-domain sentiment lexicon for restaurants. Following Turney and Littman (2003) and Mohammad et al. (2013), we calculated a sentiment score for each term w in the corpus:

$$score\,(w) = PMI\,(w, pos) - PMI\,(w, neg) \quad (1)$$

where *pos* denotes positive reviews and *neg* denotes negative reviews. PMI stands for pointwise mutual information:

$$PMI\,(w, pos) = log_2\,\frac{freq\,(w, pos) * N}{freq\,(w) * freq\,(pos)} \quad (2)$$

where *freq* (*w*, *pos*) is the number of times a term w occurs in positive reviews, *freq* (*w*) is the total frequency of term w in the corpus, *freq* (*pos*) is the total number of tokens in positive reviews, and N is the total number of tokens in the corpus. $PMI\,(w, neg)$ was calculated in a similar way. Since PMI is known to be a poor estimator of association for low-frequency events, we ignored terms that occurred less than five times in each (positive and negative) groups of reviews.

A positive sentiment score indicates a greater overall association with positive sentiment, whereas a negative score indicates a greater association with negative sentiment. The magnitude is indicative of the degree of association.

Negation words (e.g., *not*, *never*) can significantly affect the sentiment of an expression (Zhu et al., 2014). Therefore, when generating the sentiment lexicons we distinguished terms appearing in negated contexts (defined as text spans between a negation word and a punctuation mark) and affirmative (non-negated) contexts. The sentiment scores were then calculated separately for the two types of contexts. For example, the term *good* in affirmative contexts has a sentiment score of 1.2 whereas the same term in negated contexts has a score of -1.4. We built two lexicons, *Yelp Restaurant Sentiment AffLex* and *Yelp Restaurant Sentiment NegLex*, as described in (Kiritchenko et al., 2014).

Similarly, we generated in-domain sentiment lexicons from the Amazon laptop reviews corpus.

In addition, we employed existing out-of-domain sentiment lexicons: (1) large-coverage automatic tweet sentiment lexicons, Hashtag Sentiment lexicons and Sentiment140 lexicons (Kiritchenko et al., 2014), and (2) three manually created sentiment lexicons, NRC Emotion Lexicon (Mohammad and Turney, 2010), Bing Liu's Lexicon (Hu and Liu, 2004), and the MPQA Subjectivity Lexicon (Wilson et al., 2005).

Yelp Restaurant Word–Aspect Association Lexicon: The Yelp restaurant reviews corpus was also used to generate a lexicon of terms associated with the aspect categories of food, price, service, ambiance, and anecdotes. Each sentence of the corpus was labeled with zero, one, or more of the five aspect categories by our aspect category classification system (described in Section 5). Then, for each term w and each category c an association score was calculated as follows:

$$score\,(w, c) = PMI\,(w, c) - PMI\,(w, \neg c) \quad (3)$$

2.3 Word Clusters

Word clusters can provide an alternative representation of text, significantly reducing the sparsity of the token space. Using Brown clustering algorithm (Brown et al., 1992), we generated 1,000 word clusters from the Yelp restaurant reviews corpus. Additionally, we used publicly available

[1] http://www.yelp.com/dataset_challenge

word clusters generated from 56 million English-language tweets (Owoputi et al., 2013).

3 Subtask 1: Aspect Term Extraction

The objective of this subtask is to detect aspect terms in sentences. We approached this problem using in-house entity-recognition software, very similar to the system used by de Bruijn et al. (2011) to detect medical concepts. First, sentences were tokenized to split away punctuation, and then the token sequence was tagged using a semi-Markov tagger (Sarawagi and Cohen, 2004). The tagger had two possible tags: O for *outside*, and T for *aspect term*, where an aspect term could tag a phrase of up to 5 consecutive tokens. The tagger was trained using the structured Passive-Aggressive (PA) algorithm with a maximum step-size of $C = 1$ (Crammer et al., 2006).

Our features can be divided into two categories: emission and transition features. Emission features couple the tag sequence y to the input w. Most of these work on the token level, and conjoin features of each token with the tag covering that token. If a token is the first or last token covered by a tag, then we produce a second copy of each of its features to indicate its special position. Let w_i be the token being tagged; its token feature templates are: token-identity within a window $(w_{i-2} \ldots w_{i+2})$, lower-cased token-identity within a window $(lc(w_{i-2}) \ldots lc(w_{i+2}))$, and prefixes and suffixes of w_i (up to 3 characters in length). There are only two phrase-level emission feature templates: the cased and uncased identity of the entire phrase covered by a tag, which allow the system to memorize complete terms such as, "getting a table" or "fish and chips." Transition features couple tags with tags. Let the current tag be y_j. Its transition feature templates are short n-grams of tag identities: y_j; y_j, y_{j-1}; and y_j, y_{j-1}, y_{j-2}.

During development, we experimented with the training algorithm, trying both PA and the simpler structured perceptron (Collins, 2002). We also added the lowercased back-off features. In Table 2, we re-test these design decisions on the test set, revealing that lower-cased back-off features made a strong contribution, while PA training was perhaps not as important. Our complete system achieved an F1-score of 80.19 on the restaurant domain and 68.57 on the laptop domain, ranking third among 24 teams in both.

	Restaurants		
System	**P**	**R**	**F1**
NRC-Canada (All)	**84.41**	**76.37**	**80.19**
All − lower-casing	83.68	75.49	79.37
All − PA + percep	83.37	76.45	79.76
	Laptops		
System	**P**	**R**	**F1**
NRC-Canada (All)	**78.77**	**60.70**	**68.57**
All − lower-casing	78.11	60.55	68.22
All − PA + percep	77.76	61.47	68.66

Table 2: Test set ablation experiments for Subtask 1: Aspect Term Detection.

4 Subtask 2: Aspect Term Polarity

In this subtask, the goal is to detect sentiment expressed towards a given aspect term. For example, in sentence "The asian salad is barely eatable." the aspect term *asian salad* is referred to with negative sentiment. There were defined four categories of sentiment: positive, negative, neutral, or conflict. The conflict category is assigned to cases where an aspect term is mentioned with both positive and negative sentiment.

To address this multi-class classification problem, we trained a linear SVM classifier using the LibSVM software (Chang and Lin, 2011). Sentences were first tokenized and parsed with the Stanford CoreNLP toolkits[2] to obtain part-of-speech (POS) tags and (collapsed) typed dependency parse trees (de Marneffe et al., 2006). Then, features were extracted from (1) the target term itself; (2) its *surface context*, i.e., a window of n words surrounding the term; (3) the *parse context*, i.e., the nodes in the parse tree that are connected to the target term by at most three edges.

Surface features: (1) unigrams (single words) and bigrams (2-word sequences) extracted from a term and its surface context; (2) context-target bigrams (i.e., bigrams formed by a word from the surface context and a word from the term itself).

Lexicon features: (1) the number of positive/negative tokens; (2) the sum of the tokens' sentiment scores; (3) the maximal sentiment score. The lexicon features were calculated for each manually and automatically created sentiment lexicons described in Section 2.2.

Parse features: (1) word- and POS-ngrams in

[2]http://nlp.stanford.edu/software/corenlp.shtml

System	Laptops Acc.	Rest. Acc.
NRC-Canada (All)	**70.49**	**80.16**
All – sentiment lexicons	63.61	77.13
All – Yelp lexicons	68.65	77.85
All – Amazon lex.	68.13	80.11
All – manual lexicons	67.43	78.66
All – tweet lexicons	69.11	78.57
All – parse features	69.42	78.40

Table 3: Test set ablation experiments for Subtask 2: Aspect Term Polarity.

	Restaurants		
System	P	R	F1
NRC-Canada (All)	**91.04**	**86.24**	**88.58**
All – lex. resources	86.53	78.34	82.23
All – W–A lexicon	88.47	80.10	84.08
All – word clusters	90.84	86.15	88.43
All – post-processing	91.47	84.78	88.00

Table 4: Test set ablation experiments for Subtask 3: Aspect Category Detection. 'W–A lexicon' stands for Yelp Restaurant Word–Aspect Association Lexicon.

the parse context; (2) context-target bigrams, i.e., bigrams composed of a word from the parse context and a word from the term; (3) all paths that start or end with the root of the target terms. The idea behind the use of the parse features is that sometimes an aspect term is separated from its modifying sentiment phrase and the surface context is insufficient or even misleading for detecting sentiment expressed towards the aspect. For example, in sentence "The food, though different from what we had last time, is actually great" the word *great* is much closer to the word *food* in the parse tree than in the surface form. Furthermore, the features derived from the parse context can help resolve local syntactic ambiguity (e.g., the word *bad* in the phrase "a bad sushi lover" modifies *lover* and not *sushi*).

Table 3 presents the results of our official submission on the test sets for the laptop and restaurant domains. On the laptop dataset, our system achieved the accuracy of 70.49 and was ranked first among 32 submissions from 29 teams. From the ablation experiments we see that the most significant gains come from the use of the sentiment lexicons; without the lexicon features the performance of the system drops by 6.88 percentage points. Observe that the features derived from the out-of-domain Yelp Restaurant Sentiment lexicon are very helpful on the laptop domain. The parse features proved to be useful as well; they contribute 1.07 percentage points to the final performance. On the restaurant data, our system obtained the accuracy of 80.16 and was ranked second among 36 submissions from 29 teams.

5 Subtask 3: Aspect Category Detection

The objective of this subtask is to detect aspect categories discussed in a given sentence. There are 5 pre-defined categories for the restaurant domain: food, price, service, ambience, and anecdotes/miscellaneous. Each sentence can be labeled with one or more categories from the pre-defined set. No aspect categories were defined for the laptop domain.

We addressed the subtask as a multi-class multi-label text classification problem. Five binary one-vs-all Support Vector Machine (SVM) classifiers were built, one for each category. The parameter C was optimized through cross-validation separately for each classifier. Sentences were tokenized and stemmed with Porter stemmer (Porter, 1980). Then, the following sets of features were generated for each sentence: ngrams, stemmed ngrams, character ngrams, non-contiguous ngrams, word cluster ngrams, and lexicon features. For the lexicon features, we used the Yelp Restaurant Word–Aspect Association Lexicon and calculated the cumulative scores of all terms appeared in the sentence for each aspect category. Separate scores were calculated for unigram and bigram entries. Sentences with no category assigned by any of the five classifiers went through the post-processing step. For each such sentence, a category c with the maximal posterior probability $P(c|d)$ was identified and the sentence was labeled with the category c if $P(c|d) \geq 0.4$.

Table 4 presents the results on the restaurant test set. Our system obtained the F1-score of 88.58 and was ranked first among 21 submissions from 18 teams. Among the lexical resources (lexicons and word clusters) employed in the system, the Word–Aspect Association Lexicon provided the most gains: an increase in F1-score of 4.5 points. The post-processing step also proved to be beneficial: the recall improved by 1.46 points increasing the overall F1-score by 0.58 points.

6 Subtask 4: Aspect Category Polarity

In the Aspect Category Polarity subtask, the goal is to detect the sentiment expressed towards a given aspect category in a given sentence. For each input pair (sentence, aspect category), the output is a single sentiment label: positive, negative, neutral, or conflict.

We trained one multi-class SVM classifier (Crammer and Singer, 2002) for all aspect categories. The feature set was extended to incorporate the information about a given aspect category c using a domain adaptation technique (Daumé III, 2007) as follows: each feature f had two copies, $f\_general$ (for all the aspect categories) and f_c (for the specific category of the instance). For example, for the input pair ("The bread is top notch as well.", 'food') two copies of the unigram *top* would be used: $top\_general$ and top_food. With this setup the classifier can take advantage of the whole training dataset to learn common sentiment features (e.g., the word *good* is associated with positive sentiment for all aspect categories). At the same time, aspect-specific sentiment features can be learned from the training instances pertaining to a specific aspect category (e.g., the word *delicious* is associated with positive sentiment for the category 'food').

Sentences were tokenized and part-of-speech tagged with CMU Twitter NLP tool (Gimpel et al., 2011). Then, each sentence was represented as a feature vector with the following groups of features: ngrams, character ngrams, non-contiguous ngrams, POS tags, cluster ngrams, and lexicon features. The lexicon features were calculated as described in Section 4.

A sentence can refer to more than one aspect category with different sentiment. For example, in the sentence "The pizza was delicious, but the waiter was rude.", food is described with positive sentiment while service with negative. If the words *delicious* and *rude* occur in the training set, the classifier can learn that *delicious* usually refers to food (with positive sentiment) and *rude* to service (with negative sentiment). If these terms do not appear in the training set, their polarities can still be inferred from sentiment lexicons. However, sentiment lexicons do not distinguish among aspect categories and would treat both words, *delicious* and *rude*, as equally applicable to both categories, 'food' and 'service'. To (partially) overcome this problem, we applied the Yelp Restaurant Word–Aspect Association Lexicon to collect all the terms having a high or moderate association with the given aspect category (e.g., *pizza*, *delicious* for the category 'food' and *waiter*, *rude* for the category 'service'). Then, the feature set described above was augmented with the same groups of features generated just for the terms associated with the given category. We call these features *aspect term features*.

System	Restaurants Accuracy
NRC-Canada (All)	**82.93**
All – lexical resources	74.15
All – lexicons	75.32
All – Yelp lexicons	79.22
All – manual lexicons	82.44
All – tweet lexicons	84.10
All – word clusters	82.93
All – aspect term features	82.54

Table 5: Test set ablation experiments for Subtask 4: Aspect Category Polarity.

Table 5 presents the results on the test set for the restaurant domain. Our system achieved the accuracy of 82.93 and was ranked first among 23 submissions from 20 teams. The ablation experiments demonstrate the significant impact of the lexical resources employed in the system: 8.78 percentage point gain in accuracy. The major advantage comes from the sentiment lexicons, and specifically from the in-domain Yelp Restaurant Sentiment lexicons. The out-of-domain tweet sentiment lexicons did not prove useful on this subtask. Also, word clusters did not offer additional benefits on top of those provided by the lexicons. The use of aspect term features resulted in gains of 0.39.

7 Conclusion

The paper describes supervised machine-learning approaches to detect aspect terms and aspect categories and to detect sentiment expressed towards aspect terms and aspect categories in customer reviews. Apart from common surface-form features such as ngrams, our approaches benefit from the use of existing and newly created lexical resources such as word–aspect association lexicons and sentiment lexicons. Our submissions stood first on 3 out of 4 subtasks, and within the top 3 best results on all 6 task-domain evaluations.

References

Peter F Brown, Peter V Desouza, Robert L Mercer, Vincent J Della Pietra, and Jenifer C Lai. 1992. Class-based n-gram models of natural language. *Computational linguistics*, 18(4):467–479.

Chih-Chung Chang and Chih-Jen Lin. 2011. LIBSVM: A library for support vector machines. *ACM Transactions on Intelligent Systems and Technology*, 2(3):27:1–27:27.

Michael Collins. 2002. Discriminative training methods for hidden markov models: Theory and experiments with perceptron algorithms. In *Proceedings of the Conference on Empirical Methods in Natural Language Processing*.

Koby Crammer and Yoram Singer. 2002. On the algorithmic implementation of multiclass kernel-based vector machines. *The Journal of Machine Learning Research*, 2:265–292.

Koby Crammer, Ofer Dekel, Joseph Keshet, Shai Shalev-Shwartz, and Yoram Singer. 2006. Online passive-aggressive algorithms. *Journal of Machine Learning Research*, 7:551–585.

Hal Daumé III. 2007. Frustratingly easy domain adaptation. In *Proceedings of the Annual Meeting of the Association for Computational Linguistics*, ACL '07, pages 256 – 263.

Berry de Bruijn, Colin Cherry, Svetlana Kiritchenko, Joel Martin, and Xiaodan Zhu. 2011. Machine-learned solutions for three stages of clinical information extraction: the state of the art at i2b2 2010. *Journal of the American Medical Informatics Association*, 18(5):557–562.

Marie-Catherine de Marneffe, Bill MacCartney, and Christopher D. Manning. 2006. Generating typed dependency parses from phrase structure parses. In *Proceedings of the International Conference on Language Resources and Evaluation*, LREC '06.

Kevin Gimpel, Nathan Schneider, Brendan O'Connor, Dipanjan Das, Daniel Mills, Jacob Eisenstein, Michael Heilman, Dani Yogatama, Jeffrey Flanigan, and Noah A. Smith. 2011. Part-of-speech tagging for Twitter: Annotation, features, and experiments. In *Proceedings of the Annual Meeting of the Association for Computational Linguistics*, ACL '11.

Minqing Hu and Bing Liu. 2004. Mining and summarizing customer reviews. In *Proceedings of the 10th ACM SIGKDD International Conference on Knowledge Discovery and Data Mining*, KDD '04, pages 168–177, New York, NY, USA. ACM.

Svetlana Kiritchenko, Xiaodan Zhu, and Saif M. Mohammad. 2014. Sentiment analysis of short informal texts. *Journal of Artificial Intelligence Research (to appear)*.

Julian McAuley and Jure Leskovec. 2013. Hidden factors and hidden topics: understanding rating dimensions with review text. In *Proceedings of the 7th ACM conference on Recommender systems*, pages 165–172. ACM.

Saif M. Mohammad and Peter D. Turney. 2010. Emotions evoked by common words and phrases: Using Mechanical Turk to create an emotion lexicon. In *Proceedings of the NAACL-HLT Workshop on Computational Approaches to Analysis and Generation of Emotion in Text*, LA, California.

Saif M. Mohammad, Svetlana Kiritchenko, and Xiaodan Zhu. 2013. NRC-Canada: Building the state-of-the-art in sentiment analysis of tweets. In *Proceedings of the International Workshop on Semantic Evaluation*, SemEval '13, Atlanta, Georgia, USA, June.

Olutobi Owoputi, Brendan OConnor, Chris Dyer, Kevin Gimpel, Nathan Schneider, and Noah A Smith. 2013. Improved part-of-speech tagging for online conversational text with word clusters. In *Proceedings of NAACL-HLT*, pages 380–390.

Maria Pontiki, Dimitrios Galanis, John Pavlopoulos, Harris Papageorgiou, Ion Androutsopoulos, and Suresh Manandhar. 2014. SemEval-2014 Task 4: Aspect based sentiment analysis. In *Proceedings of the International Workshop on Semantic Evaluation*, SemEval '14, Dublin, Ireland, August.

M.F. Porter. 1980. An algorithm for suffix stripping. *Program*, 3:130–137.

Sunita Sarawagi and William W Cohen. 2004. Semi-markov conditional random fields for information extraction. In *Advances in Neural Information Processing Systems*, volume 17, pages 1185–1192.

Peter Turney and Michael L Littman. 2003. Measuring praise and criticism: Inference of semantic orientation from association. *ACM Transactions on Information Systems*, 21(4).

Theresa Wilson, Janyce Wiebe, and Paul Hoffmann. 2005. Recognizing contextual polarity in phrase-level sentiment analysis. In *Proceedings of the Conference on Human Language Technology and Empirical Methods in Natural Language Processing*, HLT '05, pages 347–354, Stroudsburg, PA, USA.

Xiaodan Zhu, Hongyu Guo, Saif M. Mohammad, and Svetlana Kiritchenko. 2014. An empirical study on the effect of negation words on sentiment. In *Proceedings of the Annual Meeting of the Association for Computational Linguistics*, ACL '14.

NRC-Canada-2014: Recent Improvements in the Sentiment Analysis of Tweets

Xiaodan Zhu, Svetlana Kiritchenko, and Saif M. Mohammad
National Research Council Canada
Ottawa, Ontario, Canada K1A 0R6
{xiaodan.zhu,svetlana.kiritchenko,saif.mohammad}@nrc-cnrc.gc.ca

Abstract

This paper describes state-of-the-art statistical systems for automatic sentiment analysis of tweets. In a Semeval-2014 shared task (Task 9), our submissions obtained highest scores in the term-level sentiment classification subtask on both the 2013 and 2014 tweets test sets. In the message-level sentiment classification task, our submissions obtained highest scores on the LiveJournal blog posts test set, sarcastic tweets test set, and the 2013 SMS test set. These systems build on our SemEval-2013 sentiment analysis systems (Mohammad et al., 2013) which ranked first in both the term- and message-level subtasks in 2013. Key improvements over the 2013 systems are in the handling of negation. We create separate tweet-specific sentiment lexicons for terms in affirmative contexts and in negated contexts.

1 Introduction

Automatically detecting sentiment of tweets (and other microblog posts) has attracted extensive interest from both the academia and industry. The Conference on Semantic Evaluation Exercises (SemEval) organizes a shared task on the sentiment analysis of tweets with two subtasks. In the *message-level task*, the participating systems are to identify whether a tweet as a whole expresses positive, negative, or neutral sentiment. In the *term-level task*, the objective is to determine the sentiment of a marked target term (a single word or a multi-word expression) within the tweet. Our submissions stood first in both subtasks in 2013. This paper describes improvements over that system and the subsequent submissions to the 2014 shared task (Rosenthal et al., 2014).

Evaluation Set	Term-level Task	Message-level Task
Twt14	1	4
Twt13	1	2
Sarc14	3	1
LvJn14	2	1
SMS13	2	1

Table 1: Overall rank of NRC-Canada sentiment analysis models in Semeval-2014 Task 9 under the constrained condition. The rows are five evaluation datasets and the columns are the two subtasks.

The training data for the SemEval-2014 shared task is same as that of SemEval-2013 (about 10,000 tweets). The 2014 test set has five subcategories: a tweet set provided newly in 2014 (*Twt14*), the tweet set used for testing in the 2013 shared task (*Twt13*), a set of tweets that are sarcastic (*Sarc14*), a set of sentences from the blogging website LiveJournal (*LvJn14*), and the set of SMS messages used for testing in the 2013 shared task (*SMS13*). Instances from these categories were interspersed in the provided test set. The participants were not told about the source of the individual messages. The objective was to determine how well a system trained on tweets generalizes to texts from other domains.

Our submissions to SemEval-2014 Task 9, ranked first in five out of the ten subtask–dataset combinations. In the other evaluation sets as well, our submissions performed competitively. The results are summarized in Table 1. As we will show, automatically generated tweet-specific lexicons were especially helpful in all subtask–dataset combinations. The results also show that even though our models are trained only on tweets, they generalize well to data from other domains.

Proceedings of the 8th International Workshop on Semantic Evaluation (SemEval 2014), pages 443–447,
Dublin, Ireland, August 23-24, 2014.

Our systems are based on supervised SVMs and a number of surface-form, semantic, and sentiment features. The major improvement in our 2014 system over the 2013 system is in the way it handles negation. Morante and Sporleder (2012) define negation to be "a grammatical category that allows the changing of the truth value of a proposition". Negation is often expressed through the use of negative signals or negators, words such as *isnt* and *never*, and it can significantly affect the sentiment of its scope. We create separate tweet-specific sentiment lexicons for terms in affirmative contexts and in negated contexts. That is, we automatically determine the average sentiment of a term when occurring in an affirmative context, and separately the average sentiment of a term when occurring in a negated context.

2 Our Systems

Our SemEval-2014 systems are based on our SemEval-2013 systems (Mohammad et al., 2013). For completeness, we briefly revisit our previous approach, which uses support vector machine (SVM) as the classification algorithm and leverages the following features.

Lexicon features These features are generated by using three manually constructed sentiment lexicons and two automatically constructed lexicons. The manually constructed lexicons include the *NRC Emotion Lexicon* (Mohammad and Turney, 2010; Mohammad and Yang, 2011), the *MPQA Lexicon* (Wilson et al., 2005), and the *Bing Liu Lexicon* (Hu and Liu, 2004). The two automatically constructed lexicons, the *Hashtag Sentiment Lexicon* and the *Sentiment140 Lexicon*, were created specifically for tweets (Mohammad et al., 2013).

The sentiment score of each term (e.g., a word or bigram) in the automatically constructed lexicons is computed by measuring the PMI (pointwise mutual information) between the term and the positive or negative category of tweets using the formula:

$$SenScore\,(w) = PMI(w, pos) - PMI(w, neg) \quad (1)$$

where w is a term in the lexicons. $PMI(w, pos)$ is the PMI score between w and the positive class, and $PMI(w, neg)$ is the PMI score between w and the negative class. Therefore, a positive *SenScore* (w) suggests a stronger association of word w with positive sentiment and vice versa. The magnitude indicates the strength of association. Note that the sentiment class of the tweets used to construct the lexicons was automatically identified either from hashtags or from emoticons as described in (Mohammad et al., 2013).

With these lexicons available, the following features were extracted for a *text span*. Here a text span can be a target term, its context, or an entire tweet, depending on the task. The lexicon features include: (1) the number of sentiment tokens in a text span; sentiment tokens are word tokens whose sentiment scores are not zero in a lexicon; (2) the total sentiment score of the text span: $\sum_{w \in textSpan} SenScore\,(w)$; (3) the maximal score: $max_{w \in textSpan} SenScore\,(w)$; (4) the total positive and negative sentiment scores of the text span; (5) the sentiment score of the last token in the text span. Note that all these features are generated, when applicable, by using each of the sentiment lexicons mentioned above.

Ngrams We employed two types of ngram features: word ngrams and character ngrams. The former reflect the presence or absence of contiguous or non-contiguous sequences of words, and the latter are sequences of prefix/suffix characters in each word. These features are same as in our last year's submission.

Negation The number of negated contexts. Our definition of a *negated context* follows Pang et al. (2002), which will be described in more details below in Section 2.1.

POS The number of occurrences of each part-of-speech tag. We tokenized and part-of-speech tagged the tweets with the Carnegie Mellon University (CMU) Twitter NLP tool (Gimpel et al., 2011).

Cluster features The CMU POS-tagging tool provides the token clusters produced with the Brown clustering algorithm from 56 million English-language tweets. These 1,000 clusters serve as an alternative representation of tweet content, reducing the sparsity of the token space.

Encodings The encoding features are derived from hashtags, punctuation marks, emoticons, elongated words, and uppercased words.

For the term-level task, all the above features are extracted for target terms and their context, where a *context* is a window of words surrounding a target term. For the message-level task, the features are extracted from the whole tweet.

In the term-level task, we used the LIBSVM (Chang and Lin, 2011) tool with the following parameters: *-t 0 -b 1 -m 1000*. The total number of features is about 115,000. In the message-level task, we used an in-house implementation of SVM with a linear kernel. The parameter C was set to 0.005. The total number of features was about 1.5 million.

2.1 Improving Lexicons and Negation Models

An important advantage of our SemEval-2013 systems comes from the use of the two high-coverage tweet-specific sentiment lexicons. In the SemEval-2014 submissions, we improve these lexicons by incorporating negation modeling into the lexicon generation process.

2.1.1 Improving Sentiment Lexicons

A word in a negated context has a different evaluative nature than the same word in an affirmative (non-negated) context. We have proposed a lexicon-based approach (Kiritchenko et al., 2014) to determining the sentiment of words in these two situations by automatically creating separate sentiment lexicons for the affirmative and negated contexts. In this way, we do not need to employ any explicit assumptions to model negation.

To achieve this, a tweet corpus is split into two parts: *Affirmative Context Corpus* and *Negated Context Corpus*. Following the work of Pang et al. (2002), we define a negated context as a segment of a tweet that starts with a negation word (e.g., *no, shouldn't*) and ends with one of the punctuation marks: ',', '.', ':', ';', '!', '?'. The list of negation words was adopted from Christopher Potts' sentiment tutorial.[1] Thus, part of a tweet that is marked as negated is included into the negated context corpus while the rest of the tweet becomes part of the affirmative context corpus. The sentiment label for the tweet is kept unchanged in both corpora. Then, we generate an affirmative context lexicon from the affirmative context corpus and a negated context lexicon from the negated context corpus using the technique described in (Kiritchenko et al., 2014).

Furthermore, we refined the method of constructing the negated context lexicons by splitting a negated context into two parts: the *immediate context* consisting of a *single* token that directly follows a negation word, and the *distant context* consisting of the rest of the tokens in the negated context. This has two benefits. Intuitively, negation affects words *directly* following the negation words more strongly than more distant words. Second, immediate-context scores are less noisy. Our simple negation scope identification algorithm can at times fail and include parts of a tweet that are not actually negated (e.g., if a punctuation mark is missing). Overall, a sentiment word can have up to three scores, one for affirmative context, one for immediate negated context, and one for distant negated context.

We reconstructed the *Hashtag Sentiment Lexicon* and the *Sentiment140 Lexicon* with this approach and used them in our SemEval-2014 systems.

2.1.2 Discriminating Negation Words

Different negation words, e.g., *never* and *didn't*, can have different effects on sentiment (Zhu et al., 2014; Taboada et al., 2011). In our SemEval-2014 submission, we discriminate negation words in the term-level models. For example, the word *acceptable* appearing in a sentence *this is never acceptable* is marked as *acceptable_beNever*, while in the sentence *this is not acceptable*, it is marked as *acceptable_beNot*. In this way, different negators (e.g., *be_not* and *be_never*) are treated differently. Note that we do not differentiate the *tense* and *person* of auxiliaries in order to reduce sparseness (e.g., *was not* and *am not* are treated in the same way). This new representation is used to extract ngrams and lexicon-based features.

3 Results

Overall performance The evaluation metric used in the competition is the macro-averaged F-measure calculated over the positive and negative categories. Table 2 presents the overall performance of our models. NRC13 and NRC14 are the systems we submitted to SemEval-2013 and SemEval-2014, respectively. The integers in the brackets are our official ranks in SemEval-2014 under the constrained condition.

In the term-level task, our submission ranked first on the two Tweet datasets among 14 teams. The results show that we achieved significant improvements over our last year's submission: the F-score improves from 85.19 to 86.63 on the Twt14 data and from 89.10 to 90.14 on the Twt13 data. More specifically, on the Twt14 data, the approach described in Section 2.1.1 improved our F-score

[1] http://sentiment.christopherpotts.net/lingstruc.html

	Term-level		Message-level	
	NRC13	NRC14	NRC13	NRC14
Twt14	85.19	**86.63**(1)	68.88	**69.85**(4)
Twt13	89.10	**90.14**(1)	69.02	**70.75**(2)
Sarc14	78.16	**77.13**(3)	47.64	**58.16**(1)
LvJn14	84.96	**85.49**(2)	74.01	**74.84**(1)
SMS13	88.34	**88.03**(2)	68.34	**70.28**(1)

Table 2: Overall performance of the NRC-Canada sentiment analysis systems.

from 85.19 to 86.37, and discriminating negation words (discussed in Section 2.1.2) further improved the F-score from 86.37 to 86.63.

Our system ranked second on the LvJn14 and SMS13 dataset. Note that the term-level system that ranked first on LvJn14 performed worse than our system on SMS13 and the system that ranked first on SMS13 showed worse results than ours on LvJn14, indicating that our term-level models in general have good generalizability on these two out-of-domain datasets.

On the message-level task, again the NRC14 system showed significant improvements over the last year's system on all five datasets. It achieved the second best result on the Twt13 data and the fourth result on the Twt14 data among 42 teams. It was also the best system to predict sentiment in sarcastic tweets (Sarc14). Furthermore, the system proved to generalize well to other types of short informal texts; it placed first on the two out-of-domain datasets: SMS13 and LvJn14. We observe a major improvement of our message-level model on Sarc14 over our last year's model, but as the size of Sarc14 is small (86 tweets), more data and analysis would be desirable to help better understand this phenomenon.

Contribution of features Table 3 presents the results of ablation experiments on all five test sets for the term-level task. The features derived from the manual and automatic lexicons proved to be useful on four datasets. The only exception is the Sarc14 data where removing lexicon features results in no performance improvement. Considering that this test set is very small (only about 100 test terms), further investigation would be desirable if a larger dataset becomes available. Also, in sarcasm the real sentiment of a text span may be different from its literal sentiment. In such a situation, a system that correctly recognizes the literal sentiment may actually make mistakes in capturing the real sentiment. The last two rows in Table 3 show the results obtained when the features are extracted only from the target (and not from its context) and when they are extracted only from the context of the target (and not from the target itself). Observe that even though the context may influence the polarity of the target, using target features alone is substantially more useful than using context features alone. Nonetheless, adding context features improves the F-scores in general.

On the message-level task (Table 4), the features derived from the sentiment lexicons and, in particular, from our large-coverage tweet-specific lexicons turned out to be the most influential. The use of the lexicons provided consistent gains of 9–11 percentage points not only on tweet datasets, but also on out-of-domain SMS and LiveJournal data. Note that removing the features derived from the manual lexicons as well as removing the ngram features improves the performance on the Twt14 dataset. However, this effect is not observed on the Twt13 and the out-of-domain test sets. The possible explanation of this phenomenon is minor overfitting on the tweet data.

4 Conclusions

We presented supervised statistical systems for message-level and term-level sentiment analysis of tweets. They incorporate many surface-form, semantic, and sentiment features. Among submissions from over 40 teams in the Semeval-2014 shared task "Sentiment Analysis in Twitter", our submissions ranked first in five out of the ten subtask-dataset combinations. The single most useful set of features are those obtained from automatically generated tweet-specific lexicons. We obtained significant improvements over our previous system (which ranked first in the 2013 shared task) notably by estimating the sentiment of words in affirmative and negated contexts separately. Also, since different negation words impact sentiment differently, we modeled different negation words separately in our term-level system. This too led to an improvement in F-score. The results on different kinds of evaluation sets show that even though our systems are trained only on tweets, they generalize well to text from other domains such as blog posts and SMS messages. Many of the resources we created and used are made freely available.[2]

[2]www.purl.com/net/sentimentoftweets

Experiment	Twt14	Twt13	Sarc14	LvJn14	SMS13
all features	86.63	90.14	77.13	85.49	88.03
all - lexicons	81.98	86.25	80.74	80.00	83.91
all - manu. lex.	86.08	89.25	75.32	84.13	87.69
all - auto. lex.	86.05	88.32	80.38	83.96	86.18
all - ngrams	83.31	86.67	72.95	81.58	82.41
all - target	72.93	74.19	63.09	72.21	69.34
all - context	84.40	88.83	77.22	82.99	87.97

Table 3: Term-level Task: The macro-averaged F-scores obtained on the 5 test sets with one of the feature groups removed.

Experiment	Twt14	Twt13	Sarc14	LvJn14	SMS13
all features	69.85	70.75	58.16	74.84	70.28
all - lexicons	60.59	60.04	47.17	65.80	60.56
all - manu. lex.	71.84	69.84	53.34	73.41	66.60
all - auto. lex.	63.40	65.08	47.57	71.76	66.94
all - ngrams	70.02	67.90	44.58	74.43	68.45

Table 4: Message-level Task: The macro-averaged F-scores obtained on the 5 test sets with one of the feature groups removed.

Acknowledgments

We thank Colin Cherry for providing his SVM code and for helpful discussions.

References

Chih-Chung Chang and Chih-Jen Lin. 2011. LIBSVM: A library for support vector machines. *ACM Transactions on Intelligent Systems and Technology*, 2(3):27:1–27:27.

Kevin Gimpel, Nathan Schneider, Brendan O'Connor, Dipanjan Das, Daniel Mills, Jacob Eisenstein, Michael Heilman, Dani Yogatama, Jeffrey Flanigan, and Noah A. Smith. 2011. Part-of-speech tagging for Twitter: Annotation, features, and experiments. In *Proceedings of ACL.*

Minqing Hu and Bing Liu. 2004. Mining and summarizing customer reviews. In *Proceedings of KDD*, pages 168–177, New York, NY, USA. ACM.

Svetlana Kiritchenko, Xiaodan Zhu, and Saif Mohammad. 2014. Sentiment analysis of short informal texts. *(To appear) Journal of Artificial Intelligence Research.*

Saif M. Mohammad and Peter D. Turney. 2010. Emotions evoked by common words and phrases: Using Mechanical Turk to create an emotion lexicon. In *Proceedings of the NAACL-HLT Workshop on Computational Approaches to Analysis and Generation of Emotion in Text*, LA, California.

Saif M. Mohammad and Tony (Wenda) Yang. 2011. Tracking sentiment in mail: How genders differ on emotional axes. In *Proceedings of the ACL Workshop on Computational Approaches to Subjectivity and Sentiment Analysis*, Portland, OR, USA.

Saif Mohammad, Svetlana Kiritchenko, and Xiaodan Zhu. 2013. NRC-Canada: Building the state-of-the-art in sentiment analysis of tweets. In *Proceedings of the International Workshop on Semantic Evaluation*, SemEval '13, Atlanta, Georgia, USA, June.

Roser Morante and Caroline Sporleder. 2012. Modality and negation: An introduction to the special issue. *Computational linguistics*, 38(2):223–260.

Bo Pang, Lillian Lee, and Shivakumar Vaithyanathan. 2002. Thumbs up?: Sentiment classification using machine learning techniques. In *Proceedings of EMNLP*, pages 79–86, Philadelphia, PA.

Sara Rosenthal, Preslav Nakov, Alan Ritter, and Veselin Stoyanov. 2014. SemEval-2014 Task 9: Sentiment Analysis in Twitter. In *Proceedings of SemEval-2014*, Dublin, Ireland.

Maite Taboada, Julian Brooke, Milan Tofiloski, Kimberly Voll, and Manfred Stede. 2011. Lexicon-based methods for sentiment analysis. *Computational Linguistics*, 37(2):267–307.

Theresa Wilson, Janyce Wiebe, and Paul Hoffmann. 2005. Recognizing contextual polarity in phrase-level sentiment analysis. In *Proceedings of HLT-EMNLP*, HLT '05, pages 347–354, Stroudsburg, PA, USA.

Xiaodan Zhu, Hongyu Guo, Saif Mohammad, and Svetlana Kiritchenko. 2014. An empirical study on the effect of negation words on sentiment. In *Proceedings of ACL*, Baltimore, Maryland, USA, June.

NTNU: Measuring Semantic Similarity with Sublexical Feature Representations and Soft Cardinality

André Lynum, Partha Pakray, Björn Gambäck
{andrely,parthap,gamback}@idi.ntnu.no
Norwegian University of Science and Technology
Trondheim, Norway

Sergio Jimenez
sgjimenezv@unal.edu.co
Universidad Nacional de Colombia
Bogotá, Colombia

Abstract

The paper describes the approaches taken by the NTNU team to the SemEval 2014 Semantic Textual Similarity shared task. The solutions combine measures based on lexical soft cardinality and character n-gram feature representations with lexical distance metrics from TakeLab's baseline system. The final NTNU system is based on bagged support vector machine regression over the datasets from previous shared tasks and shows highly competitive performance, being the best system on three of the datasets and third best overall (on weighted mean over all six datasets).

1 Introduction

The Semantic Textual Similarity (STS) shared task aims at providing a unified framework for evaluating textual semantic similarity, ranging from exact semantic equivalence to completely unrelated texts. This is represented by the prediction of a similarity score between two sentences, drawn from a particular category of text, which ranges from 0 (different topics) to 5 (exactly equivalent) through six grades of semantic similarity (Agirre et al., 2013). This paper describes the NTNU submission to the SemEval 2014 STS shared task (Task 10). The approach is based on the lexical and distributional features of the baseline TakeLab system from the 2012 shared task (Šarić et al., 2012), but improves on it in three ways: by adding two new categories of features and by using a bagging regression model to predict similarity scores.

The new feature categories added are based on soft cardinality and character n-grams, described in Section 2. The parameters of the two categories are optimised over several corpora and the features are combined through support vector regression (Section 3) to create the actual systems (Section 4). As Section 5 shows, the new measures give the baseline system a substantial boost, leading to very competitive results in the shared task evaluation.

2 Feature Generation Methods

The methods used for creating new features utilise soft cardinality and character n-grams. Soft cardinality (Jimenez et al., 2010) was used successfully for the STS task in previous SemEval editions (Jimenez et al., 2012a; Jimenez et al., 2013a). The NTNU systems utilise an ensemble of such 18 measures, based only on surface text information, which were extracted using soft cardinality with different similarity functions, as further described in Section 2.1.

Section 2.2 then introduces the similarity measures based on character n-gram feature representations, which proved themselves as the strongest features in the STS 2013 task (Marsi et al., 2013). The measures used here replace character n-gram features with cluster frequencies or vector values based on the n-gram collocational structure learned in an unsupervised manner from text data. A variety of n-gram feature representations were trained on subsets of Wikipedia and the best performing ones were used for the new measures, which are based on cosine similarity between the document vectors derived from each sentence in a given pair.

2.1 Soft Cardinality Measures

Soft cardinality resembles classical set cardinality as it is a method for counting the number of elements in a set, but differs from it in that similarities among elements are being considered for the "soft counting". The soft cardinality of a set of words

Proceedings of the 8th International Workshop on Semantic Evaluation (SemEval 2014), pages 448–453,
Dublin, Ireland, August 23-24, 2014.

$A = \{a_1, a_2, .., a_{|A|}\}$ (a sentence) is defined by:

$$|A|_{sim} = \sum_{i=1}^{|A|} \frac{w_{a_i}}{\sum_{j=1}^{|A|} sim(a_i, a_j)^p} \quad (1)$$

Where p is a parameter that controls the cardinality's softness (p's default value is 1) and w_{a_i} are weights for each word, obtained through inverse document frequency (*idf*) weighting. $sim(a_i, a_j)$ is a similarity function that compares two words a_i and a_j using the symmetrized Tversky's index (Tversky, 1977; Jimenez et al., 2013a) representing them as sets of 3-grams of characters. That is, $a_i = \{a_{i,1}, a_{i,2}, ..., a_{i,|a_i|}\}$ where $a_{i,n}$ is the nth character trigram in the word a_i in A. Thus, the proposed word-to-word similarity is given by:

$$sim(a_i, a_j) = \frac{|c|}{\beta(\alpha|a_{min}| + (1-\alpha)|a_{max}|) + |c|} \quad (2)$$

$$\begin{cases} |c| & = |a_i \cap a_j| + bias_{sim} \\ |a_{min}| & = \min\{|a_i \setminus a_j|, |a_j \setminus a_i|\} \\ |a_{max}| & = \max\{|a_i \setminus a_j|, |a_j \setminus a_i|\} \end{cases}$$

The sim function is equivalent to the Dice's coefficient if the three parameters are given their default values, namely $\alpha = 0.5$, $\beta = 1$ and $bias = 0$.

The soft cardinalities of any pair of sentences A, B and $A \cup B$ can be obtained using Eq. 1. The soft cardinality of the intersection is approximated by $|A \cap B|_{sim} = |A|_{sim} + |B|_{sim} - |A \cup B|_{sim}$. These four basic soft cardinalities are algebraically recombined to produce an extended set of 18 features as shown in Table 1. The feature $\mathbf{STS_{sim}}$ is a parameterized similarity function built by reusing at word level the symmetrized Tversky's index (Eq. 2), whose parameters are tuned from training data (as further described in Subsection 3.2).

Although this method is based purely on string matching, the soft cardinality has been shown to be a very strong baseline for semantic textual comparison. The word-to-word similarity sim in Eq. 1 could be replaced by other similarity functions based on semantic networks or any distributional representation making this method able to capture more complex semantic relations among words.

2.2 Sublexical Feature Representations

We have created a set of similarity measures based on induced representations of character n-grams. The measures are based on similarity between document vectors, here the centroid of the individual term vector representations, which are trained on character n-grams rather than full words. The vector representations are induced in an unsupervised manner from large unannotated corpora using word clustering, topic learning and word representation learning methods.

$\mathbf{STS_{sim}}$	$(\|A\|-\|A\cap B\|)/\|A\|$
$\|A\|$	$(\|A\|-\|A\cap B\|)/\|A\cup B\|$
$\|B\|$	$\|B\|/\|A\cup B\|$
$\|A \cap B\|$	$(\|B\|-\|A\cap B\|)/\|B\|$
$\|A \cup B\|$	$(\|B\|-\|A\cap B\|)/\|A\cup B\|$
$\|A\| - \|A \cap B\|$	$\|A\cap B\|/\|A\|$
$\|B\| - \|A \cap B\|$	$\|A\cap B\|/\|B\|$
$\|A \cup B\| - \|A \cap B\|$	$\|A\cap B\|/\|A\cup B\|$
$\|A\|/\|A\cup B\|$	$(\|A\cup B\|-\|A\cap B\|)/\|A\cap B\|$

NB: in this table only, $|*|$ is short for $|*|_{sim}$

Table 1: Soft cardinality features.

In this paper, three different methods have been used for creating the character n-gram feature representations: Brown Clusters (Brown et al., 1992), Latent Semantic Indexing (LSI) topics (Deerwester et al., 1990), and log linear skip-gram models (Mikolov et al., 2013). The Brown clusters were trained using the implementation by Liang (2005), while the LSI topic vectors and log linear skip-gram representations were trained using the Gensim topic modelling framework (Řehůřek and Sojka, 2010). In addition, *tf-idf* (Term-Frequency Inverse Document Frequency) weighting was used when training LSI topic models. We used a cosine distance measure between document vectors consisting of the centroid of the term representation vectors. For Brown clusters, the normalized term frequency vectors were used with the cluster IDs instead of the terms themselves. For LSI topic representations, the *tf-idf* weighted topic mixture for each term was used as the term representation. For the log linear skip-grams, the word representations were extracted from the model weight matrix.

3 Feature and Parameter Optimisation

The extracted features and the parameters for the two methods described in the previous section were optimised over several sets of training data. As no training data was explicitly provided for the STS evaluation campaign this year, we used different training sets from past campaigns and from Wikipedia for the new test sets.

Test set	Training set
deft-forum	MSRvid 2012 train and test + OnWN 2012 and 2013 test
deft-news	MSRvid 2012 train + test
headlines	headlines 2013 test
images	MSRvid 2012 train + test
OnWN	OnWN 2012 and 2013 test
tweet-news	SMTeuroparl 2012 test + SMTnews 2012 test

Table 2: Training-test set pairs.

3.1 Training Data and Pre-processing

The training-test sets pairs used for optimising the parameters of the soft cardinality methods were selected from the STS 2012 and STS 2013 task, as shown in Table 2. The character n-gram representation vectors were trained in an unsupervised manner on two subsets of Wikipedia consisting, respectively, of the first 12 million words (10^8 characters, hence referred to as *Wiki8*) and of 125 million words (10^9 characters; *Wiki9*).

First, however, the training data had to be pre-processed. Thus, before extracting the *idf* weights and the soft cardinality features, all the texts shown in Table 2 were passed through the following four pre-processing steps:

(i) tokenization and stop-word removal (provided by NLTK, Bird et al. (2009)),[1]

(ii) conversion to lowercase characters,

(iii) punctuation and special character removal (e.g., ".", ";", "$", "&"), and

(iv) Porter stemming.

Character n-grams including whitespace were generated from the Wikipedia texts, which in contrast only were pre-processed in a 3-step chain:

(i) removal of punctuation and extra whitespace,

(ii) replacing numbers with their single digit word ('one', 'two', etc.), and

(iii) lowercasing all text.

[1] http://www.nltk.org/

Data	α	β	$bias$	p	α'	β'	$bias'$
deft-forum	1.01	-1.01	0.24	0.93	-2.71	0.42	1.63
deft-news	3.36	-0.64	1.37	0.44	2.36	0.72	0.02
headlines	0.36	-0.29	4.17	0.85	-4.50	0.43	0.19
images	1.12	-1.11	0.93	0.64	-0.98	0.50	0.11
OnWN	0.53	-0.53	1.01	1.00	-4.89	0.52	0.46
tweet-news	0.13	0.14	2.80	0.01	2.66	1.74	0.45

Table 3: Optimal parameters used for each dataset.

3.2 Soft Cardinality Parameter Optimisation

The first feature in Table 1, $\mathbf{STS_{sim}}$, was used to optimise the four parameters α, β, *bias*, and p in the following way. First, we built a text similarity function reusing Eq. 2 for comparing two sets of words (instead of two sets of character 3-grams) and replacing the classic cardinality $|*|$ by the soft cardinality $|*|_{sim}$ from Eq. 1. This text similarity function adds three parameters (α', β', and $bias'$) to the initial four parameter set (α, β, *bias*, and p).

Second, these seven parameters were set to their default values and the scores obtained from this function for each pair of sentences were compared to the gold standards in the training data using Pearson's correlation. The parameter search space was then explored iteratively using hill-climbing until reaching optimal Pearson's correlation. The criterion for assignment of training-test set pairs was by closeness of average character length. The optimal training parameters are shown in Table 3.

3.3 Parameters for N-gram Feature Training

The character n-gram feature representation vectors were trained while varying the parameters of n-gram size, cluster size, and term frequency cut-offs for all models. For the log linear skip-gram models, our intuition is that a larger skip-gram context is needed than the 5 or 10 wide skip-grams used to train word-based representations due to the smaller term vocabulary and dependency between adjacent n-grams, so instead we trained models using skip-gram widths of 25 or 50 terms. Term frequency cut-offs were set to limit the model size, but also potentially serve as a regularization on the resulting measure. In detail, the following sub-lexical representation measures are used:

- Log linear skip-gram representations of character 3- and 4-grams of size 1000 and 2000, respectively. Trained on the Wiki8 corpus using a skip gram window of size 25 and 50, and frequency cut-off of 5.

- Brown clusters with size 1024 of character 4-grams using a frequency cut-off of 20.

- Brown clusters of character 3-, 4- and 5-grams with cluster sizes of resp. 1024, 2048 and 1024. The representations are trained on the Wiki9 corpus with successively increasing frequency cut-offs of 20, 320 and 1200.

- LSI topic vectors based on character 4-grams of size 2000. Trained on the Wiki8 corpus using a frequency cut-off of 5.

- LSI topic vectors based on character 4-grams of size 1000. Trained on the Wiki9 corpus using a frequency cut-off of 80.

3.4 Similarity Score Regression

The final sentence pair similarity score is predicted by a Support Vector Regression (SVR) model with a Radial Basis (RBF) kernel (Vapnik et al., 1997). The model is trained on all the test data for the 2013 STS shared task combined with all the trial and test data of the 2012 STS shared task.

The combined dataset hence consists of about 7,500 sentence pairs from nine different text categories: five sets from the annotated data supplied to STS 2012, based on Microsoft Research Paraphrase and Video description corpora (MSRpar and MSvid), statistical machine translation system output (SMTeuroparl and SMTnews), and sense mappings between OntoNotes and WordNet (OnWN); and four sets from the STS 2013 test data: headlines (news headlines), SMT, OnWN, and FNWM (mappings of sense definitions from FrameNet and WordNet).

The SVR model was trained as a bagged classifier, that is, for each run, 100 regression models were trained with 80% of the samples and features of the original training set drawn with replacement. The outputs of all models were then averaged into a final prediction. This bagged training procedure adds extra regularization, which can reduce the instability of prediction accuracy between different test data categories.

The prediction pipeline was implemented with the Scikit-learn software framework (Pedregosa et al., 2011), and the SVR models were trained with the implementation's default parameters: cost penalty (C) 1.0, margin (ϵ) 0.1, and RBF precision (γ) $1/|featurecount|$.

We were unable to improve the performance over these defaults by cross validation parameter search unless the models were trained for specific text categories. Consequently no parameter optimization was performed during training of the final systems.

4 Submitted Systems

The three submitted systems consist of one using only the soft cardinality features described in Section 3.2 (**NTNU-run1**), one system using a baseline set of lexical measures and WordNet augmented similarity in addition to the new sublexical representation measures (**NTNU-run2**), and one (**NTNU-run3**) which combines the output from the other two systems by taking the mean of the two sets of predictions. NTNU-run3 thus represents a combination of the measures and methods introduced by NTNU-run1 and NTNU-run2.

In addition to the sublexical feature measures described in Section 3.3, NTNU-run2 uses the following baseline features adapted from the TakeLab 2012 system submission (Šarić et al., 2012).

- Simple lexical features: Relative document length differences, number overlap, case overlap, and stock symbol named entity recognition.

- Lemma and word n-gram overlap of orders 1-3, frequency weighted lemma and word overlap, and WordNet augmented overlap.

- Cosine similarity between the summed word representation vectors from each sentence using LSI models based on large corpora with or without frequency weighting.

The specific measures used in the submitted systems were found by training the regression model on the STS 2012 shared task data and evaluating on the STS 2013 test data. We used a stepwise forward feature selection method by comparing mean (but unweighted) correlation on the four test categories in order to identify the subset of measures to include in the final system.

The system composes a feature set of similarity scores from these 20 baseline measures and the nine sublexical representation measures, and uses these to train a bagged SVM regressor as described in Section 3.4 in order to predict the final semantic similarity score for new sentence pairs.

Dataset	NTNU-run1 r	rank	NTNU-run2 r	rank	NTNU-run3 r	rank	Best r
deft-forum	0.4369	16	0.5084	2	0.5305	1	0.5305
deft-news	0.7138	14	0.7656	6	0.7813	2	0.7850
headlines	0.7219	17	0.7525	13	0.7837	1	0.7837
images	0.8000	9	0.8129	4	0.8343	1	0.8343
OnWN	0.8348	7	0.7767	20	0.8502	4	0.8745
tweet-news	0.4109	33	0.7921	1	0.6755	13	0.7921
mean	0.6531	20	0.7347	4	0.7426	2	0.7429
weighted mean	0.6631	21	0.7491	4	0.7549	3	0.7610

Table 4: Final evaluation results for the submitted systems.

5 Results and Discussion

The final evaluation results for the three submitted systems are shown in Table 4, where the rightmost column ('Best') for comparison displays the performance figures obtained by any of the 38 systems on each dataset.

The systems using sublexical representation based measures show competitive performance, ranking third and fourth among the submitted systems with a weighted mean correlation of $\sim$0.75. They also produced the best result in four out of the six text categories in the evaluation dataset, with NTNU-run3 being the #1 system on deft-forum, headlines and images, #2 on deft-news, and #4 on OnWN. It would thus have been the clear winner if it had not been for its sub-par performance on the tweet-news dataset, which on the other hand is the category NTNU-run2 was the best of all systems on.

The system based solely on soft cardinality features, NTNU-run1, displays more modest performance ranking at 21st place (of the in total 38 submitted systems) with $\sim$0.66 correlation. This is a bit surprising, since this method for obtaining features from pairs of texts was used successfully in other SemEval tasks such as cross-lingual textual entailment (Jimenez et al., 2012b) and student response analysis (Jimenez et al., 2013b). Similarly, Croce et al. (2012) used soft cardinality representing text as a bag of dependencies (syntactic soft cardinality) obtaining the best results in the typed-similarity task (Croce et al., 2013).

From our results it can be noted that for most categories the sublexical representation measures show strong performance in NTNU-run2, with a significantly better result for the combined system NTNU-run3. This indicates that while the soft cardinality features are weaker predictors overall, they are complimentary to the sublexical and lexical features of NTNU-run2. It is also indicative that this is not the case for the tweet-news category, where the text is more "free form" and less normative, so it would be expected that sublexical approaches should have stronger performance.

Acknowledgements

This work was made possible with the support from Department of Computer and Information Science, Norwegian University of Science and Technology.

Partha Pakray was 2013–2014 supported by an ERCIM Alain Bensoussan Fellowship.

The NTNU systems are partly based on code made available by the Text Analysis and Knowledge Engineering Laboratory, Department of Electronics, Microelectronics, Computer and Intelligent Systems, Faculty of Electrical Engineering and Computing, University of Zagreb.

References

Eneko Agirre, Daniel Cer, Mona Diab, Aitor Gonzalez-Agirre, and Weiwei Guo. 2013. *SEM 2013 shared task: Semantic textual similarity. In *Second Joint Conference on Lexical and Computational Semantics (*SEM), Volume 1: Proceedings of the Main Conference and the Shared Task: Semantic Textual Similarity*, pages 32–43, Atlanta, Georgia, USA, June.

Steven Bird, Ewan Klein, and Edward Loper. 2009. *Natural Language Processing with Python*. O'Reilly Media, Inc.

Peter F Brown, Peter V Desouza, Robert L Mercer, Vincent J Della Pietra, and Jenifer C Lai. 1992. Class-based n-gram models of natural language. *Computational linguistics*, 18(4):467–479.

Danilo Croce, Valerio Storch, P. Annesi, and Roberto Basili. 2012. Distributional compositional semantics and text similarity. In *2012 IEEE Sixth International Conference on Semantic Computing (ICSC)*, pages 242–249, September.

Danilo Croce, Valerio Storch, and Roberto Basili. 2013. UNITOR-CORE TYPED: Combining text similarity and semantic filters through SV regression. In *Second Joint Conference on Lexical and Computational Semantics (*SEM), Volume 1: Proceedings of the Main Conference and the Shared Task: Semantic Textual Similarity*, pages 59–65, Atlanta, Georgia, USA, June.

Scott C. Deerwester, Susan T Dumais, Thomas K. Landauer, George W. Furnas, and Richard A. Harshman. 1990. Indexing by latent semantic analysis. *JASIS*, 41(6):391–407.

Sergio Jimenez, Fabio Gonzalez, and Alexander Gelbukh. 2010. Text comparison using soft cardinality. In Edgar Chavez and Stefano Lonardi, editors, *String Processing and Information Retrieval*, volume 6393 of *LNCS*, pages 297–302. Springer, Berlin, Heidelberg.

Sergio Jimenez, Claudia Becerra, and Alexander Gelbukh. 2012a. Soft cardinality: A parameterized similarity function for text comparison. In *Proceedings of the Sixth International Workshop on Semantic Evaluation (SemEval 2012)*, Montréal, Canada, 7-8 June.

Sergio Jimenez, Claudia Becerra, and Alexander Gelbukh. 2012b. Soft cardinality+ ML: Learning adaptive similarity functions for cross-lingual textual entailment. In *Proceedings of the Sixth International Workshop on Semantic Evaluation (SemEval 2012)*, Montréal, Canada, 7-8 June.

Sergio Jimenez, Claudia Becerra, and Alexander Gelbukh. 2013a. SOFTCARDINALITY-CORE: Improving text overlap with distributional measures for semantic textual similarity. In *Second Joint Conference on Lexical and Computational Semantics (*SEM), Volume 1: Proceedings of the Main Conference and the Shared Task: Semantic Textual Similarity*, Atlanta, Georgia, USA, June.

Sergio Jimenez, Claudia Becerra, and Alexander Gelbukh. 2013b. SOFTCARDINALITY: Hierarchical text overlap for student response analysis. In *Second Joint Conference on Lexical and Computational Semantics (*SEM), Volume 1: Proceedings of the Main Conference and the Shared Task: Semantic Textual Similarity*, Atlanta, Georgia, USA, June.

Percy Liang. 2005. *Semi-supervised learning for natural language*. Ph.D. thesis, Massachusetts Institute of Technology.

Erwin Marsi, Hans Moen, Lars Bungum, Gleb Sizov, Björn Gambäck, and André Lynum. 2013. NTNU-CORE: Combining strong features for semantic similarity. In *Second Joint Conference on Lexical and Computational Semantics (*SEM), Volume 1: Proceedings of the Main Conference and the Shared Task: Semantic Textual Similarity*, pages 66–73, Atlanta, Georgia, USA, June.

Tomas Mikolov, Kai Chen, Greg Corrado, and Jeffrey Dean. 2013. Efficient estimation of word representations in vector space. *arXiv preprint arXiv:1301.3781*.

F. Pedregosa, G. Varoquaux, A. Gramfort, V. Michel, B. Thirion, O. Grisel, M. Blondel, P. Prettenhofer, R. Weiss, V. Dubourg, J. Vanderplas, A. Passos, D. Cournapeau, M. Brucher, M. Perrot, and E. Duchesnay. 2011. Scikit-learn: Machine learning in Python. *Journal of Machine Learning Research*, 12:2825–2830.

Radim Řehůřek and Petr Sojka. 2010. Software Framework for Topic Modelling with Large Corpora. In *Proceedings of the LREC 2010 Workshop on New Challenges for NLP Frameworks*, pages 45–50, Valletta, Malta, May. ELRA.

Amos Tversky. 1977. Features of similarity. *Psychological Review*, 84(4):327–352, July.

Vladimir Vapnik, Steven E. Golowich, and Alex Smola. 1997. Support vector method for function approximation, regression estimation, and signal processing. In Michael C. Mozer, Michael I. Jordan, and Thomas Petsche, editors, *Advances in Neural Information Processing Systems*, volume 9, pages 281–287. MIT Press, Cambridge, Massachusetts.

Frane Šarić, Goran Glavaš, Mladen Karan, Jan Šnajder, and Bojana Dalbelo Bašić. 2012. TakeLab: Systems for measuring semantic text similarity. In *Proceedings of the Sixth International Workshop on Semantic Evaluation (SemEval 2012)*, pages 441–448, Montréal, Canada, 7-8 June.

OPI: Semeval-2014 Task 3 System Description

Marek Kozlowski
National Information Processing Institute
mkozlowski@opi.org.pl

Abstract

In this paper, we describe the OPI system participating in the Semeval-2014 task 3 Cross-Level Semantic Similarity. Our approach is knowledge-poor, there is no exploitation of any structured knowledge resources as Wikipedia, WordNet or BabelNet. The method is also fully unsupervised, the training set is only used in order to tune the system. System measures the semantic similarity of texts using corpus-based measures of termsets similarity.

1 Introduction

The task Cross-Level Semantic Similarity of SemEval-2014 aims at an evaluation for semantic similarity across different sizes of text (lexical levels). Unlike prior SemEval tasks on textual similarity that have focused on comparing similar-sized texts, the mentioned task evaluates the case where larger text must be compared to smaller text, namely there are covered four semantic similarity comparisons: paragraph to sentence, sentence to phrase, phrase to word and word to sense.

We present the method for measuring the semantic similarity of texts using a corpus-based measure of termsets (set of words) similarity. We start from preprocessing texts, identifying boundary values, computing termsets similarities and derive from them the final score, which is normalized.

The input of the task consists of two text segments of different level. We want to determine a score indicating their semantic similarity of the smaller item to the larger item. Similarity is scored from 0 to 4, when 0 means no semantic intersection, 4 means that two items have very similar meanings.

2 Related Work

There are lots of papers about measuring the similarity between documents and single words. Document-level similarity works are based on Vector Space Models (Salton and Lesk, 1971; Salton and McGill, 1983). A significant effort has also been put into measuring similarity at the word level, namely by approaches that use distributional semantics (Turney and Pantel, 2010).

Related work can be classified into four major categories: vector-based document models methods, corpus-based methods, knowledge-based methods and hybrid methods (Islam and Inkpen, 2008).

Vector-based document models represent document as a vector of words and the similarity evaluation is based on the number of words that occur in both texts. Lexical similarity methods have problems with different words sharing common sense. Next approaches, such as corpus-based and knowledge-based methods, overcome the above issues.

Corpus based methods apply scores provided by Pointwise Mutual Information (PMI) and Latent Semantic Analysis (LSA).

The Pointwise Mutual Information (PMI) (Turney, 2001) between two words w_i and w_j is:

$$PMI(w_i, w_j) = log_2 \frac{p(w_i, w_j)}{p(w_i)p(w_j)}$$

The Latent Semantic Analysis (LSA) (Landauer and Dumais, 1997; Landauer et al., 2007) is a mathematical method for modelling of the meaning of words and contexts by analysis of representative corpora. It models the meaning of words and contexts by projecting them into a vector space of reduced dimensionality, which is built up by applying singular value decomposition (SVD).

Proceedings of the 8th International Workshop on Semantic Evaluation (SemEval 2014), pages 454–458,
Dublin, Ireland, August 23-24, 2014.

Knowledge based methods apply information from semantic networks as WordNet. They exploit the structure of WordNet to compare concepts. Leacock and Chodorow (1998) proposed metric based on the length of the shortest path between two concepts. Lesk (1986) defined similarity between concepts as the intersection between the corresponding glosses. Budanitsky and Hirst (2006) conducted the research on various WordNet-based measures. Standard thesaurus-based measures of word pair similarity are based only on a single path between concepts. By contrast Hughes and Ramage (2009) used a semantic representation of texts from random walks on WordNet.

Hybrid methods use both corpus-based measures and knowledge-based measures of word semantic similarity to determine the text similarity (Islam and Inkpen, 2008). Mihalcea and Corley (2006) suggested a combined method by exploiting corpus based measures and knowledge-based measures of words semantic similarity. Another hybrid method was proposed by Li et al. (2006) that combines semantic and syntactic information.

The methods presented above are working at fixed level of textual granularity (documents, phrases, or words). Pilehvar et al. (2013) proposed a unified approach to semantic similarity that operates at multiple levels. The method builds a common probabilistic representation over word senses in order to compare different types of linguistic data. Any lexical item is represented as a distribution over a set of word senses (obtained from WordNet), named as item's semantic signature.

3 Our Approach

Our system is fully unsupervised and knowledge-poor. It exploits Wikipedia as a raw corpus for words co-occurrence estimation. The proposed method is not using any kind of textual alignment (e.g. exploiting PoS tagging or WordNet concepts).

The method consists of four steps: preprocessing, identifying boundary values, termset-to-termset similarity computation, text-to-text similarity phase, results normalization. The results from the text-to-text similarity phase are very often beyond the range 0-4, therefore we must normalize them. We evaluated two normalization approaches: linear normalization and non-linear one. The non-linear normalization is based on built clusters (referring to integer values from 0 to 4), which are created using training data set. This step will be described in details in the section 3.5.

3.1 Preprocessing

In the first step the compared texts are retrieved, and then processed into the contexts. Context is the preprocessed original text represented as a bag of words. Texts are processed using a dictionary of proper names, name entities recognizers, PoS-taggers, providing as a result the required contexts. Contexts contain nouns, adjectives, adverbs and proper names. The output of this stage is a pair of contexts passed to the next phase.

3.2 Identifying Boundary Values

This phase is introduced in order to fast detect texts, which are unrelated (0 score) or very similar (4 score). Unrelated ones are identified basing on the lack of any co-occurrences between words from compared texts. It means that any pair of words from compared contexts do not appear together in any Wikipedia paragraph. The very similar texts are identified in two steps. At first we check if all words from the shorter texts are contained in the longer one. If the first check is not fulfilled we compute: ($c_{1,2}$) as the number of Wikipedia paragraphs that contain all of words from both contexts in the nearest neighborhood (20-words window), (c_1) and (c_2) as the numbers of Wikipedia paragraphs that contain contexts within 20-words window. If the ratio $c_{1,2}/max(c_1, c_2)$ is higher than 50% then the analyzed pair of texts refers to the same concept (very similar ones). Having two texts represented by contexts we use the proximity Lucene[1] query in order to estimate the number of Wikipedia paragraphs, which contain the words from contexts within the 20-words window.

3.3 Termset-to-termset Similarity

Termset-to-termset similarity ($t2tSim$) is defined by measure similar to PMI. Given a dictionary D and two termsets (set of words) $W_i \subseteq D$ and $W_j \subseteq D$ then the measure is expressed by the formula:

$$t2tSim(W_i, W_j) = \frac{c(W_i, W_j)}{min(c(W_i), c(W_j))}$$

Here, $c(X_1, .., X_n)$ is a number of Wikipedia paragraphs that contain all terms covered by termsets

[1] http://lucene.apache.org/core/

$X_1, .., X_n$. Two input termsets are semantically close if the similarity measure $t2tSim$ is higher than the user-defined threshold (e.g. 10%). Comparing to the previous step we use the minimum operator in the formula's denominator in order to take into account even one directed relevant association. It was proved experimentally that the proposed measure leads to better results than the PMI measure using NEAR query (co-occurrence within a 10-words window). Specifically, the following formula is used to collect the PMI value between termsets using the Wikipedia as a background corpus:

$$PMI(W_i, W_j) = log_2 \frac{c(W_i, W_j) * WikiSize}{c(W_i) * c(W_j)}$$

In the performed experiments we approximated the value of $WikiSize$ to 30 millions (number of paragraphs of English articles in Wikipedia). In table 1 we present results of Spearman correlation reported by the System using different measures PMI and $t2tSim$. The second measure is slightly better therefore it was chosen as the final one. These correlations were computed after linear normalization of the output measures.

Level	Measure	Spearman correlation
word2sense	PMI	19
word2sense	t2tSim	19
phrase2word	PMI	29
phrase2word	t2tSim	29
sentence2phrase	PMI	45
sentence2phrase	t2tSim	47
paragraph2sentence	PMI	48
paragraph2sentence	t2tSim	49

Table 1: Comparison of PMI and t2tSim measures in the semantic similarity task using Spearman correlation (percentages).

3.4 Text-to-text Similarity

Given two input texts we compute the termset-to-termset similarities in order to derive the final semantic score. We attempt to model the semantic similarity of texts as a function of the semantic similarities of the component termsets. We do this by combining metrics of termset-to-termset similarities and weights into a formula that is a potentially good indicator of semantic similarity of the two input texts. Weights ($w_{m1} > w_{m2} > w_{m3}$) are experimentally set with linear scalable values $w_{m1} = 4, w_{m2} = 2, w_{m3} = 1$ respectively. The pseudo-code of this phase is in Algorithm 1.

Algorithm 1 Text-to-text similarity

Input: c_s, c_l are contexts representing shorter and longer texts respectively; w_{m1}, w_{m2}, w_{m3} as weights for different scopes of similarity comparison;
Output: m as a similarity measure

```
m = 0
m = m + t2tSim(c_s, c_l) * w_m1
for term t_i ∈ c_l do
    m = m + t2tSim(c_s, {t_i}) * w_m2
end for
for term t_j ∈ c_s do
    m = m + t2tSim(c_l, {t_j}) * w_m2
end for
for term t_i ∈ c_s do
    for term t_j ∈ c_l do
        m = m + t2tSim({t_i}, {t_j}) * w_m3
    end for
end for
return m
```

3.5 Results Normalization

The crucial part of the method is a process of normalization obtained measures into the range (0,4). The values 0 and 4 are covered by the step described in the section 3.2. We need to normalize values from the text-to-text similarity phase. This step can be done in two ways: linear normalization and non-linear one. The first one is a casual transformation defined as dividing elements by theirs maximum and scaling to 4. The second one is based on clustering training set. In other words, using training set we induce rules how reported text-to-text similarity values should be transformed into the range (0,4). We implemented hierarchical agglomerative clustering algorithm (with average linkage)[2] in order to cluster similarity measures into five distinct groups. Sorted centroids of the above created groups are labeled with values 0 to 4 respectively. For each new similarity measure (obtained in the testing phase) we measure the distance to the closest cluster's centroids. The final value is derived linearly

[2]Hierarchical Agglomerative Clustering treats initially each instance as a singleton cluster and then successively agglomerate pairs of clusters using the average distance between cluster's elements until the user defined number of clusters persist.

from the distance to the centroids (i.e. if the value is in the middle between centroids referring to 1 and 2, we assign as a final value 1.5). In the testing step we use the non-linear normalization, the evaluations on training set show that clustering based approach provides marginal improvement against linear normalization (about 1% according to Spearman rank, 4-8% according to Pearson correlation).

4 Results

In Task 3, systems were evaluated both within one of four comparison types and also across all comparison types. The system outputs and gold standard ratings are compared in two ways, using Pearson correlation and Spearman's rank correlation (rho). Pearson correlation tests the degree of similarity between the system's similarity ratings and the gold standard ratings. Spearman's rho tests the degree of similarity between the rankings of the items according to similarity. Ranks were computed by summing the correlation values across all four levels of comparisons. The sum of the Pearson correlations is used for the official rank of Task 3. However, the organizers provide a second ranking using the sum of the Spearman correlations.

Level	System	Pearson/ Spearman
word2sense	OPI	15.2/13.1
word2sense	SimCompass	35.6/34.4
word2sense	Baseline	10.9/13.0
phrase2word	OPI	21.3/18.8
phrase2word	SimCompass	41.5/42.4
phrase2word	Baseline	16.5/16.2
sentence2phrase	OPI	43.3/42.4
sentence2phrase	SimCompass	74.2/72.8
sentence2phrase	Baseline	56.2/62.6

Table 2: Results for Pearson and Spearman correlation (percentages) scored by OPI System, SimCompass (the best performing one) and the Baseline one.

We submitted only one run in three comparison types. We avoided the paragraph-to-sentence comparison. Evaluations on training set show that our method reports values below the baseline in both types: paragraph-to-sentence and sentence-to-phrase. In the testing phase we decided to perform only sentence-to-phrase comparison because it reports better values than paragraph-to-sentence according to Pearson correlation, which is used for the official rank.

The best results our algorithm scores in the category phrase-to-word. In this comparison type it was ranked at 12th position among 21 participating systems. In the word-to-sense it was at 14th position among 20 systems. The word-to-sense comparison is converted into the task similar to phrase-to-word by using glosses of target senses. Each key of WordNet sense is replaced with its gloss. It is the only situation when we use the external knowledge resources, but it is not a part of the algorithm. The last comparison (sentence-to-phrase) was our worst, because we did not beat the baseline, as we did in the previous categories. In the sentence-to-phrase comparison word alignment or syntax parsing seems to be very important, in our case none of them was applied. The main conclusion is that comparison of larger text units can not be based on bag of words approaches, where order of words is not important. Let us recall that our method is knowledge-poor, what leads to difficulties in evaluating it against knowledge-rich ones (using sense inventories e.g. WordNet). Generally, we scored better results using Pearson correlation than Spearman's one.

5 Conclusions

We presents our cross-level semantic similarity method, which is knowledge-poor (not using any kind of structured information from resources like machine-readable dictionaries, thesaurus, or ontologies) and fully unsupervised (there is no learning phase leading to models enable to categorize compared texts). The method exploits only Wikipedia as a raw corpora in order to estimate frequencies of co-occurrences. We were aimed to verify how good results can be achieved using only corpus-based approach and not including algorithms that have embedded deep language knowledge. The system scores best in the phrase-to-word (12th rank) and word-to-sense (14th rank) types of comparison with regard to Pearson correlation, while performing a little worse with the Spearman's correlation. The worst results were reported in the sentence-to-phrase category, which brings us the conclusion that larger text units demand word alignment, syntax parsing and more sophisticated text-to-text similarity models.

References

Alexander Budanitsky and Graeme Hirst. 2006. Evaluating WordNet-based measures of Lexical Semantic Relatedness. *Computational Linguistics*, 32(1): 13–47.

Thomas Hughes and Daniel Ramage. 2007. Lexical semantic relatedness with random graph walk. In *Proceedings of the Conference on Empirical Methods in Natural Language Processing*, pages 581–589.

Aminul Islam and Diana Inkpen. 2008. Semantic Text Similarity using Corpus-Based Word Similarity and String Similarity. *ACM Transactions on Knowledge Discovery from Data*, 2(2): 1–25.

Thomas Landauer and Susan Dumais. 1997. A solution to Platos problem: The latent semantic analysis theory of acquisition, induction, and representation of knowledge. *Psychological Review*, 104: 211–240.

Thomas Landauer, Danielle McNamara, Simon Dennis and Walter Kintsch. 2007. *Handbook of Latent Semantic Analysis*. Psychology Press.

Claudia Leacock and Martin Chodorow. 1998. Combining local context and WordNet sense similarity for word sense identification. In *WordNet, An Electronic Lexical Database*, pages 265–283.

Michael Lesk. 1986. Automatic sense disambiguation using machine readable dictionaries: How to tell a pine cone from an ice cream cone. In *Proceedings of the SIGDOC Conference*, pages 24–26.

Yuhua Li, David McLean, Zuhair Bandar, James O'Shea and Keeley Crockett. 2006. Sentence similarity based on semantic nets and corpus statistics. *IEEE Transactions on Knowledge and Data Engineering*, 18(8): 1138-1149.

Rada Mihalcea, Courtney Corley and Carlo Strapparava. 2006. Corpus-based and Knowledge-based Measures of Text Semantic Similarity. In *Proceedings of the American Association for Artificial Intelligence*, pages 775–780.

Mohammad Pilehvar, David Jurgens and Roberto Navigli. 2013. Align, Disambiguate and Walk: A Unified Approach for Measuring Semantic Similarity. In *Proceedings of the 51st Annual Meeting of the Association for Computational Linguistics*, pages 1341–1351.

Gerard Salton and Michael Lesk. 1971. *Computer evaluation of indexing and text processing*. Prentice-Hall, Englewood Cliffs, New Jersey.

Gerard Salton and Michael McGill. 1983. Alternation. *Introduction to modern information retrieval.* McGraw-Hill.

Peter Turney and Patrick Pantel. 2010. From frequency to meaning: Vector space models of semantics. *Journal of Articial Intelligence Research*, 37: 141–188.

Peter Turney. 2001. Mining the web for synonyms: PMI-IR versus LSA on TOEFL. In *Proceedings of the Twelfth European Conference on Machine Learning*, pages 491–502.

Peking: Profiling Syntactic Tree Parsing Techniques for Semantic Graph Parsing

Yantao Du, Fan Zhang, Weiwei Sun and **Xiaojun Wan**
Institute of Computer Science and Technology, Peking University
The MOE Key Laboratory of Computational Linguistics, Peking University
`{duyantao,ws,wanxiaojun}@pku.edu.cn`, `zhangf717@gmail.com`

Abstract

Using the SemEval-2014 Task 8 data, we profile the syntactic tree parsing techniques for semantic graph parsing. In particular, we implement different transition-based and graph-based models, as well as a parser ensembler, and evaluate their effectiveness for semantic dependency parsing. Evaluation gauges how successful data-driven dependency graph parsing can be by applying existing techniques.

1 Introduction

Bi-lexical dependency representation is quite powerful and popular to encode syntactic or semantic information, and parsing techniques under the dependency formalism have been well studied and advanced in the last decade. The major focus is limited to tree structures, which fortunately correspond to many computationally good properties. On the other hand, some leading linguistic theories argue that more general graphs are needed to encode a wide variety of deep syntactic and semantic phenomena, e.g. topicalization, relative clauses, etc. However, algorithms for statistical graph spanning have not been well explored before, and therefore it is not very clear how good data-driven parsing techniques developed for tree parsing can be for graph generating.

Following several well-established syntactic theories, SemEval-2014 task 8 (Oepen et al., 2014) proposes using graphs to represent semantics. Considering that semantic dependency parsing is a quite new topic and there is little previous work, we think it worth appropriately profiling successful tree parsing techniques for graph parsing. To this end, we build a hybrid system that combines several important data-driven parsing techniques and evaluate their impact with the given data. In particular, we implement different transition-based and graph-based models, as well as a parser ensembler.

Our experiments highlight the following facts:

- Graph-based models are more effective than transition-based models.
- Parser ensemble is very useful to boost the parsing accuracy.

2 Architecture

We explore two kinds of basic models: One is transition-based, and the other is tree approximation. Transition-based models are widely used for dependency tree parsing, and they can be adapted to graph parsing (Sagae and Tsujii, 2008; Titov et al., 2009). Here we implement 5 transition-based models for dependency graph parsing, each of which is based on different transition system.

The motivation of developing tree approximation models is to apply existing graph-based tree parsers to generate graphs. At the training time, we convert the dependency graphs from the training data into dependency trees, and train second-order arc-factored models[1]. At the test phase, we parse sentences using this tree parser, and convert the output trees back into semantic graphs. We think tree approximation can appropriately evaluate the possible effectiveness of graph-based models for graph spanning.

Finally, we integrate the outputs of different models with a simple voter to boost the performance. The motivation of using system combination and the choice of voting is mainly due to the experiments presented by (Surdeanu and Manning, 2010). When we obtain all the outputs of

[1]The mate parser (`code.google.com/p/mate-tools/`) is used.

Proceedings of the 8th International Workshop on Semantic Evaluation (SemEval 2014), pages 459–464, Dublin, Ireland, August 23-24, 2014.

these models, we combine them into a final result, which is better than any of them. For combination, we explore various systems for this task, since empirically we know that variety leads to better performance.

3 Transition-Based Models

Transition-based models are usually used for dependency tree parsing. For this task, we exploit it for dependency graph parsing.

A transition system S contains a set $\mathcal{C}$ of configurations and a set $\mathcal{T}$ of transitions. A configuration $c \in \mathcal{C}$ generally contains a stack σ of nodes, a buffer β of nodes, and a set A of arcs. The elements in A is in the form (x, l, y), which denotes a arc from x to y labeled l. A transition $t \in \mathcal{T}$ can be applied to a configuration and turn it into a new one by adding new arcs or manipulating elements of the stack or the buffer. A statistical transition-based parser leverages a classifier to approximate an oracle that is able to generate target graphs by transforming the initial configuration $c_s(x)$ into a terminal configuration $c_t \in \mathcal{C}_t$.

An oracle of a given graph on sentence x is a sequence of transitions which transform the initial configuration to the terminal configuration the arc set A_{c_t} of which is the set of the arcs of the graph.

3.1 Our Transition Systems

We implemented 5 different transition systems for graph parsing. Here we describe two of them in detail, one is the Titov system proposed in (Titov et al., 2009), and the other is our Naive system. The configurations of the two systems each contain a stack σ, a buffer β, and a set A of arcs, denoted by $\langle \sigma, \beta, A \rangle$. The initial configuration of a sentence $x = w_1 w_2 \cdots w_n$ is $c_s(x) = \langle [0], [1, 2, \cdots, n], \{\} \rangle$, and the terminal configuration set $\mathcal{C}_t$ is the set of all configurations with empty buffer. These two transition systems are shown in 1.

The transitions of the Titov system are:

- LEFT-ARC$_l$ adds an arc from the front of the buffer to the top of the stack, labeled l, into A.
- RIGHT-ARC$_l$ adds an arc from the top of the stack to the front of the buffer, labeled l, into A.
- SHIFT removes the front of the buffer and push it onto the stack;
- POP pops the top of the stack.
- SWAP swaps the top two elements of the stack.

This system uses a transition SWAP to change the node order in the stack, thus allowing some crossing arcs to be built.

The transitions of the Naive system are similar to the Titov system's, except that we can directly manipulate all the nodes in the stack instead of just the top two. In this case, the transition SWAP is not needed.

The Titov system can cover a great proportion, though not all, of graphs in this task. For more discussion, see (Titov et al., 2009). The Naive system, by comparison, covers all graphs. That is to say, with this system, we can find an oracle for any dependency graph on a sentence x. Other transition systems we build are also designed for dependency graph parsing, and they can cover dependency graphs without self loop as well.

3.2 Statistical Disambiguation

First of all, we derive oracle transition sequences for every sentence, and train *Passive-Aggressive* models (Crammer et al., 2006) to predict next transition given a configuration. When it comes to parsing, we start with the initial configuration, predicting next transition and updating the configuration with the transition iteratively. And finally we will get a terminal configuration, we then stop and output the arcs of the graph contained in the final configuration.

We extracted rich feature for we utilize a set of rich features for disambiguation, referencing to Zhang and Nivre (2011). We examine the several tops of the stack and the one or more fronts of the buffer, and combine the lemmas and POS tags of them in many ways as the features. Additionally, we also derive features from partial parses such as heads and dependents of these nodes.

3.3 Sentence Reversal

Reversing the order the words of a given sentence is a simple way to yield heterogeneous parsing models, thus improving parsing accuracy of the model ensemble (Sagae, 2007). In our experiments, one transition system produces two models, one trained on the normal corpus, and the other on the corpus of reversed sentences. Therefore we can get 10 parse of a sentence based on 5 transition systems.

LEFT-ARC$_l$	$(\sigma\|i, j\|\beta, A) \Rightarrow (\sigma\|i, j\|\beta, A \cup \{(j, l, i)\})$
RIGHT-ARC$_l$	$(\sigma\|i, j\|\beta, A) \Rightarrow (\sigma\|i, j\|\beta, A \cup \{(i, l, j)\})$
SHIFT	$(\sigma, j\|\beta, A) \Rightarrow (\sigma\|j, \beta, A)$
POP	$(\sigma\|i, \beta, A) \Rightarrow (\sigma, \beta, A)$
SWAP	$(\sigma\|i\|j, \beta, A) \Rightarrow (\sigma\|j\|i, \beta, A)$

Titov System

LEFT-ARC$_l^k$	$(\sigma\|i_k\|\ldots\|i_2\|i_1, j\|\beta, A) \Rightarrow (\sigma\|i_k\|\ldots\|i_2\|i_1, j\|\beta, A \cup \{(j, l, i_k)\})$
RIGHT-ARC$_l^k$	$(\sigma\|i_k\|\ldots\|i_2\|i_1, j\|\beta, A) \Rightarrow (\sigma\|i_k\|\ldots\|i_2\|i_1, j\|\beta, A \cup \{(i_k, l, j)\})$
SHIFT	$(\sigma, j\|\beta, A) \Rightarrow (\sigma\|j, \beta, A)$
POP^k	$(\sigma\|i_k\|i_{k-1}\|\ldots\|i_2\|i_1, \beta, A) \Rightarrow (\sigma\|i_{k-1}\|\ldots\|i_2\|i_1, \beta, A)$

Naive System

Figure 1: Two of our transition systems.

4 Tree Approximation Models

Parsing based on graph spanning is quite challenging since computational properties of the semantic graphs given by the shared task are less explored and thus still unknown. On the other hand, finding the best higher-order spanning for general graph is NP complete, and therefore it is not easy, if not impossible, to implement arc-factored models with exact inference. In our work, we use a practical idea to indirectly profile the graph-based parsing techniques for dependency graph parsing. Inspired by the PCFG approximation idea (Fowler and Penn, 2010; Zhang and Krieger, 2011) for deep parsing, we study tree approximation approaches for graph spanning.

This tree approximation technique can be applied to both transition-based and graph-based parsers. However, since transition systems that can directly handle build graphs have been developed, we only use this technique to evaluate the possible effectiveness of graph-based models for semantic parsing.

4.1 Graph-to-Tree Transformation

In particular, we develop different methods to convert a semantic graph into a tree, and use edge labels to encode dependency relations as well as structural information which helps to transform a converted tree back to its original graph. By the graph-to-tree transformation, we can train a tree parser with a graph-annotated corpus, and utilize the corresponding tree-to-graph transformation to generate target graphs from the outputs of the tree parser. Given that the tree-to-graph transformation is quite trivial, we only describe the graph-to-tree transformation approach.

We use graph traversal algorithms to convert a directed graph to a directed tree. The transformation implies that we may lose, add or modify some dependency relations in order to make the graph a tree.

4.2 Auxiliary Labels

In the transformed trees, we use auxiliary labels to carry out information of the original graphs. To encode multiple edges to one, we keep the original label on the directed edge but may add other edges' information. On the other hand, throughout most transformations, some edges must be reversed to make a tree, so we need a symbol to indicate a edge on the tree is reversed during transformation. The auxiliary labels are listed below:

- Label with following ~R: The symbol ~R means this directed edge is reversed from the original directed graph.
- Separator: Semicolon separates two encoded original edges.
- $[N]$ followed by label: The symbol $[N]$ (N is an integer) represents the head of the edge. The dependent is the current one, but the head is the dependent's N-th ancestor where 1st ancestor is its father and 2nd ancestor is its father's father.

See Figure 2 for example.

4.3 Traversal Strategies

Given directed graph (V, E), the task is to traverse all edges on the graph and decide how to change the labels or not contain the edge on the output. We use 3 strategies for traversal. Here we use $x \rightarrow_g y$ to denote the edge on graph, and $x \rightarrow_t y$ the edge on tree.

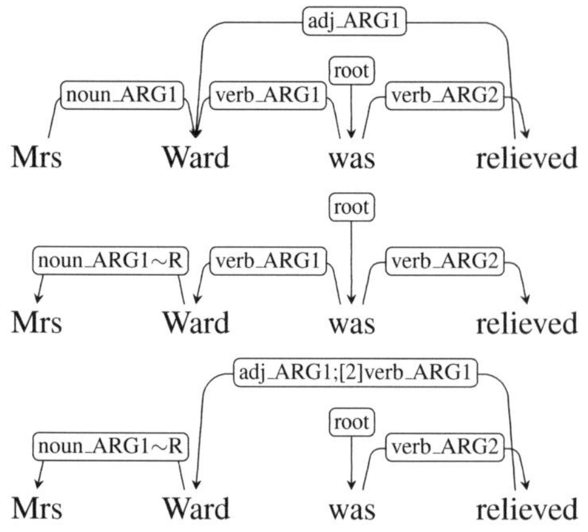

Figure 2: One dependency graph and two possible dependency trees after converting.

Depth-first-search We try graph traversal by depth-first-search starting from the root on the directed graph ignoring the direction of edges. During the traversal, we add edges to the directed tree with (perhaps new) labels. We traverse the graph recursively. Suppose the depth-first-search is running at the node x and the nodes set A which have been searched. And suppose we find node y is linked to x on the graph ($x \rightarrow_g y$ or $y \rightarrow_g x$). If $y \notin A$, we add the directed edge $x \rightarrow_t y$ to the tree immediately. In the case of $y \rightarrow_g x$, we add ~R to the edge label. If $y \in A$, then y must be one of the ancestors of x. In this case, we add this information to the label of the existing edge $z \rightarrow_t x$. Since the distance between two nodes x and y is sufficient to indicate the node y, we use the distance to represent the head or dependent of this directed edge and add the label and the distance to the label of $z \rightarrow_t x$. It is clear that the auxiliary label $[N]$ can be used for multiple edge encoding. Under this strategy, all edges can be encoded on the tree.

Breadth-first-search An alternative traversal strategy is based on breadth-first-search starting from the root. This search ignores the direction of edge too. We regard the search tree as the dependency tree. During the breadth-first-search, if (x, l, y) exists but node y has been searched, we just ignore the edge. Under this strategy, we may lose some edges.

Iterative expanding This strategy is based on depth-first-search but slightly different. The strategy only searches through the forward edges on the directed graph at first. When there is no forward edge to expend, a traversed node linked to some nodes that are not traversed must be the dependent of them. Then we choose an edge and add it (reversed) to the tree and continue to expand the tree. Also, we ignore the edges that does not satisfy the tree constraint. We call this strategy iterative expanding. When we need to expand output tree, we need to design a strategy to decide which edge to be add. The measure to decide which node should be expanded first is its possible location on the tree and the number of nodes it can search during depth-first-search. Intuitively, we want the reversed edges to be as few as possible. For this purpose, this strategy is practical but not necessarily the best. Like the Breadth-first-search strategy, this strategy may also cause edge loss.

4.4 Forest-to-Tree

After a primary searching process, if there is still edge $x \rightarrow_g y$ that has not been searched yet, we start a new search procedure from x or y. Eventually, we obtain a forest rather than a tree. To combine disconnected trees in this forest to the final dependency tree, we use edges with label *None* to link them. Let the node set W be the set of roots of the trees in the forest, which are not connected to original graph root. The mission is to assign a node $v \notin W$ for each $w \in W$. If we assign v_i for w_i, we add the edge $v_i \rightarrow w_i$ labeled by *None* to the final dependency tree. We try 3 strategies in this step:

- For each $w \in W$ we look for the first node $v \notin W$ on the left of w.
- For each $w \in W$ we look for the first node $v \notin W$ on the right of w.
- By defining the distance between two nodes as how many words are there between the two words, we can select the *nearest* node. If the distances of more than one node are equal, we choose v randomly.

We also tried to link all of the nodes in W directly to the root, but it does not work well.

5 Model Ensemble

We have 19 heterogeneous basic models (10 transition-based models, 9 tree approximation models), and use a simple voter to combine their outputs.

Algorithm	DM	PAS	PCEDT
DFS	0	0	0
BFS	0.0117	0.0320	0.0328
FEF	0.0127	0.0380	0.0328

Table 1: Edge loss of transformation algorithms.

For each pair of words of a sentence, we count the number of the models that give positive predictions. If the number is greater than a threshold, we put this arc to the final graph, and label the arc with the most common label of what the models give.

Furthermore, we find that the performance of the tree approximation models is better than the transition based models, and therefore we take weights of individual models too. Instead of just counting, we sum the weights of the models that give positive predictions. The tree approximation models are assigned higher weights.

6 Experiments

There are 3 subtasks in the task, namely DM, PAS, and PCEDT. For subtask DM, we finally obtained 19 models, just as stated in previous sections. For subtask PAS and PCEDT, only 17 models are trained due to the tight schedule.

The tree approximation algorithms may cause some edge loss, and the statistics are shown in Table 1. We can see that DFS does not cause edge loss, but edge losses of other two algorithm are not negligible. This may result in a lower recall and higher precision, but we can tune the final results during model ensemble. Edge loss in subtask DM is less than those in subtask PAS and PCEDT.

We present the performance of several representative models in Table 2. We can see that the tree approximation models performs better than the transition-based models, which highlights the effective of arc-factored models for semantic dependency parsing. For model ensemble, besides the accuracy of each single model, it is also important that the models to be ensembled are very different. As shown in Table 2, the evaluation between some of our models indicates that our models do vary a lot.

Following the suggestion of the task organizers, we use section 20 of the train data as the development set. With the help of development set, we tune the parameters of the models and ensembling. We set the weight of each transition-based model 1, and tree approximation model 2 in run 1, 3 in run 2. The threshold is set to a half of the total weight. The final results given by the organizers are shown in Table 3. Compared to Table 2 demonstrates the effectiveness of parser ensemble.

Models	DM	PAS	PCEDT
Titov	0.8468	0.8754	0.6978
Titov_r	0.8535	0.8928	0.7063
Naive	0.8481	-	-
DFS_n	0.8692	0.9034	0.7370
DFS_l	0.8692	0.9015	0.7246
BFS_n	0.8686	0.8818	0.7247
Titov vs. Titov_r	0.8607	0.8831	0.7613
Titov vs. Naive	0.9245	-	-
Titov vs. DFS_n	0.8590	0.8865	0.7650
DFS_n vs. DFS_l	0.9273	0.9579	0.8688
DFS_n vs. BFS_n	0.9226	0.9169	0.8367

Table 2: Evaluation between some of our models. Labeled f-score on test set is shown. Titov_r stands for reversed Titov, DFS_n for DFS+nearest, DFS_l for DFS+left, and BFS_n for BFS+nearest. The upper part gives the performance, and the lower part gives the agreement between systems.

Format	LP	LR	LF	LM
DM	0.9027	0.8854	0.8940	0.2982
PAS	0.9344	0.9069	0.9204	0.3872
PCEDT	0.7875	0.7396	0.7628	0.1120

Table 3: Final results of the ensembled model.

7 Conclusion

Data-driven dependency parsing techniques have been greatly advanced during the parst decade. Two dominant approaches, i.e. transition-based and graph-based methods, have been well studied. In addition, parser ensemble has been shown very effective to take advantages to combine the strengthes of heterogeneous base parsers. In this work, we propose different models to profile the three techniques for semantic dependency parsing. The experimental results suggest several directions for future study.

Acknowledgement

The work was supported by NSFC (61300064, 61170166 and 61331011) and National High-Tech R&D Program (2012AA011101).

References

Koby Crammer, Ofer Dekel, Joseph Keshet, Shai Shalev-Shwartz, and Yoram Singer. 2006. Online passive-aggressive algorithms. *JOURNAL OF MACHINE LEARNING RESEARCH*, 7:551–585.

Timothy A. D. Fowler and Gerald Penn. 2010. Accurate context-free parsing with combinatory categorial grammar. In *Proceedings of the 48th Annual Meeting of the Association for Computational Linguistics*, Uppsala, Sweden, July.

Stephan Oepen, Marco Kuhlmann, Yusuke Miyao, Daniel Zeman, Dan Flickinger, Jan Hajič, Angelina Ivanova, and Yi Zhang. 2014. SemEval 2014 Task 8: Broad-coverage semantic dependency parsing. In *Proceedings of the 8th International Workshop on Semantic Evaluation*, Dublin, Ireland.

Kenji Sagae and Jun'ichi Tsujii. 2008. Shift-reduce dependency DAG parsing. In *Proceedings of the 22nd International Conference on Computational Linguistics (Coling 2008)*, pages 753–760, Manchester, UK, August. Coling 2008 Organizing Committee.

Kenji Sagae. 2007. Dependency parsing and domain adaptation with lr models and parser ensembles. In *In Proceedings of the Eleventh Conference on Computational Natural Language Learning*.

Mihai Surdeanu and Christopher D. Manning. 2010. Ensemble models for dependency parsing: Cheap and good? In *Human Language Technologies: The 2010 Annual Conference of the North American Chapter of the Association for Computational Linguistics*, Los Angeles, California, June.

Ivan Titov, James Henderson, Paola Merlo, and Gabriele Musillo. 2009. Online graph planarisation for synchronous parsing of semantic and syntactic dependencies. In *Proceedings of the 21st international jont conference on Artifical intelligence*, IJCAI'09, pages 1562–1567, San Francisco, CA, USA. Morgan Kaufmann Publishers Inc.

Yi Zhang and Hans-Ulrich Krieger. 2011. Large-scale corpus-driven PCFG approximation of an hpsg. In *Proceedings of the 12th International Conference on Parsing Technologies*, Dublin, Ireland, October.

Yue Zhang and Joakim Nivre. 2011. Transition-based dependency parsing with rich non-local features. In *Proceedings of the 49th Annual Meeting of the Association for Computational Linguistics: Human Language Technologies*, Portland, Oregon, USA, June.

Potsdam: Semantic Dependency Parsing by Bidirectional Graph-Tree Transformations and Syntactic Parsing

Željko Agić
University of Potsdam
zagic@uni-potsdam.de

Alexander Koller
University of Potsdam
koller@ling.uni-potsdam.de

Abstract

We present the Potsdam systems that participated in the semantic dependency parsing shared task of SemEval 2014. They are based on linguistically motivated bidirectional transformations between graphs and trees and on utilization of syntactic dependency parsing. They were entered in both the closed track and the open track of the challenge, recording a peak average labeled F_1 score of 78.60.

1 Introduction

In the semantic dependency parsing (SDP) task of SemEval 2014, the meaning of a sentence is represented in terms of binary head-argument relations between the lexical units – bi-lexical dependencies (Oepen et al., 2014). Since words can be semantic dependents of multiple other words, this framework results in graph representations of sentence meaning. For the SDP task, three such annotation layers are provided on top of the WSJ text of the Penn Treebank (PTB) (Marcus et al., 1993):

- DM: the reduction of DeepBank HPSG annotation (Flickinger et al., 2012) into bi-lexical dependencies following (Oepen and Lønning, 2006; Ivanova et al., 2012),
- PAS: the predicate-argument structures derived from the training set of the Enju HPSG parser (Miyao et al., 2004) and
- PCEDT: a subset of the tectogrammatical annotation layer from the English side of the Prague Czech-English Dependency Treebank (Cinková et al., 2009).

The three annotation schemes provide three directed graph representations for each PTB sentence, with word forms as nodes and labeled dependency relations as edges pointing from functors to arguments. The SDP-annotated PTB text is split into training (sections 00–19), development (sec. 20) and testing sets (sec. 21). This in turn makes the SDP parsing task a problem of data-driven graph parsing, in which systems are to be trained for producing dependency graph representations of sentences respecting the three underlying schemes.

While a number of theoretical and preliminary contributions to data-driven graph parsing exist (Sagae and Tsujii, 2008; Das et al., 2010; Jones et al., 2013; Chiang et al., 2013; Henderson et al., 2013), our goal here is to investigate the simplest approach that can achieve competitive performance. Our starting point is the observation that the SDP graphs are relatively tree-like. On it, we build a system for data-driven graph parsing by (1) transforming dependency graphs into dependency trees in preprocessing, (2) training and using syntactic dependency parsers over these trees and (3) transforming their output back into graphs in postprocessing. This way, we inherit the accuracy and speed of syntactic dependency parsers. The secondary benefit is insight into the structure of the semantic representations, as graph-tree transformations can make the phenomena that require non-tree-like structures more explicit.

2 Data and Systems

We present the basic statistics for the SDP training sets in Table 1. The graphs contain no cycles, i.e., all SDP meaning representations are directed acyclic graphs (DAGs). DM and PAS are automatically derived from HPSG annotations, while PCEDT is based on manual tectogrammatical annotation. This is reflected in more than half of the PCEDT graphs being disjoint sets of dependency trees, i.e., forests. The number of forests in DM and PAS is negligible, on the other hand. The edge

Proceedings of the 8th International Workshop on Semantic Evaluation (SemEval 2014), pages 465–470,
Dublin, Ireland, August 23-24, 2014.

Feature	DM	PAS	PCEDT
Sentences	32,389	32,389	32,389
Tokens	742,736	742,736	742,736
Edge labels	52	43	71
Cyclic graphs	0	0	0
Forests	810	418	18,527
Treewidth (undirected)	1.30	1.71	1.45
Tree labels			
LOCAL	79	77	124
DFS	79	81	133

Table 1: Basic statistics for the training sets.

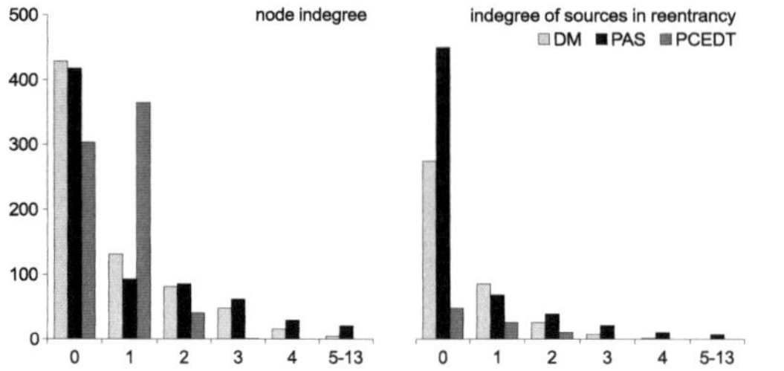

Figure 1: Distributions of node indegrees for (a) all nodes and (b) source nodes of edges participating in reentrancies.

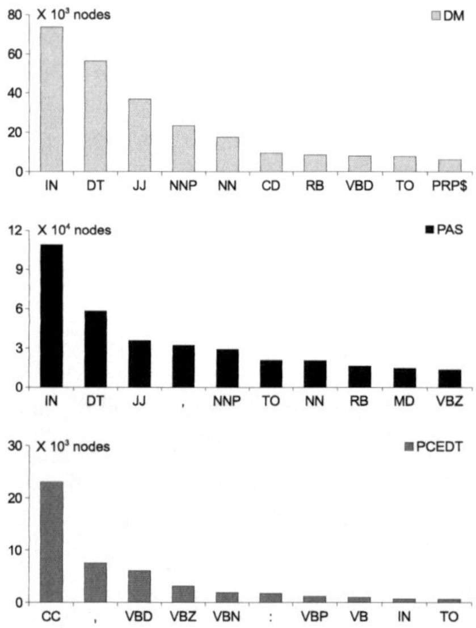

Figure 2: Distributions of parts of speech for reentrancy source nodes with zero indegree. Ten most frequent parts of speech are displayed.

label set of PCEDT is also substantially larger than the label sets of DM and PAS.

2.1 Baseline

A directed acyclic graph is a dependency tree in the sense of (Nivre, 2006) if any two nodes are connected by exactly one simple path. In other words, a DAG is a dependency tree if there are no disconnected (singleton) nodes and if there are no node reentrancies, i.e., all nodes have an indegree of 1. We calculate the average treewidth of SDP graphs by converting them to undirected graphs and applying the algorithm of (Gogate and Dechter, 2004). As we show in Table 1, the treewidth is low for all three representations. The low treewidth indicates that, even if the SDP semantic representations are graphs and not trees, these graphs are very tree-like and, as such, easily transformed into trees as there are not many edges that would require deletion. Thus, one could perform a lossy graph-to-tree conversion by (a) detecting singleton nodes and attaching them trivially and (b) detecting reentrant nodes and deleting all but one incoming edge.

The official SDP baseline system[1] (Oepen et al., 2014) is based precisely on this principle: singletons are attached to their right neighbors, only the edges to the closest predicates are kept for reentrant nodes, with a preference for leftward predicates in ties, and all remaining nodes with an indegree of 0 are attached to the root. Two dummy labels are introduced in the process: `root` for attachments to root and `null` for the remaining new attachments. The baseline is thus limited by the lossy approach to graph-to-tree reductions and the lack of linguistic motivation for these particular reduction operations. Here, we aim at introducing less lossy and more linguistically motivated reductions.

2.2 Local Edge Flipping

Furthermore, inspecting the distribution of node indegrees in the SDP data in Figure 1, we make two important observations: (1) from its left histogram, that most of the nodes in all three annotations have an indegree of 0 or 1, and (2) from its right histogram, that most source nodes of edges causing reentrancies themselves have an indegree of 0. Figure 2 deepens this observation by providing a part-of-speech distribution of source nodes in reentrancies. It shows that the edges in DM and PAS are systematically pointed from modi-

[1] `http://alt.qcri.org/semeval2014/task8/index.php?id=evaluation`

System	DM	PAS	PCEDT
BASELINE	66.19	57.66	90.70
LOCAL	89.93	88.73	91.86
DFS	95.52	93.98	92.85

Table 2: Upper bound *LF* scores on the development set for LOCAL and DFS conversion compared to the baseline. This score indicates the quality of graph-tree transformation as no parsing is done.

Dataset	*P*	*R*	F_1
DM	73.30	62.99	67.76
PAS	76.03	72.12	74.02
PCEDT	79.40	78.52	78.96

Table 3: Top node detection accuracy with CRFs on the development set for the three annotations. Precision *(P)*, recall *(R)* and the F_1 scores relate to marking tokens with the binary top node flag.

fiers to modifiees, while coordinating conjunctions in PCEDT introduce the coordinated nodes. We conclude that edges in reentrancies, for which the source nodes have zero indegree, could be flipped by changing places of their source and target nodes and encoding the switch in the edge labels by appending the suffix `flipped` to the existing labels.

This is the basis for our first system: LOCAL. In it, we locally flip all edges in reentrancies for which the source node has zero indegree and run the BASELINE conversion on the resulting graphs. We apply this conversion on the training data, use the converted training sets to train syntactic dependency parsers (Bohnet, 2010) and utilize the parsing models on the development and test data. The parsing outputs are converted back to graphs by simply re-flipping all the edges denoted as `flipped`.

2.3 Depth-first Edge Flipping

Our second system, DFS, is based on depth-first search graph traversal and edge flipping. In it, we create a undirected copy of the input graph and connect all nodes with zero indegree to the root using dummy edges. We do a depth-first traversal of this graph, starting from the root, while performing edge lookup in the original DAG. For each DFS edge traversal in the undirected copy, we check if the direction of this edge in the original DAG is identical or reversed to the traversal direction. If it is identical, we keep the existing edge. If we traverse the edge against its original direction, we

	DM		PAS		PCEDT	
closed	*LAS*	*UAS*	*LAS*	*UAS*	*LAS*	*UAS*
LOCAL	79.09	81.35	81.93	83.79	81.16	89.60
DFS	82.02	83.74	87.06	87.93	79.94	88.04
open						
LOCAL	80.86	82.73	85.16	86.18	82.04	90.79
DFS	84.23	85.77	88.42	89.26	80.82	89.02

Table 4: Syntactic dependency parsing accuracy of our systems before the tree-to-graph transformations, given as a set of labeled *(LAS)* and unlabeled *(UAS)* attachment scores. The scores are given for the development set.

reverse it. Finally, we delete the dummy edges and convert the resulting graph to a dependency tree by running the baseline, to connect the singletons to their neighbors, and to attach predicates with zero indegree and sentence-final nodes to the root.

We illustrate our graph-to-tree transformations LOCAL and DFS on a gold standard graph from the training data in Figure 3. It shows how DFS manages to preserve more edges than LOCAL by performing traversal flipping, while LOCAL flips only the edges that have source nodes with zero indegree. On the other hand, DFS performs more flipping operations than LOCAL, but as Table 1 shows, this does not result in substantial increase of the label sets.

2.4 Parsing and Top Node Detection

The same syntactic parser and top node detector are used in both LOCAL and DFS. Both systems ran in the closed SDP track, with no additional features for learning, and in the open track, where they used the SDP companion data, i.e., the outputs of a syntactic dependency parser (Bohnet and Nivre, 2012) and phrase-based parser (Petrov et al., 2006) as additional features. Our choice of parser was based on the high non-projectivity of the resulting trees, while parsers of (Bohnet and Nivre, 2012; Bohnet et al., 2013) could also be used, among others. We use the parser out of the box, i.e., without any parameter tuning or additional features other than what was previously listed for the open track.

Top node detection is implemented separately, by training a sequence labeling model (Lafferty et al., 2001; Kudo, 2005) on tokens and part-of-speech tags from the training sets. Its accuracy is given in Table 3. We use only the tokens and parts of speech as features for these models, and

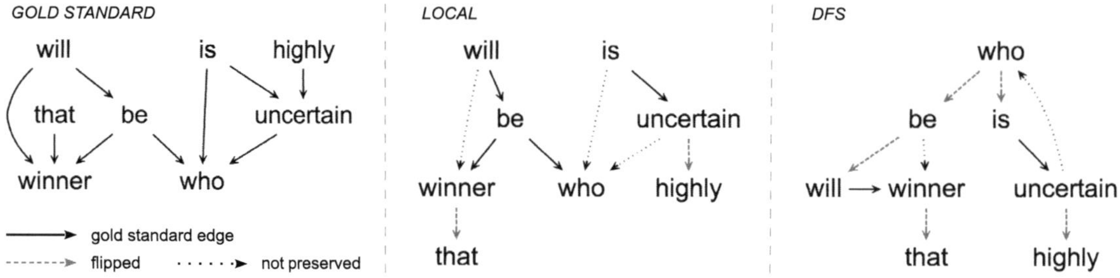

Figure 3: Illustration of graph-to-tree transformations of a gold standard graph for LOCAL and DFS. Edge labels are omitted. The sentence (PAS, #20415005): *Who that winner will be is highly uncertain.*

we design our feature set by adapting the chunking template from the CRF++ toolkit documentation.[2] We note that this model can be improved by, e.g., adding the open track companion features to the feature set, but they were not used in the experiments we present here.[3]

Our graph-to-tree conversions expand the label sets by appending the edge flip flag. The sizes of the new label sets are given in Table 1 in comparison to the original ones. The increase in size is expected to affect the parsing accuracy. The parsing accuracies on the development sets are given in Table 4. The scores correlate with the label set sizes, with a notable difference between the labeled *(LAS)* and unlabeled *(UAS)* attachment score for PCEDT. The LOCAL approach tends to outperform DFS for PCEDT, while DFS parsers also significantly outperform LOCAL for DM and PAS. The open track parsers tend to perform a little better as they make use of the additional features.

In Table 2, we measure the theoretical maximum accuracy for parsers based on our two conversions in comparison with the baseline. There, we run BASELINE, LOCAL and DFS on the development set and convert the trees back to graphs right away, i.e., without the parsing step, so as to observe the dissipation of the conversion. The scores show that LOCAL and DFS outperform BASELINE by a large margin, while the maximum accuracy for DFS is larger than the one for LOCAL, 1 point for PCEDT and around 5 points for DM and PAS. This is due to DFS performing non-local edge flipping, thus preserving more edges. The parsing scores from Table 4 and the maximum accuracy from Table 2 show that our systems are not as lossy in graph-tree conversions as the baseline, while they pay the price in the number of new labels in actual parsing and, subsequently, in the accuracy of the dependency parsers. Thus, *LAS* and *UAS* for the baseline are 1-2 points higher than the scores in Table 4 for DM and PCEDT, while our scores are 3-4 points higher for PAS.

[2] `http://crfpp.googlecode.com/svn/trunk/doc/index.html`

[3] The recall would increase by 15 points, amounting to a 10 point increase in F_1 for top node detection in DM.

	closed		*open*	
dev	*LF*	*UF*	*LF*	*UF*
LOCAL	76.70	82.01	77.87	83.19
DFS	78.49	83.78	80.03	85.31
test				
LOCAL	75.94	81.58	76.79	82.52
DFS	77.34	82.99	78.60	84.32

Table 5: Overall accuracy for our LOCAL and DFS systems, i.e., averaged labeled and unlabeled F_1 scores over the three annotations.

3 Results and Discussion

As in the official SDP scoring, we express the results in terms of labeled and unlabeled precision *(LP, UP)* and recall *(LR, UR)*, their harmonic means, the F_1 scores *(LF, UF)*, and sentence-level exact matches *(LM, UM)*. The official SDP scorer reports on two variants of these scores: the one taking into account the virtual edges to top nodes and the one excluding those edges. The former is less relaxed as it requires the top nodes to be predicted, and this is the only one we use in this report. We note that for our systems, the scores without the virtual edges are approximately 2 points higher for all the metrics.

The overall scores are given in Table 5. There, we provide the labeled and unlabeled F_1 scores on the development and test data in the closed and open track, averaged for all three annotations. The open track systems consistently score approxi-

closed track	DM				PAS				PCEDT			
	LP	*LR*	*LF*	*LM*	*LP*	*LR*	*LF*	*LM*	*LP*	*LR*	*LF*	*LM*
LOCAL	83.39	72.88	77.78	4.53	88.18	74.00	80.47	2.00	72.25	67.10	69.58	6.38
DFS	79.36	79.34	79.35	9.05	88.15	81.60	84.75	7.72	69.68	66.25	67.92	5.86
	–4.03	+6.46	+1.57	+4.52	–0.03	+7.60	+4.28	+5.72	–2.57	–0.85	–1.66	–0.52
	UP	*UR*	*UF*	*UM*	*UP*	*UR*	*UF*	*UM*	*UP*	*UR*	*UF*	*UM*
LOCAL	85.47	74.70	79.72	5.04	89.70	75.28	81.86	2.23	86.36	80.21	83.17	19.44
DFS	81.56	81.54	81.55	10.31	89.62	82.96	86.16	7.86	83.37	79.27	81.27	17.51
	–3.91	+6.84	+1.83	+5.27	–0.08	+7.69	+4.30	+5.63	–3.00	–0.94	–1.91	–1.93
open track	DM				PAS				PCEDT			
	LP	*LR*	*LF*	*LM*	*LP*	*LR*	*LF*	*LM*	*LP*	*LR*	*LF*	*LM*
LOCAL	84.54	73.80	78.80	4.53	89.72	75.08	81.75	2.00	72.52	67.33	69.83	6.08
DFS	81.32	80.91	81.11	10.46	89.41	82.61	85.88	8.46	70.35	67.33	68.80	5.79
	–3.22	+7.11	+2.31	+5.93	–0.31	+7.53	+4.13	+6.46	–2.17	+0.00	–1.03	–0.29
	UP	*UR*	*UF*	*UM*	*UP*	*UR*	*UF*	*UM*	*UP*	*UR*	*UF*	*UM*
LOCAL	86.43	75.45	80.57	5.49	90.99	76.14	82.91	2.30	87.32	81.07	84.08	19.73
DFS	83.37	82.95	83.16	11.94	90.78	83.87	87.19	8.75	84.46	80.83	82.60	18.47
	–3.06	+7.50	+2.59	+6.45	–0.22	+7.73	+4.28	+6.45	–2.86	–0.24	–1.48	–1.26

Table 6: Breakdown of the scores for our LOCAL and DFS systems on the test sets. We provide labeled and unlabeled precision *(LP, UP)*, recall *(LR, UR)*, F_1 scores *(LF, UF)* and exact matches *(LM, UM)* for all three annotations in both the closed and the open evaluation track.

mately 1 point higher than their closed track counterparts, apparently taking advantage of the additional features available in training and testing. The DFS system is 2 points better than LOCAL in all scenarios, owing to the higher maximum coverage of the original graphs in the conversions. The large label sets amount to a difference of approximately 6 points between the labeled and unlabeled accuracies in favor of the latter attachment.

Table 6 is a breakdown of the scores in Table 5 across the three annotations and the two tracks. Here, we pair the F_1 scores with the corresponding precision and recall scores. We also explicitly denote the differences in scores between LOCAL and DFS. For DM and PAS, the score patterns are very similar: due to the larger label set and less regular edge flipping, DFS has a 3-4 points lower precision than LOCAL, while its recall is 6-8 points higher, amounting to the overall improvement of approximately 4 points F_1. In contrast, on the PCEDT data, LOCAL outperforms DFS by approximately 1.5 points. We note that the label sets for PCEDT are much larger than for DM and PAS and that the favorable reentrancies in PCEDT are much less frequent to begin with (see Table 1, Table 2 and Figure 2). At 14 points F_1, the discrepancy between the labeled and unlabeled scores is much higher for PCEDT than for DM and PAS, for which we observe a 1-2 point difference.

The exact match scores *(LM, UM)* favor DFS over LOCAL by approximately 5 points for DM and PAS, while LOCAL is better than DFS for PCEDT by 1-2 points. In absolute terms, the PAS scores are higher than those for DM and PAS in both our systems. This difference between the token-level and the sentence-level scores stems from the properties of our graph-tree transformations as, e.g., certain edges in undirected cycles could not be addressed by our edge inversions.

At approximately 81, 86 and 70 points F_1 for DM, PAS and PCEDT, in this contribution we have shown that focusing on graph-tree transformations for the utilization of a syntactic dependency parser lets us achieve good overall performance in the semantic dependency parsing task. In the future, we will further investigate what transformations are appropriate for different styles of graph-based semantic representations, and what we can learn from this both for improving SDP parser accuracy and for making linguistically motivated design choices for graph-based semantic representations. Furthermore, we will extend our system to cover inherently non-tree-like structures, such as those induced by control verbs.

Acknowledgements We are grateful to Stephan Oepen for all the discussions on the properties of the SDP datasets, and for providing the infrastructure for running the systems. We also thank the anonymous reviewers for their valuable insight.

References

Bernd Bohnet and Joakim Nivre. 2012. A Transition-Based System for Joint Part-of-Speech Tagging and Labeled Non-Projective Dependency Parsing. In *Proc. EMNLP-CoNLL*, pages 1455–1465.

Bernd Bohnet, Joakim Nivre, Igor Boguslavsky, Richárd Farkas, Filip Ginter, and Jan Hajič. 2013. Joint Morphological and Syntactic Analysis for Richly Inflected Languages. *TACL*, 1:415–428.

Bernd Bohnet. 2010. Top Accuracy and Fast Dependency Parsing is not a Contradiction. In *Proc. COLING*, pages 89–97.

David Chiang, Jacob Andreas, Daniel Bauer, Karl Moritz Hermann, Bevan Jones, and Kevin Knight. 2013. Parsing Graphs with Hyperedge Replacement Grammars. In *Proc. ACL*, pages 924–932.

Silvie Cinková, Josef Toman, Jan Hajič, Kristýna Čermáková, Václav Klimeš, Lucie Mladová, Jana Šindlerová, Kristýna Tomšů, and Zdeněk Žabokrtský. 2009. Tectogrammatical Annotation of the Wall Street Journal. *The Prague Bulletin of Mathematical Linguistics*, 92:85–104.

Dipanjan Das, Nathan Schneider, Desai Chen, and Noah A. Smith. 2010. Probabilistic Frame-Semantic Parsing. In *Proc. NAACL*, pages 948–956.

Dan Flickinger, Yi Zhang, and Valia Kordoni. 2012. DeepBank: A Dynamically Annotated Treebank of the Wall Street Journal. In *Proc. TLT*, pages 85–96.

Vibhav Gogate and Rina Dechter. 2004. A Complete Anytime Algorithm for Treewidth. In *Proc. UAI*, pages 201–208.

James Henderson, Paola Merlo, Ivan Titov, and Gabriele Musillo. 2013. Multilingual Joint Parsing of Syntactic and Semantic Dependencies with a Latent Variable Model. *Computational Linguistics*, 39(4):949–998.

Angelina Ivanova, Stephan Oepen, Lilja Øvrelid, and Dan Flickinger. 2012. Who Did What to Whom? A Contrastive Study of Syntacto-Semantic Dependencies. In *Proc. Linguistic Annotation Workshop*, pages 2–11.

Bevan Keeley Jones, Sharon Goldwater, and Mark Johnson. 2013. Modeling Graph Languages with Grammars Extracted via Tree Decompositions. In *Proc. FSMNLP*, pages 54–62.

Taku Kudo. 2005. CRF++: Yet another CRF toolkit. *Software available at* `http://crfpp.sourceforge.net/`.

John Lafferty, Andrew McCallum, and Fernando Pereira. 2001. Conditional Random Fields: Probabilistic Models for Segmenting and Labeling Sequence Data. In *Proc. ICML*, pages 282–289.

Mitchell Marcus, Mary Ann Marcinkiewicz, and Beatrice Santorini. 1993. Building a Large Annotated Corpus of English: The Penn Treebank. *Computational Linguistics*, 19(2):313–330.

Yusuke Miyao, Takashi Ninomiya, and Jun'ichi Tsujii. 2004. Corpus-oriented Grammar Development for Acquiring a Head-Driven Phrase Structure Grammar from the Penn Treebank. In *Proc. IJCNLP*, pages 684–693.

Joakim Nivre. 2006. *Inductive Dependency Parsing*. Springer.

Stephan Oepen and Jan Tore Lønning. 2006. Discriminant-Based MRS Banking. In *Proc. LREC*, pages 1250–1255.

Stephan Oepen, Marco Kuhlmann, Yusuke Miyao, Daniel Zeman, Dan Flickinger, Jan Hajič, Angelina Ivanova, and Yi Zhang. 2014. SemEval 2014 Task 8: Broad-Coverage Semantic Dependency Parsing. In *Proceedings of the 8th International Workshop on Semantic Evaluation*.

Slav Petrov, Leon Barrett, Romain Thibaux, and Dan Klein. 2006. Learning Accurate, Compact, and Interpretable Tree Annotation. In *Proc. COLING-ACL*, pages 433–440.

Kenji Sagae and Jun'ichi Tsujii. 2008. Shift-Reduce Dependency DAG Parsing. In *Proc. COLING*, pages 753–760.

Priberam: A Turbo Semantic Parser with Second Order Features

André F. T. Martins[*†] **Mariana S. C. Almeida**[*†]
[*]Priberam Labs, Alameda D. Afonso Henriques, 41, 2°, 1000-123 Lisboa, Portugal
[†]Instituto de Telecomunicações, Instituto Superior Técnico, 1049-001 Lisboa, Portugal
{atm,mla}@priberam.pt

Abstract

This paper presents our contribution to the SemEval-2014 shared task on Broad-Coverage Semantic Dependency Parsing. We employ a feature-rich linear model, including scores for first and second-order dependencies (arcs, siblings, grandparents and co-parents). Decoding is performed in a global manner by solving a linear relaxation with alternating directions dual decomposition (AD^3). Our system achieved the top score in the open challenge, and the second highest score in the closed track.

1 Introduction

The last decade saw a considerable progress in statistical modeling for dependency syntactic parsing (Kübler et al., 2009). Models that incorporate rich global features are typically more accurate, even if pruning is necessary or decoding needs to be approximate (McDonald et al., 2006; Koo and Collins, 2010; Bohnet and Nivre, 2012; Martins et al., 2009, 2013). This paper applies the same rationale to **semantic dependency parsing**, in which the output variable is a **semantic graph**, rather than a syntactic tree. We extend a recently proposed dependency parser, *TurboParser* (Martins et al., 2010, 2013), to be able to perform semantic parsing using any of the three formalisms considered in this shared task (DM, PAS, and PCEDT). The result is *TurboSemanticParser*, which we release as open-source software.[1]

We describe here a **second order model** for semantic parsing (§2). We follow prior work in semantic role labeling (Toutanova et al., 2005; Johansson and Nugues, 2008; Das et al., 2012; Flanigan et al., 2014), by adding constraints and modeling interactions among arguments within the same frame; however, we go beyond such sibling interactions to consider more complex grandparent and co-parent structures, effectively correlating different predicates. We formulate parsing as a global optimization problem and solve a relaxation through AD^3, a fast dual decomposition algorithm in which several simple local subproblems are solved iteratively (§3). Through a rich set of features (§4), we arrive at top accuracies at parsing speeds around 1,000 tokens per second, as described in the experimental section (§5).

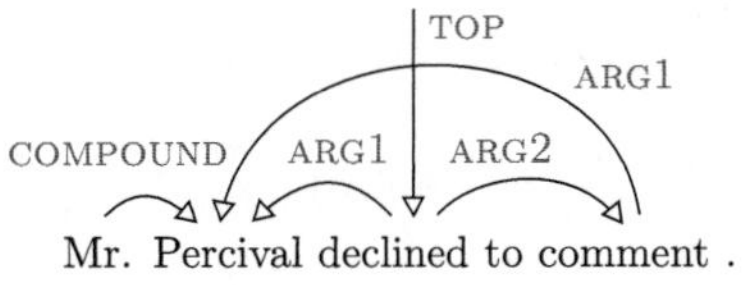

Figure 1: Example of a semantic graph in the DM formalism (sentence #22006003). We treat top nodes as a special semantic role TOP whose predicate is a dummy root symbol.

2 A Second Order Model for Parsing

Figure 1 depicts a sentence and its semantic graph. We cast semantic parsing as a structured prediction problem. Let x be a sentence and $\mathcal{Y}(x)$ the set of possible dependency graphs. We assume each candidate graph $y \in \mathcal{Y}(x)$ can be represented as a set of substructures (called **parts**) in an underlying set $\mathcal{S}$ (*e.g.*, predicates, arcs, pairs of adjacent arcs). We design a score function f which decomposes as a sum over these substructures, $f(x, y) := \sum_{s \in \mathcal{S}} f_s(x, y_s)$. We parametrize this function using a weight vector $\boldsymbol{w}$, and write each atomic function as $f_s(x, y_s) := \boldsymbol{w} \cdot \boldsymbol{\phi}_s(x, y_s)$, where $\boldsymbol{\phi}_s(x, y_s)$ is a vector of local features. The **decoding problem** consists in obtaining the best-

[1] http://labs.priberam.com/Resources/TurboSemanticParser

Proceedings of the 8th International Workshop on Semantic Evaluation (SemEval 2014), pages 471–476,
Dublin, Ireland, August 23-24, 2014.

Algorithm 1 Decoding in an Arc-Factored Model

input: Predicate scores $\sigma_P(p)$, arc scores $\sigma_A(p \rightarrow a)$, labeled arc scores $\sigma_{LA}(p \xrightarrow{r} a)$.
Initialize semantic graph $G \leftarrow \varnothing$
for $p = 0$ **to** L **do**
  Initialize $\sigma \leftarrow \sigma_P(p)$, frame $A(p) \leftarrow \varnothing$
  for $a = 1$ **to** L **do**
    Set $r' \leftarrow \arg\max_r \sigma_{LA}(p \xrightarrow{r} a)$
    if $\sigma_A(p \rightarrow a) + \sigma_{LA}(p \xrightarrow{r'} a) > 0$ **then**
      $A(p) \leftarrow A(p) \cup \{\langle p, a, r' \rangle\}$
      $\sigma \leftarrow \sigma + \sigma_A(p \rightarrow a) + \sigma_{LA}(p \xrightarrow{r'} a)$
    end if
  end for
  if $\sigma > 0$ **then** set $G \leftarrow G \cup \{\langle p, A(p) \rangle\}$
end for
output: semantic graph G.

scored semantic graph $\widehat{y}$ given a sentence x:

$$\widehat{y} = \arg \max_{y \in \mathcal{Y}(x)} f(x, y). \quad (1)$$

Our choice of parts is given in Figure 2. The second order parts are inspired by prior work in syntactic parsing, modeling interactions for pairs of (unlabeled) dependency arcs, such as **grandparents** (Carreras, 2007) and **siblings** (Smith and Eisner, 2008; Martins et al., 2009). The main novelty is *co-parent* parts, which, to the best of our knowledge, were never considered before, as they only make sense when multiple parents are allowed.

If all parts were basic, decoding could be done independently for each predicate p, as illustrated in Algorithm 1. The total runtime, for a sentence with L words, is $O(L^2|\mathcal{R}|)$, where $\mathcal{R}$ is the set of semantic roles. Adding consecutive siblings still permits independent decoding for each predicate, but dynamic programming is necessary to decode the best argument frame, increasing the runtime to $O(L^3|\mathcal{R}|)$. The addition of consecutive co-parents, grandparents, and arbitrary siblings and co-parents breaks this independency and sets a demand for approximate decoding. Even without second-order parts, the inclusion of hard constraints (such as requiring some roles to be unique, see §3) also makes the problem harder.[2]

Rather than looking for a model in which exact decoding is tractable, which could be even more stringent for parsing semantic graphs than for dependency trees, we embrace approximate decoding strategies. Namely, our approach is based on

[2]Albeit the dynamic program could still incorporate constraints for unique roles (by appending a bit-string to the state to mark semantic roles that have been filled), runtime becomes exponential in the number of unique roles, only being feasible when this number is small.

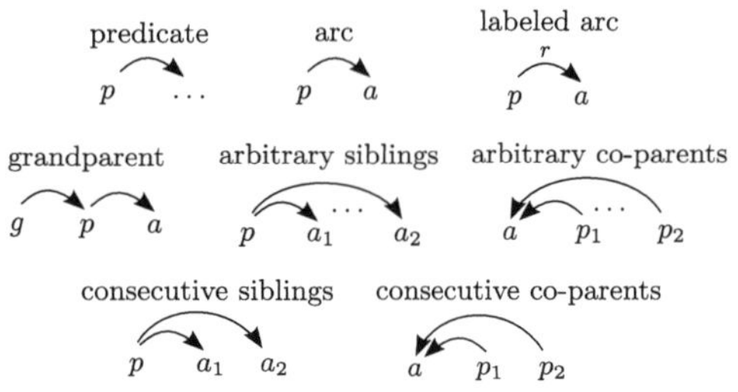

Figure 2: Parts considered in this paper. The top row illustrate the *basic parts*, representing the event that a word is a predicate, or the existence of an arc between a predicate and an argument, eventually labeled with a semantic role. Our *second-order model* looks at some pairs of arcs: arcs bearing a grandparent relationship, arguments of the same predicate, predicates sharing the same argument, and consecutive versions of these two.

dual decomposition, a class of optimization techniques that tackle the dual of combinatorial problems in a modular and extensible manner (Komodakis et al., 2007; Rush et al., 2010). We employ **alternating directions dual decomposition** (AD^3; Martins et al., 2011). Like the subgradient algorithm of Rush et al. (2010), AD^3 splits the original problem into **local subproblems**, and seeks an agreement on the overlapping variables. The difference is that the AD^3 subproblems have an additional *quadratic* term to accelerate consensus, achieving a faster convergence rate both in theory and in practice (Martins et al., 2012, 2013). For several factors (such as logic factors representing AND, OR and XOR constraints, budget constraints, and binary pairwise factors), these quadratic subproblems can be solved efficiently. For dense or structured factors, the quadratic subproblems can be solved as a sequence of local Viterbi decoding steps, via an active set method (Martins, 2014); this local decoding operation is the same that needs to be performed in the subgradient algorithm. We describe these subproblems in detail in the next section.

3 Solving the Subproblems

Predicate and Arc-Factored Parts. We capture all the basic parts with a single component. As stated in §2, local decoding in this component has a runtime of $O(L^2|\mathcal{R}|)$, by using Algorithm 1.

Unique Roles. We assume some roles are unique, *i.e.*, they can occur at most once for the same predicate.[3] To cope with unique roles, we add hard constraints of the kind

$$\sum_a \mathbb{I}(p \xrightarrow{r} a \in y) \leq 1, \; \forall p, \forall r \in \mathcal{R}_{\text{uniq}}, \quad (2)$$

where $\mathcal{R}_{\text{uniq}}$ is the set of unique roles. This set is obtained from the training data by looking at the roles that never occur multiple times in the gold argument frames.[4] The constraint above corresponds to a ATMOSTONE factor, which is built-in in AD^3 and can be decoded in linear time (rendering the runtime $O(L^2|\mathcal{R}_{\text{uniq}}|)$ when aggregating all such factors). These have also been used by Das et al. (2012) in frame-semantic parsing.

Grandparents, Arbitrary Siblings and Coparents. The second-order parts in the middle row of Figure 2 all involve the simultaneous inclusion of a pair of arcs, without further dependency on the remaining arcs. We handle each of these parts using a simple pairwise factor (called PAIR in the AD^3 toolkit). The total runtime to locally decode these factors is $O(L^3)$.

Predicate Automata. To handle consecutive siblings, we adapt the simple head automaton model (Alshawi, 1996; Smith and Eisner, 2008; Koo et al., 2010) to semantic parsing. We introduce one automaton for each predicate p and attachment direction (left or right). We describe right-side predicate automata; their left-side counterparts are analogous. Let $\langle a_0, a_1, \ldots, a_{k+1}\rangle$ be the sequence of right modifiers of p, with $a_0 =$ START and $a_{k+1} =$ END. Then, we have the following component capturing consecutive siblings:

$$f^{\text{CSIB}}_{p,\rightarrow}(p \rightarrow a_1, \ldots, p \rightarrow a_k) = \sum_{j=1}^{k+1} \sigma_{\text{CSIB}}(p, a_{j-1}, a_j). \quad (3)$$

Maximizing $f^{\text{CSIB}}_{p,\rightarrow}$ via dynamic programming has a cost of $O(L^2)$, yielding $O(L^3)$ total runtime.

Argument Automata. For consecutive coparents, we introduce another automaton which is analogous to the predicate automaton, but where arrows are reversed. Let $\langle p_0, p_1, \ldots, p_{k+1}\rangle$ be the sequence of right predicates that take a as argument (the left-side case is analagous), with $p_0 =$ START and $p_{k+1} =$ END. We define:

$$f^{\text{CCP}}_{a,\leftarrow}(a \leftarrow p_1, \ldots, a \leftarrow p_k) = \sum_{j=1}^{k+1} \sigma_{\text{CCP}}(a, p_{j-1}, p_j). \quad (4)$$

[3]Such roles have been called "deterministic" by Flanigan et al. (2014).

[4]For PAS, all 43 roles were found unique; for DM, this number is 40 out of 52, and for PCEDT only 3 out of 69.

The total runtime is also $O(L^3)$.

4 Features

We define binary features for each part represented in Figure 2. Most of the features are taken from *TurboParser* (Martins et al., 2013), while others are inspired by the semantic parser of Johansson and Nugues (2008). Those features marked with † require information from the dependency syntactic parser, and are only used in the open track.[5]

Predicate Features. Our predicate features are:

- PREDWORD, PREDLEMMA, PREDPOS. Lexical form, lemma, and POS tag of the predicate.
- PREDREL.† Syntactic dependency relation between the predicate and its head.
- PREDHEADWORD/POS.† Form and POS tag of the predicate syntactic head, conjoined with the predicate word and POS tag.
- PREDMODWORD/POS/REL.† Form, POS tag, and dependency relation of the predicate syntactic dependents, conjoined with the predicate word and POS tag.

Arc Features. All features above, plus the following (conjoined with arc direction and label):

- ARGWORD, ARGLEMMA, ARGPOS. The lexical form, lemma, and POS tag of the argument.
- ARGREL.† Syntactic dependency relation between the argument and its head.
- LEFTWORD/POS,† RIGHTWORD/POS.† Form/POS tag of the leftmost/rightmost dependent of the argument, conjoined with the predicate word and POS tag.
- LEFTSIBWORD/POS,† RIGHTSIBWORD/POS.† Form/POS tag of the left/right sibling of the argument, conjoined with the predicate tag.
- PREDCONTEXTWORD, PREDCONTEXTPOS, PREDCONTEXTLEMMA. Word, POS, and lemma on the left and right context of the predicate (context size is 2).
- PREDCONTEXTPOSBIGRAM/TRIGRAM. Bigram and trigram of POS tags on the left and right side of the predicate.
- PREDVOICE.† Predicate voice: active, passive, or none. Determined from the syntactic dependency tree as in Johansson and Nugues (2008).

[5]For the open track, the only external information used by our system were the provided automatic dependency trees.

- PREDWORDARGWORD, PREDWORDARG-POS, PREDPOSARGWORD, PREDPOSARG-POS. Predicate word/tag conjoined with argument word/tag.
- PREDARGPOSCONTEXT. Several features conjoining the POS of words surrounding the predicate and argument (similar to the contextual features in McDonald et al. (2005)).
- EXACTARCLENGTH, BINNEDARCLENGTH. Exact and binned arc length (distance between predicate and argument), conjoined with the predicate and argument POS tags.
- POSINBETWEEN, WORDINBETWEEN. POS and forms between the predicate and argument, conjoined with their own POS tags and forms.
- RELPATH,† POSPATH.† Path in the syntactic dependency tree between the predicate and the argument. The path is formed either by dependency relations or by POS tags.

Second Order Features. These involve a predicate, an argument, and a "companion word" (which can be a second argument, in the case of siblings, a second predicate, for co-parents, or the argument of another argument, for grandparents). In all cases, features are of the following kind:

- POSTRIPLET. POS tags of the predicate, the argument, and the companion word.
- UNILEXICAL. One word form (for the predicate/argument/companion) and two POS tags.
- BILEXICAL. One POS tag (for the predicate/argument/companion) and two word forms.
- PAIRWISE. Backed-off pair features for the companion word form/POS tag and the word form/POS of the predicate/argument.

5 Experimental Results

All models were trained by running 10 epochs of max-loss MIRA with $C = 0.01$ (Crammer et al., 2006). The cost function takes into account mismatches between predicted and gold dependencies, with a cost c_P on labeled arcs incorrectly predicted (false positives) and a cost c_R on gold labeled arcs that were missed (false negatives). These values were set through cross-validation in the dev set, yielding $c_P = 0.4$ and $c_R = 0.6$ in all runs, except for the DM and PCEDT datasets in the closed track, for which $c_P = 0.3$ and $c_R = 0.7$.

To speed up decoding, we discard arcs whose posterior probability is below 10^{-4}, according to a probabilistic unlabeled first-order pruner. Table 1 shows a significant reduction of the search space with a very small drop in recall.

Table 2 shows our final results in the test set, for a model trained in the train and development partitions. Our system achieved the best score in the open track (an LF score of 86.27%, averaged over DM, PAS, and PCEDT), and the second best in the closed track, after the Peking team. Overall, we observe that the precision and recall in PCEDT are far below the other two formalisms, but this difference is much smaller when looking at unlabeled scores. Comparing the results in the closed and open tracks, we observe a consistent improvement in the three formalisms of around 1% in F_1 from using syntactic information. While this confirms previous findings that syntactic features are important in semantic role labeling (Toutanova et al., 2005; Johansson and Nugues, 2008), these improvements are less striking than expected. We conjecture this is due to the fact that our model in the closed track already incorporates a variety of contextual features which are nearly as informative as those extracted from the dependency trees.

Finally, to assess the importance of the second order features, Table 3 reports experiments in the dev-set that progressively add several groups of features, along with runtimes. We can see that siblings, co-parents, and grandparents all provide valuable information that improves the final scores (with the exception of the PCEDT labeled scores, where the difference is negligible). This comes at only a small cost in terms of runtime, which is around 1,000 tokens per second for the full models.

	UR	# UA/tok	LR	# LA/tok
DM	99.33	3.5 (13.4%)	99.22	34.4 (2.5%)
PAS	99.53	3.3 (12.5%)	99.49	20.8 (1.9%)
PCEDT	99.03	2.1 (8.2%)	98.77	54.5 (3.0%)

Table 1: Pruner statistics in the dev-set, for the open track. Shown are oracle recall scores, considering both unlabeled (UR) and labeled arcs (LR); and the averaged number of unlabeled and labeled arcs per token that remained after the pruning stage (# UA/tok and # LA/tok). In brackets, we show the fraction of unlabeled/labeled arcs that survived the pruning.

	UP	UR	UF	LP	LR	LF
DM, closed	90.14	88.65	89.39	88.82	87.35	88.08
PAS, closed	93.18	91.12	92.14	91.95	89.92	90.93
PCEDT, closed	90.21	85.51	87.80	78.80	74.70	76.70
average, closed	–	–	89.77	–	–	85.24
DM, open	91.41	89.26	90.32	90.23	88.11	89.16
PAS, open	93.62	92.01	92.81	92.56	90.97	91.76
PCEDT, open	91.58	86.61	89.03	80.14	75.79	77.90
average, open	–	–	90.72	–	–	86.27

Table 2: Submitted results for the closed and open tracks. For comparison, the best-performing system in the closed track (Peking) obtained averaged UF and LF scores of 91.03% and 85.91%, respectively.

	UF	LF	Tok/sec
DM, arc-factored	89.90	88.96	1,681
DM, arc-factored, pruned	89.85	88.90	2,642
+siblings	90.34	89.34	1,838
+co-parents	90.80	89.76	1,073
+grandparent (full)	90.95	89.90	955
PAS, arc-factored	92.34	91.40	1,927
PAS, arc-factored, pruned	92.35	91.40	2,914
+siblings	92.45	91.45	2,106
+co-parents	92.71	91.71	1,104
+grandparent (full)	92.87	91.87	1,043
PCEDT, arc-factored	87.90	79.90	1,558
PCEDT, arc-factored, pruned	87.74	79.83	2,906
+siblings	88.46	79.98	2,066
+co-parents	90.17	79.90	1,531
+grandparent (full)	90.18	80.03	1,371

Table 3: Results in the dev-set for the open track, progressively adding several groups of features, until the full model is obtained. We report unlabeled/labeled F_1 and parsing speeds in tokens per second. Our speeds include the time necessary for pruning, evaluating features, and decoding, as measured on a Intel Core i7 processor @3.4 GHz.

6 Conclusions

We have described a system for broad-coverage semantic dependency parsing. Our system, which is inspired by prior work in syntactic parsing, implements a linear model with second-order features, being able to model interactions between siblings, grandparents and co-parents. We have shown empirically that second-order features have an impact in the final scores. Approximate decoding was performed via alternating directions dual decomposition (AD^3), yielding fast runtimes of around 1,000 tokens per second.

Acknowledgements

We would like to thank the reviewers for their helpful comments. This work was partially supported by the EU/FEDER programme, QREN/POR Lisboa (Portugal), under the Intelligo project (contract 2012/24803) and by a FCT grant PTDC/EEI-SII/2312/2012.

References

Hiyan Alshawi. 1996. Head automata and bilingual tiling: Translation with minimal representations. In *Proc. of Annual Meeting of the Association for Computational Linguistics*, pages 167–176.

Bernd Bohnet and Joakim Nivre. 2012. A transition-based system for joint part-of-speech tagging and labeled non-projective dependency parsing. In *Proc. of the Empirical Methods in Natural Language Processing*, pages 1455–1465.

Xavier Carreras. 2007. Experiments with a higher-order projective dependency parser. In *International Conference on Natural Language Learning*, pages 957–961.

Koby Crammer, Ofer Dekel, Joseph Keshet, Shai Shalev-Shwartz, and Yoram Singer. 2006. Online Passive-Aggressive Algorithms. *Journal of Machine Learning Research*, 7:551–585.

Dipanjan Das, André F. T. Martins, and Noah A. Smith. 2012. An Exact Dual Decomposition Algorithm for Shallow Semantic Parsing with Constraints. In *Proc. of First Joint Conference on Lexical and Computational Semantics (*SEM)*, pages 209–217.

Jeffrey Flanigan, Sam Thomson, Jaime Carbonell, Chris Dyer, and Noah A. Smith. 2014. A discriminative graph-based parser for the abstract meaning representation. In *Proc. of the Annual Meeting of the Association for Computational Linguistics*, pages 1426–1436.

Richard Johansson and Pierre Nugues. 2008. Dependency-based syntactic–semantic analysis with PropBank and NomBank. *International Conference on Natural Language Learning*, pages 183–187.

Nikos Komodakis, Nikos Paragios, and Georgios Tziritas. 2007. MRF optimization via dual decomposition: Message-passing revisited. In *Proc. of International Conference on Computer Vision*, pages 1–8.

Terry Koo and Michael Collins. 2010. Efficient third-order dependency parsers. In *Proc. of Annual Meeting of the Association for Computational Linguistics*, pages 1–11.

Terry Koo, Alexander M. Rush, Michael Collins, Tommi Jaakkola, and David Sontag. 2010. Dual decomposition for parsing with non-projective head automata. In *Proc. of Empirical Methods for Natural Language Processing*, pages 1288–1298.

Sandra Kübler, Ryan McDonald, and Joakim Nivre. 2009. *Dependency parsing*. Morgan & Claypool Publishers.

André F. T. Martins, Noah A. Smith, and Eric P. Xing. 2009. Concise Integer Linear Programming Formulations for Dependency Parsing. In *Proc. of Annual Meeting of the Association for Computational Linguistics*, pages 342–350.

André F. T. Martins, Noah A. Smith, Eric P. Xing, Pedro M. Q. Aguiar, and Mário A. T. Figueiredo. 2010. Turbo Parsers: Dependency Parsing by Approximate Variational Inference. In *Proc. of Empirical Methods for Natural Language Processing*, pages 34–44.

André F. T. Martins, Noah A. Smith, Pedro M. Q. Aguiar, and Mário A. T. Figueiredo. 2011. Dual Decomposition with Many Overlapping Components. In *Proc. of Empirical Methods for Natural Language Processing*, pages 238–249.

André F. T. Martins, Mário A. T. Figueiredo, Pedro M. Q. Aguiar, Noah A. Smith, and Eric P. Xing. 2012. Alternating directions dual decomposition. Arxiv preprint arXiv:1212.6550.

André F. T. Martins, Miguel B. Almeida, and Noah A. Smith. 2013. Turning on the turbo: Fast third-order non-projective turbo parsers. In *Proc. of the Annual Meeting of the Association for Computational Linguistics*, pages 617–622.

André F. T. Martins. 2014. AD^3: A Fast Decoder for Structured Prediction. In S. Nowozin, P. Gehler, J. Jancsary, and C. Lampert, editors, *Advanced Structured Prediction*. MIT Press, Cambridge, MA, USA.

Ryan McDonald, Koby Crammer, and Fernando Pereira. 2005. Online large-margin training of dependency parsers. In *Proc. of Annual Meeting of the Association for Computational Linguistics*, pages 91–98.

Ryan McDonald, Kevin Lerman, and Fernando Pereira. 2006. Multilingual dependency analysis with a two-stage discriminative parser. In *Proc. of International Conference on Natural Language Learning*, pages 216–220.

Alexander M. Rush, David Sontag, Michael Collins, and Tommi Jaakkola. 2010. On dual decomposition and linear programming relaxations for natural language processing. In *Proc. of Empirical Methods for Natural Language Processing*.

David A. Smith and Jason Eisner. 2008. Dependency parsing by belief propagation. In *Proc. of Empirical Methods for Natural Language Processing*, pages 145–156.

Kristina Toutanova, Aria Haghighi, and Christopher Manning. 2005. Joint learning improves semantic role labeling. In *ACL*, pages 589–596.

RelAgent: Entity Detection and Normalization for Diseases in Clinical Records: a Linguistically Driven Approach

Sv Ramanan
RelAgent Tech Pvt Ltd
Adyar, Chennai
India
ramanan@relagent.com

Senthil Nathan
RelAgent Tech Pvt Ltd
Adyar, Chennai
India
senthil@relagent.com

Abstract

We refined the performance of Cocoa/Peaberry, a linguistically motivated system, on extracting disease entities from clinical notes in the training and development sets for Task 7. Entities were identified in noun chunks by use of dictionaries, and events ('The left atrium is dilated') through our own parser and predicate-argument structures. We also developed a module to map the extracted entities to the SNOMED subset of UMLS. The module is based on direct matching against UMLS entries through regular expressions derived from a small set of morphological transformations, along with priority rules when multiple UMLS entries were matched. The performance on training and development sets was 81.0% and 83.3% respectively (Task A), and the UMLS matching scores were respectively 75.3% and 78.2% (Task B). However, the performance against the test set was low by comparison, 72.0% for Task A and 63.9% for Task B, even while the pure UMLS mapping score was reasonably high (relaxed score in Task B = 91.2%). We speculate that our moderate performance on the test set derives primarily from chunking/parsing errors.

1 Introduction

The increasing use of electronic health records, both for satisfying mandatory requirements as well as for administrative reasons, has created a need for systems to automatically tag and normalize disease/sign/symptom mentions. Statistically significant correlations extracted from automated analysis of large databases of clinical records are felt to be useful in detecting phenotype-genotype correlations (reviewed in Kohane (2011)), phenotype-phenotype correlations (Roque et al., 2011) as well as in continuous monitoring of events such as adverse reactions and even early detection of outbreaks of epidemics/infectious diseases (Botsis et al., 2013; Collier, 2012). In this context, Task 7 of SemEval 2014, which is a continuation of the ShARe/CLEF eHealth 2013 task (Pradhan et al., 2013), provides a testbed to evaluate systems that automatically tag and normalize mentions of diseases, signs and symptoms in clinical records, which include discharge summaries and echo, radiology and ECG reports.

Our system consists of (i) Cocoa, a chunk-based entity tagger and (ii) Peaberry, a parser, followed by a module for predicate-argument structure. We have tested the system in a variety of tasks, such as detecting and normalizing mentions of chemicals, proteins/genes, diseases and action terms in the BioCreative 13 Chemdner and CTD tasks (Ramanan and Senthil Nathan, 2013a; Ramanan and Senthil Nathan, 2013b), as well as in detecting cellular and pathological events in the BioNLP cancer genetics task (Ramanan and Senthil Nathan, 2013c); we also participated in the eHealth 2013 task (Ramanan et al., 2013d). Throughout, we have retained a common core platform for simultaneous detection of a multiplicity of entity types as well as for chunking and parsing; we restrict task-specific optimization primarily to post-processing modules. While this strategy may not be optimal

Proceedings of the 8th International Workshop on Semantic Evaluation (SemEval 2014), pages 477–481, Dublin, Ireland, August 23-24, 2014.

for any individual task, we feel that it is necessary for multi-document spanning tasks such as literature-based discovery (Swanson, 1988), where connections are established across a variety of scales, e.g. from molecular events to patho-physiological phenotypes. Moreover, these linkages need to be made across a multiplicity of documents from various sources, which encompass a linguistic range from complex syntactical utterances in biomedical publications to free-form phrase-centered clinical notes.

We refined performance against the provided training and development sets, with reasonable performance in Task A (relaxed $f = 0.94$, strict $f = 0.81 - 0.83$, strict recall $0.80 - 0.82$). A module to match text from gold-annotated exact spans to UMLS codes also achieved reasonable performance for Task B (relaxed accuracy $= 0.94{-}96$). However, the results against from the test set were quite low for Task A, (relaxed $f = 0.87$, strict $f = 0.72$, strict recall $= 0.70$) as well as for Task B (strict $f = 0.64$). Comparatively, the module for UMLS normalization fared better (relaxed $f = 0.91$ in Task B). We speculate that the test set contains entities that are rare in the training/development sets which were chunked incorrectly, and also that the parse errors in the test set arose from syntactic structures missing in the training sets. It is possible that a post-processing statistical module trained on a combination of gold annotations as well as linguistic output may be needed for improving the performance of our system on clinical notes.

2 System description

The basic structure of the entity-tagging system is unchanged from that used in Share/CLEF eHealth 13 (Pradhan et al., 2013) and BioNLP-ST 13. In summary, the system comprises of a sentence splitter, followed by a TBL-based POS tagger and chunker, entity tagging at the single-token level, a module to handle multi-word entities, a noun phrase coordination module, a dependency parser (Ramanan and Senthil Nathan, 2013c), and finally a semantic module to tag disease-related events.

The generic system has dictionaries and morphological rules for detecting diseases and body parts. However, there are many extensions needed for clinical notes, which (i) make extensive use of common words and phrases for describing symptoms, which requires word sense disambiguation, (ii) use unusual phrases for signs and symptoms and (iii) are full of undefined acronyms. We isolated such specialization to disease-related entities within noun phrases in clinical documents inside a subroutine in the multi-word tagger module. These were identified by a frequency-based analysis of words and phrases in the training and development corpora. Thus, a few ambiguous words and phrases such as 'crackles', 'complaints', 'mass effect' and 'focal consolidation' were tagged as disease markers regardless of context. Generally, however, even common clinical words such as 'redness' and 'swelling' were tagged only in the presence of neighboring context words. The appearance of major body parts such as 'Abdomen', 'Neck, 'Extremities' at the beginning of a line followed by a colon or a hyphen was taken as a discourse reference marker for the rest of the line to tag acronyms such as 'NT/ND' and dangling adjectives such as 'soft' and 'warm'. Very common acronyms (≈ 100) both for anatomical parts ('LUQ') and diseases ('DMII') were also tagged inside the specialized subroutine, as were common abbreviations ('regurg' for regurgitation) and words with common spelling errors. Finally, some event/process words which we found to almost always represent clinical conditions in the training text were tagged as disease markers. Examples are 'aspiration', agitation' and 'confusion'.

We also extended our generic event processing module with a task-specific routine to take into account descriptions of (mostly) signs/symptoms specific to clinical documents. These fall into several categories: (i) abnormal changes in body parts or organ systems, such as 'The left atrium was moderately enlarged', 'Nose is bloody' and 'redistribution of pulmonary blood flow' (ii) symptoms such as 'The patient was unable to walk', 'His speech was slurred', 'He had difficulty breathing' and 'alteration of consciousness' (iii) changes in parameters marked by phrases/clauses such as 'elevation of troponin', 'QR interval was prolonged' and 'decreased blood sugar'. Certain environmental conditions such as 'exposure to asbestos' were also handled. Finally, events with a default animate theme were tagged regardless of their actual arguments to handle sentences/phrases where our syntax module failed to extract the correct theme or the theme is to be inferred from the discourse; the $\approx$ 40 words in this set included verbs such as 'vomit', 'shivering', 'lethargic', 'violent' and 'somnolent'.

The above treatment served to demarcate spans for diseases that overlap with the gold annotations. The system merges words/phrases denoting a body part with adjoining words that denote diseases, and also merges words denoting severity into the disease span, since our system design strategy was to generate the longest contiguous span that can refer to a disease. However, the primary score in the shared task are with respect to exact matches with the gold annotations. We therefore wrote a small post-processing module to omit words in an approximate match that refer to severity ('acute') as well as to excise phrases dealing with intra-organ parts or their location (such as 'lobes' or 'left/right') - such words/phrases are usually omitted from the UMLS descriptions of diseases to which the gold annotations hew closely. Also, we noticed that certain words such as 'wounds' and 'lesions' do not embed an anatomical entity within their description in the gold annotations. Yet another point is that, while parameters are marked up as indicative of a symptom only when they take on abnormal values ('elevated LDL'), the direction of change is almost always omitted from the gold annotations. Descriptors of the patient ('He') are also excised. Altogether, we constructed about 40 rules to trim the approximate span into one more conformant to the exact form in the gold annotations.

Task B requires mapping diseases phrases into the SNOMED subset of UMLS as specified in the task description. We proceeded on the assumption that the exact (gold) entity spans were constructed by annotators to closely map into the UMLS descriptions. Accordingly, we used the text as defined by the gold spans and attempted to map them directly into the UMLS definitions after some preprocessing steps that constructed a regular expression: (a) common spelling errors were corrected (b) body part and disease acronyms were expanded (c) common variants were added as alternates i.e. 'tumou?rs?' were expanded into '(tumou?r|neoplasm|carcinoma)s?' (d) adjectival and nominal variants were added e.g. both 'atrium' and 'atrial' were converted into '(atri)(al?|um)', and more generally, adjectival endings were generalized, for example, the ending 'ic' was converted into '(i[ac]|ism)'. (e) singular and plural forms were converted into choices e.g. 'artery' was rendered as 'arter(y|ies)'.

Altogether, we have $\approx$ 120 rules for variant morphological forms, covering adjectives, nouns and number. The resulting regular expression was directly matched (using 'grep') against UMLS text entries. Generally, several matches were found. Matches against the defining entry (the first one) were prioritized, otherwise the entry with the largest CUID was taken. Finally, we noted that some UMLS CUID's were preferred to others; for example, 'C0007115 - Malignant neoplasm of thyroid' is preferred to 'C0549473 - Thyroid carcinoma'. The preferred choices were inferred from gold annotation frequencies, and correspond to $\approx$ 100 remapping rules.

3 Results and Discussion

With a few minor changes to the system used in the Share/CLEF 2013, we obtained a relaxed f-measure in Task A of 0.88 in the training and development sets. Thereafter we alternately refined performance in Task A against the provided training set using the development set as a testbed, or vice versa. As described in the last section, these refinements took the form of adding context-sensitive rules for disease-related words and phrases in order of their frequencies in the training/development sets. While we could thereby improve performance against both training and development sets (relaxed f = 0.94), we noticed that improvements in the performance against the training set did not correlate with better performance against the development set and vice versa, probably implying that 6% or more of the entities are unique to each set, or that we were unable to catch similarities. A similar orthogonal situation resulted in our attempt to improve performance against exact matches on the training and development sets, strict $f = 0.81 - 0.83$, strict recall $0.80 - 0.82$. The observation of orthogonal entity sets in different datasets for about 6% of entities is seemingly validated in the test set, where the results showed a relaxed $f = 0.87$, which is quite close to the baseline performance (0.88 in the Share/CLEF 2013 task); the highest scoring system had relaxed $f = 0.91$ by comparison. We speculate that our insistence on contextual clues for entity tagging is another cause for low relaxed performance on the test set.

Performance of the system for exact matches on the test set (strict $f = 0.72$) suffered greatly in comparison to the training/development sets. This could be partly ascribed to the 7% lower performance on the relaxed f-score (i.e. we missed many entities altogether) from 0.94 in training/development sets to 0.87 in the test set. Even accounting for this, there is an additional performance drop of about $3-4\%$ in exact match on the test set compared to training/development sets. One implication is that that our rule-base method for pruning approximate matches to exact spans is probably sub-optimal, and should be supplemented or replaced by a statistical algorithm. As noted earlier, gold annotations are probably made by annotators with respect to UMLS definitions, and have some degree of arbitrariness associated with them depending on the granularity of the UMLS definition e.g. in the choice of whether to remove or retain a body location in the gold span. Given the size of the UMLS definition set, a statistical approach is probably likely to do better than a rule-based system in the task of reducing approximate matches to exact spans.

The poor performance in Task A (strict recall = 0.70) directly impinges on our low 'strict' score in Task B (= 0.64); this score is simply a product of the strict recall in Task A and the accuracy of mapping to UMLS, where the latter score is given by the Task B 'relaxed' score (= 0.91). An interesting feature is the mapping accuracy for our system on the test set suffered a relatively small drop when compared to the mapping accuracies on the training and development sets, which were 0.94 and 0.96 respectively. We interpret this reasonably high figure for the mapping score (the best among the top 10+ teams in Task B) as validation of our hypothesis that gold annotations are made with respect to UMLS definitions, which also strengthens the case (made above) for the need to incorporate a (semi-)statistical approach for pruning overlap matches to exact matches in our system.

Clinical documents are terse and full of phrasal observations and incomplete sentences, often with missing punctuation. We have adapted a linguistically based system to detect disease-related entities and events with moderate performance; our observation on the training/development sets is that most errors arise from parsing/ chunking errors on grammatically incomplete phrases. The second task, namely mapping disease-related entities/events to SNOMED/UMLS, requires tagged entity spans to correspond closely to UMLS definitions; system performance in this regard can probably be usefully supplemented by statistical approaches. Given proper entity spans, a small set of morphological transformations gives high performance in mapping to UMLS ID's. We speculate that a chunk-annotated corpus of clinical records may help in improving performance for linguistically derived systems.

References

Isaac S. Kohane. 2011. *Using electronic health records to drive discovery in disease genomics.* Nat Rev Genet. 2011 Jun;12(6):417-28.

Francisco S. Roque, Peter B. Jensen, Henriette Schmock, Marlene Dalgaard, Massimo Andreatta, Thomas Hansen, Karen Soeby, Soren Bredkjor, Anders Juul, Thomas Werge, Lars J. Jensen and Soren Brunak. 2011. *Using electronic patient records to discover disease correlations and stratify patient cohorts.* PLoS Comp. Bio. 7(8):e1002141.

Sv Ramanan and Senthil Nathan. 2013. *Performance of a multi-class biomedical tagger on the BioCreative IV CTD task.* Proceedings of the Fourth BioCreative Challenge Evaluation Workshop vol. 1. Bethesda, MD.

Sv Ramanan and Senthil Nathan. 2013. *Adapting Cocoa a multi-class entity detector for the CHEMDNER task of BioCreative IV.* Proceedings of the Fourth BioCreative Challenge Evaluation Workshop vol. 2. Bethesda, MD.

Sv Ramanan and Senthil Nathan. 2013. *Performance and limitations of the linguistically motivated Cocoa/Peaberry system in a broad biomedical domain.* Proceedings of Workshop. BioNLP Shared Task 2013. ACL. Sofia.

Sv Ramanan, Shereen Broido and Senthil Nathan. 2013. *Performance of a multi-class biomedical tagger on clinical records.* Proceedings of ShARe/CLEF eHealth Evaluation Labs.

Don R. Swanson. 1988. *Migraine and Magnesium: Eleven Neglected Connections.* Persp. Bio. Med. 31(4), 526-557.

Sameer Pradhan, Noemie Elhadad, Brett R. South, David Martinez, Lee Christensen, Amy Vogel, Hanna Suominen, Wendy W. Chapman and Guergana Savova. 2013. *Online Working Notes of the CLEF 2013 Evaluation Labs and Workshop.* Proceedings of ShARe/CLEF eHealth Evaluation Labs, 23-26 September, Valencia, Spain

Taxiarchis Botsis , Michael D. Nguyen , Emily J. Woo, Marianthi Markatou and Robert Ball. 2011. *Text mining for the Vaccine Adverse Event Reporting System: medical text classification using informative feature selection.* J Am Med Inform Assoc. 2011 Sep-Oct;18(5):631-8

Nigel Collier. 2012. *Uncovering text mining: A survey of current work on web-based epidemic intelligence.* Glob Public Health. Aug 2012; 7(7): 731-749.

RoBox: CCG with Structured Perceptron for Supervised Semantic Parsing of Robotic Spatial Commands

Kilian Evang
University of Groningen
k.evang@rug.nl

Johan Bos
University of Groningen
johan.bos@rug.nl

Abstract

We use a Combinatory Categorial Grammar (CCG) parser with a structured perceptron learner to address Shared Task 6 of SemEval-2014, Supervised Semantic Parsing of Robotic Spatial Commands. Our system reaches an accuracy of 79% ignoring spatial context and 87% using the spatial planner, showing that CCG can successfully be applied to the task.

1 Introduction

When interpreting utterances, humans use world knowledge whereas most semantic parsers to date rely purely on linguistic clues. Shared Task 6 in the SemEval 2014 campaign for semantic evaluation aims to integrate reasoning about microworlds with semantic parsing. In this task, a system is given an instruction for a robot and has to produce an executable semantic representation in Robot Control Language (Dukes, 2013a, RCL). The Robot Commands Treebank (Dukes, 2013b) is used for training and evaluation. We participated in this shared task with a system rooted in Combinatory Categorial Grammar (CCG). In particular, we were interested in finding out whether existing techniques for automatically deriving categorial grammars with semantics could be moved easily to the new domain of robot commands and integrated with the provided spatial reasoning component. In this paper we outline our method and present the results for this shared task. [1]

2 Extracting a CCG from RCL

CCGs (Steedman, 2001) use a small set of atomic constituent categories such as S (sentence), NP (noun phrase) or PP (prepositional phrase). Constituents that take other constituents as arguments have complex categories describing their combinatory potential. For example, an intransitive English verb has category $S\backslash NP$, meaning that it forms a sentence by combining with an NP to its left. Similarly, *modifiers* also have complex categories. For example, a pre-sentential adverb might have category S/S because it combines with a sentence to its right to form a modified sentence. The *combinatory rules* that license these example combinations are called *backward application* and *forward application*. They and other combinatory rules also allow for constituents to be associated with semantic expressions, and specify how to form a combined semantic expression for the derived larger constituent.

In this section, we describe a process that takes an RCL corpus as input and produces a set of CCG lexical entries, i.e. natural-language words paired with categories and semantic expressions. The goal is for these lexical entries to produce the correct semantics under CCG combinatory rules also for unseen robotic commands.

2.1 Transforming the Trees

RCL expressions are rooted ordered trees whose nodes are labeled with *tags*. We will write them in the form $(t\!:\!\mathbf{h})$ where t is the root tag and $\mathbf{h}$ is the sequence of subtrees of the root's children. Leaves are abbreviated as just their tags. In each training example, each pre-terminal (parent of a leaf) can be aligned to one or more words in the corresponding natural language expression. An example is shown in Figure 1. Since the alignments to words are not crossing, we can interpret the RCL tree as a phrase structure tree for the sentence and use the algorithm of (Hockenmaier and Steedman, 2007) to translate it to CCG. We extend the algorithm with a semantic step that makes sure the derivations would produce the original RCL expressions.

[1] Our code is available at http://www.let.rug.nl/evang/RoBox.zip

Proceedings of the 8th International Workshop on Semantic Evaluation (SemEval 2014), pages 482–486, Dublin, Ireland, August 23-24, 2014.

$(event\!:\!(action\!:\!move)(entity\!:\!(color\!:\!green)(type\!:\!prism))(destination\!:\!(spatial\text{-}relation\!:\!(relation\!:\!within)(entity\!:\!(indicator\!:\!back)(indicator\!:\!left)(type\!:\!corner))))$

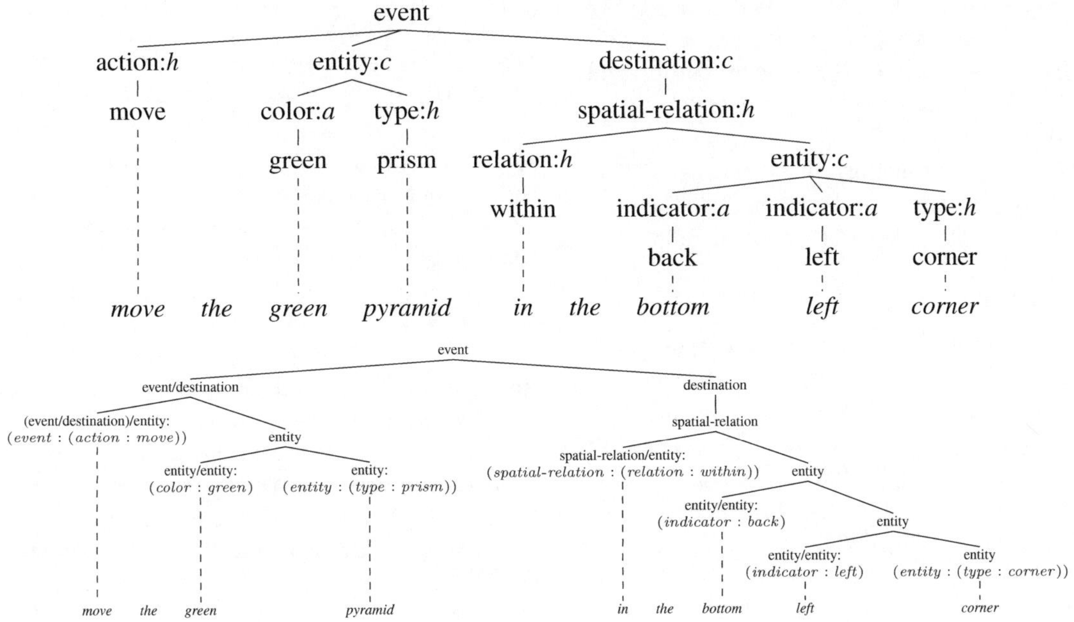

Figure 1: Top: an RCL expression. Middle: its representation as a tree diagram. Internal nodes are annotated with constituent types. Pre-terminals are aligned to words in a corresponding natural-language expression. Bottom: result of the CCG transformation.

The procedure is as follows:

1. Determine constituent types. We treat *action*, *relation* and *type* constituents as *heads*, *entity*s and *destinations* as *complements* (i.e. arguments) and *cardinal*s, *color*s, *indicator*s, *measure*s and *spatial-relation*s as *adjuncts* (i.e. modifiers). For *sequence* nodes that have multiple *event* children, we treat the first as head and the rest as adjuncts. A corresponding *constituent type label* h, a or c is added to the label of each internal node (cf. Figure 1, middle).

2. Assign lexical semantics. To the label of each pre-terminal, add an RCL expression which is a copy of a connected subgraph of the tree itself (without the constituent type labels). For a-type and c-type pre-terminals, the subgraph includes only the pre-terminal and its daughter. For h-type pre-terminals the parent is also included, as well as any subtrees with root tag *id* or *reference-id* the parent may have.To illustrate, the label of the action:h node in our example becomes action:h:$(event : (action : move))$, and color:$a$ becomes color:a:$(color\!:\!green)$. The leaves are now no longer needed, so we remove them.

3. Add sequence nodes. If the root is tagged *sequence*, add an additional node tagged *sequence* between each child and the root.

4. Binarize the tree. Each local tree with more than two daughters is binarized by inserting dummy nodes, provisionally labeled $C : h$ where C is the tag of the parent. Left adjuncts (such as the first *indicator* in Figure 1) are split off first, followed by right adjuncts (such as the *destination* in Figure 1), left complements and right complements.

5. Assign CCG categories. Starting from the root, the tag of each node is replaced by a CCG category. For simplicity, we directly use RCL tags as atomic categories rather than mapping them to standard CCG categories:

The root gets its tag (*event* or *sequence*) as category.

c-type nodes get their tag as category. Their sibling gets category P/T if it is on the left and $P\backslash T$ if it is on the right, where T is the tag of the c-type node and P is the category of the parent. For example, the *destination* node in Figure 1 gets *destination* as category, and its left sibling therefore gets $event/destination$ because the parent's category is $event$.

a-type nodes such as the two $indicator$s in Figure 1 get category P/P if they are on the left of their sibling and $P\backslash P$ if they are on its right, where P is the category of their parent. The sibling gets category P.

Nodes without siblings get their tag as category.

Constituent type labels are dropped. The result for our example is shown at the bottom of Figure 1.

2.2 The Lexicon

For each leaf in the transformed corpus that is aligned to one or more words, a lexical item is extracted containing the words, category and RCL. For single-word items, we also add part-of-speech tags, obtained using the C&C POS tagger (Curran and Clark, 2003), to reduce overgeneration. Examples of lexical items are:

- $\langle$block/NN$\rangle \vdash$ entity : $(entity : (type : (block)))$
- $\langle$on, top, of$\rangle \vdash$ spatial-relation/entity : $(spatial\text{-}relation : (relation : above))$

2.3 Combinatory Rules

Given the extracted lexical items, the corpus derivations are licensed by standard CCG rules (Steedman, 2001), using a modified semantics that keeps things simple and ensures that the semantics of (most) intermediate constituents are themselves RCL subexpressions, which is important for interfacing with the spatial planner during parsing. The most important two rules are forward and backward application:

$$(X/Y){:}f \quad Y{:}g \Rightarrow X{:}\text{FAPP}(X/Y, f, g) \qquad (>)$$
$$Y{:}g \quad (X\backslash Y){:}f \Rightarrow X{:}\text{BAPP}(X\backslash Y, g, f) \qquad (<)$$

where FAPP and BAPP are defined as follows:

$$\text{FAPP}(X/Y, \mathbf{a}, (t{:}\mathbf{h})) = (t{:}\mathbf{ah}) \text{ if } X = Y$$
$$\text{FAPP}(C, (t{:}\mathbf{h}), \mathbf{c}) = (t{:}\mathbf{hc}) \text{ otherwise}$$
$$\text{BAPP}(X\backslash Y, (t{:}\mathbf{h}), \mathbf{a}) = (t{:}\mathbf{ha}) \text{ if } X = Y$$
$$\text{BAPP}(C, \mathbf{c}, (t{:}\mathbf{h})) = (t{:}\mathbf{ch}) \text{ otherwise}$$

In words, the semantics of the adjunct or complement is added as a subtree under the root of the semantics of the head.

We also use a restricted form of the CCG rule *forward composition* to form chains of entity adjuncts:

$$(\text{entity/entity}){:}\mathbf{a} \quad (\text{entity/entity}){:}\mathbf{b}$$
$$\Rightarrow (\text{entity/entity}){:}\mathbf{ab} \qquad (>_B)$$

This is motivated by our use of the spatial planner. Without forward composition, we would, e.g., not be able to build a constituent with the semantics $(entity : (color : green)(color : red)(type : cube\text{-}group))$ in the context of a stack consisting of green and red cubes, but no stack consisting exclusively of red cubes – the planner would filter out the intermediate constituent with semantics $(entity{:}(color{:}red)(type{:}cube\text{-}group))$.

Finally, we use type-changing rules, which is standard practice in CCG parsing (Clark and Curran, 2007; Zettlemoyer and Collins, 2007). They are automatically extracted from the training data. Some of them account for unary productions within RCL expressions by introducing an additional internal node, such as the $destination$ node in Figure 1. For example:

$$\text{sp-relation}{:}\mathbf{h} \Rightarrow$$
$$\text{destination}{:}(destination{:}\mathbf{h}) \qquad (*_1)$$

Others account for RCL leaves that are not linked to any words. For example, the RCL expression for the command *take the light blue prism from the blue cube* renders the *from*-phrase as an adjunct to the $prism$ node: $(spatial\text{-}relation : (relation : above)(entity{:}(color{:}blue)(type{:}cube)))$, where $above$ is not linked. Rules like the following deal with this by not only introducing an internal node, but also a branch leading to the unlinked leaf:

$$\text{entity}{:}\mathbf{h} \Rightarrow \text{entity/entity}{:}$$
$$(sp\text{-}relation{:}(relation{:}above)\mathbf{h}) \qquad (*_2)$$

2.4 Anaphora

Anaphora are marked in RCL $entity$ expressions by the subexpression $(id : 1)$ for antecedent entities and $(reference\text{-}id : 1)$ for anaphoric entities. The latter have the special type $reference$, in which case they are typically linked to the word *it*, or $type\text{-}reference$, in which case they are typically linked to the word *one*, as in *the yellow one*. More than one anaphoric relation in a command, and thus, other IDs than 1, are possible, but extremely rare. We do not explicitly try to resolve anaphora, but merely generate versions both with and without the id subexpression for each $entity$ lexical item seen in training as an antecedent. We then rely on the parser and spatial planner to find a parse with the correct item marked as antecedent. If the spatial planner rejects a subexpression because it contains an unknown reference ID, we accept it anyway because the expression can later combine with another one that contains the antecedent. However, at the level of complete parses, those containing a $reference\text{-}id$ expression but no id expression – or vice versa – are rejected. As a heuristic, we also reject parses where $reference\text{-}id$ precedes id because we found this to be a noticeable source of errors, and no cataphora in the training data.

3 Training and Decoding

Following (Zettlemoyer and Collins, 2007), we use a CKY CCG parser in combination with simple perceptron updates: iterate over the training corpus T times, for each sentence producing all parses. Each parse is characterized by a number of features and scored using a global weight vector. The weight vector is updated by subtracting the feature vector of the highest-scoring parse and adding the feature vector of the highest-scoring correct parse. No update is performed if the highest-scoring parse is correct, or no correct parse was found. Since for the present task the training data already induces a lexicon, we treat the lexicon as fixed and perform no lexical update. We parallelize training using iterative parameter mixing (McDonald et al., 2010) with 12 shards.

3.1 Semantically Empty and Unknown Words

The parser initially considers each contiguous subsequence of words in the sentence and adds all matching lexical items to the chart. In order to allow for words that are not linked to the semantics, we simply add two additional lexical items to the chart for each word w in the sentence: $\langle w \rangle \vdash X/X : nil$ and $\langle w \rangle \vdash X \backslash X : nil$ where X is a variable that can be bound to any category during rule application. We modify the combinatory rules above to require that at least one of the input items has non-nil semantics and to use that as output semantics if the other is nil.

In decoding, the parser also has to deal with words not seen in training. For one, there are the nil items, so it is possible to treat the unknown words as semantically empty. In addition, we look at other single-word lexical items with the same POS tag and generate corresponding lexical items for the unknown word on the fly, hoping that features and the spatial planner will guide the parser to the right choice. To limit the search space, this is currently only done for nouns since we found the greatest lexical variance to occur with them.

3.2 Features

Each chart edge is characterized by the following local features:

- each lexical item $\mathbf{w} \vdash c\!:\!s$ used.
- each instance of a combinatory rule used, e.g. $>$.
- $\langle p, c, s \rangle$ for each lexical item used where p is the POS tag (or empty for multiwords). This allows to learn correlations between category/semantics pairs and particular parts of speech, primarily for unknown words.
- each instance of a type-changing rule used, together with the semantic head word of the constituent it roots, e.g. $\langle *_1, \text{in} \rangle$. This helps to learn not to use type-changing rules where they don't make sense. E.g. the word *squares* often heads entity descriptions that type-change into $measure$ phrases but the word *cube* doesn't.
- the root tag of the semantics of each constituent, together with the word to its immediate left, e.g. $\langle destination, \text{from} \rangle$. This example feature is indicative of typical erroneous parses where spatial adjuncts corresponding to *from*-phrases are misparsed as destination complements. The word *from* provides a strong clue against such a parse but would be ignored without such a feature because it is not aligned to any RCL node.
- the root tag of the semantics of each constituent, together with the first word in it, e.g. $\langle spatial\text{-}relation, \text{above} \rangle$.

3.3 The Spatial Planner

The spatial planner provided together with the treebank provides access to the context in which each command is to be interpreted, consisting of a current arrangement of bodies on a board and in the gripper of the robot being instructed. It can tell us for some RCL subexpressions, chiefly *entity* descriptions, whether they "make sense" given the context. For example, if the parser builds an edge with semantics $(entity:(type:cube)(color:red))$ but there is no red cube anywhere on the board, we can immediately reject the edge (provided no negations or hypothetical descriptions are used, which is the case for the commands in this task) and thereby avoid errors and reduce the search space. The planner also helps resolve attachment ambiguities early: in the command *put the prism on the cube*, a constituent with semantics $(entity:(type:prism)(spatial\text{-}relation:(relation:above)(entity:(type:cube))))$ is a possible but incorrect parse. If we are lucky enough that no prism is actually sitting on a cube in the microworld, the planner will weed it out.

We have not yet explored making the fullest possible use of the spatial planner for checking the validity of *event* or *sequence* expressions, which would involve simulating changing the state of the world as a sequence of *event* instructions is carried out. Currently we only filter out initial *event* instructions with action *drop* for scenes in which there is nothing initially in the robot's gripper to be dropped. RCL requires the action *move* here instead, a distinction which is often not made in the natural language commands.

4 Experiments and Results

We carried out two experiments, one using the spatial planner and one not using it. In each case, we trained on training examples shorter than 16 words to speed up training and evaluated on the full test set. In both training and decoding, a beam search strategy keeps only the 60 highest-scoring edges per chart cell. The weights of non-*nil* lexical items were initialized to 1, those of *nil* items to 0.5, all other feature weights to 0. The number of training epochs T was set to 3. These values were chosen experimentally using 80% of the training data and another 10% for testing.

Of the 909 test sentences, 720 (79.21%) were parsed exactly correctly when not using the planner, and 789 (86.80%) when using it, making third place among the six participating systems. The result shows that standard CCG-based techniques for semantic parsing can be successfully applied to the domain of robotic spatial commands and profit from the integration of a spatial planner.

A preliminary analysis suggests most errors are related to pronoun ellipsis, the ambiguous word *one*, anaphora or attachment ambiguity. We believe some further careful feature engineering and extended use of the spatial planner could go a great length to improve accuracy further.

References

Stephen Clark and James R. Curran. 2007. Wide-coverage efficient statistical parsing with CCG and log-linear models. *Computational Linguistics*, 33(4):493–552.

James R. Curran and Stephen Clark. 2003. Investigating GIS and smoothing for maximum entropy taggers. In *Proceedings of the 11th Meeting of the European Chapter of the Association for Computational Linguistics (EACL-03)*, pages 91–98, Budapest, Hungary.

Kais Dukes. 2013a. Semantic annotation of robotic spatial commands. In *Language and Technology Conference (LTC)*, Poznan, Poland.

Kais Dukes. 2013b. Train robots: A dataset for natural language human-robot spatial interaction through verbal commands. In *International Conference on Social Robotics (ICSR). Embodied Communication of Goals and Intentions Workshop*, Bristol, United Kingdom.

J. Hockenmaier and M. Steedman. 2007. CCGbank: a corpus of CCG derivations and dependency structures extracted from the Penn Treebank. *Computational Linguistics*, 33(3):355–396.

Ryan McDonald, Keith Hall, and Gideon Mann. 2010. Distributed training strategies for the structured perceptron. In *Human Language Technologies: The 2010 Annual Conference of the North American Chapter of the Association for Computational Linguistics*, HLT '10, pages 456–464, Stroudsburg, PA, USA.

Mark Steedman. 2001. *The Syntactic Process*. The MIT Press.

Luke S. Zettlemoyer and Michael Collins. 2007. Online learning of relaxed CCG grammars for parsing to logical form. In *In Proceedings of the 2007 Joint Conference on Empirical Methods in Natural Language Processing and Computational Natural Language Learning (EMNLP-CoNLL-2007)*, pages 678–687.

RTM-DCU: Referential Translation Machines for Semantic Similarity

Ergun Biçici
Centre for Global Intelligent Content
School of Computing
Dublin City University, Dublin, Ireland.
ebicici@computing.dcu.ie

Andy Way
Centre for Global Intelligent Content
School of Computing,
Dublin City University, Dublin, Ireland.
away@computing.dcu.ie

Abstract

We use referential translation machines (RTMs) for predicting the semantic similarity of text. RTMs are a computational model for identifying the translation acts between any two data sets with respect to interpretants selected in the same domain, which are effective when making monolingual and bilingual similarity judgments. RTMs judge the quality or the semantic similarity of text by using retrieved relevant training data as interpretants for reaching shared semantics. We derive features measuring the closeness of the test sentences to the training data via interpretants, the difficulty of translating them, and the presence of the acts of translation, which may ubiquitously be observed in communication. RTMs provide a language independent approach to all similarity tasks and achieve top performance when predicting monolingual cross-level semantic similarity (Task 3) and good results in semantic relatedness and entailment (Task 1) and multilingual semantic textual similarity (STS) (Task 10). RTMs remove the need to access any task or domain specific information or resource.

1 Semantic Similarity Judgments

We introduce a fully automated judge for semantic similarity that performs well in three semantic similarity tasks at SemEval-2014, Semantic Evaluation Exercises - International Workshop on Semantic Evaluation (Nakov and Zesch, 2014). RTMs provide a language independent solution for the semantic textual similarity (STS) task (Task 10) (Agirre et al., 2014), achieve top performance when predicting monolingual cross-level semantic similarity (Task 3) (Jurgens et al., 2014), and achieve good results in the semantic relatedness and entailment task (Task 1) (Marelli et al., 2014a).

Referential translation machine (Section 2) is a computational model for identifying the acts of translation for translating between any given two data sets with respect to a reference corpus selected in the same domain. An RTM model is based on the selection of interpretants, training data close to both the training set and the test set, which allow shared semantics by providing context for similarity judgments. In semiotics, an interpretant I interprets the signs used to refer to the real objects (Biçici, 2008). Each RTM model is a data translation and translation prediction model between the instances in the training set and the test set and translation acts are indicators of the data transformation and translation. RTMs present an accurate and language independent solution for making semantic similarity judgments.

We describe the tasks we participated below. Section 2 describes the RTM model and the features used. Section 3 presents the training and test results we obtain on the three tasks we competed and the last section concludes.

Task 1 Evaluation of Compositional Distributional Semantic Models on Full Sentences through Semantic Relatedness and Entailment (SRE) (Marelli et al., 2014a):

Given two sentences, produce a relatedness score indicating the extent to which the sentences express a related meaning: a number in the range $[1, 5]$.

We model the problem as a translation performance prediction task where one possible interpretation is obtained by translating S_1 (the source to translate, S) to S_2 (the target translation, T). Since linguistic processing can reveal deeper similarity relationships, we also look at the translation task at different granularities of information: plain

Proceedings of the 8th International Workshop on Semantic Evaluation (SemEval 2014), pages 487–496,
Dublin, Ireland, August 23-24, 2014.

text (R for regular) and after lemmatization (L). We lowercase all text.

Task 3 Cross-Level Semantic Similarity (CLSS) (Jurgens et al., 2014):

Given two text from different levels, produce a semantic similarity rating: a number in the range $[0, 4]$.

CLSS task targets semantic similarity comparisons between text having different levels of granularity and we address the following level crossings: paragraph to sentence, sentence to phrase, and phrase to word. We model the problem as a translation performance prediction task among text from different levels.

Task 10 Multilingual Semantic Textual Similarity (MSTS) (Agirre et al., 2014)

Given two sentences S_1 *and* S_2 *in the same language, quantify the degree of similarity: a number in the range* $[0, 5]$.

MSTS task addresses the problem in English and Spanish (score range is $[0, 4]$). We model the problem as a translation performance prediction task between S_1 and S_2.

2 Referential Translation Machine (RTM)

Referential translation machines provide a computational model for quality and semantic similarity judgments in monolingual and bilingual settings using retrieval of relevant training data (Biçici, 2011; Biçici and Yuret, 2014) as interpretants for reaching shared semantics (Biçici, 2008). RTMs are a language independent approach and achieve top performance when predicting the quality of translations (Biçici, 2013; Biçici and Way, 2014) and when predicting monolingual cross-level semantic similarity (Jurgens et al., 2014), and good performance when evaluating the semantic relatedness of sentences and their entailment (Marelli et al., 2014a), as an automated student answer grader (Biçici and van Genabith, 2013b), and when judging the semantic similarity of sentences (Biçici and van Genabith, 2013a; Agirre et al., 2014). We improve the RTM models by:

- using a parameterized, fast implementation of FDA, FDA5, and our Parallel FDA5 instance selection model (Biçici et al., 2014),
- better modeling of the language in which similarity judgments are made with improved optimization and selection of the LM data,
- using a general domain corpus to select interpretants from,
- increased feature set for also modeling the structural properties of sentences,
- extended learning models.

Algorithm 1: Referential Translation Machine

Input: Training set `train`, test set `test`, corpus $\mathcal{C}$, and learning model M.
Data: Features of `train` and `test`, $\mathcal{F}_{\texttt{train}}$ and $\mathcal{F}_{\texttt{test}}$.
Output: Predictions of similarity scores on the test $\hat{q}$.

1 FDA5($\texttt{train}, \texttt{test}, \mathcal{C}$) $\rightarrow \mathcal{I}$
2 MTPP($\mathcal{I}, \texttt{train}$) $\rightarrow \mathcal{F}_{\texttt{train}}$
3 MTPP($\mathcal{I}, \texttt{test}$) $\rightarrow \mathcal{F}_{\texttt{test}}$
4 learn($M, \mathcal{F}_{\texttt{train}}$) $\rightarrow \mathcal{M}$
5 predict($\mathcal{M}, \mathcal{F}_{\texttt{test}}$) $\rightarrow \hat{q}$

We use the Parallel FDA5 (Feature Decay Algorithms) instance selection model for selecting the interpretants (Biçici et al., 2014; Biçici and Yuret, 2014) this year, which allows efficient parameterization, optimization, and implementation of FDA, and build an MTPP model (Section 2.1). We view that acts of translation are ubiquitously used during communication:

Every act of communication is an act of translation (Bliss, 2012).

Translation need not be between different languages and paraphrasing or communication also contain acts of translation. When creating sentences, we use our background knowledge and translate information content according to the current context.

The inputs to the RTM algorithm Algorithm 1 are a training set `train`, a test set `test`, some corpus $\mathcal{C}$, preferably in the same domain as the training and test sets, and a learning model. Step 1 selects the interpretants, $\mathcal{I}$, relevant to both the training and test data. Steps 2 and 3 use $\mathcal{I}$ to map `train` and `test` to a new space where similarities between translation acts can be derived more easily. Step 4 trains a learning model M over the training features, $\mathcal{F}_{\texttt{train}}$, and Step 5 obtains the predictions. Figure 1 depicts the RTM.

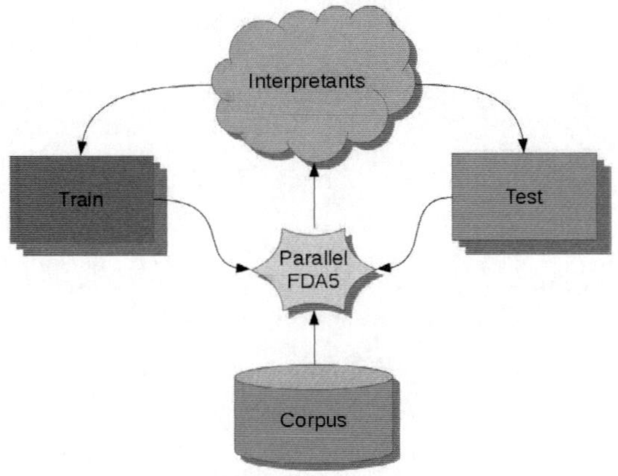

Figure 1: RTM depiction.

Our encouraging results in the semantic similarity tasks increase our understanding of the acts of translation we ubiquitously use when communicating and how they can be used to predict the semantic similarity of text. RTM and MTPP models are not data or language specific and their modeling power and good performance are applicable in different domains and tasks. RTM expands the applicability of MTPP by making it feasible when making monolingual quality and similarity judgments and it enhances the computational scalability by building models over smaller and more relevant set of interpretants.

2.1 The Machine Translation Performance Predictor (MTPP)

MTPP (Biçici et al., 2013) is a state-of-the-art and top performing machine translation performance predictor, which uses machine learning models over features measuring how well the test set matches the training set to predict the quality of a translation without using a reference translation. MTPP measures the coverage of individual test sentence features found in the training set and derives indicators of the closeness of test sentences to the available training data, the difficulty of translating the sentence, and the presence of acts of translation for data transformation.

2.2 MTPP Features for Translation Acts

MTPP feature functions use statistics involving the training set and the test sentences to determine their closeness. Since they are language independent, MTPP allows quality estimation to be performed extrinsically. MTPP uses n-gram features defined over text or common cover link (CCL) (Seginer, 2007) structures as the basic units of information over which similarity calculations are made. Unsupervised parsing with CCL extracts links from base words to head words, representing the grammatical information instantiated in the training and test data.

We extend the MTPP model we used last year (Biçici, 2013) in its learning module and the features included. Categories for the features (S for source, T for target) used are listed below where the number of features are given in brackets for S and T, {#S, #T}, and the detailed descriptions for some of the features are presented in (Biçici et al., 2013). The number of features for each task differs since we perform an initial feature selection step on the tree structural features (Section 2.3). The number of features are in the range $337-437$.

- *Coverage* $\{56, 54\}$: Measures the degree to which the test features are found in the training set for both S ($\{56\}$) and T ($\{54\}$).
- *Perplexity* $\{45, 45\}$: Measures the fluency of the sentences according to language models (LM). We use both forward ($\{30\}$) and backward ($\{15\}$) LM features for S and T.
- *TreeF* $\{0, 10\text{-}110\}$: 10 base features and up to 100 selected features of T among parse tree structures (Section 2.3).
- *Retrieval Closeness* $\{16, 12\}$: Measures the degree to which sentences close to the test set are found in the selected training set, $\mathcal{I}$, using FDA (Biçici and Yuret, 2011a) and BLEU, F_1 (Biçici, 2011), *dice*, and tf-idf cosine similarity metrics.
- *IBM2 Alignment Features* $\{0, 22\}$: Calculates the sum of the entropy of the distribution of alignment probabilities for S ($\sum_{s \in S} -p \log p$ for $p = p(t|s)$ where s and t are tokens) and T, their average for S and T, the number of entries with $p \geq 0.2$ and $p \geq 0.01$, the entropy of the word alignment between S and T and its average, and word alignment $\log$ probability and its value in terms of bits per word. We also compute word alignment percentage as in (Camargo de Souza et al., 2013) and potential BLEU, F_1, WER, PER scores for S and T.
- *IBM1 Translation Probability* $\{4, 12\}$: Calculates the translation probability of test sentences using the selected training set, $\mathcal{I}$ (Brown et al., 1993).
- *Feature Vector Similarity* $\{8, 8\}$: Calculates similarities between vector representations.

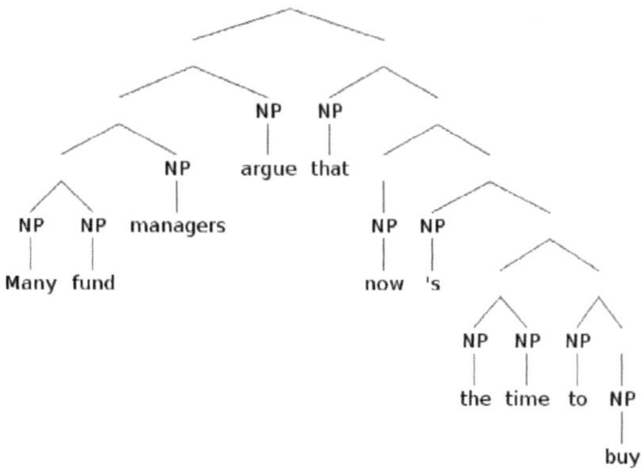

numB	depthB	CCL avg depthB	R/L	avg R/L
24.0	9.0	0.375	2.1429	3.401

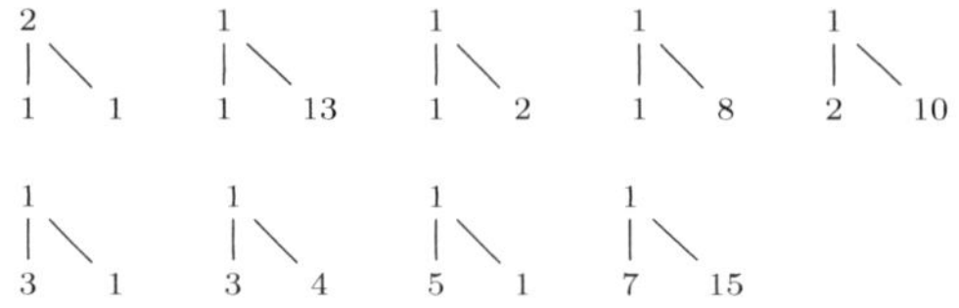

Table 1: Tree features for a parsing output by CCL (immediate non-terminals replaced with NP).

- *Entropy* {*2, 8*}*:* Calculates the distributional similarity of test sentences to the training set over top N retrieved sentences (Biçici et al., 2013).
- *Length* {*6, 3*}*:* Calculates the number of words and characters for S and T and their average token lengths and their ratios.
- *Diversity* {*3, 3*}*:* Measures the diversity of co-occurring features in the training set (Biçici et al., 2013).
- *Synthetic Translation Performance* {*3, 3*}*:* Calculates translation scores achievable according to the n-gram coverage.
- *Character n-grams* {*5*}*:* Calculates cosine between character n-grams (for n=2,3,4,5,6) obtained for S and T (Bär et al., 2012).
- *Minimum Bayes Retrieval Risk* {*0, 4*}*:* Calculates the translation probability for the translation having the minimum Bayes risk among the retrieved training instances.
- *Sentence Translation Performance* {*0, 3*}*:* Calculates translation scores obtained according to $q(T, R)$ using BLEU (Papineni et al., 2002), NIST (Doddington, 2002), or F_1 (Biçici and Yuret, 2011b) for q.
- *LIX* {*1, 1*}*:* Calculates the LIX readability score (Wikipedia, 2013; Björnsson, 1968) for S and T. [1]

2.3 Bracketing Tree Structural Features

We use the parse tree outputs obtained by CCL to derive features based on the bracketing structure. We derive 5 statistics based on the geometric properties of the parse trees: number of brackets used (numB), depth (depthB), average depth (avg depthB), number of brackets on the right branches over the number of brackets on the left (R/L) [2], average right to left branching over all internal tree nodes (avg R/L). The ratio of the number of right to left branches shows the degree to which the sentence is right branching or not. Additionally, we capture the different types of branching present in a given parse tree identified by the number of nodes in each of its children.

Table 1 depicts the parsing output obtained by CCL for the following sentence from WSJ23 [3]:

Many fund managers argue that now 's the time to buy .

We use Tregex (Levy and Andrew, 2006) for visualizing the output parse trees presented on the left. The bracketing structure statistics and features are given on the right hand side. The root node of each tree structural feature represents the number of times that feature is present in the parsing output of a document.

3 SemEval-14 Results

We develop individual RTM models for each task and subtask that we participate at SemEval-2014 with the RTM-DCU team name. The interpretants are selected from the LM corpora distributed by the translation task of WMT14 (Bojar et al., 2014) and the LM corpora provided by LDC for English (Parker et al., 2011) and Spanish (Ângelo Mendonça, 2011) [4]. We use the Stanford POS tagger (Toutanova et al., 2003) to obtain the lemmatized corpora for the SRE task. For each RTM

[1] LIX=$\frac{A}{B} + C\frac{100}{A}$, where A is the number of words, C is words longer than 6 characters, B is words that start or end with any of ".", ":", "!", "?" similar to (Hagström, 2012).

[2] For nodes with uneven number of children, the nodes in the odd child contribute to the right branches.

[3] Wall Street Journal (WSJ) corpus section 23, distributed with Penn Treebank version 3 (Marcus et al., 1993).

[4] English Gigaword 5th, Spanish Gigaword 3rd edition.

model, we extract the features both on the training set and the test set. The number of instances we select for the interpretants in each task is given in Table 2.

Task	Setting	Train	LM
Task 1, SRE	English	770	10770
Task 3, CLSS	Par2S	302	2802
Task 3, CLSS	S2Phrase	202	2702
Task 3, CLSS	Phrase2W	102	2602
Task 10, MSTS	English	504	8002
Task 10, MSTS	English OnWN	504	8004
Task 10, MSTS	Spanish	502	8002

Table 2: Number of sentences in $\mathcal{I}$ (in thousands) selected for each task.

We use ridge regression (RR), support vector regression (SVR) with RBF (radial basis functions) kernel (Smola and Schölkopf, 2004), and extremely randomized trees (TREE) (Geurts et al., 2006) as the learning models. TREE is an ensemble learning method over randomized decision trees. These models learn a regression function using the features to estimate a numerical target value. We also use these learning models after a feature subset selection with recursive feature elimination (RFE) (Guyon et al., 2002) or a dimensionality reduction and mapping step using partial least squares (PLS) (Specia et al., 2009), both of which are described in (Biçici et al., 2013). We optimize the learning parameters, the number of features to select, the number of dimensions used for PLS, and the parameters for parallel FDA5. More detailed descriptions of the optimization processes are given in (Biçici et al., 2013; Biçici et al., 2014). We optimize the learning parameters by selecting ε close to the standard deviation of the noise in the training set (Biçici, 2013) since the optimal value for ε is shown to have linear dependence to the noise level for different noise models (Smola et al., 1998). At testing time, the predictions are bounded to obtain scores in the corresponding ranges. We obtain the confidence scores using support vector classification (SVC).

3.1 Task 1: Semantic Relatedness and Entailment

MSTS contains sentence pairs from the SICK (Sentences Involving Compositional Knowledge) data set (Marelli et al., 2014b), which contain sentence pairs that contain rich lexical, syntactic and semantic phenomena. Official evaluation metric in SRE is the Pearson's correlation score, which is used to select the top systems on the training set. SRE task allows the submission of 5 entries. We present the performance of the top 5 individual RTM models on the training set in Table 3. ACC is entailment accuracy, r_P is Pearson's correlation, r_S is Spearman's correlation, MSE is mean squared error, MAE is mean absolute error, and RAE is relative absolute error. L uses the lemmatized corpora and R uses the true-cased corpora corresponding to regular. R+L correspond to the perspective using the features from both R and L, which doubles the number of features. We compute the entailment by SVC.

Data	Model	ACC	r_P	r_S	MSE	MAE	RAE
L	SVR	67.52	.7372	.6918	.6946	.5511	.6856
L	PLS-SVR	67.04	.7539	.6927	.6763	.5369	.668
R+L	PLS-SVR	66.76	.75	.6879	.6815	.539	.6705
R+L	SVR	66.66	.7295	.6814	.7027	.5591	.6956
L	PLS-RR	66.56	.7247	.6765	.7054	.5687	.7075

Table 3: SRE training results of the top 5 RTM systems selected.

SRE challenge results on the test set are given in Table 4. The setting R using PLS-SVR learning becomes the 8th out of 17 submissions when predicting the semantic relatedness and 17th out of 18 submissions when predicting the entailment.

Data	Model	ACC	r_P	r_S	RMSE	MAE	RAE
R	PLS-SVR	67.20	.7639	.6877	.655	.5246	.6645
R+L	PLS-SVR	67.65	.7688	.6918	.6492	.5194	.658
L	SVR	67.65	.7559	.6887	.664	.531	.6726
R+L	SVR	67.44	.7625	.6899	.6555	.5251	.6651
R	PLS-SVR	66.61	.7570	.6683	.6637	.5324	.6744

Table 4: RTM-DCU test results on the SRE task.

	Model	r_P	RMSE	MAE	RAE
Par2S	TREE	0.8013	0.8345	0.6277	0.5083
Par2S	PLS-TREE	0.7737	0.8824	0.673	0.5449
Par2S	SVR	0.7718	0.8863	0.6791	0.5499
S2Phrase	TREE	0.6756	0.9887	0.7746	0.6665
S2Phrase	PLS-TREE	0.6119	1.0616	0.8582	0.7384
S2Phrase	SVR	0.6059	1.0662	0.8668	0.7458
Phrase2W	TREE	0.201	1.3275	1.1353	0.9706
Phrase2W	RR	0.1255	1.3463	1.1594	0.9912
Phrase2W	SVR	0.0847	1.3548	1.1663	0.9972

Table 5: CLSS training results of the top 3 RTM systems for each subtask. Levels correspond to paragraph to sentence (Par2S), sentence to phrase (S2Phrase), and phrase to word (Phrase2W).

3.2 Task 3: Cross-Level Semantic Similarity

CLSS contains sentence pairs from different genres including text from newswire, travel, reviews, metaphoric text, community question answering sites, idiomatic text, descriptions, lexicographic text, and search. Official evaluation metric in CLSS is the sum of the Pearson's correlation scores for different levels [5]. CLSS task allows the submission of 3 entries per subtask. We present the performance of the top 3 individual RTM models on the training set in Table 5. RMSE is the root mean squared error. As the compared text size decrease, the performance decrease since it can become harder and more ambiguous to find the similarity using less context. RTM-DCU results on the CLSS challenge test set are provided in Table 6.

	Model	r_P	RMSE	MAE	RAE
Par2S	TREE	.8445	.7417	.5622	.4579
Par2S	PLS-TREE	.7847	.853	.6456	.5258
Par2S	SVR	.7858	.8428	.6539	.5325
S2Phrase	TREE	.75	.8827	.7053	.6255
S2Phrase	PLS-TREE	.6979	.9491	.7781	.69
S2Phrase	SVR	.6631	.9835	.7992	.7088
Phrase2W	TREE	.3053	1.3351	1.14	.9488
Phrase2W	RR	.2207	1.3644	1.1574	.9633
Phrase2W	SVR	.1712	1.3792	1.1792	.9815

Table 6: RTM-DCU test results on CLSS for the top 3 RTM systems for each subtask.

Table 7 lists the results along with their ranks for r_P and r_S, Spearman's correlation, out of CHECK submissions. The baseline in Table 7 is normalized longest common substring (LCS) scaled in the range $[0, 4]$. Top individual rank row lists the ranks in each subtask. We present the results for both our official and late (about 1 day) submissions including word to sense (W2S) results [6]. RTM-DCU is able to obtain the top result in Par2S in the CLSS task.

r_P	Par2S	S2Phrase	Phrase2W	W2S	Rank
LCS	0.527	0.562	0.165	0.109	25
Official	0.780	0.677	0.208		14
	0.747	0.588	0.164		19
	0.786	0.666	0.171		18
Late	0.845	0.750	0.305	0.109	6
	0.785	0.698	0.221	0.109	13
	0.786	0.663	0.171	0.109	17
Top Rank	1	5	3		
r_S	Par2S	S2Phrase	Phrase2W	W2S	Rank
LCS	0.527	0.562	0.165	0.13	23
Official	0.780	0.677	0.208		17
	0.747	0.588	0.164		22
	0.786	0.666	0.171		18
Late	0.829	0.734	0.295	0.13	8
	0.778	0.687	0.219	0.13	15
	0.778	0.667	0.166	0.13	16
Top Rank	1	5	5		

Table 7: RTM-DCU test results on CLSS.

3.3 Task 10: Multilingual Semantic Textual Similarity

MSTS contains sentence pairs from different domains: sense definitions from semantic lexical resources such as OnWN (from OntoNotes (Pradhan et al., 2007) and WordNet (Miller, 1995)) and FNWN (from FrameNet (Baker et al., 1998) and WordNet), news headlines, image descriptions, news title tweet comments, deft forum and news, paraphrases. Official evaluation metric in MSTS is the Pearson's correlation score.

MSTS task provides 7622 training instances and 3750 test instances. For the OnWN domain, 1316 training instances are available and therefore, we build a separate RTM model for this domain. Separate modeling of the OnWN dataset results with higher confidence scores on the test instances than we would obtain using the overall model to predict. MSTS task allows the submission of 3 entries per subtask. We present the performance of the top 3 individual RTM models on the training set in Table 8.

Lang		Model	r_P	RMSE	MAE	RAE
English		TREE	0.6931	1.0627	0.8058	0.6649
		PLS-TREE	0.6875	1.0753	0.8038	0.6632
		PLS-SVR	0.6884	1.0698	0.8157	0.6730
	OnWN	TREE	0.8094	0.9295	0.694	0.5245
		PLS-TREE	0.7953	0.9604	0.7203	0.5444
		PLS-SVR	0.7888	0.9779	0.7234	0.5468
Spanish		TREE	0.6513	0.7341	0.5904	0.7508
		PLS-TREE	0.4157	0.9007	0.7108	0.9039
		PLS-SVR	0.4239	1.1427	0.8293	1.0545

Table 8: MSTS training results on the English, English OnWN, and Spanish tasks.

RTM results on the MSTS challenge test set are provided in Table 9 along with the RTM results in STS 2013 (Biçici and van Genabith, 2013a). Table 10 and Table 11 lists the official results on English and Spanish tasks with rankings calculated according to weighted r_P, which weights according to the number of instances in each domain. RTM-DCU is able to become 10th in the OnWN domain and 19th overall out of 38 submissions in MSTS English and 18th out of 22 submissions in

[5] Giving advantage to participants submitting to all levels.

[6] W2S results for the late submission is obtained from the LCS baseline to calculate the ranks.

		Model	r_P	RMSE	MAE	RAE
English	deft-forum	TREE	.4341	1.4306	1.1609	1.0908
		PLS-TREE	.3965	1.4115	1.1472	1.078
		PLS-SVR	.3078	1.6277	1.3482	1.2669
	deft-news	TREE	.6974	1.1469	.9032	.8716
		PLS-TREE	.6811	1.1229	.8769	.8462
		PLS-SVR	.5562	1.2803	.9835	.9491
	headlines	TREE	.6199	1.1495	.9254	.7845
		PLS-TREE	.6125	1.1552	.9314	.7896
		PLS-SVR	.6301	1.1041	.8807	.7467
	images	TREE	.6995	1.2034	.9499	.7395
		PLS-TREE	.6656	1.2298	.9692	.7545
		PLS-SVR	.6474	1.4406	1.1057	.8607
	OnWN	TREE	.8058	1.3122	1.0028	.5585
		PLS-TREE	.7992	1.2997	.9815	.5467
		PLS-SVR	.8004	1.2913	.9449	.5263
	tweet-news	TREE	.6882	.9869	.831	.8093
		PLS-TREE	.6691	1.0101	.8433	.8213
		PLS-SVR	.5531	1.0633	.8653	.8427
Spanish	News	TREE	.7	1.5185	1.351	1.4141
		PLS-TREE	.6253	1.6523	1.4464	1.514
		PLS-SVR	.6411	1.554	1.3196	1.3813
	Wikipedia	TREE	.4216	1.5433	1.298	1.3579
		PLS-TREE	.3689	1.6655	1.4015	1.4662
		PLS-SVR	.4242	1.5998	1.3141	1.3748
STS 2013 English	headlines	L+S SVR	.6552	1.5649	1.2763	1.0231
		L+P+S SVR	.651	1.4845	1.1984	.9607
		L+P+S SVR TL	.6385	1.4878	1.2008	.9626
	OnWN	L+S SVR	.6943	1.7065	1.3545	.8255
		L+P+S SVR	.6971	1.6737	1.333	.8124
		L+P+S SVR TL	.6755	1.7124	1.3598	.8287
	SMT	L+S SVR	.3005	.8833	.6886	1.6132
		L+P+S SVR	.2861	.8810	.6821	1.598
		L+P+S SVR TL	.3098	.8635	.6547	1.5339
	FNWN	L+S SVR	.2016	1.2957	1.0604	1.2633
		L+P+S SVR	.118	1.4369	1.1866	1.4136
		L+P+S SVR TL	.1823	1.3245	1.0962	1.3059

Table 9: RTM-DCU test results on MSTS for the top 3 RTM systems for each subtask as well as RTM results in STS 2013 (Biçici and van Genabith, 2013a).

MSTS Spanish. The performance difference between MSTS English and MSTS Spanish may be due to the fewer training data available for the MSTS Spanish task, which may be decreasing the performance of our supervised learning approach.

3.4 RTMs Across Tasks and Years

We compare the difficulty of tasks according to the RAE levels achieved. RAE measures the error relative to the error when predicting the actual mean. A high RAE is an indicator that the task is hard. In Table 12, we list the RAE obtained for different tasks and subtasks, also listing RTM results in STS 2013 (Biçici and van Genabith, 2013a) and RTM results (Biçici and Way, 2014) on the quality estimation task (QET) (Bojar et al., 2014) where post-editing effort (PEE), human-targeted translation edit rate (HTER), or post-editing time (PET) of translations are predicted.

Model	Wikipedia	News	Weighted r_P	Rank
TREE	0.4216	0.7000	0.5878	18
PLS-TREE	0.3689	0.6253	0.5219	20
PLS-SVR	0.4242	0.6411	0.5537	19

Table 11: RTM-DCU test results on MSTS Spanish task. Rankings are calculated according to the weighted Pearson's correlation.

The best results are obtained for the CLSS Par2S subtask, which may be due to the larger contextual information that paragraphs can provide for the RTM models. For the SRE task, we can only reduce the error with respect to knowing and predicting the mean by about 35%. Prediction of bilingual similarity as in quality estimation of translation can be expected to be harder and RTMs achieve state-of-the-art performance in this task as well (Biçici and Way, 2014).

4 Conclusion

Referential translation machines provide a clean and intuitive computational model for automatically measuring semantic similarity by measuring the acts of translation involved and achieve to be the top on some semantic similarity tasks at SemEval-2014. RTMs make quality and semantic similarity judgments possible based on the retrieval of relevant training data as interpretants for reaching shared semantics.

Acknowledgments

This work is supported in part by SFI (07/CE/I1142) as part of the CNGL Centre for Global Intelligent Content (www.cngl.org) at Dublin City University, in part by SFI (13/TIDA/I2740) for the project "Monolingual and Bilingual Text Quality Judgments with Translation Performance Prediction" (www.computing.dcu.ie/~ebicici/Projects/TIDA_RTM.html), and in part by the European Commission through the QT-LaunchPad FP7 project (No: 296347). We also thank the SFI/HEA Irish Centre for High-End Computing (ICHEC) for the provision of computational facilities and support.

	Model	deft-forum	deft-news	headlines	images	OnWN	tweet-news	Weighted r_P	Rank
	TREE	.4341	.6974	.6199	.6995	.8058	.6882	.6706	20
	PLS-TREE	.3965	.6811	.6125	.6656	.7992	.6691	.6513	23
	PLS-SVR	.3078	.5562	.6301	.6475	.8004	.5531	.6076	27
	Top Rank	17	16	25	26	16	13		
With Conf.	TREE	.4181	.6846	.6216	.6981	.8331	.6870	.6729	19
With Conf.	PLS-TREE	.3831	.6739	.6094	.6629	.8260	.6691	.6534	23
With Conf.	PLS-SVR	.2731	.5526	.6330	.6441	.8246	.5683	.6110	26
With Conf.	Top Rank	18	18	23	27	10	14		

Table 10: RTM-DCU test results with ranks on MSTS English task.

Task	Subtask	Domain	Model	RAE
SRE	English	SICK	R PLS-SVR	.6645
			R+L PLS-SVR	.6580
			L SVR	.6726
			R+L SVR	.6651
			R PLS-SVR	.6744
CLSS	Par2S	Mixed	TREE	.4579
	S2Phrase		TREE	.6255
	Phrase2W		TREE	.9488
MSTS	English	deft-forum	PLS-TREE	1.078
		deft-news	PLS-TREE	.8462
		headlines	PLS-SVR	.7467
		images	TREE	.7395
		OnWN	PLS-SVR	.5263
		tweet-news	TREE	.8093
	Spanish	News	PLS-SVR	1.3813
		Wikipedia	TREE	1.3579
STS 2013	English	headlines	L+P+S SVR	.9607
		OnWN	L+P+S SVR	.8124
		SMT	L+P+S SVR TL	1.5339
		FNWN	L+S SVR	1.2633
QET PEE	Spanish-English	Europarl	FS-RR	.9000
	Spanish-English	Europarl	PLS-RR	.9409
	English-German	Europarl	PLS-TREE	.8883
	English-German	Europarl	TREE	.8602
	English-Spanish	Europarl	TREE	1.0983
	English-Spanish	Europarl	PLS-TREE	1.0794
	German-English	Europarl	RR	.8204
	German-English	Eurupaarl	PLS-RR	.8437
QET HTER	English-Spanish	Europarl	SVR	.8532
	English-Spanish	Europarl	TREE	.8931
QET PET	English-Spanish	Europarl	SVR	.7223
	English-Spanish	Europarl	RR	.7536

Table 12: Best RTM-DCU RAE test results for different tasks and subtasks as well as STS 2013 results (Biçici and van Genabith, 2013a) and results from quality estimation task of translation (Bojar et al., 2014; Biçici and Way, 2014).

References

Eneko Agirre, Carmen Banea, Claire Cardie, Daniel Cer, Mona Diab, Aitor Gonzalez-Agirre, Weiwei Guo, Rada Mihalcea, German Rigau, and Janyce Wiebe. 2014. SemEval-2014 Task 10: Multilingual semantic textual similarity. In *Proc. of the 8th International Workshop on Semantic Evaluation (SemEval-2014)*, Dublin, Ireland, August.

Collin F. Baker, Charles J. Fillmore, and John B. Lowe. 1998. The berkeley framenet project. In *Proc. of the 36th Annual Meeting of the Association for Computational Linguistics and 17th International Conference on Computational Linguistics - Volume 1*, ACL '98, pages 86–90, Stroudsburg, PA, USA.

Daniel Bär, Chris Biemann, Iryna Gurevych, and Torsten Zesch. 2012. Ukp: Computing semantic textual similarity by combining multiple content similarity measures. In **SEM 2012: The First Joint Conference on Lexical and Computational Semantics – Volume 1: Proc. of the main conference and the shared task, and Volume 2: Proc. of the Sixth International Workshop on Semantic Evaluation (SemEval 2012)*, pages 435–440, Montréal, Canada, 7-8 June. Association for Computational Linguistics.

Ergun Biçici and Josef van Genabith. 2013a. CNGL-

CORE: Referential translation machines for measuring semantic similarity. In **SEM 2013: The Second Joint Conference on Lexical and Computational Semantics*, Atlanta, Georgia, USA, 13-14 June. Association for Computational Linguistics.

Ergun Biçici and Josef van Genabith. 2013b. CNGL: Grading student answers by acts of translation. In **SEM 2013: The Second Joint Conference on Lexical and Computational Semantics and Proc. of the Seventh International Workshop on Semantic Evaluation (SemEval 2013)*, Atlanta, Georgia, USA, 14-15 June. Association for Computational Linguistics.

Ergun Biçici and Andy Way. 2014. Referential translation machines for predicting translation quality. In *Proc. of the Ninth Workshop on Statistical Machine Translation*, Baltimore, USA, June. Association for Computational Linguistics.

Ergun Biçici and Deniz Yuret. 2011a. Instance selection for machine translation using feature decay algorithms. In *Proc. of the Sixth Workshop on Statistical Machine Translation*, pages 272–283, Edinburgh, Scotland, July. Association for Computational Linguistics.

Ergun Biçici and Deniz Yuret. 2011b. RegMT system for machine translation, system combination, and evaluation. In *Proc. of the Sixth Workshop on Statistical Machine Translation*, pages 323–329, Edinburgh, Scotland, July. Association for Computational Linguistics.

Ergun Biçici and Deniz Yuret. 2014. Optimizing instance selection for statistical machine translation with feature decay algorithms. *IEEE/ACM Transactions On Audio, Speech, and Language Processing (TASLP)*.

Ergun Biçici, Declan Groves, and Josef van Genabith. 2013. Predicting sentence translation quality using extrinsic and language independent features. *Machine Translation*, 27:171–192, December.

Ergun Biçici, Qun Liu, and Andy Way. 2014. Parallel FDA5 for fast deployment of accurate statistical machine translation systems. In *Proc. of the Ninth Workshop on Statistical Machine Translation*, Baltimore, USA, June. Association for Computational Linguistics.

Ergun Biçici. 2011. *The Regression Model of Machine Translation*. Ph.D. thesis, Koç University. Supervisor: Deniz Yuret.

Ergun Biçici. 2013. Referential translation machines for quality estimation. In *Proc. of the Eighth Workshop on Statistical Machine Translation*, Sofia, Bulgaria, August. Association for Computational Linguistics.

Ergun Biçici. 2008. Consensus ontologies in socially interacting multiagent systems. *Journal of Multiagent and Grid Systems*.

Carl Hugo Björnsson. 1968. *Läsbarhet*. Liber.

Chris Bliss. 2012. Comedy is translation, February. http://www.ted.com/talks/chris_bliss_comedy_is_translation.html.

Ondřej Bojar, Christian Buck, Christian Federmann, Barry Haddow, Philipp Koehn, Matouš Macháček, Christof Monz, Pavel Pecina, Matt Post, Herve Saint-Amand, Radu Soricut, and Lucia Specia. 2014. Findings of the 2014 workshop on statistical machine translation. In *Proc. of the Ninth Workshop on Statistical Machine Translation*, Balrimore, USA, June. Association for Computational Linguistics.

Peter F. Brown, Stephen A. Della Pietra, Vincent J. Della Pietra, and Robert L. Mercer. 1993. The mathematics of statistical machine translation: Parameter estimation. *Computational Linguistics*, 19(2):263–311, June.

José Guilherme Camargo de Souza, Christian Buck, Marco Turchi, and Matteo Negri. 2013. FBK-UEdin participation to the WMT13 quality estimation shared task. In *Proc. of the Eighth Workshop on Statistical Machine Translation*, pages 352–358, Sofia, Bulgaria, August. Association for Computational Linguistics.

George Doddington. 2002. Automatic evaluation of machine translation quality using n-gram cooccurrence statistics. In *Proc. of the second international conference on Human Language Technology Research*, pages 138–145, San Francisco, CA, USA. Morgan Kaufmann Publishers Inc.

Pierre Geurts, Damien Ernst, and Louis Wehenkel. 2006. Extremely randomized trees. *Machine Learning*, 63(1):3–42.

Isabelle Guyon, Jason Weston, Stephen Barnhill, and Vladimir Vapnik. 2002. Gene selection for cancer classification using support vector machines. *Machine Learning*, 46(1-3):389–422.

Kenth Hagström. 2012. Swedish readability calculator. https://github.com/keha76/Swedish-Readability-Calculator.

David Jurgens, Mohammad Taher Pilehvar, and Roberto Navigli. 2014. SemEval-2014 Task 3: Cross-level semantic similarity. In *Proc. of the 8th International Workshop on Semantic Evaluation (SemEval-2014)*, Dublin, Ireland, August.

Roger Levy and Galen Andrew. 2006. Tregex and Tsurgeon: tools for querying and manipulating tree data structures. In *Proc. of the fifth international conference on Language Resources and Evaluation*.

Mitchell P. Marcus, Mary Ann Marcinkiewicz, and Beatrice Santorini. 1993. Building a large annotated corpus of english: the penn treebank. *Comput. Linguist.*, 19(2):313–330, June.

Marco Marelli, Stefano Menini, Marco Baroni, Luisa Bentivogli, Raffaella Bernardi, and Roberto Zamparelli. 2014a. SemEval-2014 Task 1: Evaluation of compositional distributional semantic models on full sentences through semantic relatedness and textual entailment. In *Proc. of the 8th International Workshop on Semantic Evaluation (SemEval-2014)*, Dublin, Ireland, August.

Marco Marelli, Stefano Menini, Marco Baroni, Luisa Bentivogli, Raffaella Bernardi, and Roberto Zamparelli. 2014b. A sick cure for the evaluation of compositional distributional semantic models. In *Proc. of LREC 2014*, Reykjavik, Iceland.

George A. Miller. 1995. WordNet: A lexical database for English. *Communications of the ACM*, 38(11):39–41, November.

Preslav Nakov and Torsten Zesch, editors. 2014. *Proc. of SemEval-2014 Semantic Evaluation Exercises - International Workshop on Semantic Evaluation*. Dublin, Ireland, 23-24 August.

Kishore Papineni, Salim Roukos, Todd Ward, and Wei-Jing Zhu. 2002. BLEU: a method for automatic evaluation of machine translation. In *Proc. of 40th Annual Meeting of the Association for Computational Linguistics*, pages 311–318, Philadelphia, Pennsylvania, USA, July.

Robert Parker, David Graff, Junbo Kong, Ke Chen, and Kazuaki Maeda. 2011. English Gigaword fifth edition, Linguistic Data Consortium.

Sameer S. Pradhan, Eduard H. Hovy, Mitchell P. Marcus, Martha Palmer, Lance A. Ramshaw, and Ralph M. Weischedel. 2007. Ontonotes: a unified relational semantic representation. *Int. J. Semantic Computing*, 1(4):405–419.

Yoav Seginer. 2007. *Learning Syntactic Structure*. Ph.D. thesis, Universiteit van Amsterdam.

Alex J. Smola and Bernhard Schölkopf. 2004. A tutorial on support vector regression. *Statistics and Computing*, 14(3):199–222, August.

A. J. Smola, N. Murata, B. Schölkopf, and K.-R. Müller. 1998. Asymptotically optimal choice of ε-loss for support vector machines. In L. Niklasson, M. Boden, and T. Ziemke, editors, *Proc. of the International Conference on Artificial Neural Networks*, Perspectives in Neural Computing, pages 105–110, Berlin. Springer.

Lucia Specia, Nicola Cancedda, Marc Dymetman, Marco Turchi, and Nello Cristianini. 2009. Estimating the sentence-level quality of machine translation systems. In *Proc. of the 13th Annual Conference of the European Association for Machine Translation (EAMT)*, pages 28–35, Barcelona, May. EAMT.

Kristina Toutanova, Dan Klein, Christopher D. Manning, and Yoram Singer. 2003. Feature-rich part-of-speech tagging with a cyclic dependency network. In *Proc. of the 2003 Conference of the North American Chapter of the Association for Computational Linguistics on Human Language Technology - Volume 1*, NAACL '03, pages 173–180, Stroudsburg, PA, USA. Association for Computational Linguistics.

Wikipedia. 2013. LIX. http://en.wikipedia.org/wiki/LIX.

David Graff Denise DiPersio Ângelo Mendonça, Daniel Jaquette. 2011. Spanish Gigaword third edition, Linguistic Data Consortium.

RTRGO: Enhancing the GU-MLT-LT System for Sentiment Analysis of Short Messages

Tobias Günther
Retresco GmbH
retresco.de
email@tobias.io

Jean Vancoppenolle
ferret go GmbH
ferret-go.com
jean.vcop@gmail.com

Richard Johansson
University of Gothenburg
www.svenska.gu.se
richard.johansson@gu.se

Abstract

This paper describes the enhancements made to our GU-MLT-LT system (Günther and Furrer, 2013) for the SemEval-2014 re-run of the SemEval-2013 shared task on sentiment analysis in Twitter. The changes include the usage of a Twitter-specific tokenizer, additional features and sentiment lexica, feature weighting and random subspace learning. The improvements result in an increase of 4.18 F-measure points on this year's Twitter test set, ranking 3rd.

1 Introduction

Automatic analysis of sentiment expressed in text is an active research area in natural language processing with obvious commercial interest. In the simplest formulation of the problem, sentiment analysis is framed as a categorization problem over documents, where the set of categories is typically a set of polarity values, such as positive, neutral, and negative. Many approaches to document-level sentiment classification have been proposed. For an overview see e.g. Liu (2012).

Text in social media and in particular microblog messages are a challenging text genre for sentiment classification, as they introduce additional problems such as short text length, spelling variation, special tokens, topic variation, language style and multilingual content. Following Pang et al. (2002), most sentiment analysis systems have been based on standard text categorization techniques, e.g. training a classifier using some sort of bag-of-words feature representation. This is also true for sentiment analysis of microblogs. Among the first to work specifically with Twitter[1] data were Go et al. (2009), who use emoticons as labels for the messages. Similarly, Davidov et al. (2010), Pak and Paroubek (2010), and Kouloumpis et al. (2011) use this method of distant supervision to overcome the data acquisition barrier. Barbosa and Feng (2010) make use of three different sentiment detection websites to label messages and use mostly non-lexical features to improve the robustness of their classifier. Bermingham and Smeaton (2010) investigate the impact of the shortness of Tweets on sentiment analysis and Speriosu et al. (2011) propagate information from seed labels along a linked structure that includes Twitter's follower graph. There has also been work on lexicon-based approaches to sentiment analysis of microblogs, such as O'Connor et al. (2010), Thelwall et al. (2010) and Zhang et al. (2011). For a detailed discussion see Günther (2013).

In 2013, the International Workshop on Semantic Evaluation (SemEval) organized a shared task on sentiment analysis in Twitter (Nakov et al., 2013) to enable a better comparison of different approaches for sentiment analysis of microblogs. The shared task consisted of two subtasks: one on recognizing contextual polarity of a given subjective expression (Task A), and one on document-level sentiment classification (Task B). For both tasks, the training sets consisted of manually labeled Twitter messages, while the test sets consisted of a Twitter part and an SMS part in order to test domain sensitivity. Among the best performing systems were Mohammad et al. (2013), Günther and Furrer (2013) and Becker et al. (2013), who all train linear models on a variety of task-specific features. In this year the corpus resources were used for a re-run of the shared task (Rosenthal et al., 2014), introducing two new Twitter test sets, as well as LiveJournal data.

[1] A popular microblogging service on the internet, its messages are commonly referred to as "Tweets."

Proceedings of the 8th International Workshop on Semantic Evaluation (SemEval 2014), pages 497–502,
Dublin, Ireland, August 23-24, 2014.

2 System Desciption

This section describes the details of our sentiment analysis system, focusing on the differences to our last year's implementation. This year we only participated in the subtask on whole message polarity classification (Subtask B).

2.1 Preprocessing

For **tokenization** of the messages we use the tokenizer of Owoputi et al. (2013)'s Twitter NLP Tools[2], which include a tokenizer and part-of-speech tagger optimized for the usage with Tweets. The tokenizer contains a regular expression grammar for recognizing emoticons, which is an especially valuable property in the context of sentiment analysis due to the high emotional expressiveness of emoticons.

It is well known that the way word tokens are represented may have a significant impact on the performance of a lexical classifier. This is particularly true in natural language processing of social media, where we run into the problem of spelling variation causing extreme lexical sparsity. To deal with this issue we **normalize** the tokens with the following technique: First, all tokens are converted to lowercase and the hashtag sign (#) is removed if present. If the token is not present in an English word list or any of the used sentiment lexica (see below), we remove all directly repeated letters after the first repetition (e.g. greeeeaaat → greeaat). If the resulting token is still not present in any of the lexical resources, we allow no direct repetition of letters at all. While this might lead to lexical collisions in some cases (e.g. goooodd → goodd → god), it is an easy and efficient way to remove some lexical sparsity. While generating all possible combinations of deletions and checking the resulting tokens against a lexical resource is another option, a correct disambiguation of the intended word would require a method making use of context knowledge (e.g. goooodd → good, vs. goooodd → god).

2.2 Features

We use the following set of features as input to our supervised classifier:

- The normalized tokens as **unigrams** and **bigrams**, where stopword and punctuation tokens are excluded from bigrams
- The **word stems** of the normalized tokens, reducing inflected forms of a word to a common form. The stems were computed using the Porter stemmer algorithm (Porter, 1980)
- The IDs of the token's **word clusters**. The clusters were generated by performing Brown clustering (Brown et al., 1992) on 56,345,753 Tweets by Owoputi et al. (2013) and are available online.[2]
- The presence of a hashtag or URL in the message (one feature each)
- The presence of a question mark token in the message
- We use the opinion lexicon by Bing Liu (Hu and Liu, 2004), the MPQA subjectivity lexicon (Wiebe et al., 2005) and the Twitrratr wordlist, which all provide a list of positive and negative words, to compute a prior polarity of the message. For each of the three **sentiment lexica** two features capture whether the majority of the tokens in the message were in the positive or negative sentiment list. The same is done for hashtags using the NRC hashtag sentiment lexicon (Mohammad et al., 2013).
- We apply special handling to features in a **negation** context. A token is considered as negated if it occurs after a negation word (up to the next punctuation). All token, stem and word cluster features are marked with a negation prefix. Additionally, the polarity for token in a negation context is inverted when computing the prior lexicon polarity.
- We use the **part-of-speech tags** computed by the part-of-speech tagger of the Twitter NLP tools by Owoputi et al. (2013) to **exclude** certain tokens. Assuming they do not carry any helpful sentiment information, no features are computed for token recognized as name (tag ^) or user mention (tag @).
- We also employ **feature weighting** to give more importance to certain features and indication of **emphasis** by the author. Normally, all features described above receive weight 1 if they are present and weight 0 if they are absent. For each of the following cases we add +1 to the weight of a token's unigram, stem and word cluster features:

[2] http://www.ark.cs.cmu.edu/TweetNLP

- The original (not normalized) token is all uppercase
- The original token has more than three adjacent repetitions of one letter
- The token is an adjective or emoticon (according to its part-of-speech tag)

Furthermore, the score of each token is divided in half, if the token occurs in a **question context**. A token is considered to be in a question context, if it occurs before a question mark (up to the next punctuation).

2.3 Machine Learning Methods

All training was done using the open-source machine learning toolkit *scikit-learn*[3] (Pedregosa et al., 2011). Just as in our last year's system we trained linear one-versus-all classifiers using stochastic gradient descent optimization with hinge loss and elastic net regularization.[4] For further details see Günther and Furrer (2013). The number of iterations was set to 1000 for the final model and 100 for the experiments.

It is widely observed that training on a lot of lexical features can lead to brittle NLP systems, that are easily overfit to particular domains. In social media messages the brittleness is particularly acute due to the wide variation in vocabulary and style. While this problem can be eased by using corpus-induced word representations such as the previously introduced word cluster features, it can also be addressed from a learning point of view. Brittleness can be caused by the problem that very strong features (e.g. emoticons) drown out the effect of other useful features.

The method of **random subspace learning** (Søgaard and Johannsen, 2012) seeks to handle this problem by forcing learning algorithms to produce models with more redundancy. It does this by randomly corrupting training instances during learning, so if some useful feature is correlated with a strong feature, the learning algorithm has a better chance to assign it a nonzero weight. We implemented random subspace learning by training the classifier on a concatenation of 25 corrupted copies of the training set. In a corrupted copy, each feature was randomly disabled with a probability of 0.2. Just as for the classifier, the hyperparameters were optimized empirically.

[3] Version 0.13.1, `http://scikit-learn.org`.

[4] `SGDClassifier(penalty='elasticnet', alpha=0.001, l1_ratio=0.85, n_iter=1000, class_weight='auto')`

3 Experiments

For the experiments and the training of the final model we used the joined training and development sets of subtask B. We were able to retrieve 10368 Tweets, of which we merged all samples labeled as objective into the neutral class. This resulted in a training set of 3855 positive, 4889 neutral and 1624 negative tweets. The results of the experiments were obtained by performing 10-fold cross-validation, predicting positive, negative and neutral class. Just as in the evaluation of the shared task the results are reported as average F-measure (F_1) between positive and negative class.

To be able to evaluate the contribution of the different features groups to the final model we perform an ablation study. By disabling one feature group at the time one can easily compare the performance of the model without a certain feature to the model using the complete feature set. In Table 1 we present the results for the feature groups bigrams (2gr), stems (stem), word clusters (wc), sentiment lexica (lex), negation (neg), excluding names and user mentions (excl), feature weighting (wei) and random subspace learning (rssl).

	Negative		**Positive**		**Avg.**
	Prec	**Rec**	**Prec**	**Rec**	$\mathbf{F_1}$
ALL	54.80	71.67	76.70	75.41	69.08
-2gr	-0.55	-0.49	-0.35	+0.20	-0.31
-stem	-1.47	-1.72	-0.49	-0.03	-0.92
-wc	-1.45	-1.60	-0.40	-1.66	-1.29
-lex	-1.73	**-5.11**	+1.06	-2.75	**-1.99**
-neg	**-1.90**	-3.14	**-1.30**	+0.36	-1.43
-excl	+0.31	-0.99	+0.59	+0.08	+0.08
-wei	-1.57	+0.43	-0.84	-0.34	-0.73
-rssl	+2.04	-4.37	+1.38	**-2.88**	-0.67

Table 1: Feature ablation study

Looking at Table 1, we can see that removing the sentiment lexica features causes the biggest drop in performance. This is especially true for the recall of the negative class, which is underrepresented in the training data and can thus profit the most from prior domain knowledge. When comparing to the features of our last year's system, it becomes clear that the used sentiment lexica can provide a much bigger gain in performance than the previously used SentiWordNet. Even though they are outperformed by the sentiment lexica, the word cluster features still provide an additional in-

	GU-MLT-LT (2013)			RTRGO (2014)		
	F_1 pos/neg	F_1 3-class	Accuracy	F_1 pos/neg	F_1 3-class	Accuracy
Twitter2013	65.42	68.13	70.42	**69.10**	70.92	72.54
Twitter2014	65.77	66.59	69.40	**69.95**	69.99	72.53
SMS2013	62.65	66.93	69.09	**67.51**	72.15	75.54
LiveJournal2014	68.97	68.42	68.39	**72.20**	72.29	72.33
Twitter2014Sarcasm	54.11	56.91	58.14	**47.09**	49.34	51.16

Table 2: Final results of our submissions on the different test sets (Subtask B)

crease in performance and can, in contrast to sentiment lexica, be learned in a completely unsupervised manner. Negation handling is an important feature to boost the precision of the classifier, while using random subspace learning increases the recall of the classes, which indicates that the technique indeed leads to more redundant models.

Another interesting question in sentiment analysis is, how machine learning methods compare to simple methods only relying on sentiment wordlists and how much training data is needed to outperform them. Figure 1 shows the results of a training size experiment, in which we tested classifiers, trained on different portions of a training set, on the same test set (10-fold cross validated). The two horizontal lines indicate the performance of two simple classifiers, using the Twitrratr wordlist (359 entries, labeled TRR) or Bing Liu opinion lexicon (6789 entries, labeled LIU) with a simple majority-vote strategy (choosing the neutral class in case of no hits or no majority and including a polarity switch for token in a negation context). The baseline of the machine learning classifiers is a logistic regression

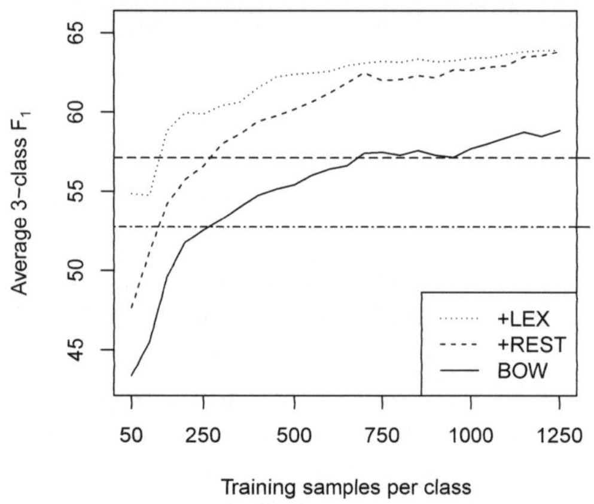

Figure 1: Training size experiment

classifier using only uni- and bigram features and negation handling (labeled BOW). To this baseline we add either the lexicon features for the Bing Liu opinion lexicon and the Twitrratr wordlist (labeled +LEX) or all other features described in section 2.2 excluding lexicon features (labeled +REST). Looking at the results, we can see that a simple bag of words classifier needs about 250 samples of each class to outperform the TRR list and about 700 samples of each class to outperform the LIU lexicon on the common test set. Adding the features that can be obtained without having sentiment lexica available (+REST) reduces the needed training samples about half. It is worth noting that from a training set size of 1250 samples per class the +REST-classifier is able to match the results of the classifier combining bag of words and lexicon features (+LEX).

4 Results and Conclusion

The results of our system are presented in Table 2, where the bold column marks the results relevant to our submission to this year's shared task. We also give results for our last year's system. Beside the average F-measure between positive and negative class, on which the shared task is evaluated, we also provide the results of both systems as average F-measure over all three classes and accuracy to create possibilities for better comparison to other research. In this paper we showed several ways to improve a machine learning classifier for the use of sentiment analysis in Twitter. Compared to our last year's system we were able to increase the performance about several F-measure points on all non-sarcastic datasets.

Acknowledgements

We would like to thank the organizers of the shared task for their effort, as well as the anonymous reviewers for their helpful comments on the paper.

References

Luciano Barbosa and Junlan Feng. 2010. Robust sentiment detection on twitter from biased and noisy data. In *Proceedings of the 23rd International Conference on Computational Linguistics: Posters*, pages 36–44. Association for Computational Linguistics.

Lee Becker, George Erhart, David Skiba, and Valentine Matula. 2013. Avaya: Sentiment analysis on twitter with self-training and polarity lexicon expansion. In *Second Joint Conference on Lexical and Computational Semantics (*SEM), Volume 2: Proceedings of the Seventh International Workshop on Semantic Evaluation (SemEval 2013)*, pages 333–340, Atlanta, Georgia, USA, June. Association for Computational Linguistics.

Adam Bermingham and Alan F Smeaton. 2010. Classifying sentiment in microblogs: is brevity an advantage? In *Proceedings of the 19th ACM international conference on Information and knowledge management*, pages 1833–1836. ACM.

Peter F Brown, Peter V Desouza, Robert L Mercer, Vincent J Della Pietra, and Jenifer C Lai. 1992. Class-based n-gram models of natural language. *Computational linguistics*, 18(4):467–479.

Dmitry Davidov, Oren Tsur, and Ari Rappoport. 2010. Enhanced sentiment learning using twitter hashtags and smileys. In *Proceedings of the 23rd International Conference on Computational Linguistics: Posters*, pages 241–249. Association for Computational Linguistics.

Alec Go, Richa Bhayani, and Lei Huang. 2009. Twitter sentiment classification using distant supervision. *CS224N Project Report, Stanford*.

Tobias Günther and Lenz Furrer. 2013. GU-MLT-LT: Sentiment analysis of short messages using linguistic features and stochastic gradient descent. In *Second Joint Conference on Lexical and Computational Semantics (*SEM), Volume 2: Proceedings of the Seventh International Workshop on Semantic Evaluation (SemEval 2013)*, pages 328–332, Atlanta, Georgia, USA, June. Association for Computational Linguistics.

Tobias Günther. 2013. Sentiment analysis of microblogs. Master's thesis, University of Gothenburg, June.

Minqing Hu and Bing Liu. 2004. Mining and summarizing customer reviews. In *Proceedings of the tenth ACM SIGKDD international conference on Knowledge discovery and data mining*, pages 168–177. ACM.

Efthymios Kouloumpis, Theresa Wilson, and Johanna Moore. 2011. Twitter sentiment analysis: The good the bad and the omg. In *Proceedings of the Fifth International AAAI Conference on Weblogs and Social Media*, pages 538–541.

Bing Liu. 2012. Sentiment analysis and opinion mining. *Synthesis Lectures on Human Language Technologies*, 5(1):1–167.

Saif Mohammad, Svetlana Kiritchenko, and Xiaodan Zhu. 2013. Nrc-canada: Building the state-of-the-art in sentiment analysis of tweets. In *Proceedings of the seventh international workshop on Semantic Evaluation Exercises (SemEval-2013)*, Atlanta, Georgia, USA, June.

Preslav Nakov, Sara Rosenthal, Zornitsa Kozareva, Veselin Stoyanov, Alan Ritter, and Theresa Wilson. 2013. Semeval-2013 task 2: Sentiment analysis in twitter. In *Second Joint Conference on Lexical and Computational Semantics (*SEM), Volume 2: Proceedings of the Seventh International Workshop on Semantic Evaluation (SemEval 2013)*, pages 312–320, Atlanta, Georgia, USA, June. Association for Computational Linguistics.

Brendan O'Connor, Ramnath Balasubramanyan, Bryan R Routledge, and Noah A Smith. 2010. From tweets to polls: Linking text sentiment to public opinion time series. In *Proceedings of the International AAAI Conference on Weblogs and Social Media*, pages 122–129.

Olutobi Owoputi, Brendan O'Connor, Chris Dyer, Kevin Gimpel, Nathan Schneider, and Noah A Smith. 2013. Improved part-of-speech tagging for online conversational text with word clusters. In *Proceedings of NAACL 2013*.

Alexander Pak and Patrick Paroubek. 2010. Twitter as a corpus for sentiment analysis and opinion mining. In *Proceedings of LREC*, volume 2010.

Bo Pang, Lillian Lee, and Shivakumar Vaithyanathan. 2002. Thumbs up?: sentiment classification using machine learning techniques. In *Proceedings of the ACL-02 conference on Empirical methods in natural language processing-Volume 10*, pages 79–86. Association for Computational Linguistics.

Fabian Pedregosa, Gaël Varoquaux, Alexandre Gramfort, Vincent Michel, Bertrand Thirion, Olivier Grisel, Mathieu Blondel, Peter Prettenhofer, Ron Weiss, Vincent Dubourg, Jake Vanderplas, Alexandre Passos, David Cournapeau, Matthieu Brucher, Matthieu Perrot, and Édouard Duchesnay. 2011. Scikit-learn: Machine learning in Python. *Journal of Machine Learning Research*, 12:2825–2830.

Martin F Porter. 1980. An algorithm for suffix stripping. *Program: electronic library and information systems*, 14(3):130–137.

Sara Rosenthal, Preslav Nakov, Alan Ritter, and Veselin Stoyanova. 2014. Semeval-2014 task 9: Sentiment analysis in twitter. In *Proceedings of the International Workshop on Semantic Evaluation (SemEval-2014)*, Dublin, Ireland, August.

Anders Søgaard and Anders Johannsen. 2012. Robust learning in random subspaces: Equipping NLP for OOV effects. In *COLING (Posters)*, pages 1171–1180.

Michael Speriosu, Nikita Sudan, Sid Upadhyay, and Jason Baldridge. 2011. Twitter polarity classification with label propagation over lexical links and the follower graph. In *Proceedings of the First Workshop on Unsupervised Learning in NLP*, pages 53–63. Association for Computational Linguistics.

Mike Thelwall, Kevan Buckley, Georgios Paltoglou, Di Cai, and Arvid Kappas. 2010. Sentiment strength detection in short informal text. *Journal of the American Society for Information Science and Technology*, 61(12):2544–2558.

Janyce Wiebe, Theresa Wilson, and Claire Cardie. 2005. Annotating expressions of opinions and emotions in language. *Language Resources and Evaluation*, 39(2-3):165–210.

Ley Zhang, Riddhiman Ghosh, Mohamed Dekhil, Meichun Hsu, and Bing Liu. 2011. Combining lexiconbased and learning-based methods for twitter sentiment analysis. *HP Laboratories, Technical Report HPL-2011-89.*

SA-UZH: Verb-based Sentiment Analysis

Nora Hollenstein, Michi Amsler, Martina Bachmann, Manfred Klenner
Institute of Computational Linguistics, University of Zurich
Binzmuehlestrasse 14, CH-8050 Zurich, Switzerland
{hollenstein,mamsler,bachmann,klenner}@ifi.uzh.ch

Abstract

This paper describes the details of our system submitted to the SemEval-2014 shared task about aspect-based sentiment analysis on review texts. We participated in subtask 2 (prediction of the polarity of aspect terms) and 4 (prediction of the polarity of aspect categories). Our approach to determine the sentiment of aspect terms and categories is based on linguistic preprocessing, including a compositional analysis and a verb resource, task-specific feature engineering and supervised machine learning techniques. We used a Logistic Regression classifier to make predictions, which were ranked above-average in the shared task.

1 Introduction

Aspect-based sentiment analysis refers to the problem of predicting the polarity of an explicit or implicit mention of a target in a sentence or text. The SemEval-2014 shared task required sentiment analysis of laptop and restaurant reviews on sentence level and comprised four subtasks (Pontiki et al., 2014). The organizers created and shared manually labelled domain-specific training and test data sets. Two of the four subtasks dealt with determining the sentiment of a given aspect term (explicitly mentioned) or aspect category (explicitly or implicitly mentioned) in a sentence. The subtasks we participated in do not include the recognition of aspects. Given the sentence *"The sushi rolls were perfect, but overall it was too expensive."*, *"sushi rolls"* is an aspect term, and the corresponding aspect categories are *"food"* and *"price"*. The correct predictions would be the following:

- Subtask 2 (aspect terms): {sushi rolls → *positive*}
- Subtask 4 (aspect categories): {food → *positive*, price → *negative*}

To solve these tasks, we introduce a Logistic Regression Model for target-specific sentiment analysis. Features are derived from a fine-grained polarity lexicon, a verb resource specifying expectations and effects of the verbs functional roles, and a compositional analysis. In our experiments on the restaurant and laptop reviews data for the SemEval-2014 shared task, we found that improvements over the baseline are possible for all classes except "conflict".

2 Related Work

We focus on the question whether fine-grained linguistic sentiment analysis improves target-specific polarity classification. Existing approaches to aspect-based sentiment detection have focused on different aspects of this task, e.g. the identification of targets and their components (Popescu and Etzioni, 2005) and sentence-level composition (Moilanen and Pulman, 2007). Ding et al. (2008) and Hu and Liu (2004) produced lexicon-based approaches, which perform quite well in a large number of domains, and Blair-Goldensohn et al. (2008) combined lexicon-based methods and supervised learning. Jiang et al. (2011) used a dependency parser to generate a set of aspect dependent features for classification. For our system we built a sentiment composition resembling the one of Läubli et al. (2012), which was developed for German. Moreover, our verb resource has some similarity with the one of Neviarouskaya et al. (2009): both rely on verb classes and utilize verb-specific

Proceedings of the 8th International Workshop on Semantic Evaluation (SemEval 2014), pages 503–507,
Dublin, Ireland, August 23-24, 2014.

behavior. However, only we specify the individual verb's (default) perspective on each role (and are, thus, able to count polar propagations). See also Reschke and Anand (2011), who describe in detail how polar (verb) complements combine to verb frame polarity (again without recording and using role perspectives as we do).

3 System Description

In this section we present the details of our sentiment analysis system. We used the same preprocessing and learning algorithm for both subtasks (2 & 4). Only the feature extraction was expanded in subtask 4 for determining the polarities of aspect categories (see section 3.3). The data sets consisted of restaurant and laptop reviews, which comprise about 3'000 manually classified target-specific sentences for each domain.

3.1 Sentiment Composition

The fundamental steps of our sentiment analysis system are parsing the sentences, rule-based sentiment analysis using a polarity lexicon and a verb resource, feature extraction and training a machine learning algorithm. In this section we will describe the composition of the lexicon as well as the structure of the sentiment composition pipeline.

Category	**Example**
POS strong	*"awesome"*
POS weak	*"adequate"*
NEG strong	*"catastrophe"*
NEG weak	*"demotivated"*
POS active	*"generous"*
POS passive	*"noteworthy"*
NEG active	*"rebellion"*
NEG passive	*"orphaned"*

Table 1: Additional categories in our fine-grained polarity lexicon

The same polarity lexicon was used for both domains. After mapping the polarities from the lexicon to the words and multi-word expressions, we calculated the polarity of nominal (NPs) and prepositional phrases (PPs) by means of lexical marking and the syntactic analysis of a dependency parser (Choi and Palmer, 2011). We did not implement any rules for neutral phrases, all words and phrases not marked as positive or negative are considered as neutral. In general, the polarities are propagated bottom-up to their respective heads of the NPs/PPs in composition with the subordinates. Shifters and negation words are also taken into account. The parser output is converted into a constraint grammar (CG) format for the subsequent analysis of words and phrases. To conduct this composition of polarity for the phrases we implemented a CG with the *vislcg3* tools (VISL-group, 2013). The next stage of our sentiment detection is the verb resource, which was also implemented with the *vislcg3* tools and will be explained in the next section.

3.2 Verb-based Sentiment Analysis

In order to combine the composition of the polar phrases with verb information, we encoded the impact of the verbs on polarity using three dimensions: effects, expectations and verb polarity. While effects should be understood as the outcome instantiated through the verb, expectations can be understood as anticipated polarities induced by the verb. Effects and expectations are assigned to subjects or objects, not to the verb itself. A positive or negative verb effect propagates from the verb to a subject or object if the latter receives the polarity of the verb. For a verb expectation, the subject or object is expected to be polar and thus receives a polarity even if the sentiment composition resulted neutral (see examples below). The verb polarity as such is the evaluation of the whole verbal phrase. Moreover, we process predicative and passive verbs, adapting the effects and expectations to the syntactic structure.

Since these effects and expectations match directly to the subject and objects of a sentence, they are of great use detecting the polarity of aspect terms (which are predominantly subjects or objects). We present the following examples extracted from the training data to illustrate three dimensions annotated by the verb analysis:

- Example of a positive effect on the direct object of a sentence induced by the verb: "I love (verb_POS) *the operating system and the preloaded software* (POS_EFF)."
- Example for a negative expectation on a prepositional object induced by the verb: "[...] the guy, who constantly complains (verb_NEG) *about the noise level* (NEG_EXP)."
- Example of positive predicative effects with an auxiliary, non-polar verb: "*Ser-*

vice (POS_predicative) is (verb_PRED) great, *takeout* (POS_predicative) is (verb_PRED) good too."

Furthermore, we make a distinction between the different prepositions a verb can invoke and the succeeding semantic changes. For example, the verb *"to die"* can be annotated in three different manners, depending on the prepositional object:

1. "My phone died (verb_NEG)."
2. "*Their pizza* (POS_EFF) is to die (verb_POS) **for**."
3. "He died (verb_NEG) **of** *cancer* (NEG_EXP)."

To summarize, in addition to verb polarity, we introduce effects and expectations to verb frames, which are determined through the syntactic pattern found, the bottom-up calculated phrase polarities and the meaning of the verb itself. We manually categorized approx. 300 of the most frequent positive and negative English verbs and their respective verb frames.

Laptop reviews

Feature	Occurrences	in %
Verbs effects	367	12.05
Verb expectations	6	0.02
Predicatives	298	9.78
Polar verbs	530	17.39

Restaurant reviews

Feature	Occurrences	in %
Verbs effects	246	8.09
Verb expectations	12	0.04
Predicatives	378	12.43
Polar verbs	521	17.13

Table 2: Occurrences and percentage of sentences of annotated polar verb features in the training data of the shared task

In table 2, we illustrate the relevance of the linguistic features of this verb resource by showing in how many sentences of the training set these annotations appear. Since we merely annotated the verb frames of the most frequent English verbs, it is conceivable that this resource may have a considerably greater effect if more domain-specific verbs are modelled.

After this final sentiment composition step, all derived polarity chunks are converted into a set of features for machine learning algorithms.

3.3 Feature Extraction

In a first step of our system, the sentences are parsed, phrase polarities are calculated and verb effects and expectations are assigned. Subsequently, a feature extractor, which extracts and aggregates polar information, operates on the output. The Simple Logistic Regression classifier from *weka* Hall et al. (2009) is then trained on these features.

We developed a feature extraction pipeline that retrieves information about various polarity levels in words, syntactic functions and phrases of the sentences in the data set. In order to use our sentiment composition approach for machine learning, we extract three different sets of features, resulting in a total of 32 features for subtask 2 and 39 features for subtask 4.

In short, the feature sets are constructed as follows:

- Lexicon-based features: These features comprise simple frequency counts of positive and negative words in the sentences and binary features showing whether any positive or negative, strong or active tokens are present at all. Furthermore, these features not only include absolute counts but also token ratios.

- Composition-based features: This feature set describes the information found in nominal, prepositional and verbal phrases, such as the number of positive/negative phrase heads or predicative verb effects found. It is also possible to distinguish between features which represent frequency counts and features which represent polarity ratios.

- Target-specific features: This set includes features from the previous two sets in connection with the aspect terms, e.g. whether the aspect term has a verb expectation or whether the aspect term is the head of a negative/positive phrase, the subject or direct object, etc. In this set we also include accumulative features that represent the complete amount of polar information in connection with an aspect term.

- *(only for subtask 4)* Category-specific features: These features are based on a cooccurrence analysis of the most frequent words used in each category. That is to say, we calculated the frequencies of all polar nouns, verbs and adjectives that appear in sentences of the same category in order to find category-specific words which have an influence on the polarity. This set includes features such as the number of category-specific words occurring in the sentence, etc.

For the classification of the aspect terms and categories of the sentences into the four classes (positive, negative, neutral and conflict), we trained a Simple Logistic Regression classifier on the features described above. We also explored other machine learning algorithms such as SVMs and artificial neural networks, however, the Logistic Regression proved to yield the best results.

4 Results & Discussion

In this section we present and discuss the results of our system in the SemEval 2014 shared task. The results of our submission for subtasks 2 and 4, compared to the majority baselines, can be found in table 3. Our system performs significantly better on restaurant reviews than on laptop reviews, probably due to the fact that our polarity lexicon comprises more restaurant-specific vocabulary than computer-specific vocabulary.

Subtask	Data	Baseline	Acc.
(2)	Laptops	47.06	58.30
(2)	Restaurants	57.8	70.98
(4)	Restaurants	59.84	73.10

Table 3: Shared-Task results for subtask 2 (aspect term polarity) and subtask 4 (aspect category polarity)

In both subtasks, calculating the polarity of the aspect terms and the aspect categories, the class *positive* scores better than the three other classes. In all data sets and all subtasks *positive* was the majority class of the four-partite classification: 42% in the aspect terms of the laptop reviews, 59% in the aspect terms and aspect categories of the laptop reviews equally (measured in the training data). Thus, it is not surprising that the most frequent error of our system is to categorize neutral aspect terms and categories as *positive*.

We do not achieve any improvements for the class *conflict*. The latter is very hard to detect, not only because this class is difficult to define but also because of the lack of training data given for this class. This could not be improved even though we included lexical features to address this particular class, for example, Boolean features showing whether an adversative conjunction is present in the sentence or whether the count of positive chunks equals the count of negative chunks in the same sentence. These features are in line with the theory that aspects are considered controversial if positive and negative occurrences are balanced and no polarity clearly prevails. Furthermore, the conflictive facet of a sentence is frequently not represented in the words (e.g. *"It has no camera, but I can always buy and install one easy."*; camera = *conflict*). Thus, it becomes challenging to generate features for this class *conflict* with a lexicon-based approach.

Furthermore, since our verb resource was newly implemented, there are still many verbs (especially domain-specific verbs) which will have to be modelled in addition to the most frequent English verbs included in the analysis by now. Another limitation of our current system is the fact that verb negation is not yet implemented: We process negation occurring in noun phrases (e.g. *"a not so tasty chicken curry"*), but not when the negation word relates to the verb (e.g. *"we didn't complain"*).

In summary, our aspect-based sentiment analysis pipeline takes into consideration many linguistic characteristics relevant for detecting opinion, and still provides the possibility to expand our compositional resources.

5 Conclusion

Given the above-average results obtained in the shared task system ranking, we conclude that the method for aspect-based sentiment analysis in review texts presented in this paper yields competitive results. We showed that the performance for this task can be improved by using linguistically motivated features for all classes except *conflict*.

We presented a supervised aspect-based sentiment analysis system to detect target-specific polarity with features derived from a fine-grained polarity lexicon, a verb resource and compositional analysis based on a dependency parser. Our results have shown that deeper linguistic analysis can positively influence the detection of target-specific polarities on sentence level in review texts.

Acknowledgements

We would like to thank the organizers of the shared task for their effort, as well as the reviewers for their helpful comments on the paper.

References

Sasha Blair-Goldensohn, Kerry Hannan, Ryan McDonald, Tyler Neylon, George A. Reis, , and Jeff Reynar. Building a sentiment summarizer for local service reviews. In *WWW Workshop on NLP in the Information Explosion Era*, 2008.

Jinho D. Choi and Martha Palmer. Getting the most out of transition-based dependency parsing. In *Proceedings of the 49th Annual Meeting of the Association for Computational Linguistics: Human Language Technologies*, HLT '11, pages 687–692, Stroudsburg, PA, USA, 2011. ACL.

Xiaowen Ding, Bing Liu, and Philip S. Yu. A holistic lexicon-based approach to opinion mining. In *Proceedings of the 2008 International Conference on Web Search and Data Mining*, WSDM '08, pages 231–240, New York, NY, USA, 2008. ACM.

Mark Hall, Eibe Frank, Geoffrey Holmes, Bernhard Pfahringer, Peter Reutemann, and Ian H. Witten. The weka data mining software: An update. *SIGKDD Explor. Newsl.*, 11(1):10–18, November 2009.

Minqing Hu and Bing Liu. Mining and summarizing customer reviews. In *Proceedings of the Tenth ACM SIGKDD International Conference on Knowledge Discovery and Data Mining*, KDD '04, pages 168–177, New York, NY, USA, 2004. ACM.

Long Jiang, Mo Yu, Ming Zhou, Xiaohua Liu, and Tiejun Zhao. Target-dependent twitter sentiment classification. In *Proceedings of the 49th Annual Meeting of the Association for Computational Linguistics*, pages 151–160. Association for Computational Linguistics, 2011.

Samuel Läubli, Mario Schranz, Urs Christen, and Manfred Klenner. Sentiment Analysis for Media Reputation Research. In *Proceedings of KONVENS 2012 (PATHOS 2012 workshop)*, pages 274–281, Vienna, Austria, 2012.

Karo Moilanen and Stephen Pulman. Sentiment composition. In *Proceedings of RANLP-2007*, pages 378–382, Borovets, Bulgaria, 2007.

Alena Neviarouskaya, Helmut Prendinger, and Mitsuru Ishizuka. *Semantically distinct verb classes involved in sentiment analysis*. IADIS AC (1), 2009.

Maria Pontiki, Dimitrios Galanis, John Pavlopoulos, Harris Papageorgiou, Ion Androutsopoulos, and Suresh Manandhar. SemEval-2014 Task 4: Aspect Based Sentiment Analysis. In *Proceedings of the 8th International Workshop on Semantic Evaluation (SemEval 2014)*, Dublin, Ireland, 2014.

Ana-Maria Popescu and Oren Etzioni. Extraction of product features and opinions from reviews. In *Proceedings of HLT-EMNLP-05*, pages 339–349, Vancouver, Canada, 2005.

Kevin Reschke and Pranav Anand. Extracting contextual evaluativity. In *Proceedings of the Ninth International Conference on Computational Semantics*, pages 370–374, 2011.

VISL-group. *http://beta.visl.sdu.dk/cg3.html*. Institute of Language and Communication (ISK), University of Southern Denmark, 2013.

SAIL-GRS: Grammar Induction for Spoken Dialogue Systems using CF-IRF Rule Similarity

Kalliopi Zervanou, Nikolaos Malandrakis and Shrikanth Narayanan
Signal Analysis and Interpretation Laboratory (SAIL),
University of Southern California, Los Angeles, CA 90089, USA
kzervanou@gmail.com, malandra@usc.edu , shri@sipi.usc.edu

Abstract

The SAIL-GRS system is based on a widely used approach originating from information retrieval and document indexing, the $TF\text{-}IDF$ measure. In this implementation for spoken dialogue system grammar induction, rule constituent frequency and inverse rule frequency measures are used for estimating lexical and semantic similarity of candidate grammar rules to a seed set of rule pattern instances. The performance of the system is evaluated for the English language in three different domains, travel, tourism and finance and in the travel domain, for Greek. The simplicity of our approach makes it quite easy and fast to implement irrespective of language and domain. The results show that the SAIL-GRS system performs quite well in all three domains and in both languages.

1 Introduction

Spoken dialogue systems typically rely on grammars which define the semantic frames and respective fillers in dialogue scenarios (Chen et al., 2013). Such systems are tailored for specific domains for which the respective grammars are mostly manually developed (Ward, 1990; Seneff, 1992). In order to address this issue, numerous current approaches attempt to infer these grammar rules automatically (Pargellis et al., 2001; Meng and Siu, 2002; Yoshino et al., 2011; Chen et al., 2013).

The acquisition of grammar rules for spoken language systems is defined as a task comprising of two subtasks (Meng and Siu, 2002; Iosif and Potamianos, 2007), the acquisition of:

(i) ***Low-level rules*** These are rules defining domain-specific entities, such as names of locations, hotels, airports, e.g. `CountryName:` "USA", `Date:` "July 15th, 2014", `CardType:` "VISA" and other common domain multi-word expressions, e.g. `DoYouKnowQ:` "do you know".

(ii) ***High-level rules*** These are larger, frame-like rule patterns which contain as semantic slot fillers multi-word entities identified by low-level rules. For example: `DirectionsQ:` "`<DoYouKnowQ>` `<where>` the `<MuseumName>` is located", `ExpressionCardProblem:` "my `<CardType>` has expired".

The shared task of *Grammar Induction for Spoken Dialogue Systems*, where our system participated, focused on the induction of high-level grammar rules and in particular on the identification and semantic classification of new rule patterns based on their semantic similarity to known rule instances.

Within this research framework, the work described in this paper proposes a methodology for estimating rule semantic similarity using a variation of the well-known measure of $TF\text{-}IDF$ as rule constituent frequency vs. inverse rule frequency, henceforth $CF\text{-}IRF$.

In the remainder of this paper, we start in Section 2 by a detailed description of our system. Subsequently, in Section 3, we present the datasets used and the evaluation process, and in Section 4 we discuss our results. We conclude in Section 5 with a summary of our observations and directions for future work.

2 System Description

The SAIL-GRS system is based on a widely used approach in information retrieval and document indexing, the $TF\text{-}IDF$ measure. $TF\text{-}IDF$ is

Proceedings of the 8th International Workshop on Semantic Evaluation (SemEval 2014), pages 508–511,
Dublin, Ireland, August 23-24, 2014.

an approach that has found numerous applications in information management applications, such as document keyword extraction, (e.g., Dillon and Gray (1983)), document clustering, summarisation, (e.g., Gong and Liu (2001)), event clustering, (e.g., De Smet and Moens (2013)). In dialogue systems, TF-IDF has been used, among other applications, for discovering local coherence (Gandhe and Traum, 2007) and for acquiring predicate-argument rule fragments in an open domain, information extraction-based spoken dialogue system (Yoshino et al., 2011). In their approach, Yoshino et al. (2011) use the TF-IDF measure to determine the importance of a given word for a given domain or topic, so as to select the most salient predicate-argument structure rule patterns from their corpus.

In our implementation for spoken dialogue system grammar induction, rule constituent frequency (CF) and inverse rule frequency (IRF) measures are used for estimating lexical and semantic similarity of candidate grammar rules to a seed set of rule pattern instances. As illustrated in Table 1, the SAIL-GRS algorithm has two main steps, the training stage and the rule induction stage.

Input: known rule pattern instances **Output:** new candidate rule patterns
Training stage:
1. Known rule instance parsing 2. Rule constituent extraction (uni-/bigrams) 3. Rule constituent frequency count (CF) 4. Inverse rule frequency count (IRF) 5. CF-IRF rule instance vector creation
Rule induction stage:
1. Unknown text fragment parsing 2. Unigram & bigram extraction 3. Uni-/bigram CF-IRF value lookup 4. Creation of CF-IRF vector for unknown text fragment 5. Estimation of cosine similarity of unknown fragment to rule instances 6. New candidate rule selection & rule semantic category classification using maximum cosine similarity

Table 1: The SAIL-GRS system algorithm.

In the first, the *Training stage*, known rule instances are parsed and, for each rule semantic category, the respective high-level rule pattern instances are acquired. These patterns are subsequently split into unigram and bigram constituents and the respective constituent frequencies and inverse rule frequencies are estimated. Finally, for each rule category, a vector representation is created for the respective rule pattern instance, based on the CF-IRF value of its unigram and bigram constituents.

In the second step, the *Rule induction stage*, the unknown text fragments are parsed and split into unigrams and bigrams. Subsequently, we lookup the known rule instance unigram and bigram representations for potential lexical matches to these new unigrams and bigrams. If these are found, then the new n-grams acquire the respective CF-IRF values found in the training instances and the respective CF-IRF vector for the unknown text fragments is created. Finally, we estimate the cosine similarity of this unknown text vector to each known rule vector. The unknown text fragments that are most similar to a given rule category are selected as candidate rule patterns and are classified in the known rule semantic category. An unknown text fragment that is selected as candidate rule pattern is assigned only to one, the most similar, rule category.

3 Experimental Setup

The overall objective in spoken dialogue system grammar induction is the fast and efficient development and portability of grammar resources. In the *Grammar Induction for Spoken Dialogue Systems* task, this challenge was addressed by providing datasets in three different domains, travel, tourism and finance, and by attempting to cover more than one language for the travel domain, namely English and Greek.

As illustrated in Table 2, the travel domain data for the two languages are comparable, with 32 and 35 number of known rule categories, for English and Greek, comprising of 982 and 956 high-level rule pattern instances respectively. The smallest dataset is the finance dataset, with 9 rule categories and 136 rule pattern instances, while the tourism dataset has a relatively low number of rule categories comprising of the highest number of rule pattern instances. Interestingly, as indicated in the column depicting the percent of unknown n-grams in the test-set, i.e. the unigrams and the bigrams without a CF-IRF value in the training data, the tourism domain test-set appears also to be the one with the greatest overlap with the training data, with a mere 0.72% and 4.84% of unknown unigrams and bigrams respectively.

For the evaluation, the system performance is estimated in terms of precision (P), recall (R) and $F\text{-}score$ measures, for the correct classification of an unknown text fragment to a given rule category cluster of pattern instances. In addition to these measures, the weighted average of the per rule scores is computed as follows:

$$P_w = \frac{\sum_{i=1}^{N-1} P_i c_i}{\sum_{i=1}^{N-1} c_i}, \quad R_w = \frac{\sum_{i=1}^{N-1} R_i n_i}{\sum_{i=1}^{N-1} n_i} \quad (1)$$

$$F_w = \frac{2 \cdot P_w \cdot R_w}{P_w + R_w} \quad (2)$$

where $N - 1$ is the total number of rule categories, P_i and R_i are the per rule i scores for precision and recall, c_i the unknown patterns correctly assigned to rule i, and n_i the total number of correct rule instance patterns for rule i indicated in the ground truth data.

4 Results

The results of the SAIL-GRS system outperform the Baseline in all dataset categories, except the Tourism domain, as illustrated in Table 3. In this domain, both systems present the highest scores compared to the other domains. The high results in the travel domain are probably due to the high data overlap between the train and the test data, as discussed in the previous section and illustrated in Table 2. However, this domain was also the one with the highest average number of rule instances per rule category, compared to the other domains, thus presenting an additional challenge in the correct classification of unknown rule fragments.

We observe that the overall higher F measures of the SAIL-GRS system in the travel and finance domains are due to higher precision scores, whereas Baseline system displays higher recall but lower precision scores and lower F-measure in these domains.

The overall lowest scores for both systems are reached in the Travel domain for Greek, which is also the dataset with the lowest overlap with the training data. However, the performance of the SAIL-GRS system does not deteriorate to the same extent as the Baseline, the precision of which falls to a mere 0.16-0.17, compared to 0.49-0.46 for the SAIL-GRS system.

5 Conclusion

In this work, we have presented the SAIL-GRS system used for the *Grammar Induction for Spoken Dialogue Systems* task. Our approach uses a fairly simple, language independent method for measuring lexical and semantic similarity of rule pattern instances. Our rule constituent frequency vs. inverse rule frequency measure, $CF\text{-}IRF$ is a modification the $TF\text{-}IDF$ measure for estimating rule similarity in the induction process of new rule instances.

The performance of our system in rule induction and rule pattern semantic classification was tested in three different domains, travel, tourism and finance in four datasets, three for English and an additional dataset for the travel domain in Greek. SAIL-GRS outperforms the Baseline in all datasets, except the travel domain for English. Moreover, our results showed that our system achieved an overall better score in precision and respective F-measure, in the travel and finance domains, even when applied to a language other than English. Finally, in cases of a larger percentage of unknown data in the test set, as in the Greek travel dataset, the smooth degradation of SAIL-GRS results compared to the Baseline indicates the robustness of our method.

A limitation of our system in its current version lies in the requirement for absolute lexical match with unknown rule unigrams and bigrams. Future extensions of the system could include rule constituent expansion using synonyms, variants or semantically or lexically similar words, so as to improve recall and the overall F-measure performance.

References

Yun-Nung Chen, William Yang Wang, and Alexander I. Rudnicky. 2013. Unsupervised induction and filling of semantic slots for spoken dialogue systems using frame-semantic parsing. In *Proceedings of the 2013 IEEE Workshop on Automatic Speech Recognition and Understanding*, pages 120–125.

Wim De Smet and Marie-Francine Moens. 2013. Representations for multi-document event clustering. *Data Mining and Knowledge Discovery*, 26(3):533–558.

Martin Dillon and Ann S. Gray. 1983. FASIT: A fully automatic syntactically based indexing system. *Journal of the American Society for Information Science*, 34(2):99–108.

Domain	High-Level Rule Categories #	Rule Patterns #		Test-set: Unknown n-grams %	
		Training-set	Test-set	Unigrams	Bigrams
Travel EN	32	982	284	5.13%	20.71%
Travel GR	35	956	324	17.26%	33.09%
Tourism EN	24	1004	285	0.72%	4.84%
Finance EN	9	136	37	12.35%	36.74%

Table 2: Characteristics of training and test datasets.

Domain	SAIL-GRS						Baseline					
	P	P_w	R	R_w	F	F_w	P	P_w	R	R_w	F	F_w
Travel EN	0.57	0.54	0.66	0.62	0.61	0.58	0.38	0.40	0.67	0.69	0.48	0.51
Travel GR	0.49	0.46	0.62	0.51	0.55	0.49	0.16	0.17	0.73	0.65	0.26	0.26
Tourism EN	0.75	0.75	0.90	0.90	0.82	0.82	0.82	0.80	0.94	0.94	0.87	0.87
Finance EN	0.67	0.78	0.62	0.78	0.65	0.78	0.40	0.48	0.63	0.78	0.49	0.60

Table 3: Evaluation results for SAIL-GRS system compared to the baseline in all four datasets in terms of per rule Precision P, Recall R, and F-score F. In the grey column, P_w, R_w, and F_w stand for the weighted average of the per rule precision, recall and F-score respectively, as defined in Equ. 1 and 2.

Sudeep Gandhe and David Traum. 2007. First steps towards dialogue modelling from an un-annotated human-human corpus. In *Proceedings of the Fifth IJCAI Workshop on Knowledge and Reasoning in Practical Dialogue Systems*, pages 22–27.

Yihong Gong and Xin Liu. 2001. Generic text summarization using relevance measure and latent semantic analysis. In *Proceedings of the 24th Annual International ACM SIGIR Conference on Research and Development in Information Retrieval*, SIGIR '01, pages 19–25, New York, NY, USA. ACM.

Elias Iosif and Alexandros Potamianos. 2007. A soft-clustering algorithm for automatic induction of semantic classes. In *Proceedings of the 8th Annual Conference of the International Speech Communication Association*, pages 1609–1612. ISCA.

Helen M. Meng and Kai-Chung Siu. 2002. Semi-automatic acquisition of semantic structures for understanding domain-specific natural language queries. *IEEE Transactions on Knowledge and Data Engineering*, 14(1):172–181.

Andrew N. Pargellis, Eric Fosler-Lussier, Alexandros Potamianos, and Chin-Hui Lee. 2001. Metrics for measuring domain independence of semantic classes. In *Proceedings of the 7th European Conference on Speech Communication and Technology*, pages 447–450. ISCA.

Stephanie Seneff. 1992. TINA: A natural language system for spoken language applications. *Computational Linguistics*, 18(1):61–86, March.

Wayne Ward. 1990. The CMU air travel information service: Understanding spontaneous speech. In *Speech and Natural Language: Proceedings of a Workshop Held at Hidden Valley, Pennsylvania*, pages 127–129.

Koichiro Yoshino, Shinsuke Mori, and Tatsuya Kawahara. 2011. Spoken dialogue system based on information extraction using similarity of predicate argument structures. In *Proceedings of the SIGDIAL 2011 Conference*, pages 59–66.

SAIL: Sentiment Analysis using Semantic Similarity and Contrast Features

Nikolaos Malandrakis, Michael Falcone, Colin Vaz, Jesse Bisogni, Alexandros Potamianos, Shrikanth Narayanan
Signal Analysis and Interpretation Laboratory (SAIL), USC, Los Angeles, CA 90089, USA
{malandra,mfalcone,cvaz,jbisogni}@usc.edu,
potam@telecom.tuc.gr, shri@sipi.usc.edu

Abstract

This paper describes our submission to SemEval2014 Task 9: Sentiment Analysis in Twitter. Our model is primarily a lexicon based one, augmented by some preprocessing, including detection of Multi-Word Expressions, negation propagation and hashtag expansion and by the use of pairwise semantic similarity at the tweet level. Feature extraction is repeated for sub-strings and contrasting sub-string features are used to better capture complex phenomena like sarcasm. The resulting supervised system, using a Naive Bayes model, achieved high performance in classifying entire tweets, ranking 7th on the main set and 2nd when applied to sarcastic tweets.

1 Introduction

The analysis of the emotional content of text is relevant to numerous natural language processing (NLP), web and multi-modal dialogue applications. In recent years the increased popularity of social media and increased availability of relevant data has led to a focus of scientific efforts on the emotion expressed through social media, with Twitter being the most common subject.

Sentiment analysis in Twitter is usually performed by combining techniques used for related tasks, like word-level (Esuli and Sebastiani, 2006; Strapparava and Valitutti, 2004) and sentence-level (Turney and Littman, 2002; Turney and Littman, 2003) emotion extraction. Twitter however does present specific challenges: the breadth of possible content is virtually unlimited, the writing style is informal, the use of orthography and grammar can be "unconventional" and there are unique artifacts like hashtags. Computation systems, like those submitted to SemEval 2013 task 2 (Nakov et al., 2013) mostly use bag-of-words models with specific features added to model emotion indicators like hashtags and emoticons (Davidov et al., 2010).

This paper describes our submissions to SemEval 2014 task 9 (Rosenthal et al., 2014), which deals with sentiment analysis in twitter. The system is an expansion of our submission to the same task in 2013 (Malandrakis et al., 2013a), which used only token rating statistics as features. We expanded the system by using multiple lexica and more statistics, added steps to the pre-processing stage (including negation and multi-word expression handling), incorporated pairwise tweet-level semantic similarities as features and finally performed feature extraction on substrings and used the partial features as indicators of irony, sarcasm or humor.

2 Model Description

2.1 Preprocessing

POS-tagging / Tokenization was performed using the ARK NLP tweeter tagger (Owoputi et al., 2013), a Twitter-specific tagger.

Negations were detected using the list from Christopher Potts' tutorial. All tokens up to the next punctuation were marked as negated.

Hashtag expansion into word strings was performed using a combination of a word insertion Finite State Machine and a language model. A normalized perplexity threshold was used to detect if the output was a "proper" English string and expansion was not performed if it was not.

Multi-word Expressions (MWEs) were detected using the MIT jMWE library (Kulkarni and Finlayson, 2011). MWEs are non-compositional expressions (Sag et al., 2002), which should be

Proceedings of the 8th International Workshop on Semantic Evaluation (SemEval 2014), pages 512–516,
Dublin, Ireland, August 23-24, 2014.

handled as a single token instead of attempting to reconstruct their meaning from their parts.

2.2 Lexicon-based features

The core of the system was formed by the lexicon-based features. We used a total of four lexica and some derivatives.

2.2.1 Third party lexica

We used three third party affective lexica.

SentiWordNet (Esuli and Sebastiani, 2006) provides continuous positive, negative and neutral ratings for each sense of every word in WordNet. We created two versions of SentiWordNet: one where ratings are averaged over all senses of a word (e.g., one ratings for "good") and one where ratings are averaged over lexeme-pos pairs (e.g., one rating for the adjective "good" and one for the noun "good").

NRC Hashtag (Mohammad et al., 2013) Sentiment Lexicon provides continuous polarity ratings for tokens, generated from a collection of tweets that had a positive or a negative word hashtag.

Sentiment140 (Mohammad et al., 2013) Lexicon provides continuous polarity ratings for tokens, generated from the sentiment140 corpus of 1.6 million tweets, with emoticons used as positive and negative labels.

2.2.2 Emotiword: expansion and adaptation

To create our own lexicon we used an automated algorithm of affective lexicon expansion based on the one presented in (Malandrakis et al., 2011; Malandrakis et al., 2013b), which in turn is an expansion of (Turney and Littman, 2002).

We assume that the continuous (in $[-1, 1]$) valence, arousal and dominance ratings of any term t_j can be represented as a linear combination of its semantic similarities d_{ij} to a set of seed words w_i and the known affective ratings of these words $v(w_i)$, as follows:

$$\hat{v}(t_j) = a_0 + \sum_{i=1}^{N} a_i \, v(w_i) \, d_{ij}, \qquad (1)$$

where a_i is the weight corresponding to seed word w_i (that is estimated as described next). For the purposes of this work, d_{ij} is the cosine similarity between context vectors computed over a corpus of 116 million web snippets (up to 1000 for each word in the Aspell spellchecker) collected using the Yahoo! search engine.

Given the starting, manually annotated, lexicon Affective Norms for English Words (Bradley and Lang, 1999) we selected 600 out of the 1034 words contained in it to serve as seed words and all 1034 words to act as the training set and used Least Squares Estimation to estimate the weights a_i. Seed word selection was performed by a simple heuristic: we want seed words to have extreme affective ratings (high absolute value) and the set to be close to balanced (sum of seed ratings equal to zero). The equation learned was used to generate ratings for any new terms.

The lexicon created by this method is task-independent, since both the starting lexicon and the raw text corpus are task-independent. To create task-specific lexica we used corpus filtering on the 116 million sentences to select ones that match our domain, using either a normalized perplexity threshold (using a maximum likelihood trigram model created from the training set tweets) or a combination of pragmatic constraints (keywords with high mutual information with the task) and perplexity threshold (Malandrakis et al., 2014). Then we re-calculated semantic similarities on the filtered corpora. In total we created three lexica: a task-independent (base) version and two adapted versions (filtered by perplexity alone and filtered by combining pragmatics and perplexity), all containing valence, arousal and dominance token ratings.

2.2.3 Statistics extraction

The lexica provide up to 17 ratings for each token. To extract tweet-level features we used simple statistics and selection criteria. First, all token unigrams and bigrams contained in a tweet were collected. Some of these n-grams were selected based on a criterion: POS tags, whether a token is (part of) a MWE, is negated or was expanded from a hashtag. The criteria were applied separately to token unigrams and token bigrams (POS tags only applied to unigrams). Then ratings statistics were extracted from the selected n-grams: length (cardinality), min, max, max amplitude, sum, average, range (max minus min), standard deviation and variance. We also created normalized versions by dividing by the same statistics calculated over all tokens, e.g., the maximum of adjectives over the maximum of all unigrams. The results of this process are features like "maximum of Emotiword valence over unigram adjectives" and "average of SentiWordNet objectivity among MWE bigrams".

2.3 Tweet-level similarity ratings

Our lexicon was formed under the assumption that semantic similarity implies affective similarity, which should apply to larger lexical units like entire tweets. To estimate semantic similarity scores between tweets we used the publicly available TakeLab semantic similarity toolkit (Šarić et al., 2012) which is based on a submission to SemEval 2012 task 6 (Agirre et al., 2012). We used the data of SemEval 2012 task 6 to train three semantic similarity models corresponding to the three datasets of that task, plus an overall model. Using these models we created four similarity ratings between each tweet of interest and each tweet in the training set. These similarity ratings were used as features of the final model.

2.4 Character features

Capitalization features are frequencies and relative frequencies at the word and letter level, extracted from all words that either start with a capital letter, have a capital letter in them (but the first letter is non-capital) or are in all capital letters.
Punctuation features are frequencies, relative frequencies and punctuation unigrams.
Character repetition features are frequencies, relative frequencies and longest string statistics of words containing a repetition of the same letter.
Emoticon features are frequencies, relative frequencies, and emoticon unigrams.

2.5 Contrast features

Cognitive Dissonance is an important phenomenon associated with complex linguistic cases like sarcasm, irony and humor (Reyes et al., 2012). To estimate it we used a simple approach, inspired by one-liner joke detection: we assumed that the final few tokens of each tweet (the "suffix") *contrast* the rest of the tweet (the "prefix") and created split versions of the tweet where the last N tokens are the suffix and all other tokens are the prefix, for $N = 2$ and $N = 3$. We repeated the feature extraction process for all features mentioned above (except for the semantic similarity features) for the prefix and suffix, nearly tripling the total number of features.

2.6 Feature selection and Training

The extraction process lead to tens of thousands of candidate features, so we performed forward stepwise feature selection using a correlation criterion (Hall, 1999) and used the resulting set of 222 features to train a model. The model chosen is a Naive Bayes tree, a tree with Naive Bayes classifiers on each leaf. The motivation comes from considering this a two stage problem: subjectivity detection and polarity classification, making a hierarchical model a natural choice. The feature selection and model training/classification was conducted using Weka (Witten and Frank, 2000).

Table 1: Performance and rank achieved by our submission for all datasets of subtasks A and B.

task	dataset	avg. F1	rank
A	LJ2014	70.62	16
	SMS2013	74.46	16
	TW2013	78.47	14
	TW2014	76.89	13
	TW2014SC	65.56	15
B	LJ2014	69.34	15
	SMS2013	56.98	24
	TW2013	66.80	10
	TW2014	67.77	7
	TW2014SC	57.26	2

Table 2: Selected features for subtask B.

Features	number
Lexicon-derived	178
By lexicon	
Ewrd / S140 / SWNet / NRC	71 / 53 / 33 / 21
By POS tag	
all (ignore tag)	103
adj / verb / proper noun	25 / 11 / 11
other tags	28
By function	
avg / min / sum / max	45 / 40 / 38 / 26
other functions	29
Semantic similarity	29
Punctuation	7
Emoticon	5
Other features	3
Contrast	72
prefix / suffix	54 / 18

3 Results

We took part in subtasks A and B of SemEval 2014 task 9, submitting constrained runs trained with the data the task organizers provided. Subtask B was the priority and the subtask A model was created as an afterthought: it only uses the lexicon-based and morphology features for the target string and the entire tweet as features of an NB Tree.

The overall performance of our submission on all datasets (LiveJournal, SMS, Twitter 2013, Twitter 2014 and Twitter 2014 Sarcasm) can be seen in Table 1. The subtask A system performed

Table 3: Performance on all data sets of subtask B after removing 1 set of features. Performance difference with the complete system listed if greater than 1%.

Features removed	LJ2014		SMS2013		TW2013		TW2014		TW2014SC	
	avg. F1	diff	avg. F1	diff	avg. F1	diff	avg. F1	diff	avg. F1	diff
None (Submitted)	69.3		57.0		**66.8**		67.8		57.3	
Lexicon-derived	43.6	-25.8	38.2	-18.8	49.5	-17.4	51.5	-16.3	43.5	-13.8
Emotiword	67.5	-1.9	56.4		63.5	-3.3	66.1	-1.7	54.8	-2.5
Base	68.4		56.3		65.0	-1.9	66.4	-1.4	**59.6**	2.3
Adapted	69.3		57.4		66.7		67.5		50.8	-6.5
Sentiment140	68.1	-1.3	54.5	-2.5	64.4	-2.4	64.2	-3.6	45.4	-11.9
NRC Tag	**70.6**	1.3	**58.5**	1.6	66.3		66.0	-1.7	55.3	-2.0
SentiWordNet	68.7		56.0		66.2		**68.1**		52.7	-4.6
per Lexeme	69.3		56.7		66.1		68.0		52.7	-4.5
per Lexeme-POS	68.8		57.1		66.7		67.4		55.0	-2.2
Semantic Similarity	69.0		58.2	1.2	64.9	-2.0	65.5	-2.2	52.2	-5.0
Punctuation	69.7		57.4		66.6		67.1		53.9	-3.4
Emoticon	69.3		57.0		**66.8**		67.8		57.3	
Contrast	69.2		57.5		66.7		67.0		51.9	-5.4
Prefix	69.5		57.2		**66.8**		67.2		47.4	-9.9
Suffix	68.6		57.2		66.5		67.9		56.3	

badly, ranking near the bottom (among 20 submissions) on all datasets, a result perhaps expected given the limited attention we gave to the model. The subtask B system did very well on the three Twitter datasets, ranking near the top (among 42 teams) on all three sets and placing second on the sarcastic tweets set, but did notably worse on the two non-Twitter sets.

A compact list of the features selected by the subtask B system can be seen in Table 2. The majority of features (178 of 222) are lexicon-based, 29 are semantic similarities to known tweets and the rest are mainly punctuation and emoticon features. The lexicon-based features mostly come from Emotiword, though that is probably because Emotiword contains a rating for every unigram and bigram in the tweets, unlike the other lexica. The most important part-of-speech tags are adjectives and verbs, as expected, with proper nouns being also highly important, presumably as indicators of attribution. Still, most features are calculated over all tokens (including stop words). Finally it is worth noting the 72 contrast features selected.

We also conducted a set of experiments using partial feature sets: each time we use all features minus one set, then apply feature selection and classification. The results are presented in Table 3. As expected, the lexicon-based features are the most important ones by a wide margin though the relative usefulness of the lexica changes depending on the dataset: the twitter-specific NRC lexicon actually hurts performance on non-tweets, while the task-independent Emotiword hurts performance on the sarcastic tweets set. Overall though using all is the optimal choice. Among the other features only semantic similarity provides a relatively consistent improvement.

A lot of features provide very little benefit on most sets, but virtually everything is important for the sarcasm set. Lexica, particularly the twitter specific ones like Sentiment 140 and the adapted version of Emotiword make a big difference, perhaps indicating some domain-specific aspects of sarcasm expression (though such assumptions are shaky at best due to the small size of the test set). The contrast features perform their intended function well, providing a large performance boost when dealing with sarcastic tweets and perhaps explaining our high ranking on that dataset.

Overall the subtask B system performed very well and the semantic similarity features and contrast features provide potential for further growth.

4 Conclusions

We presented a system of twitter sentiment analysis combining lexicon-based features with semantic similarity and contrast features. The system proved very successful, achieving high ranks among all competing systems in the tasks of sentiment analysis of generic and sarcastic tweets.

Future work will focus on the semantic similarity and contrast features by attempting more accurately estimate semantic similarity and using some more systematic way of identifying the "contrasting" text areas.

References

Eneko Agirre, Mona Diab, Daniel Cer, and Aitor Gonzalez-Agirre. 2012. SemEval-2012 Task 6: A pilot on semantic textual similarity. In *proc. SemEval*, pages 385–393.

Margaret Bradley and Peter Lang. 1999. Affective Norms for English Words (ANEW): Stimuli, instruction manual and affective ratings. technical report C-1. The Center for Research in Psychophysiology, University of Florida.

Dmitry Davidov, Oren Tsur, and Ari Rappoport. 2010. Enhanced sentiment learning using Twitter hashtags and smileys. In *Proc. COLING*, pages 241–249.

Andrea Esuli and Fabrizio Sebastiani. 2006. SENTIWORDNET: A publicly available lexical resource for opinion mining. In *Proc. LREC*, pages 417–422.

Mark A. Hall. 1999. *Correlation-based feature selection for machine learning*. Ph.D. thesis, The University of Waikato.

Nidhi Kulkarni and Mark Alan Finlayson. 2011. jMWE: A java toolkit for detecting multi-word expressions. In *proc. Workshop on Multiword Expressions*, pages 122–124.

Nikolaos Malandrakis, Alexandros Potamianos, Elias Iosif, and Shrikanth Narayanan. 2011. Kernel models for affective lexicon creation. In *Proc. Interspeech*, pages 2977–2980.

Nikolaos Malandrakis, Abe Kazemzadeh, Alexandros Potamianos, and Shrikanth Narayanan. 2013a. SAIL: A hybrid approach to sentiment analysis. In *proc. SemEval*, pages 438–442.

Nikolaos Malandrakis, Alexandros Potamianos, Elias Iosif, and Shrikanth Narayanan. 2013b. Distributional semantic models for affective text analysis. *Audio, Speech, and Language Processing, IEEE Transactions on*, 21(11):2379–2392.

Nikolaos Malandrakis, Alexandros Potamianos, Kean J. Hsu, Kalina N. Babeva, Michelle C. Feng, Gerald C. Davison, and Shrikanth Narayanan. 2014. Affective language model adaptation via corpus selection. In *proc. ICASSP*, pages 4871–4874.

Saif Mohammad, Svetlana Kiritchenko, and Xiaodan Zhu. 2013. NRC-Canada: Building the state-of-the-art in sentiment analysis of tweets. In *proc. SemEval*, pages 321–327.

Preslav Nakov, Zornitsa Kozareva, Alan Ritter, Sara Rosenthal, Veselin Stoyanov, and Theresa Wilson. 2013. SemEval-2013 Task 2: Sentiment analysis in Twitter. In *Proc. SemEval*, pages 312–320.

Olutobi Owoputi, Brendan O'Connor, Chris Dyer, Kevin Gimpel, Nathan Schneider, and Noah A. Smith. 2013. Improved part-of-speech tagging for online conversational text with word clusters. In *proc. NAACL*, pages 380–390.

Antonio Reyes, Paolo Rosso, and Davide Buscaldi. 2012. From humor recognition to irony detection: The figurative language of social media. *Data & Knowledge Engineering*, 74(0):1 – 12.

Sara Rosenthal, Preslav Nakov, Alan Ritter, and Veselin Stoyanov. 2014. SemEval-2014 Task 9: Sentiment analysis in Twitter. In *Proc. SemEval*.

Ivan A. Sag, Timothy Baldwin, Francis Bond, Ann A. Copestake, and Dan Flickinger. 2002. Multiword expressions: A pain in the neck for NLP. In *Computational Linguistics and Intelligent Text Processing*, volume 2276 of *Lecture Notes in Computer Science*, pages 189–206.

Carlo Strapparava and Alessandro Valitutti. 2004. WordNet-Affect: an affective extension of WordNet. In *Proc. LREC*, volume 4, pages 1083–1086.

Peter D. Turney and Michael L. Littman. 2002. Unsupervised learning of semantic orientation from a hundred-billion-word corpus. technical report ERC-1094 (NRC 44929). National Research Council of Canada.

Peter D. Turney and Michael L. Littman. 2003. Measuring praise and criticism: Inference of semantic orientation from association. *ACM Transactions on Information Systems*, 21:315–346.

Frane Šarić, Goran Glavaš, Mladen Karan, Jan Šnajder, and Bojana Dalbelo Bašić. 2012. Takelab: Systems for measuring semantic text similarity. In *proc. SemEval*, pages 441–448.

Ian H. Witten and Eibe Frank. 2000. *Data Mining: Practical Machine Learning Tools and Techniques*. Morgan Kaufmann.

SAP-RI: A Constrained and Supervised Approach for Aspect-Based Sentiment Analysis

Nishtha Malhotra[1,2]*, **Akriti Vij**[1,2,*], **Naveen Nandan**[1] and **Daniel Dahlmeier**[1]
[1]Research & Innovation, SAP Asia, Singapore
[2]Nanyang Technological University, Singapore
{nishtha.malhotra,akriti.vij,naveen.nandan,d.dahlmeier}@sap.com

Abstract

We describe the submission of the SAP Research & Innovation team to the SemEval 2014 Task 4: Aspect-Based Sentiment Analysis (ABSA). Our system follows a constrained and supervised approach for aspect term extraction, categorization and sentiment classification of online reviews and the details are included in this paper.

1 Introduction

The increasing popularity of the internet as a source of information, and e-commerce as a way of life, has led to a major surge in the number of reviews that can be found online, for a wide range of products and services. Consequently, more and more consumers have taken to consulting these online reviews as part of their pre-purchase research before deciding on availing services from a local business or investing in a product from a particular brand. This calls for innovative techniques for the sentiment analysis of online reviews so as to generate accurate and relevant recommendations.

Sentiment analysis has been extensively studied and applied in different domains. Predicting the sentiment polarity (*positive, negative, neutral*) of user opinions by mining user reviews (Hu and Liu, 2004; Liu, 2012; Pang and Lee, 2008; Liu, 2010) has been of high commercial and research interest. In these studies, sentiment analysis is often conducted at one of the three levels: *document level*, *sentence level* or *attribute level*.

Through the SemEval 2014 Task 4 on *Aspect Based Sentiment Analysis* (Pontiki et al., 2014), we explore sentiment analysis at the aspect level. The task consists of four subtasks: in subtask 1 *aspect term extraction*, participants need to identify the aspect terms present in a sentence and return a list containing all distinct aspect terms, in subtask 2 *aspect term polarity*, participants were to determine the polarity of each aspect term in a sentence, in subtask 3 *aspect category detection*, participants had to identify the aspect categories discussed in a given sentence, and in subtask 4 *aspect category polarity*, participants were to determine the polarity of each aspect category. The polarity classification subtasks consider sentiment analysis to be a three-way classification problem between positive, negative and neutral sentiment. On the other hand, the aspect category detection subtask is a multi-label classification problem where one sentence can be labelled with more than one aspect category.

In this paper, we describe the submission of the SAP-RI team to the SemEval 2014 Task 4. We make use of supervised techniques to extract the aspects of interest (Jakob and Gurevych, 2010), categorize them (Lu et al., 2011) and predict the sentiment of customer online reviews on *Laptops* and *Restaurants*. We developed a constrained system for aspect-based sentiment analysis of these online reviews. The system is constrained in the sense that we only use the training data that was provided by the challenge organizers and no other external data sources. Our system performed reasonably well, especially with a F_1 score of 75.61% for the aspect category polarity subtask, 79.04% F_1 score on the aspect category detection task and 66.61% F_1 score on the aspect term extraction task.

2 Subtask 1: Aspect Term Extraction

Given a review with annotated entities in the training set, the task was to extract the aspect terms for reviews in the test set. For this subtask, training, development and testing were conducted for both

* The work was done during an internship at SAP.

Proceedings of the 8th International Workshop on Semantic Evaluation (SemEval 2014), pages 517–521,
Dublin, Ireland, August 23-24, 2014.

the laptop and the restaurant domain.

2.1 Features

Each review was represented as a feature vector made up of the following features:

- **Word N-grams:** all unigrams, bigrams and trigrams from the review text
- **Casing:** presence or absence of capital case/ title case words
- **POS tags:** POS tags of a word and its neighbours
- **Parse dependencies and relations:** parse dependency relations of the aspects, i.e., presence/absence of adjectives and adverbs in the dependency parse tree
- **Punctuation Marks:** presence/absence of punctuation marks, such as *?, !*

2.2 Method

We approach the task by casting it as a sequence tagging task where each token in a candidate sentence is labelled as either *Beginning*, *Inside* or *Outside* (BIO). We then employ conditional random fields (CRF), which is a discriminative, probabilistic model for sequence data with state-of-the-art performance (Lafferty et al., 2001). A linear-chain CRF tries to estimate the conditional probability of a label sequence $\mathbf{y}$ given the observed features $\mathbf{x}$, where each label y_t is conditioned on the previous label y_{t-1}. In our case, we use BIO CoNLL-style tags (Sang and De Meulder, 2003).

During development, we split the training data in the ratio of 60:20:20 as training, development (dev) and testing (dev-test). We train the CRF model on the training set of the data, perform feature selection based on the dev set, and test the resulting model on the dev-test. In all experiments, we use the CRF++[1] implementation of conditional random fields with the parameter c=4.0. This value was chosen based on manual observation. We perform a feature ablation study and the results are reported in Table 1. Features listed in section 2.1 were those that were retained for the final run.

[1] `code.google.com/p/crfpp/`

3 Subtask 2: Aspect Term Polarity Estimation

For this subtask, the training, development and testing was done using reviews on laptops and restaurants. Given the aspect terms in a sentence, the task was to predict their sentiment polarities.

3.1 Features

For each review, we used the following features:

- **Word N-grams:** all lowercased unigrams, bigrams and trigrams from the review text
- **Polarity of neighbouring adjectives:** extracted word sentiment from SentiWordNet lexicon (Baccianella et al., 2010)
- **Neighbouring POS tags:** the POS tags of up to neighbouring 3 words
- **Parse dependencies and relations:** parse dependency relations of the aspects, i.e., presence/absence of adjectives and adverbs in the dependency parse tree

3.2 Method

For each aspect term of a sentence, the aforementioned features were extracted. For example, for the term *Sushi* in the sentence *Sushi was delicious.*, the following feature vector is constructed, {*aspect: 'sushi', advmod:'null', amod:'delicious', uni_sushi: 1, uni_was: 1, uni_delicious, uni_the: 0, ..* }.

We then treat the aspect sentiment polarity estimation as a multi-class classification task where each instance would be labelled as either *positive*, *negative* or *neutral*. For the classification task, we experimented with Naive Bayes and Support Vector Machines (SVM) – both linear and RBF kernels – and it was observed that linear SVM performed best. Hence, we use linear SVM for the classification task. Table 2 summarizes the results obtained from our experiments for various feature combinations. The classifiers used are implementations from *scikit-learn*[2], which is also used for the remaining tasks.

4 Subtask3: Aspect Category Detection

Given a review with annotated entities or aspect terms, the task was to predict the aspect categories.

[2] `scikit-learn.org/stable/`

Features	Precision	Recall	F1-Score
N-grams, POS tags	0.7655	0.4283	0.5496
N-grams, Parse relations, POS tags	0.8192	0.6641	0.7336
N-Grams, Parse relations, POS tags, casing	0.8101	0.6641	0.7299
N-grams, Parse relations, POS tags, !	0.8116	0.6641	0.7305
N-grams, Parse relations, POS tags,!, ?	0.8123	0.6672	0.7326

Table 1: Training-phase experimental results for Subtask 1 on Restaurant reviews.

Features	Laptops	Restaurants
Neighbouring words, 2,3 POS grams, bigrams, trigrams, Sentiment,1,2 ngram lower	0.4196	0.5997
Parse Relations, 2,3 POS grams, bigrams, trigrams, Sentiment, 1,2 ngram lower	0.5869	0.6375
Parse Relations, Neighbouring words, bigram, trigrams, Sentiment, 1,2 ngram lower	0.5848	0.6380
Parse Relations, 2,3 POS grams, Neighbouring words, Sentiment, 1,2 ngram lower	0.5890	0.6240
Parse Relations, 2,3 POS grams , Neighbouring words, bigram, trigrams, 1,2 ngram lower	0.5626	0.6239
Parse Relations, 2,3 POS grams , Neighbouring words, bigram, trigrams, Sentiment	0.5922	0.6409

Table 2: Training-phase experimental results (Accuracy) for Subtask 2.

As one sentence in a review could belong to multiple aspect categories, we model the task as a multi-label classification problem, i.e., given an instance, predict all labels that the instance fits to.

4.1 Features

We experimented with different features, for example unigrams, dependency tree relations, bigrams, POS tags and sentiment of the words (SentiWordNet), but using just the unigrams alone happened to yield the best result. The feature vector was merely a bag-of-words vector indicating the presence or absence of a word in an instance.

4.2 Method

The training instances were divided into 5 sets based on the aspect categories and thereby, we treated the multi-label classification task as 5 different binary classification tasks. Hence, we used an ensemble of binary classifiers for the multi-label classification. An SVM model was trained using one classifier per class to distinguish it from all other classes. For the binary classification tasks, directly estimating a linear separating function (such as linear SVM) gave better results, as shown in Table 3. Finally, the results of the 5 binary classifiers were combined to label the test instance.

The category *Miscellaneous* was observed to have the lowest accuracy, probably due to the fact that miscellaneous captures all those aspects terms that do not have a clearly defined category.

5 Subtask4 Aspect Category Polarity Detection

For each review with pre-labelled aspect categories, the task was to produce a model which predicts the sentiment polarity of each aspect category.

5.1 Features

The training data contains reviews with the polarity for the corresponding aspect category. The models performed best on using just unigram and bigram features.

5.2 Method

The training instances were split into 5 sets based on the aspect categories. We make use of the sentiment polarity classifier, as described in section 3.2, thereby, training one sentiment polarity classifier for each aspect category. Table 4 indicates the performance of different classifiers for this task, using features as discussed in section 5.1.

6 Results

Table 5 gives an overview of the performance of our system in this year's task based on the official scores from the organizers. We see that our system performs relatively well for subtasks 1, 3 and 4, while for subtask 2 the F_1 scores are behind the best system by about 12%. As observed, a sentence could have more than one aspect and each of these aspects could have different polarities expressed. Including features that preserve the context of the aspect could probably improve the performance in the subtask 2. In most cases, a simple set of features was enough to result in a

Restaurants Category	Naive Bayes	AdaBoost	LinearSVC
Food	0.7130	0.8000	0.8470
Service	0.6064	0.9137	0.8997
Miscellaneous	0.6710	0.7490	0.7890
Ambience	0.6770	0.9063	0.8940
Price	0.7608	0.8548	0.9590

Table 3: Training-phase experimental results (F_1 score) for Subtask 3.

Restaurants Category	Naive Bayes	AdaBoost	LinearSVC
Food	0.7136	0.6711	0.7417
Service	0.6733	0.5244	0.6688
Miscellaneous	0.4756	0.3170	0.4756
Ambience	0.6574	0.7232	0.6885
Price	0.7477	0.7752	0.6651

Table 4: Training-phase experimental results (F_1 score) for Subtask 4.

high F_1 score, for example, in subtask 3 a bag-of-words feature set proved to yield a relatively high F_1 score. In general, for the classification tasks, we observe that the linear SVM performs best.

Subtask	Dataset	Best score	Our score	Rank
1	Laptops	74.55	66.61	8/27
1	Restaurants	84.01	77.88	12/29
2	Laptops	70.48	58.56	18/32
2	Restaurants	80.95	69.92	22/36
3	Restaurants	88.57	79.04	7/21
4	Restaurants	82.92	75.61	5/25

Table 5: Results (F_1 score and ranking) for the Semeval-2014 test set.

7 Conclusion

In this paper, we have described the submission of the SAP-RI team to the SemEval 2014 Task 4. We model the classification tasks using linear SVM and the term extraction task using CRF in order to develop an aspect-based sentiment analysis system that performs reasonably well.

Acknowledgement

The research is partially funded by the Economic Development Board and the National Research Foundation of Singapore.

References

Stefano Baccianella, Andrea Esuli, and Fabrizio Sebastiani. 2010. SentiWordNet 3.0: An enhanced lexical resource for sentiment analysis and opinion mining. In *Proceedings of the Seventh Conference on International Language Resources and Evaluation (LREC'10)*, volume 10, pages 2200–2204.

Minqing Hu and Bing Liu. 2004. Mining and summarizing customer reviews. In *Proceedings of the tenth ACM SIGKDD International Conference on Knowledge Discovery and Data Mining*, pages 168–177.

Niklas Jakob and Iryna Gurevych. 2010. Extracting opinion targets in a single-and cross-domain setting with conditional random fields. In *Proceedings of the 2010 Conference on Empirical Methods in Natural Language Processing*, pages 1035–1045.

John Lafferty, Andrew McCallum, and Fernando Pereira. 2001. Conditional random fields: Probabilistic models for segmenting and labeling sequence data. In *Proceedings of the Eighteenth International Conference on Machine Learning*, pages 282–289.

Bing Liu. 2010. Sentiment analysis and subjectivity. In *Handbook of Natural Language Processing*, pages 627–666. Chapman & Hall, 2 edition.

Bing Liu. 2012. Sentiment analysis and opinion mining. *Synthesis Lectures on Human Language Technologies*, 5(1):1–167.

Bin Lu, Myle Ott, Claire Cardie, and Benjamin Tsou. 2011. Multi-aspect sentiment analysis with topic models. In *Proceedings of Sentiment Elicitation from Natural Text for Information Retrieval and Extraction*, pages 81–88.

Bo Pang and Lillian Lee. 2008. Opinion mining and sentiment analysis. *Foundations and trends in information retrieval*, 2(1-2):1–135.

Maria Pontiki, Dimitrios Galanis, John Pavlopoulos, Haris Papageorgiou, Ion Androutsopoulos, and Suresh Manandhar. 2014. SemEval-2014 Task 4: Aspect based sentiment analysis. In *Proceedings of the 8th International Workshop on Semantic Evaluation (SemEval 2014)*.

Erik Tjong Kim Sang and Fien De Meulder. 2003. Introduction to the CoNLL-2003 shared task: Language-independent named entity recognition. In

Proceedings of the Seventh Conference on Natural Language Learning at HLT-NAACL, pages 142–147.

SAP-RI: Twitter Sentiment Analysis in Two Days

Akriti Vij[1,2]*, **Nishtha Malhotra**[1,2]*, **Naveen Nandan**[1] and **Daniel Dahlmeier**[1]
[1]SAP Research & Innovation, Singapore
[2]Nanyang Technological University, Singapore
{akriti.vij,nishtha.malhotra,naveen.nandan,d.dahlmeier}@sap.com

Abstract

We describe the submission of the SAP Research & Innovation team to the SemEval 2014 Task 9: Sentiment Analysis in Twitter. We challenged ourselves to develop a competitive sentiment analysis system within a very limited time frame. Our submission was developed in less than two days and achieved an F_1 score of 77.26% for contextual polarity disambiguation and 55.47% for message polarity classification, which shows that rapid prototyping of sentiment analysis systems with reasonable accuracy is possible.

1 Introduction

Microblogging platforms and social networks have become increasingly popular for expressing opinions on a wide range of topics, hence making them valuable and ever-growing logs of public sentiment. This has motivated the development of automatic natural language processing (NLP) methods to analyse the sentiment expressed in these short, informal messages (Liu, 2012; Pang and Lee, 2008).

In particular, the study of sentiment and opinions in messages from the Twitter microblogging platform has attracted a lot of interest (Jansen et al., 2009; Pak and Paroubek, 2010; Barbosa and Feng, 2010; O'Connor et al., 2010; Bifet et al., 2011). However, comparative evaluations of sentiment analysis of Twitter messages have previously been hindered by the lack of a large benchmark data set. The goal of the SemEval 2013 task 2: Sentiment Analysis in Twitter (Nakov et al., 2013) and this year's continuation in the SemEval 2014 task 9: Sentiment Analysis in Twitter (Rosenthal et al., 2014) is to close this gap by hosting a shared task competition which provided a large corpus of Twitter messages which are annotated with sentiment polarity labels. The task consists of two subtasks: in subtask A *contextual polarity disambiguation*, participants need to predict the polarity of a given word or phrase in the context of a tweet message, in subtask B *message polarity classification*, participants need to predict the dominating sentiment of the complete message. Both tasks consider sentiment analysis to be a three-way classification problem between positive, negative, and neutral sentiment.

In this paper, we describe the submission of the SAP-RI team to the SemEval 2014 task 9. We challenged ourselves to develop a competitive sentiment analysis system within a very limited time frame. The complete system was implemented within only two days. Our system is based on supervised classification with support vector machines with lexical and dictionary-based features. Our system achieved an F_1 score of 77.26% for contextual polarity disambiguation and 55.47% for message polarity classification. Although our scores are about 10-20% behind the top-scoring systems, we show that it is possible to develop sentiment analysis systems via rapid prototyping with reasonable accuracy in a very short amount of time.

2 Methods

Our system is based on supervised classification with support vector machines and a variety of lexical and dictionary-based features. From the beginning, we decided to restrict ourselves to supervised classification and to focus on the constrained system setting. Experiments with more data or semi-supervised learning would have required additional time and the results of last year's task

* The work was done during an internship at SAP.

Proceedings of the 8th International Workshop on Semantic Evaluation (SemEval 2014), pages 522–526, Dublin, Ireland, August 23-24, 2014.

did not show any convincing improvements using from additional unconstrained data (Nakov et al., 2013). We cast sentiment analysis as a multi-class classification problem with three classes: *positive*, *negative*, and *neutral*. For the features, we tried to re-implement most of the features from the NRC-Canada system (Mohammad et al., 2013) which was the best performing system in last year's task. We describe the features in the following sections.

2.1 Task A : Features

For the contextual polarity disambiguation task, we extract features from the target phrase itself and from a surrounding word window of four words before and after the target phrase. To handle negation, we append the suffix *-neg* to all words in a negated context. A negated context includes any word in the target phrase or context that is following a negation word [1] up to the next following punctuation symbol.

- **Word N-grams:** all lowercased unigrams and bigrams from the target phrase and the context. We extract the lowercased full string of the target phrase as an additional feature.
- **Character N-grams:** lowercased character bigram and trigram prefixes and suffixes from all words in the target phrase and the context.
- **Elongations**: binary feature that indicates the presence of one or more words in the target phrase or context that have a letter repeated for 3 for more times e.g., *coool*.
- **Emoticons:** two binary features that indicate the presence of positive or negative emoticons in the target phrase or the context, respectively. Two additional binary features indicate the presence of positive or negative emoticons at the end of the target phrase or context[2].
- **Punctuation:** three count features for the number of tokens that consist only of exclamation marks, only of questions marks, or a mix of exclamation marks and questions marks, in the target phrase and context, receptively.
- **Casing:** two binary features that indicate the presence of at least one all upper-case word and at least one title-cased word in the target phrase or context, respectively.
- **Stop words:** a binary feature that indicates if all the words in the target phrase or context are stop words. If so, an additional feature indicates the number of stop words: 1, 2, 3, or more stop words.
- **Length:** the number of tokens in the target phrase and the context, plus a binary feature that indicates the presence of any word with more than three characters.
- **Position:** three binary features that indicate whether a target phrase is at the beginning, in the middle, or at the end of the tweet.
- **Hashtags:** all hashtags in the target phrase or the context. To handle hashtags which are formed by concatenating words, e.g., *#ihatemondays*, we additionally split hashtags using a simple dictionary-based approach and add each token of the segmented hashtag as an additional features.
- **Twitter user:** binary feature that indicates whether the context or the target phrase contain a mention of a Twitter user.
- **URL:** binary feature that indicates whether the context or the target phrase contains a URL.
- **Brown cluster:** the word cluster index for each word in the context. Cluster indexes are obtained from the Brown word clusters of the ARK Twitter tagger (Owoputi et al., 2013).
- **Sentiment lexicons:** we add the following sentiment dictionary features for the target phrase and the context for four different sentiment lexicons (NRC sentiment lexicon, NRC Hashtag lexicon (Mohammad et al., 2013), MPQA sentiment lexicon (Wilson et al., 2005), and Bing Liu lexicon (Hu and Liu, 2004)):
  - the count of words with positive sentiment score.
  - the sum of the sentiment scores for all words.

[1] `http://sentiment.christopherpotts.net/lingstruc.html`

[2] positive emoticons: :-), :), :B, :-B, :3, =), <3, :D, :-D, =D, :'), :d, ;), :}, :], :P, :-P, :-p, :p. negative emoticons: :-(, :/, :{, :[, -.-, -_-, :O, :o, :´(, :x, :X, v.v, ;(

- the maximum non-negative sentiment score for any word.
- the sentiment score of the last word with positive sentiment score.

We extract these features for both the target phrase and the context. For words that are marked as negated, the sign of the sentiment scores flipped. The MPQA lexicons requires part of speech information. We use the ARK Twitter part-of-speech tagger (Owoputi et al., 2013) to tag the input with part of speech tags.

2.2 Task B : Features

For the message polarity task, we extract features from the entire tweet message. The features are similar to the features for phrase polarity disambiguation. As before we handle negation by appending the suffix *-neg* to all words that appear in a negated context.

- **Word N-grams:** all lowercased N-grams for N=1, . . . , 4 from the message. We also include "skipgrams" for each N-gram by replacing each token in the N-gram with a asterisk place holder, e.g., *the_cat* → **_cat, the_**.
- **Character N-grams:** lowercased character level N-grams for N=3, . . . , 5 for all the words in the message. Character N-grams do not cross word boundaries.
- **Elongations**: count of words in the message which have a letter repeated for 3 for more times.
- **Emoticons:** similar to the contextual polarity disambiguation task: two binary features for presence of positive or negative emoticons in the message and two binary features indicate the presence of positive or negative emoticons at the end of the message.
- **Punctuation:** similar to the contextual polarity disambiguation task: three count features for the number of tokens that consist only of exclamation marks, only of questions marks, or a mix of exclamation marks and questions marks.
- **Hashtags:** all hashtags in the message. We do not split concatonated hashtags.

	# Tokens	# Tweets
Subtask A		
Training (SemEval 2014 train)	160,992	7,884
Development (SemEval 2013 test)	76,409	3,710
Subtask B		
Training (SemEval 2014 train)	139,128	7,112
Development (SemEval 2013 test)	47,052	2,405

Table 1: Overview of the data sets.

- **Casing:** the count of all upper-case words in the message.
- **Brown cluster:** similar to the contextual polarity disambiguation task: the cluster index for each word in the message.

3 Experiment and Results

In this section, we report experimental result for our method. We used the scikit-learn Python machine learning library (Pedregosa et al., 2011) to implement the feature extraction pipeline and the support vector machine classifier. We use a linear kernel for the support vector machine and fixed the SVM hyper-parameter C to 1.0. We found that scikit-learn allowed us to implement the system faster and resulted in much more compact code than other machine learning tools we have worked with in the past.

We used the official training set provided for the SemEval 2014 task to train our system and evaluated on the test set of the SemEval 2013 task which served as development data for this year's task [3]. Tweets in the training data that were not available any more through the Twitter API were removed from the training set. An overview of the data sets is shown in Table 1. For the evaluation, we compute precision, recall and F_1 measure for the positive, negative, and neutral sentiment tweets. Following the official evaluation metric, the overall precision, recall, and F_1 measure of the system is the average of the precision, recall, and F_1 measures for positive and negative sentiment, respectively.

Here, we report a feature ablation study: we omitted each individual feature category from the complete feature set to determine its influence on the overall performance. Table 2 summarizes the results for subtask A and B. Surprisingly many of the features do not result in a reduction of the F_1 score when removed, or even increase the score,

[3] We also did some experiments with a 60:40 training/test split of the SemEval 2014 training data which showed comparable results

Features	Positive			Negative			Neutral			Overall		
Subtask A	P	R	F_1	P	R	F_1	P	R	F_1	P	R	F_1
All features	0.86	0.87	0.86	0.78	0.78	0.78	0.23	0.13	0.17	0.82	0.83	0.82
w/o Word N-grams	0.84	0.82	0.83	0.71	0.74	0.72	0.14	0.16	0.15	0.77	0.78	0.78
w/o character N-grams	0.85	0.89	0.87	0.80	0.78	0.79	0.27	0.12	0.17	0.82	0.83	0.83
w/o elongation	0.86	0.87	0.86	0.78	0.78	0.78	0.23	0.13	0.17	0.81	0.82	0.81
w/o emoticons	0.85	0.87	0.86	0.78	0.78	0.78	0.24	0.14	0.18	0.82	0.83	0.82
w/o punctuation	0.86	0.87	0.86	0.78	0.78	0.78	0.23	0.13	0.17	0.81	0.83	0.82
w/o casing	0.86	0.87	0.87	0.78	0.78	0.78	0.23	0.13	0.17	0.82	0.83	0.82
w/o stop words	0.86	0.87	0.86	0.78	0.79	0.78	0.24	0.15	0.18	0.82	0.83	0.82
w/o length	0.86	0.87	0.86	0.78	0.78	0.78	0.23	0.14	0.17	0.82	0.83	0.82
w/o position	0.86	0.87	0.86	0.77	0.78	0.78	0.24	0.13	0.17	0.81	0.83	0.82
w/o hashtags	0.86	0.87	0.87	0.78	0.78	0.78	0.24	0.14	0.18	0.82	0.83	0.82
w/o twitter user	0.86	0.87	0.86	0.78	0.78	0.78	0.23	0.13	0.17	0.82	0.83	0.82
w/o URL	0.86	0.87	0.86	0.78	0.78	0.78	0.23	0.13	0.17	0.81	0.82	0.81
w/o Brown cluster	0.86	0.88	0.87	0.78	0.80	0.79	0.25	0.13	0.17	0.82	0.84	0.83
w/o Sentiment lexicon	0.81	0.84	0.82	0.70	0.68	0.69	0.16	0.09	0.11	0.75	0.76	0.76
Subtask B												
All features	0.81	0.54	0.65	0.66	0.34	0.44	0.59	0.89	0.71	0.74	0.44	0.54
w/o word N-grams	0.73	0.59	0.65	0.52	0.46	0.49	0.61	0.75	0.67	0.62	0.52	0.57
w/o character N-grams	0.80	0.49	0.61	0.65	0.23	0.34	0.56	0.90	0.69	0.72	0.36	0.48
w/o elongation	0.81	0.54	0.65	0.66	0.34	0.44	0.59	0.89	0.71	0.74	0.44	0.55
w/o emoticons	0.82	0.54	0.65	0.66	0.33	0.44	0.59	0.89	0.72	0.74	0.44	0.55
w/o punctuation	0.81	0.54	0.65	0.66	0.34	0.45	0.59	0.89	0.71	0.74	0.44	0.55
w/o casing	0.81	0.54	0.65	0.66	0.33	0.44	0.59	0.89	0.71	0.74	0.44	0.55
w/o hashtags	0.82	0.54	0.65	0.65	0.33	0.44	0.59	0.89	0.71	0.74	0.44	0.54
w/o Brown cluster	0.81	0.54	0.65	0.65	0.33	0.44	0.59	0.89	0.71	0.73	0.43	0.54

Table 2: Experimental Results for feature ablation study. Each row shows the precision, recall, and F_1 score for the positive, negative, and neutral class and the overall precision, recall, and F_1 score after removing the particular feature from the features set.

although not significantly. The most effective features are word N-grams and the sentiment lexicons. It is interesting that the performance for the neutral class is very low for subtask A and high for subtask B. We can also see that for subtask B, our system clearly has a problem with recall for the positive and negative sentiment.

For the performance of our system in the SemEval 2014 shared task, we report the official overall F_1 scores of our system as released by the organizers on the official test set in Table 3. The scores were reported separately for different test sets: the SemEval 2013 Twitter test set, a new SemEval 2014 Twitter test set, a new test set from LiveJournal blogs, the SMS test set from the NUS SMS corpus (Chen and Kan, 2012), and a new test set of sarcastic tweets. We also include the F_1 score of the best participating system for each test set and the rank of our system among all participating systems. The results of our system were fairly robust across different domains, with the exception of messages containing sarcasm which shows understanding sarcasm requires a deeper and more subtle understanding of the text that is not captured well in a simple linear model.

Dataset	Best score	Our score	Rank
	Subtask A		
LiveJournal 2014	85.61	77.68	18 / 27
SMS 2013	89.31	80.26	13 / 27
Twitter 2013	90.14	80.32	17 / 27
Twitter 2014	86.63	77.26	15 / 27
Twitter 2014 Sarcasm	82.75	70.64	14 / 27
	Subtask B		
LiveJournal 2014	74.84	57.86	33 / 42
SMS 2013	70.28	49.00	34 / 42
Twitter 2013	72.12	50.18	37 / 42
Twitter 2014	70.96	55.47	32 / 42
Twitter 2014 Sarcasm	58.16	48.64	15 / 42

Table 3: Official results for Semeval 2014 test set. Reported scores are overall F_1 scores.

4 Conclusion

In this paper, we have described the submission of the SAP-RI team to the SemEval 2014 task 9. We showed that is possible to develop sentiment analysis systems via rapid prototyping with reasonable accuracy within a couple of days.

Acknowledgement

The research is partially funded by the Economic Development Board and the National Research Foundation of Singapore.

References

Luciano Barbosa and Junlan Feng. 2010. Robust sentiment detection on Twitter from biased and noisy data. In *Proceedings of the 23rd International Conference on Computational Linguistics*, pages 36–44.

Albert Bifet, Geoffrey Holmes, Bernhard Pfahringer, and Ricard Gavalda. 2011. Detecting sentiment change in Twitter streaming data. *Journal of Machine LearningResearch - Proceedings Track*, 17:5–11.

Tao Chen and Min-Yen Kan. 2012. Creating a live, public short message service corpus: the NUS SMS corpus. *Language Resources and Evaluation*, pages 1–37.

Minqing Hu and Bing Liu. 2004. Mining and summarizing customer reviews. In *Proceedings of the 10th ACM SIGKDD International Conference on Knowledge Discovery and Data Mining*, pages 168–177.

Bernhard J. Jansen, Mimi Zhang, Kate Sobel, and Abdur Chowdury. 2009. Twitter power: Tweets as electronic word of mouth. *J. Am. Soc Inf. Sci. Technol.*, 60(11):2169–2188.

Bing Liu. 2012. Sentiment analysis and opinion mining. *Synthesis Lectures on Human Language Technologies*, 5(1):1–167.

Saif Mohammad, Svetlana Kiritchenko, and Xiaodan Zhu. 2013. NRC-Canada: Building the state-of-the-art in sentiment analysis of Tweets. In *Proceedings of the 7th International Workshop on Semantic Evaluation*, pages 321–327.

Preslav Nakov, Zornitsa Kozareva, Alan Ritter, Sara Rosenthal, Veselin Stoyanov, and Theresa Wilson. 2013. Semeval-2013 task 2: Sentiment analysis in Twitter. In *Proceedings of the 7th International Workshop on Semantic Evaluation*, pages 312–320.

Brendan O'Connor, Routledge Bryan R. Balasubramanyan, Ramnath, and Noah A. Smith. 2010. From Tweets to polls: Linking text sentiment to public opinion time series. In *Proceedings of the Fourth International Conference on Weblogs and Social Media (ICWSM '10)*, pages 122–129.

Olutobi Owoputi, Brendan O'Connor, Chris Dyer, Kevin Gimpel, Nathan Schneider, and Noah A. Smith. 2013. Improved part-of-speech tagging for online conversational text with word clusters. In *Proceedings of the 2013 Conference of the North American Chapter of the Association for Computational Linguistics: Human Language Technologies (NAACL-HLT)*, pages 380–390.

Alexander Pak and Patrick Paroubek. 2010. Twitter based system: Using Twitter to disambiguating sentiment ambiguous adjectives. In *Proceedings of the 8th International Workshop on Semantic Evaluation*, pages 436–439.

Bo Pang and Lillian Lee. 2008. Opinion mining and sentiment analysis. *Foundations and trends in information retrieval*, 2(1-2):1–135.

Fabian Pedregosa, Gaël Varoquaux, Alexandre Gramfort, Vincent Michel, Bertrand Thirion, Oliver Grisel, Mathieu Blondel, Peter. Prettenhofer, Ron Weiss, Vincent Dubourg, Jake Vanderplas, Alexandre Passos, David Cournapeau, Matthieu Brucher, Matthieu Perrot, and Édouard Duchesnay. 2011. Scikit-learn: Machine learning in Python. *Journal of Machine Learning Research*, 12:2825–2830.

Sara Rosenthal, Preslav Nakov, Alan Ritter, and Veselin Stoyanov. 2014. SemEval-2014 Task 9: Sentiment Analysis in Twitter. In Preslav Nakov and Torsten Zesch, editors, *Proceedings of the 8th International Workshop on Semantic Evaluation*, SemEval '14, Dublin, Ireland.

Theresa Wilson, Janyce Wiebe, and Paul Hoffmann. 2005. Recognizing contextual polarity in phrase-level sentiment analysis. In *Proceedings of Human Language Technology and Empirical Methods in Natural Language Processing (HLT-EMNLP)*, pages 307–314.

SeemGo: Conditional Random Fields Labeling and Maximum Entropy Classification for Aspect Based Sentiment Analysis

Pengfei Liu and Helen Meng
Human-Computer Communications Laboratory
Department of Systems Engineering and Engineering Management
The Chinese University of Hong Kong, Hong Kong SAR, China
{pfliu,hmmeng}@se.cuhk.edu.hk

Abstract

This paper describes our SeemGo system for the task of *Aspect Based Sentiment Analysis* in SemEval-2014. The subtask of aspect term extraction is cast as a sequence labeling problem modeled with Conditional Random Fields that obtains the F-score of 0.683 for Laptops and 0.791 for Restaurants by exploiting both word-based features and context features. The other three subtasks are solved by the Maximum Entropy model, with the occurrence counts of unigram and bigram words of each sentence as features. The subtask of aspect category detection obtains the best result when applying the Boosting method on the Maximum Entropy model, with the precision of 0.869 for Restaurants. The Maximum Entropy model also shows good performance in the subtasks of both aspect term and aspect category polarity classification.

1 Introduction

In this paper, we present the SeemGo system developed for the task of *Aspect Based Sentiment Analysis* in SemEval-2014. The task consists of four subtasks: (1) aspect term extraction (identify particular aspects of a given entity, e.g., laptop, restaurant, etc.); (2) aspect category detection (detect the category of a given sentence, e.g., food, service for a restaurant, etc.), (3) aspect term polarity, and (4) aspect category polarity. The polarity of each aspect term or aspect category includes positive, negative, neutral or conflict (i.e., both positive and negative).

In the SeemGo system, the subtask of aspect term extraction is implemented with the CRF model that shows good performance by integrating both word-based features and context features. The other subtasks of aspect category detection, aspect term/category polarity classification are all developed with the MaxEnt model with the occurrence counts of unigram and bigram words of each sentence as features. Experimental results show that MaxEnt obtains good performance in all the three subtasks. For the subtask of aspect category detection, MaxEnt obtains even better performance when combined with the Boosting method.

The rest of this paper is organized as follows: Section 2 discusses related work; Section 3 presents the architecture and the underlying models of the SeemGo system as well as the experimental results. We summarize the paper and propose future work in Section 4.

2 Related Work

The subtask of aspect term extraction is quite similar with Noun Phrase Chunking (NPC) (Sha and Pereira, 2003) and Named Entity Recognition (NER) (Finkel et al., 2005). NPC recognizes noun phrases from sentences, while NER extracts a set of entities such as *Person*, *Place*, and *Organization*. Both NPC and NER are sequential learning problems and they are typically modelled by sequence models such as Hidden Markov Model (HMM) and CRF (Finkel et al., 2005).

For the task of aspect term extraction, some related papers also model it with sequence models. Jin et al. (2009) proposed an HMM-based framework to extract product entities and associated opinion orientations by integrating linguistic features such as part-of-speech tag, lexical patterns and surrounding words/phrases. Choi et al. (2005) proposed a hybrid approach using both CRF and extraction patterns to identify sources of opinions in text. Jakob and Gurevych (2010) described a

Proceedings of the 8th International Workshop on Semantic Evaluation (SemEval 2014), pages 527–531,
Dublin, Ireland, August 23-24, 2014.

CRF-based approach for the opinion target extraction problem in both single- and cross-domain settings. Shariaty and Moghaddam (2011) used CRF for the task of identifying aspects, aspect usages and opinions in review sentences by making use of labeled dataset on aspects, opinions as well as background words in the sentences.

The task of aspect category detection is essentially a text classification problem, for which many techniques exist. Joachims (1998) explored the use of Support Vector Machines (SVM) for text categorization and obtained good performance due to their ability to generalize well in high-dimensional feature spaces. Nigam et al. (1999) proposed the MaxEnt model for document classification by estimating the conditional distribution of the class variable give the document, and showed that MaxEnt is significantly better that Naive Bayes on some datasets.

For polarity classification, Pang et al. (2002) conducted experiments on movie reviews and showed that standard machine learning techniques (e.g., Naive Bayes, SVM and MaxEnt) outperform human-produced baselines.

3 The SeemGo System

We use the CRF model (Lafferty et al., 2001) for the subtask of aspect term extraction, and adopt the MaxEnt model for the other three subtasks with the vectors of *word count* as features. Each entry in the vector represents the occurrence count of each unigram or bigram words in the sentence. Figure 1 shows the architecture and the MaxEnt and CRF models of the SeemGo system. The *label* is denoted in lowercase (e.g. y for sentiment), while *word count*, *label sequence* and *word sequence* are vectors, denoted in bold lowercase (e.g. $\mathbf{y}$ for label sequence). We developed the SeemGo system in Java based on the MALLET Toolkit (McCallum, 2002) for MaxEnt and the Stanford CRFClassifier(Finkel et al., 2005) for CRF.

3.1 Background

3.1.1 Maximum Entropy Classifier

The MaxEnt model defines the conditional distribution of the class (y) given an observation vector $\mathbf{x}$ as the exponential form in Formula 1:

$$\mathrm{P}(y|\mathbf{x}) = \frac{1}{Z(\mathbf{x})}\exp\left(\sum_{k=1}^{K}\theta_k f_k(\mathbf{x}, y)\right) \quad (1)$$

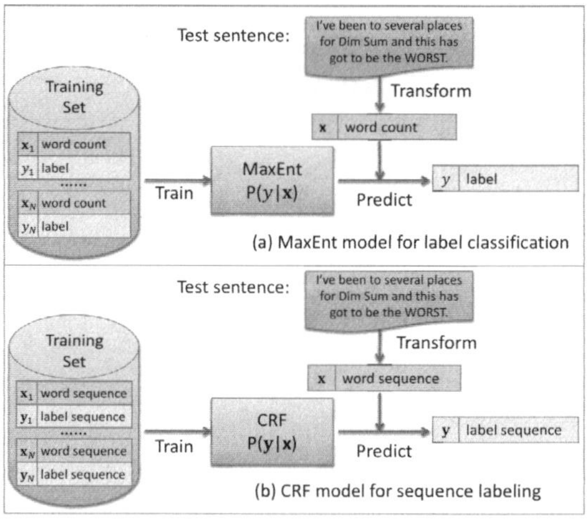

Figure 1: The Architecture, the MaxEnt and CRF Models of the SeemGo System.

where θ_k is a weight parameter to be estimated for the corresponding feature function $f_k(x, y)$, and $Z(\mathbf{x})$ is a normalizing factor over all classes to ensure a proper probability. K is the total number of feature functions.

3.1.2 Conditional Random Fields

CRF is an extension to the MaxEnt model for handling sequence data. The linear-chain CRF is a special case of CRF that obeys the Markov property between its neighbouring labels. Following McCallum and Li (2003), Formula 2 defines the linear-chain CRF: $\mathbf{y} = \{y_t\}_{t=1}^T$, $\mathbf{x} = \{x_t\}_{t=1}^T$ are label sequence and observation sequence respectively, and there are K arbitrary feature functions $\{f_k\}_{1\leq k\leq K}$ and the corresponding weight parameters $\{\theta_k\}_{1\leq k\leq K}$. $Z(\mathbf{x})$ is a normalizing factor over all label sequences.

$$P(\mathbf{y}|\mathbf{x}) = \frac{1}{Z(\mathbf{x})}\exp\left(\sum_{t=1}^{T}\sum_{k=1}^{K}\theta_k f_k(y_t, y_{t-1}, \mathbf{x}, t)\right) \quad (2)$$

In the labeling phase, the *Viterbi* decoding algorithm is applied to find the best label sequence $\mathbf{y}*$ for the observation sequence $\mathbf{x}$.

3.2 Subtask 1: Aspect Term Extraction

The datasets (Laptops and Restaurants) are provided in XML format, with each sentence and its annotations consisting of a training instance. For each instance, SeemGo first transform the sentence into a word sequence $\mathbf{x}$, and converts the corresponding annotations into the label sequence $\mathbf{y}$. SeemGo then learns a CRF model $P(\mathbf{y}|\mathbf{x})$ based on the N the training instances $\{(\mathbf{x}_n, \mathbf{y}_n)\}_{n=1}^N$.

3.2.1 IOB Labeling

Since an aspect term can contain multiple words (e.g., *hard disk*), we define the label **B-TERM** for the beginning of an aspect term, the label **I-TERM** for the subsequent inside words or end word of an aspect term and the label **O** for all other words. This definition follows the *Inside, Outside, Beginning* (IOB) labeling scheme (Ramshaw and Marcus, 1999). The subtask 1 can be viewed as a sequence labeling problem by labeling each word either as B-TERM, I-TERM or O. Figure 2 shows two example sentences labeled with the IOB2 scheme [1].

I	liked	the	service	and	the	staff.
O	O	O	B-TERM	O	O	B-TERM

The	hard	disk	is	very	noisy.
O	B-TERM	I-TERM	O	O	O

Figure 2: Example Sentences with IOB2 Labels.

3.2.2 Features for the CRF Model

In CRF, features typically refer to feature functions $\{f_k\}$, which can be arbitrary functions. In text applications, CRF features are typically binary (Sutton and McCallum, 2012). As an example for "virus protection", a binary feature function may have value 1 if and only if the label for "virus" is *B-TERM* and the current word "protection" has the suffix of "tion", and otherwise 0. Similar to the features used in Finkel et al. (2005) for the NER task, Table 1 summarizes the features for the aspect term extraction task. We call the features derived from the current word *word-based* features such as w_{id}, $w_{character}$, and the features from the surrounding words and the previous label the *contex* features ($context$).

We consider the sentence *"I've been to several places for Dim Sum and this has got to be the WORST."* as an example to explain why we choose these features: (a) word-based features: the word "Sum" is located in the middle of the sentence, with the first character capitalized. (b) context features: the previous word "Dim" is also capitalized in the first character and the label of "Dim" is assumed to be "B-TERM". By combining the word-based features and the context features, the Viterbi decoding algorithm will then label "Sum" as "I-TERM" with high degree of confidence, which is a part of the multi-word term "Dim Sum", instead of a mathematical function in some other context.

[1] With IOB2, every aspect term begins with the B label.

Table 1: Features for the CRF Model.

Feature	Description
w_{id}	word identity
$w_{character}$	whether the word characters are capitalized, hyphenated, numeric, e.g., built-in camera, BIOS, Dim Sum, Windows 7
$w_{location}$	word index in the word sequence $\mathbf{x}$
w_{ngram}	n-gram character sequences of each word with maximum length of 6, including prefixes and suffixes, e.g., **"tion"** in specification, navigation
$context$	current word w_t, its neighbouring words (w_{t-2},...,w_{t+2}) and previous label y_{t-1}
w_{pos}	part-of-speech tag of each word

3.2.3 Experimental Results

We trained the CRF model with different feature set on the training set provided by the SemEval2014 organizers, and reported the experimental results on the testing set by the evaluation tool *eval.jar*. The detailed experimental results are listed in Table 2. The *basic* feature set consists of w_{id}, $w_{character}$ and $w_{location}$. The results from one of the best systems on each dataset are also listed, marked with the star (*).

Table 2: Experimental Results on Different Feature Set for Aspect Term Extraction.

	Feature Set	Precision	Recall	F-score
Lap	$basic$	0.780 (263/337)	0.402 (263/654)	0.531
	$basic + w_{ngram}$	0.781 (375/480)	0.573 (375/654)	0.661 **(+0.13)**
	$basic + w_{context}$	0.827 (296/358)	0.453 (296/654)	0.585 **(+0.054)**
	$basic$+w_{ngram}+ $context$	0.830 (380/458)	**0.581 (380/654)**	**0.683** **(+0.152)**
	$basic$+w_{ngram}+ $context + w_{pos}$	**0.837 (365/436)**	0.558 (365/654)	0.670 **(-0.013)**
	IHS_RD_Belarus*	0.848	0.665	0.746
Res	$basic$	0.862 (692/803)	0.610 (692/1134)	0.715
	$basic + w_{ngram}$	0.838 (804/959)	0.709 (804/1134)	0.768 **(+0.053)**
	$basic + w_{context}$	0.856 (704/822)	0.621 (704/1134)	0.720 **(+0.05)**
	$basic$+w_{ngram}+ $context$	0.865 (827/956)	**0.729 (827/1134)**	**0.791** (+0.076)
	$basic$+w_{ngram}+ $context + w_{pos}$	**0.870 (806/926)**	0.711 (806/1134)	0.783 **(-0.08)**
	XRCE*	0.909	0.818	0.840

We have the following observations:

(1) Compared with using only the *basic* features, adding the feature of w_{n-gram} contributes the

greatest performance improvement, with the absolute increase of F-score by 13% for Laptops and 5.3% for Restaurants; while adding the $w_{context}$ feature *improves* the F-score by around 5% for both datasets.

(2) Combining the word-based features (*basic* and w_{ngram}) and the context-based features ($w_{context}$) lead to the best performance for both datasets in terms of recall and F-score.

(3) The POS tags lead to a *decrease* in both recall and F-score, with the absolute decrease of F-score by 1.3% for Laptops and 8% for Restaurants. The same observation is also reported by Tkachenko and Simanovsky (2012) for NER.

3.3 Subtask 3: Aspect Category Detection

We encode each sentence as a feature vector $\mathbf{x}$ with each entry representing occurrence count of each unigram word and bigram words (i.e., *word count*). All words are lowercased, while keeping the stopwords as most sentences in the datasets are short. Using the provided training set, We trained a MaxEnt classifier (ME) $P(y|\mathbf{x})$ with a Gaussian prior variance of 20 to prevent overfitting.

We also tried the Bagging (Breiman, 1996) on MaxEnt (BaggingME) and the Boosting (Freund and Schapire, 1996) on MaxEnt (BoostME). Table 3 shows the experimental results on the provided testing set. It shows that the Boosting method on MaxEnt improves both precision and recall as well as the F-score by 1.1%. The best evaluation result is by the NRC-Canada team.

Table 3: Performance of Different Classifiers for Aspect Category Detection.

Classifier	Precision	Recall	F-score
ME	0.858 (686/800)	0.669 (686/1025)	0.752
BagME	0.843 (674/800)	0.658 (674/1025)	0.739
BoostME	**0.869 (695/800)**	**0.678 (695/1025)**	**0.762**
Best*	0.910	0.862	0.886

3.4 Subtask 2 & 4: Aspect Term & Category Polarity Classification

Similar to subtask-3, we also used MaxEnt for the subtasks of 2 and 4, with word count as features. For category polarity classification, we count the words from both the sentence and the category name. For example, we count the sentence "The Dim Sum is delicious." and its category "Food" as features. This improves performance compared with counting the sentence only.

Table 4 shows the accuracy of each classifier for the subtasks of 2 and 4 on Laptops and Restaurants, including the best results from NRC-Canada (a) and DCU (b). In both datasets, the distributions of aspect term/category polarities are very imbalanced with very few sentences on *conflict* but with most sentences on *positive* or *negative*. This leads to very low classification performance for the *conflict* class, with the F-score less than 0.2. In this case, the Boosting method does not necessarily improve the performance.

Table 4: Accuracy of Different Classifiers for Aspect Term & Category Polarity Classification.

Classifier	Term		Category
	Laptops	Restaurants	(Restaurants)
ME	**0.648 (424/654)**	0.729 (827/1134)	**0.752 (771/1025)**
BagME	0.635 (415/654)	**0.732 (830/1134)**	**0.752 (771/1025)**
BoostME	0.642 (420/654)	0.730 (828/1134)	0.747 (766/1025)
Best*	0.705 (a,b) (461/654)	0.810 (b) (918/1134)	0.829 (a) (850/1025)

3.5 Evaluation Ranks

Table 5 shows the official ranks (and the new ranks in braces of the revised version after evaluation) of the SeemGo system on the two datasets. The evaluation metrics are Precision, Recall and F-score for the subtasks of 1 and 3, and Accuracy (Acc) for the subtasks of 2 and 4.

Table 5: Ranks of SeemGo on the Constrained Run (Using only the Provided Datasets).

	Subtask	Precision	Recall	F-score	Acc
Lap	1	4	12 (8)	8 (4)	-
	2	-	-	-	12 (6)
Res	1	3	11 (7)	5	-
	2	-	-	-	8 (6)
	3	3 (2)	12	8 (7)	-
	4	-	-	-	4

4 Conclusions

This paper presents the architecture, the CRF and MaxEnt models of our SeemGo system for the task of *Aspect Based Sentiment Analysis* in

SemEval-2014. For the subtask of aspect term extraction, CRF is trained with both the word-based features and the context features. For the other three subtasks, MaxEnt is trained with the features of the occurrence counts of unigram and bigram words in the sentence. The subtask of aspect category detection obtains the best performance when applying the Boosting method on MaxEnt. MaxEnt also shows good average accuracy for polarity classification, but obtains low performance for the *conflict* class due to very few training sentences.This leaves us the future work to improve classification performance for imbalanced datasets (He and Garcia, 2009).

Acknowledgements

We thank the organizers for their hard work in organizing this evaluation, and the two anonymous reviewers for their helpful comments.

References

Leo Breiman. 1996. Bagging predictors. *Machine learning*, 24(2):123–140.

Yejin Choi, Claire Cardie, Ellen Riloff, and Siddharth Patwardhan. 2005. Identifying sources of opinions with conditional random fields and extraction patterns. In *Proceedings of the Conference on Human Language Technology and Empirical Methods in Natural Language Processing*, pages 355–362.

Jenny Rose Finkel, Trond Grenager, and Christopher Manning. 2005. Incorporating non-local information into information extraction systems by gibbs sampling. In *Proceedings of the 43rd Annual Meeting on Association for Computational Linguistics*, pages 363–370.

Yoav Freund and Robert E Schapire. 1996. Experiments with a new boosting algorithm. In *International Conference on Machine Learning*, volume 96, pages 148–156.

Haibo He and Edwardo A Garcia. 2009. Learning from imbalanced data. *Knowledge and Data Engineering, IEEE Transactions on*, 21(9):1263–1284.

Niklas Jakob and Iryna Gurevych. 2010. Extracting opinion targets in a single-and cross-domain setting with conditional random fields. In *Proceedings of the Conference on Empirical Methods in Natural Language Processing*, pages 1035–1045.

Wei Jin, Hung Hay Ho, and Rohini K Srihari. 2009. A novel lexicalized HMM-based learning framework for web opinion mining. In *Proceedings of the International Conference on Machine Learning*, pages 465–472. Citeseer.

Thorsten Joachims. 1998. *Text categorization with support vector machines: Learning with many relevant features*. Springer.

John Lafferty, Andrew McCallum, and Fernando CN Pereira. 2001. Conditional random fields: Probabilistic models for segmenting and labeling sequence data.

Andrew McCallum and Wei Li. 2003. Early results for named entity recognition with conditional random fields, feature induction and web-enhanced lexicons. In *Proceedings of the seventh conference on Natural language learning at HLT-NAACL 2003-Volume 4*, pages 188–191.

Andrew Kachites McCallum. 2002. MALLET: A Machine Learning for Language Toolkit.

Kamal Nigam, John Lafferty, and Andrew McCallum. 1999. Using maximum entropy for text classification. In *IJCAI-99 workshop on machine learning for information filtering*, volume 1, pages 61–67.

Bo Pang, Lillian Lee, and Shivakumar Vaithyanathan. 2002. Thumbs up?: sentiment classification using machine learning techniques. In *Proceedings of the Conference on Empirical Methods in Natural Language Processing*, pages 79–86.

Lance A Ramshaw and Mitchell P Marcus. 1999. Text chunking using transformation-based learning. In *Natural language processing using very large corpora*, pages 157–176. Springer.

Fei Sha and Fernando Pereira. 2003. Shallow parsing with conditional random fields. In *Proceedings of the Conference of the North American Chapter of the Association for Computational Linguistics on Human Language Technology*, pages 134–141.

Shabnam Shariaty and Samaneh Moghaddam. 2011. Fine-grained opinion mining using conditional random fields. In *Data Mining Workshops (ICDMW), 2011 IEEE 11th International Conference on*, pages 109–114. IEEE.

Charles Sutton and Andrew McCallum. 2012. An introduction to conditional random fields. *Foundations and Trends in Machine Learning*, 4(4):267–373.

Maksim Tkachenko and Andrey Simanovsky. 2012. Named entity recognition: Exploring features. In *Proceedings of KONVENS*, volume 2012, pages 118–127.

SemantiKLUE: Robust Semantic Similarity at Multiple Levels Using Maximum Weight Matching

Thomas Proisl and **Stefan Evert** and **Paul Greiner** and **Besim Kabashi**
Friedrich-Alexander-Universität Erlangen-Nürnberg (FAU)
Department Germanistik und Komparatistik
Professur für Korpuslinguistik
Bismarckstr. 6, 91054 Erlangen, Germany
{thomas.proisl,stefan.evert,paul.greiner,besim.kabashi}@fau.de

Abstract

Being able to quantify the semantic similarity between two texts is important for many practical applications. SemantiKLUE combines unsupervised and supervised techniques into a robust system for measuring semantic similarity. At the core of the system is a word-to-word alignment of two texts using a maximum weight matching algorithm. The system participated in three SemEval-2014 shared tasks and the competitive results are evidence for its usability in that broad field of application.

1 Introduction

Semantic similarity measures the semantic equivalence between two texts ranging from total difference to complete semantic equivalence and is usually encoded as a number in a closed interval, e. g. $[0,5]$. Here is an example for interpreting the numeric similarity scores taken from Agirre et al. (2013, 33):

0. The two sentences are on different topics.
1. The two sentences are not equivalent, but are on the same topic.
2. The two sentences are not equivalent, but share some details.
3. The two sentences are roughly equivalent, but some important information differs/missing.
4. The two sentences are mostly equivalent, but some unimportant details differ.
5. The two sentences are completely equivalent, as they mean the same thing.

Systems capable of reliably predicting the semantic similarity between two texts can be beneficial for a broad range of NLP applications, e. g. paraphrasing, MT evaluation, information extraction, question answering and summarization.

A general system for semantic similarity aiming at being applicable in such a broad scope has to be able to adapt to the use case at hand, because different use cases might, for example, require different similarity scales: For one application, two texts dealing roughly with the same topic should get a high similarity score, whereas for another application being able to distinguish between subtle differences in meaning might be important. The three SemEval-2014 shared tasks focussing on semantic similarity (cf. Sections 3, 4 and 5 for more detailed task descriptions) provide a rich testbed for such a general system, as the individual tasks and subtasks have slightly different objectives.

In the remainder of this paper, we describe SemantiKLUE, a general system for measuring semantic similarity between texts that we built based on our experience from participating in the *SEM 2013 shared task on "Semantic Textual Similarity" (Greiner et al., 2013).

2 System Description

SemantiKLUE operates in two stages. In the first, unsupervised stage, a number of similarity measures are computed. Those measures are the same for all tasks and range from simple heuristics to distributional approaches to resource-heavy methods based on WordNet and dependency structures. The idea is to have a variety of similarity measures that can capture small differences in meaning as well as broad thematical similarities. In the second, supervised stage, all similarity measures obtained in this way are passed to a support vector regression learner that is trained on the available gold standard data in order to obtain a final semantic similarity score. This way, the proper similarity scale for a given task can be learned. The few remaining outliers in the predictions for new text pairs are cut

Proceedings of the 8th International Workshop on Semantic Evaluation (SemEval 2014), pages 532–540, Dublin, Ireland, August 23-24, 2014.

off to fit the interval required by the task definition ([0,4] or [0,5]).

Our submissions for the individual tasks were created using incomplete versions from different developmental stages of the system. In the following sections we describe the current version of the complete system for which we also report comparable results for all tasks (cf. Sections 3– 5).

The whole system is implemented in Python.

2.1 Preprocessing

We use Stanford CoreNLP[1] for part-of-speech tagging, lemmatizing and parsing the input texts. We utilize the CCprocessed variant of the Stanford Dependencies (collapsed dependencies with propagation of conjunct dependencies; de Marneffe and Manning (2008, 13–15)) to create a graph representation of the texts using the NetworkX[2] (Hagberg et al., 2008) module. All the similarity measures described below are computed on the basis of that graph representation. It is important to keep in mind that by basing all computations on the Stanford Dependencies model we effectively ignore most of the prepositions when using measures that work on tokens.[3] For some tasks, we perform some additional task-specific preprocessing steps prior to parsing, cf. task descriptions below.

2.2 Simple Measures

We use four simple heuristic similarity measures that need very little preprocessing. The first two are word form overlap and lemma overlap between the two texts. We take the sets of word form tokens/lemmatized tokens in text A and text B and calculate the Jaccard coefficient:

$$\text{overlap} = \frac{|A \cap B|}{|A \cup B|}.$$

The third is a heuristic for the difference in text length that was used by Gale and Church (1993) as a similarity measure for aligning sentences:

$$z_i = \frac{\mathrm{d}_i}{\sigma_\mathrm{d}}, \text{ where } \mathrm{d}_i = b_i - \frac{\sum_{j=1}^{N} b_j}{\sum_{j=1}^{N} a_j} a_i.$$

For each of the N text pairs we calculate the difference d_i between the observed length of text B and the expected length of text B based on the length of text A. By dividing that difference d_i by the standard deviation of all those differences, we obtain our heuristic z_i.

The fourth is a binary feature expressing whether the two texts differ in their use of negation. We check if one of the texts contains any of the lemmata *no*, *not* or *none* and the other doesn't. That feature is motivated by the comparatively large number of sentences in the SICK dataset (Marelli et al., 2014b) that mainly differ in their use of negation, e. g. sentence pair 42 in the training data that has a gold similarity score of 3.4:

- Two people are kickboxing and spectators are watching
- Two people are kickboxing and spectators are not watching

2.3 Measures Based on Distributional Document Similarity

We obtain document similarity scores from two large-vocabulary distributional semantic models (DSMs).

The first model is based on a 10-billion word Web corpus consisting of Wackypedia and ukWaC (Baroni et al., 2009), UMBC WebBase (Han et al., 2013), and UKCOW 2012 (Schäfer and Bildhauer, 2012). Target terms and feature terms are POS-disambiguated lemmata.[4] We use parameters suggested by recent evaluation experiments: co-occurrence counts in a symmetric 4-word window, the most frequent 30,000 lexical words as features, log-likelihood scores with an additional log-transformation, and SVD dimensionality reduction of L2-normalized vectors to 1000 latent dimensions. This model provides distributional representations for 150,000 POS-disambiguated lemmata as target terms.

The second model was derived from the second release of the Google Books N-Grams database (Lin et al., 2012), using the dependency pairs provided in this version. Target and feature terms are case-folded word forms; co-occurrence ounts are based on direct syntactic relations. Here, the most frequent 50,000 word forms were used as features. All other parameters are identical to the first DSM. This model provides distributional representations for 250,000 word forms.

We compute bag-of-words centroid vectors for each text as suggested by (Schütze, 1998). For each

[1] `http://nlp.stanford.edu/software/corenlp.shtml`

[2] `http://networkx.github.com/`

[3] That is because in the CCprocessed variant of the Stanford Dependencies most prepositions are "collapsed" into dependency relations and are therefore represented as edges and not as vertices in the graph.

[4] e.g. `can_N` for the noun *can*

text pair and DSM, we calculate the cosine similarity between the two centroid vectors as a measure of their semantic similarity. We also determine the number of unknown words in both texts according to both DSMs as additional features.

2.4 Alignment-based Measures

We also use features based on word-level similarity. We separately compute similarities between words using state-of-the-art WordNet similarity measures and the two distributional semantic models described above. The words from both texts are then aligned using those similarity scores to maximize the similarity total. We use two types of alignment: One-to-one alignment where some words in the longer text remain unaligned and one-to-many alignment where all words are aligned. The one-to-many alignment is based on the one-to-one alignment and aligns each previously unaligned word in the longer text to the most similar word in the shorter text. The discussion of the alignment algorithm is based on the former case.

2.4.1 Alignment via Maximum Weight Matching

We opt for a graphical solution to the alignment problem. The similarities between the words from both texts can be modelled as a bipartite graph in which every word from text A is a vertice on the left-hand side of the graph and every word from text B a vertex on the right-hand side. Weighted edges connect every word from text A to every word from text B. The weight of an edge corresponds to the similarity between the two words it connects. In order to obtain an optimal one-to-one alignment we have to select edges in such a way that no two edges share a common vertice and that the sum of the edge weights is maximized. That corresponds to the problem of finding the maximum weight matching in the graph. SemantiKLUE utilizes the NetworkX implementation of Galil's (1986) algorithms for finding that maximum weight matching.

Figure 1 visualizes the one-to-one alignment between two sentences. For the one-to-many alignment, the previously unaligned words are aligned as indicated by the dashed lines.

2.4.2 Measures Based on Distributional Word Similarities

For each of the two DSMs described in Section 2.3 we compute the best one-to-one and the best one-

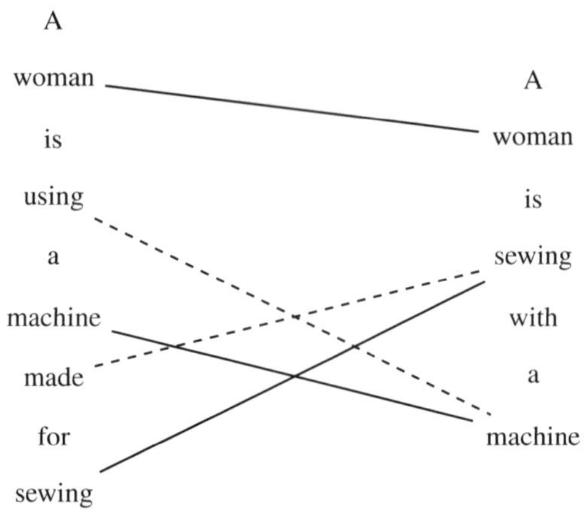

Figure 1: Alignment between a sentence pair from the SICK data set.

to-many alignment using the cosine similarity between two words as edge weight. For each of those two alignments we compute the following two similarity measures: I) the arithmetic mean of the cosines between all the aligned words from text A and text B and II) the arithmetic mean ignoring identical word pairs.

In addition to those eight measures, we use the lemma-based DSM for computing the distribution of cosines between lemma pairs. For both alignments, we categorize the cosines between aligned lemma pairs into five heuristically determined intervals ($[0.2, 0.35)$, $[0.35, 0.5)$, $[0.5, 0.7)$, $[0.7, 0.999)$, $[0.999, 1.0]$)[5] and use the proportions as features. Intuitively, the top bins correspond to links between identical words, paradigmatically related words and topically related words. All in all, we use a total of 18 features computed from the DSM-based alignments.

2.4.3 Measures Based on WordNet

We utilize two state-of-the-art (Budanitsky and Hirst, 2006) WordNet similarity measures for creating alignments: Leacock and Chodorow's (1998) normalized path length and Lin's (1998) universal similarity measure. For both of those similarity measures we compute the best one-to-one and the best one-to-many alignment. For each alignment we compute the following two similarity measures: I) the arithmetic mean of the similarities between the aligned words from text A and text B and II) the arithmetic mean ignoring identical word pairs.

[5]Values in the interval $[0.0, 0.2)$ are discarded as they would be collinear with the other features.

We also include the number of unknown words in both texts according to WordNet as additional features.

2.5 Measures Using the Dependency Structure

We expect that the information encoded in the dependency structure of the texts can be beneficial in determining the semantic similarity between them. Therefore, we use three heuristics for measuring similarity on the level of syntactic dependencies. The first simply measures the overlap of dependency relation labels between the two texts (cf. Section 2.2). The second utilizes the fact that the Stanford Dependencies are organized in a hierarchy (de Marneffe and Manning, 2008, 11–12) to compute Leacock and Chodorow's normalized path lengths between individual dependency relations. That measure for the similarity between dependency relations is then used to determine the best one-to-one alignment between dependency relations from text A and text B and to compute the arithmetic mean of the similarities between the aligned dependency relations. The third heuristic gives an indication of the quality of the one-to-one alignment and can be used to distinguish texts that contain the same words in different syntactic structures. It uses the one-to-one alignment created with similarity scores from the lemma-based DSM (cf. Section 2.4.2) to compute the average overlap of neighbors for all aligned word pairs. The overlap of neighbors is determined by computing the Jaccard coefficient of sets N_A and N_B. Set N_A contains all words from text B that are aligned to words from text A that are connected to the target word via a single dependency relation. N_B contains all words from text B that are connected to the word aligned to the target word in text A via a single dependency relation.

2.6 Experimental Features

As an experiment, we included features from a commercial text clustering software that is currently being developed by our team (Greiner and Evert, in preparation). We used this tool – which combines ideas from Latent Semantic Indexing and distributional semantics with multiple clustering steps – as a black box.

We loaded *all* training, development and test items for a given task into the system and applied the clustering algorithm. However, we did not make use of the resulting topic clusters. Instead, we computed cosine similarities for each pair (s_1, s_2) of sentences (or other textual units) based on the internal representation. In addition, we computed the average neighbour rank of the two sentences, based on the rank of s_2 among the nearest neighbours of s_1 and vice versa.

Since these features are generated from the task data themselves, they should adapt automatically to the range of meaning differences present in a given data set.

2.7 Machine Learning

Using all the features described above, we have a total of 39 individual features that measure semantic similarity between two texts (cf. Sections 2.2 to 2.5) and two experimental features (cf. Section 2.6). In order to obtain a single similarity score, we use the scikit-learn[6] (Pedregosa et al., 2011) implementation of support vector regression. In our cross-validation experiments we got the best results with an RBF kernel of degree 2 and a penalty $C = 0.7$, so those are the parameters we use in our experiments.

The SemEval-2014 Task 1 also includes a classification subtask for which we use the same $39 + 2$ features for training a support vector classifier. Cross-validation suggests that the best parameter setting is a polynomial kernel of degree 2 and a penalty $C = 2.5$.

3 SemEval-2014 Task 1

3.1 Task Description

The focus of the shared task on "Evaluation of compositional distributional semantic models on full sentences through semantic relatedness and textual entailment" (Marelli et al., 2014a) lies on the compositional nature of sentence semantics. By using a specially created data set (Marelli et al., 2014b) that tries to avoid multiword expressions and other idiomatic features of language outside the scope of compositional semantics, it provides a testbed for systems implementing compositional variants of distributional semantics. There is also an additional subtask for detecting the entailment relation (entailment, neutral, contradiction) between to sentences.

Although SemantiKLUE lacks a truly sophisticated component for dealing with compositional semantics (besides trying to incorporate the dependency structure of the texts), the system takes the seventh place in the official ranking by Pearson correlation with a correlation coefficient of 0.780

[6] `http://scikit-learn.org/`

(best of 17 systems: 0.828). In the entailment subtask, the system even takes the fourth place with an accuracy of 0.823 (best of 18 systems: 0.846).

3.2 Experiments

The official runs we submitted for this task were created by a work-in-progress version of SemantiKLUE that did not contain all the features described above. In this section, we report on some post-hoc experiments with the complete system using all the features as well as various subsets of features. See Table 1 for an overview of the results.

Run	r	ρ	MSE	Acc.
primary run	0.780	0.736	0.403	**0.823**
best run	0.782	0.738	0.398	**0.823**
complete system	0.798	0.754	0.373	0.820
no deps	0.793	0.748	0.383	0.817
no deps, no WN	0.763	0.713	0.432	0.793
complete + experimental	**0.801**	**0.757**	**0.367**	**0.823**
only DSM alignment	**0.729**	**0.670**	**0.484**	0.746
only WordNet	0.708	0.636	0.515	0.715
only simple	0.676	0.667	0.561	**0.754**
only DSM document	0.660	0.568	0.585	0.567
only deps	0.576	0.565	0.688	0.614

Table 1: Results for task 1 (Pearson's r, Spearman's ρ, mean squared error and accuracy).

The whole system as described above, without the experimental features, performs even a bit better in the semantic similarity subtask (taking place 6) and only slightly worse in the entailment subtask (still taking place 4) than the official submissions. Adding the experimental features slightly improves the results but does not lead to a better position in the ranking.

We are particularly interested in the impact of the resource-heavy features derived from the dependency structure of the texts and from WordNet. If we use the complete system without the dependency-based features (emulating the case of a language for which we have access to a WordNet-like resource but not to a parser), we get results that are only marginally worse than those for the complete system and lead to the same places in the rankings. Additionally leaving out WordNet has a bigger impact and results in places 9 and 8 in the rankings.

Regarding the individual feature groups, the DSM-alignment-based measures are the best feature group for predicting semantic similarity and the simple heuristic measures are the best feature group for predicting entailment.

4 SemEval-2014 Task 3

4.1 Task Description

Unlike the other tasks, which focus on similar-sized texts, the shared task on "Cross-Level Semantic Similarity" (Jurgens et al., 2014) is about measuring semantic similarity between textual units of different lengths. It comprises four subtasks comparing I) paragraphs to sentences, II) sentences to phrases, III) phrases to words and IV) words to word senses (taken from WordNet). Due to the nature of this task, performance in it might be especially useful as an indicator for the usefulness of a system in the area of summarization.

SemantiKLUE takes the fourth place out of 38 in both the official ranking by Pearson correlation and the alternative ranking by Spearman correlation.

4.2 Additional Preprocessing

For the official run we perform some additional preprocessing on the data for the two subtasks on comparing phrases to words and words to word senses. On the word level we combine the word with the glosses of all its WordNet senses and on the word sense level we replace the WordNet sense indication with its corresponding lemmata and gloss. As our post-hoc experiments show that has a negative effect on performance in the phrase-to-word subtask. Therefore, we skip the additional preprocessing on that level for our experiments described below.

4.3 Experiments

For each of the four subtasks, we perform the same experiments as described in Section 3.2: We compare the official run submitted from a work-in-progress version of SemantiKLUE with the results from the whole system; we see how the system performs without dependency-based features and WordNet-based features; we try out the experimental features; we determine the most important feature group for the subtask. Table 2 gives an overview of the results.

4.3.1 Paragraph to Sentence

Our submitted run takes the fifth place (ties with another system) in the official ranking by Pearson correlation with a correlation coefficient of 0.817 (best of 34 systems: 0.837) and seventh place in the alternative ranking by Spearman correlation.

Run	Paragraph to sent.		Sent. to phrase		Phrase to word		Word to sense	
	r	ρ	r	ρ	r	ρ	r	ρ
official	**0.817**	**0.802**	**0.754**	**0.739**	0.215	0.218	0.314	0.327
complete system	**0.817**	**0.802**	**0.754**	**0.739**	0.284	0.289	0.316	**0.330**
no deps	0.815	**0.802**	0.752	**0.739**	0.309	0.313	0.312	0.329
no deps, no WN	0.813	**0.802**	0.736	0.721	**0.335**	**0.335**	0.234	0.248
complete + experimental	0.816	0.800	0.752	0.738	0.292	0.298	**0.318**	**0.330**
only DSM alignment	0.799	0.789	**0.724**	**0.711**	**0.302**	**0.301**	0.216	0.216
only WordNet	0.787	0.769	0.664	0.641	0.186	0.171	**0.313**	**0.311**
only simple	**0.807**	**0.793**	0.686	0.672	0.128	0.121	0.089	0.093
only DSM document	0.629	0.624	0.546	0.558	0.247	0.240	0.144	0.148
only deps	0.655	0.621	0.449	0.440	0.036	0.057	−0.080	−0.076

Table 2: Results for task 3 (Pearson's r and Spearman's ρ).

The complete SemantiKLUE system gives identical results. Leaving out the resource-heavy features based on the dependency structure and WordNet diminishes the results only very slightly, though it still resolves the tie and puts the system on the sixth place in the Pearson ranking. Adding the experimental features to the complete system has a minor negative effect.

Probably due to the length of the texts, our simple heuristic measures surpass the DSM-alignment-based measures as the best feature group for predicting semantic similarity.

4.3.2 Sentence to Phrase

In this subtask, SemantiKLUE takes the fourth place in both the official ranking with a Pearson correlation coefficient of 0.754 (best of 34 systems: 0.777) and in the alternative ranking by Spearman correlation. The complete system performs identically to our submitted run and leaving out the dependency-based features has little impact on the results. Additionally also leaving out the WordNet-based features has more impact on the results and puts the system on the eighth place in the official ranking. Just as in the paragraph-to-sentence subtask, adding the experimental features to the complete system has a slightly negative effect.

For this subtask, the DSM-alignment-based measures are clearly the feature group that yields the best results.

4.3.3 Phrase to Word

For our submitted run we performed the additional preprocessing described in Section 4.2 resulting in the eleventh place in the official ranking with a Pearson correlation coefficient of 0.215 (best of 22 systems: 0.415) and the 14th place in the alternative ranking by Spearman correlation. For our experiments with the complete system we skip that additional preprocessing step, i. e. we do not add the WordNet glosses to the word, and drastically improve the results, putting our system on the third place in the official ranking. Even more interesting is the observation that leaving out the resource-heavy features further improves the results, putting the system on the second place. In consistency with those observations, the DSM-alignment-based measures are not only the strongest individual feature group but also yield better results when taken alone than the complete system.

In contrast to the first two subtasks, adding the experimental features to the complete systems has a slightly positive effect here.

4.3.4 Word to Sense

In the word-to-sense subtask, SemantiKLUE takes the third place in both the official ranking with a Pearson correlation coefficient of 0.316 (best of 20 systems: 0.381) and in the alternative ranking by Spearman correlation. The complete system performs slightly better than our submitted run and adding the experimental features gives another marginal improvement. Leaving out the dependency-based features has little impact but also leaving out the WordNet-based features severly hurts performance. The reason for that behaviour becomes clear when we look at the results for the individual feature groups: the WordNet-based measures are clearly the strongest feature group for predicting the semantic similarity between words and word senses.

5 SemEval-2014 Task 10

5.1 Task Description

The shared task on "Multilingual Semantic Textual Similarity" (Agirre et al., 2014) is a continuation of the SemEval-2012 and *SEM 2013 shared tasks

Run	deft-forum	deft-news	headlines	images	OnWN	tweet-news	w. mean
best run	0.349	0.643	**0.733**	0.773	0.855	0.640	0.694
complete (all training data)	0.432	0.638	0.660	0.736	0.810	0.659	0.676
best overall training data	0.464	0.672	0.657	0.771	0.836	0.690	0.700
best overall, no deps	0.457	0.675	0.636	0.764	0.834	0.690	0.694
best overall, no deps, no WN	0.426	0.653	0.617	0.719	0.780	0.636	0.654
best overall + experimental	0.466	0.674	0.673	0.772	0.849	0.687	0.706
best individual training data	**0.475**	0.706	0.711	0.788	0.852	0.715	0.727
best individ., no deps	0.465	0.700	0.699	0.781	0.848	**0.722**	0.722
best individ., no deps, no WN	0.448	**0.722**	0.677	0.752	0.791	0.706	0.697
best individ. + experimental	**0.475**	0.711	0.715	**0.795**	**0.864**	0.721	**0.733**

Table 3: Results for task 10.

on semantic textual similarity (Agirre et al., 2012; Agirre et al., 2013). It comprises two subtasks: English semantic textual similarity and Spanish semantic textual similarity. For each subtask, there are sentence pairs from various genres.

We only participate in the English subtask and take the 13th place out of 38 with a weighted mean of Pearson correlation coefficients of 0.694 (best system: 0.761).

5.2 Experiments

From participating in the *SEM 2013 shared task on semantic textual similarity (Greiner et al., 2013) we already know that the composition of the training data is one of the strongest influences on system performance in this task. As the individual data sets are not very similar to each other, we tried to come up with a good subset of the available training data for each data set. In doing so, we were moderately successful as the results in Table 3 show. Running the complete system with all of the available training data on all test data sets results in a lower weighted mean than our submitted run. If we stick to using the same training data for all test data sets and optimize the subset of the training data we use, we achieve a slightly better result than our submitted run (the optimal subset consists of the FNWN, headlines, MSRpar, MSRvid and OnWN data sets). Using that optimal subset of the training data and adding the experimental features to the complete system has a minor positive effect on the weighted mean, with the biggest impact on the headlines and OnWN data sets. Using the complete system without the dependency-based features gives roughly the same results but omitting all resource-heavy features has clearly a negative impact on the results.

In another experiment we try to optimize our strategy of finding the best subset of the training data for each test data set. Doing that gives us a considerably higher weighted mean than using the same training data for every test data set, putting our system on the eighth place. Using the complete system, we find that the best training data subsets for the individual test data sets are those shown in Table 4.

test set	training sets
deft-forum	FNWN, headlines, MSRvid
deft-news	FNWN, MSRpar, MSRvid
headlines	FNWN, headlines, MSRpar
images	FNWN, MSRpar, MSRvid
OnWN	FNWN, MSRvid, OnWN
tweet-news	FNWN, headlines, MSRpar, MSRvid

Table 4: Optimal subsets of training data for use with the complete SemantiKLUE system.

If we add the experimental features to the complete system and still optimize the training data subsets, we get a small boost to the results. Leaving out the dependency-based features does not really hurt performance but also omitting the WordNet-based features has a negative impact on the results.

6 Conclusion

SemantiKLUE is a robust system for predicting the semantic similarity between two texts that can also be used to predict entailment. The system achieves good or very good results in three SemEval-2014 tasks representing a broad variety of semantic similarity problems (cf. Table 5 for an overview of the results of all subtasks). Our two-staged strategy of computing several similarity measures and using them as input for a machine learning mechanism

Subtask	submitted run score	submitted run rank	complete system score	complete system rank	winner score
Task 1, similarity	0.780	7/17	0.798	6/17	0.828
Task 1, entailment	0.823	4/18	0.820	4/18	0.846
Task 3, par-2-sent	0.817	5/34	0.817	5/34	0.837
Task 3, sent-2-phr	0.754	4/34	0.754	4/34	0.777
Task 3, phr-2-word	0.215	11/22	0.284	3/22	0.415
Task 3, word-2-sense	0.314	3/20	0.316	3/20	0.381
Task 3 overall	N/A	4/38	N/A	3/38	N/A
Task 10, deft-forum	0.349	20/38	0.464	12/38	0.531
Task 10, deft-news	0.643	22/37	0.672	19/37	0.785
Task 10, headlines	0.733	15/37	0.657	20/37	0.784
Task 10, images	0.773	16/37	0.771	17/37	0.834
Task 10, OnWN	0.855	3/36	0.836	7/36	0.875
Task 10, tweet-news	0.640	20/37	0.690	12/37	0.792
Task 10 overall	0.694	13/38	0.700	13/38	0.761

Table 5: Overview of results.

proves itself to be adaptable to the needs of the individual tasks.

Using the maximum-weight-matching algorithm for aligning words from both texts that have similar distributional semantics leads to very sound features. Even without the resource-heavy features, the system yields competitive results. In some use cases, those expensive features are almost negligible. Without being dependent on the availability of resources like a dependency parser or a WordNet-like lexical database, SemantiKLUE can easily be adapted to other languages.

Our experimental features from the commercial topic clustering software are useful in some cases; in others at least they do not hurt performance.

We feel that the heuristics based on the dependency structure of the texts do not exhaust all the possibilities that dependency parsing has to offer. In the future we would like to try out more measures based on those structures. Probably some kind of graph edit distance incorporating the similarities between both dependency relations and words might turn out to be a powerful feature.

References

Eneko Agirre, Daniel Cer, Mona Diab, Aitor Gonzalez-Agirre, and Weiwei Guo. 2012. SemEval-2012 task 6: A pilot on semantic textual similarity. In *First Joint Conference on Lexical and Computational Semantics*, pages 385–393. ACL.

Eneko Agirre, Daniel Cer, Mona Diab, Aitor Gonzalez-Agirre, and Weiwei Guo. 2013. *SEM 2013 shared task: Semantic textual similarity. In *Second Joint Conference on Lexical and Computational Semantics (*SEM)*, volume 1: Proceedings of the Main Conference and the Shared Task, pages 32–43. ACL.

Eneko Agirre, Carmen Banea, Claire Cardie, Daniel Cer, Mona Diab, Aitor Gonzalez-Agirre, Weiwei Guo, Rada Mihalcea, German Rigau, and Janyce Wiebe. 2014. SemEval-2014 task 10: Multilingual semantic textual similarity. In *Proceedings of the 8th International Workshop on Semantic Evaluation (SemEval-2014)*.

Marco Baroni, Silvia Bernardini, Adriano Ferraresi, and Eros Zanchetta. 2009. The WaCky Wide Web: A collection of very large linguistically processed Web-crawled corpora. *Language Resources and Evaluation*, 43(3):209–226.

Alexander Budanitsky and Graeme Hirst. 2006. Evaluating WordNet-based measures of lexical semantic relatedness. *Computational Linguistics*, 32(1):13–47.

Marie-Catherine de Marneffe and Christopher D. Manning, 2008. *Stanford typed dependencies manual.* Stanford University.

William A. Gale and Kenneth W. Church. 1993. A program for aligning sentences in bilingual corpora. *Computational Linguistics*, 19(1):75–102.

Zvi Galil. 1986. Efficient algorithms for finding maximum matching in graphs. *Computing Surveys*, 18(1):23–38.

Paul Greiner and Stefan Evert. in preparation. The Klugator Engine: A distributional approach to open questions in market research.

Paul Greiner, Thomas Proisl, Stefan Evert, and Besim Kabashi. 2013. KLUE-CORE: A regression model of semantic textual similarity. In *Second Joint Conference on Lexical and Computational Semantics (*SEM)*, volume 1: Proceedings of the Main Conference and the Shared Task, pages 181–186. ACL.

Aric A. Hagberg, Daniel A. Schult, and Pieter J. Swart. 2008. Exploring network structure, dynamics, and function using NetworkX. In Gäel Varoquaux,

Travis Vaught, and Jarrod Millman, editors, *Proceedings of the 7th Python in Science Conference (SciPy2008)*, pages 11–15, Pasadena, CA.

Lushan Han, Abhay L. Kashyap, Tim Finin, James Mayfield, and Johnathan Weese. 2013. UMBC_EBIQUITY-CORE: Semantic textual similarity systems. In *Proceedings of the Second Joint Conference on Lexical and Computational Semantics*. ACL.

David Jurgens, Mohammad Taher Pilehvar, and Roberto Navigli. 2014. SemEval-2014 task 3: Cross-level semantic similarity. In *Proceedings of the 8th International Workshop on Semantic Evaluation (SemEval-2014)*.

Claudia Leacock and Martin Chodorow. 1998. Combining local context and WordNet similarity for word sense identification. In Christiane Fellbaum, editor, *WordNet: An Electronic Lexical Database*, pages 265–283. MIT Press, Cambridge, MA.

Yuri Lin, Jean-Baptiste Michel, Erez Lieberman Aiden, Jon Orwant, Will Brockman, and Slav Petrov. 2012. Syntactic annotations for the Google Books Ngram Corpus. In *Proceedings of the ACL 2012 System Demonstrations*, pages 169–174, Jeju Island, Korea. ACL.

Dekang Lin. 1998. An information-theoretic definition of similarity. In *Proceedings of the Fifteenth International Conference on Machine Learning*, pages 296–304, San Francisco, CA. Morgan Kaufmann.

Marco Marelli, Luisa Bentivogli, Marco Baroni, Raffaella Bernardi, Stefano Menini, and Roberto Zamparelli. 2014a. SemEval-2014 task 1: Evaluation of compositional distributional semantic models on full sentences through semantic relatedness and textual entailment. In *Proceedings of the 8th International Workshop on Semantic Evaluation (SemEval-2014)*.

Marco Marelli, Stefano Menini, Marco Baroni, Luisa Bentivogli, Raffaella Bernardi, and Roberto Zamparelli. 2014b. A SICK cure for the evaluation of compositional distributional semantic models. In *Proceedings of LREC 2014*, Reykjavik. ELRA.

Fabian Pedregosa, Gaël Varoquaux, Alexandre Gramfort, Vincent Michel, Bertrand Thirion, Olivier Grisel, Mathieu Blondel, Peter Prettenhofer, Ron Weiss, Vincent Dubourg, Jake Vanderplas, Alexandre Passos, David Cournapeau, Matthieu Brucher, Matthieu Perrot, and Édouard Duchesnay. 2011. Scikit-learn: Machine learning in Python. *Journal of Machine Learning Research*, 12:2825–2830.

Roland Schäfer and Felix Bildhauer. 2012. Building large corpora from the web using a new efficient tool chain. In *Proceedings of the Eighth International Conference on Language Resources and Evaluation (LREC '12)*, pages 486–493, Istanbul, Turkey. ELRA.

Hinrich Schütze. 1998. Automatic word sense discrimination. *Computational Linguistics*, 24(1):97–123.

Sensible: L2 Translation Assistance by Emulating the Manual Post-Editing Process

Liling Tan, Anne-Kathrin Schumann, Jose M.M. Martinez and Francis Bond[1]
Universität des Saarland / Campus, Saarbrücken, Germany
Nanyang Technological University[1] / 14 Nanyang Drive, Singapore
alvations@gmail.com, anne.schumann@mx.uni-saarland.de,
j.martinez@mx.uni-saarland.de, bond@ieee.org

Abstract

This paper describes the Post-Editor Z system submitted to the L2 writing assistant task in SemEval-2014. The aim of task is to build a translation assistance system to translate untranslated sentence fragments. This is not unlike the task of post-editing where human translators improve machine-generated translations. Post-Editor Z emulates the manual process of post-editing by (i) crawling and extracting parallel sentences that contain the untranslated fragments from a Web-based translation memory, (ii) extracting the possible translations of the fragments indexed by the translation memory and (iii) applying simple cosine-based sentence similarity to rank possible translations for the untranslated fragment.

1 Introduction

In this paper, we present a collaborative submission between *Saarland University* and *Nanyang Technological University* to the L2 Translation Assistant task in SemEval-2014. Our team name is *Sensible* and the participating system is Post-Editor Z (PEZ).

The L2 Translation Assistant task concerns the translation of an untranslated fragment from a partially translated sentence. For instance, given a sentence, "*Ich konnte Bärbel noch* <u>*on the border*</u> *in einen letzten S-Bahn-Zug nach Westberlin setzen.*", the aim is to provide an appropriate translation for the underline phrase, i.e. <u>*an der Grenze*</u>.

The aim of the task is not unlike the task of post-editing where human translators correct errors provided by machine-generated translations.

The main difference is that in the context of post-editing the source text is provided. A translation workflow that incorporates post-editing begins with a source sentence, e.g. "*I could still sit on the border in the very last tram to West Berlin.*" and the human translator is provided with a machine-generated translation with untranslated fragments such as the previous example and sometimes "fixing" the translation would simply require substituting the appropriate translation for the untranslated fragment.

2 Related Tasks and Previous Approaches

The L2 writing assistant task lies between the lines of machine translation and crosslingual word sense disambiguation (CLWSD) or crosslingual lexical substitution (CLS) (Lefever and Hoste, 2013; Mihalcea et al. 2010).

While CLWSD systems resolve the correct semantics of the translation by providing the correct lemma in the target language, CLS attempts to provide also the correct form of the translation with the right morphology. Machine translation tasks focus on producing translations of whole sentences/documents while crosslingual word sense disambiguation targets a single lexical item.

Previously, CLWSD systems have tried distributional semantics and string matching methods (Tan and Bond, 2013), unsupervised clustering of word alignment vectors (Apidianaki, 2013) and supervised classification-based approaches trained on local context features for a window of three words containing the focus word (van Gompel, 2010; van Gompel and van den Bosch, 2013; Rudnick et al., 2013). Interestingly, Carpuat (2013) approached the CLWSD task with a Statistical MT system .

Short of concatenating outputs of CLWSD / CLS outputs and dealing with a reordering issue

Proceedings of the 8th International Workshop on Semantic Evaluation (SemEval 2014), pages 541–545,
Dublin, Ireland, August 23-24, 2014.

and responding to the task organizers' call to avoid implementing a full machine translation system to tackle the task, we designed PEZ as an Automatic Post-Editor (APE) that attempts to resolve untranslated fragments.

3 Automatic Post-Editors

APEs target various types of MT errors from determiner selection (Knight and Chander, 1994) to grammatical agreement (Mareček et al., 2011). Untranslated fragments from machine translations are the result of out-of-vocabulary (OOV) words.

Previous approaches to the handling of untranslated fragments include using a pivot language to translate the OOV word(s) into a third language and then back into to the source language, thereby extracting paraphrases to OOV (Callison-burch and Osborne, 2006), combining sub-lexical/constituent translations of the OOV word(s) to generate the translation (Huang et al., 2011) or finding paraphrases of the OOV words that have available translations (Marton et al., 2009; Razmara et al., 2013). [1]

However the simplest approach to handle untranslated fragments is to increase the size of parallel data. The web is vast and infinite, a human translator would consult the web when encountering a word that he/she cannot translate easily. The most human-like approach to post-editing a foreign untranslated fragment is to do a search on the web or a translation memory and choose the most appropriate translation of the fragment from the search result given the context of the machine translated sentence.

4 Motivation

When post-editing an untranslated fragment, a human translator would (i) first query a translation memory or parallel corpus for the untranslated fragment in the source language, (ii) then attempt to understand the various context that the fragment can occur in and (iii) finally he/she would surmise appropriate translations for the untranslated fragment based on semantic and grammatical constraints of the chosen translations.

[1] in MT, evaluation is normally performed using automatic metrics based on automatic evaluation metrics that compares scores based on string/word similarity between the machine-generated translation and a reference output, simply removing OOV would have improved the metric "scores" of the system (Habash, 2008; Tan and Pal, 2014).

The PEZ system was designed to emulate the manual post-editing process by (i) first crawling a web-based translation memory, (ii) then extracting parallel sentences that contain the untranslated fragments and the corresponding translations of the fragments indexed by the translation memory and (iii) finally ranking them based on cosine similarity of the context words.

5 System Description

The PEZ system consists of three components, viz (i) a Web Translation Memory (`WebTM`) crawler, (ii) the `XLING` reranker and (iii) a longest ngram/string match module.

5.1 `WebTM` Crawler

Given the query fragment and the context sentence, "*Die Frau kehrte alone nach Lima zurück*", the crawler queries `www.bab.la` and returns sentences containing the untranslated fragment with various possible tranlsations, e.g:

- ***isoliert*** *: Darum sollten wir den Kaffee nicht* ***isoliert*** *betrachten.*
- ***alleine*** *: Die Kommission kann nun aber für ihr Verhalten nicht* ***alleine*** *die Folgen tragen.*
- ***Allein*** *:* ***Allein*** *in der Europischen Union sind.*

The retrieval mechanism is based on the fact that the target translations of the queried word/phrase are bolded on a web-based TM and thus they can be easily extracted by manipulating the text between `<bold>...</bold>` tags. Although the indexed translations were easy to extract, there were few instances where the translations were embedded betweeen the bold tags on the web-based TM.

5.2 `XLING` Reranker

`XLING` is a light-weight cosine-based sentence similarity script used in the previous CLWSD shared task in SemEval-2013 (Tan and Bond, 2013). Given the sentences from the WebTM crawler, the reranker first removes all stopwords from the sentences and then ranks the sentences based on the number of overlapping stems.

In situations where there are no overlapping content words from the sentences, `XLING` falls back on the most common translation of the untranslated fragment.

	en-de			en-es			fr-en			nl-en		
	acc	*wac*	*rec*	*acc*	*wac*	*rec*	*acc*	*wac*	*rec*	*acc*	*wac*	*rec*
WebTM	0.160	0.184	0.647	0.145	0.175	0.470	0.055	0.067	0.210	0.092	0.099	0.214
XLING	0.152	0.178	0.647	0.141	0.171	0.470	0.055	0.067	0.210	0.088	0.095	0.214
PEZ	**0.162**	**0.233**	**0.878**	**0.239**	**0.351**	**0.819**	**0.081**	**0.116**	**0.321**	**0.115**	**0.152**	**0.335**

Table 1: Results for *Best* Evaluation of the System Runs.

5.3 Longest Ngram/String Matches

Due to the low coverage of the indexed translations on the web TM, it is necessary to extract more candidate translations. Assuming little knowledge about the target language, human translator would find parallel sentences containing the untranslated fragment and resort to finding repeating phrases that occurs among the target language sentences.

For instance, when we query the phrase *history book* from the context "*Von ihr habe ich mehr gelernt als aus manchem* ***history book***.", the longest ngram/string matches module retrieves several target language sentences without any indexed translation:

- *Ich weise darauf hin oder nehme an, dass dies in den Geschichtsbüchern auch so erwähnt wird.*
- *Wenn die Geschichtsbücher geschrieben werden wird unser Zeitalter, denke ich, wegen drei Dingen erinnert werden.*
- *Ich bin sicher, Präsident Mugabe hat sich nun einen Platz in den Geschichtsbüchern gesichert, wenn auch aus den falschen Gründen.*
- *In den Geschichtsbüchern wird für jeden einzelnen Tag der letzten mehr als 227 Jahre an Gewalttaten oder Tragdien auf dem europäischen Kontinent erinnert.*

By simply spotting the repeating word/string from the target language sentences it is possible to guess that the possible candidates for "*history book*" are *Geschichtsbücher* or *Geschichtsbüchern*. Computationally, this can be achieved by looking for the longest matching ngrams or the longest matching string across the target language sentences fetched by the WebTM crawler.

5.4 System Runs

We submitted three system runs to the L2 writing assistant task in Semeval-2014.

1. **WebTM**: a baseline configuration which outputs the most frequent indexed translation of the untranslated fragment from the Web TM.
2. **XLING**: reranks the WebTM outputs based on cosine similarity.
3. **PEZ**: similar to the XLING but when the WebTM fetches no output, the system looks for longest common substring and reranks the outputs based on cosine similarity.

6 Evaluation

The evaluation of the task is based on three metrics, viz. absolute accuracy (*acc*), word-based accuracy (*wac*) and recall (*rec*).

Absolute accuracy measures the number of fragments that match the gold translation of the untranslated fragments. Word-based accuracy assigns a score according to the longest consecutive matching substring between output fragment and reference fragment; it is computed as such:

$$wac \quad = \quad \frac{|longestmatch(output,reference)|}{max(|output|,|reference|)}$$

Recall accounts for the number of fragments for which output was given (regardless of whether it was correct).

7 Results

Table 1 presents the results for the *best* evaluation scores of the PEZ system runs for the English to German (en-de), English to Spanish (en-es), French to English (fr-en) and Dutch to English (nl-en) evaluations. Figure 1 presents the word accuracy of the system runs for both best and out-of-five (oof) evaluation[2].

The results show that using the longest ngram/string improves the recall and subsequently the accuracy and word accuracy of the system. However, this is not true when guessing untranslated fragments from L1 English to L2. This is due to the low recall of the system when searching for the untranslated fragment in French and

[2]Please refer to http://goo.gl/y9f5Na for results of other competing systems

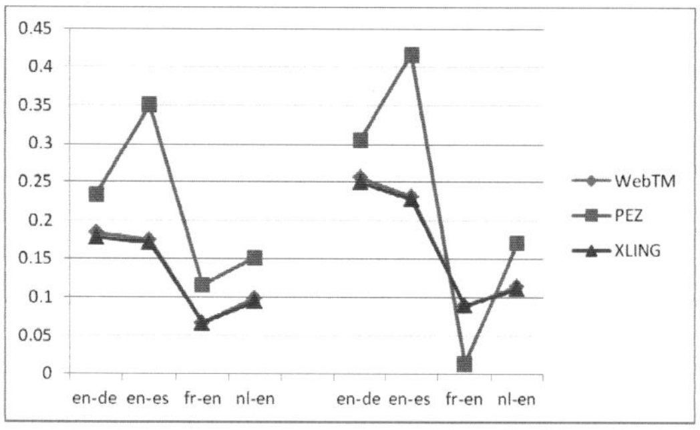

Figure 1: Word Accuracy of System Runs (*best* on the left, *oof* on the right).

Dutch, where the English words/phases indexed in the TM is much larger than other languages.

8 Error Analysis

We manually inspected the English-German outputs from the PEZ system and identified several particularities of the outputs that account for the low performance of the system for this language pair.

8.1 Weird Expressions in the TM

When attempting to translate *Nevertheless* in the context of "*Nevertheless hat sich die neue Bundesrepublik Deutschland unter amerikanischem Druck an der militrischen Einmischung auf dem Balkan beteiligt.*" where the gold translation is *Trotzdem* or *Nichtsdestotrotz*. The PEZ system retrieves the following sentence pairs that contains a rarely used expression *nichtsdestoweniger* from a literally translated sentence pair in the TM:

- **EN**: But *nevertheless* it is a fact that nobody can really recognize their views in the report.
- **DE**: Aber *nichtsdestoweniger* kann sich niemand so recht in dem Bericht wiederfinden.

Another example of weird expression is when translating "*husband*" in the context of "*In der Silvesternacht sind mein husband und ich auf die Bahnhofstraße gegangen.*". PEZ provided a lesser use yet valid translation *Gemahl* instead of the gold translation *Mann*. In this case, it is also a matter of register where in a more formal register one will use *Gemahl* instead of *Mann*.

8.2 Missing / Additional Words from Matches

When extracting candidate translations from the TM index or longest ngram/string, there are several matches where the PEZ system outputs a partial phrase or phrases with additional tokens that cause the disparity between the absolute accuracy and word accuracy. An instance of missing words is as follows:

- **Input**: Eine genetische Veranlagung *plays a decisive role*.
- **PEZ**: *Eine genetische Veranlagung eine entscheidende rolle.*
- **Gold**: *Eine genetische Veranlagung spielt (dabei) eine entscheidende rolle.*

For the addition of superfluous words is as follows:

- **Input:** *Geräte wie Handys sind not permitted wenn sie nicht unterrichtlichen Belangen dienen.*
- **PEZ**: *Geräte wie Handys sind es verboten, wenn sie nicht unterrichtlichen Belangen dienen.*
- **Gold**: *Geräte wie Handys sind verboten wenn sie nicht unterrichtlichen Belangen dienen.*

8.3 Case Sensitivity

For the English-German evaluation , there are several instances where the PEZ system produces the correct translation of the phrase but in lower cases and this resulted in poorer accuracy. This is unique to German target language and possibly contributing to the lower scores as compared to the English-Spanish evaluation.

9 Conclusion

In this paper, we presented the PEZ automatic post-editor system in the L2 writing assistant task in SemEval-2014. The PEZ post-editing system is a resource lean approach to provide translation for untranslated fragments based on no prior training data and simple string manipulations from a web-based translation memory.

The PEZ system attempts to emulate the process of a human translator post-editing out-of-vocabulary words from a machine-generated translation. The best configuration of the PEZ system involves a simple string search for the longest common ngram/string from the target language sentences without having word/phrasal alignment and also avoiding the need to handle word reordering for multi-token untranslated fragments.

Acknowledgements

The research leading to these results has received funding from the People Programme (Marie Curie Actions) of the European Union's Seventh Framework Programme FP7/2007-2013/ under REA grant agreement n ° 317471.

References

Marianna Apidianaki. 2013. Limsi : Cross-lingual word sense disambiguation using translation sense clustering. In *Second Joint Conference on Lexical and Computational Semantics (*SEM), Volume 2: Proceedings of the Seventh International Workshop on Semantic Evaluation (SemEval 2013)*, pages 178–182, Atlanta, Georgia, USA, June.

Chris Callison-burch and Miles Osborne. 2006. Improved statistical machine translation using paraphrases. In *In Proceedings of HLT/NAACL-2006*, pages 17–24.

Marine Carpuat. 2013. Nrc: A machine translation approach to cross-lingual word sense disambiguation (semeval-2013 task 10). In *Second Joint Conference on Lexical and Computational Semantics (*SEM), Volume 2: Proceedings of the Seventh International Workshop on Semantic Evaluation (SemEval 2013)*, pages 188–192, Atlanta, Georgia, USA, June.

Nizar Habash. 2008. Four techniques for online handling of out-of-vocabulary words in arabic-english statistical machine translation. In *ACL*, pages 57–60.

Chung-Chi Huang, Ho-Ching Yen, Ping-Che Yang, Shih-Ting Huang, and Jason S. Chang. 2011. Using sublexical translations to handle the oov problem in machine translation. *ACM Trans. Asian Lang. Inf. Process.*, 10(3):16.

Kevin Knight and Ishwar Chander. 1994. Automated postediting of documents. In *AAAI*, pages 779–784.

David Mareček, Rudolf Rosa, Petra Galuščáková, and Ondřej Bojar. 2011. Two-step translation with grammatical post-processing. In *Proceedings of the Sixth Workshop on Statistical Machine Translation*, WMT '11, pages 426–432, Stroudsburg, PA, USA.

Yuval Marton, Chris Callison-Burch, and Philip Resnik. 2009. Improved statistical machine translation using monolingually-derived paraphrases. In *EMNLP*, pages 381–390.

Majid Razmara, Maryam Siahbani, Reza Haffari, and Anoop Sarkar. 2013. Graph propagation for paraphrasing out-of-vocabulary words in statistical machine translation. In *Proceedings of the 51st Annual Meeting of the Association for Computational Linguistics (Volume 1: Long Papers)*, pages 1105–1115, Sofia, Bulgaria, August.

Alex Rudnick, Can Liu, and Michael Gasser. 2013. Hltdi: Cl-wsd using markov random fields for semeval-2013 task 10. In *Second Joint Conference on Lexical and Computational Semantics (*SEM), Volume 2: Proceedings of the Seventh International Workshop on Semantic Evaluation (SemEval 2013)*, pages 171–177, Atlanta, Georgia, USA, June.

Liling Tan and Francis Bond. 2013. Xling: Matching query sentences to a parallel corpus using topic models for wsd. In *Second Joint Conference on Lexical and Computational Semantics (*SEM), Volume 2: Proceedings of the Seventh International Workshop on Semantic Evaluation (SemEval 2013)*, pages 167–170, Atlanta, Georgia, USA, June.

Liling Tan and Santanu Pal. 2014. Manawi: Using multi-word expressions and named entities to improve machine translation. In *Proceedings of the Ninth Workshop on Statistical Machine Translation*, Baltimore, USA, August.

Maarten van Gompel and Antal van den Bosch. 2013. Wsd2: Parameter optimisation for memory-based cross-lingual word-sense disambiguation. In *Second Joint Conference on Lexical and Computational Semantics (*SEM), Volume 2: Proceedings of the Seventh International Workshop on Semantic Evaluation (SemEval 2013)*, pages 183–187, Atlanta, Georgia, USA, June.

Maarten van Gompel. 2010. Uvt-wsd1: A cross-lingual word sense disambiguation system. In *Proceedings of the 5th International Workshop on Semantic Evaluation*, SemEval '10, pages 238–241, Stroudsburg, PA, USA.

Senti.ue: Tweet Overall Sentiment Classification Approach for SemEval-2014 Task 9

José Saias
DI - ECT - Universidade de Évora
Rua Romão Ramalho, 59
7000-671 Évora, Portugal
`jsaias@uevora.pt`

Abstract

This document describes the `senti.ue` system and how it was used for participation in SemEval-2014 Task 9 challenge. Our system is an evolution of our prior work, also used in last year's edition of Sentiment Analysis in Twitter. This system maintains a supervised machine learning approach to classify the tweet overall sentiment, but with a change in the used features and the algorithm. We use a restricted set of 47 features in subtask B and 31 features in subtask A.

In the constrained mode, and for the five data sources, `senti.ue` achieved a score between 78,72 and 84,05 in subtask A, and a score between 55,31 and 71,39 in subtask B. For the unconstrained mode, our score was slightly below, except for one case in subtask A.

1 Introduction

This paper describes the approach taken by a team of Universidade de Évora's Computer Science Department in SemEval-2014 Task 9: Sentiment Analysis in Twitter (Rosenthal et al., 2014). SemEval-2014 Task 9 has an expression-level (subtask A) and a message-level (subtask B) polarity classification challenges. The first subtask aims to determine whether a word (or phrase) is positive, negative or neutral, within the textual context in which it appears. The second subtask concerns the classification of the overall text polarity, which corresponds to automatically detecting the sentiment expressed in a Twitter message. In both subtasks, systems can operate in constrained or unconstrained mode. Constrained means that learning is based only on provided training texts, with the possible aid of static resources such as lexicons. Extra tweets or additional annotated documents for training are permitted only in unconstrained mode.

The system we used to respond to this challenge is called `senti.ue`, and follows on from our previous work on Natural Language Processing (NLP) and Sentiment Analysis (SA). We developed work in automatic reputation assessment, using a Machine Learning (ML) based classifier for comments with impact on a particular target entity (Saias, 2013). We also participated in the previous edition of SemEval SA task, where we have implemented the basis for the current system. In last year's solution (Saias and Fernandes, 2013), we treated both subtasks using the same method (except the training set). We have updated the method for subtask A, now considering also the text around the area to classify, by dedicating new features to those preceding and following tweet parts. Text overall sentiment classification is the core objective of our system, and is performed, as before, with a supervised machine learning technique. For subtask B, we fixed some implementation issues in the previous version, and we went from 22 to 53 features, explained in Section 3.

2 Related Work

The popularity of social networks and microblogging facilitated the sharing of opinions. To know whether people are satisfied or not with a particular brand or product is of great interest to marketing companies. Much work has appeared in SA, trying to capture valuable information in expressions of contentment or discontentment.

Important international scientific events, NLP related, include SA challenges and workshops. This was the case in SemEval-2013, whose task 2 (Wilson et al., 2013) required sentiment analysis of Twitter and SMS text messages. Being the pre-

Proceedings of the 8th International Workshop on Semantic Evaluation (SemEval 2014), pages 546–550, Dublin, Ireland, August 23-24, 2014.

decessor task of the challenge for which this work was developed, it is similar to this year's Task 9. The participating systems achieved better results in contextual polarity subtask (A) than those obtained for the overall message polarity subtask (B). In that edition, the best results were obtained by systems in constrained mode. The most common method was supervised ML with features that can be related to text words, syntactic function, discourse elements relation, internet slang and symbols, or clues from sentiment lexicons. In that task, the `NRC-Canada` system (Mohammad et al., 2013) obtained the best performance, achieving an F1 of 88.9% in subtask A and 69% in subtask B. That system used one SVM classifier for each subtask, together with text surface based features, features associated with manually created and automatically generated sentiment lexicons, and n-gram features. Other systems with good results in that task were `GU-MLT-LT` (Günther and Furrer, 2013) and `AVAYA` (Becker et al., 2013). The first was implemented in the Python language. It includes features for: text tokens after normalization, stems, word clusters, and two values for the accumulated positive and accumulated negative SentiWordNet (Baccianella et al., 2010) scores, considering negation. Its machine learning classifier is based on linear models with stochastic gradient descent. The approach taken in the `AVAYA` system centers on training high-dimensional, linear classifiers with a combination of lexical and syntactic features. This system uses Bag-of-Words features, with negation represented in word suffix, and including not only the raw word forms but also combinations with lemmas and PoS tags. Then, word polarity features are added, using the MPQA lexicon (Wiebe et al., 2005), as well as syntactic dependency and PoS tag features. Other features consider emoticons, capitalization, character repetition, and emphasis characters, such as asterisks and dashes. The resulting model was trained with the LIBLINEAR (Fan et al., 2008) classification library.

Another NLP task very close to SA is polarity classification on the reputation of an entity. Here, instead the sentiment in the perspective of the opinion holder, the goal is to detect the impact of this particular opinion on some entity's reputation. The `diue` system (Saias, 2013) uses a supervised ML approach for reputation polarity classification, including Bag-of-Words and a limited set of features based on sentiment lexicons and superficial text analysis.

3 Method

This work follows on from our previous participation in SemEval-2013 SA task, where we have devoted greater effort to subtask B. We start by explaining our current approach for this subtask, and then we describe how such classifier is also used in subtask A.

3.1 Message Polarity Classification

The `senti.ue` system maintains a supervised machine learning approach to perform the overall sentiment classification. As before, Python and the Natural Language Toolkit (NLTK[1]) are used for text processing and ML feature extraction.

The first step was to obtain the tweet content and forming the instances of the training set. During the download phase, several tweets were not found. In constrained mode, we got only 7352 instances available for training.

Tweet preprocessing includes tokenization, which is punctuation and white space based, negation detection, and lemmatization, through NLTK class `WordNetLemmatizer`. After that, the system runs the ML component. Instead of the solution we used in 2013, with two differently configured classifiers in a pipeline, we chose to use a single classifier, which this year is based on `SciKit-Learn`[2], and to increase the number of features that are extracted to represent each instance. The classification algorithm was Support Vector Machines (SVM), using SVC[3] class, with a linear kernel and 10^{-5} tolerance for stopping criterion. SVC class implementation is based on `libsvm` (Chang and Lin, 2011), and uses one-against-one approach for multi-class classification. From each instance, the system extracts the 47 features in Figure 1. The first two features represent the index of the first polarized token. The following represent the repeated occurrence of a question mark, and the existence of a token with negation (*not*, *never*). Then there are two features that indicate whether there is negation before positive or negative words. The following 8 fea-

[1]Python based platform with resources and programming libraries suitable for linguistic processing (Bird, 2006).

[2]Open source tool for Machine Learning in Python - http://scikit-learn.org/

[3]http://scikit-learn.org/stable/modules/svm.html#svm-classification

tures indicate whether there are positive or negative terms, just after, or near, a question mark or an exclamation mark. We build a table with words or phrases marked as positive or negative in subtask A data. Using this resource, 4 features test the presence and the count of word n-grams marked as positive or negative. Then the *TA.alike* features represent the same, but after lemmatization and synonym verification. To find the synonyms of a term, we used the WordNet (Princeton University, 2010) resource. The probability of each word belonging to a class was calculated. There are 3 features *avgProbWordOn*, one per class, that represent the average of this probability for each instance words. Next 3 features represent the same, but focusing only on the last 5 words of each text. Then we have 6 *ProbLog2Prob* features, representing the average of $P \times \log_2(P)$, for all words, or only the latest 5 words, for all classes. P is the probability of the word belonging to one class. One feature cumulates the token polarity values, according to SentiWordNet. The final 12 features are based on sentiment lexicons: AFINN (Nielsen, 2011), Bing Liu (Liu et al., 2005), MPQA, and a custom polarity table with some manually entered entries. For each resource, we count the instance tokens with negative and positive polarity, and create a feature *direction*, having the value 1 if *countTokens.pos*>*countTokens.neg*, -1 if *countTokens.pos*<*countTokens.neg*, or 0.

For the unconstrained mode, the only difference is the use of more instances for the training set, with 3296 short texts obtained from SemEval-2014 Task 4 data[4], about laptops and restaurants.

```
firstIndexOf.{pos,neg}, hasDoubleQuestionMark,
hasNegation, hasNegationBefore.{pos,neg},
{pos,neg}.{After,Near}.Exclamation,
{pos,neg}.{After,Near}.Question,
hasTA.{pos,neg}.NGrams, countTA.{pos,neg}.NGrams,
hasTA.alike.{pos,neg}.NGrams,
countTA.alike.{pos,neg}.NGrams,
avgProbWordOn.{pos,neg,neutral},
last5AvgProbWordOn.{pos,neg,neutral},
avgW.ProbLog2Prob.{pos,neg,neutral},
last5AvgW.ProbLog2Prob.{pos,neg,neutral},
SentiWordNetAccumulatedValue,
{AFINN,Liu,MPQA,custom}.countTokens.{pos,neg},
{AFINN,Liu,MPQA,custom}.direction
```

Figure 1: features for message polarity

```
{AFINN,Liu,custom}.countTokens.{pos,neg},
{AFINN,Liu,custom}.direction,
{AFINN,Liu,custom}.sentence.countTok.{pos,neg},
{AFINN,Liu,custom}.sentence.direction,
{AFINN,Liu,custom}.left.countTokens.{pos,neg},
{AFINN,Liu,custom}.left.direction,
b.sentClass.{left,right,sentence,chosenText}
```

Figure 2: features for contextual polarity

3.2 Contextual Polarity Disambiguation

In this subtask, the download phase fetched only 6506 tweets. These instances have boundaries marking the substring to classify. Our system starts by splitting the document into text segments: *fullText, leftText, rightText, sentenceText, chosenText*. The first corresponds to the entire tweet. The following represent the text before and the text after the chosen text. Then we have the sentence where the chosen text is, and finally the text segment that systems must classify. The preprocessing described before is then applied to each of these text segments. For each instance, the system generates the 31 features listed in Figure 2. First 27 features represent 9 values for each *chosenText*, *sentenceText* and *leftText* instance segments. These values represent the count of polarized tokens, and the direction (1, 0, or -1, as before), according to 3 sentiment lexicons. The final 4 features have the overall sentiment classification, using the subtask B classifier, for each text segment: *leftText*, *rightText*, *sentenceText*, and *chosenText*. In unconstrained mode the instances used for subtask A training are the same. The difference with respect to the constrained mode is the overall sentiment classifier used for the last 4 features, which corresponds to the unconstrained classifier of subtask B.

This subtask has specific features, different from those used in the previous subtask, and after some tests with `SciKit-Learn` classifiers, we found that, in this case, our best results were not obtained with SVM. For subtask A, we chose Gradient Boosting classifier[5], an ensemble method that combines the predictions of several models, configured with deviance loss function, 0.1 for learning rate, and 100 regression estimators with individual maximum depth of 4.

[4]http://alt.qcri.org/semeval2014/task4/

[5]http://scikit-learn.org/stable/modules/generated/sklearn.ensemble.GradientBoostingClassifier.html

run	LJ'14	SMS'13	T'13	T'14	T'14s
A const.	81,90	78,72	84,05	80,54	82,75
A unc.	79,70	82,93	83,80	77,07	80,02
B const.	71,39	59,34	67,34	63,81	55,31
B unc.	68,08	56,16	65,21	61,47	54,09

Table 1: `senti.ue` score

	LJ'14	SMS'13	T'13	T'14	T'14s
A avg	77,08	77,37	79,94	76,84	68,33
A best	85,61	89,31	90,14	86,63	82,75
B avg	63,52	55,63	59,78	60,41	45,44
B best	74,84	70,28	72,12	70,96	58,16

Table 2: all systems: higher and average score

4 Results

We submitted four runs, with the system output for each subtask, and both constrained and unconstrained modes. Test set documents come from five sources: LiveJournal blogs (LJ'14), SMS test (SMS'13) and Twitter test (T'13) data from last year, a new Twitter collection (T'14), and 100 tweets whose text includes sarcasm (T'14s). The primary metric to evaluate the results is the average F-measure for positive and negative classes. Table 1 shows the score obtained by our system. In the constrained mode, and for the five data sources, `senti.ue` achieved a score between 78,72 and 84,05 in subtask A, and a score between 55,31 and 71,39 in subtask B. Comparing the evaluation between constrained and unconstrained modes, the latter was always a little below, except for one case in subtask A and SMS2013 data, where the extra training data led to a 4% score improvement. In this SA challenge there were a total of 27 submissions in subtask A and 50 submissions in subtask B. Among these, the best score and the average score for each subtask are shown in Table 2. In both subtaks, our system result is above the participating systems average score. In subtask A and the Twitter Sarcasm 2014 collection (T'14s), `senti.ue` achieved the highest score, with 82,75% in constrained mode.

For each data set, tables 3 and 4 show the precision and recall of our system result on the highest scored mode, per class. In subtask A precision is between 64 and 99% for positive and negative classes, taking the value of zero in the neutral class. For the overall sentiment subtask, precision is similar among the 3 classes, having the minimum value in the negative class of sarcasm tweets. The best recall value was obtained in the positive class of the 2014 tweet collection.

task, mode, data	Positive	Negative	Neutral
A, C, LJ'14	87,27	86,69	0,00
A, U, SMS'13	85,06	85,87	1,89
A, C, T'13	91,11	79,10	0,00
A, C, T'14	90,37	74,74	1,14
A, C, T'14s	98,78	64,86	0,00
B, C, LJ'14	65,11	80,59	67,64
B, C, SMS'13	48,98	55,08	88,73
B, C, T'13	65,65	65,39	77,99
B, C, T'14	65,89	62,87	71,00
B, C, T'14s	78,79	32,50	61,54

Table 3: `senti.ue` precision in best mode

task, mode, data	Positive	Negative	Neutral
A, C, LJ'14	80,11	74,70	0,00
A, U, SMS'13	80,62	80,48	11,54
A, C, T'13	85,05	81,16	0,00
A, C, T'14	89,09	68,25	14,29
A, C, T'14s	83,51	88,89	0,00
B, C, LJ'14	77,65	64,99	68,30
B, C, SMS'13	83,68	58,81	74,58
B, C, T'13	78,72	60,93	68,87
B, C, T'14	80,07	49,42	60,28
B, C, T'14s	55,32	76,47	36,36

Table 4: `senti.ue` recall in best mode

5 Conclusions

Continuing last year experience, we participated in SemEval-2014 Task 9 to test our approach for a real-time SA system for the English used nowadays in social media content. We changed the method for subtask A, now considering also the text around the area to classify, by dedicating new features to it, which led to good results. Our method for overall sentiment is ML based, using a restricted set of features that are dedicated to superficial text properties, negation presence, and sentiment lexicons. Without a deep linguistic analysis, our system achieved a reasonable result in subtask B. The evaluation of our solution, in both subtasks, shows an appreciable improvement, by 10% or more, when compared to our results in 2013. We believe that the additional training instances used in unconstrained mode and subtask B, about laptops and restaurants, have a writing style different from most of the test set documents. And perhaps this is the cause for lower score in the unconstrained mode, something that happened also with many systems in the past edition (Wilson et al., 2013).

This time, we implemented the contextual polarity solution based on the subtask B classifier. Given the results, we intend to do, in the near future, a new iteration of our system where the overall classifier will depend on (or receive features from) the current subtask A classifier.

It seems to us that `senti.ue` feature engineering can be improved, maintaining this line of development. Once stabilized, the introduction of named entity recognition and a richer linguistic analysis will help to identify the sentiment target entities, as the ultimate goal for this system.

References

Stefano Baccianella, Andrea Esuli and Fabrizio Sebastiani. 2010. *SentiWordNet 3.0: An Enhanced Lexical Resource for Sentiment Analysis and Opinion Mining*. In Proceedings of the Seventh conference on International Language Resources and Evaluation - LREC'10. European Language Resources Association. Malta.

Lee Becker, George Erhart, David Skiba and Valentine Matula. 2013. AVAYA: Sentiment Analysis on Twitter with Self-Training and Polarity Lexicon Expansion. In Second Joint Conference on Lexical and Computational Semantics (*SEM), Volume 2: Proceedings of the Seventh International Workshop on Semantic Evaluation (SemEval 2013). Atlanta, Georgia, USA.

Steven Bird. 2006. *NLTK: the natural language toolkit*. In Proceedings of the COLING'06/ACL on Interactive presentation sessions. Australia.

Chih-Chung Chang and Chih-Jen Lin. 2011. LIBSVM : a library for support vector machines. ACM Transactions on Intelligent Systems and Technology, 2:27:1–27:27.

Rong-En Fan, Kai-Wei Chang, Cho-Jui Hsieh, Xiang-Rui Wang, and Chih-Jen Lin. 2008. LIBLINEAR: A Library for Large Linear Classication. Journal of Machine Learning Research, 9:1871–1874.

Tobias Günther and Lenz Furrer. 2013. GU-MLT-LT: Sentiment Analysis of Short Messages using Linguistic Features and Stochastic Gradient Descent. In Second Joint Conference on Lexical and Computational Semantics (*SEM), Volume 2: Proceedings of the Seventh International Workshop on Semantic Evaluation (SemEval 2013). Atlanta, Georgia, USA.

Bing Liu, Minqing Hu and Junsheng Cheng. 2005. *Opinion Observer: Analyzing and Comparing Opinions on the Web*. In Proceedings of the 14th International World Wide Web conference (WWW-2005). Chiba, Japan.

Saif M. Mohammad, Svetlana Kiritchenko, and Xiaodan Zhu. 2013. NRC-Canada: Building the State-of-the-Art in Sentiment Analysis of Tweets. In Proceedings of the seventh international workshop on Semantic Evaluation Exercises (SemEval-2013). Atlanta, Georgia, USA.

Finn Årup Nielsen. 2011. *A New ANEW: Evaluation of a Word List for Sentiment Analysis in Microblogs*. In Proceedings, 1st Workshop on Making Sense of Microposts (#MSM2011): Big things come in small packages. pp: 93-98. Greece.

Princeton University. 2010. "About WordNet." WordNet. http://wordnet.princeton.edu

Sara Rosenthal, Alan Ritter, Veselin Stoyanov, and Preslav Nakov. 2014. SemEval-2014 Task 9: Sentiment Analysis in Twitter. In Proceedings of the Eighth International Workshop on Semantic Evaluation (SemEval'14). August 23-24, 2014, Dublin, Ireland.

José Saias. 2013. In search of reputation assessment: Experiences with polarity classification in replab 2013. In Pamela Forner, Roberto Navigli, and Dan Tufis, editors, *CLEF 2013 Evaluation Labs and Workshop Online Working Notes - Online Reputation Management (RepLab)*, Valencia, Spain, September 2013. ISBN 978-88-904810-5-5.

José Saias and Hilário Fernandes. 2013. senti.ue-en: an approach for informally written short texts in semeval-2013 sentiment analysis task. In *Second Joint Conference on Lexical and Computational Semantics (*SEM), Volume 2: Proceedings of the Seventh International Workshop on Semantic Evaluation (SemEval 2013)*, pages 508–512, Atlanta, Georgia, USA.

Janyce Wiebe, Theresa Wilson, and Claire Cardie. 2005. Annotating expressions of opinions and emotions in language. Language Resources and Evaluation, 39:165–210.

Theresa Wilson, Zornitsa Kozareva, Preslav Nakov, Alan Ritter, Sara Rosenthal and Veselin Stoyanov. 2013. SemEval-2013 task 2: Sentiment Analysis in Twitter. In *Proceedings of the 7th International Workshop on Semantic Evaluation*. ACL.

SentiKLUE: Updating a Polarity Classifier in 48 Hours

Stefan Evert and **Thomas Proisl** and **Paul Greiner** and **Besim Kabashi**
Friedrich-Alexander-Universität Erlangen-Nürnberg
Department Germanistik und Komparatistik
Professur für Korpuslinguistik
Bismarckstr. 6, 91054 Erlangen, Germany
{stefan.evert,thomas.proisl,paul.greiner,besim.kabashi}@fau.de

Abstract

SentiKLUE is an update of the KLUE polarity classifier – which achieved good and robust results in SemEval-2013 with a simple feature set – implemented in 48 hours.

1 Introduction

The SemEval-2014 shared task on "Sentiment Analysis in Twitter" (Rosenthal et al., 2014) is a rerun of the corresponding shared task from SemEval-2013 (Nakov et al., 2013) with new test data. It focuses on polarity classification in computer-mediated communication such as Twitter, other micro-blogging services, and SMS. There are two subtasks: the goal of *Message Polarity Classification* (B) is to classify an entire SMS, tweet or other message as *positive* (pos), *negative* (neg) or *neutral* (ntr); in the subtask on *Contextual Polarity Disambiguation* (A), a single word or short phrase has to be classified in the context of the whole message.

The training data are the same as in SemEval-2013. The test data from 2013 are used as a development set in order to select features and tune machine learning algorithms, but may not be included in the training data. The 2014 test set comprises the development data, new Twitter messages, LiveJournal entries as out-of-domain data, and a small number of tweets containing sarcasm (see Rosenthal et al. (2014) for further details). For subtask B, there are 10,239 training items, 5,907 items in the development set, and 3,861 additional unseen items in the new test set. For subtask A, there are 9,505 training items, 6,769 items in the development set, and 3,912 additional items in the test set.

Our team participated in the SemEval-2013 shared task with a relatively simple, but robust system (KLUE) based on a maximum entropy classifier and a small set of features (Proisl et al., 2013). Despite its simplicity, KLUE performed very well in subtask B, ranking 5th out of 36 constrained systems on the Twitter data and 3rd out of 28 on the SMS data. Results for contextual polarity disambiguation (subtask A) were less encouraging, with rank 14 out of 21 constrained systems on the Twitter data and rank 12 out of 19 on the SMS data.

This paper describes our efforts to bring the KLUE system up to date within a period of 48 hours. The results obtained by the new SentiKLUE system are summarised in Table 1, showing that the update was successful. The ranking of the system has improved substantially in subtask A, making it one of the best-performing systems in the shared task. Rankings in subtask B are similar to those of the previous year, showing that SentiKLUE has kept up with recent developments. Moreover, differences to the best-performing systems are much smaller than in SemEval-2013.

2 Updating the KLUE polarity classifier

The KLUE polarity classifier is described in detail by Proisl et al. (2013). It used the following features as input for a maximum entropy classifier:

- The AFINN sentiment lexicon (Nielsen, 2011), which provides numeric polarity scores ranging from -5 to $+5$ for 2,476 English word forms, extended with distributionally similar words. For each input message, the number of positive and negative words as well as their average polarity score were computed.
- Emoticons and Internet slang expressions that were manually classified as positive, negative or neutral. Features were generated in the same way as for the sentiment lexicon.
- A bag-of-words representation that generates a separate feature for each word form that occurs in at least 5 different messages ($f \geq 5$). Only

Proceedings of the 8th International Workshop on Semantic Evaluation (SemEval 2014), pages 551–555,
Dublin, Ireland, August 23-24, 2014.

task	subset	rank	score	best
B	LJ14	3 / 42	73.99	74.84
B	SMS13	4 / 42	67.40	70.28
B	Twit13	6 / 42	69.06	72.12
B	Twit14	10 / 42	67.02	70.96
B	Sarcasm	24 / 42	43.36	58.16
A	LJ14	1 / 20	85.61	85.61
A	SMS13	6 / 20	85.16	89.31
A	Twit13	2 / 20	90.11	90.14
A	Twit14	2 / 20	84.83	86.63
A	Sarcasm	2 / 20	79.32	82.75

Table 1: SentiKLUE results in SemEval 2014 Task 9 (among constrained systems). See Rosenthal et al. (2014) for further details and rankings including the unconstrained systems.

single words (unigrams) were used, since experiments with additional bigram features did not lead to a clear improvement.

- A negation heuristic, which inverts the polarity score of the first sentiment word within 4 tokens after a negation marker. In the bag-of-words representation, the next 3 tokens after a negation marker are prefixed with `not_`.
- For subtask A, these features were computed both for the marked word or phrase and for the rest of the message.

In order to improve the KLUE classifier, we drew inspiration from two other systems participating in the SemEval-2013 task: NRC-Canada (Mohammad et al., 2013), which won the task by a large margin over competing systems, and GU-MLT-LT (Günther and Furrer, 2013), which used similar features to our classifier, but obtained better results due to careful selection and tuning of the machine learning algorithm.

Mohammad et al. (2013) used a huge set of features, including several sentiment lexica (both manually and automatically created), word n-grams (up to 4-grams with low frequency threshold), character n-grams (3-grams to 5-grams), Twitter-derived word clusters and a negation heuristic similar to our approach. Features with the largest impact in subtask B were sentiment lexica (esp. large automatically generated word lists), word n-grams, character n-grams and the negation heuristic, in this order. NRC-Canada achieved F-scores of 68.46 (SMS) and 69.02 (Twitter) in task B, as well as 88.00 (SMS) and 88.93 (Twitter) in task A.

Günther and Furrer (2013) claim that state-of-the-art results can be obtained with a small feature set if a suitable machine learning algorithm is chosen. They used stochastic gradient descent (SGD) and tuned its parameters by grid search. GU-MLT-LT achieved scores of 62.15 (SMS) and 65.27 (Twitter) in task B, as well as 88.37 (SMS) and 85.19 (Twitter) in task A.

We therefore decided to make use of a wider range of sentiment lexica, extend the bag-of-words representation to bigrams, implement character n-gram features, and experiment with different machine learning algorithms, resulting in the SentiKLUE system described in the following section.

3 The SentiKLUE system

SentiKLUE is an improved version of the KLUE system and uses the same tokenisation, preprocessing and negation heuristics; see Proisl et al. (2013) for details. The features described below are used as input for a machine learning classifier that predicts the polarity categories *positive* (pos), *negative* (neg) or *neutral* (ntr). As in KLUE and GU-MLT-LT, the implementations of the Python library scikit-learn (Pedregosa et al., 2011)[1] are used. We tested four different learning algorithms: logistic regression (MaxEnt), stochastic gradient descent (SGD), linear SVM (LinSVM) and SVM with a RBF kernel (SVM). Parameters were tuned by grid search and the best-performing algorithm was chosen for each subtask. SentiKLUE makes use of the following features:

- Several sentiment lexica, which are treated as lists of positive and negative polarity words. Numerical scores are converted by setting appropriate cutoff thresholds. For each lexicon, we compute the number of positive and negative words occurring in a message as features, with separate counts for negated and non-negated contexts.
  - AFINN (Nielsen, 2011)[2]
  - Bing Liu lexicon (Hu and Liu, 2004)[3]
  - MPQA (Wilson et al., 2005)[4]
  - SentiWords (Guerini et al., 2013)[5]; we cre-

[1] http://scikit-learn.org/

[2] http://www2.imm.dtu.dk/pubdb/views/publication_details.php?id=6010

[3] http://www.cs.uic.edu/~liub/FBS/sentiment-analysis.html

[4] http://mpqa.cs.pitt.edu/lexicons/subj_lexicon/

[5] http://hlt.fbk.eu/technologies/sentiwords

ated two word lists with score thresholds of 0.3 and 0.1

- Sentiment140 (Mohammad et al., 2013)[6], which was compiled from a corpus of 1.6 million tweets for NRC-Canada; we created separate lists for normal words and hashtags with a score threshold of 1.0
- NRC Hashtag Sentiment Lexicon (Mohammad et al., 2013)[7], which contains words that exhibit a strong statistical association (PMI score) to positive or negative hashtags, also compiled for NRC-Canada; again, we created separate lists for normal words and hashtags with a score threshold of 0.8
- a manual extension including synonyms, antonyms and several word lists from online sources, compiled by the SNAP team (Schulze Wettendorf et al., 2014)
- an automatic extension with distributionally similar words (DSM extension), using a strategy similar to Proisl et al. (2013)

• Word form unigrams and bigrams. After some experimentation, the document frequency threshold was set to $f \geq 5$ for subtask B and $f \geq 2$ for subtask A.

• In order to include information from character n-grams, we used a Perl implementation of n-gram language models (Evert, 2008) that has already been applied successfully to text categorization tasks (boilerplate detection in the CLEANEVAL 2007 competition). We trained three separate models on positive, negative and neutral messages. We selected a 5-gram model ($n = 5$) with strong smoothing ($q = 0.7$), which minimized cross-entropy on the training data (measured by cross-validation). For each message in the training and test data, three features were generated, specifying per-character cross-entropy for each of the three n-gram models.[8]

• Counts of positive and negative emoticons using the same lists as in the KLUE system.

• The same negation heuristic as in KLUE.[9]

[6]http://www.umiacs.umd.edu/~saif/WebPages/Abstracts/NRC-SentimentAnalysis.htm

[7]ibid.

[8]Note that these features had to be generated by cross-validation on the training data to avoid catastrophic overfitting.

[9]The full list of negation markers is *not, don't, doesn't, won't, can't, mustn't, isn't, aren't, wasn't, weren't, couldn't, shouldn't, wouldn't*. To our surprise, including further negation markers such as *none*, *ain't* or *hasn't* led to a decrease in classification quality.

For subtask A, we chose a simplistic strategy and computed the same set of features for the marked word or phrase instead of the entire message. In order to take context into account, the three class probabilities assigned to the complete message by a MaxEnt classifier were included as additional features. No other features describing the context of the marked expression were used.

Optionally, features were standardized and prior class weights (2× for *positive*, 4× for *negative*) were used in order to balance the predicted labels. The best-performing machine learning algorithms on the development set were MaxEnt for subtask B (L1 penalty, $C = 0.3$) and linear SVM for subtask A (L1 penalty, L2 loss, $C = 0.5$), as shown in Table 2.

4 Experiments and conclusion

In order to determine the importance of individual features, ablation experiments were carried out for both subtasks by deactivating one group of features at a time. Tables 3 and 4 show the resulting changes in the official criterion $F_{p/n}$ separately for each subset of the development and test sets, as well as micro-averaged across the full development set (DEV) and test set (GOLD). Rows are ordered by feature impact on the full gold standard. Positive values indicate that a feature group has a negative impact on classification quality: results are improved by omitting the features (which is often the case for the Sarcasm subset).

The most important features are bag-of-words unigrams and bigrams, closely followed by sentiment lexica. Training class weights had a strong positive impact in subtask B, but decreased performance in subtask A. In our official submission, they were only used for subtask B. Full-message polarity is the third most important feature in subtask A. Other features contributed relatively small individual effects, but were necessary to achieve state-of-the-art performance in combination. They are often specific to one of the subtasks or to a particular subset of the gold standard.

The bottom half of each table shows ablation results for individual sentiment lexica, with all other features active. Key resources are the standard lexica (AFINN, Liu, MPQA) as well as Twitter-specific lexica (Sentiment140, NRC Hashtag). Noisy word lists (DSM extension, SNAP, SentiWords) have a small or even a negative effect. Surprisingly, the standard lexica seem to give misleading cues on the Twitter 2014 subset (Table 3).

task	classifier	CV	development set						test set (gold standard)					
		F_{all}	F_{pos}	F_{neg}	F_{ntr}	F_{all}	$F_{p/n}$	acc.	F_{pos}	F_{neg}	F_{ntr}	F_{all}	$F_{p/n}$	acc.
B	MaxEnt	.727	.724	.651	.772	.735	**.688**	**.734**	.731	.650	.750	.726	.691	.725
B	SGD	.725	.728	.645	.773	.736	.686	**.734**	.733	.656	.749	.727	**.695**	**.726**
B	LinSVM	.702	.687	.604	.743	.700	.646	.701	.699	.599	.716	.689	.649	.690
B	SVM	.702	.721	.631	.742	.716	.676	.712	.729	.636	.720	.709	.683	.706
A	MaxEnt	.864	.890	.872	.179	.849	.881	.863	.893	.853	.171	.841	.873	.856
A	SGD	.864	.889	.867	.223	.849	.878	.860	.891	.847	.188	.839	.869	.852
A	LinSVM	.860	.892	.876	.064	.847	**.884**	**.865**	.895	.856	.064	.838	**.875**	**.857**
A	SVM	.855	.890	.873	.024	.842	.881	.862	.892	.853	.014	.832	.872	.854

Table 2: Performance of different machine learning algorithms on the training data (CV), development set and test set (F_{all} = weighted average F-score; $F_{p/n}$ = official score; best results highlighted in bold font).

Task B	SMS	Twitter	DEV	LJ14	SMS13	Twit13	Twit14	Sarcasm	GOLD
– bag of words	−.0837	−.0322	−.0502	−.0344	−.0807	−.0316	−.0335	+.0511	**−.0430**
– sentiment lexica	−.0445	−.0354	−.0389	−.0690	−.0422	−.0372	−.0092	+.0750	**−.0363**
– training weights	−.0033	−.0413	−.0266	−.0275	−.0077	−.0482	−.0204	−.0342	**−.0294**
– emoticons	−.0071	−.0107	−.0087	−.0006	−.0067	−.0105	+.0004	+.0492	**−.0048**
– bow bigrams	−.0074	−.0005	−.0035	+.0010	−.0105	−.0012	−.0096	+.0956	**−.0028**
– feature scaling	−.0027	−.0010	−.0014	−.0021	−.0030	−.0026	−.0004	−.0034	**−.0020**
– character n-grams	+.0029	−.0068	−.0033	+.0012	+.0040	−.0044	−.0056	+.0056	**−.0015**
– negation	−.0098	+.0019	−.0014	−.0016	−.0049	+.0002	−.0012	+.0351	**−.0002**
– bow $f \geq 2$	+.0017	+.0026	+.0022	+.0004	+.0021	−.0003	+.0021	+.0171	**+.0013**
sentiment lexica:									
– standard lexica	−.0206	−.0135	−.0152	−.0245	−.0234	−.0124	+.0035	+.0586	**−.0124**
– Twitter lexica	−.0026	+.0000	−.0019	−.0118	−.0073	−.0007	−.0094	+.0034	**−.0066**
– SentiWords	−.0008	−.0010	−.0009	−.0034	−.0015	−.0005	−.0075	+.0165	**−.0017**
– hashtag lexica	−.0011	+.0021	+.0005	−.0045	−.0039	+.0035	+.0011	−.0302	**−.0005**
– DSM extension	+.0047	−.0032	−.0002	−.0070	+.0039	+.0022	−.0025	+.0392	**+.0002**
– manual extension	−.0008	−.0018	−.0011	−.0015	−.0019	+.0000	+.0041	+.0361	**+.0009**
only standard lexica	−.0124	−.0119	−.0120	−.0088	−.0101	−.0108	−.0095	+.0439	**−.0094**
only DSM extension	−.0303	−.0260	−.0262	−.0427	−.0287	−.0251	+.0021	+.0183	**−.0230**

Table 3: Results of feature ablation experiments for subtask B. Values show change in $F_{p/n}$-score if feature is excluded. Rows are sorted by impact of features on the full SemEval-2014 test data (GOLD).

Task A	SMS	Twitter	DEV	LJ14	SMS13	Twit13	Twit14	Sarcasm	GOLD
– bag of words	−.0283	−.0252	−.0256	−.0207	−.0292	−.0249	−.0411	−.0041	**−.0273**
– sentiment lexica	−.0027	−.0231	−.0151	−.0078	−.0023	−.0245	−.0144	−.0109	**−.0141**
– context (class probs)	+.0027	−.0050	−.0022	−.0105	+.0017	−.0057	−.0171	+.0390	**−.0062**
– negation	−.0081	−.0041	−.0052	−.0064	−.0063	−.0024	−.0058	+.0000	**−.0043**
– bow bigrams	−.0045	−.0009	−.0022	−.0014	−.0046	+.0007	−.0033	+.0208	**−.0014**
– character n-grams	−.0015	+.0003	−.0004	+.0003	−.0038	+.0001	−.0012	+.0085	**−.0012**
– feature scaling	+.0001	+.0001	+.0001	+.0009	+.0005	−.0002	−.0029	−.0041	**−.0004**
– emoticons	+.0023	+.0026	+.0025	+.0016	+.0038	+.0012	−.0062	+.0000	**+.0004**
bow $f \geq 5$	+.0027	+.0000	+.0009	+.0082	+.0027	+.0006	−.0025	+.0243	**+.0015**
– training weights	+.0046	+.0072	+.0059	+.0104	+.0037	+.0050	+.0000	−.0145	**+.0040**
sentiment lexica:									
– standard lexica	−.0100	−.0024	−.0050	+.0014	−.0086	−.0035	−.0055	+.0000	**−.0044**
– Twitter lexica	−.0039	−.0016	−.0024	−.0009	−.0038	−.0024	−.0052	−.0085	**−.0031**
– hashtag lexica	−.0023	−.0007	−.0012	+.0000	−.0014	−.0019	−.0030	−.0126	**−.0017**
– manual extensions	−.0016	+.0003	−.0004	+.0021	−.0025	−.0009	+.0002	+.0000	**−.0007**
– SentiWords	+.0017	+.0005	+.0010	+.0001	+.0013	−.0013	+.0001	+.0000	**−.0002**
– DSM extensions	+.0099	+.0011	+.0044	−.0008	+.0098	−.0006	−.0004	−.0085	**+.0019**
only standard lexica	+.0030	−.0038	−.0011	−.0019	+.0035	−.0048	−.0027	−.0168	**−.0019**
only DSM lexica	−.0114	−.0085	−.0094	−.0035	−.0117	−.0104	−.0057	−.0338	**−.0089**

Table 4: Results of feature ablation experiments for subtask A. Values show change in $F_{p/n}$-score if feature is excluded. Rows are sorted by impact of features on the full SemEval-2014 test data (GOLD).

References

Stefan Evert. 2008. A lightweight and efficient tool for cleaning Web pages. In *Proceedings of the 6th International Conference on Language Resources and Evaluation (LREC 2008)*, Marrakech, Morocco.

Marco Guerini, Lorenzo Gatti, and Marco Turchi. 2013. Sentiment analysis: How to derive prior polarities from SentiWordNet. In *Proceedings of the 2013 Conference on Empirical Methods in Natural Language Processing (EMNLP 2013)*, pages 1259–1269, Seattle, WA, October.

Tobias Günther and Lenz Furrer. 2013. GU-MLT-LT: Sentiment analysis of short messages using linguistic features and stochastic gradient descent. In *Second Joint Conference on Lexical and Computational Semantics (*SEM), Volume 2: Proceedings of the Seventh International Workshop on Semantic Evaluation (SemEval 2013)*, pages 328–332, Atlanta, GA.

Minqing Hu and Bing Liu. 2004. Mining and summarizing customer reviews. In *Proceedings of the 10th ACM SIGKDD International Conference on Knowledge Discovery and Data Mining (KDD '04)*, pages 168–177, Seattle, WA.

Saif Mohammad, Svetlana Kiritchenko, and Xiaodan Zhu. 2013. NRC-Canada: Building the state-of-the-art in sentiment analysis of tweets. In *Second Joint Conference on Lexical and Computational Semantics (*SEM), Volume 2: Proceedings of the Seventh International Workshop on Semantic Evaluation (SemEval 2013)*, pages 321–327, Atlanta, GA.

Preslav Nakov, Sara Rosenthal, Zornitsa Kozareva, Veselin Stoyanov, Alan Ritter, and Theresa Wilson. 2013. SemEval-2013 task 2: Sentiment analysis in Twitter. In *Proceedings of the 7th International Workshop on Semantic Evaluation (SemEval-2013)*.

Finn Årup Nielsen. 2011. A new ANEW: Evaluation of a word list for sentiment analysis in microblogs. In *Proceedings of the ESWC2011 Workshop on Making Sense of Microposts: Big things come in small packages*, number 718 in CEUR Workshop Proceedings, pages 93–98, Heraklion, Greece, May.

F. Pedregosa, G. Varoquaux, A. Gramfort, V. Michel, B. Thirion, O. Grisel, M. Blondel, P. Prettenhofer, R. Weiss, V. Dubourg, J. Vanderplas, A. Passos, D. Cournapeau, M. Brucher, M. Perrot, and E. Duchesnay. 2011. Scikit-learn: Machine learning in Python. *Journal of Machine Learning Research*, 12:2825–2830.

Thomas Proisl, Paul Greiner, Stefan Evert, and Besim Kabashi. 2013. KLUE: Simple and robust methods for polarity classification. In *Second Joint Conference on Lexical and Computational Semantics (*SEM), Volume 2: Proceedings of the Seventh International Workshop on Semantic Evaluation (SemEval 2013)*, pages 395–401, Atlanta, Georgia, USA, June. Association for Computational Linguistics.

Sara Rosenthal, Preslav Nakov, Alan Ritter, and Veselin Stoyanov. 2014. SemEval-2014 Task 9: Sentiment analysis in Twitter. In *Proceedings of the 8th International Workshop on Semantic Evaluation (SemEval-2014)*, Dublin, Ireland.

Clemens Schulze Wettendorf, Robin Jegan, Allan Körner, Julia Zerche, Nataliia Plotnikova, Julian Moreth, Tamara Schertl, Verena Obermeyer, Susanne Streil, Tamara Willacker, and Stefan Evert. 2014. SNAP: A multi-stage XML pipeline for aspect based sentiment analysis. In *Proceedings of the 8th International Workshop on Semantic Evaluation (SemEval-2014)*, Dublin, Ireland.

Theresa Wilson, Janyce Wiebe, and Paul Hoffmann. 2005. Recognizing contextual polarity in phrase-level sentiment analysis. In *Proceedings of the Human Language Technology Conference and Conference on Empirical Methods in Natural Language Processing (HLT-EMNLP 2005)*, pages 347–354, Vancouver, BC, Canada.

ShrdLite: Semantic Parsing Using a Handmade Grammar

Peter Ljunglöf
Department of Computer Science and Engineering
University of Gothenburg and Chalmers University of Technology
Gothenburg, Sweden
peter.ljunglof@cse.gu.se

Abstract

This paper describes my approach for parsing robot commands, which was task 6 at SemEval 2014. My solution is to manually create a compact unification grammar. The grammar is highly ambiguous, and relies heavily on filtering the parse results by checking their consistency with the current world.

The grammar is small, consisting of not more than 25 grammatical and 60 lexical rules. The parser uses simple error correction together with a straightforward iterative deepening search. Nevertheless, with these very basic algorithms, the system still managed to get 86.1% correctness on the evaluation data. Even more interesting is that by making the parser slightly more robust, the accuracy of the system rises to 93.5%, and by adding one single word to the lexicon, the accuracy is boosted to 98.0%.

1 Introduction

SemEval 2014, task 6, was about parsing commands to a robot operating in a blocks world. The goal is to parse utterances in natural language into commands in a formal language, the Robot Control Language (RCL). As a guide the system can use a spatial planner which can tell whether an RCL command is meaningful in a given blocks world.

The utterances are taken from the Robot Commands Treebank (Dukes, 2013), which pairs 3409 sentences with semantic annotations consisting of an RCL command together with a description of a world where the command is meaningful. The corpus was divided into 2500 training sentences and 909 evaluation sentences.

The system that is described in this paper, together with the evaluation data, is available online from GitHub:

https://github.com/heatherleaf/semeval-2014-task6

2 System Description

The Shrdlite system is based on a small unification grammar, together with a naive robust parser implemented using iterative deepening. After parsing, the resulting parse trees are modified according to six extra-grammatical semantic rules.

The grammar and the semantic rules were handcrafted using manual analysis of the available 2500 training sentences, and an incremental and iterative process to select and fine-tune the grammar. The total amount of work for creating the grammar consisted of about 3–4 days for one person. This excludes programming the robust parser and the rest of the system, which took another 2–3 days.

I did not have any access to the 909 evaluation sentences while developing the grammar or the other parts of the system.

2.1 Grammar

The grammar is a Prolog DCG unification grammar (Pereira and Warren, 1980) which builds a semantic parse tree during parsing. The core grammar is shown in figure 1. For presentation purposes, the DCG arguments (including the semantic parse trees) are left out of the figure. The lexicon consists of ca 150 surface words (or multi-word units) divided into 23 lexical categories. The lexical categories are the lowercase italic symbols in the core grammar.

Proceedings of the 8th International Workshop on Semantic Evaluation (SemEval 2014), pages 556–559,
Dublin, Ireland, August 23-24, 2014.

Main	⟶	Event ?*periods*
Event	⟶	*take-verb* Entity *take-suffix*
	|	*drop-verb* Entity *drop-suffix*
	|	*move-verb* Entity ?*commas* *move-suffix* Destination
	|	*take-verb* Entity *take-suffix* *and-then* *move-verb* RefEntity *move-suffix* Destination
RefEntity	⟶	?*reference-pronoun*
Destination	⟶	SpatialRelation
SpatialRelation	⟶	(Measure | *entity-relation* | Measure *entity-relation*) Entity
RelativeClause	⟶	?*commas* *relative-pronoun* SpatialRelation
Measure	⟶	Entity
Entity	⟶	?*determiner* BasicEntity
BasicEntity	⟶	(*cardinal* | *indicator* | *color* | *cube-group-indicator*) BasicEntity
	|	(*type* | *one*) ?RelativeClause
	|	?(*its* | *the*) *region-indicator* ?*of-board*

Figure 1: The core grammar. Lowercase italic symbols are lexicon entries, and a question mark indicates that the following symbol is optional. DCG arguments (semantic trees and syntactic coordination) are left out for presentation reasons.

2.2 Semantic Modifications After Parsing

After parsing, each resulting semantic parse tree is modified according to the following rules. Most of these rules should be possible to implement as grammar rules, but I felt that this would make the grammar unnecessarily complicated.

- If a color is specified before an indicator, change the order between them.
- If an entity of type CUBE is described using two colours, its type is changed to CUBE-GROUP.
- Relation words such as *"above"*, *"opposite"*, *"over"*, etc., correspond to the relation WITHIN() if the entity is of type CORNER or REGION; for all other entities the relation will be ABOVE().
- The relation FRONT() is changed to FORWARD() if the entity is of type TILE.
- Add a reference id to the subject of a TAKE-AND-DROP command sequence, unless it already has a reference id.
- If the destination of a move command is of type TYPE-REFERENCE or TYPE-REFERENCE-GROUP, add a reference id to the subject; unless the subject is of type PRISM and it has a spatial relation, in which case the reference id is added to its spatial relation instead.

2.3 Robust Parsing

The parser is a standard Prolog recursive-descent parser, augmented with simple support for handling robustness. The algorithm is shown in figure 2.

2.3.1 Misspellings and Junk Words

The parser tries to compensate for misspellings and junk words. Any word can be recognized as a misspelled word, penalized using the Levenshtein edit distance (Levenshtein, 1966), or it can be skipped as a junk word with a fixed penalty.[1] The parser first tries to find an exact match of the sentence in the grammar, then it gradually allows higher penalties until the sentence is parsed. This is done using iterative deepening on the edit penalty of the sentence, until it reaches the maximum edit penalty – if the sentence still cannot be parsed, it fails. In the original evaluation I used a maximum edit penalty of 5, but by just increasing this penalty, the accuracy was boosted considerably as discussed in sections 2.4 and 3.1.

2.3.2 Filtering Through the Spatial Planner

The parser uses the spatial planner that was distributed together with the task as a black box. It takes a semantic parse tree and the current world configuration, and decides if the tree is meaningful in the given world.

When the sentence is recognized, all its parse trees are filtered through the spatial planner. If

[1] The penalty of skipping over a word is 3 if the word is already in the lexicon, and 2 otherwise.

```
function robust-parse(sentence, world):
    for penalty in 0...5:
        trees = { t' | t ∈ parse-dcg(sentence, edit-penalty=penalty),
                       t' = modify-tree(t),
                       spatial-planner(t', world) = MEANINGFUL }
        if trees ≠ ∅:
            return min(trees, key=treesize)
    return FAILURE
```

Figure 2: The robust parsing algorithm.

none of the trees are meaningful in the world, the parser tries to parse the sentence with a higher edit penalty.

2.3.3 Selecting the Best Tree

If there is more than one possible semantic tree, the system returns the tree with the smallest number of nodes.

2.4 Minor Modifications After Evaluation

As explained in section 3.1, the error analysis of the final evaluation revealed one construction and one lexical item that did not occur in the training corpus:

- Utterances can start with 2–3 periods. The reason why this was not caught by the robust parser is that each of these periods are considered a word of its own, and as mentioned in section 2.3.1, the penalty for skipping a lexicon word is 3 which means that the penalty for parsing a sentence with 2–3 initial periods is 6 or 9. Unfortunately I had chosen a maximum penalty of 5 which meant that the original evaluation missed all these sentences.

  By just increasing the maximum penalty from 5 to 9, the accuracy increased from 86.1% to 93.5%.

- The word *"cell"* occurs in the evaluation data as a synonym for the entity type TILE, in addition to the existing tile words *"square"*, *"grid"*, *"space"*, etc. Unfortunately, the parser tries to correct *"cell"* into the Levenshtein-similar *"cube"*, giving the wrong semantics.

  By adding *"cell"* to the lexicon, the accuracy increased further from 93.5% to 98.0%.

The results of these minimal modifications are substantial, and are discussed further in section 3.2.

3 Evaluation

The system was evaluated on 909 sentences from the treebank, and I only tested for exact matches. The result of the initial evaluation was that 86% of the sentences returned a correct result, when using the spatial planner as a guide for selecting parses. Without the planner, the accuracy was only 51%. The results are shown in the top rows in tables 1 and 2.

The grammar is ambiguous and the system relies heavily on the spatial planner to filter out candidates. Without the planner, 42% of the utterances are ambiguous returning between 2 and 18 trees, but with the planner, only 4 utterances are ambiguous (i.e., 0.4%).

3.1 Error Analysis

As already mentioned in section 2.4, almost all of the errors that the system makes are of two forms that are very easy to correct:

- None of the training sentences start with a sequence of periods, but 58 of the evaluation sentences do. This was solved by increasing the maximum edit penalty to 9.
- The word *"cell"* does not occur in the training sentences, but in does appear in 45 of the evaluation sentences. To solve this error I just added that word to the lexicon.

3.2 Evaluation Results

As already mentioned, the accuracy of the initial grammar was 86.1% with the spatial planner. The two minor modifications described in section 2.4 improve the results significantly, as can be seen in table 1. Increasing the maximum edit penalty solves 67 of the 126 failing sentences, and adding the word *"cell"* solves 41 of the remaining sentences. These two improvements together solve 108 sentences, leaving only 18 failing sentences.

	Max. penalty	Correct			Incorrect			
		Unique	Ambiguous	Total	Ambiguous	Miss	Fail	Total
Original grammar	5	782	1	86.1%	0	19	107	13.9%
Original grammar	9	845	5	93.5%	0	50	9	6.5%
Adding *"cell"*	9	886	5	98.0%	0	10	8	2.0%

Table 1: Evaluation results *with* the spatial planner.

	Max. penalty	Correct			Incorrect			
		Unique	Ambiguous	Total	Ambiguous	Miss	Fail	Total
Original grammar	5	450	18	51.5%	315	64	62	48.5%
Original grammar	9	493	20	56.4%	330	65	1	43.6%
Adding *"cell"*	9	498	24	57.4%	366	20	1	42.6%

Table 2: Evaluation results *without* the spatial planner.

The final accuracy was therefore boosted to an impressive 98.0%.

The columns in the result tables are as follows: *Unique* are the number of sentences for which the system returns one single tree which is correct. *Ambiguous* are the number of sentences where the parser returns several trees, and the correct tree is among them: if the tree that the system selects (i.e., the smallest tree) is correct, it is counted as a correct ambiguous sentence, otherwise it is counted as incorrect. *Miss* are the number of sentences where all the returned trees are incorrect, and *Fail* are the sentences for which the system could not find a tree at all.

Table 2 shows that the modifications also improve the accuracy when the spatial planner is not used, but the improvement is not as impressive. The reason for this is that many of the failed sentences become ambiguous, and since the planner cannot be used for disambiguation, there is still a risk that the returned tree is not the correct one. The number of sentences for which the system returns the correct tree somewhere among the results is the sum of all unique and ambiguous sentences, which amounts to $450+18+315=783$ (i.e., 86.1%) for the original grammar and $498+24+366=888$ (i.e., 97.7%) for the updated grammar. Note that these are almost the same results as in table 1, which is consistent with the fact that the system uses the planner to filter out incorrect interpretations.

4 Discussion

In this paper I have showed that a traditional symbol-based grammatical approach can be as good as, or even superior to, a data-based machine learning approach, in specific domains where the language and the possible actions are restricted. The grammar-based system gets an accuracy of 86.1% on the evaluation data. By increasing the penalty threshold the accuracy rises to 93.5%, and with a single addition to the lexicon it reaches 98.0%.

This suggests that grammar-based approaches can be useful when developing interactive systems for limited domains. In particular it seems that a grammar-based system could be well suited for systems that are built using an iterative and incremental development process (Larman and Basili, 2003), where the system is updated frequently and continuously evaluated by users.

References

Kais Dukes. 2013. Semantic annotation of robotic spatial commands. In *Proceedings of LTC'13: 6th Language and Technology Conference*, Poznań, Poland.

Craig Larman and Victor R. Basili. 2003. Iterative and incremental development: A brief history. *Computer*, 36(6):47–56.

Vladimir I. Levenshtein. 1966. Binary codes capable of correcting deletions, insertions, and reversals. *Soviet Physics Doklady*, 10(8):707–710.

Fernando C. N. Pereira and David H. D. Warren. 1980. Definie clause grammars for language analysis. *Artificial Intelligence*, 13:231–278.

SimCompass: Using Deep Learning Word Embeddings to Assess Cross-level Similarity

Carmen Banea, Di Chen, Rada Mihalcea*
University of Michigan
Ann Arbor, MI

Claire Cardie
Cornell University
Ithaca, NY

Janyce Wiebe
University of Pittsburgh
Pittsburgh, PA

Abstract

This article presents our team's participating system at SemEval-2014 Task 3. Using a meta-learning framework, we experiment with traditional knowledge-based metrics, as well as novel corpus-based measures based on deep learning paradigms, paired with varying degrees of context expansion. The framework enabled us to reach the highest overall performance among all competing systems.

1 Introduction

Semantic textual similarity is one of the key components behind a multitude of natural language processing applications, such as information retrieval (Salton and Lesk, 1971), relevance feedback and text classification (Rocchio, 1971), word sense disambiguation (Lesk, 1986; Schutze, 1998), summarization (Salton et al., 1997; Lin and Hovy, 2003), automatic evaluation of machine translation (Papineni et al., 2002), plagiarism detection (Nawab et al., 2011), and more.

To date, semantic similarity research has primarily focused on comparing text snippets of similar length (see the semantic textual similarity tasks organized during **Sem 2013* (Agirre et al., 2013) and *SemEval 2012* (Agirre et al., 2012)). Yet, as new challenges emerge, such as augmenting a knowledge-base with textual evidence, assessing similarity across different context granularities is gaining traction. The SemEval Cross-level semantic similarity task is aimed at this latter scenario, and is described in more details in the task paper (Jurgens et al., 2014).

* {carmennb,chenditc,mihalcea}@umich.edu

2 Related Work

Over the past years, the research community has focused on computing semantic relatedness using methods that are either knowledge-based or corpus-based. Knowledge-based methods derive a measure of relatedness by utilizing lexical resources and ontologies such as WordNet (Miller, 1995) or Roget (Rog, 1995) to measure definitional overlap, term distance within a graphical taxonomy, or term depth in the taxonomy as a measure of specificity. There are many knowledge-based measures that were proposed in the past, e.g., (Leacock and Chodorow, 1998; Lesk, 1986; Resnik, 1995; Jiang and Conrath, 1997; Lin, 1998; Jarmasz and Szpakowicz, 2003; Hughes and Ramage, 2007).

On the other side, corpus-based measures such as Latent Semantic Analysis (LSA) (Landauer and Dumais, 1997), Explicit Semantic Analysis (ESA) (Gabrilovich and Markovitch, 2007), Salient Semantic Analysis (SSA) (Hassan and Mihalcea, 2011), Pointwise Mutual Information (PMI) (Church and Hanks, 1990), PMI-IR (Turney, 2001), Second Order PMI (Islam and Inkpen, 2006), Hyperspace Analogues to Language (Burgess et al., 1998) and distributional similarity (Lin, 1998) employ probabilistic approaches to decode the semantics of words. They consist of unsupervised methods that utilize the contextual information and patterns observed in raw text to build semantic profiles of words. Unlike knowledge-based methods, which suffer from limited coverage, corpus-based measures are able to induce the similarity between any two words, as long as they appear in the corpus used for training.

3 System Description

3.1 Generic Features

Our system employs both knowledge and corpus-based measures as detailed below.

Proceedings of the 8th International Workshop on Semantic Evaluation (SemEval 2014), pages 560–565,
Dublin, Ireland, August 23-24, 2014.

Knowledge-based features
Knowledge-based metrics were shown to provide high correlation scores with the goldstandard in text similarity tasks (Agirre et al., 2012; Agirre et al., 2013). We used three WordNet-based similarity measures that employ information content. We chose these metrics because they are able to incorporate external information derived from a large corpus: Resnik (Resnik, 1995) (RES), Lin (Lin, 1998) (LIN), and Jiang & Conrath (Jiang and Conrath, 1997) (JCN).

Corpus based features
Our corpus based features are derived from a deep learning vector space model that is able to "understand" word meaning without human input. Distributed word embeddings are learned using a skip-gram recurrent neural net architecture running over a large raw corpus (Mikolov et al., 2013b; Mikolov et al., 2013a). A primary advantage of such a model is that, by breaking away from the typical n-gram model that sees individual units with no relationship to each other, it is able to generalize and produce word vectors that are similar for related words, thus encoding linguistic regularities and patterns (Mikolov et al., 2013b). For example, vec(Madrid)-vec(Spain)+vec(France) is closer to vec(Paris) than any other word vector (Mikolov et al., 2013a). We used the pre-trained Google News word2vec model (WTV) built over a 100 billion words corpus, and containing 3 million 300-dimension vectors for words and phrases. The model is distributed with the word2vec toolkit. [1]

Since the methods outlined above provide similarity scores at the sense or word level, we derive text level metrics by employing two methods.

VectorSum. We add the vectors corresponding to the non-stopwords tokens in bag of words (BOW) A and B, resulting in vectors V_A and V_B, respectively. The assumption is that these vectors are able to capture the semantic meaning associated with the contexts, enabling us to gauge their relatedness using cosine similarity.

Align. Given two BOW A and B as input, we compare them using a word-alignment-based similarity measure (Mihalcea et al., 2006). We calculate the pairwise similarity between the words in A and B, and match each word in A with its most similar counterpart in B. For corpus-based features, the similarity measure represents the average over these scores, while for knowledge-based measures, we consider the top 40% ranking pairs.

We use the DKPro Similarity package (Bär et al., 2013) to compute knowledge-based metrics, and the word2vec implementation from the Gensim toolkit (Rehurek and Sojka, 2010).

3.2 Feature Variations

Since our system participated in all four lexical levels evaluations, we describe below the modifications pertaining to each.

word2sense. At the word2sense level, we employ both knowledge and corpus-based features. Since the information available in each pair is extremely limited (only a word and a sense key) we infuse contextual information by drawing on WordNet (Miller, 1995). In WordNet, the sense of each word is encapsulated in a uniquely identifiable synset, consisting of the definition (gloss), usage examples and its synonyms. We can derive three variations (where the *word* and *sense* components are represented by BOW A and B, respectively): **a) no expansion** (A={*word*}, B={*sense*}), **b) expand right (R)** (A={*word*}, B={*sense* gloss & example}), **c) expand left (L) & right (R)** (A={*word* glosses & examples}, B={*sense* gloss & example}). After applying the Align method, we obtain measures JNC, LIN, RES and $WTV1$; VectorSum results in $WTV2$.

phrase2word. As this lexical level also suffers from low context, we adapt the above variations, where the *phrase* and *word* components are represented by BOW A and BOW B, respectively. Thus, we have: **a) no expansion** (A={*phrase*}, B={*word*}), **b) expand R** (A={*phrase*}, B={*word* glosses and examples}), **c) expand L & R** (A={*phrase* glosses & examples}, B={*word* glosses and examples}). We extract the same measures as for *word2sense*.

sentence2phrase. For this variation, we use only corpus based measures; BOW A represents the *sentence* component, B, the *phrase*. Since there is sufficient context available, we follow the **no expansion** variation, and obtain metrics $WTV1$ (by applying Align) and $WTV2$ (using VectorSum).

paragraph2sentence. At this level, due to the long context that entails one-to-many mappings between the words in the *sentence* and those in the *paragraph*, we use a text clustering technique prior to calculating the features' weights.

[1] https://code.google.com/p/word2vec/

a) no clustering. We use only corpus based measures, where the *paragraph* represents BOW A, and the *sentence* represents BOW B. Then we apply Align and VectorSum, resulting in $WTV1$ and $WTV2$, respectively.

b) paragraph centroids extraction. Since the longer text contains more information compared to the shorter one, we extract k topic vectors after K-means clustering the left context.[2] These centroids are able to model topics permeating across sentences, and by comparing them with the word vectors pertaining to the short text, we seek to capture how much of the information is covered in the shorter text. Each word is paired with the centroid that it is closest to, and the average is computed over these scores, resulting in $WTV3$.

c) sentence centroids extraction. Under a different scenario, assuming that one sentence covers only a few strongly expressed topics, unlike a paragraph that may digress and introduce unrelated noise, we apply clustering on the short text. The centroids thus obtained are able to capture the essence of the sentence, so when compared to every word in the paragraph, we can gauge how much of the short text is reflected in the longer one. Each centroid is paired with the word that it is most similar to, and we average these scores, thus obtaining $WTV4$. In a way, methods b) and c) provide a macro, respectively micro view of how the topics are reflected across the two spans of text.

3.3 Meta-learning

The measures of similarity described above provide a single score per each *long text - short text* pair in the training and test data. These scores then become features for a meta-learner, which is able to optimize their impact on the prediction process. We experimented with multiple regression algorithms by conducting 10 fold cross-validation on the training data. The strongest performer across all lexical levels was Gaussian processes with a radial basis function (RBF) kernel. Gaussian processes regression is an efficient probabilistic prediction framework that assumes a Gaussian process prior on the unobservable (latent) functions and a likelihood function that accounts for noise. An individual classifier[3] was trained for each lexical level and applied to the test data sets.

[2] Implementation provided in the Scikit library (Pedregosa et al., 2011), where k is set to 3.

[3] Implementation available in the WEKA machine learning software (Hall et al., 2009) using the default parameters.

4 Evaluations & Discussion

Our system participated in all cross-level subtasks under the name *SimCompass*, competing with 37 other systems developed by 20 teams.

Figure 1 highlights the Pearson correlations at the four lexical levels between the gold standard and each similarity measure introduced in Section 3, as well as the predictions ensuing as a result of meta-learning. The left and right histograms in each subfigure present the scores obtained on the train and test data, respectively.

In the case of *word2sense* train data, we notice that expanding the context provides additional information and improves the correlation results. For corpus-based measures, the correlations are stronger when the expansion involves only the right side of the tuple, namely the *sense*. We notice an increase of 0.04 correlation points for WTV1 and 0.09 for WTV2. As soon as the *word* is expanded as well, the context incorporates too much noise, and the correlation levels drop. In the case of knowledge-based measures, expanding the context does not seem to impact the results. However, these trends do not carry out to the test data, where the corpus-based features without expansion reach a correlation higher than 0.3, while the knowledge-based features score significantly lower (by 0.16). Once all these measures are used as features in a meta learner (*All*) using Gaussian processes regression (GP), the correlation increases over the level attained by the best performing individual feature, reaching 0.45 on the train data and 0.36 on the test data. SimCompass ranks second in this subtask's evaluations, falling short of the leading system by 0.025 correlation points.

Turning now to the *phrase2word* subfigure, we notice that the context already carries sufficient information, and expanding it causes the performance to drop (the more extensive the expansion, the steeper the drop). Unlike the scenario encountered for *word2sense*, the trend observed here on the training data also gets mirrored in the test data. Same as before, knowledge-based measures have a significantly lower performance, but deep learning-based features based on word2vec (WTV) only show a correlation variation by at most 0.05, proving their robustness. Leveraging all the features in a meta-learning framework enables the system to predict stronger scores for both the train and the test data (0.48 and 0.42, respectively). Actually, for this variation, SimCompass

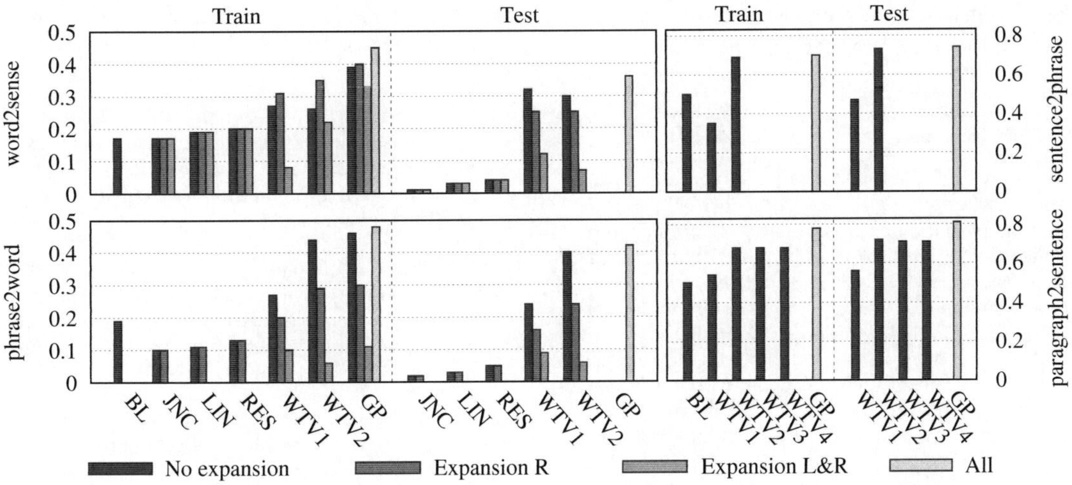

Figure 1: Pearson correlation of individual measures on the train and test data sets. As these measures become features in a regression algorithm (GP), prediction correlations are included as well. BL represents the baseline computed by the organizers.

obtains the highest score among all competing systems, surpassing the second best by 0.10.

Noticing that expansion is not helpful when sufficient context is available, for the next variations we use the original tuples. Also, due to the reduced impact of knowledge-based features on the training outcome, we only focus on deep learning features (*WTV1*, *WTV2*, *WTV3*, *WTV4*).

Shifting to *sentence2phrase*, *WTV2* (constructed using VectorSum) is the top performing feature, surpassing the baseline by 0.19, and attaining 0.69 and 0.73 on the train and test sets, respectively. Despite also considering a lower performing feature (*WTV1*), the meta-learner maintains high scores, surpassing the correlation achieved on the train data by 0.04 (from 0.70 to 0.74). In this variation, our system ranks fifth, at 0.035 from the top system.

For the *paragraph2sentence* variation, due to the availability of longer contexts, we introduce *WTV3* and *WTV4* that are based on clustering the left and the right sides of the tuple, respectively. *WTV2* fares slightly better than *WTV3* and *WTV4*. *WTV1* surpasses the baseline this time, leaving its mark on the decision process. When training the GP learner on all features, we obtain 0.78 correlation on the train data, and 0.81 on test data, 0.10 higher than those attained by the individual features alone. SimCompass ranks seventh in performance on this subtask, at 0.026 from the first.

Considering the overall system performance, SimCompass is remarkably versatile, ranking among the top at each lexical level, and taking the first place in the SemEval Task 3 overall evaluation with respect to both Pearson (0.58 average correlation) and Spearman correlations.

5 Conclusion

We described SimCompass, the system we participated with at SemEval-2014 Task 3. Our experiments suggest that traditional knowledge-based features are cornered by novel corpus-based word meaning representations, such as word2vec, which emerge as efficient and strong performers under a variety of scenarios. We also explored whether context expansion is beneficial to the cross-level similarity task, and remarked that only when the context is particularly short, this enrichment is viable. However, in a meta-learning framework, the information permeating from a set of similarity measures exposed to varying context expansions can attain a higher performance than possible with individual signals. Overall, our system ranked first among 21 teams and 38 systems.

Acknowledgments

This material is based in part upon work supported by National Science Foundation CAREER award #1361274 and IIS award #1018613 and by DARPA-BAA-12-47 DEFT grant #12475008. Any opinions, findings, and conclusions or recommendations expressed in this material are those of the authors and do not necessarily reflect the views of the National Science Foundation or the Defense Advanced Research Projects Agency.

References

Eneko Agirre, Daniel Cer, Mona Diab, and Aitor Gonzalez-Agirre. 2012. SemEval-2012 Task 6: A pilot on semantic textual similarity. In *Proceedings of the 6th International Workshop on Semantic Evaluation (SemEval 2012), in conjunction with the First Joint Conference on Lexical and Computational Semantics (*SEM 2012)*, Montreal, Canada.

Eneko Agirre, Daniel Cer, Mona Diab, Aitor Gonzalez-Agirre, and Weiwei Guo. 2013. *SEM 2013 Shared Task: Semantic Textual Similarity, including a Pilot on Typed-Similarity. In *The Second Joint Conference on Lexical and Computational Semantics (*SEM 2013)*.

Daniel Bär, Torsten Zesch, and Iryna Gurevych. 2013. DKPro Similarity: An open source framework for text similarity. In *Proceedings of the 51st Annual Meeting of the Association for Computational Linguistics: System Demonstrations*, pages 121–126, Sofia, Bulgaria.

Curt Burgess, Kay Livesay, and Kevin Lund. 1998. Explorations in context space: words, sentences, discourse. *Discourse Processes*, 25(2):211–257.

Kenneth Church and Patrick Hanks. 1990. Word association norms, mutual information, and lexicography. *Computational Linguistics*, 16(1):22–29.

Evgeniy Gabrilovich and Shaul Markovitch. 2007. Computing semantic relatedness using Wikipedia-based explicit semantic analysis. In *Proceedings of the 20th International Joint Conference on Artificial Intelligence*, pages 1606–1611, Hyderabad, India.

Mark Hall, Eibe Frank, Geoffrey Holmes, Bernhard Pfahringer, Peter Reutemann, and Ian H. Witten. 2009. The WEKA Data Mining Software: An Update. *SIGKDD Explorations*, 11(1).

Samer Hassan and Rada Mihalcea. 2011. Measuring semantic relatedness using salient encyclopedic concepts. *Artificial Intelligence, Special Issue*.

Thad Hughes and Daniel Ramage. 2007. Lexical semantic knowledge with random graph walks. In *Proceedings of the Conference on Empirical Methods in Natural Language Processing*, Prague, Czech Republic.

Aminul Islam and Diana Zaiu Inkpen. 2006. Second order co-occurrence PMI for determining the semantic similarity of words. In *Proceedings of the Fifth Conference on Language Resources and Evaluation*, volume 2, pages 1033–1038, Genoa, Italy, July.

Mario Jarmasz and Stan Szpakowicz. 2003. Roget's thesaurus and semantic similarity. In *Proceedings of the conference on Recent Advances in Natural Language Processing RANLP-2003*, Borovetz, Bulgaria, September.

Jay J. Jiang and David W. Conrath. 1997. Semantic similarity based on corpus statistics and lexical taxonomy. In *Proceeding of the International Conference Research on Computational Linguistics (ROCLING X)*, Taiwan.

David Jurgens, Mohammad Taher Pilehvar, and Roberto Navigli. 2014. SemEval-2014 Task 3: Cross-Level Semantic Similarity. In *Proceedings of the 8th International Workshop on Semantic Evaluation (SemEval-2014)*, Dublin, Ireland.

Thomas K. Landauer and Susan T. Dumais. 1997. A solution to plato's problem: The latent semantic analysis theory of acquisition, induction, and representation of knowledge. *Psychological Review*, 104.

Claudia Leacock and Martin Chodorow. 1998. Combining local context and WordNet sense similarity for word sense identification. In *WordNet, An Electronic Lexical Database*. The MIT Press.

Michael E. Lesk. 1986. Automatic sense disambiguation using machine readable dictionaries: How to tell a pine cone from an ice cream cone. In *Proceedings of the SIGDOC Conference 1986*, Toronto, June.

Chin-Yew Lin and Eduard Hovy. 2003. Automatic evaluation of summaries using n-gram cooccurrence statistics. In *Proceedings of Human Language Technology Conference (HLT-NAACL 2003)*, Edmonton, Canada, May.

Dekang Lin. 1998. An information-theoretic definition of similarity. In *Proceedings of the Fifteenth International Conference on Machine Learning*, pages 296–304, Madison, Wisconsin.

Rada Mihalcea, Courtney Corley, and Carlo Strapparava. 2006. Corpus-based and knowledge-based measures of text semantic similarity. In *American Association for Artificial Intelligence (AAAI-2006)*, Boston, MA.

Tomas Mikolov, Kai Chen, Greg Corrado, and Jeffrey Dean. 2013a. Distributed Representations of Words and Phrases and their Compositionality . In *NIPS*, pages 3111–3119.

Tomas Mikolov, Wen-tau Yih, and Geoffrey Zweig. 2013b. Linguistic regularities in continuous space word representations. In *NAACL HLT*, pages 746–751, Atlanta, GA, USA.

George A. Miller. 1995. WordNet: a Lexical database for English. *Communications of the Association for Computing Machinery*, 38(11):39–41.

Rao Muhammad Adeel Nawab, Mark Stevenson, and Paul Clough. 2011. External plagiarism detection using information retrieval and sequence alignment:

Notebook for PAN at CLEF 2011. In *Proceedings of the 5th International Workshop on Uncovering Plagiarism, Authorship, and Social Software Misuse (PAN 2011)*.

Kishore. Papineni, Salim Roukos, Todd Ward, and Wei-Jing Zhu. 2002. Bleu: A method for automatic evaluation of machine translation. In *Proceedings of the 40th Annual Meeting of the Association for Computational Linguistics*, pages 311–318, Philadelphia, PA.

Fabian Pedregosa, Gaël Varoquaux, Alexandre Gramfort, Vincent Michel, Bertrand Thirion, Olivier Grisel, Mathieu Blondel, Peter Prettenhofer, Ron Weiss, Vincent Dubourg, Jake Vanderplas, Alexandre Passos, David Cournapeau, Matthieu Brucher, Matthieu Perrot, and Édouard Duchesnay. 2011. Scikit-learn: Machine learning in Python. *The Journal of Machine Learning Research*, 12:2825–2830.

Radim Rehurek and Petr Sojka. 2010. Software framework for topic modelling with large corpora. In *Proceedings of the LREC 2010 Workshop on New Challenges for NLP Frameworks*, pages 45–50, Valletta, Malta, May. ELRA.

Philip Resnik. 1995. Using information content to evaluate semantic similarity in a taxonomy. In *Proceedings of the 14th International Joint Conference on Artificial Intelligence*, pages 448–453, Montreal, Quebec, Canada. Morgan Kaufmann Publishers Inc.

J. Rocchio, 1971. *Relevance feedback in information retrieval*. Prentice Hall, Ing. Englewood Cliffs, New Jersey.

1995. *Roget's II: The New Thesaurus*. Houghton Mifflin.

Gerard Salton and Michael E. Lesk, 1971. *The SMART Retrieval System: Experiments in Automatic Document Processing*, chapter Computer evaluation of indexing and text processing. Prentice Hall, Ing. Englewood Cliffs, New Jersey.

Gerard Salton, Amit Singhal, Mandar Mitra, and Chris Buckley. 1997. Automatic text structuring and summarization. *Information Processing and Management*, 2(32).

Hinrich Schutze. 1998. Automatic word sense discrimination. *Computational Linguistics*, 24(1):97–124.

Peter D. Turney. 2001. Mining the Web for Synonyms: PMI-IR versus LSA on TOEFL. In *Proceedings of the 12th European Conference on Machine Learning (ECML'01)*, pages 491–502, Freiburg, Germany.

SINAI: Voting System for Aspect Based Sentiment Analysis

Salud María Jiménez-Zafra, Eugenio Martínez-Cámara,
M. Teresa Martín-Valdivia, L. Alfonso Ureña-López
SINAI Research Group
University of Jaén
E-23071, Jaén (Spain)
{sjzafra, emcamara, maite, laurena}@ujaen.es

Abstract

This paper describes the participation of the SINAI research group in Task 4 of the 2014 edition of the International Workshop SemEval. This task is concerned with Aspect Based Sentiment Analysis and its goal is to identify the aspects of given target entities and the sentiment expressed towards each aspect.

1 Introduction

The web has evolved progressively since its beginning in 1990. At first, the user was almost a passive subject who received the information or published it, without many possibilities to generate an interaction. The emergence of the Web 2.0 was a social revolution, because it offered users the possibility of producing and sharing contents, opinions, experiences, etc.

Some years ago it was common to ask family and friends to know their opinion about a particular topic, but after the emergence of the Web 2.0, the number of Internet users has been greatly increased. The exponential growth of the subjective information in the last years has created a great interest in the treatment of this information.

Opinion Mining (OM), also known as Sentiment Analysis (SA) is the discipline that focuses on the computational treatment of opinion, sentiment and subjectivity in texts (Pang and Lee, 2008). Currently, OM is a trendy task in the field of Natural Language Processing due mainly to the fact of the growing interest in the knowledge of the opinion of people from different sectors of the society. However, the study on Opinion Mining goes back to 2002 when two of the most cited articles in this task were published (Pang et al., 2002) (Turney, 2002).

OM or SA can be divided into two subtasks that are known as subjectivity classification and polarity classification. Subjectivity classification is the task concentrated on the identification of subjectivity in texts, that is, these systems are binary classifiers that separate the documents in two classes, objective and subjective ones. On the other hand, polarity classification is the task of determining the semantic orientation of a subjective text. The ideal OM system has to be composed by a subjectivity classifier and a polarity classifier. However, most of the works in the field of OM are carried out considering the documents as subjective, so polarity classification systems have been more studied than subjectivity classification ones. The reader can find a complete overview about the research in OM in (Pang and Lee, 2008) and (Liu, 2012).

As Liu asserts in (Liu, 2012), the polarity classification systems can be divided into three levels:

- **Document level polarity classification:** This kind of systems assumes that each document expresses an opinion on a single entity (Pang et al., 2002) (Turney, 2002).

- **Sentence level polarity classification:** In this case the polarity classification systems are focused on the identification of the level of polarity of each sentence of the document (Wilson et al., 2005) (Yu and Hatzivassiloglou, 2003).

- **Entity and Aspect level polarity classification:** These systems accomplish a finer-grained sentiment classification. Whereas the document-level and sentiment-level only discover the overall sentiment expressed by the author, the goal of the entity and aspect polarity classification is the identification of the

Proceedings of the 8th International Workshop on Semantic Evaluation (SemEval 2014), pages 566–571,
Dublin, Ireland, August 23-24, 2014.

sentiment of the author towards each entity or aspect.

An entity usually is composed by several aspects, for example a telephone is formed by a headset, which also consists of a speaker and an earphone. An entity can be regarded as a hierarchy of all the aspects whose head is the entity, so the entity can also be considered as an aspect or general aspect. Therefore, the task "entity and aspect level polarity classification" can be called "aspect polarity classification".

The main objective of OM at aspect level is to discover every quintuple (e_i, a_{ij}, s_{ijkl}, h_k, t_l) in a given document, where e_i is the entity, a_{ij} is one of the aspects of the entity or the entity and s_{ijkl} is the orientation of the opinion expressed by the opinion holder h_k in a certain moment t_l. To achieve the objective of populate the quintuple is needed the splitting of the task into several subtasks that correspond with the identification of the aspect, the author or the holder of the opinion and the moment when the opinion is expressed or posted. But in a real scenario, OM at aspect level is also limited like OM at sentence and document level, and most of the research works are only focused on the identification of the aspect and in the calculation of the level of intensity of the sentiment stated about the aspect. However, there are some papers that are closely to the goal of finding out each of the components of the quintuple (Kim and Hovy, 2004) (Kim and Hovy, 2006).

The task four of the 2014 edition of SemEval workshop aims to promote the research polarity classification systems at aspect level. The task is divided into four subtasks, two of them related to the aspect identification and the other with the polarity classification. Due to the fact that OM is a domain-dependent task, the organization proposes the four subtasks in two different domains, Restaurants and Laptops. Task one and three are the ones linked to the aspect identification. Subtask one is focused on the identification of the aspects in each review of the two given corpus. Subtask three goes one step further, in which the main objective is for a given predefined set of aspect categories, identify the aspect categories discussed in the given sentence. Subtask two proposes the classification of the sentiment expressed by the author about each of the aspects extracted, and subtask four has as challenge the classification of the polarity of each of the categories of the aspects. A wider description of the task and the datasets used can be found in the task description paper (Pontiki et al., 2014).

The rest of the paper is organized as follows. Section two outlines the two main parts of our proposed system, firstly the strategy to solve the subtask 1 and 2 and then the method used to resolve the subtask 3 and 4. To sum up the paper, an analysis of the results and the conclusion of this work are shown in section three and four respectively.

2 System description

The guidelines of this task indicate that each team may submit two runs: constrained (using only the provided training data and other resources, such as lexicons) and unconstrained (using additional data for training). We decided to follow an unsupervised approach that we present below.

Our system is divided into two subsystems (Figure 1). The aim of the first subsystem is to extract the aspect terms related to a given target entity (subtask 1) and calculate the sentiment expressed towards each aspect in the opinion (subtask 2). The goal of the second is, for a given set of categories, to identify the categories discussed in the review (subtask 3) and determine its polarity (subtask 4).

2.1 Subsystem 1: Aspects Identification and Polarity Classification

To identify the aspects related with the target entity (laptops or restaurants) we decided to use a bag of words built from all the aspect terms present in the training data. But this method only detects previously tagged aspect in the training data, so, we enriched the list of words with data automatically extracted from the collaborative knowledge base Freebase[1], in order to improve the identification. For this, we obtained all categories in restaurants domain and in computers domain[2] (types in a domain) using MQL[3] (Metaweb Query Language) (Figure 2).

Then, for each domain category we extracted all terms (instances of a type) to enrich the bag. In Figure 3 we can see an example to get all terms of

[1]http://www.freebase.com/

[2]Nowadays, Freebase has more than 70 different domains. But, for this task, we are only interested in these two.

[3]MQL is a language which is used to express Metaweb queries. This allows you to incorporate knowledge from the Freebase database into your own applications and websites.

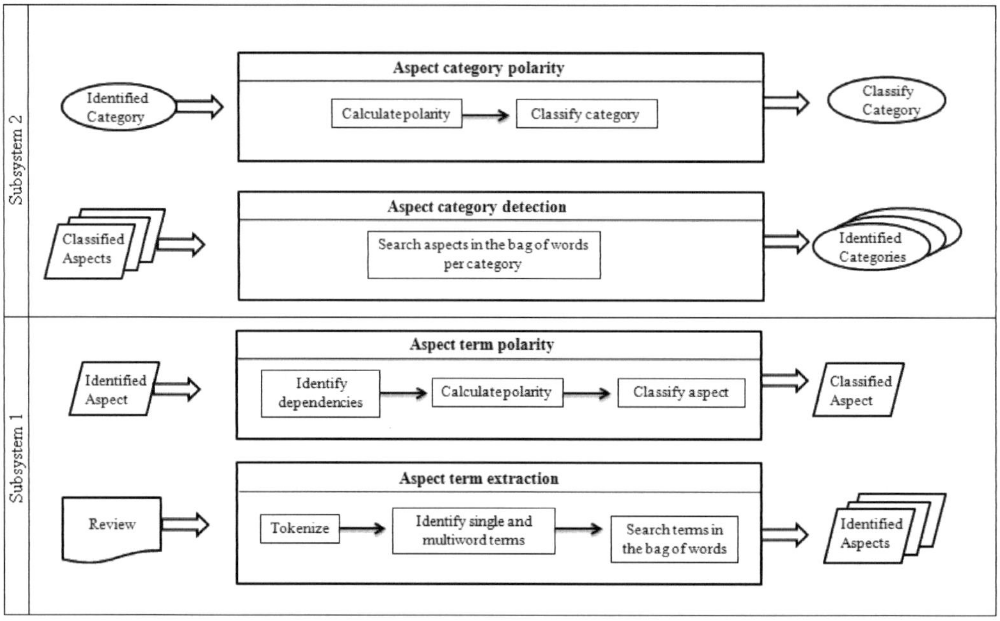

Figure 1: Arquitecture of the system.

```
[{
  "id": null,
  "name": null,
  "type": "/type/type",
  "domain": "/food"
}]
```

Figure 2: Query for list all categories in food domain.

a category, in particular cheese category of food domain.

```
[{
  "id": null,
  "name": null,
  "type": "/food/cheese"
}]
```

Figure 3: Query for list all term in cheese category.

In this way, given a review of the test data, the first step is to tokenize it to get a vector of unigrams with all single words in the text (we do not divide the reviews into sentences because there is only one sentence per review). The second step is to represent each review as a list of n lists of unigrams, bigrams, ..., n-grams where n is the number of tokens in the sentence. This is because an aspect term can be a nominal phrase, a word formed from a verb but functioning as a different part of speech (e.g. gerunds and participles) or a simple term. For example, the review "The salad was excellent as was the lamb chettinad" is represented as shown in Figure 4.

After obtaining the possible terms of a review, the next step is to go over the list of lists to extract the aspects. Each list is traversed backwards matching each term with each aspect from the bag. When an aspect is found or the top of the list is reached the search begins in the next list. In the review showed in Figure 4, the system will identify two aspects: **salad** and **lamb chettinad**. The search in this example begins in the list 1 with "The salad was excellent as was the lamb chettinad", ends with "The" and continues with the next list, because the top of the list is reached. The search in the list 2 begins with "salad was excellent as was the lamb chettinad", ends with "salad" because it is an aspect and continues with the list 3 and so on. At last, the search in the list 8 begins with the term "lamb chettinad", ends with it because it is an aspect presents in the bag of words and continues with the list 9.

Once extracted the aspects related with the target entity, the next step is to determine the words that modify each aspect. For this, we have used the Stanford Dependencies Parser[4]. This parser

[4] http://nlp.stanford.edu/software/lex-parser.shtml

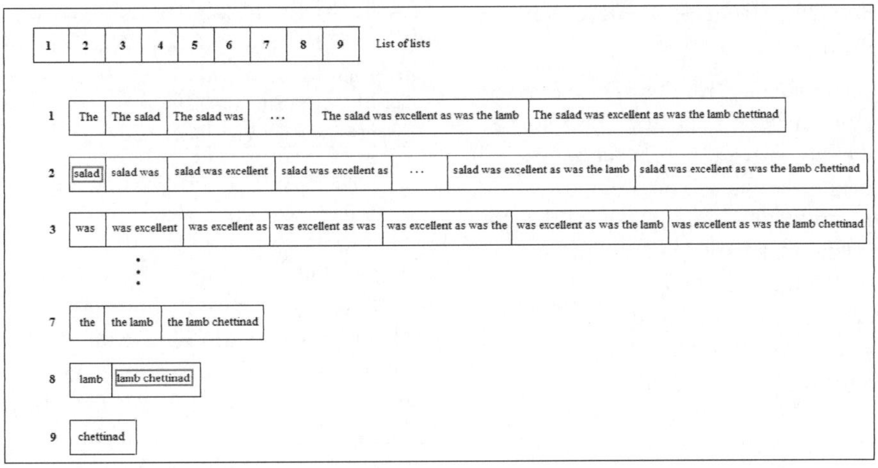

Figure 4: Possible terms of the sentence "The salad was excellent as was the lamb chettinad".

was designed to provide a simple description of the grammatical relationships in a sentence that can easily be understood and effectively used by people without linguistic expertise who want to extract textual relations (De Marneffe and Manning, 2008). It represents all sentence relationships uniformly as typed dependency relations. In this work, we have considered the main relationships for expressing opinion about an aspect: using a verb ("nsubj" or "nsubjpass"), an adjectival modifier ("amod") or a dependency relation with another word ("dep"). In the review "The salad was excellent as was the lamb chettinad", the system will identify two modifiers words: the adjective **excellent** that expresses how is the **salad** through the relationship **"nsubj"** and the adjective **excellent** that also modified the aspect **lamb chettinad** through the relationship **"dep"** Figure 5.

To determine the sentiment expressed over an aspect we have calculated the polarity of each word that modifies it through a voting system based on three classifiers: Bing Liu Lexicon (Hu and Liu, 2004), SentiWordNet (Baccianella et al., 2010) and MPQA (Wilson et al., 2005). The Bing Liu Lexicon is a list of 2006 positive words and another with 4783 negative ones. MPQA is also a subjectivity lexicon with positive and negative words and has extra information about each one: the part-of-speech, the strength, etc. Finally, SentiWordNet is a lexical resource that assigns to each synset of WordNet three sentiment scores: positivity, negativity and objectivity. Therefore, an aspect is positive/negative if there are at least two classifiers that tag it as positive/negative and neutral in another case. It may happen that a word is affected by negation, to treat this problem we have used a straightforward method, the fixed window size method. We have considered the negative particles: "not", "n't", "no", "never". So if any of the preceding or following 3 words to one aspect is one of these negative particles, the aspect polarity is reversed (positive —> negative, negative —> positive, neutral —> neutral).

In the example showed in Figure 5, the aspect salad is modified by the word excellent that also modified the aspect lamb chettinad. This adjective is part of the Bing Liu positive list, MPQA classifies it as positive and SentiWordNet assigns it the scores: 1 (positivity), 0(objectivity), 0 (objectivity). Then, the aspects **salad** and **lamb chettinad** are classified as **positive** by the voting system.

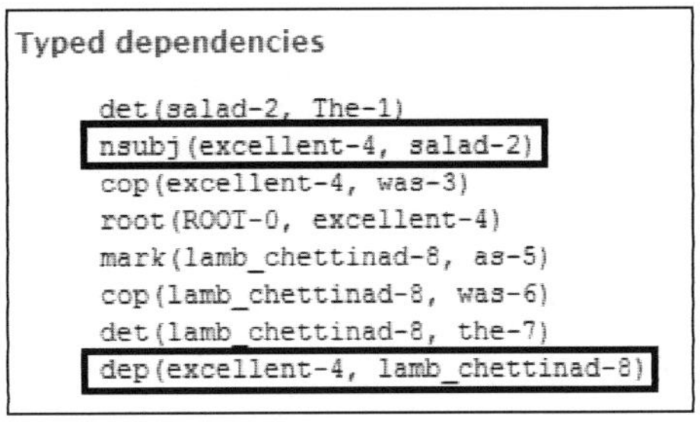

Figure 5: Dependency analysis of the sentence: "The salad was excellent as was the lamb chettinad".

2.2 Subsystem 2: Categories Identification and Polarity Classification

As we have mentioned above, this subsystem focuses on the treatment of the categories and has been used only with the dataset of restaurants.

On the one hand, we have built a bag of words for each of the given categories related to the target entity (restaurants). We have tagged manually each aspect of the bag of words, built for the first subsystem, in one of the categories of the given set (food, service, price, ambience, anecdotes/miscellaneous). Thus, to determine the categories that are referenced in a review we have searched each aspect identified with the first subsystem in each bag, if the aspect belongs to any category then this category is identified. If any aspect belongs to a category, then the category allocated is "anecdotes/miscellaneous".

On the other hand, the sentiment expressed about each category has been calculated as the most frequent polarity of the aspects that belongs to this category. In case of a tie between positive and negative values, the polarity value conflict is assigned to the category. If any aspect belongs to the category, then the polarity value of the review is assigned to the category.

In the above example, the aspects salad and lamb chettinad belong to food's bag of words, so that the system will identify that the **category food** is discussed in this review and will assign it the **polarity** value **positive**, because the sentiment expressed about the two aspects that belongs to this category is positive.

3 Analysis of the results

The aim of this section is to provide a meaningful report of the results obtained after participation in the task related to Aspect Based Sentiment Analysis (ABSA). Table 1 shows the evaluation results for the aspect extraction subtask. As we can see, the recall overcomes the mean value of results of participants in both domains (laptops and restaurants), that is, the system identifies quite aspects of the corpus. However, the precision is lower because the system identifies aspects that are not considered by the organization, due to the fact that our bag of words contains more aspects than the tagged by the organization.

The results reached in the aspect term extraction subtask are similar (Table 2). It should be taken into account that the system is a general-domain sentiment classifier, so it does not use specific knowledge for each of the domains. This fact can be shown in the results reached in the task of polarity classification for the two domains, which are similar. Therefore, this subtask could be improved by taking into account the domain and other relationships for expressing opinion about an aspect apart from that we have treated ("nsubj", "nsubjpass", "amod", "dep").

	Laptops		Restaurants	
	SINAI	Average	SINAI	Average
Precision	0.3729	0.6890	0.5961	0.7674
Recall	0.5765	0.5045	0.72487	0.6726
F-score	0.4529	0.5620	0.6542	0.7078

Table 1: Aspect Term Extraction results.

	Laptops		Restaurants	
	SINAI	Average	SINAI	Average
Accuracy	0.5872	0.5925	0.5873	0.6910

Table 2: Aspect Term Polarity results.

On the other hand, the results in the identification of the categories discussed in a review have been high (Table 3) and even overcome the average recall of the participating systems. At last, Table 4 shows the result evaluation of the aspect category polarity subtask that are slightly lower than the average. These tables show that is possible to reach good results using a simple approach as described in subsection 2.2.

	Restaurants	
	SINAI	Average
Precision	0.6659	0.76
Recall	0.8244	0.7226
F-score	0.7367	0.7379

Table 3: Aspect Category Detection results.

4 Conclusion and future works

In SA can be differentiated three levels of study of a text: document level, sentence level and aspect level. The document level analysis determines the overall sentiment expressed in a review, while the sentence level analysis specifies for each sentence of a text, whether express a positive, negative or neutral opinion. However, these two types of anal-

	Restaurants	
	SINAI	**Average**
Accuracy	0.6030	0.6951

Table 4: Aspect Category Polarity results.

ysis do not reach the level of detail that an user wants when searches for information about a product. The fact that the overall sentiment of a product is positive does not mean that the author has a positive opinion about all aspects of that product, or the fact that is negative does not involve that everything about the product is bad.

In addition, the large amount of sources and the high volume of texts with reviews, make difficult for the user to select information of interest. Therefore, it is necessary to develop classification systems at aspect level that help users to make decisions and, on the other hand, that show companies the opinion that consumers have about their products, in order to help them to decide what to keep, what to delete and what to improve.

In this paper we have presented our first approach for the Aspect Based Sentiment Analysis that has been developed for the task four of the 2014 edition of SemEval workshop. After analyzing the evaluation results we consider that is possible to introduce some improvements we are currently working: domain adaptation in the polarity calculation, consideration of other relationships to determine which words modify an aspect and treatment of negation (in the system proposed we have used the fixed window size method). Also, in a near future we will try to extrapolate it to Spanish reviews.

Acknowledgments

This work has been partially supported by a grant from the Fondo Europeo de Desarrollo Regional (FEDER), ATTOS project (TIN2012-38536-C03-0) from the Spanish Government, AORESCU project (P11-TIC-7684 MO) from the regional government of Junta de Andalucía and CEATIC-2013-01 project from the University of Jaén.

References

Stefano Baccianella, Andrea Esuli, and Fabrizio Sebastiani. 2010. Sentiwordnet 3.0: An enhanced lexical resource for sentiment analysis and opinion mining. In *LREC*, volume 10, pages 2200–2204.

Marie-Catherine De Marneffe and Christopher D Manning. 2008. Stanford typed dependencies manual.

Minqing Hu and Bing Liu. 2004. Mining and summarizing customer reviews. In *Proceedings of the Tenth ACM SIGKDD International Conference on Knowledge Discovery and Data Mining*, KDD '04, pages 168–177, New York, NY, USA. ACM.

Soo-Min Kim and Eduard Hovy. 2004. Determining the sentiment of opinions. In *Proceedings of the 20th International Conference on Computational Linguistics*, COLING '04, Stroudsburg, PA, USA.

Soo-Min Kim and Eduard Hovy. 2006. Extracting opinions, opinion holders, and topics expressed in online news media text. In *Proceedings of the Workshop on Sentiment and Subjectivity in Text*, SST '06, pages 1–8, Stroudsburg, PA, USA.

Bing Liu. 2012. Sentiment analysis and opinion mining. *Synthesis Lectures on Human Language Technologies*, 5(1):1–167.

Bo Pang and Lillian Lee. 2008. Opinion mining and sentiment analysis. *Found. Trends Inf. Retr.*, 2(1-2):1–135, January.

Bo Pang, Lillian Lee, and Shivakumar Vaithyanathan. 2002. Thumbs up?: Sentiment classification using machine learning techniques. In *Proceedings of the ACL-02 Conference on Empirical Methods in Natural Language Processing - Volume 10*, EMNLP '02, pages 79–86, Stroudsburg, PA, USA.

Maria Pontiki, Dimitrios Galanis, John Pavlopoulos, Harris Papageorgiou, Ion Androutsopoulos, and Suresh Manandhar. 2014. Semeval-2014 task 4: Aspect based sentiment analysis. In *Proceedings of the International Workshop on Semantic Evaluation (SemEval)*.

Peter D. Turney. 2002. Thumbs up or thumbs down?: Semantic orientation applied to unsupervised classification of reviews. In *Proceedings of the 40th Annual Meeting on Association for Computational Linguistics*, ACL '02, pages 417–424, Stroudsburg, PA, USA.

Theresa Wilson, Janyce Wiebe, and Paul Hoffmann. 2005. Recognizing contextual polarity in phrase-level sentiment analysis. In *Proceedings of the Conference on Human Language Technology and Empirical Methods in Natural Language Processing*, HLT '05, pages 347–354, Stroudsburg, PA, USA.

Hong Yu and Vasileios Hatzivassiloglou. 2003. Towards answering opinion questions: Separating facts from opinions and identifying the polarity of opinion sentences. In *Proceedings of the 2003 Conference on Empirical Methods in Natural Language Processing*, EMNLP '03, pages 129–136, Stroudsburg, PA, USA.

SINAI: Voting System for Twitter Sentiment Analysis

Eugenio Martínez-Cámara, Salud María Jiménez-Zafra,
M. Teresa Martín-Valdivia, L. Alfonso Ureña-López
SINAI Research Group
University of Jaén
E-23071, Jaén (Spain)
{emcamara, sjzafra, maite, laurena}@ujaen.es

Abstract

This article presents the participation of the SINAI research group in the task Sentiment Analysis in Twitter of the SemEval Workshop. Our proposal consists of a voting system of three polarity classifiers which follow a lexicon-based approach.

1 Introduction

Opinion Mining (OM) or Sentiment Analysis (SA) is the task focuses on the computational treatment of opinion, sentiment and subjectivity in texts (Pang and Lee, 2008). Currently, OM is a trendy task in the field of Natural Language Processing due mainly to the fact of the growing interest in the knowledge of the opinion of people from different sectors of the society.

The interest in the research community for the extraction of the sentiment in Twitter posts is reflected in the organization of several workshops with the aim of promoting the research in this task. Two are the most relevant, the first is the task Sentiment Analysis in Twitter celebrated within the SemEval workshop whose first edition was in 2013 (Nakov et al., 2013). The second is the workshop TASS[1] , which is a workshop for promoting the research in sentiment analysis in Spanish in Twitter. The first edition of the workshop took place in 2012 (Villena-Román et al., 2013).

The 2014 edition of the task Sentiment Analysis in Twitter proposes a first subtask, which has as challenge the sentiment classification at entity level, and a second subtask that consists of the polarity classification at document or tweet level. The training corpus is the same than the former edition, but this year the test corpus is considerably bigger than the prior one. A wider description of the task and the corpus can be read in (Rosenthal et al., 2014).

We present an unsupervised polarity classification system for the subtask B of the task Sentiment Analysis in Twitter. The system is based on a voting strategy of three lexicon-based sentiment classifiers. The sentiment analysis research community broadly knows the lexicons selected. They are, SentiWordNet (Baccianella et al., 2010), the lexicon developed by Hu and Liu (Hu and Liu, 2004) and the MPQA lexicon (Wilson et al., 2005).

The rest of the paper is organized as follows. The following section focuses on the description of the different sentiment resources used for developing the sentiment classifiers. The subsequent section outlines the system proposed for the 2014 edition of the task. The last section exposes the analysis of the results reached this year.

2 Sentiment lexical resources

Sentiment lexicons are lexical resources composed of opinion-bearing words and some of them also of sentiment phrases of idioms. Most of the sentiment lexicons are formed by a list of words without any additional information.

A sentiment classifier based on list of opinion-bearing words usually consists of finding out the words of the list in a given document. This method can be considered very simple for the complexity of OM, but it has reached acceptable results in different domains and also is applied in real systems like Trayt.com[2].

Our experience in the field of SA allows us to assert that sentiment lexicons can be divided depending on the information linked to each word,

[1] http://www.daedalus.es/TASS

[2] Trayt.com is a search engine of reviews of restaurants. The polarity classifier of Tryt.com is a lexicon-based system which uses the opinion list compiled by Bing Liu.

Proceedings of the 8th International Workshop on Semantic Evaluation (SemEval 2014), pages 572–577,
Dublin, Ireland, August 23-24, 2014.

so three groups can be found:

- List of opinion-bearing words: These lexicons are usually two lists of polar words, one of them of positive words and another one of negative terms. Some examples of this kind of sentiment lexicons are for English the one compiled by (Hu and Liu, 2004), and for Spanish, the iSOL lexicon (Molina-González et al., 2013).

- List of opinion-bearing words with syntactic information: As it is wider known, OM is a domain-dependent task and can be also said that a context-dependent task. Thus, some lexicons add syntactic information with the aim of offering some information for disambiguating the term, and also provide a different orientation of the word depending on its POS-tags. One example of this kind of lexicon is MPQA subjectivity lexicon (Wilson et al., 2005).

- Knowledge base sentiment lexicons: These lexicons usually indicate the semantic orientation of the different senses of each word, whereas the previous lexicons only indicate the polarity of each word. Also, it is very common that in the knowledge base sentiment lexicons each sense is linked to the likelihood of being positive, negative and neutral. One example of this kind of polar lexicon is SentiWordNet (Baccianella et al., 2010).

In the polarity classifier developed for the workshop a lexicon of each type has been utilised. The sentiment linguistic resources used has been:

- Sentiment lexicon compiled by Bing Liu: The lexicon was used the first time in (Hu and Liu, 2004). Since then, the authors have been updating the list, and currently the list is formed by 2006 positive words and 4783 negative words. Also, the lexicon includes some misspellings with the aim of better representing the language used in the Internet.

- MPQA Subjectivity lexicon (Wilson et al., 2005): The lexicon is formed by over 8000 subjectivity clues. Subjectivity clues are words and phrases that have subjective usages. The lexicon was developed joining words compiled by the authors and with words taken from General Inquirer. Each word is linked with its grade of subjectivity, with its part of speech tag and with its semantic orientation. Due to the fact that each word has its POS-tag there are some words that depending on its POS have a different semantic orientation.

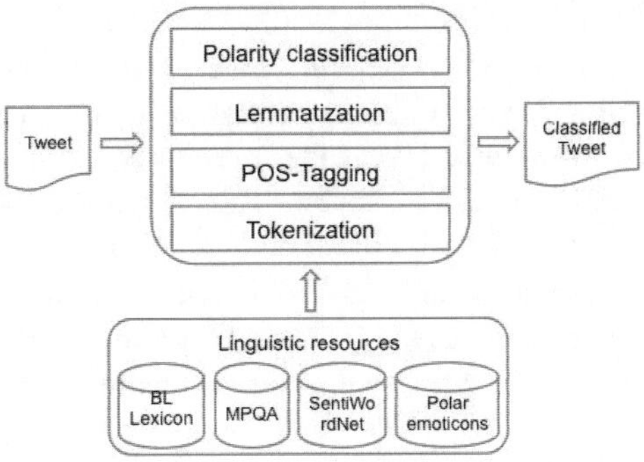

Figure 1: Architecture of the system.

- SentiWordNet 3.0 (Baccianella et al., 2010): is a lexical resource which assigns three sentiment scores to each synset of WordNet: positivity, negativity and objectivity.

3 Polarity classification

We wanted to take advantage from our experience in meta-classification in OM for the 2014 edition of the task, Sentiment Analysis in Twitter. We have reached good results in OM using meta-classifiers in different domains (Perea-Ortega et al., 2013) and (Martín-Valdivia et al., 2013). Therefore, we propose a voting system that combines three polarity classifiers. The general architecture of the system is shown in Figure 1.

Tokenization is a common step of the three classifiers. Due to the specific characteristics of the language used in Twitter, a specific tokenizer for Twitter was preferred to use. The tokenizer published by Christopher Potts[3] was selected and updated, with the aim of recognizing a wider range of tokens.

When the tweet is tokenized, the following step is discover its polarity. Each of the three polarity classifiers follows the same strategy for the classification, but they perform different operations on each tweet. The classifier based on the lexicon compiled by Bing Liu (C_BingL) consists of seeking each token in the opinion-bearing words

[3]http://sentiment.christopherpotts.net/tokenizing.html

list. Therefore, after the tokenization, any linguistic operation has to be performed on the tweet. This classifier classifies a tweet as positive if the number of positive tokens is greater or equal than the number of negative tokens. If there are not polar tokens, the polarity of the tweet is neutral.

The second polarity classifier is the based on MPQA lexicon (C_MPQA). Some of the words that are in the MPQA lexicon are lemmatized, and also the sentiment depends on their POS-tag. Thus, to take advantage of all the information offered by MPQA is needed to perform a morphological analysis to each tweet. The morphological analysis firstly identifies the POS-tag of each token of the tweet, and then the lemmatizer extracts the lemma of the token.

Recently, some linguistic tools have been published to carry out linguistic analysis in tweets. Currently, two POS-taggers for Twitter are available. One of them, is the described in (Gimpel et al., 2011) and the second one in (Derczynski et al., 2013). Although the authors of the two systems are competing for which of the two taggers are better, our selection was based on the usability of the two systems. To use the tagger developed by Gimpel et al. is needed to download their software, meanwhile the one developed by Derczynski et al. can be integrated in other taggers. On our point of view, the tagger of Derczynski et al. has the advantage of offering the training model of the tagger[4], which allows us to integrate it in other POS-tagging tools. The training model of the tagger was integrated in the Stanford Part-of-Speech Tagger[5]. When each token of the tweet is associated with its corresponding POS-tag, the lemmatizer is run over the tweet. The lemmatizer used is the offered by the toolkit for Natural Language Processing, NLTK (Bird et al., 2009). When each token is accompanied by its corresponding POS-tag and lemma, the polarity classifier can seek each token in the MPQA subjective lexicon.

Besides the label of the polar class (positive or negative), each entry in the MPQA corpus has a field called type, which indicates whether the term is considered strongly subjective or the term is considered weakly subjective. Thus, in the calculation of the polarity score these two levels of subjectivity are considered, so when the term is strong subjective it is considered to have a score of 1, and when the term is weak subjective the system considers the term as less important and its score is 0.75.

The polarity classifier based on the use of SentiWordNet (C_SWN) needs that each word of the tweet is linked with its POS-tag and its lemma, so the same pipeline that the classifier based on MPQA follows is also followed by the classifier based on SentiWordNet.

In the bibliography about OM can be found different ways to calculate the polarity class when SentiWordNet is used as a sentiment knowledge base. Some works perform a disambiguation method with the aim of selecting only the synset that corresponds with the sense of the word in the context of the given document. But there are other works that do not perform any disambiguation method, and also reach good results. Denecke in (Denecke, 2008) describes a very simple method to calculate the polarity of each of the words of a document without the need of a disambiguation process. The method consists of calculating per each word in the document, which is in SentiWordNet, the arithmetic mean of the positive, negative and neutral score of each of the synsets that the word has in SentiWordNet. When the scores of each word are calculated, the score of the document is determined as the arithmetic mean of each score of the words. The class of the document is corresponded with the greatest polar score (positive, negative, neutral). Due to the acceptable results that the Denecke formula reaches, we have introduced a soft disambiguation process with the aim of improving the classification accuracy. This soft disambiguation process consist of only taking those synsets corresponding with POS-tag of the word whose polarity are being calculated. For example, the word "good" can do the function of an adverb, a noun or an adjective. In SentiWordNet, there are two synsets of "good" as an adverb, four synset of "good" as a noun, and twenty-one synsets as an adjective. If the polarity score is calculated with the Denecke formula, the twenty-seven synsets are used. Meanwhile, if it used our proposal, and the word "good" in the given sentence is acting as an adverb, then only the two synsets of the word "good" when it is adverb are considered to calculate the polarity score.

During the development of the system, we noticed that synsets have a lower probability to be positive or negative, and most of them in Senti-

[4] https://gate.ac.uk/wiki/twitter-postagger.html

[5] http://nlp.stanford.edu/software/tagger.shtml

WordNet are neutral. With the aim of boosting the likelihood to be positive or negative, the polarity classifier does not consider the neutral score of the synset. If the positive score is greater than the negative score and greater than 0.15 then the term is positive. If the negative score is greater than the positive score and greater than 0.15 then the word is negative, in other case the word is neutral.

Each of the polarity classifiers take into consideration the presence of emoticons, the expressions of laughing and negation. The emoticons are processed as words, so for determining their polarity a sentiment lexicon of emoticons was built. The polar lexicon of emoticons consists of fifty-eight positive emoticons and forty-four negative ones. Laughing expressions usually express a positive sentiment, so when a laughing expression is detected the counter of positive words is increased by one. The strategy for negation identification is a bit straightforward but effective. Due to the specific linguistic characteristics of tweets, a strategy based on windows of words has been implemented. When a polar word is identified, it is sought in the previous three words whether there is a negative particle. In those cases that a negative particle is found, the polarity of the sentiment word is reversed, that it to say if a positive (negative) word is negated the system considers it as negative (positive).

The last step of the polarity classifier is the running of a voting system among the three polarity classifiers. Three are the possible output values of the three base classifiers {negative, neutral, positive}. When the majority class is positive, the tweet is classified as positive, when the majority class is negative then negative is the class assigned to the tweet and when majority class is neutral or there is not a majority class then the tweet is classified as neutral.

4 Analysis of the results

Before showing the results reached in the evaluation of the task, the results accomplished in the development phase of the system will be shown. Three main systems were assessed during the development phase:

- Baseline (BL): The three base classifiers compose the baseline system, but the three polarity scores of SentiWordNet are considered and negation is not taken into account.
- Neutral scores are not considered (NN): It is the same than the Baseline system but the neutral scores of SentiWordNet are not considered.
- Negation identification (NI): The neutral scores of SentiWordNet are not taken into account and the negation is identified.

The results are show in Table 1.

	Precision	Recall	F1	Accuracy	Improve (Acc.)
BL	55.85%	52.02%	53.87%	60.32%	-
NN	56.03%	52.27%	54.09%	60.46%	0.23%
NI	57.22%	53.41%	55.25%	61.12%	1.33%

Table 1: Results achieved during the developing phase.

As can be seen in Table 1 the systems (NN) and (NI) reach better results than the baseline, so all the modifications to the baseline are good for the polarity classification process. The results confirm our hypothesis that the neutral score of the synsets in SentiWordNet are not contributing positively to the sentiment classification. Also, a straightforward strategy for identifying the scope of the negation improves the accuracy of the classification. The results help us to choose the final configuration of the system. As is described in the former section the final polarity classification system follows a voting scheme of three base lexicon-based polarity classifiers. The three base classifiers take into consideration the presence of emoticons, laughing expressions, identifies the scope of negation, and the classifier based on SentiWordNet does not take into consideration the neutral score of the synsets.

The edition 2014 of the task Sentiment Analysis in Twitter has assessed the systems with five different corpus tests: LiveJournal2014, SMS2013, Twitter2013, Twitter2014, Twitter2014Sarcasm. The results reached with each of the test corpus are shown in Table 2.

Some of the results shown in Table 2 are much closed to the results reached during the development phase, because all of the F1 scores are closed to 55%. The lower results have been reached with the corpus Twitter2014 and Twitter2014Sarcasm. The poor results in Twitter2014Sarcasm are due to the lack of a module in the system for the detection of sarcasm. A sarcastic sentence is usually a sentence with a sentiment that expresses the opposite

		Precision	Recall	F1
LiveJournal2014	Positive	60.19%	76.95%	67.54%
	Negative	36,51%	75,00%	49.12%
	Neutral	82.48%	51.36%	63.31%
	Overall	–	–	58.33%
SMS2013	Positive	63.01%	60.19%	61.57%
	Negative	42.13%	71.86%	53.12%
	Neutral	82.27%	73.72%	77,76%
	Overall	–	–	57.34%
Twitter2013	Positive	60.56%	70.15%	65.01%
	Negative	28.29%	50.15%	36.17%
	Neutral	73.66%	57.06%	64.31%
	Overall	–	–	50.59%
Twitter2014	Positive	57.13%	77.49%	65.77%
	Negative	27.23%	42.64%	33.23%
	Neutral	73.54%	49.20%	58.96%
	Overall	–	–	49.50%
Twitter2014Sarcasm	Positive	57.58%	48.72%	52.78%
	Negative	5.00%	100.00%	9.52%
	Neutral	84.62%	24.44%	37.93%
	Overall	–	–	31.15%

Table 2: Results reached with the test corpus.

		F1		
		C_BingL	C_SWN	C_MPQA
LiveJournal2014	Positive	68.11%	42.62%	65.20%
	Negative	55.43%	39.81%	49.60%
	Neutral	64.03%	58.07%	58.43%
	Overall	61.77%	41.21%	57.40%
SMS2013	Positive	61.67%	43.53%	53.56%
	Negative	54.19%	28.79%	52.678%
	Neutral	76.00%	75.85%	68.38%
	Overall	57.93%	36.16%	53.12%
Twitter2013	Positive	68.30%	23.40%	62.37%
	Negative	46.20%	11.60%	37.75%
	Neutral	61.17%	62.11%	57.39%
	Overall	57.25%	17.50%	50.06%
Twitter2014	Positive	69.33%	22.17%	66.74%
	Negative	41.55%	9.79%	33.00%
	Neutral	53.25%	55.63%	52.76%
	Overall	55.44%	15.98%	49.87%
Twitter2014Sarcasm	Positive	56.10%	27.27%	52.06%
	Negative	17.78%	9.52%	8.51%
	Neutral	44.44%	30.24%	30.77%
	Overall	36.94%	18.40%	30.28%

Table 3: Results reached by each base classifier with the test corpus.

sentiment, so a polarity classifier without a specific module to treat this linguistic phenomenon will be probably misclassified the sarcastic sentences. The results for Twitter2014Sarcasm for the negative class indicate this problem. The low value of the precision and the high value of the recall in the negative class mean that a high number of negative sentences have been classified as positive.

The analysis of the results is completed with the assessment of our method. We proceed from the hypothesis that a combination of several classifiers will improve the final classification. Our hypothesis is based on own previous publications, (Perea-Ortega et al., 2013) and (Martín-Valdivia et al., 2013). We have classified the test corpus with each of the three base classifiers, with the aim of knowing the performance of each one. The results are shown in Table 3.

Table 3 shows that the classifier C_BingL reaches better results than the combination of the three classifiers. The first conclusion we draw from this fact is that the good performance of meta-classifiers with large opinions is not achieved with the short texts of Twitter. But, this conclusion is preliminary, because the lower results of the voting system may be due to a not good combination of the three classifiers. So we have to continue working in the analysis on how to build a meta-classifier for OM in Twitter. The rest of the classifiers reached lower results than the voting system. Another reason that the voting system achieved lower results than C_BingL may because the three classifiers are not heterogeneous, in other words, when one of the systems misclassified a document the other ones classify it correctly, so the base classifiers help each other, and the combination of systems reaches better results than the individual systems. But, in our case may be that the systems are not heterogeneous, so our ongoing work is the study of the heterogeneity between the three classifiers.

If we focus only in the results achieved by C_BingL, it is remarkable that the higher difference is in the negative class. C_BingL reaches greater results than the voting system in negative class, and it has the same negation treatment module that the voting system. This fact allow us to say that the low results in the negative class reached by the voting system is not due to the negation treatment module, and may because by the own combination method.

To sum up, after analysing the results, we have noticed that the same meta-classifier methodology that we usually apply to large reviews cannot be directly apply to tweets. Therefore, our ongoing work is focused firstly on conducting a deep analysis of the results presented in this work, and secondly in the study on how to improve of polarity classification in Twitter following a unsupervised methodology, and thirdly on how to build a good meta-classifier for OM in Twitter.

Acknowledgements

This work has been partially supported by a grant from the Fondo Europeo de Desarrollo Regional

(FEDER), ATTOS project (TIN2012-38536-C03-0) from the Spanish Government, AORESCU project (P11-TIC-7684 MO) from the regional government of Junta de Andalucía and CEATIC-2013-01 project from the University of Jaén.

References

Stefano Baccianella, Andrea Esuli, and Fabrizio Sebastiani. 2010. SentiWordnet 3.0: An enhanced lexical resource for sentiment analysis and opinion mining. In *Proceedings of the Seventh International Conference on Language Resources and Evaluation (LREC'10)*, Valletta, Malta, may. European Language Resources Association (ELRA).

Steven Bird, Ewan Klein, and Edward Loper. 2009. *Natural language processing with Python*. O'Reilly Media, Inc.

Kerstin Denecke. 2008. Using SentiWordnet for multilingual sentiment analysis. In *Data Engineering Workshop, 2008. ICDEW 2008. IEEE 24th International Conference on*, pages 507–512, April.

Leon Derczynski, Alan Ritter, Sam Clark, and Kalina Bontcheva. 2013. Twitter part-of-speech tagging for all: Overcoming sparse and noisy data. In *Proceedings of the International Conference Recent Advances in Natural Language Processing RANLP 2013*, pages 198–206, Hissar, Bulgaria, September. INCOMA Ltd. Shoumen, BULGARIA.

Kevin Gimpel, Nathan Schneider, Brendan O'Connor, Dipanjan Das, Daniel Mills, Jacob Eisenstein, Michael Heilman, Dani Yogatama, Jeffrey Flanigan, and Noah A. Smith. 2011. Part-of-speech tagging for Twitter: Annotation, features, and experiments. In *Proceedings of the 49th Annual Meeting of the ACL: Human Language Technologies: Short Papers - Volume 2*, HLT '11, pages 42–47, Stroudsburg, PA, USA. ACL.

Minqing Hu and Bing Liu. 2004. Mining and summarizing customer reviews. In *Proceedings of the Tenth ACM SIGKDD International Conference on Knowledge Discovery and Data Mining*, KDD '04, pages 168–177, New York, NY, USA. ACM.

María-Teresa Martín-Valdivia, Eugenio Martínez-Cámara, Jose-M. Perea-Ortega, and L. Alfonso Ureña López. 2013. Sentiment polarity detection in Spanish reviews combining supervised and unsupervised approaches. *Expert Syst. Appl.*, 40(10):3934–3942, August.

M. Dolores Molina-González, Eugenio Martínez-Cámara, Maria Teresa Martín-Valdivia, and José M. Perea-Ortega. 2013. Semantic orientation for polarity classification in spanish reviews. *Expert Syst. Appl.*, 40(18):7250–7257.

Preslav Nakov, Sara Rosenthal, Zornitsa Kozareva, Veselin Stoyanov, Alan Ritter, and Theresa Wilson. 2013. Semeval-2013 task 2: Sentiment analysis in Twitter. In *Second Joint Conference on Lexical and Computational Semantics (*SEM), Volume 2: Proceedings of the Seventh International Workshop on Semantic Evaluation (SemEval 2013)*, pages 312–320, Atlanta, Georgia, USA, June. ACL.

Bo Pang and Lillian Lee. 2008. Opinion mining and sentiment analysis. *Foundations and Trends in Information Retrieval*, 2(1-2):1–135, January.

José M. Perea-Ortega, M. Teresa Martín-Valdivia, L. Alfonso Ureña López, and Eugenio Martínez-Cámara. 2013. Improving polarity classification of bilingual parallel corpora combining machine learning and semantic orientation approaches. *Journal of the American Society for Information Science and Technology*, 64(9):1864–1877.

Sara Rosenthal, Preslav Nakov, Alan Ritter, and Veselin Stoyanov. 2014. SemEval-2014 Task 9: Sentiment Analysis in Twitter. In Preslav Nakov and Torsten Zesch, editors, *Proceedings of the 8th International Workshop on Semantic Evaluation*, SemEval '14, Dublin, Ireland.

Julio Villena-Román, Sara Lana-Serrano, Eugenio Martínez-Cámara, and José Carlos González-Cristóbal. 2013. TASS - Workshop on sentiment analysis at SEPLN. *Procesamiento del Lenguaje Natural*, 50.

Theresa Wilson, Janyce Wiebe, and Paul Hoffmann. 2005. Recognizing contextual polarity in phrase-level sentiment analysis. In *Proceedings of the Conference on Human Language Technology and Empirical Methods in Natural Language Processing*, HLT '05, pages 347–354, Stroudsburg, PA, USA. ACL.

SNAP: A Multi-Stage XML-Pipeline for Aspect Based Sentiment Analysis

Clemens Schulze Wettendorf and **Robin Jegan** and **Allan Körner** and **Julia Zerche** and **Nataliia Plotnikova** and **Julian Moreth** and **Tamara Schertl** and **Verena Obermeyer** and **Susanne Streil** and **Tamara Willacker** and **Stefan Evert**

Friedrich-Alexander-Universität Erlangen-Nürnberg
Department Germanistik und Komparatistik
Professur für Korpuslinguistik
Bismarckstr. 6, 91054 Erlangen, Germany

{clemens.schulze.wettendorf, robin.jegan, allan.koerner, julia.zerche, nataliia.plotnikova, julian.moreth, tamara.schertl, verena.obermeyer, susanne.streil, tamara.willacker, stefan.evert}@fau.de

Abstract

This paper describes the SNAP system, which participated in Task 4 of SemEval-2014: *Aspect Based Sentiment Analysis*. We use an XML-based pipeline that combines several independent components to perform each subtask. Key resources used by the system are Bing Liu's sentiment lexicon, Stanford CoreNLP, RFTagger, several machine learning algorithms and WordNet. SNAP achieved satisfactory results in the evaluation, placing in the top half of the field for most subtasks.

1 Introduction

This paper describes the approach of the SemaNtic Analyis Project (SNAP) to Task 4 of SemEval-2014: *Aspect Based Sentiment Analysis* (Pontiki et al., 2014). SNAP is a team of undergraduate students at the Corpus Linguistics Group, FAU Erlangen-Nürnberg, who carried out this work as part of a seminar in computational linguistics.

Task 4 was divided into the four subtasks *Aspect term extraction* (1), *Aspect term polarity* (2), *Aspect category detection* (3) and *Aspect category polarity* (4), which were evaluated in two phases (A: subtasks 1/3; B: subtasks 2/4). Subtasks 1 and 3 were carried out on two different datasets, one of laptop reviews and one of restaurant reviews. Subtasks 2 and 4 only made use of the latter.

Task	Dataset	Rank	Score	Best
1	Lap	10 of 21	**0.624**	*0.746*
1	Res	20 of 21	**0.465**	*0.840*
3	Res	6 of 15	**0.782**	*0.886*
2	Lap	7 of 23	**0.641**	*0.705*
2	Res	12 of 24	**0.708**	*0.810*
4	Res	11 of 18	**0.696**	*0.829*

Table 1: Ranking among constrained systems.

The developed system consists of one module per subtask, in addition to a general infrastructure and preprocessing module, All modules accept training and test data in the XML format specfied by the task organizers. The modules can be combined into a pipeline, where each step adds new annotation corresponding to one of the four subtasks.

Table 1 shows our ranking among all constrained systems (counting only the best run from each team), the score achieved by SNAP (accuracy or F-score, depending on subtask), and the score achieved by the best system in the respective subtask. Because of a preprocessing mistake that was only discovered after phase A of the evaluation had ended, results for subtasks 1 and 3 are significantly lower than the results achieved during development of the system.

2 Sentiment lexicon

Early on in the project it was decided that a comprehensive, high-quality sentiment lexicon would play a crucial role in building a successful system. After a review of several existing lexica, Bing

Proceedings of the 8th International Workshop on Semantic Evaluation (SemEval 2014), pages 578–584, Dublin, Ireland, August 23-24, 2014.

Liu's sentiment word list (Hu and Liu, 2004) was taken as a foundation and expanded with extensive manual additions.

The first step was an exhaustive manual web-search to find additional candidates for the lexicon. The candidates were converted to a common format, and redundant entries were discareded. The next step consisted of further expansion with the help of online thesauri, from which large number of synonyms and antonyms for existing entries were obtained. Since the coverage of the lexicon was still found to be insufficient, it was further complemented with entries from two other existing sentiment lexica, AFINN (Nielsen, 2011) and MPQA (Wilson et al., 2005).

Finally the augmented lexicon was compared with the original word lists from AFINN, MPQA and Bing Liu in order to measure the reliabilty of the entries. The reliability score of each entry is the number of sources in which it is found.

3 Infrastructure and preprocessing

Within the scope of Task 4 – but not one of the official subtasks – the goal of the infrastructure module was (i) to support the other modules with a set of project-specific tools and (ii) to provide a common API to the training and test data augmented with several layers of linguistic annotation. In order to roll out the required data as quick as possible, the Stanford CoreNLP suite[1] was used as an off-the-shelf tool. The XML files provided by the task organizers were parsed with the *xml.etree.ElementTree* API, which is part of the standard library of Python 2.7.

Since the module for subtask 1 was pursuing an IOB-tagging approach for aspect term identification, the part-of-speech tags provided by CoreNLP had to be extended. During the process of merging the original XML files with the CoreNLP annotations, IOB tags were generated indicating whether each token is part of an aspect term or not. See Section 4 for further information.

For determining the polarity of an aspect term, the subtask 2 module made use of syntactic dependencies between words (see Section 5 for details). For this purpose, the dependency trees produced by CoreNLP were converted into a more accessible format with the help of the Python software package *NetworkX*.[2].

[1]http://nlp.stanford.edu/software/corenlp.shtml

[2]http://networkx.github.io/

4 Aspect term extraction

The approach chosen by the aspect term extraction module (subtask 1) was to treat aspect term extraction as a tagging task. We used a standard IOB tagset indicating whether each token is at the beginning of an aspect term (`ATB`), inside an aspect term (`ATI`), or not part of an aspect term at all (`ATX`).

First experiments were carried out with unigram, bigram and trigram taggers implemented in NLTK (Bird et al., 2009), which were trained on IOB tags derived from the annotations in the Task 4 gold standard (comprising both trial and training data). We also tested higher-order n-gram taggers and the NLTK implementation of the Brill tagger (Brill, 1992).

For a more sophisticated approach we used RFTagger (Schmid and Laws, 2008), which extends the standard HMM tagging model with complex hidden states that consist of features corresponding to different pieces of information. RFTagger was developed for morphological tagging, where complex tags such as `N.Reg.Nom.Sg.Neut` are decomposed into the main syntactic category (`N`) and additional morpho-syntactic features representing case (`Nom`), number (`Sg`), etc.

In our case, the tagger was used for joint annotation of part-of-speech tags and IOB tags for the aspect term boundaries, based on the rationale that the additional information encoded in the hidden states (compared to a simple IOB tagger) would allow RFTagger to learn more meaningful aspect term patterns. We decided to encode the IOB tags as the main category and the part-of-speech tags as additional features, since changing these categories, meaning POS tags as the main category and IOB tags as additional features, had resulted in lesser performance. The training data were thus converted into word-annotation pairs such as `screen_AT/ATB.NN` or `beautiful/ATX.JJ`. Note that known aspect terms from the gold standard (as well as additional candidates that were generated through comparisons of known aspect terms with lists from WordNet) were extended with the suffix `_AT` in a preprocessing step. Our intention was to enable the tagger to learn directly that tokens with this suffix are likely to be aspect terms.

Table 2 shows tagging accuracy for different algorithms, computed by ten-fold cross-validation over a gold standard comprising the training and

Tagger	Rest.	Laptops
Unigram	83.41%	83.91%
Bigram (backoff: U)	85.37%	85.74%
Trigram (backoff: U+Bi)	85.41%	86.33%
Brill (backoff: U+Bi+T)	85.48%	86.47%
RFTagger	**95.20%**	**96.47%**

Table 2: Accuracy of different aspect term taggers.

trial data sets. The table shows that the bigram, trigram and Brill taggers achieve only marginal improvements over a simplistic unigram tagger, even when they are combined through back-off linking. The RFTagger achieved by far the best accuracy on both data sets.

4.1 Results and debugging

Our final results for the full aspect term extraction procedure are shown in Table 3.

Score	Rest.	Laptops
Precision	57.14%	64.54%
Recall	39.15%	60.40%
F_1-Score	46.47%	62.40%

Table 3: Aspect term extraction results.

The huge difference between tagging accuracy achieved in the development phase and the aspect term extraction quality obtained on the SemEval-2014 test set is caused by different factors. First, Table 2 shows the tagging accuracy across all tokens, not limited to aspect terms. A tagger that works particularly well for many irrelevant tokens (punctuation, verbs, etc.), correctly marking them `ATX`, may achieve high accuracy even if it has low recall on tokens belonging to aspect terms. Second, the official scores only consider an aspect term candidate to be a true positive if it covers exactly the same tokens as the gold standard annotation. If the tagger disagrees with the human annotators on whether an adjective or determiner should be considered part of an aspect term, this will be counted as a mistake despite the overlap. Thus, even a relatively small number of tagging mistakes near aspect term boundaries will be punished severly in the evaluation. Unseen words as well as long or unusual noun phrases turned out to be particularly difficult.

Table 3 indicates a serious problem with the restaurant data, which has surprisingly low recall, resulting in an F_1-score almost 16 percent points lower than for the laptop data. A careful examination of the trial, training and test data revealed an early mistake in the preprocessing code as the main culprit. Once this mistake was corrected, the recall score for restaurants was similar to the score for laptops.

5 Aspect term polarity

Subtask 2 is concerned with opinion sentences, i.e. sentences that contain one or more aspect terms and express subjective opinions about (some of) these aspects. Such opinions are expressed through opinion words; common opinion words with their corresponding confidence values (numeric values from 1 to 6 expressing the level of certainty that a word is positive or negative, cf. Sec. 2) are collected in sentiment lexica.

The preprocessing stage in this subtask starts with a sentence segmentation step that uses the output of the Stanford CoreNLP parser.[3] All dependencies map onto a directed graph representation where words of each sentence are nodes in the graph and grammatical relations are edge labels. All aspect terms (Sec. 2) are marked in each dependency graph. When processing such a graph we extract all positive and negative opinion words occurring in each sentence by comparing them with word lists contained in our sentiment lexica. A corresponding confidence value from lexica is assigned for each opinion word, the number of positive and negative aspect terms occurring in each sentence are counted and their confidence values are summed up. These values serve as features for supervised machine learning using algorithms implemented in scikit-learn (Pedregosa et al., 2011).

All opinion words that build a dependency with an aspect term are stored for each sentence. A dominant word of each dependency is stored as a governor, whereas a subordinate one is stored as a dependent. Both direct and indirect dependencies are processed. If there are several indirect dependencies to an aspect term, they are processed recursively. Using lists of extracted dependencies between opinion words and aspect terms handwriten rules assign corresponding confidence values to aspect terms.

[3] nlp.stanford.edu/software/dependencies_manual.pdf

5.1 Features based on a sentiment lexica

The extended sentiment dictionaries were used to extract five features: I) tokens expressing a positive sentiment belonging to one aspect term, II) tokens expressing a negative sentiment, III) confidence values of positive tokens, IV) confidence values of negative tokens, V) a sum of all confidence values for all positive and all negative opinion words occurring in a sentence.

5.2 Features based on hand-written rules

We made use of direct and indirect negation markers, so that all opinion words belonging to a negated aspect term swap their polarity signs. We added rules for negative particles *not* and *no* that directly precede an opinion word, for adverbs *barely*, *scarcely* and *too*, for such constructions as *could have been* and *wish* in the subjunctive mood. After swapping polarity signs of opinion words, a general set of hand-written rules was applied to the graph dependencies. The rules follow the order of importance of dependencies scaling from least important up to most important. We placed the dependencies in the following order: *acomp*, *advmod*, *nsubjpass*, *conj_and*, *amod*, *prep_of*, *prep_worth*, *prep_on*, *prep_in*, *nsubj*, *infmod*, *dobj*, *xcomp*, *rcmod*, *conj_or*, *appos*. All dependencies can be grouped into three categories based on the direction of the polarity assignment. The first group (*acomp*, *advmod*, *amod*, *rcmod*, *prep_in*) includes dependencies where a governor of a dependency takes over polarity of a dependent if the latter is defined. The second group (*infmod*, *conj_or*, *prep_on*, *prep_worth*, *prep_of*, *conj_and*) covers dependencies in which a dependent element takes over polarity of a governor if the latter is defined. The third group (*dobj*, *xcomp*) is for cases when both governor and dependent are defined. Here a governor takes over polarity of a dependent.

5.3 Experiments

In this section we compare two approches to aspect term polarity detection. The first approach simply counts all positive and negative words in each sentence and then assigns a label based on which of the two counts is larger. It does not make use of machine learning techniques and its accuracy is only about 54%. Results improve significantly with supervised machine learning based on the feature sets described above. We experimented with different classifiers (Maximum Entropy, Linear SVM and SVMs with RBF kernel) and various subsets of features. By default, we worked on the level of single opinion words that express a positive or negative polarity (sg). We added the following features in different combinations: an extended list of opinion words (ex) obtained from a distribution semantic model, based on nearest neighbours of known opinion words (Proisl et al., 2013); potential misspellings of know opinion words, within a maximal Levenshtein distance of 1 (lv); word combinations and fixed phrases (ml) containing up to 3 words (e.g., *good mannered, put forth, tried and true, up and down*); and the sums of positive and negative opinion words in the whole sentence (st). The best results for the laptops data were achieved with a Maximum Entropy classifier, excluding misspellings (lv) and word combinations (ml); the corresponding line in Table 4 is highlighted in bold font. Even though MaxEnt achieved the best results during development, we decided to use SVM with a RBF kernel for the test set, assuming that it would be able to exploit interdependencies between features. The accuracy achieved by the submitted system is highlighted in italics in the table. The training test data provided for restaurants and laptops categories were split equally into two sets where the first set (first half) was used for training a model and the second set was used for the test and evaluation stages. Experiments on the restaurants data produced similar results.

classifier	sg	ex	lv	ml	st	Acc
MaxEnt	+	+	–	–	–	0.5589
MaxEnt	+	+	+	–	–	0.4905
MaxEnt	+	+	–	+	–	0.5479
MaxEnt	+	+	–	–	+	**0.6506**
MaxEnt	+	+	–	+	+	0.5742
SVM_{rbf}	+	+	–	–	–	0.5581
SVM_{rbf}	+	+	+	–	–	0.4905
SVM_{rbf}	+	+	–	+	–	0.5479
SVM_{rbf}	+	+	–	–	+	*0.6402*
SVM_{rbf}	+	+	–	+	+	0.5717

Table 4: Results for laptops category on train set.

6 Aspect category detection

Subtask 3 deals with determining which aspect categories out of a predefined set occur in a given sentence. The developed module consists of two independent parts – one based on machine learning, the other on similarities between WordNet synsets ("synonym sets", roughly corresponding to concepts). While both approaches achieved similar performance during development, combining them resulted in overall better scores. However, the success of this method crucially depends on accurate indentification of aspect terms.

6.1 A WordNet-based approach[4]

The WordNet-based component operates on previously identified aspect terms (from the gold standard in the evaluation, but from the module described in Sec. 4 in a real application setting). For each term, it finds all synsets and compares them to a list of "key synsets" that characterize the different aspect categories (e.g. the category *food* is characterized by the key synset *meal.n.01*, among others). The best match is chosen and added to an internal lexicon, which maps each unique phrase appearing as an aspect term to exactly one aspect category. As a similarity measure for synsets we used path similarity, which determines the length of the shortest path between two synsets in the WordNet hypernym/hyponym taxonomy. Key synsets were extracted from a list of high frequency terms and tested manually to create an accurate represenation for each category.

In the combined approach this component was taken as a foundation and was augmented by high-confidence suggestions from the machine learning component (see below).

Additional extensions include a high-confidence lexicon based on nearest neighbours from a distributional semantic model, a rudimentary lexicon of international dishes, and the application of a spellchecker; together, they accounted only for a small increase in F-score on the development data (from 0.758 to 0.768).

6.2 A machine learning approach[5]

The machine learning component is essentially a basic bag-of-words model. It employs a multinomial Naive Bayes classifier in a one-vs-all setup to achieve multi-label classification. In addition to tuning of the smoothing parameters, a probability threshold was introduced that every predicted category has to pass to be assigned to a sentence.

[4]We used the version of WordNet included in NLTK 2.0.4 (Bird et al., 2009), accessed through the NLTK API.

[5]We used machine learning algorithms implemented in scikit-learn 0.14.1 (Pedregosa et al., 2011).

Test	Train	AT	Mode	F_1
SE14	Dev	Sub1	All	0.782
SE14	Dev*	Sub1	WN	0.666
SE14	Dev	Sub1*	ML	**0.788**
SE14	Dev	Gold	All	**0.848**
SE14	Dev*	Gold	WN	0.829
SE14	Dev	Gold*	ML	0.788
Dev (cv)	Dev	Gold	All	**0.800**
Dev (cv)	Dev*	Gold	WN	0.768
Dev (cv)	Dev	Gold*	ML	0.769

*indicates data sets not used by a given component

Table 5: Aspect category detection results.

Different thresholds were used for the stand-alone component ($th = 0.625$) and the combined approach ($th = 0.9$). In the latter case all predicitions of the WordNet-based component were accepted, but only high-confidence predictions from the Naive Bayes classifier were added.

6.3 Results

Table 5 summarizes the results of different experiments with aspect category detection. In all cases the training data consisted of the combined official train and trial sets (Dev). The last three rows show results obtained by ten-fold cross-validation in the development phase, the other rows show the corresponding results on the official test set (SE14). The first three rows are based on automatically detected aspect terms from the module described in Sec. 4 (Sub 1), the other rows used gold standard aspect terms. Separate results are provided for the combined approach (Mode: All) as well as for the two individual components (WN = WordNet, ML = machine learning). Note that the WN component does not require any training data, while the ML component does not make use of aspect terms marked in the input.

With gold standard aspect terms, the WordNet-based approach is equal to or better than the Naive Bayes classifier, and best results are achived by a combination of the two components. However, the poor accuracy of the automatic aspect term extraction (cf. Table 3) has a disastrous effect: even the combined approach used in the official submission performs less well than the ML component alone. Nevertheless the experiment with gold standard aspect terms suggests that the matching from aspect term to category works quite well, with a small additional improvement from the Naive

Bayes bag-of-words model.

7 Aspect category polarity

The general approach was to allocate each aspect term to the corresponding aspect categories. A simple rule set was then used to determine the polarity of each aspect category based on the polarities of the aligned aspect terms. In cases where no aspect terms are marked (but sentences are still labelled with aspect categories), the idea was to fall back on the sentiment values for the entire sentences provided by the CoreNLP suite.[6]

7.1 Term / category alignment

To establish a basis for creating the mapping rules, the first step was to work out the distribution of aspect terms and aspect categories in the training data. The most common case is that an aspect category aligns with a single aspect term (1476×); there are also many aspect categories with multiple aspect terms (1179×) and some aspect categories without any aspect terms. Since the WordNet-Approach from Sec. 6 showed relatively good results (especially if gold standard aspect terms are available, which is the case here), a modified version was used to assign each aspect term to one of the annotated categories.

7.2 Polarity allocation

After the assignment of aspect terms to their according aspect category – if needed – the aspect category polarity can be determined. For this, the polarity values of all aspect terms assigned to this category were collected, and duplicates were removed in order to produce a *unique set* (e.g. 1, 1, -1, 0, 0 would be reduced to 1, -1, 0). A set with both negative and positive polarity values indicates a conflict for the corresponding aspect category, while a neutral polarity value would be ignored, if positive or negative polarity values occur. Our method achieved an accuracy of 89.16% for sentences annotated with just a single aspect category. In cases where only one aspect term had been assigned to a aspect category the accuracy was unsuprisingly high (96.61%), whereas the accuracy decreased in cases of multiple assigned aspect terms (78.44%). For aspect categories without aligned aspect terms, as well as the category *anecdotes/miscellaneous*, the sentiment values of the CoreNLP sentiment analysis tool had to be used, which led to a poor accuracy in those cases, namely 52.74%.

[6]http://nlp.stanford.edu/software/corenlp.shtml

7.3 Results

On the official test set, the module for subtask 4 achieved an accuracy of 69.56%. An important factor is the very low accuracy in cases where the CoreNLP sentiment value for the entire sentence had to be used. We expect a considerable improvement from using a modified version of the subtask 2 module (Sec. 5) to compute overall sentence polarity.

8 Conclusion

We have shown a modular system working as a pipeline that modifies the input sentences step by step by adding new information as XML tags. Aspect term extraction was handled as a tagging task that utilized an IOB tagset to find aspect terms with the final version relying on Schmid's RFTagger. Determination of aspect term polarity was achieved through a machine learning approach that uses SVMs with RBF kernel. This was supported by an augmented sentiment lexicon based on several different sources, which was expanded manually by a team of students. Aspect category detection in turn employs a combination approach of an algorithm depending on WordNet synsets and a bag-of-words Naive Bayes classifier. Finally aspect category polarity was calculated by combining the results from the last two modules.

Overall results were satisfactory, being mostly in the top half of submitted systems. During phase A of testing (subtasks 1 and 3), a preprocessing error caused a massive drop in performance in aspect term extraction. This carried over to the other subtask, because the module uses aspect terms among other features to identify aspect categories. Scores for phase B (subtasks 2 and 4) were very close to test results during development with the exception of cases where the CoreNLP sentiment value for an entire sentence had to be used.

References

Steven Bird, Ewan Klein, and Edward Loper. 2009. *Natural Language Processing with Python*. O'Reilly Media.

Eric Brill. 1992. A simple rule-based part of speech tagger. In *Proceedings of the Third Conference on Applied Natural Language Processing*, pages 152–155, Trento, Italy.

Minqing Hu and Bing Liu. 2004. Mining and summarizing customer reviews. In *Proceedings of the 10th ACM SIGKDD International Conference on Knowledge Discovery and Data Mining (KDD '04)*, pages 168–177, Seattle, WA.

Finn Årup Nielsen. 2011. A new ANEW: Evaluation of a word list for sentiment analysis in microblogs. In *Proceedings of the ESWC2011 Workshop on Making Sense of Microposts: Big things come in small packages*, number 718 in CEUR Workshop Proceedings, pages 93–98, Heraklion, Greece, May.

Fabian Pedregosa, Gaël Varoquaux, Alexandre Gramfort, Vincent Michel, Bertrand Thirion, Olivier Grisel, Mathieu Blondel, Peter Prettenhofer, Ron Weiss, Vincent Dubourg, Jake Vanderplas, Alexandre Passos, David Cournapeau, Matthieu Brucher, Matthieu Perrot, and Édouard Duchesnay. 2011. Scikit-learn: Machine learning in Python. *Journal of Machine Learning Research*, 12:2825–2830.

Maria Pontiki, Dimitrios Galanis, John Pavlopoulos, Harris Papageorgiou, Ion Androutsopoulos, and Suresh Manandhar. 2014. SemEval-2014 task 4: Aspect based sentiment analysis. In *Proceedings of the 8th International Workshop on Semantic Evaluation (SemEval 2014)*, Dublin, Ireland.

Thomas Proisl, Paul Greiner, Stefan Evert, and Besim Kabashi. 2013. KLUE: Simple and robust methods for polarity classification. In *Second Joint Conference on Lexical and Computational Semantics (*SEM), Volume 2: Proceedings of the Seventh International Workshop on Semantic Evaluation (SemEval 2013)*, pages 395–401, Atlanta, Georgia, USA, June. Association for Computational Linguistics.

Helmut Schmid and Florian Laws. 2008. Estimation of conditional probabilities with decision trees and an application to fine-grained POS tagging. In *Proceedings of the 22nd International Conference on Computational Linguistics*, volume 1, pages 777–784.

Theresa Wilson, Janyce Wiebe, and Paul Hoffmann. 2005. Recognizing contextual polarity in phrase-level sentiment analysis. In *Proceedings of the Human Language Technology Conference and Conference on Empirical Methods in Natural Language Processing (HLT-EMNLP 2005)*, pages 347–354, Vancouver, BC, Canada.

SSMT: A Machine Translation Evaluation View to Paragraph-to-Sentence Semantic Similarity

Pingping Huang
Department of Linguistic Engineering
School of Software and Microelectronics
Peking University, China
girlhpp@163.com

Baobao Chang
Key Laboratory of Computational Linguistics, Ministry of Education
Institute of Computational Linguistics
Peking University, China
chbb@pku.edu.cn

Abstract

This paper presents the system SSMT measuring the semantic similarity between a paragraph and a sentence submitted to the SemEval 2014 task3: Cross-level Semantic Similarity. The special difficulty of this task is the length disparity between the two semantic comparison texts. We adapt several machine translation evaluation metrics for features to cope with this difficulty, then train a regression model for the semantic similarity prediction. This system is straightforward in intuition and easy in implementation. Our best run gets 0.808 in Pearson correlation. METEOR-derived features are the most effective ones in our experiment.

1 Introduction

Cross level semantic similarity measures the similarity between different levels of text unit, for example, between a document and a paragraph, or between a phrase and a word.

Paragraph and sentence are the natural language units to convey opinions or state events in daily life. We can see posts on forums, questions and answers in Q&A communities and customer reviews on E-commerce websites, are mainly organised in these two units. Better similarity measurement across them will be helpful in clustering similar answers or reviews.

The paragraph-to-sentence semantic similarity subtask in SemEval2014 task3 (Jurgens et al., 2014) is the first semantic similarity competition across these two language levels. The special difficulty of this task is the length disparity between the compared pair: a paragraph contains 3.67 times the words of a sentence on average in the training set.

Semantic similarity on different levels, for example, on word level (Mikolov et al., 2013), sentences level (Bär et al., 2012), document level (Turney and Pantel, 2010), have been well studied, yet methods on one level can hardly be applied to a different level, let alone be applied for the cross-level tasks. The work of Pilehvar et al.(2013) was an exception. They proposed a unified method for semantic comparison at multi-levels all the way from comparing word senses to comparing text documents

Our work is inspired by automatic machine translation(MT) evaluation, in which different metrics are designed to compare the adequacy and fluency of a MT system's output, called hypothesis, against a gold standard translation, called reference. As MT evaluation metrics measure sentence pair similarity, it is a natural idea to generalize them for paragraph-sentence pair.

In this paper, we follow the motivations of several MT evaluation metrics yet made adaption to cope with the length disparity difficulty of this task, and combine these features in a regression model. Our system SSMT (**S**emantic **S**imilarity in view of **M**achine **T**ranslation evaluation) involves no extensive resource or strenuous computation, yet gives promising result with just a few simple features.

2 Regression Framework

In our experiment, we use features adapted from some MT evaluation metrics and combine them in a regression model for the semantic similarity measurement. We exploit the following two simple models:

A linear regression model is presented as:

$$y = w_1 x_i + w_2 x_i .. + w_n x_n + \varepsilon$$

Proceedings of the 8th International Workshop on Semantic Evaluation (SemEval 2014), pages 585–589, Dublin, Ireland, August 23-24, 2014.

A log-linear model is presented as:

$$y = x_1^{w_1} \cdot x_2^{w_2} .. \cdot x_n^{w_n} \cdot e^{\varepsilon}$$

Where y is the similarity score, $\{x_1, x_2.., x_n\}$ are the feature values.

We can see that in a log-linear model, if any feature x_i get a value of 0, the output y will suck in 0 forever no matter what the values other features get. In our experiment we resort to smoothing to avoid this "0-trap" for some features (Section 4.3).

3 Features

MT evaluation metrics vary from lexical level to syntactic level to semantic level. We consider only lexical ones to avoid complicated steps like parsing or semantic role labelling, which are computational expensive and may bring extra noise.

But instead of directly using the MT evaluation metrics, we use the factors in them as features, the idea is that the overall score of the original metric is highly related to the length of both of the compared pair, but its factors are often related to the length of just one side yet still carry useful similarity information.

3.1 BLEU-Derived Features

As the most wildly used MT evaluation metric, BLEU (Papineni et al., 2002) uses the geometric mean of *n*-gram precisions to measure the hypotheses against references. It is a corpus-based and precision-based metric, and uses "*brevity penalty*" as a replacement for recall. Yet this *penalty* is meaningless on sentence level. Therefore we considers only the precision factors in BLEU:

$$P_{n_{BLEU}} = \frac{Ngram_{ref} \cap Ngram_{hyo}}{Ngram_{ref}}$$

We use the modified *n*-gram precision here and regard "paragraph" as "reference", and "sentence" as the "hypothesis". N= 1,2,3,4. We call these four features BLEU-derived features.

3.2 ROUGE-L-Derived Features

ROUGE-L (Lin and Och, 2004) measures the largest common subsequence(LCS) between a compared pair. BLEU implies the *n*-gram to be consecutive, yet ROUGE-L allows for gaps between them. By considering only in-sequence words, ROUGE-L captures sentence level structure in a natural way, then:

$$\begin{aligned} R_{lcs} &= \frac{LCS(ref, hyo)}{length(hyo)} \\ P_{lcs} &= \frac{LCS(ref, hyo)}{length(ref)} \\ F_{lcs} &= \frac{(1+\beta^2)R_{lcs}P_{lcs})}{R_{lcs} + \beta^2 P_{lcs}} \end{aligned}$$

Where $LCS(ref, hoy)$ is the length of LCS of the compared pair. We set $\beta = 1$, which means we don't want to make much distinction between the "reference" and "hypothesis" here. We call these three features ROUGE-L-derived features.

3.3 ROUGE-S-Derived Features

ROUGE-S (Lin and Och, 2004) uses skip-bigram co-occurrence statistics for similarity measurement. One advantage of skip-bigram over BLEU is that it does not require consecutive matches but is still sensitive to word order. Given the reference of length n, and hypothesis of length m, then:

$$\begin{aligned} P_{skip2} &= \frac{skip2(ref, hyo)}{C(m, 2)} \\ R_{skip2} &= \frac{skip2(ref, hyo)}{C(n, 2)} \\ F_{skip2} &= \frac{(1+\beta^2)P_{skip2}R_{skip2}}{R_{skip2} + \beta^2 P_{skip2}} \end{aligned}$$

Where C is combination, and $skip2(ref, hyo)$ is the number of common skip-bigrams. We also set $\beta = 1$ here, and call these three indicators ROUGE-S-derived features.

3.4 METEOR-Derived Features

METEOR (Banerjee and Lavie, 2005) evaluates a hypothesis by aligning it to a reference translation and gives sentence-level similarity scores. It uses a generalized concept of unigram mapping that matches words in the following types: exact match on words surface forms , stem match on words stems, synonym match according to the synonym sets in WordNet, and paraphrase match (Denkowski and Lavie, 2010).

METEOR also makes distinction between content words and function words. Each type of match m_i is weighted by w_i, let $(m_i(h_c), m_i(h_f))$ be the number of content and function words covered by this type in the hypothesis, and

$(m_i(r_c), m_i(r_f))$ be the counts in the reference, then:

$$P = \frac{\sum_{i=1} w_i \cdot (\delta \cdot m_i(h_i) + (1-\delta) \cdot m_i(h_f))}{\delta \cdot \mid h_c \mid + (1-\delta) \cdot \mid h_f \mid}$$

$$R = \frac{\sum_{i=1} w_i \cdot (\delta \cdot m_i(r_i) + (1-\delta) \cdot m_i(r_f))}{\delta \cdot \mid r_c \mid + (1-\delta) \cdot \mid r_f \mid}$$

$$F_{mean} = \frac{P \cdot R}{\alpha P + (1-\alpha) R}$$

To account for word order difference, the fragmentation penalty is calculated using the total number of matched words(m) and the number of chunks[1](ch) in the hypothesis:

$$Pen = \gamma \cdot \left(\frac{ch}{m}\right)^{\beta}$$

And the final METEOR score is:

$$Score = (1 - Pen) \cdot F_{mean}$$

Parameters $\alpha, \beta, \gamma, \delta$and $w_i ... w_n$ are tuned to maximize correlation with human judgements (Denkowski and Lavie, 2014). We use Meteor1.5 system[2] for scoring. Parameters are tuned on WMT12, and the paraphrase table is extracted on the WMT data.

We use the p, r, $frag(frag = ch/m)$ and $score$ as features and call them METEOR-derived features.

4 Experiment and Discussion

4.1 Data Set

The SemEval2014 task3 subtask gives a training set of 500 paragraph-sentence pairs, with human annotated continuous score of $0 - 4$. These pairs are labelled with genres of "Newswire/ cqa[3]/ metaphoric/ scientific/ travel/ review". Systems are asked to predict the similarity scores for 500 pairs in the test set. Performance is evaluated in Pearson correlation and Spearman correlation.

4.2 Data Processing

To avoid meaningless n-gram match "*the a*", or words surface form difference, we employ very simple data processings here: for features derived from BLEU, ROUGE-L and ROUGE-S, we remove stop words and stem the sentences with coreNLP[4]. For METEOR-derived features, we use the tool's option for text normalization before matching.

4.3 Result

Though texts with different genres may have different regression parameters, we just train one model for all for simplicity. Table 1 compares the result. Run1 is submitted as SSMT in the official evaluation. It's a log-linear model. We choose more dense features for log-linear model and use smoothing to avoid the "0-trap" mentioned in (Section 2). The features include $P_{1,2_{BLEU}}$,$P_{ROUGE-L}$,$P_{ROUGE-S}$ 4 features, and 4 METEOR-derived features, altogether 8 features. When calculation the first 4 features, we plus 1 to both numerator and denominator as smoothing. Run2 is a linear-regression model with the same features as Run1. Run3 is a simple linear regression model, which is free from the "0-trap", thus we use all the 14 features without smoothing. We use Matlab for regression. The baseline is officially given using LCS.

Run	Regression	Pearson	Spearman
Baseline	LCS	0.527	0.613
run1	log-linear	0.789	0.777
run2	linear	0.794	0.777
run3	linear	**0.808**	**0.792**

Table 1: System Performance.

4.4 System Analysis

We compares the effectiveness of different features in a linear regression model. Table 2 shows the result. "All" refers to all the features, "-METEOR" means the feature set excludes METEOR-derived features. We can see the METEOR-derived features are the most effective ones here.

Figure 1 shows the performance of our system submitted as SSMT in the SemEval2014 task3 competition. It shows quite good correlation with the gold standard.

A well predicted example is the #trial-p2s-5 pair in the trial set:

Paragraph: *Olympic champion Usain Bolt regained his 100m world title and won a fourth individual World Championships gold with a season's best of 9.77 seconds in Moscow. In heavy*

[1]Chunk is defined as a series of matched unigrams that is contiguous and identically ordered in both sentences

[2]https://www.cs.cmu.edu/ alavie/METEOR/

[3]cqa:Community Question Answering site text

[4]http://nlp.stanford.edu/software/corenlp.shtml

Feature	Pearson	Spearman
All	0.808	0.792
- METEOR	**0.772**	**0.756**
- ROUGE-L	0.802	0.789
- ROUGE-S	0.807	0.793
- BLEU	0.807	0.790

Table 2: Effectiveness of Different Features. "-METEOR" means the feature set excluding METEOR-derived features.

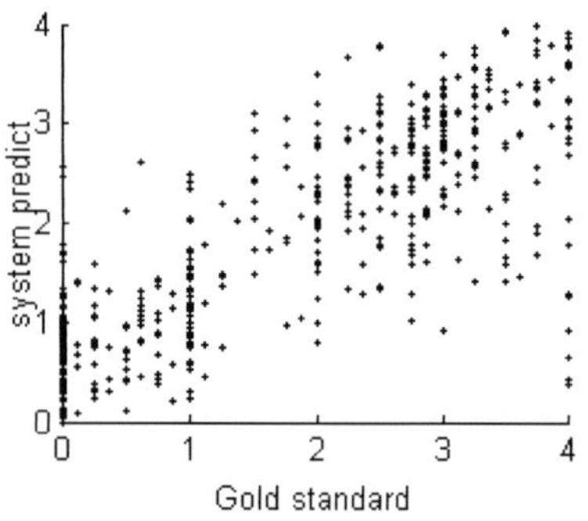

Figure 1: Result Scatter of SSMT.

rain, the 26-year-old Jamaican made amends for his false start in Daegu two years ago and further cemented his status as the greatest sprinter in history. The six-time Olympic champion overtook Justin Gatlin in the final stages, forcing the American to settle for silver in 9.85. Bolt's compatriot Nesta Carter (9.95) claimed bronze, while Britain's James Dasaolu was eighth (10.21).

Sentence: *Germany's Robert Harting beats Iran's Ehsan Hadadi and adds the Olympic discus title to his world crown.*

The system gives a prediction of 1.253 against the gold standard 1.25. We can see that topic words like "*Olympic*" , "*world crown*", "*beats*" in the short text correspond to expressions of "*world title* " , "*champion*" across several sentences in the long text, but this pair of texts are not talking about the same event. The model captures and models this commonness and difference very well .

But Figure 1 also reveals an interesting phenomenon: the system seldom gives the boundary scores of 0 or 4. In other words, it tends to overscore or underscore the boundary conditions. An example in point is the #trial-p2s-17 pair in the trial data, it is actually the worst predicted pair by our system in the trail set:

Paragraph: *A married couple who met at work is not a particularly rare thing. Three in ten workers who have dated a colleague said in a recent survey by CareerBuilder.com that their office romance eventually led to marriage.*

Sentence: *Marrying a coworker isn't uncommon given that 30% of workers who dated a coworker ended up marrying them.*

The system gives a 1.773 score against the gold standard of 4. It should fail to detect the equality of expressions between "*three in ten*" and "*30%*". Thus better detection of phrase similarity is desired. We think this is the main reason to underscore the similarity. For test pairs with the genre of "Metaphoric", the system almost underscores all of them. This failure has been expected, though. Because "Metaphoric" pairs demand full understanding of the semantic meaning and paragraph structure, which is far beyond the reach of lexical match metrics.

5 Conclusion

MT evaluation metrics have been directly used as features in paraphrase (Finch et al., 2005) detection and sentence pair semantic comparison (Souza et al., 2012). But paragraph-to-sentence pair faces significant length disparity, we try a way out to alleviate this impact yet still follow the motivations underlying these metrics. By factorizing down the original metrics, the linear model can flexibly pick out factors that are not sensitive to the length disparity problem.

We derive features from BLEU, ROUGE-L, ROUGE-S and METEOR, and show that METEOR-derived features make the most significant contributions here. Being easy and light, our submitted SSMT achieves 0.789 in Pearson and 0.777 in Spearman correlation, and ranks 11 out of the 34 systems in this subtask. Our best try achieves 0.808 in Pearson and 0.786 in Spearman correlation.

Acknowledgements

This work is supported by National Natural Science Foundation of China under Grant No.61273318 and National Key Basic Research Program of China 2014CB340504.

References

Andrew Finch, Yong S. Hwang, Eiichiro Sumita. Using machine translation evaluation techniques to determine sentence-level semantic equivalence. *Proceedings of the Third International Workshop on Paraphrasing(IWP2005)*, 2005: 17-24.

Chin Y. Lin,Franz J. Och. Automatic evaluation of machine translation quality using longest common subsequence and skip-bigram statistics. *Proceedings of the 42nd Annual Meeting on Association for Computational Linguistics. ACL*, 2004: 605.

Daniel Bär, Chris Biemann, Iryna Gurevych, et al. Ukp: Computing semantic textual similarity by combining multiple content similarity measures. *Proceedings of the First Joint Conference on Lexical and Computational Semantics-Volume 1: Proceedings of the main conference and the shared task, and Volume 2: Proceedings of the Sixth International Workshop on Semantic Evaluation. ACL*, 2012: 435-440.

David Jurgens, Mohammad Taher Pilehvar, and Roberto Navigli. SemEval-2014 Task 3: Cross-Level Semantic Similarity. *In Proceedings of the 8th International Workshop on Semantic Evaluation (SemEval-2014).*, August 23-24, 2014, Dublin, Ireland.

George Miller,Christiane Fellbaum. WordNet. http://wordnet.princton.edu/, 2007.

José G C de Souza, Matteo Negri, Yashar Mehdad. FBK: machine translation evaluation and word similarity metrics for semantic textual similarity. *Proceedings of the First Joint Conference on Lexical and Computational Semantics-Volume 1: Proceedings of the main conference and the shared task, and Volume 2: Proceedings of the Sixth International Workshop on Semantic Evaluation. ACL*, 2012: 624-630.

Kishore Papineni, Salim Roukos, Todd Ward, et al. BLEU: a method for automatic evaluation of machine translation. *Proceedings of the 40th annual meeting on association for computational linguistics. ACL*, 2002: 311-318.

Michael Denkowski, Alon Lavie. Extending the METEOR machine translation evaluation metric to the phrase level. *Human Language Technologies: The 2010 Annual Conference of the North American Chapter of the Association for Computational Linguistics. ACL*, 2010: 250-253.

Michael Denkowski, Alon Lavie. Meteor Universal: Language Specific Translation */Evaluation for Any Target Language translation. Proceedings of the EACL 2014 Workshop on Statistical Machine Translation*, 2014.

Mohammad T Pilehvar, David Jurgens, Roberto Navigli. Align, Disambiguate and Walk: A Unified Approach for Measuring Semantic Similarity *Proceedings of the 51st Annual Meeting of the Association for Computational Linguistics,ACL*, 2013: 1341-1351.

Peter D. Turney and Patrick Pantel. From frequency to meaning: Vector space models of semantics *Artificial Intelligence Research*, 2010. 37(1): 141-188

Satanjeev Banerjee, Alon Lavie. METEOR: an automatic metric for MT Evaluation with improved correlation with human judgements. *Proceedings of the ACL Workshop on Intrinsic and Extrinsic Evaluation Measures for Machine Translation and/or Summarization.*, 2005: 65-72.

Tomas Mikolov, Kai Chen, Greg Corrado, et al. Efficient estimation of word representations in vector space. 2013. *arXiv preprint arXiv:1301.3781*,

SU-FMI: System Description for SemEval-2014 Task 9 on Sentiment Analysis in Twitter

Boris Velichkov[*], **Borislav Kapukaranov**[†], **Ivan Grozev**[‡], **Jeni Karanesheva**[§], **Todor Mihaylov**[¶], **Yasen Kiprov**[||], **Georgi Georgiev**[**], **Ivan Koychev**[†,†], **Preslav Nakov**[‡‡]

Abstract

We describe the submission of the team of the Sofia University to SemEval-2014 Task 9 on Sentiment Analysis in Twitter. We participated in *subtask B*, where the participating systems had to predict whether a Twitter message expresses positive, negative, or neutral sentiment. We trained an SVM classifier with a linear kernel using a variety of features. We used publicly available resources only, and thus our results should be easily replicable. Overall, our system is ranked 20th out of 50 submissions (by 44 teams) based on the average of the three 2014 evaluation data scores, with an F1-score of 63.62 on general tweets, 48.37 on sarcastic tweets, and 68.24 on LiveJournal messages.

1 Introduction

We describe the submission of the team of the Sofia University, Faculty of Mathematics and Informatics (SU-FMI) to SemEval-2014 Task 9 on Sentiment Analysis in Twitter (Rosenthal et al., 2014).

[*]Sofia University, bobby.velichkov@gmail.com
[†]Sofia University, b.kapukaranov@gmail.com
[‡]Sofia University, iigrozev@gmail.com
[§]Sofia University, j.karanesheva@gmail.com
[¶]Sofia University, tbmihailov@gmail.com
[||]Sofia University, yasen.kiprov@gmail.com
[**]Ontotext, g.d.georgiev@gmail.com
[††]Sofia University, koychev@fmi.uni-sofia.bg
[‡‡]Qatar Computing Research Institute, pnakov@qf.org.qa

This SemEval challenge had two subtasks:

- *subtask A* (term-level) asks to predict the sentiment of a phrase inside a tweet;
- *subtask B* (message-level) asks to predict the overall sentiment of a tweet message.

In both subtasks, the sentiment can be positive, negative, or neutral. Here are some examples:

- *positive*: Gas by my house hit $3.39!!!! I'm going to Chapel Hill on Sat. :)
- *neutral*: New York Giants: Game-by-Game Predictions for the 2nd Half of the Season http://t.co/yK9VTjcs
- *negative*: Why the hell does Selma have school tomorrow but Parlier clovis & others don't?
- *negative (sarcastic)*: @MetroNorth wall to wall people on the platform at South Norwalk waiting for the 8:08. Thanks for the Sat. Sched. Great sense

Below we first describe our preprocessing, features and classifier in Section 2. Then, we discuss our experiments, results and analysis in Section 3. Finally, we conclude with possible directions for future work in Section 4.

2 Method

Our approach is inspired by the highest scoring team in 2013, NRC Canada (Mohammad et al., 2013). We reused many of their resources.[1]

Our system consists of two main submodules, (i) feature extraction in the framework of GATE (Cunningham et al., 2011), and (ii) machine learning using SVM with linear kernels as implemented in LIBLINEAR[2] (Fan et al., 2008).

[1]http://www.umiacs.umd.edu/~saif/WebPages/Abstracts/NRC-SentimentAnalysis.htm

[2]http://www.csie.ntu.edu.tw/~cjlin/liblinear/

Proceedings of the 8th International Workshop on Semantic Evaluation (SemEval 2014), pages 590–595, Dublin, Ireland, August 23-24, 2014.

2.1 Preprocessing

We integrated a pipeline of various resources for tweet analysis that are already available in GATE (Bontcheva et al., 2013) such as a Twitter tokenizer, a sentence splitter, a hashtag tokenizer, a Twitter POS tagger, a morphological analyzer, and the Snowball[3] stemmer.

We further implemented in GATE some shallow text processing components in order to handle negation contexts, emoticons, elongated words, all-caps words and punctuation. We also added components to find words and phrases contained in sentiment lexicons, as well as to annotate words with word cluster IDs using the lexicon built at CMU,[4] which uses the Brown clusters (Brown et al., 1992) as implemented[5] by (Liang, 2005).

2.2 Features

2.2.1 Sentiment lexicon features

We used several preexisting lexicons, both manually designed and automatically generated:

- Minqing Hu and Bing Liu opinion lexicon (Hu and Liu, 2004): 4,783 positive and 2,006 negative terms;
- MPQA Subjectivity Cues Lexicon (Wilson et al., 2005): 8,222 terms;
- Macquarie Semantic Orientation Lexicon (MSOL) (Mohammad et al., 2009): 30,458 positive and 45,942 negative terms;
- NRC Emotion Lexicon (Mohammad et al., 2013): 14,181 terms with specified emotion.

For each lexicon, we find in the tweet the terms that are listed in it, and then we calculate the following features:

- Negative terms count;
- Positive terms count;
- Positive negated terms count;
- Positive/negative terms count ratio;
- Sentiment of the last token;
- Overall sentiment terms count.

[3]http://snowball.tartarus.org/

[4]http://www.ark.cs.cmu.edu/TweetNLP/cluster_viewer.html

[5]http://github.com/percyliang/brown-cluster

We further used the following lexicons:

- NRC Hashtag Sentiment Lexicon: list of words and their associations with positive and negative sentiment (Mohammad et al., 2013): 54,129 unigrams, 316,531 bigrams, 480,010 pairs, and 78 high-quality positive and negative hashtag terms;
- Sentiment140 Lexicon: list of words with associations to positive and negative sentiments (Mohammad et al., 2013): 62,468 unigrams, 677,698 bigrams, 480,010 pairs;
- Stanford Sentiment Treebank: contains 239,231 evaluated words and phrases. If a word or a phrase was found in the tweet, we took the given sentiment label.

For the NRC Hashtag Sentiment Lexicon and the Sentiment140 Lexicon, we calculated the following features for unigrams, bigrams and pairs:

- Sum of positive terms' sentiment;
- Sum of negative terms' sentiment;
- Sum of the sentiment for all terms in the tweet;
- Sum of negated positive terms' sentiment;
- Negative/positive terms ratio;
- Max positive sentiment;
- Min negative sentiment;
- Max sentiment of a term.

We used different features for the two lexicon groups because their contents differ. The first four lexicons provide a discrete sentiment value for each word. In contrast, the following two lexicons offer numeric sentiment scores, which allows for different feature types such as sums and min/max scores.

Finally, we manually built a new lexicon with all emoticons we could find, where we assigned to each emoticon a positive or a negative label. We then calculated four features: number of positive and negative emoticons in the tweet, and whether the last token is a positive or a negative emoticon.

2.2.2 Tweet-level features

We use the following tweet-level features:

- **All caps:** the number of words with all characters in upper case;

- **Hashtags:** the number ot hashtags in the tweet;

- **Elongated words:** the number of words with character repetitions.

2.2.3 Term-level features

We used the following term-level features:

- **Word n-grams**: presence or absence of 1-grams, 2-grams, 3-grams, 4-grams, and 5-grams. We add an `NGRAM` prefix to each n-gram. Unfortunately, the n-grams increase the feature space greatly and contribute to higher sparseness. They also slow down training dramatically. That is why our final submission only includes 1-grams.

- **Character n-grams**: presence or absence of one, two, three, four and five-character prefixes and suffixes of all words. We add a `PRE` or `SUF` prefix to each character n-gram.

- **Negations:** the number of negated contexts. We define a negated context as a segment of a tweet that starts with a negation word (e.g., *no*, *shouldnt*) from our custom gazetteer and ends with one of the punctuation marks: ,, ., :, ;, !, ?. A negated context affects the n-gram and the lexicon features: we add a `NEG` suffix to each word following the negation word, e.g., *perfect* becomes *perfect_NEG*.

- **Punctuation:** the number of contiguous sequences of exclamation marks, of question marks, of *either* exclamation or question marks, and of *both* exclamation and question marks. Also, whether the last token contains an exclamation or a question mark (excluding URLs).

- **Stemmer:** the stem of each word, excluding URLs. We add a `STEM` prefix to each stem.

- **Lemmatizer:** the lemma of each word, excluding URLs. We add a `LEMMA` prefix to each lemma. We use the built-in GATE Morphological analyser as our lemmatizer.

- **Word and word bigram clusters:** word clusters have been shown to improve the performance of supervised NLP models (Turian et al., 2010). We use the word clusters built by CMU's NLP toolkit, which were produced over a collection of 56 million English tweets (Owoputi et al., 2012) and built using the Percy Liang's HMM-based implementation[6] of Brown clustering (Liang, 2005; Brown et al., 1992), which group the words into 1,000 hierarchical clusters. We use two features based on these clusters:
  - presence/absence of a word in a word cluster;
  - presence/absence of a bigram in a bigram cluster.

- **POS tagging:** Social media are generally hard to process using standard NLP tools, which are typically developed with newswire text in mind. Such standard tools are not a good fit for Twitter messages, which are too brief, contain typos and special wordforms. Thus, we used a specialized POS tagger, TwitIE, which is available in GATE (Bontcheva et al., 2013), and which we integrated in our pipeline. It provides (i) a tokenizer specifically trained to handle smilies, user names, URLs, etc., (ii) a normalizer to correct slang and misspellings, and (iii) a POS tagger that uses the Penn Treebank tagset, but is optimized for tweets. Using the TwitIE toolkit, we performed POS tagging and we extracted all POS tag types that we can find in the tweet together with their frequencies as features.

2.3 Classifier

For classification, we used the above features and a support vector machine (SVM) classifier as implemented in LIBLINEAR. This is a very scalable implementation of SVM that does not support kernels, and is suitable for classification on large datasets with a large number of features. This is particularly useful for text classification, where the number of features is very large, which means that the data is likely to be linearly separable, and thus using kernels is not really necessary. We scaled the SVM input and we used L2-regularization during training.

[6] `https://github.com/percyliang/brown-cluster`

3 Experiments, Results, Analysis

3.1 Experimental setup

At development time, we trained on train-2013, tuned the C value of SVM on dev-2013, and evaluated on test-2013 (Nakov et al., 2013). For our submission, we trained on train-2013+dev-2013, and we evaluated on the 2014 test dataset provided by the organizers. This dataset contains two parts and a total of five datasets: (a) progress test (the Twitter and SMS test datasets for 2013), and (b) new test datasets (from Twitter, from Twitter with sarcasm, and from LiveJournal). We used C=0.012, which was best on development.

3.2 Official results

Due to our very late entering in the competition, we have only managed to perform a small number of experiments, and we only participated in subtask B. We were ranked 20th out of 50 submissions; our official results are shown in Table 1. The numbers after our score are the delta to the best solution. We have also included a ranking among 2014 participant systems on the 2013 data sets, released by the organizers.

Data Category	F1-score (best)	Ranking
tweets2014	63.62 (6.23)	23
sarcasm2014	48.34 (9.82)	19
LiveJournal2014	68.23 (6.60)	21
tweets2013	60.96 (9.79)	29
SMS2013	61.67 (8.61)	16
2014 mean	60.07 (7.55)	20

Table 1: Our submitted system for subtask B.

3.3 Analysis

Tables 2 and 3 analyze the impact of the individual features. They show the F1-scores and the loss when a feature or a group of features is removed; we show the impact on all test datasets, both from 2013 and from 2014. The exception here is the *all + ngrams* row, which contains our scores if we had used the n-grams feature group.

The features are sorted by their impact on the Twitter2014 test set. We can see that the three most important feature groups are POS tags, word/bigram clusters, and lexicons.

We can further see that although the overall lexicon feature group is beneficial, some of the lexicons actually hurt the 2014 score and we would have been better off without them.

These are the Sentiment140 lexicon, the Stanford Sentiment Treebank and the NRC Emotion lexicon. The highest gain we get is from the lexicons of Minqing Hu and Bing Liu. It must be noted that using lexicons with good results apparently depends on the context, e.g., the Sentiment140 lexicon seems to be helping a lot with the LiveJournal test dataset, but it hurts the Sarcasm score by a sizeable margin.

Another interesting observation is that even though including the n-gram feature group is performing notably better on the Twitter2013 test dataset, it actually worsens performance on all 2014 test sets. Had we included it in our results, we would have scored lower.

The negation context feature brings little in regards to regular tweets or LiveJournal text, but it heavily improves our score on the Sarcasm tweets.

It is unclear why our results differ so much from those of the NRC-Canada team in 2013 since our features are quite similar. We attribute the difference to the fact that some of the lexicons we use actually hurt our score as we mentioned above. Another difference could be that last year's NRC system uses n-grams, which we have disabled as they lowered our scores. Last but not least, there could be bugs lurking in our feature representation that additionally lower our results.

3.4 Post-submission improvements

First, we did more extensive experiments to validate our classifier's C value. We found that the best value for C is actually 0.08 instead of our original proposal 0.012.

Then, we experimented further with our lexicon features and we removed the following ones, which resulted in significant improvement over our submitted version:

- Sentiment of the last token for NRC Emotion, MSOL, MPQA, and Bing Liu lexicons;
- Max term positive, negative and sentiment scores for unigrams of Sentiment140 and NRC Sentiment lexicons;
- Max term positive, negative and sentiment scores for bigrams of Sentiment140 and NRC Sentiment lexicons;
- Max term positive, negative and sentiment scores for hashtags of Sentiment140 and NRC Sentiment lexicons.

Feature Diff	SMS2013	SMS2013 delta	Twitter2013	Twitter2013 delta
submitted features	**61.67**		**60.96**	
no POS tags	54.73	-6.94	52.32	-8.64
no word clusters	58.06	-3.61	55.44	-5.52
all lex removed	59.94	-1.73	58.35	-2.61
no Hu-Liu lex	60.56	-1.11	60.10	-0.86
all + ngrams	61.37	-0.30	62.22	1.26
no NRC #lex	61.35	-0.32	60.66	-0.30
no MSOL lex	61.88	0.21	61.35	0.39
no Stanford lex	61.84	0.17	61.02	0.06
no negation cntx	61.94	0.27	60.88	-0.08
no encodings	61.74	0.07	60.92	-0.04
no NRC emo lex	61.67	0.00	60.96	0.00
no Sent140 lex	61.61	-0.06	60.32	-0.64

Table 2: Ablation experiments on the 2013 test sets.

Feature Diff	LiveJournal	LJ delta	Twitter	Twitter delta	Sarcasm	Sarcasm delta
submitted features	**68.23**		**63.62**		**48.34**	
no POS tags	62.28	-5.95	59.00	-4.62	43.70	-4.64
no word clusters	65.08	-3.15	59.82	-3.80	43.96	-4.38
all lex removed	66.16	-2.07	60.73	-2.89	49.59	1.25
no Hu-Liu lex	66.44	-1.79	62.15	-1.47	46.72	-1.62
all + ngrams	67.79	-0.44	62.96	-0.66	47.82	-0.52
no NRC #lex	66.81	-1.42	63.25	-0.37	47.54	-0.80
no MSOL lex	68.50	0.27	63.54	-0.08	48.34	0.00
no Stanford lex	67.86	-0.37	63.70	0.08	48.34	0.00
no negation cntx	68.09	-0.14	63.62	0.00	46.37	-1.97
no encodings	68.23	0.00	63.64	0.02	47.54	-0.80
no NRC emo lex	68.24	0.01	63.62	0.00	48.34	0.00
no Sent140 lex	67.32	-0.91	63.94	0.32	49.47	1.13

Table 3: Ablation experiments on the 2014 test sets.

The improved scores are shown in Table 4, with the submitted and the best system results.

Test Set	New F1	Old F1	Best
tweets2014	66.23	63.62	69.85
sarcasm2014	50.00	48.34	58.16
LiveJournal2014	69.41	68.24	74.84
tweets2013	63.08	60.96	70.75
SMS2013	62.28	61.67	70.28
2014 mean	62.20	60.07	67.62

Table 4: Our post-submission results.

4 Conclusion and Future Work

We have described the system built by the team of SU-FMI for SemEval-2014 task 9. Due to our late entering in the competition, we were only ranked 20th out of 50 submissions (from 44 teams).

We have made some interesting observations about the impact of the different features. Among the best-performing feature groups were POS-tag counts, word cluster presence and bigrams, the Hu-Liu lexicon and the NRC Hashtag Sentiment lexicon. These had the most sustainable performance over the 2013 and the 2014 test datasets. Others we did not use, seemingly more context dependent, seem to have been more suited for the 2013 test sets like the n-grams feature group.

Even though we made some improvements after submitting our initial version, we feel there is more to gain and optimize. There seem to be several low-hanging fruits based on our experiments data, which could add few points to our F1-scores.

Going forward, our goal is to extend our experiments with more feature sub- and super-sets and to turn our classifier into a state-of-the-art performer.

Acknowledgments

This work is partially supported by the FP7-ICT Strategic Targeted Research Project PHEME (No. 611233), and by the European Social Fund through the Human Resource Development Operational Programme under contract BG051PO001-3.3.06-0052 (2012/2014).

References

Kalina Bontcheva, Leon Derczynski, Adam Funk, Mark Greenwood, Diana Maynard, and Niraj Aswani. 2013. TwitIE: An open-source information extraction pipeline for microblog text. In *Proceedings of the International Conference on Recent Advances in Natural Language Processing*, RANLP '13, pages 83–90, Hissar, Bulgaria.

Peter Brown, Peter deSouza, Robert Mercer, Vincent Della Pietra, and Jenifer Lai. 1992. Class-based n-gram models of natural language. *Computational Linguistics*, 18:467–479.

Hamish Cunningham, Diana Maynard, and Kalina Bontcheva. 2011. *Text Processing with GATE*. Gateway Press CA.

Rong-En Fan, Kai-Wei Chang, Cho-Jui Hsieh, Xiang-Rui Wang, and Chih-Jen Lin. 2008. LIBLINEAR: A library for large linear classification. *J. Mach. Learn. Res.*, 9:1871–1874.

Minqing Hu and Bing Liu. 2004. Mining and summarizing customer reviews. In *Proceedings of the Tenth ACM SIGKDD International Conference on Knowledge Discovery and Data Mining*, KDD '04, pages 168–177, New York, NY, USA.

Percy Liang. 2005. Semi-supervised learning for natural language. Master's thesis, Massachusetts Institute of Technology.

Saif Mohammad, Cody Dunne, and Bonnie Dorr. 2009. Generating high-coverage semantic orientation lexicons from overtly marked words and a thesaurus. In *Proceedings of the Conference on Empirical Methods in Natural Language Processing: Volume 2*, EMNLP '09, pages 599–608, Singapore.

Saif Mohammad, Svetlana Kiritchenko, and Xiaodan Zhu. 2013. NRC-Canada: Building the state-of-the-art in sentiment analysis of tweets. In *Proceedings of the Seventh International Workshop on Semantic Evaluation Exercises*, SemEval '13, Atlanta, Georgia, USA.

Preslav Nakov, Sara Rosenthal, Zornitsa Kozareva, Veselin Stoyanov, Alan Ritter, and Theresa Wilson. 2013. SemEval-2013 task 2: Sentiment analysis in Twitter. In *Second Joint Conference on Lexical and Computational Semantics (*SEM), Volume 2: Proceedings of the Seventh International Workshop on Semantic Evaluation*, SemEval '13, pages 312–320, Atlanta, Georgia, USA.

Olutobi Owoputi, Brendan O'Connor, Chris Dyer, Kevin Gimpel, and Nathan Schneider. 2012. Part-of-speech tagging for Twitter: Word clusters and other advances. Technical Report CMU-ML-12-107, Carnegie Mellon University.

Sara Rosenthal, Alan Ritter, Veselin Stoyanov, and Preslav Nakov. 2014. SemEval-2014 task 9: Sentiment analysis in Twitter. In *Proceedings of the Eighth International Workshop on Semantic Evaluation*, SemEval '14, Dublin, Ireland.

Joseph Turian, Lev Ratinov, and Yoshua Bengio. 2010. Word representations: A simple and general method for semi-supervised learning. In *Proceedings of the 48th Annual Meeting of the Association for Computational Linguistics*, ACL '10, pages 384–394, Uppsala, Sweden.

Theresa Wilson, Janyce Wiebe, and Paul Hoffmann. 2005. Recognizing contextual polarity in phrase-level sentiment analysis. In *Proceedings of the Conference on Human Language Technology and Empirical Methods in Natural Language Processing*, HLT '05, pages 347–354, Vancouver, British Columbia, Canada.

Supervised Methods for Aspect-Based Sentiment Analysis

Hussam Hamdan*,,*****
*LSIS
Aix-Marseille Université CNRS
Av. Esc. Normandie Niemen,
13397 Marseille Cedex 20,
France
hussam.hamdan@lsis.org

Patrice Bellot*,**
**OpenEdition
Aix-Marseille Université CNRS
3 pl. V. Hugo, case n°86
13331 Marseille Cedex 3,
France
patrice.bellot@lsis.org

Frederic Béchet***
***LIF
Aix-Marseille Université CNRS
Avenue de Luminy
13288 Marseille Cedex 9,
France
frederic.bechet@lif.univ-mrs.fr

Abstract

In this paper, we present our contribution in SemEval2014 ABSA task, some supervised methods for Aspect-Based Sentiment Analysis of restaurant and laptop reviews are proposed, implemented and evaluated. We focus on determining the aspect terms existing in each sentence, finding out their polarities, detecting the categories of the sentence and the polarity of each category. The evaluation results of our proposed methods exhibit a significant improvement in terms of accuracy and f-measure over all four subtasks regarding to the baseline proposed by SemEval organisers.

1 Introduction

The increasing amount of user-generated textual data has increased the need of efficient techniques for analysing it. Sentiment Analysis (SA) has become more and more interesting since the year 2000 (Liu 2012), many techniques in Natural Language Processing have been used to understand the expressed sentiment on an entity.

Many levels of granularity have been also distinguished: Document Level SA considers the whole document is about an entity and classifies whether the expressed sentiment is positive, negative or neutral; Sentence Level SA determines the sentiment of each sentence, some works have been done on Clause Level SA but they are still not enough; Entity or Aspect-Based SA performs finer-grained analysis in which all entities and their aspects should be extracted and the sentiment on them should also be determined.

Aspect-Based SA task consists of several subproblems, the document is about many entities which could be for example *a restaurant, a laptop, a printer*. Users may refer to an entity by different writings but normally there are not a lot of variations to indicate the same entity, each entity has many aspects which could be its parts or attributes, some aspects could be another entity such as *screen of laptop*, but most works did not take this case into account. Therefore, we could define the opinion by the quintuple (Liu 2012) (e_i, a_{ij}, s_{ijkl}, h_k, t_l) where e_i is the entity i, a_{ij} are the aspects of the entity i, s_{ijkl} is the expressed sentiment on the aspect at the time t_l, h_k the holder which created the document or the text.

This definition does not take into account that the entity has aspects that could have also other aspects which leads to an aspect hierarchy, in order to avoid this information loss, few works have handled this issue, they proposed to represent the aspect as a tree of aspect terms (Wei and Gulla 2010; Kim, Zhang et al. 2013).

Supervised and unsupervised methods have been used for handling this task, in this paper, we propose supervised methods and test them over two datasets related to laptop reviews and restaurant reviews provided by the ABSA task of SemEval2014 (Pontiki, Galanis et al. 2014). We tackle four subtasks:

1. Aspect term extraction: CRF model is proposed.
2. Aspect Term Polarity Detection: Multinomial Naive-Bayes classifier with some features such as Z-score, POS and prior polarity extracted from Subjectivity

Proceedings of the 8th International Workshop on Semantic Evaluation (SemEval 2014), pages 596–600, Dublin, Ireland, August 23-24, 2014.

Lexicon (Wilson, Wiebe et al. 2005) and Bing Liu's Opinion Lexicon[1].

3. Category Detection:
   Z-score model for category detection has been used.
4. Category Polarity Detection:
   The same model proposed for aspect term polarity detection has been adopted.

2 Related works

Several methods concerning the ABSA have been proposed, some of them are supervised, and others unsupervised. The earliest work on aspect detection from on-line reviews presented by Hu and Liu used association rule mining based on Apriori algorithm to extract frequent noun phrases as product features, they used two seed sets of 30 positive and negative adjectives, then WordNet has been used to find and add the seed words synonyms. Infrequent aspects had been processed by finding the noun related to an opinionated word (Hu and Liu 2004).

Opinion Digger (Moghaddam and Ester 2010) used also Apriori algorithm to extract the frequent aspects then it filters the non-aspects by applying a constraint -learned from the training data- on the extracted aspects. KNN algorithm is applied to estimate the aspect rating scaling from 1 to 5 stands for (Excellent, Good, Average, Poor, Terrible), assuming that the sentiment is expressed by the nearest adjectives to the aspect term in the sentence segment, WordNet is used for finding the synonyms of sentiment word in order to use them to estimate the distance between it and the words of rating scale.

Some unsupervised methods based on LDA (Latent Dirichlet allocation) were proposed. Brody and Elhadad used LDA to find the aspects, determined the number of topics by applying a clustering method (Brody and Elhadad 2010), then they used a similar method proposed by Hatzivassiloglou and McKeown (Hatzivassiloglou and McKeown 1997) to extract the conjunctive adjectives but not the disjunctive due to the specificity of the domain, seed sets were used and assigned scores, these scores were propagated using propagation method through the aspect-sentiment graph building from the pairs of aspect and related adjectives.

Other works make one LDA based model for the aspect and sentiment extraction. Lin and He (Lin and He 2009)proposed Joint model of Sentiment and Topic (JST) which extends the state-of-the-art topic model, Latent Dirichlet Allocation (LDA) by adding a sentiment layer, this model is fully unsupervised and it can detect sentiment and topic simultaneously.

Wei and Gulla (Wei and Gulla 2010) modelled the hierarchical relation between product aspects. They defined SOT Sentiment Ontology Tree to formulate the knowledge of hierarchical relationships among product attributes and tackle the problem of sentiment analysis as a hierarchical classification problem. Unsupervised hierarchical aspect

Sentiment model (HASM) was proposed by Kim et al (Kim, Zhang et al. 2013) to discover a hierarchical structure of aspect-based sentiments from unlabelled online reviews.

Supervised methods uses normally a CRF or HMM models. Jin and Ho (Jin and Ho 2009) applied a lexicalized HMM model to extract aspects using the words and their part-of-speech tags in order to learn a model, then unsupervised algorithm for determining the aspect sentiment using the nearest opinion word to the aspect and taking into account the polarity reversal words (such as not). CRF model was used by Jakob and Gurevych (Jakob and Gurevych 2010) with these features: tokens, POS tags, syntactic dependency (if the aspect has a relation with the opinionated word), word distance (the distance between the word in the closest noun phrase and the opinionated word), and opinion sentences (each token in the sentence containing an opinionated expression is labelled by this feature), the input of this method is also the opinionated expressions, they use these expressions for predicting the aspect sentiment using the dependency parsing for retrieving the pair aspect-expression from the training set.

Our method for aspect extraction is closed to (Jakob and Gurevych 2010), where we used CRF model with different features for aspect extraction, but another method for sentiment detection.

The second and fourth subtasks are concerning the polarity detection, so besides to all previous discussed works, we can handle them as sentence level SA. We choose to use Multinomial Naive Bayes with some features (POS, Z-score, prepolarity). The most related work is (Hamdan, Béchet et al. 2013) where they used Naive Bays with WordNet, DBpedia and SentiWordNet features.

[1] http://www.cs.uic.edu/~liub/FBS/sentiment-analysis.html#lexicon

3 The System

Our system is composed of four subtasks:

3.1 Subtask1: Aspect Terms Extraction

The objective of this subtask is to extract all aspect terms in the review sentence, aspect terms could be a word or multiple words. For this purpose we have used CRF (**C**onditional **R**andom **F**ield) which have been used for information extraction. We choose the IOB notation, therefore we distinguish the terms at the **B**eginning, the **I**nside and the **O**utside of aspect term expression. Then, we propose 16 features, for each term we extract the following features:

- Its root (Porter Stemmer);
- Its POS tag;
- The stemming roots for all three words before and after the term;
- The POS tags for all three words before and after the term;
- A feature indicates if the word starts with capital letter;
- A feature indicates if the word is capitalised.

For example, for this review "But the staff was so horrible to us." Where *staff* is the aspect term, the target of each word will be:

But:O the:O staff:B was:O so:O horrible:O to:O us:O.

3.2 Subtask2: Aspect Term Polarity Detection

This subtask can be seen as sentence level or phrase level sentiment Analysis, the first step (1) we should detect the context or the words related to the aspect term, then to compute its polarity according to these words. Dependency parsing could be used to determine these words or simple distance function. We extract the context of aspect term according to the syntax and other aspect terms. Therefore, the context is the term itself and all the surrounding terms enclosed between two separators (commas in general), if another aspect is also enclosed by these separators we consider it as a separator instead of the comma, and we do not take the terms after it or before it (according to its direction to the aspect term). If the sentence has only an aspect term the separators will be the beginning and the end of the sentence. For example, for this review "*It took half an hour to get our check, which was perfect since we could sit, have drinks and talk!*" where we have two aspect terms *drinks* and *check*, the context of *check* will be "*It took half an hour to get our check*" and the context of *drinks* will be "*have drinks and talk!*". Another example, "*All the money went into the interior decoration, none of it went to the chefs.*" The context for *interior decoration* will be "*All the money went into the interior decoration*" and the context for *chefs* will be "*none of it went to the chefs*".

The second step (2) we should determine the polarity, which could be positive, negative, neutral or conflict. We propose to use Multinomial Naive-Bayes for learning a classifier based on different features:

- The terms in the sentence (term frequency);
- The POS features (the number of adjectives, adverbs, verbs, nouns, connectors)
- The pre-polarity features (the number of positive and negative words in the sentence extracted from Subjectivity lexicon and Bing Liu's Opinion Lexicon);
- Z-score features (the number of words which have Z-score more than three in each sentiment class), Z_score is described in 3.3.

3.3 Subtask3: Category Detection

Determining the categories of each sentence can be seen as a multi-label classification problem at sentence level.

We propose to use Z-score which is capable of distinguishing the importance of a term in a category. The more the term is important in a category the more its Z-score is high in this category and low in other categories in which it is not important. Thus, we compute the Z-score for all terms using the annotated data, then for each given sentence, the sum of Z-score over each category is computed if the Z-score of term in a category is less than zero, we ignore it in this category because it is not important, the sentence will be attributed to the category having the highest Z-score, if some categories have the same Z-scores the sentence will be attributed to the both. The algorithm steps:

For each tem t in the sentence:
  For each category c:
    If z-score(t,c)>0:
      Z_sc[c]+= z-score(t,c)
Categories=max(Z_sc)

We assume that the term frequency follows the multinomial distribution. Thus, Z_score can be seen as a standardization of the term frequency. We compute Z score for each term t_i in a class C_j (t_{ij}) by calculating its term relative frequency tfr_{ij} in a particular class C_j, as well as the mean

($mean_i$) which is the term probability over the whole corpus multiplied by n_j the number of terms in the class C_j, and standard deviation (sd_i) of term ti according to the underlying corpus (see Eq. (1,2)).

$$Z_{score(t_{ij})} = \frac{tfr_{ij} - mean_i}{sdi} \text{Eq. (1)}$$

$$Z_{score(t_{ij})} = \frac{tfr_{ij} - n_j * p(ti)}{\sqrt{nj * p(ti) * (1 - p(ti))}} \text{Eq. (2)}$$

Z_score was exploited for SA by (Zubaryeva and Savoy 2010), they choose a threshold (Z>2) for selecting the number of terms having Z_score more than the threshold, then they used a logistic regression for combining these scores. We use Z_score as added features for multinomial Naive Bayes classifier.

3.4 Subtask4: Category Polarity Detection

We have used Multinomial Naive-Bayes as in the subtask2 step (2) with the same features, but the different that we add also the name of the category as a feature. Thus, for each sentence having *n* category we add *n* examples to the training set, the difference between them is the feature of the category.

4 Experiments and Evaluations

We tested our system using the training and testing data provided by SemEval 2014 ABSA task. Two data sets were provided; the first contains3Ksentences of restaurant reviews annotated by the aspect terms, their polarities, their categories, the polarities of each category. The second contains of 3K sentences of laptop reviews annotated just by the aspect terms, their polarities.

The evaluation process was done in two steps. First step is concerning the subtasks 1 and 3 which involves the aspect terms extraction and category detection, we were provided with restaurant review and laptop review sentences and we had to extract the aspect terms for both data sets and the categories for the restaurant one. Baseline methods were provided; Table1 demonstrates the results of these subtasks in terms of precision *P*, recall *R* and f-measure *F* for our system and the baseline[2].

We remark that our system is 24% and 21% above the baseline for aspect terms extraction in restaurant and laptop reviews respectively, and above 3% for category detection in restaurant reviews.

Data	subtask		P	R	F
Res	1	Baseline	0,52	0,42	0,47
		System	**0.81**	**0.63**	**0.71**
	3	Baseline	0,73	0,59	0,65
		System	**0.77**	**0.60**	**0.68**
Lap	1	Baseline	0,44	0,29	0,35
		System	**0.76**	**0.45**	**0.56**

Table 1. Results of subtask 1, 2 for restaurant reviews, subtask 1 for laptop reviews

The second step involves the evaluation of subtask 2 and 4, we were provided with(1) restaurant review sentences annotated by their aspect terms, and categories, we had to determine the polarity for each aspect term and category; (2) laptop review sentences annotated by aspect terms and we had to determine the aspect term polarity. Table 2 demonstrates the results of our system and the baseline (A: accuracy, R: number of true retrieved examples, All: number of all true examples).

Data	subtask		R	All	A
Res	2	Baseline	673	1134	0,64
		System	**818**	**1134**	**0.72**
	4	Baseline	673	1025	0,65
		System	**739**	**1025**	**0.72**
Lap	2	Baseline	336	654	0,51
		System	**424**	654	**0,64**

Table 2. Results of subtask 2, 4 for restaurant reviews, subtask 2 for laptop reviews

We remark that our system is 8% and 13% above the baseline for aspect terms polarity detection in restaurant and laptop reviews respectively, and 7% above for category polarity detection in restaurant reviews.

5 Conclusion

We have built a system for Aspect-Based Sentiment Analysis; we proposed different supervised methods for the four sub-tasks. Our results are always above the baseline proposed by the organiser of SemEval. We proposed to use CRF for aspect term extraction, Z-score model for category detection, Multinomial Naive-Bayes with some new features for polarity detection. We find that the use of Z-score is useful for the category and polarity detection, we are going to test it in another sentiment analysis tasks of another domains.

[2]http://alt.qcri.org/semeval2014/task4/data/uploads/baselinesystemdescription.pdf

Reference

Samuel Brody and Noemie Elhadad (2010). An unsupervised aspect-sentiment model for online reviews. Human Language Technologies: The 2010 Annual Conference of the North American Chapter of the Association for Computational Linguistics. Los Angeles, California, Association for Computational Linguistics: 804-812.

Hussam Hamdan,Frederic Béchet and Patrice Bellot (2013). Experiments with DBpedia, WordNet and SentiWordNet as resources for sentiment analysis in micro-blogging. Proceedings of the Seventh International Workshop on Semantic Evaluation (SemEval 2013), Atlanta, Georgia, USA.

Vasileios Hatzivassiloglou and Kathleen R Mckeown (1997). Predicting the semantic orientation of adjectives. Proceedings of the 35th Annual Meeting of the Association for Computational Linguistics and Eighth Conference of the European Chapter of the Association for Computational Linguistics, Association for Computational Linguistics.

Minqing Hu and Bing Liu (2004). Mining and summarizing customer reviews. Proceedings of the tenth ACM SIGKDD international conference on Knowledge discovery and data mining. Seattle, WA, USA, ACM: 168-177.

Niklas Jakob and Iryna Gurevych (2010). Extracting opinion targets in a single- and cross-domain setting with conditional random fields. Proceedings of the 2010 Conference on Empirical Methods in Natural Language Processing. Cambridge, Massachusetts, Association for Computational Linguistics: 1035-1045.

Wei Jin and Hung Hay Ho (2009). A novel lexicalized HMM-based learning framework for web opinion mining. Proceedings of the 26th Annual International Conference on Machine Learning. Montreal, Quebec, Canada, ACM: 465-472.

Suin Kim,Jianwen Zhang,Zheng Chen,Alice Oh and Shixia Liu (2013). A Hierarchical Aspect-Sentiment Model for Online Reviews.

Chenghua Lin and Yulan He (2009). Joint sentiment/topic model for sentiment analysis. Proceedings of the 18th ACM conference on Information and knowledge management. Hong Kong, China, ACM: 375-384.

Bing Liu (2012). Sentiment Analysis and Opinion Mining, Morgan & Claypool Publishers.

Samaneh Moghaddam and Martin Ester (2010). Opinion digger: an unsupervised opinion miner from unstructured product reviews. Proceedings of the 19th ACM international conference on Information and knowledge management. Toronto, ON, Canada, ACM: 1825-1828.

Maria Pontiki,Dimitrios Galanis,John Pavlopoulos,Harris Papageorgiou,Ion Androutsopoulos and Suresh Manandhar. (2014). "SemEval-2014 Task 4: Aspect Based Sentiment Analysis." Proceedings of the International Workshop on Semantic Evaluation (SemEval).

Wei Wei and Jon Atle Gulla (2010). Sentiment learning on product reviews via sentiment ontology tree. Proceedings of the 48th Annual Meeting of the Association for Computational Linguistics. Uppsala, Sweden, Association for Computational Linguistics: 404-413.

Theresa Wilson,Janyce Wiebe and Paul Hoffmann (2005). Recognizing contextual polarity in phrase-level sentiment analysis. Proceedings of the conference on Human Language Technology and Empirical Methods in Natural Language Processing. Vancouver, British Columbia, Canada, Association for Computational Linguistics: 347-354.

Olena Zubaryeva and Jacques Savoy (2010). "Opinion Detection by Combining Machine Learning & Linguistic Tools." In Proceedings of the 8th NTCIR, Workshop Meeting on Evaluation of Information Access Technologies: InformationRetrieval, Question Answering and Cross-Lingual Information Access.

Swiss-Chocolate: Sentiment Detection using Sparse SVMs and Part-Of-Speech n-Grams

Martin Jaggi
ETH Zurich
Zürich, Switzerland
jaggi@inf.ethz.ch

Fatih Uzdilli and **Mark Cieliebak**
Zurich University of Applied Sciences
Winterthur, Switzerland
{ uzdi, ciel } @zhaw.ch

Abstract

We describe a classifier to predict the message-level sentiment of English micro-blog messages from Twitter. This paper describes the classifier submitted to the SemEval-2014 competition (Task 9B). Our approach was to build up on the system of the last year's winning approach by NRC Canada 2013 (Mohammad et al., 2013), with some modifications and additions of features, and additional sentiment lexicons. Furthermore, we used a sparse (ℓ_1-regularized) SVM, instead of the more commonly used ℓ_2-regularization, resulting in a very sparse linear classifier.

1 Introduction

With the immense growth of user generated text online, the interest in automatic sentiment analysis of text has greatly increased recently in both academia and industry.

In this paper, we describe our approach for a modified SVM based classifier for short text as in Twitter messages. Our system has participated in the SemEval-2014 Task 9 competition, "Sentiment Analysis in Twitter, Subtask–B Message Polarity Classification" (Rosenthal et al., 2014). The goal is to classify a tweet (on the full message level) into the three classes positive, negative, and neutral. An almost identical competition was already run in 2013.

Our Results in the Competition. Our approach was ranked on the 8th place out of the 50 participating submissions, with an F1-score of 67.54 on the Twitter-2014 test set. The 2014 winning team obtained an average F1-score of 70.96.

(The more detailed rankings of our approach were 4th rank on the LiveJournal data, 5th on the SMS data (2013), 18th on Twitter-2013, and 16th on Twitter Sarcasm, see (Rosenthal et al., 2014) for full details and all results).

Data. In the competition, the tweets for training and development were only provided as tweet IDs. A fraction (10-15%) of the tweets were no longer available on twitter, which makes the results of the competition not fully comparable. For testing, in addition to last years data (tweets and SMS), new tweets and data from a surprise domain were provided. An overview of the data, which we were able to download, is shown in Table 1.

Table 1: Overview of the data we found available for training, development and testing.

Dataset	Total	Positive	Negative	Neutral
Train (Tweets)	8224	3058	1210	3956
Dev (Tweets)	1417	494	286	637
Test: Twitter2014	1853	982	202	669
Test: Twitter2013	3813	1572	601	1640
Test: SMS2013	2093	492	394	1207
Test: Tw2014Sarcasm	86	33	40	13
Test: LiveJournal2014	1142	427	304	411

2 Description of Our Approach

Compared to the previous NRC Canada 2013 approach (Mohammad et al., 2013), our main changes are the following three: First we use sparse linear classifiers instead of classical dense ones. Secondly, we drop n-gram features completely, in favor of what we call *part-of-speech n-grams*, which are n-grams where up to two tokens are the original ones, and the rest of the tokens is replaced by their corresponding POS tag (noun, verb, punctuation etc). Third, we added two new sentiment lexicons, containing numerical scores associated for all 3 classes (positive, neutral, negative), instead of just 2 as in classical po-

Proceedings of the 8th International Workshop on Semantic Evaluation (SemEval 2014), pages 601–604,
Dublin, Ireland, August 23-24, 2014.

larity lexicons. All changes are described in more detail in Sections 4 and 3 below.

Performance. We tried to reproduce the same classifier as in (Mohammad et al., 2013) as a baseline for comparison.

Trying to quantify our contributions, when adding all our additional features and tricks described below, the score of our method increases from the baseline of 63.25 to 64.81 (on the Twitter-2013 test set), which is a gain of 1.56 points in F1.

Baseline Approach by NRC Canada 2013. Unfortunately our replica system of Mohammad et al. (2013) only achieved an F1-score of 63.25 on the Twitter-2013 test set, while their score in the 2013 competition on the same test set was 69.02, nearly 6 points higher in F1.

Part of this big difference might be explained by the fact that the exact same training sets are not available anymore. Other possibly more important differences are the SVM classifier variant used and class weighting (described in Section 4). Furthermore, we didn't implement all features in the exactly same way, see the more detailed description in Section 3.1.2 below. Although we had the impression that these changes individually had only a relatively minor effect, it might be that the changes together with the different training set add up to the difference in score.

3 Features

Before we describe the linear classifier in Section 4, we detail the used features for each tweet message. On average, we generated 843 features per tweet. For comparison, the average in our NRC Canada 2013 replica system was only 285. Most of the increase in features comes from the fact that we allowed for slightly longer n-grams (6 instead of 4), and substrings (length 6 instead of 5).

3.1 New Features

3.1.1 Part of Speech n-grams

We used the ArkTweetNLP structured prediction POS tagger provided by Owoputi et al. (2013) together with their provided standard model (model.20120919) suitable for twitter data.

Part of speech n-grams are n-grams where up to two tokens are kept as the original ones, and all other tokens are replaced by their corresponding POS tag (noun, verb, punctuation etc). We generated these modified n-grams for all possible positions of the one or two original tokens within the n positions, for $3 \leq n \leq 6$.

As features for a classifier, we found POS n-grams at least as useful (with some more robustness) as the n-grams themselves. In our final approach, we dropped the use of n-grams completely, and only used POS n-grams instead. The idea of replacing some of the tokens by their POS tag is also investigated by Joshi and Penstein-Rosé (2009), where the authors used $n \leq 3$.

3.1.2 Various Changes Compared to NRC Canada 2013

- We do not allow n-grams (or POS n-grams) to span over sentence boundaries.
- Substrings of length up to 6 (instead of 5).
- Substring features are weighted increasingly by their length (weights $0.7 \cdot \{1.0, 1.1, 1.2, 1.4, 1.6, 1.9\}$ for lengths $3, 4, \dots$)
- Instead of the score itself, we used the sigmoid value $s(t) = 1/(1 + e^{-t}))$ of each lexicon score. For each lexicon, the 4 scores were the same as in (Mohammad et al., 2013), i.e. per tweet, we use the number of tokens appearing in the lexicon, the sum and the max of the scores, and the last non-zero score.

We skipped some features from the baseline approach (because their effect was not significant in our setting): Elongated words (number of words with one character repeated more than two times), and word clustering. Also, we had a slightly simplified variant of how to use the lexicon scores. We didn't count the lexicon scores separately per emotion (pos and neg), but only altogether.

3.2 Existing Features

Text Preprocessing. A good tokenization seems very important for twitter data. We used the popular tokenizer ArkTweetNLP (Owoputi et al., 2013) which is suitable for tweets. All text was transformed to lowercase (except for those features in (Mohammad et al., 2013) which use case information). As usual, URLs were normalized to http://someurl and twitter user IDs to @someuser.

We also employed the usual marking of negated contexts of a sentence as in (Pang et al., 2002), using the list of negation words from Christopher Potts' sentiment tutorial[1].

4 Classifier

We used a linear support vector machine (SVM) classifier, which is standard for text data. The LibLinear package (Fan et al., 2008) was employed for training the multi-class classifier.

Multi-Class Formulation, and Class Weights. We found significant performance changes depending on which type of multi-class SVM, and also which regularizer (ℓ_1- or ℓ_2-norm) is used. For the multi-class variant, we found the *one-against-all* models to perform slightly better than the Crammer and Singer (2001) formulation.

More importantly, since the 3 classes (positive, negative and neutral) are quite unbalanced in size in the training set, it is crucial to set a good weight for each class in the SVM. We used $(4.52, 1.38, 1.80)$, which corresponds to the twice the ratio of each class compared to the average class size.

Sparse Linear Classifiers. In our setting, an ℓ_1-regularized squared loss SVM (one-against-all) performed best (this is mode L1R_L2LOSS_SVC in LibLinear), despite the fact that ℓ_2-regularization is generally more commonly used in text applications. We used $C = 0.055$ for the regularization parameter, and $\varepsilon = 0.003$ as the optimization stopping criterion. We did not employ any kernel, but always used linear classifiers.

Another benefit of the ℓ_1-regularization is that the resulting classifier is extremely sparse and compact, which significantly accelerates the evaluation of the classifier on large amounts of text, e.g. for testing. Our final classifier only uses 1985 non-zero features (1427 unigram/substrings, and 558 other features, such as lexicon scores, n-grams, POS n-grams, as explained in the previous Section 3).

As the resulting classifier is so small, it is also relatively easy to read and interpret. We have made our final classifier weights publicly available for download as a text file[2] . Every line contains the feature description followed by the 3 weights corresponding to the 3 sentiment classes.

Our final classifier was trained on 9641 tweets, which are all we could download from the IDs given in this years train and dev set.

5 Lexicons

A sentiment lexicon is a mapping from words (or n-grams) to an association score corresponding to positive or negative sentiment. Such lists can be constructed either from manually labeled data (supervised), or automatically labeled data (unsupervised) as for example tweets with a positive or negative smiley. We used the same set of lexicons as in (Mohammad et al., 2013), with one addition:

5.1 A Lexicon for 3-Class Classification

Our main new addition was another type of lexicon, which not only provides one score per word, but 3 of them, (being the association to positive, negative and neutral). The idea here is to improve on the discrimination quality, especially for neutral text, and treat all 3 labels in this multi-class task the same way, instead of just 2 as in the previous approaches.

Data. We found it challenging to find good datasets to build such a lexicon. We again used the Sentiment140 corpus (Go et al., 2009) (containing tweets with positive or negative emoticons). Using a subset of 100k positive and 100k negative ones, we added a set of 100k arbitrary (hopefully neutral) tweets. The neutral set was chosen randomly from the thinknook.com dataset[3] of 1.5mio tweets (from which we ignored the provided labels, and counted the tweets as neutral).

We did the same with the movie reviews from the recent kaggle competition on annotated reviews from the rotten-tomatoes website[4]. We automatically built a lexicon from 100k texts in this dataset, with the data balanced equally for the three classes.

Features Used in the Lexicon. To construct the lexicon, we extracted the POS n-grams (as we described in Section 3.1.1 above) from all texts. In comparison, Mohammad et al. (2013) used non-contiguous n-grams (unigram–unigram, unigram–bigram, and bigram–bigram pairs). We only used POS n-grams with 2 tokens kept original, and the

[1] http://sentiment.christopherpotts.net/lingstruc.html

[2] http://www.m8j.net/sentiment/

[3] http://thinknook.com/twitter-sentiment-analysis-training-corpus-dataset-2012-09-22/

[4] http://www.kaggle.com/c/sentiment-analysis-on-movie-reviews/data

remaining ones replaced by their POS tag, with n ranging from 3 to 6.

Building the Lexicon. While in (Mohammad et al., 2013), the score for each n-gram was computed using point-wise mutual information (PMI) with the labels, we trained a linear classifier on the same labels instead. The lexicon weights are set as the resulting classifier weights for our (POS) n-grams. We used the same type of sparse SVM trained with LibLinear, for 3 classes, as in the final classifier.

Download of the Lexicons. We built 4 lexicons as described above. Thanks to the sparsity of the linear weights from the SVM, they are again relatively small, analogous to the final classifier. We also provide the lexicons for download as text files[5].

5.2 Existing Lexicons

Lexicons from Manually Labeled Data. We used the same 3 existing sentiment lexicons as in (Mohammad et al., 2013). All lexicons give a single score for each word (if present in the lexicon). Those existing lexicons are: NRC Emotion Lexicon (about 14k words), the MPQA Lexicon (about 8k words), and the Bing Liu Lexicon (about 7k words).

Lexicons from Automatically Labeled Data. The NRC hashtag sentiment lexicon was generated automatically from a set of 775k tweets containing a hashtag of a small predefined list of positive and negative hashtags (Mohammad et al., 2013). Lexicon scores were trained via PMI (point-wise mutual information). Scores are not only available for words, but also unigram–unigram, unigram–bigram, and bigram–bigram pairs (that can be non-contiguous in the text).

The Sentiment140 lexicon (Go et al., 2009) was generated automatically from a set of 1.6 million tweets containing a positive or negative emoticon. This uses the same features and scoring as above.

6 Conclusion

We have described an SVM classifier to detect the sentiment of short texts such as tweets. Our system is built up on the approach of NRC Canada (Mohammad et al., 2013), with several modifications and extensions (e.g. sparse linear classifiers, POS-n-grams, new lexicons). We have seen that our system significantly improves the baseline approach, achieving a gain of 1.56 points in F1 score.

We participated in the SemEval-2014 competition for Twitter polarity classification, and our system was among the top ten out of 50 submissions, with an F1-score of 67.54 on tweets.

For future work, it would be interesting to incorporate our improvements into the most recent version of NRC Canada or similar systems, to see how much one could gain there.

[5] http://www.m8j.net/sentiment/

References

Crammer, K. and Singer, Y. (2001). On the Algorithmic Implementation of Multiclass Kernel-based Vector Machines. *JMLR*, 2:265–292.

Fan, R.-E., Chang, K.-W., Hsieh, C.-J., Wang, X.-R., and Lin, C.-J. (2008). LIBLINEAR: A Library for Large Linear Classification. *JMLR*, 9:1871–1874.

Go, A., Bhayani, R., and Huang, L. (2009). Twitter Sentiment Classification using Distant Supervision. Technical report, The Stanford Natural Language Processing Group.

Joshi, M. and Penstein-Rosé, C. (2009). Generalizing dependency features for opinion mining. In *Proceedings of the ACL-IJCNLP 2009 Conference Short Papers*, p 313–316, Singapore. Association for Computational Linguistics.

Mohammad, S. M., Kiritchenko, S., and Zhu, X. (2013). NRC-Canada: Building the State-of-the-Art in Sentiment Analysis of Tweets. In *SemEval-2013 - Proceedings of the International Workshop on Semantic Evaluation*, pages 321–327, Atlanta, Georgia, USA.

Owoputi, O., O'Connor, B., Dyer, C., Gimpel, K., Schneider, N., and Smith, N. A. (2013). Improved Part-Of-Speech Tagging for Online Conversational Text with Word Clusters. In *Proceedings of NAACL-HLT*, pages 380–390.

Pang, B., Lee, L., and Vaithyanathan, S. (2002). Thumbs up? Sentiment Classification using Machine Learning Techniques. In *ACL-02 conference*, pages 79–86, Morristown, NJ, USA. Association for Computational Linguistics.

Rosenthal, S., Ritter, A., Nakov, P., and Stoyanov, V. (2014). SemEval-2014 Task 9: Sentiment Analysis in Twitter. In *SemEval 2014 - Proceedings of the Eighth International Workshop on Semantic Evaluation*, Dublin, Ireland.

Synalp-Empathic: A Valence Shifting Hybrid System for Sentiment Analysis

Alexandre Denis, Samuel Cruz-Lara, Nadia Bellalem and Lotfi Bellalem
LORIA/University of Lorraine
Nancy, France
{alexandre.denis, samuel.cruz-lara, nadia.bellalem, lotfi.bellalem}@loria.fr

Abstract

This paper describes the *Synalp-Empathic* system that competed in SemEval-2014 Task 9B Sentiment Analysis in Twitter. Our system combines syntactic-based valence shifting rules with a supervised learning algorithm (Sequential Minimal Optimization). We present the system, its features and evaluate their impact. We show that both the valence shifting mechanism and the supervised model enable to reach good results.

1 Introduction

Sentiment Analysis (SA) is the determination of the polarity of a piece of text (positive, negative, neutral). It is not an easy task, as proven by the moderate agreement between human annotators when facing this task. Their agreement varies whether considering document or sentence level sentiment analysis, and different domains may show different agreements as well (Bermingham and Smeaton, 2009).

As difficult the task is for human beings, it is even more difficult for machines which face syntactic, semantic or pragmatic difficulties. Consider for instance irrealis phenomena such as "*if this is good*" or "*it would be good if*" that are both neutral. Irrealis is also present in questions ("*is this good?*") but presupposition of existence does matter: "*can you fix this terrible printer?*" would be polarized while "*can you give me a good advice?*" would not. Negation and irrealis interact as well, compare for instance "*this could be good*" (neutral or slightly positive) and "*this could not be good*" (clearly negative). Other difficult phenomena include semantic or pragmatic effects, such as point of view ("*Israel failed to defeat Hezbollah*", negative for Israel, positive for Hezbollah), background knowledge ("*this car uses a lot of gas*"), semantic polysemy ("*this vacuum cleaner sucks*" vs "*this movie sucks*"), etc.

From the start, machine learning has been the widely dominant approach to sentiment analysis since it tries to capture these phenomena alltogether (Liu, 2012). Starting from simple n-grams (Pang et al., 2002), more recent approaches tend to include syntactic contexts (Socher et al., 2011). However these supervised approaches all require a training corpus. Unsupervised approaches such as the seminal paper of (Turney, 2002) require training corpus as well but do not require annotations. We propose in this paper to look first at approaches that *do not* require any corpus because annotating a corpus is in general costly, especially in sentiment analysis in which several annotators are required to maintain a high level of agreement[1]. Nevertheless supervised machine learning can be useful to *adapt* the system to a particular domain and we will consider it as well.

Hence, we propose in this paper to first consider a domain independent sentiment analysis tool that does not require any training corpus (section 2). Once the performance of this tool is assessed (section 2.4) we propose to consider how the system can be extended with machine learning in section 3. We show the results on the SemEval 2013 and 2014 corpora in section 4.

2 Sentiment Analysis without Corpus

We present here a system that does sentiment analysis without requiring a training corpus. We do so in three steps: we first present a raw lexical baseline that naively considers average valence taking the prior valence of words from polarity lexicons.

[1] as done in SemEval2013 SA task (Nakov et al., 2013)

Proceedings of the 8th International Workshop on Semantic Evaluation (SemEval 2014), pages 605–609,
Dublin, Ireland, August 23-24, 2014.

We then show how to adapt this baseline to the Twitter domain. Finally, we describe a method wich takes into account the syntactic context of polarized words. All methods and strategies are then evaluated.

2.1 Raw Lexical Baseline

The raw lexical baseline is a simple system that only relies on polarity lexicons and takes the average valence of all the words. The valence is modeled using a continuous value in $[0,1]$, 0.5 being neutral. The algorithm is as follows:

1. perform part of speech tagging of the input text using the Stanford CoreNLP tool suite,
2. for all words in the input text, retrieve their polarity from the lexicons using lemma and part of speech information. If the word is found in several lexicons, return the average of the found polarities. Otherwise if the word is not found, return 0.5.
3. then for the tweet, simply compute the average valence among all words.

We tried several lexicons but ended with focusing on the Liu's lexicon (Hu and Liu, 2004) which proved to offer the best results. However Liu's lexicon is missing slang or bad words. We therefore extended the lexicon using the *onlineslangdictionary.com* website which provides a list of slang words expressing either positive or negative properties. We extracted around 100 words from this lexicon which we call *urban lexicon*.

2.2 Twitter Adaptations

From this lexical base we considered several small improvements to adapt to the Twitter material. We first observed that the Stanford part of speech tagger had a tendency to mistag the first position in the sentence as proper noun. Since in tweets this position is often in fact a common noun, we systematically retagged these words as common nouns. Second, we used a set of 150 hand written rules designed to handle chat colloquialism i.e., abbreviations ("*wtf*" → "*what the f****", twitter specific expressions ("*mistweet*" → "*regretted tweet*"), missing apostrophe ("*isnt*" → "*isn't*"), and smileys. Third, we applied hashtag splitting (e.g. "*#ihatemondays*" → "*i hate mondays*"). Finally we refined the lexicon lookup strategy to handle discrepancies between lexicon and part of speech tagger. For instance, while the part of speech tagger may tag *stabbed* as an adjective with lemma *stabbed*, the lexicon might list it as a verb with lemma *stab*. To improve robustness we therefore look first for the inflected form then for the lemma.

2.3 Syntactic Enhancements

Valence Shifting Valence shifting refers to the differential between the *prior polarity* of a word (polarity from lexicons) and its contextual polarity (Polanyi and Zaenen, 2006). Following (Moilanen and Pulman, 2007), we apply polarity rewriting rules over the parsing structure. However we differ from them in that we consider dependency rather than phrase structure trees.

The algorithm is as follows:

1. perform dependency parsing of the text (with Stanford CoreNLP)
2. annotate each word with its prior polarity as found in polarity lexicons
3. rewrite prior polarities using dependency matching, hand-crafted rules
4. return the root polarity

Table 1 shows example rules. Each rule is composed of a matching part and a rewriting part. Both parts have the form (N, L_G, P_G, L_D, P_D) where N is the dependency name, L_G and L_D are respectively the lemmas of the governor and dependent words, P_G and P_D are the polarity of the governor and dependent words. We write the rules in short form by prefixing them with the name of the dependency and either the lemma or the polarity for the arguments, e.g. $N(P_G, P_D)$. For instance, the *inversion* rule "neg(P_G, P_D) → neg(!P_G, P_D)" inverts the polarity of the governor P_G for dependencies named *neg*. One important rule is the *propagation* rule "N(0.5, P_D) → N(P_D,P_D)" which propagates the polarity of the dependent word P_D to the governor only if it is neutral. Another useful rule is the *overwrite* rule "amod(1,0) → amod(0,0)" which erases for *amod* dependencies, the positive polarity of the governor given a negative modifier.

The main algorithm for rule application consists in testing all rules (in a fixed order) on all dependencies iteratively. Whenever a rule fires, the whole set of rules is tested again. Potential looping

Rule	Example
neg(P_G, P_D) → neg(!P_G, P_D)	he's not happy
det(P_G, "no") → det(!P_G,"no")	there is no hate
amod(1,0) → amod(0,0)	a missed opportunity
nsubj(0,1) → nsubj(0,0)	my dreams are crushed
nsubj(1,0) → nsubj(1,1)	my problem is fixed
$N(0.5, P_D) \rightarrow N(P_D,P_D)$	(propagation)

Table 1: Excerpt of valence shifting rules.

is prevented because (i) the dependency graph returned by the Stanford Parser is a directed acyclic graph (de Marneffe and Manning, 2008) and (ii) the same rule cannot apply twice to the same dependency.

For instance, in the sentence "*I do not think it is a missed opportunity*", the verb "*missed*" has negative polarity and the noun "*opportunity*" has positive polarity. The graph in Figure 1 shows different rules application: first the *overwrite* rule (1.) changes the positive polarity of "*opportunity*" to a negative polarity which is then transferred to the main verb "*think*" thanks to the *propagation* rule (2.). Finally, the *inversion* rule (3.) inverts the negative polarity of *think*. As a result, the polarity of the sentence is positive.

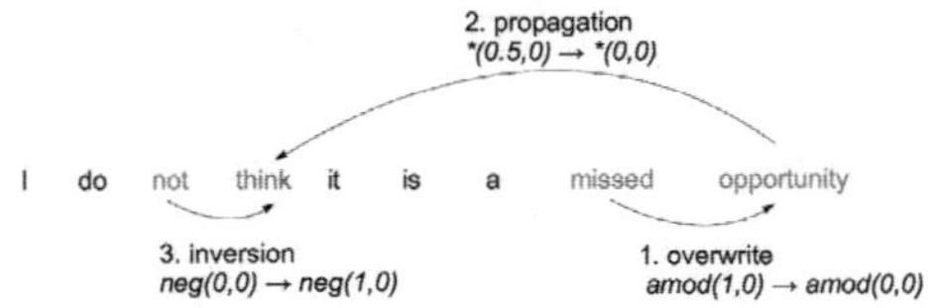

Figure 1: Rules application example.

Various Phenomena Several other phenomena need to be taken into account when considering the co-text. Because of irrealis phenomena mentioned in the introduction, we completely ignored questions. We also ignored proper nouns (such as in "*u need 2 c the documentary* The Devil Inside") which were a frequent source of errors. These two phenomena are labeled *Ignoring forms* in Table 2. Finally since our approach is sentence-based we need to consider valence of tweets with several sentences and we simply considered the average.

2.4 Results on SemEval2013

We measure the performance of the different strategies on the 3270 tweets that we downloaded from the SemEval 2013 Task 2 (Nakov et al., 2013) test corpus[2]. The used metrics is the same than SemEval 2013 one, an unweighted average between positive and negative F-score.

System	F-score	Gain
Raw lexical baseline	54.75	
+ Part of speech fix	55.00	+0.25
+ Colloqualism rewriting	57.66	**+2.66**
+ Hashtag splitting	57.80	+0.14
+ Lexicon fetch strategy	58.25	+0.45
+ Valence shifting	62.37	**+4.12**
+ Ignoring forms	62.97	+0.60

Table 2: Results of syntactic system.

As shown in Table 2, the raw lexical baseline starts at 54.75% F-score. The two best improvements are *Colloquialism rewriting* (+2.66) that seems to capture useful polarized elements and *Valence shifting* (+4.12) which provides an accurate account for shifting phenomena. Overall other strategies taken separately do not contribute much but enable to have an accumulated +1.44 gain of F-score. The final result is 62.97%, and we will refer to this first system as the *Syntactic system*.

3 Machine Learning Optimization

The best F-score attained with the syntactic system (62.97%) is still below the best system that participated in SemEval2013 (69.02%)[3]. To improve performance, we input the valence computed by the syntactic system as a feature in a supervised machine learning (ML) algorithm. While there exists other methods such as (Choi and Cardie, 2008) which incorporates syntax at the heart in the machine algorithm, this approach has the advantage to be very simple and independent of any specific ML algorithm. We chose the Sequential Minimal Optimization (SMO) which is an optimization of Support Vector Machine (Platt, 1999) since it was shown (Balahur and Turchi, 2012) to have good results that we observed ourselves.

In addition to the valence output by our syntactic system, we considered the following additional low level features:

- *1-grams words*: we observed lower results with n-grams ($n > 1$) and decided to keep 1-grams only. The words were lemmatized and no tf-idf weighting was applied since it showed lower results.
- *polarity counts*: it is interesting to include low level polarity counts in case the

[2]Because of Twitter policy the test corpus is not distributed by organizers but tweets must be downloaded using their identifiers, resulting in discrepancies from the official campaign (3814 tweets).

[3]Evaluated on full 3814 tweets corpus

syntactic system does not correctly capture valence shifts. We thus included independent features counting the number of positive/negative/neutral words according to several lexicons: Liu's lexicon (Hu and Liu, 2004), our *urban* lexicon, SentiWordnet (Baccianella et al., 2010), QWordnet (Agerri and Garca-Serrano, 2010) and MPQA lexicon (Wilson et al., 2005).

- *punctuation count*: exclamation and interrogation marks are important, so we have an independent feature counting occurrences of "?", "!", "?!", "!?".

Thanks to the ML approach, we can obtain for a given tweet the different probabilities for each class. We were then able to adapt each probabilities to favor the SemEval metrics by weighting the probabilities thanks to the SemEval 2013 training and development corpus using 10-fold cross validation (the weights were trained on 90% and evaluated on 10%). The resulting weights reduce the probability to assign the neutral class to a given tweet while raising the positive/negative probabilities. This optimization is called *metrics weighting* in Table 3.

4 Optimization Results

We describe here the results of integrating the syntactic system as a feature of the SMO along with other low level features. The SemEval 2014 gold test corpus was not available at the time of this writing hence we detail the features only on the SemEval 2013 gold test corpus.

4.1 On SemEval 2013

The results displayed in Table 3 are obtained with the SMO classifier trained using the WEKA library (Hall et al., 2009) on our downloaded SemEval 2013 development and training corpora (7595 tweets). As before, the given score is the average F-score computed on the SemEval 2013 test corpus. Note that the gain of each feature must be interpreted in the context of other features (e.g. *Polarity counts* needs to be understood as *Words+Polarity Counts*).

The syntactic system feature, that is considering only one training feature which is the valence annotated by the syntactic system, starts very low (33.69%) since it appears to systematically favor positive and neutral classes. However adding the 1-gram lemmatized words raises the result to 63.03%, slightly above the syntactic system alone (62.97%). Considering polarity counts raises the F-score to 65.02% showing that the syntactic system does not capture correctly all valence shifts (or valence neutralizations). Considering an independent feature for punctuation slightly raises the result. Metrics weighting, while not being a training feature per se, provides an important boost for the final F-score (67.83%).

Features	F-score	Gain
Syntactic system	33.69	
+ Words	63.03	+29.34
+ Polarity counts	65.02	+1.99
+ Punctuation	65.65	+0.63
+ Metrics weighting	67.83	+2.18

Table 3: Detailed results on SemEval 2013.

4.2 On SemEval 2014

We participated to SemEval 2014 task B as the *Synalp-Empathic* team (Rosenthal et al., 2014). The results are 67.43% on the Twitter 2014 dataset, 3.53 points below the best system. Interestingly the score obtained on Twitter 2014 is very close to the score we computed ourselves on Twitter 2013 (67.83%) suggesting no overfitting to our training corpus. However, we observed a big drop in the Twitter 2013 evaluation as carried out by organizers (63.65%), we assume that the difference in results could be explained by difference in datasets coverage caused by Twitter policy.

5 Discussion and Conclusion

We presented a two-steps approach for sentiment analysis on Twitter. We first developed a lexico-syntactic approach that does not require any training corpus and enables to reach 62.97% on SemEval 2013. We then showed how to adapt the approach given a training corpus which enables reaching 67.43% on SemEval 2014, 3.53 points below the best system. We further showed that the approach is not sensitive to overfitting since it proved to be as efficient on the SemEval 2013 and the SemEval 2014 test corpus. In order to improve the performance, it could be possible adapt the lexicons to the specific Twitter domain (Demiroz et al., 2012). It may also be possible to investigate how to learn automatically the valence shifting rules, for instance with Monte Carlo methods.

Acknowledgements

This work was conducted in the context of the ITEA2 1105 Empathic Products *project, and is supported by funding from the French Services, Industry and Competitivity General Direction. We would like to thank Christophe Cerisara for the insights regarding the machine learning system and Claire Gardent for her advices regarding the readability of the paper.*

References

Rodrigo Agerri and Ana Garca-Serrano. 2010. Q-wordnet: Extracting polarity from wordnet senses. In *Proceedings of the Seventh International Conference on Language Resources and Evaluation (LREC'10)*, Valletta, Malta, may. European Language Resources Association (ELRA).

Stefano Baccianella, Andrea Esuli, and Fabrizio Sebastiani. 2010. Sentiwordnet 3.0: An enhanced lexical resource for sentiment analysis and opinion mining. In *Proceedings of the Seventh International Conference on Language Resources and Evaluation (LREC'10)*, Valletta, Malta, may. European Language Resources Association (ELRA).

Alexandra Balahur and Marco Turchi. 2012. Multilingual sentiment analysis using machine translation? In *Proceedings of the 3rd Workshop in Computational Approaches to Subjectivity and Sentiment Analysis*, WASSA '12, pages 52–60, Stroudsburg, PA, USA.

Adam Bermingham and Alan F. Smeaton. 2009. A study of inter-annotator agreement for opinion retrieval. In James Allan, Javed A. Aslam, Mark Sanderson, ChengXiang Zhai, and Justin Zobel, editors, *SIGIR*, pages 784–785. ACM.

Yejin Choi and Claire Cardie. 2008. Learning with compositional semantics as structural inference for subsentential sentiment analysis. In *Proceedings of the Conference on Empirical Methods in Natural Language Processing*, EMNLP '08, pages 793–801, Stroudsburg, PA, USA.

Marie-Catherine de Marneffe and Christopher D. Manning. 2008. Stanford typed dependencies manual. Technical report.

Gulsen Demiroz, Berrin Yanikoglu, Dilek Tapucu, and Yücel Saygin. 2012. Learning domain-specific polarity lexicons. In *Proceedings of the 12th International Conference of Data Mining Workshops (ICDMW)*, pages 674–679, Dec.

Mark Hall, Eibe Frank, Geoffrey Holmes, Bernhard Pfahringer, Peter Reutemann, and Ian H. Witten. 2009. The WEKA data mining software: An update. *SIGKDD Explor. Newsl.*, 11(1):10–18, November.

Minqing Hu and Bing Liu. 2004. Mining and summarizing customer reviews. In *Proceedings of the 10th International Conference on Knowledge Discovery and Data Mining*, pages 168–177.

Bing Liu, 2012. *Sentiment Analysis and Opinion Mining*. Morgan & Claypool Publishers, May.

Karo Moilanen and Stephen Pulman. 2007. Sentiment composition. In *Proceedings of Recent Advances in Natural Language Processing (RANLP 2007)*, pages 378–382, September 27-29.

Preslav Nakov, Sara Rosenthal, Zornitsa Kozareva, Veselin Stoyanov, Alan Ritter, and Theresa Wilson. 2013. SemEval-2013 task 2: sentiment analysis in twitter. In *Proceedings of the 7th International Workshop on Semantic Evaluation.*

Bo Pang, Lillian Lee, and Shivakumar Vaithyanathan. 2002. Thumbs up? Sentiment classication using machine learning techniques. In *Proceedings of the 2002 Conference on Empirical Methods in Natural Language Processing*, pages 79–86, Philadelphia, PA.

John C. Platt. 1999. Fast training of support vector machines using sequential minimal optimization. In *Advances in Kernel Methods*, pages 185–208. MIT Press, Cambridge, MA, USA.

Livia Polanyi and Annie Zaenen. 2006. Contextual valence shifters. In JamesG. Shanahan, Yan Qu, and Janyce Wiebe, editors, *Computing Attitude and Affect in Text: Theory and Applications*, volume 20 of *The Information Retrieval Series*, pages 1–10. Springer Netherlands.

Sara Rosenthal, Preslav Nakov, Alan Ritter, and Veselin Stoyanov. 2014. SemEval-2014 task 9: Sentiment analysis in twitter. In *Proceedings of the 8th International Workshop on Semantic Evaluation.*

Richard Socher, Jeffrey Pennington, Eric H. Huang, Andrew Y. Ng, and Christopher D. Manning. 2011. Semi-supervised recursive autoencoders for predicting sentiment distributions. In *Proceedings of the 2011 Conference on Empirical Methods in Natural Language Processing*, pages 151–161, Edinburgh.

Peter Turney. 2002. Thumbs up or thumbs down? semantic orientation applied to unsupervised classication of reviews. In *Proceedings of the 40th Annual Meeting of the Association for Computational Linguistics*, pages 417–424, Philadelphia, PA.

Theresa Wilson, Janyce Wiebe, and Paul Hoffmann. 2005. Recognizing Contextual Polarity in Phrase-Level Sentiment Analysis. In *Proceedings of Human Language Technologies Conference/Conference on Empirical Methods in Natural Language Processing (HLT/EMNLP 2005)*, Vancouver, CA.

SZTE-NLP: Aspect Level Opinion Mining Exploiting Syntactic Cues

Viktor Hangya[1], **Gábor Berend**[1], **István Varga**[2]*, **Richárd Farkas**[1]
[1]University of Szeged
Department of Informatics
{hangyav,berendg,rfarkas}@inf.u-szeged.hu
[2]NEC Corporation, Japan
Knowledge Discovery Research Laboratories
vistvan@az.jp.nec.com

Abstract

In this paper, we introduce our contributions to the SemEval-2014 Task 4 – *Aspect Based Sentiment Analysis* (Pontiki et al., 2014) challenge. We participated in the *aspect term polarity* subtask where the goal was to classify opinions related to a given aspect into positive, negative, neutral or conflict classes. To solve this problem, we employed supervised machine learning techniques exploiting a rich feature set. Our feature templates exploited both phrase structure and dependency parses.

1 Introduction

The booming volume of user-generated content and the consequent popularity growth of online review sites has led to vast amount of user reviews that are becoming increasingly difficult to grasp. There is desperate need for tools that can automatically process and organize information that might be useful for both users and commercial agents.

Such early approaches have focused on determining the overall polarity (e.g., positive, negative, neutral, conflict) or sentiment rating (e.g., star rating) of various entities (e.g., restaurants, movies, etc.) cf. (Ganu et al., 2009). While the overall polarity rating regarding a certain entity is, without question, extremely valuable, it fails to distinguish between various crucial dimensions based on which an entity can be evaluated. Evaluations targeting distinct key aspects (i.e., functionality, price, design, etc) provide important clues that may be targeted by users with different priorities concerning the entity in question, thus holding much greater value in one's decision making process.

In this paper, we introduce our contribution to the SemEval-2014 Task 4 – *Aspect Based Sentiment Analysis* (Pontiki et al., 2014) challenge. We participated in the *aspect term polarity* subtask where the goal was to classify opinions which are related to a given aspect into positive, negative, neutral or conflict classes. We employed supervised machine learning techniques exploiting a rich feature set for target polarity detection, with a special emphasis on features that deal with the detection of aspect scopes. Our system achieved an accuracy of 0.752 and 0.669 for the restaurant and laptop domains, respectively.

2 Approach

We employed a four-class supervised (positive, negative, neutral and conflict) classifier here. As a normalization step, we converted the given texts into their lowercased forms. Bag-of-words features comprised the basic feature set for our maximum entropy classifier, which was shown to be helpful in polarity detection (Hangya and Farkas, 2013).

In the case of aspect-oriented sentiment detection, we found it important to locate text parts that refer to particular aspects. For this, we used several syntactic parsing methods and introduced parse tree based features.

2.1 Distance-weighted Bag-of-words Features

Initially, we used n-gram token features (unigrams and bigrams). It could be helpful to take into consideration the distance between the token in question and the mention of the target aspect. The closer a token is to an entity the more plausible that the given token is related to the aspect.

*The work was done while this author was working as a guest researcher at the University of Szeged

Proceedings of the 8th International Workshop on Semantic Evaluation (SemEval 2014), pages 610–614,
Dublin, Ireland, August 23-24, 2014.

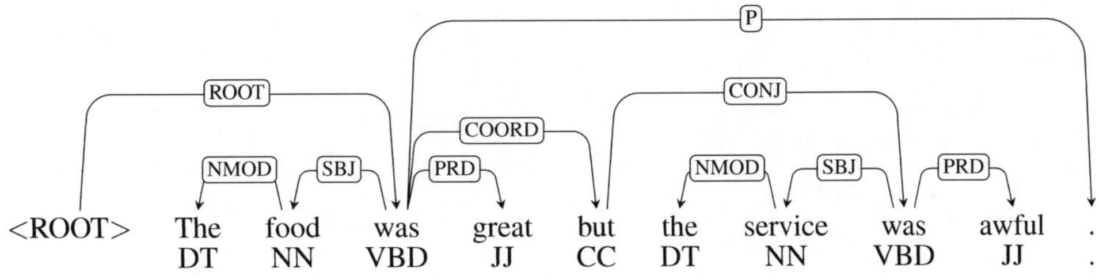

Figure 1: Dependency parse tree (MATE parser).

For this we used weighted feature vectors, and weighted each n-gram feature by its distance in tokens from the mention of the given aspect:

$$\frac{1}{e^{\frac{1}{n}|i-j|}},$$

where n is the length of the review and the values i, j are the positions of the actual word and the mentioned aspect.

2.2 Polarity Lexicon

To examine the polarity of the words comprising a review, we incorporated the SentiWordNet sentiment lexicon (Baccianella et al., 2010) into our feature set.

In this resource, synsets – i.e. sets of word forms sharing some common meaning – are assigned positivity, negativity and objectivity scores. These scores can be interpreted as the probabilities of seeing some representatives of the synsets in a positive, negative and neutral meaning, respectively. However, it is not unequivocal to determine automatically which particular synset a given word belongs to with respect its context. Consider the word form *great* for instance, which might have multiple, fundamentally different sentiment connotations in different contexts, e.g. in expressions such as *"great food"* and *"great crisis"*.

We determined the most likely synset a particular word form belonged to based on its contexts by selecting the synset, the members of which were the most appropriate for the lexical substitution of the target word. The extent of the appropriateness of a word being a substitute for another word was measured relying on Google's N-Gram Corpus, using the indexing framework described in (Ceylan and Mihalcea, 2011).

We look up the frequencies of the n-grams that we derive from the context by replacing the target words with its synonyms(*great*) from various synsets, e.g. *good* versus *big*. We count down the frequency of the phrases *food is good* and *food is big* in a huge set of in-domain documents (Ceylan and Mihalcea, 2011). Than we choose the meaning which has the highest probability, *good* in this case. This way we assign a polarity value for each word in a text and created three new features for the machine learning algorithm, which are the number of positive, negative and objective words in the given document.

2.3 Negation Scope Detection

Since negations are quite frequent in user reviews and have the tendency to flip polarities, we took special care of negation expressions. We collected a set of negation expressions, like *not*, *don't*, etc. and a set of delimiters *and*, *or*, etc. It is reasonable to think that the scope of a negation starts when we detect a negation word in the sentence and it lasts until the next delimiter. If an n-gram was in a negation scope we added a *NOT* prefix to that feature.

2.4 Syntax-based Features

It is very important to discriminate between text fragments that are referring to the given aspect and the fragments that do not, within the same sentence. To detect the relevant text fragments, we used dependency and constituency parsers. Since adjectives are good indicators of opinion polarity, we add the ones to our feature set which are in close proximity with the given aspect term. We define proximity between an adjective and an aspect term as the length of the non-directional path between them in the dependency tree. We gather adjectives in proximity less than 6.

Another feature, which is not aspect specific but can indicate the polarity of an opinion, is the polarity of words' modifiers. We defined a feature template for tokens whose syntactic head is present in

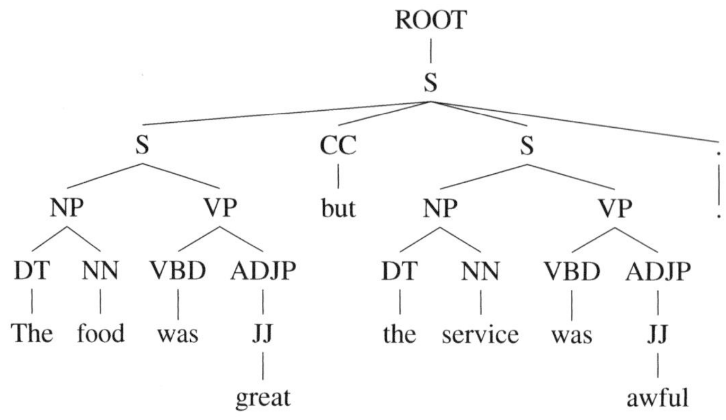

Figure 2: Constituency parse tree (Stanford parser).

our positive or negative lexicon. For dependency parsing we used the MATE parser (Bohnet, 2010) trained on the Penn Treebank (penn2malt conversion), an example can be seen on Figure 1.

Besides using words that refer to a given aspect, we tried to identify subsentences which refers to the aspect mention. In a sentence we can express our opinions about more than one aspect, so it is important not to use subsentences containing opinions about other aspects. We developed a simple rule based method for selecting the appropriate subtree from the constituent parse of the sentence in question (see Figure 2). In this method, the root of this subtree is the leaf which contains the given aspect initially. In subsequent steps the subtree containing the aspect in its yield gets expanded until the following conditions are met:

- The yield of the subtree consists of at least five tokens.
- The yield of the subtree does not contain any other aspect besides the five-token window frame relative to the aspect in question.
- The current root node of the subtree is either the non-terminal symbol `PP` or `S`.

Relying on these identified subtrees, we introduced a few more features. First, we created new n-gram features from the yield of the subtree. Next, we determined the polarity of this subtree with a method proposed by Socher et al. () and used it as a feature. We also detected those words which tend to take part in sentences conveying subjectivity, using the χ^2 statistics calculated from the training data. With the help of these words, we counted the number of opinion indicator words in the subtree as additional features. We used the Stanford constituency parser (Klein and Manning, 2003) trained on the Penn Treebank for these experiments.

2.5 Clustering

Aspect mentions can be classified into a few distinct topical categories, such as aspects regarding the *price*, *service* or *ambiance* of some product or service. Our hypothesis was that the distribution of the sentiment categories can differ significantly depending on the aspect categories. For instance, people might tend to share positive ideas on the price of some product rather than expressing negative, neutral or conflicting ideas towards it. In order to make use of this assumption, we automatically grouped aspect mentions based on their contexts as different aspect target words can still refer to the very same aspect category (e.g. "delicious food" and "nice dishes").

Clustering of aspect mentions was performed by determining a vector for each aspect term based on the words co-occurring with them. $6,485$ distinct lemmas were found to co-occur with any of the aspect phrases in the two databases, thus context vectors originally consisted of that many elements. Singular value decomposition was then used to project these aspect vectors into a lower dimensional 'semantic' space, where k-means clustering (with $k = 10$) was performed over the data points. For each classification instance, we regarded the cluster ID of the particular aspect term as a nominal feature.

3 Results

In this section, we will report our results on the shared task database which consists of English product reviews. There are $3,000$ laptop and restaurant related sentences, respectively. Aspects were annotated in these sentences, resulting in a total of $6,051$ annotated aspects. In our experiments, we used maximum entropy classifier with the default parameter settings of the Java-based machine learning framework MALLET (McCallum,).

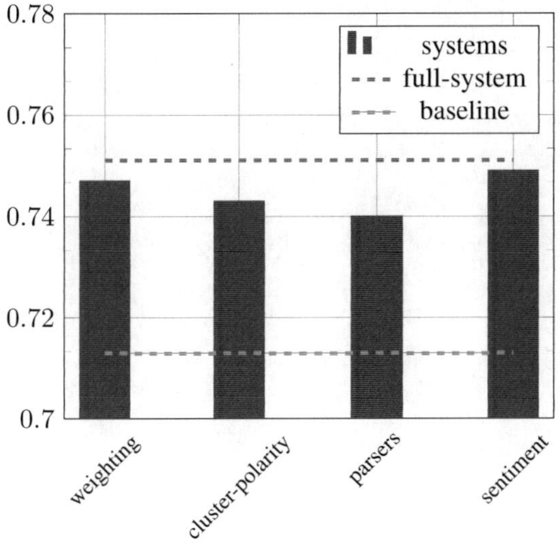

Figure 3: Accuracy on the restaurant test data.

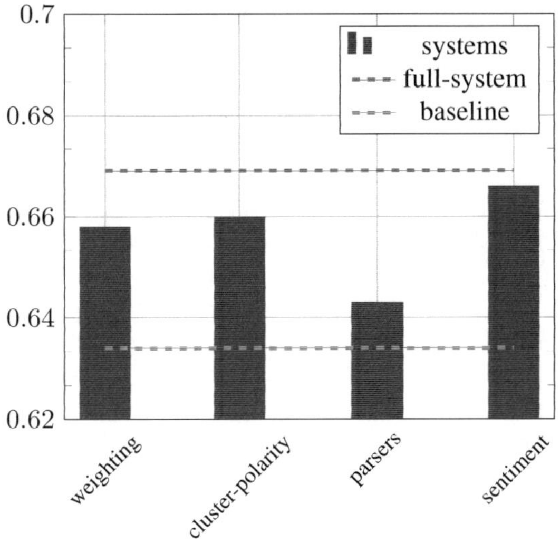

Figure 4: Accuracy on the laptop test data.

Our accuracy measured on the restaurant and laptop test databases can be seen on figures 3 and 4. On the x-axis the accuracy loss can be seen comparing to our *baseline* (n-gram features only) and *full-system*, while turning off various sets of features. Firstly, the *weighting* of n-gram features are absent, then features based on aspect clustering and words which indicate polarity in texts. Afterwards, features that are created using dependency and constituency parsing are turned off and lastly sentiment features based on the SentiWordNet lexicon are ignored. It can be seen that omitting the features based on parsing results in the most serious drop in performance. We achieved 1.1 and 2.6 error reduction on the restaurant and laptop test data using these features, respectively.

In Table 1 the results of several other participating teams can be seen on the restaurant and laptop test data. There were more than 30 submissions, from which we achieved the sixth and third best results on the restaurants and laptop domains, respectively. At the bottom of the table the official baselines for each domain can be seen.

Team	restaurant	laptop
DCU	0.809	0.704
NRC-Canada	0.801	0.704
SZTE-NLP	0.752	0.669
UBham	0.746	0.666
USF	0.731	0.645
ECNU	0.707	0.611
baseline	0.642	0.510

Table 1: Accuracy results of several other participants. Our system is named SZTE-NLP.

4 Conclusions

In this paper, we presented our contribution to the aspect term polarity subtask of the SemEval-2014 Task 4 – *Aspect Based Sentiment Analysis* challenge. We proposed a supervised machine learning technique that employs a rich feature set targeting aspect term polarity detection. Among the features designed here, the syntax-based feature group for the determination of the scopes of the aspect terms showed the highest contribution. In the end, our system was ranked as 6th and 3rd, achieving an 0.752 and 0.669 accuracies for the restaurant and laptop domains, respectively.

Acknowledgments

Viktor Hangya and István Varga were funded in part by the European Union and the European Social Fund through the project FuturICT.hu (TÁMOP-4.2.2.C-11/1/KONV-2012-0013).
Gábor Berend and Richárd Farkas was partially funded by the "Hungarian National Excellence Program" (TÁMOP 4.2.4.A/2-11-1-2012-0001), co-financed by the European Social Fund.

References

Stefano Baccianella, Andrea Esuli, and Fabrizio Sebastiani. 2010. SentiWordNet 3.0: An Enhanced Lexical Resource for Sentiment Analysis and Opinion Mining. In *Proceedings of the Seventh International Conference on Language Resources and Evaluation (LREC'10)*.

Bernd Bohnet. 2010. Top accuracy and fast dependency parsing is not a contradiction. In *Proceedings of the 23rd International Conference on Computational Linguistics (Coling 2010)*, pages 89–97, Beijing, China, August. Coling 2010 Organizing Committee.

Hakan Ceylan and Rada Mihalcea. 2011. An efficient indexer for large n-gram corpora. In *ACL (System Demonstrations)*, pages 103–108. The Association for Computer Linguistics.

Gayatree Ganu, Noemie Elhadad, and Amelie Marian. 2009. Beyond the stars: Improving rating predictions using review text content. In *WebDB*.

Viktor Hangya and Richard Farkas. 2013. Target-oriented opinion mining from tweets. In *Cognitive Infocommunications (CogInfoCom), 2013 IEEE 4th International Conference on*, pages 251–254. IEEE.

Dan Klein and Christopher D. Manning. 2003. Accurate unlexicalized parsing. In *Proceedings of the 41st ACL*, pages 423–430.

Andrew Kachites McCallum. Mallet: A machine learning for language toolkit.

Maria Pontiki, Dimitrios Galanis, John Pavlopoulos, Harris Papageorgiou, Ion Androutsopoulos, and Suresh Manandhar. 2014. Semeval-2014 task 4: Aspect based sentiment analysis. In *Proceedings of the International Workshop on Semantic Evaluation*, SemEval '14.

Richard Socher, Alex Perelygin, Jean Wu, Jason Chuang, Christopher D. Manning, Andrew Y. Ng, and Christopher Potts. In *Proceedings of the 2013 Conference on Empirical Methods in Natural Language Processing*, October.

SZTE-NLP: Clinical Text Analysis with Named Entity Recognition

Melinda Katona and Richárd Farkas
Department of Informatics
University of Szeged
Árpád tér 2., Szeged, 6720, Hungary
{mkatona,rfarkas}@inf.u-szeged.hu

Abstract

This paper introduces our contribution to the SemEval-2014 Task 7 on "Analysis of Clinical Text". We implemented a system which combines MetaMap taggings and Illinois NER Tagger. MetaMap is developed to link the text of medical documents to the knowledge embedded in UMLS Metathesaurus. The UMLS contains a very rich lexicon while the promise of a NER system is to carry out context-sensitive tagging. Our system's performance was 0.345 F-measure in terms of strict evaluation and 0.551 F-measure in terms of relaxed evaluation.

1 Introduction

Clinical notes and discharge summaries from the patient's medical history contain a huge amount of useful information for medical researchers and also for hospitals. The automatic identification of these unstructured information is an important task for analysis of free-text electronic health records. Natural Language Processing (NLP) techniques provide a solution to process clinical documents and to help patients understand the contents of their clinical records (Tang et al., 2012; Lee et al., 2004).

In this paper we introduce an approach which discovers mentions of disorders in the free-text of discharge summaries. The system participated in the *SemEval-2014 Task 7: Analysis of Clinical Text, Task A.*

Task A aims at the identifying of mention concepts that belong to the UMLS (Bodenreider, 2004) semantic group "disorders" and Task B is for mapping from each mention to a unique UMLS/SNOMED-CT CUI (Concept Unique Identifiers). Here are a few examples from the task description:

- The rhythm appears to be **atrial fibrillation.**

  „atrial fibrillation" is a mention of type disorders with CUI C0004238

- The **left atrium** is moderately **dilated.**

  „left atrium [...] dilated" is a mention of type disorders with CUI C0344720

- 53 year old man s/p **fall from ladder.**

  „fall from ladder" is a mention of type disorders with CUI C0337212

Many approaches have been published to solve these problems cf. (Skeppstedt et al., 2012; Pestian et al., 2007).

2 Approach

After a text-normalization step we run a Named Entity Recogniser (NER) on the documents. This NER model was trained on the training set of the shared task. It also employs a dictionary gathered from UMLS through MetaMap tagging. Our initial experiments revealed that MetaMap (Aronson and Lang, 2010) in its own gives a very poor precision hence we decided to investigate a NER approach which takes the context also into account.

2.1 Normalization

Clinical reports contain numerous special annotations, such as anonymized data (for example patient name), etc. We made the following steps to normalize texts:

- We removed the unnecessary characters, such as . , ! ? # : ; — = + * ^
- Then replaced the [****] anonymized tags with REPLACED_ANONYMOUS_DATA notation.

Proceedings of the 8th International Workshop on Semantic Evaluation (SemEval 2014), pages 615–618,
Dublin, Ireland, August 23-24, 2014.

2.2 UMLS Dictionary

Our NER system constructs features from dictionaries as well. We created a dictionary from UMLS with the help of MetaMap for incorporating external knowledge into the NER. The use of a specialized dictionary is important because it contains phrases that occur in clinical texts.

MetaMap (Aronson and Lang, 2010) is developed to link the text of medical documents to the knowledge embedded in UMLS Metathesaurus. MetaMap employs natural language processing techniques working at the lexical/syntactic levels, for example handling acronyms/abbrevations, POS tagging, word sense disambiguation and so on.

Both the test and training datasets were used for creating our dictionary. We used MetaMap to collect disorders from raw texts. After that, we removed the redundant and most frequently used common words, based on a list of the 5000 most frequent English words according to the Google's n-gram corpus[1].

2.3 Named Entity Recognition

In the task "Analysis of Clinical Text", our task is to recognize mentions of concepts that belong to the UMLS semantic group "disorder", which can be viewed as a subclass of named entities, so NER approach is effective for this assignment.

For training, we used the Illinois Named Entity Recognition (Ratinov and Roth, 2009) system. By default, Illinois NER contains Wikipedia gazetters and categories, but in this task, we need one or more dictionary which contains disorders and other clinical text terminology.

NER is typically viewed as a sequence labeling problem. The typical models include HMM (Rabiner, 1989), CRF (Lafferty et al., 2001) and sequential application of Perceptron or Winnow (Collins, 2002). Illinois NER has several inference algorithms: Viterbi, beamsearch, greedy left-to-right decoding. In our approach, we used beamsearch. The beamsize was 3. Initially, we used bigger beamsize, but our empirical studies showed that applying a small beamsize is more effective.

Beside the decoding algorithm, an important question that has been studied extensively in the context of shallow parsing which was somewhat overlooked in the NER literature is the representation of text segments. Illinois NER contains several representation schemes such as BIO and BILOU - two of the most popular schemes. The BIO scheme is employed to train classifiers that identify **B**eginning, the **I**nside and the **O**utside of the text segment. The BILOU scheme is employed to train classifiers that identify the **B**eginning, the **I**nside and the **L**ast tokens of multi-token chunks as well as **U**nit-length chunks. We used the BILOU scheme.

The key intuition behind non-local features in NER has been that identical tokens should have identical label assignments. Ratinov and Roth (2009) consider three approaches proposed in the literature namely context aggregation, two-stage prediction aggregation and extended prediction history. The combination of these approaches is more stable and better than any approach taken alone.

In our experiments we used the combination of context aggregation and two-stage prediction aggregation. Context aggregation is the following approach in Illinois NER: for each token instance x_i we used the tokens in the window of size two around it as features: $c_i = x_{i-2}, x_{i-1}, x_i, x_{i+1}, x_{i+2}$. If the same token ($t$) appears in several locations in the text for each instance x_{i_j} (x_{i_1}, x_{i_2}, ..., x_{i_N}). We also aggregated the context across all instances within 200 tokens.

Context aggregation as done above can lead to an excessive number of features. Some instances of a token appear in easily-identifiable contexts. The resulting predictions were used as features at a second level of inference. This is a two-stage prediction aggregation.

3 Experimental Results

Our system was developed and trained only on the training set provided by the organizers and was evaluated on the test set. The performance was evaluated by Precision, Recall and F-measure in both "strict" and "relaxed" modes. "Strict" means that a concept is recognized correctly if the starting and ending offsets are the same as in gold standard and "relaxed" means that a disorder mention is correctly recognized as long as it overlaps with the gold standard disorder mention.

3.1 Dataset

For training and testing, we used the datasets provided by the shared task organisers. The train-

[1] http://storage.googleapis.com/books/ngrams/books/datasetsv2.html

	Strict			Relaxed		
	P	R	F	P	R	F
original NER	0.508	0.225	0.312	0.874	0.378	0.528
NER with normalization	0.509	0.229	0.316	0.875	0.383	0.528
NER with normalization and full dictionary	0.512	0.226	0.313	0.878	0.378	0.533
NER with normalization and filtered dictionary	0.516	0.232	0.320	0.890	0.390	0.542

Table 1: Evaluation results of our system on the training set (**P** - Precision, **R** - Recall, **F** - F-score).

ing dataset contains of 398 notes from different clinical documents including radiology reports, discharge summaries, and ECG/ECHO reports. For each note, disorder entities were annotated based on a pre-defined guideline and then mapped to SNOMED-CT concepts represented by UMLS CUIs. The reference UMLS version was 2012AB. If a disorder entity could not be found, it was marked as CUI-less, otherwise marked with CUI identifier.

The training set was used for system development, and we evaluated the system on the test set of 133 notes.

3.2 Results

We examined the contribution of our systems' steps. Table 1 summarizes the results where the first column contains result of named entity tagger without any modification. Normalization gave only a marginal improvement in accuracy. Next, we employed all MetaMap matches as a feature for the NER module. This decreased recall, because NER identified a lot of unnecessary expression. In our final and submitted system, we filtered this dictionary as described in the previous section.

Lastly, Table 2 shows our official evaluation results.

	Strict	Relaxed
Precision	0.547	0.884
Recall	0.252	0.401
F-score	0.345	0.551

Table 2: Results of our submission on the test set.

4 Error Analysis

In both strict and relaxed evaluation modes, precision is high but recall is low. We have found three important source of errors:

- multiple meaning words
- unknown disorders
- discontinuous phrases

A named entity tagger with context-aggregation mode does not monitor multiple meanings, so if a word has more occurrence, but in other meaning, it will be a bad tagging. For example

*"**Seizure-like** activity with clamped jaw and left lip twitching was then noted after several days of treatment. [...] Despite these therapies, she failed to recover, and began to show further signs of increasing intracranial pressure with increasing **seizure** activity and posturing [...]"*

Our sequence labeling approach cannot recognize discontinuous phrases. Even when every token was marked, we took only continuous sequences as named entity mentions. For example the sentence

*"The left **ventricular cavity** is moderately **dilated**."*

yields three errors in the strict evaluation scenario. We did not recognise the three token-long phrase while predicted two false positive mentions. We also note that this shortcoming of our approach is the reason for the huge difference between the achieved strict and relaxed scores.

The last error category is unrecognised disorders. For instance,

*"The PICC line was trimmed to the appropriate length and advanced over the 0.018 wire with the tip int the **axillary vein**"*

Named entity tagger identified hepatitis B, but hepatitis C not because dictionary does not contain it. Expansion of dictionary increase accuracy.

5 Conclusion

In this paper we examined a machine learning based disorder recognition system using MetaMap and Illinois Named Entity Recognition. Illinois NER uses different dictionaries for training. We created a new filtered in-domain dictionary and we showed that this dictionary is an important factor for accuracy. The results achieved on the training set and the test set show that the proposed clinical dictionary creation procedure is efficient.

Acknowledgements

Melinda Katona is supported by the European Union and co-funded by the European Social Fund. Project title: "Telemedicine-focused research activities on the field of Matematics, Informatics and Medical sciences" (project number: TÁMOP-4.2.2.A-11/1/KONV-2012-0073). Richárd Farkas was partially funded by the "Hungarian National Excellence Program" (TÁMOP 4.2.4.A/2-11-1-2012-0001), co-financed by the European Social Fund.

References

Alan R. Aronson and Franois-Michel Lang. 2010. An Overview of MetaMap: Historical Perspective and Recent Advances. *JAMIA*, 17:229–236.

Olivier Bodenreider. 2004. The Unified Medical Language System (UMLS): Integrating Biomedical Terminology. *Nucleic Acids Research*, 32:267–270.

Michael Collins. 2002. Discriminative Training Methods for Hidden Markov Models: Theory and Experiments with Perceptron Algorithms. In *Proceedings of the ACL-02 Conference on Empirical Methods in Natural Language Processing - Volume 10*, pages 1 – 8.

John D. Lafferty, Andrew McCallum, and Fernando C. N. Pereira. 2001. Conditional Random Fields: Probabilistic Models for Segmenting and Labeling Sequence Data. In *Proceedings of the Eighteenth International Conference on Machine Learning*, pages 282 – 289.

Chih Lee, Wen-Juan Hou, and Hsin-Hsi Chen. 2004. Annotating Multiple Types of Biomedical Entities: A Single Word Classification Approach. In *Proceedings of the International Joint Workshop on Natural Language Processing in Biomedicine and Its Applications*, JNLPBA '04, pages 80–83.

John P. Pestian, Christopher Brew, Pawel Matykiewicz, D. J. Hovermale, Neil Johnson, K. Bretonnel Cohen, and Wlodzislaw Duch. 2007. A Shared Task Involving Multi-label Classification of Clinical Free Text. In *Proceedings of the Workshop on BioNLP 2007: Biological, Translational, and Clinical Language Processing*, pages 97–104.

Lawrence Rabiner. 1989. A Tutorial on Hidden Markov Models and Selected Applications in Speech recognition. *Proceedings of the IEEE*, 77:257–286.

L. Ratinov and D. Roth. 2009. Design Challenges and Misconceptions in Named Entity Recognition. In *CoNLL*, 6.

Maria Skeppstedt, Maria Kvist, and Hercules Dalianis. 2012. Rule-based Entity Recognition and Coverage of SNOMED CT in Swedish Clinical Text. In *Proceedings of the Eight International Conference on Language Resources and Evaluation (LREC'12)*.

Buzhou Tang, Hongxin Cao, Yonghui Wu, Min Jiang, and Hua Xu. 2012. Clinical Entity Recognition Using Structural Support Vector Machines with Rich Features. In *Proceedings of the ACM Sixth International Workshop on Data and Text Mining in Biomedical Informatics*, DTMBIO '12, pages 13–20.

TCDSCSS: Dimensionality Reduction to Evaluate Texts of Varying Lengths - an IR Approach

Arun Jayapal
Dept of Computer Science
Trinity College Dublin
jayapala@cs.tcd.ie

Martin Emms
Dept of Computer Science
Trinity College Dublin
martin.emms@cs.tcd.ie

John D.Kelleher
School of Computing
Dublin Institute of Technology
john.d.kelleher@dit.ie

Abstract

This paper provides system description of the cross-level semantic similarity task for the SEMEVAL-2014 workshop. Cross-level semantic similarity measures the degree of relatedness between texts of varying lengths such as *Paragraph to Sentence* and *Sentence to Phrase*. *Latent Semantic Analysis* was used to evaluate the cross-level semantic relatedness between the texts to achieve above baseline scores, tested on the training and test datasets. We also tried using a bag-of-vectors approach to evaluate the semantic relatedness. This bag-of-vectors approach however did not produced encouraging results.

1 Introduction

Semantic relatedness between texts have been dealt with in multiple situations earlier. But it is not usual to measure the semantic relatedness of texts of varying lengths such as *Paragraph to Sentence* (P2S) and *Sentence to Phrase* (S2P). This task will be useful in natural language processing applications such as *paraphrasing* and *summarization*. The working principle of information retrieval system is the motivation for this task, where the queries are not of equal lengths compared to the documents in the index. We attempted two ways to measure the semantic similarity for P2S and S2P in a scale of 0 to 4, 4 meaning both texts are similar and 0 being dissimilar. The first one is Latent Semantic Analysis (LSA) and second, a bag-of-vecors (BV) approach. An example of target similarity ratings for comparison type *S2P* is provided in table 1.

Sentence: *Schumacher was undoubtedly one of the very greatest racing drivers there has ever been, a man who was routinely, on every lap, able to dance on a limit accessible to almost no-one else.*

Score	Phrase
4	the unparalleled greatness of Schumachers driving abilities
3	driving abilities
2	formula one racing
1	north-south highway
0	orthodontic insurance

Table 1: An Example - *Sentence to Phrase* similarity ratings for each scale

2 Data

The task organizers provided training data, which included 500 pairs of *P2S*, *S2P*, *Phrase to Word* (P2W) and their similarity scores. The training data for *P2S* and *S2P* included text from different genres such as Newswire, Travel, Metaphoric and Reviews. In the training data for *P2S*, newswire text constituted 36% of the data, while reviews constituted 10% of the data and rest of the three genres shared 54% of the data.

Considering the different genres provided in the training data, a chunk of data provided for NIST TAC's Knowledge Base Population was used for building a term-by-document matrix on which to base the LSA method. The data included newswire text and web-text, where the web-text included data mostly from blogs. We used 2343 documents from the NIST dataset[1], which were available in eXtended Markup Language format.

Further to the NIST dataset, all the paragraphs in the training data[2] of *paragraph to sentence* were added to the dataset. To add these paragraphs to the dataset, we converted each paragraph into a

[1]Distributed by LDC (Linguistic Data Consortium)
[2]provided by the SEMEVAL task-3 organizers

Proceedings of the 8th International Workshop on Semantic Evaluation (SemEval 2014), pages 619–623,
Dublin, Ireland, August 23-24, 2014.

new document and the documents were added to the corpus. The unique number of words identified in the corpus were approximately 40000.

3 System description

We tried two different approaches for evaluating the P2S and S2P. Latent Semantic Analysis (LSA) using SVD worked better than the Bag-of-Vectors (BV) approach. The description of both the approaches are discussed in this section.

3.1 Latent Semantic Analysis

LSA has been used for information retrieval allowing retrieval via vectors over latent, arguably conceptual, dimensions, rather than over surface word dimensions (Deerwester et al., 1990). It was thought this would be of advantage for comparison of texts of varying length.

3.1.1 Representation

The data corpus was converted into a mxn term-by-document matrix, A, where the counts ($c_{m,n}$) of all terms (w_m) in the corpus are represented in rows and the respective documents (d_n) in columns:

$$A = \begin{array}{c} \\ w_1 \\ w_2 \\ \vdots \\ w_m \end{array} \begin{array}{c} \begin{array}{cccc} d_1 & d_2 & \cdots & d_n \end{array} \\ \begin{pmatrix} c_{1,1} & c_{1,2} & \cdots & c_{1,n} \\ c_{2,1} & c_{2,2} & \cdots & c_{2,n} \\ \vdots & \vdots & \ddots & \vdots \\ c_{m,1} & c_{m,2} & \cdots & c_{m,n} \end{pmatrix} \end{array}$$

The document indexing rules such as text tokenization, case standardization, stop words removal, token stemming, and special characters and punctuations removal were followed to get the matrix A.

Singular Value Decomposition (SVD) decomposes the matrix into U, Σ and V matrices (ie., $A = U\Sigma V^T$) such that U and V are orthonormal matrices and Σ is a diagonal matrix with singular values. Retaining just the first k columns of U and V, gives an approximation of A

$$A \approx A_k = U_k \Sigma_k V_k^T \tag{1}$$

According to LSA, the columns of U_k are thought of as representing latent, *semantic* dimensions, and an arbitrary m-dimensional vector $\vec{v}$ can be projected onto this semantic space by taking the dot-product with each column of U_k; we will call the result $\overrightarrow{v_{sem}}$.

In the experiments reported later, the m-dimensional vector $\vec{v}$ is sometimes a vector of word counts, and sometimes a thresholded or 'boolean' version, mapping all non-zero numbers to 1.

3.1.2 Similarity Calculation

To evaluate the similarity of a paragraph, p, and a sentence, s, first these are represented as vectors of word counts, $\vec{p}$ and $\vec{s}$, then these are projected in the latent semantic space, to give $\overrightarrow{p_{sem}}$ and $\overrightarrow{s_{sem}}$, and then between these the cosine similarity metric is calculated:

$$cos(\overrightarrow{p_{sem}}.\overrightarrow{s_{sem}}) = \frac{\overrightarrow{p_{sem}}.\overrightarrow{s_{sem}}}{|\overrightarrow{p_{sem}}|.|\overrightarrow{s_{sem}}|} \tag{2}$$

The cosine similarity metric provides a similarity value in the range of 0 to 1, so to match the target range of 0 to 4, the cosine values were multiplied by 4. Exactly the same procedure is used for the sentence to phrase comparison.

Further, the number of retained dimensions of U_k was varied, giving different dimensionalities of the LSA space. The results of testing at the reduced dimensions are discussed in 4.1

3.2 Bag-of-Vectors

Another method we experimented on could be termed a 'bag-of-vectors' (BV) approach: each word in an item to be compared is replaced by a vector representing its co-occurrence behavior and the obtained bags of vectors enter into the comparison process.

3.2.1 Representation

For the BV approach, the same data sources as was used for the LSA approach is turned into a $m \times m$ term-by-term co-occurrence matrix C:

$$C = \begin{array}{c} \\ w_1 \\ w_2 \\ \vdots \\ w_m \end{array} \begin{array}{c} \begin{array}{cccc} w_1 & w_2 & \cdots & w_m \end{array} \\ \begin{pmatrix} c_{1,1} & c_{1,2} & \cdots & c_{1,m} \\ c_{2,1} & c_{2,2} & \cdots & c_{2,m} \\ \vdots & \vdots & \ddots & \vdots \\ c_{m,1} & c_{m,2} & \cdots & c_{m,m} \end{pmatrix} \end{array}$$

The same preprocessing steps as for the LSA approach applied (text tokenization, case standardization, stop words removal, special characters and punctuations removal). Via C, if one has a bag-of-words representing a paragraph, sentence or phrase, one can replace it by a bag-of-vectors, replacing each word w_i by the corresponding row of C – we will call these rows word-vectors.

3.2.2 Similarity Calculation

For calculating P2S similarity, the procedure is as follows. The paragraph and sentence are tokenized, and stop-words were removed and are represented as two vectors $\vec{p}$ and $\vec{s}$.

For each word p_i from $\vec{p}$, its word vector from C is found, and this is compared to the word vector for each word s_i in $\vec{s}$, via the cosine measure. The highest similarity score for each word p_i in $\vec{p}$ is stored in a vector $\vec{S_p}$ shown in (3). The overall semantic similarity score between paragraph and sentence is then the mean value of the vector $\vec{S_p} \times 4$ – see (4).

$$S_p = \begin{bmatrix} S_{p_1} & S_{p_2} & \cdots & S_{p_i} \end{bmatrix} \quad (3)$$

$$S_{sim} = \frac{\sum_{i=1}^{n} S_{p_i}}{n} \times 4 \quad (4)$$

Exactly corresponding steps are carried out for the *S2P* similarity. Although experiments were carried out this particular BV approach, the results were not encouraging. Details of the experiments carried out are explained in 4.2.

4 Experiments

Different experiments were carried out using LSA and BV systems described in sections 3.1 and 3.2 on the dataset described in section 2. Pearson correlation and Spearman's rank correlation were the metrics used to evaluate the performance of the systems. Pearson correlation provides the degree of similarity between the system's score for each pair and the gold standard's score for the said pair while Spearman's rank correlation provides the degree of similarity between the rankings of the pairs according to similarity.

4.1 LSA

The LSA model was used to evaluate the semantic similarity between *P2S* and *S2P*.

4.1.1 Paragraph to Sentence

An initial word-document matrix A was built by extracting tokens just based on spaces, stop words removed and tokens sorted in alphabetical order. As described in 3.1.1, via the SVD of A, a matrix U_k is obtained which can be used to project an m dimensional vector into a k dimensional one. In one setting the paragraph and sentence vectors which are projected into the LSA space have unique word counts for their dimensions. In another setting before projection, these vectors are thresholded into 'boolean' versions, with 1 for every non-zero count.

Dimensions	100%	90%	50%	30%	10%
Basic word-doc representation	0.499	-	0.494	0.484	0.426
Evaluation-boolean counts	0.548	-	0.533	0.511	0.420
Constrained tokenization	0.368	0.564	0.540	0.516	0.480
Added data	0.461	0.602	0.568	0.517	0.522

Table 2: Pearson scores at different dimensions - *Paragraph to Sentence*

The Pearson scores for these settings are in the first and second rows of table 2. They show the variation with the number of dimensions of the LSA representation (that is the number of columns of U that are kept)[3]. An observation is that the usage of boolean values instead of word counts showed improved results.

Further experiments were conducted, retaining the boolean treatment of the vectors to be projected. In a new setting, further improvements were made to the pre-processing step, creating a new word-document matrix A using constrained tokenization rules, removing unnecessary spaces and tabs, and tokens stemmed[4]. The performance of the similarity calculation is shown as the third row of Table 2: there is a trend of increase in correlation scores with respect to the increase in dimensionality up to a maximum of 0.564, reached at 90% dimension.

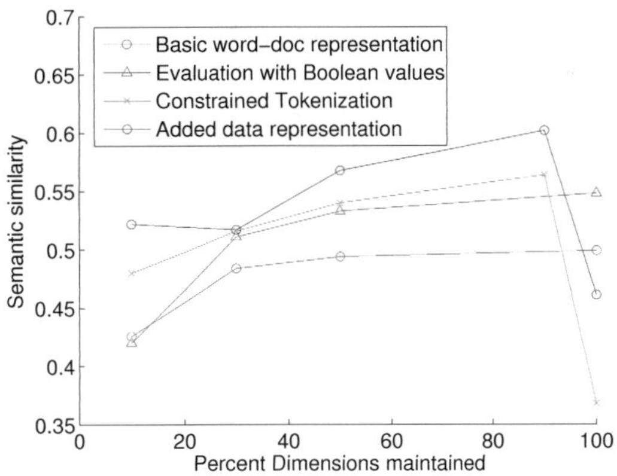

Figure 1: Paragraph to Sentence - Pearson correlation scores for four different experiments at different dimensions[3] (represented in percent) of U_k

Not convinced with the pearson scores, more

[3]Here, the dimension $X\%$ means $k = (X/100) \times N$, where N is the total number of columns in A in the unreduced SVD.

[4]Stemmed using Porter Stemmer module availabe from http://tartarus.org/~martin/PorterStemmer/

documents were added to the dataset to build a new word-document matrix representation A. The documents included all the paragraphs from the training set. Each paragraph provided in the training set was added to the dataset as a separate document. The experiment was performed maintaining the settings from the previous experiment and the results are shown in the fourth row of table 2. The increase in trend of correlation scores with respect to the increase in dimensionality is followed by the new U produced from A after applying SVD. Figure 2 provides the distribution of similarity scores evaluated at 90% dimension of the model with respect to the gold standard.

Further to compare the performance of different experiments, all the experiment results are plotted in Figure 1. It can be observed that every subsequent model built has shown improvements in performance. The first two experiments shown in the first two rows of table 2 are shown in red and blue lines in the figure. It can be observed that in both the settings, the pearson correlation scores were increasing as the the number of dimensions maintained also increased, whereas in the other two settings, the pearson correlation scores reached their maximum at 90% and came down at 100% dimension, which is unexpected and so is not justified. It is observed from Figure 2 that the scores

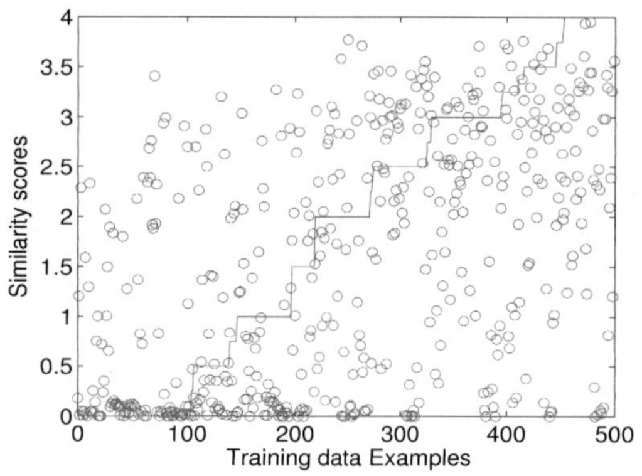

Figure 2: Semantic similarity scores - Gold standard (Line plot) vs System scores (Scatter plot) for examples in training data

of the system in scatter plot are not always clustered around the gold standard scores, plotted as a line. As the gold standard score goes up, the system prediction accuracy has come down. One reason for this pattern can be attributed to the training set which had data mostly data from Newswire

Dimensions	100%	90%	70%	50%	30%	10%
Basic word-doc representation	0.493	-	-	0.435	0.423	0.366
Evaluation boolean counts	0.472	-	-	0.449	0.430	0.363
Constrained tokenization	0.498	0.494	0.517	0.485	0.470	0.434
Added data	0.493	0.504	0.498	0.498	0.488	0.460

Table 3: Pearson scores at different dimensions[3]- *Sentence to Phrase*

and webtext. Therefore, during evaluation all the words from paragraph and/or sentence would not have got a position while getting projected on the latent semantic space, which we believe has pulled down the accuracy.

4.1.2 Sentence to Phrase

The experiments carried out for *P2S* provided in 4.1.1 were conducted for *S2P* examples as well. The pearson scores produced by different experiments at different dimensions are provided in table 3. This table shows that the latest word-document representation made with added documents, did not have any impact on the correlation scores, while the earlier word-document representation provided in 3rd row, which used the original dataset preprocessed with constrained tokenization rules, removing unnecessary spaces and tabs, and tokens stemmed, provided better correlation score at 70% dimension. Further the comparison of different experiments carried out at different settings are plotted in Figure 3.

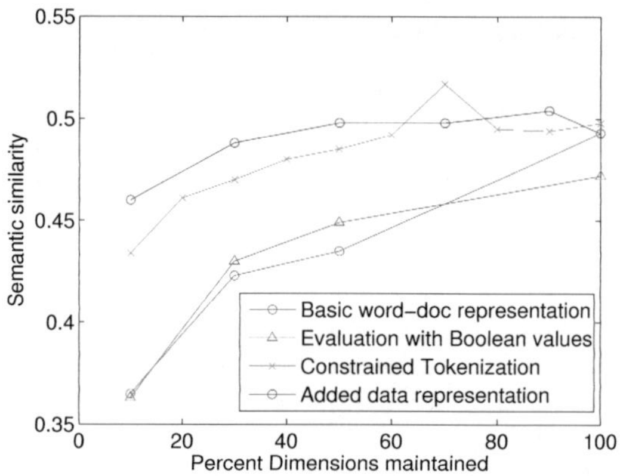

Figure 3: Sentence to Phrase - Pearson correlation scores for four different experiments at different dimensions[3] (represented in percentage) of U_k

4.2 Bag of Vectors

BV was tested in two different settings. The first representation was created with bi-gram co-occurance count as mentioned in section 3.2.1 and experiments were carried out as mentioned in section 3.2.2. This produced negative Pearson correlation scores for *P2S* and *S2P*. Then we created another representation by getting co-occurance count in a window of 6 words in a sentence, on evaluation produced correlation scores of 0.094 for *P2S* and 0.145 for *S2P*. As BV showed strong negative results, we did not continue using the method for evaluating the test data. But we strongly believe that the BV approach can produce better results if we could compare the sentence to the paragraph rather than the paragraph to the sentence as mentioned in section 3.2.2. During similarity calculation, when comparing sentence to the paragraph, for each word in the sentence, we look for the best semantic match from the paragraph, which would increase the mean value by reducing the number of divisions representing the number of words in the sentence. In the current setting, it is believed that while computing the similarity for the paragraph to sentence, the words in the paragraph (longer text) will consider a few words in the sentence to be similar multiple times. This could not be right when we compare the texts of varying lengths.

5 Conclusion and Discussion

On manual verification, it was identified that the dataset used to build the representation did not have documents related to the genres Metaphoric, CQA and Travel. The original dataset mostly had documents from Newswire text and blogs which included reviews as well. Further, it can be identified from tables 2 and 3, the word-document representation with added documents from the training set improved Pearson scores. This allowed to assume that the dataset did not have completely relevant set of documents to evaluate the training set which included data from different genres. For evaluation of the model on test data, we submitted two runs and best of them reported Pearson score of 0.607 and 0.552 on *P2S* and *S2P* respectively. In the future work, we should be able to experiment with more relevant data to build the model using LSI and also use statistically strong unsupervised classifier pLSI (Hofmann T, 2001) for the same task. Further to this, as discussed in 4.2 we would be able to experiment with the BV approach by comparing the sentence to the paragraph, which we believe will yield promising results to compare the texts of varying lengths.

References

Scott Deerwester, Susan T. Dumais, George W. Furnas, Thomas K. Landauer and Richard Harshman 1990. *Indexing by latent semantic analysis* Journal of the American society for information science, 41(6):391–401

Thomas Hofmann 2001. *Unsupervised Learning by Probabilistic Latent Semantic Analysis* Journal Machine Learning, Volume 42 Issue 1-2, January-February 2001 Pages 177 - 196

Team Z: Wiktionary as a L2 Writing Assistant

Anubhav Gupta
UFR SLHS
Université de Franche-Comté
anubhav.gupta@edu.univ-fcomte.fr

Abstract

This paper presents a word-for-word translation approach using Wiktionary for SemEval-2014 Task 5. The language pairs attempted for this task were English-Spanish and English-German. Since this approach did not take context into account, it performed poorly.

1 Introduction

The objective of SemEval-2014 Task 5 is to translate a few words or a phrase from one language (L1) into another (L2). More specifically, a sentence containing primarily L2 and a few L1 words is provided, and the task is to translate the L1 words into the L2. This task is similar to the previous cross-linguistic SemEval tasks involving lexical substitution (Mihalcea et al., 2010) and word-sense disambiguation (Lefever and Hoste, 2013).

For example, consider the following sentence, written entirely in German except for one English word: *Aber auf diesem Schiff wollen wir auch Ruderer sein, wir sitzen im selben Boot und wollen mit Ihnen **row***. Here, the word **row** is polysemous and can be translated as the verb **rudern** or as the noun **Reihe** depending on context. The words to be translated can also form an idiomatic expression, such as **in exchange** in *die 1967 eroberten arabischen Gebiete **in exchange** gegen Frieden.* These examples reveal that this is not a straightforward task, as word-for-word translation may give inaccurate results.

Wiktionary is a multilingual dictionary containing word-sense, examples, sample quotations, collocations, usage notes, proverbs and translations (Torsten et al., 2008; Meyer and Gurevych, 2012). Since Wiktionary data have previously been used for translations (Orlandi and Passant, 2010), it was chosen for looking up the translation of source language (L1) words. However, the translation approach was word-for-word and ignored the target language (L2) context, i.e., the context in which the text fragment to be translated is found. The Wiktionary-based solution is for English-to-Spanish and English-to-German language translation though four language pairs were provided in this shared task.

2 Wiktionary

For a given word, the English version of Wiktionary gives not only its definition but also possible translations. The translations are divided based on part of speech (PoS) and word sense and at times also encode gender and number information. For example, the German and Spanish translations for the English word **book** are stored in Wiktionary as follows:

```
====Noun====
{{en-noun}}

=====Translations=====
{{trans-top|collection of sheets
of paper bound together
containing printed or written
material}}
* German: {{t+|de|Buch|n}}
* Spanish: {{t+|es|libro|m}}

{{trans-top|record of betting}}
* German: {{t|de|Wettliste|f}}
{{trans-top|convenient collection
of small paper items, such as
stamps}}
* German: {{t+|de|Album|n}}
* Spanish: {{t+|es|álbum|m}}

{{trans-top|major division of
a published work, larger than
```


Proceedings of the 8th International Workshop on Semantic Evaluation (SemEval 2014), pages 624–627,
Dublin, Ireland, August 23-24, 2014.

```
a chapter}}

{{trans-top|script of a musical}}
* Spanish: {{t+|es|libreto|m}}

{{trans-top|usually in plural:
records of the accounts of
a business}}
* German: {{t+|de|Bücher|n-p}}

{{trans-top|ebook}}
* German: {{t+|de|E-Book|n}}

====Verb====
{{en-verb}}

=====Translations=====
{{trans-top|to reserve}}
* German: {{t+|de|buchen}},
{{t+|de|reservieren}}
* Spanish: {{t|es|reservar}}

{{trans-top|to write down,
register, record}}
* German: {{t+|de|notieren}},
{{t+|de|schreiben}}
* Spanish: {{t+|es|anotar}}

{{trans-top|to record the details
of}}
* {{ttbc|de}}: {{t+|de|bestrafen}}

{{trans-top|sports: to issue with
a caution}}

{{trans-top|slang: to travel
very fast}}
* German: {{t+|de|rasen}}
* {{ttbc|es}}: {{t|es|multar}}
```

The Wiktionary dump[1] is an XML file containing the word in the `<title>` tag and its description under the `<text>` tag. The translation of the word is indicated by `{{t|` or `{{t+|` followed by two letters to denote the target language (*es* for Spanish and *de* for German). This is followed by the translation and gender information in the case of nouns.

The information in Wiktionary was converted into a multidimensional hash table consisting of English words as key and PoS and translations in Spanish and German as the values. This table was used to look up the translations for the task.

Wiktionary also contains lists of the 10000 most frequent words in Spanish and of the 2000 most frequent words in German. This information was used to sort the target language words in the hash table in decreasing order of frequency. The translations absent from these frequency lists were kept in the hash table in the order that they were extracted from Wiktionary.

[1]For this task the 17 Dec 2013 version was used.

3 Translation

TreeTagger PoS	Wiktionary PoS
DT	Determiner, Article
NC, NN, NNS	Noun
IN, TO	Preposition
VB, VBG,VBZ, MD	Verb
RB, RBR, RP, WRB	Adverb
CD	Numeral
CC	Conjunction
PP, PRP, WP	Pronoun
JJ, JJS	Adjective

Table 1: PoS Mapping

The TreeTagger (Schmid, 1994) was used to parse the English (L1) phrases to obtain the PoS of each word along with the lemma. The PoS tags returned by the TreeTagger were mapped to the PoS used in Wiktionary as shown in Table 1. The word and its PoS were searched for in the hash table. If the translation was not found, then the lemma and its PoS were looked up. If the lemma lookup also failed then the phrase was not translated.

Once the L2 words were obtained for all the L1 words in the phrase, the L2 words were matched based on the gender and number information provided. For example, for the phrase **this question**, Wiktionary offered **este | m** and **esta | f** as Spanish translations of **this**, and **interrogante | m pregunta | f duda | f cuestión | f incógnita | f** for **question**. The translations were paired based on gender agreement rules (e.g. *este interrogante*, where both are masculine, and *esta pregunta*, where both are feminine) and provided as solutions.

3.1 Rules for English-to-Spanish Translation

Wiktionary only provides translations for the citation form of a word (even though other forms exist in WIktionary as valid entries), which is prob-

Language Pair	Dataset	Approach	Evaluation	Accuracy	Word Accuracy	Recall
en-es	Trial	Word-by-Word	Best	0.278	0.372	0.876
			Oof	0.382	0.471	0.876
		Word-by-Word + Rules	Best	0.340	0.434	0.844
			Oof	0.444	0.535	0.844
	Test	Word-by-Word	Best	0.200	0.308	0.785
			Oof	0.246	0.356	0.785
		Word-by-Word + Rules	Best	0.223	0.333	0.751
			Oof	0.277	0.386	0.751
en-de	Trial	Word-by-Word	Best	0.210	0.306	0.900
			Oof	0.316	0.422	0.900
	Test	**Word-by-Word**	Best	0.218	0.293	0.851
			Oof	0.307	0.385	0.851

Table 2: Performance of the System.

lematic when translating plural nouns or conjugated (finite) verbs. Lack of this inflectional information degraded the overall performance of both English-to-Spanish and English-to-German translations. Two rules were included in an attempt to improve the English-to-Spanish translations: (1) plural nouns and adjectives were formed by adding **-s** or **-es**, and (2) where a noun was preceded by an adjective in a L1 phrase, after the translation, the positions of the noun and the adjective were switched to respect the noun-adjective word order that is more commonly found in Spanish.

4 Results and Conclusions

Table 2 shows the performance of the system for the English-to-Spanish and English-to-German translations. The approach in bold was submitted for evaluation. The accuracy refers to the percentage of the fragments that were predicted accurately, whereas word accuracy measures the partially correct solutions. For each fragment, up to 5 translations could be submitted with one considered as the best answer and the rest regarded as alternatives. The *best* evaluation considered only the best answers. On the other hand, *oof* (out-of-five) evaluation considered the alternative answers to calculate the scores if the best answer was incorrect.

A context-independent, word-for-word translation approach to L2 Writing Assistant was proposed. The mediocre performance was due to the fact the approach was very basic. The system can be significantly improved by using the Spanish and German versions of Wiktionary to make up for the translations missing from the English version and by considering the L2 context provided. One such example in the German Wiktionary is the `{{Charakteristische Wortkombinationen}}` tag, which refers to the possible collocations. For example, one of the translations of the English word **exchange** in German is **Austausch**, which is most often collocated with **im** or **als**. Also, using a tool like JWKTL[2] would improve the quality of information extracted from Wiktionary.

References

Els Lefever and Véronique Hoste. 2013. SemEval-2013 Task 10: Cross-lingual Word Sense Disambiguation. In *Proceedings of the Seventh International Workshop on Semantic Evaluation (SemEval 2013)*. Atlanta, Georgia, USA.

Christian M. Meyer and Iryna Gurevych. 2012. Wiktionary: A New Rival for Expert-Built Lexicons? Exploring the Possibilities of Collaborative Lexicography. In *Electronic Lexicography*, edited by Sylviane Granger and Magali Paquot, 259–91. Oxford: Oxford University Press.

Rada Mihalcea, Ravi Sinha, and Diana McCarthy. 2010. Semeval 2010 Task 2: Cross-lingual Lexical Substitution. In *Proceedings of the 5th International Workshop on Semantic Evaluations (SemEval-2010)*. Uppsala, Sweden.

Fabrizio Orlandi and Alexandre Passant. 2010. Semantic Search on Heterogeneous Wiki Systems. In *Proceedings of the 6th International Symposium on Wikis and Open Collaboration*, 4:1–4:10. WikiSym '10. New York, NY, USA: ACM.

Helmut Schmid. 1994. Probabilistic Part-of-Speech Tagging Using Decision Trees. In *Proceedings of*

[2]https://code.google.com/p/jwktl/

International Conference on New Methods in Language Processing. Manchester, UK.

Torsten Zesch, Christof Müller, and Iryna Gurevych. 20008. Extracting Lexical Semantic Knowledge from Wikipedia and Wiktionary. In *Proceedings of the 6th International Conference on Language Resources and Evaluation*. Marrakech, Morocco.

TeamX: A Sentiment Analyzer with Enhanced Lexicon Mapping and Weighting Scheme for Unbalanced Data

Yasuhide Miura
Fuji Xerox Co., Ltd. / Japan
yasuhide.miura@fujixerox.co.jp

Shigeyuki Sakaki
Fuji Xerox Co., Ltd. / Japan
sakaki.shigeyuki@fujixerox.co.jp

Keigo Hattori
Fuji Xerox Co., Ltd. / Japan
keigo.hattori@fujixerox.co.jp

Tomoko Ohkuma
Fuji Xerox Co., Ltd. / Japan
ohkuma.tomoko@fujixerox.co.jp

Abstract

This paper describes the system that has been used by TeamX in SemEval-2014 Task 9 Subtask B. The system is a sentiment analyzer based on a supervised text categorization approach designed with following two concepts. Firstly, since lexicon features were shown to be effective in SemEval-2013 Task 2, various lexicons and pre-processors for them are introduced to enhance lexical information. Secondly, since a distribution of sentiment on tweets is known to be unbalanced, an weighting scheme is introduced to bias an output of a machine learner. For the test run, the system was tuned towards Twitter texts and successfully achieved high scoring results on Twitter data, average F_1 70.96 on Twitter2014 and average F_1 56.50 on Twitter2014Sarcasm.

1 Introduction

The growth of social media has brought a rising interest to make natural language technologies that work with informal texts. Sentiment analysis is one such technology, and several workshops such as SemEval-2013 Task 2 (Nakov et al., 2013), CLEF 2013 RepLab 2013 (Amigó et al., 2013), and TASS 2013 (Villena-Román and García-Morera, 2013) have recently targeted tweets or cell phone messages as analysis text. This paper describes a system that has submitted a sentiment analysis result to Subtask B of SemEval-2014 Task9 (Rosenthal et al., 2014). SemEval-2014 Task9 is a rerun of SemEval-2013 Task 2 with different test data, and Subtask B is a task of message polarity classification.

The system we prepared is a sentiment analyzer based on a supervised text categorization approach. Various features and their extraction methods are integrated in the system following the works presented in SemEval-2013 Task 2. Additionally to these features, we assembled following notable functionalities to the system:

1. Processes to enhance word-to-lemma mapping.
   (a) A spelling corrector to normalize out-of-vocabulary words.
   (b) Two Part-of-Speech (POS) taggers to realize word-to-lemma mapping in two perspectives.
   (c) A word sense disambiguator to obtain word senses and their confidence scores.
2. An weighting scheme to bias an output of a machine learner.

Functionalities 1a to 1c are introduced to enhance information based on lexical knowledge, since features based on lexicons are shown to be effective in SemEval-2013 Task 2 (Mohammad et al., 2013). Functionality 2 is introduced to make the system adjustable to polarity unbalancedness known to exists in Twitter data (Nakov et al., 2013).

The accompanying sections of this papers are organized as follows. Section 2 describes resources such as labeled texts and lexicons used in our system. Section 3 explains the details of the system. Section 4 discusses the submission test run and some extra test runs that we performed after the test data release. Finally, section 5 concludes the paper.

2 Resources

2.1 Sentiment Labeled Data

The system is a constrained system, therefore only the sentiment labeled data distributed by the task

Proceedings of the 8th International Workshop on Semantic Evaluation (SemEval 2014), pages 628–632, Dublin, Ireland, August 23-24, 2014.

Type	#Used	#Full	%
Twitter(train)	6949	9684	71.8
Twitter(dev)	1066	1654	64.4
Twitter(dev-test)	3269	3813	85.7
SMS(dev-test)	2094	2094	100

Table 1: The numbers of messages for each type. 'train', 'dev', and 'dev-test' denote training, development, and development-test respectively. #Used is the number of messages that we were able to obtain, and #Full is the maximum number of messages that were provided.

Criterion	Lexicon
FORMAL	General Inquirer MPQA Subjectivity Lexicon SentiWordNet
INFORMAL	AFINN-111 Bing Liu's Opinion Lexicon NRC Hashtag Sentiment Lexicon Sentiment140 Lexicon

Table 2: The seven sentiment lexicons and their criteria.

organizers were used. However, due to accessibility changes in tweets, a subset of the training, the development, and the development-test data were used. Table 1 shows the numbers of messages for each type.

2.2 Sentiment Lexicons

The system includes seven sentiment lexicons namely: AFINN-111 (Nielsen, 2011), Bing Liu's Opinion Lexicon[1], General Inquirer (Stone et al., 1966), MPQA Subjectivity Lexicon (Wilson et al., 2005), NRC Hashtag Sentiment Lexicon (Mohammad et al., 2013), Sentiment140 Lexicon (Mohammad et al., 2013), and SentiWordNet (Baccianella et al., 2010). We categorized these seven lexicons to two criteria: 'FORMAL' and 'INFORMAL'. Lexicons that include lemmas of erroneous words (e.g. misspelled words) were categorized to 'INFORMAL'. Table 2 illustrates the criteria of the seven lexicons. These criteria are used in the process of word-to-lemma mapping processes and will be explained in Section 3.1.3.

3 System Details

The system is a modularized system consisting of a variety of pre-processors, feature extractors, and a machine learner. Figure 1 illustrates the overview of the system.

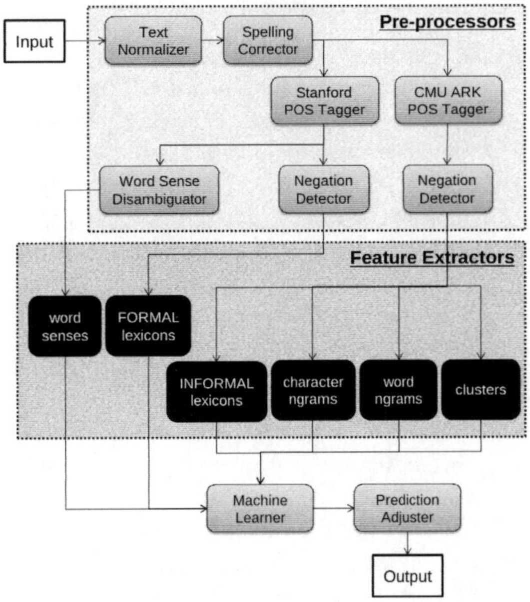

Figure 1: An overview of the system.

3.1 Pre-processors

3.1.1 Text Normalizer

The text normalizer performs following three rule-based normalization of an input text:

- Unicode normalization in form NFKC[2].
- All upper case letters are converted to lower case ones (ex. 'GooD' to 'good').
- URLs are exchanged with string 'URL's (ex. 'http://example.org' to 'URL').

3.1.2 Spelling Corrector

A spelling corrector is included in the system to normalize misspellings. We used Jazzy[3], an open source spell checker with US English dictionaries provided along with Jazzy. Jazzy combines DoubleMetaphone phonetic matching algorithm and a near-miss match algorithm based on Levenshtein distance to correct a misspelled word.

3.1.3 POS Taggers

The system includes two POS taggers to realize word-to-lemma mapping in two perspectives.

Stanford POS Tagger Stanford Log-linear Part-of-Speech Tagger (Toutanova et al., 2003) is one POS tagger which is used to map words

[1] `http://www.cs.uic.edu/~liub/FBS/sentiment-analysis.html`

[2] `http://www.unicode.org/reports/tr15/`

[3] `http://jazzy.sourceforge.net/`

to lemmas of 'FORMAL' criterion lexicons, and to extract word sense features. A finite-state transducer based lemmatizer (Minnen et al., 2001) included in the POS tagger is used to obtain lemmas of tokenized words.

CMU ARK POS Tagger A POS tagger for tweets by CMU ARK group (Owoputi et al., 2013) is another POS tagger used to map words to lemmas of 'INFORMAL' criterion lexicons, and to extract ngram features and a cluster feature.

3.1.4 Word Sense Disambiguator

A word sense disambiguator is included in the system to determine a sense of a word. We used UKB[4] which implements graph-based word sense disambiguation based on Personalized PageRank algorithm (Agirre and Soroa, 2009) on a lexical knowledge base. As a lexical knowledge base, WordNet 3.0 (Fellbaum, 1998) included in the UKB package is used.

3.1.5 Negation Detector

The system includes a simple rule-based negation detector. The detector is an implementation of the algorithm on Christopher Potts' Sentiment Symposium Tutorial[5]. The algorithm is a simple algorithm that appends a negation suffix to words that appear within a negation scope surrounded by a negation key (ex. 'no') and a certain punctuation (ex. ':').

3.2 Features

The followings are the features used in the system.

word ngrams Contiguous 1, 2, 3, and 4 grams of words, and non-contiguous 3 and 4 grams of words are extracted from a given words. Non-contiguous ngram are ngrams where one of words are replaced with a wild card word '*'. Example of contiguous 3 grams is 'by_the_way', and the corresponding noncontiguous variation is 'by_*_way'.

character ngrams Contiguous 3, 4, and 5 grams of characters with in a word are extracted from given words.

lexicons Words are mapped to seven lexicons of section 2.2. For two sentiment labels (positive and negative) in each lexicon, following four values are extracted: total matched word count, total score, maximal score, and last word score[6]. For lexicons without sentiment scores, score 1.0 is used for all entries. Note that different POS taggers are used in word-to-lemma mapping as described in Section 3.1.3.

clusters Words are mapped to Twitter Word Clusters of CMU ARK group[7]. The largest clustering result consisting of 1000 clusters from approximately 56 million tweets is used as clusters.

word senses A result of the word sense disambiguator is extracted as weighted features according to their scores. Figure 2 shows an example of this feature.

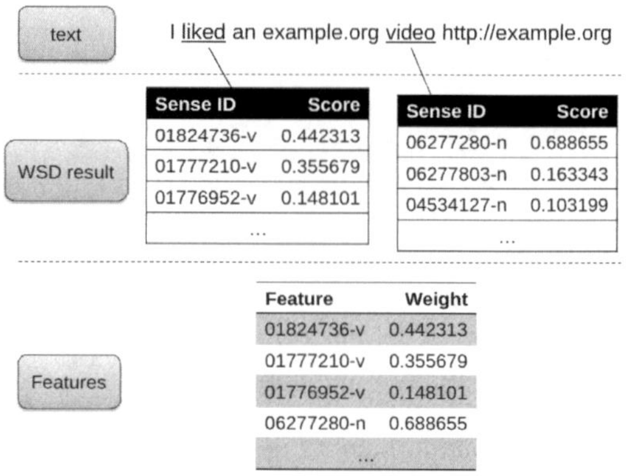

Figure 2: An example of word senses feature.

The ngram features are introduced as basic bag-of-words features in a supervised text categorization approach. Lexicon features are designed to strengthen the lexical features of Mohammad et al. (2013) which have been shown to be effective in the last year's task. Cluster features are implemented as an improvement for an supervised NLP system following the work of Turian et al. (2010). Word sense features are utilized to help subjectivity analysis and contextual polarity analysis (Akkaya et al., 2009).

3.3 Machine Learner

Logistic Regression is utilized as an algorithm of a supervised machine learning method. As an implementation of Logistic Regression, LIBLINEAR (Fan et al., 2008) is used. A Logistic Regression is trained using the features of Section 3.2 with the three polarities (positive, negative, and neutral) as labels.

[4] http://ixa2.si.ehu.es/ukb/

[5] http://sentiment.christopherpotts.net/lingstruc.html#negation

[6] The total number of lexical features is $7 \times 2 \times 4 = 56$.

[7] http://www.ark.cs.cmu.edu/TweetNLP/

Parameter Selection Source	Parameters			Sources				
	C	w_{pos}	w_{neg}	LiveJournal 2014	SMS 2013	Twitter 2013	Twitter 2014	Twitter2014 Sarcasm
Twitter(train)+Twitter(dev)	0.07	1.7	2.6	71.23	62.33	71.28	70.40	53.32
Twitter(dev-test)*	0.03	2.4	3.3	69.44	57.36	72.12	70.96	56.50
SMS(dev-test)	0.80	1.1	1.2	72.99	68.92	65.65	66.66	48.24
SMS(dev-test)+Twitter(dev-test)	0.07	1.9	2.0	72.54	65.44	70.41	69.80	51.09

Table 3: The scores for each source in the test runs. The run with asterisk (*) denotes the submission run. The values in the 'Sources' columns represent scores in SemEval-2014 Task 9 metric (the average of positive F_1 and negative F_1).

3.4 Prediction Adjuster

Since the labels in the tweets data are unbalanced (Nakov et al., 2013), we prepared a prediction adjuster for Logistic Regression output. For each polarity l, an weighting factor w_l that adjusts a probability output $Pr(l)$ is introduced. An updated prediction label is decided by selecting an l that maximizes $score(l)$ which can be expressed as equation 1.

$$\arg\max_{l \in \{pos,neg,neu\}} \quad score(l) = w_l Pr(l) \tag{1}$$

The approach we took in this prediction adjuster is a simple approach to bias an output of Logistic Regression, but may not be a typical approach to handle unbalanced data. For instance, LIBLINEAR includes the weighting option '-wi' which enables a use of different cost parameter C for different classes. One advantage of our approach is that the change in w_l does not require a training of Logistic Regression. Various values of w_l can be tested with very low computational cost, which is helpful in a situation like SemEval tasks where the time for development is limited.

4 Test Runs

4.1 Submission Test Run

The system was trained using the 8,015 tweets included in Twitter(train) and Twitter(dev) described in Section 2.1. Three parameters: cost parameter C of Logistic Regression, weight w_{pos} of the prediction adjuster, and weight w_{neg} of the prediction adjuster, were considered in the submission test run. For the w_{neu} of the prediction adjuster, a fixed value of 1.0 was used.

Prior to the submission test run, the following two steps were performed to select a parameter combination for the submission run.

Step 1 The system with all combinations of C in range of $\{0.01$ to 0.09 by step 0.01, 0.1 to 0.9 by step 0.1, 1 to 10 by step $1\}$, w_{pos} in range of $\{1.0$ to 5.0 by step $0.1\}$, and w_{neg} in range of $\{1.0$ to 5.0 by step $0.1\}$ were prepared[8].

Step 2 The performances of the system for all these parameter combinations were calculated using Twitter(dev-test) described in Section 2.1.

As a result, the parameter combination $C = 0.03$, $w_{pos} = 2.4$, and $w_{neg} = 3.3$ which performed best in Twitter(dev-test) was selected as a parameter combination for the submission run.

Finally, the system with the selected parameters was applied to the test set of SemEval-2014 Task 9. 'Twitter(dev-test)' in Table 3 shows the values of this submission run. The system achieved high performances on Twitter data: 72.12, 70.96, and 56.50 on Twitter2013, Twitter2014, and Twitter2014Sarcasm respectively.

4.2 Post-Submission Test Runs

The system performed quite well on Twitter data but not so well on other data on the submission run. After the release of the gold data of the 2014 test tun, we conducted several test runs using different parameter combinations. 'Twitter(train)+Twitter(dev)', 'SMS(dev-test)', and 'SMS(dev-test)+Twitter(dev-test)' are the results of test runs with different data sources used for the parameter selection process. In 'Twitter(train)+Twitter(dev)', the parameter combination that maximizes a micro-average score of 5-fold cross validation was chosen since the training data and the parameter selection are equivalent.

The parameter combination selected with 'Twitter(train)+Twitter(dev)' showed similar result as the submission run, which is high performances on Twitter data. In the case of 'SMS(dev-test)', the system performed well on 'LiveJournal2014' and 'SMS(dev-test)' namely 72.99 and 68.92. How-

[8]The total number of parameter combination is $29 \times 51 \times 51 = 75429$.

ever, in this parameter combination the scores on Twitter data were clearly lower than the submission run. Finally, 'SMS(dev-test)+Twitter(dev-test)' resulted to a mid performing result, where scores for each source marked in-between values of 'Twitter(dev-test)' and 'SMS(dev-test)'.

5 Conclusion

We proposed a system that is designed to enhance information based on lexical knowledge and to be adjustable to unbalanced training data. With parameters tuned towards Twitter data, the system successfully achieved high scoring results on Twitter data, average F_1 70.96 on Twitter2014 and average F_1 56.50 on Twitter2014Sarcasm.

Additional test runs with different parameter combination showed that the system can be tuned to perform well on non-Twitter data such as blogs or short messages. However, the limitation of our approach to directly weight a machine learner's output was shown, since we could not find a general purpose parameter combination that can achieve high scores on any types of data.

Acknowledgements

We would like to thank the anonymous reviewers for their valuable comments to improve this paper.

References

Eneko Agirre and Aitor Soroa. 2009. Personalizing PageRank for word sense disambiguation. In *Proceedings of EACL 2009*, pages 33–41.

Cem Akkaya, Janyce Wiebe, and Rada Mihalcea. 2009. Subjectivity word sense disambiguation. In *Proceedings of EMNLP 2009*, pages 190–199.

Enrique Amigó, Jorge Carrillo de Albornoz, Irina Chugur, Adolfo Corujo, Julio Gonzalo, Tamara Martín, Edgar Meij, Maarten de Rijke, and Damiano Spina. 2013. Overview of RepLab 2013: Evaluating online reputation monitoring systems. In *CLEF 2013 Evaluation Labs and Workshop, Online Working Notes*.

Stefano Baccianella, Andrea Esuli, and Fabrizio Sebastiani. 2010. SentiWordNet 3.0: An enhanced lexical resource for sentiment analysis and opinion mining. In *Proceedings of LREC 2010*, pages 2200–2204.

Rong-En Fan, Kai-Wei Chang, Cho-Jui Hsieh, Xiang-Rui Wang, and Chih-Jen Lin. 2008. LIBLINEAR: A library for large linear classification. In *Journal of Machine Learning Research*, volume 9, pages 1871–1874.

Christiane Fellbaum, editor. 1998. *WordNet: An Electronic Lexical Database*. MIT Press.

Guido Minnen, John Carroll, and Darren Pearce. 2001. Applied morphological processing of English. *Natural Language Engineering*, 7(3):207–223.

Saif Mohammad, Svetlana Kiritchenko, and Xiaodan Zhu. 2013. NRC-Canada: Building the state-of-the-art in sentiment analysis of tweets. In *Proceedings of the seventh international workshop on Semantic Evaluation Exercises (SemEval-2013)*, pages 321–327.

Preslav Nakov, Sara Rosenthal, Zornitsa Kozareva, Veselin Stoyanov, Alan Ritter, and Theresa Wilson. 2013. SemEval-2013 task 2: Sentiment analysis in Twitter. In *Proceedings of the seventh international workshop on Semantic Evaluation Exercises (SemEval-2013)*, pages 312–320.

Finn Årup Nielsen. 2011. A new ANEW: Evaluation of a word list for sentiment analysis in microblogs. In *Proceedings of the ESWC2011 Workshop on 'Making Sense of Microposts': Big things come in small packages*, pages 93–98.

Olutobi Owoputi, Brendan O'Connor, Chris Dyer, Kevin Gimpel, Nathan Schneider, and Noah A. Smith. 2013. Improved part-of-speech tagging for online conversational text with word clusters. In *Proceedings of NAACL 2013*, pages 380–390.

Sara Rosenthal, Alan Ritter, Preslav Nakov, and Veselin Stoyanov. 2014. SemEval-2014 task 9: Sentiment analysis in Twitter. In *Proceedings of the eighth international workshop on Semantic Evaluation Exercises (SemEval-2014)*.

Philip Stone, Dexter Dunphy, Marshall Smith, and Daniel Ogilvie. 1966. *General Inquirer: A Computer Approach to Content Analysis*. MIT Press.

Kristina Toutanova, Dan Klein, Christopher Manning, and Yoram Singer. 2003. Feature-rich part-of-speech tagging with a cyclic dependency network. In *Proceedings of HLT-NAACL 2003*, pages 252–259.

Joseph Turian, Lev Ratinov, and Yoshua Bengio. 2010. Word representations: A simple and general method for semi-supervised learning. In *Proceedings of ACL 2010*, pages 384–394.

Julio Villena-Román and Janine García-Morera. 2013. TASS 2013 - Workshop on sentiment analysis at SEPLN 2013: An overview. In *Proceedings of the TASS workshop at SEPLN 2013*.

Theresa Wilson, Janyce Wiebe, and Paul Hoffmann. 2005. Recognizing contextual polarity in phrase-level sentiment analysis. In *Proceedings of HLT-EMNLP 2005*, pages 347–354.

TeamZ: Measuring Semantic Textual Similarity for Spanish Using an Overlap-Based Approach

Anubhav Gupta
UFR SLHS
Université de Franche-Comté
anubhav.gupta@edu.univ-fcomte.fr

Abstract

This paper presents an overlap-based approach using bag of words and the Spanish WordNet to solve the STS-Spanish subtask (STS-Es) of SemEval-2014 Task 10. Since bag of words is the most commonly used method to ascertain similarity, the performance is modest.

1 Introduction

The objective of STS-Es is to score a pair of sentences in Spanish on the scale of 0 (the two sentences are on different topics) to 4 (the two sentences are completely equivalent, as they mean the same thing) (Agirre et al., 2014). The textual similarity finds its utility in various NLP applications such as information retrieval, text categorisation, word sense disambiguation, text summarisation, topic detection, etc. (Besançon et al., 1999; Mihalcea et al., 2006; Islam and Inkpen, 2008).

The method presented in this paper calculates the similarity based on the number of words that are common in two given sentences. This approach, being simplistic, suffers from various drawbacks. Firstly, the semantically similar sentences need not have many words in common (Li et al., 2006). Secondly, even if the sentences have many words in common, the context in which they are used can be different (Sahami and Heilman, 2006). For example, based on the bag of words approach, the sentences in Table 1 would be scored the same:

No.	Spanish	English
1	Él es listo.	He is clever.
2	Él está listo.	He is ready.
3	Él está preparado.	He is prepared.

Table 1: Examples.

However, only sentences [2] and [3] mean the same.

Despite the flaws, this approach was used because of the Basic Principle of Compositionality (Zimmermann, 2011), which states that the meaning of a complex expression depends upon the meaning of its components and the manner in which they are composed. Furthermore, mainly nouns were considered in the bag of words because Spanish is an exocentric language, and nouns contain more specific, concrete semantic information than verbs (Michael Herslund, 2010; Michael Herslund, 2012).

2 Methodology

The training dataset provided for the task consisted of 65 pairs of sentences along with their corresponding similarity scores. There were two test sets: one consisted of 480 sentence pairs from a news corpus, and the other had 324 sentence pairs taken from Wikipedia.

The approach consisted of learning the scoring with the help of linear regression. Two runs were submitted as solutions. The first run used three-feature vectors, whereas the second one used four-feature vectors. The features are the Jaccard indices for the lemmas, noun lemmas, synsets, and noun subjects in each sentence pair. For both runs, the sentence pairs were parsed using the TreeTagger (Schmid, 1994). The TreeTagger was used because it provides the part-of-speech tag and lemma for each word of a sentence.

Run 1 used these features:

- The fraction of lemmas that were common between the two sentences. In other words, the number of unique lemmas common between the sentences divided by the total number of unique lemmas of the two sentences.

Proceedings of the 8th International Workshop on Semantic Evaluation (SemEval 2014), pages 633–635,
Dublin, Ireland, August 23-24, 2014.

- The fraction of noun lemmas common between the two sentences.

- The fraction of synsets common between the two sentences. For each noun, its corresponding synset[1] was extracted from the Spanish WordNet (spaWN) of the Multilingual Central Repository[2] (MCR 3.0) (Gonzalez-Agirre et al., 2012).

Run 2 employed one more feature in addition to the aforementioned, which was the fraction of synsets of noun subjects that were common for each sentence pair. The subject nouns were extracted from the sentences after parsing them with the MaltParser (Nivre et al., 2007). Since the TreeTagger PoS tagset[3] differed from the EAGLES (Expert Advisory Group on Language Engineering Standards) tagset[4] required by the MaltParser, rules were written to best translate the TreeTagger tags into EAGLES tags. However, one-to-one mapping was not possible: EAGLES tags are seven characters long and encode number and gender, whereas TreeTagger tags do not. For example, using the EAGLES tagset, the masculine singular common noun *árbol* 'tree' is tagged as NCMS000, whereas the feminine singular common noun *hoja* 'leaf' is tagged as NCFS000; TreeTagger, on the other hand, tags both as NC.

3 Results and Conclusions

Table 2 presents the performance, measured using the Pearson correlation, of the approach. **Run 1** achieved a weighted correlation of 0.66723 and ranked 15th among 22 submissions to the task.

Dataset	Run 1	Run 2
Training	0.83693	0.83773
Wikipedia (Test)	0.61020	0.60425
News (Test)	0.71654	0.70974

Table 2: Performance of the Approach.

Given that the approach relied mostly on bag of words, a modest performance was expected. The performance was also affected by the fact that the spaWN did not have synsets for most of the words. Finally, converting TreeTagger tags to those required by the MaltParser instead of using a parser which annotates with EAGLES tags may also have contributed to the relatively low **Run 2** score. However, the confidence intervals of the two runs obtained after bootstrapping overlapped. Thus, the difference between the two runs for both the datasets is not statistically significant.

[1]stored as synset offset in wei_spa-30_variant.tsv

[2]The resource can be obtained from http://grial.uab.es/descarregues.php

[3]http://www.cis.uni-muenchen.de/~schmid/tools/TreeTagger/data/spanish-tagset.txt

[4]http://nlp.lsi.upc.edu/freeling/doc/tagsets/tagset-es.html

Acknowledgements

I would like to thank Vlad Niculae, Àngels Catena and Calvin Cheng for their inputs and feedback.

References

Eneko Agirre, Carmen Banea, Claire Cardie, Daniel Cer, Mona Diab, Aitor Gonzalez-Agirre, Weiwei Guo, Rada Mihalcea, German Rigau, and Janyce Wiebe. 2014. "SemEval-2014 Task 10: Multilingual Semantic Textual Similarity." In *Proceedings of the 8th International Workshop on Semantic Evaluation* (SemEval-2014). Dublin, Ireland.

Romaric Besançon, Martin Rajman, and Jean-Cédric Chappelier. 1999. Textual Similarities Based on a Distributional Approach. In *Proceedings of the 10th International Workshop on Database & Expert Systems Applications.* 180–184. DEXA '99. Washington, DC, USA: IEEE Computer Society.

Aitor Gonzalez-Agirre, Egoitz Laparra, and German Rigau. 2012. Multilingual Central Repository version 3.0: upgrading a very large lexical knowledge base. In *Proceedings of the Sixth International Global WordNet Conference (GWC '12).*

Aminul Islam and Diana Inkpen. 2008. Semantic Text Similarity Using Corpus-Based Word Similarity and String Similarity. *ACM Transactions on Knowledge Discovery from Data* 2 (2): 1–25.

Michael Herslund. 2010. Predicati e sostantivi complessi. In *Language, Cognition and Identity*, eds. Irn Korzen and Emanuela Cresti. 1–9. Strumenti per La Didattica E La Ricerca. Firenze University Press.

Michael Herslund. 2012. Structures lexicales et typologie. In *Sémantique et lexicologie des langues d'Europe*, eds. Louis Begioni and Christine Bracquenier. 35–52. Rivages Linguistiques. Presses Universitaires de Rennes.

Rada Mihalcea, Courtney Corley, and Carlo Strapparava. 2006. Corpus-Based and Knowledge-Based Measures of Text Semantic Similarity. In *Proceedings of the 21st National Conference on Artificial Intelligence.* 775–80. AAAI'06. Boston, Massachusetts: AAAI Press.

Yuhua Li, David McLean, Zuhair A. Bandar, James D. O'Shea, and Keeley Crockett. 2006. Sentence Similarity Based on Semantic Nets and Corpus Statistics.

IEEE Transactions on Knowledge and Data Engineering, 18 (8): 1138–50.

Joakim Nivre, Johan Hall, Jens Nilsson, Atanas Chanev, Gülşen Eryiğit, Sandra Kübler, Svetovlas Marinov, and Erwin Marsi. 2007. MaltParser: A language-independent system for data-driven dependency parsing. *Natural Language Engineering*, 13 (2): 95–135.

Mehran Sahami and Timothy D. Heilman. 2006. A Web-Based Kernel Function for Measuring the Similarity of Short Text Snippets. In *Proceedings of the 15th International Conference on World Wide Web*, 377–86. WWW '06. New York, NY, USA: ACM.

Helmut Schmid. 1994. Probabilistic Part-of-Speech Tagging Using Decision Trees. *Proceedings of International Conference on New Methods in Language Processing*. Manchester, UK.

Thomas Ede Zimmermann. 2011. Model-theoretic semantics. *Semantics. An International Handbook of Natural Language Meaning*. edited by Claudia Maienborn, Klaus von Heusinger, and Paul Portner. Vol. 1. Berlin, Boston: De Gruyter Mouton.

The Impact of Z_score on Twitter Sentiment Analysis

Hussam Hamdan*,,*****
*LSIS
Aix-Marseille Université CNRS
Av. Esc. Normandie Niemen,
13397 Marseille Cedex 20,
France
hussam.hamdan@lsis.org

Patrice Bellot*,**
**OpenEdition
Aix-Marseille Université CNRS
3 pl. V. Hugo, case n°86
13331 Marseille Cedex 3,
France
patrice.bellot@lsis.org

Frederic Béchet***
***LIF
Aix-Marseille Université CNRS
Avenue de Luminy
13288 Marseille Cedex 9,
France
frederic.bechet@lif.univ-mrs.fr

Abstract

Twitter has become more and more an important resource of user-generated data. Sentiment Analysis in Twitter is interesting for many applications and objectives. In this paper, we propose to exploit some features which can be useful for this task; the main contribution is the use of Z-scores as features for sentiment classification in addition to pre-polarity and POS tags features. Our experiments have been evaluated using the test data provided by SemEval 2013 and 2014. The evaluation demonstrates that Z_scores features can significantly improve the prediction performance.

1 Introduction

The interactive Web has changed the relation between the users and the web. Users have become an important source of content. They express their opinion towards different issues. These opinions are important for others who are interested in understanding users' interests such as buyers, sellers and producers.

Twitter is one of the most important platforms in which the users express their opinions. Many works have exploited this media for predicting valuable issues depending on Sentiment Analysis (SA). The authors in (Asur and Huberman 2010) predicted the box-office revenues of movies in advance of their releases using the tweets talking about them. In (Bae and Lee 2012) Sentiment Analysis has been used to study the impact of 13 twitter accounts of famous persons on their followers and also for forecasting the interesting tweets which are more probably to be reposted by the followers (Naveed, Gottron et al. 2011).

Sentiment Analysis can be done in different levels; Document level; Sentence level; Clause level or Aspect-Based level. SA in Twitter can be seen as a sentence level task, but some limitations should be considered in such sentences. The size of tweets is limited to 140 characters, informal language, emotion icons and non-standard expressions are commonly used, and many spelling errors can be found due to the absence of correctness verification.

Three different approaches can be identified in the literature of Sentiment Analysis in Twitter, the first approach is lexicon based, using specific types of lexicons to derive the polarity of a text, this approach suffers from the limited size of lexicon and requires human expertise to build manual lexicon (Joshi, Balamurali et al. 2011), in the other hand the automatic lexicons are not so efficient. The second one is machine learning approach which uses annotated texts with a given labels to learn a classification model, an early work was done on a movie review dataset (Pang, Lee et al. 2002). Both lexicon and machine learning approaches can be combined to achieve a better performance (Khuc, Shivade et al. 2012). These two approaches are used for SA task but the third one is specific for Twitter or social content, the social approach exploits social network properties and data for enhancing the accuracy of the classification (Speriosu, Sudan et al. 2011).

In this paper, we exploit machine learning algorithm with the aid of some features:

- The original Terms: the terms representing the tweet after the tokenization and stemming;

Proceedings of the 8th International Workshop on Semantic Evaluation (SemEval 2014), pages 636–641,
Dublin, Ireland, August 23-24, 2014.

- Pre-polarity features: the number of negative, positive and neutral words extracted from two sentiment lexicons;
- POS tags: the number of adjectives, connectors, verbs, nouns, adverbs in the tweet;
- Z-score: The numbers of terms having Z-score value more than three for each class positive, negative and neutral.

We extended the original terms with these last features. We also constructed a dictionary for the abbreviations and the slang words used in Twitter in order to overcome the ambiguity of the tweets. We tested the performance of every possible combination of these features.

The rest of this paper is organized as follows. Section 2 outlines previous work that focused on sentiment analysis in Twitter. Section 3 presents the Z_score features and the others which we used for training a classifier. Our experiments are described in section 4, conclusion and future work is presented in section 5.

2 Related Works

We can identify three main approaches for sentiment analysis in Twitter. The lexicon based approaches which depend on sentiment lexicons containing positive, negative and neutral words or expressions; they calculate the polarity according to the number of common opinionated words between the lexicons and the text. Many dictionaries have been created manually such as ANEW (Affective Norms for English Words) or automatically such as SentiWordNet (Baccianella, Esuli et al. 2010). Four lexicon dictionaries were used to overcome the lack of words in each one (Joshi, Balamurali et al. 2011; Mukherjee, Malu et al. 2012). Automatically construction of a Twitter lexicon was implemented by (Khuc, Shivade et al. 2012).

Machine learning approaches were employed from annotated tweets by using Naive Bayes, Maximum Entropy *MaxEnt* and Support Vector Machines (SVM). The authors (Go, Bhayani et al. 2009) reported that SVM outperforms other classifiers. They tried a unigram and a bigram model in conjunction with parts-of-speech (POS) features; they noted that the unigram model outperforms all other models when using SVM and that POS features decrease the quality of results. The authors in (Kouloumpis, Wilson et al. 2011) found that N-gram with lexicon features and micro-blogging features are useful but POS features are not. In contrast, in (Pak and Paroubek 2010) they reported that POS and bigrams both help. In (Barbosa and Feng 2010) the authors proposed the use of syntax features of tweets like retweet, hashtags, link, punctuation and exclamation marks in conjunction with features like prior polarity of words and POS tags, in (Agarwal, Xie et al. 2011) this approach was extended by using real valued prior polarity and by combining prior polarity with POS. Authors in (Saif, He et al. 2012) proposed to use the semantic features, therefore they extracted the named entities in the tweets. Authors in (Hamdan, Béchet et al. 2013) used the concepts extracted from DBpedia and the adjectives from WordNet, they reported that the DBpedia concepts are useful with Naïve-Bayes classifier but less useful with SVM.

The third main approach takes into account the influence of users on their followers and the relation between the users and the tweets they wrote. It assumes that using the Twitter follower graph might improve the polarity classification. In (Speriosu, Sudan et al. 2011) they demonstrated that using label propagation with Twitter follower graph improves the polarity classification. In (Tan, Lee et al. 2011) they employed social relation for user-level sentiment analysis. In (Hu, Tang et al. 2013) a Sociological Approach to handling the Noisy and short Text (SANT) for supervised sentiment classification is used; they reported that social theories such as Sentiment Consistency and Emotional Contagion could be helpful for sentiment analysis.

3 Feature Selection

We used different types of features in order to improve the accuracy of sentiment classification.

- Bag of words (Terms)

The most commonly used features in text analysis are the bag of words which represent a text as unordered set of words or terms. It assumes that words are independent from each other and also disregards their order of appearance. We stemmed the words using Porter Stemmer and used them as a baseline features.

- Z_score Features (Z)

We suggest using a new type of features for Sentiment Analysis, Z_score can distinguish the importance of each term in each class. We compute the number of terms having Z_score more than three for each class over each tweet. We assume that the term frequencies follow the multinomial distribution. Thus, Z_score can be seen as a standardization of the term. We compute the

Z_score for each term t_i in a class Cj (t_{ij}) by calculating its term relative frequency tfr_{ij} in a particular class C_j, as well as the mean ($mean_i$) which is the term probability over the whole corpus multiplied by n_j the number of terms in the class C_j, and standard deviation (sd_i) of term t_i according to the underlying corpus (see Eq. (1,2)).

$$Z_{score(t_{ij})} = \frac{tfr_{ij} - mean_i}{sdi} \quad \text{Eq. (1)}$$

$$Z_{score(t_{ij})} = \frac{tfr_{ij} - n_j * p(ti)}{\sqrt{nj * p(ti) * (1 - p(ti))}} \quad \text{Eq. (2)}$$

The term which has salient frequency in a class in compassion to others will have a salient Z_score. Z_score was exploited for SA by (Zubaryeva and Savoy 2010) , they choose a threshold (>2) for selecting the number of terms having Z_score more than the threshold, then they used a logistic regression for combining these scores. We use Z_scores as added features for classification because the tweet is too short, therefore many tweets does not have any words with salient Z_score. The three following figures 1,2,3 show the distribution of Z_score over each class, we remark that the majority of terms has Z_score between -1.5 and 2.5 in each class and the rest are either vey frequent (>2.5) or very rare (<-1.5). It should indicate that negative value means that the term is not frequent in this class in comparison with its frequencies in other classes. Table1 demonstrates the first ten terms having the highest Z_scores in each class. We have tested to use different values for the threshold, the best results was obtained when the threshold is 3.

positive	Z_score	negative	Z_score	Neutral	Z_score
Love	14.31	Not	13.99	Httpbit	6.44
Good	14.01	Fuck	12.97	Httpfb	4.56
Happy	12.30	Don't	10.97	Httpbnd	3.78
Great	11.10	Shit	8.99	Intern	3.58
Excite	10.35	Bad	8.40	Nov	3.45
Best	9.24	Hate	8.29	Httpdlvr	3.40
Thank	9.21	Sad	8.28	Open	3.30
Hope	8.24	Sorry	8.11	Live	3.28
Cant	8.10	Cancel	7.53	Cloud	3.28
Wait	8.05	stupid	6.83	begin	3.17

Table1. The first ten terms having the highest Z_score in each class

- Sentiment Lexicon Features (POL)

We used two sentiment lexicons, MPQA Subjectivity Lexicon(Wilson, Wiebe et al. 2005) and Bing Liu's Opinion Lexicon which is created by (Hu and Liu 2004) and augmented in many latter works. We extract the number of positive, negative and neutral words in tweets according to these lexicons. Bing Liu's lexicon only contains negative and positive annotation but Subjectivity contains negative, positive and neutral.

- Part Of Speech (POS)

We annotate each word in the tweet by its POS tag, and then we compute the number of adjectives, verbs, nouns, adverbs and connectors in each tweet.

4 Evaluation

4.1 Data collection

We used the data set provided in SemEval 2013 and 2014 for subtask B of sentiment analysis in Twitter(Rosenthal, Ritter et al. 2014) (Wilson, Kozareva et al. 2013). The participants were provided with training tweets annotated as positive, negative or neutral. We downloaded these tweets using a given script. Among 9646 tweets, we could only download 8498 of them because of protected profiles and deleted tweets. Then, we used the development set containing 1654 tweets for evaluating our methods. We combined the development set with training set and built a new model which predicted the labels of the test set 2013 and 2014.

4.2 Experiments

Official Results

The results of our system submitted for SemEval evaluation gave 46.38%, 52.02% for test set 2013 and 2014 respectively. It should mention that these results are not correct because of a software bug discovered after the submission deadline, therefore the correct results is demonstrated as non-official results. In fact the previous results are the output of our classifier which is trained by all the features in section 3, but because of index shifting error the test set was represented by all the features except the terms.

Non-official Results

We have done various experiments using the features presented in Section 3 with Multinomial Naïve-Bayes model. We firstly constructed feature vector of tweet terms which gave 49%, 46% for test set 2013, 2014 respectively. Then, we augmented this original vector by the Z_score features which improve the performance by 6.5% and 10.9%, then by pre-polarity features which also improve the f-measure by 4%, 6%, but the extending with POS tags decreases the f-measure. We also test all combinations with these previous features, Table2 demonstrates the results of each combination, we remark that POS tags are not useful over all the experiments, the best result is obtained by combining Z_score and pre-polarity features. We find that Z_score features improve significantly the f-measure and they are better than pre-polarity features.

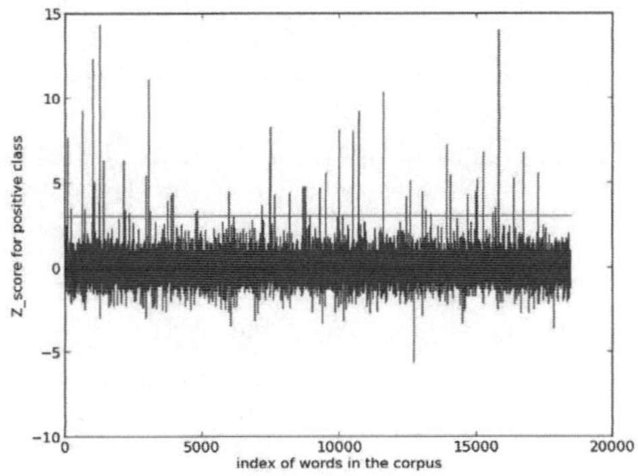

Figure 1 Z_score distribution in positive class

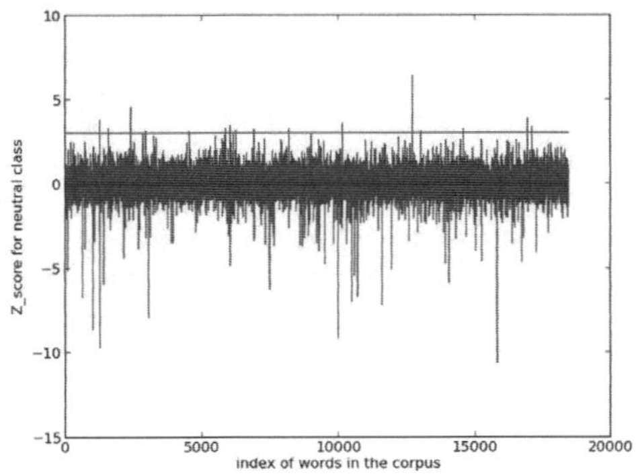

Figure 2 Z_score distribution in neutral class

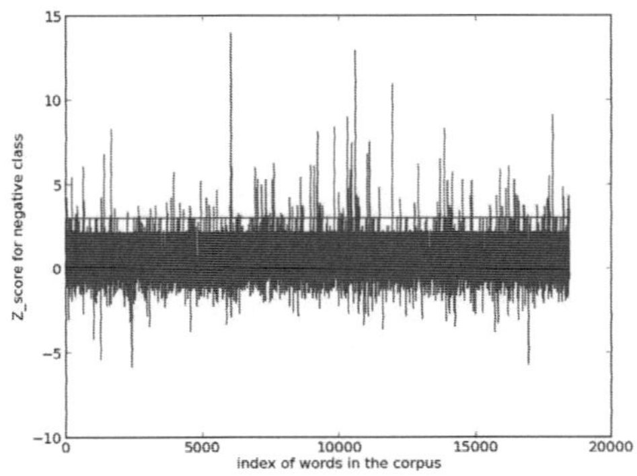

Figure 3 Z_score distribution in negative class

Features	F-measure	
	2013	2014
Terms	49.42	46.31
Terms+Z	55.90	57.28
Terms+POS	43.45	41.14
Terms+POL	53.53	52.73
Terms+Z+POS	52.59	54.43
Terms+Z+POL	**58.34**	**59.38**
Terms+POS+POL	48.42	50.03
Terms+Z+POS+POL	55.35	58.58

Table 2. Average f-measures for positive and negative classes of SemEval2013 and 2014 test sets.

We repeated all previous experiments after using a twitter dictionary where we extend the tweet by the expressions related to each emotion icons or abbreviations in tweets. The results in Table3 demonstrate that using that dictionary improves the f-measure over all the experiments, the best results obtained also by combining Z_scores and pre-polarity features.

Features	F-measure	
	2013	2014
Terms	50.15	48.56
Terms+Z	57.17	58.37
Terms+POS	44.07	42.64
Terms+POL	54.72	54.53
Terms+Z+POS	53.20	56.47
Terms+Z+POL	**59.66**	**61.07**
Terms+POS+POL	48.97	51.90
Terms+Z+POS+POL	55.83	60.22

Table 3. Average f-measures for positive and negative classes of SemEval2013 and 2014 test sets after using a twitter dictionary.

5 Conclusion

In this paper we tested the impact of using Twitter Dictionary, Sentiment Lexicons, Z_score features and POS tags for the sentiment classification of tweets. We extended the feature vector of tweets by all these features; we have proposed new type of features Z_score and demonstrated that they can improve the performance.

We think that Z_score can be used in different ways for improving the Sentiment Analysis, we are going to test it in another type of corpus and using other methods in order to combine these features.

Reference

Apoorv Agarwal,Boyi Xie,Ilia Vovsha,Owen Rambow and Rebecca Passonneau (2011). Sentiment analysis of Twitter data. Proceedings of the Workshop on Languages

in Social Media. Portland, Oregon, Association for Computational Linguistics: 30-38.
Sitaram Asur and Bernardo A. Huberman (2010). Predicting the Future with Social Media. Proceedings of the 2010 IEEE/WIC/ACM International Conference on Web Intelligence and Intelligent Agent Technology - Volume 01, IEEE Computer Society: 492-499.
Stefano Baccianella,Andrea Esuli and Fabrizio Sebastiani (2010). SentiWordNet 3.0: An Enhanced Lexical Resource for Sentiment Analysis and Opinion Mining. Proceedings of the Seventh Conference on International Language Resources and Evaluation (LREC'10), European Language Resources Association (ELRA).
Younggue Bae and Hongchul Lee (2012). "Sentiment analysis of twitter audiences: Measuring the positive or negative influence of popular twitterers." J. Am. Soc. Inf. Sci. Technol. **63**(12): 2521-2535.
Luciano Barbosa and Junlan Feng (2010). Robust sentiment detection on Twitter from biased and noisy data. Proceedings of the 23rd International Conference on Computational Linguistics: Posters. Beijing, China, Association for Computational Linguistics: 36-44.
Alec Go,Richa Bhayani and Lei Huang Twitter Sentiment Classification using Distant Supervision.
Hussam Hamdan,Frederic Béchet and Patrice Bellot (2013). Experiments with DBpedia, WordNet and SentiWordNet as resources for sentiment analysis in micro-blogging. Proceedings of the Seventh International Workshop on Semantic Evaluation (SemEval 2013), Atlanta, Georgia, USA.
Minqing Hu and Bing Liu (2004). Mining and summarizing customer reviews. Proceedings of the tenth ACM SIGKDD international conference on Knowledge discovery and data mining. Seattle, WA, USA, ACM: 168-177.
Xia Hu,Lei Tang,Jiliang Tang and Huan Liu (2013). Exploiting social relations for sentiment analysis in microblogging. Proceedings of the sixth ACM international conference on Web search and data mining. Rome, Italy, ACM: 537-546.
Aditya Joshi,A. R. Balamurali,Pushpak Bhattacharyya and Rajat Mohanty (2011). C-Feel-It: a sentiment analyzer for micro-blogs. Proceedings of the 49th Annual Meeting of the Association for Computational Linguistics: Human Language Technologies: Systems Demonstrations. Portland, Oregon, Association for Computational Linguistics: 127-132.
Vinh Ngoc Khuc,Chaitanya Shivade,Rajiv Ramnath and Jay Ramanathan (2012). Towards building large-scale distributed systems for twitter sentiment analysis. Proceedings of the 27th Annual ACM Symposium on Applied Computing. Trento, Italy, ACM: 459-464.
E. Kouloumpis,T. Wilson and J. Moore (2011). Twitter Sentiment Analysis: The Good the Bad and the OMG! Fifth International AAAI Conference on Weblogs and Social Media.
Subhabrata Mukherjee,Akshat Malu,Balamurali A.R. and Pushpak Bhattacharyya (2012). TwiSent: a multistage system for analyzing sentiment in twitter. Proceedings of the 21st ACM international conference on Information and knowledge management. Maui, Hawaii, USA, ACM: 2531-2534.
Nasir Naveed,Thomas Gottron,J\'Er\^Ome Kunegis and Arifah Che Alhadi (2011). Bad News Travels Fast: A Content-based Analysis of Interestingness on Twitter. Proc. Web Science Conf.
Alexander Pak and Patrick Paroubek (2010). Twitter as a Corpus for Sentiment Analysis and Opinion Mining. Proceedings of the Seventh conference on International Language Resources and Evaluation (LREC'10), Valletta, Malta, European Language Resources Association (ELRA).
Bo Pang,Lillian Lee and Shivakumar Vaithyanathan (2002). Thumbs up?: sentiment classification using machine learning techniques. Proceedings of the ACL-02 conference on Empirical methods in natural language processing - Volume 10, Association for Computational Linguistics: 79-86.
Sara Rosenthal,Alan Ritter,Veselin Stoyanov and Preslav Nakov (2014). "SemEval-2014 Task 9: Sentiment Analysis in Twitter." In Proceedings of the Eighth International Workshop on Semantic Evaluation (SemEval'14).August 23-24, Dublin, Ireland.
Hassan Saif,Yulan He and Harith Alani (2012). Semantic sentiment analysis of twitter. Proceedings of the 11th international conference on The Semantic Web - Volume Part I. Boston, MA, Springer-Verlag: 508-524.
Michael Speriosu,Nikita Sudan,Sid Upadhyay and Jason Baldridge (2011). Twitter polarity classification with label propagation over lexical links and the follower graph. Proceedings of the First Workshop on Unsupervised Learning in NLP. Edinburgh, Scotland, Association for Computational Linguistics: 53-63.
Chenhao Tan,Lillian Lee,Jie Tang,Long Jiang,Ming Zhou and Ping Li (2011). User-level

sentiment analysis incorporating social networks. Proceedings of the 17th ACM SIGKDD international conference on Knowledge discovery and data mining. San Diego, California, USA, ACM: 1397-1405.
Theresa Wilson,Zornitsa Kozareva,Preslav Nakov,Alan Ritter,Sara Rosenthal and Veselin Stoyanov (2013). "SemEval-2013 Task 2: Sentiment Analysis in Twitter." Proceedings of the 7th International Workshop on Semantic Evaluation. Association for Computational Linguistics.
Theresa Wilson,Janyce Wiebe and Paul Hoffmann (2005). Recognizing contextual polarity in phrase-level sentiment analysis. Proceedings of the conference on Human Language Technology and Empirical Methods in Natural Language Processing. Vancouver, British Columbia, Canada, Association for Computational Linguistics: 347-354.
Olena Zubaryeva and Jacques Savoy (2010). "Opinion Detection by Combining Machine Learning & Linguistic Tools." In Proceedings of the 8th NTCIR, Workshop Meeting on Evaluation of Information Access Technologies: InformationRetrieval, Question Answering and Cross-Lingual Information Access.

The Meaning Factory: Formal Semantics for Recognizing Textual Entailment and Determining Semantic Similarity

Johannes Bjerva
Univ. of Groningen
j.bjerva@rug.nl

Johan Bos
Univ. of Groningen
johan.bos@rug.nl

Rob van der Goot
Univ. of Groningen
r.van.der.goot@rug.nl

Malvina Nissim
Univ. of Bologna
malvina.nissim@unibo.it

Abstract

Shared Task 1 of SemEval-2014 comprised two subtasks on the same dataset of sentence pairs: recognizing textual entailment and determining textual similarity. We used an existing system based on formal semantics and logical inference to participate in the first subtask, reaching an accuracy of 82%, ranking in the top 5 of more than twenty participating systems. For determining semantic similarity we took a supervised approach using a variety of features, the majority of which was produced by our system for recognizing textual entailment. In this subtask our system achieved a mean squared error of 0.322, the best of all participating systems.

1 Introduction

The recent popularity of employing distributional approaches to semantic interpretation has also lead to interesting questions about the relationship between classic formal semantics (including its computational adaptations) and statistical semantics. A promising way to provide insight into these questions was brought forward as Shared Task 1 in the SemEval-2014 campaign for semantic evaluation (Marelli et al., 2014). In this task, a system is given a set of sentence pairs, and has to predict for each pair whether the sentences are somehow related in meaning. Interestingly, this is done using two different metrics: the first stemming from the formal tradition (contradiction, entailed, neutral), and the second in a distributional fashion (a similarity score between 1 and 5). We participated in this shared task with a system rooted in formal semantics. In particular, we were interested in finding out whether paraphrasing techniques could increase the accuracy of our system, whether meaning representations used for textual entailment are useful for predicting semantic similarity, and conversely, whether similarity features could be used to boost accuracy of recognizing textual entailment. In this paper we outline our method and present the results for both the textual entailment and the semantic similarity task.[1]

2 Recognizing Textual Entailment

2.1 Overview

The core of our system for recognizing textual entailment works as follows: (i) produce a formal semantic representation for each sentence for a given sentence pair; (ii) translate these semantic representations into first-order logic; (iii) use off-the-shelf theorem provers and model builders to check whether the first sentence entails the second, or whether the sentences are contradictory. This is essentially an improved version of the framework introduced by Bos & Markert (2006).

To generate background knowledge that could assist in finding a proof we used the lexical database WordNet (Fellbaum, 1998). We also used a large database of paraphrases (Ganitkevitch et al., 2013) to alter the second sentence in case no proof was found at the first attempt, inspired by Bosma & Callison-Burch (2006). The core system reached high precision on entailment and contradiction. To increase recall, we used a classifier trained on the output from our similarity task system (see Section 3) to reclassify the "neutrals" into possible entailments.

2.2 Technicalities

The semantic parser that we used is Boxer (Bos, 2008). It is the last component in the pipeline of the C&C tools (Curran et al., 2007), comprising a tokenizer, POS-tagger, lemmatizer (Minnen et

[1]To reproduce these results in a linux environment (with SWI Prolog) one needs to install the C&C tools (this includes Boxer and the RTE system), the Vampire theorem prover, the two model builders Paradox and Mace-2, and the PPDB-1.0 XL database. Detailed instructions can be found in the `src/scripts/boxer/sick/README` folder of the C&C tools.

Proceedings of the 8th International Workshop on Semantic Evaluation (SemEval 2014), pages 642–646, Dublin, Ireland, August 23-24, 2014.

al., 2001), and a robust parser for CCG (Steedman, 2001). Boxer produces semantic representations based on Discourse Representation Theory (Kamp and Reyle, 1993). We used the standard translation from Discourse Representation Structures to first-order logic, rather than the one based on modal first-order logic (Bos, 2004), since the shared task data did not contain any sentences with propositional argument verbs.

After conversion to first-order logic, we checked with the theorem prover Vampire (Riazanov and Voronkov, 2002) whether a proof could be found for the first sentence entailing the second, and whether a contradiction could be detected for the conjunction of both sentences translated into first-order logic. If neither a proof nor a contradiction could be found within 30 seconds, we used the model builder Paradox (Claessen and Sörensson, 2003) to produce a model of the two sentences separately, and one of the two sentences together. However, even though Paradox is an efficient piece of software, it does not always return minimal models with respect to the extensions of the non-logical symbols. Therefore, in a second step, we asked the model builder Mace-2 (McCune, 1998) to construct a minimal model for the domain size established by Paradox. These models are used as features in the similarity task (Section 3).

Background knowledge is important to increase recall of the theorem prover, but hard to acquire automatically (Bos, 2013). Besides translating hypernym relations of WordNet to first-order logic axioms, we also reasoned that it would be beneficial to have a way of dealing with multi-word expressions. But instead of translating paraphrases into axioms, we used them to rephrase the input sentence in case no proof or contradiction was found for the original sentence pair. Given a paraphrase SRC$\mapsto$TGT, we rephrased the first sentence of a pair only if SRC matches with up to four words, no words of TGT were already in the first sentence, and every word of TGT appeared in the second sentence. The paraphrases themselves were taken from PPDB-1.0 (Ganitkevitch et al., 2013). In the training phrase we found that the XL version (comprising o2m, m2o, phrasal, lexical) gave the best results (using a larger version caused a strong decrease in precision, while smaller versions lead to a decrease in recall).

We trained a separate classifier in order to reclassify items judged by our RTE system as being neutral. This classifier uses a single feature, namely the relatedness score for each sentence pair. As training material, we used the gold relatedness scores from the training and trial sets. For classification of the test set, we used the relatedness scores obtained from our Semantic Similarity system (see Section 3). The classifier is a Support Vector Machine classifier, in the implementation provided by *Scikit-Learn* (Pedregosa et al., 2011), based on the commonly used implementation *LIBSVM* (Chang and Lin, 2011). We used the implementation's standard parameters.

2.3 Results

We submitted two runs. The first (primary) run was produced by a configuration that included reclassifying the 'neutrals'. The second run is without the reclassification of the neutrals. After submission we ran a system that did not use the paraphrasing technique in order to measure what influence the PPDB had on our performance. The results are summarized in Table 1. In the training phase we got the best results for the configuration using the PPDB and reclassication, which was submitted as our primary run.

Table 1: Results on the entailment task for various system configurations.

System Configuration	**Accuracy**
most frequent class baseline	56.7
−PPDB, −reclassification	77.6
+PPDB, −reclassification	79.6
+PPDB, +reclassification	81.6

In sum, our system for recognizing entailment performed well reaching 82% accuracy and by far outperforming the most-frequent class baseline (Table 1). We show some selected examples illustrating the strengths of our system below.

Example 1627 (ENTAILMENT)
A man is mixing a few ingredients in a bowl
Some ingredients are being mixed in a bowl by a person

Example 2709 (CONTRADICTION)
There is no person boiling noodles
A woman is boiling noodles in water

Example 9051 (ENTAILMENT)
A pair of kids are sticking out blue and green colored tongues
Two kids are sticking out blue and green colored tongues

A proof for entailment is found for Ex. 1627, because for passive sentences Boxer produces a meaning representation equivalent to their active variants. A contradiction is detected for Ex. 2709 because of the way negation is handled by Boxer. Both examples trigger background knowledge from WordNet hyperonyms (man $\rightarrow$ person; woman $\rightarrow$ person) that is used in the proofs.[2] Ex. 9051 shows how paraphrasing helps, here "a pair of" $\mapsto$ "two".

3 Determining Semantic Similarity

3.1 Overview

The Semantic Similarity system follows a supervised approach to solving the regression problem of determining the similarity between each given sentence pair. The system uses a variety of features, ranging from simpler ones such as word overlap, to more complex ones in the form of deep semantic features and features derived from a compositional distributional semantic model. The majority of these features are derived from the models from our RTE system (see Section 2).

3.2 Technicalities

3.2.1 Regressor

The regressor used is a Random Forest Regressor in the implementation provided by *Scikit-Learn* (Pedregosa et al., 2011). Random forests are robust with respect to noise and do not overfit easily (Breiman, 2001). These two factors make them a highly suitable choice for our approach, since we are dealing with a relatively large number of weak features, i.e., features which may be seen as individually containing a rather small amount of information for the problem at hand.

Our parameter settings for the regressor is follows. We used a total of 1000 trees, with a maximum tree depth of 20. At each node in a tree the regressor looked at maximum 3 features in order to decide on the split. The quality of each such split is determined using mean squared error as measure. These parameter values were optimised when training on the training set, with regards to performance on the trial set.

3.2.2 Feature overview

We used a total of 32 features for our regressor. Due to space constraints, we have sub-divided our features into groups by the model/method involved. For all features we compared the outcome of the original sentence pair with the outcome of the paraphrased sentence pairs (see Section 2.2)[3]. If the paraphrased sentence pair yielded a higher feature overlap score than the original sentence pair, we utilized the former. In other words, we assume that the sentence pair generated with paraphrases is a good representation of the original pair, and that similarities found here are an improvement on the original score.

Logical model We used the logical models created by Paradox and Mace for the two sentences separately, as well as a combined model (see Section 2.2). The features extracted from this model are the proportion of overlap between the instances in the domain, and the proportion of overlap between the relations in the model.

Noun/verb overlap We first extracted and lemmatised all nouns and verbs from the sentence pairs. With these lemmas we calculated two new separate features, the overlap of the noun lemmas and the overlap of the verb lemmas.

Discourse Representation Structure (DRS) The two most interesting pieces of information which easily can be extracted from the DRS models are the agents and patients. We first extracted the agents for both sentences in a sentence pair, and then computed the overlap between the two lists of agents. Secondly, since all sentences in the corpus have exactly one patient, we extracted the patient of each sentence and used this overlap as a binary feature.

Wordnet novelty We build one tree containing all WordNet concepts included in the first sentence, and one containing all WordNet concepts of both sentences together. The difference in size between these two trees is used as a feature.

RTE The result from our RTE system (entailment, neutral or contradiction) is used as a feature.

Compositional Distributional Semantic Model Our CDSM feature is based on word vectors derived using a Skip-Gram model (Mikolov et al., 2013a; Mikolov et al., 2013b). We used the publicly available *word2vec*[4] tool to calculate these vectors. We trained the tool on a data set consisting of the first billion characters of Wikipedia[5] and the English part of the French-English 10^9 corpus used in the wmt11 translation task[6]. The Wikipedia section of the data was pre-processed using a script[7] which made the text lower case, removed tables etc. The second section of the data was also converted to lower case prior to training.

We trained the vectors using the following parameter settings. Vector dimensionality was set

[2] In the training data around 20% of the proofs for entailment were established with the help of WordNet, but only 4% for detecting contradictions.

[3] In addition to the PPDB we added handling of negations, by removing some negations {not, n't} and substituting others {no:a, none:some, nobody:somebody}.

[4] code.google.com/p/word2vec/

[5] mattmahoney.net/dc/enwik9.zip

[6] statmt.org/wmt11/translation-task.html#download

[7] mattmahoney.net/dc/textdata.html

Table 2: Pearson correlation and MSE obtained on the test set for each feature group in isolation.

Feature group	p [−PPDB]	p [+PPDB]	MSE [−PPDB]	MSE [+PPDB]
Logical model	0.649	0.737	0.590	0.476
Noun/verb overlap	0.647	0.676	0.592	0.553
DRS	0.634	0.667	0.610	0.569
Wordnet novelty	0.652	0.651	0.590	0.591
RTE	0.621	0.620	0.626	0.627
CDSM	0.608	0.609	0.681	0.679
IDs	0.493	0.493	0.807	0.807
Synset	0.414	0.417	0.891	0.889
Word overlap	0.271	0.340	0.944	0.902
Sentence length	0.227	0.228	0.971	0.971
All with IDs	0.836	0.842	0.308	0.297
All without IDs	0.819	**0.827**	0.336	**0.322**

to 1600 with a context window of 10 words. The skip-gram model with hierarchical softmax, and a negative sampling of $1e$-3 was used.

To arrive at the feature used for our regressor, we first calculated the element-wise sum of the vectors of each word in the given sentences. We then calculated the cosine distance between the sentences in the sentence pair.

IDs One surprisingly helpful feature was each sentence pair's ID in the corpus.[8] Since this feature clearly is not representative of what one would have access to in a real-world scenario, it was not included in the primary run.

Synset Overlap We built one set for each sentence pair consisting of each possible lemma form of all possible noun synsets for each word. The proportion of overlap between the two resulting sets was then used as a feature. Given cases where relatively synonymous words are used (e.g. *kid* and *child*), these will often belong to the same synset, thus resulting in a high overlap score.

Synset Distance We first generated each possible word pair consisting of one word from each sentence. Using these pairings, we calculated the maximum *path similarity* between the noun synsets available for these words. This calculation is restricted so that each word in the first sentence in each pair is only used once.

Word overlap Our word overlap feature was calculated by first creating one set per sentence, containing each word occurring in that sentence. The four most common words in the corpus were used as a stop list, and removed from each set. The proportion of overlap between the two sets was then used as our word overlap feature.

Sentence Lengths The difference in length between the sentence pairs proved to be a somewhat useful feature. Although mildly useful for this particular data set, we do not expect this to be a particularly helpful feature in real world applications.

3.3 Results

We trained our system on 5000 sentence pairs, and evaluated it on 4927 sentence pairs. Table 2 contains our scores for the evaluation, broken up per feature group. Our relatedness system yielded the highest scores compared to all other systems in this shared task, as measured by MSE and Spearman correlation scores. Although our system performed slightly worse as measured by Pearson correlation, there is no significant difference to the scores obtained by the two higher ranked systems.

4 Conclusion

Our work shows that paraphrasing techniques can be used to improve the results of a textual entailment system. Additionally, the scores from our semantic similarity measure could be used to improve the scores of the textual entailment system. Our work also shows that deep semantic features can be used to predict semantic relatedness.

Acknowledgements

We thank Chris Callison-Burch, Juri Ganitkevitch and Ellie Pavlick for getting the most out of PPDB. We also thank our colleagues Valerio Basile, Harm Brouwer, Kilian Evang and Noortje Venhuizen for valuable comments and feedback.

[8] We discovered that the ordering of the entire data set was informative for the prediction of sentence relatedness. We have illustrated this by using the ordering of the sentences (i.e. the sentence IDs) as a feature in our model, and thereby obtaining better results. Relying on such a non-natural ordering of the sentences would be methodologically flawed, and therefore this feature was not used in our primary run.

References

Johan Bos and Katja Markert. 2006. Recognising textual entailment with robust logical inference. In Joaquin Quinonero-Candela, Ido Dagan, Bernardo Magnini, and Florence d'Alché Buc, editors, *Machine Learning Challenges, MLCW 2005*, volume 3944 of *LNAI*, pages 404–426.

Johan Bos. 2004. Computational Semantics in Discourse: Underspecification, Resolution, and Inference. *Journal of Logic, Language and Information*, 13(2):139–157.

Johan Bos. 2008. Wide-Coverage Semantic Analysis with Boxer. In J. Bos and R. Delmonte, editors, *Semantics in Text Processing. STEP 2008 Conference Proceedings*, volume 1 of *Research in Computational Semantics*, pages 277–286. College Publications.

Johan Bos. 2013. Is there a place for logic in recognizing textual entailment? *Linguistic Issues in Language Technology*, 9(3):1–18.

Wauter Bosma and Chris Callison-Burch. 2006. Paraphrase substitution for recognizing textual entailment. In *Proceedings of CLEF*.

Leo Breiman. 2001. Random forests. *Machine learning*, 45(1):5–32.

Chih-Chung Chang and Chih-Jen Lin. 2011. LIBSVM: a library for support vector machines. *ACM Transactions on Intelligent Systems and Technology (TIST)*, 2(3):27.

K. Claessen and N. Sörensson. 2003. New techniques that improve mace-style model finding. In P. Baumgartner and C. Fermüller, editors, *Model Computation – Principles, Algorithms, Applications (Cade-19 Workshop)*, pages 11–27, Miami, Florida, USA.

James Curran, Stephen Clark, and Johan Bos. 2007. Linguistically Motivated Large-Scale NLP with C&C and Boxer. In *Proceedings of the 45th Annual Meeting of the Association for Computational Linguistics Companion Volume Proceedings of the Demo and Poster Sessions*, pages 33–36, Prague, Czech Republic.

Christiane Fellbaum, editor. 1998. *WordNet. An Electronic Lexical Database*. The MIT Press.

Juri Ganitkevitch, Benjamin VanDurme, and Chris Callison-Burch. 2013. PPDB: The paraphrase database. In *Proceedings of the 2013 Conference of the North American Chapter of the Association for Computational Linguistics (NAACL 2013)*, Atlanta, Georgia, June. Association for Computational Linguistics.

Hans Kamp and Uwe Reyle. 1993. *From Discourse to Logic; An Introduction to Modeltheoretic Semantics of Natural Language, Formal Logic and DRT*. Kluwer, Dordrecht.

M. Marelli, L. Bentivogli, M. Baroni, R. Bernardi, S. Menini, and R. Zamparelli. 2014. Semeval-2014 task 1: Evaluation of compositional distributional semantic models on full sentences through semantic relatedness and textual entailment. In *Proceedings of SemEval 2014: International Workshop on Semantic Evaluation*.

W. McCune. 1998. Automatic Proofs and Counterexamples for Some Ortholattice Identities. *Information Processing Letters*, 65(6):285–291.

Tomas Mikolov, Kai Chen, Greg Corrado, and Jeffrey Dean. 2013a. Efficient estimation of word representations in vector space. *arXiv preprint arXiv:1301.3781*.

Tomas Mikolov, Ilya Sutskever, Kai Chen, Greg S Corrado, and Jeff Dean. 2013b. Distributed representations of words and phrases and their compositionality. In *Advances in Neural Information Processing Systems*, pages 3111–3119.

Guido Minnen, John Carroll, and Darren Pearce. 2001. Applied morphological processing of english. *Journal of Natural Language Engineering*, 7(3):207–223.

F. Pedregosa, G. Varoquaux, A. Gramfort, V. Michel, B. Thirion, O. Grisel, M. Blondel, P. Prettenhofer, R. Weiss, V. Dubourg, J. Vanderplas, A. Passos, D. Cournapeau, M. Brucher, M. Perrot, and E. Duchesnay. 2011. Scikit-learn: Machine learning in Python. *Journal of Machine Learning Research*, 12:2825–2830.

A. Riazanov and A. Voronkov. 2002. The Design and Implementation of Vampire. *AI Communications*, 15(2–3):91–110.

Mark Steedman. 2001. *The Syntactic Process*. The MIT Press.

Think Positive: Towards Twitter Sentiment Analysis from Scratch

Cícero Nogueira dos Santos
Brazilian Research Lab
IBM Research
ciceron s@br.ibm.com

Abstract

In this paper we describe a Deep Convolutional Neural Network (DNN) approach to perform two sentiment detection tasks: message polarity classification and contextual polarity disambiguation. We apply the proposed approach for the SemEval-2014 Task 9: Sentiment Analysis in Twitter. Despite not using any handcrafted feature or sentiment lexicons, our system achieves very competitive results for Twitter data.

1 Introduction

In this work we apply a recently proposed deep convolutional neural network (dos Santos and Gatti, 2014) that exploits from character- to sentence-level information to perform sentiment analysis of Twitter messages (tweets). The network proposed by dos Santos and Gatti (2014), named Character to Sentence Convolutional Neural Network (CharSCNN), uses two convolutional layers to extract relevant features from words and messages of any size.

We evaluate CharSCNN in the unconstrained track of the SemEval-2014 Task 9: Sentiment Analysis in Twitter (Rosenthal et al., 2014). Two subtasks are proposed in the SemEval-2014 Task 9: the contextual polarity disambiguation (SubtaskA), which consists in determining the polarity (positive, negative, or neutral) of a marked word or phrase in a given message; and the message polarity classification (SubtaskB), which consists in classifying the polarity of the whole message. We use the same neural network to perform both tasks. The only difference is that in SubtaskA, CharSCNN is fed with a text segment composed by the words in a context window centered at the target word/phrase. While in SubtaskB, CharSCNN is fed with the whole message.

The use of deep neural networks for sentiment analysis has been the focus of recent research. However, instead of convolutional neural network, most investigation has been done in the use of recursive neural networks (Socher et al., 2011; Socher et al., 2012; Socher et al., 2013).

2 Neural Network Architecture

Given a segment of text (e.g. a tweet), CharSCNN computes a score for each sentiment label $\tau \in T = \{positive, negative, neutral\}$. In order to score a text segment, the network takes as input the sequence of words in the segment, and passes it through a sequence of layers where features with increasing levels of complexity are extracted. The network extracts features from the character-level up to the sentence-level.

2.1 Initial Representation Levels

The first layer of the network transforms words into real-valued feature vectors (embeddings) that capture morphological, syntactic and semantic information about the words. We use a fixed-sized word vocabulary V^{wrd}, and we consider that words are composed of characters from a fixed-sized character vocabulary V^{chr}. Given a sentence consisting of N words $\{w_1, w_2, ..., w_N\}$, every word w_n is converted into a vector $u_n = [r^{wrd}; r^{wch}]$, which is composed of two subvectors: the *word-level embedding* $r^{wrd} \in \mathbb{R}^{d^{wrd}}$ and the *character-level embedding* $r^{wch} \in \mathbb{R}^{cl_u^0}$ of w_n. While word-level embeddings are meant to capture syntactic and semantic information, character-level embeddings capture morphological and shape information.

Proceedings of the 8th International Workshop on Semantic Evaluation (SemEval 2014), pages 647–651,
Dublin, Ireland, August 23-24, 2014.

2.1.1 Word-Level Embeddings

Word-level embeddings are encoded by column vectors in an embedding matrix $W^{wrd} \in \mathbb{R}^{d^{wrd} \times |V^{wrd}|}$. Each column $W_i^{wrd} \in \mathbb{R}^{d^{wrd}}$ corresponds to the word-level embedding of the i-th word in the vocabulary. We transform a word w into its word-level embedding r^{wrd} by using the matrix-vector product:

$$r^{wrd} = W^{wrd} v^w \quad (1)$$

where v^w is a vector of size $|V^{wrd}|$ which has value 1 at index w and zero in all other positions. The matrix W^{wrd} is a parameter to be learned, and the size of the word-level embedding d^{wrd} is a hyper-parameter to be chosen by the user.

2.1.2 Character-Level Embeddings

In the task of sentiment analysis of Twitter data, important information can appear in different parts of a hash tag (e.g., "*#SoSad*", "*#ILikeIt*") and many informative adverbs end with the suffix "*ly*" (e.g. "*beautifully*", "*perfectly*" and "*badly*"). Therefore, robust methods to extract morphological and shape information from this type of tokens must take into consideration all characters of the token and select which features are more important for sentiment analysis. Like in (dos Santos and Zadrozny, 2014), we tackle this problem using a convolutional approach (Waibel et al., 1989), which works by producing local features around each character of the word and then combining them using a max operation to create a fixed-sized character-level embedding of the word.

Given a word w composed of M characters $\{c_1, c_2, ..., c_M\}$, we first transform each character c_m into a character embedding r_m^{chr}. Character embeddings are encoded by column vectors in the embedding matrix $W^{chr} \in \mathbb{R}^{d^{chr} \times |V^{chr}|}$. Given a character c, its embedding r^{chr} is obtained by the matrix-vector product:

$$r^{chr} = W^{chr} v^c \quad (2)$$

where v^c is a vector of size $|V^{chr}|$ which has value 1 at index c and zero in all other positions. The input for the convolutional layer is the sequence of character embeddings $\{r_1^{chr}, r_2^{chr}, ..., r_M^{chr}\}$.

The convolutional layer applies a matrix-vector operation to each window of size k^{chr} of successive windows in the sequence $\{r_1^{chr}, r_2^{chr}, ..., r_M^{chr}\}$. Let us define the vector $z_m \in \mathbb{R}^{d^{chr} k^{chr}}$ as the concatenation of the character embedding m, its $(k^{chr} - 1)/2$ left neighbors, and its $(k^{chr} - 1)/2$ right neighbors:

$$z_m = \left(r^{chr}_{m-(k^{chr}-1)/2}, ..., r^{chr}_{m+(k^{chr}-1)/2}\right)^T$$

The convolutional layer computes the j-th element of the vector r^{wch}, which is the character-level embedding of w, as follows:

$$[r^{wch}]_j = \max_{1<m<M} \left[W^0 z_m + b^0\right]_j \quad (3)$$

where $W^0 \in \mathbb{R}^{cl_u^0 \times d^{chr} k^{chr}}$ is the weight matrix of the convolutional layer. The same matrix is used to extract local features around each character window of the given word. Using the max over all character windows of the word, we extract a "global" fixed-sized feature vector for the word.

Matrices W^{chr} and W^0, and vector b^0 are parameters to be learned. The size of the character vector d^{chr}, the number of convolutional units cl_u^0 (which corresponds to the size of the character-level embedding of a word), and the size of the character context window k^{chr} are hyper-parameters.

2.2 Sentence-Level Representation and Scoring

Given a text segment x with N words $\{w_1, w_2, ..., w_N\}$, which have been converted to joint word-level and character-level embedding $\{u_1, u_2, ..., u_N\}$, the next step in CharSCNN consists in extracting a segment-level representation r_x^{seg}. Methods to extract a segment-wide feature set most deal with two main problems: text segments have different sizes; and important information can appear at any position in the segment. A convolutional approach is a good option to tackle this problems, and therefore we use a convolutional layer to compute the segment-wide feature vector r^{seg}. This second convolutional layer works in a very similar way to the one used to extract character-level features for words. This layer produces local features around each word in the text segment and then combines them using a max operation to create a fixed-sized feature vector for the segment.

The second convolutional layer applies a matrix-vector operation to each window of size k^{wrd} of successive windows in the sequence $\{u_1, u_2, ..., u_N\}$. Let us define the vector $z_n \in \mathbb{R}^{(d^{wrd}+cl_u^0)k^{wrd}}$ as the concatenation of a sequence of k^{wrd} embeddings, centralized in the n-th word[1]:

$$z_n = \left(u_{n-(k^{wrd}-1)/2}, \ldots, u_{n+(k^{wrd}-1)/2}\right)^T$$

The convolutional layer computes the j-th element of the vector r^{seg} as follows:

$$[r^{seg}]_j = \max_{1<n<N} \left[W^1 z_n + b^1\right]_j \quad (4)$$

where $W^1 \in \mathbb{R}^{cl_u^1 \times (d^{wrd}+cl_u^0)k^{wrd}}$ is the weight matrix of the convolutional layer. The same matrix is used to extract local features around each word window of the given segment. Using the max over all word windows of the segment, we extract a "global" fixed-sized feature vector for the segment. Matrix W^1 and vector b^1 are parameters to be learned. The number of convolutional units cl_u^1 (which corresponds to the size of the segment-level feature vector), and the size of the word context window k^{wrd} are hyper-parameters to be chosen by the user.

Finally, the vector r_x^{seg}, the "global' feature vector of text segment x, is processed by two usual neural network layers, which extract one more level of representation and compute a score for each sentiment label $\tau \in T$:

$$s(x) = W^3 h(W^2 r_x^{seg} + b^2) + b^3 \quad (5)$$

where matrices $W^2 \in \mathbb{R}^{hl_u \times cl_u^1}$ and $W^3 \in \mathbb{R}^{|T| \times hl_u}$, and vectors $b^2 \in \mathbb{R}^{hl_u}$ and $b^3 \in \mathbb{R}^{|T|}$ are parameters to be learned. The transfer function $h(.)$ is the hyperbolic tangent. The size of the number of hidden units hl_u is a hyper-parameter to be chosen by the user.

2.3 Network Training

Our network is trained by minimizing a negative likelihood over the training set D. Given a text segment x, the network with parameter set θ computes a score $s_\theta(x)_\tau$ for each sentiment label $\tau \in T$. In order to transform this score into a conditional probability $p(\tau|x,\theta)$ of the label given the segment and the set of network parameters θ, we apply a softmax operation over all tags:

$$p(\tau|x,\theta) = \frac{e^{s_\theta(x)_\tau}}{\sum_i e^{s_\theta(x)_i}} \quad (6)$$

Taking the log, we arrive at the following conditional log-probability:

$$\log p(\tau|x,\theta) = s_\theta(x)_\tau - \log\left(\sum_{\forall i \in T} e^{s_\theta(x)_i}\right) \quad (7)$$

We use stochastic gradient descent (SGD) to minimize the negative log-likelihood with respect to θ:

$$\theta \mapsto \sum_{(x,y)\in D} -\log p(y|x,\theta) \quad (8)$$

where (x, y) corresponds to a text segment (e.g. a tweet) in the training corpus D and y represents its respective sentiment class label.

We use the backpropagation algorithm to compute the gradients of the network (Lecun et al., 1998; Collobert, 2011). We implement the CharSCNN architecture using the automatic differentiation capabilities of the *Theano* library (Bergstra et al., 2010).

3 Experimental Setup and Results

3.1 Unsupervised Learning of Word-Level Embeddings

Unsupervised pre-training of word embeddings has shown to be an effective approach to improve model accuracy (Collobert et al., 2011; Luong et al., 2013; Zheng et al., 2013). In our experiments, we perform unsupervised learning of word-level embeddings using the *word2vec* tool[2].

We use two Twitter datasets as sources of unlabeled data: the Stanford Twitter Sentiment corpus (Go et al., 2009), which contains 1.6 million tweets; and a dataset containing 10.4 million tweets that were collected in October 2012 for a previous work by the author (Gatti et al., 2013). We tokenize these corpora using Gimpel et al.'s (2011) tokenizer, and removed messages that are less than 5 characters long (including white spaces) or have less than 3 tokens. Like in (Collobert et al., 2011) and (Luong et al., 2013), we lowercase all words and substitute each numerical digit by a 0 (e.g., *1967* becomes *0000*). The resulting corpus contains about 12 million tweets.

We do not perform unsupervised learning of character-level embeddings, which are initialized by randomly sampling each value from an uniform distribution: $\mathcal{U}(-r, r)$, where $r = \sqrt{\frac{6}{|V^{chr}| + d^{chr}}}$. The character vocabulary is

[1]We use a special *padding token* for the words with indices outside of the text segment boundaries.

[2]https://code.google.com/p/word2vec/

constructed by the (not lowercased) words in the training set, which allows the neural network to capture relevant information about capitalization.

3.2 Sentiment Corpora and Model Setup

SemEval-2014 Task 9 is a rerun of the SemEval-2013 Task 2 (Nakov et al., 2013), hence the training set used in 2014 is the same of the 2013 task. However, as we downloaded the Twitter training and development sets in 2014 only, we were not able to download the complete dataset since some tweets have been deleted by their respective creators. In Table 1, we show the number of messages in our SemEval-2013 Task 2 datasets.

Dataset	SubtaskA	SubtaskB
Train	7390	8213
Dev.	904	1415
Twitter2013 (test)	3491	3265
SMS2013 (test)	2,334	2,093

Table 1: Number of tweets in our version of SemEval-2013 Task2 datasets.

In SemEval-2014 Task 9, three different test sets are used: Twitter2014, Twitter2014Sarcarm and LiveJournal2014. While the two first contain Twitter messages, the last one contains sentences from LiveJournal blogs. In Table 2, we show the number of messages in the SemEval-2014 Task 9 test datasets.

Test Dataset	SubtaskA	SubtaskB
Twitter2014	2597	1939
Twitter2014Sarcasm	124	86
LiveJournal2014	1315	1142

Table 2: Number of tweets in the SemEval-2014 Task9 test datasets.

We use the copora Twitter2013 (test) and SMS2013 to tune CharSCNN's hyper-parameter values. In Table 3, we show the selected hyper-parameter values, which are the same for both SubtaskA and SubtaskB. We concatenate the SemEval-2013 Task 2 training and development sets to train the submitted model.

Parameter	Parameter Name	Value
d^{wrd}	Word-Level Emb. dim.	100
k^{wrd}	Word Context window	3
d^{chr}	Char. Emb. dim.	5
k^{chr}	Char. Context window	5
cl_u^0	Char. Convol. Units	30
cl_u^1	Word Convol. Units	100
hl_u	Hidden Units	300
λ	Learning Rate	0.02

Table 3: Neural Network Hyper-Parameters.

3.3 Sentiment Prediction Results

In Table 4, we present the official results of our submission to the SemEval-2014 Task9. In SubtaskB, CharSCNN's result for the Twitter2014 test corpus is the top 11 out of 50 submissions, and is 3.9 F-measure points from the top performing system. In the SubtaskA, CharSCNN's result for the Twitter2014 test corpus is the top 6 out of 27 submissions. These are very promising results, since our approach do not use any handcrafted features or lexicons, all features (representations) are automatically learned from unlabeled and labeled data.

Nevertheless, our system result for the LiveJournal2014 corpus in SubtaskB is regular. For this dataset CharSCNN achieves only the top 25 out of 50 submissions, and is 7.9 F-measure points behind the top performing system. We believe the main reason for this poor result is the exclusive use of Twitter data in the unsupervised pre-training.

Test Subset	SubtaskA	SubtaskB
Twitter2014	82.05	67.04
Twitter2014Sarcasm	76.74	47.85
LiveJournal2014	80.90	66.96
Twitter2013	88.06	68.15
SMS2013	87.65	63.20

Table 4: Average F-measure of CharSCNN for different test sets.

4 Conclusions

In this work we describe a sentiment analysis system based on a deep neural network architecture that analyses text at multiple levels, from character-level to sentence-level. We apply the proposed system to the SemEval-2014 Task 9 and achieve very competitive results for Twitter data in both contextual polarity disambiguation and message polarity classification subtasks. As a future work, we would like to investigate the impact of the system performance for the LiveJournal2014 corpus when the unsupervised pre-training is performed using in-domain texts.

References

James Bergstra, Olivier Breuleux, Frédéric Bastien, Pascal Lamblin, Razvan Pascanu, Guillaume Desjardins, Joseph Turian, David Warde-Farley, and Yoshua Bengio. 2010. Theano: a CPU and GPU math expression compiler. In *Proceedings of the Python for Scientific Computing Conference (SciPy)*.

Ronan Collobert, Jason Weston, Léon Bottou, Michael Karlen, Koray Kavukcuoglu, and Pavel Kuksa. 2011. Natural language processing (almost) from scratch. *Journal of Machine Learning Research*, 12:2493–2537.

Ronan Collobert. 2011. Deep learning for efficient discriminative parsing. In *Proceedings of the Fourteenth International Conference on Artificial Intelligence and Statistics (AISTATS)*, pages 224–232.

Cícero Nogueira dos Santos and Maíra Gatti. 2014. Deep convolutional neural networks for sentiment analysis of short texts. In *Proceedings of the 25th International Conference on Computational Linguistics (COLING)*, Dublin, Ireland.

Cícero Nogueira dos Santos and Bianca Zadrozny. 2014. Learning character-level representations for part-of-speech tagging. In *Proceedings of the 31st International Conference on Machine Learning (ICML), JMLR: W&CP volume 32*, Beijing, China.

Maíra Gatti, Ana Paula Appel, Cícero Nogueira dos Santos, Claudio Santos Pinhanez, Paulo Rodrigo Cavalin, and Samuel Martins Barbosa Neto. 2013. A simulation-based approach to analyze the information diffusion in microblogging online social network. In *Winter Simulation Conference*, pages 1685–1696.

Kevin Gimpel, Nathan Schneider, Brendan O'Connor, Dipanjan Das, Daniel Mills, Jacob Eisenstein, Michael Heilman, Dani Yogatama, Jeffrey Flanigan, and Noah A. Smith. 2011. Part-of-speech tagging for twitter: Annotation, features, and experiments. In *Proceedings of the 49th Annual Meeting of the Association for Computational Linguistics: Human Language Technologies: Short Papers - Volume 2*, pages 42–47.

Alec Go, Richa Bhayani, and Lei Huang. 2009. Twitter sentiment classification using distant supervision. Technical report, Stanford University.

Yann Lecun, Lon Bottou, Yoshua Bengio, and Patrick Haffner. 1998. Gradient-based learning applied to document recognition. In *Proceedings of the IEEE*, pages 2278–2324.

Minh-Thang Luong, Richard Socher, and Christopher D. Manning. 2013. Better word representations with recursive neural networks for morphology. In *Proceedings of the Conference on Computational Natural Language Learning*, Sofia, Bulgaria.

Preslav Nakov, Sara Rosenthal, Zornitsa Kozareva, Veselin Stoyanov, Alan Ritter, and Theresa Wilson. 2013. Semeval-2013 task 2: Sentiment analysis in twitter. In *Second Joint Conference on Lexical and Computational Semantics (*SEM), Volume 2: Proceedings of the Seventh International Workshop on Semantic Evaluation (SemEval 2013)*, pages 312–320, Atlanta, Georgia, USA, June. Association for Computational Linguistics.

Sara Rosenthal, Preslav Nakov, Alan Ritter, and Veselin Stoyanov. 2014. SemEval-2014 Task 9: Sentiment Analysis in Twitter. In Preslav Nakov and Torsten Zesch, editors, *Proceedings of the 8th International Workshop on Semantic Evaluation*, SemEval'14, Dublin, Ireland.

Richard Socher, Jeffrey Pennington, Eric H. Huang, Andrew Y. Ng, and Christopher D. Manning. 2011. Semi-supervised recursive autoencoders for predicting sentiment distributions. In *Proceedings of the Conference on Empirical Methods in Natural Language Processing*, pages 151–161.

Richard Socher, Brody Huval, Christopher D. Manning, and Andrew Y. Ng. 2012. Semantic compositionality through recursive matrix-vector spaces. In *Proceedings of theConference on Empirical Methods in Natural Language Processing*, pages 1201–1211.

Richard Socher, Alex Perelygin, Jean Wu, Jason Chuang, Christopher D. Manning, Andrew Y. Ng, and Christopher Potts. 2013. Recursive deep models for semantic compositionality over a sentiment treebank. In *Proceedings of the Conference on Empirical Methods in Natural Language Processing*, pages 1631–1642.

Alexander Waibel, Toshiyuki Hanazawa, Geoffrey Hinton, Kiyohiro Shikano, and Kevin J. Lang. 1989. Phoneme recognition using time-delay neural networks. *IEEE Transactions on Acoustics, Speech and Signal Processing*, 37(3):328–339.

Xiaoqing Zheng, Hanyang Chen, and Tianyu Xu. 2013. Deep learning for chinese word segmentation and pos tagging. In *Proceedings of the Conference on Empirical Methods in NLP*, pages 647–657.

ThinkMiners: Disorder Recognition using Conditional Random Fields and Distributional Semantics

Ankur Parikh **Avinesh PVS** **Joy Mustafi** **Lalit Agarwalla** **Ashish Mungi**
IBM India Pvt Ltd, IBM Software Group, Watson
{anparikh,pavinesh,jmustafi,lalit.agarwalla,r1amungi}@in.ibm.com

Abstract

In 2014, SemEval organized multiple challenges on natural language processing and information retrieval. One of the task was analysis of the clinical text. This challenge is further divided into two tasks. The task A of the challenge was to extract disorder mention spans in the clinical text and the task B was to map each of the disorder mentions to a unique Unified Medical Language System Concept Unique Identifier. We participated in the task A and developed a clinical disorder recognition system. The proposed system consists of a Conditional Random Fields based approach to recognize disorder entities. The SemEval challenge organizers manually annotated disorder entities in 298 clinical notes, of which 199 notes were used for training and 99 for development. On the test data, our system achieved the F-measure of 0.844 for entity recognition in relaxed and 0.689 in strict evaluation.

Keywords: medical language processing, clinical concept extraction, conditional random fields.

1 Introduction

Mining concepts from the electronic medical records such as clinical reports, discharge summaries as well as large number of doctor's notes has become an utmost important task for automatic analysis in the medical domain. Identification and mapping of the concepts like symptoms, disorders, surgical procedures, body sites to a normalized standards are usually the first steps towards understanding natural language text in the medical records.

In this paper, we describe a machine learning based disorder recognition system for the Task 7A of 2014 SemEval challenge. In Section 2 we give a background of the existing solutions to tackle the problem. Section 3 covers our approach in detail, followed by evaluation and conclusion in Section 4 and Section 5 respectively.

2 Background

In recent times, many systems have been developed to extract clinical concepts from various types of clinical notes. The earlier natural language processing (NLP) systems were mainly built heavily using domain knowledge i.e. medical dictionaries. These systems include MetaMap (Aronson and Lang, 2010), HiTEX (Zeng et al., 2006), KnowledgeMap (Denny et al., 2003), MedLEE (Friedman et al., 1994), SymText (Koehler, 1994) and Mplus (Christensen et al., 2002). In the past couple of years, researchers have been exploring the use of machine learning algorithms in the clinical concept detection. To promote the research in this field many organizations such as ShARe/CLEF, SemEval have organized a few clinical NLP challenges. In CLEF 2013 (Pradhan et al., 2013), the challenge was to recognize medication-related concepts. Both rule-based (Fan et al., 2013; Ramanan et al., 2013; Wang and Akella, 2013) and machine learning based methods as well as hybrid methods (Xia et al., 2013; Osborne et al., 2013; Hervas et al., 2013) were developed. In this shared-task sequential labeling algorithms (i.e., Conditional Random Fields (CRF)) (Gung, 2013; Patrick et al., 2013; Bodnari et al., 2013; Zuccon et al., 2013) and machine learning methods (i.e., Support Vector Machine (SVM)) (Cogley et al., 2013) have been demonstrated to achieve promising performance when provided with a large annotated corpus for

Proceedings of the 8th International Workshop on Semantic Evaluation (SemEval 2014), pages 652–656,
Dublin, Ireland, August 23-24, 2014.

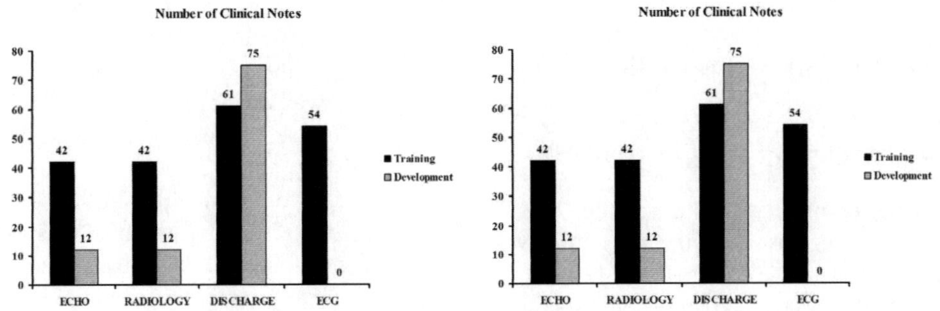

Figure 1: Dataset distribution

training.

3 Approach

Entity recognition has been tried in various domains like news articles, Wikipedia, sports articles, financial reports and clinical texts. In clinical text, entities can vary from medical procedures, disorders, body site indicators etc. Clinical text also presents with a peculiar concept of disjoint disorders/entities. This phenomenon is common in clinical domain compared to others and further complicates entity extraction from clinical notes.

3.1 Data

The data consisted of around 298 notes from different clinical types including radiology reports, discharge summaries, ECG and ECHO reports. For each note, disorder entities were annotated based on a pre-defined guidelines. The data set was further divided into two, with 199 notes in the training set and 99 notes in the development set. The training set contains 5811 disorders where as the development contained 5340 disorders. Figure 1 shows the distribution of the training and development set respectively.

3.2 Data Preprocessing

In the pre-processing step we tokenized, lemmatized and tagged the text with part of speech using the Apache cTAKES[1] (Savova et al., 2010). Further, section and source meta data extraction is done for the text in the documents.

In Named Entity Recognition (NER), when solved using machine learning, the text is typically converted to BIO format (Beginning, Inside and Outside the entity). BIO representation means the words in the text are assigned one of the following tags B - begin, I - inside and O - outside of the entity i.e. in this case a disorder. So now the task of NER is a sequence labeling problem to assign the labels to the tokens. Especially in the medical domain, the challenge is more complicated due to the presence of disjoint disorders (<10%), which could not be solved using the traditional BIO-notation. BIO approach works well with entities which are consecutive. So, we took an enhanced approach (Tang et al., 2013a) where the consecutive disorders are assigned traditional BIO tags and for disjoint disorders we create two tag sets a) D{B,I} : for disjoint entity words which are not shared by multiple concepts; and b) H{B,I}: for disjoint entity words which belong to more than one disjoint concept.

The following examples show the annotations of consecutive as well as disjoint disorders.

1: "The **left atrium** is moderately **dilated**."
"The/O left/DB atrium/DI is/O moderately/O dilated/DB ./O"

2: "The **left** & **right atrium** are moderately **dilated**."
"The/O left/DB &/O right/DB atrium/HB are/O moderately/O dilated/HB ./O"

3.3 Sequence Labeling

We have used Conditional Random Fields (CRF), a popular approach to solve sequence labeling tasks. CRF++[2] was used as an implementation of CRF for our purpose.

[1] https://ctakes.apache.org/

[2] http://crfpp.googlecode.com/svn/trunk/doc/index.html

Feature set used for the learning algorithm:

- **Word level features**: words [-2,2], suffix and prefix.
- **Syntactic features**: parts-of-speech(POS).
- **Discourse features**: source & section. Sentence containing disorder mentions usually have similar syntactic patterns based on sections (ex: 'Past Medical History') and source type (ex: discharge summary, radiology report). To capture this, source and section meta data have been provided as a feature.
- **Distributional semantics**: We used a contextual similarity based approach from the popular concept called NC-value (Frantzi et al., 2000).

  We followed the following steps to encapsulate the distributional semantics into the learning model:

  - For all the disorders in the training data we created two sets of contextual words namely context before ($CB_a train$) and context after ($CA_a train$). These words belong to open class (Noun, Verb, Adjective, Adverb) allocated for each section (S_j).
  - Weights are calculated for the contextual words.

    $$\text{Weight}(b_{train}) = \frac{freq(disorders,b)}{freq(disorders)}$$

  - For each word in the test data we created a similar sets of contextual words(CB_a, CA_a) as above.
  - Two scores are calculated for each token based on the product of frequency of the contextual word per section S_j with weight calculated of that word in the training set.

    For each section (S_j):

    $$NC\text{-}value_B(a) = \sum_{b \epsilon CB_a, S_j} f_a(b_{test}) * weight(b_{train}) \quad (1)$$

    $$NC\text{-}value_A(a) = \sum_{b \epsilon CA_a, S_j} f_a(b_{test}) * weight(b_{train}) \quad (2)$$

    where
    a is the candidate term,
    CB_a is the set of context words of "a" in a window of [-2,0],
    CA_a is the set of context words of "a" in a window of [0,2],
    S_j is a section like "Past Medical History", "Lab Reports" etc.
    b is a word from CB_a or CA_a,
    $f_a(b_{test})$ is the frequency of b as a term context word of "a" in the test set,
    $weight(b_{train})$ is the weight of b as term context word of a disorder in the training set,
    $NC\text{-}value_B(a)$ is the distributional semantic score of contextual words ***before*** the candidate term,
    $NC\text{-}value_A(a)$ is the distributional semantic score of contextual words ***after*** the candidate term.
  - Further a similarity class is calculated based on a set of thresholds on the NC-value namely High-Sim, Med-Sim, Low-Sim and assigned to the tokens.

Most of the features were similar to that of the previous approaches (Tang et al., 2013a; Tang et al., 2012; Tang et al., 2013; Jiang et al., 2011) with an addition of an innovative distributional semantics based features (Nc-value$_B$, NC-value$_A$), which we have tried and tested for concept mining in clinical text.

4 Evaluation

The evaluation was done in two categories a) strict evaluation: exact match, which requires the starting and ending of the concept to be the same as the gold standard data b) relaxed evaluation: here the concepts don't match exactly with the start and end of the concept but may overlap.

In the strict and relaxed evaluation, the best F-measure among our system was 0.689, 0.844 without the distributional semantics where as best Precision was 0.907, 0.749 with the distributional semantics as a feature. Table 1. shows the detailed result.

5 Conclusion

Extraction of the concepts from the medical text is the fundamental task in the process of analysing patient data. In this paper we have tried a CRF based approach to mine the disorder terms from the clinical free text. We have tried various word

SemEval-2014 Shared Task 7A	Strict			Relaxed		
	Precision	Recall	F-measure	Precision	Recall	F-measure
Disorder Recognition without Distributional Semantics Feature	0.734	0.65	0.689	0.892	0.802	0.844
Disorder Recognition with Distributional Semantics Feature	0.749	0.617	0.677	0.907	0.758	0.826

Table 1: Results of the system on test set

level, syntactic, discourse and distributional semantic based features as adapted to the medical domain.

We have observed an increase (+1.5%) in precision but a drastic fall (-4.4%) in recall while using the distributional semantic feature. Ideally this feature has to improve the results because it takes contextual features into consideration. In our opinion inappropriate scaling of the feature values might have caused the drop. Further we would like to investigate the use of large unlabeled data, dependency tree based context and more experiments have to be carried out like threshold setting, feature value scaling to show better results. Also due to license issues we could not use UMLS dictionary. From our survey we figured out that 2-3% of improvement has been observed when the concepts from the dictionary are used.

References

B. Tang, H. Cao, Y. Wu, M. Jiang, and H. Xu. 2013. *Recognizing clinical entities in hospital discharge summaries using Structural Support Vector Machines with word representation features*. BMC Med Inform Decis Mak, vol. 13 Suppl 1, p. S1.

M. Jiang, Y. Chen, M. Liu, S. T. Rosenbloom, S. Mani, J. C. Denny, and H. Xu. 2011. *A study of machine-learning-based approaches to extract clinical entities and their assertions from discharge summaries*. J Am Med Inform Assoc, vol. 18, no. 5, pp. 601606.

B. Tang, Y. Wu, M. Jiang, Y. Chen, J. C. Denny, and H. Xu. 2013. *A hybrid system for temporal information extraction from clinical text*. J Am Med Inform Assoc.

B. Tang, H. Cao, Y. Wu, M. Jiang, and H. Xu. 2012. *Clinical entity recognition using structural support vector machines with rich features*. in Proceedings of the ACM sixth international workshop on Data and text mining in biomedical informatics, New York, NY, USA, pp. 1320.

C. Friedman, P. O. Alderson, J. H. Austin, J. J. Cimino, and S. B. Johnson. 1994. *A general natural-language text processor for clinical radiology*. J Am Med Inform Assoc, vol. 1, no. 2, pp. 161174.

S. B. Koehler. 1994. *SymText: a natural language understanding system for encoding free text medical data*. University of Utah.

L. M. Christensen, P. J. Haug, and M. Fiszman. 2002. *MPLUS: a probabilistic medical language understanding system*. in Proceedings of the ACL-02 workshop on Natural language processing in the biomedical domain - Volume 3, Stroudsburg, PA, USA, pp. 2936.

J. C. Denny, P. R. Irani, F. H. Wehbe, J. D. Smithers, and A. Spickard. 2003. *The KnowledgeMap Project: Development of a Concept-Based Medical School Curriculum Database*. AMIA Annu Symp Proc, vol. 2003, pp. 195199.

G. K. Savova, J. J. Masanz, P. V. Ogren, J. Zheng, S. Sohn, K. C. Kipper Schuler, and C. G. Chute. 2010. *Mayo clinical Text Analysis and Knowledge Extraction System (cTAKES): architecture, component evaluation and applications*. J Am Med Inform Assoc, vol. 17, no. 5, pp. 507513.

Q. T. Zeng, S. Goryachev, S. Weiss, M. Sordo, S. N. Murphy, and R. Lazarus. 2006. *Extracting principal diagnosis, co-morbidity and smoking status for asthma research: evaluation of a natural language processing system*. BMC Med Inform Decis Mak, vol. 6, p. 30.

A. R. Aronson and F. M. Lang. 2010. *An overview of MetaMap: historical perspective and recent advances*. J Am Med Inform Assoc, vol. 17, no. 3, pp. 229236.

. Uzuner, I. Solti, and E. Cadag. 2010. *Extracting medication information from clinical text*. J Am Med Inform Assoc, vol. 17, no. 5, pp. 514518.

Katerina Frantzi, Sophia Ananiadou, and Hideki Mima 2000. *Automatic recognition of multi-word terms:. the C-value/NC-value method*. International Journal on Digital Libraries 3(2):115–130.

James Cogley, Nicola Stokes and Joe Carthy. 2013. *Medical Disorder Recognition with Structural Support Vector Machines*. Online Working Notes of the CLEF 2013 Evaluation Labs and Workshop, 23 - 26 September, Valencia - Spain.

Robert Leaman, Ritu Khare and Zhiyong Lu. 2013. *NCBI at 2013 ShARe/CLEF eHealth Shared Task: Disorder Normalization in Clinical Notes with Dnorm*. Online Working Notes of the CLEF 2013 Evaluation Labs and Workshop, 23 - 26 September, Valencia - Spain.

James Gung. 2013. *Using Relations for Identification and Normalization of Disorders: Team CLEAR in the ShARe/CLEF 2013 eHealth Evaluation Lab*. Online Working Notes of the CLEF 2013 Evaluation Labs and Workshop, 23 - 26 September, Valencia - Spain.

Hongfang Liu, Kavishwar Wagholikar, Siddhartha Jonnalagadda and Sunghwan Sohn. 2013. *Integrated cTAKES for Concept Mention Detection and Normalization*. Online Working Notes of the CLEF 2013 Evaluation Labs and Workshop, 23 - 26 September, Valencia - Spain.

Jon D. Patrick, Leila Safari and Ying Ou. 2013. *ShARe/CLEF eHealth 2013 Named Entity Recognition and Normalization of Disorders Challenge*. Online Working Notes of the CLEF 2013 Evaluation Labs and Workshop, 23 - 26 September, Valencia - Spain.

Andreea Bodnari, Louise Deleger, Thomas Lavergne, Aurelie Neveol and Pierre Zweigenbaum. 2013. *A Supervised Named-Entity Extraction System for Medical Text*. Online Working Notes of the CLEF 2013 Evaluation Labs and Workshop, 23 - 26 September, Valencia - Spain.

Guido Zuccon, Alexander Holloway, Bevan Koopman and Anthony Nguyen. 2013. *Identify Disorders in Health Records using Conditional Random Fields and Metamap AEHRC at ShARe/CLEF 2013 eHealth Evaluation Lab Task 1*. Online Working Notes of the CLEF 2013 Evaluation Labs and Workshop, 23 - 26 September, Valencia - Spain.

Jung-wei Fan, Navdeep Sood and Yang Huang. 2013. *Disorder Concept Identification from Clinical Notes An Experience with the ShARe/CLEF 2013 Challenge*. Online Working Notes of the CLEF 2013 Evaluation Labs and Workshop, 23 - 26 September, Valencia - Spain.

S. V. Ramanan, Shereen Broido and P. Senthil Nathan. 2013. *Performance of a multi-class biomedical tagger on clinical records*. Online Working Notes of the CLEF 2013 Evaluation Labs and Workshop, 23 - 26 September, Valencia - Spain.

Chunye Wang and Ramakrishna Akella. 2013. *Performance of a multi-class biomedical tagger on clinical records*. Online Working Notes of the CLEF 2013 Evaluation Labs and Workshop, 23 - 26 September, Valencia - Spain.

Yunqing Xia, Xiaoshi Zhong, Peng Liu, Cheng Tan, Sen Na, Qinan Hu and Yaohai Huang. 2013. *Combining MetaMap and cTAKES in Disorder Recognition: THCIB at CLEF eHealth Lab 2013 Task 1*. Online Working Notes of the CLEF 2013 Evaluation Labs and Workshop, 23 - 26 September, Valencia - Spain.

John David Osborne, Binod Gyawali and Thamar Solorio. 2013. *Evaluation of YTEX and MetaMap for clinical concept recognition*. Online Working Notes of the CLEF 2013 Evaluation Labs and Workshop, 23 - 26 September, Valencia - Spain.

Lucia Hervas, Victor Martinez, Irene Sanchez and Alberto Diaz. 2013. *UCM at CLEF eHealth 2013 Shared Task1*. Online Working Notes of the CLEF 2013 Evaluation Labs and Workshop, 23 - 26 September, Valencia - Spain.

Sameer Pradhan, Noemie Elhadad, Brett R. South, David Martinez, Lee Christensen, Amy Vogel, Hanna Suominen, Wendy W. Chapman and Guergana Savova. 2013. *Task 1: ShARe/CLEF eHealth Evaluation Lab 2013*. Online Working Notes of the CLEF 2013 Evaluation Labs and Workshop, 23 - 26 September, Valencia - Spain.

TJP: Identifying the Polarity of Tweets from Context

Tawunrat Chalothorn
Department of Computer Science and Digital Technologies
University of Northumbria at Newcastle, Pandon Building, Camden Street
Newcastle Upon Tyne, NE2 1XE, UK
tawunrat.chalothorn@northumbria.ac.uk

Jeremy Ellman
Department of Computer Science and Digital Technologies
University of Northumbria at Newcastle, Pandon Building, Camden Street
Newcastle Upon Tyne, NE2 1XE, UK
jeremy.ellman@northumbria.ac.uk

Abstract

The TJP system is presented, which participated in SemEval 2014 Task 9, Part A: Contextual Polarity Disambiguation. Our system is 'constrained', using only data provided by the organizers. The goal of this task is to identify whether marking contexts are positive, negative or neutral. Our system uses a support vector machine, with extensive pre-processing and achieved an overall F-score of 81.96%.

1 Introduction

The aim of sentiment analysis is to identify whether the subject of a text is intended to be viewed positively of negatively by a reader. Such emotions are sometimes hidden in long sentences and are difficult to identify. Consequently sentiment analysis is an active research area in natural language processing.

Sentiment is currently conceived terms of polarity. This has numerous interesting applications. For example, Grabner et al. (2012) used sentiment analysis to classify customers' reviews of hotels by using a star rating to categorize the reviews as bad, neutral and good. Similarly, Tumasjan et al. (2010) tried to predict the outcome of the German federal election through the analysis more than 100,000 tweets posted in the lead up. Sentiment analysis has also used to classify whether dreams are positive or negative (Nadeau et al. 2006).

This paper presents the TJP system which was submitted to SemEval 2014 Task 9, Part A: Contextual Polarity Disambiguation (Rosenthal et al., 2014). TJP focused on the 'Constrained' task.

The 'Constrained' task only uses data provided by the organizers. That is, external resources such as sentiment inventories (e.g. Sentiwordnet (Esuli, and Sebastiani 2006) are excluded. The objective of the TJP system was to use the results for comparison with our previous experiment (Chalothorn and Ellman, 2013). More details of these can be found in section 5.

The TJP system was implemented using a support vector machine (SVM, e.g. Joachims, 1999) with the addition of extensive preprocessing such as stopword removal, negation, slang, contraction, and emoticon expansions.

The remainder of this paper is constructed as follows: firstly, related work is discussed in section 2; the methodology, the experiment and results are presented in sections 3 and 4,

Proceedings of the 8th International Workshop on Semantic Evaluation (SemEval 2014), pages 657–662,
Dublin, Ireland, August 23-24, 2014.

respectively. Finally a discussion and future work are given in section 5.

2 Related Work

Twitter is a popular social networking and microblogging site that allows users to post messages of up to 140 characters; known as 'Tweets'. Tweets are extremely attractive to the marketing sector, since tweets may be searched in real-time. This means marketing can find customer sentiment (both positive and negative) far more quickly than through the use of web pages or traditional media. Consequently analyzing the sentiment of tweets is currently active research task.

The word 'emoticon' is a neologistic contraction of 'emotional icon'. It refers specifically to the use of combinations of punctuation characters to indicate sentiment in a text. Well known emoticons include :) to represent a happy face, and :(a sad one. Emoticons allow writers to augment the impact of limited texts (such as in SMS messages or tweets) using few characters.

Read (2005) used emoticons from a training set downloaded from Usenet newsgroups as annotations (positive and negative). Using the machine learning techniques of Naïve Bayes and SVM, Read (2005) achieved up to 61.50 % and 70.10%, accuracy respectively in determining text polarity from the emoticons used.

Go et al. (2009) used distant supervision to classify sentiment of Twitter, similar to Read (2005). Emoticons were used as noisy labels in training data. This allowed the performance of supervised learning (positive and negative) at a distance. Three classifiers were used: Naïve Bayes, Maximum Entropy and SVM. These classifiers were able to obtain more than 81.30%, 80.50% and 82.20%, respectively accuracy on their unigram testing data .

Aramaki et al. (2011) classified contexts on Twitter related to influenza using a SVM. The training data was annotated with the polarity label by humans, whether they are positive or negative. The contexts will be labelled as positive if the contexts mention the user or someone close to them has the flu, or if they mention a time when they caught the flu. The results demonstrated that they obtained a 0.89 correction ratio for their testing data against a gold standard.

Finally, a well known paper by Bollen and Mao (2011) identified a correlation between the movements of the Dow Jones stock market index, and prevailing sentiment as determined from twitter's live feed. This application has prompted considerable work such as Makrehchi et al (2013) that has attempted to create successful trading strategies from sentiment analysis of tweets.

These work both the wide ranging applications of analysing twitter data, and the importance of Sentiment Analysis. We now move on to look at our approach to SemEval 2014 task 9.

3 Methodology

3.1 Corpus

The training and development dataset of SemEval was built using Tweets from more than one thousand pieces of context. The contexts have various features often used in Tweets, such as emoticons, tags, usernames etc. These features were extracted from the datasets before training for the supervised machine learning model.

During initial pre-processing of the datasets, emoticons were labelled by matching with the emoticons that have been collect manually from the dataset. Those labelled were matched against a well-known collection of emoticons[†].

Subsequently, negative contractions[‡] were expanded in place and converted to full form (e.g. don't -> do not). Moreover, the features of

[†]http://en.wikipedia.org/wiki/List_of_emoticons
[‡]http://en.wikipedia.org/wiki/English_auxiliaries_and_contractions#Negative_contractions

twitters were also removed or replaced by words such as twitter usernames, URLs and hashtags.

A Twitter username is a unique name that shows in the user's profile and may be used for both authentication and identification. This is shown by prefacing the username with an @ symbol. When a tweet is directed at an individual or particular entity this can be shown in the tweet by including @username. For example a tweet directed at 'tawunrat' would include the text @tawunrat. Before URLs are posted in twitter they are shortened automatically to use the t.co domain whose modified URLs are at most 22 characters. However, both features have been removed from the datasets. For the hashtags, they are used for represent keyword and topics in twitter by using # follow by words or phrase such as #newcastleuk. This feature has been replaced with the following word after # symbol. For example, #newcastleuk was replaced by newcastleuk.

Frequently repeated letters are used in tweets for emphasis. These were reduced and replaced using a simple regular expression by two of the same character. For example, happpppppy will be replaced with happy, and coollllll will be replaced by cooll. Next, special character such as [,],{,},?,and ! were also removed. Slang and contracted words were converted to their full form. E.g. 'fyi' was converted to 'for your information'. Finally, NLTK (Bird et al. 2009) stopwords such as 'a', 'the', etc., were removed from the datasets.

3.2 Classifier

Our system uses the SVM classifier model (Hearst et al., 1998, Cristianini and Shawe-Taylor, 2000), which is based on SVM-light (Joachims, 1999). SVM is a binary linear classification model with the learning algorithm for classification and regression analyzing the data and recognizing the pattern.

Training SVMLight requires data to be formulated into vectors of attribute value pairs preceded by a numeric value. For example,

<target> <feature>:<value> <feature>:<value> ... <feature>:<value> # <info>

Here, 'target' represents the polarity of a sentence or tweet; 'feature' refers to a term in the document, and 'value' refers to a feature weight. This could be used as the relative frequency of a term in the set of documents, or Tf-Idf. Tf-idf is the combination of term frequency (tf) and inverse document frequency (idf), is a weight value often used in text mining and information retrieval. This weight is a statistical measure used to evaluate the relative important of word in a document in the collection (Manning et al., 2008).

$$tf - idf_{t,d} = tf_{t,d} * idf_t \quad (1)$$

where $tf - idf_{t,d}$ is the weighting the scheme assigns to term t in document d

Term frequency (tf) is used to measure how frequent the term appears in the document.

$$tf_{t,d} = \frac{n_{t,d}}{\sum_k n_{k,d}} \quad (2)$$

where $n_{t,d}$ is the number of term t appears in a document d. $\sum_k n_{k,d}$ is the total number of terms k in the document d.

Inverse document frequency (idf) is used to measure how important the term is – i.e. whether the term is common or rare in the collection.

$$idf_t = \log \frac{D}{d_t} \quad (3)$$

where D is the total number of documents in the collection in corpus. d_t is the number of documents d which term t appears.

Therefore, we chose to work with both of these to observe which yielded the best results in the polarity classification.

The default settings of SVMLight were used throughout. This meant that we used a linear kernel that did not require any parameters.[§]

4 Experiment and Results

In our experiment, we used the datasets and evaluated the system using the F-score measurement. During pre-processing features were extracted from both datasets. First, we used a frequency of word as a featured weight by calculating the frequency of word in the dataset and, during pre-processing, we labelled the emotions in both datasets. The results revealed a lower than average F-score at 34.80%. As this was quite low we disregarded further use of term frequency as a feature weight. We moved on to use Tf-Idf as the feature weight and, again, emoticons in both datasets were labelled. The score of 78.10% was achieved. Then, we kept the prepossessing of the training set stable by combining the features to extract from the testing data. These results are presented in Table 1[**].

The highest score of 81.96% was recorded when all the features were combined and extracted from both datasets.

The lowest score of 36.48% was recorded when emoticons were extracted from testing data and all features were extracted from training datasets. The results of the highest scoring experiment were submitted to the task organizers.

Following solution submissions, the task organizers announced the scores by separating the data into the following five groups: LiveJournal2014; SMS2013; Twitter2013; Twitter2014; and Twitter2014 Sarcasm. This would allow the identification of any domain dependent effects. However, the results showed that we achieved above average in all the datasets, as illustrated in Figure 1.

§Based on SVMLight
**The results in the table are from the test set 2014 in task 2A.

5 Conclusion and Future Work

The TJP system participated in SemEval 2014 Task 9, Part A: Contextual Polarity Disambiguation. The system exploited considerable preprocessing, before using the well known, SVMLight machine learning algorithm (Joachims. 1999). The pre-processing used several twitter specific features, such as hashtags and ids, in addition to more traditional Information Retrieval concepts such as the Tf-Idf heuristic (Manning et al., 2008). The results showed that the combination of all features in both datasets achieved the best results, at 81.96%.

An aspect of this contribution is the comparative analysis of feature effectiveness. That is, we attempted to identify which factor(s) made the most significant improvement to system performance. It is clear the pre-processing had a considerable effect on system performance. The use of a different learning algorithm also contributed to performance since, on this task, SVMLight performed better than the Naive Bayes algorithm that was used by our team in 2013.

Sentiment resources was not been used in our system in SemEval 2014 as same as in SemEval 2013 whilst other user groups have employed a variety of resources of different sizes, and accuracy (Wilson et al., 2013). These points lead to the following plan for future activities.

Our future work is to rigorously investigate the success factors for sentiment analysis, especially in the twitter domain. More specifically, we have formulated the following research questions as a result of our participation in SemEval

- Are Sentiment resources essential for the Sentiment Analysis task?
- Can the accuracy and effectiveness of sentiment lexicons be measured? If so, which feature of the resource (accuracy vs. coverage) is the most effective metric.
- Might it be more effective to use a range of sentiments (e.g. [-1.0 .. 1.0]), rather

than binary approach(e.g. positive and negative) taken in SemEval 2013, and 2014?

- Is one machine learning algorithm sufficient, and if so which is it? Or, alternately would an ensemble approach (Rokach, 2005) significantly improve performance?

Training \ Testing	Emoticon	Negation	@user URL	HashTag	Repeated letters	Special characters	Slang	Stopwords
Emoticon	78.10%	75.18%	75.18%	75.25%	75.25%	76.35%	76.26%	68.19%
Negation	63.56%	79.06%	79.06%	75.25%	79.14%	80.07%	80.00%	69.70%
@user, URL	63.54%	79.05%	79.05%	79.12%	79.14%	80.07%	80.00%	69.70%
HashTag	63.59%	79.08%	79.08%	79.11%	79.18%	80.10%	80.03%	69.67%
Repeated letters	63.60%	79.08%	79.10%	79.14%	79.18%	80.11%	80.02%	69.74%
Special characters	67.87%	79.10%	78.55%	79.17%	78.62%	80.82%	80.69%	69.62%
Slang	68.39%	78.39%	78.39%	78.62%	78.45%	80.70%	80.85%	69.56%
Stopwords	36.48%	64.67%	64.67%	78.45%	64.67%	64.82%	64.82%	81.96%

Table 1: The results of each feature analyzed in the approach of TF-IDF

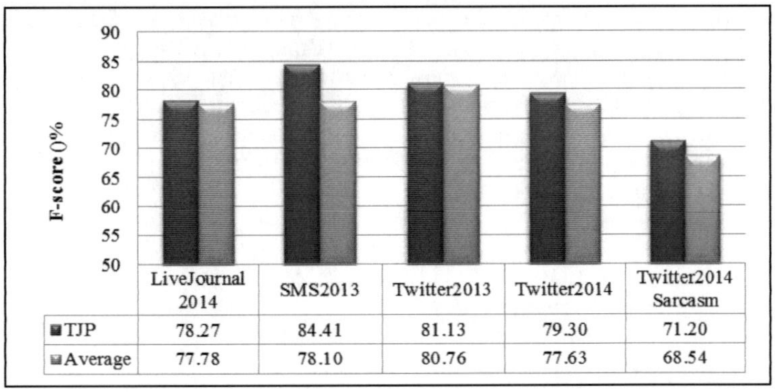

Figure 1: The comparison of TJP and average scores

References

Alec Go, Richa Bhayani and Lei Huang. 2009. Twitter sentiment classification using distant supervision. *CS224N Project Report, Stanford*, 1-12.

Andrea Esuli, Fabrizio Sebastiani 2006 "SENTIWORDNET: A Publicly Available Lexical Resource for Opinion Mining" in Proceedings of the 5th Conference on Language Resources and Evaluation, LREC (2006), pp. 417-422

Andranik Tumasjan, Timm O. Sprenger, Philipp G. Sandner and Isabell M. Welpe. 2010. "Predicting elections with twitter: What 140 characters reveal about political sentiment," in *Proceedings of the Fourth International AAAI Conference on Weblogs and Social Media*, pp. 178-185.

Christopher D. Manning, Prabhakar Raghavan and Hinrich Schütze, *Introduction to Information Retrieval*, Cambridge University Press. 2008. ISBN: 0521865719.

David Nadeau, Catherine Sabourin, Joseph De Koninck, Stan Matwin and Peter D. Turney. 2006.

"Automatic dream sentiment analysis," presented at the In: *Proceedings of the Workshop on Computational Aesthetics at the Twenty-First National Conference on Artificial Intelligence*, Boston, Massachussetts, USA.

Dietmar Grabner, Markus Zanker, Gunther Fliedl and Matthias Fuchs. 2012."Classification of customer reviews based on sentiment analysis," *presented at the 19th Conference on Information and Communication Technologies in Tourism (ENTER)*, Helsingborg, Sweden.

Eiji Aramaki, Sachiko Maskawa and Mizuki Morita. 2011. Twitter catches the flu: detecting influenza epidemics using Twitter. *Proceedings of the Conference on Empirical Methods in Natural Language Processing.* Edinburgh, United Kingdom: Association for Computational Linguistics.

Johan. Bollen and Huina. Mao. Twitter mood as a stock market predictor. IEEE Computer, 44(10):91–94.

Jonathon Read. 2005. Using emoticons to reduce dependency in machine learning techniques for sentiment classification. *Proceedings of the ACL Student Research Workshop.* Ann Arbor, Michigan: Association for Computational Linguistics.

Lior Rokach. 2005. Chapter 45 Ensemble Methods for Classifiers. *In:* Oded Maimon and Lior Rokach (eds.) *Data Mining and Knowledge Discovery Handbook.* Springer US.

Marti A. Hearst, Susan T. Dumais, Edgar Osman, John Platt and Bernhard Scholkopf. 1998. Support vector machines. *IEEE, Intelligent Systems and their Applications,* 13, 18-28.

Masoud Makrehchi, Sameena Shah and Wenhui Liao. 2013. Stock Prediction Using Event-Based Sentiment Analysis. Web Intelligence (WI) and Intelligent Agent Technologies (IAT), 2013 IEEE/WIC/ACM International Joint Conferences on,. 337-342.

Nello Cristianini and John Shawe-Taylor. 2000. *An introduction to support vector machines and other kernel-based learning methods*, Cambridge university press.

Sara Rosenthal, Preslav Nakov, Alan Ritter and Veselin Stoyanov. 2014. SemEval-2014 Task 9: Sentiment Analysis in Twitter. *International Workshop on Semantic Evaluation (SemEval-2014).* Dublin, Ireland.

Steven Bird, Ewan Klein and Edward Loper. 2009. *NLTK: Natural language processing with Python*, O'Reilly.

Takeshi Sakaki, Makoto Okazaki and Yutaka Matsuo. 2010. Earthquake shakes Twitter users: real-time event detection by social sensors. *Proceedings of the 19th international conference on World wide web.* Raleigh, North Carolina, USA: ACM.

Tawunrat Chalothorn and Jeremy Ellman. 2013. TJP: Using Twitter to Analyze the Polarity of Contexts. *Second Joint Conference on Lexical and Computational Semantics (*SEM), Volume 2: Proceedings of the Seventh International Workshop on Semantic Evaluation (SemEval 2013).* Atlanta, Georgia, USA: Association for Computational Linguistics.

Theresa Wilson, Zornitsa Kozareva, Preslav Nakov, Alan Ritter, Sara Rosenthal and Veselin Stoyanov. 2013. SemEval-2013 Task 2: Sentiment Analysis in Twitter. *Proceedings of the 7th International Workshop on Semantic Evaluation.* Association for Computational Linguistics.

Thorsten Joachims. 1999. Making large-scale support vector machine learning practical. *Advances in kernel methods.* MIT Press.

TMUNSW: Disorder Concept Recognition and Normalization in Clinical Notes for SemEval-2014 Task 7

Jitendra Jonnagaddala
Translational Cancer Research Network, University of New South Wales, Sydney 2031, Australia
z3339253@unsw.edu.au

Manish Kumar
Krishagni Solutions Pty Ltd, Armadale 6112, Australia
manish.kumar@krishagni.com

Hong-Jie Dai* **Enny Rachmani** **Chien-Yeh Hsu**
Graduate Institute of Biomedical Informatics, College of Medical Science and Technology
Taipei Medical University, Taipei City 110, Taiwan
{hjdai, d610101005, cyhsu}@tmu.edu.tw

Abstract

We present our participation in Task 7 of SemEval shared task 2014. The goal of this particular task includes the identification of disorder named entities and the mapping of each disorder to a unique Unified Medical Language System concept identifier, which were referred to as Task A and Task B respectively. We participated in both of these subtasks and used YTEX as a baseline system. We further developed a supervised linear chain Conditional Random Field model based on sets of features to predict disorder mentions. To take benefit of results from both systems we merged these results. Under strict condition our best run evaluated at 0.549 F-measure for Task A and an accuracy of 0.489 for Task B on test dataset. Based on our error analysis we conclude that recall of our system can be significantly increased by adding more features to the Conditional Random Field model and by using another type of tag representation or frame matching algorithm to deal with the disjoint entity mentions.

*Corresponding author

1 Introduction

Clinical notes are rich sources of valuable patient's information. These clinical notes are often plain text records containing important entity mentions such as clinical findings, procedures and disease mentions (Jimeno et al., 2008). Using automated tools to extract the aforementioned information can undoubtedly help researchers and clinicians with better decision making. An important subtask of information extraction called named entity recognition (NER) can recognize the boundary of named entity mention and classify it into a certain semantic group.
The focus of the SemEval-2104 task 7 is recognition and normalization of disorder entities mentioned in clinical notes. As such, this task was further divided into two parts: first, task A which includes recognition of mention of concepts that belong to UMLS (Unified Medical Language System) semantic group *disorders* (Bodenreider, 2004). The concepts considered in Task A include the following eleven UMLS semantic types: Congenital Abnormality; Acquired Abnormality; Injury or Poisoning; Pathologic Function; Disease or Syndrome; Mental or Behavioral Dysfunction; Cell or Molecular Dysfunction; Experimental Model of Disease; Anatomical Abnormality; Neoplastic Process; and Signs and Symptoms. Second, task B referred to as task of normalization involves the mapping of each disorder mention to a UMLS concept unique identifier (CUI).The mapping was limited to UMLS CUI of SNOMED clinical term codes (Spackman, Campbell, & CÃ, 1997). We participated in both tasks and devel-

Proceedings of the 8th International Workshop on Semantic Evaluation (SemEval 2014), pages 663–667,
Dublin, Ireland, August 23-24, 2014.

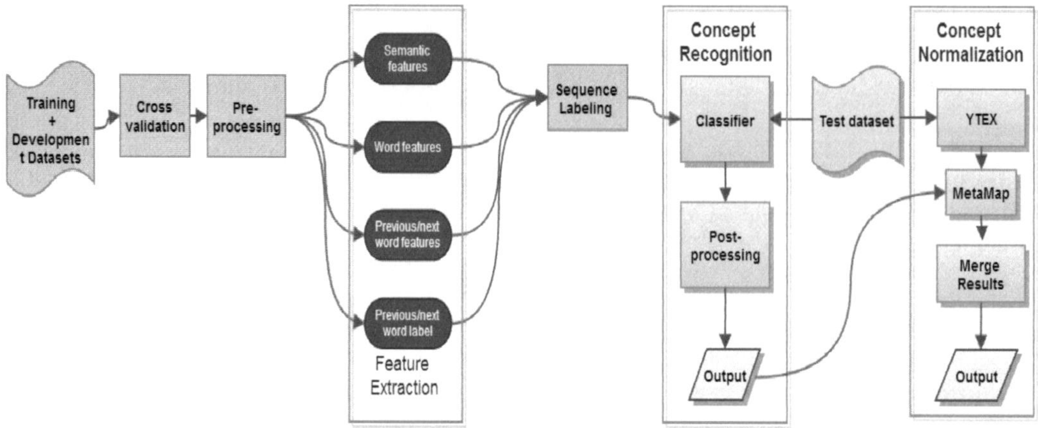

Fig. 1: TMUNSW system design for SemEval-2014 Task 7.

oped a disorder concept recognition/normalization system based on several openly available tools and machine learning algorithms.

2 Methods

2.1 System Design

For both task A and B, YTEX (Garla et al., 2011) system was employed as a baseline system. We chose to use YTEX since it is specifically designed for processing clinical notes with improvements to cTAKES's dictionary lookup algorithm and word sense disambiguation feature. The pre-processing involves sentence detection, tokenization and part-of-speech (POS) tagging(Fiscus, 1997). Based on the tokenized tokens, several features along with the corresponding part-of-speech tags were extracted for the supervised learning algorithm–conditional random field (CRF) model (Lafferty, McCallum, & Pereira, 2001). After training, the CRF model was used for recognizing disorder mentions. Furthermore the recognized disorder concepts were sent to MetaMap (Aronson & Lang, 2010) to look for their corresponding CUIs for generating normalized results. The results were finally merged with the output of YTEX. A high level diagram of the developed system is schematized in Figure 1.

2.2 Disorder Concept Recognition

The task A involves detecting boundaries of entity that belongs to UMLS semantic group, disorders. We used the sequence tagging tool based on Mallet's implementation of the supervised linear chain CRF model to perform this task. We followed the traditional BIO format to formulate the disorder concept recognition task as a sequential labelling task, wherein each token was assigned a label such as B is indicated the Beginning of entity, I is indicated the Inside an entity, or O is indicated the Outside of an entity. Thus, the model assigns each of the word into one of the above three labels. We investigated various types of features proposed in previous works (Jiang et al., 2011; Li, Kipper-Schuler, & Savova, 2008; Tang, Cao, Wu, Jiang, & Xu, 2013), like semantic feature which includes UMLS semantic group and semantic type, to develop our classifier. We also investigated various word features like POS, capitalization, and 'position of word' in the sentence. We also used 'previous word', 'next word' and 'label of these words' as a feature for developing our classifier.

2.3 Disorder Concept Normalization

Each disorder concept recognized by our recognition system was passed to a local installation of MetaMap using MetaMap Java API to obtain its candidate CUI. To increase the recall, we merged results from both YTEX and MetaMap systems. Output from YTEX baseline system was merged to the output from our CRF model with MetaMap. This method was used because it was observed that our CRF/MetaMap model has higher precision while YTEX baseline system has higher recall.

3 Results

3.1 Datasets

For Task A and Task B, the training and development datasets provided by the SemEval task 7 organizers were used. Both were derived from ShARe corpus containing de-identified plain text clinical notes from MIMIC II database (Suominen et al., 2013). These clinical notes were manually annotated for disorder mention and normalized to an UMLS CUI when possible. The corpus consisted of four types of clinical notes: discharge summaries, electrocardiogram, echocardiogram, and radiology reports. As the dataset, we included different types of clinical notes, further we trained a CRF model for each type and evaluated its performance on the corresponding development data. However, test set from task organizers contained discharge summaries only. Hence, the model developed for discharge summary was selected for evaluation on the test set.

3.2 Evaluation Metrics

The official evaluation script provided by organizers of the shared task was used to evaluate our system ability to correct an identify spans of text that belongs to semantic group disorders and to normalize them to the corresponding CUIs.

We calculated the evaluation measures under two settings-strict and relaxed. The strict setting matches exact boundaries with the gold standard, while relaxed setting matches overlapping boundaries in the gold standard. The evaluation measures were calculated using the commonly used evaluation measures including recall (R), precision (P), and F-measure (F) (Powers, 2007).

3.3 System Configurations

We used YTEX V0.8 with cTAKES V2.5.0 as the baseline system for performance comparison. All default settings for YTEX, including the concept window of the length 10, were adopted. We submit two runs for both tasks. For Task A, the first run, denoted as Run0, used the developed CRF model to recognize the disorder concepts. The second run was denoted as Run1, which merged the results of CRF model with YTEX. Similarly, for Task B, Run0 used the MetaMap 2012 version to normalize the candidate disorder concepts recognized by our CRF model. For Run1, we merged normalized annotation results of YTEX with Run0.

3.4 System Performance Comparison

We performed a ten-fold cross validation on the combination of the training and development datasets for examining the recognition and normalization performance of the developed CRF model combined with MetaMap (Run0), and compared with the YTEX as the baseline system. Table 1 summarized the results for Task A and B.

The results showed, for both tasks, Run0 significantly outperformed YTEX in the strict setting. The higher F-score of Run0 can be attributed by the fact that Run0 is developed based on the released corpus and the machine learning algorithm which is better suited for NER task as compared to the rule based YTEX system. In the relaxed setting, for Task A, Run0 also has significantly higher F-score than the YTEX baseline system. However, in case of Task B accuracy of YTEX is significantly greater than Run0. We believe that the higher accuracy of the baseline system can be attributed by the word sense disambiguation feature within YTEX.

Task A	**YTEX**		**Run0**	
	Strict	**Relaxed**	**Strict**	**Relaxed**
P	0.524	0.917	**0.771**	**0.978**
R	0.469	0.670	**0.615**	**0.811**
F	0.495	0.774	**0.682**	**0.884**
Task B	**YTEX**		**Run0**	
	Strict	**Relaxed**	**Strict**	**Relaxed**
Accuracy	0.469	**1.000**	**0.684**	0.752

Table 1. Summary of Training Set Evaluation Results.

3.5 Official Evaluation Results

Table 2 shows the official evaluation results of the submitted two configurations, Run0 and Run1. Under the strict setting, Run1 achieves the better performance with an F-measure of 0.549 for Task A and an accuracy of 0.489 for Task B on test dataset. Our best run for Task A was ranked 15 out of 21 participants, while for Task B it was ranked 9 out of 18 participants.

Task A	**Run0**		**Run1**	
	Strict	**Relaxed**	**Strict**	**Relaxed**
P	**0.622**	0.899	0.524	**0.914**
R	0.429	0.652	**0.576**	**0.765**
F	0.508	0.756	**0.549**	**0.833**
Task B	**Run0**		**Run1**	
	Strict	**Relaxed**	**Strict**	**Relaxed**
Accuracy	0.358	0.834	**0.489**	**0.849**

Table 2. Summary of Test Set Evaluation Results.

Table 2 shows that Run1 has higher F-score than Run0 because of its high recall. On the other hand, Run0 achieves significantly higher precision compared to Run1 for Task A. The result is in accordance with our expectation, because Run1 integrated the results from YTEX to improve the recall of Run0 at the cost of the decrease in precision. The trade-off seems acceptable because it can significantly improve the accuracy in normalizing disorder concepts.

4 Discussion

We performed error analysis on development dataset and found that the lower recall of Run0 derived from the miss of many disjoint entities (where the tokens comprising the entity string are non-adjacent), which cannot be captured by the current BIO tag set. For example, consider the sentence "*Abdomen is soft, nontender, nondistended, negative bruits.*" For this sentence the gold annotations contain three entities as "*Abdomen bruits*-CUI= C0221755", "*Abdomen nontender*-CUI=CUI-less" and "*nondistended*-CUI=CUI-less". In the current BIO formulation, all of the above three disjoint entities cannot be correctly recognized. There are also abbreviations which were rarely seen in the training dataset but appeared more in the development/test sets. So when we test our developed model on test set the abbreviations which are not part of training and development set must have been missed by our system. We believe that by incorporating medical abbreviations database into our model development, the performance of our overall system would have been better. Also, the precision in Task A of Run1 was lower than Run0 because of some disjoint annotations.

5 Conclusion

We present a clinical NER system based on Mallet's implementation of CRF and a hybrid normalization system using MetaMap and YTEX. We developed our system with limited features due to the time constraint. We can conclude from error analysis that recall of this system could be significantly increased by adding more features to it. We plan to extend our system in future by using another type of tag representation or frame-based pattern matching algorithm to handle disjoint named entities. Similarly missing abbreviations can be handled by employing external resources such as abbreviation recognition tools.

Acknowledgements

This project was supported by a Cancer Institute NSW's translational cancer research centre program grant, and the research grant TMU101-AE1-B55 of Taipei Medical University.

References

Aronson, A. R., & Lang, F. M. (2010). An overview of MetaMap: historical perspective and recent advances. *J Am Med Inform Assoc, 17*(3), 229-236. doi: 10.1136/jamia.2009.002733

Bodenreider, O. (2004). The unified medical language system (UMLS): integrating biomedical terminology. *Nucleic acids research, 32*(suppl 1), D267-D270.

Fiscus, J. G. (1997). *A post-processing system to yield reduced word error rates: Recognizer output voting error reduction (ROVER).* Paper presented at the Automatic Speech Recognition and Understanding, 1997. Proceedings., 1997 IEEE Workshop on.

Garla, V., Re, V. L., Dorey-Stein, Z., Kidwai, F., Scotch, M., Womack, J., . . . Brandt, C. (2011). The Yale cTAKES extensions for document classification: architecture and application. *Journal of the American Medical Informatics Association, 18*(5), 614-620.

Jiang, M., Chen, Y., Liu, M., Rosenbloom, S. T., Mani, S., Denny, J. C., & Xu, H. (2011). A study of machine-learning-based approaches to extract clinical entities and their assertions from discharge summaries. *Journal of the American Medical Informatics Association, 18*(5), 601-606.

Jimeno, A., Jimenez-Ruiz, E., Lee, V., Gaudan, S., Berlanga, R., & Rebholz-Schuhmann, D. (2008). Assessment of disease named entity recognition on a corpus of annotated sentences. *BMC Bioinformatics, 9 Suppl 3*, S3. doi: 10.1186/1471-2105-9-S3-S3

Lafferty, J., McCallum, A., & Pereira, F. (2001). *Conditional random fields: Probabilistic models for segmenting and labeling sequence data.* Paper presented at the Proceedings of the 18th International Conference on Machine Learning (ICML).

Li, D., Kipper-Schuler, K., & Savova, G. (2008). *Conditional random fields and support vector machines for disorder named entity recognition in clinical texts.* Paper presented at the Proceedings of the workshop on current trends in biomedical natural language processing.

Powers, D. M. W. (2007). Evaluation: From Precision, Recall and F-Factor to ROC, Informedness, Markedness & Correlation. *Journal of Machine Learning Technologies, 2*(1), 37-63. doi: citeulike-article-id:10061513

Spackman, K. A., Campbell, K. E., & CÃ, R. (1997). *SNOMED RT: a reference terminology for health care.* Paper presented at the Proceedings of the AMIA annual fall symposium.

Suominen, H., Salanterä, S., Velupillai, S., Chapman, W. W., Savova, G., Elhadad, N., . . . Jones, G. J. (2013). Overview of the ShARe/CLEF eHealth Evaluation Lab 2013 *Information Access Evaluation. Multilinguality, Multimodality, and Visualization* (pp. 212-231): Springer.

Tang, B., Cao, H., Wu, Y., Jiang, M., & Xu, H. (2013). Recognizing clinical entities in hospital discharge summaries using Structural Support Vector Machines with word representation features. *BMC medical informatics and decision making, 13*(1), 1-10.

tucSage: Grammar Rule Induction for Spoken Dialogue Systems via Probabilistic Candidate Selection

Arodami Chorianopoulou[†], **Georgia Athanasopoulou**[†], **Elias Iosif**[‡ †],
Ioannis Klasinas[†], **Alexandros Potamianos**[*]
[†] School of ECE, Technical University of Crete, Chania 73100, Greece
[*] School of ECE, National Technical University of Athens, Zografou 15780, Greece
[‡] "Athena" Research Center, Marousi 15125, Greece
{achorianopoulou,gathanasopoulou,iklasinas}@isc.tuc.gr
iosife@telecom.tuc.gr, apotam@gmail.com

Abstract

We describe the grammar induction system for Spoken Dialogue Systems (SDS) submitted to SemEval'14: Task 2. A statistical model is trained with a rich feature set and used for the selection of candidate rule fragments. Posterior probabilities produced by the fragment selection model are fused with estimates of phrase-level similarity based on lexical and contextual information. Domain and language portability are among the advantages of the proposed system that was experimentally validated for three thematically different domains in two languages.

1 Introduction

A critical task for Spoken Dialogue Systems (SDS) is the understanding of the transcribed user input, that utilizes an underlying domain grammar. An obstacle to the rapid deployment of SDS to new domains and languages is the time-consuming development of grammars that require human expertise. Machine-assisted grammar induction has been an open research area for decades (K. Lari and S. Young, 1990; S. F. Chen, 1995) aiming to lower this barrier. Induction algorithms can be broadly distinguished into resource-based, e.g., (A. Ranta, 2004), and data-driven, e.g., (H. Meng and K.-C. Siu, 2002). The main drawback of the resource-based paradigm is the requirement of pre-existing knowledge bases. This is addressed by the data-driven paradigm that relies (mostly) on plain corpora. SDS grammars are built by utilizing low- and high-level rules. Low-level rules are similar to gazetteers consisting of terminal entries, e.g., list of city names. High-level rules can be lexicalized as textual fragments (or chunks), which are semantically defined on top of low-level rules, e.g., `'depart from <City>'`. The data-driven induction of low-level rules is a well-researched area enabled by various technologies including web harvesting for corpora creation (Klasinas et al., 2013), term extraction (K. Frantzi and S. Ananiadou, 1997), word-level similarity computation (Pargellis et al., 2004) and clustering (E. Iosif and A. Potamianos, 2007). High-level rule induction is a less researched area that poses two main challenges: 1) the extraction and selection of salient candidate fragments from a corpus that convey semantics relevant to the domain of interests and 2) the organization of such fragments (e.g., via clustering) according to their semantic similarity. Despite the recent interest on phrase (J. Mitchell and M. Lapata, 2010) and sentence similarity, each respective problem remains open.

Next, our submission[1] for the SemEval'14: Task2 is briefly described, which constitutes a data-driven approach for inducing high-level SDS grammar rules. At the system's core lies a statistical model for the selection of textual fragments based on a rich set of features. This set includes various lexical features, augmented with statistics from n-gram language models, as well as with heuristic features. The candidate selection model posterior is fused with a phrase-level semantic similarity metric. Two different approaches are used for similarity computation relying on the overlap of character bigrams or context-based similarity according to the distributional hypothesis of meaning. The domain and language portability of the proposed system is demonstrated by its successful application across three different domains and

[1]Please note that the last three authors of this submission are among the organizers of this task.

Proceedings of the 8th International Workshop on Semantic Evaluation (SemEval 2014), pages 668–672,
Dublin, Ireland, August 23-24, 2014.

two languages. All the four subtasks defined by the organizers were completed with very good performance that exceeds the baseline.

2 System Description

The basic functionality of the proposed system is the mapping (assignment) of unknown textual fragments into known high-level grammar rules. Let E be the set of unknown fragments, while the set of known rules is denoted by R. Each unknown fragment $f \in E$ is allowed to be mapped to a single high-level rule $r_s \in R$, where $1 \leq s \leq m$ and m is the total number of rules in the grammar.

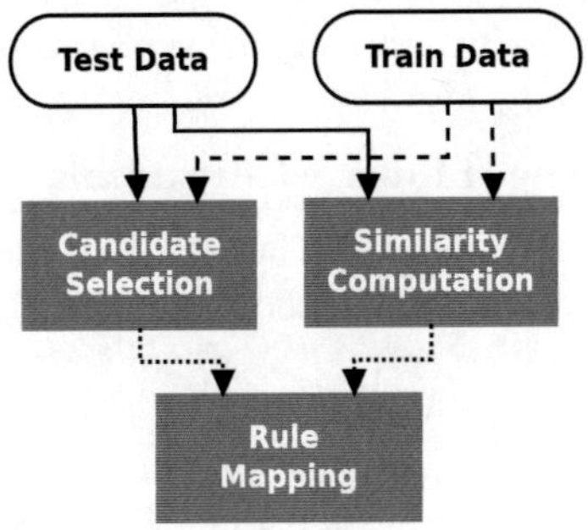

Figure 1: Overview of system architecture.

The system consists of three major components as shown at the system architecture diagram in Fig. 1, specifically: 1) candidate selection: a set of classifiers is built, one for each r_s to select whether $f \in E$ is a candidate member of the specific rule[2], 2) similarity computation between f and r_s, and 3) mapping f to a high-level rule r_s (denoted as $f \mapsto r_s$) according to the following model:

$$\underset{s}{\operatorname{argmax}}\{p(r_s|f)^w S(f, r_s)\} : f \mapsto r_s \quad (1)$$

where $p(r_s|f)$ stands for the probability of f belonging to rule r_s and it is estimated via the respective classifier. The similarity between f and r_s is denoted by $S(f|r_s)$, while w is a fixed weight taking values in the interval $[0\ \infty)$. The fusion weight w controls the relative importance of the candidate selection and semantic similarity modules, e.g., for $w = 0$ only the similarity metric $S(f, r_s)$ is used in the decision. For example, consider the fragment f `'leaving <City>'`. Also, assume two high-level rules, namely, `<ArrCity>={'arrive at <City>',...}` and `<DepCity>= {'depart <City>',...}`. According to (1) f is mapped to the `<DepCity>` rule.

[2]The requirement for building a classifier for each grammar rule is realistic for the case of SDS, especially for the typical iterative human-in-the-loop grammar development scenario.

2.1 Candidate Selection

In this section, the features used for building the candidate selection module for each $r_s \in R$ are briefly described. Given a pair (f, r_s) a two-class statistical classification model that corresponds to r_s is used for estimating $p(r_s|f)$ in (1).

Definitions. A high-level rule r_s can be considered as a set of fragments, e.g.,`'depart <City>'`, `'leaving <City>'`. For each fragment there are two types of constituents, namely, lexical (e.g., `'depart'`,`'leaving'`) and low-level rules (e.g., `'<City>'`). The following features are extracted for r_s considering its respective fragments, as well as for f.

Shallow features. 1) the number of constituents (i.e., tokens), 2) the count of lexical constituents to the number of tokens, 3) the count of low-level rules to the number of tokens, 4) the count of lexical constituents that follow the right-most low-level rule of the fragment, and 5) the count of low-level rules that appear twice in a fragment.

Perplexity-based features. A fragment $\tilde{f}$ can be represented as a sequence of tokens as $w_1\ w_2\ ...\ w_z$. The perplexity of $\tilde{f}$ is defined as $PP(\tilde{f}) = 2^{H(\tilde{f})}$, where $H(\tilde{f}) = \frac{1}{z}\log(p(\tilde{f}))$. $p(\tilde{f})$ stands for the probability of $\tilde{f}$ estimated using an n-gram language model. Two PP values were used as features computed for $n = 2, 3$.

Features of lexical similarity. Four scores of lexical similarity computed between f and r_s were used as features. Let N_s denote the set of fragments that are included in the training set of each rule r_s. The following metrics were employed for computing the similarity between the unknown fragment f and a fragment $f_s \in N_s$: 1) the normalized longest common subsequence (Stoilos et al., 2005) denoted as S_C, 2) the normalized overlap in character bigrams that is denoted as S_B and it is defined in (2), 3) a proposed variation of the Levenshtein distance, S_L, defined as $S_L(f, f_s) = \frac{l_1 - L(f, f_s)}{l_1 + d}$, where l_1 and l_2 are the lengths (in characters) of the lengthiest and the shortest fragment between f and f_s, respectively, while $d = l_1 - l_2$. $L(.)$ stands for the Levenshtein distance (V. I. Levenshtein, 1966; R. A. Wagner and M. J. Fischer, 1974). 4) if f and f_s differ by one token exactly S_L is applied, otherwise their similarity is set to 0. Regarding S_C and S_B, the similarity between

f and r_s was estimated as the maximum similarity yielded when computing the similarities between f and each $f_s \in N_s$. For the rest metrics, the similarity between f and r_s was estimated by averaging the $|N_s|$ similarities computed between f and each $f_s \in N_s$.

Heuristic features. Considering an unknown fragment f and the set of training fragments N_s corresponding to rule r_s, in total nine features were used: 1) the difference between the average length (in tokens) of fragments in N_s and the length of f, 2) the difference between the average number of low-level rules in N_s and the number of low-level rules in f, 3) as 2) but considering the lexical constituents instead of low-level rules, 4) the number of low-level rules shared between N_s and f, 5) as 4) but considering the lexical constituents instead of low-level rules, 6) a boolean function that equals 1 if f is a substring of at least one $f_s \in N_s$, 7) a boolean function that equals 1 if f shares the same lexical constituents at least one $f_s \in N_s$, 8) a boolean function that equals 1 if f is shorter by one token compared to any $f_s \in N_s$, 9) a boolean function that equals 1 if f is lengthier by one token compared to any $f_s \in N_s$.

Selection. The aforementioned features are used for building a binary classifier for each $r_s \in R$, where $1 \leq s \leq m$, for deciding whether f can be regarded as a candidate member of r_s or not. Given an unknown fragment f these classifiers are employed for estimating in total m probabilities $p(r_s|f)$.

2.2 Similarity Metrics

Here, two types of similarity metrics are defined, which are used for estimating $S(f, r_s)$ in (1).

String-based similarity. Consider two fragments f_i and f_j whose sets of character bigrams are denoted as M_i and M_j, respectively. Also, $M_{min} = \min(|M_i|, |M_j|)$ and $M_{max} = \max(|M_i|, |M_j|)$. The similarity between f_i and f_j is based on the overlap of their respective character bigrams defined as (Jimenez et al., 2012):

$$S_B(f_i, f_j) = \frac{|M_i \cap M_j|}{\alpha M_{max} + (1-\alpha) M_{min}}, \quad (2)$$

where $0 \leq \alpha \leq 1$, while, here we use $\alpha = 0.5$. The similarity between a fragment f and a rule r_s is computed by averaging the similarities computed between f and each $f_s \in N_s$.

Context-based similarity. This is a corpus-based metric relying on the distributional hypothesis of meaning suggesting that *similarity of context implies similarity of meaning* (Z. Harris, 1954). A contextual window of size $2K+1$ words is centered on the fragment of interest f_i and lexical features are extracted. For every instance of f_i in the corpus the K words left and right of f_i formulate a feature vector v_i. For a given value of K the context-based semantic similarity between two fragments, f_i and f_j, is computed as the cosine of their feature vectors: $S^K(f_i, f_j) = \frac{v_i . v_j}{||v_i|| \, ||v_j||}$. The elements of feature vectors can be weighted according various schemes (E. Iosif and A. Potamianos, 2010), while, here we use a binary scheme. The similarity between a fragment f and a rule r_s is computed by averaging the similarities computed between f and each $f_s \in N_s$.

2.3 Mapping of Unknown Fragments

The output of the described system is the mapping of a fragment f to a single (i.e., one-to-one assignment) high-level rule $r_s \in R$, where $1 \leq s \leq m$. This is achieved by applying (1). The $p(r_s|f)$ probabilities were estimated as described in Section 2.1. The $S(f, r_s)$ similarities were estimated using either S^K or S_B defined in Section 2.2.

3 Datasets and Experiments

Datasets. The data was organized with respect to three different domains: 1) air travel (flight booking, car rental etc.), 2) tourism (information for city guide), and 3) finance (currency exchange). In total, there are four separate datasets: two datasets for the air travel domain in English (EN) and Greek (GR), one dataset for the tourism domain in English, and one dataset for the finance domain in English.

The number of high-level rules for each dataset are shown in Table 1, along with the number of fragments included in training and test data.

Domain	#rules	#train frag.	#test frag.
Travel:EN	32	982	284
Travel:GR	35	956	324
Tourism:EN	24	1004	285
Finance:EN	9	136	37

Table 1: Number of rules and train/test fragments.

Experiments. Regarding the computation of perplexity-based features (defined in Section 2.1) the SRILM toolkit (A. Stolcke, 2002) was used. The n-gram probabilities were estimated over a corpus that was created by aggregating all the valid fragments included in the training data. For the computation of the context-based similarity metric S^K (defined in Section 2.2) a corpus of web-harvested data was created for each domain/language. The context window size K was set to 1. The size of the used corpora are presented Table 2, while the process of corpus creation is detailed in (Klasinas et al., 2013). The classifiers used for the candidate selection module, described in Section 2.1 were random forests with 50 trees (L. Breiman, 2001).

Domain	# sentences
Travel:EN	5721
Travel:GR	6359
Tourism:EN	829516
Finance:EN	168380

Table 2: Size of corpora used in S^K metric.

4 Evaluation Metrics and Results

The proposed model defined by (1) was evaluated in terms of weighted F-measure, (FM). Initially, we run our system using the training and development set provided by the task organizers, in order to tune the w and K parameters. The tuning was conducted on the Travel English domain, while the respective evaluation results are shown in Table 3 in terms of FM. We observe that the best results are achieved for $w = 1$ and $w = 500$. In the case where $w = 0$ the rule mapping relies only on the similarity metric. In addition, we experimented with various values the context window size K of the context-based similarity metric S^K: $K = 1, 3, 7$. For all values of K similar performance was obtained (0.70). Given the aforementioned tuning the following values were selected for the official runs: $w = 1$, $w = 500$ and $K = 1$. In total, three system runs were submitted:

Weight w	0	1	50	500
FM	0.68	0.72	0.70	0.72

Table 3: Results for the tuning of w.

Domains	Baseline	Run 1	Run 2	Run 3
Travel:EN	0.51	0.66	0.65	**0.68**
Travel:GR	0.26	**0.52**	0.49	0.49
Tourism:EN	**0.87**	0.86	0.85	0.86
Finance:EN	0.60	**0.70**	0.63	0.58
UA	0.56	**0.69**	0.66	0.65
WA	0.52	**0.66**	0.64	0.65

Table 4: Official results.

Run 1. The character bigram similarity metric was used, while w was set to 1.
Run 2. The context-based similarity metrics was used with $K = 1$, while w was set to 1.
Run 3. The character bigram similarity metric was used, while w was set to 500.
The results for the aforementioned runs, along with the baseline performance are shown in Table 4. An overview of the participating systems suggests that our submission achieved the highest performance for almost all domains and languages. The weighted (WA) and unweighted (UA) average across the 4 datasets are also presented, where the weight depends on the number of rules in the dataset. Using these measures, our main run (Run 1) obtained the best results. We observe that the performance is consistently worse for Runs 2 and 3, with the exception of the Travel English dataset. Comparing the performance of Runs 1 and 2, we observe that the character bigram metric consistently outperforms the context-based one. For individual datasets, our system underperforms for the Finance (in Run 3) and the Tourism domain (in all Runs). For the case of the Finance domain this may be attributed to the relatively limited training data.

5 Conclusions

We proposed a supervised grammar induction system using the fusion of a grammar fragment selection and similarity estimation modules. The best configuration of our system was Run 1 which achieved the highest performance compared to other submissions, in almost all domains. To summarize, 1) the selection module boost the system's performance significanlty, 2) the high performance in different domains is a promising indicator for domain and language portability. Future work should involve the implementation of more complex features for the candidate selection algorithm and further investigation of phrase level similarity metrics.

Acknowledgements

This work has been partially funded by the projects: 1) SpeDial, and 2) PortDial, supported by the EU Seventh Framework Programme (FP7), with grant number 611396 and 296170, respectively.

References

Elias Iosif and Alexandros Potamianos. 2010. *Unsupervised semantic similarity computation between terms using web documents.* IEEE Transactions on Knowledge and Data Engineering, 22(11), pp. 1637-1647.

Sergio Jimenez, Claudia Becerra and Alexander Gelbukh. 2012. *Soft Cardinality: A parameterized similarity function for text comparison.* In Proceedings of the First Joint Conference on Lexical and Computational Semantics (*SEM), pp. 449-453

Ioannis Klasinas, Alexandros Potamianos, Elias Iosif, Spyros Georgiladakis and Gianluka Mameli. 2013. *Web data harvesting for speech understanding grammar induction.* in Proceedings of the Interspeech.

Helen M. Meng and Kai-Chung Siu 2002. *Semi-automatic acquisition of semantic structures for understanding domain-specific natural language queries.* IEEE Transactions on Knowledge and Data Engineering, 14(1), pp. 172-181.

PortDial Project free data deliverable D3.1. https://sites.google.com/site/portdial2/deliverables-publication

Andreas Stolcke 2002 *Srilm-an extensible language modeling toolkit* in Proceedings of the Interspeech 2002

Karim Lari and Steve J. Young 2002. *The estimation of stochastic context-free grammars using the inside-outside algorithm.* Computer Speech and Language, 4(1), pp. 35-56.

Stanley F. Chen 1995. *Bayesian grammar induction for language modeling.* in Proceedings of the 33rd annual meeting of ACL

Zellig Harris 1954. *Distributional structure.* Word, 10(23), pp. 146-162.

Rebecca Hwa 1999. *Supervised grammar induction using training data with limited constituent information.* in Proceedings of the 37th annual meeting of ACL

Matthew Lease, Eugene Charniak, and Mark Johnson 2005. *Parsing and its applications for conversational speech.* in Proceedings of Acoustics, Speech, and Signal Processing (ICASSP)

Vladimir I. Levenshtein 1966. *Binary codes capable of correcting deletions, insertions and reversals.* in Soviet physics doklady, 10(8), pp. 707-710.

Leo Breiman 2001. *Random forests.* in Machine Learning, 45(1), pp. 5-32.

Dan Jurafsky and James H. Martin 2009. *Speech and language processing an introduction to natural language processing, computational linguistics, and speech.* Pearson Education Inc

Giorgos Stoilos, Giorgos Stamou, and Stefanos Kollias 2005. *A string metric for ontology alignment.* in The Semantic WebISWC, pp. 624637

Robert A. Wagner and Michael J. Fisher 1974. *The string-to-string correction problem.* Journal of the ACM (JACM), 21(1), pp. 168-173

Katerina Frantzi and Sophia Ananiadou 1997. *Automatic term recognition using contextual cues.* in Proceedings of International Joint Conferences on Artificial Intelligence

Elias Iosif and Alexandros Potamianos 2007. *A soft-clustering algorithm for automatic induction of semantic classes.* in Proceedings of Interspeech

Jeffrey Mitchell and Mirela Lapata 2010. *Composition in distributional models of semantics.* Cognitive Science, 34(8):1388-1429.

Ye-Yi Wang and Alex Acero 2006. *Rapid development of spoken language understanding grammars.* Speech Communication, 48(3), pp. 360-416.

Eric Brill 1992. *A simple rule-based part of speech tagger.* in Proceedings of the workshop on Speech and Natural Language

Alexander Clark 2001. *Unsupervised induction of stochastic context-free grammars using distributional clustering.* in Proceedings of the 2001 workshop on Computational Natural Language Learning

Benjamin Snyder, Tahira Naseem, and Regina Barzilay 2009. *Unsupervised multilingual grammar induction.* in Proceedings of the Joint Conference of the 47th Annual Meeting of the ACL

Aarne Ranta 2009. *Grammatical framework: A type-theoretical grammar formalism.* Journal of Functional Programming: 14(2), pp. 145-189

Andrew Pargellis, Eric Fosler-Lussier, Chin Hui Lee, Alexandros Potamianos and Augustine Tsai 2009. *Auto-induced Semantic Classes.* Speech Communication: 43(3), pp. 183-203

Eneko Agirre, Daniel Cer, Mona Diab, and Aitor Gonzalez-Agirre 2012. *SemEval-2012 Task 6: A Pilot on Semantic Textual Similarity.* in Proceedings of the First Joint Conference on Lexical and Computational Semantics (*Sem), pp. 385-393

TUGAS: Exploiting Unlabelled Data for Twitter Sentiment Analysis

Silvio Amir[+], Miguel Almeida[*†], Bruno Martins[+], João Filgueiras[+], and Mário J. Silva[+]
[+]INESC-ID, Instituto Superior Técnico, Universidade de Lisboa, Portugal
[*]Priberam Labs, Alameda D. Afonso Henriques, 41, 2°, 1000-123 Lisboa, Portugal
[†]Instituto de Telecomunicações, Instituto Superior Técnico, Universidade de Lisboa, Portugal
samir@inesc-id.pt, miguel.almeida@priberam.pt, bruno.g.martins@tecnico.ulisboa.pt
jfilgueiras@inesc-id.pt, mjs@inesc-id.pt

Abstract

This paper describes our participation in the message polarity classification task of SemEval 2014. We focused on exploiting unlabeled data to improve accuracy, combining features leveraging word representations with other, more common features, based on word tokens or lexicons. We analyse the contribution of the different features, concluding that unlabeled data yields significant improvements.

1 Introduction

Research in exploiting social media for measuring public opinion, evaluating popularity of products and brands, anticipating stock-market trends, or predicting elections showed promising results (O'Connor et al., 2010; Mitchell et al., 2013). However, this type of content poses a particularly challenging problem for text analysis systems. Typical messages show heavy use of Internet slang, emoticons and other abbreviations and discourse conventions. The lexical variation introduced by this creative use of language, together with the unconventional spelling and occasional typos, leads to very large vocabularies. On the other hand, messages are very short, and therefore word feature representations tend to become very sparse, degrading the performance of machine learned classifiers.

The growing interest in this problem motivated the creation of a shared task for Twitter Sentiment Analysis in the 2013 edition of SemEval. The **Message Polarity Classification** task was formalized as follows: *Given a message, decide whether the message is of positive, negative, or neutral sentiment. For messages conveying both a positive and negative sentiment, whichever is the stronger sentiment should be chosen* (Nakov et al., 2013).

	Positive	Neutral	Negative
Train 2014	3230	4109	1265
Tweets 2013	1572	1640	601
Tweets 2014	982	669	202
SMS 2013	492	1207	394
Tweets Sarcasm 2014	33	13	40
LiveJournal 2014	427	411	304

Table 1: Number of examples per class in each SemEval dataset. The first row represents all training data; the other rows are sets used for testing.

We describe our participation on the 2014 edition of this task, for which a set of manually labelled messages was created. Complying with the Twitter policies for data access, the corpus was distributed as a list of message IDs and each participant was responsible for downloading the actual tweets. Using the provided script, we collected a training set with 8604 tweets. After submission, the 2014 test sets were also made available. Along with the Tweets 2014 test set, evaluation was also performed on a set of tweets with sarcasm, on a set of LiveJournal blog entries, and on sets of tweets and SMS messages from the 2013 edition of the task. Table 1 shows the class distribution for each of these datasets.

In the 2013 edition (task 2B), the NRC-Canada system (Mohammad et al., 2013) earned first place by scoring 69.02% on the Official SemEval metric (see Section 4) with a significant margin with respect to the other systems: the second (Günther and Furrer, 2013) and third (Reckman et al., 2013) best systems scored 65.27% and 64.86%, respectively. The main novelty in the NRC-Canada system was the use of sentiment lexicons, specific for the Twitter domain, generated from unlabeled tweets using emoticons and hashtags as indicators of sentiment. They found that these lexicons had a strong impact on the results – more than word and

Proceedings of the 8th International Workshop on Semantic Evaluation (SemEval 2014), pages 673–677,
Dublin, Ireland, August 23-24, 2014.

character n-grams.

The automatically induced lexicons are a way to use information from unlabeled data to aid in the classification task. In our approach, we take this reasoning further, and focus on the impact of various ways to incorporate knowledge from unlabeled data. This allows us to mimic many real-world scenarios where labelled data is scarce but unlabeled data is plentiful.

2 Word Representations

In text classification it is common to represent documents as bags-of-words, i.e., as unordered collections of words. However, in the case of very short social media texts, these representations become less effective, as they lead to increased data sparseness. We focused our experiments in comparing and complementing these approaches with denser representations, which we now describe.

2.1 Bag-Of-Words and ΔBM25

In a representation based on bags-of-words, each message is represented as a vector $\mathbf{m} = \{w_1, w_2, ..., w_n\} \in \mathbb{R}^V$, where V is the size of the vocabulary. In order to have weights that reflect how relevant a word is to each of the classes, we weighted the individual terms according to the ΔBM25 heuristic (Paltoglou and Thelwall, 2010):

$$\Delta\text{BM25}(\text{w}_\text{i}) = tf_i \times \log\left(\frac{(N_p - df_{i,p} + s) \cdot df_{i,n} + s}{(N_n - df_{i,n} + s) \cdot df_{i,p} + s}\right), \quad (1)$$

where tf_i represents the frequency of term i in the message, N_a is the size of corpus a, $df_{i,a}$ is the document frequency of term i in the corpus a (i.e., in one of two subsets for the training data, corresponding to either positive or negative messages), and s is a smoothing constant, which we set to 0.5. This term weighting function was previously shown to be effective for sentiment analysis.

2.2 Brown Clusters

Brown et al. (1992) proposed a greedy agglomerative hierarchical clustering procedure that groups words to maximize the mutual information of bigrams. Clusters are initialized as consisting of a single word each, and are then greedily merged according to a mutual information criterion, to form a lower-dimensional representation of a vocabulary. The hierarchical nature of the clustering allows words to be represented at different levels in the hierarchy. This approach provides a denser representation of the messages, mitigating the feature sparseness problem. We used a publicly available[1] set of 1000 Brown clusters induced from a corpus of 56 million Twitter messages.

We leveraged the word clusters by mapping each word to the corresponding cluster, and we then represented each message as a bag-of-clusters vector in $\mathbb{R}^K$, where $K = 1000$ is the number of clusters. These word cluster features were also weighted with the ΔBM25 scheme.

2.3 Concise Semantic Analysis

Concise Semantic Analysis is a form of term and document representation that assigns, to each term, its weight on each of the classes (Li et al., 2011). These weights, computed from the frequencies of the term on the training data, reflect how associated the term is to each class. The weight of term j in class c is given by (Lopez-Monroy et al., 2013):

$$w_{cj} = \sum_{k \in P_c} \log_2 \left(1 + \frac{tf_{kj}}{\text{len}(k)}\right), \quad (2)$$

where P_c is the set of documents with label c and tf_{kj} is the term frequency of term j in document k. To prevent labels with a higher number of examples, or terms with higher frequencies, to have stronger weights, an additional normalization step is performed to obtain nw_{cj}, the normalized weight of term j in class c:

$$nw_{cj} = \frac{w_{cj}}{\sum_{l \in L} w_{lj} \times \sum_{t \in T} w_{ct}}. \quad (3)$$

In the formula, L is the set of class labels and T is the set of terms, making w_{lj} the weight of term j for a class l, and w_{ct} the weight of a term t in class c. After defining every term as a vector $\mathbf{t}_j = \{nw_{1j}, \ldots, nw_{Cj}\} \in \mathbb{R}^C$, where C is the number of classes, each message m is represented by summing each of its terms' weight vectors:

$$\mathbf{m}_{csa} = \sum_{j \in m} \frac{tf_j}{\text{len}(m)} \times \mathbf{t}_j. \quad (4)$$

In the formula, tf_j is the frequency of term j in m.

2.4 Dense Word Vectors

Efficient approaches have recently been introduced to train neural networks capable of producing continuous representations of words (Mikolov

[1] http://www.ark.cs.cmu.edu/TweetNLP/

Lexicon	#1-grams	#2-grams	#pairs
Bing Liu	6789	-	-
MPQA	8222	-	-
SentiStrength	2546	-	-
NRC EmoLex	14177	-	-
Sentiment140	62468	677698	480010
NRC HashSent	54129	316531	308808

Table 2: Number of unigrams, bigrams, and collocation pairs, in the lexicons used in our system.

et al., 2013). These approaches allow fast training of projections from a representation based on bags-of-words, where vectors have very high dimension (of the order of 10^4), but are also very sparse and integer-valued, to vectors of much lower dimensions (of the order of 10^2), with full density and continuous values.

To induce word embeddings, a corpus of 17 million Twitter messages was collected with the Twitter crawler of Boanjak et al. (2012). Then, using *word2vec*[2], we induced representations for the word tokens occurring in the messages. All the tokens were represented as vectors $\mathbf{w}_j \in \mathbb{R}^n$, with $n = 100$. A message was modeled as the sum of the vector representations of the individual words:

$$\mathbf{m}_{vec} = \sum_{j \in m} \mathbf{w}_j. \quad (5)$$

We also created a *polarity class vector* $\mathbf{p_c}$ for each class c, defined as:

$$\mathbf{p}_c = \frac{1}{N_c} \sum_{m \in c} \mathbf{m}_{vec}, \quad (6)$$

where m is a message of class c and N_c is the total number of instances in class c. These vectors can be interpreted as prototypes of their classes, and are used in the **classVec** features described below.

3 The TUGAS System

We now describe the TUGAS approach, detailing the considered features and our modeling choices.

3.1 Word Features

To reduce the feature space of the model, messages were lower-cased, Twitter user mentions (*@username*) were replaced with the token <USER> and URLs were replaced with the <URL> token. We also normalized words to include at most 3 repeated characters (*e.g.*, *"helloooooo!"* to *"hellooo!"*). Following Pang et al. (2002), negation was directly integrated into the word representations. All the tokens occurring between a negation word and the next punctuation mark, were suffixed with the **_NEG** annotation.

We used the following groups of features:

- **bow-uni**: vector of word unigrams
- **bow-bc**: vector of Brown word clusters
- **csa**: Concise Semantic Analysis vector $\mathbf{m}_{csa}$
- **wordVec**: *word2vec* message vector $\mathbf{m}_{vec}$
- **classVec**: Euclidean distance between message vector $\mathbf{m}_{vec}$ and each class vector $\mathbf{p}_c$

3.2 Lexicon Features

The document model was enriched with features that take into account the presence of words with a known prior polarity, such as *happy* or *sad*. We included words from manually annotated sentiment lexicons: Bing Liu Opinion Lexicon (Hu and Liu, 2004), MPQA (Wilson et al., 2005) and the NRC Emotion Lexicon (Mohammad and Turney, 2013). We also used the two automatically generated lexicons from Mohammad et al. (2013): the NRC Hashtag Sentiment Lexicon and the Sentiment140 Lexicon. Table 2 summarizes the number of terms of each lexicon.

As Mohammad et al. (2013), we added the following set of **lexicon** features, for each lexicon, and for each combination of negated/non-negated words and positive/negative polarity.

- The sum of the sentiment scores of all (negated/non-negated) terms with (positive/negative) sentiment
- The largest of those scores
- The sentiment score of the last word in the message that is also present in the lexicon
- The number of terms within the lexicon

Notice that terms can be unigrams, bigrams, and collocations pairs. A group of these features was computed for each of the sentiment lexicons.

3.3 Syntactic Features

We extracted **syntactic** features aimed at the Twitter domain, such as the use of heavy punctuation, emoticons and character repetition. Concretely, the following features were computed from the original Twitter messages:

- Number of words originally with more than 3 repeated characters
- Number of sequences of exclamation marks and/or question marks

[2] https://code.google.com/p/word2vec/

	Tweets Test 2013			Tweets Test 2014			SMS 2013			Live Journal 2014			Tweets Sarcasm 2014		
Features	**Acc**	**F1**	**Official**	**Acc**	**F1**	**Official**	**Acc**	**F1**	**Official**	**Acc**	**F1**	**Official**	**Acc**	**F1**	**Official**
bow-uni	65.62	59.30	54.60	69.94	66.30	**65.60**	68.80	62.40	54.90	60.42	58.30	56.60	47.67	43.90	41.50
submitted	**69.55**	**67.50**	**65.60**	**71.45**	**69.00**	**69.00**	**70.57**	**67.60**	**62.70**	**68.21**	**68.20**	**69.80**	**53.49**	**50.10**	**52.90**
- lexicons	66.90	64.30	61.70	70.37	67.00	**66.40**	66.46	63.50	58.30	64.27	64.20	65.50	48.84	45.10	47.00
- classVec	69.37	67.30	65.40	71.83	69.30	**69.60**	69.14	66.60	62.10	67.51	67.50	69.30	53.49	50.10	52.90
- wordVec	69.63	67.70	66.00	70.32	67.70	**68.00**	66.79	64.90	60.90	68.04	68.00	69.70	53.49	50.50	53.50
- bow-bc	68.06	66.40	65.10	67.40	64.30	**65.30**	67.89	65.20	60.40	68.30	68.30	70.00	52.33	49.90	49.90
+ syntactic	69.58	67.60	65.70	71.24	68.30	**68.50**	70.38	67.40	62.40	67.95	68.00	69.70	52.33	48.80	50.00
+ csa	67.45	63.70	60.50	70.10	67.30	**67.50**	71.48	67.60	62.10	66.11	66.00	68.30	53.49	51.30	50.30
+ bow-uni	67.69	62.50	58.50	70.64	67.30	**66.70**	72.77	67.10	60.40	67.60	67.20	67.10	51.16	48.00	43.90

Table 3: Impact of removing or adding groups of features. The row marked as submitted, in bold, is the one that we submitted to the shared task. The bold column is the official score used to rank participants.

- Number of positive/negative emoticons, detected with a pre-existing regular expression[3]
- Number of capitalized words

3.4 Model Training

We used the L2-regularized logistic regression implementation from *scikit-learn*[4]. Given a set of m instance-label pairs $(\mathbf{x_i}, y_i)$, with $i = 1, \ldots, m$, $\mathbf{x_i} \in \mathbb{R}^n$, and $y_i \in \{-1, +1\}$, learning the classifier involves solving the following optimization problem, where $C > 0$ is a penalty parameter.

$$\min_{w} \frac{1}{2}\mathbf{w}'\mathbf{w} + C\sum_{i=1}^{m} \log(1 + e^{-y_i w' \mathbf{x_i}}). \quad (7)$$

In *scikit-learn*, the problem is solved through a trust region Newton method, using a wrapper over the implementation available in the *liblinear*[5] package. For multi-class problems, *scikit-learn* uses the one-vs-the-rest strategy. This particular implementation also suports the introduction of class weights, which we set to be inversely proportional to the class frequency in the training data, thus making each class equally important.

The selection of groups of features to be included in the submitted run, as well as the tuning of the regularization constant, were obtained by cross-validation on the training dataset.

4 Results

We report results using the following metrics:

- **Accuracy**, defined as the percentage of tweets correctly classified.
- Overall **F1**, computed by averaging the F1 score of all three classes.
- The **Official** SemEval score, computed by averaging the F1 scores of the positive and negative classes (Nakov et al., 2013).

[3] http://sentiment.christopherpotts.net/
[4] http://scikit-learn.org/
[5] http://www.csie.ntu.edu.tw/~cjlin/liblinear/

Feature group	Acc	F1	Official
bow-bc	66.33	63.30	60.30
wordVec	62.34	60.00	57.90
bow-uni	65.62	59.30	54.60
csa	61.58	56.70	52.90

Table 4: Performance comparison using different word representations in isolation.

We tried including or excluding various groups of features, and obtained the best results on the training set using Brown clusters (**bow-bc**), lexicon features (**lexicon**), word2vec word representations (**wordVec**), and the Euclidean distance between the word2vec representation and each class vector (**classVec**). These features were the ones used in our submission. Inclusion of syntactic features (**syntactic**), Concise Semantic Analysis (**csa**), and word unigrams (**bow-uni**) was found to decrease performance during cross-validation, and thus these features were not included.

Table 4 shows the results on the Twitter 2014 test set using only a single group of word representation features to train the model, from each of the techniques introduced in Section 2. This table suggests that exploiting unlabeled data is beneficial, as representing words through their Brown clusters (**bow-bc**) or through word2vec (**wordVec**) yields better results than unigrams or CSA.

Table 3 shows results on five different test sets, including two from the 2013 challenge (Nakov et al., 2013), when features are added or removed from the official submission, one group at a time. Adding representations like **bow-uni** or **csa** actually *hurts* the performance, suggesting that, given the relatively small set of training instances, using coarse-level features in isolation, such as Brown clusters, can yield better results.

More importantly, we verify that lexicon-based and Brown cluster features have the largest impact

(2.6% and 3.7%, respectively, in the official metric). These results indicate that leveraging unlabeled data yields significant improvements.

5 Conclusions

This paper describes the participation of the TUGAS team in the message polarity classification task of SemEval 2014. We showed that there are significant gains in leveraging unlabeled data for the task of classifying the sentiment of Twitter texts. Our score of 69% ranks at fifth place in 42 submissions, roughly 2% points below the top score of 70.96%. We believe that the direction of leveraging unlabeled data is still vastly unexplored and, for future work, we intend to: (a) experiment with semi-supervised learning approaches, further exploiting unlabeled tweets; and (b) make use of domain adaptation strategies to leverage on labelled non-Twitter data.

Acknowledgements

This work was partially supported by the EU/FEDER programme, QREN/POR Lisboa (Portugal), under the Intelligo project (contract 2012/24803). The researchers from INESC-ID were supported by Fundação para a Ciência e Tecnologia (FCT), through contracts Pest-OE/EEI/LA0021/2013, EXCL/EEI-ESS/0257/2012 (DataStorm), project grants PTDC/CPJ-CPO/116888/2010 (POPSTAR), and EXPL/EEI-ESS/0427/2013 (KD-LBSN), and Ph.D. scholarship SFRH/BD/89020/2012.

References

Matko Boanjak, Eduardo Oliveira, José Martins, Eduarda Mendes Rodrigues, and Luís Sarmento. 2012. Twitterecho: a distributed focused crawler to support open research with twitter data. In *21st International Conference Companion on World Wide Web*, pages 1233–1240.

Peter F. Brown, Peter V. Desouza, Robert L. Mercer, Vincent J. Della Pietra, and Jenifer C. Lai. 1992. Class-based n-gram models of natural language. *Computational Linguistics*, 18(4):467–479.

Tobias Günther and Lenz Furrer. 2013. GU-MLT-LT: Sentiment analysis of short messages using linguistic features and stochastic gradient descent. In *7th International Workshop on Semantic Evaluation*, pages 328–332.

Minqing Hu and Bing Liu. 2004. Mining and summarizing customer reviews. In *10th ACM SIGKDD International Conference on Knowledge Discovery and Data Mining*, pages 168–177.

Zhixing Li, Zhongyang Xiong, Yufang Zhang, Chunyong Liu, and Kuan Li. 2011. Fast text categorization using concise semantic analysis. *Pattern Recognition Letters*, 32(3):441–448.

Ádrian Pastor Lopez-Monroy, Manuel Montes-y Gomez, Hugo Jair Escalante, Luis Villasenor-Pineda, and Esaú Villatoro-Tello. 2013. INAOE's participation at PAN'13: Author profiling task. In *CLEF 2013 Evaluation Labs and Workshop*.

Tomas Mikolov, Ilya Sutskever, Kai Chen, Greg Corrado, and Jeffrey Dean. 2013. Distributed representations of words and phrases and their compositionality. In *27th Annual Conference on Neural Information Processing Systems*, pages 3111–3119.

Lewis Mitchell, Kameron Decker Harris, Morgan R Frank, Peter Sheridan Dodds, and Christopher M Danforth. 2013. The geography of happiness: connecting twitter sentiment and expression, demographics, and objective characteristics of place. *PLoS ONE*, 8(5):e64417.

Saif M Mohammad and Peter D Turney. 2013. Crowdsourcing a word–emotion association lexicon. *Computational Intelligence*, 29(3):436–465.

Saif Mohammad, Svetlana Kiritchenko, and Xiaodan Zhu. 2013. NRC-Canada: building the state-of-the-art in sentiment analysis of tweets. In *7th International Workshop on Semantic Evaluation*, pages 321–327.

Preslav Nakov, Sara Rosenthal, Zornitsa Kozareva, Veselin Stoyanov, Alan Ritter, and Theresa Wilson. 2013. SemEval-2013 task 2: Sentiment analysis in Twitter. In *7th International Workshop on Semantic Evaluation*, pages 312–320.

Brendan O'Connor, Ramnath Balasubramanyan, Bryan R Routledge, and Noah A Smith. 2010. From tweets to polls: Linking text sentiment to public opinion time series. In *4th International AAAI Conference on Weblogs and Social Media*, pages 122–129.

Georgios Paltoglou and Mike Thelwall. 2010. A study of information retrieval weighting schemes for sentiment analysis. In *48th Annual Meeting of the Association for Computational Linguistics*, pages 1386–1395.

Bo Pang, Lillian Lee, and Shivakumar Vaithyanathan. 2002. Thumbs up?: sentiment classification using machine learning techniques. In *ACL-02 Conference on Empirical Methods in Natural Language Processing*, pages 79–86.

Hilke Reckman, Baird Cheyanne, Jean Crawford, Richard Crowell, Linnea Micciulla, Saratendu Sethi, and Fruzsina Veress. 2013. teragram: Rule-based detection of sentiment phrases using SAS sentiment analysis. In *7th International Workshop on Semantic Evaluation*, pages 513–519.

Theresa Wilson, Janyce Wiebe, and Paul Hoffmann. 2005. Recognizing contextual polarity in phrase-level sentiment analysis. In *Conference on Human Language Technology and Empirical Methods in Natural Language Processing*, pages 347–354.

Turku: Broad-Coverage Semantic Parsing with Rich Features

Jenna Kanerva*
Department of Information Technology
University of Turku
Finland
jmnybl@utu.fi

Juhani Luotolahti*
Department of Information Technology
University of Turku
Finland
mjluot@utu.fi

Filip Ginter
Department of Information Technology
University of Turku
Finland
figint@utu.fi

Abstract

In this paper we introduce our system capable of producing semantic parses of sentences using three different annotation formats. The system was used to participate in the SemEval-2014 Shared Task on broad-coverage semantic dependency parsing and it was ranked third with an overall F_1-score of 80.49%. The system has a pipeline architecture, consisting of three separate supervised classification steps.

1 Introduction

In the SemEval-2014 Task 8 on semantic parsing, the objective is to extract for each sentence a rich set of typed semantic dependencies in three different formats: *DM*, *PAS* and *PCEDT*. These formats differ substantially both in the assignment of semantic heads as well as in the lexicon of semantic dependency types. In the open track of the shared task, participants were encouraged to use all resources and tools also beyond the provided training data. To improve the comparability of the systems, the organizers provided ready-to-use dependency parses produced using the state-of-the-art parser of Bohnet and Nivre (2012).

In this paper we describe our entry in the open track of the shared task. Our system is a pipeline of three support vector machine classifiers trained separately for detecting semantic dependencies, assigning their roles, and selecting the top nodes of semantic graphs. In this, we loosely follow the architecture of e.g. the TEES (Björne et al., 2012) and EventMine (Miwa et al., 2012) systems, which were found to be effective in the structurally related task of biomedical event extraction. Similar classification approach is shown to be effective also in semantic parsing by e.g. Zhao et al. (2009), the winner of the CoNLL'09 Shared Task on Syntactic and Semantic Dependencies in Multiple Languages (SRL-only subtask) (Hajič et al., 2009), where semantic parsing is approached as a word-pair classification problem and semantic arguments and their roles are predicted simultaneously. In preliminary experiments, we also developed a joint approach to simultaneously identify semantic dependencies and assign their roles, but found that the performance of the joint prediction was substantially worse than for the current pipeline approach. As the source of features, we rely heavily on the syntactic parses as well as other external resources such as vector space representations of words and large-scale syntactic n-gram statistics.

In the following sections, we describe the three individual classification steps of our semantic parsing pipeline.

2 Detecting Semantic Dependencies

The first step of our semantic parsing pipeline is to detect semantic dependencies, i.e. governor-dependent pairs which has a semantic relation between them. The first stage covers only the identification of such dependencies; the labels describing the semantic roles of the dependents are assigned in a later stage.

The semantic dependencies are identified using a binary support vector machine classifier from the *LIBSVM* package (Chang and Lin, 2011). Each possible combination of two tokens in the sentence is considered to be a candidate for a semantic dependency in both directions, and thus also included as a training example. No beforehand pruning of possible candidates is performed during training. However, we correct for the overwhelming number of negative training examples

*These authors contributed equally.

Proceedings of the 8th International Workshop on Semantic Evaluation (SemEval 2014), pages 678–682, Dublin, Ireland, August 23-24, 2014.

by setting the weights of positive and negative examples used during training, so as to maximize the unlabeled F_1-score on the development set.

Increasing the recall of semantic dependency detection can be beneficial for the overall performance of the pipeline system, since a candidate lost in the dependency detection stage cannot be recovered later. We therefore tested the approach applied, among others by Björne et al. (2012), whereby the dependency detection stage heavily overgenerates candidates and the next stage in the pipeline is given the option to predict a negative label, thus removing a candidate dependency. In preliminary experiments we tried to explicitly overgenerate the dependency candidates by altering the classifier threshold, but noticed that heavy overgeneration of positive examples leads to a decreased performance in the role assigning stage. Instead, the above-mentioned optimization of the example weights during training results in a classifier which overgenerates positive examples by 4.4%, achieving the same objective and improving the overall performance of the system.

Features used during the dependency identification are derived from tokens and the syntactic parse trees provided by the organizers. Our primary source of features are the syntactic trees, since 73.2% of semantic dependencies have a corresponding undirected syntactic dependency in the parse tree. Further, the syntactic dependency path between the governor and the dependent is shorter than their linear distance in 48.8% of cases (in 43.4% of cases the distance is the same). The final feature set used in the identification is optimized by training models with different combinations of features and selecting the best combination based on performance on the held-out development set. Interestingly, the highest performance is achieved with a rather small set of features, whose full listing is shown in Table 1. The feature vectors are normalized to unit length prior to classification and the SVM regularization parameter c is optimized separately for each annotation format.

3 Role Assignment

After the semantic governor-dependent pairs are identified, the next step is to assign a role for each pair to constitute a full semantic dependency. This is done by training a multiclass support vector machine classifier implemented in the *SVM-multiclass* package by Joachims (1999). We it-

Feature	D	R	T
arg.pos	X	X	
arg.deptype	X	X	
arg.lemma	X	X	
pred.pos	X	X	X
pred.deptype	X	X	X
pred.lemma	X	X	X
pred.is_predicate		X	X
arg.issyntaxdep		X	
arg.issyntaxgov		X	
arg.issyntaxsibling		X	
path.length	X	X	
undirected_path.deptype	X	X	
directed_path.deptype	X	X	
undirected_path.pos	X	X	
extended_path.deptype	X	X	
simplified_path.deptype with len		X	
simplified_path.deptype wo len		X	
splitted_undirected_path.deptype	X		
arg.prev.pos	X	X	
arg.next.pos	X	X	
arg.prev+arg.pos	X	X	
arg.next+arg.pos	X	X	
arg.next+arg+arg.prev.pos	X	X	
pred.prev.pos	X	X	
pred.next.pos	X	X	
pred.prev+pred.pos	X	X	
pred.next+pred.pos	X	X	
pred.next+pred+pred.prev.pos	X	X	
linear_route.pos	X		
arg.child.pos		X	
arg.child.deptype		X	
arg.child.lemma		X	
pred.child.pos		X	
pred.child.deptype		X	X
pred.child.lemma		X	
syntaxgov.child.deptype		X	
vector_similarities		X	
n-gram_frequencies		X	
pred.sem_role			X
pred.child.sem_role			X
pred.syntaxsibling.deptype			X
pred.semanticsibling.sem_role			X

Table 1: Features used in the detection of semantic dependencies (D), assigning their roles (R) and top node detection (T). *path* refers to syntactic dependencies between the argument and the predicate, and *linear route* refers to all tokens between the argument and the predicate. In top node detection, where only one token is considered at a time, the *pred* is used to represent that token.

erate through all identified dependencies, and for each assign a role, or alternatively classify it as a negative example. This is to account for the 4.4% of overgenerated dependencies. However, the proportion of negative classifications should stay relatively low and to ensure this, we downsample the number of negative examples used in training to contain only 5% of all negative examples. The downsampling ratio is optimized on the development set using grid search and downsampled training instances are chosen randomly.

The basic features, shown in Table 1, follow the same style as in dependency identification. We also combine some of the basic features by creating all possible feature pairs in a given set, but do not perform this with the full set of features. In the open track, participants are also allowed to use additional data and tools beyond the official training data. In addition to the parse trees, we include also features utilizing syntactic n-gram frequencies and vector space similarities.

Google has recently released a large corpus of syntactic n-grams, a collection of dependency subtrees with frequency counts (Goldberg and Orwant, 2013). The syntactic n-grams are induced from the Google Books collection, a 350B token corpus of syntactically parsed text. In this work we are interested in *arcs*, which are $(governor, dependent, syntactic\ relation)$ triplets associated with their count.

For each governor-dependent pair, we generate a set of n-gram features by iterating through all known dependency types and searching from the syntactic n-grams how many times (if any) the governor-dependent pair with the particular dependency type is seen. A separate feature is then created for each dependency type and the counts are encoded in feature weights compressed using $w = \log_{10}(count)$. This approach gives us an opportunity to include statistical information about word relations induced from a very large corpus. Information is captured also outside the particular syntactic context, as we iterate through all known dependency types during the process.

Another source of additional data used in role classification is a publicly available Google News vector space model[1] representing word similarities. The vector space model is induced from the Google News corpus with the *word2vec* software (Mikolov et al., 2013) and negative sampling architecture, and each vector have 300 dimensions. The vector space representation gives us an opportunity to measure word similarities using the standard cosine similarity function.

The approach to transforming the vector representations into features varies with the three different annotation formats. On *DM* and *PAS*, we follow the method of Kanerva and Ginter (2014), where for each role an average argument vector is calculated. This is done by averaging all word vectors seen in the training data as arguments for the given predicate with a particular role. For each candidate argument, we can then establish a set of similarity values to each possible role by taking the cosine similarity of the argument vector to the role-wise average vectors. These similarities are then turned into separate features, where the similarity values are encoded as feature weights.

On *PCEDT*, preliminary experiments showed that the best strategy to include word vectors into classification is by turning them directly into features, so that each dimension of the word vector is represented as a separate feature. Thus, we iterate through all 300 vector dimensions and create a separate feature representing the position and value of a particular dimension. Values are again encoded in feature weights. These features are created separately for both the argument and the predicate. The word vectors are pre-normalized to unit length, so no additional normalization of feature weights is needed.

Both the n-gram– and vector similarities–based features give a modest improvement to the classification performance.

4 Detecting Top Nodes

The last step in the pipeline is the detection of *top nodes*. A top node is the semantic head or the structural root of the sentence. Typically each sentence annotated in the *DM* and *PAS* formats contains one top node, whereas *PCEDT* sentences have on average 1.12 top nodes per sentence.

As in the two previous stages, we predict top nodes by training a support vector machine classifier, with each token being considered a candidate. Because the top node prediction is the last step performed, in addition to the basic information available in the two previous steps, we are able to use also predicted arguments as features. Otherwise, the feature set used in top node detection follows the same style as in the two previous

[1] `https://code.google.com/p/word2vec/`

	LP	LR	LF	UF
DM	80.94	82.14	81.53	83.48
PAS	87.33	87.76	87.54	88.97
PCEDT	72.42	72.37	72.40	85.86
Overall	80.23	80.76	80.49	86.10

Table 2: Overall scores of whole task as well as separately for each annotation format in terms of labeled precision (LP), recall (LR) and F_1-score (LF) as well as unlabeled F_1-score (UF).

tasks, but is substantially smaller (see Table 1). We also create all possible feature pairs prior to classification to simulate the use of a second-degree polynomial kernel.

For each token in the sentence, we predict whether it is a top node or not. However, in *DM* and *PAS*, where typically only one top node is allowed, we choose only the token with the maximum positive value to be the final top node. In *PCEDT*, we simply let all positive predictions act as top nodes.

5 Results

The primary evaluation measure is the labeled F_1-score of the predicted dependencies, where the identification of top nodes is incorporated as an additional dummy dependency. The overall semantic F_1-score of our system is 80.49%. The prediction performance in *DM* is 81.53%, in *PAS* 87.54% and in *PCEDT* 72.40%. The top nodes are identified with an overall F_1-score of 87.05%. The unlabeled F_1-score reflects the performance of the dependency detection in isolation from labeling task and by comparing the labeled and unlabeled F_1-scores from Table 2 we can see that the most common mistake relates to the identification of correct governor-dependent pairs. This is especially true with the *DM* and *PAS* formats where the difference between labeled and unlabeled scores is very small (1.9pp and 1.4pp), reflecting high performance in assigning the roles. Instead, in *PCEDT* the role assignment accuracy is substantially below the other two and the difference between unlabeled and labeled F_1-score is as much as 13.5pp. One likely reason is the higher number of possible roles defined in the *PCEDT* format.

5.1 Discussion

Naturally, our system generally performs better with frequently seen semantic roles than roles that are seen rarely. In the case of *DM*, the 4 most common semantic roles cover over 87% of the gold standard dependencies and are predicted with a macro F_1-score of 85.3%, while the remaining 35 dependency labels found in the gold standard are predicted at an average rate of 49.4%. To give this a perspective, the most common 4 roles have on average 121K training instances, while the remaining 35 roles have on average about 2000 training instances. For *PAS*, the 9 most common labels, which comprise over 80% of all dependencies in the gold standard data and have on average about 66K training instances per role, are predicted with an F_1-score of 87.6%, while the remaining 32 labels have on average 4200 training instance and are predicted with an F_1-score of 57.8%. The *PCEDT* format has the highest number of possible semantic roles and also lowest correlation between the frequency in training data and F_1-score. For *PCEDT*, the 11 most common labels, which cover over 80% of all dependencies in the gold standard, are predicted with an F_1-score of 69.6%, while the remaining 53 roles are predicted at an average rate of 46.6%. The higher number of roles also naturally affects the number of training instances and the 11 most common labels in *PCEDT* have on average 35K training instances, while the remaining 53 roles have on average 1600 instances per role.

Similarly, the system performs better with semantic arguments which are nearby the governor. This is true for both linear distance between the two tokens and especially for distance measured by syntactic dependency steps. For example in the case of *DM*, semantic dependencies shorter than 3 steps in the syntactic tree cover more than 95% of the semantic dependencies in the gold standard and have an F_1-score of 75.1%, while the rest have only 32.6%. The same general pattern is also evident in the other formats.

6 Conclusion

In this paper we presented our system used to participate in the SemEval-2014 Shared Task on broad-coverage semantic dependency parsing. We built a pipeline of three supervised classifiers to identify semantic dependencies, assign a role for each dependency and finally, detect the top nodes.

In addition to basic features used in classification we have shown that additional information, such as frequencies of syntactic n-grams and word similarities derived from vector space representations, can also positively contribute to the classification performance.

The overall F_1-score of our system is 80.49% and it was ranked third in the open track of the shared task.

Acknowledgments

This work was supported by the Emil Aaltonen Foundation and the Kone Foundation. Computational resources were provided by CSC – IT Center for Science.

References

Jari Björne, Filip Ginter, and Tapio Salakoski. 2012. University of Turku in the BioNLP'11 shared task. *BMC Bioinformatics*, 13(Suppl 11):S4.

Bernd Bohnet and Joakim Nivre. 2012. A transition-based system for joint part-of-speech tagging and labeled non-projective dependency parsing. In *Proceedings of the 2012 Joint Conference on Empirical Methods in Natural Language Processing and Computational Natural Language Learning*, pages 1455–1465.

Chih-Chung Chang and Chih-Jen Lin. 2011. LIBSVM: A library for support vector machines. *ACM Transactions on Intelligent Systems and Technology*, 2:27:1–27:27.

Yoav Goldberg and Jon Orwant. 2013. A dataset of Syntactic-Ngrams over time from a very large corpus of English books. In *Second Joint Conference on Lexical and Computational Semantics (*SEM), Volume 1: Proceedings of the Main Conference and the Shared Task: Semantic Textual Similarity*, pages 241–247.

Jan Hajič, Massimiliano Ciaramita, Richard Johansson, Daisuke Kawahara, Maria Antònia Martí, Lluís Màrquez, Adam Meyers, Joakim Nivre, Sebastian Padó, Jan Štěpánek, et al. 2009. The CoNLL-2009 shared task: Syntactic and semantic dependencies in multiple languages. In *Proceedings of the Thirteenth Conference on Computational Natural Language Learning: Shared Task*, pages 1–18.

Thorsten Joachims. 1999. Making large-scale SVM learning practical. In *Advances in Kernel Methods - Support Vector Learning*, pages 169–184. MIT Press.

Jenna Kanerva and Filip Ginter. 2014. Post-hoc manipulations of vector space models with application to semantic role labeling. In *Proceedings of the 2nd Workshop on Continuous Vector Space Models and their Compositionality (CVSC)@ EACL*, pages 1–10.

Tomas Mikolov, Kai Chen, Greg Corrado, and Jeffrey Dean. 2013. Efficient estimation of word representations in vector space. In *Workshop Proceedings of International Conference on Learning Representations*.

Makoto Miwa, Paul Thompson, John McNaught, Douglas Kell, and Sophia Ananiadou. 2012. Extracting semantically enriched events from biomedical literature. *BMC Bioinformatics*, 13(1):108.

Hai Zhao, Wenliang Chen, Chunyu Kit, and Guodong Zhou. 2009. Multilingual dependency learning: a huge feature engineering method to semantic dependency parsing. In *Proceedings of the Thirteenth Conference on Computational Natural Language Learning: Shared Task*, pages 55–60.

UBham: Lexical Resources and Dependency Parsing for Aspect-Based Sentiment Analysis

Viktor Pekar
School of Computer Science
University of Birmingham
Birmingham, UK
v.pekar@cs.bham.ac.uk

Naveed Afzal
FCIT, North Branch
King Abdulaziz University
Jeddah, KSA
nafzal@kau.edu.sa

Bernd Bohnet
School of Computer Science
University of Birmingham
Birmingham, UK
b.bohnet@cs.bham.ac.uk

Abstract

This paper describes the system developed by the UBham team for the SemEval-2014 Aspect-Based Sentiment Analysis task (Task 4). We present an approach based on deep linguistic processing techniques and resources, and explore the parameter space of these techniques applied to the different stages in this task and examine possibilities to exploit interdependencies between them.

1 Introduction

Aspect-Based Sentiment Analysis (ASBA) is concerned with detection of the author's sentiment towards different issues discussed in a document, such as aspects or features of a product in a customer review. The specific ASBA scenario we address in this paper is as follows. Given a sentence from a review, identify (1) *aspect terms*, specific words or multiword expressions denoting aspects of the product; (2) *aspect categories*, categories of issues being commented on; (3) *aspect term polarity*, the polarity of the sentiment associated with each aspect term; and (4) *aspect category polarity*, the polarity associated with each aspect category found in the sentence. For example, in:

I liked the service and the staff, but not the food.

aspect terms are *service*, *staff* and *food*, where the first two are evaluated positively and the last one negatively; and aspect categories are SERVICE and FOOD, where the former is associated with positive sentiment and the latter with negative. It should be noted that a given sentence may contain one, several, or no aspect terms, one, several, or no aspect categories, and may express either positive, negative, neutral, or conflicted sentiment.

While the ASBA task is usually studied in the context of documents (e.g., online reviews), peculiarities of this scenario are short input texts, complex categorization schemas, and a limited amount of annotated data. Therefore we focused on ways to exploit deep linguistic processing techniques, which we use for both creating complex classification features and rule-based processing.

The research was partially supported by FP7 ICT project "Workbench for Interactive Contrastive Analysis of Patent Documentation" under grant no. FP7-SME-606163.

2 Related Work

2.1 Aspect Term Extraction

To recognize terms that express key notions in a product or service review, a common general approach has been to extract nouns and noun phrases as potential terms and then apply a certain filtering technique to ensure only the most relevant terms remain. These techniques include statistical association tests (Yi et al., 2003), associative mining rules with additional rule-based post-processing steps (Hu and Liu, 2004), and measures of association with certain pre-defined classes of words, such as part-whole relation indicators (Popescu and Etzioni, 2005).

2.2 Aspect Category Recognition

Aspect category recognition is often addressed as a text classification problem, where a classifier is learned from reviews manually tagged for aspects (e.g., Snyder and Barzilay, 2007, Ganu et al., 2009). Titov and McDonald (2008) present an approach which jointly detects aspect categories and their sentiment using a classifier trained on topics discovered via Multi-Grain LDA and star ratings available in training data. Zhai et al. (2010) presented an approach based on Expectation-Maximization to group aspect expressions into user-defined aspect categories.

Proceedings of the 8th International Workshop on Semantic Evaluation (SemEval 2014), pages 683–687,
Dublin, Ireland, August 23-24, 2014.

2.3 Sentence Sentiment

Lexicon-based approaches to detecting sentiment in a sentence rely on a lexicon where words and phrases are provided with sentiment labels as well as on techniques to recognize "polarity shifters", phrases causing the polarity of a lexical item to reverse. Early work on detection of polarity shifters used surface-level patterns (Yu and Hatzivassilouglu, 2003; Hu and Liu, 2004). Moilanen and Pulman (2007) provide a logic-oriented framework to compute the polarity of grammatical structures, that is capable of dealing with phenomena such as sentiment propagation, polarity reversal, and polarity conflict. Several papers looked at different ways to use syntactic dependency information in a machine learning framework, to better account for negations and their scope (Nakagawa et al., 2010; Socher et al., 2013).

To adapt a generic sentiment lexicon to a new application domain, previous work exploited semantic relations encoded in WordNet (Kim and Hovy, 2006), unannotated data (Li et al, 2012), or queries to a search engine (Taboada et al., 2006).

3 Our Approach

In the following sections, we will describe our approach to each stage of the Shared Task, reporting experiments on the provided training data using a 10-fold cross-validation.

3.1 Aspect Term Extraction

During pre-processing training data was parsed using a dependency parser (Bohnet and Nivre, 2012), and sentiment words were recognized in it using a sentiment lexicon (see Section 6.1). Candidate terms were extracted as single nouns, noun phrases, adjectives and verbs, enforcing certain exceptions as detailed in the annotation guidelines for the Shared Task (Pontiki et al., 2014), namely:

- Sentiment words were not allowed as part of terms;
- Noun phrases with all elements capitalized and acronyms were excluded, under the assumption they refer to brands rather than product aspects;
- Nouns referring to the product class as a whole ("restaurant", "laptop", etc) were excluded.

Candidate terms that exactly overlapped with manually annotated terms were discarded, while those that did not were used as negative examples of aspect terms.

In order to provide the term extraction process with additional lexical knowledge, from the training data we extracted those manually annotated terms that corresponded to a single aspect category. Then the set of terms belonging to each category was augmented using WordNet: first we determined the 5 most prominent hyperonyms of these terms in the WordNet hierarchy using Resnik (1992)'s algorithm for learning a class in a semantic hierarchy that best represents selectional preferences of a verb, additionally requiring that each hypernym is at least 7 nodes away from the root, to make them sufficiently specific. Then we obtained all lexical items that belong to children synsets of these hypernyms, and further extended these lexical items with their meronyms and morphological derivatives. The resulting set of lexical items was later used as an extended aspect term lexicon. We additionally created a list of all individual lemmas of content words found in this lexicon.

For each term, we extracted the following features to be used for automatic classification:

- **Normalized form**: the surface form of the term after normalization;
- **Term lemmas**: lemmas of content words found in the term;
- **Lexicon term**: if the term is in the lexicon;
- **Lexicon lemmas ratio**: the ratio of lexicon lemmas in the term;
- **Unigram**: 3 unigrams on either side of the term;
- **Bigrams**: The two bigrams around the term;
- **Adj+term**: If an adjective depends on the term[1] or related to it via a link verb ("be", "get", "become", etc);
- **Sentiment+term**: If a sentiment word depends on the term or related via a link verb;
- **Be+term**: If the term depends on a link verb;
- **Subject term**: If the term is a subject;

[1]In case the term was a multi-word expression, the relation to the head of the phrase was used.

- **Object term**: If the term is an object.

We first look at how well the manually designed patterns extracted potential terms. We are primarily interested in recall at this stage, since after that potential terms are classified into terms and non-terms with an automatic classifier. The recall on the restaurants was 70.5, and on the laptops – 56.9. These are upper limits on recall for the overall task of aspect term recognition.

Table 1 and Table 2 compare the performance of several learning algorithms on the restaurants and the laptops dataset, respectively[2].

	P	R	F
Linear SVM	94.42	95.51	94.96
Decision Tree	94.24	92.90	93.56
Naïve Bayes	84.97	95.67	89.99
kNN (k=5)	82.71	93.50	87.76

Table 1: Learning algorithms on the aspect term extraction task, restaurants dataset.

	P	R	F
Linear SVM	88.14	94.07	91.00
Naïve Bayes	93.61	79.46	85.92
Decision Tree	83.87	82.99	83.39
kNN (k=5)	82.83	83.31	83.03

Table 2: Learning algorithms on the aspect term extraction task, laptops dataset.

On both datasets, linear SVMs performed best, and so they were used in the subsequent experiments on term recognition. To examine the quality of each feature used for term classification, we ran experiments where a classifier was built and tested without that feature, see Tables 3 and 4, for the restaurants and laptops datasets respectively, where a greater drop in performance compared to the entire feature set, indicates a more informative feature.

The results show the three most useful features are the same in both datasets: the occurrence of the candidate term in the constructed sentiment lexicon, the lemmas found in the term, and the normalized form of the term account.

We ran further experiments manually selecting several top-performing features, but none of the configurations produced significant improvements on the use of the whole feature set.

[2]This and the following experiments were run on the train data supplied by the shared task organizers using 10-fold cross-validation.

	P	R	F
Lexicon term	91.74	95.01	93.33
Term lemmas	92.43	95.00	93.69
Normalized form	93.45	95.36	94.39
Be+term	93.99	95.28	94.63
Left bigram	94.21	95.09	94.64
All features	94.42	95.51	94.96

Table 3: Top 5 most informative features for the term extraction subtask, restaurants dataset.

	P	R	F
Lexicon term	88.82	88.61	88.69
Term lemmas	85.02	95.16	89.79
Normalized form	87.79	92.13	89.89
Left bigram	87.83	93.62	90.62
Term is obj	87.79	94.43	90.97
All features	88.14	94.07	91.00

Table 4: Top 5 most informative features for the term extraction subtask, laptops dataset.

Table 5 shows the results of evaluation of the aspect term extraction on the test data of the Shared Task (baseline algorithms were provided by the organizers). The results correspond to what can be expected based on the upper limits on recall for the pattern-based extraction of candidate terms as well as precision and recall for the classifier.

	P	R	F
Restaurants	77.9	61.1	68.5
Restaurants, baseline	53.9	51.4	52.6
Laptops	60.3	39.1	47.5
Laptops, baseline	40.1	38.1	39.1

Table 5: Aspect term extraction on the test data of the Shared Task.

3.2 Aspect Category Recognition

To recognize aspect categories in a sentence, we classified individual clauses found in it, assuming that each aspect category would be discussed in a separate clause. Features used for classification were lemmas of content words; to account for the fact that aspect terms are more indicative of aspect categories than other words, we additionally used entire terms as features, weighting them twice as much as other features. Table 6 compares the performance of several learning algorithms when automatically recognized aspect terms were not used as an additional feature; Table 7 shows results when terms were used as features.

	P	R	F
Linear SVM	66.37	58.07	60.69
Decision Tree	58.07	51.22	53.05
Naïve Bayes	74.34	46.07	48.63
kNN (*k*=5)	58.65	43.77	46.57

Table 6: Learning algorithms on the aspect category recognition task, aspect terms not weighted.

	P	R	F
Linear SVM	67.23	59.43	61.90
Decision Tree	64.41	55.84	58.36
Naïve Bayes	78.02	49.57	52.87
kNN (*k*=5)	67.92	47.91	51.94

Table 7: Learning algorithms on the aspect category recognition task, aspect terms weighted.

The addition of aspect terms as separate features increased F-scores for all the learning methods, sometimes by as much as 5%. Based on these results, we used the linear SVM method for the task submission. Table 8 reports results achieved on the test data of the Shared Task.

	P	R	F
Restaurants	81.8	67.9	74.2
Baseline	64.8	52.5	58.0

Table 8: Aspect category extraction on the test data of the Shared Task.

3.3 Aspect Term Sentiment

To recognize sentiment in a sentence, we take a lexicon-based approach. The sentiment lexicon we used encodes the lemma, the part-of-speech tag, and the polarity of the sentiment word. It was built by combining three resources: lemmas from SentiWordNet (Baccianella et al., 2010), which do not belong to more than 3 synsets; the General Inquirer lexicon (Stone et al., 1966), and a subsection of the Roget thesaurus annotated for sentiment (Heng, 2004). In addition, we added sentiment expressions that are characteristic of the restaurants and laptop domains, obtained based on manual analysis of the restaurants corpus used in (Snyder and Barzilay (2007) and the laptop reviews corpus used in (Jindal and Liu, 2008).

To detect negated sentiment, we used a list of negating phrases such as "not", "never", etc., and two types of patterns to determine the scope of a negation. The first type detected negations on the sentence level, checking for negative phrases at the start of the sentence; negations detected on the sentence level were propagated to the clause level. The second type of patterns detected negated sentiment within a clause, using patterns specific to the part-of-speech of the sentiment word (e.g., "AUXV + negation + VB + MAINV", where MAINV is a sentiment verb). The output of this algorithm is the sentence split into clauses, with each clause being assigned one of four sentiment labels: "positive", "negative", "neutral", "conflict". Thus, each term was associated with the sentiment of the clause it appeared in.

On the test data of the Shared Task, the algorithm achieved the accuracy scores of 76.0 (the restaurants data, for the baseline of 64.3) and 63.6 (the laptops data, for the baseline of 51.1).

3.4 Category Sentiment

Recall that aspect categories were recognized in a sentence by classifying its individual clauses. Category sentiment was determined from the sentiment of the clauses where the category was found. In case more than one clause was assigned to the same category and at least one clause expressed positive sentiment and at least one – negative, such cases were classified as conflicted sentiment. This method achieved the accuracy of 72.8 (on the restaurants data), with the baseline being 65.65.

4 Conclusion

Our study has shown that aspect terms can be detected with a high accuracy using a domain lexicon derived from WordNet, and a set of classification features created with the help of deep linguistic processing techniques. However, the overall accuracy of aspect term recognition is greatly affected by the extraction patterns that are used to extract initial candidate terms. We also found that automatically extracted aspect terms are useful features in the aspect category recognition task. With regards to sentiment detection, our results suggest that reasonable performance can be achieved with a lexicon-based approach coupled with carefully designed rules for the detection of polarity shifts.

References

Stefano Baccianella, Andrea Esuli, and Fabrizio Sebastiani. 2010. *SENTIWORDNET 3.0: An Enhanced Lexical Resource for Sentiment Analysis and Opinion Mining*. Proceedings of LREC-2010.

Bernd Bohnet and Joakim Nivre. 2012. *A Transition-Based System for Joint Part-of-Speech Tagging and Labeled Non-Projective Dependency Parsing*. Proceedings of EMNLP-CoNLL.

Gayatree Ganu, Noémie Elhadad, and Amelié Marian. 2009. *Beyond the Stars: Improving Rating Predictions using Review Text Content*. Proceedings of Twelfth International Workshop on the Web and Databases (WebDB 2009).

Adrian Heng. 2004. *An exploratory study into the use of faceted classification for emotional words*. Master Thesis. Nanyang Technological University, Singapore.

Minqing Hu and Bing Liu. 2004. *Mining opinion features in customer reviews*. Proceedings of the 9th National Conference on Artificial Intelligence (AAAI-2004).

Nitin Jindal and Bing Liu. 2008. *Opinion Spam and Analysis* Proceedings of WWW-2008.

Soo-Min Kim and Eduard Hovy. 2006. *Identifying and analyzing judgment opinions*. Proceedings of HLT/NAACL-2006.

Fangtao Li, Sinno Jialin Pan, Ou Jin, Qiang Yang and Xiaoyan Zhu. 2012. *Cross-Domain Co-Extraction of Sentiment and Topic Lexicons*. Proceedings of ACL-2012.

Tetsuji Nakagawa, Kentaro Inui, and Sadao Kurohashi. 2010. *Dependency tree-based sentiment classification using CRFs with hidden variables*. Proceedings of NAACL/HLT-2010.

Karo Moilanen and Stephen Pulman. 2007. *Sentiment composition*. Proceedings of the Recent Advances in Natural Language Processing (RANLP 2007).

Maria Pontiki, Dimitrios Galanis, John Pavlopoulos, Haris Papageorgiou, Ion Androutsopoulos, and Suresh Manandhar. 2014. *SemEval-2014 Task 4: Aspect Based Sentiment Analysis*. Proceedings of the 8th International Workshop on Semantic Evaluation (SemEval 2014).

Ana-Maria Popescu and Oren Etzioni. 2005. *Extracting product features and opinions from reviews*. Proceedings HLT/EMNLP-2005.

Philip Resnik. 1992. *A class-based approach to lexical discovery* Proceedings of the Proceedings of the 30th Annual Meeting of the Association for Computational Linguists.

Benjamin Snyder and Regina Barzilay 2007. *Multiple Aspect Ranking using the Good Grief Algorithm*. Proceedings of NAACL-2007.

Richard Socher, Alex Perelygin, Jean Y. Wu, Jason Chuang, Christopher D. Manning, Andrew Y. Ng and Christopher Potts 2013. *Recursive Deep Models for Semantic Compositionality Over a Sentiment Treebank*. Proceedings of EMNLP-2013.

Philip J. Stone, Dexter C. Dunphy, Marshall S. Smith, and Daniel M. Ogilvie. 1966. *The General Inquirer: A Computer Approach to Content Analysis*. Cambridge, MA: The MIT Press.

Maite Taboada, Caroline Anthony, and Kimberly Voll. 2006. *Creating semantic orientation dictionaries* Proceedings of 5th International Conference on Language Resources and Evaluation (LREC).

Ivan Titov and Ryan McDonald. 2008. *A joint model of text and aspect ratings for sentiment summarization*. Proceedings of ACL-2008.

Liheng Xu, Kang Liu, Siwei Lai, Yubo Chen and Jun Zhao. 2013. *Mining Opinion Words and Opinion Targets in a Two-Stage Framework*. Proceedings of ACL-2013.

Jeonghee Yi, Tetsuya Nasukawa, Razvan Bunescu, and Wayne Niblack. 2003. *Sentiment analyzer: Extracting sentiments about a given topic using natural language processing techniques*. Proceedings of the 3rd IEEE International Conference on Data Mining (ICDM-2003), pp. 423-434.

Hong Yu and Vasileios Hatzivassiloglou. 2003. *Towards Answering Opinion Questions: Separating Facts from Opinions and Identifying the Polarity of Opinion Sentences*. Proceedings of EMNLP-03.

Zhongwu Zhai, Bing Liu, Hua Xu and Peifa Jia. 2011. *Clustering product features for opinion mining*. Proceedings of the 4th ACM International Conference on Web Search and Data Mining, ACM, pp 347354.

UEdin: Translating L1 Phrases in L2 Context using Context-Sensitive SMT

Eva Hasler
ILCC, School of Informatics
University of Edinburgh
e.hasler@ed.ac.uk

Abstract

We describe our systems for the SemEval 2014 Task 5: *L2 writing assistant* where a system has to find appropriate translations of L1 segments in a given L2 context. We participated in three out of four possible language pairs (English-Spanish, French-English and Dutch-English) and achieved the best performance for all our submitted systems according to word-based accuracy. Our models are based on phrase-based machine translation systems and combine topical context information and language model scoring.

1 Introduction

In the past years, the fields of statistical machine translation (SMT) and word sense disambiguation (WSD) have developed largely in parallel, with each field organising their own shared tasks aimed at improving translation quality (Bojar et al., 2013) and predicting word senses, e.g. Agirre et al. (2010). Because sense disambiguation is a central problem in machine translation, there has been work on integrating WSD classifiers into MT systems (Carpuat and Wu, 2007a; Carpuat and Wu, 2007b; Chan et al., 2007). However, one problem with the direct integration of WSD techniques into MT has been the mismatch between word predictions of WSD systems and the phrase segmentations of MT system. This problem was adressed in Carpuat and Wu (2007b) by extending word sense disambiguation to phrase sense disambiguation. The relation between word sense distinctions and translation has also been explored in past SemEval tasks on *cross-lingual word sense disambiguation*, where senses are not defined in terms of WordNet senses as in previous tasks, but instead as translations to another language (Lefever and Hoste, 2010; Lefever and Hoste, 2013).

This year's *L2 writing assistant* task is similar to the cross-lingual word sense disambiguation task but differs in the context provided for disambiguation and the length of the fragments (source phrases instead of words). While in other translation and disambiguation tasks the source language context is given, the *L2 writing assistant* task assumes a given target language context that constrains the possible translations of L1 fragments. This is interesting from a machine translation point-of-view because it allows for a direct comparison with systems that exploit the target context using a language model. As language models have become more and more powerful over the years, mostly thanks to increased computing power, new machine translation techniques are also judged by their ability to improve performance over a baseline system with a strong language model. Another difference to previous SemEval tasks is the focus on both lexical and grammatical forms, while previous tasks have mostly focused on lexical selection.

2 Translation Model for L1 Fragments in L2 Context

Our model for translating L1 fragments in L2 context is a phrase-based machine translation system with an additional context similarity feature. We aim to resolve lexical ambiguities by taking the entire topical L2 context of an L1 fragment into account rather than only relying on the phrasal L1 context. We do not explicitly model the grammaticality of target word forms but rather use a standard 5-gram language model to score target word sequences. We describe the context similarity feature in the following section.

Proceedings of the 8th International Workshop on Semantic Evaluation (SemEval 2014), pages 688–693, Dublin, Ireland, August 23-24, 2014.

2.1 Context Similarity Feature

The context similarity feature is derived from the phrase pair topic model (PPT) described in Hasler et al. (2014). At training time, this model learns topic distributions for all phrase pairs in the phrase table in an unsupervised fashion, using a variant of Latent Dirichlet Allocation (LDA). The underlying assumption is that all phrase pairs share a set of global topics of predefined size, thus each phrase pair is assigned a distribution over the same set of global topics. This is in contrast to Word Sense Induction (WSI) methods which typically learn a set of topics or senses for each word type, for example in Lau et al. (2010).

The input to the model are distributional profiles of words occurring in the context of each phrase pair, thus, the model learns lower-dimensional representations of the likely context words of a phrase pair. While in a normal machine translation setup the source sentence context is given, it is straightforward to replace source language words with target language words as given in the L2 context for each test example. At test time, the topic model is applied to the given L2 context to infer a topic distribution of the test context. The topic distribution of an applicable phrase pair is compared to the topic distribution of a given test context (defined as all L2 words in the same sentence as the L1 fragment, excluding stop words) using cosine similarity.

To adapt the translation system to the context of each test sentence, the phrase table is filtered per test sentence and each applicable phrase pair receives one additional feature that expresses its topical similarity with the test context. While the baseline system (the system without similarity feature) translates the entire test set with the same translation model, the context-sensitive system loads an adapted phrase table for each test sentence. While the phrase pair topic model can also deal with document-level context, here we consider only sentence-level context as no wider context was available. We evaluate three variations of the context similarity feature on top of a standard phrase-based MT system:

- **50-topics** The cosine similarity according to the PPT model trained with 50 topics (submitted as run1)
- **mixture:geoAvg** The geometric average of the cosine similarities according to PPT models trained with 20, 50 and 100 topics (submitted as run2)
- **mixture:max** For each source phrase, the cosine similarity according to the PPT model that yields the lowest entropy (out of the models with 20, 50 and 100 topics) when converting the similarities into probabilities (submitted as run3)

2.2 Language Model Scoring of L2 Context

On top of using the words in the L2 context for computing the similarity feature described above, we introduce a simple method for using a language model to score the target sequence that includes the translated L1 segments and the words to the left and right of the translated segments. In order to use the language model scoring implemented in the Moses decoder, we present the decoder with an input sentence that contains the L1 fragment as well as the L2 context with XML markup. While the L1 fragments are translated without special treatment, the L2 tokens are passed through untranslated by specifying the identity translation as markup. The XML markup also includes reordering walls to prevent the decoder from reordering the L2 context. An example input sentence with markup (French-English) is shown below:

```
<wall/>les manifesteurs<wall/>
<np translation="want">want</np><wall/>
<np translation="to">to</np><wall/>
<np translation="replace">replace</np><wall/>
<np translation="the">the</np><wall/>
<np translation="government">government</np><wall/>
<np translation=".">.</np><wall/>
```

3 Experimental Setup

Although the task is defined as building a *translation assistance system* rather than a full machine translation system, we use a standard machine translation setup to translate L1 phrases. We used the Moses toolkit (Koehn et al., 2007) to build phrase-based translation systems for the language pairs English-Spanish, French-English and Dutch-English[1]. For preprocessing, we applied punctuation normalisation, truecasing and tokenisation using the scripts provided with the Moses toolkit. The model contains the following standard features: direct and inverse phrase translation probabilities, lexical weights, word and phrase penalty, lexicalised reordering and distortion features and a 5-gram language model with modified Kneser-Ney smoothing. In addition, we add the context similarity feature described in Section 2.1.

[1] We left out the English-German language pair for time reasons.

Training data	English-Spanish	French-English	Dutch-English
Europarl	1.92M	1.96M	1.95M
News Commentary	192K	181K	n/a
TED	157K	159K	145K
News	2.1G	2.1G	2.1G
Commoncrawl	50M	82M	-

Table 1: Overview of parallel and monolingual training data (top/bottom, in number of sentences/words).

3.1 Training Data

Most of the training data was taken from the WMT13 shared task (Bojar et al., 2013), except where specified otherwise. For the English-Spanish and French-English systems, we used parallel training data from the Europarl and News Commentary corpora, as well as the TED corpus (Cettolo et al., 2012). For Dutch-English, we used parallel data from the Europarl and TED corpus. The language models were trained on the target sides of the parallel data and additional news data from the years 2007-2012. For English-Spanish and French-English, we used additional language model data from the Commoncrawl corpus[2]. Separate language models were trained for each corpus and interpolated on a development set. An overview of the training data is shown in Table 1.

3.2 Tuning Model Parameters

The parameters of the baseline MT excluding the similarity feature were tuned with kbest-mira (Cherry and Foster, 2012) on mixed development sets containing the trial data (500 sentence pairs with XML markup) distributed for the task as well as development data from the news and TED corpora for the English-Spanish and French-English systems and development data from the TED corpus for the Dutch-English system. Because the domain(s) of the test examples was not known beforehand, we aimed for learning model weights that would generalise across domains by using rather diverse tuning sets. In total, the development sets consisted of 3435, 3705 and 3516 sentence pairs, respectively. We did not tune the weight of the similarity feature automatically, but set it to an empirically determined value instead.

3.3 Simulating Ambiguous Development Data

When developing our systems using the trial data supplied by the task organisers, we noticed that the context similarity feature did not add much to the overall performance, which we attributed to the small number of ambiguous examples in the trial data. Therefore, we extracted a set of 1076 development instances containing 14 ambiguous French words and their English translations from a mixed corpus containing data from the News Commentary, TED and Commoncrawl corpora as used in Hasler et al. (2014). Examples of ambiguous source words and their translations in that de-

[2] For the Dutch-English system, the Commoncrawl data did not seem to improve performance.

Source words	Translations
chaîne	chain, string, channel, station
matière	matter, material, subject
flux	stream, flow, feed
démon	demon, daemon, devil
régime	regime, diet, rule

Table 2: Examples of ambiguous source words and their different translations in the simulated development set.

System	French-English
Baseline	0.314
+ LM context	0.726
20-topics	0.603
+ LM context	0.845
50-topics	**0.674**
+ LM context	**0.886**
100-topics	0.628
+ LM context	0.872
mixture:arithmAvg	0.650
+ LM context	0.869
mixture:geoAvg	**0.670**
+ LM context	**0.883**
mixture:max	**0.690**
+ LM context	**0.889**

Table 3: Word accuracy (best) on the simulated development set for the smaller baseline system and the systems with added context similarity feature, with and without language model context.

velopment set are shown in Table 2.

Translating the L1 fragments in the simulated development set using a smaller baseline system trained on this mixed data set yields the results at the top of Table 3. Note that even though the instances were extracted from the training set, this does not affect the translation model since the L1 fragments contain only the ambiguous source words and no further source context that could be memorised.

The bottom part of Table 3 shows the performance of the three context similarity features described in Section 2.1 plus some further variants (the models with 20 and 100 topics as well as the arithmetic average of the cosine similarities of models trained with 20, 50 and 100 topics). First, we observe that each of the features clearly outperforms the baseline system without language model context. Second, each context similarity feature together with the language model context still outperforms the *Baseline + LM context*. Even though the gain of the context similarity features is smaller when the target context is scored with a language model, the topical context still provides additional information that improves lexical choice. We trained versions of the three best models from Table 3 (in bold) for our submissions on the official test sets.

4 Results and Discussion

In this section we report the experimental results of our systems on the official test sets. The results without scoring the L2 context with a language model are shown in Table 4 and including language model scoring of L2 context in Table 5. We limit the reported scores to word accuracy and do not report recall because our systems produce output for every L1 phrase.

In Table 4, we compare the performance of the baseline MT system to systems including one of three variants of the similarity feature as described in Section 2.1, according to the 1-best translation (best) as well as the 5-best translations (out-of-five) in a distinct n-best list. For five out of the six tasks, at least one of the systems including the similiary feature yields better performance than the baseline system. Only for French-English *best*, the baseline system yields the best word accuracy. Among the three variants, 50-topics and mixture:geoAvg perform slightly better than mixture:max in most cases.

Table 5 shows the results of our submitted runs

Input:	There are many ways of cooking <f>des œufs</f> for breakfast.
Reference:	There are many ways of cooking <f>eggs</f> for breakfast.
Input:	I loved animals when I was <f>un enfant</f>.
Reference:	I loved animals when I was <f>a kid<alt>a child</alt></f>.

Figure 1: Examples of official test instances.

(run1-run3) as well as the baseline system, all with language model scoring of L2 context via XML markup. The first thing to note in comparison to Table 4 is that providing the L2 context for language model scoring yields quite substantial improvements (0.165, 0.101 and 0.073, respectively). Again, in five out of six cases at least one of the systems with context similarity feature performs better than the baseline system. Only for Spanish-English *best*, the baseline system yields higher word accuracy than the three submitted runs. As before, 50-topics and mixture:geoAvg perform slightly better than mixture:max, with a preference for 50-topics. For comparison, we also show the word accuracies of the 2nd-ranked system for both tasks and each language pair. We note that the distance to the respective runner-up system is largest for French-English and on average larger for the *out-of-five* task than for the *best* task.

As a general observation, we can state that although the similarity feature improves performance in most cases, the improvements are small compared to the improvements achieved by scoring the L2 language model contexts. We suspect two reasons for this effect: first, we do not explicitly model grammaticality of word forms. Therefore, our system relies on the language model to choose the best word form for those test examples that do not contain any lexical ambiguity. Second, we have noticed that for some of the test examples, the correct translations do not depend particularly on words in the L2 context, as shown in Figure 1 where the most common translations of the source phrases without context would match the reference translations. These are cases where we do not expect much of an improvement in translation by taking the L2 context into account.

Since in Section 3.3 we have provided evidence that topical similarity features can improve lexical choice over simply using a target language model, we believe that the lower performance of the similarity features on the official test set is caused by

System	English-Spanish		French-English		Dutch-English	
	best	oof	best	oof	best	oof
Baseline	0.674	0.854	**0.722**	0.884	0.613	0.750
50-topics	**0.682**	0.860	0.719	**0.896**	0.616	**0.759**
mixture:geoAvg	0.677	**0.863**	0.715	**0.896**	**0.619**	0.756
mixture:max	0.679	0.860	0.712	0.887	0.618	0.753

Table 4: Word accuracy (best and out-of-five) of the baseline system and the systems with added context similarity feature. All systems were run without scoring the language model context.

System	English-Spanish		French-English		Dutch-English	
	best	oof	best	oof	best	oof
Baseline + LM context	**0.839**	0.944	0.823	0.934	0.686	0.809
run1: 50-topics + LM context	0.827	0.946	**0.824**	0.938	**0.692**	**0.811**
run2: mixture:geoAvg + LM context	0.827	0.944	0.821	**0.939**	0.688	0.808
run3: mixture:max + LM context	0.820	**0.949**	0.816	0.937	0.688	0.808
2nd-ranked systems	0.809[1]	0.887[2]	0.694[2]	0.839[2]	0.679[3]	0.753[3]

Table 5: Word accuracy (best and out-of-five) of all submitted systems (runs 1-3) as well as the baseline system without the context similarity feature. All systems were run with the language model context provided via XML input. Systems on 2nd rank: [1]UNAL-run2, [2]CNRC-run1, [3]IUCL-run1

different levels of ambiguity in the simulated development set and the official test set. For the simulated development set, we explicitly selected ambiguous source words in contexts which trigger multiple different translations, while the official test set also contains examples where the focus is on correct verb forms. It further contains examples where the baseline system without context information could easily provide the correct translation, as shown above. Thus, the performance of our topical context models should ideally be evaluated on test sets that contain a sufficient number of ambiguous source phrases in order to measure its ability to improve lexical selection.

Finally, in Figure 2 we show some examples where the 50-topics system (with LM context) produced semantically better translations than the baseline system and where words in the L2 context would have helped in promoting them over the choice of the baseline system.

Input:	Why has Air France authorised <f>les appareils électroniques</f> at take-off?
Baseline:	.. <f>the electronics</f> ..
50-topics:	.. <f>electronic devices</f> ..
Reference:	.. <f>electronic devices</f> ..
Input:	This project represents one of the rare advances in strenghtening <f>les liens</f> between Brazil and the European Union.
Baseline:	.. <f>the links</f> ..
50-topics:	.. <f>the ties</f> ..
Reference:	.. <f>the ties<alt>relations</alt><alt> the bonds</alt></f> ..

Figure 2: Examples of improved translation output with the context similarity feature.

5 Conclusion

We have described our systems for the SemEval 2014 Task 5: *L2 writing assistant* which achieved the best performance for all submitted language pairs and both the *best* and *out-of-five* tasks. All systems are based on phrase-based machine translation systems with an added context similarity feature derived from a topic model that learns topic distributions for phrase pairs. We show that the additional similarity feature improves performance over our baseline models and that further gains can be achieved by passing the L2 context through the decoder via XML markup, thereby producing language model scores of the sequences of L2 context words and translated L1 fragments. We also provide evidence that the relative performance of the context similarity features depends on the level of ambiguity in the L1 fragments.

Acknowledgements

This work was supported by funding from the Scottish Informatics and Computer Science Alliance and funding from the European Union Seventh Framework Programme (FP7/2007-2013) under grant agreement 287658 (EU BRIDGE).

References

Eneko Agirre, Oier Lopez De Lacalle, Christiane Fellbaum, Maurizio Tesconi, Monica Monachini, Piek Vossen, and Roxanne Segers. 2010. SemEval-2010 Task 17: All-words Word Sense Disambiguation on a Specific Domain. In *Proceedings of the 5th International Workshop on Semantic Evaluation*.

Ondrej Bojar, Christian Buck, Chris Callison-Burch, Christian Federmann, Barry Haddow, Philipp Koehn, Christof Monz, Matt Post, Radu Soricut, and Lucia Specia. 2013. Findings of the 2013 workshop on statistical machine translation. In *Proceedings of WMT 2013*.

Marine Carpuat and Dekai Wu. 2007a. How Phrase Sense Disambiguation outperforms Word Sense Disambiguation for Statistical Machine Translation. In *International Conference on Theoretical and Methodological Issues in MT*.

Marine Carpuat and Dekai Wu. 2007b. Improving Statistical Machine Translation using Word Sense Disambiguation. In *Proceedings of EMNLP*, pages 61–72.

Mauro Cettolo, Christian Girardi, and Marcello Federico. 2012. WIT3: Web Inventory of Transcribed and Translated Talks. In *Proceedings of EAMT*.

Yee Seng Chan, Hwee Tou Ng, and David Chiang. 2007. Word Sense Disambiguation Improves Statistical Machine Translation. In *Proceedings of ACL*.

Colin Cherry and George Foster. 2012. Batch Tuning Strategies for Statistical Machine Translation. In *Proceedings of NAACL*.

Eva Hasler, Barry Haddow, and Philipp Koehn. 2014. Dynamic Topic Adaptation for SMT using Distributional Profiles. In *Proceedings of the 9th Workshop on Statistical Machine Translation*.

Philipp Koehn, Hieu Hoang, Alexandra Birch, Chris Callison-Burch, Marcello Federico, Nicola Bertoldi, Brooke Cowan, Wade Shen, Christine Moran, Richard Zens, Chris Dyer, Ondrej Bojar, Alexandra Constantin, and Evan Herbst. 2007. Moses: Open source toolkit for SMT. In *Proceedings of ACL: Demo and poster sessions*.

Jey Han Lau, Paul Cook, Diana Mccarthy, David Newman, and Timothy Baldwin. 2010. Word Sense Induction for Novel Sense Detection. In *Proceedings of EACL*.

Els Lefever and Veronique Hoste. 2010. SemEval-2010 Task 3: Cross-lingual Word Sense Disambiguation. In *Proceedings of the 5th International Workshop on Semantic Evaluation*.

Els Lefever and Veronique Hoste. 2013. SemEval-2013 Task 10: Cross-lingual Word Sense Disambiguation. In *Proceedings of the 7th International Workshop on Semantic Evaluation, in Conjunction with the Second Joint Conference on Lexical and Computational Semantics*.

ÚFAL: Using Hand-crafted Rules in Aspect Based Sentiment Analysis on Parsed Data

Kateřina Veselovská, Aleš Tamchyna
Charles University in Prague, Faculty of Mathematics and Physics
Institute of Formal and Applied Linguistics
Malostranské náměstí 25, Prague, Czech Republic
{veselovska,tamchyna}@ufal.mff.cuni.cz

Abstract

This paper describes our submission to SemEval 2014 Task 4[1] (aspect based sentiment analysis). The current work is based on the assumption that it could be advantageous to connect the subtasks into one workflow, not necessarily following their given order. We took part in all four subtasks (aspect term extraction, aspect term polarity, aspect category detection, aspect category polarity), using polarity items detection via various subjectivity lexicons and employing a rule-based system applied on dependency data. To determine aspect categories, we simply look up their WordNet hypernyms. For such a basic method using no machine learning techniques, we consider the results rather satisfactory.

1 Introduction

In a real-life scenario, we usually do not have any golden aspects at our disposal. Therefore, it could be practical to be able to extract both aspects and their polarities at once. So we first parse the data, bearing in mind that it is very difficult to detect both sources/targets and their aspects on plain text corpora. This holds especially for pro-drop languages, e.g. Czech (Veselovská et al., 2014) but the proposed method is still language independent to some extent. Secondly, we detect the polarity items in the parsed text using a union of two different existing subjectivity lexicons (see Section 2). Afterwards, we extract the aspect terms in the dependency structures containing polarity expressions. In this task, we employ several hand-crafted rules detecting aspects based on syntactic features of the evaluative sentences, inspired by the method by Qiu et al. (2011). Finally, we identify aspect term categories with the help of the English WordNet and derive their polarities based on the polarities of individual aspects. The obtained results are discussed in Section 4.

2 Related Work

This work is related to polarity detection based on a list of evaluative items, i.e. subjectivity lexicons, generally described e.g. in Taboada et al. (2011). The English ones we use are minutely described in Wiebe et al. (2005) and several papers by Bing Liu, starting with Hu and Liu (2004). Inspired by Kobayashi et al. (2007), who make use of evaluative expressions when learning syntactic patterns obtained via pattern mining to extract aspect-evaluation pairs, we use the opinion words to detect evaluative structures in parsed data. The issue of target extraction in sentiment analysis is discussed in articles proposing different methods, mainly tested on product review datasets (Popescu and Etzioni, 2005; Mei et al., 2007; Scaffidi et al., 2007). Some of the authors take into consideration also product aspects (features), defined as product components or product attributes (Liu, 2006). Hu and Liu (2004) take as the feature candidates all noun phrases found in the text. Stoyanov and Cardie (2008) see the problem of target extraction as part of a topic modelling problem, similarly to Mei et al. (2007). In this contribution, we follow the work of Qiu et al. (2011) who learn syntactic relations from dependency trees.

3 Pipeline

Our workflow is illustrated in Figure 1. We first pre-process the data, then mark all aspects seen in the training data (still on plain text). The rest of the pipeline is implemented in Treex (Popel and

[1] http://alt.qcri.org/semeval2014/task4/

Proceedings of the 8th International Workshop on Semantic Evaluation (SemEval 2014), pages 694–698,
Dublin, Ireland, August 23-24, 2014.

Pattern			Example sentence
Subj_{aspect}	Pred_{copula}	PAdj	The food was great.
Subj_{aspect}	Pred_{copula}	PNoun	The coconut juice is the MUST!
Subj_{aspect}	Pred Adv_{eval}		The pizza tastes so good.
Attr_{eval}	Noun_{aspect}		Nice value.
Subj_{aspect}	Pred_{eval}		Their wine sucks.
Subj_{source}	Pred_{eval}	Obj_{aspect}	I liked the beer selection.

Table 1: Syntactic rules.

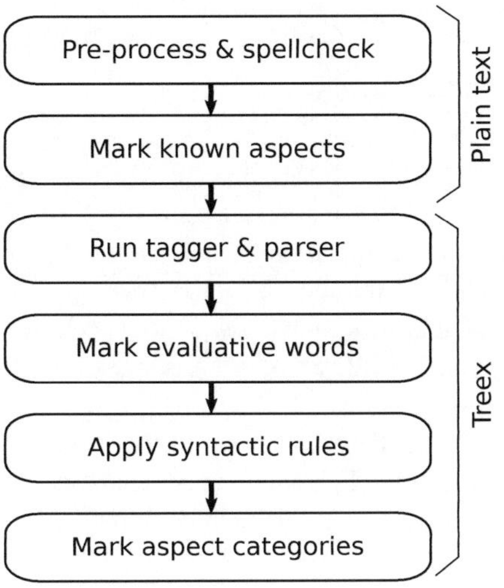

Figure 1: Overall schema of our approach.

Žabokrtský, 2010) and consists of linguistic analysis (tagging, dependency parsing), identification of evaluative words, and application of syntactic rules to find the evaluated aspects. Finally, for restaurants, we also identify aspect categories and their polarity.

3.1 Data

We used the training and trial data provided by the organizers. During system development, we used the trial section as a held-out set. In the final submission, both datasets are utilized in training.

3.2 Pre-processing

The main phase of pre-processing (apart from parsing the input files and other simple tasks) is running a spell-checker. As data for this task comes from real-world reviews, it contains various typos and other small errors. We therefore implemented a statistical spell-checker which works in two stages:

1. Run Aspell[2] to detect typos and obtain suggestions for them.
2. Select the appropriate suggestions using a language model (LM).

We trained a trigram LM from the English side of CzEng 1.0 (Bojar et al., 2012) using SRILM (Stolcke, 2002). We binarized the LM and use the Lazy decoder (Heafield et al., 2013) for selecting the suggestions that best fit the current context. Our script is freely available for download.[3]

We created a list of exceptions (domain-specific words, such as "netbook", are unknown to Aspell's dictionary) which should not be corrected and also skip named entities in spell-checking.

3.3 Marking Known Aspects

Before any linguistic processing, we mark all words (and multiword expressions) which are marked as aspects in the training data. For our final submission, the list also includes aspects from the provided development sets.

3.4 Morphological Analysis and Parsing

Further, we lemmatize the data and parse it using Treex (Popel and Žabokrtský, 2010), a modular framework for natural language processing (NLP). Treex is focused primarily on dependency syntax and includes blocks (wrappers) for taggers, parsers and other NLP tools. Within Treex, we used the Morče tagger (Hajič et al., 2007) and the MST dependency parser (McDonald et al., 2005).

3.5 Finding Evaluative Words

In the obtained dependency data, we detect polarity items using MPQA subjectivity lexicon (Wiebe et al., 2005) and Bing Liu's subjectivity clues.[4]

[2] http://aspell.net/

[3] https://redmine.ms.mff.cuni.cz/projects/staspell

[4] http://www.cs.uic.edu/~liub/FBS/sentiment-analysis.html#lexicon

	Task 1: aspect extraction			Task 2: aspect polarity	Task 3: category detection			Task 4: category polarity
	prec	recall	F-measure	accuracy	prec	recall	F-measure	accuracy
UFAL	0.50	0.72	0.59	0.67	0.57	0.74	0.65	0.63
best	0.91	0.82	0.84	0.81	0.91	0.86	0.88	0.83

Table 2: Results of our system on the Restaurants dataset as evaluated by the task organizers.

	Task 1: aspect extraction			Task 2: aspect polarity
	prec	recall	F-measure	accuracy
UFAL	0.39	0.66	0.49	0.57
best	0.85	0.67	0.75	0.70

Table 3: Results of our system on the Laptops dataset as evaluated by the task organizers.

We lemmatize both lexicons and look first for matching surface forms, then for matching lemmas. (English lemmas as output by Morče are sometimes too coarse, eliminating e.g. negation – we can mostly avoid their matching by looking at surface forms first.)

3.6 Syntactic Rules

Further, we created six basic rules for finding aspects in sentences containing evaluative items from the lexicons, e.g. *"If you find an adjective which is a part of a verbonominal predicate, the subject of its governing verb should be an aspect."*, see Table 1. Situational functions are marked with subscript, PAdj and PNoun stand for adjectival and nominal predicative expressions.

Moreover, we applied three more rules concerning coordinations. We suppose that if we find an aspect, every member of a given coordination must be an aspect too.

The excellent mussels, puff pastry, goat cheese and salad.

Concerning but-clauses, we expect that if there is no other aspect in the second part of the sentence, we assign the conflict value to the identified aspect.

The food was pretty good, but a little flavorless.

If there are two aspects identified in the but-coordination, they should be marked with opposite polarity.

The place is cramped, but the food is fantastic!

3.7 Aspect Categories

We collect a list of aspects from the training data and find all their hypernyms in WordNet (Fellbaum, 1998). We hand-craft a list of typical hypernyms for each category (such as "cooking" or "consumption" for the category "food"). Moreover, we look at the most frequent aspects in the training data and add as exceptions those for which our list would fail.

We rely on the output of aspect identification for this subtask. For each aspect marked in the sentence, we look up all its hypernyms in WordNet and compare them to our list. When we find a known hypernym, we assign its category to the aspect. Otherwise, we put the aspect in the "anecdotes/miscellaneous" category. For category polarity assignment, we combine the polarities of all aspects in that category in the following way:

- all positive → positive
- all negative → negative
- all neutral → neutral
- otherwise → conflict

4 Results and Discussion

Table 2 and Table 3 summarize the results of our submission. We do not achieve the best performance in any particular task, our system overall ranked in the middle.

We tend to do better in terms of recall than precision. This effect is mainly caused by our decision to also automatically mark all aspects seen in the training data.

4.1 Effect of the Spell-checker

We evaluated the performance of our system with and without the spell-checker. Overall, the impact is very small (f-measure stays within 2-decimal rounding error). In some cases its corrections are useful ("convienent" → "convenient parking"), sometimes its limited vocabulary harms our system ("fettucino alfredo" → "fitting Alfred"). This issue could be mitigated by providing a custom lexicon to Aspell.

4.2 Sources of Errors

As we always extract aspects that were observed in the training data, our system often marks them in non-evaluative contexts, leading to a considerable number of false positives. However, using this approach improves our f-measure score due to the limited recall of the syntactic rules.

The usefulness of our rules is mainly limited by the (i) sentiment lexicons and (ii) parsing errors.

(i) Since we used the lexicons directly without domain adaptation, many domain-specific terms are missed ("flavorless", "crowded") and some are matched incorrectly.

(ii) Parsing errors often confuse the rules and negatively impact both recall and precision. Often, they prevented the system from taking negation into account, so some of the negated polarity items were assigned incorrectly.

The "conflict" polarity value was rarely correct – all aspects and their polarity values need to be correctly discovered to assign this value. However, this type of polarity is infrequent in the data, so the overall impact is small.

Having participated in all four tasks, our system can be readily deployed as a complete solution which covers the whole process from plain text to aspects and aspect categories annotated with polarity. Considering the number of tasks covered and the fact that our system is entirely rule-based, the achieved results seem satisfactory.

5 Conclusion and Future Work

In our work, we developed a purely rule-based system for aspect based sentiment analysis which can both detect aspect terms (and categories) and assign polarity values to them. We have shown that even such a simple approach can achieve relatively good results.

In the future, our main plan is to involve machine learning in our system. We expect that outputs of our rules can serve as useful indicator features for a discriminative learning model, along with standard features such as bag-of-words (lemmas) or n-grams.

6 Acknowledgements

The research described herein has been supported by the by SVV project number 260 140 and by the LINDAT/CLARIN project funded by the Ministry of Education, Youth and Sports of the Czech Republic, project No. LM2010013.

This work has been using language resources developed and/or stored and/or distributed by the LINDAT/CLARIN project of the Ministry of Education, Youth and Sports of the Czech Republic (project LM2010013).

References

Ondřej Bojar, Zdeněk Žabokrtský, Ondřej Dušek, Petra Galuščáková, Martin Majliš, David Mareček, Jiří Maršík, Michal Novák, Martin Popel, and Aleš Tamchyna. 2012. The Joy of Parallelism with CzEng 1.0. In *Proc. of LREC*, pages 3921–3928. ELRA.

Christiane Fellbaum. 1998. *WordNet: An Electronic Lexical Database*. Bradford Books.

Jan Hajič, Jan Votrubec, Pavel Krbec, Pavel Květoň, et al. 2007. The best of two worlds: Cooperation of statistical and rule-based taggers for czech. In *Proceedings of the Workshop on Balto-Slavonic Natural Language Processing: Information Extraction and Enabling Technologies*, pages 67–74.

Kenneth Heafield, Philipp Koehn, and Alon Lavie. 2013. Grouping language model boundary words to speed k-best extraction from hypergraphs. In *Proceedings of the 2013 Conference of the North American Chapter of the Association for Computational Linguistics: Human Language Technologies*, pages 958–968, Atlanta, Georgia, USA, June.

Minqing Hu and Bing Liu. 2004. Mining and summarizing customer reviews. In *Proceedings of the Tenth ACM SIGKDD International Conference on Knowledge Discovery and Data Mining*, KDD '04, pages 168–177, New York, NY, USA. ACM.

Nozomi Kobayashi, Kentaro Inui, and Yuji Matsumoto. 2007. Extracting aspect-evaluation and aspect-of relations in opinion mining. In *Proceedings of the 2007 Joint Conference on Empirical Methods in Natural Language Processing and Computational Natural Language Learning (EMNLP-CoNLL)*.

Bing Liu. 2006. *Web Data Mining: Exploring Hyperlinks, Contents, and Usage Data (Data-Centric Systems and Applications)*. Springer-Verlag New York, Inc., Secaucus, NJ, USA.

Ryan McDonald, Fernando Pereira, Kiril Ribarov, and Jan Hajič. 2005. Non-projective dependency parsing using spanning tree algorithms. In *Proceedings of the conference on Human Language Technology and Empirical Methods in Natural Language Processing*, pages 523–530.

Qiaozhu Mei, Xu Ling, Matthew Wondra, Hang Su, and ChengXiang Zhai. 2007. Topic sentiment mixture: Modeling facets and opinions in weblogs. In *Proceedings of the 16th International Conference on World Wide Web*, WWW '07, pages 171–180, New York, NY, USA. ACM.

Martin Popel and Zdeněk Žabokrtský. 2010. TectoMT: Modular NLP Framework. In Hrafn Loftsson, Eirikur Rögnvaldsson, and Sigrun Helgadottir, editors, *IceTAL 2010*, volume 6233 of *Lecture Notes in Computer Science*, pages 293–304. Iceland Centre for Language Technology (ICLT), Springer.

Ana-Maria Popescu and Oren Etzioni. 2005. Extracting product features and opinions from reviews. In *Proceedings of the Conference on Human Language Technology and Empirical Methods in Natural Language Processing*, HLT '05, pages 339–346, Stroudsburg, PA, USA.

Guang Qiu, Bing Liu, Jiajun Bu, and Chun Chen. 2011. Opinion word expansion and target extraction through double propagation. *Comput. Linguist.*, 37(1):9–27, March.

Christopher Scaffidi, Kevin Bierhoff, Eric Chang, Mikhael Felker, Herman Ng, and Chun Jin. 2007. Red opal: Product-feature scoring from reviews. In *Proceedings of the 8th ACM Conference on Electronic Commerce*, EC '07, pages 182–191, New York, NY, USA. ACM.

Andreas Stolcke. 2002. SRILM – An Extensible Language Modeling Toolkit. In *Proc. Intl. Conf. on Spoken Language Processing*, volume 2, pages 901–904.

Veselin Stoyanov and Claire Cardie. 2008. Topic identification for fine-grained opinion analysis. In *Proceedings of the 22Nd International Conference on Computational Linguistics - Volume 1*, COLING '08, pages 817–824, Stroudsburg, PA, USA.

Maite Taboada, Julian Brooke, Milan Tofiloski, Kimberly Voll, and Manfred Stede. 2011. Lexicon-based methods for sentiment analysis. *Comput. Linguist.*, 37(2):267–307, June.

Kateřina Veselovská, Jan Mašek, and Vladislav Kuboň. 2014. Sentiment detection and annotation in a treebank.

Janyce Wiebe, Theresa Wilson, and Claire Cardie. 2005. Annotating expressions of opinions and emotions in language. *Language resources and evaluation*, 39(2-3):165–210.

UIO-Lien: Entailment Recognition using Minimal Recursion Semantics

Elisabeth Lien
Department of Informatics
University of Oslo, Norway
elien@ifi.uio.no

Milen Kouylekov
Department of Informatics
University of Oslo, Norway
milen@ifi.uio.no

Abstract

In this paper we present our participation in the Semeval 2014 task *"Evaluation of compositional distributional semantic models on full sentences through semantic relatedness and textual entailment"*. Our results demonstrate that using generic tools for semantic analysis is a viable option for a system that recognizes textual entailment. The invested effort in developing such tools allows us to build systems for reasoning that do not require training.

1 Introduction

Recognizing textual entailment (RTE) has been a popular area of research in the last years. It has appeared in a variety of evaluation campaigns as both monolingual and multilingual tasks. A wide variety of techniques based on different levels of text interpretation has been used, e.g., lexical distance, dependency parsing and semantic role labeling (Androutsopoulos and Malakasiotis, 2010).

Our approach uses a semantic representation formalism called Minimal Recursion Semantics (MRS), which, to our knowledge, has not been used extensively in entailment decision systems. Notable examples of systems that use MRS are Wotzlaw and Coote (2013), and Bergmair (2010). In Wotzlaw and Coote (2013), the authors present an entailment recognition system which combines high-coverage syntactic and semantic text analysis with logical inference supported by relevant background knowledge. MRS is used as an intermediate format in transforming the results of the linguistic analysis into representations used for logical reasoning. The approach in Bergmair (2010) uses the syllogism as an approximation of natural language reasoning. MRS is used as a step in the translation of natural language sentences into logical formulae that are suitable for processing. Both works describe approaches that can be adapted to RTE, but no empirical evaluation is included to demonstrate the potential of the proposed approaches.

In contrast to these approaches, our system bases entailment decision directly on the MRS representations. Graph alignment over MRS representations forms the basis for entailment recognition. If key nodes in the hypothesis MRS can be aligned to nodes in the text MRS, this is treated as an indicator of entailment.

This paper represents our first attempt to evaluate a system based on logical-form semantic representations in a RTE competition. Using a state-of-the-art semantic analysis component, we have created a generic rule-based system for recognizing textual entailment that obtains competitive results on a real evaluation dataset. Our approach does not require training. We confront it with a strong baseline provided by the EDITS system (Kouylekov et al., 2011).

In Section 2 we describe the computational semantics framework that forms the basis of our approach. Section 3 details our entailment system, and in Section 4 we analyze our results from the task evaluation.

2 Minimal Recursion Semantics

Minimal Recursion Semantics (MRS) (Copestake et al., 2005) is a framework for computational semantics which provides expressive representations with a clear interface with syntax. MRS allows underspecification of scope, in order to capture the different readings of a sentence with a single MRS representation. We use the MRS analyses that are produced by the HPSG English Resource Grammar (ERG) (Flickinger, 2000).

Proceedings of the 8th International Workshop on Semantic Evaluation (SemEval 2014), pages 699–703,
Dublin, Ireland, August 23-24, 2014.

The core of an MRS representation is a multiset of relations, called *elementary predications* (EPs). An EP represents a single lexeme, or general grammatical features. Each EP has a *predicate symbol*, and a *label* (also called *handle*) that identifies the EPs position within the MRS structure. Each EP contains a list of numbered arguments: `ARG0`, `ARG1`, etc., whose values are scopal or non-scopal variables. The `ARG0` value is called the EP's *distinguished variable*, and denotes an event or state, or an entity.

Finally, an MRS has a set of *handle constraints* which describe how the scopal arguments of the EPs can be equated with EP labels. A constraint $h_i =_q h_j$ denotes equality modulo quantifier insertion. EPs are directly and indirectly linked through handle constraints and variable sharing, and the resulting MRS forms a connected graph.

In Figure 1, we see an MRS for the sentence *A woman is cutting a potato*. The topmost EP, `_cut_v_1`, has a list of three argument-value pairs: its distinguished variable e_3 denotes an event, and the variables x_6 and x_9 refer to the entities filling the agent and patient roles in the verb event. x_6 and x_9 are in turn the distinguished variables of the EPs that represent *a woman* and *a potato*, respectively.

3 System Description

In the following, T_{sent} and H_{sent} refer to the text and hypothesis sentence, and T_{mrs} and H_{mrs} to their MRS representations.

The core of our system is a rule based component, which bases entailment decision on graph alignment over MRS structures. An earlier version of the system is described in Lien (2014). The earlier version was developed on the data set from the SemEval-2010 shared task Parser Evaluation using Textual Entailment (PETE) (Yuret et al., 2010). Using no external linguistic resources, the system output positive entailment decisions for sentence pairs where core nodes of the H_{mrs} could be aligned to nodes in T_{mrs} according to a set of heuristic matching rules. The system we present in this paper extends the earlier version by adding support for contradiction recognition, and by using lexical relations from WordNet.

For our participation in the entailment recognition task, first, we did an analysis of the SICK trial data. In the ENTAILMENT pairs, H_{sent} is a paraphrase over the whole or part of the text sentence. The changes from T_{sent} to H_{sent} can be syntactic (e.g., active-passive conversion), lexical (e.g., synonymy, hyponymy-hypernymy, multiword expressions replaced by single word), or T_{sent} contains some element that does not appear in H_{sent} (e.g., T_{sent} is a conjunction and H_{sent} one of its conjuncts, a modifier in T_{sent} is left out of H_{sent}). In the CONTRADICTION category, the sentences of a pair are also basically the same or paraphrases, and a negation or a pair of antonymous expressions create the contradiction. The NEUTRAL pairs often have a high degree of word overlap, but H_{sent} cannot be inferred from T_{sent}. Our system accounts for many of these characteristics.

The system bases its decision on the results of two procedures: a) an *event relation match* which searches for an alignment between the MRSs, and b) a *contradiction cue* check. After running these procedures, the system outputs

1. ENTAILMENT, if the event relation matching procedure found an alignment, and no contradiction cues were found,
2. CONTRADICTION, if contradiction cues were found,
3. NEUTRAL, if neither of the above conditions are met.

The *event relation matching procedure* extends the one developed in Lien (2014) to account for the greater lexical variation in the SICK data. The procedure selects all the EPs in T_{mrs} and H_{mrs} that have an *event variable* as their `ARG0`—we call them *event relations*. These event relations mainly represent verbs, verb conjunctions, adjectives, and prepositions. For each event relation H_{event} in the hypothesis the procedure tries to find a matching relation T_{event} among the text event relations. We say that H_{event} matches T_{event} if:

1. they represent the same lexeme with the same part-of-speech, or if both are verbs and H_{event} is a synonym or hypernym of T_{event}, and
2. all their arguments match. Two event relation arguments in the same argument position match if:
    - they are the same or synonymous, or the H_{event} argument is a hypernym of the T_{event} argument, or

$\langle\, h_1,$
h_4:_a_q⟨0:1⟩(ARG0 x_6, RSTR h_7, BODY h_5),
h_8:_woman_n_1⟨2:7⟩(ARG0 x_6),
h_2:_cut_v_1⟨11:18⟩(ARG0 e_3, ARG1 x_6, ARG2 x_9),
h_{10}:_a_q⟨19:20⟩(ARG0 x_9, RSTR h_{12}, BODY h_{11}),
h_{13}:_potato_n_1⟨21:28⟩(ARG0 x_9)
$\{\, h_{12} =_q h_{13},\, h_7 =_q h_8,\, h_1 =_q h_2 \,\}\,\rangle$

Figure 1: MRS for *A woman is cutting a potato* (pair 4661, SICK trial data).

- the argument in T_{event} represents a noun phrase and the argument in H_{event} is an underspecified pronoun like *somebody*, or
- the argument in T_{event} is either a scopal relation or a conjunction relation, and one of its arguments matches that of H_{event}, or
- the argument in H_{event} is not expressed (i.e., it matches the T_{event} argument by default)

The matching procedure does not search for more than one alignment between the event relations of H_{mrs} and T_{mrs}.

The *contradiction cue procedure* checks whether the MRS pairs contain relations expressing negation. The quantifier _no_q_rel negates an entity (e.g., *no man*), whereas neg_rel denotes sentence negation. If a negation relation appears in one but not the other MRS, we treat this as an indicator of CONTRADICTION.

Example: Figure 1 shows the MRS analysis of the hypothesis in the entailment pair *A woman is slicing a potato* ⇒ *A woman is cutting a potato*. There is only one event relation in H_{mrs}: _cut_v_1. T_{mrs} is an equivalent structure with one event relation _slice_v_1. Using WordNet, the system finds that _cut_v_1 is a hypernym of _slice_v_1. Then, the system compares the ARG1 and ARG2 values of the event relations. The arguments match since they are the same relations. There are no contradiction cues in either of the MRSs, so the system correctly outputs ENTAILMENT.

If we look at the rule based component's output (Table 1) for the 481 of the 500 SICK trial sentence pairs for which the ERG produced MRSs, we get a picture of how well it covers the phenomena in the data set:

Of the 134 ENTAILMENT pairs, 59 were paraphrases where the variation was relatively limited and could be captured by looking for synonyms, hyponyms, and treating the hypothesis as a subgraph of the text. The simple contradiction cue check, which looks for negation relations, covered 51 of 73 CONTRADICTION pairs.

	gold ENT	gold CON	gold NEU
sys ENT	**59**	0	1
sys CON	0	**51**	14
sys NEU	75	22	**259**

Table 1: Output for the system on SICK trial data.

75 ENTAILMENT and 22 CONTRADICTION pairs were not captured by the matching and contradiction cue procedures. Almost 30% of the ENTAILMENT pairs had word pairs whose lexical relationship was not recognized using WordNet (e.g.: *playing a guitar* ⇒ *strumming a guitar*). In the other pairs there were alternations between simple and more complex noun phrases (*protective gear* ⇒ *gear used for protection*), change of part-of-speech from T_{sent} to H_{sent} for the same meaning entities (*It is raining on a walking man* ⇒ *A man is walking in the rain*); some pairs required reasoning, and in some cases H_{sent} contained information not present in T_{sent}. In some cases, entailment recognition fails because the MRS analysis is not correct (e.g., misrepresentation of passive constructions).

The contradiction cue check did not look for antonymous words and expressions, and this accounts for almost half of the missing CONTRADICTION pairs. The rest contained negation, but were misclassified either because an incorrect MRS analysis was chosen by the parser or because synonymous words within the scope of the negation were not recognized.

EDITS We used a backoff-system for the pairs when the rule-based system fails to produce re-

System	1	2	3	4	5
	Rules Only	Rules Only	Combined	Combined	Edits
Training	76.13	75.4	76.62	76.62	74.78
Test	77.0	76.35	77.12	77.14	74.79

Table 2: Submitted system accuracy on training and test set.

sults. Our choice was EDITS[1] as it provides a strong baseline system for recognizing textual entailment (Kouylekov et al., 2011). EDITS (Kouylekov and Negri, 2010) is an open source package which offers a modular, flexible, and adaptable working environment for experimenting with the RTE task over different datasets. The package allows to: *i)* create an entailment engine by defining its basic components; *ii)* train this entailment engine over an annotated RTE corpus to learn a model and *iii)* use the entailment engine and the model to assign an entailment judgment and a confidence score to each pair of an unannotated test corpus.

We used two strategies for combining the rule-based system with EDITS: Our first strategy was to let the rule-based system classify those sentence pairs for which the ERG could produce MRSs, and use EDITS for the pairs were we did not have MRSs (or processing failed due to errors in the MRSs) . The second strategy was to mix the output from both systems when they disagree. In this case we took the ENTAILMENT decisions from the rule-based, and EDITS contributes with CONTRADICTION and NEUTRAL.

4 Analysis

We have submitted the results obtained from five system configurations. The first four used the rule-based system as the core. The fifth was a system obtained by training EDITS on the training set. We use the fifth system as a strong baseline. In the few cases in which the rule-based system did not produce result (2% of the test set pairs) EDITS judgments were used in the submission. In *System 1* and *System 2* we have used the first combination strategy described in the end of section 3. In *System 4* and *System 5* the entailment decisions are a combination of the results from the rule-based system and EDITS as described in the second strategy in the same section. The rule-based component in *System 1* and *System 3* has more fine-grained negation rules so that `_no_q_rel` is not treated as a contradiction cue in different contexts (e.g., *No woman runs* does not contradict *A woman sings*). Table 2 shows the results for the five submitted systems.

[1] http://edits.sf.net

	Precision	Recall	F-Measure
Contradiction	0.8422	0.7264	0.78
Entailment	0.9719	0.4158	0.5825
Neutral	0.7241	0.9595	0.8254

Table 3: Performance of System 1.

The results demonstrate that the rule-based system can be used as a general system for recognizing textual entailment. It surpasses with 3 points of accuracy EDITS, which is an established strong baseline system. We are quite content with the results obtained as we did not use the training dataset to create the rules, but only the trial dataset. The combination of the two systems brings a slight improvement.

Overall the rule-based system is quite precise as demonstrated in Table 3. The numbers in the table correspond to *System 1* but are comparable to the other rule-based systems 2, 3 and 4. The system achieves an excellent precision on the entailment and contradiction relations. It is almost always correct when assigning the entailment relation. And it also obtains a decent recall, correctly assigning almost half of the entailment pairs. On the contradiction relation the system also obtained a decent result, capturing most of the negation cases.

5 Conclusions

Using a state-of-the-art semantic analysis component, we have created a generic rule-based system for recognizing textual entailment that obtains competitive results on a real evaluation dataset. An advantage of our approach is that it does not require training. The precision of the approach makes it an excellent candidate for a system that uses textual entailment as the core of an intelligent search engine.

References

Ion Androutsopoulos and Prodromos Malakasiotis. 2010. A Survey of Paraphrasing and Textual Entailment Methods. *J. Artif. Intell. Res. (JAIR)*, 38:135–187.

Richard Bergmair. 2010. *Monte Carlo Semantics: Robust Inference and Logical Pattern Processing with Natural Language Text*. Ph.D. thesis, University of Cambridge.

Ann Copestake, Dan Flickinger, Carl Pollard, and Ivan A. Sag. 2005. Minimal Recursion Semantics: An Introduction. *Research on Language & Computation*, 3(2):281–332.

Dan Flickinger. 2000. On Building a More Effcient Grammar by Exploiting Types. *Natural Language Engineering*, 6(1):15–28.

Milen Kouylekov and Matteo Negri. 2010. An Open-Source Package for Recognizing Textual Entailment. In *48th Annual Meeting of the Association for Computational Linguistics (ACL 2010) ,Uppsala, Sweden*, pages 42–47.

Milen Kouylekov, Yashar Mehdad, and Matteo Negri. 2011. Is it Worth Submitting this Run? Assess your RTE System with a Good Sparring Partner. In *Proceedings of the TextInfer 2011 Workshop on Textual Entailment, Edinburgh Scotland*, pages 30–34.

Elisabeth Lien. 2014. Using Minimal Recursion Semantics for Entailment Recognition. In *Proceedings of the Student Research Workshop at the 14th Conference of the European Chapter of the Association for Computational Linguistics*, pages 76–84, Gothenburg, Sweden, April.

Andreas Wotzlaw and Ravi Coote. 2013. A Logic-based Approach for Recognizing Textual Entailment Supported by Ontological Background Knowledge. *CoRR*, abs/1310.4938.

Deniz Yuret, Aydin Han, and Zehra Turgut. 2010. SemEval-2010 Task 12: Parser Evaluation using Textual Entailments. In *Proceedings of the 5th International Workshop on Semantic Evaluation*, pages 51–56.

UKPDIPF: A Lexical Semantic Approach to Sentiment Polarity Prediction in Twitter Data

Lucie Flekova[†‡], **Oliver Ferschke**[†‡] **and Iryna Gurevych**[†‡]
[†] Ubiquitous Knowledge Processing Lab (UKP-TUDA)
Computer Science Department, Technische Universität Darmstadt
[‡] Ubiquitous Knowledge Processing Lab (UKP-DIPF)
German Institute for Educational Research
http://www.ukp.tu-darmstadt.de

Abstract

We present a sentiment classification system that participated in the SemEval 2014 shared task on sentiment analysis in Twitter. Our system expands tokens in a tweet with semantically similar expressions using a large novel distributional thesaurus and calculates the semantic relatedness of the expanded tweets to word lists representing positive and negative sentiment. This approach helps to assess the polarity of tweets that do not directly contain polarity cues. Moreover, we incorporate syntactic, lexical and surface sentiment features. On the message level, our system achieved the 8th place in terms of macro-averaged F-score among 50 systems, with particularly good performance on the Life-Journal corpus (F_1=71.92) and the Twitter sarcasm (F_1=54.59) dataset. On the expression level, our system ranked 14 out of 27 systems, based on macro-averaged F-score.

1 Introduction

Microblogging sites, such as Twitter, have become an important source of information about current events. The fact that users write about their experiences, often directly during or shortly after an event, contributes to the high level of emotions in many such messages. Being able to automatically and reliably evaluate these emotions in context of a specific event or a product would be highly beneficial not only in marketing (Jansen et al., 2009) or public relations, but also in political sciences (O'Connor et al., 2010), disaster management, stock market analysis (Bollen et al., 2011) or the health sector (Culotta, 2010).

Due to its large number of applications, sentiment analysis on Twitter is a very popular task. Challenges arise both from the character of the task and from the language specifics of Twitter messages. Messages are normally very short and informal, frequently using slang, alternative spelling, neologism and links, and mostly ignoring the punctuation.

Our experiments have been carried out as part of the SemEval 2014 Task 9 - Sentiment Analysis on Twitter (Rosenthal et al., 2014), a rerun of a SemEval-2013 Task 2 (Nakov et al., 2013). The datasets are thus described in detail in the overview papers. The rerun uses the same training and development data, but new test data from Twitter and a "surprise domain". The task consists of two subtasks: an expression-level subtask (Subtask A) and a message-level subtask (Subtask B). In subtask A, each tweet in a corpus contained a marked instance of a word or phrase. The goal is to determine whether that instance is positive, negative or neutral in that context. In subtask B, the goal is to classify whether the entire message is of positive, negative, or neutral sentiment. For messages conveying both a positive and negative sentiment, the stronger one should be chosen.

The key components of our system are the sentiment polarity lexicons. In contrast to previous approaches, we do not only count exact lexicon hits, but also calculate explicit semantic relatedness (Gabrilovich and Markovitch, 2007) between the tweet and the sentiment list, benefiting from resources such as Wiktionary and WordNet. On top of that, we expand content words (adjectives, adverbs, nouns and verbs) in the tweet with similar words, which we derive from a novel corpus of more than 80 million English Tweets gathered by the Language Technology group[1] at TU Darm-

[1] http://www.lt.informatik.tu-darmstadt.de

Proceedings of the 8th International Workshop on Semantic Evaluation (SemEval 2014), pages 704–710,
Dublin, Ireland, August 23-24, 2014.

stadt.

2 Experimental setup

Our experimental setup is based on an open-source text classification framework *DKPro TC*[2] (Daxenberger et al., 2014), which allows to combine NLP pipelines into a configurable and modular system for preprocessing, feature extraction and classification. We use the *unit classification* mode of DKPro TC for Subtask A and the *document classification* mode for Subtask B.

2.1 Preprocessing

We customized the message reader for Subtask B to ignore the first part of the tweet when the word *but* is found. This approach helps to reduce the misleading positive hits when a negative message is introduced positively (*It'd be good, but*).

For preprocessing the data, we use components from DKPro Core[3]. Preprocessing is the same for subtasks A and B, with the only difference that in the subtask A the target expression is additionally annotated as *text classification unit*, while the rest of the tweet is considered to be a document context. We first segment the data with the Stanford Segmenter[4], apply the Stanford POS Tagger with a Twitter-trained model (Derczynski et al., 2013), and subsequently apply the Stanford Lemmatizer[4], TreeTagger Chunker (Schmid, 1994), Stanford Named Entity Recognizer (Finkel et al., 2005) and Stanford Parser (Klein and Manning, 2003) to each tweet. After this linguistic preprocessing, the token segmentation of the Stanford tools is removed and overwritten by the ArkTweet Tagger (Gimpel et al., 2011), which is more suitable for recognizing hashtags and smileys as one particular token. Finally, we expand the tweet and proceed to feature extraction as described in detail in Section 3.

2.2 Classification

We trained our system on the provided training data only, excluding the `dev` data. We use classifiers from the WEKA (Hall et al., 2009) toolkit, which are integrated in the DKPro TC framework. Our final configuration consists of a SVM-SMO classifier with a gaussian kernel. The optimal hyperparameters have been experimentally derived and finally set to C=1 and G=0.01. The resulting model was wrapped in a cost sensitive meta classifier from the WEKA toolkit with the error costs set to reflect the class imbalance in the training set.

[2] http://code.google.com/p/dkpro-tc

[3] http://code.google.com/p/dkpro-core-asl

[4] http://nlp.stanford.edu/software/corenlp.shtml

3 Features used

We now describe the features used in our experiments. For Subtask A (contextual polarity), we extracted each feature twice - once on the tweet level and once on the focus expression level. Only n-gram features were extracted solely from the expressions. For Subtask B (tweet polarity), we extracted features on tweet level only. In both cases, we use the Information Gain feature selection approach in WEKA to rank the features and prune the feature space with a threshold of T=0.005.

3.1 Lexical features

As a basis for our similarity and expansion experiments (sections 3.4 and 3.5), we use the binary sentiment polarity lexicon by Liu (2012) augmented with the smiley polarity lexicon by Becker et al. (2013) and an additional swear word list[5] [further as $Liu_{augmented}$]. We selected this augmented lexicon for two reasons: firstly, it was the highest ranked lexical feature on the development-test and crossvalidation experiments, secondly it consists of two plain word lists and therefore does not introduce another complexity dimension for advanced feature calculations.

We further measure lexicon hits normalized per number of tweet tokens for the following lexicons: Pennebaker's Linguistic Inquiry and Word Count (LIWC) (Pennebaker et al., 2001), the NRC Emotion Lexicon (Mohammad and Turney, 2013), the NRC Hashtag Emotion Lexicon (Mohammad et al., 2013) and the Sentiment140 lexicon (Mohammad et al., 2013). We use an additional lexicon of positive, negative, very positive and very negative words, diminishers, intensifiers and negations composed by Steinberger et al. (2012), where we calculate the polarity score as described in their paper.

In a complementary set of features we combine each of the lexicons above with a list of weighted intensifying expressions as published by Brooke (2009). The intensity of any polar word found in any of the emotion lexicons used is intensified or diminished by a given weight if an intensifier (*a*

[5] based on http://www.youswear.com

bit, very, slightly...) is found within the preceding three tokens.

Additionally, we record the overall counts of lexicon hits for positive words, negative words and the difference of the two. In one set of features we consider only lexicons clearly meant for binary polarity, while a second set of features also includes other emotions, such as fear or anger, from the NRC and the LIWC corpora.

3.2 Negation

We handle negation in two ways. On the expression level (Subtask A) we rely on the negation dependency tag provided by the Stanford Dependency Parser. This one captures verb negations rather precisely and thus helps to handle emotional verb expressions such as *like* vs *don't like*. On the tweet level (all features of Subtask B and entire-tweet-level features of Subtask A) we adopt the approach of Pang et al. (2002), considering as a negation context any sequence of tokens between a negation expression and the end of a sentence segment as annotated by the Stanford Segmenter. The negation expressions *(don't, can't...)* are represented by the list of invertors from Steinberger's lexicon (Steinberger et al., 2012). We first assign polarity score to each word in the tweet based on the lexicon hits and then revert it for the words lying in the negation context. This approach is more robust than the one of the dependency governor but is error-prone in the area of overlapping (cascaded) negation contexts.

3.3 N-gram features

We extract the 5,000 most frequent word unigrams, bigrams and trigrams cleaned with the Snowball stopword list[6] as well as the same amount of skip-n-grams and character trigrams. These are extracted separately on the target expression level for subtask A and on document level for subtask B. On the syntactic level, we monitor the most frequent 5,000 part-of-speech ngrams with the size up to part-of-speech quadruples. Additionally, as an approximation for exploiting the key message of the sentence, we extract from the tweets a verb chunk and its left and right neighboring noun chunks, obtaining combinations such as *we-go-cinema*. The 1,000 most frequent chunk triples are then used as features similarly to ngrams.

[6] http://snowball.tartarus.org/algorithms/english/stop.txt

Word	Score	Word (continued)	Score
awesome	1,000	fun	60
amazing	194	sexy	59
great	148	cold	59
cool	104	crazy	57
good	96	fantastic	56
best	93	bored	55
beautiful	93	excited	54
nice	87	true	53
funny	84	stupid	53
cute	81	gr8	52
perfect	70	entertaining	52
wonderful	67	favorite	52
lovely	66	talented	49
tired	65	other	49
annoying	63	depressing	48
Great	63	flawless	48
new	62	inspiring	47
hilarious	62	incredible	46
bad	61	complicated	46
hot	61	gorgeous	45

Table 1: Unsupervised expansion of '*awesome*'

3.4 Tweet expansion

We expanded the content words in a tweet, i.e. nouns, verbs, adjectives and adverbs, with similar words from a word similarity thesaurus that was computed on 80 million English tweets from 2012 using the JoBim contextual semantics framework (Biemann and Riedl, 2013). Table 1 shows an example for a lexical expansion of the word *awesome*. The score was computed using left and right neighbor bigram features for the holing operation. The value hence shows how often the word appeared in the same left and right context as the original word. The upper limit of the score is set to 1,000.

We then match the expanded tweet against the $Liu_{augmented}$ positive and negative lexicons. We assign to the lexicon hits of the expanded words their (contextual similarity) expansion score, using a score of 1,000 as an anchor-value for the original tweet, setting an expansion cut at 100. The overall tweet score is then normalized by the sum of word expansion scores.

3.5 Semantic similarity

Tweet messages are short and each emotional word is very valuable for the task, even when it may not be present in a specific lexicon. Therefore, we calculate a semantic relatedness score between the tweet and the positive or negative word list. We use the ESA similarity measure (Gabrilovich and Markovitch, 2007) as implemented in the DKPro similarity software package (Bär et al., 2013), calculated on English Wiktionary and WordNet as two separate concept spaces. The ESA vectors are freely available[7]. This way we obtain in total six features: *sim(original tweet word list, positive word list)*, *sim(original tweet word list, negative word list)*, difference between the two, *sim(expanded tweet word list, positive word list)*, *sim(expanded tweet word list, negative word list)* and difference between the two. Our SemEval run was submitted using WordNet vectors mainly for the shorter computation time and lower memory requirements. However, in our later experiments Wiktionary performed better. We presume this can be due to a better coverage for the Twitter corpus, although detailed analysis of this aspect is yet to be performed.

3.6 Other features

Pak and Paroubek (2010) pointed out a relation between the presence of different part-of-speech types and sentiment polarity. We measure the ratio of each part-of-speech type to each chunk. We furthermore count the occurrences of the dependency tag for negation. We use the Stanford Named Entity Recognizer to count occurrence of persons, organizations and locations in the tweet. Additionaly, beside basic surface metrics, such as the number of tokens, characters and sentences, we measure the number of elongated words (such as *coool*) in a tweet, ratio of sentences ending with exclamation, ratio of questions and number of positive and negative smileys and their proportion. We capture the smileys with the following two regular expressions for positive, respectively negative ones: `[<>]?[:;=8][-o*']?[)]dDpPxXoO0*}]`, `[<>]?[:;=8][-o*']?[([/:{|]`. We also separately measure the sentiment of smileys at the end of the tweet body, i.e. followed only by a hashtag, hyperlink or nothing.

4 Results

In Subtask A, our system achieved an averaged F-score of 81.42 on the LiveJournal corpus and 79.67 on the Twitter 2014 corpus. The highest scores achieved in related work were 85.61 and 86.63 respectively. For subtask B, we scored 71.92 on LifeJournal and 63.77 on Twitter 2014, while the highest F-scores reported by related work were 74.84 and 70.96.

[7] https://code.google.com/p/dkpro-similarity-asl/downloads/list

Features with the highest Information Gain were the ones based on $Liu_{augmented}$. Adding the weighted intensifiers of Brooke to the sentiment lexicons did not outperform the simple lexicon lookup. They were followed by features derived from the lexicons of Steinberger, which includes invertors, intensifiers and four polarity levels of words. On the other hand, adding the weighted intensifiers of Brooke to lexicons did not outperform the simple lexicon lookup. Overall, lexicon-based features contributed to the highest performance gain, as shown in Table 3. The negation approach based on the Stanford dependency parser was the most helpful, although it tripled the runtime. Using the simpler negation context as suggested in Pang et al. (2002) performed still on average better than using none.

When using WordNet, semantic similarity to lexicons did not outperform direct lexicon hits. Usage of Wiktionary instead lead to major improvement (Table 3), unfortunately after the SemEval challenge.

Tweet expansion appears to improve the classification performance, however the threshold of 100 that we used in our setup was chosed too conservatively, expanding mainly stopwords with other stopwords or words with their spelling alternatives, resulting in a noisy, little valuable feature (`expansion full` in Table 3). Setting up the threshold to 50 and cleaning up both the tweet and the expansion with Snowball stopword list (`expansion clean` in Table 3), the performance increased remarkably.

Amongst other prominent features were parts of lexicons such as LIWC Positive emotions, LIWC Affect, LIWC Negative emotions, NRC Joy, NRC Anger and NRC Disgust. Informative were also the proportions of nouns, verbs and adverbs, the exclamation ratio or number of positive and negative smileys at the end of the tweet.

Feature(s)	ΔF_1 **Twitter2014**	ΔF_1 **LifeJournal**
Similarity Wikt.	0.56	3.65
Similarity WN	0.0	2.61
Expansion full	0.0	0.0
Expansion clean	0.59	3.82
Lexical negation	0.24	0.13
N-gram features	0.30	0.32
Lexicon-based f.	7.85	4.74

Table 3: Performance increase where feature added to the full setup

#	Gold label	Prediction	Message
1	negative	positive	Your plans of attending the **Great** Yorkshire Show may have been washed out because of the weather, so how about...
2	neutral	positive	sitting here with my belt in jean shorts watching Cena win his first title. I think we tie for 1st my friend **xD**
3	neutral	positive	saw your LJ post ... yay for Aussies **;)**
4	positive	negative	haha , that **sucks** , because the drumline will be just fine
5	positive	negative	...woah, Deezer. Babel only came out on Monday, can you leave it up for longer than a day to give slow people like me a chance?
6	positive	negative	Yeah so much has changed for the 6th. Lots of combat **fighting**. And inventory is different.
7	positive	negative	just finish doing it and tomorrow I'm going to the celtics game and don't **fucking** say "thanks for the invite" it's **annoying**
8	positive	negative	Haha... Yup hopefully we will **lose** a few kg by mon. after hip hop can go orchard and weigh
9	positive	negative	U r just like my friends? I made them feel warm, happy, then make them angry and they cry? Finally they left me? Will u leave 2? I hope not. Really hope so.

Table 2: Examples of misclassified messages

5 Error analysis

Table 2 lists a sample of misclassified messages. The majority of errors resulted from misclassifying neutral tweets as emotionally charged. This was partly caused by the usage of emoticons and expressions such as *haha* in a neutral context, such as in examples 2 and 3. Other errors were cause by lexicon hits of proper nouns (example 1), or by using negative words and swearwords in overall positive tweet (examples 4, 7, 9). Some tweets contained domain specific vocabulary that would hit the negative lexicon, e.g., discussing fighting and violence in computer games would, in contrast to other topic domains, usually have positive polarity (example 6). Similar domain-specific polarity distinction could be applied to certain verbs, e.g., *lose weight* vs. *lose a game* (example 8).

Another challenge for the system was the nonstandard language in twitter with a large number of spelling variants, which was only partly captured by the emotion lexicons tailored for this domain. A twitter-specific lemmatizer, which would group all variations of a misspelled word into one, could help to improve the performance.

The length of the negation context window does not suit all purposes. Also double negations such as *I don't think he couldn't...* can easily misdirect the polarity score.

6 Conclusion

We presented a sentiment classification system that can be used on both message level and expression level with only small changes in the framework configuration. We employed a contextual similarity thesaurus for the lexical expansion of the messages. The expansion was not efficient without an extensive stopword cleaning, overweighting more common words and introducing noise. Utilizing the semantic similarity of tweets to lexicons instead of a direct match improves the score only with certain lexicons, possibly dependent on the coverage. Negation by dependency parsing was more beneficial to the classifier than the negation by keyword span annotation. Naive combination of sentiment lexicons was not more helpful than using individual ones separately. Among the common source of errors were laughing signs used in neutral messages and swearing used in positive messages. Even within Twitter, same words can have different polarity in different domains (*lose weight, lose game, game with nice violent fights...*). Deeper semantic insights are necessary to distinguish between polar words in context.

7 Acknowledgement

This work has been supported by the Volkswagen Foundation as part of the Lichtenberg-Professorship Program under grant No. I/82806. We warmly thank Chris Biemann, Martin Riedl and Eugen Ruppert of the Language Technology group at TU Darmstadt for providing us with the Twitter-based distributional thesaurus.

References

Daniel Bär, Torsten Zesch, and Iryna Gurevych. 2013. Dkpro similarity: An open source framework for text similarity. In *Proceedings of the 51st Annual Meeting of the Association for Computational Linguistics: System Demonstrations*, pages 121–126, Sofia, Bulgaria.

Lee Becker, George Erhart, David Skiba, and Valentine

Matula. 2013. Avaya: Sentiment analysis on twitter with self-training and polarity lexicon expansion. *Atlanta, Georgia, USA*, page 333.

Chris Biemann and Martin Riedl. 2013. Text: Now in 2d! a framework for lexical expansion with contextual similarity. *Journal of Language Modelling*, 1(1):55–95.

Johan Bollen, Huina Mao, and Xiaojun Zeng. 2011. Twitter mood predicts the stock market. *Journal of Computational Science*, 2(1):1 – 8.

Julian Brooke. 2009. A semantic approach to automated text sentiment analysis.

Aron Culotta. 2010. Towards detecting influenza epidemics by analyzing twitter messages. In *Proceedings of the First Workshop on Social Media Analytics*, pages 115–122, New York, NY, USA.

Johannes Daxenberger, Oliver Ferschke, Iryna Gurevych, and Torsten Zesch. 2014. Dkpro tc: A java-based framework for supervised learning experiments on textual data. In *Proceedings of the 52nd Annual Meeting of the Association for Computational Linguistics. System Demonstrations*, page (to appear), Baltimore, MD, USA.

Leon Derczynski, Alan Ritter, Sam Clark, and Kalina Bontcheva. 2013. Twitter part-of-speech tagging for all: Overcoming sparse and noisy data. In *Proceedings of the International Conference on Recent Advances in Natural Language Processing*, Hissar, Bulgaria.

Jenny Rose Finkel, Trond Grenager, and Christopher Manning. 2005. Incorporating non-local information into information extraction systems by gibbs sampling. In *Proceedings of the 43nd Annual Meeting of the Association for Computational Linguistics (ACL 2005)*, pages 363–370.

Evgeniy Gabrilovich and Shaul Markovitch. 2007. Computing semantic relatedness using wikipedia-based explicit semantic analysis. In *Proceedings of the 20th International Joint Conference on Artificial Intelligence*, volume 7, pages 1606–1611, Hyderabad, India.

Kevin Gimpel, Nathan Schneider, Brendan O'Connor, Dipanjan Das, Daniel Mills, Jacob Eisenstein, Michael Heilman, Dani Yogatama, Jeffrey Flanigan, and Noah A Smith. 2011. Part-of-speech tagging for twitter: Annotation, features, and experiments. In *Proceedings of the 49th Annual Meeting of the Association for Computational Linguistics: Human Language Technologies: short papers-Volume 2*, pages 42–47.

Mark Hall, Eibe Frank, Geoffrey Holmes, Bernhard Pfahringer, Peter Reutemann, and Ian H Witten. 2009. The weka data mining software: an update. *ACM SIGKDD Explorations Newsletter*, 11(1):10–18.

Bernard J. Jansen, Mimi Zhang, Kate Sobel, and Abdur Chowdury. 2009. Twitter power: Tweets as electronic word of mouth. *Journal of the American Society for Information Science and Technology*, 60(11):2169–2188.

Dan Klein and Christopher D Manning. 2003. Accurate unlexicalized parsing. In *Proceedings of the 41st Annual Meeting on Association for Computational Linguistics-Volume 1*, pages 423–430.

Bing Liu. 2012. Sentiment analysis and opinion mining. *Synthesis Lectures on Human Language Technologies*, 5(1):1–167.

Saif M Mohammad and Peter D Turney. 2013. Crowdsourcing a word–emotion association lexicon. *Computational Intelligence*, 29(3):436–465.

Saif Mohammad, Svetlana Kiritchenko, and Xiaodan Zhu. 2013. Nrc-canada: Building the state-of-the-art in sentiment analysis of tweets. In *Proceedings of the seventh international workshop on Semantic Evaluation Exercises (SemEval-2013)*, Atlanta, Georgia, USA.

Preslav Nakov, Sara Rosenthal, Zornitsa Kozareva, Veselin Stoyanov, Alan Ritter, and Theresa Wilson. 2013. Semeval-2013 task 2: Sentiment analysis in twitter. In *Second Joint Conference on Lexical and Computational Semantics (*SEM), Volume 2: Proceedings of the Seventh International Workshop on Semantic Evaluation (SemEval 2013)*, pages 312–320, Atlanta, Georgia, USA.

Brendan O'Connor, Ramnath Balasubramanyan, Bryan R Routledge, and Noah A Smith. 2010. From tweets to polls: Linking text sentiment to public opinion time series. In *Fourth International AAAI Conference on Weblogs and Social Media*, pages 122–129.

Alexander Pak and Patrick Paroubek. 2010. Twitter as a corpus for sentiment analysis and opinion mining. In Nicoletta Calzolari (Conference Chair), Khalid Choukri, Bente Maegaard, Joseph Mariani, Jan Odijk, Stelios Piperidis, Mike Rosner, and Daniel Tapias, editors, *Proceedings of the Seventh International Conference on Language Resources and Evaluation (LREC'10)*, Valletta, Malta.

Bo Pang, Lillian Lee, and Shivakumar Vaithyanathan. 2002. Thumbs up?: sentiment classification using machine learning techniques. In *Proceedings of the ACL-02 conference on Empirical methods in natural language processing-Volume 10*, pages 79–86.

James W Pennebaker, Martha E Francis, and Roger J Booth. 2001. Linguistic inquiry and word count: Liwc 2001. *Mahway: Lawrence Erlbaum Associates*, 71:2001.

Sara Rosenthal, Preslav Nakov, Alan Ritter, and Veselin Stoyanov. 2014. SemEval-2014 Task 9: Sentiment Analysis in Twitter. In Preslav Nakov and

Torsten Zesch, editors, *Proceedings of the 8th International Workshop on Semantic Evaluation*, Dublin, Ireland.

Helmut Schmid. 1994. Probabilistic part-of-speech tagging using decision trees. In *Proceedings of international conference on new methods in language processing*, volume 12, pages 44–49.

Josef Steinberger, Mohamed Ebrahim, Maud Ehrmann, Ali Hurriyetoglu, Mijail Kabadjov, Polina Lenkova, Ralf Steinberger, Hristo Tanev, Silvia Vázquez, and Vanni Zavarella. 2012. Creating sentiment dictionaries via triangulation. *Decision Support Systems*, 53(4):689–694.

ULisboa: Identification and Classification of Medical Concepts

André Leal[+], Diogo Gonçalves[+], Bruno Martins[*], and Francisco M. Couto[+]
[+]LASIGE, Faculdade de Ciências, Universidade de Lisboa, 1749-016 Lisboa, Portugal.
[*]INESC-ID, Instituto Superior Técnico, Universidade de Lisboa, Portugal
{aleal,dgoncalves}@lasige.di.fc.ul.pt, bruno.g.martins@ist.ul.pt, fcouto@di.fc.ul.pt

Abstract

This paper describes our participation on Task 7 of SemEval 2014, which focused on the recognition and disambiguation of medical concepts. We used an adapted version of the Stanford NER system to train CRF models to recognize textual spans denoting diseases and disorders, within clinical notes. We considered an encoding that accounts with non-continuous entities, together with a rich set of features (i) based on domain specific lexicons like SNOMED CT, or (ii) leveraging Brown clusters inferred from a large collection of clinical texts. Together with this recognition mechanism, we used a heuristic similarity search method, to assign an unambiguous identifier to each concept recognized in the text.

Our best run on Task A (i.e., in the recognition of medical concepts in the text) achieved an F-measure of 0.705 in the strict evaluation mode, and a promising F-measure of 0.862 in the relaxed mode, with a precision of 0.914. For Task B (i.e., the disambiguation of the recognized concepts), we achieved less promising results, with an accuracy of 0.405 in the strict mode, and of 0.615 in the relaxed mode.

1 Introduction

Currently, many off-the-shelf named entity recognition solutions are available, and these can be used to recognize mentions in clinical notes denoting diseases and disorders. We decided to use the Stanford NER tool (Finkel et al., 2005) to train CRF models based on annotated biomedical text.

The use of unsupervised methods for inferring word representations is nowadays also known to increase the accuracy of entity recognition models (Turian et al., 2010). Thus, we also used Brown clusters (Brown et al., 1992; Turian et al., 2009) inferred from a large collection of non-annotated clinical texts, together with domain specific lexicons, to build features for our CRF models.

An important challenge in entity recognition relates to the recognition of overlapping and non-continuous entities (Alex et al., 2007). In this paper, we describe how we modified the Stanford NER system to be able to recognize non-continuous entities, through an adapted version of the SBIEO scheme (Ratinov and Roth, 2009).

Besides the recognition of medical concepts, we also present the strategy used to map each of the recognized concepts into a SNOMED CT identifier (Cornet and de Keizer, 2008). This task is particularly challenging, since there are many ambiguous cases. We describe our general approach to address the aforementioned CUI mapping problem, based on similarity search and on the information content of SNOMED CT concept names.

2 Task and Datasets

Task 7 of SemEval 2014 actually consisted of two smaller tasks: recognition of mentions of medical concepts (Task A) and mapping each medical concept, recognized in clinical notes, to a unique UMLS CUI (Task B). In the first task, recognition of medical concepts, systems have to detect continuous and discontinuous medical concepts that belong to the UMLS semantic group *disorders*. The second task, concerning with normalization and mapping, is limited to UMLS CUIs of SNOMED CT codes (i.e., although the UMLS meta-thesaurus integrates several resources, we are only interested in SNOMED CT). Each concept that was previously recognized can have a unique CUI associated to it, or none at all (CUI-

Proceedings of the 8th International Workshop on Semantic Evaluation (SemEval 2014), pages 711–715,
Dublin, Ireland, August 23-24, 2014.

LESS). The goal here is to disambiguate the concepts and choose the right CUI for each case. For supporting the recognition and CUI mapping of medical concepts, we retrieved the disorders subset of SNOMED CT directly from UMLS[1].

The evaluation can be done in a strict or a in a relaxed way. For the case of strict evaluation, an exact match must be achieved in the recognition, by having correct start and end offsets, within the text, for the continuous concepts, and a correct set of start and end offsets for the discontinuous concepts. In the relaxed evaluation, there is some space for errors in the offset values from the recognition task. If there is some overlap between the concepts, then the result is considered a partial match, otherwise it is a recognition error.

A set of annotated biomedical texts was given to the participants, separated in three categories: trial, development and training. We also received a final test set, and a large set of non-annotated texts. All the provided texts were initially converted into a common tokenized format, to be used as input to the tools that we considered for developing our approach. After processing, we converted the results back into the format used by SemEval 2014, this way generating the official runs.

3 Entity Recognition

Our entity recognition approach was based on the usage of the Stanford NER software, which employs a linear chain Conditional Random Field (CRF) approach for building probabilistic models based on training data (Finkel et al., 2005). In Stanford NER, model training is based on the L-BFGS algorithm, and model decoding is made through the Viterbi algorithm.

This tool requires all input texts to be tokenized and encoded according to a named entity recognition scheme such as SBIEO (Ratinov and Roth, 2009), characterized by only being able to recognize continuous entities. As we also need to recognize non-continuous entities, we modified the Stanford NER software to use a SBIEON encoding scheme. This new scheme has the following specific token-tag associations:

- **S:** *Single*, that indicates if the token individually constitutes an entity to be recognized.
- **B:** *Begin*, identifying the beginning of the entity. This tag is only given to the first word of the entity, being followed is most cases by tokens labeled as being *inside* the entity.
- **I:** *Inside*, representing the continuation of a non single word entity (i.e., the middle tokens).
- **E:** *Ending*, representing the last word in the case of entities composed by more than one word.
- **N:** *Non-Continuous*, which identifies all the words that are between the beginning and the end of an entity, but that do not belong to it. This label specifically allows us to model the in-between tokens of non-continuous entities.
- **O:** *Other*, which is associated to all other words that are not part of entities.

We developed a Java parser that converts the biomedical text, provided to the participants, into a tokenized format. This tokenized format, in the case of the annotated texts, associates individual tokens to their SBIEON or SBIEO tags, so that the datasets can be used as input to train CRF models.

3.1 Concept Recognition Models

As we said, SBIEON tokenization differs from SBIEO by the fact that the first one gives support to non-continuous entities. Based on these two input schemes, we generated two different models:

Only continuous entities: A 2nd-order CRF model was trained based on the SBIOE entity encoding scheme, which only recognizes continuous entities. Non-continuous and overlapping entities will thus, in this case, only be partially modeled (i.e., we only considered the initial span of text associated to the non-continuous entities).

Non-continuous entities: A 2nd-order CRF model was trained based on the SBIOEN entity encoding scheme, accepting continuous and non-continuous entities, although still not supporting the case of overlapping entities. In these last cases, only the first entity in each of the overlapping groups will be modeled correctly, while the others will only be partially modeled (i.e., by only considering the non-overlapping spans).

Our CRF models relied on a standard set of feature templates that includes (i) word tokens within a window of size 2, (ii) the token shape (e.g., if it is uppercased, capitalized, numeric, etc.), (iii) token prefixes and suffixes, (iv) token position (e.g., at the beginning or ending of a sentence), and (v) conjunctions of the current token with the previous 2 tags. Besides these standard features, we also considered (a) domain-specific lexicons, and (b) word representations based on Brown clusters.

[1] http://www.nlm.nih.gov/research/umls/

3.2 Word Clusters

In addition to the annotated *training* dataset, participants were also provided with 403876 non-annotated texts, containing a total of 828509 tokens. We used this information to induce generalized cluster-based word representations.

Brown et al. proposed a greedy agglomerative hierarchical clustering procedure that groups words to maximize the mutual information of bi-grams (Brown et al., 1992). According to Brown's clustering procedure, clusters are initialized as consisting of a single word each, and are then greedily merged according to a mutual information criterion, based on bi-grams, to form a lower-dimensional representation of a vocabulary that can mitigate the feature sparseness problem. In the context of named entity recognition studies, several authors have previously noted that using these types of cluster-based word representations can indeed result in improvements (Turian et al., 2009). The hierarchical nature of the clustering allows words to be represented at different levels in the hierarchy and, in our case, we considered 1000 different clusters of similar words.

We specifically used the set of training documents, together with the non-annotated documents that were provided by the organizers, to induce word representations based on Brown's clustering procedure, using an open-source implementation that follows the description given by (Turian et al., 2010). The word clusters are latter used as features within the Stanford NER package, by considering that each word can be replaced by the corresponding cluster, this way adding some other *back-off* features to the models (i.e., features that are less sparse, in the sense that they will appear more frequently associated to some of the instances).

4 Disambiguating Concepts

For mapping entities to concept IDs (Task B), we used a heuristic method based on similarity search, supported on Lucene indexes (MacCandless et al., 2010). We look for SNOMED CT concepts that have a high n-gram overlap with the entity name occurring in the text, together with the information content of each SNOMED CT concept.

In our implementation, we used Lucene to retrieve candidate SNOMED CT concepts according to different string distance algorithms: the NGram distance (Kondrak, 2005) first, then according to the Jaro-Winkler distance (Winkler, 1990), and finally according to the Levenshtein distance. The most similar candidate is chosen as the disambiguation. The specific order for the similarity metrics was based on the intuition that metrics based on individual character-level matches are probably not as informative as metrics based on longer sequences of characters, although they can be useful for dealing with spelling variations. However, for future work, we plan to explore more systematic approaches (e.g., based on learning to rank) for combining multiple similarity metrics.

Additionally to the aforementioned similarity metrics, a measure of the Information Content (IC) of each SNOMED CT concept was also employed, to further disambiguate the mappings (i.e., to select the SNOMED CT identifier that is more general, and thus more likely to be associated to a particular concept descriptor). Notice that the IC of a concept corresponds to a measure of its specificity, where higher values correspond to more specific concepts, and lower values to more general ones. Given the frequency $\mathrm{freq}(c)$ for each concept c in a corpus (i.e., the same corpus that was used to infer the word clusters), the information content of this concept can be computed from the ratio between its frequency (including its descendants) and the maximum frequency of all concepts (Resnik, 1995):

$$\mathrm{IC}(c) = -\log\left(\frac{\mathrm{freq}(c)}{\mathrm{maxFreq}}\right)$$

In the formula, $\mathrm{maxFreq}$ represents the maximum frequency of a concept, i.e. the frequency of the *root* concept, when it exists. The frequency of a concept can be computed using an extrinsic approach that counts the exact matches of the concept names on a large text corpus.

5 Evaluation Experiments

We submitted three distinct runs to the SemEval competition. These runs were as follows:

Run 1: A SBIOEN model was used to recognize non-continuous entities. This model was trained using only the annotated texts from the provided training set. We also used some domain specific lexicons like SNOMED CT, or lists with names for drugs and diseases retrieved from DBPedia. Finally, the recognition model also used Brown clusters generated from the non-annotated datasets provided in the competition.

For assigning a SNOMED CT identifier to each entity, we used the disambiguation technique supported by Lucene indexes. In this specific run we used all the considered heuristics for similarity search.

Run 2: A simpler model based on the SBIOE scheme was used in this case, which can only recognize continuous entities. The same features from Run 1 were used for training the recognition model.

For assigning the SNOMED CT identifier to each entity, we also used the same strategy that was presented for Run 1.

Run 3: A similar SBIOE model to that from Run 2 was used for the recognition.

For assigning the corresponding SNOMED CT identifier to each entity, we in this case limited the heuristic rules that were used. Instead of using the string similarity algorithms, we used only exact matches, together with the information content measure and the neighboring terms for disambiguation.

6 Results and Discussion

We present our official results in Table 1, which highlights our best results for each task.

Specifically in Task A, we achieved encouraging results. Run 1 achieved an F-measure of 0.705 in the strict evaluation, and of 0.862 in the relaxed evaluation. Since Runs 2 and 3 used the same recognition strategy (i.e., models that attempted to capture only the continuous entities), we obtained the same results for Task A in both these runs. Table 1 also shows that our performance in Task B was significantly lower than in Task A.

As we can see in the table, our first run was the one with the best results for Task A. The model used on this run recognizes non-continuous entities, and this is perhaps the main reason for the higher results (i.e., the other two runs used the same features for the recognition models).

On what concerns the results of Task B, it is important to notice the distinct results from the first and second runs, which used exactly the same disambiguation strategy. The differences in the results are a consequence from the use of a different recognition model in Task A. We can see that the ability to recognize non-continuous entities leads to the generation of worse mappings, when considering our specific disambiguation strategy. Our last run is the best in terms of the performance over Task B, but the difference is subtle.

7 Conclusions and Future Work

This paper described our participation in Task 7 of the SemEval 2014 competition, which was divided into two subtasks, namely (i) the recognition of continuous and non-continuous medical concepts, and (ii) the mapping of each recognized concept to a SNOMED CT identifier.

For the first task, we used the Stanford NER software (Finkel et al., 2005), modified by us to recognize not only continuous, but also non-continuous entities. This was possible by introducing the SBIEON scheme, derived from the traditional SBIEO encoding. To increase the accuracy and precision of the recognition we have also used domain specific lexicons and Brown clusters inferred from non-annotated documents.

For the second task, we used a heuristic method based on similarity search, for matching concepts in the text against concepts from SNOMED CT, together with a measure of information content to disambiguate the cases of term polysemy in SNOMED CT. We implemented our disambiguation approach through the Lucene software framework (MacCandless et al., 2010).

In the first task (Task A) we achieved some particularly encouraging results, showing that an off-the-shelf NER system can be easily adapted to the recognition of medical concepts in biomedical text. Our specific modifications to the Stanford NER system, in order to support the recognition of non-continuous entity names, indeed increased the precision and recall on Task A. However, our approach for the disambiguation of the recognized concepts (Task B) performed much worse, achieving an accuracy of 0.615 in the case of the relaxed evaluation. Future developments will therefore focus on improving the component that addressed the entity disambiguation subtask.

Specifically on what regards future work, we plan to experiment with the usage of machine learning methods for the disambiguation subtask, instead of relying on a purely heuristic approach. We are interested in experimenting with the usage of Learning to Rank (L2R) methods, similar to those employed on the DNorm system (Leaman et al., 2013), to optimally combine different heuristics such as the ones that were used in our current approach. A L2R model can be used to rank candi-

Run	Task A: Strict Evaluation Precision	Recall	F-measure	Task A: Relaxed Evaluation Precision	Recall	F-measure	Task B: Strict Accuracy	Relaxed Accuracy
1	**0.753**	**0.663**	**0.705**	**0.914**	**0.815**	**0.862**	0.402	0.606
2	0.752	0.660	0.703	0.909	0.806	0.855	0.404	0.612
3	0.752	0.660	0.703	0.909	0.806	0.855	**0.405**	**0.615**

Table 1: Our official results for Tasks A and B of the SemEval challenge focusing on clinical text.

date disambiguations (e.g., retrieved through similarity search with basis on Lucene) according to a combination of multiple criteria, and we can then choose the top candidate as the disambiguation.

Additionally, we plan to use ontology-based similarity measures to validate and improve the mappings (Couto and Pinto, 2013). For example, by assuming that all entities in a given span of text are semantically related with each other, we can use ontology relations to filter likely misannotations (Grego and Couto, 2013; Grego et al., 2013).

Acknowledgments

The authors would like to thank Fundação para a Ciência e Tecnologia (FCT) for the financial support of SOMER (PTDC/EIA-EIA/119119/2010), LASIGE (PEst-OE/EEI/UI0408/2014) and INESC-ID (Pest-OE/EEI/LA0021/2013).

We also would like to thank our colleagues Berta Alves, for her support in evaluating development errors, and Luís Atalaya, for the development of some of the data pre-processing scripts.

References

Beatrice Alex, Barry Haddow, and Claire Grover. 2007. Recognising nested named entities in biomedical text. In *Proceedings of the ACL-07 Workshop on Biological, Translational, and Clinical Language Processing*, pages 65–72.

Peter F. Brown, Peter V. deSouza, Robert L. Mercer, Vincent J. Della Pietra, and Jenifer C. Lai. 1992. Class-based n-gram models of natural language. *Computational linguistics*, 18(4):467–479.

Ronald Cornet and Nicolette de Keizer. 2008. Forty years of SNOMED: A literature review. *BMC Medical Informatics and Decision Making*, 8(Suppl 1:S2):1–6.

Francisco M. Couto and Helena Sofia Pinto. 2013. The next generation of similarity measures that fully explore the semantics in biomedical ontologies. *Journal of Bioinformatics and Computational Biology*, 11(05):1–11.

Jenny Rose Finkel, Trond Grenager, and Christopher Manning. 2005. Incorporating non-local information into information extraction systems by Gibbs sampling. In *Proceedings of the 43rd Annual Meeting on Association for Computational Linguistics*, pages 363–370.

Tiago Grego and Francisco M Couto. 2013. Enhancement of chemical entity identification in text using semantic similarity validation. *PloS ONE*, 8(5):1–9.

Tiago Grego, Francisco Pinto, and Francisco Couto. 2013. LASIGE: using conditional random fields and chebi ontology. In *Proceedings of the 7th International Workshop on Semantic Evaluation*, pages 660–666.

Grzegorz Kondrak. 2005. N-gram similarity and distance. In *Proceedings of the 12th International Conference String Processing and Information Retrieval*, pages 115–126.

Robert Leaman, Rezarta Islamaj Doğan, and Zhiyong Lu. 2013. DNorm: disease name normalization with pairwise learning to rank. *Bioinformatics*, 29(22):2909–2917.

Michael MacCandless, Erik Hatcher, and Otis Gospodnetić. 2010. *Lucene in Action*. Manning Publications Company.

Lev Ratinov and Dan Roth. 2009. Design challenges and misconceptions in named entity recognition. In *Proceedings of the 13th Conference on Computational Natural Language Learning*, pages 147–155.

Philip Resnik. 1995. Using information content to evaluate semantic similarity in a taxonomy. In *Proceedings of the 14th International Joint Conference on Artificial Intelligence*, pages 448–453.

Joseph Turian, Lev Ratinov, Yoshua Bengio, and Dan Roth. 2009. A preliminary evaluation of word representations for named-entity recognition. In *Proceedings of the NIPS-09 Workshop on Grammar Induction, Representation of Language and Language Learning*, pages 1–8.

Joseph Turian, Lev Ratinov, and Yoshua Bengio. 2010. Word representations: A simple and general method for semi-supervised learning. In *Proceedings of the 48th Annual Meeting of the Association for Computational Linguistics*, pages 384–394.

William E Winkler. 1990. String comparator metrics and enhanced decision rules in the Fellegi-Sunter model of record linkage. In *Proceedings of the Section on Survey Research of the American Statistical Association*, pages 354–359.

UMCC_DLSI_SemSim: Multilingual System for Measuring Semantic Textual Similarity

Alexander Chávez
Héctor Dávila
DI, University of Matanzas, Cuba.
{alexander.chavez, hector.davila}@umcc.cu

Yoan Gutiérrez
Antonio Fernández-Orquín
Andrés Montoyo
Rafael Muñoz
DLSI, University of Alicante, Spain.
{ygutierrez montoyo,rafael}@dlsi.ua.es,
antonybr@yahoo.com

Abstract

In this paper we describe the specifications and results of UMCC_DLSI system, which was involved in Semeval-2014 addressing two subtasks of Semantic Textual Similarity (STS, Task 10, for English and Spanish), and one subtask of Cross-Level Semantic Similarity (Task 3). As a supervised system, it was provided by different types of lexical and semantic features to train a classifier which was used to decide the correct answers for distinct subtasks. These features were obtained applying the Hungarian algorithm over a semantic network to create semantic alignments among words. Regarding the Spanish subtask of Task 10 two runs were submitted, where our Run2 was the best ranked with a general correlation of 0.807. However, for English subtask our best run (Run1 of our 3 runs) reached 16th place of 38 of the official ranking, obtaining a general correlation of 0.682. In terms of Task 3, only addressing Paragraph to Sentence subtask, our best run (Run1 of 2 runs) obtained a correlation value of 0.760 reaching 3rd place of 34.

1 Introduction

Many applications of language processing rely on measures of proximity or remoteness of various kinds of linguistic units (words, meanings, sentences, documents). Thus, issues such as disambiguation of meanings, detection of lexical chains, establishing relationships between documents, clustering, etc., require accurate similarity measures.

The problem of formalizing and quantifying an intuitive notion of similarity has a long history in philosophy, psychology, artificial intelligence, and through the years has followed many different perspectives (Hirst, 2001). Recent research in the field of Computational Linguistics has emphasized the perspective of semantic relations between two lexemes in a lexical resource, or its inverse, semantic distance. The similarity of sentences is a confidence score that reflects the relationship between the meanings of two sentences. This similarity has been addressed in the literature with terminologies such as affinity, proximity, distance, difference and divergence (Jenhani, et al., 2007). The different applications of text similarity have been separated into a group of similarity tasks: between two long texts, for document classification; between a short text with a long text, for Web search; and between two short texts, for paraphrase recognition, automatic machine translation, etc. (Han, et al., 2013).

At present, the calculation of the similarity between texts has been tackled from different points of views. Some have opted for a single measure to capture all the features of texts and other models have been trained with various measures to take text features separately. In this work, we addressed the combination of several measures using a Supervised Machine Learning (SVM) approach. Moreover, we intend to introduce a new approach to calculate textual similarities using a knowledge-based system, which is based on a set of cases composed by a vector with values of several measures. We also combined both approaches.

Proceedings of the 8th International Workshop on Semantic Evaluation (SemEval 2014), pages 716–721, Dublin, Ireland, August 23-24, 2014.

After this introduction, the rest of the paper is organized as follows. Section 2 shows the Pre-processing stage. Subsequently, in Section 3 we show the different features used in our system. In Section 4 we describe our knowledge-based system. Tasks and runs are provided in Section 5. Finally, the conclusions and further work can be found in Section 6.

2 Pre-processing

Below are listed the pre-processing steps performed by our system. In bold we emphasize some cases which were used in different tasks.

- All brackets were removed.
- The abbreviations were expanded to their respective meanings. It was applied using a list of the most common abbreviations in English, with 819 and Spanish with 473. Phrases like "The G8" and "The Group of Eight" are detected as identical.
- Deletion of hyphen to identify words forms. For example, "well-studied" was replaced by "well studied". Example taken from line 13 of MSRpar corpus in test set of Semeval STS 2012 (Agirre, et al., 2012).
- The sentences were tokenized and POS-tagged using Freeling 3.0 (Padró and Stanilovsky, 2012).
- All contractions were expanded. For example: *n't*, *'m*and *'s*. In the case of *'s* was replaced with "is" or "of", "Tom's bad" to "Tom is bad" and "Tom's child" by "Child of Tom". (**Only for English tasks**).
- Punctuation marks were removed from the tokens except for the decimal point in numbers.
- Stop words were removed. We used a list of the most common stop words. (28 for English and 48 for Spanish).
- The words were mapped to the most common sense of WordNet 3.0. (**Only for Spanish task**).
- A syntactic tree was built for every sentence using Freeling 3.0.

3 Features Extraction

Measures of semantic similarity have been traditionally used between words or concepts, and much less between text segments, (i.e. two or more words). The emphasis on word to word similarity is probably due to the availability of resources that specifically encode relations between words or concepts (e.g. WordNet) (Mihalcea, et al., 2006). Following we describe the similarity measures used in this approach.

3.1 Semantic Similarity of Words

A relatively large number of word to word similarity metrics have previously been proposed in the literature, ranging from distance-oriented measures computed on semantic networks, to metrics based on models of distributional similarity learned from large text collections (Mihalcea, et al., 2006).

3.2 Corpus-based Measures

Corpus-based measures of word semantic similarity try to identify the degree of similarity between words using information exclusively derived from large corpora (Mihalcea, et al., 2006). We considered one metric named Latent Semantic Analysis (LSA) (Landauer, et al., 1998).

Latent Semantic Analysis: The Latent semantic analysis (LSA) is a corpus/document based measure proposed by Landauer in 1998. In LSA term co-occurrences in a corpus are captured by means of a dimensionality reduction operated by singular value decomposition (SVD) on the term-by-document matrix *T* representing the corpus (Mihalcea, et al., 2006). There is a variation of LSA called HAL (*Hyperspace Analog to Language*) (Burgess, et al., 1998) that is based on the co-occurrence of words in a common context. The variation consists of counting the number of occurrences in that two words appear at *n*[1] distance (called windows).

For the co-occurrence matrix of words we took as core the UMBC WebBase corpus[2] (Han, et al., 2013), which is derived from the Stanford WebBase project[3]. For the calculation of HAL measure we used the Cosine Similarity between the vectors for each pair of words.

[1] The windows is the number of intermediate words between two words.

[2] Dataset of high quality English paragraphs containing over three billion words and it is available in http://ebiquity.umbc.edu/resource/html/id/351

[3] Stanford WebBase 2001. http://bit.ly/WebBase.

3.3 Knowledge-based Measures

There are many measures developed to quantify the degree of semantic relation between two words senses using semantic network information. For example:

Leacock & Chodorow Similarity: The Leacock & Chodorow (LC) similarity is determined as follows:

$$Sim_{lc} = -\log\left(\frac{length}{2*D}\right) \quad (1)$$

Where *length* is the length of the shortest path between senses using node-counting and *D* is the maximum depth of the taxonomy (Leacock and Chodorow, 1998)

Wu and Palmer: The Wu and Palmer similarity metric (Wup) measures the depth of two given senses in the WordNet taxonomy, and the depth of the least common subsumer (LCS), and combine them into a similarity score (Wu and Palmer, 1994):

$$Sim_{Wup} = \frac{2*depth(LCS)}{depth(sense_1)+depth(sense_2)} \quad (2)$$

Resnik: The Resnik similarity (Res) returns the information content (IC) of the LCS of two senses:

$$Sim_{Res} = IC(LCS) \quad (3)$$

Where IC is defined as:

$$IC(c) = -\log P(c) \quad (4)$$

And *P(c)* is the probability of encountering an instance of sense *c* in a large corpus (Resnik, 1995) (Mihalcea, et al., 2006).

Lin: The Lin similarity builds on Resnik's measure and adds a normalization factor consisting of the information content of the two inputs senses (Lin, 1998):

$$Sim_{Lin} = \frac{2*IC(LCS)}{IC(sense)+IC(sense_2)} \quad (5)$$

Jiang & Conrath: The Jiang and Conrath similarity (JC) is defined as follows (Jiang and Conrath, 1997):

$$Sim_{jc} = \frac{1}{IC(sense_1)+IC(sense_2)-2*IC(LCS)} \quad (6)$$

PathLen: The PathLen similarity (Len) involves the path lengths between two senses in the taxonomy (Pedersen, et al., 2004).

$$Sim_{Path} = -\log pathlen(sense_1, sense_1) (7)$$

Where $pathlen(sense_1, sense_1)$ is the number of edges in the shortest path between $sense_1$and $sense_2$.

Word Similarity: In order to calculate the similarity between two words (WS) we used the following expression:

$$WS(w1, w2) = max_{\substack{s1 \in senses(w1) \\ s2 \in senses(w2)}} sim(s1, s2) \quad (8)$$

Where $sim(s1, s2)$ is one of the similarity metrics at sense level previously described.

3.4 Lexical Features

We used a well-known lexical attributes similarity measures based on distances between strings. Dice-Similarity, Euclidean-Distance, Jaccard-Similarity, Jaro-Winkler, Levenstein Distance, Overlap-Coefficient, QGrams Distance, Smith-Waterman, Smith-Waterman-Gotoh, Smith-Waterman-Gotoh-Windowed-Affine.

These metrics have been obtained from an API (Application Program Interface) SimMetrics library v1.5 for.NET[4] 2.0.

3.5 Word Similarity Models

With the purpose of calculating the similarity between two words, we developed two models involving the previous word similarity metrics. These were defined as:

Max Word Similarity: The Max Word Similarity (MaxSim) is defined as follows:

$$MaxSim(w1, w2) = \begin{cases} 1 & if QGDistance(w1, w2) = 1 \\ Max\left(Sim_{Hal}(w1, w2), Sim_{Wup}(w1, w2)\right) \end{cases} \quad (9)$$

Where $QGDistance(w1, w2)$ is the QGram-Distance between *w1* and *w2*.

Statistics **and Weight Ratio:** For calculating the weight ratio in this measure of similarity was used WordNet 3.0 and it was defined in (10):

$$StaWeiRat\ (w1, w2) = \frac{\left(Sim_{Hal}(w1, w2) + \left(\frac{1}{WeiRat(w1, w2)}\right)\right)}{2} \quad (10)$$

[4] Copyright (c) 2006 by Chris Parkinson, available in http://sourceforge.net/projects/simmetrics/

Where $WeiRat(w1, w2)$ takes a value based on the type of relationship between *w1* and *w2*. The possible values are defined in Table 1.

Value	Relation between $w1$ and $w2$
10	Antonym.
1	Synonym.
2	Direct Hypernym, Similar_To or Derivationally Related Form.
3	Two-links indirect Hypernym, Similar_To or Derivationally Related Form.
3	One word is often found in the gloss of the other.
9	Otherwise.

Table 1: Values of Weight Ratio.

3.6 Sentence Alignment

In the recognition of texts' similarities, several methods of lexical alignment have been used and can be appreciated by different point of views (Brockett, 2007) (Dagan, et al., 2005). Glickman (2006) used the measurement of the overleap grade between bags of words as a form of sentence alignment. Rada et al. (2006) made reference to an all-for-all alignment, leaving open the possibility when the same word of a sentence is aligned with several sentences. For this task, we used the Hungarian assignment algorithm as a way to align two sentences (Kuhn, 1955). Using that, the alignment cost between the sentences was reduced. To increase the semantic possibilities we used all word similarity metrics (including the two word similarity models) as a function cost.

3.7 N-Grams Alignment

Using the Max Word Similarity model, we calculated three features based on 2-gram, 3-gram and 4-gram alignment with the Hungarian algorithm.

4 Knowledge-based System

For similarity calculation between two phrases, we developed a knowledge-based system using SemEval-2012, SemEval-2013 and SemEval-2014 training corpus (Task 10 and Task 1 for the last one). For each training pair of phrases we obtained a vector with all measures explained above. Having it, we estimated the similarity value between two new phrases by applying the Euclidian distance between the new vector (made with the sentence pair we want to estimate the similarity value) and each vector in the training corpus. Then, the value of the instance with minor Euclidian Distance was assigned to the new pair of phrases.

5 Tasks and runs

Our system participated in Sentence to Phrase subtask of Task 3: "Cross-Level Semantic Similarity" (Jurgens, et al., 2014) and in two subtasks of Task 10: "Multilingual Semantic Textual Similarity" of SemEval-2014. It is important to remark that our system, using SVM approach, did not participate in Task 1: "Evaluation of compositional distributional semantic models on full sentences through semantic relatedness and textual entailment", due to deadline issues. We compared our system results with the final ranking of Task 1 and we could have reached the 6th place of the ranking for Relatedness Subtask with a 0.781 of correlation coefficient, and the 9th place for Entailment Subtask with an accuracy of 77.41%.

	Task 10 Sp		Task 10 En			Task 3 Sentence to Phrase	
Features/Runs	1	2	1	2	3	1	2
PathLenAlign	x		x	x		x	x
ResAlign	x		x	x		x	x
LcAlign	x		x	x		x	x
WupAlign	x		x	x		x	x
Res	x		x	x		x	x
Lc	x		x	x		x	x
DiceSimilarity	x	x	x	x		x	x
EuclideanDistance	x	x	x	x		x	x
JaccardSimilarity	x	x	x	x		x	x
JaroWinkler	x	x	x	x		x	x
Levenstein	x	x	x	x		x	x
Overlap-Coefficient	x	x	x	x		x	x
QGramsDistance	x	x	x	x		x	x
SmithWaterman	x	x	x	x		x	x
SmithWatermanGotoh	x	x	x	x		x	x
SmithWatermanGotoh-WindowedAffine	x	x	x	x		x	x
BiGramAlingHungMax	x		x	x		x	x
TriGramAlingHungMax	x		x	x		x	x
TetraGramAlingHungMax	x		x	x		x	x
WordAlingHungStatWeigthRatio	x		x	x		x	x
SentenceLengthPhrase1	x		x	x		x	x
SentenceLengthPhrase2	x		x	x		x	x

Table 2: Features and runs. Spanish (Sp) and English (En).

In Table 2 is important to remark the following situations:

- In Task 10 Spanish (two runs), we used the training corpus of Task 10 English.

- In Run2 of Task 10 English, the similarity score was replaced for the knowledge-based system value if Euclidean Distance of the most similar case was less than 0.30.
- Run3 of Task 10 English was a knowledge-based system.
- In Run1 of Sentence to Phrase of Task 3, we trained the SVM model using only the training corpus of this task.
- In Run2 of Sentence to Phrase of Task 3, we trained the SVM model using the training corpus of this task and the training corpus of Task 10 English.

6 Conclusion

In this paper we introduced a new framework for recognizing Semantic Textual Similarity, involving feature extraction for SVM model and a knowledge-based system. We analyzed different ways to estimate textual similarities applying this framework. We can see in Table 3 that all runs obtained encouraging results. Our best run was first position of the ranking for task 10 (Spanish) and other important positions were reached in the others subtasks. According to our participation, we used a SVM which works with features extracted from six different strategies: String-Based Similarity Measures, Semantic Similarity Measures, Lexical-Semantic Alignment, Statistical Similarity Measures and Semantic Alignment. Finally, we can conclude that our system achieved important results and it is able to be applied on different scenarios, such as task 10, task 3.1 and task 1. See Table 3 and the beginning of Section 5.

Subtask	Run	SemEval-2014 Position
Task 10-Spanish	Run1	4
	Run2	1
Task 10-English	Run1	16
	Run2	18
	Run3	33
Task-3	Run1	3
	Run2	16

Table 3: SemEval-2014 results.

As further work, we plan to analyze the main differences between task 10 for Spanish and English in order to homogenise both system's results.

Acknowledgments

This research work has been partially funded by the University of Alicante, Generalitat Valenciana, Spanish Government and the European Commission through the projects, "Tratamiento inteligente de la información para la ayuda a la toma de decisiones" (GRE12-44), ATTOS (TIN2012-38536-C03-03), LEGOLANG (TIN2012-31224), SAM (FP7-611312), FIRST (FP7-287607) and ACOMP/2013/067.

Reference

Eneko Agirre, Mona Diab, Daniel Cer and Aitor Gonzalez-Agirre, 2012. *SemEval 2012 Task 6: A Pilot on Semantic Textual Similarity.*. s.l., First Join Conference on Lexical and Computational Semantic (*SEM), Montréal, Canada. 2012., pp. 385-393.

Chris Brockett, 2007. *Aligning the RTE 2006 Corpus.* Microsoft Research, p. 14.

Curt Burgess, Kay Livesay and Kevin Lund, 1998. *Explorations in Context Space: Words, Sentences, Discourse.* Discourse Processes, Issue 25, pp. 211 - 257.

Ido Dagan, Oren Glickman and Bernardo Magnini, 2005. *The PASCAL Recognising Textual Entailment Challenge.* En: Proceedings of the PASCAL Challenges Workshop on Recognising Textual Entailment.

Oren Glickman, Ido Dagan and Moshe Koppel, 2006. *A Lexical Alignment Model for Probabilistic Textual Entailment.* In: Proceedings of the First International Conference on Machine Learning Challenges: Evaluating Predictive Uncertainty Visual Object Classification, and Recognizing Textual Entailment. Southampton, UK: Springer-Verlag, pp. 287--298.

Lushan Han et al., 2013. *UMBC_EBIQUITY-CORE: Semantic Textual Similarity Systems.* s.l., s.n.

Alexander B. Hirst and Graeme, 2001. *Semantic distance in WordNet: An experimental, application-oriented evaluation of five measures.*

Ilyes Jenhani, Nahla Ben Amor and Zi Elouedi, 2007. *Information Affinity: A New Similarity Measure for Possibilistic Uncertain Information.* En: Symbolic and Quantitative Approaches to Reasoning with Uncertainty. s.l.:Springer Berlin Heidelberg, pp. 840-852.

Jay Jiang and David Conrath, 1997. *Semantic similarity based on corpus statistics and lexical taxonomy.* s.l., Proceedings of the International Conference on Research in Computational Linguistics.

David Jurgens, Mohammad Taher and Roberto Navigli, 2014. *SemEval-2014 Task 3: Cross-*

Level Semantic Similarity. Dublin, Ireland, In Proceedings of the 8th International Workshop on Semantic Evaluation., pp. 23-24.

Harold W. Kuhn, 1955. *The Hungarian Method for the assignment problem.* Naval Research Logistics Quarterly.

Thomas K. Landauer, Peter W. Foltz and Darrell Laham, 1998. *Introduction to latent semantic analysis.* Discourse Processes, Issue 25, pp. 259-284.

Claudia Leacock and Martin Chodorow, 1998. *Combining local context and WordNet sense similarity for word sense identification.* s.l.:s.n.

Lin Dekang, 1998. *An information-theoretic definition of similarity.* s.l., Proceedings of the International Conf. on Machine Learning.

Rada Mihalcea, Courtney Corley and Carlo Strapparava, 2006. *Corpus-based and knowledge-based measures of text semantic similarity.* In: IN AAAI'06. s.l.:21st National Conference on Artificial Intelligence, pp. 775--780.

Luís Padró and Evgeny Stanilovsky, 2012. *FreeLing 3.0: Towards Wider Multilinguality.* Istanbul, Turkey, Proceedings of the Language Resources and Evaluation Conference (LREC 2012) ELRA.

Ted Pedersen, Siddharth Patwardhan and Jason Michelizzi, 2004. *WordNet::Similarity - Measuring the Relatedness of Concepts.* American Association for Artificial Intelligence.

Philip Resnik, 1995. *Using information content to evaluate semantic similarity.* s.l., Proceedings of the 14th International Joint Conference on Artificial Intelligence.

Zhibiao Wu and Martha Palmer, 1994. *Verb semantics and lexical selection.*

UMCC_DLSI_Prob: A Probabilistic Automata for Aspect Based Sentiment Analysis

Yenier Castañeda
Armando Collazo
Elvis Crego
Jorge L. Garcia
DI, University of Matanzas
Matanzas, Cuba
{yenier.castaneda, armando.collazo}@umcc.cu, elvis.crego@mtz.cu, jorge.garcia@infonet.umcc.cu

Yoan Gutiérrez
David Tomás
Andrés Montoyo
Rafael Muñoz
DLSI, University of Alicante
Alicante, Spain
{ygutierrez,dtomas,montoyo, rafael}@dlsi.ua.es

Abstract

This work introduces a new approach for aspect based sentiment analysis task. Its main purpose is to automatically assign the correct polarity for the aspect term in a phrase. It is a probabilistic automata where each state consists of all the nouns, adjectives, verbs and adverbs found in an annotated corpora. Each one of them contains the number of occurrences in the annotated corpora for the four required polarities (i.e. positive, negative, neutral and conflict). Also, the transitions between states have been taken into account. These values were used to assign the predicted polarity when a pattern was found in a sentence; if a pattern cannot be applied, the probabilities of the polarities between states were computed in order to predict the right polarity. The system achieved results around 66% and 57% of recall for the restaurant and laptop domain respectively.

1 Introduction

Sentiment analysis is increasingly viewed as a vital task from both an academic and a commercial standpoint. Textual information has become one of the most important sources of data to extract useful and heterogeneous knowledge. "*Texts can provide factual information, such as: descriptions, lists of characteristics, or even instructions to opinion-based information, which would include reviews, emotions, or feelings. These facts have motivated dealing with the identification and extraction of opinions and sentiments in texts that require special attention.*" (Gutiérrez, et al., 2014). Sentiment Analysis or "Subjectivity Analysis" in (Liu, 2010) is defined as the computational treatment of opinions, sentiments and emotions expressed in a text. In order to automatically treat the subjectivity, we need lexical resources that allow the detection and evaluation of the affective/ subjective charges in texts, its polarity and intensity.

Regarding research carried out for linguistic patterns identification and its polarity in texts, it is worth mentioning works on: adjectives (Hatzivassiloglou and McKeown, 1997) (Wiebe, 2000); adjectives and verbs (Turney, 2002) (Wilson, et al., 2005) (Takamura, et al., 2007); and also verbs and names (Esuli and Sebastini, 2006). WordNet (Fellbaum, 1998) has also been used for the collection of opinion adjectives and verbs (Kim and Hovy, 2005) to determine the semantic orientation of the terms depending on their notes (Esuli and Sebastiani, 2005), for the adjective extraction (Andreevskaia and Bergler, 2006) or opinion mining (Esuli and Sebastiani, 2007).

Inspired on Hidden Markov models (Baum and Petrie, 1966) and following the idea that words combinations are finite in an evaluation text, we decided to create a finite automata in graph form to represent all these relations extracted from a training corpus. For the creation of this automata we utilised different resources, such as WordNet and OpinionFinder Subjectivity Lexicon. Also, different extracted patterns based on (Cazabón, 1973) were applied.

This paper is structured as follows: In section 1.1 is described the task 4 of SemEval2014 (Pontiki, et al., 2014) where this system was presented. Section 2 presents the description of the automata and how it was built. The polarity assignation method using the trained automata is

Proceedings of the 8th International Workshop on Semantic Evaluation (SemEval 2014), pages 722–726,
Dublin, Ireland, August 23-24, 2014.

described in section 3. Finally, in section 4 and 5 are shown the results and conclusions, respectively.

1.1 Task Description

The SemEval2014 task 4 (Pontiki, et al., 2014) was divided into four subtasks: 4.1 Aspect term extraction; 4.2 Aspect term polarity; 4.3 Aspect category detection; and 4.4 Aspect category polarity.

This paper is focused on subtask 4.2 which is described as follows:

Given one or more Aspect Terms within a sentence, it is necessary to determine whether the polarity of each Aspect Term is positive, negative, neutral or conflict (i.e., both positive and negative). For example:

```
"I loved their fajitas" →
"fajitas": positive
"I hated their fajitas, but
their salads were great" →
"fajitas": negative,
"salads": positive
"The fajitas are their first
plate" → "fajitas": neutral
"The fajitas were great to
taste, but not to see" →
"fajitas": conflict.
```

Each participant was permitted to submit two kinds of runs for this task:

Constrained: Using only the provided training data and other resources, such as lexicons.

Unconstrained: Using additional data for training. Teams were asked to report what resources they used for each submitted run.

The training dataset, provided by the organiser of the Task 4 challenge, consists of two domain-specific datasets which contain over 6,500 sentences with fine-grained aspect-level human-authored annotations. These domains are:

Restaurant reviews: This dataset consists of over 3000 English sentences from the restaurant reviews of (Ganu, et al., 2009) that were adapted to the task.

Laptop reviews: This dataset consists of over 3000 English sentences extracted from customer reviews of laptops.

2 The automata

The automata was represented as a graph $G = (S, T)$ whose vertexes constitute the group of finite states $S = [s_1, s_2, s_3, \dots, s_n]$ while the edges represent the transitions $T = [t_1, t_2, t_3, \dots, t_n]$ of going from one state to another.

Our finite automata involves the following features:

1. Group of finite states: all the verbs, nouns, adverbs, adjectives that were extracted from the training dataset (see Section 2.1) using Freeling 3.1 language analyser (Atserias, et al., 2006), or Aspect Terms (that may be formed by several words). In every state the automata stores the occurrences W_i^p, where p is one of the following polarity classes: positive, negative, neutral, conflict or undefined, i being the index of the current state in the graph.
2. Finite alphabet: a sentences set which contains one or more Aspect Terms to which should be assigned a polarity.
3. Initial state: first word of the sentence.
4. Transition state ($Ts_{i,j}$ and $Ts_{j,i}$): each transition between two states contains $W_{i,j}^p$ and $W_{j,i}^p$, where p is positive, negative, neutral or conflict, i is the current state, and j is the next state.
5. End state: last word of the sentence.

If we could not determine the polarity classification for a state or transition, then we set it as *undefined polarity*.

2.1 Training the automata

In order to create the automata the training dataset provided for the SemEval2014 taks 4[1] was used.

In the automata, each word of a sentence forms a state which is connected to the following word. This connection forms a transition between the two words. This method is repeated until the last word of the sentence is reached. If the word already exists in the automata, both its state and all the transitions (from and to that word) are adjusted, increasing in one the W_i^p, $W_{i,j}^p$ and $W_{j,i}^p$ of the polarity value initially assigned in the corpus.

The transitions from words to Aspect Terms with their respective polarities allow to go through those words with undefined polarities to the target Aspect Terms. This event is done for finding the most probably polarity according to the training discoveries. Same thing happens with transitions from an Aspect Term to a word, but in this case from the polarity of the Aspect Term to *undefined polarity*.

[1]http://alt.qcri.org/semeval2014/task4/

On the other hand, if the word is not an Aspect Term its state do not change at all, since the dataset only annotates the Aspect Terms, so we do not know the polarity of those words that are not an Aspect Term.

To solve this issue we decided to make use of other resources to enhance the automata, so that the probability for finding a polarity for a word in the automata increases with the expansion of the dictionary. We used the Opinion Finder Subjectivity Lexicon (OFSL) (Wilson, et al., 2005) to adjust the state and transitions of the words in the automata. To address the adjustment, for every word of OFSL (according to the classification of the sentiment polarity) that exists in the graph represented by automata, the respective value of polarity of W_i^p, $W_{i,j}^p$ and $W_{j,i}^p$ is increased in one. We also used WordNet 3.0 to obtain the synonyms and antonyms of the words in the automata to form new states and transitions. Synonyms were given the same polarity as the related word, whereas antonyms took the opposite polarity. The subjectivity clues extracted by the patterns detected in the training dataset were used as well (See section 3.2).

In Table 1 we show the terminology used for the patterns.

Symbol	Description
[]	Optional word
/!	Subjectivity clue
/l	Compare by lemma
AT	Aspect Term

Table 1: Pattern symbols

Examples:

```
[DT] AT [PRP] [RB] be/l [VBG/!]
RB/! [JJ/!] [RB/!]
[RB/!] [DT] JJS/! [DT] [NN] AT [VB]
[NN/!]
[DT] JJ/! NN PRP VBD VB [DT] AT
AT be/l [DT/!] JJ/! [PRP/!] [RB/!]
```

Note the use of the POS tags such as DT, NN, VBD, and others were taken from the result of the pos-tagging process performed by Freeling 3.1. Using this tool the incoming texts were split into parts (sentences) for the following processes.

For instance, in the sentence "This MacBook Pro is excellent" the subjectivity clue for the Aspect Term **MacBook Pro** is **excellent**; so its states and transitions get adjusted the same way as the Aspect Term. Figure 1 describes this example, where p_i is W_i^p , p_{ij} is $W_{i,j}^p$ and p_{ji} is $W_{j,i}^p$ means the occurrence for positive polarity (negative, neutral and conflict polarities were omitted by lack of space). Both states and transitions are represented.

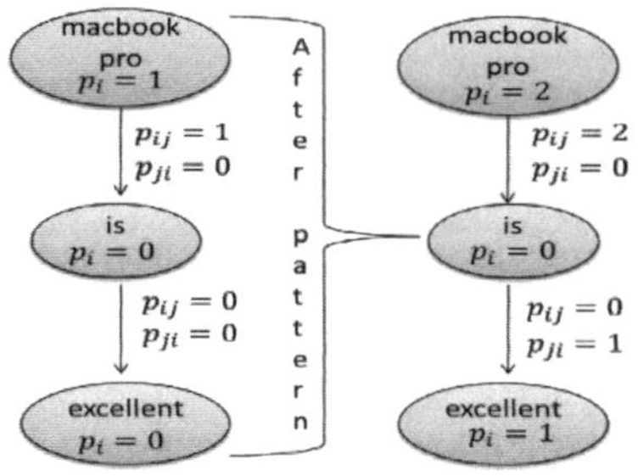

Figure 1: Adjusting states and transitions after pattern analysis.

3 Polarity Assignation

Before predicting the polarity of the Aspect Terms, each sentence is divided by its connectors (conjunctions, prepositions and adverbs, extracted using Freeling), forming the corresponding phrases. For instance, the sentence "Where Gabriela personally greets you **and** recommends you what to eat" is divided into the phrase "Where Gabriela personally greets you" and the phrase "recommends you what to eat" by connector **and**.

3.1 Selection criteria

If only one polarity is found then that is the polarity for the Aspect Term. On the other hand, if more than one polarity is found, the polarity for the Aspect Term is the most repeated one.

Note that if both positive and negative are the most repeated polarities we set conflict as the polarity for the Aspect Term.

If no polarities are found at all, we assignee neutral to the Aspect Term.

3.2 Assigning polarity using patterns

We detected different patterns which allowed us to extract those words that influence on the Aspect Term polarity in the phrase (See section 2.1).

For each phrase subjectivity clue i, we calculate the most probable polarity $Pp_i = max_p(W_i^p)$, if i has a state in the automata. After that, we apply our selection criteria described in section 3.1.

If no polarities are found at all, we process the phrase in the next steps.

3.3 Assigning polarity using the automata

For each Aspect Term in the phrase we get the sentence it belongs to and we calculate $Pt_{i,j} = \frac{W_{i,j}^p}{\sum W_{i,j}^p}$ in that sentence, where $Pt_{i,j}$ is the most probable polarity of $Ts_{i,j}$ (j being the Aspect Term), if such a transition existed. If no polarity is found, then we calculate $Pt_{j,i}=\frac{w_{j,i}^{p}}{\sum w_{j,i}^{p}}$ again if such a transition existed.

In case of applying aforementioned processes without finding out a concrete polarity for the target Aspect Terms, we perform other steps to try to find one or more polarities for the Aspect Term.

First, we verify whether the Aspect Term is part of a phrase which was matched to a pattern but no polarity was found as explained in section 3.2, if so we get the subjectivity clues of the phrase and for each subjectivity clue we calculate $Ts_{i,j}$, where i is the Aspect Term index and j corresponds to the subjectivity clue index. If no polarity is found, then we calculate $Ts_{j,i}$.

If no polarities are found after this step, we proceed to do the same as above, but this time for each word in the sentence.

Lastly, if no polarities are found, Pp_i is obtained for each word i in the sentence if i has a state in the automata.

After performing these steps we apply our selection criteria to assign the polarity to the Aspect Term in question. As can be seen, our proposal is focused on the application of an exhaustive exploration of the automata in order to classify Aspect Terms with the target polarities.

4 Results and Discussion

In order to evaluate the accuracy of the system several tests were run. Table 2 shows some of the tests using SemEval2014 task4 Baseline for the Restaurant reviews. We did the same evaluation for Laptop reviews and the results obtained were very similar to those shown in Table 2 for Restaurant. We used **semeval_base.py**[2] script to split the dataset into a train and a test part using an 80:20 ratio. Despite tests 1, 2 and 3 results do not vary much, it is evident that using the three training resources yields our best accuracy.

Training				Evaluation		
Test	Patterns	WordNet	OFSL	Pattern/Automata only	Automata only	Accuracy (%)
1	X	X	X	X		58.0
2	X			X		57.9
3	X		X	X		57.9
4	X	X	X		X	54.0

Table 2: Evaluation over restaurant domain

With test 4 it is evident that it is better to use two methods combined than only one of them, since the patterns indicate the words that assign polarity to the Aspect Term, making the automata more precise with this information at the time of assigning the correct polarity. Otherwise, if a pattern is not encountered we need to analyse the words that are closer to the Aspect Term determining the polarity according to the context. In addition, not always is assigned a polarity to it in case of the pattern found in the context is empty. Table 3 shows the results of our system in comparison with the best of the challenge SemEval2014 subtask 4.2.

Test	Constrained	Unconstrained
Rest	66.5	66.8
Laptop	56.1	57.0
BRR	80.9	77.6
BRL	70.4	66.6

Table 3: Test subtask 4.2 (BRR: Best Ranked for Restaurant; BRL Best Ranked for Laptop)

The system behaved the same as the training stage on the competition although the accuracy increased.

5 Conclusions and future works

This work introduces a new approach for aspect based sentiment analysis. For that, a probabilistic automata was created where the states are formed by the nouns, adjectives, verbs and adverbs found in the annotated corpora, based on their occurrence. The transitions between states are also taken into account. A set of patterns were defined in order to extract the words that influence on an Aspect Term, also known as subjectivity clues, and then we predicted their polarity using the automata's probabilities. A system was developed following this approach to participate on SemEval2014 competition, obtaining an accuracy of 66% for restaurant reviews and 57% for laptop reviews.

As future works we plan to deal with the fact that this automata only involves states represented by the words lack extracted from the training data. So, the previously unseen aspect terms which do not correspond to any state in the automata, are not recognised in many cases as far as the polarity is concerned. To address this issue we plan to

[2] http://alt.qcri.org/semeval2014/task4/data/semeval14-absa-base-eval-valid.zip

expand the aspect term dictionary using Wikipedia definitions. On the other hand, we plan to use a disambiguation method to select the exact WordNet synset and then to reduce the polysemy of the automata's words. Finally, to smooth the probabilities it would be interesting to study different balances in order to get new improvements for the system.

Acknowledgments

This research work has been partially funded by the University of Alicante, Generalitat Valenciana, Spanish Government and the European Commission through the projects, "Tratamiento inteligente de la información para la ayuda a la toma de decisiones" (GRE12-44), ATTOS (TIN2012-38536-C03-03), LEGOLANG (TIN2012-31224), SAM (FP7-611312), FIRST (FP7-287607) and ACOMP/2013/067.

References

Alina Andreevskaia and Sabine Bergler, 2006. *Mining WordNet for Fuzzy Sentiment: Sentiment Tag Extraction from WordNet Glosses.* Trento, Italia, s.n.

Jordi Atserias et al., 2006. *FreeLing 1.3: Syntactic and semantic services in an opensource NLP library.* Genoa, Italy, s.n.

Leonard Baum and Ted Petrie, 1966. Statistical Inference for Probabilistic Functions of Finite State Markov Chains. *The Annals of Mathematical Statistics,* pp. 1554--1563.

María Cazabón, 1973. *Patterns of English.* s.l.:Editorial Pueblo y Educación.

Andrea Esuli and Fabrizio Sebastiani , 2005. Determining the semantic orientation of terms through gloss classification. *Proceedings of the 14th ACM International Conference on Information and Knowledge Management,* pp. 617-624.

Andrea Esuli and Fabrizio Sebastiani, 2007. *PageRanking WordNet Synsets: An Application to Opinion Mining.* Prague, Czeck Republic, s.n., pp. 424-431.

Andrea Esuli and Fabrizio Sebastiani, 2006. *SentiWordNet: A Publicly Available Lexical Resource for Opinion Mining.* Genova, IT, s.n., pp. 417-422.

Christiane Fellbaum, 1998. *WordNet. An Electronic Lexical Database.* University of Cambridge: s.n.

Gayatree Ganu, Noemie Elhadad and Amélie Marian, 2009. *Beyond the stars: Improving rating predictions using review text content.* Rhode Island, s.n.

Yoan Gutiérrez, Andy González, Roger Pérez, José I. Abreu, Antonio Fernández Orquín, Alejandro Mosquera, Andrés Montoyo, Rafael Muñoz and Franc Camara, 2014. UMCC_DLSI-(SA): Using a ranking algorithm and informal features to solve Sentiment Analysis in Twitter. *Second Joint Conference on Lexical and Computational Semantics (*SEM), Volume 2: Proceedings of the Seventh International Workshop on Semantic Evaluation (SemEval 2013),* pp. 443--449.

Vasileios Hatzivassiloglou and Kathleen McKeown, 1997. *Predicting the Semantic Orientation of Adjectives.* Madrid, Spain, s.n., pp. 174-181.

Soo-Min Kim and Eduard Hovy, 2005. *Automatic Detection of Opinion Bearing Words and Sentences.* Jeju Island, Republic of Korea, s.n.

Bing Liu, 2010. Sentiment Analysis and Subjectivity. In: *Handbook of Natural Language Processing.* Boca Raton: s.n., pp. 627-666.

Maria Pontiki, Dimitrios Galanis, John Pavlopoulos, Haris Papageorgiou, Ion Androutsopoulos, and Suresh Manandhar, 2014. SemEval-2014 Task 4: Aspect Based Sentiment Analysis. *In Proceedings of the 8th International Workshop on Semantic Evaluation (SemEval 2014),* Dublin, Ireland.

Hiroya Takamura, Takashi Inui and Manabu Okumura, 2007. *Extracting Semantic Orientations of Phrases from Dictionary.* s.l., s.n., pp. 292-299.

Peter Turney, 2002. *Thumbs up or thumbs down? Semantic orientation applied to unsupervised classification of reviews.* Philadelphia, Pennsylvania, s.n., pp. 417-424.

Janyce Wiebe, 2000. *Learning Subjective Adjectives from Corpora.* Austin, Texas, s.n.

Theresa Wilson, Janyce Wiebe, and Paul Hoffmann, 2005. *Recognizing Contextual Polarity in Phrase-Level Sentiment Analysis.* Vancouver, Canada., s.n.

UMCC_DLSI: Sentiment Analysis in Twitter using Polirity Lexicons and Tweet Similarity

Pedro Aniel Sánchez-Mirabal,
Yarelis Ruano Torres,
Suilen Hernández Alvarado
University of Matanzas / Cuba
pedroasm@umcc.cu
yara@umcc.cu
suilen.alvarado@umcc.cu

Yoan Gutiérrez,
Andrés Montoyo,
Rafael Muñoz
University of Alicante/Spain
ygutierrez@dlsi.ua.es
montoyo@dlsi.ua.es
rafael@dlsi.ua.es

Abstract

This paper describes a system submitted to *SemEval-2014 Task 4B: Sentiment Analysis in Twitter*, by the team **UMCC_DLSI_Sem** integrated by researchers of the University of Matanzas, Cuba and the University of Alicante, Spain. The system adopts a cascade classification process that uses two classifiers, K-NN using the lexical Levenshtein metric and a Dagging model trained over attributes extracted from annotated corpora and sentiment lexicons. Phrases that fit the distance thresholds were automatically classified by the KNN model, the others, were evaluated with the Dagging model. This system achieved over 52.4% of correctly classified instances in the Twitter message-level subtask.

1 Introduction

Nowadays, one of the most important sources of data to extract useful and heterogeneous knowledge is Textual Information. Daily, millions of Tweets, SMS and blog comments increase the huge volume of information available for researchers. Texts can provide factual information, such as: descriptions, lists of characteristics, or even instructions to opinion-based information, which would include reviews, emotions, or feelings (Gutiérrez et al., 2013). These facts have motivated that dealing with the identification and extraction of opinions and sentiments in texts requires special attention. Applications of Sentiment Analysis are now more common than ever in fields like politics and business. More than 50 systems participating in this task, clearly indicate the increase of interest in the scientific community.

Twitter messages can be found among of the most used corpora nowadays for Sentiment Analysis (SA). This kind of messages involves an evident informality which has been addressed in different ways. For example, there are some works like (Gutiérrez et al., 2013) that apply normalisation textual tools to reduce the informality of the twitter messages. Authors such as (Go et al., 2009), (Gutiérrez et al., 2013), (Fernández et al., 2013) and others are focused on the application of preprocessing processes and feature reduction to be able to standardise twitter messages and reduce different types of elements like hashtags, user nicks, urls, etc.

In terms of those techniques that can be used for SA, we can cite (Pang et al., 2002) who built a lexicon with associated polarity value, starting with a set of classified seed adjectives and using conjunctions (and) disjunctions (or, but) to deduce the orientation of new words in a corpus. This research was based on machine learning techniques to address Sentiment Classification. Other interesting research is (Turney, 2002), which classifies words according to their polarity based on the idea that terms with similar orientation tend to co-occur in documents. There are a large quantity of approaches to deal with SA, and basically most of them are based on word bags and/or annotated corpora as knowledge base. Based on this information the SA systems are able to apply different types of evaluation techniques such as machine learning or statistic formulas to predict the correct classification. As part of machine learning approaches we would like to mention those works such as (Go et al., 2009), (Mohammad et al., 2013) and others that were based on feature vectors and which cover a wide range settings of SA. As a starting point, we based this work on the (Mohammad et al., 2013) approach, adding

Proceedings of the 8th International Workshop on Semantic Evaluation (SemEval 2014), pages 727–731,
Dublin, Ireland, August 23-24, 2014.

new features extracted from the sentiment repositories Sentiment 140 [1] and NRC-Hashtag Sentiment (Mohammad and Turney, 2013).

The remainder of this paper is structured as follows: section 2 describes in detail the approach presented. In section 3 we explain the experiments we carried out. Finally in section 4 conclusions and future works are expounded.

2 System Description

In this section we present our system in detail which is able to classify the polarity of tweets as positive, negative, or neutral.

The system is structured in two main stages. The first stage consists of classifying a given tweet. For that, we first recovered all the tweets from the training corpus that have a similarity value greater than a fixed threshold T. The second stage consists of classifying using the K-NN rule (Coomans and Massart, 1982), considering as K all tweets recovered. The process begins with $T = 0.9$ decreasing it until $T = 0.6$. In section 3 we will explain how these values were determined.

As similarity metric we use the Levenshtein (Levenshtein, 1966) lexical distance. In case that we cannot find any tweet fulfilling the condition, the tweet polarity is assigned using a second classifier trained using **Dagging** which combines several **Logistic** classifiers set by **WEKA** as default.

2.1 Preprocessing

The first step in our system is to pre-process all tweets. The following operations were applied in the given order.

- Replacing emoticons: Each emoticon is replaced by a word according to a lexicon of emoticons. The meanings of the emoticons were taken from `http://en.wikipedia.org/wiki/List_of_emoticons`.

- Replacing acronyms: Each acronym is replaced by its meaning. The meanings of the acronyms were taken from `http://www.acronymfinder.com/`.

- Cleaning text: Remove not alphanumeric characters from the tweet.

- Replacing abbreviations: Each abbreviation is replaced by its respective words. The abbreviations were taken from `http://en.wikipedia.org/wiki/Abbreviation`.

- Lemmatising: Each word is replaced by its lemma. We use Freeling 3.0 (Padró and Stanilovsky, 2012) for this purpose. We only retain lemmas corresponding to adjectives, adverbs, interjections, nouns and verbs.

- Expanding contractions: Each contraction is replaced by its respective word. The contractions were taken from `http://www.softschools.com/language_arts/grammar/contractions/contractions_list/`.

- Deleting punctuation marks.

- Deleting stop words. The stop words were taken from `http://www.ranks.nl/stopwords`.

2.2 Recovering tweets from similarity

As it was explained before, in a first step we tried to classify tweets using the K-NN rule. To recover the K similar tweets we used the Levenshtein metric (Levenshtein, 1966). This measure allows to compute the similarity of two strings of symbols counting the minimum number of deletions, substitutions and insertions necessary to transform one string into another. In our case, each word in the string is considered as a symbol. In the future we plan to improve this metric using Levenshtein at word level and then at sentence level. This metric is known as DLED (Double Levenshteins Edit Distance) and will be taken from (Fernández et al., 2012).

2.3 Features for Dagging classifier

We represented each tweet as a vector of features based in (Mohammad et al., 2013) plus other new ones. Also we used the lexicons **Sentiment 140** and **NRC-Hashtag Sentiment** as it was defined by Mohammad.

Also two new lexicons, named **NRC Emotion Lexicon 1.0** and **NRC Emotion Lexicon 2.0** were derived from the **NRC Emotion Lexicon** (Mohammad and Turney, 2013). In the first case we associated to each word just the values in the columns *positive* and *negative* of **NRC Emotion Lexicon**, thus, no sentiment score was computed.

[1] http://cs.stanford.edu/people/alecmgo/trainingandtestdata.zip

For the second lexicon, the *positive* score was calculated as the sum of the values for the classifications *positive*, *anticipation*, *joy*, *surprise* and *trust*. On the other hand, the negative score was computed as the sum of the values for the classifications *negative*, *anger*, *disgust*, *fear*, *sadness* and *trust*.

In each case we computed the following attributes:

- Pos: Sum of the positive scores of each token in the tweet over the number of tokens in the tweet.

- Neg: Sum of the negative scores of each token in the tweet over the number of tokens in the tweet.

- PercentPos: $\frac{100*Pos}{Pos+Neg}$

- MissNGram: Percent of tokens in the tweet that were not found in the lexicon.

For the **Sentiment 140** and **NRC-Hashtag Sentiment** lexicons we also computed the feature:

- SSE: Sum of the sentiment score of each token in the tweet over the number of tokens in the tweet.

Based on the information involved into Sentiment 140 and NRC-Hashtag Sentiment lexicons, unigrams, bigrams and pairs were tokenised involving any non-contiguous combination of the previous n-grams. With respect to the pairs extraction were considered the following possibilities: unigram-unigram, unigram-bigram and bigram-bigram. Similar to (Mohammad et al., 2013) different set of attributes were generated for each type of token. As result an initial set of 50 attributes were obtained.

In the case of the new lexicons (NRC Emotion Lexicon 1.0 and NRC Emotion Lexicon 2.0), only unigrams were considered. Moreover, the feature **SSE** was not computed. So, another 8 features were taken into account with respect to these lexicons.

Finally we computed:

- NCL: Percent of tokens in capital letters.

- NoE: Number of emoticons in the tweet.

- NoA: Number of acronyms in the tweet.

In general the system works with a total of 61 attributes.

2.4 Classifier Design

As training set, we joined the preprocessed tweets from both the *train* and *development* sets provided by the Task9B of Semeval-2014. The Dagging classifier was trained using this set with the following parameters **-F 15 -S 1 -W weka.classifiers.functions.Logistic – -R 1.0E-8 -M -1** using a 10 fold cross-validation as evaluation method.

3 Experiments

The experiments were evaluated over the training dataset provided by Task 9: Sentiment Analysis in Twitter, subtask B. Based on the explanation provided in section 2 according to the initialisation of the threshold T to ensure that the K similar tweets are in fact similar enough, we carried out an experiment for different values of T. These experiments refer an analysis to know how the variation of T affects the classification results.

T	% CCI
0.9	86.7
0.8	83.3
0.7	74.1
0.6	67.2
0.5	61.1
0.4	55.0
0.3	56.0

Table 1: Results of the K-NN classifier using Levenshtein metric.

T	% CCI
0.9	81.2
0.8	83.3
0.7	74.1
0.6	66.7
0.5	63.1
0.4	60.6
0.3	54.2

Table 2: Results of the K-NN classifier using Matching Coefficient metric.

The first stage of the system was applied to compute the number of instances which have at least one instance with a similarity value greater than T. We computed the percent of instances correctly classified ($\%CCI$). Table 1 shows the behaviour of the system when T changes. Table 2 shows the results of the K-NN classifier using

System	LiveJournal2014	SMS2013	Twitter2013	Twitter2014	Twitter2014Sarcasm
Best result	74.8	70.3	72.1	71.0	58.2
Average result	63.5	55.6	59.8	60.6	45.4
UMCC-DLSI-Sem	**53.1**	**50.0**	**52.0**	**55.4**	**42.8**
Worse result	29.3	24.6	34.2	33.0	29.0

Table 3: Results in the SemEval-2014 Task 4B.

Matching Coefficient metric (`http://www.coli.uni-saarland.de/courses/LT1/2011/slides/stringmetrics.pdf`). This metric counts the quantity of matched symbols (words in this case) between two sentences.

Furthermore, we repeated this experiment using the Matching Coefficient similarity metric to better tunning the algorithm and to evaluate if the results behave in a similar way when T changes. In both cases, we use the implementation provided in the **SimMetrics** library.

As those results shows, when T decrease the accuracy decrease too. In practice, for the values of T lower than 0.6 the results are worse than 61.4% using the Dagging classifier in the 10 fold cross-validation. For that reason, as was mentioned in 2, we only tried to apply the first stage for values of $T \geq 0.6$.

We evaluated our system in the challenge Task 4B: Sentiment Analysis in Twitter, using the provided training and test data of this challenge. Based on the classifier obtained in the training process we tested our system over the test dataset achieving values of $\%CCI$ up to 55.4. Table 3 show detailed results for each of the 5 different sources.

4 Conclusions and Future Works

Our system was based on an approach that follows two stages to classify the polarity of tweets. Regardless the fact that our system behaves worse than the average, we consider that the approach is suitable to deal with SA, since our results are close to the average. As future works we will study other approaches in order to encourage further developments of this proposal. Several issues could be adjusted, for example, other distances should be tested and evaluated such as DLED (Double Levenshteins Edit Distance) (Fernández et al., 2012). Also, features that encode information about the presence of negation and opposition words could be very useful.

Acknowledgements

This research work has been partially funded by the University of Alicante, Generalitat Valenciana, Spanish Government and the European Commission through the projects, "Tratamiento inteligente de la informacin para la ayuda a la toma de decisiones" (GRE12-44), ATTOS (TIN2012-38536-C03-03), LEGOLANG (TIN2012-31224), SAM (FP7-611312), FIRST (FP7-287607) and ACOMP/2013/067.

References

D. Coomans and D.L. Massart. 1982. Alternative k-nearest neighbour rules in supervised pattern recognition : Part 1. k-nearest neighbour classification by using alternative voting rules. *Analytica Chimica Acta*, 136(0):15–27.

Antonio Fernández, Yoan Gutiérrez, Héctor Dávila, Alexander Chávez, Andy González, Rainel Estrada, Yenier Castañeda, Sonia Vázquez, Andrés Montoyo, and Rafael Muñoz. 2012. Umcc_dlsi: Multidimensional lexical-semantic textual similarity. In **SEM 2012: The First Joint Conference on Lexical and Computational Semantics – Volume 1: Proceedings of the main conference and the shared task, and Volume 2: Proceedings of the Sixth International Workshop on Semantic Evaluation (SemEval 2012)*, pages 608–616, Montréal, Canada, 7-8 June. Association for Computational Linguistics.

Javi Fernández, Yoan Gutiérrez, José M Gómez, Patricio Martınez-Barco, Andrés Montoyo, and Rafael Munoz. 2013. Sentiment analysis of spanish tweets using a ranking algorithm and skipgrams. *Proc. of the TASS workshop at SEPLN 2013. IV Congreso Español de Informática*, pages 17–20.

Alec Go, Richa Bhayani, and Lei Huang. 2009. Twitter sentiment classification using distant supervision. *Processing*, pages 1–6.

Yoan Gutiérrez, Andy González, Roger Pérez, José I. Abreu, Antonio Fernández Orquín, Alejandro Mosquera, Andrés Montoyo, Rafael Muñoz, and Franc Camara. 2013. Umcc_dlsi-(sa): Using a ranking algorithm and informal features to solve sentiment analysis in twitter. In *Second Joint Conference on Lexical and Computational Semantics (*SEM), Volume 2: Proceedings of the Seventh International*

Workshop on Semantic Evaluation (SemEval 2013), pages 443–449, Atlanta, Georgia, USA, June. Association for Computational Linguistics.

Vladimir Levenshtein. 1966. Binary codes capable of correcting deletions, insertions, and reversals. *Cybernetics and Control Theory*, 10(8):707–710. Original in *Doklady Akademii Nauk SSSR* 163(4): 845–848 (1965).

Saif M. Mohammad and Peter D. Turney. 2013. Crowdsourcing a word-emotion association lexicon. 29(3):436–465.

Saif M. Mohammad, Svetlana Kiritchenko, and Xiaodan Zhu. 2013. Nrc-canada: Building the state-of-the-art in sentiment analysis of tweets. *CoRR*, abs/1308.6242.

Lluís Padró and Evgeny Stanilovsky. 2012. Freeling 3.0: Towards wider multilinguality. In *Proceedings of the Language Resources and Evaluation Conference (LREC 2012)*, Istanbul, Turkey, May. ELRA.

Bo Pang, Lillian Lee, and Shivakumar Vaithyanathan. 2002. Thumbs up?: Sentiment classification using machine learning techniques. In *Proceedings of the ACL-02 Conference on Empirical Methods in Natural Language Processing - Volume 10*, EMNLP '02, pages 79–86, Stroudsburg, PA, USA. Association for Computational Linguistics.

Peter D. Turney. 2002. Thumbs up or thumbs down?: Semantic orientation applied to unsupervised classification of reviews. In *Proceedings of the 40th Annual Meeting on Association for Computational Linguistics*, ACL '02, pages 417–424, Stroudsburg, PA, USA. Association for Computational Linguistics.

UNAL-NLP: Combining Soft Cardinality Features for Semantic Textual Similarity, Relatedness and Entailment

Sergio Jimenez, George Dueñas,
and **Julia Baquero**
Universidad Nacional de Colombia
Ciudad Universitaria, edificio 453,
oficina 114, Bogotá, Colombia
[sgjimenezv,geduenasl,
jmbaquerov]@unal.edu.co

Alexander Gelbukh
Center for Computing Research (CIC),
Instituto Politécnico Nacional (IPN),
Av. Juan Dios Bátiz, Av. Mendizábal,
Col. Nueva Industrial Vallejo,
Mexico City, Mexico
www.gelbukh.com

Abstract

This paper describes our participation in the SemEval-2014 tasks 1, 3 and 10. We used an uniform approach for addressing all the tasks using the soft cardinality for extracting features from text pairs, and machine learning for predicting the gold standards. Our submitted systems ranked among the top systems in all the task and sub-tasks in which we participated. These results confirm the results obtained in previous SemEval campaigns suggesting that the soft cardinality is a simple and useful tool for addressing a wide range of natural language processing problems.

1 Introduction

The semantic textual similarity is a core problem in the computational linguistic field. Consequently, the previous evaluation campaigns of this task in SemEval have attracted the attention of many research groups worldwide (Agirre et al., 2012; Agirre et al., 2013).This year, 3 tasks related to this problem have been proposed exploring different facets such as semantic relatedness, entailment , multilingualism, lack of training data and imbalance in the amount of information.

The soft cardinality (Jimenez et al., 2010) is a simple concept that generalizes the classical set cardinality by considering the similarities among the elements in a collection for a more intuitive quantification of the number of elements in that collection. This approach can be applied to text applications representing texts as collections of words and providing a similarity function that compares two words. Varying this word-to-word similarity function the soft cardinality can reflect notions of syntactic similarity, semantic relatedness, among others. We (and others) have used this approach to address with success the semantic textual similarity and other tasks in previous SemEval editions (Jimenez et al., 2012b; Jimenez et al., 2012a; Jimenez et al., 2013a; Jimenez et al., 2013b; Jimenez et al., 2013c; Croce et al., 2013).

In this paper we describe our participating systems in the SemEval-2014 tasks 1, 3, and 10, which used the soft cardinality as core approach.

2 Features from Soft Cardinalities

The cardinality of a collection of elements is the counting of non-repeated elements in it. This definition is intrinsically associated with the notion of set, which is a collection of non-repeated elements.Thus, the cardinality of a collection or set A is denoted as $|A|$. Clearly, the cardinality of a collection with repeated elements treats groups of identical elements as a single instance contributing only with a unit (1) to the element counting. Jimenez et al. (2010) proposed the *soft cardinality* that uses a notion of similarity among elements for grouping not only identical elements but similar too. That notion of similarity among elements is provided by a similarity function that compares two elements a_i and a_j and returns a score in [0,1] interval, having $sim(a_i, a_i) = 1$. Although, it is not necessary that sim fulfills another metric properties aside of identity, symmetry is also desirable. Thus, the soft cardinality of a collection A, whose elements $a_1, a_2, \ldots, a_{|A|}$ are comparable with a similarity function $sim(a_i, a_j)$, is denoted as $|A|_{sim}$. This soft cardinality is given by the following expression:

$$|A|_{sim} = \sum_{i=1}^{|A|} \frac{w_{a_i}}{\sum_{j=1}^{|A|} sim(a_i, a_j)^p} \quad (1)$$

It is trivial to see that $|A| = |A|_{sim}$ either if $p \to \infty$ or when the function sim is a crisp com-

Proceedings of the 8th International Workshop on Semantic Evaluation (SemEval 2014), pages 732–742,
Dublin, Ireland, August 23-24, 2014.

Basic	Derived
$\|A\|$	$\|A \cap B\| = \|A\| + \|B\| - \|A \cup B\|$
$\|B\|$	$\|A \triangle B\| = \|A \cup B\| - \|A \cap B\|\|$
$\|A \cup B\|$	$\|A \setminus B\| = \|A\| - \|A \cap B\|$
	$\|B \setminus A\| = \|B\| - \|A \cap B\|$

Table 1: The 7 basic and derived cardinalities for two sets comparison.

parator, i.e. one that returns 1 for identical elements and 0 otherwise. This property shows that the soft cardinality generalizes the classical cardinality and that the parameter p controls its degree of "softness", whose default value is 1. The values w_{a_i} are optional "importance" weights associated with each element a_i, by default those weights can be assigned to 1.

For the tasks at hand, we represent each short text (lets say A) as a collection of words a_i and the sim function can be any operator that compares pairs of words. The motivation for using the soft cardinality is that the sim function can reflect any dimension of word similarity (e.g. syntactic, semantic) and the soft cardinality projects that notion at sentence level. For instance, if sim provides the degree of semantic relatedness between two words using WordNet, two texts A and B could be compared by computing $|A|_{sim}$, $|B|_{sim}$ and $|A \cup B|_{sim}$. Given that $A \cap B$ could be empty, the soft cardinality of the intersection must be approximated by $|A \cap B|_{sim} \approx |A|_{sim} + |B|_{sim} - |A \cup B|_{sim}$ instead of being computed directly from $A \cap B$ using equation 1. Using that approximation, the commonality (intersection) between A and B is induced by the pair-wise similarities provided by sim among the words in A and B.

Since more than a century when Jaccard (1901) proposed his well-known index, the classical set cardinality has been used to build similarity functions for set comparison. Any binary-cardinality-based similarity function is an algebraic combination of $|A|$, $|B|$ and either $|A \cap B|$ or $|A \cup B|$ (e.g. Jaccard, Dice, Tversky, overlap and cosine indexes). These three cardinalities describes unambiguously all the regions in the Venn's diagram when comparing two sets. Thus, in this scenario 4 possible cardinalities can be derived from these 3 basic cardinalities, see Table 1. Clearly, the same set of cardinalities can be obtained for the soft cardinality.

When training data is available, which is the case for tasks 1, 3 and 10 in SemEval 2014, it is possible to think that instead of using an ad-hoc expression (e.g. Jaccard, Dice) the similarity function can be obtained using the cardinalities in Table 1 as features for a machine-learning regression algorithm. Our hypothesis is that such learnt function should predict in a more accurate way the gold standard variable than any other ad-hoc function. However, these cardinality features are intrinsically correlated with the length of the texts where they were obtained. This correlation makes that the performance of the learnt similarity function could be dependent of the length of the texts. For instance, if the function was trained using long texts it is plausible to think that this function would be more effective when tested with long texts than with shorter ones. Having this in mind, an extended set of rational features is proposed, whose values are standardized in [0,1] interval aiming to reduce the effect of the length of the texts. These features are presented in Table 2.

#	Feature expression
1	$\|A\|/\|A \cup B\|$
2	$\|A\| - \|A \cap B\|/\|A\|$
3	$\|A\| - \|A \cap B\|/\|A \cup B\|$
4	$\|B\|/\|A \cup B\|$
5	$\|B\| - \|A \cap B\|/\|B\|$
6	$\|B\| - \|A \cap B\|/\|A \cup B\|$
7	$\|A \cap B\|/\|A\|$
8	$\|A \cap B\|/\|B\|$
9	$\|A \cap B\|/\|A \cup B\|$
10	$\|A \cup B\| - \|A \cap B\|/\|A \cap B\|$

Table 2: Extended set of 10 rational features.

The soft cardinality has proven to overcome the classic cardinality in the semantic textual similarity (STS) task in previous SemEval campaigns (Jimenez et al., 2012b; Jimenez et al., 2013a). Even using a simplistic function sim based on q-grams of characters, the soft cardinality method ranked third among 89 participating systems (Agirre et al., 2012). Thus, our participating systems in the SemEval 2014 campaign were based on the previously described set of 17 features, obtained from the soft cardinality with different sim functions for comparing pairs of words. Each sim function produced a different set of features, which were combined with a regression algorithm for similarity and relatedness tasks. Similarly, a classification algorithm was used for the entailment task.

3 Systems Description

In this section the different feature sets used for each submitted system to the different task and subtask are described. Besides, the data used for training, parameters and other preprocessing details are described for each system.

3.1 Task 1: Textual Relatedness and Entailment

The task 1 is based on the SICK (Sentences Involving Compositional Knowledge) data set (Marelli et al., 2014), which contains nearly 10,000 pairs of sentences manually labeled by relatedness and entailment. The relatedness gold labels range from 1 to 5, having 1 the minimum level of relatedness between the texts and 5 for the maximum. The entailment labels have three categorical values: *neutral*, *contradiction* and *entailment*. The two sub tasks consist of predicting the relatedness and entailment gold standards using approximately the 50% of the text pairs as training and the other part as test bed.

Our overall approach consists in extracting 4 different sets of features using the method presented in section 2 and training a machine learning algorithm for predicting the gold standard labels in the test data. Each feature set is described in the following 4 subsections and the subsection 3.1.6 provides details of the used combination of features, machine learning algorithm and preprocessing details.

3.1.1 String-Matching Features

First, all texts in the SICK data set where preprocessed by lower casing, tokenizing and stop-word removal (using the NLTK[1]). Then each word was reduced to its stem using the Porter's algorithm (Porter, 1980) and a *idf* weight (Jones, 2004) was associated to each stem (w_{a_i} weights in eq. 1) using the very SICK data set as document collection. Next, for each instance in the data, which is composed of two texts A and B, the 17 features listed in Tables 1 and 2 where extracted using eq.1. The used word-to-word similarity function sim decomposes each word in bags of 3-grams of characters, which are compared using the symmetrical Tversky's index (Tversky, 1977; Jimenez et al., 2013a). Thus, the similarity between two pairs of words w_1 and w_2, represented each one as a collection of 3-grams of characters, is given by the following expression:

$$sim(w_1, w_2) = \frac{|c|}{\beta(\alpha|w_{min}| + (1-\alpha)|w_{max}|) + |c|} \quad (2)$$

$$|c| = |w_1 \cap w_2| + bias_{sim},$$

$$|w_{min}| = \min[|w_1 \setminus w_2|, |w_2 \setminus w_1|],$$

$$|w_{max}| = \max[|w_1 \setminus w_2|, |w_2 \setminus w_1|].$$

The values used for the parameters were $\alpha = 1.9$, $\beta = 2.36$, $bias = -0.97$, and $p = 0.39$ (where p corresponds to eq.1). The motivation and justification for these parameters can be found in (Jimenez et al., 2013a). These values were obtained by building a text similarity function using the Dice's coefficient and the soft cardinalities plugging eq.2 in eq.1. Next, this text similarity function is evaluated in the 5,000 training text pairs and the obtained scores are compared against the relatedness gold-standard using the Pearson's correlation.

w_{a_i} are not training parameters, but they are weights associated with the words. These weights could have been obtained from a larger corpus, but we use the training texts to obtain them. This process is repeated iteratively exploring the search space defined by these 4 parameters using a hill-climbing approach until a maximum correlation is reached. We observe that the optimal values of the parameters p, α, β, and $bias$ vary considerably between the data sets and for the different *sim* functions of word-to-word similarity. We do not yet understand from which factors of the data and the *sim* functions depend on these parameters. This issue will be the objective of further research.

Henceforth, the set of 17 string-based features described in this subsection will be referred as SM.

3.1.2 ESA Features

For this set of features we used the idea proposed by Gabrilovich and Markovitch (2007) of enriching the representation of a text by representing each word by its textual definition in a knowledge base, i.e. explicit semantic analysis (ESA). For that, we used as knowledge base the synset's textual definitions provided by WordNet. First, in order to determine the textual definition associated to each word, the texts were tagged using

[1] http://www.nltk.org/

the maximum entropy POS tagger included in the NLTK. Next, the adapted Lesk algorithm (Banerjee and Pedersen, 2002) for word sense disambiguation was applied in the texts disambiguating one word at the time. The software package used for this disambiguation process was *pywsd*[2]. The arguments needed for the disambiguation of each word are the POS tag of the target word and the entire sentence as context. Once all the words are disambiguated with their corresponding WordNet synsets, each word is replaced by all the words in their textual definition jointly with the same word and its lemma. The final result of this stage is that each text in the data set is replaced by a longer text including the original text and some related words. The motivation of this procedure is that the extended versions of each pair of texts have more chance of sharing common words that the original texts.

The extended versions of these texts were used to obtain another 17 features with the same procedure described in the previous subsection (3.1.1). This feature subset will henceforth be referred as **ESA**.

3.1.3 Features for each part-of-speech category

This set of features is motivated by the idea proposed by Corley and Mihalcea (2005) of grouping words by their POS category before being compared for semantic textual similarity. Our approach consist in provide a version of each text pair in the data set for each POS category including only the words belonging to that category. For instance, the pair of texts {"*A beautiful girl is playing tennis*", "*A nice and handsome boy is playing football*"} produce new pairs such as: {"*beautiful*", "*nice handsome*"} for the ADJ tag, {"*girl tennis*", "*boy football*"} for NOUN and {"*is playing*", "*is playing*"} for VERB.

Again, the POS tags were provided by the NLTK's max entropy tagger. The 28 POS categories were simplified to 9 categories in order to avoid an excessive number of features and hence sparseness; the used mapping is shown in Table 3. Next, for each one of the 9 new POS categories a set of 17 features (SM) is extracted reusing again the method proposed in subsection 3.1.1. The only difference with the method described in that subsection is that the stop-words were not removed and the stemming process was not performed. The motivation for generating this feature sets by POS category is that the machine learning algorithms could weight differently each category. The intuition behind this is that it is reasonable that categories such as VERB and NOUN could play a more important role for the task at hand than others such as ADJ or PREP. Using these categorized features, such discrimination among POS categories can be discovered from the training data.

Reduced tag set	NLTK's POS tag set
ADJ	JJ,JJR,JJS
NOUN	NN,NNP,NNPS,NNS
ADV	RB,RBR,RBS,WRB
VERB	VB,VBD,VBG,VBN,VBP,VBZ
PRO	WP,WP$,PRP,PRP$
PREP	RP,IN
DET	PDT,DT,WDT
EX	EX
CC	CC

Table 3: Mapping reduction of the POS tag set.

Finally, the total number of features in this set is 153 (17 features $\times$ 9 POS categories). This feature set will be referred as **POS**.

3.1.4 Features From Dependencies

The *syntactic soft cardinality* (Croce et al., 2012; Croce et al., 2013) extend the soft cardinality approach by representing texts as bags of dependencies instead of bags of words. Each dependency is a 3-tuple composed of two syntactically related words and the type of their relationship. For instance, the sentence "*The boy plays football*" can be represented with 3 dependencies: [**det**,"*boy*","*The*"], [**subj**,"*plays*","*boy*"] and [**obj**,"*plays*","*football*"]. Clearly, this representation distinguish pairs of texts such as {"*The dog bites a boy*","*The boy bites a* dog"}, which are indistinguishable when they are represented as bags of words. This representation can be obtained automatically using the Stanford Parser (De Marneffe et al., 2006), which in addition provides a dependency identifying the root word in a sentence. We used the version 3.3.1[3] of that parser to obtain such representation.

Once the texts are represented as bags of dependencies, it is necessary to provide a similarity function between two dependency tuples in or-

[2]https://github.com/alvations/pywsd

[3]http://nlp.stanford.edu/software/lex-parser.shtml

der to use the soft cardinality (eq. 1) and hence to obtain the 17 cardinality features in Tables 1 and 2. Such function can be obtained using the sim function (eq. 2) for comparing the first and second words between the dependencies and even the labels of the dependency types. Let's consider two dependencies tuples $d = [d_{dep}, d_{w_1}, d_{w_2}]$ and $p = [p_{dep}, p_{w_1}, p_{w_2}]$ where d_{dep} and p_{dep} are the labels of the dependency type; d_{w_1} and p_{w_1} are the first words on each dependency tuple; and d_{w_2} and p_{w_2} are the second words. The similarity function for comparing two dependency tuples can be a linear combination of the sim scores between the corresponding elements of the dependency tuples by the following expression:

$$sim_{dep}(d,p) = \gamma sim(d_{dep}, p_{dep}) + \delta sim(d_{w_1}, p_{w_2}) + \lambda sim(d_{w_2}, p_{w_2})$$

Although, it is unusual to compare the dependencies' type labels d_{dep} and p_{dep} with a similarity function designed for words, we observed experimentally that this approach yield better overall performance in the relatedness task in comparison with a simple crisp comparison. The optimal values for the parameters $\gamma = -3$, $\delta = 10$ and $\lambda = 3$ were determined with the same methodology used in subsection 3.1.1 for determining α, β and $bias$. Clearly, the fact that $\delta > \lambda$ means that the first words in the dependency tuples plays a more important role than the second ones for the task at hand. However, the fact that $\gamma < 0$ is counter intuitive because it means that the lower the similarity between the dependency type labels is, the larger the similarity between the two dependencies. Up to date we have been unable to find a plausible explanation for this phenomenon. This set of 17 features will be referred hereinafter as **DEP**.

3.1.5 Additional Features

In addition to the feature sets based in soft cardinality, we designed some features aimed to address linguistic phenomena such as antonymy, hypernymy and negation.

Antonymy: Consider the following text pair from the test data {"*A man is emptying a container made of plastic*","*A man is filling a container made of plastic*" }, which is labeled as a *contradiction* with a relatedness score of 3.91. Clearly, these labels are explained by the antonymy relation between "*emptying*" and "*filling*". Given that none of the features presented above address this issue, a list of 11,028 pairs of antonym words was gathered from several web sites (see Table 4) and from the antonymy relationships in WordNet, in order to detect these cases. That list was used to count the number of occurrences of pairs antonym words between pairs of texts and in each one of the texts. Thus, for any pair of texts A and B (represented as sets of words), three features (referred henceforth as **ANT**) were extracted:

antonym_AB Counts the number of occurrences of pairs of antonyms in $A \times B$ (Cartesian product) or in $B \times A$.

antonym_AA Counts the number of occurrences of pairs of antonyms in $A \times A$.

antonym_BB Counts the number of occurrences of pairs of antonyms in $B \times B$.

Hypernymy: Consider the following text pair from the test data {"*A man is sitting comfortably at a table*","*A person is sitting comfortably at the table*" }, which is labeled as an *entailment* with a relatedness score of 3.96. In this case, the entailment is based on the hypernymy between "*person*" and "*man*". In order to capture this linguistic factor 3 features similar to the previously described antonym features were proposed. First, word sense disambiguation was performed (as described in subsection 3.1.2) for obtaining a synset label for each word. Secondly, we build a binary function $hyp(ss_1, ss_2)$ that takes two WordNet synsets as arguments and returns 1 if ss_1 is a hypernym of ss_2 with a maximum depth in the WordNet's is-a hierarchy of 6 steps, and 0 otherwise. This hypernymy function was build using the WordNet interface provided by the NLTK. Next, based on that synset-to-synset function, a text-to-text function that captures the degree or hypernymy in a text or in a pair of texts was build using the Monge-Elkan measure (Monge and Elkan, 1996). Thus, for two texts A and B represented as sets of synset labels, the following expression measures their degree of hypernymy:

$$HYP(A,B) = \frac{1}{|A|}\sum_{i=1}^{|A|}\max_{j=1}^{|B|} hyp(a_i, b_j)$$

Using the function $HYP(*,*)$, 3 features are extracted from each pair of text (referred henceforth as **HYP**):

hypernym_AB from $HYP(A, B)$

http://www.myenglishpages.com/site_php_files/vocabulary-lesson-opposites-adjectives.php
http://www.allaboutspace.com/wordlist/opposites.shtml
http://www.michigan-proficiency-exams.com/antonym-list.html
http://examples.yourdictionary.com/examples-of-antonyms.html
http://www.synonyms-antonyms.com/antonyms.html
http://englishwilleasy.com/word-must-know/vocabulary/vocabulary-list-by-opposites-or-antonyms/
http://www.meridianschools.org/staff/districtcurriculum/moreresources/languagearts/all grades/antonyms.doc
http://mrsbrower.weebly.com/uploads/1/3/2/4/13243672/antonymlist.pdf
https://foxhugh.wordpress.com/word-lists/list-of-antonyms/
http://www.paulnoll.com/Books/Clear-English/English-antonyms-1.html
http://wordnet.princeton.edu/wordnet/download/

Table 4: URLs used for the list of 11,028 antonym pairs (accessed on March 20, 2014).

hypernym_AA from $HYP(A, A)$

hypernym_BB from $HYP(B, B)$

Negation: Negations play an important role in the task at hand. For instance, consider this pair of texts {"*A person is rinsing a steak with water*","*A man is not rinsing a large steak*"} labeled as a *contradiction*. In that example the negation of the verb "*rising*" is the main factor of contradiction. In order to capture this linguistic feature we build a simple function that detects the occurrence of a verb negation if the text contains one of the following words: "*not*", "*n't*", "*nor*", "*null*", "*neither*", "*either*", "*barely*", "*scarcely*" and "*hardly*". Similarly, noun negation is detected looking for the words: "*no*", "*none*", "*nobody*", "*nowhere*", "*nothing*" and "*never*". Thus, for two texts A and B, 4 features are extracted (referred henceforth as **NEG**):

verb_neg_A if verb negation is detected in A

verb_neg_B if verb negation is detected in B

noun_neg_A if noun negation is detected in A

noun_neg_B if noun negation is detected in B

3.1.6 Submitted Runs and Results

RUN1 (PRIMARY) This system produced predictions by extracting all the features described previously (**SM**, **ESA**, **POS**, **DEP**, **ANT**, **HYP** and **NEG**) from all the texts in the SICK data set. Next, two machine learning models were obtained (WEKA (Hall et al., 2009) was used for that) using the training part of SICK, one for regression (relatedness) and another for classification (entailment). The regression model was a *reduced-error pruning tree* (*REPtree*) (Quinlan, 1987) boosted with 20 iterations of *bagging (Breiman, 1996)*. The classification model was a *J48Graft* tree also boosted with 20 bagging iterations. These two models produced the predictions for the test part of SICK.

RUN2 This system is similar to the one used in RUN1, but it used only the feature sets **SM** and **NEG**. Another difference is that a linear regression was used instead of the *REPtree* and no *bagging* was performed.

RUN3 The same as RUN1, but again, linear regression was used instead of the *REPtree* and no *bagging* was performed.

RUN4 The same as RUN2, but the models were boosted with 20 iterations of *bagging*.

RUN5 The same as RUN3, but 30 iterations of bagging were used instead of 20.

The official results obtained by these systems (prefixed UNAL-NLP) are shown in Table 5 jointly with those obtained by other 3 top systems among the 18 participating systems. Our primary run (RUN1) obtained pretty competitive results ranking 3th and 4th in the entailment and relatedness tasks. The RUN4 obtained a remarkable performance (it would be ranked 6th for entailment and 8th for relatedness) in spite of the fact that is a system purely based on string matching. The comparison of our runs 1, 3 and 5, which mainly differs by the use of *bagging*, shows that this boosting method provides considerable improvements. In fact, comparing RUN3 (all features, no bagging) and RUN4 (SM and NEG feature sets boosted with bagging), they performed similarly in spite of the considerable larger number of features used in RUN3. Besides, the RUN5 slightly outperformed our primary run (RUN1) us-

	Entailment		Relatedness			
system	accuracy	official rank	Pearson	Spearman	MSE	official rank
UNAL-NLP_run1 (primary)	83.05%	3rd/18	0.8043	0.7458	0.3593	4th/17
UNAL-NLP_run2	79.81%	-	0.7482	0.7033	0.4487	-
UNAL-NLP_run3	80.15%	-	0.7747	0.7286	0.4081	-
UNAL-NLP_run4	80.21%	-	0.7662	0.7142	0.4210	-
UNAL-NLP_run5	83.24%	-	0.8070	0.7489	0.3550	-
ECNU_run1	83.64%	2nd/18	**0.8280**	**0.7689**	0.3250	1st/17
Stanford_run5	74.49%	12th/18	0.8272	0.7559	**0.3230**	2nd/17
Illinois-LH_run1	**84.58%**	1st/18	0.7993	0.7538	0.3692	5th/17

Table 5: Results for task 1.

ing 10 additional iterations of bagging.

3.1.7 Error Analysis

Our primary run for the task 1 failed in 835 pairs of sentences out of 4,927 in the entailment subtask. We wanted to understand in why our system failed in these 835 instances, so we classified manually these instances in 4 error categories (each instance could be assigned to several categories).

Paraphrase not detected (NP): example={"*Two groups of people are playing football*", "*Two teams are competing in a football match*"}, gold standard=*entailment*, prediction=*neutral*, number of occurrences= 420 (50.3%). The system failed to detect the paraphrase between "*groups of people*" and "*teams*".

Negation not detected (NN) : example={"*There is no one playing the guitar*", "*Someone is playing the guitar*"}, gold standard=*contradiction*, prediction=*neutral*, number of occurrences=94 (11.3%). The system failed to detect that the contradiction is due to the negation in the first text.

False similarity between words (NSS) : example={"*Two dogs are playing by a tree*", "*Two dogs are sleeping by a tree*"}, gold standard=*neutral*, prediction=*entailment*, number of occurrences=413 (49.5%). The only difference between these 2 sentences is the gerund "*playing*" vs. "*sleeping*", which the system erroneously considered as similar.

Antonym not detected (NA): example={"*Three children are running down hill*", "*Three children are running up hill*"}, gold standard=*contradiction*, prediction=*entailment*, number of occurrences=40 (4.8%). The only difference between these 2 sentences is the words "*down*" vs. "*up*". In spite that this pair of antonyms was included in the antonym list, the system failed to distinguish the contradiction between the texts.

Error category	NP	NN	NSS	NA
NP	420	5	125	0
NN	-	94	1	0
NSS	-	-	413	22
NA	-	-	-	40

Table 6: Co-ocurrences of types of errors in RUN1 (task1).

The matrix in Table 6 reports the number of co-occurrences of error categories in the 835 instances erroneously classified.

3.2 Task 3: Cross-level Semantic Similarity

The SemEval 2014 task 3 (cross-level semantic similarity) (Jurgens et al., 2014) proposed the semantic textual similarity task but across different textual levels, namely *paragraph-to-sentence*, *sentence-to-phrase*, *phrase-to-word* and *word-to-sense*. As usual, the goal is to predict the gold similarity scores for each pair of texts. For each one of these cross-level comparison types there were proposed a separated training and test data sets. Basically, we addressed this task using the set of features SM presented in subsection 3.1.1 in combination with a text expansion approach similar to the method presented in subsection 3.1.2.

3.2.1 Paragraph-to-sentence and Sentence-to-phrase

For these two cross-level comparison types we extracted the SM feature set using the provided texts. The model parameters obtained for paragraph-to-sentence were $\alpha = 0.1$, $\beta = 1.75$, $bias = -1.35$, $p = 1.55$; and for sentence-to-phrase were $\alpha = 0.68$, $\beta = 0.92$, $bias = -0.92$, $p = 2.49$.

The system for the RUN2 used the **SM** feature set and a machine learning model build with the provided training data for generating the similarity score predictions for the test data. For the paragraph-to-sentence data set the model was a *REPtree* for regression boosted with 40 *bagging* iterations. Similarly, the model for the sentence-to-phrase data set was a linear regressor also boosted with 40 *bagging* iterations.

Unlike RUN2, RUN1 does not make use of any machine learning algorithm. Instead, we used the only the basic cardinalities (see Table 1) from the **SM** feature set in combination with an ad-hoc resemblance coefficient, i.e. the Dice's coefficient $2|A \cap B|/|A|+|B|$ for the paragraph-to-sentence data set. In turn, for sentence-to-phrase the overlap coefficient, i.e. $|A \cap B|/\min[|A|,|B|]$, was used.

3.2.2 Phrase-to-word and Word-to-sense

Before applying the same procedure used in the previous subsection, the texts in the phrase-to-word and word-to-sense data sets were expanded with a similar approach to that was used in subsection 3.1.2.

Phrase-to-word expansion: First, the "word" was expanded finding its corresponding WordNet synset using the adapted Lesk's algorithm providing as context the "phrase". Then, once the word's synset is obtained, the "word" text is extended with the textual definition of the synset. Similarity, this procedure is repeated for each word in the "phase" obtaining and extended version of the phrase. Finally, these two texts are used for extracting the **SM** feature set. The model parameters were $\alpha = 0.8$, $\beta = 1.9$, $bias = -0.8$, $p = 1.5$.

Word-to-sense expansion: First, the "sense" (i.e. synset) is replaced by its textual definition and its lemma. At this point the pair word-sense becomes a pair word-sentence. Then, the synset of the "word" is obtained performing the adapted Lesk's algorithm. Next, the "word" is extended with textual definition of the synset. Finally, these two texts are used for extracting the **SM** feature set obtaining the following model parameters were $\alpha = 0.59$, $\beta = 0.9$, $bias = -0.89$, $p = 3.91$.

3.2.3 Results

The official results obtained by the two submitted runs jointly with other 3 top systems are shown in Table 7. Our submissions (prefixed with UNAL-NLP) ranked 3rd and 5th among 38 participating systems, showing that the **SM** (string-matching) feature set is effective for the prediction of similarity scores. Particularly, in the paragraph-to-sentence data set, which has the longest text, RUN2 obtained the best official score. In contrast, the scores obtained for the phrase-to-word and word-to-sense data sets were considerably lower in comparison with the top system, but still competitive against most of the other participating systems.

test data	train data
OnWN (en)	OnWN 2012/2013 test
headlines (en)	headlines 2013 test
images (en)	MSRvid 2012 train and test
deft-news (en)	MSRpar 2013 train and test
deft-forum (en)	MSRvid 2012 train and test OnWN 2012/2013 test
tweet-news (en)	SMTeuroparl 2012 test SMTnews 2012 test
Wikipedia (es)	SMTeuroparl 2012 train
news (es)	SMTeuroparl 2012 train

Table 8: Training data used for the STS-2014 data sets (task 10).

3.3 Task 10: Multilingual Semantic Similarity

The SemEval-2014 task 10 (multilingual semantic similarity) (Agirre et al., 2014) is the sequel of the semantic textual similarity (STS) evaluations at SemEval in the past two years (Agirre et al., 2012; Agirre et al., 2013). This year 6 test data sets were proposed in English and 2 data sets in Spanish. Similarly to the 2013 campaign, there is not explicit training data for each data set. Consequently, different data sets from the previous STS evaluations were selected to be used as training data for the new data sets. The selection criterion was the average character length and type of the texts. The Table 8 shows the training data used for each test data set.

3.3.1 English Subtask

The RUN1 for the English data sets was produced with a parameterized similarity function based on the **SM** feature set and the symmetrized Tversky's index (Tversky, 1977; Jimenez et al., 2013a). For a detailed description of this function and its parameters, please refer to the $\mathbf{STS}_{\mathrm{sim}}$ feature in the system description paper of the NTNU team (Lynum et al., 2014). The parameters used in that

System	Para-2-Sent	Sent-2-Phr	Phr-2-Word	Word-2-Sense	Official Rank
SimCompass_run1	0.811	0.742	**0.415**	**0.356**	1st/38
ECNU_run1	0.834	**0.771**	0.315	0.269	2nd/38
UNAL-NLP_run2	**0.837**	0.738	0.274	0.256	3rd/38
SemantiKLUE_run1	0.817	0.754	0.215	0.314	4th/38
UNAL-NLP_run1	0.817	0.739	0.252	0.249	5th/38

Table 7: Official results for task 3 (Pearson's correlation).

Data	α	β	$bias$	p	α'	β'	$bias'$
OnWN	0.53	-0.53	1.01	1.00	-4.89	0.52	0.46
headlines	0.36	-0.29	4.17	0.85	-4.50	0.43	0.19
images	1.12	-1.11	0.93	0.64	-0.98	0.50	0.11
deft-news	3.36	-0.64	1.37	0.44	2.36	0.72	0.02
deft-forum	1.01	-1.01	0.24	0.93	-2.71	0.42	1.63
tweet-news	0.13	0.14	2.80	0.01	2.66	1.74	0.45

Table 9: Optimal parameters used for task 10 in English.

function are reported in Table 9. Unlike subsection 3.1.1 where the Dice's coefficient was used as the text similarity function, here the symmetrical Tversky's index (eq. 2) was reused generating the three additional parameters marked with apostrophe (α', β' and $bias'$).

For the RUN2 the **SM** feature set was extracted from all the data sets in English (en) listed in Table 8. Then, a *REPtree* (Quinlan, 1987) boosted with 50 *bagging* iterations (Breiman, 1996) was trained using the training data sets selected for each test data set. Finally, these machine learning models produced the similarity score predictions for each test data set.

The RUN3 was identical to the RUN2 but included additional feature sets apart from **SM**, namely: **ESA**, **POS** and **WN**. The **WN** feature set is the same as **SM**, but replacing the word-to-word similarity function in eq. 2 by the *path* measure from the WordNet::Similarity package (Pedersen et al., 2004).

3.3.2 Spanish Subtask

The Spanish system was based entirely in the **SM** feature set with some small changes for adapting the system to Spanish. Basically, the list of English stop-words was replaced by the Spanish stop-words provided by the NLTK. In addition, the Porter stemmer was replaced by its Spanish equivalent, i.e. the Snowball stemmer for Spanish. The RUN1 is equivalent to the RUN1 for the English subtask described in the previous subsection. The parameters used for the text similarity function were $\alpha = 1.16$, $\beta = 1.08$, $bias = 0.02$, $p = 1.02$, $\alpha' = 1.54$, $\beta' = 0.08$ and $bias' = 1.37$. The description and meaning of these parameters can be found in (Lynum et al., 2014) associated to the $\mathbf{STS_{sim}}$ feature.

data set	run1	run2	run3
deft-forum	0.5043	0.3826	0.4607
deft-news	0.7205	0.7305	0.7216
headlines	0.7616	0.7645	0.7605
images	0.8071	0.7706	0.7782
OnWN	0.7823	0.8268	0.8426
tweet-news	0.6145	0.4028	0.6583
mean (en)	0.7113	0.6573	0.7209
official rank (en)	12th/38	22th/38	9th/38
Wikipedia	**0.7804**	0.7566	0.6894
news	0.8154	0.7829	0.7965
mean (es)	0.8013	0.7723	0.7533
official rank (es)	3rd/22	9th/22	12th/22

Table 10: Official results for the task 10 (Pearson's correlation).

The RUN2 was obtained using the **SM** feature set and a linear regressor for generating the similarity score predictions. Similarity, RUN3 used the same feature set SM in combination with a *REPtree* boosted with 30 *bagging* iterations.

3.3.3 Results

The results for the 3 submitted runs corresponding to the 2 sub tasks (English and Spanish) are shown in Table 10. It is important to note that the RUN1 for the Wikipedia data set in Spanish was the top system among 22 participating systems. This result is remarkable given that this system was trained with a data set in English showing the domain adaptation ability of the soft cardinality approach.

4 Conclusions

We participated in the SemEval-2014 task 1, 3 and 10 with an uniform approach based on soft cardinality features, obtaining pretty satisfactory results in all data sets, tasks and sub tasks. This approach has been used since SemEval-2012 in all versions of the following tasks: semantic textual similarity (Jimenez et al., 2012b; Jimenez et al., 2013a), typed similarity (Croce et al., 2013), cross-lingual textual entailment (Jimenez et al., 2012a; Jimenez et al., 2013c), student response analysis (Jimenez et al., 2013b), and multilingual semantic textual similarity (Lynum et al., 2014). In the majority of the cases, the systems based on soft cardinality, built by us and other teams, have been among the top systems. Given the uniformity of the approach, the consistency of the results, the few computational resources required and the overall conceptual simplicity, the soft cardinality is established as a useful tool for a wide spectrum of applications in natural language processing.

References

Eneko Agirre, Daniel Cer, Mona Diab, and Gonzalez-Agirre Aitor. 2012. SemEval-2012 task 6: A pilot on semantic textual similarity. In *Proceedings of the 6th International Workshop on Semantic Evaluation (SemEval@*SEM 2012)*, Montreal,Canada.

Eneko Agirre, Daniel Cer, Mona Diab, Aitor Gonzalez-Agirre, and Weiwei Guo. 2013. *SEM 2013 shared task: Semantic textual similarity, including a pilot on typed-similarity. Atlanta, Georgia, USA.

Eneko Agirre, Carmen Banea, Claire Cardie, Daniel Cer, Mona Diab, Aitor Gonzalez-Agirre, Weiwei Guo, Rada Mihalcea, German Rigau, and Janyce Weibe. 2014. SemEval-2014 task 10: Multilingual semantic textual similarity. In *Proceedings of the 8th International Workshop on Semantic Evaluation (SemEval-2014)*, Dublin, Ireland, August.

Satanjeev Banerjee and Ted Pedersen. 2002. An adapted lesk algorithm for word sense disambiguation using WordNet. In *Computational linguistics and intelligent text processing*, page 136–145. Springer.

Leo Breiman. 1996. Bagging predictors. *Machine Learning*, 24(2):123–140.

Courtney Corley and Rada Mihalcea. 2005. Measuring the semantic similarity of texts. In *Proceedings of the ACL Workshop on Empirical Modeling of Semantic Equivalence and Entailment*, EMSEE '05, page 13–18, Stroudsburg, PA, USA.

Danilo Croce, Valerio Storch, P. Annesi, and Roberto Basili. 2012. Distributional compositional semantics and text similarity. In *2012 IEEE Sixth International Conference on Semantic Computing (ICSC)*, pages 242–249, September.

Danilo Croce, Valerio Storch, and Roberto Basili. 2013. UNITOR-CORE TYPED: Combining text similarity and semantic filters through SV regression. In *Second Joint Conference on Lexical and Computational Semantics (*SEM), Volume 1: Proceedings of the Main Conference and the Shared Task: SemanticTextual Similarity*, page 59, Atlanta, Georgia, USA.

Marie-Catherine De Marneffe, Bill MacCartney, and Christopher D. Manning. 2006. Generating typed dependency parses from phrase structure parses. In *Proceedings of LREC*, volume 6, page 449–454, Genoa, Italy, May.

Evgeniy Gabrilovich and Shaul Markovitch. 2007. Computing semantic relatedness using wikipedia-based explicit semantic analysis. In *Proceedings of the 20th International Joint Conference on Artifical Intelligence*, IJCAI'07, page 1606–1611, San Francisco, CA, USA. Morgan Kaufmann Publishers Inc.

Mark Hall, Frank Eibe, Geoffrey Holmes, and Bernhard Pfahringer. 2009. The WEKA data mining software: An update. *SIGKDD Explorations*, 11(1):10–18.

Paul Jaccard. 1901. Etude comparative de la distribution florare dans une portion des alpes et des jura. *Bulletin de la Société Vaudoise des Sciences Naturelles*, pages 547–579.

Sergio Jimenez, Fabio Gonzalez, and Alexander Gelbukh. 2010. Text comparison using soft cardinality. In Edgar Chavez and Stefano Lonardi, editors, *String Processing and Information Retrieval*, volume 6393 of *LNCS*, pages 297–302. Springer, Berlin, Heidelberg.

Sergio Jimenez, Claudia Becerra, and Alexander Gelbukh. 2012a. Soft cardinality: A parameterized similarity function for text comparison. In *SemEval 2012*, Montreal, Canada.

Sergio Jimenez, Claudia Becerra, and Alexander Gelbukh. 2012b. Soft cardinality+ ML: Learning adaptive similarity functions for cross-lingual textual entailment. In *SemEval 2012*, Montreal, Canada.

Sergio Jimenez, Claudia Becerra, and Alexander Gelbukh. 2013a. SOFTCARDINALITY-CORE: Improving text overlap with distributional measures for semantic textual similarity. In **SEM 2013*, Atlanta, Georgia, USA, June.

Sergio Jimenez, Claudia Becerra, and Alexander Gelbukh. 2013b. SOFTCARDINALITY: Hierarchical text overlap for student response analysis. In *SemEval 2013*, Atlanta, Georgia, USA, June.

Sergio Jimenez, Claudia Becerra, and Alexander Gelbukh. 2013c. SOFTCARDINALITY: Learning to identify directional cross-lingual entailment from cardinalities and SMT. In *SemEval 2013*, Atlanta, Georgia, USA, June.

Karen Spärck Jones. 2004. A statistical interpretation of term specificity and its application in retrieval. *Journal of Documentation*, 60(5):493–502, October.

David Jurgens, Mohammad T. Pilehvar, and Roberto Navigli. 2014. SemEval-2014 task 3: Cross-level semantic similarity. In *Proceedings of the 8th International Workshop on Semantic Evaluation (SemEval-2014)*, Dublin, Ireland, August.

André Lynum, Partha Pakray, Björn Gambäck, and Sergio Jimenez. 2014. NTNU: Measuring semantic similarity with sublexical feature representations and soft cardinalty. In *Proceedings of the 8th International Workshop on Semantic Evaluation (SemEval-2014)*, Dublin, Ireland, August.

Marco Marelli, Stefano Menini, Marco Baroni, Lucia Bentivogli, Raffaella Bernardi, and Roberto Zamparelli. 2014. A SICK cure for the evaluation of compositional distributional semantic models. In *Proceedings of LREC*, Reykjavik, Iceland, May.

Alvaro E. Monge and Charles Elkan. 1996. The field matching problem: Algorithms and applications. In *Proceeding of the 2nd International Conference on Knowledge Discovery and Data Mining (KDD-96)*, pages 267–270, Portland, OR.

Ted Pedersen, Siddharth Patwardhan, and Jason Michelizzi. 2004. WordNet::similarity: measuring the relatedness of concepts. In *Proceedings HLT-NAACL–Demonstration Papers*, Stroudsburg, PA, USA.

Martin Porter. 1980. An algorithm for suffix stripping. *Program*, 3(14):130–137, October.

J. Ross Quinlan. 1987. Simplifying decision trees. *International journal of man-machine studies*, 27(3):221–234.

Amos Tversky. 1977. Features of similarity. *Psychological Review*, 84(4):327–352, July.

UNAL-NLP: Cross-Lingual Phrase Sense Disambiguation with Syntactic Dependency Trees

Emilio Silva-Schlenker
Departamento de Lingüística
Universidad Nacional de Colombia
Departamento de Ingeniería de Sistemas
Universidad de los Andes,
Bogotá D.C., Colombia
esilvas@unal.edu.co

Sergio Jimenez and Julia Baquero
Universidad Nacional de Colombia,
Bogotá D.C., Colombia
sgjimenezv@unal.edu.co
jmbauqerov@unal.edu.co

Abstract

In this paper we describe our participation in the SemEval 2014, Task 5, consisting of the construction of a *translation assistance system* that translates L1 fragments, written in L2 context, to their correct L2 translation. Our approach consists of a bilingual parallel corpus, a system of syntactic features extraction and a statistical memory-based classification algorithm. Our system ranked 4th and 6th among the 10 participating systems that used the English-Spanish data set.

1 Introduction

An L2 writing assistant is a tool intended for language learners who need to improve their writing skills. This tool lets them write a text in L2, but fall back to their native L1 whenever they are not sure about a certain word or expression. In these cases, the assistant automatically translates this text for them (van Gompel et al., 2014).

Although at first glance this may be seen as a classification problem, it might be better fulfilled by a cross-lingual word sense disambiguation (WSD) approach, which takes context into account by means of contextual features used in a machine learning setting. The main differences between this and previous approaches to cross-lingual WSD are the bilingual nature of the input sentences (see section 2.3) and the annotation of target phrases, rather than single words.

The remainder of this article is organized as follows. Section 2 describes the proposed method. A description of the system we submitted, the obtained results and an error analysis are discussed in section 3. In section 4 we present a brief discussion about the results. Finally, in section 5 we make some concluding remarks.

2 Method Description

The core of the proposed system uses techniques from memory-based classification to find the most appropriate translation of a target phrase in a given context. It receives an input as in (1) and yields an output as in (2).

(1) No creo que ella *is coming*.
(2) No creo que ella *venga*.

It does so on the basis of a syntactic selection of context features, a large bilingual parallel corpus and a classifier built using the Tilburg Memory-Based Learner, TiMBL (Daelemans et al., 2010).

The proposed system consists of several stages. First, a large bilingual corpus is aligned at word and phrase level. Next, an index is built by each phrase in the L1 side of the corpus to retrieve efficiently the occurrences of a particular L1 phrase in the aligned corpus along with their translations and contexts in L2 (subsection 2.1). Second, the relevant contexts for each L1 phrase in the test set (example sentences) are retrieved from the corpus and a set of syntactic features are extracted from each sentence (subsection 2.2). Third, a special two-stage process is used to extract the same features from the sentences in the test set to deal with the fact that these sentences were written in two languages (subsection 2.3). Finally, each target phrase is translated using the IBL algorithm and the translations were incorporated in the original test sentences (subsection 2.4).

Proceedings of the 8th International Workshop on Semantic Evaluation (SemEval 2014), pages 743–747,
Dublin, Ireland, August 23-24, 2014.

Input sentence	Parallel example sentences	
No creo que las necesidades afectivas de las personas estén necesariamente *linked* al matrimonio.	He said Boyd already *linked* him to Brendan.	Dijo que Boyd ya le había *relacionado* con Brendan.
	The three things are inextricably *linked*, and I have the formula right here.	Las tres cosas están estrechamente *vinculadas*, y tengo la fórmula aquí.

Table 1: An input sentence and 2 example sentences from Linguee.com.

2.1 Parallel Corpus Selection and Preparation

As no training corpus was given prior to developing this system, finding and processing the most suitable corpus for this task was paramount. As the purpose of this system is to help language students, the corpus needs to account for simple yet correct everyday speech.

In an initial stage of development we opted to use the 70-million sentences OpenSubtitles.org corpus compiled by the Opus Project (Tiedemann, 2012), which includes many informal everyday utterances, at the expense of a less accurate translation quality[1]. Although the use of this training corpus yielded over 95% of recall on the trial corpus given by the task organizers, only 80% of the trial sentences had enough (>100) training examples in order to produce a quality translation. To solve this issue, an ad-hoc corpus compilation mechanism was created by using the Linguee.com. Thus, a set of parallel example sentences is retrieved from Linguee.com by querying all the L1 target phrases from the evaluation data (see an example in Table 1).

The corpus preparation procedure consisted of several steps. The first step was to clean the corpus with the Moses cleaning script (Koehn et al., 2007). Next, the corpus was tokenized and PoS-tagged using FreeLing (Padró and Stanilovsky, 2012) (HMM tagger was used). After that, the corpus was word-aligned using Giza++ (Och and Ney, 2003) over Moses (Koehn et al., 2007). The resulting alignment was then combined with the tagged version of the corpus. Finally, a phrase index was built using a SMT phrase extraction algorithm (Ling et al., 2010) including for each phrase pointers to all its occurrences in the corpus for further retrieval.

[1]The EPPS corpus (Lambert et al., 2005) was very useful as a training corpus in the developing stages of this system. It was however not used in the final system training.

2.2 Syntactic Feature Extraction

The syntactic tags feature is a novel feature we are introducing for the CLWSD problem (Lefever and Hoste, 2013). They are linearizations of syntactic dependency trees. These trees were built by Freeling's Txala Parser (Lloberes et al., 2010) and were introduced as individual tags in a sentence analysis by parsing the tree and mapping its leaves with their corresponding order in the source sentence. Then, each leaf's label and parent number was extracted. For the root, the special parent tag 'S' was used.

The WSD literature commonly distinguishes between local and global context features (Martinez and Agirre, 2001). The former are extracted from the neighboring words and the latter are extracted from words of the whole context provided using some heuristic to select relevant. Unlike global features, the relevance of the surrounding words is not put into question or are weighted by the degree of relevance according to their position in the sentence and lexicographic distance from the target phrase (van Gompel, 2010). There is a linguistic explanation as to why surrounding words play a significant role in determining the target's translation. Often, these words have a direct dependency relation with the target. Indeed, physical closeness is an approximation of syntactic relatedness. What we propose in this paper is that the relevance of the context words for determining a correct translation is proportional to their syntactic relatedness to the target, rather than their physical closeness in the sentence. Unlike Martinez et al. (2002), what we propose here is to use syntax as a feature selector, rather than as a feature itself.

Instead of defining a local and a global set of relevant words, we selected a single set of relevant words according to their syntactic relation to the target phrase. This set consisted of all the children of the target words, and the parents of the main target words. The main target words are the subset

	0	1	2	3	4	5	6
Forms	Las	tres	cosas	están	estrechamente	vinculadas	.
Lemmas	el	3	cosa	estar	estrechamente	vincular	.
PoS Tags	DA0FP0	Z	NCFP000	VAIP3P0	RG	VMP00PF	Fp
Syn Tags	espec:1	espec:2	subj:3	co-v:7	espec:5	att:3	?:7

Table 2: Tagging of the sentence *"Las tres cosas están estrechamente vinculadas."*

of words with the highest number of (nested) children within the target phrase. Table 3 features the rules used for selecting the relevant words.

This Feature Extraction method uses the dependency labels as a means of selecting only relevant examples. Take for instance the example sentences in Table 1. Given that the target word is an attribute, the subject is included as a relevant feature, as per the last rule in Table 3. Any example sentence in which there is no subject as the sibling of the target word (as is the case for the first example sentence in Table 1) will have an empty feature, which increases its likelihood of not being included in the training set of this sentence.

2.3 Test Data Pre-processing

The test data for this task is composed of bilingual input sentences, making it impossible to obtain a correct tagging or parsing. To overcome this issue, a two-stage process wherein the first stage obtains translations for the L1 portions was performed. These plausible translations are obtained by TiMBL using as features the neighboring words of the target phrases. Once the sentences are in a single language (L2) they are tagged and parsed syntactically. Finally, the second stage consists in applying the same feature selection algorithm proposed in subsection 2.2.

2.4 Translation Selection

The processing of each sentence consists of several steps. In the first step, the L1 target phrase is searched for in the phrase index Given an L1 phrase, a binary search algorithm iterates through the phrase index and returns an array of pointers[2] to the corpus. Then, a multi-threaded subroutine reads the word-aligned bilingual corpus and extracts all the referenced sentences. Thus, for each input sentence, a set of example bilingual word-aligned sentences is extracted from the corpus. Relevant features are extracted according to a syntactic analysis as explained in subsection 2.2, and written to text files in the C4.5 format. The features extracted from the example sentences, as well as the L2 translations of the target phrases in each sentence, are used as the training set for TiMBL, while the features extracted from the input sentence are used as its (singleton) test set.

The L2 translations of each target phrase in the example sentences are used as the classes for the training set, in order to turn a bilingual disambiguation problem into a machine learning classification problem. TiMBL learns how to classify the training feature vectors into their corresponding classes and then predicts the class for the test set feature vector, i.e. its most likely translation using an IBL algorithm (Aha et al., 1991), which is a variation of the k-nearest neighbor classifier.

3 System Submissions

We submitted three result sets for the English-Spanish language pair. Two of them were submitted for the 'Best' evaluation type, and the other one was submitted for the 'out-of-five' evaluation type. The difference between these two evaluation types is that out-of-five evaluation expects up to five different translations for every target phrase, while 'best' only accepts one. The evaluation metrics include accuracy and recall, and also a word-based special type of accuracy, which takes into account partially correct translations.

Of the two runs submitted in the 'Best' evaluation type, **Run1-best** (see table 4) used our proposed syntactic feature extraction method, while **Run2-best** used a regular 2-word window around the target phrase. For the **Run1-oof** we combined the two methods mentioned above with different values of k.

3.1 Results

The test data consisted in 500 sentences written in Spanish, with target English phrases. The official results obtained by our runs are shown in Table 4.

Our control run, **Run2-best**, yielded slightly

[2] Given that line breaks are just regular characters, what is actually referenced in the phrase index are byte offsets.

Case	Rule	Example
One of the *target words* is a subject.	Include any **sibling** which is an auxiliary or modal verb.	*Our cat* **quiere** comerse la ensalada.
The parent of one of the main *target words* is a coordinative conjunction.	Include its closest **sibling**.	No quería ni *eat*, ni **dormir**.
The parent of one of the main *target words* is a relative pronoun.	Include its **grandparent**.	No **creo** que ella *is coming*.
One of the *target words* is an attribute.	Include any **sibling** which is subject.	Mis **tías** están *very tired*.

Table 3: Relevant word selection rules.

better results than our experimental run, **Run1-best**. This means that our method of syntactic features extraction did not improve translation quality.

3.2 Error Analysis

By analyzing our results, we detected three groups of recurrent errors. The first group of errors is related to verb morphology, in which a single English verbal form corresponds to many Spanish verbal forms. In these cases, our system often outputs an infinitive form or a past participle instead of a finite verb.

The second group of errors we detected comprises incomplete translations. In these cases, a single word in English has a multiword Spanish translation, but our system often outputs a single-word translation.

The third group of errors are related to English words with multiple possible parts of speech, as 'flood', which can be a noun but also a verb. Our system tends to output nouns instead of verbs and vice versa.

4 Discussion

There are two main reasons as to why the syntactic feature extraction method did not work. The first reason is related to the nature of the task; the second is related to the scope of the method.

The fact that this task involved analyzing sentences partly written in two languages made syntactic analysis extremely difficult as dependencies span all over the bilingual sentence. The best solution we found for this was to divide the operation of the system in two stages, where the first one did not involve syntactic dependencies and provided a working translation, and the second one used this first translation to perform a syntactic analysis and then rerun the classification step. This, however, favored error propagation. Although translation quality did improve between the two stages, there were many cases in which a bad initial translation involved a bad syntactic analysis, which in turn resulted in a bad final translation.

A more sophisticated version of his method was initially developed for the English-Spanish language pair and involved several language-specific rules. However, we decided to make this method language-independent, so we simplified it to its actual version. This simplified version uses syntactic dependencies as feature selectors, but the features themselves are regular lemma/PoS combinations, which is not always the best feature choice.

5 Conclusion

Syntactic dependency relations are an important means of analyzing the internal structure of a sentence and can successfully be used to improve the feature selection process in WSD. However, syntactic parsing is far away from optimal in Spanish, a fortiori if it involves sentences written in two languages. For this kind of task, perhaps a statistical language model of L2 would have yielded better results.

Acknowledgments

We would like to specially thank Professor Silvia Takahashi of Universidad de los Andes for her continued advice and support. We would also like to thank Pedro Rodríguez for his development of the Linguee crawler, María De-Arteaga, Alejandro Riveros and David Hoyos for their useful suggestions in the conception and development of this project, and the rest of the UNAL-NLP team for

Run	Recall	Accuracy	Word Accuracy	Rank (runs)	Rank (systems)
Run1-best	0.993	0.721	0.794	5	2
Run2-best	0.993	0.733	0.809	4	2
Run1-oof	0.993	0.823	0.880	6	3

Table 4: Official results.

their interest and encouragement. Many thanks to Jay C. Soper for proof-reading this article.

References

David W. Aha, Dennis Kibler, and Marc K. Albert. 1991. Instance-based learning algorithms. *Machine Learning*, 6:37–66.

Walter Daelemans, Jakub Zavrel, Ko Van der Sloot, and Antal Van den Bosch. 2010. Timbl: Tilburg memory-based learner. reference guide. ILK Research Group, Tilburg University.

Philipp Koehn, Hieu Hoang, Alexandra Birch, Chris Callison-Burch, Marcello Federico, Nicola Bertoldi, Brooke Cowan, Wade Shen, Christine Moran, and Richard Zens. 2007. Moses: Open source toolkit for statistical machine translation. In *Proceedings of the 45th Annual Meeting of the ACL on Interactive Poster and Demonstration Sessions*, page 177–180.

Patrik Lambert, Adrià Gispert, Rafael Banchs, and José B. Mariño. 2005. Guidelines for word alignment evaluation and manual alignment. *Language Resources and Evaluation*, 39(4):267–285, December.

Els Lefever and Véronique Hoste. 2013. Semeval-2013 task 10: Cross-lingual word sense disambiguation. In *Second joint conference on lexical and computational semantics*, volume 2, page 158–166.

Wang Ling, Tiago Luís, João Graça, Luısa Coheur, and Isabel Trancoso. 2010. Towards a general and extensible phrase-extraction algorithm. In *IWSLT'10: International Workshop on Spoken Language Translation*, page 313–320.

Marina Lloberes, Irene Castellón, and Lluís Padró. 2010. Spanish FreeLing dependency grammar. In *LREC*, volume 10, page 693–699.

David Martinez and Eneko Agirre. 2001. Decision lists for english and basque. In *The Proceedings of the Second International Workshop on Evaluating Word Sense Disambiguation Systems*, page 115–118.

David Martínez, Eneko Agirre, and Lluís Màrquez. 2002. Syntactic features for high precision word sense disambiguation. In *Proceedings of the 19th international conference on Computational linguistics-Volume 1*, page 1–7.

Franz Josef Och and Hermann Ney. 2003. A systematic comparison of various statistical alignment models. *Computational linguistics*, 29(1):19–51.

Lluís Padró and Evgeny Stanilovsky. 2012. Freeling 3.0: Towards wider multilinguality. In *Proceedings of the Language Resources and Evaluation Conference*, pages 2473–2479, Istambul, Turkey, May.

Jörg Tiedemann. 2012. Parallel data, tools and interfaces in OPUS. In *Proceedings of the Language Resources and Evaluation Conference*, page 2214–2218, Istambul, Turkey, May.

Maarten van Gompel, Iris Hendrickx, Antal van den Bosh, Els Lefever, and Véronique Hoste. 2014. Semeval-2014 task 5: L2 writing assistant. In *Proceedings of the 8th International Workshop on Semantic Evaluation (SemEval-2014)*, Dublin, Ireland, August.

Maarten van Gompel. 2010. UvT-WSD1: a cross-lingual word sense disambiguation system. In *Proceedings of the 5th international workshop on semantic evaluation*, page 238–241, Uppsala, Sweden.

UNIBA: Combining Distributional Semantic Models and Word Sense Disambiguation for Textual Similarity

Pierpaolo Basile and **Annalina Caputo** and **Giovanni Semeraro**
Department of Computer Science
University of Bari Aldo Moro
Via, E. Orabona, 4 - 70125 Bari (Italy)
{firstname.surname}@uniba.it

Abstract

This paper describes the UNIBA team participation in the Cross-Level Semantic Similarity task at SemEval 2014. We propose to combine the output of different semantic similarity measures which exploit Word Sense Disambiguation and Distributional Semantic Models, among other lexical features. The integration of similarity measures is performed by means of two supervised methods based on Gaussian Process and Support Vector Machine. Our systems obtained very encouraging results, with the best one ranked 6th out of 38 submitted systems.

1 Introduction

Cross-Level Semantic Similarity (CLSS) is the task of computing the similarity between two text fragments of different sizes. The task focuses on the comparison between texts at different *lexical levels*, i.e. between a larger and a smaller text. The task comprises four different levels: 1) paragraph to sentence; 2) sentence to phrase; 3) phrase to word; 4) word to sense. The task objective is to provide a framework for evaluating general vs. level-specialized methods.

Our general approach consists in combining scores coming from different semantic similarity algorithms. The combination is performed by a supervised method using the training data provided by the task organizers. The data set comprises pairs of text fragments that can be rated with a score between 0 and 4, where 4 indicates the maximum level of similarity.

We select algorithms which provide similarities at different levels of semantics: surface (or string-based), lexical (word sense disambiguation), and distributional level. The idea is to combine in a unique system the semantic aspects that pertain text fragments.

The following section gives more details about the similarity measures and their combination in a unique score through supervised methods (Section 2). Section 3 describes the system set up for the evaluation and comments on the reported results, while Section 4 concludes the paper.

2 System Description

The idea behind our system is to combine the output of several similarity measures/features by means of a supervised algorithm. Those features were grouped in three main categories. The following three sub-sections describe in detail each feature exploited by the system.

2.1 Distributional Semantics Level

Distributional Semantic Models (DSM) are an easy way for building geometrical spaces of concepts, also known as *Semantic* (or *Word*) *Spaces*, by skimming through huge corpora of text in order to learn the context of word usage. In the resulting space, semantic relatedness/similarity between two words is expressed by the opposite of the distance between points that represent those words. Thus, the semantic similarity can be computed as the cosine of the angle between the two vectors that represent the words. This concept of similarity can be extended to whole sentences by combining words through vector addition (+), which corresponds to the point-wise sum of the vector components. Our DSM measure (**DSM**) is based on a *SemanticSpace*, represented by a co-occurrences matrix M, built by analysing the distribution of words in the British National Corpus (BNC). Then, M is reduced using the Latent Semantic Analysis (LSA) (Landauer and Dumais, 1997). Vector addition and cosine similarity are

Proceedings of the 8th International Workshop on Semantic Evaluation (SemEval 2014), pages 748–753,
Dublin, Ireland, August 23-24, 2014.

then used for building the vector representation of each text fragment and computing their pairwise similarity, respectively.

2.2 Lexical Semantics Level

Word Sense Disambiguation. Most of our measures rely on the output of a Word Sense Disambiguation (WSD) algorithm. Our newest approach to WSD, recently presented in Basile et al. (2014), is based on the simplified Lesk algorithm (Vasilescu et al., 2004). Each word w_i in a sequence $w_1 w_2 ... w_n$ is disambiguated individually by choosing the sense that maximizes the similarity between the gloss and the context of w_i (i.e. the whole text where w_i occurs). To boost the overlap between the context and the gloss, this last is expanded with glosses of related meanings, following the approach described in Banerjee and Pedersen (2002). As sense inventory we choose BabelNet 1.1, a huge multilingual semantic network which comprises both WordNet and Wikipedia (Navigli and Ponzetto, 2012). The algorithm consists of the following steps:

1. *Building the glosses.* We retrieve all possible word meanings for the target word w_i that are listed in BabelNet. BabelNet mixes senses in WordNet and Wikipedia. First, senses in WordNet are searched for; if no sense is found (as often happens with named entities), senses for the target word are sought in Wikipedia. We preferred that strategy rather than retrieving senses from both sources at once because this last approach produced worse results when tuning the system. Once the set of senses $S_i = \{s_{i1}, s_{i2}, ..., s_{ik}\}$ associated to the target word w_i has been retrieved, gloss expansion occurs. For each sense s_{ij} of w_i, the algorithm builds the sense extended gloss g^*_{ij} by appending the glosses of meanings related to s_{ij} to its original gloss g_{ij}. The related meanings, with the exception of "antonym" senses, are the output of the BabelNet function "getRelatedMap". Moreover, each word in g^*_{ij} is weighted by a function inversely proportional to the distance between s_{ij} and its related meaning. The distance d is computed as the number of edges linking two senses in the graph. The function takes also into account the frequencies of the words in all the glosses giving more emphasis to the most discriminative words; this can be considered as a variation of the inverse document frequency (*idf*) for retrieval that we named inverse gloss frequency (*igf*). The *igf* for a word w_k occurring gf^*_k times in the set of extended glosses for all the senses in S_i, the sense inventory of w_i, is computed as $IGF_k = 1 + log_2 \frac{|S_i|}{gf^*_k}$. The final weight for the word w_k appearing h times in the extended gloss g^*_{ij} is given by:

$$weight(w_k, g^*_{ij}) = h \times IGF_k \times \frac{1}{1+d} \quad (1)$$

2. *Building the context.* The context C for the word w_i is represented by all the words that occur in the text.

3. *Building the vector representations.* The context C and each extended gloss g^*_{ij} are represented as vectors in the *SemanticSpace* built through the DSM described in Subsection 2.1.

4. *Sense ranking.* The algorithm computes the cosine similarity between the vector representation of each extended gloss g^*_{ij} and that of the context C. Then, the cosine similarity is linearly combined with the probability $p(s_{ij}|w_i)$, which takes into account the sense distribution of s_{ij} given the word w_i. The sense distribution is computed as the number of times the word w_i was tagged with the sense s_{ij} in SemCor, a collection of 352 documents manually annotated with WordNet synsets. T he additive (Laplace) smoothing prevents zero probabilities, which can occur when some synsets do not appear in SemCor. The probability is computed as follows:

$$p(s_{ij}|w_i) = \frac{t(w_i, s_{ij}) + 1}{\#w_i + |S_i|} \quad (2)$$

The output of this step is a ranked list of synsets.

The WSD measure (**WSD**) is computed on the top of the output of the last step. For each text fragment, we build a Bag-of-Synset (BoS) as the sum, over the whole text, of the weighted synsets associated with each word. Then, we compute the WSD similarity as the cosine similarity between the two BoS.

Graph. A sub-graph of BabelNet is built for each text fragment starting from the synsets provided by the WSD algorithm. For each word the synset with the highest score is selected, then this initial set is expanded with the related synsets in BabelNet. We apply the Personalized Page Rank (Haveliwala, 2002) to each sub-graph where the synset scores computed by the WSD algorithm are exploited as prior probabilities. The weighted rank of synsets provided by Page Rank is used to build the BoS of the two text fragments, then the Personalized Page Rank (**PPR**) is computed as the cosine similarity between them.

Synset Distributional Space. Generally, similarity measures between synsets rely on the synsets hierarchy in a semantic network (e.g. WordNet). We define a new approach that is completely different, and represents synsets as points in a geometric space that we call SDS (Synset Distributional Space). SDS is generated taking into account the synset relationships, and similarity is defined as the synsets closeness in the space. We build a symmetric matrix S which contains synsets on both rows and columns. Each cell in the matrix is set to one if a semantic relation exists between the corresponding synsets. The relationships are extracted from BabelNet limiting synsets to those occurring also in WordNet, while synsets coming from Wikipedia are removed to reduce the size of S. The method for building the matrix S relies on Reflective Random Indexing (RRI) (Cohen et al., 2010), a variation of the Random Indexing technique for matrix reduction (Kanerva, 1988). RRI retains the advantages of RI which incrementally builds a reduced space where distance between points is nearly preserved. Moreover, cyclical training, i.e. the retraining of a new space exploiting the RI output as basis vectors, makes indirect inference to emerge. Two different similarity measures can be defined by exploiting this space for representing synsets: **WSD-SDS** and **PPR-SDS**, based on **WSD** and **PPR** respectively. Each BoS is represented as the sum of the synset vectors in the SDS space. Then, the similarity is computed as the cosine similarity between the two vector representations.

2.3 Surface Level

At the surface level, we compute the following features:

EDIT The edit, or Levenshtein, distance between the two texts;

MCS The most common subsequence between the two texts;

2-gram, 3-gram For each text fragment, we build the *Bag-of-n-$gram$* (with n varying in $\{2, 3\}$); then we compute the cosine similarity between the two *Bag-of-n-$gram$* representations.

BOW For each tokenized text fragment, we build its Bag-of-Word, and then compute the cosine similarity between the two BoW.

L1 The length in characters of the first text fragment;

L2 The length in caracters of the second text fragment;

DIFF The difference between **L1** and **L2**.

2.4 Word to Sense

The *word to sense* level is different from the other ones: in this case the similarity is computed between a word and a particular word meaning. Since a word meaning is not a text fragment, this level poses a new challenge with respect to the classical text similarity task. In this case we decide to consider the word on its own as the first text fragment, while for the second text fragment we build a dummy text using the BabelNet gloss assigned to the word sense. In that way, the distributional and the lexical measures (WSD, Graph, and DSM) can be applied to both fragments. Table 1 recaps the features used for each task.

3 Evaluation

Dataset Description. The SemEval-2014 Task 3 *Cross-Level Semantic Similarity* is designed for evaluating systems on their ability to capture the semantic similarity between lexical items of different length (Jurgens et al., 2014). To this extent, the organizers provide four different levels of comparison which correspond to four different datasets: 1) Paragraph to Sentence (*Par2Sent*); 2) Sentence to Phrase (*Sent2Ph*); 3) Phrase to Word (*Ph2W*); and 4) Word to Sense (*W2Sense*).

For each dataset, the organizer released trial, training and test data. While the trial includes a few examples (approximately 40), both training and test data comprise 500 pairs of text fragments.

Run	*Par2Sent*	*Sent2Ph*	*Ph2W*	*W2Sense*	*Official Rank*	*Spearman Correlation*
bestTrain	.861	.793	.555	.420	-	-
LCS	*.527*	*.562*	*.165*	*.109*	-	-
run1	.769	.729	.229	.165	7	10
run2	.784	.734	.255	.180	6	8
run3	.769	.729	.229	.165	8	11

Table 2: Task results.

Feature	*Par2Sent Sent2Ph Ph2W*	*W2Sense*
DSM	√	√
WSD	√	√
PPR	√	√
WSD-SDS	√	√
PPR-SDS	√	√
EDIT	√	-
MCS	√	-
2-*gram*	√	-
3-*gram*	√	-
BOW	√	-
L1	√	-
L2	√	-
DIFF	√	-

Table 1: Features per task.

Each pair is associated with a human-assigned similarity score, which varies from 4 (very similar) to 0 (unrelated). Organizers provide the normalized Longest Common Substring (LCS) as baseline. The evaluation is performed through the Pearson (official rank) and the Spearman's rank correlation.

System setup. We develop our system in JAVA relying on the following resources:

- Stanford CoreNLP to pre-process the text: tokenization, lemmatization and PoS-tagging are applied to the two text fragments;
- BabelNet 1.1 as knowledge-base in the WSD algorithm;
- JAVA JUNG library for Personalized Page Rank;
- British National Corpus (tokenized text with stop word removal) and SVDLIB to build the *SemanticSpace* described in Subsection 2.1;
- A proprietary implementation of Reflective Random Indexing to build the distributional space based on synsets (SDS) extracted from BabelNet (we used two cycles of retraining);
- Weka for the supervised approach.

After a tuning step using both training and trial data provided by organizers, we selected three different supervised systems: Gaussian Process with Puk kernel ($run1$), Gaussian Process with RBF kernel ($run2$), and Support Vector Machine Regression with Puk kernel ($run3$). All the systems are implemented with the default parameters set by Weka. We trained a different model on each dataset. The DSM is built using the $100,000$ most frequent terms in the BNC, while the co-occurrences are computed on a window size of 5 words. The vector dimension is set to 400, the same value is adopted for building the SDS, where the number of seeds (no zero components) generated in the random vectors is set to 10 with one step of retraining. The total number of synset vectors in the SDS is $576,736$. In the WSD algorithm, we exploited the whole sentence as context. The linear combination between the cosine similarity and the probability $p(s_{ij}|w_i)$ is performed with a factor of 0.5. The distance for expanding a synset with its related meaning is set to one. The same depth is used for building the graph in the PPR method, where we fixed the maximum number of iterations up to 50 and the dumpling factor to 0.85.

Results. Results of our three systems for each similarity level are reported in Table 2 with the baseline provided by the organizer (LCS). Our three systems always outperform the LCS baseline. Table 2 also shows the best results ($bestTrain$) obtained on the training data by a Gaussian Process with Puk kernel and a 10-fold cross-validation. Support Vector Machine and Gaussian Process with Puk kernel, $run1$ and $run3$ respectively, produce the same results. Comparing

Task	*DSM*	*WSD*	*PPR*	*WSD-SDS*	*PPR-SDS*	*EDIT*	*MCS*	*2-gram*	*3-gram*	*BOW*	*L1*	*L2*	*DIFF*
Par2Sent	.612	.697	.580	.129	.129	.461	.44	.630	.478	.585	.002	.231	.116
Sent2Ph	.540	.649	.641	.110	.110	.526	.474	.376	.236	.584	.069	.357	.218
Ph2W	.228	.095	.094	.087	.087	.136	.120	-	-	.095	.079	.013	.071
W2Sense	.147	.085	-.062	.084	.062								

Table 3: Individual measures for each task.

these figures with those obtained on training data (*run*1 and *run*3 vs. *bestTrain*), we can observe that the Puk kernel tends to over-fit on training data, while RBF kernel seems to be less sensitive to this problem.

We analysed also the performance of each measure on its own; results in Table 3 are obtained by training the best supervised system (*run*2) with default parameters on each feature individually. WSD obtains the best results in the first two levels, while DSM is the best method in the last two ones. This behaviour can be ascribed to the size of the text fragments. In large text fragments the WSD algorithm can rely on wider contexts to obtain good performance; while in short texts information about context is poor. At the *W*2*Sense* level, the measure based on the Personalized Page Rank obtains the worst results; however, we noticed that the ablation of that feature causes a drop in performance of the supervised systems.

After the submission deadline, we noticed that sometimes PoS-tagging produced wrong results on small texts. This incorrect behaviour influenced negatively the correct retrieval of synsets from BabelNet. Thus, we decided to exclude PoS-tagging for text fragments with less than three words. In such a case, all the synsets for a given word are retrieved. Making this adjustment, we were able to obtain the improvements ($\Delta\%$) with respect to the submitted runs reported on Table 4.

Run	*Ph2W*	$\Delta\%$	*W2Sense*	$\Delta\%$
run1	.263	+14.85	.242	+46.67
run2	.257	+ 0.78	.237	+31.67
run3	.263	+14.85	.242	+46.66

Table 4: Results after PoS-tagging removal for short text ($<$ 3 words).

4 Conclusions

We have reported the results of our participation in the cross-level semantic similarity task of SemEval-2014. Our systems combine different similarity measures based on string-matching, word sense disambiguation and distributional semantic models. Our best system ranks *6th* out of the 38 participants in the task with respect to the Pearson correlation, while it ranks *8th* when Spearman was used. These results suggest that our methods are robust with respect to the evaluation measures.

Acknowledgments

This work fulfils the research objectives of the PON 02_00563_3470993 project "VINCENTE - A Virtual collective INtelligenCe ENvironment to develop sustainable Technology Entrepreneurship ecosystems" funded by the Italian Ministry of University and Research (MIUR).

References

Satanjeev Banerjee and Ted Pedersen. 2002. An adapted lesk algorithm for word sense disambiguation using wordnet. In *Computational linguistics and intelligent text processing*, pages 136–145. Springer.

Pierpaolo Basile, Annalina Caputo, and Giovanni Semeraro. 2014. An Enhanced Lesk Word Sense Disambiguation algorithm through a Distributional Semantic Model. In *Proceedings of COLING 2014*, Dublin, Ireland, August. (http://www.coling-2014.org/accepted-papers.php, in press).

Trevor Cohen, Roger Schvaneveldt, and Dominic Widdows. 2010. Reflective random indexing and indirect inference: A scalable method for discovery of implicit connections. *Journal of Biomedical Informatics*, 43(2):240 – 256.

Taher H. Haveliwala. 2002. Topic-sensitive pagerank. In *Proceedings of the 11th International Conference on World Wide Web*, WWW '02, pages 517–526, New York, NY, USA. ACM.

David Jurgens, Mohammad Taher Pilehvar, and Roberto Navigli. 2014. Semeval-2014 task 3: Cross-level semantic similarity. In *Proceedings of the 8th International Workshop on Semantic Evaluation (SemEval-2014)*, Dublin, Ireland, August 23–24.

Pentti Kanerva. 1988. *Sparse Distributed Memory*. MIT Press.

Thomas K. Landauer and Susan T. Dumais. 1997. A Solution to Plato's Problem: The Latent Semantic Analysis Theory of Acquisition, Induction, and Representation of Knowledge. *Psychological Review*, 104(2):211–240.

Roberto Navigli and Simone Paolo Ponzetto. 2012. BabelNet: The automatic construction, evaluation and application of a wide-coverage multilingual semantic network. *Artificial Intelligence*, 193:217–250.

Florentina Vasilescu, Philippe Langlais, and Guy Lapalme. 2004. Evaluating variants of the lesk approach for disambiguating words. In *Proceedings of the Conference on Language Resources and Evaluation (LREC)*, pages 633–636.

UniPi: Recognition of Mentions of Disorders in Clinical Text

Giuseppe Attardi, Vittoria Cozza, Daniele Sartiano
Dipartimento di Informatica
Università di Pisa
Largo B. Pontecorvo, 3
I-56127 Pisa, Italy
`{attardi, cozza, sartiano}@di.unipi.it`

Abstract

The paper describes our experiments addressing the SemEval 2014 task on the Analysis of Clinical text. Our approach consists in extending the techniques of NE recognition, based on sequence labelling, to address the special issues of this task, i.e. the presence of overlapping and discontiguous mentions and the requirement to map the mentions to unique identifiers. We explored using supervised methods in combination with word embeddings generated from unannotated data.

1 Introduction

Clinical records provide detailed information on examination and findings of a patient consultation expressed in a narrative style. Such records abound in mentions of clinical conditions, anatomical sites, medications, and procedures, whose accurate identification is crucial for any further activity of text mining. Many different surface forms are used to represent the same concept and the mentions are interleaved with modifiers, e.g. adjectives, verb or adverbs, or are abbreviated involving implicit terms.

For example, in

```
Abdomen is soft, nontender,
nondistended, negative bruits
```

the mention occurrences are "`Abdomen nontender`" and "`Abdomen bruits`", which refer to the disorders: "`nontender abdomen`" and "`abdomininal bruit`", with only the second having a corresponding UMLS Concept Unique Identifier (CUI). In this case the two mentions overlap and both are interleaved with other terms, not part of the mentions.

Secondly, mentions can be nested, as in this example:

```
left pleural and parenchymal
calcifications
```

where the mention `calcifications` is nested within `pleural calcifications.`

Mentions of this kind are a considerable departure from those dealt in typical Named Entity recognition, which are contiguous and non-overlapping, and therefore they represents a new challenge for text analysis.

The analysis of clinical records poses additional difficulties with respect to other biomedical NER tasks, which use corpora from the medical literature. Clinical records are entered by medical personnel on the fly and so they contain misspellings and inconsistent use of capitalization.

The task 7 at SemEval 2014, Analysis of Clinical Text, addresses the problem of recognition of mentions of disorders and is divided in two parts:

A. *recognition of mentions* of bio-medical concepts that belong to the UMLS semantic group *disorders*;
B. *mapping* of each *disorder* mention to a unique UMLS CUI (Concept Unique Identifiers).

The challenge organizers provided the following resources:

- A training corpus of clinical notes from MIMIC II database manually annotated for disorder mentions and normalized to an UMLS CUI, consisting of 9432 sentences, with 5816 annotations.
- A collection of unannotated notes, consisting of 1,611,080 sentences.

Proceedings of the 8th International Workshop on Semantic Evaluation (SemEval 2014), pages 754–760,
Dublin, Ireland, August 23-24, 2014.

We also had access to the UMLS ontology (Bodenreider, 2004).

Our approach to portion A of the task was to adapt a sequence labeller, which provides good accuracy in Named Entity recognition in the newswire domain, to handle the peculiarities of the clinical domain.

We performed mention recognition in two steps:

1. identifying contiguous portions of a mention;
2. combining separated portions of mentions into a full mention.

In order to use a traditional sequence tagger for the first step, we had to convert the input data into a suitable format, in particular, we dealt with nested mentions by transforming them into non-overlapping sequences, through replication.

For recombining discontiguous mentions, we employed a classifier, trained to recognize whether pairs of mentions belong to the same entity. The classifier was trained using also features extracted from the dependency tree of a sentence, in particular the distance of terms along the tree path. Terms related by a dependency have distance 1 and terms having a common head have distance 2. By limiting the pairs[1] to be considered for combination to those within distance 3, we both ensure that only plausible combinations are performed and reduce the cost of the algorithm.

For dealing with portion B of the task, we apply fuzzy matching (Fraiser, 2011) between the extracted mentions and the textual description of entities present in selected sections of UMLS disorders. The CUI from the match with highest score is chosen.

In the following sections, we describe how we carried out the experiments, starting with the preprocessing of the data, then with the training of several versions of NE recognizer, the training of the classifier for mention combination. We then report on the results and discuss some error analysis on the results.

2 Preprocessing of the annotated data

The training data was pre-processed, in order to obtain corpora in a suitable format for:

1. training a sequence tagger
2. training the classifier for mention combination.

Annotations in the training data adopt a pipe-delimited stand-off character-offset format. The example in the introduction has these annotations:

```
00098-016139-
DISCHARGE_SUMMARY.txt || Dis-
ease_Disorder || C0221755 ||
1141 || 1148 || 1192 || 1198
00098-016139-
DISCHARGE_SUMMARY.txt || Dis-
ease_Disorder || CUI-less ||
1141 || 1148 || 1158 || 1167
```

The first annotation marks `Disease_Disorder` as annotation type, `C0221755` as CUI, while the remaining pairs of numbers represent character offsets within the original text that correspond to spans of texts containing the mention, i.e. `Abdomen nondistended`. The second annotation is similar and refers to `Abdomen bruits`.

In order to prepare the training corpus for a NE tagger, the data had to be transformed and converted into IOB[2] notation. However a standard IOB notation does not convey information about overlapping or discontiguous mentions.

In order to deal with overlapping mentions, as is the case for word "`Abdomen`" in our earlier example, multiple copies of the sentence are produced, each one annotated with disjoint mentions. If two mentions overlap, two versions are generated, one annotated with just the first mention and one with the second. If several overlapping mentions are present in a sentence, copies are generated for all possible combinations of non-overlapping mentions.

For dealing with discontiguous mentions, each annotated entity is assigned an id, uniquely identifying the mention within the sentence. This id is added as an extra attribute to each token, represented as an extra column in the tab separated IOB file format for the NE tagger.

We processed with the Tanl pipeline (Attardi et al., 2009; Attardi et al., 2010). We first extracted the text from the training corpus in XML format and added the mentions annotations as tags enclosing them, with spans and mentions id as attributes. We then applied sentence splitting, tokenization, PoS tagging and dependency parsing using DeSR (Attardi, 2006).

The tags were converted to IOB format.

Here are two sample tokens in the resulting annotation, with attributes id, form, pos, head, deprel, entity, entity id:

[1] Not implemented in the submitted runs.

[2] http://en.wikipedia.org/wiki/Inside_Outside_Beginning

```
1 Abdomen NNP 2 SBJ B-DISO 1
...
5 nontender NN 10 NMOD B-DISO 1
```

3 Named Entity Tagging

The core of our approach relies on an initial stage of Named Entity recognition. We performed several experiments, using different NE taggers in different configurations and using both features from the training corpus and features obtained from the unannotated data.

3.1 Tanl NER

We performed several experiments using the Tanl NE Tagger (Attardi et al., 2009), a generic, customizable statistical sequence labeller, suitable for many tasks of sequence labelling, such as POS tagging or Named Entity Recognition.

The tagger implements a Conditional Markov Model and can be configured to use different classification algorithms and to specify feature templates for extracting features. In our experiments we used a linear SVM classification algorithm.

We experimented with several configurations, all including a set of word *shape* features, as in (Attardi et al., 2009): (1) the previous word is capitalized; (2) the following word is capitalized; (3) the current word is in upper case; (4) the current word is in mixed case; (5) the current word is a single uppercase character; (6) the current word is a uppercase character and a dot; (7) the current word contains digits; (8) the current word is two digits; (9) the current word is four digits; (10) the current word is made of digits and "/"; (11) the current word contains "$"; (12) the current word contains "%"; (13) the current word contains an apostrophe; (14) the current word is made of digits and dots.

A number of dictionary features were also used, including prefix and suffix dictionaries, bigrams, last words, first word and frequent words, all extracted from the training corpus.

Additionally, a dictionary of disease terms was used, consisting of about 22,000 terms extracted from the preferred terms for CUIs belonging to the UMLS semantic type "Disease or Syndrome".

The first character of the POS tag was also used as feature, extracted from a window of tokens before and after the current token.

Finally *attribute features* are extracted from attributes (Form, PoS, Lemma, NE, Disease) of surrounding tokens, denoted by their relative position to the current token. The best combination of Attribute features obtained with runs on the development set was the following:

Feature	Tokens
POS[0]	$w_{i-2}\ w_{i-1}\ w_i\ w_{i+1}$
DISEASE	$w_i\ w_{i+1}\ w_{i+2}$

Table 1. *Attribute features* used in the runs.

3.2 Word Embeddings

We explored ways to use the unannotated data in NE recognition by exploiting word embeddings (Collobert et al, 2011). In a paper published after our submission, Tang et al. (2014) show that word embeddings are beneficial to Biomedical NER.

We used the word embeddings for 100,000 terms created through deep learning on the English Wikipedia by Al-Rfou et al. (2013). We then built, with the same procedure, embedding for terms from the supplied unlabelled data. The corpus was split, tokenized and normalized and a vocabulary was created with the most frequent words not already present among the Wikipedia word embeddings. Four versions of the embeddings were created, varying the size of the vocabulary and the size of the context window, as described in Table 1.

	Run1	Run2	Run3	Run4
Vocabulary size	50,000	50,000	30,000	30,000
Context	5	2	5	2
Hidden Layers	32	32	32	32
Learning Rate	0.1	0.1	0.1	0.1
Embedding size	64	64	64	64

Table 2. Word Embedding Parameters.

We developed and trained a Deep Learning NE tagger (nlpnet, 2014) based on the SENNA architecture (SENNA, 2011) using these word embeddings.

As an alternative to using the embeddings directly as features, we created clusters of word embeddings using the Dbscan algorithm (Ester et al., 1996) implemented in the sklearn library. We carried out several experiments, varying the parameters of the algorithm. The configuration that produced the largest number of clusters had 572 clusters. The clusters turned out not to be much significant, since a single cluster had about 29,000 words, another had 5,000 words, and the others had few, unusual words.

We added the clusters as a dictionary feature to our NE tagger. Unfortunately, most of the terms fell within 4 clusters, so the feature turned out to be little discriminative.

3.3 Stanford NER

We performed experiments also with a tagger based on a different statistical approach: the Stanford Named Entity Recognizer. This tagger is based on the Conditional Random Fields (CRF) statistical model and uses Gibbs sampling instead of other dynamic programming techniques for inference on sequence models (Finkel et al., 2005). This tagger normally works well enough using just the form of tokens as feature and we applied it so.

3.4 NER accuracy

We report the accuracy of the various NE taggers we tested on the development set, using the scorer from the CoNLL Shared Task 2003 (Tjong Kim Sang and De Meulder, 2003).

We include here also the results with CRFsuite, the CRF tagger used in (Tang et al., 2014).

NER	Precision	Recall	F- score
Tanl	80.41	65.08	71.94
Tanl+clusters	80.43	64.48	71.58
nlpnet	80.29	62.51	70.29
Stanford	80.30	64.89	71.78
CRFsuite	79.69	61.97	69.72

Table 3. Accuracy of various NE taggers on the development set.

Based on these results we chose the Tanl tagger and the Stanford NER for our submitted runs.

All these taggers are known to be capable of achieving state of the art performance or close to it (89.57 F1) in the CoNLL 2003 shared task on the WSJ Penn Treebank.

The accuracy on the current benchmark is much lower, despite the fact that there is only one category and the terminology for disorders is drawn from a restricted vocabulary.

It has been noted by Dingare et al. (2005) that NER over biomedical texts achieves lower accuracy compared to other domains, quite within the range of the above results. Indeed, compared with the newswire domain or other domains, the entities in the biomedical domain tend to be more complex, without the distinctive shape features of the newswire categories.

4 Discontiguous mentions

Discontiguous mention detection can be formulated as a problem of deciding whether two contiguous mentions belong to the same mention. As such, it can be cast into a classification problem. A similar approach was used successfully for the coreference resolution task at SemEval 2010 (Attardi, Dei Rossi et al., 2010)

4.1 Mentions detection

We trained a Maximum Entropy classifier (Ratnaparkhi, 1996) to recognize whether two terms belong to the same mention.

The training instances for the pair-wise learner consist of each pair of terms within a sentence annotated as disorders. A positive instance is created if the terms belong to the same mention, negative otherwise.

The classifier was trained using the following features, extracted for each pair of words for diseases.

Distance features

- *Token distance:* quantized distance between the two words;
- *Ancestor distance:* quantized distance between the words in the parse tree if one is the ancestor of the other

Syntax features

- *Head:* whether the two words have the same head;
- *DepPath:* concatenation of the dependency relations of the two words to their common parent

Dictionary features

- UMLS: whether the two words are both present in an UMLS definition

The last feature is motivated by the fact that, according to the task description, most of the disorder mentions correspond to diseases in the SNOMED terminology.

4.2 Merging of mentions

The mentions detected in the first phase are merged using the following process. Sentence are parsed and then for each pair of words that are tagged as disorder, features are extracted and passed to the classifier.

If the classifier assigns a probability greater than a given threshold the two words are combined into a larger mention. The process is then repeated trying to further extend each mention with additional terms by combining mentions that share a word.

5 Mapping entities to CUIs

Task B requires mapping each recognized entity to a concept in the SNOMED-CT terminology, assigning to it a unique UMLS CUI, if possible, or else marking it as `CUI-less`. The CUIs are limited to those corresponding to SNOMED codes and belonging to the following UMLS semantic types: "Acquired Abnormality" or "Congenital Abnormality", "Injury or Poisoning", "Pathologic Function", "Disease or Syndrome", "Mental or Behavioral Dysfunction", "Cell or Molecular Dysfunction", "Experimental Model of Disease" or "Anatomical Abnormality", "Neoplastic Process" or "Sign or Symptom".

In order to speed up search, we created two indices: an inverted index from words in the definition of a CUI to the corresponding CUI and a forward index from a CUI to its definition.

For assigning a CUI to a mention, we search in the dictionary of CUI preferred terms, first for an exact match, then for a normalized mention and finally for a fuzzy match (Fraiser, 2011). Normalization entails dropping punctuation and stop words. Fuzzy matching is sometimes too liberal, for example it matches "`chronic obstructive pulmonary`" with "`chronic obstructive lung disease`"; so we also put a ceiling on the edit distance between the phrases.

The effectiveness of the process is summarized in these results on the development set:

Exact matches	Normalized matches	Fuzzy matches	No matches
1352	868	304	5488

Table 4. CUI identifications on the devel set.

6 Experiments

The training corpus for the submission consisted of the merge of the train and development sets.

We submitted three runs, using different or differently configured NE tagger.

Two runs were submitted using the Tanl tagger using the features listed in Table 5, where DISEASE and CLUSTER meaning is explained earlier.

Feature	UniPI_run0	UniPI_run1
POS[0]	$w_{i-2}\ w_{i-1}\ w_i\ w_{i+1}$	$w_{i-2}\ w_{i-1}\ w_i\ w_{i+1}$
CLUSTER	$w_i\ w_{i+1}$	$w_i\ w_{i+1}$
DISEASE	$w_i\ w_{i+1}\ w_{i+2}$	

Table 5. *Attribute features* used in the runs.

Since the clustering produced few large clusters, the inclusion of this feature did not affect substantially the results.

A third run (UniPi_run_2) was performed using the Stanford NER with default settings.

7 Results

The results obtained in the three submitted runs, are summarized in Table 6, in terms of accuracy, precision, recall and F-score. For comparison, also the results obtained by the best performing systems are included.

Run	Precision	Recall	F- score
	Task A		
Unipi_run0	0.539	0.684	0.602
Unipi_run1	0.659	0.612	0.635
Unipi_run2	0.712	0.601	0.652
SemEval best	**0.843**	**0.786**	**0813**
	Task A relaxed		
Unipi_run0	0.778	0.885	0.828
Unipi_run1	0.902	0.775	0.834
Unipi_run2	0.897	0.766	0.826
SemEval best	**0.936**	**0.866**	**0.900**

Table 6. UniPI Task A results, compared to the best submission.

Run	Accuracy
Task B	
Unipi_run0	0.467
Unipi_run1	0.428
Unipi_run2	0.417
SemEval best	**0.741**
Task B relaxed	
Unipi_run0	0.683
Unipi_run1	0.699
Unipi_run2	0.693
SemEval best	**0.873**

Table 7. UniPI Task B results, compared to the best submission.

8 Error analysis

Since the core step of our approach is the NE recognition, we tried to analyze possible causes of its errors.

Some errors might be due to mistakes by the POS tagger. For example, often some words occur in full upper case, leading to classify adjectives like `ABDOMINAL` as `NNP` instead of `JJ`. Training our POS tagger on the GENIA corpus or using the GENIA POS tagger might have helped a little. Spelling errors like `abdominla` instead of `abdominal` could also have been corrected.

Another choice that might have affected the NER accuracy was our decision to duplicate the sentences in order to remove mention overlaps. An alternative solution might have been to use two categories in the IOB annotation: one category for full contiguous disorder mentions and another for partial disorder mentions. This might have reduced the confusion in the tagger, since isolated words like `abdomen` get tagged as disorder, having been so annotated in the training set. Distinguishing the two cases, `abdomen` would become a disorder mention in the step of mention merging. Counting the errors in the development set we found that 939 out of the 1757 errors were indeed individual words incorrectly identified as disorders.

8.1 After submission experiments

After the submission, we changed the algorithm for merging mentions, in order to avoid nested spans, retaining only the larger one. Tests on the development set show that this change leads to a small improvement in the strict evaluation:

Run	Precision	Recall	F- score
	Task A		
devel_run1	0.596	**0.653**	0.624
devel run1_after	**0.668**	0.637	**0.652**
	Task A relaxed		
devel_run1	**0.865**	**0.850**	**0.858**
devel run1_after	0.864	0.831	0.847

Table 8. UniPI Task A post submission results.

9 Conclusions

We reported our participation to SemEval 2014 on the Analysis of Clinical Text. Our approach is based on using a NER, for identifying contiguous mentions and on a Maximum Entropy classifier for merging discontiguous ones.

The training data was transformed into a format suitable for a standard NE tagger, that does not accept discontiguous or nested mentions. Our measurements on the development set showed that different NE tagger reach a similar accuracy.

We explored using word embeddings as features, generated from the unsupervised data provided, but they did not improve the accuracy of the NE tagger.

Acknowledgements

Partial support for this work was provided by project RIS (POR RIS of the Regione Toscana, CUP n° 6408.30122011.026000160).

References

Rami Al-Rfou', Bryan Perozzi, and Steven Skiena. 2013. Polyglot: Distributed Word Representations for Multilingual NLP. In *Proceedings of Conference on Computational Natural Language Learning*, CoNLL '13, pages 183-192, Sofia, Bulgaria.

Giuseppe Attardi. 2006. Experiments with a Multilanguage Non-Projective Dependency Parser. In *Proceedings of the Tenth Conference on Natural Language Learning,* CoNLL '06, pages 166-170, New York, NY.

Giuseppe Attardi et al., 2009. Tanl (Text Analytics and Natural Language Processing). SemaWiki project: http://medialab.di.unipi.it/wiki/SemaWiki.

Giuseppe Attardi, Stefano Dei Rossi, Felice Dell'Orletta and Eva Maria Vecchi. 2009. The Tanl Named Entity Recognizer at Evalita 2009. In *Proceedings of Workshop Evalita'09 - Evaluation of NLP and Speech Tools for Italian*, Reggio Emilia, ISBN 978-88-903581-1-1.

Giuseppe Attardi, Felice Dell'Orletta, Maria Simi and Joseph Turian. 2009. Accurate Dependency Parsing with a Stacked Multilayer Perceptron. In *Proceedings of Workshop Evalita'09 - Evaluation of NLP and Speech Tools for Italian*, Reggio Emilia, ISBN 978-88-903581-1-1.

Giuseppe Attardi, Stefano Dei Rossi and Maria Simi. 2010. The Tanl Pipeline. In *Proceedings of LREC Workshop on Web Services and Processing Pipelines in HLT, WSPP*, La Valletta, Malta, pages 14-21

Giuseppe Attardi, Stefano Dei Rossi and Maria Simi. 2010. TANL-1: Coreference Resolution by Parse Analysis and Similarity Clustering. In *Proceedings of the 5th International Workshop on Semantic Evaluation, SemEval 2010*, Uppsala, Sweden, pages 108-111

Olivier Bodenreider. 2004. The Unified Medical Language System (UMLS): integrating biomedical terminology. *Nucleic Acids Research*, vol. 32, no. supplement 1, pages D267–D270.

Ronan Collobert et al. 2011. Natural Language Processing (Almost) from Scratch. *Journal of Machine Learning Research*, 12, pages 2461–2505.

Shipra Dingare, Malvina Nissim, Jenny Finkel, Christopher Manning and Claire Grover. 2005. A System for Identifying Named Entities in Biomedical Text: how Results From two Evaluations Reflect on Both the System and the Evaluations. *Comp Funct Genomics*. Feb-Mar; 6(1-2): pages 77–85.

Martin Ester, et al. 1996. A density-based algorithm for discovering clusters in large spatial databases with noise. In *Proceedings of 2nd International Conference on Knowledge Discovery and Data Mining,* KDD 96, pages 226–231.

Jenny Rose Finkel, Trond Grenager and Christopher Manning 2005. Incorporating Non-local Information into Information Extraction Systems by Gibbs Sampling. In *Proceedings of the 43nd Annual Meeting of the Association for Computational Linguistic*s, 2005, pages 363–370.

Neil Fraser. 2011. Diff, Match and Patch libraries for Plain Text. (Based on Myer's diff algorithm).

Adwait Ratnaparkhi. 1996. A Maximum Entropy Part-Of-Speech Tagger. In *Proceedings of the Empirical Methods in Natural Language Processing Conference, EMNLP '96*, pages 17-18.

Buzhou Tang, Hongxin Cao, Xiaolong Wang, Qingcai Chen, and Hua Xu. 2014. Evaluating Word Representation Features in Biomedical Named Entity Recognition Tasks. *BioMed Research International*, Volume 2014, Article ID 240403.

Erik F. Tjong Kim Sang and Fien De Meulder 2003. Introduction to the CoNLL '03 Shared Task: Language-Independent Named Entity Recognition. In: *Proceedings of CoNLL '03*, Edmonton, Canada, pages 142-147.

SENNA. 2011. http://ml.nec-labs.com/senna/

nlpnet. 2014. https://github.com/attardi/nlpnet

UNITOR: Aspect Based Sentiment Analysis with Structured Learning

Giuseppe Castellucci[(†)], **Simone Filice**[(‡)], **Danilo Croce**[(⋆)], **Roberto Basili**[(⋆)]

(†) Dept. of Electronic Engineering
(‡) Dept. of Civil Engineering and Computer Science Engineering
(⋆) Dept. of Enterprise Engineering
University of Roma, Tor Vergata, Italy
{castellucci,filice}@ing.uniroma2.it; {croce,basili}@info.uniroma2.it

Abstract

In this paper, the UNITOR system participating in the SemEval-2014 Aspect Based Sentiment Analysis competition is presented. The task is tackled exploiting Kernel Methods within the Support Vector Machine framework. The Aspect Term Extraction is modeled as a sequential tagging task, tackled through SVM^{hmm}. The Aspect Term Polarity, Aspect Category and Aspect Category Polarity detection are tackled as a classification problem where multiple kernels are linearly combined to generalize several linguistic information. In the challenge, UNITOR system achieves good results, scoring in almost all rankings between the 2nd and the 8th position within about 30 competitors.

1 Introduction

In recent years, many websites started offering a high level interaction with users, who are no more a passive audience, but can actively produce new contents. For instance, platforms like Amazon[1] or TripAdvisor[2] allow people to express their opinions on products, such as food, electronic items or clothes. Obviously, companies are interested in understanding what customers think about their brands and products, in order to implement corrective strategies on products themselves or on marketing solutions. Performing an automatic analysis of user opinions is then a very hot topic. The automatic extraction of subjective information in text materials is generally referred as *Sentiment Analysis* or *Opinion Mining* and it is performed via natural language processing, text analysis and computational linguistics techniques. Task 4 in SemEval 2014 edition[3] (Pontiki et al., 2014) aims at promoting research on *Aspect Based Opinion Mining* (Liu, 2007), which is approached as a cascade of 4 subtasks. For example, let us consider the sentence:

The fried rice is amazing here. (1)

The *Aspect Term Extraction* (ATE) subtask aims at finding words suggesting the presence of aspects on which an opinion is expressed, e.g. fried rice in sentence 1. In the *Aspect Term Polarity* (ATP) task the polarity evoked for each aspect is recognized, i.e. a positive polarity is expressed with respect to fried rice. In the *Aspect Category Detection* (ACD) task the category evoked in a sentence is identified, e.g. the food category in sentence 1). In the *Aspect Category Polarity* (ACP) task the polarity of each expressed category is recognized, e.g. a positive category polarity is expressed in sentence 1.

Different strategies have been experimented in recent years. Classical approaches are based on machine learning techniques and rely on simple representation features, such as unigrams, bigrams, Part-Of-Speech (POS) tags (Pang et al., 2002; Pang and Lee, 2008; Wiebe et al., 1999). Other approaches adopt sentiment lexicons in order to exploit some sort of prior knowledge about the polar orientation of words. These resources are usually semi-automatically compiled and provide scores associating individual words to sentiments or polarity orientation.

In this paper, the UNITOR system participating to the SemEval-2014 *Aspect Based Sentiment Analysis* task (Pontiki et al., 2014) is presented. The ATE task is modeled as a sequential labeling problem. A sentence is considered as a sequence of tokens: a Markovian algorithm is adopted in

[1] http://www.amazon.com

[2] http://www.tripadvisor.com

[3] http://alt.qcri.org/semeval2014/task4/

Proceedings of the 8th International Workshop on Semantic Evaluation (SemEval 2014), pages 761–767,
Dublin, Ireland, August 23-24, 2014.

order to decide what is an aspect term . All the remaining tasks are modeled as multi-kernel classification problems based on Support Vector Machines (SVMs). Various representation have been exploited using proper kernel functions (Shawe-Taylor and Cristianini, 2004a). Tree Kernels (Collins and Duffy, 2001; Moschitti et al., 2008; Croce et al., 2011) are adopted in order to capture structural sentence information derived from the parse tree. Moreover, corpus-driven methods are used in order to acquire meaning generalizations in an unsupervised fashion (e.g. see (Pado and Lapata, 2007)) through the analysis of distributions of word occurrences in texts. It is obtained by the construction of a Word Space (Sahlgren, 2006), which provides a distributional model of lexical semantics. Latent Semantic Kernel (Cristianini et al., 2002) is thus applied within such space.

In the remaining, in Section 2 and 3 we will explain our approach in more depth. Section 4 discusses the results in the SemEval-2014 challenge.

2 Sequence Labeling for ATE

The Aspect Term Extraction (ATE) has been modeled as a *sequential tagging* process. We consider each token representing the *beginning* (B), the *inside* (I) or the *outside* (O) of an argument. Following this IOB notation, the resulting ATE representation of a sentence like "*The [fried rice]*$_{\text{ASPECTTERM}}$ *is amazing here*" can be expressed by labeling each word according to its relative position, i.e.: [*The*]$_{\text{O}}$ [*fried*]$_{\text{B}}$ [*rice*]$_{\text{I}}$ [*is*]$_{\text{O}}$ [*amazing*]$_{\text{O}}$ [*here*]$_{\text{O}}$.

The ATE task is thus a labeling process that determines the individual (correct IOB) class for each token. The labeling algorithm used is SVM^{hmm} (Altun et al., 2003)[4]: it combines both a discriminative approach to estimate the probabilities in the model and a generative approach to retrieve the most likely sequence of tags that explains a sequence. Given an input sequence $\mathbf{x} = (x_1 \dots x_l) \in \mathcal{X}$ of feature vectors $x_1 \dots x_l$, the model predicts a tag sequence $\mathbf{y} = (y_1 \dots y_l) \in \mathcal{Y}$ after learning a linear discriminant function $F : \mathcal{X} \times \mathcal{Y} \rightarrow \mathbb{R}$ over input-output pairs. The labeling $f(\mathbf{x})$ is thus defined as: $f(\mathbf{x}) = \arg\max_{\mathbf{y}\in\mathcal{Y}} F(\mathbf{x}, \mathbf{y}; \mathbf{w})$ and it is obtained by maximizing F over the response variable, $\mathbf{y}$, for a specific given input $\mathbf{x}$. F is linear in some combined feature representation of inputs and outputs $\Phi(\mathbf{x}, \mathbf{y})$, i.e. $F(\mathbf{x}, \mathbf{y}; \mathbf{w}) = \langle \mathbf{w}, \Phi(\mathbf{x}, \mathbf{y}) \rangle$.

In SVM^{hmm} the observations $x_1 \dots x_l$ can be naturally expressed in terms of feature vectors. In particular, we modeled each word through a set of lexical and syntactic features, as described in the following section.

2.1 Modeling Features for ATE

In the discriminative view of SVM^{hmm}, each word is represented by a feature vector, describing its different observable properties. For instance, the word *rice* in the example 1 is modeled through the following features: *Lexical features*: its lemma (*rice*) and POS tag (*NN*); *Prefixes and Suffixes*: the first n and the last m characters of the word ($n = m = 3$) (e.g. *ric* and *ice*); *Contextual features*: the left and right lexical contexts represented by the 3 words before (*BEGIN*::BB *the*::DT *fried*::JJ) and after (*is*::VBZ *amazing*::JJ *here*::RB); the left and right syntactic contexts as the POS bi-grams and tri-grams occurring *before* (i.e. BB_DT DT_JJ BB_DT_JJ) and *after* (i.e. VBZ_JJ JJ_RB VBZ_JJ_RB) the word; *Grammatical features*: features derived from the dependency graph associated to the sentence, i.e. boolean indicators that capture if the token is involved in a *Subj*, *Obj* or *Amod* relation in the corresponding graph.

3 Multiple Kernel Approach for Polarity and Category Detection

We approached the remaining three subtasks of the pipeline as classification problems with multiple kernels, in line with (Castellucci et al., 2013). We used Support Vector Machines (SVMs) (Joachims, 1999), a maximum-margin classifier that realizes a linear discriminative model. The kernelized version of SVM learns from instances x_i exploiting rich similarity measures (i.e.the kernel functions) $K(x_i, x_j) = \langle \phi(x_i) \cdot \phi(x_j) \rangle$. In this way projection functions $\phi(\cdot)$ can be implicitly used in order to transform the initial feature space into a more expressive one, where a hyperplane that separates the data with the widest margin can be found. Kernels can directly operate on variegate forms of representation, such as feature vectors, trees, sequences or graphs. Then, modeling instances in different representations, specific kernels can be defined in order to explore different linguistic information. These variety of kernel functions

[4] www.cs.cornell.edu/People/tj/svm_light/svm_hmm.html

$K_1 \ldots K_n$ can be independently defined and the combinations $K_1 + K_2 + \ldots$ of multiple functions can be integrated into SVM as they are still kernels. The next section describes the representations as well as the kernel functions.

3.1 Representing Lexical Information

The **Bag of Word** (BoW) is a simple representation reflecting the lexical information of the sentence. Each text is represented as a vector whose dimensions correspond to different words, i.e. they represent a boolean indicator of the presence or not of a word in the text. The resulting kernel function is the cosine similarity (or linear kernel) between vector pairs, i.e. $\mathbf{lin_{BoW}}$. In line with (Shawe-Taylor and Cristianini, 2004b) we investigated the contribution of the Polynomial Kernel of degree 2, $\mathbf{poly^2_{BoW}}$ as it defines an implicit space where also feature pairs, i.e. words pairs, are considered.

In the polarity detection tasks, several polarity lexicons have been exploited in order to have useful hints of the intrinsic polarity of words. We adopted MPQA Subjectivity Lexicon[5] (Wilson et al., 2005) and NRC Emotion Lexicon (Mohammad and Turney, 2013): they are large collection of words provided with the underlying emotion they generally evoke. While the former considers only positive and negative sentiments, the latter considers also eight primary emotions, organized in four opposing pairs, joy-sadness, anger-fear, trust-disgust, and anticipation-surprise. We define the **Lexicon Based** (LB) vectors as follows. For each lexicon, let $E = \{e_1, ..., e_{|E|}\}$ be the emotion vocabulary defined in it. Let $w \in s$ be a word occurring in sentence s, with $I(w, i)$ being the indicator function whose output is 1 if w is associated to the emotion label e_i, or 0 otherwise. Then, given a sentence s, each e_i, i.e. a dimension of the emotional vocabulary E, receives a score $s_i = \sum_{w \in s} I(w, i)$. Each sentence produces a vector $\vec{s} \in \mathbb{R}^{|E|}$, for each lexicon, on which a linear kernel $\mathbf{lin_{LB}}$ is applied.

3.2 Generalizing Lexical Information

Another representation is used to generalize the lexical information of each text, without exploiting any manually coded resource. Basic lexical information is obtained by a co-occurrence **Word Space** (WS) built accordingly to the methodology described in (Sahlgren, 2006) and (Croce and Previtali, 2010). A word-by-context matrix M is obtained through a large scale corpus analysis. Then the *Latent Semantic Analysis* (Landauer and Dumais, 1997) technique is applied as follows. The matrix M is decomposed through Singular Value Decomposition (SVD) (Golub and Kahan, 1965) into the product of three new matrices: U, S, and V so that S is diagonal and $M = USV^T$. M is then approximated by $M_k = U_k S_k V_k^T$, where only the first k columns of U and V are used, corresponding to the first k greatest singular values. This approximation supplies a way to project a generic word w_i into the *k*-dimensional space using $W = U_k S_k^{1/2}$, where each row corresponds to the representation vector $\vec{w_i}$. The result is that every word is projected in the reduced Word Space and a sentence is represented by applying an additive model as an unbiased linear combination. We adopted these vector representations using a linear kernel, as in (Cristianini et al., 2002), i.e. $\mathbf{lin_{WS}}$ and a Radial Basis Function Kernel $\mathbf{rbf_{WS}}$.

In Aspect Category Detection, and more generally in topic classification tasks, some specific words can be an effective indicator of the underlying topic. For instance, in the restaurant domain, the word *tasty* may refer to the quality of food. These kind of word-topic relationships can be automatically captured by a Bag-of-Word approach, but with some limitations. As an example, a BoW representation may not capture synonyms or semantically related terms. This lack of word generalization is partially compensated by the already discussed Word Space. However, this last representation aims at capturing the sense of an overall sentence, and no particular relevance is given to individual words, even if they can be strong topic indicators. To apply a modeling more focused on topics, we manually selected m seed words $\{\sigma_1, \ldots, \sigma_m\}$ that we consider reliable *topic-indicators*, for example *spaghetti* for `food`. Notice that for every seed σ_i, as well as for every word w the similarity function $sim(\sigma_i, w)$ can be derived from the Word Space representations $\vec{\sigma_i}$ and $\vec{w}$, respectively. What we need is a specific seed-based representation reflecting the similarity between topic indicators and sentences s. Given the words w occurring in s, the **Seed-Oriented** (SO) representation of s is an m-dimensional vector $\vec{so}(s)$ whose components are: $so_i(s) = \max_{w \in s} sim(\sigma_i, w)$. Alternatively, as

[5] http://mpqa.cs.pitt.edu/lexicons/subj_lexicon

seeds σ refer to a set of evoked topics (i.e. aspect categories such as food) $\Sigma_1, ..., \Sigma_t$, we can define a t-dimensional vector $\vec{to}(s)$ called **Topic-Oriented** (TO) representation for s, whose features are: $to_i(s) = \max_{w \in s, \sigma_k \in \Sigma_i} \; sim(\sigma_k, w)$.

The adopted word similarity function $sim(\cdot, \cdot)$ over $\vec{so}(s)$ and $\vec{to}(s)$ depends on the experiments. In the unconstrained setting, i.e. the Word Space Topic Oriented **WSTO** system, $sim(\cdot, \cdot)$ consists in the dot product over the Word Space representations $\vec{\sigma_i}$ and $\vec{w}$. In the constrained case $sim(\cdot, \cdot)$ corresponds to the Wu & Palmer similarity based on WordNet (Wu and Palmer, 1994), in the so called WordNet Seed Oriented **WNSO** system. The Radial Basis Function (RBF) kernel is then applied onto the resulting feature vectors $\vec{to}(s)$ and $\vec{so}(s)$ in the **rbf$_{\mathbf{WSTO}}$** and **rbf$_{\mathbf{WNSO}}$**, respectively.

3.3 Generalizing Syntactic Information

In order to exploit the syntactic information, *Tree Kernel* functions proposed in (Collins and Duffy, 2001) are adopted. Tree kernels exploit syntactic similarity through the idea of convolutions among syntactic tree substructures. Any tree kernel evaluates the number of common substructures between two trees T_1 and T_2 without explicitly considering the whole fragment space. Many tree representations can be derived to represent the syntactic information, according to different syntactic theories. For this experiment, dependency formalism of parse trees is employed to capture sentences syntactic information. As proposed in (Croce et al., 2011), the kernel function is applied to examples modeled according the Grammatical Relation Centered Tree representation from the original dependency parse structures, shown in Fig. 1: non-terminal nodes reflect syntactic relations, such as NSUBJ, pre-terminals are the Part-Of-Speech tags, such as nouns, and leaves are lexemes, such as *rice::n* and *amazing::j*[6]. In each example, the aspect terms and the covering nodes are enriched with a a suffix and all lexical nodes are duplicated by the node asp in order to reduce data sparseness. Moreover, prior information derived by the lexicon can be injected in the tree, by duplicating all lexical nodes annotated in the MPQA Subjectivity Lexicon, e.g. the adjective *amazing*, with a node expressing the polarity (pos).

Given two tree structures T_1 and T_2, the

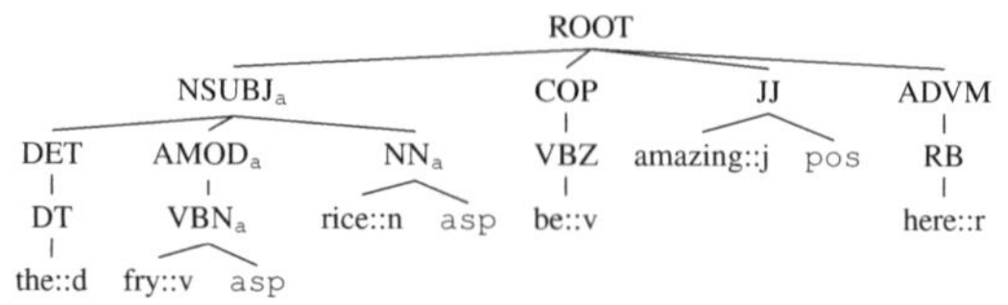

Figure 1: Tree representation of the sentence 1.

Tree Kernel formulation is reported hereafter: $TK(T_1, T_2) = \sum_{n_1 \in N_{T_1}} \sum_{n_2 \in N_{T_2}} \Delta(n_1, n_2)$ where N_{T_1} and N_{T_2} are the sets of the T_1's and T_2's nodes, respectively and $\Delta(n_1, n_2)$ is equal to the number of common fragments rooted in the n_1 and n_2 nodes. The function Δ determines the nature of the kernel space. In the constrained case the Partial Tree Kernel formulation (Moschitti, 2006) is used, i.e. **ptk$_{\mathbf{GRCT}}$**. In the unconstrained setting the Smoothed Partial Tree Kernel formulation (Croce et al., 2011) is adopted to emphasizes the lexicon in the Word Space, i.e. the **sptk$_{\mathbf{GRCT}}$**. It computes the similarity between lexical nodes as the similarity between words in the Word Space. So, this kernel allows a generalization both from a syntactic and lexical point of view.

4 Results

In this Section the experimental results of the UNITOR system in the four different subtasks of Semeval 2014 competition are discussed. Teams were allowed to submit two different outcomes for each task: *constrained* submissions (expressed by the suffix C in all the tables) are intended to measure systems ability to learn sentiment analysis models only over the provided data; *unconstrained* (expressed by the suffix U in all the tables) submissions allows teams to exploit additional training data. The first two tasks, i.e. ATE and ATP, are defined on the *laptop* and *restaurant* domains, while the last two tasks, i.e. ACD and ACP, are defined for the *restaurant* dataset only.

The unconstrained versions are derived by exploiting word vectors derived in an unsupervised fashion through the analysis of large scale corpora. All words in a corpus occurring more than 100 times (i.e. the *targets*) are represented through vectors. The original space dimensions are generated from the set of the 20,000 most frequent words (i.e. *features*) in the corpus. One dimension describes the Point-wise Mutual Information score between one feature, as it occurs on a left or right window of 3 tokens around a target. Left contexts of targets are distinguished from the right ones, in order to capture asymmetric syntactic behaviors

[6]Each word is lemmatized to reduce data sparseness, but they are enriched with POS tags.

(e.g., useful for verbs): 40,000 dimensional vectors are thus derived for each target. The Singular Value Decomposition is applied and the space dimensionality is reduced to $k = 250$. Two corpora are used for generating two different Word Spaces, one for the laptop and one for the restaurant domain. The Opinosis dataset (Ganesan et al., 2010) is used to build the electronic domain Word Space, while the restaurant domain corpus adopted is the TripAdvisor dataset[7]. Both provided data and in-domain data are first pre-processed through the Stanford Parser (Klein and Manning, 2003) in order to obtain POS tags or Dependency Trees.

A modified version of LibSVM has been adopted to implement Tree Kernel. Parameters such as the SVM regularization coefficient C, the kernel parameters (for instance the degree of the polynomial kernel) have been selected after a tuning stage based on a 5-fold cross validation.

4.1 Aspect Term Extraction

The Aspect Term Extraction task is modeled as a sequential labeling problem. The feature representation described in Section 2.1, where each token is associated to a specific target class according to the `IOB` notation, is used in the SVM^{hmm} learning algorithm. In the constrained version of the `UNITOR` system only the training data are used to derive features. In the unconstrained case the `UNITOR` system exploits lexical vectors derived from a Word Space. Each token feature representation is, in this sense, augmented through distributional vectors derived from the Word Spaces described above. Obviously, the Opinosis Word Space is used in the laptop subtask, while the TripAdvisor Word Space is used in the restaurant subtask. These allow the system to generalize the lexical information, enabling a smoother match between words during training and test phases, hopefully capturing similarity phenomena such as the relation between *screen* and *monitor*.

In Table 1 results in the laptop case are reported. Our system performed quite well, and ranked in 6th and 10th position over 28 submitted systems. In this case, the use of the Word Space is effective, as noticed by the 4 position gain in the final ranking (almost 2 points in F1-measure). In Table 2 results in the restaurant case are reported. Here, the use of Word Space does not give an improvement in the final performance.

[7] `http://sifaka.cs.uiuc.edu/~wang296/Data/index.html`

Table 1: Aspect Term Extraction Results - Laptop.

System (Rank)	P	R	F1
UNITOR-C (10/28)	.7741	.5764	.6608
UNITOR-U (6/28)	.7575	.6162	.6795
Best-System-C (1/28)	.8479	.6651	.7455
Best-System-U (2/28)	.8251	.6712	.7403

Table 2: Aspect Term Extraction - Restaurants.

System (Rank)	P	R	F1
UNITOR-C (5/29)	.8244	.7786	.8009
UNITOR-U (6/29)	.8131	.7865	.7996
Best-System-C (2/29)	.8624	.8183	.8398
Best-System-U (1/29)	.8535	.8271	.8401

In both cases, we observed that most of the errors were associated to aspect terms composed by multiple words. For example, in the sentence *The portions of the food that came out were mediocre* the gold aspect term is `portions of the food` while our system was able only to retrieve *food* as aspect term. The system is mainly able to recognize single word aspect terms and, in most of the cases, double words aspect terms.

4.2 Aspect Term Polarity

The Aspect Term Polarity subtask has been modeled as a multi-class classification problem: for a given set of aspect terms within a sentence, it aims at determining whether the polarity of each aspect term is *positive*, *negative*, *neutral* or *conflict*. It has been tackled using multi-kernel SVMs in a One-vs-All Schema. In the constrained setting, the linear combination of the following kernel functions have been used: ptk_{GRCT}, $poly^2_{BoW}$ that consider all the lemmatized terms in the sentence, a $poly^2_{BoW}$ that considers only the aspect terms, $poly^2_{BoW}$ of the terms around the aspect terms in a window of size 5, lin_{LB} derived from the Emolex lexicon. In the unconstrained setting the $sptk_{GRCT}$ replaces the ptk counterpart and the rbf_{WS} is added by linearly combining Word Space vectors for verbs, nouns adjective and adverbs. Results in Table 3 show that the proposed kernel combination allows to achieve the 8th position with the unconstrained system in the *restaurant* domain. The differences with the constrained setting demonstrate the contribution of the Word Space acquired from the TripAdvisor corpus. Unfortunately, it is not true in the laptop domain, as shown in Table 4. The use of the Opinosis corpus lets to a performance drop of the unconstrained setting. An error analysis shows that the main limitation of the proposed model is the inability to capture deep semantic phenomena such as irony, as in the negative sentence "*the two waitress's looked like they had been sucking on lemons*".

Table 3: Aspect Term Polarity Results - Restaurant.

System (Rank)	Accuracy
UNITOR-C (12/36)	.7248
UNITOR-U (8/36)	.7495
Best-System-C (1/36)	.8095
Best-System-U (5/36)	.7768

Table 4: Aspect Term Polarity Results - Laptop.

System (Rank)	Accuracy
UNITOR-C (10/32)	.6299
UNITOR-U (17/32)	.5856
Best-System-C (1/32)	.7048
Best-System-U (5/32)	.6666

4.3 Aspect Category Detection

The Aspect Category Detection has been modeled as a multi-label classification task where 5 categories (*ambience*, *service*, *food*, *price*, *anecdotes/miscellaneous*) must be recognized. In the constrained version, each class has been tackled using a binary multi-kernel SVM equipped with a linear combination of $poly^2_{BoW}$ and rbf_{WNSO}. A category is assigned if the SVM classifiers provides a positive prediction. The anecdotes/miscellaneous acceptance threshold has been set to 0.3 (it has been estimated over a development set) due to its poor precision observed during the tuning phase. Moreover, considering each sentence is always associated to at least one category, if no label has been assigned, then the sentence is labelled with the category associated to the highest prediction.

In the unconstrained case, each class has been tackled using an ensemble of a two binary SVM-based classifiers. The first classifier is a multi-kernel SVM operating on a linear combination of rbf_{WS} and $poly^2_{BoW}$. The second classifier is a SVM equipped with a rbf_{WSTO}. A sentence is labelled with a category if at least one of the two corresponding classifiers predicts that label. The first classifier assigns a label if the corresponding prediction is positive. A more conservative strategy is applied to the second classifier, and a category is selected if its corresponding prediction is higher than 0.3; again this threshold has been estimated over a development set. As in the constrained version, we observed a poor precision in the anecdotes/miscellaneous category, so we increased the first classifier acceptance threshold to 0.3, while the second classifier output is completely ignored. Finally, if no label has been assigned, the sentence is labelled with the category associated to the highest prediction of the first classifier.

Table 5: Aspect Category Detection Results.

System (Rank)	P	R	F1
UNITOR-C (6/21)	.8368	.7804	.8076
UNITOR-U (2/21)	.8498	.8556	.8526
Best-System-C (1/21)	.9104	.8624	.8857
Best-System-U (4/21)	.8435	.7892	.8155

Table 5 reports the achieved results. Considering the simplicity of the proposed approach, the results are impressive. The ensemble schema, adopted in the unconstrained version, is very useful in improving the recall and allows the system to achieve the second position in the competition.

4.4 Aspect Category Polarity

The Aspect Category Polarity subtask has been modeled as a multi-class classification problem: given a set of pre-identified aspect categories for a sentence, it aims at determining the polarity (*positive*, *negative*, *neutral* or *conflict*) of each category. It has been tackled using multi-kernel SVMs in a One-vs-All Schema. In the constrained setting, the linear combination of the following kernel functions has been used: ptk_{GRCT}, $poly^2_{BoW}$ that consider all the lemmatized terms in the sentence, a $poly^2_{BoW}$ that considers only verbs, nouns adjective and adverbs in the sentence, lin_{LB} derived from the MPQA sentiment lexicon. In the unconstrained case the $sptk_{GRCT}$ replaces the ptk counterpart and the rbf_{WS} is added by linearly combining Word Space vectors for verbs, nouns adjective and adverbs.

Again, results shown in Table 6 suggest the positive contribution of the lexical generalization provided by the Word Space (in the $sptk_{GRCT}$ and rbf_{WS}) allows to achieve a good rank, i.e. the 4th position with the unconstrained system in the *restaurant* domain. The error analysis underlines that the proposed features do not capture irony.

Table 6: Aspect Category Polarity Results.

System (Rank)	Accuracy
UNITOR-C (7/25)	.7307
UNITOR-U (4/25)	.7629
Best-System-C (1/25)	.8292
Best-System-U (9/25)	.7278

References

Yasemin Altun, I. Tsochantaridis, and T. Hofmann. 2003. Hidden Markov support vector machines. In *Proceedings of the International Conference on Machine Learning*.

Giuseppe Castellucci, Simone Filice, Danilo Croce, and Roberto Basili. 2013. Unitor: Combining syntactic and semantic kernels for twitter sentiment analysis. In *Second Joint Conference on Lexical and Computational Semantics (*SEM), Volume 2: Proceedings of the Seventh International Workshop on Semantic Evaluation (SemEval 2013)*, pages 369–374, Atlanta, Georgia, USA, June. ACL.

Michael Collins and Nigel Duffy. 2001. Convolution kernels for natural language. In *Proceedings of Neural Information Processing Systems (NIPS'2001)*, pages 625–632.

Nello Cristianini, John Shawe-Taylor, and Huma Lodhi. 2002. Latent semantic kernels. *J. Intell. Inf. Syst.*, 18(2-3):127–152.

Danilo Croce and Daniele Previtali. 2010. Manifold learning for the semi-supervised induction of framenet predicates: an empirical investigation. In *GEMS 2010*, pages 7–16, Stroudsburg, PA, USA. ACL.

Danilo Croce, Alessandro Moschitti, and Roberto Basili. 2011. Structured lexical similarity via convolution kernels on dependency trees. In *Proceedings of EMNLP*, Edinburgh, Scotland, UK.

Kavita Ganesan, ChengXiang Zhai, and Jiawei Han. 2010. Opinosis: a graph-based approach to abstractive summarization of highly redundant opinions. In *Proceedings of the 23rd International Conference on Computational Linguistics*, pages 340–348. ACL.

Gene Golub and W. Kahan. 1965. Calculating the singular values and pseudo-inverse of a matrix. *Journal of the Society for Industrial and Applied Mathematics: Series B, Numerical Analysis*, 2(2):pp. 205–224.

Thorsten Joachims. 1999. *Making large-Scale SVM Learning Practical.* MIT Press, Cambridge, MA.

Dan Klein and Christopher D. Manning. 2003. Accurate unlexicalized parsing. In *Proceedings of ACL'03*, pages 423–430.

Tom Landauer and Sue Dumais. 1997. A solution to plato's problem: The latent semantic analysis theory of acquisition, induction and representation of knowledge. *Psychological Review*, 104.

Bing Liu. 2007. *Web data mining*. Springer.

Saif Mohammad and Peter D. Turney. 2013. Crowdsourcing a word-emotion association lexicon. *Computational Intelligence*, 29(3):436–465.

Alessandro Moschitti, Daniele Pighin, and Robert Basili. 2008. Tree kernels for semantic role labeling. *Computational Linguistics*, 34.

Alessandro Moschitti. 2006. Efficient convolution kernels for dependency and constituent syntactic trees. In *ECML*, Berlin, Germany, September.

Sebastian Pado and Mirella Lapata. 2007. Dependency-based construction of semantic space models. *Computational Linguistics*, 33(2).

Bo Pang and Lillian Lee. 2008. Opinion mining and sentiment analysis. *Found. Trends Inf. Retr.*, 2(1-2):1–135, January.

Bo Pang, Lillian Lee, and Shivakumar Vaithyanathan. 2002. Thumbs up?: sentiment classification using machine learning techniques. In *EMNLP*, volume 10, pages 79–86, Stroudsburg, PA, USA. ACL.

Maria Pontiki, Dimitrios Galanis, John Pavlopoulos, Harris Papageorgiou, Ion Androutsopoulos, and Suresh Manandhar. 2014. Semeval-2014 task 4: Aspect based sentiment analysis. In *Proceedings of the International Workshop on Semantic Evaluation (SemEval)*.

Magnus Sahlgren. 2006. *The Word-Space Model.* Ph.D. thesis, Stockholm University.

John Shawe-Taylor and Nello Cristianini. 2004a. *Kernel Methods for Pattern Analysis.* Cambridge University Press, New York, NY, USA.

John Shawe-Taylor and Nello Cristianini. 2004b. *Kernel Methods for Pattern Analysis.* Cambridge University Press.

Janyce M. Wiebe, Rebecca F. Bruce, and Thomas P. O'Hara. 1999. Development and use of a gold-standard data set for subjectivity classifications. In *Proceedings of the 37th annual meeting of the ACL on Computational Linguistics*, pages 246–253, Stroudsburg, PA, USA. ACL.

Theresa Wilson, Janyce Wiebe, and Paul Hoffmann. 2005. Recognizing contextual polarity in phrase-level sentiment analysis. In *Proceedings of Human Language Technologies Conference/Conference on Empirical Methods in Natural Language Processing (HLT/EMNLP 2005)*, Vancouver, CA.

Zhibiao Wu and Martha Palmer. 1994. Verbs semantics and lexical selection. In *Proceedings of the 32Nd Annual Meeting of ACL*, ACL '94, pages 133–138, Stroudsburg, PA, USA. ACL.

University_of_Warwick: SENTIADAPTRON - A Domain Adaptable Sentiment Analyser for Tweets - Meets SemEval

Richard Townsend
University of Warwick
Richard.Townsend@warwick.ac.uk

Aaron Kalair
University of Warwick
Aaron.Kalair@warwick.ac.uk

Ojas Kulkarni
University of Warwick
Ojas.Kulkarni@warwick.ac.uk

Rob Procter
University of Warwick
Rob.Procter@warwick.ac.uk

Maria Liakata
University of Warwick
M.Liakata@warwick.ac.uk

Abstract

We give a brief overview of our system, SentiAdaptron, a domain-sensitive and domain adaptable system for twitter analysis in tweets, and discuss performance on SemEval (in both the constrained and unconstrained scenarios), as well as implications arising from comparing the intra- and inter- domain performance on our twitter corpus.

1 Introduction

A domain is broadly defined as a set of documents demonstrating a similar distribution of words and linguistic patterns. Task 9 of *SemEval* treats Twitter as a single domain with respect to sentiment analysis. However previous research has argued for the topic-specific treatment of sentiment given domain-specific nuances and the over-generality of current sentiment analysis systems with respect to applications in the social sciences (Thelwall and Buckley, 2013). Thelwal's method - manually extending a sentiment lexicon for a particular topic or domain - highlights that expression of sentiment varies from one domain to another. Rather than relying on the manual extension of lexica, we developed an approach to Twitter sentiment classification that is domain sensitive. To this effect we gathered tweets from three primary domains - financial news, political opinion, technology companies and their products - and trained our system on one domain while adapting to the other. Using this methodology we obtained both intrinsic as well as extrinsic evaluation of the system on real world applications with promising results. As our approach to sentiment analysis has been influenced by the task description of SemEval 2013 we decided to also evaluate the system on SemEval's data, since it provides a well established benchmark. In the following we briefly describe our system and corpus and discuss our approach for the SemEval submission.

	Positive	Negative	Neutral	Objective
SemEval	11610	6332	905	189887
Our corpus	10725	17837	3514	36904

(a) Contextual polarity.

	Positive	Negative	Neutral	Objective
SemEval	4215	1798	4082	1243
Our corpus	1090	1711	1191	-

(b) Message polarity.

Table 1: The distribution of sentiment classes between SemEval and our corpus at word and tweet level.

2 A Corpus of Three Domains: Source of Unconstrained Data

Our goal in developing SentiAdaptron was domain adaptive tweet-level classification. We decided to follow SemEval 2013 and collect both word-level as well as message level annotations. We prepared a corpus of 4000 tweets with a balanced coverage of financial, political and technology related tweets. Tweets were collected using keywords from domain-specific websites: the final list was chosen after evaluating each candidate keyword's popularity using a third-party service[1]. Each tweet is tagged with multiple candidate domains, based on a hierarchy of terms generated from the original keyword list and tweets are filtered using a clustering methodology based on the DBSCAN clustering algorithm to remove robotic and repetitive tweets. We performed domain disambiguation for annotation through keyword filtering and also by picking a number of synsets from WordNet and computing the tweet's mean semantic distance using the NLTK toolkit. Tweets which didn't contain

[1] http://topsy.com

Proceedings of the 8th International Workshop on Semantic Evaluation (SemEval 2014), pages 768–772,
Dublin, Ireland, August 23-24, 2014.

any words associated with a score of less than 0.3 in SentiWordNet were removed, in a manner similar to Nakov et al (2013). After further manual relevance checks, the remaining tweets were submitted to Amazon's Mechanical Turk service for message and phrase-level annotation. We initially used the form demonstrated by Nakov et al., although we later redesigned it with a dramatic improvement in annotator performance and annotation quality. Each tweet was annotated by four workers and annotation sparsity at the phrase level was addressed by taking the majority of annotations following the precedence neutral $>$ pos $>$ neg $>$ other. This is in contrast to the approach used by Nakov et al. for SemEval which intersects annotations. Annotations at the tweet level were aggregated using a majority vote. We found that using the proportion of positive, negative and neutral words in a tweet is a surprisingly robust feature for cross-domain classification, and boosted our performance when using bigrams.

3 Subjectivity Detection and Contextual Polarity Disambiguation (Subtask A)

Sentiment lexicons such as SentiWordNet (Esuli and Sebastiani, 2006), the NRC emotions lexicon (Mohammad and Turney, 2010), the MPQA lexicon (Wilson et al., 2005) and the Bing Liu Lexicon (Hu and Liu, 2004) have been used for determining whether a phrase should be labelled as positive, negative or neutral within a tweet or sentence (contextual polarity). However, lexical resources are by nature non-contextual and may not have good coverage over a given domain. We instead considered how to infer contextual polarity purely from the data available.

To address the problem of class imbalance in the tweets, we break the problem of contextual polarity detection into two stages: (i) we first determine whether a given word should be assigned a positive, negative or neutral annotation (*subjectivity detection*) and (ii) distinguish subjective tweets into positive, negative neutral.

3.1 Contextual Subjectivity Detection

Task A asks participants to predict the contextual subjectivity annotation of a text span at a given offset: our extrinsic applications don't have this fundamental structure, so we considered whether it was possible to automatically separate the content of input documents into those regions which should be assigned an annotation and those which should not. We considered a unigram and a bigram baseline using a naive Bayes classifier, which gave an F1 score of 0.640 and 0.520 respectively on our in domain data (under 10-fold cross-validation). We followed a number of approaches to subjectivity detection to try and improve on the baseline including sequential modelling using linear-chain Conditional Random Fields (CRFs) with CRF-suite (Okazaki, 2007) and lexical inference using semantically disambiguated WordNet (Miller, 1995) synsets in conjunction with their occurrence in a subjective context.

We found that the observed subjective proportion of a given word alongside its successor and predecessor[2] was a viable feature engineering scheme, which we call *neighbouring subjectivity proportions*. This gave the best subjectivity performance on our in-domain data when fed to a *voted perceptron* (Freund and Schapire, 1999), an ensemble approach which assigns particularly predictive iterations of an incrementally trained perceptron a greater weight when deciding the final classification, and offers wide-margin classification akin to support vector machines whilst also requiring less parameter exploration. We used the implementation provided by the WEKA machine-learning environment (Hall et al., 2009), which achieved an F1-score of 0.740 (again under 10-fold cross validation) for our in-domain data, but performance dropped to an F1-score of 0.323 on the SemEval 2013 training and development data. Table 1 indicates that the proportion of objective features in SemEval is much greater than that seen within our own corpus, likely due to the differences in the way we processed annotations (outlined in Section 2).

3.2 Contextual Polarity

We considered a naive Bayes unigram baseline, (similar approaches have proven popular with SemEval 2013 participants for Task A) and achieved an F1-measure of 0.662 when training using SemEval's 2014 training and development data and evaluating on SemEval's 2013 gold-standard annotations. However we could not detect the neutral class, and the test did not consider the objective class.

[2] As an example, if we observe 14 total occurrences of the word "heartbreaking", and 13 of them appear with a positive, negative or neutral label, the subjective proportion computed would be 13/14.

	F1-score				Precision			Recall		
	P	N	E	Overall	P	N	E	P	N	E
Task A (constrained)	85.5	49.0	9.84	67.3	91.1	41.4	3.8	80.6	60.2	16.7
Task A (unconstrained)	85.1	49.2	12.2	67.2	89.8	43.4	8.0	80.9	59.8	25.9
Finance	78.0	83.1	51.2	78.0	77.3	81.7	58.7	78.7	45.5	84.6
Politics	67.3	83.3	42.1	74.3	70.9	79.7	50.3	64.1	87.2	36.3
Technology	75.1	85.6	47.4	77.8	77.8	81.8	56.7	89.8	89.8	40.7

(a) Performance on word-level contextual annotation tasks.

	F1-score				Precision			Recall		
	P	N	E	Overall	P	N	E	P	N	E
Task B (constrained)	57.1	34.0	57.0	45.6	46.1	42.6	68.8	75.0	28.3	48.7
Task B (unconstrained)	57.2	33.0	57.7	45.1	46.2	36.1	72.1	74.9	30.4	47.9
Finance	78.7	78.9	64.6	73.8	77.9	79.5	64.8	78.3	79.5	64.5
Politics	80.8	75.0	61.9	72.3	78.4	74.8	63.7	83.3	75.1	60.2
Technology	73.2	78.2	58.0	70.1	69.7	76.3	62.9	76.9	80.2	53.7

(b) Performance on document-level annotation tasks.

Table 2: Classifier metrics obtained from 4-fold intra-domain cross-validation (using reference annotations) and results for subtasks A and B of SemEval task 9 (computed using reference scorer).

	Tech	Politics	Finance
Unigrams	0.53	0.35	0.53
Bigrams	0.38	0.31	0.52
Bigrams + SP	0.77	0.65	0.78
Unigrams + SP	0.68	0.62	0.76

Table 3: F1-scores achieved for each domain on our corpus (naive Bayes, 10-fold cross validation) using reference annotations with and without subjective (positive, negative, neutral) proportions (SP).

We improved on this baseline by combining unigrams with information from the wider context of the tweet. The algorithm first runs subjectivity detection on the entire document and then, for each word we need to classify (or otherwise each word detected as subjective), effectively generates two bags of words consisting of the subjective words before and after that word (we also included any adverbs as annotated by the Gimpel tagger (2011) in this bag to improve robustness). We output the word itself as a further feature, and use a random forest classifier (10 trees, $\log_2 N + 1$ features) to generate the annotation. We found this approach outperformed the other approaches we tried (including Naive Bayes and OneR) and also gave us better F1-scores on the neutral class. Results from this approach for our in-domain data and the SemEval 2014 data can be seen in Table 2a. The drop in performance from our in-domain data to SemEval 2014 can be explained by the different class distribution observed in SemEval (Table 1). Subjectivity detection was used to generate features for subtask B, but not subtask A, where the target subjective phrases are already given.

4 Message Polarity Classification (Subtask B)

We tried various different combinations of features to discover the best intra-domain classification approach for our corpus and found that the proportion of positive, negative and neutral words within a tweet boosted performance using bigram binary features (Table 3). This involves first running the contextual polarity detection component as described in Section 3 and feeding in the results as features (together with bigrams) into a naive Bayes classifier for tweet level sentiment detection. However, one of our hypotheses was that domain adaptation could help improve performance when moving from one domain to another, effectively allowing us to port our classifier from our own corpus to SemEval.

4.1 Cross-Domain Adaptation

Our research in domain adaptation uses and extends the technique described by Blitzer and Pereira (2007) called Structural Correspondence Learning (SCL), which derives a relationship (or correspondence) between features from two different domains. This is done via *pivot features* selected from the intersection of features from both domains which have been ranked according to mutual information. The technique then uses N pivot features from both the seen and unseen domains to learn a set of binary problems corresponding to whether a given pivot exists in a target document. A perceptron is then used to train each of the binary problems, giving a matrix of weights (where a weight represents covariance of non pivot features with pivot features). We extended Blitzer's technique to encompass the neutral class and gave a wider notion of domain than previously found in the literature. As an example Liu et al. (2013) use

Training domains	Test	Accuracy	Precision	Recall	F-measure
Tech & Finance	Politics	0.76	0.52	0.40	0.45
Tech & Politics	Finance	0.69	0.51	0.78	0.61
Finance & Politics	Tech	0.63	0.53	0.58	0.55

Table 4: Binary class metrics with structural correspondence learning on our own corpus.

			F-measure			**Precision**			**Recall**		
Train	**Test**	**Accuracy (SP)**	**SP**	**Baseline**(Bigrams)	**Loss**	**SP**	**Baseline (Bigrams)**	**Loss**	**SP**	**Baseline (Bigrams)**	**Loss**
Tech	**Politics**	69.74%	0.67	0.24	0.43	0.64	0.19	0.45	0.71	0.33	0.38
Tech	**Finance**	72.28%	0.78	0.20	0.58	0.74	0.15	0.59	0.83	0.33	0.50
Politics	**Tech**	72.40%	0.76	0.21	0.55	0.71	0.25	0.46	0.82	0.33	0.49
Politics	**Finance**	73.06%	0.79	0.22	0.57	0.77	0.16	0.61	0.82	0.33	0.49
Finance	**Politics**	68.39%	0.66	0.23	0.43	0.67	0.18	0.49	0.66	0.33	0.33
Finance	**Tech**	71.92%	0.76	0.22	0.54	0.71	0.16	0.55	0.82	0.33	0.49
Tech & Finance	**Politics**	69.17%	0.63	0.23	0.40	0.61	0.18	0.43	0.67	0.33	0.34
Tech & Politics	**Finance**	70.49%	0.63	0.20	0.43	0.61	0.15	0.46	0.64	0.33	0.31
Finance & Politics	**Tech**	72.88%	0.77	0.22	0.55	0.72	0.16	0.56	0.84	0.33	0.51

Table 5: Classifier metrics from training and testing on different domains, with and without proportions of positive, negative and neutral phrases from the source domain (Subjective Proportions SP).

an SVM-derived technique to adapt on domains containing terms relevant to *Google* and *Twitter*, which are both considered part of the technology domain in our corpus, whereas we attempted to adapt from technology topics to financial news and political opinions.

We found that the amount of mutual information in our three domains was very low and was practically zero for the three class version of our problem. The results for the binary version of the classifier generated poorer results (Table 4) than those produced by our back-up classifier (based on the naive Bayes bigrams and subjective phrase proportions from the source domain, see Table 5, last three rows). Therefore we generated our submission to SemEval 2014 based on bigrams and subjective proportions rather than SCL, since we found that the proportion of pos/neg/neutral phrases is a robust feature across domains (as long as it can be reliably predicted during the contextual polarity prediction stage, which was the case for our data). Our results for SemEval task B using the subjective phrase proportions can be found in Table 2b. Our unconstrained performance indicates that whilst this classifier provides reasonable cross domain performance for our own data (Table 5), it is very sensitive to the performance of subjectivity and contextual polarity detection, which is lower for SemEval than it is for our own corpus. Presumably the reason for this is the different assumptions in annotations in the two cases and the differences in the class distributions between SemEval and our own data. This meant that our performance was lower than systems that had specifically trained on the SemEval data.

5 Conclusions

Our goal was to demonstrate the potential of domain sensitivity and domain adaptability for sentiment analysis in tweets - a task which brings challenges defying the use of fixed lexica. We found that the proportions of positive, negative and neutral tweets are quite robust cross-domain features, although we do think that domain adaptation techniques such as Structural Correspondence Learning merit further investigation in the context of sentiment analysis for Twitter.

Access to the source code of this submission

The source code of the applications used to gather and prepare our corpus, conduct CRFsuite and structural correspondence learning, and the Java-based environment used to generate our final submission are available at `https://github.com/Sentimentron/Nebraska-public`[3] and `https://github.com/Sentimentron/PRJ9081`[4].

Acknowledgements

Warwick Research Development Fund grant RD13129 provided funding for crowdsourced annotations. We thank our partners at CUSP, NYU for enabling us to use Amazon Mechanical Turk for this process.

[3] `http://dx.doi.org/10.5281/zenodo.9906`
[4] `http://dx.doi.org/10.5281/zenodo.9904`

References

Martin Ester, Hans-Peter Kriegel, Jörg Sander, and Xiaowei Xu. 1996. A density-based algorithm for discovering clusters in large spatial databases with noise. In *KDD*, volume 96, pages 226–231.

Andrea Esuli and Fabrizio Sebastiani. 2006. SentiWordNet: A publicly available lexical resource for opinion mining. In *Proceedings of LREC*, volume 6, pages 417–422.

Yoav Freund and Robert E Schapire. 1999. Large margin classification using the perceptron algorithm. *Machine learning*, 37(3):277–296.

Kevin Gimpel, Nathan Schneider, Brendan O'Connor, Dipanjan Das, Daniel Mills, Jacob Eisenstein, Michael Heilman, Dani Yogatama, Jeffrey Flanigan, and Noah A. Smith. 2011. Part-of-speech tagging for Twitter: annotation, features, and experiments. In *Proceedings of the 49th Annual Meeting of the Association for Computational Linguistics: Human Language Technologies: short papers - Volume 2*, HLT '11, pages 42–47.

Mark Hall, Eibe Frank, Geoffrey Holmes, Bernhard Pfahringer, Peter Reutemann, and Ian H Witten. 2009. The WEKA data mining software: an update. *ACM SIGKDD explorations newsletter*, 11(1):10–18.

Minqing Hu and Bing Liu. 2004. Mining and summarizing customer reviews. In *Proceedings of the tenth ACM SIGKDD international conference on Knowledge discovery and data mining*, pages 168–177.

Mark Dredze John Blitzer and Fernando Pereira. 2007. Biographies, bollywood, boom-boxes and blenders: Domain adaptation for sentiment classification. In *Proceedings of the 45th Annual Meeting of the Association of Computational Linguistics*, pages 440–447.

Shenghua Liu, Fuxin Li, Fangtao Li, Xueqi Cheng, and Huawei Shen. 2013. Adaptive co-training SVM for sentiment classification on tweets. In *Proceedings of the 22nd ACM international conference on Conference on information & knowledge management*, pages 2079–2088.

George A Miller. 1995. WordNet: a lexical database for english. *Communications of the ACM*, 38(11):39–41.

Saif M Mohammad and Peter D Turney. 2010. Emotions evoked by common words and phrases: Using Mechanical Turk to create an emotion lexicon. In *Proceedings of the NAACL HLT 2010 Workshop on Computational Approaches to Analysis and Generation of Emotion in Text*, pages 26–34.

Preslav Nakov, Sara Rosenthal, Zornitsa Kozareva, Veselin Stoyanov, Alan Ritter, and Theresa Wilson. 2013. SemEval-2013 Task 2: Sentiment Analysis in Twitter. pages 312–320, June.

Naoaki Okazaki. 2007. CRFsuite: a fast implementation of Conditional Random Fields (CRFs). [ONLINE] `http://www.chokkan.org/software/crfsuite/` (Retrieved: July 16, 2014).

Mike Thelwall and Kevan Buckley. 2013. Topic-based sentiment analysis for the social web: The role of mood and issue-related words. *Journal of the American Society for Information Science and Technology*, 64(8):1608–1617.

Theresa Wilson, Paul Hoffmann, Swapna Somasundaran, Jason Kessler, Janyce Wiebe, Yejin Choi, Claire Cardie, Ellen Riloff, and Siddharth Patwardhan. 2005. OpinionFinder: A system for subjectivity analysis. In *Proceedings of HLT/EMNLP on Interactive Demonstrations*, pages 34–35.

UO_UA: Using Latent Semantic Analysis to Build a Domain-Dependent Sentiment Resource

Reynier Ortega
Adrian Fonseca
Carlos Muñiz
CERPAMID
Ave Patricio Lumumba, S/N
Santigo de Cuba, Cuba
reynier.ortega@cerpamid.co.cu
adrian@cerpamid.co.cu

Yoan Gutiérrez
Andrés Montoyo
DLSI, University of Alicante
Carretera de San Vicente, S/N
Alicante, Spain
ygutierrez@dlsi.ua.es
montoyo@dlsi.ua.es

Abstract

In this paper we present our contribution to *SemEval-2014 Task 4: Aspect Based Sentiment Analysis (Pontiki et al., 2014), Subtask 2: Aspect Term Polarity* for Laptop domain. The most outstanding feature in this contribution is the automatic building of a domain-depended sentiment resource using Latent Semantic Analysis. We induce, for each term, two real scores that indicate its use in positive and negative contexts in the domain of interest. The aspect term polarity classification is carried out in two phases: opinion words extraction and polarity classification. The opinion words related with an aspect are obtained using dependency relations. These relations are provided by the Stanford Parser[1]. Finally, the polarity of the feature, in a given review, is determined from the positive and negative scores of each word related to it. The results obtained by our approach are encouraging if we consider that the construction of the polarity lexicon is performed fully automatically.

1 Introduction

Hundreds of millions of people and thousands of companies around the world, actively use Social Media[2]. Every day are more amazing websites and applications (Facebook, Twitter, MySpace, Amazon, etc.) that allow the easy sharing of information in near real time. For this reason, at present, the Web is flooded with subjective, personal and affective data. Mining this huge volume of information offer both interesting challenges and useful intelligent applications such as recommendation systems (Dong et al., 2013; Sun et al., 2009) and customer's reviews summarization (Bafna and Toshniwal, 2013; Balahur and Montoyo, 2008).

Nowadays, companies have redirected their marketing strategies toward the Web. Each one of them advertises that their products are the best, amazing, easy to use, long lasting and cheap. But are these advertisements really true? Obviously, not everything is true. The companies usually exaggerate the product's quality and in many cases tend not to advertise the limitations of their products. Therefore, taking a rational decision about which product is the best among the variety of existing options can be very stressful.

To avoid this situation, frequently we trust in the experiences gained by others who have purchased the product of our interest, or one similar. The existence of websites like Ciao[3], Epinions[4] and Cnet[5] make possible to the customers to interchange their experiences about a specific product, and to future clients avoid products advertising

However, the existence of a large volume of reviews entails that it is impossible to conduct an effective exploration before making a final decision. The most important benefit of having that amount of user-generated content on hand, specifically product's reviews, is that, these data can be explored by a computer system to obtain information about products and their features.

The task of aspect-based sentiment analysis (Liu, 2012) is a fine-grained level of Sentiment Analysis (Pang and Lee, 2008). This aim to identify the aspects (*e.g., battery, screen, food, service, size, weight, time-life*) of given target entities

[1] http://nlp.stanford.edu:8080/parser/

[2] http://en.wikipedia.org/wiki/Social_media

[3] www.ciao.com

[4] www.epinions.com

[5] www.cnet.com

Proceedings of the 8th International Workshop on Semantic Evaluation (SemEval 2014), pages 773–778,
Dublin, Ireland, August 23-24, 2014.

(*e.g., laptops, restaurants, camera*) and the sentiment expressed towards each aspect (*e.g., positive, negative, neutral*). This are composed by two basic phases: feature extraction and feature polarity classification.

In this paper we present our contribution for *SemEval-2014 Task 4: Aspect Based Sentiment Analysis (Pontiki et al., 2014), Subtask 2: Aspect Term Polarity*. In this approach we only focus on the polarity classification problem. For this, we induce a domain-dependent sentiment lexicon applying Latent Semantic Analysis (LSA) on product reviews corpus, gathered from Ciao. The classification phase is carried out as follow: the opinion words related with the product aspect are draw out using the dependency relations provided by Stanford Parser, then the polarity of the extracted words are combined to obtain overall aspect polarity.

The paper is organized as follows. Section 2 describes our approach. Further on, in Section 3, we discuss the results obtained in the SemEval 2014 Task No. 4 subtask 2. Finally, section 4 provides concluding remarks.

2 UO_UA System

One of major challenge in sentiment analysis into product reviews, is dealing with a quite domain dependence. For instance, the word *"unpredictable"* can be considered as positive in Movie domain, however it is very negative in Airplane domain. For this reason, we propose to create a specific sentiment lexicon for addressing aspect based sentiment analysis in reviews.

Our proposal is divided in two main phases. The first one aims to build a domain-dependent sentiment resource for Laptop domain applying LSA. The second phase obtains the words related by means of some dependency relation with the aspect, and later, the polarity of these words are obtained from induced polarity lexicon and combined for computing overall aspect polarity.

2.1 Domain-Dependent Polarity Lexicon

The use of sentiment resource has been proven to be useful to build, train, and evaluate systems for sentiment analysis (Gutiérrez et al., 2013; Balahur, 2011). In order to build sentiment resource, several approach has been presented. In one of the first works, presented by (Hatzivassiloglou and McKeown, 1997), was proposed to take into account if adjectives are linked by adversative or copulative conjunctions for detecting its polarity. In (Turney and Littman, 2003) the authors exposed a method for inferring the semantic orientation of a word from its statistical association with a set of positive and negative paradigm words, measured by point-wise mutual information (PMI). In (2004), Hu and Liu suggested a technique to expand the lexicon using the relations of synonymy and antonym provided by WordNet (Fellbaum, 1998). In (2009), Cruz et al., created a sentiment resource based on a graph, constructed from conjunctive expressions between pairs of adjectives, observed in a review corpus. PageRank algorithm (Page et al., 1999) was adapted to be used on graphs with positive and negative edges, in order to obtain the semantic orientation of words.

Despite the wide range of existing proposals for resources construction, the results achieved with them are far from expected. As we have already seen, in aspect based sentiment analysis, the polarity of a word is heavily dependent on the domain; and general propose sentiment resource such as General Inquirer (Stone et al., 1966), WordNet-Affect(Strapparava and Valitutti, 2004), SentiWordNet(Baccianella et al., 2010) or HowNet (Dong et al., 2010) do not capture this dependency. On the other hand, the human annotators can not create specific sentiment resources for each new product launched to market. Therefore, propose methods to create these resources is a challenging task.

In this paper we address this task, presenting a framework for building domain-dependent sentiment resource. Our proposal is compounded of four phases. (See figure 1).

Firstly, review pages about the product of interest can be retrieved from different websites, for instance, Ciao, Epinions and Cnet (in this work we only use reviews from Ciao). This reviews are parsed and cleaned (this time we use Python XML Parser[6]). For each page we extract: pros, cons, title, full review and rating. In this work we have only focus on the pros and cons attributes because they are usually very brief, consist of short phrases or sentence segments and give a positive and negative evaluation about the product aspects. Each pros and cons in remainder paper will be considered as positive and negative samples, respectively.

[6]https://docs.python.org/2/library/xml.html

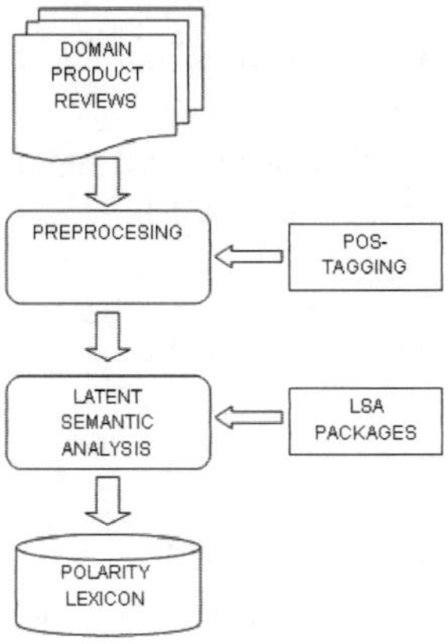

Figure 1: Building domain-dependent sentiment resource.

Subsequently, the samples are preprocessed, applying a POS-Tagging tool (Padró and Stanilovsky, 2012) to convert all words in lemmas. After that, the stopwords are removed from text. Afterward each sample is represented using the classic vector space model (Salton et al., 1975). Intending to measure the association between term and class we add a special term to the vectors. In positive samples the term t_{pos} is added whereas in the negative samples the term t_{neg} is aggregated.

Later, we apply a Latent Semantic Analysis (this time we use, Gensim python package) to calculate the strength of the semantic association between words and classes. LSA uses the Singular Value Decomposition (SVD) to analyze the statistical relationships among words in a corpus.

The first step is construct a matrix $M_{n \times m}$, in which the row vectors v_i represent lemmas and the column vectors s_i the positive and negative sample (pros and cons). In each cell t_{ij}, we have the TF score (Term Frequency) of the ith lemma in j^{th} sample. The next step is apply Singular Value Decomposition to matrix $M_{n \times m}$ to decompose it into a product of three matrices $U \Sigma V^T$, then, we select the k largest singular values, and their corresponding singular vectors from U and V, obtained an approximation $\hat{M} = U_k \Sigma_k V_k^T$ of rank k to original matrix $M_{n \times m}$. After LSA is performed, we use the new matrix $\hat{M}$ to measure the association between lemmas l_i and l_j computing the cosine measure between vectors v_i and v_j, with the equation 1.

$$LSA_{score}(l_i, l_j) = \frac{< v_i, v_j >}{\| v_i \| \cdot \| v_j \|} \quad (1)$$

Finally, the polarity lexicon contains lemmas l_i and its positive and negative scores. This values are computed using $LSA_{score}(l_i, t_{pos})$ and $LSA_{score}(l_i, t_{neg})$ respectively. The table 1 show some top positive and negative words computed with this strategy.

Positive	**Score**	**Negative**	**Score**
sturdy	0.8249	*prone*	0.8322
superb	0.7293	*weak*	0.8189
durable	0.7074	*disaster*	0.8120
sexy	0.6893	*erm*	0.8118
powerfull	0.6700	*ill*	0.8107
robust	0.6686	*uncomfortable*	0.8084
affordable	0.6630	*noisy*	0.7917
suuupeerrr	0.6550	*overwhelm*	0.7514
lighweight	0.6550	*unsturdy*	0.7491
unbreakable	0.6542	*lousy*	0.7143

Table 1: Examples of positive and negative words.

With aim to do our contribution to *SemEval-2014, Task 4: Aspect Based Sentiment Analysis (Pontiki et al., 2014), Subtask 2: Aspect Term Polarity*, we gathered 3010 Laptop Reviews, from Ciao and create a corpus with 6020 samples, 3010 positives (Pros) and 3010 negatives (Cons). This corpus was used as input in the developed framework (See figure 1). In this time we utilize Freeling[7] as POS-Tagging tool and Gensim Python Packages[8] to perform LSA (only the most 100 most significant eigenvalue are used). After that, a domain-dependent sentiment resource (DLSR) with 4482 term was created for Laptop reviews.

2.2 Aspect Polarity Classification

In order to exploit our domain-dependent sentiment resource building for Laptop domain, we develop an unsupervised method based on language rule to classify the product aspect. The basic rules are used to find dependency relation between aspect and their attributes. The figure 2 show the architecture of our proposal.

The proposed method receive as input a tuple $(P_{feature}, R)$, where $P_{feature}$ represent the aspect to evaluate, and R is the context (review) in it appears.

[7] http://nlp.lsi.upc.edu/freeling/

[8] https://pypi.python.org/pypi/gensim

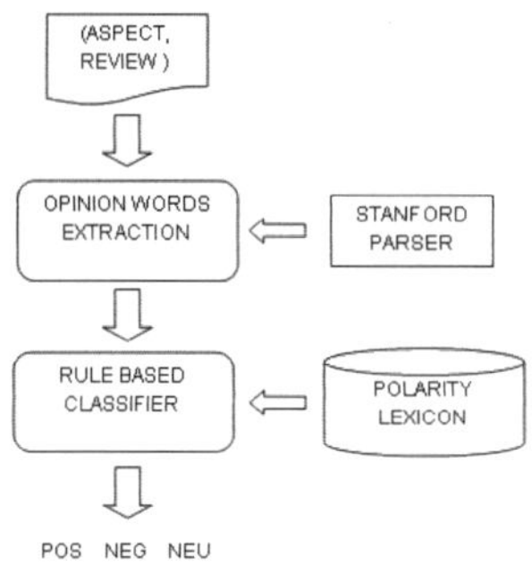

Figure 2: Apect polarity classification.

The dependency parsed is applied to review R, using Stanford Parser. Following that, we extract a set of tuples W, each tuple is represented as a pair (Att, Mod) where Att is a word related with the aspect $P_{feature}$ through some dependency relations shown in Table 2, and Mod is a integer value indicating if Att is modified by a valence shifter (Polanyi and Zaenen, 2004), (we only consider negation words, e.g., *never, no, not, don't, nothing,* etc.) , and default value of 0 is assign, in case that, the Att is modified by a valence shifter, we assign value of -1.

Dependency relations		
mod	subj	nsubj
amod	csub	csubpass
advmod	obj	dobj
vmod	iobj	pobj
rcmod	npadvmod	nn
subj	xcomp	advcl

Table 2: Stanford Parser dependency relations.

Once, the set of pairs W was obtained, the polarity of the feature $P_{feature}$ is determined from the scores of the attributes (related words) that describe it. To sum up, for each pair $(Att, Mod) \in W$, the positive $Pos((Att, Mod))$ and negative $Neg((Att, Mod))$ scores are calculated as:

$$Neg((Att, Mod)) = \begin{cases} -N(Att)\, if\, Mod < 0 \\ N(Att)\, otherwise \end{cases} \quad (2)$$

$$Pos((Att, Mod)) = \begin{cases} -P(Att)\, if\, Mod < 0 \\ P(Att)\, otherwise \end{cases} \quad (3)$$

Where $P(Att)$ and $N(Att)$ are the positive and negative score for Att in domain-dependent sentiment resource DLSR.

Finally, the global positive and negative scores (SO_{pos}, SO_{neg}) are calculated as:

$$SO_{pos}(P_{feature}) = \sum_{w \in W} Pos(w) \quad (4)$$

$$SO_{neg}(P_{feature}) = \sum_{w \in W} Neg(w) \quad (5)$$

If SO_{pos} is greater than SO_{neg} then the aspect is considered as positive. On the contrary, if SO_{pos} is less than SO_{neg} the aspect is negative. Finally, if SO_{pos} is equal to SO_{neg} the aspect is considered as neutral.

3 Results

In this section we present the evaluation of our system in the context of *SemEval-2014, Task 4: Aspect Based Sentiment Analysis (Pontiki et al., 2014), Subtask 2: Aspect Term Polarity.* For evaluating the participant's system two unlabeled domain-specific datasets for laptops and restaurants were distributed. For each dataset two runs can be submitted, the first (constrained), the system can only be used the provided training data and other resources such as lexicons. In the second (unconstrained), the system can use additional data for training. We send one run for laptop dataset and it only use external data retrieved from Ciao website (the training data was not used) (unconstrained).

The results achieve by our method are illustrate in Table 3. As may be observed, the accuracy

Label	Pr	Rc	F1
conflict	0.0	0.0	0.0
negative	**0,5234**	0,3764	0,4379
neutral	0,4556	0,4074	0,4302
positive	**0,6364**	**0,7561**	**0,6911**
Accuracy		0.55198777	

Table 3: Results in aspect polarity classification for laptop dataset.

achieve by UA_OU was 0.55, and F1 measure for negative, neutral and positive were 0,4379, 0,4302 and 0,6911 respectively. In case of conflict polarity we reached a 0.0 F1 value because our system not handle this situation. For this subtask (Laptop domain) a total of 32 runs was submitted by all systems participant's and our run was ranked as 25th. The results despite not achieving expected, are encouraging. These evidence the feasibility of building resources from data available on the web, for aspect-based sentiment analysis.

4 Conclusions

In this article, we presented and evaluated the approach considered for our participation in *SemEval-2014 Task 4: Aspect Based Sentiment Analysis (Pontiki et al., 2014), Subtask 2: Aspect Term Polarity*, specifically for Laptop Domain. We present a framework for building domain-dependent sentiment resources applying Latent Semantic Analysis and build a special resource for polarity classification in Laptop domain. This resource was combined into unsupervised method to compute the polarity associated to different aspect in reviews. The results obtained by our approach are encouraging if we consider that the construction of the polarity lexicon is performed fully automatically.

Acknowledgements

This research work has been partially funded by the University of Alicante, Generalitat Valenciana, Spanish Government and the European Commission through the projects, "Tratamiento inteligente de la información para la ayuda a la toma de decisiones" (GRE12-44), ATTOS (TIN2012-38536-C03-03), LEGOLANG (TIN2012-31224), SAM (FP7-611312), FIRST (FP7-287607) and ACOMP/2013/067.

References

Stefano Baccianella, Andrea Esuli, and Fabrizio Sebastiani. 2010. SentiWordnet 3.0: An enhanced lexical resource for sentiment analysis and opinion mining. *Proceedings of the Seventh International Conference on Language Resources and Evaluation*, LREC '10, Valletta, Malta, May.

Kushal Bafna and Durga Toshniwal. 2013. Feature based summarization of customers' reviews of online products. *Procedia Computer Science*, 22(0):142 – 151. 17th International Conference in Knowledge Based and Intelligent Information and Engineering Systems - KES2013.

Alexandra Balahur and Andrés Montoyo. 2008. Multilingual feature-driven opinion extraction and summarization from customer reviews. In Epaminondas Kapetanios, Vijayan Sugumaran, and Myra Spiliopoulou, editors, *Natural Language and Information Systems*, volume 5039 of *Lecture Notes in Computer Science*, pages 345–346. Springer Berlin Heidelberg.

Alexandra Balahur. 2011. *Methods and Resources for Sentiment Analysis in Multilingual Documents of Different Text Types*. Ph.D. thesis, Department of Software and Computing Systems. Alcalant, Alcalant University.

Fermín Cruz, José Antonio Troyano, Francisco Javier Ortega, and Carlos García Vallejo. 2009. Inducción de un lexicón de opinión orientado al dominio. *Procesamiento del Lenguaje Natural*, 43:5–12.

Zhendong Dong, Qiang Dong, and Changling Hao. 2010. HowNet and its computation of meaning. In *Proceedings of the 23rd International Conference on Computational Linguistics: Demonstrations*, COLING'10, pages 53–56, Stroudsburg, PA, USA.

Ruihai Dong, Markus Schaal, Michael P. O'Mahony, Kevin McCarthy, and Barry Smyth. 2013. Opinionated product recommendation. In Sarah Jane Delany and Santiago Ontañón, editors, *Case-Based Reasoning Research and Development*, volume 7969 of *Lecture Notes in Computer Science*, pages 44–58. Springer Berlin Heidelberg.

Christiane Fellbaum, editor. 1998. *WordNet: An Electronic Lexical Database*. MIT Press.

Yoan Gutiérrez, Andy González, Roger Pérez, José Abreu, Antonio Fernández Orquín, Alejandro Mosquera, Andrés Montoyo, Rafael Muñoz, and Franc Camara. 2013. UMCC_DLSI-(SA): Using a ranking algorithm and informal features to solve sentiment analysis in Twitter. *Atlanta, Georgia, USA*, page 443.

Vasileios Hatzivassiloglou and Kathleen McKeown. 1997. Predicting the semantic orientation of adjectives. In *Proceedings of the Joint ACL/EACL Conference*, pages 174–181.

Minqing Hu and Bing Liu. 2004. Mining opinion features in customer reviews. In *Proceedings of AAAI*, pages 755–760.

Bing Liu. 2012. Sentiment Analysis and Opinion Mining. *Synthesis Lectures on Human Language Technologies*, 5(1):1–167.

Lluís Padró and Evgeny Stanilovsky. 2012. Freeling 3.0: Towards wider multilinguality. *Proceedings of the Eight International Conference on Language Resources and Evaluation (LREC'12)*, Istanbul, Turkey, May. European Language Resources Association (ELRA).

Lawrence Page, Sergey Brin, Rajeev Motwani, and Terry Winograd. 1999. The PagerRank Citation Ranking: Bringing Order to the Web.

Bo Pang and Lillian Lee. 2008. Opinion Mining and Sentiment Analysis.

Livia Polanyi and Annie Zaenen. 2004. Contextual lexical valence shifters. In Yan Qu, James Shanahan, and Janyce Wiebe, editors, *Proceedings of the AAAI Spring Symposium on Exploring Attitude and Affect in Text: Theories and Applications*. AAAI Press. AAAI technical report SS-04-07.

Maria Pontiki, Dimitrios Galanis, John Pavlopoulos, Harris Papageorgiou, Ion Androutsopoulos, and Suresh Manandhar. 2014. Semeval-2014 task 4: Aspect Based Sentiment Analysis. In *International Workshop on Semantic Evaluation (SemEval), 2014*.

Gerard Salton, Andrew Wong, and Chung Shu Yang. 1975. A vector space model for automatic indexing. *Communications of the ACM*, 18(11):613–620.

Philip James Stone, Dexter Colboyd Dunphy, Marshall Smith, and Daniel Ogilvie. 1966. *The General Inquirer: A Computer Approach to Content Analysis*. MIT Press, Cambridge, MA.

Carlo Strapparava and Alessandro Valitutti. 2004. WordNet-Affect: an affective extension of WordNet. In *In Proceedings of the 4th International Conference on Language Resources and Evaluation*, LREC, pages 1083–1086, Lisbon, Portugal, May 26-28. European Language Resources Association.

Jianshu Sun, Chong Long, Xiaoyan Zhu, and Minlie Huang. 2009. Mining reviews for product comparison and recommendation. *Polibits*, pages 33 – 40, 06.

Peter Turney and Michael Lederman Littman. 2003. Measuring praise and criticism: Inference of semantic orientation from association. *ACM Transactions on Information Systems (TOIS)*, 21(4):315–346.

UoW: Multi-task Learning Gaussian Process for Semantic Textual Similarity

Miguel Rios
Research Group in Computational Linguistics
University of Wolverhampton
Stafford Street, Wolverhampton,
WV1 1SB, UK
M.Rios@wlv.ac.uk

Lucia Specia
Department of Computer Science
University of Sheffield
Regent Court, 211 Portobello,
Sheffield, S1 4DP, UK
L.Specia@sheffield.ac.uk

Abstract

We report results obtained by the UoW method in SemEval-2014's Task 10 – Multilingual Semantic Textual Similarity. We propose to model Semantic Textual Similarity in the context of Multi-task Learning in order to deal with inherent challenges of the task such as unbalanced performance across domains and the lack of training data for some domains (i.e. unknown domains). We show that the Multi-task Learning approach outperforms previous work on the 2012 dataset, achieves a robust performance on the 2013 dataset and competitive results on the 2014 dataset. We highlight the importance of the challenge of unknown domains, as it affects overall performance substantially.

1 Introduction

The task of Semantic Textual Similarity (STS) (Agirre et al., 2012) is aimed at measuring the degree of semantic equivalence between a pair of texts. Natural Language Processing (NLP) applications such as Question Answering (Lin and Pantel, 2001), Text Summarisation (Lin and Hovy, 2003) and Information Retrieval (Park et al., 2005) rely heavily on the ability to measure semantic similarity between pairs of texts. The STS evaluation campaign provides datasets that consist of pairs of sentences from different NLP domains such as paraphrasing, video paraphrasing, and machine translation (MT) evaluation. The participating systems are required to predict a graded similarity score from 0 to 5, where a score of 0 means that the two sentences are on different topics and a score of 5 means that the two sentences have exactly the same meaning.

Methods for STS are commonly based on computing various types of similarity metrics between the pair of sentences, where the similarity scores are used as features to train regression algorithms. Bär et al. (2012) use similarity metrics of varying complexity. The range of features goes from simple string similarity metrics to complex vector space models. The method yielded the best average results based on the official evaluation metrics, despite not having achieved the best results in all individual domains. Šarić et al. (2012) use a similar set up, extracting features from similarity metrics, where these features are based on word-overlap and syntax similarity. The method was among the best for domains related to paraphrasing. It also achieved a high correlation between the training and test data. In contrast, for the machine translation data the performance in the test set was lower than the one over the training data. A possible reason for the poor results on this domain is the difference in length between the training and test sentences, as in the test data the pairs tend to be short and share similar words. Šarić et al. (2012) claim that these differences show that the MT training data is not representative of the test set given their choice of features.

Most of the participating systems in the STS challenges achieve good results on certain domains (i.e. STS datasets), but poor results on others. Even the most robust methods still show a big gap in performances for different datasets. In the second evaluation campaign of STS a new challenge was proposed: domains for which no training sets are provided, but only test sets. Heilman and Madnani (2013) propose to incorporate domain adaptation techniques (Daumé et al., 2010) for STS to generalise models to new domains. They add new features into the model, where the feature set contains domain specific features plus

Proceedings of the 8th International Workshop on Semantic Evaluation (SemEval 2014), pages 779–784, Dublin, Ireland, August 23-24, 2014.

general task features. The machine learning algorithm infers the extra weights of each specific domain and of the general domain. When an instance of a specific domain is to be predicted, only the copy of the features of that domain will be active; if the domain is unknown, the general features will be active. Severyn et al. (2013) propose to use meta-classification to cope with domain adaptation. They merge each pair into a single text and extract meta-features such as bag-of-words and syntactic similarity scores. The meta-classification model predicts, for each instance, its most likely domain based on these features.

A possible solution to alleviate unbalanced performances on different domains is to model STS in the context of Multi-task Learning (MTL). The motivation behind MTL is that by learning multiple related tasks simultaneously the model performance may improve compared to the case where the tasks are learnt separately. MTL is based on the assumption that related tasks can be clustered and inter-task correlations between tasks within the same cluster can be transferred.

We propose to model STS using MTL based on a state-of-the-art STS feature set (Šarić et al., 2012). As algorithm we use a non-parametric Bayesian approach, namely Gaussian Processes (GP) (Rasmussen, 2006). We show that the MTL model outperforms previous work on the 2012 datasets and leads to robust performance on the 2013 datasets. On the STS 2014 challenge, our method shows competitive results.

2 Experimental Setting

We apply MTL to cope with the challenge of unbalanced performances across domains and unknown domains present in the STS datasets.

2.1 TakeLab Features

We use the features from one the top performing system in STS 2012: the TakeLab[1] system, which is publicly available. It extracts the following types of features:

N-gram overlap is the harmonic mean of the degree of matching between the first and second texts, and vice-versa. The overlap is computed for unigrams, bigrams, and trigrams.

WordNet-augmented word overlap is the partial WordNet path length similarity score assigned to words that are not common to both texts.

Vector space sentence similarity is the representation of each text as a distributional vector by summing the distributional (i.e., LSA) vectors of each word in the text and taking the cosine distance between these texts vectors.

Shallow NE similarity is the matching between Named Entities (NE) that indicates whether they were found in both texts.

Numbers overlap is an heuristic that penalises differences between numbers in texts.

Altogether, these features make up a vector of 21 similarity scores.

2.2 Multi-task Gaussian Processes

Gaussian Processes (Rasmussen, 2006) is a Bayesian non-parametric machine learning framework based on kernels for regression and classification. In GP regression, for the inputs x we want to learn a function f that is inferred from a GP prior:

$$f(x) \sim GP(m(x), k(x, x\prime)), \tag{1}$$

where $m(x)$ defines a 0 mean and $k(x, x\prime)$ defines the covariance or kernel functions. In the single output case, the random variables are associated to a process f evaluated at different values of the input x. In the multiple output case, the random variables are associated to different processes and evaluated at different values of x.

We are interested in the intrinsic coregionalization model for GP. A coregionalization model is a *heterotopic* MTL model in which each output is associated with a different set of inputs. In our case the different set of inputs are the STS domains (i.e. datasets). The intrinsic coregionalization model (i.e. MTL-GP) is based on a separable multi-task kernel (Álvarez et al., 2012) of the form

$$K(X, X) = B \otimes k(X, X), \tag{2}$$

where $k(X, X)$ is a standard kernel over the input points and B is a positive semi-definite matrix encoding task covariances, called coregionalization matrix. B is built from other matrices $B = WW^\top + diag(k)$, where W is a matrix that determines the correlations between the different outputs and k is a matrix which allows the outputs

[1] http://takelab.fer.hr/sts/

(i.e. tasks) to behave independently. The representation of data points is augmented with task ids and given the id of a pair of data points the covariance from the standard kernel between them is multiplied by a corresponding covariance from B, which modifies the data points' covariance depending on whether they belong to the same task or different tasks.

The coregionalization matrix B allows us to control the amount of inter and intra task transfer of learning among tasks. Cohn and Specia (2013) propose different types of B matrices to model the problem of predicting the quality of machine translations. They developed B matrices that represent an explicit intra-task transfer to be a part of the parameterised kernel function. We use a default B where the weights of the matrix are learnt along with the hyper-parameters by the GP tool.

For training our method we use the GPy toolkit[2] with a combination of RBF and coregionalization kernels. The parameters used to build the coregionalization matrix are the number of outputs to coregionalize and the rank of W. For example, in the 2012 training set, the number of outputs to coregionalize is 3, given that we have three tasks/domains. The B matrix and the RBF kernel hyper-parameters are jointly optimised. Each instance of the training data is then augmented with the id of their corresponding task. During testing a new instance has to be matched to a specific task/domain id from the training data. In the case of an unknown test domain, we match it to a training domain which is similar, given the description of the test dataset.

For the STS 2014 dataset, given the large number of training instances, we train a sparse GP model within GPy. The main limitation of the GP model is the that memory demands grow $O(n^2)$, and the computational demands grow $O(n^3)$, with n equals the number of training instances. Sparse methods (e.g. (Titsias, 2009)) try to overcome this limitation by constructing an approximation of the full model on a smaller set of m support or inducing instances that allow the reduction of computational demands to $O(nm^2)$. For the sparse GP we use the same combination of kernels as the full model, where we chose empirically the number of inducing instances m and the GP tool randomly selects the instances from the training data.

[2] https://github.com/SheffieldML/GPy

3 Results and Discussion

In what follows we show a comparison with previous work on the STS 2012 and 2013 datasets, and the official results for English and Spanish STS 2014 datasets.

3.1 STS 2012 and STS 2013

For training we use the STS 2012 training datasets and we compare the results on the STS 2012 with publicly available systems and with the official Baseline, which is based on the cosine metric computed over word overlaps. The official evaluation metric is Pearson's correlation. We match the unknown domain OnWN to MSRpar given that the domain of paraphrasing is that of news from the web, which potentially contains a broad enough vocabulary to cover OnWN.

Table 3.1 shows a comparison of the MTL-GP with previous work on the STS 2012 data, where our method outperforms them for most of the domains. Our method improves the results of TakeLab with the same feature set. In other words, the transfer learning improves over (Šarić et al., 2012), which is trained with a separate Support Vector Regression model for each domain. We note that we can only compare our method against the simpler version of TakeLab that is available. A different version using syntactic features was also proposed, where most results do not show a significant variation, except for an improvement of r=0.4683 in the SMTnews dataset. For the complete alternative results we refer the reader to (Šarić et al., 2012).

On the STS 2013 dataset, we compare our method with work based on domain adaptation and the official baseline. We use the 2012 data for training as no additional training data is provided in 2013. Table 3.1 shows all the possible matching combinations between the STS 2013 test sets and STS 2012 training sets. The best results are given by matching the STS 2013 test sets with the MSRvid domain, where all 2013 sets achieve their best results.

In Table 3.1, we show the comparison with previous work on the 2013 datasets, where we use the best matching result from Table 3.1 (MSRvid). Our method shows very competitive results but only with the correct matching of domains, whereas the worst performed matching (SMTeuroparl, Table 3.1) shows results that are closer to the official Baseline. In previous work

Method	MSRpar	MSRvid	SMTeuroparl	SMTnews	OnWN
Šarić et al. (2012)	**0.7343**	0.8803	0.4771	0.3989	0.6797
Bär et al. (2012)	0.68	0.8739	0.5280	0.4937	0.6641
MTL-GP	0.7324	**0.8877**	**0.5615**	**0.6053**	**0.7256**
Baseline	0.4334	0.2996	0.4542	0.3908	0.5864

Table 1: Comparison with previous work on the STS 2012 test datasets.

(Heilman and Madnani, 2013), domain adaptation is performed with the addition of extra features and the subsequent extra parameters to the model, where in the MTL-GP the transfer learning is done with the coregionalization matrix and does not depend on large amounts of data.

3.2 English STS 2014

The training dataset consists of the combination of each English training and test STS datasets from 2012 and 2013, which results in 7 domains. For testing, in our first run we matched similar domains with each other and the unknown domain with MSRpar. For our second run, we matched the unknown domains with a similar one. The domain matching (test/training) was done as follows: deft-forum/MSRpar, deft-news/SMTnews, tweet-news/SMTnews and images/MSRvid. For our third run, the difference in matching is for deft-news/headlines and tweet-news/headlines, where the other domains remain with the same matching. Table 3.2 shows the official STS 2014 results where our best method (i.e. run3) achieves rank 10.

In Table 3.2, we show the comparison of the MTL-GP and the sparse MTL-GP with the best 2014 system (DLSCU run2). For both MTL methods we match the 2014 domains with the training domain *headlines*. For the sparse MTL-GP, we chose empirically a number m of 500 randomly induced points. For reference, the correlation of sparse MTL-GP with 50 points on deft-forum is r=0.4691 obtained in 0.23 hours, with 100 points, r=0.4895, with 500 points, r=0.4912, and with 1000 points, r=0.4911. The sparse MTL-GP with 500 points runs in 1.38 hours, compared to 2.39 hours for the full MTL-GP[3]. Additionally, the sparse version achieves similar results to the full model and very competitive performance compared to the best STS 2014 system. However, the result for OnWN is substantially lower than the best system. This result can be highly improved (r=0.7990) if the test set is matched with the correspondent training domain.

Test \ Train	MSRvid	MSRpar	SMTeuroparl
Headlines	**0.6666**	0.6595	0.5693
OnWN	**0.6516**	0.4635	0.4113
FNWN	**0.4062**	0.3217	0.2344

Table 2: Matching of new 2013 domains with 2012 training data.

3.3 Spanish STS 2014

For the Spanish STS subtask we use both simple and state-of-the-art (SoA) features to train the MTL-GP. The simple features are similarity scores from string metrics such as Levenshtein, Gotoh, Jaro, etc.[4] The SoA similarity features come again from TakeLab. The training dataset consists of the combination of each English STS domains from 2012 and 2013 and the Spanish trial dataset with task-id matching each instance to a given domain. We represent the feature vectors with sparse features for the English and Spanish training datasets, where in English the pairs have simple and SoA features, and for Spanish, only the simple features. In other words, the feature vectors have the same number of features (34): 13 simple features and 21 SoA features. However, for Spanish the SoA features are set to 0 in training and testing. The motivation to use SoA and simple features in English is that the extra information will improve the transfer learning on the English domains and discriminate between the English domains and the Spanish domain, which only contains simple features. For testing we only extracted the simple features; the SoA features were set to 0. For the coregionalization matrix we set the number of domains to be the English STS domains from 2012 and 2013, plus the Spanish trial, where the Spanish is treated as an additional domain, which results in 8 domains. In the first run of testing, we matched the test datasets to the Spanish domain, and in the second run we matched the datasets to the English MSRpar do-

[3] Intel Xeon(R) at 2.67GHz with 24 cores

[4] https://github.com/Simmetrics/simmetrics

Method	Headlines	OnWN	FNWN
Heilman and Madnani (2013)	**0.7601**	0.4631	0.3516
Severyn et al. (2013)	0.7465	0.5572	0.3875
MTL-GP	0.6666	**0.6516**	**0.4062**
Baseline	0.5399	0.2828	0.2146

Table 3: Comparison between best matching MTL-GP (MSRvid) and previous work on the STS 2013 test datasets.

Run	deft-forum	deft-news	headlines	images	OnWN	tweet-news	Weighted mean	rank
UoW run1	0.3419	0.7512	0.7535	0.7763	0.7990	0.7368	0.7143	11
UoW run2	0.3419	0.5875	0.7535	0.7877	0.7990	0.6281	0.6817	17
UoW run3	0.3419	0.7634	0.7535	0.7877	0.7990	0.7529	0.7207	10

Table 4: Official English STS 2014 results.

main. Table 3.3 shows the official results for the Spanish subtask, where our method achieves competitive performance, placed 7 in the systems ranking. We only show the results for the first run as both runs achieved the same performance.

Run	Wikipedia	News	Weighted mean	rank
UoW	0.7483	0.8001	0.7792	7

Table 6: Official Spanish STS 2014 results.

Table 3.3 shows the comparison of the best Spanish STS 2014 system (UMCC_DLSI run2) against two different sparse MTL-GP matched with the Spanish trial with 500 inducing points. Sparse MTL-GP run1 uses the sparse features described above, while run2 uses a modification of the feature set consisting in specific features for each type of domain. For the English domains the simple features are set to 0, and for Spanish the SoA are still set to 0. The difference between sparse MTL-GP models is very small, where the use of all the features on the English domains improves the results. However, the performance of both models is still substantially lower than that of the best system.

Run	Wikipedia	News
UMCC_DLSI run2	0.7802	0.8254
Sparse MTL-GP run1	0.7468	0.7959
Sparse MTL-GP run2	0.7380	0.7878

Table 7: Comparison of best system against sparse MTL-GP STS 2014 results.

4 Conclusions

We propose the use of MTL for STS. We show that MTL improves the results of one of the best STS systems, TakeLab. However, the matching of an unknown domain during testing proved a key challenge that affects performance significantly. Given the results of STS 2013 and 2014, our method tends to achieve best results when known/unknown domains are matched to the same training domains (i.e. *MSRpar* for 2013 and *headlines* for 2014). The sparse MTL-GP shows similar performance to the full GP model, but takes half the time to be trained. In the Spanish subtask, we train our method with English datasets and the Spanish trial data as an additional domain. For this subtask our method also shows competitive results. Future work involves the automatic matching of unknown domains at test time via meta-classification (Severyn et al., 2013).

Acknowledgments

This work was supported by the Mexican National Council for Science and Technology (CONACYT), scholarship reference 309261, and by the QTLaunchPad (EU FP7 CSA No. 296347) project.

References

Eneko Agirre, Mona Diab, Daniel Cer, and Aitor Gonzalez-Agirre. 2012. Semeval-2012 task 6: A pilot on semantic textual similarity. In *Proceedings of the First Joint Conference on Lexical and Computational Semantics*, SemEval '12, pages 385–393, Stroudsburg, PA, USA.

Mauricio A. Álvarez, Lorenzo Rosasco, and Neil D. Lawrence. 2012. Kernels for vector-valued functions: A review. *Found. Trends Mach. Learn.*, 4(3):195–266, March.

Daniel Bär, Chris Biemann, Iryna Gurevych, and Torsten Zesch. 2012. Ukp: Computing semantic textual similarity by combining multiple content similarity measures. In *Proceedings of the First*

Run	deft-forum	deft-news	headlines	images	OnWN	tweet-news
DLSCU run2	0.4828	**0.7657**	**0.7646**	**0.8214**	**0.8589**	**0.7639**
Best matching MTL-GP	0.4903	0.7633	0.7535	0.8063	0.7222	0.7528
Sparse MTL-GP	**0.4910**	0.7642	0.7540	0.8057	0.7276	0.7539

Table 5: Comparison between best matching MTL-GP (headlines), Sparse MTL-GP and best STS 2014 system.

Joint Conference on Lexical and Computational Semantics, SemEval '12, pages 435–440, Stroudsburg, PA, USA.

Trevor Cohn and Lucia Specia. 2013. Modelling annotator bias with multi-task gaussian processes: An application to machine translation quality estimation. In *51st Annual Meeting of the Association for Computational Linguistics*, ACL-2013, pages 32–42, Sofia, Bulgaria.

Hal Daumé, III, Abhishek Kumar, and Avishek Saha. 2010. Frustratingly easy semi-supervised domain adaptation. In *Proceedings of the 2010 Workshop on Domain Adaptation for Natural Language Processing*, DANLP 2010, pages 53–59, Stroudsburg, PA, USA.

Michael Heilman and Nitin Madnani. 2013. Henry-core: Domain adaptation and stacking for text similarity. In *Second Joint Conference on Lexical and Computational Semantics (*SEM)*, pages 96–102, Atlanta, Georgia, USA, June.

Chin-Yew Lin and Eduard Hovy. 2003. Automatic evaluation of summaries using n-gram co-occurrence statistics. In *Proceedings of the 2003 Conference of the North American Chapter of the Association for Computational Linguistics on Human Language Technology - Volume 1*, NAACL '03, pages 71–78, Stroudsburg, PA, USA.

Dekang Lin and Patrick Pantel. 2001. Discovery of inference rules for question-answering. *Nat. Lang. Eng.*, 7(4):343–360.

Eui-Kyu Park, Dong-Yul Ra, and Myung-Gil Jang. 2005. Techniques for improving web retrieval effectiveness. *Inf. Process. Manage.*, 41(5):1207–1223.

Carl Edward Rasmussen. 2006. Gaussian processes for machine learning. MIT Press.

Aliaksei Severyn, Massimo Nicosia, and Alessandro Moschitti. 2013. ikernels-core: Tree kernel learning for textual similarity. In *Second Joint Conference on Lexical and Computational Semantics (*SEM)*, pages 53–58, Atlanta, Georgia, USA, June.

Michalis Titsias. 2009. Variational Learning of Inducing Variables in Sparse Gaussian Processes. In *the 12th International Conference on Artificial Intelligence and Statistics (AISTATS)*.

Frane Šarić, Goran Glavaš, Mladen Karan, Jan Šnajder, and Bojana Dalbelo Bašić. 2012. Takelab: Systems for measuring semantic text similarity. In *Proceedings of the First Joint Conference on Lexical and Computational Semantics*, SemEval '12, pages 441–448, Stroudsburg, PA, USA.

UoW: NLP Techniques Developed at the University of Wolverhampton for Semantic Similarity and Textual Entailment

Rohit Gupta, Hanna Béchara, Ismail El Maarouf and **Constantin Orăsan**
Research Group in Computational Linguistics,
Research Institute of Information and Language Processing,
University of Wolverhampton, UK
{R.Gupta, Hanna.Bechara, I.El-Maarouf, C.Orasan}@wlv.ac.uk

Abstract

This paper presents the system submitted by University of Wolverhampton for SemEval-2014 task 1. We proposed a machine learning approach which is based on features extracted using Typed Dependencies, Paraphrasing, Machine Translation evaluation metrics, Quality Estimation metrics and Corpus Pattern Analysis. Our system performed satisfactorily and obtained 0.711 Pearson correlation for the semantic relatedness task and 78.52% accuracy for the textual entailment task.

1 Introduction

The SemEval task 1 (Marelli et al., 2014a) involves two subtasks: predicting the degree of relatedness between two sentences and detecting the entailment relation holding between them. The task uses SICK dataset (Marelli et al., 2014b), consisting of 10000 pairs, each annotated with relatedness in meaning and entailment relationship holding between them. Similarity measures between sentences are required in a wide variety of NLP applications. In applications like Information Retrieval (IR), measuring similarity is a vital step in order to determine the best result for a related query. Other applications such as Paraphrasing and Translation Memory (TM) rely on similarity measures to weight results. However, computing semantic similarity between sentences is a complex and difficult task, due to the fact that the same meaning can be expressed in a variety of ways. For this reason it is necessary to have more than a surface-form comparison.

We present a method based on machine learning which exploits available NLP technology. Our approach relies on features inspired by deep semantics (such as parsing and paraphrasing), machine translation quality estimation, machine translation evaluation and Corpus Pattern Analysis (CPA[1]).

We use the same features to measure both semantic relatedness and textual entailment. Our hypothesis is that each feature covers a particular aspect of implicit similarity and entailment information contained within the pair of sentences. Training is performed in a regression framework for semantic relatedness and in a classification framework for textual entailment.

The remainder of the paper is structured as follows. In Section 2, we review the work related to our study and the existing NLP technologies used to measure sentence similarity. In Sections 3 and 4, we describe our approach and the similarity measures we used. In Section 5, we present the results and an analysis of our runs based on the test and training data provided by the SemEval-2014 task. Finally, our work is summed up in Section 6 with perspectives for future work we would like to explore.

2 Related Work

The areas of semantic relatedness and entailment have received extensive interest from the research community in the last decade. Earlier work in relatedness (Banerjee and Pedersen, 2003; Li et al., 2006) exploited WordNet in various ways to extract the semantic relatedness. Banerjee and Pedersen (2003) presented a measure using extended gloss overlap. This measure takes two WordNet synsets as input and uses the overlap of their WordNet glosses to compute their degree of semantic relatedness. Li et al. (2006) presented a semantic similarity metric based on the semantic similarity of words in a sentence. Recently, Wang and Cer (2012) presented an ap-

[1] http://pdev.org.uk

Proceedings of the 8th International Workshop on Semantic Evaluation (SemEval 2014), pages 785–789,
Dublin, Ireland, August 23-24, 2014.

proach that uses probabilistic edit-distance to measure semantic similarity. The approach uses probabilistic finite state and pushdown automata to model weighted edit-distance where state transitions correspond to edit-operations. In some aspects, our work is similar to Bär et al. (2012), who presented an approach which combines various text similarity measures using a log-linear regression model.

Entailment has been modelled using various approaches. The main approaches are based on logic inferencing (Moldovan et al., 2003), machine learning (Hickl et al., 2006; Castillo, 2010) and tree edit-distance (Kouylekov and Magnini, 2005). Most of the recent approaches employ various syntactic or tree edit models (Heilman and Smith, 2010; Mai et al., 2011; Rios and Gelbukh, 2012; Alabbas and Ramsay, 2013). Recently, Alabbas and Ramsay (2013) presented a modified tree edit distance approach, which extends tree edit distance to the level of subtrees. The approach extends Zhang-Shasha's algorithm (Zhang and Shasha, 1989).

3 Features

Our system uses the same 31 features for both subtasks. This section explains them and the code which implements most of them can be found on GitHub[2].

3.1 Language Technology Features

We used existing language processing tools to extract features. Stanford CoreNLP[3] toolkit provides lemma, parts of speech (POS), named entities, dependencies relations of words in each sentence.

We calculated Jaccard similarity on surface form, lemma, dependencies relations, POS and named entities to get the feature values. The Jaccard similarity computes sentence similarity by dividing the overlap of words on the total number of words of both sentences.

$$Sim(s1, s2) = \frac{|s1 \cap s2|}{|s1 \cup s2|} \quad (1)$$

where in equation (1), $Sim(s1, s2)$ is the Jaccard similarity between sets of words $s1$ and $s2$.

We used the same toolkit to identify coreference relations and determine clusters of coreferential entities. The coreference feature value was calculated using clusters of coreferential entities. The intuition is that sentences containing coreferential entities should have some semantic relatedness. In order to extract clusters of coreferential entities, the pair of sentences was treated as a document. The coreference feature value using these clusters was calculated as follows:

$$Value_{coref} = \frac{CC}{TC} \quad (2)$$

where CC is the number of clusters formed by the participation of entities (at least one entity from each sentence of the pair) in both sentences and TC is the total number of clusters.

We calculated two separate feature values for dependency relations: the first feature concatenated the words involved in a dependency relation and the second used grammatical relation tags. For example, for the sentence pair "the kids are playing outdoors" and "the students are playing outdoors" the Jaccard similarity is calculated based on concatenated words "kids::the, playing::kids, playing::are, ROOT::playing, playing::outdoors" and "students::the, playing::students, playing::are, ROOT::playing, playing::outdoors" to get the value for the first feature and "det, nsubj, aux, root, dobj" and "det, nsubj, aux, root, dobj" to get the value for the second feature.

These language technology features try to capture the token based similarity and grammatical similarity between a pair of sentences.

3.2 Paraphrasing Features

We used the PPDB paraphrase database (Ganitkevitch et al., 2013) to get the paraphrases. We used lexical and phrasal paraphrases of "L" size. For each sentence of the pair, we created two sets of bags of n-grams ($1 \leq n \leq$ length of the sentence). We extended each set with paraphrases for each n-gram available from paraphrase database. We then calculated the Jaccard similarity (see Section 3.1) between these extended bag of n-grams to get the feature value. This feature capture the cases where one sentence is a paraphrase of the other.

3.3 Negation Feature

Our system does not attempt to model similarity with negation, but since negation is an important feature for contradiction in textual entailment, we designed a non-similarity feature. The system checks for the presence of a negation word such as 'no', 'never' and 'not' in the pair of sentences and

[2]https://github.com/rohitguptacs/wlvsimilarity

[3]http://nlp.stanford.edu/software/corenlp.shtml

returns "1" ("0" otherwise) if both or none of the sentences contain any of these words.

3.4 Machine Translation Quality Estimation Features

Seventeen of the features consist of Machine Translation Quality Estimation (QE) features, based on the work of (Specia et al., 2009) and used as a baseline in recent QE tasks (such as (Callison-Burch et al., 2012)). We extracted these features by treating the first set of sentences as the Machine Translation (MT) "source", and the second set of sentences as the MT "target". In Machine Translation, these features are used to access the quality of MT "target". The QE features include shallow surface features such as the number of punctuation marks, the average length of words, the number of words. Furthermore, these features include n-gram frequencies and language model probabilities. A full list of the QE features is provided in the documentation of the QE system[4] (Specia et al., 2009).

QE features relate to well-formedness and syntax, and are not usually used to compute semantic relatedness between sentences. We have used them in the hope that the surface features at least will show us some structural similarity between sentences.

3.5 Machine Translation Evaluation Features

Additionally, we used BLEU (Papineni et al., 2002), a very popular machine translation evaluation metric, as a feature. BLEU is based on n-gram counts. It is meant to capture the similarity between translated text and references for machine translation evaluation. The BLEU score over surface, lemma and POS was calculated to get three feature values. In a pair of sentences, one side was treated as a translation and another as a reference. We applied it at the sentence level to capture the similarity between two sentences.

3.6 Corpus Pattern Analysis Features

Corpus Pattern Analysis (CPA) (Hanks, 2013) is a procedure in corpus linguistics that associates word meaning with word use by means of semantic patterns. CPA is a new technique for mapping meaning onto words in text. It is currently being used to build a "Pattern Dictionary of English Verbs"(PDEV[5]). It is based on the Theory of Norms and Exploitations (Hanks, 2013).

There are two features extracted from PDEV. They both make use of a derived resource called the CPA network (Bradbury and El Maarouf, 2013). The CPA network links verbs according to similar semantic patterns (e.g. both 'pour' and 'trickle' share an intransitive use where the subject is "liquid").

The first feature value compares the main verbs in both sentences. When both verbs share a pattern, the system returns a value of "1" (otherwise "0"). The second feature extends the CPA network to compute the probability of a PDEV pattern, given a word. This probability is computed over the portion of the British National Corpus which is manually tagged with PDEV patterns. The probability of a pattern given each word of a sentence of the dataset is obtained by the product of those probabilities. The feature value is the (normalised) number of common patterns from the three most probable patterns in each sentence. These features try to capture similarity based on semantic patterns.

4 Predicting Through Machine Learning

4.1 Model Description

We used a support vector machine in order to build a regression model to predict semantic relatedness and a classification model to predict textual entailment. For the actual implementation we used LibSVM[6] (Chang and Lin, 2011).

We used a regression model for the relatedness task that estimates a continuous score between 1 and 5 for each sentence. For the entailment task, we trained a classification model which assigns one of three different labels (ENTAILMENT, CONTRADICTION, NEUTRAL) to each sentence pair. We trained both systems on the 4500 sentence training set, augmented with the 500 sentence trial data. The values of C and γ have been optimised through a grid-search which uses a 5-fold cross-validation method.

The RBF kernel proved to be the best for both tasks.

5 Results and Analysis

We submitted 4 runs of our system (Run-1 to Run-4). Run-1 was submitted as primary run. Run-2, Run-3 and Run-4 systems were identical except

[4]https://github.com/lspecia/quest

[5]http://pdev.org.uk

[6]http://www.csie.ntu.edu.tw/ cjlin/libsvm/

	Run-1	Run-2	Run-3	Run-4
C	8	8	2	2
γ	0.0441	0.0441	0.125	0.125
Pearson	0.7111	0.7166	0.6968	0.6975

Table 1: Results: Relatedness.

	Run-1	Run-2	Run-3	Run-4
C	16	16	8	8
γ	0.0625	0.0625	0.5	0.5
Accuracy	78.526	78.526	78.343	78.343

Table 2: Results: Entailment.

for some parameter differences for SVM training and the replacement of the values which were outside the boundaries (1-5). If relatedness values predicted by the system were less than 1 or greater than 5, these values were replaced by 1 and 5 respectively for Run-1, Run-2 and Run-4 and 1.5 and 4.5 respectively for Run-3. Our primary run also used one extra feature for relatedness, which was obtained by considering entailment judgement as a feature. Our hypothesis was that entailment judgement may help in measuring relatedness. In the actual test this feature was not helpful and we obtained Pearson correlation of 0.711 for the primary run, compared to 0.716 for Run-2. The details of runs are given in Table 1 and 2.

After training both models, we ran a feature selection algorithm to determine which features yielded the highest accuracy, and therefore had the highest impact on our system. Perhaps unsurprisingly, the QE features were not very useful in predicting semantic similarity or entailment. However, despite their focus on fluency rather than semantic correctness, the QE features still managed to contribute to some improvements in the textual entailment task (increasing accuracy by 1%), and the semantic relatedness task (0.027 increase in Pearson correlation).

In the entailment (classification) task, the strongest feature proved to be the negation feature with 70% accuracy (on the training set) when training on this feature only. This suggests that some measure of negation is crucial in determining whether a sentence contradicts or entails another sentence. Other strong features were lemma, paraphrasing and dependencies.

In the relatedness (regression) task, the lemma, surface, paraphrasing, dependencies, PDEV features were the strongest contributors to accuracy.

6 Conclusion and Future Work

We have presented an efficient approach to calculate semantic relatedness and textual entailment. One noticeable point of our approach is that we have used the same features for both tasks and our system performed well in each of these tasks. Therefore, our system captures reasonably good models to compute semantic relatedness and textual entailment.

In the future we would like to explore more features and particularly those based on tree edit distance, WordNet and PDEV. Our intuition suggests that tree edit distance seems to be more helpful for entailment, whereas WordNet and PDEV seem to be more helpful for similarity measurement. Additionally, we would like to combine our techniques for measuring relatedness and entailment with MT evaluation techniques. We would further like to apply these techniques cross-lingually, moving into other areas like machine translation evaluation and quality estimation.

Acknowledgement

The research leading to these results has received funding from the People Programme (Marie Curie Actions) of the European Union's Seventh Framework Programme FP7/2007-2013/ under REA grant agreement no. 317471 and partly supported by an AHRC grant "Disambiguating Verbs by Collocation project, AH/J005940/1, 2012-2015".

References

Maytham Alabbas and Allan Ramsay. 2013. Natural language inference for Arabic using extended tree edit distance with subtrees. *Journal of Artificial Intelligence Research*, 48:1–22.

Satanjeev Banerjee and Ted Pedersen. 2003. Extended gloss overlaps as a measure of semantic relatedness. In *IJCAI*, volume 3, pages 805–810.

Daniel Bär, Chris Biemann, Iryna Gurevych, and Torsten Zesch. 2012. Ukp: Computing semantic textual similarity by combining multiple content similarity measures. In *First Joint Conference on*

Lexical and Computational Semantics, Association for Computational Linguistics, pages 435–440.

Jane Bradbury and Ismaïl El Maarouf. 2013. An empirical classification of verbs based on Semantic Types: the case of the 'poison' verbs. In *Proceedings of the Joint Symposium on Semantic Processing. Textual Inference and Structures in Corpora*, pages 70–74.

Chris Callison-Burch, Philipp Koehn, Christof Monz, Matt Post, Radu Soricut, and Lucia Specia, editors. 2012. *Proceedings of the Seventh Workshop on Statistical Machine Translation*. Association for Computational Linguistics, Montréal, Canada, June.

Julio J. Castillo. 2010. Recognizing textual entailment: experiments with machine learning algorithms and RTE corpora. *Special issue: Natural Language Processings and its Applications, Research in Computing Science*, 46:155–164.

Chih-Chung Chang and Chih-Jen Lin. 2011. LIBSVM: A library for support vector machines. *ACM Transactions on Intelligent Systems and Technology*, 2:27:1–27:27.

Juri Ganitkevitch, Van Durme Benjamin, and Chris Callison-Burch. 2013. Ppdb: The paraphrase database. In *Proceedings of NAACL-HLT*, pages 758–764, Atlanta, Georgia.

Patrick Hanks. 2013. *Lexical Analysis: Norms and Exploitations*. Mit Press.

Michael Heilman and Noah A. Smith. 2010. Tree edit models for recognizing textual entailments, paraphrases, and answers to questions. In *The 2010 Annual Conference of the North American Chapter of the ACL*, number June, pages 1011–1019.

Andrew Hickl, Jeremy Bensley, John Williams, Kirk Roberts, Bryan Rink, and Ying Shi. 2006. Recognizing textual entailment with LCC's GROUNDHOG system. In *Proceedings of the Second PASCAL Challenges Workshop*.

Milen Kouylekov and Bernardo Magnini. 2005. Recognizing textual entailment with tree edit distance algorithms. In *Proceedings of the First Challenge Workshop Recognising Textual Entailment*, pages 17–20.

Yuhua Li, David McLean, Zuhair A Bandar, James D O'shea, and Keeley Crockett. 2006. Sentence similarity based on semantic nets and corpus statistics. *Knowledge and Data Engineering, IEEE Transactions on*, 18(8):1138–1150.

Zhewei Mai, Y Zhang, and Donghong Ji. 2011. Recognizing text entailment via syntactic tree matching. In *Proceedings of NTCIR-9 Workshop Meeting*, pages 361–364, Tokyo, Japan.

Marco Marelli, Luisa Bentivogli, Marco Baroni, Raffaella Bernardi, Stefano Menini, and Roberto Zamparelli. 2014a. Semeval-2014 task 1: Evaluation of compositional distributional semantic models on full sentences through semantic relatedness and textual entailment. In *Proceedings of the 8th International Workshop on Semantic Evaluation (SemEval-2014)*.

Marco Marelli, Stefano Menini, Marco Baroni, Luisa Bentivogli, Raffaella Bernardi, and Roberto Zamparelli. 2014b. A sick cure for the evaluation of compositional distributional semantic models. In *Proceedings of LREC 2014*.

Dan Moldovan, Christine Clark, Sanda Harabagiu, and Steve Maiorano. 2003. COGEX : A Logic Prover for Question Answering. In *Proceedings of HLT-NAACL*, number June, pages 87–93.

Kishore Papineni, Salim Roukos, Todd Ward, and Wei-Jing Zhu. 2002. Bleu: a method for automatic evaluation of machine translation. In *Proceedings of the ACL*, pages 311–318.

Miguel Rios and Alexander Gelbukh. 2012. Recognizing Textual Entailment with a Semantic Edit Distance Metric. In *11th Mexican International Conference on Artificial Intelligence*, pages 15–20. IEEE.

Lucia Specia, Marco Turchi, Nicola Cancedda, Marc Dymetman, and Nello Cristianini. 2009. Estimating the sentence-level quality of machine translation systems. In *13th Conference of the European Association for Machine Translation*, pages 28–37.

Mengqiu Wang and Daniel Cer. 2012. Stanford: probabilistic edit distance metrics for STS. In *Proceedings of the First Joint Conference on Lexical and Computational Semantics*, pages 648–654.

Kaizhong Zhang and Dennis Shasha. 1989. Simple Fast Algorithms for the Editing Distance between Trees and Related Problems. *SIAM Journal on Computing*, 18(6):1245–1262.

USF: Chunking for Aspect Term Identification & Polarity Classification

Cindi Thompson
University of San Francisco
2130 Fulton St, HR 240 San Francisco, CA 94117
cathompson4@usfca.edu

Abstract

This paper describes the systems submitted by the University of San Francisco (USF) to Semeval-2014 Task 4, Aspect Based Sentiment Analysis (ABSA), which provides labeled data in two domains, laptops and restaurants. For the constrained condition of both the aspect term extraction and aspect term polarity tasks, we take a supervised machine learning approach using a combination of lexical, syntactic, and baseline sentiment features. Our extraction approach is inspired by a chunking approach, based on its strong past results on related tasks. Our system performed slightly below average compared to other submissions, possibly because we use a simpler classification model than prior work. Our polarity labeling approach uses two baseline hand-built sentiment classifiers as features in addition to lexical and syntactic features, and performed in the top ten of other constrained systems on both domains.

1 Introduction

As stated in the call for participation for this Semeval task, sentiment analysis focusing on overall polarity of a document, sentence, or similar context has been well studied in recent years (Liu, 2010; Pang and Lee, 2008; Tsytsarau and Palpanas, 2012). However, there is less prior work examining finer levels of granularity associated with individual entities and their characteristics or attributes, which the organizers for this task call *aspects*. The aspect based sentiment analysis task (ABSA) has the goal of identifying aspects of stated or implied target entities and the sentiment expressed towards each aspect. This problem has not been deeply studied in prior literature due to the lack, until now, of a large gold standard dataset. This Semeval task has provided two such datasets, in the domains of laptops and restaurants. A full description of the task and data is presented with this volume (Pontiki et al., 2014).

In this paper, we discuss our approach to the first two subtasks of the Semeval ABSA Task, those of aspect term extraction and aspect term polarity. In aspect term extraction the domain (restaurants or laptops) is known and the goal is to identify terms in a sentence that are features commonly associated with that domain, such as service and staff in the case of restaurants or size and speed in the case of laptops. In the polarity subtask, the aspect terms for a given sentence are already identified and the sentiment polarity (positive, negative, conflict, or neutral) must be assigned.

We approach both subtasks using supervised machine learning with background knowledge of sentiment lexicons and syntax included in our feature set. Our goal was to investigate whether techniques that have been successful in similar tasks would perform well on this newly created data set. We did not use additional corpus-based resources, so qualified for the constrained (versus unconstrained) version of the task. The remainder of the paper details related work, our approach, and experiments and the results we obtained.

2 Related Work

We divide related work into two areas: research related to aspect and aspect term identification, and research related to sentiment classification for aspect terms. We note that aspects have also been called topics and features in prior work. Until more recently, the community lacked a corpus

Proceedings of the 8th International Workshop on Semantic Evaluation (SemEval 2014), pages 790–795, Dublin, Ireland, August 23-24, 2014.

of gold-standard labeled data that focuses on aspect terms, rather than more general expressions of subjectivity or other private states. Thus, early work focused on learning or identifying aspects in an unsupervised (Hu and Liu, 2004) or semi-supervised setting (Moghaddam and Ester, 2010; Zhai et al., 2011). The earliest work on aspect detection focused on identifying frequently occurring noun phrases using information extraction (IE) techniques (Hu and Liu, 2004). Unsupervised techniques include clustering (Fahrni and Klenner, 2008; Popescu and Etzioni, 2005) and topic models (Titov and McDonald, 2008).

The benchmark corpus for sentiment analysis from Wiebe et al. (2005) inspired much work on learning subjective phrases in a supervised setting. The nature of the data and annotation differ from the data for this Semeval task, as it focuses on news articles and identifying an entire opinion phrase, including the source of the opinion, and only recently added aspect annotations. However, the techniques used by others to learn to extract this data and the associated polarity inspired our own approach. These include extraction-like approaches, usually using sequence modeling (Breck et al., 2007; Jin et al., 2009; Johansson and Moschitti, 2013; Li et al., 2010; Mitchell et al., 2013; Yang and Cardie, 2013) and semantic dependency or semantic parsing approaches (Kim and Hovy, 2006; Kobayashi et al., 2007; Wu et al., 2009) sometimes using background knowledge from sentiment lexicons (Zhang et al., 2009). The main differences between our approach and that of Breck et al. (2007) and Mitchell et al. (2013) are the classifier used and some of the features; they both use CRFs versus our Maximum entropy classifier, and they used a wider range of syntactic and dictionary-based features.

A second related corpus which includes more aspect information is that developed by Kim and Hovy (2006). This corpus also focuses on news articles rather than reviews, but does expand the types of aspects identified. The main focus of that work is on the identification, using FrameNet role labels, of the holder and target of an opinion, while the opinion itself is provided to the system.

The restaurant reviews used in this Semeval task are a 3000-plus sentence subset of those harvested by Ganu et al. (2009), plus newly annotated sentences used for test data. The original corpus contains over 50,000 structured restaurant reviews including restaurant information and a star rating. The original star rating was not made available for the Semeval tasks, and the aspect term annotations and their associated sentiment were added for this task; the original sentence-level sentiment annotations were not provided. Most of the work exploring this corpus to date uses unsupervised (Brody and Elhadad, 2010) or semi-supervised (Mukherjee and Liu, 2012) approaches.

As there has been an explosion of research in sentiment classification, it is impossible to review all of the related work. See Tsytsarau and Palpanas (2012) for a recent survey. We will note that our approach follows a somewhat standard machine learning approach inspired by that of Wilson et al. (2005), but with a different feature set. We did not thoroughly explore as many classifiers as this work and others have done. Finally, we note that some work has investigated the joint task of identifying opinion phrases or targets simultaneously with polarity (Choi and Cardie, 2009; Johansson and Moschitti, 2013; Mitchell et al., 2013).

3 Approach

For both subtasks, we take a supervised machine learning approach, examining several classifiers and their variants, and converging on feature sets which performed best in small-scale cross-validation experiments. After the official competition ended, we continued to examine different variants and discuss alternative approaches and their accuracy in the experimental results section. For all tasks we use the Maximum Entropy classifier, "iib" variant from the Natural Language Toolkit (NLTK) in Python (Bird et al., 2009). We experimented with several other classifiers from NLTK and found that Maximum Entropy performed best on a hold out set of data. We had originally planned to use a Conditional Random Field (CRF) model (Lafferty et al., 2001) because of its strong performance on similar tasks, but met with time limitations when converting the data to the appropriate format (there is no CRF provided with NLTK at this time). We had also planned to try classifiers from the scikit-learn toolkit (Pedregosa et al., 2011), but again met with time constraints due to the necessity to manually convert the features to a binary representation.

We first preprocess the data using NLTK's tokenization and part-of-speech tagging modules and align the results with the aspect terms in the data, as detailed further below. The sentiment lexicon we use as the basis of all sentiment features discussed below combines two standard lexicons (Liu et al., 2005; Wilson et al., 2005).

3.1 Aspect Term Extraction

While it is difficult to give a precise definition of aspect, it can be roughly thought of as a characteristic of a target concept such as a restaurant or laptop. Examples include the italicized terms in the following:

- I liked the *service* and the *staff*, but not the *food*.
- The *hard disk* is very noisy.

We use a sequence labeling approach, which can also be thought of as a tagging or chunking approach, to identify the aspect terms in each sentence. Specifically, and similar to Breck et al. (2007) and Mitchell et al. (2013), as the target class for each token, we use the IOB2 sequence labeling scheme (Tjong et al., 2000), where the aspect terms are considered as the chunks to be labeled. Using this approach, each token is tagged as either Beginning an aspect term, being In an aspect term, or being Outside an aspect term. We also experimented with an IO labeling scheme as discussed in the experimental results section, in which each token is tagged as being either In or Outside an aspect term. Here is an example of a sentence with its IOB tags:

- The-O pizza-B is-O the-O best-O if-O you-O like-O thin-B crusted-I pizza-I .-O

Of course, unlike an HMM or CRF, a standard classifier such as Maximum entropy does not label entire sequences. Therefore, each example presented to our classifier represents a single token from the sentence being labeled, and the target label is the IOB tag of that token. Further, we present the tokens of a given sentence in order from the first word in the sentence to the last.

The features used for each token are derived from the token, the prior token, and the next token in the sentence (thus using a three-token window). In addition, we include the IOB tag of the prior token, using the gold standard at training time and the classifier's output at testing time, even if it is incorrect. For each token we extract the word, its stem, its part-of-speech (POS) tag, its polarity from the sentiment dictionary, and whether the word is objective or subjective, from the same sentiment dictionary. We use dummy values for the prior and next words of the first and last token in a sentence, respectively. All feature-value pairs are converted to binary features automatically by NLTK.

Because we believed that the data would prove to be sparse and that new words would appear in the testing data, we also include an unknown word feature, replacing the 50% least frequent words in the training data with the "UNK" token, and doing the same for both these words and unseen words in the test set. However, we later found that we should have used cross-validation to support our hypothesis, and that using the full vocabulary would have improved our results, as shown in the experimental results section.

3.2 Polarity

In the polarity subtask, the aspect terms are provided, and the goal is to classify them as positive, negative, conflict, or neutral. In this case, we use a simple classification approach that includes features of the aspect term and surrounding tokens (again in a three-token window), and also some simple baseline sentiment classification features. First, we use similar features as for the aspect term extraction task, with changes to incorporate the fact that aspect terms are occasionally *phrases*, not single words. In fact, we hypothesize that features of the words before and after an aspect phrase could be more useful than the words prior to and after a particular *word* in the phrase.

Thus, instead of using features from the three-token window including the current token, we use features from the words on each side of the aspect phrase, and use the head of the aspect phrase and its features as the middle of the window. This approach is similar to that of Johansson and Moschitti (2013), who use features from the words before and after opinion expressions. In our case, these features are again the word, its POS tag, its sentiment polarity and objectivity, and its IOB tag. Note that in this case we use the IOB tag from all terms in the window, since the aspect term extraction task is treated as a prerequisite to the polarity classification task.

In addition to these word-based features, we add four higher-level features. The first is an indicator of the number of aspect terms in the entire sentence, since this might indicate a more detailed sentence, and we believe that more specific sentences might correlate with positive sentiment. The other three features are baselines connected to the estimated sentiment of the sentence or phrase. First, we apply a hand-built sentence level sentiment classifier that follows a now standard baseline approach (Zhu et al., 2009): using a sentiment lexicon (Liu's), it counts the number of positive and negative sentiment words in the sentence, flipping polarity when negation words are encountered, and discontinuing the polarity flip when punctuation is encountered. This results in a "high level sentiment" feature consisting of the number of positive sentiment words minus the number of negative sentiment words.

Our other two sentiment features provide finer granularity information, based on the sentiment of the "chunks" in which an aspect term appears. First, we use the punctuation within the sentence to divide it into punctuation-separated chunks. Then, we calculate the number of positive and negative sentiment words within each chunk, again flipping polarity after the presence of a negation word. The positive and negative counts associated with the chunk within which an aspect phrase appears are then used as features when classifying the phrase. We also experimented with using conjunctions (and, or, but, etc.) as chunk boundaries, but preliminary results indicated that this resulted in reduced accuracy.

4 Experimental Results & Analysis

In this section we report our results and some additional analysis for the ABSA subtasks 1 and 2. Please refer to Pontiki et al. (2014) for details on the tasks, corpora, and evaluation criteria. We chose the constrained condition, which allows the use of sentiment lexicons in addition to the training data provided, but no additional data such as other reviews.

Aspect term extraction is evaluated using Precision, Recall, and F-measure on an unseen set of sentences. Table 1 shows our results[1] on both domains, the top results,[2] and the mean score of all constrained submissions (21 entries). Note that for Restaurants, COMMIT-P1WP3 had the best Precision, at 0.909, but XRCE had the best F-measure, so we show their three scores. Our results were close to the mean for both corpora and quite a bit above the lowest scoring submissions and the baseline provided by the organizers; the latter is also shown in the Table.

[1]Rank averaged over P, R, and F for USF

[2]We abbreviate IHS_RD_Belarus as Belarus.

	System	P	R	F1	Rank
Lap	Belarus	0.848	0.665	0.746	1
	mean	*0.760*	*0.503*	*0.562*	*11*
	USF	0.754	0.404	0.526	14.7
	baseline	*0.443*	*0.298*	*0.356*	
Rest	XRCE	0.862	0.818	0.840	1
	mean	*0.770*	*0.649*	*0.693*	*11*
	USF	0.783	0.645	0.707	14.3
	baseline	*0.525*	*0.428*	*0.472*	

Table 1: Aspect Term Extraction Results, Constrained.

	Approach	P	R	F1
Lap	FV-No-Snt	0.724	**0.622**	**0.669**
	Full Voc.	**0.733**	0.601	0.660
	Original	0.715	0.493	0.583
	IO	0.696	0.501	0.582
Rest	Full Voc.	**0.792**	0.704	**0.746**
	FV-No-Snt	0.784	**0.710**	0.745
	Original	0.777	0.657	0.711
	IO	0.769	0.660	0.710

Table 2: Aspect Term Extraction Cross-Validation Results.

After the submission deadline, we continued to experiment with alternative approaches using 5-fold cross validation on the training set, shown in Table 2. We found that using the full vocabulary was better than our original approach of only using the top 50% occurring words, even with 28% unseen words in the restaurant test set and 21% in laptops. We also found that leaving out the polarity feature while using all vocabulary words (FV-No-Snt) improved our F-measure score to 0.669 for laptops but reduced it slightly to 0.745 for restaurants. Finally, using IO versus IOB tagging did not influence the F-measure significantly. About 25% of the aspect terms in the restaurant training set have length greater than one, and 37% of the laptop terms.

Aspect term polarity is evaluated on accuracy over all labels: positive, negative, neutral, or conflict. Table 3 shows our results on both domains, the top results, the mean score of all constrained submissions (24 entries for laptops, 28 for restaurants), and the baseline accuracy. In this case our scores are above average in all cases.

	System	Acc	Rank
Lap	NRC-Canada	0.705	1
	USF	0.645	6
	mean	*0.604*	*12.5*
	baseline	*0.514*	
Rest	DCU	0.810	1
	USF	0.732	9
	mean	*0.702*	*14.5*
	baseline	*0.643*	

Table 3: Aspect Term Polarity Results, Constrained.

5 Conclusions

In conclusion, we show that a chunking approach to supervised learning works fairly well in the aspect term extraction task, and that local sentence features and a baseline sentiment classifier work well for aspect term polarity classification. Our systems for both tasks performed reasonably well considering the relatively simple classification techniques and features incorporated. In future work, we plan to apply more sophisticated classifiers which have shown to be accurate on related tasks, including CRFs and Support Vector Machines. We also would like to experiment with variants of the features used here, such as the exploration of smaller or larger context windows, or the usefulness of stemming compared to the original tokens. We also believe that more sophisticated syntactic or semantic features, or topic models, could improve results on one or both tasks.

We thank the organizers for the provision of this interesting dataset.

Acknowledgements

The author thanks her spring 2014 research assistant, Hao Chen, for his help in preparing some of the code used in the experiments.

References

Steven Bird, Edward Loper, and Ewan Klein. 2009. *Natural Language Processing with Python*. O'Reilly Media Inc.

Eric Breck, Yejin Choi, and Claire Cardie. 2007. Identifying expressions of opinion in context. In *Twentieth International Joint Conference on Artificial Intelligence*, pages 2683–2688.

Samuel Brody and Noemie Elhadad. 2010. An unsupervised aspect-sentiment model for online reviews. In *Human Language Technologies: The 2010 Annual Conference of the North American Chapter of the Association for Computational Linguistics*, pages 804–812.

Yejin Choi and Claire Cardie. 2009. Adapting a polarity lexicon using integer linear programming for domain-specific sentiment classification. In *Proceedings of the 2009 Conference on Empirical Methods in Natural Language Processing*, pages 590–598.

Angela Fahrni and Manfred Klenner. 2008. Old wine or warm beer: Target-specific sentiment analysis of adjectives. In *Proc. of the Symposium on Affective Language in Human and Machine, AISB*, pages 60–63.

Gayatree Ganu, Noemie Elhadad, and Amelie Marian. 2009. Beyond the stars: Improving rating predictions using review text content. In *12th International Workshop on the Web and Databases*, pages 1–6.

Minqing Hu and Bing Liu. 2004. Mining and summarizing customer reviews. In *Proceedings of the tenth ACM SIGKDD international conference on Knowledge discovery and data mining*, pages 168–177. ACM.

Wei Jin, Hung Hay Ho, and Rohini K Srihari. 2009. A novel lexicalized HMM-based learning framework for web opinion mining. In *Proceedings of the 26th Annual International Conference on Machine Learning*, pages 465–472.

Richard Johansson and Alessandro Moschitti. 2013. Relational features in fine-grained opinion analysis. *Computational Linguistics*, 39(3):473–509.

Soo-min Kim and Eduard Hovy. 2006. Extracting opinions, opinion holders, and topics expressed in online news media text. In *Workshop on Sentiment and Subjectivity in Text*, pages 1–8.

Nozomi Kobayashi, Kentaro Inui, and Yuji Matsumoto. 2007. Extracting aspect-evaluation and aspect-of relations in opinion mining. In *EMNLP-CoNLL*, pages 1065–1074.

John Lafferty, Andrew McCallum, and Fernando Pereira. 2001. Conditional random fields: Probabilistic models for segmenting and labeling sequence data. In *Proceedings of International Conference on Machine Learning*, pages 282–289.

Fangtao Li, Chao Han, Minlie Huang, and Xiaoyan Zhu. 2010. Structure-aware review mining and summarization. In *Proceedings of the 23rd International Conference on Computational Linguistics*, pages 653–661.

Bing Liu, Minqing Hu, and Junsheng Cheng. 2005. Opinion observer: Analyzing and comparing opinions on the web. In *Proceedings of the 14th International World Wide Web conference*, pages 342–351. ACM.

Bing Liu. 2010. Sentiment analysis and subjectivity. In *Handbook of Natural Language Processing 2*, pages 627–666. CRC Press.

Margaret Mitchell, Jacqueline Aguilar, Theresa Wilson, and Benjamin Van Durme. 2013. Open domain targeted sentiment. In *EMNLP*, pages 1643–1654.

Samaneh Moghaddam and Martin Ester. 2010. Opinion digger: An unsupervised opinion miner from unstructured product reviews. In *Proceedings of the 19th ACM international conference on Information and knowledge management*, pages 1825–1828. ACM.

Arjun Mukherjee and Bing Liu. 2012. Aspect extraction through semi-supervised modeling. In *Proceedings of the 50th Annual Meeting of the Association for Computational Linguistics*, pages 339–348.

Bo Pang and Lillian Lee. 2008. Opinion mining and sentiment analysis. *Foundations and Trends in Information Retrieval*, 2(1-2):1–135.

Fabian Pedregosa, Gaël Varoquaux, Alexandre Gramfort, Vincent Michel, Bertrand Thirion, Olivier Grisel, Mathieu Blondel, Peter Prettenhofer, Ron Weiss, Vincent Dubourg, Jake Vanderplas, Alexandre Passos, David Cournapeau, Matthieu Brucher, Matthieu Perrot, and Édouard Duchesnay. 2011. Scikit-learn: Machine learning in Python. *Journal of Machine Learning Research*, 12:2825–2830.

Maria Pontiki, Dimitrios Galanis, John Pavlopoulos, Harris Papageorgiou, Ion Androutsopoulos, and Suresh Manandhar. 2014. Semeval-2014 task 4: Aspect based sentiment analysis. In *Proceedings of the 8th International Workshop on Semantic Evaluation (SemEval 2014)*.

Ana-maria Popescu and Oren Etzioni. 2005. Extracting product features and opinions from reviews. In *Proceedings of Human Language Technology Conference and Conference on Empirical Methods in Natural Language Processing*, pages 339–346.

Ivan Titov and Ryan McDonald. 2008. Modeling online reviews with multi-grain topic models. In *Proceeding of the 17th international conference on World Wide Web*, pages 111–120, New York, New York, USA. ACM.

Erik F Tjong, Kim Sang, Walter Daelemans, Rob Koeling, Yuval Krymolowski, Vasin Punyakanok, Dan Roth, Millers Yard, Mill Lane, and Ramat Gan. 2000. Applying system combination to base noun phrase identification. In *Proceedings of the 18th conference on Computational linguistics*, pages 857–863.

Mikalai Tsytsarau and Themis Palpanas. 2012. Survey on mining subjective data on the web. *Data Mining and Knowledge Discovery*, 24(3):478–514.

Janyce Wiebe, Theresa Wilson, and Claire Cardie. 2005. Annotating expressions of opinions and emotions in language. *Language Resources and Evaluation*, 39(2-3):165–210.

Theresa Wilson, Janyce Wiebe, and Paul Hoffmann. 2005. Recognizing contextual polarity in phrase-level sentiment analysis. In *Proceedings of the conference on Human Language Technology and Empirical Methods in Natural Language Processing*, pages 347–354.

Yuanbin Wu, Qi Zhang, Xuanjing Huang, and Lide Wu. 2009. Phrase dependency parsing for opinion mining. In *Proceedings of the 2009 Conference on Empirical Methods in Natural Language Processing*, pages 1533–1541.

Bishan Yang and Claire Cardie. 2013. Joint inference for fine-grained opinion extraction. In *Proceedings of ACL*, pages 16550–1649.

Zhongwu Zhai, Bing Liu, Hua Xu, and Peifa Jia. 2011. Clustering product features for opinion mining. In *Proceedings of the fourth ACM international conference on Web search and data mining*, pages 347–354, New York, New York, USA. ACM.

Qi Zhang, Yuanbin Wu, Tao Li, Mitsunori Ogihara, Joseph Johnson, and Xuanjing Huang. 2009. Mining product reviews based on shallow dependency parsing. In *Proceedings of the 32nd international ACM SIGIR conference on Research and development in information retrieval*, pages 726–727. ACM.

Jingbo Zhu, Muhua Zhu, Huizhen Wang, and Benjamin Tsou. 2009. Aspect-based sentence segmentation for sentiment summarization. In *Proceedings of the 1st international CIKM workshop on Topic-sentiment analysis for mass opinion*, pages 65–72. ACM.

UTexas: Natural Language Semantics using Distributional Semantics and Probabilistic Logic

Islam Beltagy*, **Stephen Roller***, **Gemma Boleda**†, **Katrin Erk**†, **Raymond J. Mooney***
* Department of Computer Science
† Department of Linguistics
The University of Texas at Austin
{beltagy, roller, mooney}@cs.utexas.edu
gemma.boleda@upf.edu, katrin.erk@mail.utexas.edu

Abstract

We represent natural language semantics by combining logical and distributional information in probabilistic logic. We use Markov Logic Networks (MLN) for the RTE task, and Probabilistic Soft Logic (PSL) for the STS task. The system is evaluated on the SICK dataset. Our best system achieves 73% accuracy on the RTE task, and a Pearson's correlation of 0.71 on the STS task.

1 Introduction

Textual Entailment systems based on logical inference excel in correct reasoning, but are often brittle due to their inability to handle soft logical inferences. Systems based on distributional semantics excel in lexical and soft reasoning, but are unable to handle phenomena like negation and quantifiers. We present a system which takes the best of both approaches by combining distributional semantics with probabilistic logical inference.

Our system builds on our prior work (Beltagy et al., 2013; Beltagy et al., 2014a; Beltagy and Mooney, 2014; Beltagy et al., 2014b). We use Boxer (Bos, 2008), a wide-coverage semantic analysis tool to map natural sentences to logical form. Then, distributional information is encoded in the form of inference rules. We generate lexical and phrasal rules, and experiment with symmetric and asymmetric similarity measures. Finally, we use probabilistic logic frameworks to perform inference, Markov Logic Networks (MLN) for RTE, and Probabilistic Soft Logic (PSL) for STS.

2 Background

2.1 Logical Semantics

Logic-based representations of meaning have a long tradition (Montague, 1970; Kamp and Reyle, 1993). They handle many complex semantic phenomena such as relational propositions, logical operators, and quantifiers; however, they can not handle "graded" aspects of meaning in language because they are binary by nature.

2.2 Distributional Semantics

Distributional models use statistics of word co-occurrences to predict semantic similarity of words and phrases (Turney and Pantel, 2010; Mitchell and Lapata, 2010), based on the observation that semantically similar words occur in similar contexts. Words are represented as vectors in high dimensional spaces generated from their contexts. Also, it is possible to compute vector representations for larger phrases compositionally from their parts (Mitchell and Lapata, 2008; Mitchell and Lapata, 2010; Baroni and Zamparelli, 2010). Distributional similarity is usually a mixture of semantic relations, but particular *asymmetric* similarity measures can, to a certain extent, predict hypernymy and lexical entailment distributionally (Kotlerman et al., 2010; Lenci and Benotto, 2012; Roller et al., 2014). Distributional models capture the graded nature of meaning, but do not adequately capture logical structure (Grefenstette, 2013).

2.3 Markov Logic Network

Markov Logic Networks (MLN) (Richardson and Domingos, 2006) are a framework for probabilistic logic that employ weighted formulas in first-order logic to compactly encode complex undirected probabilistic graphical models (i.e., Markov networks). Weighting the rules is a way of softening them compared to hard logical constraints.

Proceedings of the 8th International Workshop on Semantic Evaluation (SemEval 2014), pages 796–801,
Dublin, Ireland, August 23-24, 2014.

MLNs define a probability distribution over possible worlds, where the probability of a world increases exponentially with the total weight of the logical clauses that it satisfies. A variety of inference methods for MLNs have been developed, however, computational overhead is still an issue.

2.4 Probabilistic Soft Logic

Probabilistic Soft Logic (PSL) is another recently proposed framework for probabilistic logic (Kimmig et al., 2012). It uses logical representations to compactly define large graphical models with continuous variables, and includes methods for performing efficient probabilistic inference for the resulting models. A key distinguishing feature of PSL is that ground atoms (i.e., atoms without variables) have soft, continuous truth values on the interval [0, 1] rather than binary truth values as used in MLNs and most other probabilistic logics. Given a set of weighted inference rules, and with the help of Lukasiewicz's relaxation of the logical operators, PSL builds a graphical model defining a probability distribution over the continuous space of values of the random variables in the model (Kimmig et al., 2012). Then, PSL's MPE inference (Most Probable Explanation) finds the overall interpretation with the maximum probability given a set of evidence. This optimization problem is a second-order cone program (SOCP) (Kimmig et al., 2012) and can be solved in polynomial time.

2.5 Recognizing Textual Entailment

Recognizing Textual Entailment (RTE) is the task of determining whether one natural language text, the *premise*, Entails, Contradicts, or is not related (Neutral) to another, the *hypothesis*.

2.6 Semantic Textual Similarity

Semantic Textual Similarity (STS) is the task of judging the similarity of a pair of sentences on a scale from 1 to 5 (Agirre et al., 2012). Gold standard scores are averaged over multiple human annotations and systems are evaluated using the Pearson correlation between a system's output and gold standard scores.

3 Approach

3.1 Logical Representation

The first component in the system is Boxer (Bos, 2008), which maps the input sentences into logical form, in which the predicates are words in the sentence. For example, the sentence "A man is driving a car" in logical form is:

$\exists x, y, z.\ man(x) \wedge agent(y, x) \wedge drive(y) \wedge patient(y, z) \wedge car(z)$

3.2 Distributional Representation

Next, distributional information is encoded in the form of weighted inference rules connecting words and phrases of the input sentences T and H. For example, for sentences T: "A man is driving a car", and H: "A guy is driving a vehicle", we would like to generate rules like $\forall x.\ man(x) \Rightarrow guy(x) \mid w_1, \forall x. car(x) \Rightarrow vehicle(x) \mid w_2$, where w_1 and w_2 are weights indicating the similarity of the antecedent and consequent of each rule.

Inferences rules are generated as in Beltagy et al. (2013). Given two input sentences T and H, for all pairs (a, b), where a and b are words or phrases of T and H respectively, generate an inference rule: $a \rightarrow b \mid w$, where the rule weight w is a function of $sim(\vec{a}, \vec{b})$, and sim is a similarity measure of the distributional vectors $\vec{a}, \vec{b}$. We experimented with the symmetric similarity measure $cosine$, and $asym$, the supervised, asymmetric similarity measure of Roller et al. (2014).

The $asym$ measure uses the vector difference $(\vec{a} - \vec{b})$ as features in a logistic regression classifier for distinguishing between four different word relations: hypernymy, cohyponymy, meronomy, and no relation. The model is trained using the noun-noun subset of the BLESS data set (Baroni and Lenci, 2011). The final similarity weight is given by the model's estimated probability that the word relationship is either hypernymy or meronomy: $asym(\vec{a}, \vec{b}) = P(hyper(a, b)) + P(mero(a, b))$.

Distributional representations for words are derived by counting co-occurrences in the ukWaC, WaCkypedia, BNC and Gigaword corpora. We use the 2000 most frequent content words as basis dimensions, and count co-occurrences within a two word context window. The vector space is weighted using Positive Pointwise Mutual Information.

Phrases are defined in terms of Boxer's output to be more than one unary atom sharing the same variable like "a little kid" $(little(k) \wedge kid(k))$, or two unary atoms connected by a relation like "a man is driving" $(man(m) \wedge agent(d, m) \wedge drive(d))$. We compute vector representations of phrases using vector addition across the component predicates. We also tried computing phrase vectors using component-wise vector multiplication (Mitchell and Lapata, 2010), but found it performed marginally worse than addition.

3.3 Probabilistic Logical Inference

The last component is probabilistic logical inference. Given the logical form of the input sentences, and the weighted inference rules, we use them to build a probabilistic logic program whose solution is the answer to the target task. A probabilistic logic program consists of the evidence set E, the set of weighted first order logical expressions (rule base RB), and a query Q. Inference is the process of calculating $Pr(Q|E, RB)$.

3.4 Task 1: RTE using MLNs

MLNs are the probabilistic logic framework we use for the RTE task (we do not use PSL here as it shares the problems of fuzzy logic with probabilistic reasoning). The RTE classification problem for the relation between T and H can be split into two inference tasks. The first is testing if T entails H, $Pr(H|T, RB)$. The second is testing if the negation of the text $\neg T$ entails H, $Pr(H|\neg T, RB)$. In case $Pr(H|T, RB)$ is high, while $Pr(H|\neg T, RB)$ is low, this indicates Entails. In case it is the other way around, this indicates Contradicts. If both values are close, this means T does not affect the probability of H and indicative of Neutral. We train an SVM classifier with LibSVM's default parameters to map the two probabilities to the final decision.

The MLN implementation we use is Alchemy (Kok et al., 2005). Queries in Alchemy can only be ground atoms. However, in our case the query is a complex formula (H). We extended Alchemy to calculate probabilities of queries (Beltagy and Mooney, 2014). Probability of a formula Q given an MLN K equals the ratio between the partition function Z of the ground network of K with and without Q added as a hard rule (Gogate and Domingos, 2011)

$$P(Q \mid K) = \frac{Z(K \cup \{(Q, \infty)\})}{Z(K)} \quad (1)$$

We estimate Z of the ground networks using SampleSearch (Gogate and Dechter, 2011), an advanced importance sampling algorithm that is suitable for ground networks generated by MLNs.

A general problem with MLN inference is its computational overhead, especially for the complex logical formulae generated by our approach. To make inference faster, we reduce the size of the ground network through an automatic type-checking technique proposed in Beltagy and Mooney (2014). For example, consider the evidence ground atom $man(M)$ denoting that the constant M is of type man. Then, consider another predicate like $car(x)$. In case there are no inference rule connecting $man(x)$ and $car(x)$, then we know that M which we know is a man cannot be a car, so we remove the ground atom $car(M)$ from the ground network. This technique reduces the size of the ground network dramatically and makes inference tractable.

Another problem with MLN inference is that quantifiers sometimes behave in an undesirable way, due to the Domain Closure Assumption (Richardson and Domingos, 2006) that MLNs make. For example, consider the text-hypothesis pair: “There is a black bird” and “All birds are black”, which in logic are $T : bird(B) \wedge black(B)$ and $H : \forall x.\ bird(x) \Rightarrow black(x)$. Because of the Domain Closure Assumption, MLNs conclude that T entails H because H is true for all constants in the domain (in this example, the single constant B). We solve this problem by introducing extra constants and evidence in the domain. In the example above, we introduce evidence of a new bird $bird(D)$, which prevents the hypothesis from being true. The full details of the technique of dealing with the domain closure is beyond the scope of this paper.

3.5 Task 2: STS using PSL

PSL is the probabilistic logic we use for the STS task since it has been shown to be an effective approach for computing similarity between structured objects. We showed in Beltagy et al. (2014a) how to perform the STS task using PSL. PSL does not work “out of the box” for STS, because Lukasiewicz's equation for the conjunction is very restrictive. We address this by replacing Lukasiewicz's equation for conjunction with an averaging equation, then change the optimization problem and grounding technique accordingly.

For each STS pair of sentences S_1, S_2, we run PSL twice, once where $E = S_1$, $Q = S_2$ and another where $E = S_2$, $Q = S_1$, and output the two scores. The final similarity score is produced from an Additive Regression model with WEKA's default parameters trained to map the two PSL scores to the overall similarity score (Friedman, 1999; Hall et al., 2009).

3.6 Task 3: RTE and STS using Vector Spaces and Keyword Counts

As a baseline, we also attempt both the RTE and STS tasks using only vector representations and unigram counts. This baseline model uses a supervised regressor with features based on vector similarity and keyword counts. The same input features are used for performing RTE and STS, but a SVM classifier and Additive Regression model is trained separately for each task. This baseline is meant to establish whether the task truly requires the sophisticated logical inference of MLNs and PSL, or if merely checking for logical keywords and textual similarity is sufficient.

The first two features are simply the *cosine* and *asym* similarities between the text and hypothesis, using vector addition of the unigrams to compute a single vector for the entire sentence.

We also compute vectors for both the text and hypothesis using vector addition of the mutually exclusive unigrams (MEUs). The MEUs are defined as the unigrams of the premise and hypothesis with common unigrams removed. For example, if the premise is "A dog chased a cat" and the hypothesis is "A dog watched a mouse", the MEUs are "chased cat" and "watched mouse." We compute vector addition of the MEUs, and compute similarity using both the *cosine* and *asym* measures. These form two features for the regressor.

The last feature of the model is a keyword count. We count how many times 13 different keywords appear in either the text or the hypothesis. These keywords include negation (*no*, *not*, *nobody*, etc.) and quantifiers (*a*, *the*, *some*, etc.) The counts of each keyword form the last 13 features as input to the regressor. In total, there are 17 features used in this baseline system.

4 Evaluation

The dataset used for evaluation is **SICK**: Sentences Involving Compositional Knowledge dataset, a task for SemEval 2014 (Marelli et al., 2014a; Marelli et al., 2014b). The dataset is 10,000 pairs of sentences, 5000 training and 5000 for testing. Sentences are annotated for both tasks.

	SICK-RTE	SICK-STS
Baseline	70.0	71.1
MLN/PSL + Cosine	72.8	68.6
MLN/PSL + Asym	73.2	68.9
Ensemble	73.2	71.5

Table 1: Test RTE accuracy and STS Correlation.

4.1 Systems Compared

We compare multiple configurations of our probabilistic logic system.

- **Baseline**: Vector- and keyword-only baseline described in Section 3.6;
- **MLN/PSL + Cosine**: MLN and PSL based methods described in Sections 3.4 and 3.5, using *cosine* as a similarity measure;
- **MLN/PSL + Asym**: MLN and PSL based methods described in Sections 3.4 and 3.5, using *asym* as a similarity measure;
- **Ensemble**: An ensemble method which uses all of the features in the above methods as inputs for the RTE and STS classifiers.

4.2 Results and Discussion

Table 1 shows our results on the held-out test set for SemEval 2014 Task 1.

On the RTE task, we see that both the MLN + Cosine and MLN + Asym models outperformed the Baseline, indicating that textual entailment requires real inference to handle negation and quantifiers. The MLN + Asym and Ensemble systems perform identically on RTE, further suggesting that the logical inference subsumes keyword detection.

The MLN + Asym system outperforms the MLN + Cosine system, emphasizing the importance of asymmetric measures for predicting lexical entailment. Intuitively, this makes perfect sense: *dog* entails *animal*, but not vice versa.

In an error analysis performed on a development set, we found our RTE system was extremely conservative: we rarely confused the Entails and Contradicts classes, indicating we correctly predict the direction of entailment, but frequently misclassify examples as Neutral. An examination of these examples showed the errors were mostly due to missing or weakly-weighted distributional rules.

On STS, our vector space baseline outperforms both PSL-based systems, but the ensemble outperforms any of its components. This is a testament to the power of distributional models in their ability to predict word and sentence similarity. Surprisingly, we see that the PSL + Asym system slightly outperforms the PSL + Cosine system. This may indicate that even in STS, some notion of asymmetry plays a role, or that annotators may have been biased by simultaneously annotating both tasks. As with RTE, the major bottleneck of our system appears to be the knowledge base, which is built solely using distributional inference rules.

Results also show that our system's performance is close to the baseline system. One of the reasons behind that could be that sentences are not exploiting the full power of logical representations. On RTE for example, most of the contradicting pairs are two similar sentences with one of them being negated. This way, the existence of any negation cue in one of the two sentences is a strong signal for contradiction, which what the baseline system does without deeply representing the semantics of the negation.

5 Conclusion & Future Work

We showed how to combine logical and distributional semantics using probabilistic logic, and how to perform the RTE and STS tasks using it. The system is tested on the SICK dataset.

The distributional side can be extended in many directions. We would like to use longer phrases, more sophisticated compositionality techniques, and contextualized vectors of word meaning. We also believe inference rules could be dramatically improved by integrating from paraphrases collections like PPDB (Ganitkevitch et al., 2013).

Finally, MLN inference could be made more efficient by exploiting the similarities between the two ground networks (the one with Q and the one without). PLS inference could be enhanced by using a learned, weighted average of rules, rather than the simple mean.

Acknowledgements

This research was supported by the DARPA DEFT program under AFRL grant FA8750-13-2-0026. Some experiments were run on the Mastodon Cluster supported by NSF Grant EIA-0303609. The authors acknowledge the Texas Advanced Computing Center (TACC)[1] for providing grid resources that have contributed to these results. We thank the anonymous reviewers and the UTexas Natural Language and Learning group for their helpful comments and suggestions.

[1] `http://www.tacc.utexas.edu`

References

Eneko Agirre, Daniel Cer, Mona Diab, and Aitor Gonzalez-Agirre. 2012. Semeval-2012 task 6: A pilot on semantic textual similarity. In *Proceedings of Semantic Evaluation (SemEval-12)*.

Marco Baroni and Alessandro Lenci. 2011. How we BLESSed distributional semantic evaluation. In *Proceedings of the GEMS 2011 Workshop on GEometrical Models of Natural Language Semantics*, pages 1–10, Edinburgh, UK, July. Association for Computational Linguistics.

Marco Baroni and Roberto Zamparelli. 2010. Nouns are vectors, adjectives are matrices: Representing adjective-noun constructions in semantic space. In *Proceedings of Conference on Empirical Methods in Natural Language Processing (EMNLP-10)*.

Islam Beltagy and Raymond J. Mooney. 2014. Efficient Markov logic inference for natural language semantics. In *Proceedings of AAAI 2014 Workshop on Statistical Relational AI (StarAI-14)*.

Islam Beltagy, Cuong Chau, Gemma Boleda, Dan Garrette, Katrin Erk, and Raymond Mooney. 2013. Montague meets Markov: Deep semantics with probabilistic logical form. In *Proceedings of the Second Joint Conference on Lexical and Computational Semantics (*SEM-13)*.

Islam Beltagy, Katrin Erk, and Raymond Mooney. 2014a. Probabilistic soft logic for semantic textual similarity. In *Proceedings of Association for Computational Linguistics (ACL-14)*.

Islam Beltagy, Katrin Erk, and Raymond Mooney. 2014b. Semantic parsing using distributional semantics and probabilistic logic. In *Proceedings of ACL 2014 Workshop on Semantic Parsing (SP-2014)*.

Johan Bos. 2008. Wide-coverage semantic analysis with Boxer. In *Proceedings of Semantics in Text Processing (STEP-08)*.

J.H. Friedman. 1999. Stochastic gradient boosting. Technical report, Stanford University.

Juri Ganitkevitch, Benjamin Van Durme, and Chris Callison-Burch. 2013. PPDB: The paraphrase database. In *Proceedings of North American Chapter of the Association for Computational Linguistics: Human Language Technologies (NAACL-HLT-13)*.

Vibhav Gogate and Rina Dechter. 2011. Samplesearch: Importance sampling in presence of determinism. *Artificial Intelligence*, 175(2):694–729.

Vibhav Gogate and Pedro Domingos. 2011. Probabilistic theorem proving. In *27th Conference on Uncertainty in Artificial Intelligence (UAI-11)*.

Edward Grefenstette. 2013. Towards a formal distributional semantics: Simulating logical calculi with tensors. In *Proceedings of Second Joint Conference on Lexical and Computational Semantics (*SEM 2013)*.

Mark Hall, Eibe Frank, Geoffrey Holmes, Bernhard Pfahringer, Peter Reutemann, and Ian H. Witten. 2009. The weka data mining software: an update. *SIGKDD Explor. Newsl.*, 11(1):10–18.

Hans Kamp and Uwe Reyle. 1993. *From Discourse to Logic*. Kluwer.

Angelika Kimmig, Stephen H. Bach, Matthias Broecheler, Bert Huang, and Lise Getoor. 2012. A short introduction to Probabilistic Soft Logic. In *Proceedings of NIPS Workshop on Probabilistic Programming: Foundations and Applications (NIPS Workshop-12)*.

Stanley Kok, Parag Singla, Matthew Richardson, and Pedro Domingos. 2005. The Alchemy system for statistical relational AI. Technical report, Department of Computer Science and Engineering, University of Washington. `http://www.cs.washington.edu/ai/alchemy`.

Lili Kotlerman, Ido Dagan, Idan Szpektor, and Maayan Zhitomirsky-Geffet. 2010. Directional distributional similarity for lexical inference. *Natural Language Engineering*, 16(4):359–389.

Alessandro Lenci and Giulia Benotto. 2012. Identifying hypernyms in distributional semantic spaces. In *Proceedings of the first Joint Conference on Lexical and Computational Semantics (*SEM-12)*.

Marco Marelli, Luisa Bentivogli, Marco Baroni, Raffaella Bernardi, Stefano Menini, and Roberto Zamparelli. 2014a. SemEval-2014 task 1: Evaluation of compositional distributional semantic models on full sentences through semantic relatedness and textual entailment. In *Proceedings of the 8th International Workshop on Semantic Evaluation (SemEval-2014)*, Dublin, Ireland.

Marco Marelli, Stefano Menini, Marco Baroni, Luisa Bentivogli, Raffaella Bernardi, and Roberto Zamparelli. 2014b. A sick cure for the evaluation of compositional distributional semantic models. In Nicoletta Calzolari (Conference Chair), Khalid Choukri, Thierry Declerck, Hrafn Loftsson, Bente Maegaard, Joseph Mariani, Asuncion Moreno, Jan Odijk, and Stelios Piperidis, editors, *Proceedings of the Ninth International Conference on Language Resources and Evaluation (LREC'14)*, Reykjavik, Iceland, may. European Language Resources Association (ELRA).

Jeff Mitchell and Mirella Lapata. 2008. Vector-based models of semantic composition. In *Proceedings of Association for Computational Linguistics (ACL-08)*.

Jeff Mitchell and Mirella Lapata. 2010. Composition in distributional models of semantics. *Cognitive Science*, 34(3):1388–1429.

Richard Montague. 1970. Universal grammar. *Theoria*, 36:373–398.

Matthew Richardson and Pedro Domingos. 2006. Markov logic networks. *Machine Learning*, 62:107–136.

Stephen Roller, Katrin Erk, and Gemma Boleda. 2014. Inclusive yet selective: Supervised distributional hypernymy detection. In *Proceedings of the Twenty Fifth International Conference on Computational Linguistics (COLING-14)*, Dublin, Ireland.

Peter Turney and Patrick Pantel. 2010. From frequency to meaning: Vector space models of semantics. *Journal of Artificial Intelligence Research*, 37(1):141–188.

UTH_CCB: A Report for SemEval 2014 – Task 7 Analysis of Clinical Text

Yaoyun Zhang[1] Jingqi Wang[1] Buzhou Tang[2] Yonghui Wu[1] Min Jiang[1] Yukun Chen[3] Hua Xu[1*]

[1]University of Texas School of Biomedical Informatics at Houston Houston, TX, 77030, USA

[2]Harbin Institute of Technology Shenzhen Graduate School Shenzhen, 518055, China

[3]Vanderbilt University Department of Biomedical Informatics Nashville, TN, 37240, USA

{Yaoyun.Zhang, Yonghui.Wu, Min.Jiang, Hua.Xu} @uth.tmc.edu
tangbuzhou@gmail.com yukun.chen@Vanderbilt.Edu

Abstract

This work describes the participation of the University of Texas Health Science Center at Houston (UTHealth) team on the SemEval 2014 – Task 7 analysis of clinical text challenge. The task consisted of two subtasks: (1) disorder entity recognition, recognizing mentions of disorder concepts; (2) disorder entity encoding, mapping each mention to a unique Concept Unique Identifier (CUI) defined in Unified Medical Language System (UMLS). We developed three ensemble learning approaches for recognizing disorder entities and a Vector Space Model based method for encoding. Our approaches achieved top rank in both subtasks, with the best F measure of 0.813 for entity recognition and the best accuracy of 74.1% for encoding, indicating the proposed approaches are promising.

1 Introduction

In recent years, clinical natural language processing (NLP) has received great attention for its critical role in unlocking information embedded in clinical documents. Leveraging such information can facilitate the secondary use of electronic health record (EHR) data to promote clinical and translational research. Clinical entity recognition, which recognizes mentions of clinically relevant concepts (e.g., disorders, procedures, drugs etc.) in narratives, and clinical entity encoding, which maps the recognized entities to concepts in standard vocabularies (e.g., UMLS CUI (Bodenreider, 2004)), are among the fundamental tasks in clinical NLP research.

Many systems have been developed to extract clinical concepts from various types of clinical notes in last two decades, ranging from early symbolic NLP systems heavily dependent on domain knowledge to machine learning algorithm based systems driven by increasingly available annotated clinical corpora. The representative systems include MedLEE (Friedman et al., 1994), MetaMap (Aronson and Lang, 2010), KnowledgeMap (Denny et al., 2003), cTAKES (Savova et al., 2010), etc. Clinical NLP challenges organized by the Center for Informatics for Integrating Biology & the Beside (i2b2) have promoted research using machine learning algorithms to recognize clinical entities (Uzuner et al., 2010; Uzuner et al., 2011).

Unlike the previous i2b2 challenges, the ShARe/CLEF challenge of clinical disorder extraction and encoding held in 2013 took the initiative to recognize disjoint entities, in addition to entities made up of consecutive words (Chapman et al., 2013). ShARe/CLEF challenge also required encoding of the disorder entities to Systematized Nomenclature Of Medicine Clinical Terms (SNOMED-CT) (using UMLS CUIs).

Proceedings of the 8th International Workshop on Semantic Evaluation (SemEval 2014), pages 802–806, Dublin, Ireland, August 23-24, 2014.

In this paper, we describe our system for Task 7 of SemEval 2014, which followed the requirements of 2013 ShARe/CLEF challenge. Our system employed ensemble learning based approaches for disorder entity recognition and a Vector Space Model (VSM) based method for mapping extracted entities to CUIs of SNOMED-CT concepts. Our system was top-ranked among all participating teams according to evaluation by the organizer.

2 Method

Our end-to-end system for Task 7 of SemEval 2014 consists of two components: disorder entity recognition and encoding. The raw clinical notes first went through the pre-processing modules for rule-based sentence boundary detection and tokenization. Extracted features were then used to train two machine learning algorithm-based entity recognition models, Conditional Random Fields (CRFs) (Lafferty et al., 2001) and Structural Support Vector Machines (SSVMs) (Tsochantaridis et al., 2005), respectively. These two models were ensembled with MetaMap, a symbolic biomedical NLP system, by three different approaches. Recognized entities were mapped to SNOWMED-CT CUIs in the encoding component. Detailed information of the components are presented in the following sections.

2.1 Dataset

The training and test sets of 2013 ShARe/CLEF challenge were used as the training and development sets respectively for system development in SemEval 2014 Task 7. The training set consists of 199 notes and the development set has 99 notes, both of which were collected from four types of clinical notes including discharge summaries (DIS), radiology reports (RAD), and ECG/ECHO reports. Based on a pre-defined guideline, disorder entities were annotated for each note and then mapped to UMLS CUIs of SNOMED-CT concepts. Disorder entities not found in SNOMED-CT were marked as "CUI-less". The training set contained 5811 disorder entities which were mapped to 1007 unique CUIs or CUI-less. The development set contained 5340 disorder entities mapped to 795 CUIs or CUI-less. The test set contained 133 notes, all of which were discharge summaries. As the gold-standard annotation of the test set is not released by the organizer, the detailed annotation information of the test set is not available. Table 1 shows the total counts of notes, entities and CUIs in the three datasets.

Dataset	Type	Note	Entity	CUI	CUI-less
Train	ALL	199	5816	4177	1639
	ECHO	42	828	662	166
	RAD	42	555	392	163
	DIS	61	3589	2646	943
	ECG	54	193	103	90
Dev	ALL	99	5340	3619	1721
	ECHO	12	338	241	97
	RAD	12	162	126	36
	DIS	75	4840	3252	1588
	ECG	0	0	0	
Test	ALL	133	-	-	
	DIS	133	-	-	

Table 1. Statistics of the dataset.

2.2 Disorder entity recognition

The disorder entity recognition component consists of two modules: 1) the machine learning (e.g., CRF and SSVM) based named entity recognition (NER) module and 2) the ensemble learning module. For the challenge of this year, we mainly focused on the second ensemble learning module.

Machine learning based NER Module. This module was built based on our previous challenge participation in the 2013 ShARe/CLEF challenge (Tang et al., 2013). Annotated data were typically converted into a BIO format in machine learning-based NER systems. Each word was assigned one of the three labels: B for beginning of an entity, I for inside an entity, and O for outside of an entity. A unique challenge of this task is the high frequency (>10%) of disjoint disorders. For example, in the sentence "*the left atrium is not moderately dilated*", the discontinuous phrase "*left atrium...dilated*" is defined as a disjoint disorder. Such entities could not be directly represented using the traditional BIO approach. Therefore, in addition to traditional BIO tags used for labeling words in the consecutive disorder entities, two sets of tags were created for disjoint entities: (1) D{B, I} was used to label disjoint entity words that are not shared by multiple concepts; and (2) H{B, I} was used to label head words that belonged to more than two disjoint concepts. Ultimately, we assigned one of the seven labels {B, I, O, DB, DI, HB, HI} to each word. A few simple rules were then defined to convert labeled words to entities (Tang et al., 2013).

We exploited two state-of-the-art machine learning algorithms for disorder entity recognition, namely CRF (Lafferty et al., 2001) and SSVM (Tsochantaridis et al., 2005). CRFsuite and SVM^{hmm} were used to implement CRF and SSVM respectively.

For features, we used bag-of-word, part-of-speech from Stanford tagger, type of notes, section information, word representation from Brown clustering (Brown et al., 1992), random indexing (Lund and Burgess, 1996) and semantic categories of words based on UMLS lookup, MetaMap, and cTAKES outputs. More detailed information of this module can be found in our paper for 2013 ShARe/CLEF challenge (Tang et al., 2013).

One thing to note is that for word representation features like Brown clustering and random indexing, we only use the combination of traning and development and test datasets for feature extraction. The non-annotated corpus provided by the SemEval organizers was not employed currently. We do plan to pre-generate word clusters and random indexing using the provided corpus in the near future.

Ensemble Learning Module. Three approaches were employed to consolidate the CRF-model, SSVM-model and the MetaMap outputs, namely machine learning classifier based ensemble ($ensemble^{ML}$), majortiy voting based ensemble ($ensemble^{MV}$) and direct merging of the entity recognition results from the three models ($ensemble^{DM}$).

In the $ensemble^{ML}$ approach, a binary classifier was trained to determine if the entities recognized by the CRF-model, SSVM-model and MetaMap were true positives. A new set of features were then extracted for each candidate entity, that included the specific models recognizing the entity, the entity itself, n-gram and word shape features of the first/last word of the entity. A sliding window based feature was extracted to check whether there was any recognized entity within 20 characters before the first and after the last word. Some features extracted from the first module were also employed. We used the open source toolkit Liblinear (Fan et al., 2008), to build the binary classifier for $ensemble^{ML}$.

2.3 Disorder Entity Encoding

We developed a Vector Space Model (VSM) based approach to find the most suitable CUI for a given disorder entity. The disorder entity was used as query and all the UMLS terms were treated as documents. We used the cosine-similarity score to rank the candidate terms. For post-processing, if the top-ranked CUI was not a disorder CUI, it was replaced with 'CUI-less'. 'CUI-less' was also assigned to entities without any retrieved candidate CUI.

2.4 Experiments and Evaluation

Our system was developed and trained using the enlarged training set by merging the 199 notes in the training set and the 99 notes in the development set. All parameters of CRF, SSVM and Liblinear were optimized by 10-fold cross-validation on the enlarged training dataset. The performance of disorder entity recognition was evaluated by precision, recall and F-measure, which were measured in both "strict" and "relaxed" modes. The "strict" mode was defined as follows: a concept is correctly recognized if and only if it can be matched exactly to a disorder mention in the gold standard, and the "relaxed" mode means that a disorder mention is correctly recognized if it overlaps with any disorder mention in the gold standard. For entity encoding, all participating systems were evaluated using accuracy, in "strict" and "relaxed" modes, as defined in (Suominen et al., 2013).

3 Results

Table 2 and Table 3 show the best performance of our systems in the SemEval 2014 Task 7 as reported by the organizers, where "P", "R", "F" denote precision, recall and F-measure respectively. For disorder entity recognition, the $ensemble^{ML}$ based system outperformed the other two ensemble approaches, achieving the best F-measure of 0.813 under "strict" criterion and was ranked first in the challenge. For encoding, our system achieved an accuracy of 0.741 by $ensemble^{DM}$ under "strict" criterion and was again ranked first in the challenge.

	Strict			Relaxed		
	P	R	F	P	R	F
$ensemble^{ML}$	84.3	78.6	81.3	93.6	86.6	90.0

Table 2. The disorder recognition performance of our system for the SemEval 2014 task 7 (%).

	Accuracy	
	Strict	Relaxed
$ensemble^{DM}$	0.741	0.873

Table 3. The SNOMED encoding performance of our system for the SemEval 2014 task 7.

4 Discussion

In this study, we developed an ensemble learning-based approach to recognize disorder entities and a vector space model-based method to encode disorders to UMLS CUIs. Our system was top-ranked among all participating teams. However, there are still expectations for further improvement.

For disorder entity recognition, directly merging the entity recognition results of the three models (ensemble^{DM}) achieved the highest encoding accuracy of 0.741. This shows the great potential of performance enhancement by combining different models. However, the precision of ensemble^{DM} was much lower than the current machine learning-based ensemble approach ensemble^{ML}. ensemble^{ML} improved the precision to 84.3%, with the lowest recall of 78.6% among the three ensemble approaches. Further investigations for balancing and enhancing both precision and recall simultaneously by combining different models will be pursued in the follow-up studies.

For encoding, when a disorder entity can be labelled with multiple CUIs in different contexts, a more effective disambiguation model could be exploited. Further, query expansion techniques may be helpful and worth investigating. The above methods should be potentially helpful to address the problems caused by synonyms or spelling variants.

5 Conclusion

We developed a clinical disorder recognition and encoding system that consists of a ensemble learning-based approach to recognize disorder entities and a vector space model-based method to encode the identified disorders to UMLS CUIs of SNOMED-CT concepts. The performance of our system was top-ranked in the SemEval 2014 Task 7, indicating that our approaches are promising. However, further improvements are needed in order to enhance performance on concept extraction and encoding in clinical text.

Acknowledgments

This study is supported in part by grants from NLM R01LM010681, NCI 1R01CA141307, NIGMS 1R01GM102282 and CPRIT R1307 (H.X).

Reference

Aronson, A. R., & Lang, F.-M. (2010). An overview of MetaMap: historical perspective and recent advances. *Journal of the American Medical Informatics Association: JAMIA*, *17*(3), 229–236.

Bodenreider, O. (2004). The unified medical language system (UMLS): integrating biomedical terminology. *Nucleic Acids Research*, *32*(suppl 1), 267–270.

Brown, P. F., deSouza, P. V., Mercer, R. L., Pietra, V. J. D., & Lai, J. C. (1992). Class-Based n-gram Models of Natural Language. *Computational Linguistics*, *18*, 467–479.

Denny, J. C., Irani, P. R., Wehbe, F. H., Smithers, J. D., & Spickard, A. (2003). The KnowledgeMap Project: Development of a Concept-Based Medical School Curriculum Database. *AMIA Annual Symposium Proceedings*, *2003*, 195–199.

Fan, R.-E., Chang, K.-W., Hsieh, C.-J., Wang, X.-R., & Lin, C.-J. (2008). LIBLINEAR: A library for large linear classification. *The Journal of Machine Learning Research*, *9*, 1871–1874.

Friedman, C., Alderson, P. O., Austin, J. H., Cimino, J. J., & Johnson, S. B. (1994). A general natural-language text processor for clinical radiology. *Journal of the American Medical Informatics Association*, *1*(2), 161–174.

Lafferty, J., McCallum, A., & Pereira, F. C. N. (2001). Conditional Random Fields: Probabilistic Models for Segmenting and Labeling Sequence Data. *Departmental Papers (CIS)*.

Lund, K., & Burgess, C. (1996). Producing high-dimensional semantic spaces from lexical co-occurrence. *Behavior Research Methods, Instruments, & Computers*, *28*(2), 203–208.

Savova, G. K., Masanz, J. J., Ogren, P. V., Zheng, J., Sohn, S., Kipper-Schuler, K. C., & Chute, C. G. (2010). Mayo clinical Text Analysis and Knowledge Extraction System (cTAKES): architecture, component evaluation and applications. *Journal of the American Medical Informatics Association: JAMIA*, *17*(5), 507–513.

Suominen, H., SalanterÃ, S., Velupillai, S., Chapman, W. W., Savova, G., & Elhadad, N. (2013). Overview of the ShARe/CLEF eHealth Evaluation Lab 2013. *Information Access Evaluation. Multilinguality, Multimodality, and Visualization*, *2013*, 212–231.

Tang, B., Cao, H., Wu, Y., Jiang, M., & Xu, H. (2013). Recognizing and Encoding Discorder Concepts in Clinical Text using Machine Learning and Vector Space Model. *Workshop of ShARe/CLEF eHealth Evaluation Lab 2013*.

Tsochantaridis, I., Joachims, T., Hofmann, T., & Altun, Y. (2005). Large margin methods for structured and interdependent output variables. *Journal of Machine Learning Research*, *6*, 1453–1484.

Uzuner, Ã., Solti, I., & Cadag, E. (2010). Extracting medication information from clinical text. *Journal of the American Medical Informatics Association*, *17*(5), 514–518.

Uzuner, Ã., South, B. R., Shen, S., & DuVall, S. L. (2011). 2010 i2b2/VA challenge on concepts, assertions, and relations in clinical text. *Journal of the American Medical Informatics Association: JAMIA*, *18*(5), 552–556.

UTU: Disease Mention Recognition and Normalization with CRFs and Vector Space Representations

Suwisa Kaewphan[1,2,3*], **Kai Hakaka**[1*], **Filip Ginter**[1]
[1] Dept. of Information Technology, University of Turku, Finland
[2] Turku Centre for Computer Science (TUCS), Turku, Finland
[3] The University of Turku Graduate School (UTUGS), University of Turku, Finland
sukaew@utu.fi, kahaka@utu.fi, ginter@cs.utu.fi

Abstract

In this paper we present our system participating in the SemEval-2014 Task 7 in both subtasks A and B, aiming at recognizing and normalizing disease and symptom mentions from electronic medical records respectively. In subtask A, we used an existing NER system, NERsuite, with our own feature set tailored for this task. For subtask B, we combined word vector representations and supervised machine learning to map the recognized mentions to the corresponding UMLS concepts. Our system was placed 2nd and 5th out of 21 participants on subtasks A and B respectively showing competitive performance.

1 Introduction

The SemEval 2014 task 7 aims to advance the development of tools for analyzing clinical text. The task is organized by providing the researchers annotated clinical records to develop systems that can detect the mentions of diseases and symptoms in medical records. In particular, the SemEval task 7 comprises two subtasks, recognizing the mentions of diseases and symptoms (task A) and mapping the mentions to unique concept identifiers that belong to the semantic group of disorders in the Unified Medical Language System (UMLS).

Our team participated in both of these subtasks. In subtask A, we used an existing named entity recognition (NER) system, NERsuite, supplemented with UMLS dictionary and normalization similarity features. In subtask B, we combined compositional word vector representations with supervised machine learning to map the recognized mentions from task A to the UMLS concepts. Our best systems, evaluated on strict matching criteria, achieved F-score of 76.6% for the subtask A and accuracy of 60.1% for the subtask B, showing competitive performance in both tasks.

2 Task A: Named Entity Recognition with NERSuite

The ML approach based on conditional random fields (CRFs) has shown to have state-of-the-art performance in recognizing the biological entities. We thus performed task A by using NERsuite, an existing NER toolkit with competitive performance on biological entity recognition (Campos et al., 2013).

NERsuite is a NER system that is built on top of the CRFsuite (Okazaki, 2007). It consists of three language processing modules: a tokenizer, a modified version of the GENIA tagger and a named entity recognizer. NERsuite allows user-implemented features in addition to dictionary matching and features shown to benefit the systems such as raw token, lemma, part-of-speech (POS) and text chunk.

Prior to detecting the disease mentions by the recognizer module of NERsuite, the clinical text is split into sentences by using GENIA Sentence Splitter, a supervised ML system that is known to be well optimized for biomedical texts (Sætre et al., 2007). The sentences are subsequently tokenized and POS tagged.

To represent the positive entities, the "BIO" model was used in our system. The first tokens of positive mentions are labeled with "B" and the rest with "I". Negative examples, non-entities, are thus labeled with "O". This model was used for both contiguous and discontiguous entities.

The features include the normalization similarity (see Section 3.3), types of medical records (*discharge*, *echo*, *radiology* and *ecg*), and UMLS dic-

*These authors contributed equally.

Proceedings of the 8th International Workshop on Semantic Evaluation (SemEval 2014), pages 807–811, Dublin, Ireland, August 23-24, 2014.

Trained Model	Precision	Recall	F-score
train + positive samples	77.3%	72.4%	74.8%
train + development	76.7 %	76.5%	76.6%

Table 1: The results of our different NERsuite models, announced by the organizers.

tionary matching in addition to NERsuite's own feature generation.

The UMLS dictionary is prepared by extracting the UMLS database for the semantic types demanded by the task. In addition to those 11 semantic types, "Finding" was also included in our dictionary since, according to its definition, the concept is also deemed relevant for the task. Due to the common use of acronyms, which are not extensively provided by UMLS, we also extended the coverage of our prepared UMLS dictionary by extracting medical acronyms from the UMLS database using regular expression.

We assessed the effect of dictionary matching by training the models with and without the compiled UMLS dictionary and evaluating against the development set. The model trained with dictionary features outperformed the one without. The best model was obtained by training the NERsuite with UMLS dictionary in case-number-symbol normalization mode. In this mode, all letters, numbers and symbols are converted to lower case, zero (0) and underscore (_) respectively.

The regularization parameter (C2) was selected by using development set to evaluate the best model. The default parameter (C2 = 1.0) gave the best performing system and thus was used throughout the work.

Finally, for the NER task, we submitted two models. The first model was trained with the original training data and duplicates of sentences with at least one entity mention. The second model was trained by using the combination of the first model's training data and development set.

2.1 Results and Discussions

Our NER system from both submissions benefited from the increased number of training examples while the more diverse training data set gave a better performance. The official results are shown in table 1.

The analysis of our best performing NER system is not possible since the gold standard of the test data is not publicly available. We thus simply analyze our second NER system based on the evaluation on the development data. The F-score of the system was 75.1% and 88.0% for the strict and relaxed evaluation criteria respectively. Among all the mistakes made by the system, the discontiguous entities were the most challenging ones for the NERsuite. In development data, the discontiguous entities contribute about 10% of all entities, however, only 2% were recognized correctly. On the contrary, the system did well for the other types as 73% were correctly recognized under strict criteria. This demonstrates that the "BIO" model has limitations in representing the discontiguous entities. Improving the model to better represent the discontiguous entities can possibly boost the performance of the NER system significantly.

3 Task B: Normalization with Compositional Vector Representations

Our normalization approach is based on continuous distributed word vector representations, namely the state-of-the-art method *word2vec* (Mikolov et al., 2013a). Our word2vec model was trained on a subset of abstracts and full articles from the PubMed and PubMed Central resources. This data was used as it was readily available to us from the EVEX resource (Van Landeghem et al., 2013). Before training, all non-alphanumeric characters were removed and all tokens were lower-cased. Even though a set of unannotated clinical reports was provided in the task to support unsupervised learning methods, our experiments on the development set showed better performance with the model trained with PubMed articles. This might be due to the size of the corpora, as the PubMed data included billions of tokens whereas the provided clinical reports totaled in over 200 million tokens.

The dimensionality of the word vectors was set to 300 and we used the continuous skip-gram approach. For other word2vec parameters default values were used.

One interesting feature demonstrated by Mikolov et al. (2013b; 2013c) is that the vectors conserve some of the semantic characteristics in element-wise addition and subtraction. In this task we used the same approach of simply summing the word-level vectors to create compositional vectors for multi-word entities and concepts, i.e. we looked up the vectors for every token appearing in a concept name or entity and summed them to form a vector to represent the whole phrase.

We then formed a lexicon including all preferred terms and synonyms of all the concepts in the subset of UMLS defined in the task guidelines. This lexicon is a mapping from the compositional vector representations of the concept names into the corresponding UMLS identifiers. To select the best concept for a recognized entity we calculated cosine similarity between the vector representation of the given entity and all the concept vectors in the lexicon and the concept with the highest similarity was chosen.

Word2vec is generally able to relate different forms of the same word to each other, but we noticed a small improvement in accuracy when possessive suffixes were removed and all tokens were lemmatized.

3.1 Detecting CUI-less Mentions

As some of the mentions in the training data do not have corresponding concepts in the semantic categories listed in the task guidelines, they are annotated as "CUI-less". However, our normalization approach will always find the nearest matching concept, thus getting penalized for wrong predictions in the official evaluation. To overcome this problem, we implemented three separate steps for detecting the "CUI-less" mentions. As the simplest approach we set a fixed cosine similarity threshold and if the maximal similarity falls below it, the mention is normalized to "CUI-less". The threshold value was selected using a grid search to optimize the performance on the official development set. Although this method resulted in decent performance, it is not capable of coping with cases where the mention has very high similarity or even exact match with a concept name. For instance our system normalized "aspiration" mentions into UMLS concept "Pulmonary aspiration" which has a synonym "Aspiration", thus resulting in an exact match. To resolve this kind of cases, we used similar approach as in the DNorm system (Leaman et al., 2013b), where the "CUI-less" mentions occurring several times in the training data were added to the concept lexicon with concept ID "CUI-less". As the final step we trained a binary SVM classifier to distinguish the "CUI-less" mentions. The classifier utilized bag-of-word features as well as the compositional vectors. The performance improvement provided by each of these steps is presented in table 2. This evaluation shows that each step increases the performance considerably, but the overall performance is still 3.9pp below perfect detection.

Method	Strict accuracy
B	43.6
T	48.4
T + L	53.5
T + L + C	55.4
O	59.3

Table 2: Evaluation of the different approaches to detect CUI-less entities on the official development set compared to a baseline without CUI-less detection and an oracle method with perfect detection. This evaluation was done with the entities recognized by our NER system instead of the gold standard entities. B = baseline without CUI-less detection, T = similarity threshold, L = Lexicon-based method, C = classifier, O = Oracle.

3.2 Acronym Resolution

Abbreviations, especially acronyms, form a considerable portion of the entity mentions in clinical reports. One of the problems in normalizing the acronyms is disambiguation as one acronym can be associated with multiple diseases. Previous normalization systems (Leaman et al., 2013b) handle this by selecting the matching concept with most occurrences in the training data. However, this approach does not resolve the problem of non-standard acronyms, i.e. acronyms that are not known in the UMLS vocabulary or in other medical acronym dictionaries. Our goal was to resolve both of these problems by looking at the other entities found in the same document instead of matching the acronym against the concept lexicon. With this approach for instance entity mention "CP" was on multiple occasions correctly normalized into the concept "Chest Pain", even though UMLS is not aware of this acronym for the given concept and in fact associates it with several other concepts such as "Chronic Pancreatitis" and "Cerebral Palsy". However, the overall gain in accuracy obtained from this method was only minor.

3.3 Normalization Feedback to Named Entity Recognition

While basic exact match dictionary features provide usually a large improvement in NER performance, they are prone to bias the system to high precision and low recall. As both noun and adjective forms of medical concepts, e.g. "atrium" and "atrial", are commonly used in clinical texts, the entities may not have exact dictionary matches. Moreover the different forms of medical terms may not share a common morphological root discovered by simple stemming methods, thus complicating approximate matching. In this task we tried to boost the recall of our entity recognition by feeding back the normalization similarity information as features. These features included the maximum similarity between the token and the UMLS concepts as a numerical value as well as a boolean feature describing whether the similarity exceeded a certain threshold.

In addition we experimented by calculating the similarities for bigrams and trigrams in a sliding window around the tokens, but these features did not provide any further performance improvements.

3.4 Other Directions Explored

The DNorm system utilizes TF-IDF vectors to represent the entities and concepts but instead of calculating cosine similarity, the system trains a ranking algorithm to measure the maximal similarity (Leaman et al., 2013a). Their evaluation, carried out on the NCBI disease corpus (Doğan et al., 2014), showed a notable improvement in performance compared to cosine similarity. In our analysis we noticed that in 39% of the false predictions made by our normalization system, the correct concept was in the top 10 most similar concepts. This strongly suggested that a similar ranking method might be beneficial with our system as well. To test this we trained a linear SVM to rerank the top 10 concepts with highest cosine similarity, but we were not able to increase the overall performance of the system. However, due to the strict time constraints of the task, we cannot conclude whether this approach is feasible or not.

As our compositional vectors are formed by summing the word vectors, each word has an equal weight in the sum. Due to this our system made various errors where the entity was a single word matching closely to several concepts with longer names. For instance entity "hypertensive" was falsely normalized to concept "Hypertensive cardiopathy" whereas the correct concept was "Hypertensive disorder". These mistakes could have been prevented to some extent if the more important words had had a larger weight in the sum, e.g. word "disorder" is of low significance when trying to distinguish different disorders. However, weighting the word vectors with their IDF values, document in this case being an UMLS concept, did not improve the performance.

Team	Strict accuracy	Relaxed accuracy
UTH_CCB	74.1	87.3
UWM	66.0	90.9
RelAgent	63.9	91.2
IxaMed	60.4	86.2
UTU	60.1	78.3

Table 3: Official evaluation results for the top 5 teams in the normalization task.

3.5 Results

The official results for the normalization task are shown in table 3. Our system achieved accuracy of 60.1% when evaluated with the official strict evaluation metric. This result suggests that compositional vector representations are a competitive approach for entity normalization. However, the best performing team surpassed our performance by 14.0pp, showing that there is plenty of room for other teams to improve. It is worth noting though that their recall in the NER task tops ours by 8.2pp thus drastically influencing the normalization results as well. To evaluate the normalization systems in isolation from the NER task, a separate evaluation set with gold standard entities should be provided.

4 Conclusions

Overall, our NER system can perform well with the same default settings of NERsuite for gene name recognition. The performance improves when relevant features, such as UMLS dictionary matching and word2vec similarity are added. We speculated that representing the nature of the data with more suitable model can improve the system performance further. As a part of a combined system, the improvement on NER system can result in the increased performance of normalization system.

Our normalization system showed competitive results as well, indicating that word2vec-based vector representations are a feasible way of solving the normalization task. As future work we would like to explore different methods for creating the compositional vectors and reassess the applicability of the reranking approach described in section 3.4.

Acknowledgements

Computational resources were provided by CSC — IT Center for Science Ltd, Espoo, Finland. This work was supported by the Academy of Finland.

References

David Campos, Sérgio Matos, and José Luís Oliveira. 2013. Gimli: open source and high-performance biomedical name recognition. *BMC bioinformatics*, 14(1):54.

Rezarta Islamaj Doğan, Robert Leaman, and Zhiyong Lu. 2014. NCBI disease corpus: a resource for disease name recognition and concept normalization. *Journal of Biomedical Informatics*, 47:1–10, Feb.

Robert Leaman, Rezarta Islamaj Doğan, and Zhiyong Lu. 2013a. DNorm: disease name normalization with pairwise learning to rank. *Bioinformatics*, 29(22):2909–2917.

Robert Leaman, Ritu Khare, and Zhiyong Lu. 2013b. NCBI at 2013 ShARe/CLEF eHealth Shared Task: Disorder normalization in clinical notes with DNorm. In *Proceedings of the Conference and Labs of the Evaluation Forum*.

Tomas Mikolov, Kai Chen, Greg Corrado, and Jeffrey Dean. 2013a. Efficient estimation of word representations in vector space. In *ICLR Workshop*.

Tomas Mikolov, Ilya Sutskever, Kai Chen, Gregory S. Corrado, and Jeffrey Dean. 2013b. Distributed representations of words and phrases and their compositionality. In *NIPS*, pages 3111–3119.

Tomas Mikolov, Wen tau Yih, and Geoffrey Zweig. 2013c. Linguistic regularities in continuous space word representations. In *HLT-NAACL*, pages 746–751.

Naoaki Okazaki. 2007. CRFsuite: a fast implementation of conditional random fields (CRFs). http://www.chokkan.org/software/crfsuite/.

Rune Sætre, Kazuhiro Yoshida, Akane Yakushiji, Yusuke Miyao, Y Matsubyashi, and Tomoko Ohta. 2007. AKANE system: protein-protein interaction pairs in BioCreAtIvE2 challenge, PPI-IPS subtask. In *Proceedings of the BioCreative II*, pages 209–212.

Sofie Van Landeghem, Jari Björne, Chih-Hsuan Wei, Kai Hakala, Sampo Pyysalo, Sophia Ananiadou, Hung-Yu Kao, Zhiyong Lu, Tapio Salakoski, Yves Van de Peer, and Filip Ginter. 2013. Large-scale event extraction from literature with multi-level gene normalization. *PLoS ONE*, 8(4):e55814.

UW-MRS: Leveraging a Deep Grammar for Robotic Spatial Commands

Woodley Packard
University of Washington
sweaglesw@sweaglesw.org

Abstract

This paper describes a deep-parsing approach to SemEval-2014 Task 6, a novel context-informed supervised parsing and semantic analysis problem in a controlled domain. The system comprises a hand-built rule-based solution based on a pre-existing broad coverage deep grammar of English, backed up by a off-the-shelf data-driven PCFG parser, and achieves the best score reported among the task participants.

1 Introduction

SemEval-2014 Task 6 involves automatic translation of natural language commands for a robotic arm into structured "robot control language" (**RCL**) instructions (Dukes, 2013a). Statements of RCL are trees, with a fixed vocabulary of content words like `prism` at the leaves, and markup like `action:` or `destination:` at the nonterminals. The yield of the tree largely aligns with the words in the command, but there are frequently substitutions, insertions, and deletions.

A unique and interesting property of this task is the availability of highly relevant machine-readable descriptions of the spatial context of each command. Given a candidate RCL fragment describing an object to be manipulated, a spatial planner provided by the task organizers can automatically enumerate the set of task-world objects that match the description. This information can be used to resolve some of the ambiguity inherent in natural language.

The commands come from the Robot Commands Treebank (Dukes, 2013a), a crowdsourced corpus built using a *game with a purpose* (von Ahn, 2006). Style varies considerably, with missing determiners, missing or unexpected punctuation, and missing capitalization all common (Dukes, 2013b). Examples (1) and (2) show typical commands from the dataset.

(1) drop the blue cube

(2) Pick yellow cube and drop it on top of blue cube

Although the natural language commands vary in their degree of conformance to what might be called standard English, the hand-built gold standard RCL annotations provided with them (e.g. Figure 1) are commendable in their uniformity and accuracy, in part because they have been automatically verified against the formal *before* and *after* scene descriptions using the spatial planner.

```
(event: (action: drop)
        (entity: (color: blue)
                 (type: cube))
```

Figure 1: RCL corresponding to Example (1).

2 Related Work

Automatic interpretation of natural language is a difficult and long-standing research problem. Some approaches have taken a relatively shallow view; for instance, ELIZA (Weizenbaum, 1966) used pattern matching to somewhat convincingly participate in an English conversation. Approaches taking a deeper view tend to parse utterances into structured representations. These are usually abstract and general-purpose in nature, e.g. the syntax trees produced by mainstream PCFG parsers and the DRS produced by the Boxer system (Bos, 2008). As a notable exception, Dukes (2014) presents a novel method to produce RCL output directly.

The English Resource Grammar (**ERG**; Flickinger, 2000) employed as a component in the present work is a broad-coverage precision hand-written unification grammar of English, following the Head-driven Phrase Structure Grammar theory of syntax (Pollard & Sag, 1994). The ERG produces Minimal Recursion Semantics

Proceedings of the 8th International Workshop on Semantic Evaluation (SemEval 2014), pages 812–816,
Dublin, Ireland, August 23-24, 2014.

(**MRS**; Copestake et al., 2005) analyses, which are flat structures that explicitly encode predicate argument relations (and other data). A simplified MRS structure is shown in Figure 2. With minor modifications to allow determinerless NPs and some unexpected measure noun lexemes (as in "two *squares* to the left", etc), the ERG yields analyses for 99% of the commands in the training portion of the Robot Command Treebank.

$$\big(\text{INDEX} = e, \big\{\texttt{pron}(x), \texttt{cube\_n}(y), \texttt{drop\_v\_cause}(e, x, y), \texttt{blue\_a}(\_, y)\big\}\big)$$

Figure 2: Highly simplified view of the MRS produced by the ERG for Example (1).

3 ERG-based RCL Synthesis

This section outlines the method my system employs to synthesize RCL outputs from the MRS analyses produced by the ERG. The ERG provides a ranked list of candidate MRS analyses for each input. As a first step, grossly inappropriate analyses are ruled out, e.g. those proposing non-imperative main verbs or domain-inappropriate parts of speech ("block" as a verb). An attempt is made to convert each remaining analysis into a candidate RCL statement. If conversion is successful, the result is tested for coherence with respect to the known world state, using the supplied spatial planner. An RCL statement is incoherent if it involves picking up or moving an entity which does not exist, or if its command type (`take`, `move`, `drop`) is incompatible with the current state of the robot arm, e.g. `drop` is incoherent when the robot arm is not holding anything. Processing stops as soon as a coherent result is found.[1]

3.1 From MRS to RCL

Given an individual (imperative) MRS structure, the first step in conversion to RCL is to identify the sequence of top-level verbal predications. The `INDEX` property of the MRS provides an entry point. In a simple command like Example (1), the `INDEX` will point to a single verbal predication, whereas in a compound command such as Example (2), the `INDEX` will point to a coordination predication, which itself will have left and right arguments which must be visited recursively. Each verbal predication visited in this manner generates an `event:` RCL statement whose `action:` property is determined by a looking up the verbal predicate in a short hand-written table (e.g. `drop_v_cause` maps to `action: drop`). If the predicate is not found in the table, the most common action `move` is guessed.

Every RCL `event:` element must have an `entity:` subelement, representing the object to be moved by the action. Although in principle MRS makes no guarantees about the generalizability of the semantic interpretation of argument roles across different predicates, in practice the third argument of every verbal predicate relevant to this domain represents the object to be moved; hence, synthesis of an `event:` proceeds by inspecting the third argument of the MRS predicate which gave rise to it. Some types of `event:` also involve a `destination:` subelement, which encodes the location where the entity should come to rest. When present, a verbal predicate's *fourth* argument almost always identifies a prepositional predication holding this information, although there are exceptions (e.g. for `_move_v_from-to_rel` it is the fifth). When no such resultative role is present, the first prepositional modifier (if any) of the verbal event variable is used for the `destination:` subelement.

Synthesis of an `entity:` element from a referential index like y in Figure 2 or a `spatial-relation:` element from a prepositional predication proceeds in much the same way: the RCL `type:` or `relation:` is determined by a simple table lookup, and subelements are built based on connections indicated in the MRS. One salient difference is the treatment of predicates that are not found in their respective lookup tables. Whereas unknown command predicates default to the most common action `move`, unknown modifying spatial relations are simply dropped,[2] and unknown entity types cause conversion to fail, on the theory that an incorrect parse is likely. Prudent rejection of suspect parses only rarely eliminates all available analyses, and generally helps to find the most appropriate one. On development data, the first analysis produced by the ERG was

[1]Practically speaking, conversion from MRS to RCL is accomplished by a relatively short C program embodying these rules and steps (about 1500 lines in the final version): http://sweaglesw.org/svn/semeval-2014-task6/tags/dublin

[2]If the spatial relation is part of a mandatory `destination:` element, this can then cause conversion to fail.

convertible for 87% of commands, and the first RCL hypothesis was spatially coherent for 96% of commands. These numbers indicate that the parse ranking component of the ERG works quite well.

3.2 Polishing the Rules

I split the 2500 task-supplied annotated commands into a randomly-divided training set (2000 commands) and development set (500 commands). Throughout this work, the development set was only used for estimating performance on unseen data and tuning system combination settings; the contents of the development set were never inspected for rule writing or error analysis purposes. Although the conversion architecture outlined above constitutes an effective framework, there were quite a few details to be worked through, such as the construction of the lookup tables, identification of cases requiring special handling, elimination of undesirable parses, modest extension of the ERG, etc. An error-analysis tool which performed a fine-grained comparison of the synthesized RCL statements with the gold-standard ones and agglomerated common error types proved invaluable when writing rules. [3] Polishing the system in this manner took about two weeks of part-time effort; I maintained a log giving a short summary of each tweak (e.g. "map `_center_n_of_rel` to `type: region`"). These tweaks required varying amounts of time to implement, from a few seconds up to perhaps an hour; system accuracy as a function of the number of such tweaks is shown in Figure 3.

3.3 Anaphora and Ellipsis

Some commands use anaphora to evoke the identity or type of previously mentioned entities. Typically, the pronoun "it" refers to a specific entity while the pronoun "one" refers to the type of an entity (e.g. "Put the red cube on the blue one."). Empirically, the antecedent is nearly always the first `entity:` element in the RCL statement, and this heuristic works well in the system. A small fraction of commands ($< 0.5\%$ of the training data) elide the pronoun, in commands like "Take the blue tetrahedron and place in front left corner." In principle these could be detected and accommodated through the addition of a simple mal-rule to

[3]The error-analysis tool walks the system and gold RCL trees in tandem, recording differences and printing the most common mismatches. It consists of about 100 lines of Python and shell script, and took perhaps an hour to build.

Figure 3: Tuning the MRS-to-RCL conversion system by tweaking/adding rules. Development-set accuracy was only checked occasionally during rule-writing to avoid over-fitting.

the ERG (Bender et al., 2004), but for simplicity my system ignores this problem, leading to errors.

4 Robustness Strategies

If none of the analyses produced by the ERG result in coherent RCL statements, the system produces no output. On the one hand this results in quite a high precision: on the training data, 96.75% of the RCL statements produced are exactly correct. On the other hand, in some scenarios a lower precision result may be preferable to no result. The ERG-based system fails to produce any output for 3.1% of the training data inputs, a number that should be expected to increase for unseen data (since conversion can sometimes fail when the MRS contains unrecognized predicates).

In order to produce a best-guess answer for these remaining items, I employed the Berkeley parser (Petrov et al., 2006), a state-of-the-art data-driven system that induces a PCFG from a user-supplied corpus of strings annotated with parse trees. The RCL treebank is not directly suitable as training material for the Berkeley parser, since the yield of an RCL tree is not identical to (or even in 1-to-1 correspondence with) the words of the input utterance. In the interest of keeping things simple, I produced a phrase structure translation of the RCL treebank by simply discarding the elements of the RCL trees that did not correspond to any input, and inserting `(X word)` nodes for input words that were not aligned to any RCL fragment. The question of where in the tree to insert these `X` nodes is presumably of considerable importance, but again in the interest of simplicity I simply clustered them together with the first RCL-

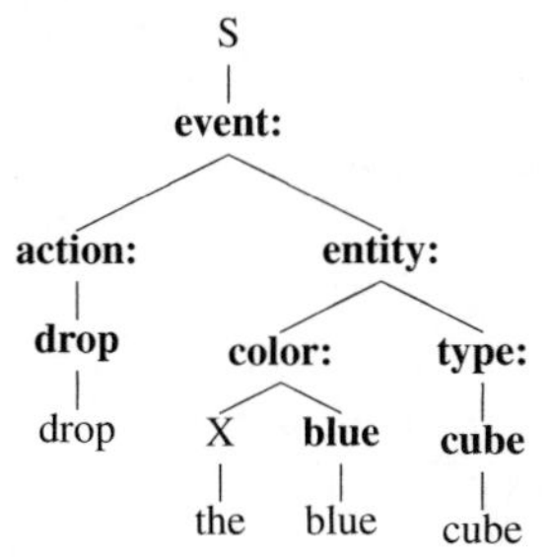

Figure 4: Automatic phrase structure tree translation of the RCL statement shown in Figure 1.

System	Dev P	Dev R	Eval P	Eval R
MRS-only (−**SP**)	90.7	88.0	92.1	80.3
MRS-only (+**SP**)	95.4	92.2	96.1	82.4
Robust-only (−**SP**)	88.2	88.2	81.5	81.5
Combined (−**SP**)	90.8	90.8	90.5	90.5
Combined (+**SP**)	95.0	95.0	92.5	92.5
ERG coverage		98.6		91.0

Figure 5: Evaluation results. ±**SP** indicates whether or not spatial planning was used. The robust and combined systems always returned a result, so P = R.

aligned word appearing after them. Unaligned input tokens at the end of the sentence were added as siblings of the root node. Figure 4 shows the phrase structure tree resulting from the translation of the RCL statement shown in Figure 1.

Using this phrase structure treebank, the Berkeley parser tools make it possible to automatically derive a similar phrase structure tree for any input string, and indeed when the input string is a command such as the ones of interest in this work, the resulting tree is quite close to an RCL statement. Deletion of the `X` nodes yields a robust system that frequently produces the exact correct RCL, at least for those items where only input-aligned RCL leaves are required. The most common type of non-input-aligned RCL fragment is the `id:` element, identifying the antecedent of an anaphor. As with the ERG-based system, a heuristic selecting the first `entity` as the antecedent whenever an anaphor is present works quite well.

Improving the output of the statistical system via tweaks of the type used in the ERG-based system was much more challenging, due to the relative impoverishedness of the information made available by the parser. Accurately detecting situations to improve without causing collateral damage proved difficult. However, the base accuracy of the statistical system was quite good, and when used as a back-off it improved overall system scores considerably, as shown in Table 5.

5 Results and Discussion

The combined system performs best on both portions of the data. Over the development data, the MRS-based system performs considerably better than the statistical system, in part due to the use of spatial planning in the MRS-based system (time did not permit adding spatial planning to the statistical system). The statistical system has a slightly higher recall than the MRS-only system without spatial planning, but the MRS-only system has a higher precision — markedly so on the evaluation data. This is consistent with previous findings combining precision grammars with statistical systems (Packard et al., 2014).

ERG coverage dropped precipitously from roughly 99% on the development data to 91% on the evaluation data. This is likely the major cause of the 10% absolute drop in the recall of the MRS-only system. The fact that the robust statistical system encounters a comparable drop on the evaluation data suggests that the text is qualitatively different from the (also held-out) development data. One possible explanation is that whereas the development data was randomly selected from the 2500 task-provided training commands, the evaluation data was taken as the sequentially following segment of the treebank, resulting in the same distribution of game-with-a-purpose participants (and hence writing styles) between the training and development sets but a different distribution for the evaluation data. [4]

Dukes (2014) reports an accuracy of 96.53%, which appears to be superior to the present system; however, that system appears to have used more training data than was available for the shared task, and averaged scores over the entire treebank, making direct comparison difficult.

Acknowledgements

I am grateful to Dan Flickinger, Emily Bender and Stephan Oepen for their many helpful suggestions.

[4]Reviewers suggested dropping sentence initial punctuation and reading "cell" as "tile." This trick boosts the MRS-only recall to 91.1% and the combined system to 94.5%, demonstrating both the frailty of NLP systems to unexpected inputs and the presence of surprises in the evaluation data. ERG coverage rose from 91.0% to 98.6%.

References

Bender, E. M., Flickinger, D., Oepen, S., Walsh, A., & Baldwin, T. (2004). Arboretum: Using a precision grammar for grammar checking in CALL. In *Instil/icall symposium 2004*.

Bos, J. (2008). Wide-coverage semantic analysis with boxer. In J. Bos & R. Delmonte (Eds.), *Semantics in text processing. step 2008 conference proceedings* (pp. 277–286). College Publications.

Copestake, A., Flickinger, D., Pollard, C., & Sag, I. (2005). Minimal recursion semantics: An introduction. *Research on Language & Computation*, *3*(2), 281–332.

Dukes, K. (2013a). Semantic annotation of robotic spatial commands. In *Language and Technology Conference (LTC)*. Poznan, Poland.

Dukes, K. (2013b). Train robots: A dataset for natural language human-robot spatial interaction through verbal commands. In *International Conference on Social Robotics (ICSR). Embodied Communication of Goals and Intentions Workshop.*

Dukes, K. (2014). Contextual Semantic Parsing using Crowdsourced Spatial Descriptions. *Computation and Language. arXiv:1405.0145 [cs.CL].*

Flickinger, D. (2000). On building a more efficient grammar by exploiting types. *Natural Language Engineering*, *6*(01), 15-28.

Packard, W., Bender, E. M., Read, J., Oepen, S., & Dridan, R. (2014). Simple negation scope resolution through deep parsing: A semantic solution to a semantic problem. In *Proceedings of the 52nd annual meeting of the Association for Computational Linguistics.* Baltimore, USA.

Petrov, S., Barrett, L., Thibaux, R., & Klein, D. (2006). Learning accurate, compact, and interpretable tree annotation. In *Proceedings of the 21st International Conference on Computational Linguistics and the 44th annual meeting of the Association for Computational Linguistics* (pp. 433–440).

Pollard, C., & Sag, I. A. (1994). *Head-Driven Phrase Structure Grammar*. Chicago, USA: The University of Chicago Press.

von Ahn, L. (2006). Games with a purpose. *Computer*, *39*(6), 92–94.

Weizenbaum, J. (1966). ELIZA — a computer program for the study of natural language communication between man and machine. *Communications of the ACM*, *9*(1), 36–45.

UWB: Machine Learning Approach to Aspect-Based Sentiment Analysis

Tomáš Brychcín
NTIS – New Technologies for the Information Society,
Faculty of Applied Sciences,
University of West Bohemia,
Univerzitní 8, 306 14 Plzeň
Czech Republic
brychcin@kiv.zcu.cz

Michal Konkol
NTIS – New Technologies for the Information Society,
Faculty of Applied Sciences,
University of West Bohemia,
Univerzitní 8, 306 14 Plzeň
Czech Republic
konkol@kiv.zcu.cz

Josef Steinberger
Department of Computer Science and Engineering,
Faculty of Applied Sciences,
University of West Bohemia,
Univerzitní 8, 306 14 Plzeň
Czech Republic
jstein@kiv.zcu.cz

Abstract

This paper describes our system participating in the aspect-based sentiment analysis task of Semeval 2014. The goal was to identify the aspects of given target entities and the sentiment expressed towards each aspect. We firstly introduce a system based on supervised machine learning, which is strictly constrained and uses the training data as the only source of information. This system is then extended by unsupervised methods for latent semantics discovery (LDA and semantic spaces) as well as the approach based on sentiment vocabularies. The evaluation was done on two domains, restaurants and laptops. We show that our approach leads to very promising results.

1 Introduction

The majority of current sentiment analysis approaches tries to detect the overall polarity of a sentence (or a document) regardless of the target entities (e.g. restaurants) and their aspects (e.g. food, price). By contrast, the ABSA (aspect based sentiment analysis) task is concerned with identifying the aspects of given target entities and estimating the sentiment polarity for each mentioned aspect.

The aspect scenario can be decomposed into two tasks: aspect extraction and aspect sentiment classification (Liu, 2012).

The task of aspect extraction is to recognize aspects of the entity and more generally can be seen as an information extraction task. The basic approach is finding frequent nouns and noun phrases (Liu et al., 2005; Blair-Goldensohn et al., 2008; Moghaddam and Ester, 2010; Long et al., 2010). Aspect extraction can be also seen as a special case of the general information extraction problem. The most dominant methods are based on sequential learning (e.g. HMM – Hidden Markov Models (Rabiner, 2010) or CRF – Conditional Random Fields (Lafferty et al., 2001)). Another group of methods use topic models (Mei et al., 2007; Titov and McDonald, 2008; Blei et al., 2003).

Aspect sentiment classification determines whether the opinions on different aspects are positive, negative, or neutral. While lexicon-based approaches use a list of aspect-related sentiment phrases as the core resource (Ding et al., 2008; Hu and Liu, 2004), the key issue for learning methods is to determine the scope of each sentiment expression, i.e., whether it covers the aspect in the sentence (Jiang et al., 2011; Boiy and Moens, 2009).

The most of the research in aspect-level sentiment analysis has been done in English, however, there were some attempts to tackle the aspect-level task in other languages (e.g. in Czech (Steinberger et al., 2014)).

The rest of the article is organized as follows. In Section 2, we summarize the ABSA shared task (Pontiki et al., 2014). Then, we give a description of our participating system (Section 3). In Section 4, we discuss our results in the task. We participated with both the constrained and the unconstrained variants of the system.

2 The ABSA task

Datasets consisting of customer reviews with human-authored annotations identifying the mentioned aspects of the target entities and the sentiment polarity of each aspect were provided. The experiments were run in two domains: restaurant and laptop reviews.

Proceedings of the 8th International Workshop on Semantic Evaluation (SemEval 2014), pages 817–822,
Dublin, Ireland, August 23-24, 2014.

Each team could submit two versions of systems – constrained and unconstrained. The constrained system uses only the training data and other resources (such as lexicons) for training. The unconstrained system can use additional data.

We use another definition of these types, which is not against the rules. Our constrained systems are based purely on ABSA training data, without any external knowledge such as dictionaries or rules. Our unconstrained systems use additional dictionaries, rule-based extensions and unlabeled data. From our point of view, hand-crafted dictionaries and rules are external knowledge and thus it is the same as adding external data.

The task consists of the four subtasks.

2.1 Subtask 1: Aspect term extraction

Given a set of sentences with pre-identified entities (restaurants or laptops), the task is to identify the aspect terms present in the sentence and return a list containing all the distinct aspect terms.

I liked the service and the staff, but not the food. $\rightarrow$ {service, staff, food}

2.2 Subtask 2: Aspect term polarity

For a given set of aspect terms within a sentence, the task is to determine the polarity of each aspect term: positive, negative, neutral or conflict (i.e., both positive and negative).

I hated their fajitas, but their salads were great. $\rightarrow$ {fajitas: negative, salads: positive}

2.3 Subtask 3: Aspect category detection

Given a predefined set of aspect categories, the task is to identify the aspect categories discussed in a given sentence. Aspect categories are typically coarser than the aspect terms of Subtask 1, and they do not necessarily occur as terms in the given sentence.

For example, the following categories were defined for the restaurants' domain: food, service, price, ambience and anecdotes/miscellaneous.

The restaurant was expensive, but the menu was great. $\rightarrow$ {price, food}

2.4 Subtask 4: Aspect category polarity

Given a set of pre-identified aspect categories, the task is to determine the polarity (positive, negative, neutral or conflict) of each aspect category.

The restaurant was expensive, but the menu was great. $\rightarrow$ *{price: negative, food: positive}*

3 System description

We use machine learning approach to all subtasks. For aspect term extraction we use CRF. For the other three tasks we use the Maximum Entropy classifier. We use the Brainy (Konkol, 2014) implementation of these algorithms.

During the data preprocessing, we use simple word tokenizer based on regular expressions. All tokens are lowercased for tasks 2 and 4.

We will firstly describe all the features used in this paper because the tasks share some of them. These features are then referenced in the descriptions of individual subtasks.

Words (W) – Word occurrence on a given position in the context window.

Bag of Words (BoW) – Occurrence of a word in a sentence (or context window).

Bigrams (B) – Bigram occurrence on a given position in the context window.

Bag of Bigrams (BoB) – Occurrence of a bigram in a sentence (or context window).

Tf-idf – Term frequency–inverse document frequency for all tokens in the sentence.

Learned Dictionary (LD) – Dictionary of terms based on training data.

Suffixes (S) – Suffix of a word (2-4 characters).

Sentiment Dictionary (SD) – Dictionary created using semi-automatic triangulation method (Steinberger et al., 2012). The score is normalized.

Senti Wordnet (SW) – See (Baccianella et al., 2010).

LDA – See Section 3.1.

Word Clusters (WC) – See Section 3.2. Cluster occurrence on a given position in the context window.

Bag of Clusters (BoC) – Same as word clusters, but without information about position.

We use two features that are not in common use in similar tasks – Latent Dirichlet Allocation and word clusters based on semantic spaces. Both these features use large amount of unlabeled data to discover latent semantics. We downloaded the restaurant reviews from `http://opentable.com`. This corpus consists of 409,665 reviews (documents) with about 27 million words. The *opentable* corpus is used as the training data for these features. Unfortunately, we did not find any large corpus for laptop domain, thus presented unsupervised features are used in restaurant domain only.

We devote the following two subsections to describe these features. Then we introduce our approach to the individual tasks.

3.1 Latent Dirichlet Allocation

The Latent Dirichlet Allocation (LDA) (Blei et al., 2003) is a topic model that is assumed to provide useful information for particular subtasks. We use LDA implementation from the MALLET (McCallum, 2002) software package. For each experiment we always train the 400 topics LDA (no significant difference was observed between different numbers of topics) with 1,000 iterations of Gibbs sampling. The hyperparameters of Dirichlet distributions were initially set to $\alpha = 50/K$, where K is the number of topics and $\beta = 0.1$. This setting is recommended by (Griffiths and Steyvers, 2004). The topic probabilities are directly used as new features to the classifier.

3.2 Word clusters

We use same approach as presented in (Brychcín and Konopík, 2014), where word clusters derived from semantic spaces improved language modeling. As recommended by these authors, we use COALS (Correlated Occurrence Analogue to Lexical Semantics) (Rohde et al., 2004) and HAL (Hyperspace Analogue to Language) (Lund and Burgess, 1996) for representing the word meaning and the Repeated Bisection algorithm for clustering. Similar approach has been already used for sentiment analysis in (Habernal and Brychcín, 2013) and (Brychcín and Habernal, 2013).

The parameters of semantic spaces are set as follows. For both semantic spaces we use a four-word context window (in both directions). HAL uses a matrix consisting of 50,000 columns, which keeps the largest amount of information. COALS uses a matrix with only 14,000 columns (as recommended by the authors of the algorithm). The SVD reduction was not used in our experiments.

Implementation of the HAL, COALS algorithms is available in an open source package S-Space (Jurgens and Stevens, 2010). For clustering, we use the implementation from the CLUTO software package (Karypis, 2003). As a measure of the similarity between two words, we use the cosine similarity of word vectors.

For both semantic spaces the word vectors are clustered into four different depths: 100, 500, 1,000, and 5,000 clusters (i.e. eight different cluster sets). The occurrences of particular clusters represent additional features to the classifiers.

3.3 Aspect term extraction

Our approach for aspect term extraction is based on Conditional Random Fields (CRF). The choice was based on similarity with the named entity recognition task, where CRF are regarded as the current state of the art (Konkol and Konopík, 2013). We use the BIO model for representing aspect terms (Ramshaw and Marcus, 1999).

The constrained feature set consists of: *W, BoW, B, LD, S*. It is extended by *WC* for the unconstrained case.

3.4 Aspect term polarity

During the detection of the aspect term polarities, the words affecting the sentiment of the aspect term are assumed to be close in most of cases. Thus we use a context window of 10 words in both directions around the target aspect term. We assume the further the word or bigram is from the target aspect term, the lower impact it has on the polarity label. To model this assumption we use a weight for each word and bigram feature taken from the Gaussian distribution according to the distance from the aspect term. The mean is set to 0 and the variance is optimized on training data.

As a feature set for the constrained approach we use only *BoW, BoB* and for the unconstrained approach we use *BoC, SD, SW* above that.

3.5 Aspect category detection

Aspect category detection is based on a set of binary Maximum Entropy classifiers, one for each class. The final decision is simply assembled from decisions of individual classifiers.

For this task we use *BoW, Tf-Idf* for the constrained approach and add *LDA, BoC* for unconstrained approach.

		Team	Const.	Rank	$P[\%]$	$R[\%]$	$F_1[\%]$	Rank	$ACC[\%]$
Aspect terms	Restaurants	Best	–	1.	85.35	82.71	84.01	1.	80.95
		UWB	U	7.	82.70	76.28	79.36	4.	77.69
		UWB	C	12.	83.28	70.28	76.23	12.	72.13
		Average	–	14-15.	76.74	67.26	70.78	18.	69.15
		Semeval Baseline	–	–	–	–	47.15	–	64.28
	Laptops	Best	–	1.	84.80	66.51	74.55	1.	70.49
		UWB	U	–	–	–	–	4.	66.67
		UWB	C	14.	77.33	49.54	60.39	10.	62.54
		Average	–	14.	68.97	50.45	56.20	16.	59.01
		Semeval Baseline	–	–	–	–	35.64	–	51.07
Aspect	categories	Best	–	1.	91.04	86.24	87.58	1.	82.92
		UWB	U	4.	84.36	78.93	81.55	8.	72.78
		UWB	C	5.	85.09	77.37	81.04	9.	72.78
		Average	–	11.	76.00	72.26	73.79	12-13.	69.51
		Semeval Baseline	–	–	–	–	63.89	–	65.66

Table 1: Comparison of our constrained (C) and unconstrained (U) system with Semeval baseline, best and average results. P, R, and F_1 denote the precision, recall and F-measure, respectively, used for measuring aspect term and category detection. ACC denotes the accuracy, used for measuring aspect term and category sentiment polarity detection.

3.6 Aspect category polarity

For this task we always take the whole sentence into account. We cannot take a limited window as we do not know where exactly the category is mentioned in the sentence. Moreover, it can be at several positions. To distinguish between different categories we again use standalone Maximum Entropy classifier for each category.

The constrained feature set consists of: *BoW, BoB, Tf-Idf*. It is extended by *BoC, LDA, SD, SW* for the unconstrained case.

4 Results

The ABSA task was a competition between research teams from around the world. There were 21 to 32 submitted systems for individual tasks.

We have submitted both constrained (no external knowledge, dictionaries or rules) and unconstrained systems for all tasks, except unconstrained system for aspect term extraction in the laptops domain.

Table 1 shows results of our systems (UWB) and compares them with the best and average systems as well as with the Semeval baseline. The average system is not any particular system. It is represented by average rank and metrics (metrics are averaged separately).

Our systems performed quite well. In all tasks, we outperform the Semeval baseline system. Moreover, we are always above average (F-measure and accuracy) in all tasks. We were three times in the fourth place and our unconstrained systems were always in top ten.

Table 2 presents the 10-fold cross-validation results on restaurant training data. We can clearly see, that any of our extension (LDA, clusters, sentiment vocabularies) brings at least some improvement.

5 Conclusion

This paper covers our participation in the ABSA task of Semeval 2014. The ABSA task consists of 4 subtasks. For each subtask we propose both constrained (no external knowledge) and unconstrained approach. The constrained versions of our system are based purely on machine learning techniques. The unconstrained versions extend the constrained feature set by LDA, semantic spaces and sentiment dictionaries.

The proposed approaches achieved very good results. The constrained versions were always above average, often by a large margin. The unconstrained versions were ranked among the best systems.

	$P[\%]$	$R[\%]$	$F_1[\%]$
Constrained	68.72	82.14	74.83
Constrained + WC	76.77	82.51	79.53

(a) Aspect term extraction

	$ACC[\%]$
Constrained	65.91
Constrained+BoC	70.05
Constrained+SD+SW	68.13
All	71.02

(b) Aspect term polarity

	$P[\%]$	$R[\%]$	$F_1[\%]$
Constrained	74.56	80.69	77.51
Constrained + LDA	75.96	81.94	78.84
Constrained + BoC	77.01	81.42	79.16
All	77.28	81.62	79.39

(c) Aspect category extraction

	$ACC[\%]$
Constrained	66.69
Constrained+LDA	67.85
Constrained+BoC	68.61
Constrained+SD+SW	69.28
All	70.20

(d) Aspect category polarity

Table 2: 10 fold cross-validation results on the restaurants training data for individual features. P, R, and F_1 denote the precision, recall and F-measure, respectively, used for measuring aspect term and category detection. ACC denotes the accuracy, used for measuring aspect term and category sentiment polarity detection.

Acknowledgements

This work was supported by grant no. SGS-2013-029 Advanced computing and information systems, by the European Regional Development Fund (ERDF) and by project "NTIS - New Technologies for Information Society", European Centre of Excellence, CZ.1.05/1.1.00/02.0090, and by project MediaGist, EU's FP7 People Programme (Marie Curie Actions), no. 630786.

References

Stefano Baccianella, Andrea Esuli, and Fabrizio Sebastiani. 2010. Sentiwordnet 3.0: An enhanced lexical resource for sentiment analysis and opinion mining. In Nicoletta Calzolari (Conference Chair), Khalid Choukri, Bente Maegaard, Joseph Mariani, Jan Odijk, Stelios Piperidis, Mike Rosner, and Daniel Tapias, editors, *Proceedings of the Seventh International Conference on Language Resources and Evaluation (LREC'10)*, Valletta, Malta, may. European Language Resources Association (ELRA).

Sasha Blair-Goldensohn, Kerry Hannan, Ryan McDonald, Tyler Neylon, George Reis, and Jeff Reynar. 2008. Building a sentiment summarizer for local service reviews. In *Proceedings of WWW-2008 workshop on NLP in the Information Explosion Era*.

David M. Blei, Andrew Y. Ng, and Michael I. Jordan. 2003. Latent dirichlet allocation. *Journal of Machine Learning Research*, 3:993–1022.

Erik Boiy and Marie-Francine Moens. 2009. A machine learning approach to sentiment analysis in multilingual web texts. *Information retrieval*, 12(5):526–558.

Tomáš Brychcín and Ivan Habernal. 2013. Unsupervised improving of sentiment analysis using global target context. In *Proceedings of the International Conference Recent Advances in Natural Language Processing RANLP 2013*, pages 122–128, Hissar, Bulgaria, September. INCOMA Ltd. Shoumen, BULGARIA.

Tomáš Brychcín and Miloslav Konopík. 2014. Semantic spaces for improving language modeling. *Computer Speech & Language*, 28(1):192 – 209.

Xiaowen Ding, Bing Liu, and Philip S. Yu. 2008. A holistic lexicon-based approach to opinion mining. In *Proceedings of the Conference on Web Search and Web Data Mining*.

Thomas L. Griffiths and Mark Steyvers. 2004. Finding scientific topics. *Proceedings of the National Academy of Sciences of the United States of America*, 101(Suppl 1):5228–5235, April.

Ivan Habernal and Tomáš Brychcín. 2013. Semantic spaces for sentiment analysis. In *Text, Speech and Dialogue*, volume 8082 of *Lecture Notes in Computer Science*, pages 482–489, Berlin Heidelberg. Springer.

Minqing Hu and Bing Liu. 2004. Mining and summarizing customer reviews. In *Proceedings of the tenth ACM SIGKDD international conference on Knowledge discovery and data mining*, KDD '04, pages 168–177, New York, NY, USA. ACM.

Long Jiang, Mo Yu, Ming Zhou, Xiaohua Liu, and Tiejun Zhao. 2011. Target-dependent twitter sentiment classification. In *Proceedings of the 49th Annual Meeting of the Association for Computational Linguistics*.

David Jurgens and Keith Stevens. 2010. The s-space package: An open source package for word space models. In *In Proceedings of the ACL 2010 System Demonstrations*.

George Karypis. 2003. Cluto - a clustering toolkit.

Michal Konkol and Miloslav Konopík. 2013. Crf-based czech named entity recognizer and consolidation of czech ner research. In Ivan Habernal and Václav Matoušek, editors, *Text, Speech and Dialogue*, volume 8082 of *Lecture Notes in Computer Science*, pages 153–160. Springer Berlin Heidelberg.

Michal Konkol. 2014. Brainy: A machine learning library. In Leszek Rutkowski, Marcin Korytkowski, Rafa Scherer, Ryszard Tadeusiewicz, Lotfi A. Zadeh, and Jacek M. Zurada, editors, *Artificial Intelligence and Soft Computing*, volume 8468 of *Lecture Notes in Computer Science*. Springer Berlin Heidelberg.

John Lafferty, Andrew McCallum, and Fernando Pereira. 2001. Conditional random fields: Probabilistic models for segmenting and labeling sequence data. In *Proceedings of International Conference on Machine Learning*.

Bing Liu, Minqing Hu, and Junsheng Cheng. 2005. Opinion observer: Analyzing and comparing opinions on the web. In *Proceedings of International Conference on World Wide Web*.

Bing Liu. 2012. *Sentiment Analysis and Opinion Mining*. Morgan & Claypool Publishers.

Chong Long, Jie Zhang, and Xiaoyan Zhu. 2010. A review selection approach for accurate feature rating estimation. In *Proceedings of Coling 2010: Poster Volume*.

Kevin Lund and Curt Burgess. 1996. Producing high-dimensional semantic spaces from lexical co-occurrence. *Behavior Research Methods Instruments and Computers*, 28(2):203–208.

Andrew Kachites McCallum. 2002. Mallet: A machine learning for language toolkit.

Qiaozhu Mei, Xu Ling, Matthew Wondra, Hang Su, and ChengXiang Zhai. 2007. Topic sentiment mixture: modeling facets and opinions in weblogs. In *Proceedings of International Conference on World Wide Web*.

Samaneh Moghaddam and Martin Ester. 2010. Opinion digger: an unsupervised opinion miner from unstructured product reviews. In *Proceeding of the ACM conference on Information and knowledge management*.

Maria Pontiki, Dimitrios Galanis, John Pavlopoulos, Harris Papageorgiou, Ion Androutsopoulos, and Suresh Manandhar. 2014. Semeval-2014 task 4: Aspect based sentiment analysis. In *Proceedings of the International Workshop on Semantic Evaluation (SemEval 2014)*, Dublin, Ireland.

Lawrence Rabiner. 2010. A tutorial on hidden markov models and selected applications in speech recognition. In *Proceedings of the IEEE*, pages 257–286.

Lance A Ramshaw and Mitchell P Marcus. 1999. Text chunking using transformation-based learning. In *Natural language processing using very large corpora*, pages 157–176. Springer.

Douglas L. T. Rohde, Laura M. Gonnerman, and David C. Plaut. 2004. An improved method for deriving word meaning from lexical co-occurrence. *Cognitive Psychology*, 7:573–605.

Josef Steinberger, Mohamed Ebrahim, Maud Ehrmann, Ali Hurriyetoglu, Mijail Kabadjov, Polina Lenkova, Ralf Steinberger, Hristo Tanev, Silvia Vzquez, and Vanni Zavarella. 2012. Creating sentiment dictionaries via triangulation. *Decision Support Systems*, 53(4):689 – 694.

Josef Steinberger, Tomáš Brychcín, and Michal Konkol. 2014. Aspect-level sentiment analysis in czech. In *Proceedings of the 5th Workshop on Computational Approaches to Subjectivity, Sentiment and Social Media Analysis*, Baltimore, USA, June. Association for Computational Linguistics.

Ivan Titov and Ryan McDonald. 2008. Modeling online reviews with multi-grain topic models. In *Proceedings of International Conference on World Wide Web*.

UWM: Applying an Existing Trainable Semantic Parser to Parse Robotic Spatial Commands

Rohit J. Kate
University of Wisconsin-Milwaukee
Milwaukee, WI
katerj@uwm.edu

Abstract

This paper describes Team UWM's system for the Task 6 of SemEval 2014 for doing supervised semantic parsing of robotic spatial commands. An existing semantic parser, KRISP, was trained using the provided training data of natural language robotic spatial commands paired with their meaning representations in the formal robot command language. The entire process required very little manual effort. Without using the additional annotations of word-aligned semantic trees, the trained parser was able to exactly parse new commands into their meaning representations with 51.18% best F-measure at 72.67% precision and 39.49% recall. Results show that the parser was particularly accurate for short sentences.

1 Introduction

Semantic parsing is the task of converting natural language utterances into their complete formal meaning representations which are executable for some application. Example applications of semantic parsing include giving natural language commands to robots and querying databases in natural language. Some old semantic parsers were developed manually to work for specific applications (Woods, 1977; Warren and Pereira, 1982). However, such semantic parsers were generally brittle and building them required a lot of manual effort. In addition, these parsers could not be ported to any other application without again putting significant manual effort.

More recently, several semantic parsers have been developed using machine learning (Zelle and Mooney, 1996; Ge and Mooney, 2005; Zettlemoyer and Collins, 2005; Wong and Mooney, 2006; Kate and Mooney, 2006; Lu et al., 2008; Kwiatkowski et al., 2011). In this approach, training data is first created for the domain of interest. Then using one of the many machine learning methods and semantic parsing frameworks, a semantic parser is automatically learned from the training data (Mooney, 2007). The trained semantic parser is then capable of parsing new natural language utterances into their meaning representations. Semantic parsers built using machine learning tend to be more robust and can be easily ported to other application domains with appropriate domain-specific training data.

The Task 6 of SemEval 2014 provided a new application domain for semantic parsing along with training and test data. The domain involved giving natural language commands to a robotic arm which would then move blocks on a board (Dukes, 2013). The domain was inspired from the classic AI system SHRDLU (Winograd, 1972). The training data contained 2500 examples of sentences paired with their meaning representations in the Robot Command Language (RCL) which was designed for this domain (Dukes, 2013). The test data contained 909 such example pairs.

We trained an existing and freely available[1] semantic parser KRISP (Kate and Mooney, 2006) using the training data for this domain. Besides changing the format of the data for running KRISP and writing a context-free grammar for the meaning representation language RCL, the entire process required minimal manual effort. The author spent less than a week's time for participating in the Task 6, and most of it was spent in running the experiments. This demonstrates that trainable semantic parsers like KRISP can be rapidly adopted to new domains. In the Results section we show different precisions and recalls it ob-

[1] http://www.cs.utexas.edu/users/ml/krisp/

Proceedings of the 8th International Workshop on Semantic Evaluation (SemEval 2014), pages 823–827,
Dublin, Ireland, August 23-24, 2014.

tained at different confidence levels in the form of a precision-recall curve. The results also show that the parser was particularly accurate on shorter sentences. Two major reasons that prevented KRISP from performing better on this domain were - its high computational demand for memory which prevented it from being trained beyond 1500 training examples, and some variability in the meaning representation language RCL that negatively affected training as well as evaluation.

2 Background: KRISP Semantic Parser

KRISP (Kernel-based Robust Interpretation for Semantic Parsing) is a trainable semantic parser (Kate and Mooney, 2006) that uses Support Vector Machines (SVMs) (Cristianini and Shawe-Taylor, 2000) as the machine learning method with string-subsequence kernel (Lodhi et al., 2002). It takes natural language utterances and their corresponding formal meaning representation as the training data along with the context-free grammar of the meaning representation language (MRL). The key idea in KRISP is that every production of the MRL is treated as a semantic concept. For every MRL production, an SVM classifier is trained so that it can give for any input natural language substring of words the probability that it expresses the corresponding semantic concept. Once these classifiers are trained, parsing a sentence reduces to finding the most probable semantic derivation of the sentence in which different productions cover different parts of the sentence and together form a complete meaning representation. Figure 1 shows an example semantic derivation of a robotic spatial command. Productions of RCL grammar (Table 1) are shown at tree nodes depicting different parts of the sentence they cover.

Since the training data is not in the form of such semantic derivations, an EM-like iterative algorithm is used to collect appropriate positive and negative examples in order to train the classifiers (Kate and Mooney, 2006). Positive examples are collected from correct semantic derivations derived by the parser learned in the previous iteration, and negative examples are collected from the incorrect semantic derivations.

KRISP was shown to work well on the US geography database query domain (Tang and Mooney, 2001) as well as on the RoboCup Coach Language (CLang) domain (Kate et al., 2005). It was also shown to be particularly robust to noise in

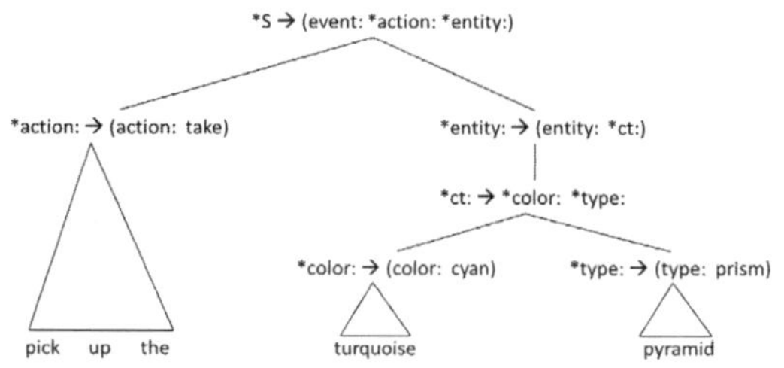

Figure 1: Semantic derivation of the robotic spatial command *"pick up the turquoise pyramid"* obtained by KRISP during testing which gives the correct RCL representation *(event: (action: take) (entity: (color: cyan) (type: prism)))*.

the natural language utterances (Kate and Mooney, 2006). KRISP was later extended to do semi-supervised semantic parsing (Kate and Mooney, 2007b), to learn from ambiguous supervision in which multiple sentences could be paired with a single meaning representation in the training data (Kate and Mooney, 2007a), and to transform the MRL grammar to improve semantic parsing (Kate, 2008).

3 Methods

In order to apply KRISP to the Task 6 of SemEval 2014, the format of the provided data was first changed to the XML-type format that KRISP accepts. The data contained several instances of co-references which was also part of RCL, but KRISP was not designed to handle co-references and expects them to be pre-resolved. We observed that almost all co-references in the meaning representations, indicated by "reference-id" token, resolved to the first occurrence of an "entity" element in the meaning representation. This was found to be true for more than 99% of the cases. We used this observation to resolve co-references during semantic parsing in the following way. As a pre-processing step, we first remove from the meaning representations all the "id:" tokens (these resolve the references) but keep the "reference-id:" tokens (these encode presence of co-references). The natural language sentences are not modified in any way and the parser learns from the training data to relate words like "it" and "one" to the RCL token "reference-id". After KRISP generates a meaning representation during testing, as a post-processing step, "id: 1" is added to the first "entity" element in the meaning representation if it contains the "reference-id:" token.

The context-free grammar for RCL was not provided by the Task organizers. There are multiple ways to write a context-free grammar for a meaning representation language and those that conform better to natural language work better for semantic parsing (Kate, 2008). We manually wrote grammar for RCL which mostly followed the structure of the meaning representations as they already conformed highly to natural language commands and hence writing the grammar was straightforward. KRISP runs faster if there are fewer non-terminals on the right-hand-side (RHS) of the grammar because that makes the search for the most probable semantic derivation faster. Hence we kept non-terminals on RHS as few as possible while writing the grammar. Table 1 shows the entire grammar for RCL that we wrote which was given to KRISP. The non-terminals are indicated with a "*" in their front. We point out that KRISP needs grammar only for the meaning representation language (an application will need it anyway if the statements are to be executed) and not for the natural language.

KRISP's training algorithm could be aided by providing it with information about which natural language words are usually used to express the concept of a production. For example, word "red" usually expresses "*color: → (color: red)". The data provided with the Task 6 came with the word-aligned semantic trees which indicated which natural language words corresponded to which meaning representation components. This information could have been used to aid KRISP, however, we found many inconsistencies and errors in the provided word-aligned semantic trees and chose not to use them. In addition, KRISP seemed to learn most of that information on its own anyway.

The Task 6 also included integrating semantic parsing with spatial planning. This meant that if the semantic parser generates an RCL representation that does not make sense for the given block configuration on the board, then it could be dismissed and the next best RCL representation could be considered. Besides generating the best meaning representation for a natural language utterance, KRISP is also capable of generating multiple possible meaning representations sorted by their probabilities. We could have used this capability to output only the best RCL representation that is valid for the given board configuration. Unfortunately, unfamiliarity with the provided Java API for the spatial planner and lack of time prevented us from doing this.

*action: → (action: move)
*action: → (action: drop)
*action: → (action: take)
*cardinal: → (cardinal: 1)
*cardinal: → (cardinal: 2)
*cardinal: → (cardinal: 3)
*cardinal: → (cardinal: 4)
*color: → (color: magenta)
*color: → (color: red)
*color: → (color: white)
*color: → (color: cyan)
*color: → (color: green)
*color: → (color: yellow)
*color: → (color: blue)
*color: → (color: gray)
*indicator: → (indicator: rightmost)
*indicator: → (indicator: back)
*indicator: → (indicator: center)
*indicator: → (indicator: right)
*indicator: → (indicator: leftmost)
*indicator: → (indicator: individual)
*indicator: → (indicator: nearest)
*indicator: → (indicator: front)
*indicator: → (indicator: left)
*reference-id: → (reference-id: 1)
*relation: → (relation: right)
*relation: → (relation: forward)
*relation: → (relation: within)
*relation: → (relation: above)
*relation: → (relation: nearest)
*relation: → (relation: adjacent)
*relation: → (relation: front)
*relation: → (relation: left)
*relation: → (relation: backward)
*type: → (type: type-reference-group)
*type: → (type: board)
*type: → (type: prism)
*type: → (type: cube)
*type: → (type: type-reference)
*type: → (type: cube-group)
*type: → (type: corner)
*type: → (type: robot)
*type: → (type: stack)
*type: → (type: edge)
*type: → (type: region)
*type: → (type: tile)
*type: → (type: reference)
*indicator: → *indicator: *indicator:
*color: → *color: *color:
*ct: → *color: *type:
*ict: → *indicator: *ct:
*ctr: → *ct: *reference-id:
*cct: → *cardinal: *ct:
*ed: → *entity: (destination: *spatial-relation:)
*entity: → (entity: *type:)
*entity: → (entity: *type: *reference-id:)
*entity: → (entity: *type: *spatial-relation:)
*entity: → (entity: *ct:)
*entity: → (entity: *indicator: *type:)
*entity: → (entity: *ict:)
*entity: → (entity: *ict: *spatial-relation:)
*entity: → (entity: *cardinal: *type:)
*entity: → (entity: *cct:)
*entity: → (entity: *cct: *spatial-relation:)
*entity: → (entity: *ctr:)
*entity: → (entity: *ct: *spatial-relation:)
*entity: → (entity: *ctr: *spatial-relation:)
*measure: → (measure: *entity:)
*mr: → *measure: *relation:
*spatial-relation: → (spatial-relation: *relation: *entity:)
*spatial-relation: → (spatial-relation: *mr:)
*spatial-relation: → (spatial-relation: *mr: *entity:)
*S → (sequence: *S *S)
*S → (event: *action: *ed:)
*S → (event: *action: *entity:)

Table 1: Grammar for the Robot Command Language (RCL) given to KRISP for semantic parsing. The non-terminals are indicated with a "*" in their front. The start symbol is *S.

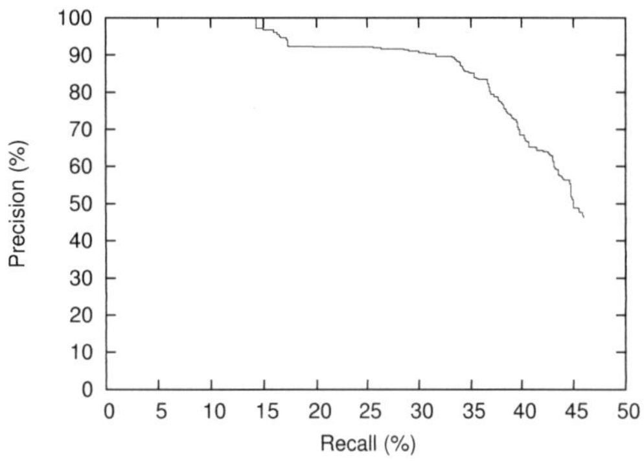

Figure 2: Precision-recall curve for the semantic parsing output on test sentences.

Sentence length	Accuracy (Correct/Total)
1-3	100.00% (15/15)
4-7	71.20% (136/191)
8-11	51.76% (147/284)
12-15	41.80% (79/189)
16-19	22.22% (28/126)
20-23	15.71% (11/70)
24-27	3.23% (1/31)
28-31	33.33% (1/3)
All	45.98% (418/909)

Table 2: Accuracy of semantic parsing across test sentences of varying lengths.

4 Results

We found that KRISP could not be trained beyond 1500 examples in this domain because the number of negative examples that are generated during the training process would become too large for the available memory size. This is something that could be fixed in the future by suitably sampling negative examples. Using the first 1500 training examples, we evaluated KRISP's performance on the provided 909 test examples. A generated RCL representation is considered correct only if it exactly matches the correct answer; no partial credit is given. In order to avoid generating incorrect meaning representations when it is not confident, KRISP uses a threshold and if the confidence (probability) of the best semantic derivation is below this threshold, it does not generate any meaning representation. This threshold was set to 0.05 as was previously done for other domains.

Performance was measured in terms of precision (the percentage of generated meaning representations that were correct) and recall (the percentage of all sentences for which correct meaning representations were obtained). Given that KRISP also gives confidences with its output meaning representations, we can compute precisions and recalls at various confidence levels. Figure 2 shows the entire precision-recall curve thus obtained. The best F-measure (harmonic mean of precision and recall) on this curve is 51.18% pdf at 72.67% precision and 39.49% recall. The precision at the highest recall was 45.98% which we had reported as our official evaluation result for the SemEval Task 6.

We further analyzed the results according to the lengths of the sentences and found that KRISP was very accurate with shorter sentences and became progressively less accurate as the lengths of the sentences increase. Table 2 shows these results. This could be simply because the longer the sentence, the more the likelihood of making an error, and since no partial credit is given, the entire output meaning representation is deemed incorrect.

On further error analysis we observed that there was some variability in the meaning representations. The "move" and "drop" actions seemed to mean the same thing and were used alternatively. For example in the training data, the utterance *"place the red block on single blue block"* had "(action: drop)" in the corresponding meaning representation, while *"place red cube on grey cube"* had "(action: move)", but there is no apparent difference between the two cases. There were many such instances. This was confusing KRISP's training algorithm because it would collect the same phrase sometimes as a positive example and sometimes as a negative example. This also affected the evaluation, because KRISP would generate "move" which won't match "drop", or vice-versa, and the evaluator will call it an error.

5 Conclusions

We participated in the SemEval 2014 Task 6 of supervised semantic parsing of robotic spatial commands. We used an existing semantic parser learner, KRISP, and trained it on this domain which required minimum time and effort from our side. The trained parser was able to map natural language robotic spatial commands into their formal robotic command language representations with good accuracy, particularly for shorter sentences.

References

Nello Cristianini and John Shawe-Taylor. 2000. *An Introduction to Support Vector Machines and Other Kernel-based Learning Methods*. Cambridge University Press.

Kais Dukes. 2013. Semantic annotation of robotic spatial commands. In *Proceedings of the Language and Technology Conference (LTC-2013)*, Poznan, Poland.

Ruifang Ge and Raymond J. Mooney. 2005. A statistical semantic parser that integrates syntax and semantics. In *Proceedings of the Ninth Conference on Computational Natural Language Learning (CoNLL-2005)*, pages 9–16, Ann Arbor, MI, July.

Rohit J. Kate and Raymond J. Mooney. 2006. Using string-kernels for learning semantic parsers. In *Proceedings of the 21st International Conference on Computational Linguistics and 44th Annual Meeting of the Association for Computational Linguistics (COLING/ACL-06)*, pages 913–920, Sydney, Australia, July.

Rohit J. Kate and Raymond J. Mooney. 2007a. Learning language semantics from ambiguous supervision. In *Proceedings of the Twenty-Second Conference on Artificial Intelligence (AAAI-07)*, pages 895–900, Vancouver, Canada, July.

Rohit J. Kate and Raymond J. Mooney. 2007b. Semi-supervised learning for semantic parsing using support vector machines. In *Proceedings of Human Language Technologies: The Conference of the North American Chapter of the Association for Computational Linguistics (NAACL-HLT-07)*, pages 81–84, Rochester, NY, April.

Rohit J. Kate, Yuk Wah Wong, and Raymond J. Mooney. 2005. Learning to transform natural to formal languages. In *Proceedings of the Twentieth National Conference on Artificial Intelligence (AAAI-05)*, pages 1062–1068, Pittsburgh, PA, July.

Rohit J. Kate. 2008. Transforming meaning representation grammars to improve semantic parsing. In *Proceedings of the Twelfth Conference on Computational Natural Language Learning (CoNLL-2008)*, pages 33–40. Association for Computational Linguistics.

Tom Kwiatkowski, Luke Zettlemoyer, Sharon Goldwater, and Mark Steedman. 2011. Lexical generalization in CCG grammar induction for semantic parsing. In *Proceedings of the Conference on Empirical Methods in Natural Language Processing (EMNLP-2011)*, pages 1512–1523. Association for Computational Linguistics.

Huma Lodhi, Craig Saunders, John Shawe-Taylor, Nello Cristianini, and Chris Watkins. 2002. Text classification using string kernels. 2:419–444.

Wei Lu, Hwee Tou Ng, Wee Sun Lee, and Luke S. Zettlemoyer. 2008. A generative model for parsing natural language to meaning representations. In *Proceedings of the 2008 Conference on Empirical Methods in Natural Language Processing (EMNLP-08)*, Honolulu, HI, October.

Raymond J. Mooney. 2007. Learning for semantic parsing. In A. Gelbukh, editor, *Computational Linguistics and Intelligent Text Processing: Proceedings of the 8th International Conference (CICLing-2007), Mexico City*, pages 311–324. Springer Verlag, Berlin.

Lappoon R. Tang and Raymond J. Mooney. 2001. Using multiple clause constructors in inductive logic programming for semantic parsing. In *Proceedings of the 12th European Conference on Machine Learning (ECML-2001)*, pages 466–477, Freiburg, Germany.

David H. D. Warren and Fernando C. N. Pereira. 1982. An efficient easily adaptable system for interpreting natural language queries. *American Journal of Computational Linguistics*, 8(3-4):110–122.

Terry Winograd. 1972. *Understanding Natural Language*. Academic Press, Orlando, FL.

Yuk Wah Wong and Raymond J. Mooney. 2006. Learning for semantic parsing with statistical machine translation. In *Proceedings of Human Language Technology Conference / North American Chapter of the Association for Computational Linguistics Annual Meeting (HLT-NAACL-06)*, pages 439–446, New York City, NY.

William A. Woods. 1977. Lunar rocks in natural English: Explorations in natural language question answering. In Antonio Zampoli, editor, *Linguistic Structures Processing*. Elsevier North-Holland, New York.

John M. Zelle and Raymond J. Mooney. 1996. Learning to parse database queries using inductive logic programming. In *Proceedings of the Thirteenth National Conference on Artificial Intelligence (AAAI-96)*, pages 1050–1055, Portland, OR, August.

Luke S. Zettlemoyer and Michael Collins. 2005. Learning to map sentences to logical form: Structured classification with probabilistic categorial grammars. In *Proceedings of 21st Conference on Uncertainty in Artificial Intelligence (UAI-2005)*, Edinburgh, Scotland, July.

UWM: Disorder Mention Extraction from Clinical Text Using CRFs and Normalization Using Learned Edit Distance Patterns

Omid Ghiasvand
University of Wisconsin-Milwaukee
Milwaukee, WI
ghiasva2@uwm.edu

Rohit J. Kate
University of Wisconsin-Milwaukee
Milwaukee, WI
katerj@uwm.edu

Abstract

This paper describes Team UWM's system for the Task 7 of SemEval 2014 that does disorder mention extraction and normalization from clinical text. For the disorder mention extraction (Task A), the system was trained using Conditional Random Fields with features based on words, their POS tags and semantic types, as well as features based on MetaMap matches. For the disorder mention normalization (Task B), variations of disorder mentions were considered whenever exact matches were not found in the training data or in the UMLS. Suitable types of variations for disorder mentions were automatically learned using a new method based on edit distance patterns. Among nineteen participating teams, UWM ranked third in Task A with 0.755 strict F-measure and second in Task B with 0.66 strict accuracy.

1 Introduction

Entity mention extraction is an important task in processing natural language clinical text. Disorders, medications, anatomical sites, clinical procedures etc. are among the entity types that predominantly occur in clinical text. Out of these, the Task 7 of SemEval 2014 concentrated on extracting (Task A) and normalizing (Task B) disorder mentions. Disorder mention extraction is particularly challenging because disorders are frequently found as discontinuous phrases in clinical sentences. The extracted mentions were then to be normalized by mapping them to their UMLS CUIs if they were in the SNOMED-CT part of UMLS and belonged to the "disorder" UMLS semantic group, otherwise they were to be declared as "CUI-less". This normalization task is challenging because disorder names are frequently mentioned in modified forms which prevents their exact matching with concept descriptions in UMLS.

Our team, UWM, participated in both Task A and Task B. We modelled disorder mention extraction as a standard sequence labeling task. The model was trained using Conditional Random Fields (Lafferty et al., 2001) with various types of lexical and semantic features that included MetaMap (Aronson, 2001) matches. The model was also inherently capable of extracting discontinuous disorder mentions. To normalize disorder mentions, our system first looked for exact matches with disorder mentions in the training data and in the UMLS. If no exact match was found, then suitable variations of the disorder mentions were generated based on the commonly used variations of disorder mentions learned from the training data as well as from the UMLS synonyms. We developed a novel method to automatically learn such variations based on edit distances (Levenshtein, 1966) which is described in the next section.

Our Team ranked third on Task A and second on Task B in the official SemEval 2014 Task 7 evaluation (considering only the best run for each team). We also present results of ablation studies we did on the development data in order to determine the contributions of various features and components of our system.

2 Methods

2.1 Task A: Disorder Mention Extraction

We modelled disorder mention extraction as a sequence labeling task with the standard "BIO" (Begin, Inside, Outside) scheme of output labels for sentence tokens. The tokens labelled "I" following the latest "B" token are extracted together as

Proceedings of the 8th International Workshop on Semantic Evaluation (SemEval 2014), pages 828–832,
Dublin, Ireland, August 23-24, 2014.

a disorder. For example, in the following labelled sequence "the/O left/B atrium/I is/O moderately/O dilated/I", "left atrium dilated" will be extracted as a disorder. The labeling scheme thus naturally models discontinuously mentioned disorders which is one challenging aspect of the disorder mention extraction task.

The sequence labeling model is trained using Condition Random Fields (CRFs) (Lafferty et al., 2001) using the five group of features shown in Table 1. The clinical reports are first pre-processed using Stanford CoreNLP[1] for tokenization, sentence segmentation and part-of-speech (POS) tagging which help in obtaining the lexical features (Group 1). The semantic features (Group 2) are obtained by matching the tokens, along with bigrams and trigrams in UMLS. For the first three features in Group 2, only the eleven semantic types under the "disorder" semantic group are considered.[2] If a token is a concept in UMLS with "disorder" semantic group then its feature is assigned the value of its semantic type (for example "congenital abnormality", "Neoplastic process", etc.) otherwise it is assigned the value "Null". The next three features in Group 2 take Boolean values depending upon whether the bigram or trigram is present in UMLS as a concept or not. The last feature in Group 2 takes CUI as its value if the word is a concept in UMLS otherwise it takes "Null" as the value.

The features in Group 3 are obtained by running MetaMap (Aronson, 2001). The lemmatized version of word obtained using Stanford CoreNLP is used as an additional feature in Group 4. Finally, if the word is an abbreviation according to a list of clinical abbreviations[3] then its full-form is obtained.[4] The full-form, whether it is in UMLS, and its semantic type (out of "disorder group") are used as features under Group 5. We used the CRFsuite (Okazaki, 2007) implementation of CRFs.

Group 1: Lexical
Word
Next word
Previous word
POS tag of word
POS tag of next word
POS tag of previous word
Next to next word
Previous to previous word
Length of the word
Group 2: Semantic
UMLS semantic type of word
UMLS semantic type of next word
UMLS semantic type of previous word
Bigram with next word is in UMLS
Reverse bigram with next word is in UMLS
Trigram with next two words is in UMLS
CUI of the word
Group 3: MetaMap
Word tagged as disorder by MetaMap
Next word tagged as disorder by MetaMap
Previous word tagged as disorder by MetaMap
Group 4: Lemmatization
Lemmatized version of the word
Group 5: Abbreviation
Full-form
Full-form is in UMLS
UMLS semantic type of full-form

Table 1: Features used to train the CRF model for disorder mention extraction.

2.2 Task B: Disorder Mention Normalization

The extracted disease mentions from Task A are normalized in Task B as follows. As a first step, our system tries to exactly match the disease mentions in the training data. If they match, then the corresponding CUI or CUI-less is the output. If no match is found in the training data, then the system tries to exactly match names of concepts in UMLS including their listed synonyms.[5] If a match is found then the corresponding CUI is the output. If the mention does not match either in the training data or in the UMLS and if it is an abbreviation according to the abbreviation list (same as used in Task A), then its full-form is used to exactly match in the training data and in UMLS. However, what makes the normalization task challenging is that exact matching frequently fails. We employed a novel method that learns to do approximate matching for this task.

We found that most failures in exact matching were because of minor typographical variations due to morphology, alternate spellings or typos. In order to automatically learn such variations, we developed a new method based on edit distance which is a measure of typographical similarity between two terms. We used a particular type of well-known edit distance called Levenshtein dis-

[1] http://nlp.stanford.edu/software/corenlp.shtml

[2] We found that using all semantic groups negatively affected the performance.

[3] http://en.wikipedia.org/wiki/List_of_medical_abbreviations

[4] If multiple full-forms were present then only the first one was used. In the future, one could improve this through abbreviation disambiguation (Xu et al., 2012).

[5] In accordance to the task definition, only the concepts listed in SNOMED CT and of the UMLS semantic group "disorder" are considered in this step.

Learned Edit Distance Pattern	**Comments**
SAME o INSERT u SAME r	Change American spelling to British
INSERT s SAME space	Pluralize by adding "s" before space
DELETE i DELETE e SUBSTITUTE s/y	Example: "Z-plasties" → "Z-plasty"
START SAME h INSERT a SAME e SAME m SAME o	Variation: "hemo..." → "haemo..."
DELETE space DELETE n DELETE o DELETE s END	Drop " nos" in the end
SAME s SUBSTITUTE i/e SAME s	Example: "metastasis" → "metastases"

Table 2: A few illustrative edit distance patterns that were automatically learned from UMLS and the training data.

Data used for training	Task A						Task B	
	Strict			Relaxed			Strict	Relaxed
	P	R	F	P	R	F	Accuracy	Accuracy
Training + Development	0.787	0.726	0.755	0.911	0.856	0.883	0.660	0.909
Training	0.775	0.679	0.724	0.909	0.812	0.858	0.617	0.908

Table 3: SemEval 2014 Task 7 evaluation results for our system. Precision (P), recall (R) and F-measure (F) were measured for Task A while accuracy was measured for Task B.

tance (Levenshtein, 1966) which is defined as the minimum number of edits needed to convert one term into another. The edits are in the form of insertions, deletions and substitution of characters. For example, the term "cyanotic" can be converted into "cyanosis" in minimum two steps by substituting "t" for "s" and "c" for "s", hence the Levenshtein edit distance between these terms is two. There is a fast dynamic programming based algorithm to compute this. The algorithm also gives the steps to change one term into another, which for the above example will be "START SAME c SAME y SAME a SAME n SAME o SUBSTITUTE t/s SAME i SUBSTITUTE c/s END". We will call such a sequence of steps as an *edit distance pattern*.

Our method first computes edit distance patterns between all synonyms of the disorder concepts is UMLS[6] as well as between their mentions in the training data and the corresponding tagged concepts in UMLS. But these patterns are very specific to the terms they are derived from and will not directly apply to other terms. Hence these patterns are generalized next. We define generalization of two edit distance patterns as their largest contiguous common part that includes all the edit operations of insertions, deletions and substitutions (i.e. generalization can only remove "SAME", "START" and "END" steps). For example, the generalized edit distance pattern of "cyanotic → cyanosis" and "thrombotic → thrombosis" will be "SAME o SUBSTITUTE t/s SAME i SUBSTITUTE c/s END", essentially meaning that a term that ends with "otic" can be changed to end with "osis". Our method generalizes every pair of edit distance patterns as well as repeatedly further generalizes every pair of generalization patterns.

Not all generalization patterns may be good because some may change the meaning of terms when applied. Hence our method also evaluates the goodness of these patterns by counting the number of *positives* and *negatives*. When a pattern is applied to a UMLS term and the resultant term has the same CUI then it is counted as a positive. But if the resultant term has a different CUI then it is counted as a negative. Our system heuristically only retains patterns that have the number of positives more than the number of negatives and have at least five positives. Our method learned total 554 edit distance patterns, Table 2 shows a few illustrative ones.

These patterns are used as follows to normalize disease mentions. When exact matching for a disease mention in the training data and the UMLS fails, then our system generates its variations by applying the learned edit distance patterns. These variations are then searched for exact matching in the UMLS. If even the variations fail to match then the variations of possible full-forms (according to the abbreviation list) are tried, otherwise the mention is declared CUI-less. Note that while our method learns variations only for disorder mentions, it is general and could be used to learn variations for terms of other types. Finally, because it is a learning method and it also learns variations used in the training data, it is capable of learning variations that are specific to the style or genre of the clinical notes that constitute the training data. We note that the problem of matching variations is analogous to the duplicate detection problem

[6]Due to the large size of UMLS, we restricted to the second of the two concept files in the 2013 UMLS distribution.

in database records (Bilenko and Mooney, 2003). But to the our best knowledge, no one has used an approach to learn patterns of variations based on edit distances. We used the edit-distance patterns only for Task B in this work, in future we plan to also use them in Task A for the features that involve matching with UMLS.

3 Results

The organizers of the SemEval 2014 Task 7 provided the training, the development and the test data containing 199, 99 and 133 clinical notes respectively that included de-identified discharge summaries, electrocardiogram, echocardiogram and radiology reports (Pradhan et al., 2013). The extraction performance in Task A was evaluated in terms of precision, recall and F-measure for strict (exact boundaries) and relaxed (overlapping boundaries) settings. The normalization performance in Task B was evaluated in terms of strict accuracy (fraction of correct normalizations out of all gold-standard disease mentions) and relaxed accuracy (fraction of correct normalizations out of the correct disease mentions extracted in Task A). Note that a system's strict accuracy in Task B depends on its performance in Task A because if it misses to extract a disease mention in Task A then it will get zero score for its normalization.

Table 3 shows the performance of our system as determined through the official evaluation by the organizers. The systems were evaluated on the test data when trained using both the training and the development data as well as when trained using just the training data. When trained using both the training and the development data, our team ranked third in Task A and second in Task B considering the best run of each team if they submitted multiple runs. The ranking was according to the strict F-measure for Task A and according to the strict accuracy for Task B. When trained using just the training data, our team ranked second in Task A and first in Task B.

We also performed ablation study to determine the contribution of different components of our system towards its performance. Since the gold-standard annotations for the test data were not made available to the participants, we used the development data for testing for the ablation study. Table 4 shows the results (strict) for Task A when various groups of features (shown in Table 1) are excluded one at a time. It can be noted that lexical group of features were most important without which the performance drops significantly. MetaMap matches were the next most important group of features. Each of the remaining feature groups improves the performance by only small amount.

Features	P	R	F
All	0.829	0.673	0.743
All - Lexical	0.779	0.569	0.658
All - Semantic	0.824	0.669	0.738
All - MetaMap	0.810	0.648	0.720
All - Lemmatization	0.825	0.666	0.737
All - Abbreviations	0.828	0.668	0.740

Table 4: Ablation study results for Task A showing how the performance is affected by excluding various feature groups (shown in Table 1). Development data was used for testing. Only strict precision (P), recall (R) and F-measure (F) are shown.

Component	Accuracy
Training	78.1
UMLS	83.8
Training + UMLS	88.8
Training + Patterns	86.3
UMLS + Patterns	85.2
Training + UMLS + Patterns	89.5

Table 5: Performance on Task B obtained by combinations of exactly matching the mentions in the training data, exactly matching in the UMLS and using learned edit distance patterns for approximately matching in the UMLS. Development data was used for testing with gold-standard disease mentions.

Table 5 shows the performance on Task B when disease mentions are exactly matched in the training data, exactly matched in the UMLS and approximately matched in the UMLS using edit distance patterns, as well as their combinations. In order to evaluate the performance of our system on Task B independent of its performance on Task A, we used gold-standard disease mentions in the development data as input for Task B in which case the strict and relaxed accuracies are equal. It may be noted that adding edit distance patterns improves the performance in each case.

4 Conclusions

We participated in the SemEval 2014 Task 7 of disorder mention extraction and normalization from clinical text. Our system used conditional random fields as the learning method for the extraction task with various lexical, semantic and MetaMap based features. We introduced a new method to do approximate matching for normalization that learns general patterns of variations using edit distances. Our system performed competitively on both the tasks.

References

Alan R Aronson. 2001. Effective mapping of biomedical text to the UMLS Metathesaurus: the MetaMap program. In *Proceedings of the AMIA Symposium*, page 17. American Medical Informatics Association.

Mikhail Bilenko and Raymond J Mooney. 2003. Adaptive duplicate detection using learnable string similarity measures. In *Proceedings of the ninth ACM SIGKDD international conference on Knowledge discovery and data mining*, pages 39–48. ACM.

John Lafferty, Andrew McCallum, and Fernando Pereira. 2001. Conditional Random Fields: Probabilistic models for segmenting and labeling sequence data. In *Proceedings of 18th International Conference on Machine Learning (ICML-2001)*, pages 282–289, Williamstown, MA.

Vladimir I Levenshtein. 1966. Binary codes capable of correcting deletions, insertions and reversals. In *Soviet physics doklady*, volume 10, page 707.

Naoaki Okazaki. 2007. CRFsuite: A fast implementation of Conditional Random Fields (CRFs), http://www.chokkan.org/software/crfsuite/.

Sameer Pradhan, Noemie Elhadad, B South, David Martinez, Lee Christensen, Amy Vogel, Hanna Suominen, W Chapman, and Guergana Savova. 2013. Task 1: ShARe/CLEF eHealth Evaluation Lab 2013. *Online Working Notes of CLEF, CLEF*, 230.

Hua Xu, Peter D Stetson, and Carol Friedman. 2012. Combining corpus-derived sense profiles with estimated frequency information to disambiguate clinical abbreviations. In *AMIA Annual Symposium Proceedings*, volume 2012, page 1004. American Medical Informatics Association.

V3: Unsupervised Generation of Domain Aspect Terms for Aspect Based Sentiment Analysis

Aitor García-Pablos,
Montse Cuadros, Seán Gaines
Vicomtech-IK4 research centre
Mikeletegi 57, San Sebastian, Spain
{agarciap,mcuadros}@vicomtech.org

German Rigau
IXA Group
Euskal Herriko Unibertsitatea,
San Sebastian, Spain
german.rigau@ehu.es

Abstract

This paper presents V3, an unsupervised system for aspect-based Sentiment Analysis when evaluated on the SemEval 2014 Task 4. V3 focuses on generating a list of aspect terms for a new domain using a collection of raw texts from the domain. We also implement a very basic approach to classify the aspect terms into categories and assign polarities to them.

1 Introduction

The automatic analysis of opinions, within the framework of opinion mining or sentiment analysis, has gained a huge importance during the last decade due to the amount of review web sites, blogs and social networks producing everyday a massive amount of new content (Pang and Lee, 2008; Liu, 2012; Zhang and Liu, 2014). This content usually contains opinions about different entities, products or services. Trying to cope with this large amounts of textual data is unfeasible without the help of automatic Opinion Mining tools which try to detect, identify, classify, aggregate and summarize the opinions expressed about different topics (Hu and Liu, 2004) (Popescu and Etzioni, 2005) (Wu et al., 2009) (Zhang et al., 2010). In this framework, aspect based opinion mining systems aim to detect the sentiment at "aspect" level (i.e. the precise feature being opinionated in a clause or sentence).

In this paper we describe our system presented in the SemEval 2014 task 4[1] *Aspect Based Sentiment Analysis* (Pontiki et al., 2014), which focuses on detecting opinionated aspect terms (e.g. *wine list* and *menu* in restaurant domain, and *hard disk* and *battery life* in laptop domain), their categories and polarities in customer review sentences.

The task provides two training datasets, one of restaurant reviews and other of laptop reviews. The restaurant review dataset consists of over 3,000 English sentences from restaurant reviews borrowed from (Ganu et al., 2009). The laptop review dataset consists of over 3,000 English sentences extracted from customer reviews. The task is divided in four different subtasks: subtask 1 aspect term extraction, subtask 2 aspect term polarity detection, subtask 3 aspect category detection, subtask 4 aspect category polarity detection. Our system mainly focused on subtask 1, but we have also participated in the other subtasks.

The paper is organized as follows: section 2 presents our approach, section 3 details the improvement methods used for the aspects term selection and section 4 focus on category and polarity tagging. Finally section 5 presents the results obtained and section 6 draws the conclusions and future work.

2 Our approach

We have adapted the double-propagation technique described in (Qiu et al., 2009; Qiu et al., 2011). This method consists of using a minimal seed list of aspect terms and opinion words and propagate them through an unlabelled domain-related corpus using a set of propagation rules. The goal is to obtain an extended aspect term and opinion word lists. (Qiu et al., 2009) define opinion words as words that convey some positive or negative sentiment polarities. They only extract nouns as aspect terms and adjectives as opinion words, and we assume the same restriction.

The propagation rules have the form of dependency relations and some part-of-speech restrictions. Some rules extract new aspect terms, and others extract new opinion words. Table 1 shows

[1] http://alt.qcri.org/semeval2014/task4/

Proceedings of the 8th International Workshop on Semantic Evaluation (SemEval 2014), pages 833–837,
Dublin, Ireland, August 23-24, 2014.

the rules used in our approach, similar to those detailed in (Qiu et al., 2011) with some modifications. In this table, T stands for *aspect term* (i.e. a word already in the aspect terms set) and O for *opinion word* (i.e. a word already in the opinion words set). W means *any word*. The dependency types used are *amod*, *dobj*, *subj* and *conj*, which stand for *adjectival modifier*, *direct object*, *subject* and *conjunction* respectively. Additional restrictions on the Part-Of-Speech (POS) of the words present in the rule are shown in the third column of the table. The last column indicates to which set (aspect terms or opinion words) the new word is added.

To obtain the dependency trees and word lemmas and POS tags, we use the Stanford NLP tools[2] (De Marneffe et al., 2006). Our initial seed words are just the adjectives *good* and *bad*, which are added to the initial opinion words set. The initial aspect terms set starts empty. Each sentence in the dataset is analysed to obtain its dependency tree and the rules are checked sequentially. If rule is triggered, then the word indicated by that rule is added to the corresponding set (aspect terms or opinion words, depending on the rule). These new words can be then used to trigger the propagation rules later. After the last sentence the process starts from the beginning to check the rules with the newly added words. The process stops when no more words have been added during a full dataset iteration.

3 Selecting aspect term candidates

The double-propagation process populates both sets of domain aspect terms and domain opinion words, but we focus our attention in the aspect terms set. Due to the nature of the process it tends to generate hundreds of different potential aspect terms, many of them being incorrect. We apply some additional processes to improve the list.

3.1 Ranking the aspect terms

One way to reduce the undesired terms is to rank them, pushing the incorrect aspect terms to the bottom of the list and using only a certain subset of top ranked terms. In order to rank this list we have modelled the double-propagation process as a undirected graph population process. Each new aspect term or opinion word discovered by applying a propagation rule is added as a vertex to the graph. The rule used to extract the new word is added as an edge to the graph, connecting the original word and the newly discovered word.

We have applied the well-known PageRank algorithm (Brin and Page, 1998) to score the vertices of the graph. To calculate the PageRank scores we have used the JUNG framework[3] (OMadadhain et al., 2005), a set of Java libraries to work with graphs. The value of the alpha parameter that represents the probability of a random jump to any node of the graph has been left at 0.15 (in the literature it is recommended an alpha value between 0.1 and 0.2). The aspect terms are then ordered using their associated score, being the most relevant aspect term, the one with the highest score. Then the list can be trimmed to a certain amount of top ranked terms, trying to balance the precision and recall of the resulting list.

3.2 Filtering undesired words

The double-propagation method always introduces many undesired words. Some of these undesired words appear very frequently and are combined with a large number of words. So, they tend to also appear in high positions in the ranking. Many of these words are easy to identify, and they are not likely to be useful aspect terms in any domain. Examples of these words are: *nothing*, *everything*, *thing*, *anyone*, *someone*, *somebody*, etc. In this work we use a domain agnostic stop word list to deal with this kind of words. The authors of the original double-propagation approach use some clause and frequency based heuristics that we do not employ here.

3.3 Detecting multiword terms

Many aspect terms are not just single words, but compounds and multiword terms (e.g. *wine list*, *hard disk drive*, *battery life*, etc.). In the original double-propagation paper, the authors consider adjacent nouns to a given aspect term as multiword terms and perform an *a posteriori* pruning based on the frequency of the combination. We have tried to add multiword terms without increasing the amount of noise in the resulting list. One of the approaches included in the system exploits WordNet [4] (Fellbaum, 1999), and the following simple rules:

[2]http://nlp.stanford.edu/software/lex-parser.shtml

[3]http://jung.sourceforge.net

[4]http://wordnet.princeton.edu/

Rule	Observations	Constraints	Action
R11	O → amod→W	W is a noun	W→T
R12	O→dobj→W1 ←subj←W2	W2 is a noun	W2→T
R21	T ← amod ← W	W is an adjective	W→O
R22	T → subj → W1 ← dobj ← W2	W2 is an adjective	W2→ O
R31	T → conj → W	W is a noun	W → T
R32	T → subj → W1 ← dobj ← W2	W2 is a noun	W → T
R41	O → conj → W	W is an adjective	W→ O
R42	O → Dep1 → W1 ← Dep2 ← W2	Dep1==Dep2, W2 is an adjective	W2→ O

Table 1: Propagation rules.

- If word N and word N+1 are nouns, and the combination is an entry in WordNet (or in Wikipedia, see below). E.g.: *battery life*
- If word N is an adjective and word N+1 is a noun, and the combination is an entry in WordNet. E.g.: *hot dog*, *happy hour*
- If word N is an adjective, word N+1 is a noun, and word n is a relational adjective in WordNet (lexical file 01). E.g.: *Thai food*

In order to improve the coverage of the WordNet approach, we also check if a combination of two consecutive nouns appears as a Wikipedia article title. Wikipedia articles refer to real word concepts and entities, so if a combination of words is a title of a Wikipedia article it is very likely that this word combination is also meaningful (e.g. *DVD player*, *USB port*, *goat cheese*, *pepperoni pizza*). We limit the lookup in Wikipedia titles just to combination of nouns to avoid the inclusion of incorrect aspect terms.

4 Assigning categories and polarities

Despite we have focused our attention on acquiring aspect terms from a domain, we have also participated in the rest of subtasks: grouping aspect terms into a fixed set of categories, and assigning polarities to both aspect terms and categories.

To group the aspect terms into categories, we have employed WordNet similarities. The idea is to compare the detected aspect terms against a term or group of terms representative of the target categories. In this case the categories (only for restaurants) were *food*, *service*, *price*, *ambience* and *anecdotes/miscellaneous*.

Initially, the representative word for each category (except for the *anecdotes/miscellaneous*) was the name of the category itself. We use the similarity measure described by (Wu and Palmer, 1994). Detected aspect terms are compared to the set of representative words on each category, and they are assigned to the category with a higher similarity result. For example using this approach, the similarity between *food* and *cheese* is 0.8, while similarity between *service* and *cheese* is 0.25, and between *price* and *cheese* is 0.266. Thus, in this case *cheese* is assigned to the category *food*.

If the similarity does not surpass a given minimum threshold (manually set to 0.7), the current aspect term is not assigned to the category to avoid assigning a wrong category just because the other were even less similar. After classifying the aspect terms of a given sentence into categories, we assign those categories to the sentence. If no category has been assigned, then we use the *anecdotes/miscellaneous* category as the default one.

This approach is quite naive and it has many limitations. It works quite well for the category *food*, classifying ingredients and meals, but it fails when the category or the aspect terms are more vague or abstract. In addition, we do not perform any kind of word sense disambiguation or sense pruning, which probably would discard unrelated senses.

For detecting the polarity we have used the SentiWords (Guerini et al., 2013; Warriner et al., 2013) as a polarity lexicon. Using direct dependency relations between aspect terms and polarity bearing words we assign the polarity value from the lexicon to the aspect term. We make a simple count of the polarities of the aspect terms classified under a certain category to assign the polarity of that category in a particular sentence.

5 Evaluation

The run submitted to the SemEval task 4 competition was based on 25k unlabelled sentences extracted from domain related reviews (for restaurants and laptops) obtained by scraping different websites. We used these unlabelled sentences to execute our unsupervised system to generate and

Restaur. aspect terms	Precision	Recall	F-score
SemEval Baseline	0.525	0.427	0.471
V3 (S)	**0.656**	0.562	0.605
V3 (W)	0.571	0.641	0.604
V3 (W+S)	0.575	**0.645**	**0.608**

Table 2: Results on the restaurant review test set.

Laptops aspect terms	Precision	Recall	F-score
SemEval Baseline	**0.443**	0.298	0.356
V3 (S)	0.265	0.276	0.271
V3 (W)	0.321	0.425	**0.366**
V3 (W+S)	0.279	**0.444**	0.343

Table 3: Results on the laptop review test set.

rank the aspect term lists. Then we used those aspect term lists to annotate the sentences using a simple lemma matching approach between the words. The generated aspect term lists were limited to the first ranked 550 items after some initial experiments with the SemEval training sets.

The SemEval test datasets (restaurants and laptops) contain about 800 sentences each. The restaurant dataset contains 1,134 labelled gold aspect term spans, and the laptop dataset contains 634 labelled gold aspect term spans. We compare the results against the SemEval baseline which is calculated using the scripts provided by the SemEval organizers. This baseline splits the dataset into *train* and *test* subsets, and uses all the labelled aspect terms in the *train* subset to build a dictionary of aspect terms. Then it simply uses that dictionary to label the test subset for evaluation.

Tables 2 and 3 show the performance of our system with respect to the baselines in both datasets. "V3 (S)" stands for our system only using the SemEval test data (as our approach is unsupervised it learns from the available texts for the task). (W) refers to the results using our own dataset scraped from the Web. Finally (W+S) refers to the results using both SemEval and our Web dataset mixed together. The best results are highlighted in bold. For subtask 1, although our system outperforms the baseline in terms of F-score in both datasets, in the competition our system obtained quite modest results ranking 24th and 26th out of 29 participants for restaurants and laptops respectively.

Restaur. categories	Precision	Recall	F-score
SemEval Baseline	**0.671**	**0.602**	**0.638**
V3	0.638	0.569	0.602

Table 4: Results on restaurant category detection using the test set.

Polarity detection accuracy	Baseline	V3
Restaur. aspect terms	**0.642**	0.597
Restaur. categories	**0.656**	0.472
Laptop aspect terms	0.510	**0.538**

Table 5: Results for the polarity classification subtasks (subtasks 2 and 4).

One of the most important source of errors are the multiword aspect term detection. In the SemEval datasets, about the 25% of the gold aspect terms are multiword terms. In both datasets we find a large number of names of recipes and meals, composed by two, three or even more words, which cannot appear in our aspect term lists because we limit the multiword length up to two words.

As mentioned in the introduction our approach focuses mainly in the aspects so the approach for detecting categories and polarities needs more attention. Table 4 presents our results on category detection and table 5 our results on polarities. The results are quite poor so we do not comment on them here. We will address these subtasks in future work.

6 Conclusions and future work

In this paper we propose a simple and unsupervised system able to bootstrap and rank a list of domain aspect terms from a set of unlabelled domain texts. We use a double-propagation approach, and we model the obtained terms and their relations as a graph. Then, we apply the PageRank algorithm to score the obtained terms. Despite the modest results, our unsupervised system for detecting aspect terms performs better than the supervised baseline. In our future work we will try to improve the way we deal with multiword terms to reduce the amount of incorrect aspect terms and generate a better ranking. We also plan to try different methods for the category grouping, and explore knowledge-based word sense disambiguation methods for improving the current system.

Acknowledgements

This work has been partially funded by SKaTer (TIN2012-38584-C06-02) and OpeNER (FP7-ICT-2011-SME- DCL-296451).

References

Sergey Brin and Lawrence Page. 1998. The anatomy of a large-scale hypertextual web search engine. *Computer networks and ISDN systems*, 30(1):107–117.

Marie-Catherine De Marneffe, Bill MacCartney, Christopher D Manning, et al. 2006. Generating typed dependency parses from phrase structure parses. In *Proceedings of LREC*, volume 6, pages 449–454.

Christiane Fellbaum. 1999. *WordNet*. Wiley Online Library.

Gayatree Ganu, N Elhadad, and A Marian. 2009. Beyond the Stars: Improving Rating Predictions using Review Text Content. *WebDB*, (WebDB):1–6.

Marco Guerini, Lorenzo Gatti, and Marco Turchi. 2013. Sentiment analysis: How to derive prior polarities from sentiwordnet. *arXiv preprint arXiv:1309.5843*.

Minqing Hu and Bing Liu. 2004. Mining opinion features in customer reviews. *AAAI*.

Bing Liu. 2012. Sentiment analysis and opinion mining. *Synthesis Lectures on Human Language Technologies*, 5(1):1–167.

Joshua OMadadhain, Danyel Fisher, Padhraic Smyth, Scott White, and Yan-Biao Boey. 2005. Analysis and visualization of network data using jung. *Journal of Statistical Software*, 10(2):1–35.

Bo Pang and Lillian Lee. 2008. Opinion mining and sentiment analysis. *Foundations and trends in information retrieval*, 2(1-2):1–135.

Maria Pontiki, Dimitrios Galanis, John Pavlopoulos, Harris Papageorgiou, Ion Androutsopoulos, and Suresh Manandhar. 2014. Semeval-2014 task 4: Aspect based sentiment analysis. *Proceedings of the International Workshop on Semantic Evaluation (SemEval)*.

AM Popescu and Oren Etzioni. 2005. Extracting product features and opinions from reviews. *Natural language processing and text mining*, (October):339–346.

Guang Qiu, Bing Liu, Jiajun Bu, and Chun Chen. 2009. Expanding Domain Sentiment Lexicon through Double Propagation. *IJCAI*.

Guang Qiu, Bing Liu, Jiajun Bu, and Chun Chen. 2011. Opinion word expansion and target extraction through double propagation. *Computational linguistics*, (July 2010).

Amy Beth Warriner, Victor Kuperman, and Marc Brysbaert. 2013. Norms of valence, arousal, and dominance for 13,915 english lemmas. *Behavior research methods*, 45(4):1191–1207.

Zhibiao Wu and Martha Palmer. 1994. Verbs semantics and lexical selection. In *Proceedings of the 32nd annual meeting on Association for Computational Linguistics*, pages 133–138. Association for Computational Linguistics.

Yuanbin Wu, Qi Zhang, Xuanjing Huang, and Lide Wu. 2009. Phrase dependency parsing for opinion mining. In *Proceedings of the 2009 Conference on Empirical Methods in Natural Language Processing: Volume 3-Volume 3*, pages 1533–1541. Association for Computational Linguistics.

Lei Zhang and Bing Liu. 2014. Aspect and Entity Extraction for Opinion Mining. *Data Mining and Knowledge Discovery for Big Data*.

L Zhang, Bing Liu, SH Lim, and E O'Brien-Strain. 2010. Extracting and ranking product features in opinion documents. *Proceedings of the 23rd International Conference on Computational Linguistics*, (August):1462–1470.

XRCE: Hybrid Classification for Aspect-based Sentiment Analysis

Caroline Brun, Diana Nicoleta Popa, Claude Roux
Xerox Research Centre Europe
6, chemin de Maupertuis
38240 Meylan, France
{caroline.brun, diana.popa, claude.roux}@xrce.xerox.com

Abstract

In this paper, we present the system we have developed for the SemEval-2014 Task 4 dedicated to Aspect-Based Sentiment Analysis. The system is based on a robust parser that provides information to feed different classifiers with linguistic features dedicated to aspect categories and aspect categories polarity classification. We mainly present the work which has been done on the restaurant domain[1] for the four subtasks, aspect term and category detection and aspect term and category polarity.

1 Introduction

Aspect Based Sentiment Analysis aims at discovering the opinions or sentiments expressed by a user on the different aspects of a given entity ((Hu and Liu, 2004); (Liu, 2012)). A wide range of methods and techniques have been proposed to address this task, among which systems that use syntactic dependencies to link source and target of the opinion, such as in (Kim and Hovy, 2004), (Bloom et al., 2007), or (Wu et al., 2009). We have developed a system that belongs to this family, (Brun, 2011), as we believe that syntactic processing of complex phenomena (negation, comparison, ...) is a crucial step to perform aspect-based opinion mining. In this paper, we describe the adaptations we have made to this system for SemEval, and the way it is applied to category and polarity classification.

[1]We have not performed any domain adapation for the laptop corpus and only submitted a run for the subtask 1, term detection.

2 Description of the System

In this section, we describe the different components of the system.

2.1 Existing System

In order to tackle the Semeval'14 Task 4, (Pontiki et al., 2014), we used our existing aspect-based opinion detection system. The opinion detection system we built relies on a robust deep syntactic parser, (Ait-Mokhtar et al., 2001), as a fundamental component, from which semantic relations of opinion are calculated. Parsing here includes tokenization, morpho-syntactic analysis, tagging which is performed via a combination of hand-written rules and HMM, Named Entity Detection, chunking and finally, extraction of dependency relations between lexical nodes. These relations are labeled with deep syntactic functions. More precisely, a predicate (verbal or nominal) is linked with what we call its deep subject (SUBJ-N), its deep object (OBJ-N), and modifiers. In addition, the parser calculates more sophisticated and complex relations using derivational morphologic properties, deep syntactic properties (subject and object of infinitives in the context of control verbs), and some limited lexical semantic coding.

Syntactic relations already extracted by a general dependency grammar, lexical information about word polarities, sub categorization information and syntactic dependencies are all combined within our robust parser to extract the semantic relations. The polarity lexicon has been built using existing resources and also by applying classification techniques over large corpora, while the semantic extraction rules are handcrafted, see (Brun, 2011) and (Brun, 2012) for the complete description of these different components. The system outputs a semantic dependency called SENTIMENT which can be binary, i.e. linking opinionated terms and their targets, or unary, i.e. just the polar term in case the target of the

Proceedings of the 8th International Workshop on Semantic Evaluation (SemEval 2014), pages 838–842,
Dublin, Ireland, August 23-24, 2014.

opinion hasn't been detected. For example, when parsing *I was highly disappointed by their service and food.*, the systems outputs the following dependencies:

SUBJ_N(disappointed,food)
SUBJ_N(disappointed,service)
OBJ_N(disappointed,I)
MANNER_PRE(disappointed,highly)
SENTIMENT_NEGATIVE(disappointed,service)
SENTIMENT_NEGATIVE(disappointed,food)

In this system, aspects terms are not explicitly extracted, however all non-polar arguments of the SENTIMENT dependency are potential aspect terms. Moreover, this system considers only positive and negative opinions, but does not cover the neutral and conflict polarities.

2.2 System Adaptation

The opinion detection system described in the previous section has been adapted for the SemEval2014 Task4, in two ways: some lexical acquisition has been performed in order to detect the terms of the domain, and some rules have been developed to detect multi-word terms and to output semantic dependencies associating their polarity to terms and categories.

2.2.1 Lexical Enrichment and Term Detection

As said before, the existing system encodes a reasonable amount of polar vocabulary. However, as the task implies domain knowledge to detect the terms, we have first extracted the terms from the training corpus and encoded their words into our lexicons, assigning to them the semantic features food, service, ambiance and price. We have then extended the list with Wordnet synonyms. To improve coverage, we have also extracted and filtered food term lists from Wikipedia pages and encoded them. More precisely, the list of food terms has been extracted from the Wikipedia "Food Portal", from the category "Lists_of_foods"[2]. At the end of this process, our lexicon has the following coverage: Polar words: 1265 negative, 1082 positive and Domain words: 761 food words, 31 price words, 105 ambiance words, 42 service words.

In order to detect the terms, some local grammar rules (based on regular expressions) have been developed taking into account the lexical semantic information encoded in the previous step. These rules detect the multi-words terms, e.g. *pastrami sandwiches*, group them under the appropriate syntactic category (noun, verb) and associate them with the corresponding lexical semantic feature, *food*, *service*, *ambiance*, *price*. In addition to this, in order to prepare the aspect category classification (c.f. section 2.3.3), a layer of semantic dependencies has been added to the grammar: If a domain term is detected in a sentence, a unary dependency corresponding to its category (FOOD, SERVICE, PRICE, AMBIANCE) is built.

2.2.2 Grammar Adaptation for Polarity Detection

The English grammar, which had been previously developed to detect sentiments, has also been adapted in order to extract the opinions associated to the terms and categories detected at the previous step.

If an aspect term is the second argument of a SENTIMENT relation, 2 dependencies, one for the term (OPINION_ON_TERM) and one for the corresponding category (OPINION_ON_CATEGORY) are built. They inherit the polarity (positive or negative) of the SENTIMENT dependency. If these dependencies target the same term and category and if they have opposite polarity, they are modified in order to bear the feature "conflict".

Then, if a sentence contains a term and if no SENTIMENT dependency has been detected, the OPINION_ON_TERM and OPINION_ON_CATEGORY are created with the polarity "neutral". Finally, if no terms have been detected in a sentence, there are two cases: (1) a SENTIMENT dependency has been detected somewhere in the sentence, the dependency OPINION_ON_CATEGORY(anecdote/misc), is created with the corresponding polarity (positive or negative); (2) no SENTIMENT dependency has been detected, the dependency OPINION_ON_CATEGORY(anecdote/misc), is created with polarity "neutral".

The dependency OPINION_ON_TERM links the terms to their polarities in the sentences and serves as input for the subtasks 1 and 3.

2.3 Classification

2.3.1 KiF (*Knowledge in Frame*)

The whole system, training and prediction, has been implemented in KiF (*Knowledge in Frame*), a script language that has been implemented into

[2]http://en.wikipedia.org/wiki/Category:Lists_of_foods

the very fabric of the rule-based Xerox Incremental Parser (XIP). KiF offers a very simple way to hybridize a rule-based parser with machine learning technique. For instance, a KiF function, which evaluates a set a features to predict a class, can be called from a rule, which could then be fired along the output of that function. KiF is a multi-threaded programming language, which is available for all platforms (Windows, Mac OS, Linux). It provides all the necessary objects (strings, containers or classes) and many encapsulations of dynamic libraries from different C programs such as classifiers (liblinear and libsvm), database (SQLite), or XML (libxml2), which can be loaded on the fly. All internal XIP linguistic structures are wrapped up into KiF objects. For example, linguistic features are available as maps, which can be modified and re-injected into their own syntactic nodes. The language syntax is a mix between Java (types are static) and Python (in the way containers are handled), but provides many implicit conversions to avoid code overloading with too many functions. KiF allows for an efficient integration of all aspects of linguistic analysis into a very simple framework, where XML documents can be analyzed and modified both with linguistic parsing and classifiers into a few hundred lines of code.

2.3.2 General Methodology

We focus on four main tasks: detecting the aspect terms and aspect categories and their corresponding polarities. While the detection of aspect terms and their corresponding polarities occurs at the grammar level, for the detection of aspect categories and their corresponding polarities we make use of the liblinear library (Fan et al., 2008) to train our models. We train one classifier for detecting the categories and further, for each category we train a separate classifier for detecting the polarities corresponding to that particular category. For both settings, we use 10-fold cross-validation. The two modules for aspect category classification and aspect category polarity classification are described in details further.

2.3.3 Aspect Category Classification

The sentence classification module is used to assign aspect categories to sentences. For each sentence, the module takes as input features the bag of words in the sentence as well as the information provided by the syntactic parser. The output consists of a list of categories corresponding to each sentence.

In the pre-processing stage stop words are removed (determinants, conjunctions). Further, we use the L2-regularized logistic regression solver from the liblinear library to train a model. The features considered are the word lemmas from the sentence along with their frequencies (term frequency). Apart from this, the information provided by the rule based component is also taken into account to increase the term frequency for terms belonging to the detected categories.

Such information can consist of: dependencies denoting the category to which a detected aspect term belongs (Food, Service, Price, Ambiance) and dependencies denoting the opinions on the detected aspect terms and categories (OPINION_ON_CATEGORY, OPINION_ON_TERM). For example for the following sentence: *"Fabulous service, fantastic food, and a chilled out atmosphere and environment"*, the salient dependencies produced by the syntactic parser are:

FOOD(food), AMBIANCE(atmosphere),
SERVICE(service), AMBIANCE(environment),
OPINION_ON_CATEGORY_POSITIVE(food),
OPINION_ON_CATEGORY_POSITIVE(service),
OPINION_ON_CATEGORY_POSITIVE(ambiance),
OPINION_ON_TERM_POSITIVE(food),
OPINION_ON_TERM_POSITIVE(service),
OPINION_ON_TERM_POSITIVE(atmosphere).

This yields the following features having an increase in their frequencies: food (+3), service (+3), atmosphere (+2), environment (+1), ambiance (+1).

Once the logistic regression is performed, each category is predicted with a certain probability. Since in one sentence there may be entities that refer to different categories, we set a threshold with respect to the probability values to be taken into account. We have tried different approaches to set this threshold. The best results on the training and trial data were obtained with a threshold of 0.25, (i.e. we kept only the categories with a probability over 0.25).

2.3.4 Aspect Category Polarity Classification

The approach to predict the polarity for each category is similar to the one predicting the categories for each sentence, with some differences as will be further detailed. The classification uses for features, the bag of words (term frequency), but also the polarity provided by XIP by the following dependencies: OPINION_ON_CATEGORY and SENTIMENT. Whenever these dependencies are detected, a feature is added to the classification of the form *polarity_category*. Thus for the previous example sentence: *Fabulous service, fantastic food, and a chilled out atmosphere and environment*, the additional dependencies considered are SENTIMENT_POSITIVE(atmosphere, chilled out), SENTIMENT_POSITIVE(food, fantastic), SENTIMENT_POSITIVE(service, Fabulous). After mapping back the terms to their corresponding categories, the added features are: *positive_ambiance*, *positive_food* and *positive_service*. Since the dependency OPINION_ON_CATEGORY is also detected by the parser for these categories, each of the above mentioned features will have a frequency of 2 in this case. Moreover, the polarity alone is also added as a feature. The training is performed using the L2-regularized L2-loss support vector classification solver from the same library (liblinear) and a model is generated for each category. Thus, depending on the categories detected within a certain sentence, the corresponding model is used to make the prediction regarding their polarities. The classifier's output represents the predicted polarity for one given category.

3 Evaluation

The corpus used for evaluating the system contains 800 sentences, 1134 aspect term occurrences, 1025 aspect category occurrences, 5 different aspect categories and 555 distinct aspect terms. All these belong to the restaurant domain.

3.1 Terms and Category Detection

When evaluating aspect terms and aspect categories detection, three measures were taken into account: precision, recall and the f1-measure.

For both aspect term extraction and aspect category detection, the baseline methodologies are presented in (Pontiki et al., 2014). Table 1 shows the results obtained using our approach as compared to the baseline for aspect term detection, whereas Table 2 outlines the results regarding aspect category detection in terms of the previously mentioned measures.

Furthermore, it is interesting to notice the increase in performance obtained by combining the bag-of-words features with the output of the parser as opposed to just using the bag-of words. These differences are outlined for aspect category detection in Table 2, where BOW denotes the system using the same settings, but just the bag-of-words features and XRCE denotes the submitted system where the bag-of-words features are augmented with parser output features.

Method	Precision	Recall	F-Measure
Baseline	0.627329	0.376866	0.470862
XRCE	0.862453	0.818342	0.839818

Table 1: Aspect term detection.

Method	Precision	Recall	F-Measure
Baseline	0.637500	0.483412	0.549865
BOW	0.77337	0.799024	0.785988
XRCE	0.832335	0.813658	0.822890

Table 2: Aspect category detection.

For both tasks of aspect term and aspect category detection, our system clearly outperforms the baseline, resulting in being ranked among the first 3 in the competition for the restaurant corpus.

3.2 Terms and Category Polarity Detection

Similarly, Table 3 shows the results in terms of accuracy on aspect term polarity detection and on aspect category polarity detection. Here, baseline methodologies are similar to the ones used for aspect category detection and also described in (Pontiki et al., 2014). Again, our system ranks high in the competition, achieving an overall accuracy of 0.77 for aspect term polarity detection and 0.78 for aspect category polarity detection. Furthermore, a comparison is also made between the current system and one that, using the same settings, would not take into account the features provided by the parser (BOW). The results emphasize the importance of using the merged version.

Method	Task	Accuracy
Baseline	Term polarity	0.552239
XRCE	Term polarity	0.776895
Baseline	Category polarity	0.563981
BOW	Category polarity	0.681951
XRCE	Category polarity	0.781463

Table 3: Aspect term and aspect category polarity.

Label	Precision	Recall	F-measure
conflict	NaN	0	NaN
negative	0.7857	0.7296	0.7566
neutral	0.5833	0.3214	0.4145
positive	0.7998	0.9272	0.8588

Table 4: Aspect term polarity (2).

Label	Precision	Recall	F-measure
conflict	0.5333	0.1538	0.2388
negative	0.726	0.6802	0.7023
neutral	0.5119	0.4574	0.4831
positive	0.8343	0.9117	0.8713

Table 5: Aspect category polarity (2).

3.3 Error Analysis

The results obtained with our system are unarguably competitive, but some remarks can be made regarding the most frequent causes of errors. In the task of aspect category classification, the choice of the threshold (0.25) may have constituted a factor impacting the performance. In the task of aspect term detection, the lexical coverage is one of the factors to explain the difference in performance between training/trial data and test data.

Table 4 contains the results obtained in terms of precision, recall and F-measure for each of the possible polarities for terms (positive, negative, neutral and conflict) and similarly does Table 5 for category polarities. In both cases we notice a clear decrease for these measures when predicting the *conflict* and *neutral* classes, with a higher decrease in the case of aspect term polarity detection. This can be explained by the fact that the syntactic parser was primarily customized to detect the *negative* and *positive* labels. This obviously had an impact on the final results as the information from the parser constituted some of the input features for the classification.

4 Conclusion

The combination of a symbolic parser, customized with specialized lexicons, with SVM classifiers proved to be an interesting platform to implement a category/polarity detection system. The symbolic parser on the one hand provides a versatile architecture to add lexical and multi-words information, augmented with specific rules, in order to feed classifiers with high quality features. However, some work will be needed to improve performances on the neutral and conflict polarities, which rely less on specific words, than on a more global interpretation of the content.

Acknowledgements

We would like to thank the Semeval task 4 organizers, as well as our colleague, Vassilina Nikoulina, for her help on this project.

References

Salah Ait-Mokhtar, Jean-Pierre Chanod, and Claude Roux. 2001. A multi-input dependency parser. In *IWPT*.

Kenneth Bloom, Navendu Garg, and Shlomo Argamon. 2007. Extracting appraisal expressions. In *In HLT-NAACL 2007*, pages 308–315.

Caroline Brun. 2011. Detecting opinions using deep syntactic analysis. In *RANLP*, pages 392–398.

Caroline Brun. 2012. Learning opinionated patterns for contextual opinion detection. In *COLING*, pages 165–174.

Rong-En Fan, Kai-Wei Chang, Cho-Jui Hsieh, Xiang-Rui Wang, and Chih-Jen Lin. 2008. Liblinear: A library for large linear classification. *Journal of Machine Learning Research*, 9:1871–1874.

Minqing Hu and Bing Liu. 2004. Mining and summarizing customer reviews. In *KDD*, pages 168–177.

Soo-Min Kim and Eduard Hovy. 2004. Determining the sentiment of opinions. In *Proceedings of the 20th International Conference on Computational Linguistics*, COLING '04, Stroudsburg, PA, USA.

Bing Liu. 2012. *Sentiment Analysis and Opinion Mining*. Synthesis Lectures on Human Language Technologies. Morgan & Claypool Publishers.

Maria Pontiki, Dimitrios Galanis, John Pavlopoulos, Harris Papageorgiou, Ion Androutsopoulos, and Suresh Manandhar. 2014. Semeval-2014 task 4: Aspect based sentiment analysis. In *International Workshop on Semantic Evaluation (SemEval)*.

Yuanbin Wu, Qi Zhang, Xuanjing Huang, and Lide Wu. 2009. Phrase dependency parsing for opinion mining. In *EMNLP*, pages 1533–1541. ACL.

Author Index